AMERICAN CRIMINAL PROCEDURE: ADJUDICATIVE

CASES AND COMMENTARY

[from AMERICAN CRIMINAL PROCEDURE:
CASES AND COMMENTARY,
ELEVENTH EDITION]

■ ■ ■

Stephen A. Saltzburg

Wallace and Beverley Woodbury University Professor of Law
Co-Director of the Litigation and Dispute Resolution Program
The George Washington University Law School

Daniel J. Capra

Reed Professor of Law
Fordham University School of Law

AMERICAN CASEBOOK SERIES®

American Casebook Series is a trademark registered in the U.S. Patent and Trademark Office.

© West, a Thomson business, 2007
© 2010 Thomson Reuters
© 2014 LEG, Inc. d/b/a West Academic
© 2018 LEG, Inc. d/b/a West Academic
     444 Cedar Street, Suite 700
     St. Paul, MN 55101
     1-877-888-1330

Printed in the United States of America

ISBN: 978-1-68328-986-9

To the women we love,
Susan Lee and Anne Capra

PREFACE

This book is a complete, unchanged reprint of Chapters 6–13 of Saltzburg & Capra, American Criminal Procedure (11th ed. 2018).

This Eleventh Edition plays to what we feel were the strengths of the first ten editions. While the predominant focus is on Supreme Court jurisprudence, we have tried wherever possible to give the reader a sense of what the lower courts are doing with the interesting and exciting issues that abound in criminal procedure. The lower courts are where the day-to-day law is made, and where many of the most interesting fact situations arise. Since our topic is "American" Criminal Procedure, we have made an effort to include cases from all the circuits and state courts throughout the book. As with prior editions, extensive commentary and interesting fact situations are included to assist in doctrinal development. We have also added extensive academic commentary on some of the cutting issues in criminal procedure. Finally, the book covers all problems of criminal investigation and adjudication. It is not limited to constitutional issues. Yet despite the breadth of the book, we have made a special effort to keep it to a manageable and readable length.

The format of the book is the same as the prior editions, although much of the material has been reorganized and updated. Citations to Supreme Court opinions are limited to United States Reports, unless the case is so recent that the U.S. cite is not available. Certiorari denied citations are omitted on the ground that they unnecessarily clutter a book that is primarily for classroom use. Citations included in cases are often omitted without so specifying. Lettered footnotes are from the original materials. Numbered footnotes are ours. Omissions from the text of original material are indicated by asterisks and brackets. We have added more than 1000 headnotes in an effort to make the book as user friendly as possible.

This Edition gives special treatment to some of the more active areas of criminal procedure in the past few years, including important developments after the terrorist attack on 9/11/2001, as well as problems created by developing technology, such as GPS tracking, cellphone tracking and searches, and searches of computer hard-drives. Racially-based stops and encounters are discussed in Chapter 2. Important questions concerning the right to retained counsel and to counsel's role are also explored in Chapter 10. The fundamental changes wrought in sentencing under the Supreme Court's *Apprendi* line of cases, are explored in Chapters 10 and 11.

Because every criminal procedure teacher likes to cover different material, we have tried to divide the book into numerous subdivisions to

v

enable teachers to pick and choose the subjects they most want to cover. We think that an advanced criminal procedure course is a useful and popular addition to the curriculum. If an advanced course is contemplated, Chapters 9 through 13 could be reserved for that course. An alternative approach is to include Chapter 9 in the basic course and move Chapters 8 and 5 into the advanced course. A third approach is to cover parts of all, or almost all, chapters in the basic course, and to finish them in the advanced course. We believe and hope that the material lends itself to several different divisions that all work well in class and make either a single course or a tandem interesting for all students.

STEPHEN A. SALTZBURG
Washington, D.C.

DANIEL J. CAPRA
New York, N.Y.

April, 2018

INTRODUCTION

Criminal procedure is one of the courses in law school that generates classroom excitement that continues from the first to the last day of class. Whether it is the opportunity to compare the Warren, Burger and Rehnquist Courts or to predict the likely course of the Roberts Court, criminal procedure as a subject of study is almost always on the cutting edge of the law. It involves the battle between government and individual and the true adversary clash that often results. People like to talk and argue about criminal procedure, and they mind studying it less than they mind studying many other things.

As excited as students of criminal procedure are, too often they leave their courses feeling somewhat frustrated. They have learned a lot of recent law and they know what the latest decisions of the Supreme Court are, but they do not feel comfortable in their understanding of the criminal justice system (to the extent that it is accurate to call the way criminal cases are handled a system) as a whole, or in their knowledge of the doctrinal roots of the numerous concepts that they have examined. This book is an effort to remove some of that frustration, to clarify the way in which the parts of the criminal justice system relate to one another, and to explain how we arrived where we now find ourselves.

To accomplish this task, the book utilizes far more original text and scholarly commentary than is typically found in casebooks on the subject. The text attempts to develop the history of the rules discussed, to point out how judicial treatment of various concepts has changed over time, and to indicate the vices and the virtues of various approaches, past and present. An effort is made to provide students with citations to law journals, books and cases not presented in this book so that those who are interested can examine topics more fully on their own with easy access to the relevant literature.

When a subject is examined, an effort is made to point out inadequacies in judicial opinions or legislative reactions to judicial opinions. Sometimes our own views are stated, either explicitly or implicitly, in an effort to stimulate thinking about new approaches to familiar problems. Where appropriate, students are asked to think about the concepts they have learned in connection with problems that encourage them to develop their own ideas about how best to handle hard cases and close questions.

An effort has been made to reproduce in case form only those Supreme Court cases that are most important. Less important cases are discussed in the textual material. Some of the cases that are offered are not yesterday's Supreme Court decisions, but those of a more distant Court, because the important opinions may be those that were seminal.

The emphasis on the development of concepts over time indicates a bias that should be confessed here: We believe that the judiciary, especially the Supreme Court, and legislatures, to the extent that they become involved in establishing procedures for criminal cases, attempt to articulate and apply doctrines that will hold their own over time. In other words, we believe that they struggle "to get it right" eventually, if not always at the first crack.

This is not to suggest that right answers are clear or easy to ascertain. In many instances, reasonable minds will differ on the proper solution to questions, and often reasonable minds will find proper solutions to be elusive. We suggest only that approaches that are plainly defective are almost always abandoned or changed, and that it seems that courts and legislatures do attempt to refine the procedures that govern criminal investigations and prosecutions as a result of experience.

Like most criminal procedure books, this one places much emphasis on constitutional rules. This hardly can be avoided, because the Constitution as now interpreted does set minimum standards for many parts of the criminal justice system. But, an attempt is made to indicate when nonconstitutional rules may be more important or more useful than constitutional ones.

To sum up, this book combines elements of traditional casebooks with textual material that might more typically be found in a treatise or hornbook, and it intersperses problems in many chapters. Overall, the idea is to identify clearly the problems of criminal procedure, to offer various ideas about how to handle the problems, and to describe the work that still needs to be done if criminal cases are to be processed fairly.

Some comments on the particular chapters of the book may help to explain how we have approached various topics.

Chapter 1 begins with a development of the criminal justice system. The importance of constitutional rules is discussed, and the incorporation and retroactivity doctrines are examined, since they arise again and again in the cases that are discussed in the following chapters.

Chapter 2 examines all aspects of Fourth Amendment law. It begins with a careful examination of the Amendment's language—including the threshold requirement of "search" or "seizure"—and an exploration of the relationship between the warrant clause and the reasonableness clause. The concepts of probable cause, valid warrants, arrest, stop and frisk, and scrutiny by a detached magistrate are all covered at length. Eavesdropping and wiretapping, and NSA bulk data collection are looked at afterwards. The chapter reserves an examination of the exclusionary rule until the end and attempts thereby to promote an understanding of what the rule is and what its true costs are. This is the longest chapter of the book, covering the many facets of search and seizure law.

Chapter 3 covers self-incrimination and confessions. More than usual attention is paid to traditional Fifth Amendment law and how it relates to the law of confessions. Much space is devoted to laying the historical foundation for present law. Only then are *Miranda, Thompkins, Massiah, Brewer, Henry* and other major cases discussed.

Identification evidence is scrutinized in Chapter 4. The major Supreme Court cases take up most of the chapter, but an attempt is made to point out the shortcomings in the Court's work and to suggest how identification procedures might be improved and how fairer trials might result. The chapter also discusses some of the scientific findings on what factors can render an identification unreliable, and analyzes some non-constitutional remedies for guaranteeing the reliability of identifications.

Chapter 5 is about the right to counsel. As the right to counsel may be important in connection with confessions and identifications, as well as later in the process, it might seem strange for this chapter to follow the previous ones. But we believe that the order works and that it is helpful to treat the counsel cases in one place—at the point at which counsel is likely to be involved for the remainder of the process. The doctrines of ineffective assistance and self-representation are not treated here, but are reserved for Chapter 10.

Chapter 6 looks at the decision whether or not to charge a suspect. The roles of the police, the prosecutor and the grand jury are examined, and an effort is made to show how interdependent they are. The current controversy over the utility of the grand jury as a screening device and the dangers of the grand jury serving as an arm of the executive are described and discussed. Preliminary hearings and their relationship to grand juries and charging decisions generally are considered in some detail.

Chapter 7 covers bail and pretrial release. Both constitutional and nonconstitutional rules, especially the 1984 Federal Bail Reform Act, are analyzed. The purposes of bail and the controversy over preventive detention are discussed. Some emphasis is placed on the traditional role of the bondsman and the need for bail reform.

Chapter 8 presents criminal discovery. After a general overview, attention is paid to what the defendant can get from the prosecutor and what the prosecutor can get from the defendant without violating the Constitution. Proposals for liberalizing discovery are considered.

Chapter 9 is devoted to guilty pleas and plea bargaining. An extensive excerpt from a comprehensive study of plea bargaining in the United States begins the chapter. It is followed by a scholarly debate about the merits of plea bargaining, and then by a discussion of the requirements of a valid plea and an analysis of the finality of a plea.

Trial and trial-related rights are treated in Chapter 10. Among the topics covered are speedy trial, joinder of defendants and charges, burdens of persuasion, jury trial, fair-trial—free press conflicts, and effective representation and self-representation. This is the second longest chapter in the book. It addresses in the context of criminal trials many issues that are considered in the context of civil trials in the typical course in Civil Procedure.

Sentencing is the exclusive concern of Chapter 11. Basic options in sentencing are described, as are the roles of judge and jury. The determinate versus indeterminate sentencing controversy is explored, and the Federal Sentencing Guidelines are carefully examined. Also, the procedures that are generally employed in sentencing, and the applicable constitutional rules are set forth.

Chapter 12 covers all aspects of double jeopardy. Most attention is paid to recent decisions of the Supreme Court that clarify (or further confuse, depending on how the decisions are read) a subject that has been puzzling criminal procedure students for years. Collateral estoppel and vindictive prosecutorial conduct also are discussed.

Finally, Chapter 13 focuses on post-trial motions, appeals, and collateral attacks on convictions. An effort is made to examine all important post-sentencing challenges that can be made to a conviction. The section on collateral attack endeavors to explain the development of habeas corpus by the Supreme Court and Congress and the high points of the debate over how much post-conviction attack is desirable in a criminal justice system.

It should be obvious that we have tried to cover all of the significant parts of the criminal justice system and to do so in a reasonable number of pages. To accomplish this, we have worked hard to make the textual portions of the book as informative as possible. This Edition cannot be called a short book, but criminal procedure is not a subject that is easily confined to a few pages. To make the length somewhat more tolerable, we have endeavored to use headnotes as well as several different typesizes, not only for purposes of emphasis, but also to break the monotony of the printed page. To make the book easier to read, we also delete most internal citations in material that we quote from other sources. Thus, most internal cites in the Supreme Court opinions found throughout the book are missing. Footnotes in quoted material generally are deleted also. When we leave internal citations and original footnotes in the quoted material, we do so in the belief that they make a contribution to the overall coverage of the materials. Footnotes that are taken from the original source all have small letters to identify them—i.e., a, b, c, etc. Our own footnotes are identified by number—i.e., 1, 2, 3, etc. We hope that these choices enhance the "readability" of the book, and that by choosing to delete unnecessary baggage in quoted material, we have been able to pay more attention to the important and interesting questions that make criminal procedure a joy to study.

STEPHEN A. SALTZBURG
Washington, D.C.

DANIEL J. CAPRA
New York, N.Y.

April, 2018

SUMMARY OF CONTENTS

TABLE OF CONTENTS

TABLE OF CASES

The principal cases are in bold type.

———

TABLE OF AUTHORITIES

AMERICAN CRIMINAL PROCEDURE: ADJUDICATIVE

CASES AND COMMENTARY

[from AMERICAN CRIMINAL PROCEDURE:
CASES AND COMMENTARY,
ELEVENTH EDITION]

CHAPTER 6

THE SCREENING AND CHARGING PROCESS

■ ■ ■

I. CRIMINAL JUSTICE CHOICES

A. CONTROLLED AND UNCONTROLLED CHOICES

Choices must be made at all levels of our criminal justice system. The police must decide whether to arrest or to investigate. Prosecutors must decide whether to initiate cases, what charges to file, and whether to plea bargain. Magistrates issuing search and arrest warrants, or sitting in preliminary hearings, must decide whether probable cause exists or whether a suspect should be released on bail or pursuant to other conditions of pre-trial release. Grand juries must decide whether to indict, and prosecutors must decide whether to take cases to grand juries or to bring charges when grand jury indictments are not required. Trial judges must decide whether there is enough evidence for cases to go to petit juries, and petit juries must decide whether to convict or acquit. Judges or juries must determine the sentences to be imposed on convicted offenders. Correctional authorities must decide how to treat incarcerated offenders, and parole or pardon authorities must determine whether to release offenders before their formal sentences have been served.

Some of these choices are controlled by standards—e.g., whether probable cause exists, whether there is enough evidence to go to a jury, and how convinced the jury must be before it convicts—and the task of government officials or jurors is to apply the standards to particular facts. Other choices—sentencing is an example—might be controlled by minimum and maximum provisions but provide the decisionmaker some latitude in choosing where to settle within the permissible range. Still other choices are essentially discretionary. The screening and charging process involves many uncontrolled choices, and these are a cause of concern. As you proceed in this chapter, keep in mind what choices are possible and what controls, if any, are placed upon them by the agency making the choice, or by some external authority.

B. LESS THAN FULL ENFORCEMENT OF THE LAW

One of the realities of law enforcement is that not all crimes are investigated, not all criminals are prosecuted, and not all laws are enforced. Nowhere in the United States is there a full enforcement policy—i.e., one that seeks to impose a sanction on every criminal act that occurs.

There is no such thing as full enforcement because it would be too costly. We are not willing to pay for the police, the prosecutors, the public defenders, the judges, the courtrooms, and the penal institutions that would be required to punish all criminal acts that occur. But apart from economics, there are reasons why choices are made in the processing of cases. The notion of individualized justice runs deep in this country. Actions that technically fall under the same statutory proscription may not be equally reprehensible.

Moreover, legislative "overcriminalization" has resulted in criminal codes that, if they were fully enforced, might be intolerable. Laws are sometimes passed as "state-declared ideals," such as adultery statutes, which are "unenforced because we want to continue our conduct, and unrepealed because we want to preserve our morals."[1] Other laws like gambling laws might be drafted broadly for administrative convenience but never intended to be fully enforced because the legislature never really wanted to prohibit private poker games among friends. Outdated laws, which would cause public outrage were they enforced, remain unrepealed, sometimes because legislators do not want to go on record as having repealed *any* criminal law for fear of being labelled as "soft on crime."[2]

It seems, then, that legislatures pass and refuse to repeal statutes that invite choices by those who screen cases and make charging decisions. See Misner, note 2 supra (arguing that legislatures, "by creating too many policy choices, have effectively abdicated policy-making to the prosecutor since it is the prosecutor, and not the legislature, that has the final decision in determining which public policy, if any, is breached by an individual's conduct."). See also Richman and Stuntz, Al Capone's Revenge: An Essay on the Political Economy of Pretextual Prosecution, 105 Colum. L.Rev. 583 (2005) (arguing that the "overexpansion of the federal criminal code" has invited "pretextual enforcement" whereby a prosecutor who suspects a person of one crime can "charge and convict him of a different crime, unrelated to and less severe than the first.").

Some other countries purport to operate on the principle that the police and prosecutor have no discretion to exercise at all. If the case is one in which there is sufficient evidence to prosecute, it must be prosecuted.

---

[1]   LaFave, The Prosecutor's Discretion in the United States, 18 J.Am.Comp.L. 532, 533 (1970).

[2]   An example of this problem is mentioned in Misner, Recasting Prosecutorial Discretion, 86 J.Crim.L. & Crim. 717 (1996). When the Arizona legislature adopted its revised criminal code, a majority of legislators refused to go on record as voting for a repeal of any of the old sex offense statutes, even if they had become outmoded or superfluous. So that left two sets of sex offense statutes, using different terminology and imposing different punishment—thus increasing prosecutorial discretion.

Whether these systems operate in practice as they are designed to in theory is questionable. Two observers make the following comment:

> The principle of compulsory prosecution which formally permeates the German and Italian systems, and informally the French, demands the impossible: full enforcement of the law in a time of rising crime and fierce competition for resources. Inevitably, adjustments must be made in the way in which the principle is to be applied; where formal law or ideology does not permit these adjustments, informal processes are created that do.[3]

This observation serves as a reminder that it may be more difficult to make a mandatory system of prosecutions work in practice than it is to posit such a system in theory.

Judge Miner, in The Consequences of Federalizing Criminal Law, 4 Crim.Just. 16 (1989) argues that a prosecutor's decision not to prosecute someone who is guilty of a crime invades the province of the jury and creates a public perception of unfairness. Professor Green, in "Hare and Hounds": The Fugitive Defendant's Constitutional Right to be Pursued, 56 Brooklyn L.Rev. 439 (1990), disagrees with Judge Miner and argues that it makes sense that the prosecutor enjoys "virtually unfettered discretion in deciding how to allocate investigative and prosecutorial resources." Professor Green contends that the prosecutor is in the "best position" to decide how to use the finite resources allocated to prosecuting crime.

II. SCREENING BY THE POLICE

A. THE NATURE OF POLICE CHOICES

Before reaching the question of what choices should be available to those responsible for charging suspects with criminal offenses, it is necessary to focus on the police. Generally, officials who have the ultimate responsibility for charging decisions do not themselves investigate criminal conduct—other than through grand jury investigations. Obviously, then, if the police do not turn information over to the charging officials, it is unlikely that those officials will have any real choice to make.

In Chapter 2, the restrictions on police investigations, arrests, and searches were examined. The assumption there was that the police wanted to proceed against citizens, and the question was what limits, if any, should be placed on police activity. Sometimes, though, the police decide they do not want to take action against individuals, even though such action might be permissible under the rules previously discussed. When the police decide

---

[3] Goldstein & Marcus, The Myth of Judicial Supervision in Three Inquisitorial Systems: France, Italy, and Germany, 87 Yale L.J. 240, 280 (1977).

not to act, the effect is usually to screen cases from the criminal justice process.

The Choice Not to Arrest

The first level of screening occurs when the police decide whom to arrest. Although a decision to make an arrest must be reviewed by an impartial magistrate, either before or after the arrest is made, a decision *not to arrest* is essentially unreviewable.

The suggestion has been made that police cannot properly be given the choice whether or not to arrest, and that they must arrest when they have probable cause to do so.[4] In fact, police in all American jurisdictions make decisions not to arrest people whom they could arrest. Several explanations can be offered for this phenomenon.

Were the police to arrest every suspect who they reasonably believed committed a crime, an already overburdened judicial system would be further burdened. Thus, we tolerate choices by the police because we are not prepared to handle more cases. Actually, the police themselves are not prepared to handle more cases. If they spent more time in processing cases, they would have less time to spend on the street to deal with crimes that they view as more serious than the ones they now choose to ignore.

Also, police officers learn that courts and prosecutors will not proceed very far in processing certain kinds of cases. Rather than initiating a process that they know will be shortlived, the police may decide not to make arrests for certain crimes and to devote their energies to other activities. For an interesting discussion of the interrelationship between the police investigatory function and the prosecutor's function, see Richman, Prosecutors and Their Agents: Agents and Their Prosecutors, 103 Colum.L.Rev. 749 (2003).

Police also might refrain from an arrest when they are engaged in a community caretaking function, in which case they need to maintain good relations with community elements who might resent the filing of criminal charges in some instances. The police officer may approach a disruptive incident "not in terms of enforcing the law but in terms of handling the situation."[5] Arrest is only one of several tools that the officer may use to maintain order and protect the public. The officer may rely on personal qualities and an aura of authority, rather than the arrest power, to maintain and restore order.

Police officers are also aware that complete enforcement of certain crimes by arrest would create a public backlash. If police officers arrested every driver who drove 56 miles per hour in a 55 mile per hour zone, it is

---

[4]   Hall, Police and Law in a Democratic Society, 28 Ind.L.J. 133, 155 (1953).

[5]   J. Wilson, Varieties of Police Behavior 33 (1968).

clear that the police would hear about it. Upset drivers might create a risk of violence during the arrest for such a minimal offense. (Witness Walter White's reaction to simply being ticketed for a cracked windshield in "Breaking Bad"). Requiring police officers to arrest whenever they have probable cause of a violation of any of the thousands of offenses that legislatures have enacted would simply be unworkable.

That said, there is an undeniable problem in the police having virtually unfettered discretion in determining whom to arrest and whom not to arrest. Professor Davis, in Prosecution and Race: The Power and Privilege of Discretion, 67 Fordham L.Rev. 13 (1998), notes the racial impact that such discretion can have:

> Because police officers are not required to make an arrest when they observe conduct creating probable cause, their discretion may result in the failure to detain or arrest whites who commit acts for which their African American counterparts would often be detained or arrested.

As an illustration, Professor Davis notes an event in Prince George's County, Maryland, "where white officers observed three white adults smoking crack cocaine in a car with a baby and neither made arrest nor filed charges." If someone can prove that police arrest racial minorities but not white suspects for particular crimes, an equal protection violation may be established. But, as we shall see later in this Chapter, it is difficult to gather sufficient evidence to prove racial discrimination.

B. SOME TYPICAL CASES

Consider the following situations that a police officer might expect to confront, and in which a choice to arrest or not will be made.

1. An officer responds to a call from a woman who says her husband is going to beat her. When the officer arrives, the woman has a broken nose and several facial bruises, but she refuses to sign a complaint. Should the officer arrest the husband anyway? Should the officer suggest that the couple see a marriage counselor? Should the decision be affected by whether the couple has children who witnessed the beating?

2. Suppose two officers are operating a speed trap and a car whizzes by at 30 miles per hour over the speed limit. They usually make an arrest of anyone speeding more than 15 miles over the limit. Should they make an arrest if the driver is a parent rushing to the hospital to see an ill child? If the driver is an employee who is late to work and may be facing the loss of a job if tardy one more time? If the driver is from out of town and did not realize that he was speeding?

3. Officers enter a house without a warrant believing that they will find illegal narcotics. They find the drugs they were looking for but have

grave reservations about whether they had exigent circumstances excusing the warrantless entry. Should the officers arrest the occupants and let the prosecution and the court figure it out? Or should they just seize and destroy the narcotics as an informal sanction? Does it matter if the officers believe that if they make an arrest, a motion to suppress will likely follow that will probably lead to a conclusion that the officers violated the Fourth Amendment and could be disciplined for the warrantless entry?

4.   The U.S. Department of Justice at various time encourages and even insists that state and local law enforcement authorities assist in determining the immigration status of those who are stopped or arrested. The state and local authorities in many jurisdictions believe that if they appear to be an arm of immigration officials, potential witnesses and actual victims might be discouraged from reporting criminal acts and cooperating in bringing offenders to justice. See, e.g., Yee and Ruiz, Sessions Once Again Threatens Sanctuary Cities, N.Y. Times, July 26, 2017, https://www.nytimes.com/2017/07/26/us/politics/sessions-sanctuary-cities.html?_r=0.

The clash between the Department of Justice and some state and local jurisdictions raises constitutional issues that are beyond the scope of this course. Federal immigration officials believe they need help in doing their job, while law enforcement officials believe that by providing such help they make it more difficult to do their own jobs. So the questions in the end are which function is more important and who decides.

Is police rulemaking a means by which an officer's discretion to arrest or not to arrest can be limited? Would rulemaking make decisions easier in the first three examples set forth above? Ironically, if police departments contemplate adopting rules that would indicate circumstances in which an arrest could, but probably ought not be, made, they may be criticized. There would be no deterrent effect to a law that the police have advertised will not be enforced. Yet, without rules, decisions are left to individual officers at the lowest enforcement level.

III.   THE PROSECUTORIAL DECISION WHETHER TO CHARGE

A. THE POWER OF THE PROSECUTOR

While discretion runs through the criminal justice system, it is the discretionary decisions made by the prosecutor that have the most impact. Professor Misner, supra note 2, notes the awesome authority granted to prosecutors—authority that has increased over time.

The prosecutor's authority is evident in bail hearings, grants of immunity, and in trial strategy. But in the areas of charging, bargaining, and sentencing, it has become clear that the prosecutor plays the pivotal role in the criminal justice process. Despite criticism, plea bargaining continues unabated. While a few courts have rather unsuccessfully attempted to formulate "a common law of prosecutorial discretion," the authority of the prosecutor continues to grow.

Three closely related trends have been at work to promote the authority of the prosecutor. First, current criminal codes contain so many overlapping provisions that the choice of how to characterize conduct as criminal has passed to the prosecutor. In many cases the legislature has effectively delegated its prerogative to define the nature and severity of criminal conduct to the prosecutor. Legislative mandates regarding sentencing maxima, sentencing minima, and sentencing guidelines are dependent upon the substantive charge chosen by the prosecutor. In addition, prosecutors have the untrammeled authority to select the number of separate criminal acts for which the defendant will be charged. The prosecutors also determine whether to seek sentencing enhancements.

Second, the increase in reported crime without a concomitant increase in resources dedicated to the prosecution and defense of criminal conduct has resulted in a criminal process highly dependent upon plea bargaining. There are very few restraints placed upon the prosecutor in the bargaining process.

Third, the development of sentencing guidelines and a growth of statutes with mandatory minimum sentences have increased the importance of the charging decision since the since the charging decision can affect the range of sentences available to the court. * * *

The American Bar Association approved a resolution (10B) on August 15, 2017 expressing disapproval of mandatory minimum sentences and urging their repeal. In the report accompanying the resolution, the authors focus on the extent to which these sentences take discretion from judges and give it to prosecutors:

Mandatory minimums undermine judicial discretion and disturb a just allocation of authority among the parties. In the United States adversarial criminal justice system, the judge serves as an impartial arbiter of the case, neither on the side of the prosecution nor the defense. Because of this, judges are entrusted to determine appropriate sentences. Mandatory minimum sentencing regimes, however, deprive judges of the discretion they need to fashion sentences tailored to the circumstances of the offense and the offender. And while judges are stripped of the discretion they need to do justice, at the same time, mandatory minimums often shift that discretion to prosecutors, who do not have the incentive, training or even the appropriate information to properly consider a defendant's mitigating circumstances at the initial charging stage of a case. To give prosecutors such unchecked authority dangerously disturbs the balance of power between the parties in an adversarial system, and deprives defendants of access to an impartial decision-maker in the all-important area of sentencing.

B. THE NATURE OF THE CHARGING DECISION

The prosecutor's decision whether to charge a suspect with a crime is of a different character than the officer's decision whether to arrest. While the officer usually must make an on-the-spot decision, the prosecutor has time, a fuller knowledge of the facts, and the opportunity to consult with colleagues. The consequences of a decision to charge are far greater than those of the decision to arrest. A decision to charge constitutes a finding that the suspect should bear the monetary and social costs of trial and, in some cases, that the suspect's freedom should either be conditioned on payment of bail or suspended as a means of preventive detention. That the defendant may reduce some of these costs by pleading guilty to a lesser charge only makes the prosecutor's decision more consequential.

Professor Davis, in Prosecution and Race: The Power and Privilege of Discretion, 67 Fordham L.Rev. 13 (1998), describes the importance of the prosecutor's decision to charge a person with a crime:

> The first and most important function exercised by a prosecutor is the charging decision. Although police officers decide whether to arrest a suspect, the prosecutor decides whether he should be formally charged with a crime and what the charge should be. This decision is entirely discretionary. Even if there is probable cause to believe the suspect has committed a crime, the prosecutor may decide to dismiss the case and release the suspect. She may also file a charge that is either more or less serious than that recommended by the police officer, as long as there is probable cause to believe the suspect committed the crime. Other than a constitutional challenge by a criminal defendant, there is very little process for review of these decisions.

> The charging decision is one of the most important decisions a prosecutor makes. In conjunction with the plea bargaining process, the charging decision almost predetermines the outcome of a criminal case, because the vast majority of criminal cases result in guilty pleas or guilty verdicts. The charge also often determines the sentence that the defendant will receive * * *.

At the outset, does it trouble you that the prosecutor's decision to charge, carrying the grave consequences that it does, is largely discretionary? If you think the prosecutor's unfettered discretion is a problem, what safeguards would you impose?

C. THE FACTORS THAT ARE CONSIDERED

The prosecutor must decide whether to charge and what crime to charge. The decision whether to charge depends on the prosecutor's belief that (1) the suspect is guilty, (2) the evidence is sufficient to secure conviction, and (3) it is in the community's best interest to prosecute the suspect. General criteria to be employed by the prosecutor are set forth in the ABA Standards for Criminal Justice: The Prosecution Function (4th edition).

Standard 3–4.4 Discretion in Filing, Declining, Maintaining, and Dismissing Criminal Charges

(a) In order to fully implement the prosecutor's functions and duties, including the obligation to enforce the law while exercising sound discretion, the prosecutor is not obliged to file or maintain all criminal charges which the evidence might support. Among the factors which the prosecutor may properly consider in exercising discretion to initiate, decline, or dismiss a criminal charge, even though it meets the requirements of Standard 3–4.3, are:

(i)   the strength of the case;

(ii)   the prosecutor's doubt that the accused is in fact guilty;

(iii)   the extent or absence of harm caused by the offense;

(iv)   the impact of prosecution or non-prosecution on the public welfare;

(v)   the background and characteristics of the offender, including any voluntary restitution or efforts at rehabilitation;

(vi)   whether the authorized or likely punishment or collateral consequences are disproportionate in relation to the particular offense or the offender;

(vii)   the views and motives of the victim or complainant;

(viii) any improper conduct by law enforcement;

(ix)   unwarranted disparate treatment of similarly situated persons;

(x)   potential collateral impact on third parties, including witnesses or victims;

(xi)   cooperation of the offender in the apprehension or conviction of others;

(xii)   the possible influence of any cultural, ethnic, socioeconomic or other improper biases;

(xiii) changes in law or policy;

(xiv) the fair and efficient distribution of limited prosecutorial resources;

(xv)   the likelihood of prosecution by another jurisdiction; and

(xvi) whether the public's interests in the matter might be appropriately vindicated by available civil, regulatory, administrative, or private remedies.

(b) In exercising discretion to file and maintain charges, the prosecutor should not consider:

(i)   partisan   or   other   improper   political   or   personal considerations;

(ii)   hostility or personal animus towards a potential subject, or any other improper motive of the prosecutor; or

(iii)   the impermissible criteria described in Standard 1.6 above [Improper Bias Prohibited].

(c)   A prosecutor may file and maintain charges even if juries in the jurisdiction have tended to acquit persons accused of the particular kind of criminal act in question.

(d)   The prosecutor should not file or maintain charges greater in number or degree than can reasonably be supported with evidence at trial and are necessary to fairly reflect the gravity of the offense or deter similar conduct.

(e)   A prosecutor may condition a dismissal of charges, *nolle prosequi*, or similar action on the accused's relinquishment of a right to seek civil redress only if the accused has given informed consent, and such consent is disclosed to the court. A prosecutor should not use a civil waiver to avoid a bona fide claim of improper law enforcement actions, and a decision not to file criminal charges should be made on its merits and not for the purpose of obtaining a civil waiver.

(f)   The prosecutor should consider the possibility of a noncriminal disposition, formal or informal, or a deferred prosecution or other diversionary disposition, when deciding whether to initiate or prosecute criminal charges. The prosecutor should be familiar with the services and resources of other agencies, public or private, that might assist in the evaluation of cases for diversion or deferral from the criminal process.

––––––––––––

Professor Fairfax discusses a number of nonevidentiary factors that the prosecutor may consider in a charging decision, including:

whether the defendant is a recidivist or is likely to offend again, whether the prosecutor has a heavy caseload at the time, whether the type of case is career-advancing, whether the investigating law enforcement agency is pleasant to work with, whether the case has jury appeal, whether a matter is more appropriately prosecuted by a different sovereign or handled as a civil matter, and whether the criminal conduct is a priority area for the prosecutor's superiors.

Fairfax, Grand Jury Discretion and Constitutional Design, 93 Cornell L. Rev. 703, 735 (2008). See also Green and Zacharias, Prosecutorial Neutrality, 2004 Wis. L.Rev. 837 (discussing criteria for a charging decision and the difficulty of crafting clear standards given the need for prosecutorial discretion in charging).

Sample Cases

Using the criteria from the standards set forth above, consider whether the prosecutor should have brought the following cases:

1.   Congressman Mel Reynolds, an African-American, was charged and convicted of statutory rape and obstruction of justice. The evidence showed that he had a long-term sexual relationship with a teenage girl, and that he tried to cover-up the relationship when an investigation began. The relationship was consensual and the girl was at best a reluctant witness against him. In such a case, should the prosecutor take into account (a) the fact that Reynolds is an elected official, and (b) the attempted cover-up? If so, how important are these factors?

2.   In the Southern District of New York, the U.S. Attorney promulgated a "Federal Tuesday" program, in which low-level drug dealers were arrested on the streets while making narcotics transactions. These low-level dealers were prosecuted under the federal narcotics laws, and given much harsher sentences than they would have received had they been prosecuted in the state system. Does deterrence justify prosecuting ordinary dealers caught on one week day in federal court while similarly situated dealers arrested every other day are prosecuted in state court?

3.   Leona Helmsley was charged and convicted of tax fraud. The government proved that she evaded taxes by charging renovations to her home as business expenses. On balance, however, Ms. Helmsley paid millions of dollars a year in taxes—the amount of evasion was a rather small percentage of the amount she paid. Mrs. Helmsley was a well-known hotelier. Assuming that a prosecutor would not ordinarily bring a criminal prosecution for a relatively small amount of unjustified deductions, is a prosecution justifiable if it focuses public attention on tax evasion and the possible consequences?

4.   Los Angeles police officers Stacy Koon and Lawrence Powell were convicted in federal court for violating the civil rights of Rodney King. The convictions arose out of the use of excessive force after the officers had

lawfully pursued King in a high-speed chase and stopped and arrested him. The Rodney King beating was on videotape. A state prosecution had already been brought, resulting in acquittal on most of the counts and a hung jury on one count. The case was highly publicized and was widely watched both in Los Angeles and around the nation. Should a federal prosecutor consider filing federal charges if she believes that the acquittals were largely attributable to the fact that the entire jury was white while the victim in the case was black?

5.   The accused snipers who tormented Maryland, Virginia and the District of Columbia for three weeks in October 2002, John Muhammad and Lee Malvo, were going to be tried in Maryland, where most of the sniper attacks occurred. But the Justice Department intervened to assure that the defendants would be prosecuted in Virginia. The apparent reason for this decision was that prosecutors could seek the death penalty for Malvo in Virginia but not in Maryland (because Malvo was a juvenile at the time of the crimes, and Maryland does not permit the use of the death penalty when the crime is committed by a juvenile). Should the Department of Justice be deciding whether Maryland or Virginia has the better criminal justice policy when it comes to juveniles and the death penalty?

6.   Arthur Anderson, the accounting firm, was indicted for destroying records that were pertinent to the SEC investigation of Enron. The indictment essentially resulted in the dissolution of the firm. The conviction, which was based on a single e-mail from a single lawyer concerning records destruction, was overturned by the Supreme Court, but by that time the firm was all but destroyed. Should a prosecutor consider the effects of a conviction on a partnership or corporation in deciding whether to charge the entity along with or in lieu of individuals?

7.   Beau Bergdahl was an army soldier stationed in Afghanistan when he left his post and was captured by the Taliban in 2009. President Obama announced his release in exchange for the release of five Guantanamo detainees in 2014. A Major General investigated why Bergdahl left his post, determined that he did so to call attention to poor leadership in his unit, and testified at a preliminary hearing that jail time would be inappropriate. The presiding officer at the preliminary hearing agreed and recommended that Bergdahl's case be handled by a special court martial with no jail time. But, the Commander of U.S. Army Forces Command rejected the recommendation and ordered Bergdahl's case to a general court-martial for trial on charges of desertion and misbehavior before the enemy. Then-candidate for President Donald Trump called Bergdahl a "dirty rotten traitor," and on Inauguration Day Bergdahl's lawyers moved to dismiss the charges on the ground that the President's earlier comments had made a fair trial impossible. The motion was denied, and ultimately Bergdahl elected a trial before a military judge. https://en.

wikipedia.org/wiki/Bowe_Bergdahl. Ultimately, he pled guilty to desertion and misbehavior before the enemy and was sentenced to a dishonorable discharge but no prison time.

The Commander, almost certainly a non-lawyer who sent the case to a general court martial, had discretion to reject the recommendation of the presiding officer at the preliminary hearing. In the military justice system commanders have Judge Advocate General lawyers to advise them, but they have the ultimate decision-making power. There are those who believe that charging decisions should rest with lawyers, not commanders. See, e.g., Rustico, Note: Overcoming OverCorrection: Towards Holistic Military Sexual Assault Reform, 102 Va. L. Rev. 2027 (2016) (discussing proposals in Congress to shift the charging function from commanders to JAGs). Military commanders historically used the military justice system as a mechanism (a) to promote good order and discipline in the ranks and (b) to impose proper punishment for criminal acts. The question is whether these goals are complementary or conflicting. Should an exceptionally good soldier get more favorable consideration as to charges than an ordinary soldier?

Politics, and the Chance of a Favorable Outcome

Of course, an important factor in a prosecutor's decision to prosecute is whether the prosecutor thinks a case can be won. A prosecutor with a high conviction rate is not only more likely to be successful in a reelection bid (in jurisdictions where prosecutors are elected), but also will have enhanced credibility when she does file charges. Therefore, she is likely to want to carry all the way to trial only those cases that are supported by a great deal of evidence to which the judge and jury will be sympathetic.

Problems can arise, however, if charging decisions are dominated by politics and the goal of maintaining high conviction rates. Prosecutors could become less concerned about the danger of convicting innocent persons. Conviction rates could be reached by offering very favorable plea bargains to people against whom the evidence is quite weak and who might well be acquitted at trial. Or, prosecutors could decline to pursue hard cases, which might lead to (a) wealthy litigants going free because prosecutors do not want to face well paid defense counsel who will pull out all stops to defend their clients; and (b) serious offenses going unprosecuted despite sufficient evidence to support convictions because plausible defenses exist and prosecutors do not want to risk defeat. In short, it is not clear that a prosecutor's office should be judged on the basis of its rate of conviction. But the reality is that it often will be—largely because ordinary voters have few ways to assess the performance of prosecutors' offices.

D. THE DECISION NOT TO PROSECUTE

A prosecutor's decision not to prosecute a suspect is generally protected from judicial review. This means that the effect of a prosecutor's decision not to charge a suspect is a final resolution of the case in favor of the suspect. Of course, the prosecutor may change her mind and decide to charge the suspect within the time prescribed by the applicable statute of limitations, but few mechanisms exist that compel the prosecutor to pursue charges.

Even when statutory language appears to make prosecution of all violations of a statute mandatory, courts have been extremely reluctant to *require* prosecution where the prosecutor has decided against it. See, e.g., Inmates of Attica v. Rockefeller, 477 F.2d 375 (2d Cir.1973) (statutory language that prosecutor is "required" to institute prosecutions "has never been thought to exclude the exercise of prosecutorial discretion"). The court in *Attica* relied on separation of powers principles and refused to order the prosecutor to instigate prosecutions against state officials.

Refusing to Prosecute a Certain Type of Crime

In some situations, a prosecutor might decide that a certain type of crime will not be prosecuted. A prosecutor's decision not to prosecute a certain type of crime is often based on a judgment that the violation of law involved is simply not worth the resources that would have to be expended in a prosecution. Prosecutors might also be concerned about a public backlash in prosecuting certain crimes. Local and cultural conditions might be involved as well.

Kamin, Prosecutorial Discretion in the Context of Immigration and Marijuana Law Reform: The Search for a Limiting Principle, 14 Ohio St. J. Crim. L. 183 (2016), discusses the Obama Administration's decision not to fully enforce particular federal laws:

> To the extent that marijuana and immigration policy are mentioned together on the national stage, it is usually in the context of pointing out that, despite the relaxation or elimination of many states' marijuana prohibitions, marijuana possession and manufacture can still be grounds for the deportation of migrants otherwise in the country lawfully. However, these two seemingly disparate policy arenas share one other important thing in common: in the enforcement of both federal marijuana law and immigration policy, the Obama administration has quite publicly promulgated a policy of limited and selective enforcement of federal law. * * *

* * *

Thus, we can imagine two extreme views of prosecutorial discretion, both of which are untenable. On the one hand, the power to completely invalidate a criminal statute by categorically refusing to enforce a validly enacted law is clearly beyond the authority of a prosecutor. Such a policy would be a clear usurpation of the legislative prerogative, tantamount to allowing a prosecutor to substitute her own views regarding the wisdom of criminal laws for those of a duly elected legislative body. On the other hand, the conception that prosecutorial discretion should, or even could, be completely legislated away is a fallacy. For better or for worse, and in a world of limited resources, any sensible criminal justice system will always rely in part on the wisdom and judgment of those charged with enforcing the laws.

Of course, the trick lies in determining how far toward one of these extremes executive policy may stray in practice. * * *

Overriding the Grand Jury's Decision to Indict

No federal prosecutor can lawfully sign an indictment not approved by the grand jury, but he or she may *decline* to sign off on charges that the grand jury wishes to file. See, e.g., United States v. Navarro-Vargas, 408 F.3d 1184 (9th Cir. 2005) ("The prosecutor has no obligation to prosecute the [grand jury's] presentment, to sign the return of an indictment, or even to prosecute an indictment properly returned.").

It is unusual for prosecutors and the grand juries with which they work to be at odds, but it does happen. A dozen grand jurors in Colorado rebelled against a prosecutor's decision not to indict Rockwell International for polluting a site with nuclear waste. During its term, the grand jury heard from more than 100 witnesses and examined hundreds of thousands of documents. The evidence indicated that the cost of the clean-up at the site would be $2 billion. But the prosecutor pulled the plug on the grand jury by entering into a deal whereby Rockwell would pay an $18 million fine. The grand jurors made statements to the press that they wanted to indict Rockwell but were overruled by the prosecutor. They then wrote a report about their findings and sent it to a federal judge, requesting judicial intervention. The judge not only refused to intervene in the prosecutor's decision; he asked the U.S. Attorney General to determine whether criminal charges could be brought against the grand jurors for violation of grand jury secrecy. The foreman of the grand jury was quoted as saying: "The judge's instructions were very vivid and clear to us. He said that we were not to be a rubber stamp for the prosecutor. What we've done is in the best interest of the prosecutor and the nation." Subsequently the grand jurors brought a petition to release materials associated with the grand jury's investigation. See In re Special Grand Jury, 450 F.3d 1159 (10th Cir. 2006).

Explaining the Decision Not to Prosecute

The public is rarely made aware of a prosecutor's decision not to bring charges. In highly publicized cases, however, prosecutors may have to worry about public opinion. Some prosecutors have found it necessary to explain their decisionmaking process when they decide not to charge in a high profile case.

For example, U.S. Attorney Otto Obermaier decided not to bring charges against Salomon Brothers, a Wall Street Brokerage house, in connection with Salomon's admission of submitting false bids in treasury securities auctions. He made a public statement explaining why he decided not to seek charges. Obermaier singled out four pertinent factors: (1) Salomon's extensive cooperation with the authorities; (2) Salomon's replacement of those senior management officials who had failed to promptly report the offenses to the authorities after first learning of it; (3) heavy fines and other punishments imposed as part of Salomon's civil settlement with the SEC, the Federal Reserve Bank, and the Treasury Department; and (4) the "negative effect on the company's innocent employees and shareholders" that would have resulted from criminal charges against the corporation. Obermaier, Drafting Companies to Fight Crime, New York Times, May 24, 1992, sec. 3, p.11, col.2.

The most controversial example of an explanation of a decision not to prosecute arose when FBI Director James Comey (1) explained publicly in July 2016 why the government declined to prosecute former Secretary of State (and then Presidential candidate) Hillary Clinton for her use of a private e-mail server during her service as Secretary; (2) informed Congress shortly before the November 2016 election that the FBI was investigating whether any classified information was contained in e-mails on the computer of her assistant who shared a computer with her husband, former Congressman Anthony Weiner; and (3) a few days later announced that the newly discovered e-mails were duplicates of e-mails the FBI had previously examined. Questions arose as to Director Comey's motives and judgment. McLean, The True Story of the Comey Letter Debacle, https://www.vanityfair.com/news/2017/02/james-comey-fbi-director-letter.

In Secretary Clinton's case the public was aware of an investigation into her handling of e-mails. In such circumstances is it proper to announce that no charges will be brought? Should a government representative explain the decision not to prosecute? Once the decision not to prosecute is made, is it fair to a candidate to have the electorate believe that the investigation is ongoing? What if the public is unaware of an investigation but it is possible that charges might be brought against a candidate after the election? Is it fair for a prosecutor to remain silent? Is it fair for the prosecutor to reveal the investigation before a decision to charge has been made? Does a prosecutor have any good options?

E. PROSECUTORIAL RULEMAKING

Just as there have been numerous calls for rulemaking by the police, there have been a number of suggestions that chief prosecutorial officers should formulate regulations to govern the conduct of their offices. See, e.g., ALI Model Code of Pre-Arraignment Procedure § 10.3 (calling for regulations); ABA Standards, The Prosecution Function § 3–2.4 ("[e]ach prosecutor's office should seek to develop general policies to guide the exercise of prosecutorial discretion, and standard operating procedures for the office").

Some guidelines have been drafted, but they leave much room for individualized charging judgment on the part of particular prosecutors. See, e.g., U.S. Dept. of Justice, Materials Relating to Prosecutorial Discretion. See also Baker, A View to the Future of Judicial Federalism: "Neither Out Far Nor In Deep," 45 Case W. Res. L. Rev. 705, 749 (1995) (discussing the process by which "the Department of Justice and the typical U.S. Attorney's Office have written prosecution guidelines, often labeled 'declination policies,' that describe principles for informed exercise of federal prosecutorial discretion."). The arguments for prosecutorial rulemaking are similar to those made in favor of police rulemaking, but they are even stronger, because policy-making executive officials are likely to be trusted with greater power to make enforcement decisions than are lower level police officers.

Arguments against prosecutorial rulemaking have been made, however. They are the following:

- the application of rules in particular cases would be challenged, thus raising the costs of the criminal process;

- rules would reduce the deterrent effect of the criminal law by announcing which laws would not be vigorously enforced;

- individual treatment would be sacrificed in order to have uniformity;

- problems in law enforcement change rapidly (e.g., post-September 11) and rulemaking would inhibit a rapid prosecutorial response to new problems; and

- adequate rules cannot be devised because discretion cannot be controlled by any clear criteria.[6]

---

[6] See generally, Beck, The Administrative Law of Criminal Prosecution: The Development of Prosecutorial Policy, 27 Am.U.L.Rev. 310, 337–80 (1978). See also, Vorenberg, Decent Restraint of Prosecutorial Discretion, 94 Harv.L.Rev. 1521 (1981), which suggests appropriate ways of controlling discretion. Frase, The Decision to File Federal Criminal Charges: A Quantitative Study of Prosecutorial Discretion, 47 U.Chi.L.Rev. 246 (1980), focuses on one United States Attorney's office and documents the tremendous discretion afforded federal prosecutors and the factors they most often consider in exercising it.

Are these arguments persuasive? For an argument that internal standards are critical to assure the public integrity of a prosecutor's decisions, see Green and Zacharias, Prosecutorial Neutrality, 2004 Wis. L.Rev. 837.

F. SELECTIVE ENFORCEMENT

Whether by rules or by ad hoc decisions, prosecutors operating in a world of partial enforcement must somehow choose whom to prosecute. The selection of a certain type of case or person for enforcement may raise questions of arbitrariness and even equal protection. Understandably, however, courts are reluctant to regulate the traditional discretion of the prosecutor to charge. As Judge Posner has stated:

> A judge in our system does not have the authority to tell prosecutors which crimes to prosecute or when to prosecute them. Prosecutorial discretion resides in the executive, not in the judicial, branch, and that discretion, though subject of course to judicial review, is not reviewable for a simple abuse of discretion.

United States v. Giannattasio, 979 F.2d 98 (7th Cir.1992).[7]

1. Charges on Collateral Matters

It should be no surprise that a disproportionate number of prosecutions are brought against career offenders, members of organized crime, and suspected terrorists. Often prosecutors hunt to bring a charge that will "stick," even if the crime charged might be considered collateral to the central criminal activity of the defendant. The classic example is the successful prosecution of Al Capone for tax violations. Should a prosecutor be able to tell law enforcement officials to "go after X who I believe is an organized crime official. Check his tax records, his business dealings, everything"? Professors Richman and Stuntz, in Al Capone's Revenge: An Essay on the Political Economy of Pretextual Prosecution, 105 Colum. L.Rev. 583 (2005), argue that pretextual decisions to charge create social costs:

> There is a strong social interest in non-pretextual prosecution, and that interest is much more important than the "fairness to defendants" argument that has preoccupied the literature on this subject. Criminal charges are not only a means of identifying and punishing criminal conduct. They are also a means by which prosecutors send signals to their superiors, including the voters to whom they are ultimately responsible. When a murderer is brought to justice for murder rather than for tax evasion, voters learn some

---

[7]   In Imbler v. Pachtman, 424 U.S. 409 (1976), the Court held that a prosecutor has absolute immunity from liability for all claims concerning the initiation of charges and the trying of the case. See also Buckley v. Fitzsimmons, 509 U.S. 259 (1993) (prosecutor entitled to absolute immunity for charging decisions, but receives only qualified immunity for statements to the media and for actions taken during the preliminary investigation of an uncharged crime).

important things about their community and about the justice system: that a given homicide has been committed in a particular way * * * ; that the crime has been solved; that the police and prosecution have done a good job of assembling evidence against the killer, and so forth. If there is a legislative body that oversees the relevant law enforcement agencies, those same signals are sent to the legislative overseers. When a prosecutor gets a conviction * * * for an unrelated lesser crime than the one that motivated the investigation, the signals are muddied. They may disappear altogether. * * *

Another audience also gets a muddied signal: would-be criminals. Instead of sending the message that running illegal breweries and bribing local cops would lead to a term in a federal penitentiary, the Capone prosecution sent a much more complicated and much less helpful message: If you run a criminal enterprise, you should keep your name out of the newspapers and at least pretend to pay your taxes. * * * [T]he political economy of criminal law enforcement depends on a reasonably good match between the charges that motivate prosecution and the charges that appear on defendants' rap sheets. When crimes and charges do not coincide, no one can tell whether law enforcers are doing their jobs. The justice system loses the credibility it needs, and voters lose the trust they need to have in the justice system. Individual agents and prosecutors pay only a tiny fraction of that price, which is why they continue to follow the Capone strategy. The larger price is paid only over time—by crime victims, by law enforcement agencies, and (not least) by the voting public.

2. Constitutional Limitations on the Charging Decision

The following case sets forth strict requirements for proving a constitutional claim of selective prosecution.

UNITED STATES V. ARMSTRONG
Supreme Court of the United States, 1996.
517 U.S. 456.

CHIEF JUSTICE REHNQUIST delivered the opinion of the Court.

In this case, we consider the showing necessary for a defendant to be entitled to discovery on a claim that the prosecuting attorney singled him out for prosecution on the basis of his race. We conclude that respondents failed to satisfy the threshold showing: They failed to show that the Government declined to prosecute similarly situated suspects of other races.

In April 1992, respondents were indicted in the United States District Court for the Central District of California on charges of conspiring to possess with intent to distribute more than 50 grams of cocaine base (crack) and conspiring to distribute the same, in violation of 21 U.S.C. §§ 841 and 846, and federal firearms offenses. * * * On seven separate occasions * * * informants had bought a total of 124.3 grams of crack from respondents and witnessed respondents carrying firearms during the sales. * * *

[R]espondents filed a motion for discovery or for dismissal of the indictment, alleging that they were selected for federal prosecution because they are black. In support of their motion, they offered only an affidavit [alleging] that, in every one of the 24 §§ 841 or 846 cases closed by the office during 1991, the defendant was black. Accompanying the affidavit was a "study" listing the 24 defendants, their race, whether they were prosecuted for dealing cocaine as well as crack, and the status of each case.

The Government opposed the discovery motion, arguing, among other things, that there was no evidence or allegation "that the Government has acted unfairly or has prosecuted non-black defendants or failed to prosecute them." The District Court granted the motion. It ordered the Government (1) to provide a list of all cases from the last three years in which the Government charged both cocaine and firearms offenses, (2) to identify the race of the defendants in those cases, (3) to identify what levels of law enforcement were involved in the investigations of those cases, and (4) to explain its criteria for deciding to prosecute those defendants for federal cocaine offenses.

The Government moved for reconsideration of the District Court's discovery order. With this motion it submitted affidavits and other evidence to explain why it had chosen to prosecute respondents and why respondents' study did not support the inference that the Government was singling out blacks for cocaine prosecution. The federal and local agents participating in the case alleged in affidavits that race played no role in their investigation. An Assistant United States Attorney explained in an affidavit that the decision to prosecute met the general criteria for prosecution, because

> "there was over 100 grams of cocaine base involved, over twice the threshold necessary for a ten year mandatory minimum sentence; there were multiple sales involving multiple defendants, thereby indicating a fairly substantial crack cocaine ring; . . . there were multiple federal firearms violations intertwined with the narcotics trafficking; the overall evidence in the case was extremely strong, including audio and videotapes of defendants; . . . and several of the defendants had criminal histories including narcotics and firearms violations."

The Government also submitted sections of a published 1989 Drug Enforcement Administration report which concluded that "large-scale, interstate trafficking networks controlled by Jamaicans, Haitians and Black street gangs dominate the manufacture and distribution of crack."

In response, one of respondents' attorneys submitted an affidavit alleging that an intake coordinator at a drug treatment center had told her that there are "an equal number of caucasian users and dealers to minority users and dealers." Respondents also submitted an affidavit from a criminal defense attorney alleging that in his experience many nonblacks are prosecuted in state court for crack offenses, and a newspaper article reporting that Federal "crack criminals . . . are being punished far more severely than if they had been caught with powder cocaine, and almost every single one of them is black," Newton, Harsher Crack Sentences Criticized as Racial Inequity, Los Angeles Times, Nov. 23, 1992, p. 1.

The District Court denied the motion for reconsideration. When the Government indicated it would not comply with the court's discovery order, the court dismissed the case.

A divided three-judge panel of the Court of Appeals for the Ninth Circuit reversed, holding that, because of the proof requirements for a selective-prosecution claim, defendants must "provide a colorable basis for believing that 'others similarly situated have not been prosecuted'" to obtain discovery. (Quoting United States v. Wayte, 710 F.2d 1385, 1387 (C.A.9 1983), aff'd, 470 U.S. 598 (1985)). The Court of Appeals voted to rehear the case en banc, and the en banc panel affirmed the District Court's order of dismissal, holding that "a defendant is not required to demonstrate that the government has failed to prosecute others who are similarly situated." We granted certiorari to determine the appropriate standard for discovery for a selective-prosecution claim.

[The Court held that Federal Rule of Criminal Procedure 16 did not mandate disclosure of material supporting a selective prosecution claim. That Rule requires disclosure of documents "material to the preparation of the defendant's defense" and the Court construed that phrase to refer to a defense that was responsive to the government's case-in-chief (e.g., that the defendant is not guilty). A selective prosecution attack was not material to the "defense" in this sense. See the discussion of this aspect of the opinion in Chapter 8, infra.]

* * *

A selective-prosecution claim is not a defense on the merits to the criminal charge itself, but an independent assertion that the prosecutor has brought the charge for reasons forbidden by the Constitution. Our cases delineating the necessary elements to prove a claim of selective prosecution have taken great pains to explain that the standard is a demanding one.* * *

A selective-prosecution claim asks a court to exercise judicial power over a "special province" of the Executive. The Attorney General and United States Attorneys retain broad discretion to enforce the Nation's criminal laws. * * * In the ordinary case, so long as the prosecutor has probable cause to believe that the accused committed an offense defined by statute, the decision whether or not to prosecute, and what charge to file or bring before a grand jury, generally rests entirely in his discretion.

Of course, a prosecutor's discretion is subject to constitutional constraints. One of these constraints, imposed by the equal protection component of the Due Process Clause of the Fifth Amendment, is that the decision whether to prosecute may not be based on "an unjustifiable standard such as race, religion, or other arbitrary classification," Oyler v. Boles, 368 U.S. 448, 456 (1962). A defendant may demonstrate that the administration of a criminal law is "directed so exclusively against a particular class of persons . . . with a mind so unequal and oppressive" that the system of prosecution amounts to "a practical denial" of equal protection of the law. Yick Wo v. Hopkins, 118 U.S. 356, 373 (1886).

In order to dispel the presumption that a prosecutor has not violated equal protection, a criminal defendant must present "clear evidence to the contrary." We explained in *Wayte* why courts are "properly hesitant to examine the decision whether to prosecute." Judicial deference to the decisions of these executive officers rests in part on an assessment of the relative competence of prosecutors and courts. "Such factors as the strength of the case, the prosecution's general deterrence value, the Government's enforcement priorities, and the case's relationship to the Government's overall enforcement plan are not readily susceptible to the kind of analysis the courts are competent to undertake." It also stems from a concern not to unnecessarily impair the performance of a core executive constitutional function. "Examining the basis of a prosecution delays the criminal proceeding, threatens to chill law enforcement by subjecting the prosecutor's motives and decisionmaking to outside inquiry, and may undermine prosecutorial effectiveness by revealing the Government's enforcement policy."

The requirements for a selective-prosecution claim draw on ordinary equal protection standards. The claimant must demonstrate that the federal prosecutorial policy had a discriminatory effect and that it was motivated by a discriminatory purpose. To establish a discriminatory effect in a race case, the claimant must show that similarly situated individuals of a different race were not prosecuted. * * *

The similarly situated requirement does not make a selective-prosecution claim impossible to prove. [In Yick Wo v. Hopkins], we invalidated an ordinance, * * * adopted by San Francisco, that prohibited the operation of laundries in wooden buildings. The plaintiff in error successfully demonstrated that the ordinance was applied against Chinese nationals but not against other laundry-shop operators. The authorities had denied the applications of 200 Chinese subjects for permits to operate shops in wooden buildings, but granted the applications of 80 individuals who were not Chinese subjects to operate laundries in wooden buildings "under similar conditions."

* * *

Having reviewed the requirements to prove a selective-prosecution claim, we turn to the showing necessary to obtain discovery in support of such a claim. If discovery is ordered, the Government must assemble from its own files documents which might corroborate or refute the defendant's claim. Discovery thus imposes many of the costs present when the Government must respond to a prima facie case of selective prosecution. It will divert prosecutors' resources and may disclose the Government's prosecutorial strategy. The justifications for a rigorous standard for the elements of a selective-prosecution claim thus require a correspondingly rigorous standard for discovery in aid of such a claim.

The parties, and the Courts of Appeals which have considered the requisite showing to establish entitlement to discovery, describe this showing with a variety of phrases, like "colorable basis," "substantial threshold showing," "substantial and concrete basis," or "reasonable likelihood". However, the many labels for this showing conceal the degree of consensus about the evidence necessary to meet it. The Courts of Appeals "require some evidence tending to show the existence of the essential elements of the defense," discriminatory effect and discriminatory intent. United States v. Berrios, 501 F.2d 1207, 1211 (C.A.2 1974).

In this case we consider what evidence constitutes "some evidence tending to show the existence" of the discriminatory effect element. The Court of Appeals held that a defendant may establish a colorable basis for discriminatory effect without evidence that the Government has failed to prosecute others who are similarly situated to the defendant. We think it was mistaken in this view. The vast majority of the Courts of Appeals require the defendant to produce some evidence that similarly situated defendants of other races could have been prosecuted, but were not, and this requirement is consistent with our equal protection case law. As the three-judge panel explained," selective prosecution implies that a selection has taken place."

The Court of Appeals reached its decision in part because it started "with the presumption that people of all races commit all types of crimes—not with the premise that any type of crime is the exclusive province of any particular racial or ethnic group." It cited no authority for this proposition, which seems contradicted by the most recent statistics of the United States Sentencing Commission. Those statistics show that: More than 90% of the persons sentenced in 1994 for crack cocaine trafficking were black; 93.4% of convicted LSD dealers were white.; and 91% of those convicted for pornography or prostitution were white (Table 13). Presumptions at war with presumably reliable statistics have no proper place in the analysis of this issue.

The Court of Appeals also expressed concern about the "evidentiary obstacles defendants face." But all of its sister Circuits that have confronted the issue have required that defendants produce some evidence of differential treatment of similarly situated members of other races or protected classes. In the present case, if the claim of selective prosecution were well founded, it should not have been an insuperable task to prove that persons of other races were being treated differently than respondents. For instance, respondents could have investigated whether similarly situated persons of other races were prosecuted by the State of California, were known to federal law enforcement officers, but were not prosecuted in federal court. We think the required threshold—a credible showing of different treatment of similarly situated persons—adequately balances the Government's interest in vigorous prosecution and the defendant's interest in avoiding selective prosecution.

In the case before us, respondents' "study" did not constitute "some evidence tending to show the existence of the essential elements of" a selective-prosecution claim. The study failed to identify individuals who were not black, could have been prosecuted for the offenses for which respondents were charged, but were not so prosecuted. This omission was not remedied by respondents' evidence in opposition to the Government's motion for reconsideration. The newspaper article, which discussed the discriminatory effect of federal drug sentencing laws, was not relevant to an allegation of discrimination in decisions to prosecute. Respondents' affidavits, which recounted one attorney's conversation with a drug treatment center employee and the experience of another attorney defending drug prosecutions in state court, recounted hearsay and reported personal conclusions based on anecdotal evidence. The judgment of the Court of Appeals is therefore reversed, and the case is remanded for proceedings consistent with this opinion.

[The concurring opinions of JUSTICES SOUTER, GINSBURG and BREYER are omitted.]

JUSTICE STEVENS, dissenting.

* * *

[I]t is undisputed that the brunt of the elevated federal penalties [for crack cocaine] falls heavily on blacks. While 65% of the persons who have used crack are white, in 1993 they represented only 4% of the federal offenders convicted of trafficking in crack. Eighty-eight percent of such defendants were black.. * * *

The extraordinary severity of the imposed penalties and the troubling racial patterns of enforcement give rise to a special concern about the fairness of charging practices for crack offenses. * * * In my view, the District Judge, who has sat on both the federal and the state benches in Los Angeles, acted well within her discretion to call for the development of facts that would demonstrate what standards, if any, governed the choice of forum where similarly situated offenders are prosecuted.

Critique of Armstrong

Professor Davis, in Prosecution and Race: The Power and Privilege of Discretion, 67 Fordham L.Rev. 13 (1998), provides the following critique on the intent-based test of selective prosecution set forth by the Court in *Armstrong*:

> * * * Instead of focusing on the harm experienced by African Americans as a result of actions by state actors, the Court has focused on whether the act itself is inherently invidious and whether the actor intended to cause the harm. In addition, the Court has placed the burden of proving intent on the shoulders of the victim. * * *

> The main problem with this intent-focused analysis is that it is backward-looking. Although perhaps adequate in combating straightforward and explicit discrimination as it existed in the past, it is totally deficient as a remedy for the more complex and systemic discrimination that African Americans currently experience. When state actors openly expressed their racist views, it was easy to identify and label the invidious nature of their actions. But today, with some notable exceptions, most racist behavior is not openly expressed. More significantly, some racist behavior is committed unconsciously, and many who engage in this behavior are well-intentioned people who would be appalled by the notion that they would be seen as behaving in a racist or discriminatory manner.

> Unconscious racism, although arguably less offensive than purposeful discrimination, is no less harmful. In fact, in many ways it is more perilous because it is often unrecognizable to the victim as well as the perpetrator. And the Court, by focusing on intent rather than harm, has refused to recognize, much less provide a remedy for, this most common and widespread form of racism. * * *

For another critique of the *Armstrong* standards, see McAdams, Race and Selective Prosecution: Discovering the Pitfalls of *Armstrong*, 73 Chicago-Kent L.Rev. 605 (1998).

Unprosecuted Similar Conduct

In United States v. Parham, 16 F.3d 844 (8th Cir.1994), the defendants were African-Americans who were convicted of voting more than once in the same Arkansas election. The defendants, pursuing selective prosecution claims, proffered evidence of numerous voter irregularities attributable to whites that went unprosecuted. These included episodes where African-American disabled or elderly voters were refused assistance while whites were helped, and cases of intimidation of African-American voters by whites brandishing guns. While the court found that these acts by whites warranted prosecution, they were held irrelevant to the defendants' selective prosecution claims. This is because the acts by whites were

> not sufficiently similar to the acts of voter fraud for which Parham and Johnson were prosecuted to constitute a prima facie case of selective prosecution. Parham and Johnson were in effect charged with forging names on absentee ballots. They presented no evidence that other's acts of absentee ballot forgery or fraud were tolerated without prosecution. Where a defendant cannot show anyone in a similar situation who was not prosecuted, he has not met the threshold point of showing that there has been selectivity in prosecution.

Judge Heaney dissented in *Parham*, reasoning that the defendant need only establish that unprosecuted crimes are *similar*, not that they are identical.

Example of a Case in Which Discovery Was Ordered on a Selective Prosecution Claim

United States v. Jones, 159 F.3d 969 (6th Cir.1998), is one of the rare cases in which discovery was ordered to permit investigation of a selective prosecution claim, after the defendant was convicted of drugs and weapons offenses. The shocking facts were related by the court as follows:

> Jones argues on appeal that he was prosecuted based on his race, citing to the Government's decision to prosecute him in federal court instead of state court and the egregious and unprofessional conduct of the arresting local law enforcement officers, Kerry Nelson and Terry Spence.
>
> The conduct of officers Nelson and Spence was undeniably shameful. Prior to the planned arrest of Jones and his wife, the two officers had t-shirts made with Jones's picture emblazoned on the front accompanied by the printed words, "See ya, wouldn't want to be ya" above the picture, and below, "going back to prison." On the back of the t-shirts appeared a picture of Jones's wife, a co-defendant, with the words, "wait on me, Slow, [Jones' nickname was "Slow Motion"] I am

coming, too." The two officers were wearing the t-shirts when they arrested Jones in August of 1995. Over one year later, while on a Caribbean cruise, Officer Spence mailed a postcard purchased in Jamaica to Jones while he was in custody awaiting trial. Jones regards Spence's mailing of the postcard, that pictured a black woman with a basket of bananas on her head, as a racial insult. On the postcard, postmarked from Cozumel, Mexico on October 24, 1996, appeared the following handwritten message:

> Slow Motion. What's up? Haven't talked to you since you were in court and lost all your motions. Sorry, but life goes on. Just wanted to drop you a line and let you know that Cozumel, Mexico is beautiful. I'm on vacation and I'll be back Monday for trial, and chances are good you're going to jail for a long time. See ya, Officer Spence.

Spence testified that he sent the postcard to relieve "stress I was feeling while I was on the cruise." Regarding the t-shirts, Spence explained that "It was just—I took pride in arresting [Jones]." Nelson also testified that he wore the t-shirt to demonstrate "a great deal of pride in Mr. Jones's arrest."

In addition, there was testimony at the hearing with respect to Jones's claim that local law enforcement agents improperly referred his case for federal prosecution based on his race. [Federal prosecution subjected to the defendants to much harsher sentencing penalties]. The testimony showed that the Murfreesboro Police Department had referred fourteen defendants, including Jones and his Caucasian co-defendant, Donnie Billings, for federal prosecution in the preceding five years. Of those fourteen defendants, four were African-American, two were Columbian, two were Lebanese, one was Israeli and five were Caucasian. Of the cases referred for federal prosecution in the preceding five years, however, only Jones's and Billings's prosecutions involved crack cocaine. Further, Jones presented evidence of eight non-African-American defendants prosecuted for crack cocaine offenses who were not referred for federal prosecution.

The court found that Jones had established a prima facie case of discriminatory intent, which is the first part of the intent/impact test imposed by *Armstrong*.

The court found, however, that there was not enough evidence of discriminatory impact to require dismissal of the indictment. Yet there was enough to justify further discovery.

3. Choice of Forum

In the American system of dual sovereignty, the same criminal conduct is often prosecutable under either federal or state law. It is also possible for the choice of forum to be outcome-determinative. For example, in drug cases—as indicated in *Jones* above—the relevant sentencing laws generally provide for much harsher sentences than could be given for the same conduct in a state prosecution. Suppose that the defendant can show that a federal prosecution was brought in order to trigger the harsher federal sentences—but unlike in *Jones, supra,* there is no allegation that the decision was based on racial or other discriminatory grounds. Is the defendant entitled to relief?

A typical response to a challenge to the prosecutor's choice of forum is found in United States v. Jacobs, 4 F.3d 603 (8th Cir.1993), a case in which the defendant would have received probation had he been convicted on state charges, but instead received a five-year prison sentence after being convicted in federal court. As the court noted:

> Prosecutors have broad discretion in making prosecutive decisions. So long as the prosecutor has probable cause to believe that the accused committed an offense defined by statute, the decision whether or not to prosecute, and what charge to file, generally rests entirely in his discretion. In exercising this discretion, the prosecutor may take into account the penalties available upon conviction. The prosecutor may not, of course, base the decision to prosecute upon impermissible factors such as race, religion, or other arbitrary and unjustifiable classifications. Likewise the prosecutor may not file charges out of vindictiveness nor in retaliation for a defendant's exercise of legal rights.

> The fact that the federal government prosecutes a federal crime in a federal court that could have been or has been prosecuted as a state crime in a state court does not itself violate due process. Choice of forum lies within the realm of prosecutorial discretion.

See also United States v. Dockery, 965 F.2d 1112 (D.C.Cir.1992) (it was permissible for the U.S. Attorney in the District of Columbia to terminate prosecutions in the D.C. Superior Court and reinstitute them in the U.S. District Court a block away to take advantage of the sterner penalties set by the federal sentencing law; defendant received a ten-year minimum sentence, which would have been 1–5 years in the Superior Court); United States v. Williams, 963 F.2d 1337 (10th Cir.1992) (defendant received 20 years under federal law, and would have received 5 years under state law: "prosecution in a federal rather than a state court does not violate due process despite the absence of guidelines for such referral"); United States v. Ucciferri, 960 F.2d 953 (11th Cir.1992) (it was irrelevant that a federal prosecution was motivated by a desire to avoid more rigorous state constitutional protections).

4. Choice of Crime

What if two criminal statutes cover the same conduct—does the prosecutor have the discretion to charge under the statute resulting in the longer prison sentence? In United States v. Batchelder, 442 U.S. 114 (1979), Justice Marshall wrote for the Court as it held that a defendant who was convicted of receiving a firearm that had traveled in interstate commerce could be sentenced to five years' imprisonment, the maximum term under the statute, and that he was not entitled to be sentenced under another statute that punished felons for transporting firearms with a maximum penalty of two years. Justice Marshall reasoned that a wrongdoer has notice that more than one statute covers his conduct. Thus, the fact that conduct violates two statutes does not require a prosecution under the more lenient of them. The Court emphasized the deference due to the prosecutor in making a charging decision and reiterated that a defendant's sole complaint is against invidious discrimination.

Prosecutors may, however, be limited in their ability to charge a defendant in a certain way as punishment for a defendant's exercise of constitutional rights. The subject of vindictive prosecutions is considered in Chapter 12, infra.

IV.   THE GRAND JURY

The American criminal justice system, like the American political system, has checks and balances to prevent against too much centralized authority being placed in the hands of the executive. In some instances, depending on the jurisdiction and the seriousness of the crime, the grand jury operates as a check on the prosecutor's decision to charge. In other instances, the preliminary hearing serves this function. In some rare instances, both checks are available. Where a minor offense is charged, it is possible that no pretrial screening procedure will be utilized. This section will focus on the grand jury and how it operates.

A.   BACKGROUND ON THE GRAND JURY

The Ninth Circuit, in United States v. Navarro-Vargas, 408 F.3d 1184 (9th Cir. 2005) provides a good summary of the history and purpose of the grand jury, and addresses critiques about its modern function. The court relies on an extensive list of sources, most of which are deleted from the entry below.

The Historical Role of the Grand Jury

1.   The Early English Grand Jury: Quasi-Prosecutor

The modern grand jury is a direct descendant of the English grand jury first employed more than 800 years ago. Its origins belie its modern role as intermediary between the people and their government. The earliest grand juries were the tool of the Crown. In 1164, anxious to consolidate power held by the church and feudal barons, King Henry II signed the Constitutions of Clarendon, which created a jury to charge all laity who were to be tried in ecclesiastical courts. Two years later he established the Assize of Clarendon, which was composed of twelve men who would "present" those suspected of crimes to the royal courts. These acts reasserted the King's power over his subjects and filled his coffers with the proceeds from chattels confiscated after conviction.

During its first hundred years, * * * the English grand jury was somewhat like a quasi-prosecutor for the King. Indeed, grand juries were expected to bring charges based on their own knowledge, as well as consider charges brought by prosecutors. * * *

The first real evidence of the grand jury acting as a shield to protect the accused was in 1681 when two London grand juries refused to indict the Earl of Shaftesbury and his follower Stephen Colledge, the political enemies of King Charles II. The King wanted them held over for public proceedings before the grand jury, but the grand jury insisted on conducting its inquiry in private. Given its powerful influence, the Crown expected a quick indictment pursuant to its charges. However, the grand jury returned the equivalent of a no-bill in the matter, defying the Crown's will both in holding private proceedings and in its ultimate decision not to indict. The Shaftesbury and Colledge cases established grand jury secrecy, which continues to be a crucial element in grand juries serving as an independent screen. * * *

2. The Colonial Grand Jury: Quasi-Legislative, Quasi-Administrative

American colonists adopted the grand jury as integral to the common law system. * * * In America, the institution gained broad powers to propose legislation and perform various administrative tasks. Grand juries "exercised broad, unorthodox powers," inspecting roads, jails, and other public buildings; monitoring public works expenditures, construction and maintenance; proposing new legislation; and criticizing poor administration. The colonial grand jury still performed a quasi-prosecutorial role by accusing individuals suspected of crimes, but colonial grand juries demonstrated greater independence than their English counterparts, due in part to the relatively weak position of colonial governments. With their expanding quasi-legislative and quasi-administrative roles, grand juries acquired greater popularity because they were regarded as more representative of the people. * * * [T]he American grand jury in effect enjoyed a roving commission to ferret out official malfeasance or self-dealing of any sort and bring it to the attention of the public at large * * *. Following the English traditions established in the Shaftesbury and Colledge cases, grand jury secrecy remained an important part of grand jury proceedings in the colonies. Grand jurors pledged to an oath of secrecy, and its violation was both a contempt and a crime.

While Colonial grand juries continued to serve as accusatory bodies, they occasionally refused to return indictments in high-profile cases. The most celebrated example in American history is that of John Peter Zenger, a newspaper publisher charged with libel after criticizing the Governor of New York. Based on the jury instructions, it seems clear that Zenger was guilty of the crime of libel. Nevertheless, three grand juries refused to indict not because of insufficient evidence but rather because the jurors were politically opposed to the prosecutions. As the Revolutionary War drew closer, the grand jury became popular at least as much from its success as a political weapon as from its role in the criminal justice system. * * * Grand jurors, selected from the public, frustrated prosecutors loyal to the king by refusing to indict those charged under unpopular laws imposed by the Crown, often on the urging of colonial judges. Grand jury presentments served an additional function during this time: they became excellent mediums of propaganda as grand juries issued stinging denunciations of Great Britain and stirring defenses of their rights as Englishmen. * * *

* * * In early debates over the ratification of the Constitution, before the Bill of Rights had been written, some feared that "there is no provision . . . to prevent the attorney-general from filing information against any person, whether he is indicted by the grand jury or not; in consequence of which the most innocent person in the commonwealth may be taken by virtue of a warrant issued in consequence of such information. . . ." Because of this fear, the Grand Jury Clause, located in the Fifth Amendment, was adopted with little debate or discussion.

3.   The Post-Revolutionary and Nineteenth Century Grand Jury: Screening Function

As they had in colonial times, nineteenth century grand juries occasionally asserted their independence by refusing to indict under unpopular laws, even when the grand jury was instructed to indict if the facts satisfied the law. Prominently, grand juries in Kentucky and Mississippi refused to indict former Vice President Aaron Burr, although he was finally indicted in Virginia; refused to indict Americans who aided French privateers in violation of the Neutrality Proclamation of 1793; and resisted indicting those accused of violating the controversial Alien and Sedition Acts. Throughout the nineteenth century, courts continued to recognize the necessity of secrecy in grand jury proceedings. This secrecy allowed grand juries to independently determine whether to indict, despite a judge's instructions.

* * *

The political potential in the screening function of the grand jury was * * * manifest during the Civil War era. Prior to the war, Southern grand juries readily indicted those involved in crimes related to abolition of the slave trade, while Northern grand juries were slow to indict those charged with violations of the fugitive slave laws. Following the Civil War, Southern grand juries frustrated enforcement of Reconstruction-era laws by refusing to indict Ku Klux Klan members and others accused of committing crimes against newly-freed blacks. * * *

4.   *The Modern Grand Jury*

By the twentieth century, dramatic confrontations between prosecutors and jurors in grand jury proceedings had become rare. Currently, grand jurors no longer perform any other function but to investigate crimes and screen indictments, and they tend to indict in the overwhelming number of cases brought by prosecutors. Because of this, many criticize the modern grand jury as no more than a "rubber stamp" for the prosecutor. *See* Federal Justice Statistics Resource Center, Federal Justice Statistics Database, *at* http://fjsrc.urban.org (noting that federal grand juries returned only twenty-one no-bills in 2001). * * * As the grand jury's tendency to indict has become more pronounced, some commentators claim that the modern grand jury has lost its independence. * * * Against this criticism, the Supreme Court has steadfastly insisted that the grand jury remains as a shield against unfounded prosecutions.

So as a historical matter, the grand jury served two major functions. On one hand, it was a "buffer" protecting citizens from unjust prosecution by the state. On the other hand, it served an enforcement function by investigating incidents or offenses that the grand jurors thought suspicious. These functions were considered so important that they are expressed in the Fifth Amendment, which states in relevant part:

> No person shall be held to answer for a capital, or otherwise infamous crime, unless on a presentment or indictment of a Grand Jury, except in cases arising in the land or naval forces, or in the Militia, when in actual service in time of War or public danger; * * *.

The Supreme Court has stated that the grand jury's dual historic functions "survive to this day. Its responsibilities continue to include both the determination whether there is probable cause to believe a crime has been committed and the protection of citizens against unfounded criminal prosecutions." United States v. Calandra, 414 U.S. 338 (1974).

Many observers, however, see the modern grand jury as performing only the first (prosecutorial) function and ignoring the second (protective) function. For example, Hafetz and Pellettieri conclude that

> whatever its historic antecedents, the grand jury has long ceased to function as an independent entity acting both as shield for the citizenry as well as sword for the prosecutor. * * * [T]he grand jury functions as an investigative tool of the prosecutor. Employing the power of compulsory process in a secret proceeding the prosecutor investigates and determines with virtually no check by the grand jury who gets indicted and for what.

Time to Reform the Grand Jury, The Champion, at 12 (Jan. 1999).

As you read the materials in this Chapter, consider whether the assessment of the grand jury as only a tool for the prosecutor is correct, and if so, whether reforms can be instituted to return the grand jury to its role as protector of citizens from unfounded prosecutions.

A Right Not Incorporated

Unlike most other provisions of the Bill of Rights examined thus far, the right to a grand jury indictment does not extend to defendants accused of state crimes. In Hurtado v. California, 110 U.S. 516 (1884), the Supreme Court held that the right to a grand jury indictment is not incorporated in the Due Process Clause of the Fourteenth Amendment. Today, slightly less than half the states require prosecution by indictment for serious crimes as a matter of state constitutional or statutory law. The majority of the states use the alternatives of preliminary hearing and the filing of an information, methods of charging discussed later in this Chapter.

What Is an Infamous Crime?

The Fifth Amendment requires a grand jury indictment for the prosecution of an "infamous crime." Courts have held that a crime is "infamous" only if it can result in either hard labor or imprisonment in a penitentiary. Ex parte Wilson, 114 U.S. 417 (1885). Thus, the court in United States v. Armored Transport, Inc., 629 F.2d 1313 (9th Cir.1980), held that an indictment was not constitutionally required for a corporation to be convicted of an antitrust felony—a corporation is subject only to a fine and a fine is not an infamous punishment. See also United States v. Colt, 126 F.3d 981 (7th Cir.1997) (no right to grand jury indictment where statute authorized imprisonment in a federal prison camp, but not in a federal penitentiary: "The distinction between penitentiaries and other places of imprisonment survives in today's federal prison system. * * * Only eight of the Bureau of Prisons' institutions are designated as U.S. Penitentiaries, which feature the highest security and the closest control of prisoner actions.").

How the Grand Jury Works

The court in In re Motions of Dow Jones & Co., 142 F.3d 496 (D.C.Cir.1998), provided this summary of the operation of the grand jury:

> Grand juries summon witnesses and documents with subpoenas. Witnesses, including custodians of documents, report on the scheduled date not to a courtroom, but to a hallway outside the room where the grand jury is sitting. The witness must enter the grand jury room alone, without his or her lawyer. No judge presides and none is present. See Beale et al., Grand Jury Law and Practice § 4.10, at 4–44 (2d ed.1997). Inside the grand jury room are sixteen to twenty-three grand jurors, one or more prosecuting attorneys, and a court reporter. 18 U.S.C. § 3321; Fed.R.Crim.P. 6. The witness is sworn, and questioning commences, all to the end of determining whether "there is adequate basis for bringing a criminal charge." United States v. Williams, 504 U.S. 36 (1992). Other than witnesses, each person present in the grand jury room or otherwise assisting the prosecutor is forbidden from disclosing matters occurring before the grand jury, Fed.R.Crim.P. 6.

The court explained judicial oversight of the grand jury in the following paragraph:

> Although the grand jury normally operates, of course, in the courthouse and under judicial auspices, its institutional relationship with the Judicial Branch has traditionally been, so to speak, at arm's length. Still, at many points, from service of the subpoena through the completion of the witness's grand jury appearance, judicial proceedings relating to the grand jury may take place. The judge may be called upon to decide a witness's motion to postpone the date of testimony or to quash the subpoena. If a witness refuses to answer questions on the basis of a testimonial privilege, such as attorney-client or husband-wife, the grand jury may seek a court order compelling the witness to answer. This may be done forthwith, through an oral presentation to the court, or upon the filing of pleadings, followed by a hearing. A hearing will also be needed if a witness asserts his or her privilege against self-incrimination, and the prosecutor seeks an order from the court granting the witness immunity. See 18 U.S.C. § 6003(a).

B. THE CHARGE TO THE GRAND JURY

What follows are excerpts from the Model Grand Jury Charge approved by the Judicial Conference of the United States. It provides a useful introduction to the work of the grand jury and the expectations that the community has for this body. The charge is given by the judge who empanels and supervises the grand jury. https://cldc.org/wp-content/uploads/2012/10/model-gj-charge.pdf.

MODEL GRAND JURY CHARGE

Ladies and Gentlemen:

1.   Now that you have been empaneled and sworn as a Grand Jury, it is the Court's responsibility to instruct you as to the law which should govern your actions and your deliberations as Grand Jurors.

2.   * * * The purpose of the Grand Jury is to determine whether there is sufficient evidence to justify a formal accusation against a person—that is, to determine if there is "probable cause" to believe the person committed a crime. If law enforcement officials were not required to submit to an impartial grand jury proof of guilt as to a proposed charge against a person suspected of having committed a crime, they would be free to arrest a suspect and bring that suspect to trial no matter how little evidence existed to support the charge.

3.   The Grand Jury is an independent body and does not belong to any branch of the government. As members of the Grand Jury, you, in a very real sense, stand between the government and the person being investigated by the government. A federal grand jury must never be made an instrument of private prejudice, vengeance, or malice. It is your duty to see to it that indictments are returned only against those who you find probable cause to believe are guilty and to see to it that the innocent are not compelled to go to trial.

4.   A member of the Grand Jury who is related by blood or marriage to a person under investigation, or who knows that person well enough to have a biased state of mind as to that person, or is biased for any reason, should not participate in the investigation of that person or in the return of the indictment. This does not mean that if you have an opinion you should not participate in the investigation. However, it does mean that if you have a fixed opinion before you hear any evidence, either on a basis of friendship or ill will or some other similar motivation, you should not participate in that investigation and in voting on the indictment.

5.   Sixteen of the twenty-three members of the Grand Jury constitute a quorum and must be present for the transaction of any business. If fewer than this number are present, even for a moment, the proceedings of the Grand Jury must stop.

Limitation on the Power of the Grand Jury

6. Although as Grand Jurors you have extensive powers, they are limited in several important respects.

7. You can only investigate conduct which violates federal criminal laws. Criminal activity which violates state law is outside your inquiry. Sometimes, though, the same conduct violates both federal and state law, and this you may properly consider.

8. There is also a geographic limitation on the scope of your inquiries in the exercise of your power. You may inquire only to federal offenses committed in this district.

9. You cannot judge the wisdom of the criminal laws enacted by Congress, that is, whether or not there should or should not be a federal law designating certain activity as criminal. That is to be determined by Congress and not by you.[8]

10. Furthermore, when deciding whether or not to indict, you should not consider punishment in the event of conviction.

The Grand Jury Procedures

11. The cases which you will hear will come before you in various ways. Frequently, suspects are arrested during or shortly after the commission of an alleged crime, and they are taken before a Magistrate Judge, who then holds a preliminary hearing to determine whether there is probable cause to believe that the person has committed a crime. If the Magistrate Judge finds such probable cause, he or she will direct that the person be held for the action of the Grand Jury so that you can independently consider whether there should be an indictment.

12. Other cases will be brought before you by a government attorney—the U.S. Attorney or an Assistant U.S. Attorney before an arrest but after an investigation has been conducted by a governmental agency such as the Federal Bureau of Investigation, the Treasury Department, the Drug Enforcement Administration, Postal Authorities, or other federal law enforcement officials.

13. Since the government attorney has the duty of prosecuting persons charged with the commission of federal crimes, the government attorney will present the matters which the government desires to have you consider. The government will point out to you the laws which it believes have been violated, and will subpoena for testimony before you such witnesses as the government attorney may

---

[8] The court in United States v. Navarro-Vargas, 408 F.3d 1184 (9th Cir. 2005), rejected the defendants' claim that this charge unconstitutionally impinged upon the grand jury's independence. See the discussion on grand jury nullification later in this Chapter.

consider important and necessary and also any other witnesses that you may request or direct be called before you.

14. If during the course of your hearings, a different crime other than the one you are investigating surfaces, you have the right to pursue this new crime. Although you can subpoena new witnesses and documents, you have no power to employ investigators or to expend federal funds for investigative purposes. If the government attorney refuses to assist you or if you believe he or she is not acting impartially, you may take it up with me or any Judge of this Court. You may use this power even over the active opposition of the government's attorneys, if you believe it is necessary to do so in the interest of justice.

Evidence

15. The evidence you will consider will normally consist of oral testimony of witnesses and written documents. Each witness will appear before you separately. When the witness first appears before you, the Grand Jury foreperson will administer the witness an oath or affirmation, to testify truthfully. After this has been accomplished, the witness may be questioned. Ordinarily, the government attorney questions the witness first. Next, the foreperson may question the witness, and then any other members of the Grand Jury may ask questions. In the event a witness does not speak or understand the English language, an interpreter may be brought into the Grand Jury room to assist in the questioning.

16. Witnesses should be treated courteously and questions put to them in an orderly fashion. If you have any doubt whether it is proper to ask a particular question, ask the government attorney for advice. If necessary, a ruling may be obtained from the court.

17. You alone decide how many witnesses you want to hear. You can subpoena witnesses from anywhere in the country, directing the government attorney to issue necessary subpoenas. However, persons should not ordinarily be subjected to disruption of their daily lives, harassed, annoyed, or inconvenienced, nor should public funds be expended to bring in witnesses unless you believe they can provide meaningful evidence which will assist you in your investigation.

18. Every witness has certain rights when appearing before a Grand Jury. Witnesses have the right to refuse to answer any question if the answer would tend to incriminate them and the right to know that anything they say may be used against them. The Grand Jury should hold no prejudice against a witness who exercises the right against compulsory self-incrimination, and this can play no part in the return of any indictment.

19. Although witnesses are not permitted to have a lawyer present with them in the Grand Jury room, the law permits witnesses to confer with their lawyer outside of the Grand Jury room. Since an appearance before a Grand Jury may present complex legal problems requiring the assistance of a lawyer, you also can not hold it against a witness if a witness chooses to exercise this right and leaves the Grand Jury room to confer with an attorney.

20. Ordinarily, neither the person being investigated by the government nor any witnesses on behalf of that person will testify before the Grand Jury. Upon his or her request, preferably in writing, you may afford that person an opportunity to appear before you. Because the appearance of the person being investigated before you may raise complicated legal problems, you should seek the government attorney's advice and, if necessary, the Court's ruling before his or her appearance is permitted. Before that person testifies, he or she must be advised of his or her rights and required to sign a formal waiver. You should be completely satisfied that the person being investigated understands what he or she is doing. * * *

21. The determination of whether a witness is telling the truth is something that you must decide. * * * You may consider in that regard whether the witnesses are personally interested in the outcome of the investigation, whether their testimony has been corroborated or supported by other witnesses or circumstances, what opportunity they have had for observing or acquiring knowledge concerning the matters about which they testify, the reasonableness or probability of the testimony they relate to you, and their manner and demeanor in testifying before you.

22. Hearsay is testimony as to facts not known by the witness of the witness's own personal knowledge but which have been told or related to the witness by persons other than the person being investigated. Hearsay testimony, if deemed by you to be persuasive, may in itself provide a basis for returning an indictment. You must be satisfied only that there is evidence against the accused showing probable cause, even if such evidence is composed of hearsay testimony that might or might not be admissible in evidence at a trial.

23. Frequently, charges are made against more than one person. It will be your duty to examine the evidence as it relates to each person, and to make your finding as to each person. In other words, where charges are made against more than one person, you may indict all of the persons or only those persons who you believe properly deserve indictment.

Deliberation and Vote

24. After you have heard all the evidence you wish to hear in a particular matter, you will then proceed to deliberate as to whether the person being investigated should be indicted. No one other than your own members or an interpreter necessary to assist a juror who is hearing or speech impaired is to be present while you are deliberating or voting.

25. To return an indictment charging an individual with an offense, it is not necessary that you find that individual guilty beyond a reasonable doubt. You are not a trial jury and your task is not to decide the guilt or innocence of the person charged. Your task is to determine whether the government's evidence as presented to you is sufficient to cause you to conclude that there is probable cause to believe that the person being investigated committed the offense charged. To put it another way, you should vote to indict where the evidence presented to you is sufficiently strong to warrant a reasonable person's belief that the person being investigated is probably guilty of the offense charged.

26. Each juror has the right to express his or her view of the matter under consideration. Only after all Grand Jurors have been given full opportunity to be heard will a vote be taken. You may decide after deliberation among yourselves that further evidence should be considered before a vote is taken. In such case you may direct to subpoena the additional documents or witnesses you desire to consider.

27. When you have decided to vote, the foreperson shall designate a juror as secretary who will keep a record of the vote, which shall be filed with the Clerk of Court. The record does not include the names of the jurors but only the number of those voting for the indictment. Remember, at least sixteen jurors must be present at all times, and at least twelve members must vote in favor of an indictment before one may be returned.

28. If twelve or more members of the Grand Jury, after deliberation, believe that an indictment is warranted, then you will request the government attorney to prepare the formal written indictment if one has not already been prepared and presented to you. The indictment will set forth the date and place of the alleged offense, will assert the circumstances making the alleged conduct criminal, and will identify the criminal statute violated. The foreperson will sign the indictment as a true bill, in the space followed by the word "foreperson." It is the duty of the foreperson to sign every indictment, whether the foreperson voted for or against. If less than twelve members of the Grand Jury vote in favor of an indictment which has

been submitted to you for your consideration, the foreperson will endorse the indictment "Not a True Bill" and return it to the Court and the Court will impound it.

29. Indictments which have been signed as a true bill will be presented to a Judge [or a Magistrate Judge] in open court by your foreperson at the conclusion of each deliberative session of the Grand Jury. In the absence of the foreperson, a deputy foreperson may act in place of the foreperson and perform all functions and duties of the foreperson.

Independence of the Grand Jury

30. It is extremely important for you to realize that * * * the Grand Jury is independent of the United States Attorney and is not an arm or agent of the Federal Bureau of Investigation, the Drug Enforcement Administration, the Internal Revenue Service, or any governmental agency charged with prosecuting a crime. Simply put, as I have already told you, the Grand Jury is an independent body and does not belong to any branch of the government.

31. However, as a practical matter you must work closely with the government attorneys. They will provide you with important service in helping you to find your way when confronted with complex legal matters. It is entirely proper that you should receive this assistance. If past experience is any indication of what to expect in the future, then you can expect candor, honesty and good faith in matters presented by the government attorneys.[9] However, ultimately, you must depend on your own independent judgment, never becoming an arm of the United States Attorney's office. The government attorneys are prosecutors. You are not. If the facts suggest that you should not indict, then you should not do so, even in the face of the opposition or statements of the government attorney. You would violate your oath if you merely "rubber-stamped" indictments brought before you by the government representatives.

* * *

The Obligation of Secrecy

33. Your proceedings are secret and must remain secret permanently unless and until the Court decrees otherwise. You cannot relate to your family, to the news or television reporters, or to anyone that which transpired in the Grand Jury room. There are several

---

[9] In *United States v. Navarro-Vargas*, 408 F.3d 1184 (9th Cir. 2005), the defendants challenged this instruction because it amounted to a "vote of confidence" by the judge on the honesty of government attorneys and therefore undermined the independence of the grand jury. The court rejected the defendants' argument by looking to the instruction as a whole, reasoning that the passage would be problematic if it stated that the Grand Jury was an agent of the U.S. Attorney—but it did not.

important reasons for this requirement. A premature disclosure of Grand Jury action may frustrate the ends of justice by giving an opportunity to the person being investigated to escape and become a fugitive or to destroy evidence. Also, if the testimony of a witness is disclosed, the witness may be subject to intimidation, retaliation, bodily injury, or other tampering before testifying at trial. Thirdly, the requirement of secrecy protects an innocent person who may have come under investigation but has been cleared by the actions of the Grand Jury. In the eyes of some, investigation by a Grand Jury alone carries with it a suggestion of guilt. Thus great injury can be done to a person's good name even though the person is not indicted. And fourth, the secrecy requirement helps to protect the members of the grand jury themselves from improper contacts by those under investigation. For all these reasons, therefore, the secrecy requirement is of the utmost importance and must be regarded by you as an absolute duty. If you violate your oath of secrecy, you may be subject to punishment.

34. To insure the secrecy of Grand Jury proceedings, the law provides that only authorized persons may be in the Grand Jury room while evidence is being presented. Only the members of the Grand Jury, the government attorney, the witness under examination, the court reporter, and an interpreter, if required, may be present.

* * *

C. THE PROCEDURES OF THE GRAND JURY

Rule 6 of the Federal Rules of Criminal Procedure illustrates typical procedures of the grand jury—providing for number of jurors (16 to 23), provisions on secrecy, and the process and requirements for handing down an indictment. State grand juries may have fewer members and operate somewhat differently. But, the limitations on who can be present in the grand jury room and other aspects of Rule 6 are common to most grand juries. See Fed.R.Crim.P. 6 in the Statutory Supplement.

Discriminatory Selection of Grand Jurors

The Equal Protection Clause prohibits racial or ethnic discrimination in the selection of grand jurors. See Rose v. Mitchell, 443 U.S. 545 (1979) (racial discrimination in the selection of grand jurors is a valid ground for setting aside a criminal conviction, even where the defendant has been found guilty beyond a reasonable doubt by a properly constituted petit jury at a trial that was free from other constitutional error). In Castaneda v. Partida, 430 U.S. 482 (1977), the Court established that statistics could be used to make out a prima facie case of discrimination against Mexican-Americans, even where a majority of a county's population were Mexican-Americans. Challenges under the Fourteenth Amendment are like all of the challenges to government action on the basis of suspect classifications. See also Jefferson v. Morgan, 962 F.2d 1185 (6th Cir.1992) (statistical evidence, adjusted by standard deviation, shows systematic exclusion of African-Americans from grand jury; conviction reversed and indictment dismissed; error was not harmless simply because the defendant was convicted at trial).

Discriminatory Selection of Grand Jury Forepersons

Chief Justice Burger wrote for the Court in Hobby v. United States, 468 U.S. 339 (1984), as it held that discrimination in the selection of grand jury forepersons and deputy forepersons in a federal district did not require reversal of a conviction. Chief Justice Burger condemned all discrimination in the selection of grand jurors, but found that the ministerial functions of the foreperson and the deputy added little to the role that any particular grand juror plays. Thus, as long as the grand jury itself was validly selected, discrimination in the selection of the two ministerial leaders did not prejudice the defendant.

Secrecy of Grand Jury Proceedings

The Supreme Court has consistently recognized the importance of grand jury secrecy:

> First, if preindictment proceedings were made public, many prospective witnesses would be hesitant to come forward voluntarily, knowing that those against whom they testify would be aware of that testimony. Moreover, witnesses who appeared before the grand jury would be less likely to testify fully and frankly, as they would be open to retribution as well as to inducements. There also would be the risk that those about to be indicted would flee, or would try to influence individual grand jurors to vote against indictment. Finally, by preserving the secrecy of the proceedings, we assure that persons who are accused but exonerated by the grand jury will not be held up to public ridicule.

Douglas Oil Co. v. Petrol Stops N.W., 441 U.S. 211 (1979).

Grand Jury Witnesses and Secrecy

Note that Federal Rule 6 does not require grand jury witnesses to maintain secrecy as to their own testimony. The argument has been made that a secrecy requirement for the witness's own testimony would be impractical. Do you agree with this? If witnesses are free to talk, how effective do you think the secrecy rule is likely to be?

D. THE RELATIONSHIP OF THE GRAND JURY TO THE PROSECUTOR AND TO THE COURT

The roles played by the prosecutor, the court, and the grand jury are not exactly the same in all jurisdictions. However, it is common for courts to view the prosecutor's relationship to the grand jury as subject to little, if any, judicial scrutiny. United States v. Chanen, 549 F.2d 1306 (9th Cir.1977), illustrates this. The government presented its case three times to a federal grand jury. The first time the government did not ask for an indictment, and no vote was taken before the grand jury was discharged. A second grand jury indictment was dismissed because no transcript was made, and the government failed to present the jury with the evidence presented to the first grand jury. On the third attempt, the government secured an indictment against defendants for statutory fraud. The government presented its evidence to the third grand jury by reading testimony from its first grand jury presentation. The district court quashed the indictment because the judge felt that where the first grand jury failed to indict on the basis of live testimony, a subsequent grand jury should hear live testimony as well. The court of appeals reversed. It held that the prosecutor's action was not "fundamentally unfair" and therefore did not constitute a basis for dismissal. It reasoned as follows:

As a practical matter, the grand jury generally relies on the prosecutor to determine what witnesses to call. Also, in practice the prosecutor conducts the examination of the witnesses and otherwise determines what evidence to present before the grand jury. In addition, it is the prosecutor who normally prepares the indictment, although of course the grand jury must review the indictment and adopt it as its own. Some of these functions—such as initiating a criminal case by presenting evidence before the grand jury—qualifies as an executive function within the exclusive prerogative of the Attorney General.

The court, on the other hand, exercises its power to summon witnesses to attend and to give testimony before the grand jury. Also, it is the court which must compel a witness to testify if, after appearing, he refuses to do so. In addition, the court exercises a form of authority over the grand jury when, for example, it dismisses an indictment for failure to charge all elements of the offense or to warn the defendant fairly of the charge against which he must defend. Likewise, the court exercises authority over the prosecutor when it dismisses an indictment because of prosecutorial misconduct. * * *

Nevertheless, given the constitutionally-based independence of each of the three actors—court, prosecutor and grand jury—we believe a court may not exercise its "supervisory power" in a way which encroaches on the prerogatives of the other two unless there is a clear basis in fact and law for doing so. If the district courts were not required to meet such a standard, their "supervisory power" could readily prove subversive of the doctrine of separation of powers.

Application of this standard to the present case requires reversal. The asserted legal basis for the district court's interference with a standard prosecutorial decision—what evidence to present to the grand jury and how to present it—is the need to preserve the integrity of the judicial process and to avoid any fundamental unfairness. But it is far from clear that the prosecutor's decision in this case regarding the presentation of evidence to the third grand jury implicates any of those interests.

See also United States v. Strouse, 286 F.3d 767 (5th Cir. 2002) (federal court does not have supervisory power to dismiss a grand jury indictment based on perjured testimony, unless it is shown that the prosecutor knew that the testimony was perjurious: "a rule allowing dismissal of an indictment without a showing of government misconduct would open the door to attacks on grand jury evidence for which there are large incentives including discovery by the accused").[10]

Role of the Prosecutor

The role of the prosecutor may vary somewhat from place to place in grand jury proceedings, but generally she serves the following functions:

(a) She is the legal advisor to the grand jury. Many critics maintain that the grand jury should have separate counsel at its disposal to reduce the prosecutor's control over the grand jury. But traditionally the prosecutor is also the grand jury's counsel. See Mogul Bent on Grand Jury Reform, Nat.L.J. July 27, 1998, p. A10 (discussing an "Open Letter" sent to grand jurors suggesting that grand jurors should retain their own counsel, as "a simple way to the Grand Jury to reclaim its legal independence").

(b) She presents evidence to the grand jury. The grand jury can always hear any additional evidence that it requests, but as a practical matter grand juries usually rely on the prosecutor to explain criminal offenses and to present the evidence that the grand jury considers. The prosecutor can subpoena witnesses to attend grand jury hearings, and once the witnesses are present the grand jury will hear them.

(c) The prosecutor may negate a grand jury's decision to return an indictment by refusing to sign the indictment, or by nolle prosequi, which dismisses the charges. And a grand jury decision not to indict can be

---

[10] United States v. McKenzie, 678 F.2d 629 (5th Cir.1982), indicates that an indictment will be quashed because of prosecutorial misconduct before a grand jury "only when prosecutorial misconduct amounts to overbearing the will of the grand jury so that the indictment is, in effect, that of the prosecutor rather than the grand jury." The court indicated that a prosecutor could tell the grand jury that the evidence shows the defendant is guilty.

circumvented if the prosecutor resubmits the case to another grand jury. In some jurisdictions such action requires court approval.

E. THE GRAND JURY AS A PROTECTION AGAINST UNJUST PROSECUTION

The traditional view of the grand jury as a protection against unwarranted prosecution has been described by the Supreme Court as follows:

> Historically, this body has been regarded as a primary security to the innocent against hasty, malicious and oppressive persecution; it serves the invaluable function in our society of standing between the accuser and the accused, whether the latter be an individual, minority group, or other, to determine whether a charge is founded upon reason or was dictated by an intimidating power or by malice and personal ill will.

Wood v. Georgia, 370 U.S. 375, 390 (1962).

More recently this view has been challenged. Commentators and courts now see a grand jury indictment as little more than a rubber stamp for the prosecutor's decision to go forward. See Leipold, Why Grand Juries Do Not (And Cannot) Protect the Accused, 80 Cornell L.Rev.260 (1995) (noting that during 1984, federal grand juries returned 17,419 indictments and only sixty-eight no bills, a success rate of 99.6%). In Hawkins v. Superior Court, 22 Cal.3d 584, 150 Cal.Rptr. 435, 586 P.2d 916 (1978), the California Supreme Court expressed its somewhat cynical view of the modern grand jury:

> The prosecuting attorney is typically in complete control of the total process in the grand jury room: he calls the witnesses, interprets the evidence, states and applies the law, and advises the grand jury on whether a crime has been committed. The grand jury is independent only in the sense that it is not formally attached to the prosecutor's office; though legally free to vote as they please, grand jurors virtually always assent to the recommendations of the prosecuting attorney, a fact borne out by available statistical and survey data. * * * The contemporary grand jury investigates only those whom the prosecutor asks to be investigated, and by and large indicts those whom the prosecutor wants to be indicted. * * *

> The domination of grand jury proceedings by the prosecuting attorney no doubt derives at least in part from the grand jury's institutional schizophrenia: it is expected to serve two distinct and largely inconsistent functions—accuser and impartial factfinder. * * *

The high proportion of true bills (i.e., decisions to charge) compared to no bills is not surprising. The grand jury is a body that hears only one side of a case. And it reacts to that side. Moreover the relevant standard of proof for issuing an indictment is low.

The principal function of the grand jury today probably is not to refuse indictment, but rather to force the prosecution to gather and to offer evidence in some systematic way before a charge is brought. What often is overlooked in discussions of grand juries is the fact that when the evidence, once put together, turns out to be weak, prosecutors sometimes decide not to ask for indictments or to seek indictments on lesser offenses than they might have charged on their own.

F. THE EVIDENCE BEFORE THE GRAND JURY

One reason that the screening function of the grand jury does not work better than it otherwise could is that prosecutors are permitted to offer a good deal of evidence to grand juries that could not be offered at trials. The next case is an illustration.

COSTELLO v. UNITED STATES
Supreme Court of the United States, 1956.
350 U.S. 359.

JUSTICE BLACK delivered the opinion of the Court.

We granted certiorari in this case to consider a single question: "May a defendant be required to stand trial and a conviction be sustained where only hearsay evidence was presented to the grand jury which indicted him?"

Petitioner, Frank Costello, was indicted for wilfully attempting to evade payment of income taxes due the United States for the years 1947, 1948 and 1949. * * * Petitioner promptly filed a motion for inspection of the minutes of the grand jury and for a dismissal of the indictment. His motion was based on an affidavit stating that he was firmly convinced there could have been no legal or competent evidence before the grand jury which indicted him since he had reported all his income and paid all taxes due. The motion was denied. At the trial which followed the Government offered evidence designed to show increases in Costello's net worth in an attempt to prove that he had received more income during the years in question than he had reported. To establish its case the Government called and examined 144 witnesses and introduced 368 exhibits. * * * The prosecution concluded its case by calling three government agents. Their investigations had produced the evidence used against petitioner at the trial. They were allowed to summarize the vast amount of evidence already heard and to introduce computations showing, if correct, that petitioner and his wife had received far greater income than they had reported.

* * *

Counsel for petitioner asked each government witness at the trial whether he had appeared before the grand jury which returned the indictment. This cross-examination developed the fact that the three investigating officers had been the only witnesses before the grand jury. After the Government concluded its case, petitioner again moved to dismiss the indictment on the ground that the only evidence before the grand jury was "hearsay," since the three officers had no firsthand knowledge of the transactions upon which their computations were based. Nevertheless the trial court again refused to dismiss the indictment, and petitioner was convicted. * * *

* * * [N]either the Fifth Amendment nor any other constitutional provision prescribes the kind of evidence upon which grand juries must act. * * * There is every reason to believe that our constitutional grand jury was intended to operate substantially like its English progenitor. The basic purpose of the English grand jury was to provide a fair method for instituting criminal proceedings against persons believed to have committed crimes. Grand jurors were selected from the body of the people and their work was not hampered by rigid procedural or evidential rules. * * *

* * * If indictments were to be held open to challenge on the ground that there was inadequate or incompetent evidence before the grand jury, the resulting delay would be great indeed. The result of such a rule would be that before trial on the merits a defendant could always insist on a kind of preliminary trial to determine the competency and adequacy of the evidence before the grand jury. This is not required by the Fifth Amendment. An indictment returned by a legally constituted and unbiased grand jury, like an information drawn by the prosecutor, if valid on its face, is enough to call for trial of the charge on the merits. * * *

* * * In a trial on the merits, defendants are entitled to a strict observance of all the rules designed to bring about a fair verdict. Defendants are not entitled, however, to a rule which would result in interminable delay but add nothing to the assurance of a fair trial.

[JUSTICE CLARK and JUSTICE HARLAN took no part in the consideration or decision of this case.]

[The concurring opinion of JUSTICE BURTON is omitted.]

Analysis of Costello

Aside from historical justifications, several arguments can be offered in support of *Costello*. First, inadmissible evidence often has probative value, and the grand jury's function is *investigative,* not adjudicative. Second, many evidentiary rules are designed to ensure fairness in an *adversary proceeding*, and the grand jury is not adversarial. See Federal Rule of Evidence 1101 (providing that the Rules of Evidence, except those related to privilege, are not applicable in grand jury proceedings). Evidence rules operate by way of objection; a prosecutor cannot be expected to object to her own evidence. Third, any misleading effect of inadmissible evidence will be remedied at trial. Fourth, grand jury proceedings would be greatly burdened if the rules of evidence were applicable to them. The court would have to review decisions as to the admissibility of evidence, because defense counsel would not be there to object. In order to make relevance and other rulings, supervising courts would have to ask grand juries why they wanted certain evidence, and this might infringe upon the independence of the grand jury.

Note that the fact situation of *Costello* was rather unique because defense counsel was able, by questioning witnesses at trial, to determine that hearsay statements were the only evidence presented to the grand jury. More commonly, the defendant will never know the degree to which hearsay and other inadmissible evidence is considered by the grand jury. Grand jury minutes are exempt from disclosure under Fed.R.Crim.P. 6. And the witnesses who render hearsay and other inadmissible testimony might not, for that very reason, testify at trial. As long as a defendant is convicted at trial on the basis of admissible evidence, he cannot complain that what occurred before the grand jury somehow affecte the trial. See United States v. Mechanik, 475 U.S. 66 (1986) (challenge to indictment based upon prosecutorial misconduct was rendered moot by conviction at a fairly conducted trial).

Use of Illegally Obtained Evidence

In Chapter 2, we saw that illegally seized evidence can be used in the grand jury proceeding. United States v. Calandra, 414 U.S. 338 (1974). The Court in *Calandra* reasoned that applying the exclusionary rule "would unduly interfere with the effective and expeditious discharge of the grand jury's duties" and that sufficient deterrence of illegal police activity would flow from the fact that the tainted evidence could not be used at trial.

Exculpatory Evidence: United States v. Williams

Does the prosecutor have an obligation to present all relevant evidence to the grand jury—including evidence that would exculpate the accused? Justice Scalia wrote for the Court in United States v. Williams, 504 U.S. 36 (1992), as it rejected a Tenth Circuit supervisory rule that required prosecutors to present "substantial exculpatory evidence" to the grand jury. He concluded that a rule requiring the prosecutor to present all substantially exculpatory evidence exceeded the courts' supervisory authority, because "the grand jury is an institution separate from the courts, over whose functioning the courts [do] not preside."

Justice Scalia stated that "any power federal courts may have to fashion, on their own initiative, rules of grand jury procedure is a very limited one, not remotely comparable to the power they maintain over their own proceedings." He asserted that the Tenth Circuit's rule was far from so limited, because it would result in the "judicial reshaping of the grand jury institution, substantially altering the traditional relationships between the prosecutor, the constituting court, and the grand jury itself." Justice Scalia reasoned that "requiring the prosecutor to present exculpatory as well as inculpatory evidence would alter the grand jury's historical role, transforming it from an accusatory to an adjudicatory body." He explained as follows:

> It is axiomatic that the grand jury sits not to determine guilt or innocence, but to assess whether there is adequate basis for bringing a criminal charge. That has always been so; and to make the assessment it has always been thought sufficient to hear only the prosecutor's side. * * *

> Imposing upon the prosecutor a legal obligation to present exculpatory evidence in his possession would be incompatible with this system. If a "balanced" assessment of the entire matter is the objective, surely the first thing to be done—rather than requiring the prosecutor to say what he knows in defense of the target of the investigation—is to entitle the target to tender his own defense. To require the former while denying (as we do) the latter would be quite absurd. It would also be quite pointless, since it would merely invite the target to circumnavigate the system by delivering his exculpatory evidence to the prosecutor, whereupon it would *have* to be passed on to the grand jury * * *

Justice Scalia observed that the grand jury itself might choose not to hear more evidence than that which suffices to support an indictment. That is, the grand jury is free on its own to refuse to consider evidence that exculpated the target. He reasoned that if "the grand jury has no obligation to consider all substantial exculpatory evidence, we do not understand how the prosecutor can be said to have a binding obligation to present it." The Court thus rejected "the attempt to convert a nonexistent duty of the grand jury itself into an obligation of the prosecutor."

Justice Stevens, joined by Justices Blackmun and O'Connor and in relevant part by Justice Thomas, dissented. Justice Stevens stated that he was "unwilling to hold that countless forms of prosecutorial misconduct must be tolerated—no matter how prejudicial they may be, or how seriously they may distort the legitimate function of the grand jury— simply because they are not proscribed by Rule 6 of the Federal Rules of

Criminal Procedure or a statute that is applicable in grand jury proceedings."

As to the scope of the prosecutor's duty to disclose exculpatory evidence to the grand jury, the dissenters endorsed the position expressed in the Department of Justice's United States Attorneys' Manual, Title 9, ch. 7, par. 9–11.233,88: "When a prosecutor conducting a grand jury inquiry is personally aware of substantial evidence which directly negates the guilt of a subject of the investigation, the prosecutor must present or otherwise disclose such evidence to the grand jury before seeking an indictment against such a person."

G. THE GRAND JURY'S POWERS OF INVESTIGATION

The Supreme Court has emphasized that the role of the grand jury is to investigate any and all potential criminal conduct, and that the power to obtain information is broad. See, e.g., Branzburg v. Hayes, 408 U.S. 665 (1972) (grand jury has a right to disclosure of journalist's sources); United States v. Nixon, 418 U.S. 683 (1974) (communications protected by executive privilege must be disclosed to the grand jury). To understand how broadly the grand jury can sweep, it is helpful to think back to the search and seizure material in Chapter 2. You will recall that the government generally cannot search for evidence unless it has probable cause, and the government cannot arrest a person without probable cause. This is in sharp contrast with the standards used by a grand jury. The grand jury can call anyone to testify before it upon the hint of suspicion or on the basis of a prosecutor's speculation about possible criminal activity. People called before the grand jury can be directed to bring documents and other tangible objects with them. Although certain privileges (such as Fifth Amendment and attorney-client) can be raised before the grand jury, the burden is on the person called to raise them and sometimes to be willing to litigate in order to preserve them. Any aspect of a person's life that might shed light on some criminal activity by somebody is within the proper scope of a grand jury inquest. See, e.g., In re Grand Jury, 286 F.3d 153 (3d Cir. 2002) (grand jury has the power to demand the production of material even where it is covered by a protective order in a civil case).

Grand Jury Subpoena Power

The scope of the subpoena power of a federal grand jury is nationwide, which means that the burden of traveling to testify can be considerable. The state grand jury has no such nationwide reach, but it too can impose travel burdens on witnesses. When it is recognized that often the prosecutor subpoenas witnesses without prior consultation with the grand jurors, it is apparent that a prosecutor can call witnesses who are considerably burdened by the duty of responding to a subpoena but who might end up having little to tell the grand jury.

For example, one of the cases consolidated for hearing in Branzburg v. Hayes, supra, involved Earl Caldwell, a New York Times reporter who covered the Black Panther Party. Caldwell claimed that his appearance before the grand jury would compromise his relationship with the Party. The Supreme Court held that this risk of harm gave him neither the right to refuse to appear before the grand jury nor the right to refuse to answer questions based on information related to him in confidence. Under the Court's opinion, even if the grand jury did not have any significant need for answers to questions, and even if, by answering, Caldwell's ability to function as a reporter covering the Party would be destroyed, the grand jury had a right to the information.

The breadth of grand jury power was evidenced once again in the grand jury investigation into charges of impropriety by then-President Clinton. The grand jury subpoenaed information from a bookstore concerning a purchase made by Monica Lewinsky. Despite the First Amendment ramifications, the subpoena was found valid. See Stout, Lewinsky's Bookstore Purchases Are Now Subject of a Subpoena, N.Y. Times, March 26, 1998, at A16 (quoting a legal director for the ACLU as stating that "people in this country ought to have the right to buy books without government scrutiny").

In Blair v. United States, 250 U.S. 273 (1919), the Supreme Court established the appropriate degree of deference to be accorded grand jury subpoenas by judicial officers:

> [T]he giving of testimony and the attendance upon court or grand jury in order to testify are public duties which every person within the jurisdiction of the Government is bound to perform upon being properly summoned, and for performance of which he is entitled to no further compensation than that which the statutes provide. The personal sacrifice involved is a part of the necessary contribution of the individual to the welfare of the public. The duty, so onerous at times, yet so necessary to the administration of justice * * * is subject to mitigation in exceptional circumstances; there is a constitutional exemption from being compelled in any criminal case to be a witness against oneself, entitling the witness to be excused from answering anything that will tend to incriminate him; some confidential matters are shielded from considerations of policy, and perhaps in other cases for special reasons a witness may be excused from telling all that he knows.
>
> But, aside from exceptions and qualifications—and none such is asserted in the present case—the witness is bound not only to attend

but to tell what he knows in answer to questions framed for the purpose of bringing out the truth of the matter under inquiry.

* * *

[The grand jury] is a grand inquest, a body with powers of investigation and inquisition, the scope of whose inquiries is not to be limited narrowly by questions of propriety or forecasts of the probable result of the investigation, or by doubts whether any particular individual will be found properly subject to an accusation of crime. As has been said before, the identity of the offender, and the precise nature of the offense, if there be one, normally are developed at the conclusion of the grand jury's labors, not at the beginning.

Grand Jury Cattle Call: United States v. Dionisio

An objection to the breadth of a grand jury investigation, and correspondingly to the broad use of its subpoena power, is ordinarily dismissed out of hand. A case in point is United States v. Dionisio, 410 U.S. 1 (1973). The next excerpt contains the Court's description of the facts and the Court's deferential approach to grand jury subpoenas.

A special grand jury was convened in the Northern District of Illinois in February 1971, to investigate possible violations of federal criminal statutes relating to gambling. In the course of its investigation, the grand jury received in evidence certain voice recordings that had been obtained pursuant to court orders.

The grand jury subpoenaed approximately 20 persons, including the respondent Dionisio, seeking to obtain from them voice exemplars for comparison with the recorded conversations that had been received in evidence. Each witness was advised that he was a potential defendant in a criminal prosecution. Each was asked to examine a transcript of an intercepted conversation, and to go to a nearby office of the United States Attorney to read the transcript into a recording device. * * * Dionisio and other witnesses refused to furnish the voice exemplars * * *.

* * *

The Court of Appeals found critical significance in the fact that the grand jury had summoned approximately 20 witnesses to furnish voice exemplars. We think that fact is basically irrelevant to the constitutional issues here. The grand jury may have been attempting to identify a number of voices on the tapes in evidence, or it might have summoned the 20 witnesses in an effort to identify one voice. But whatever the case, a grand jury's investigation is not fully carried out until every available clue has been run down and all witnesses examined in every proper way to find if a crime has been committed

* * *. The grand jury may well find it desirable to call numerous witnesses in the course of an investigation. It does not follow that each witness may resist a subpoena on the ground that too many witnesses have been called.

In dissent, Justice Marshall argued that some protection against prosecutorial control of the grand jury is necessary. Justice Marshall urged that the government should have to make a showing of reasonableness before real evidence is gathered by the grand jury over the objection of a witness.

Minimal Limits on Grand Jury Subpoenas: United States v. R. Enterprises, Inc.

The Court in United States v. Nixon, 418 U.S. 683 (1974), held that a *trial* subpoena must satisfy a three pronged test of relevancy, admissibility, and specificity. However, in United States v. R. Enterprises, Inc., 498 U.S. 292 (1991), the Court rejected the application of the *Nixon* standards to grand jury subpoenas. Justice O'Connor, writing for a unanimous Court on this point, stressed the distinction between a grand jury investigation and a trial proceeding. She stated that "the Government cannot be required to justify the issuance of a grand jury subpoena by presenting evidence sufficient to establish probable cause because the very purpose of requesting the information is to ascertain whether probable cause exists." The Court also noted that the multifactor *Nixon* test would produce unacceptable procedural delays that would frustrate the grand jury's investigation.

Justice O'Connor noted, however, that the grand jury's investigatory powers are "not unlimited." Under Federal Rule of Criminal Procedure 17(c), subpoenas may be quashed if compliance would be "unreasonable or oppressive." The Court held that a subpoena would be unreasonable under Rule 17(c) only if "there is no reasonable possibility that the category of materials the Government seeks will produce information relevant to the general subject of the grand jury's investigation." Justice O'Connor recognized that this standard would be extraordinarily difficult to meet in practice, especially given the difficult position of subpoena recipients, who may have no knowledge of the government's purpose in seeking production of the requested information. The Court suggested that an *in camera* proceeding should be employed in cases where the recipient of the subpoena is unaware of the nature of the investigation.

Warnings to Witnesses Testifying Before the Grand Jury

Witnesses can be called to testify before the grand jury without being told why they are being called, what the purpose of the inquiry is, or whether they are suspected of criminal wrongdoing. Ignorance of the nature of the inquiry is compounded by the absence of counsel for the witness in the federal grand jury room (as well as in many states). Because grand jurors and prosecutors can ask leading questions, a witness who might be a target of the grand jury has good reason to fear that a slip of the tongue may come back to haunt her. Yet, the witness will have difficulty in answering carefully without knowledge of what the investigation is all about. Without a lawyer present to assist, vague or confusing questions may be asked, and a witness may later discover that what she said to the grand jury can be cast in a more negative light than she would have supposed while testifying.

In response to concerns about the possible unfair treatment of grand jury witnesses, the Department of Justice has added to the guidelines for United States Attorneys, found in the United States Attorney's Manual,[11] sections that require that a witness be advised of several things before testifying: of the general subject matter of the grand jury's inquiry (to the extent that an investigation would not be compromised); that the witness may refuse to answer questions that would tend to incriminate; that any answers may be used against the witness; and that the witness may step outside the grand jury room to consult with counsel. The guidelines provide that a target of an investigation may be subpoenaed, but known targets should be advised that they are targets and should be invited to testify voluntarily; if they refuse, a subpoena should be issued only after the grand jury and the responsible prosecutor have approved the subpoena. The prosecutor is encouraged to offer a target an opportunity to testify before the grand jury hands down an indictment.

It is notable, however, that there is no private right of action for violation of the DOJ guidelines on warnings. If they are ignored by the prosecutor, the most that will occur is a referral by the court to the Justice Department for internal (and confidential) discipline. See United States v. Gillespie, 974 F.2d 796 (7th Cir.1992) (asserting that judicial enforcement might deter the DOJ from adopting such rules in the first place). It should also be noted that a witness before the grand jury is not entitled to *Miranda* warnings, even if he is a target or subject of the investigation; such a witness is not in custody within the meaning of *Miranda*. See United States v. Mandujano, 425 U.S. 564 (1976).

Counsel in the Grand Jury Room

As discussed above, under Federal practice, a witness has no right to counsel while in the grand jury room. The Supreme Court reaffirmed the nonexistence of any right to counsel in Conn v. Gabbert, 526 U.S. 286 (1999). The plaintiff in *Conn* was a criminal defense attorney. He sued

---

[11] United States Department of Justice, United States Attorneys' Manual, Title 9, Ch.11, ¶ 9–11.50.

prosecutors and others for subjecting him to a search while his client was testifying before a grand jury. Before the Supreme Court, the attorney did not press a Fourth Amendment claim. Rather, he argued that the search "interfered with his client's right to have him outside the grand jury room and available to consult with her." Chief Justice Rehnquist, writing for the Court, analyzed this claim in the following passage:

> A grand jury witness has no constitutional right to have counsel present during the grand jury proceeding, and no decision of this Court has held that a grand jury witness has a right to have her attorney present outside the jury room. We need not decide today whether such a right exists, because Gabbert clearly had no standing to raise the alleged infringement of the rights of his client Tracy Baker.

Thus, the Court in *Conn* does not even concede that a grand jury witness has a right to have counsel *outside* the room, much less inside. In practice, counsel is permitted to park herself outside the grand jury room, and the witness can excuse himself for consultation.[12]

A number of states permit witnesses to be accompanied by counsel in the grand jury room. A subcommittee of the Judicial Conference Advisory Committee on Criminal Rules considered making such a change in federal procedure, and ultimately decided against it. The Report of the Subcommittee reasons that allowing counsel to be present before the grand jury would create the following problems:

1.   Loss of spontaneity of testimony.

2.   Transforming the grand jury investigation into an adversary proceeding.

3.   Loss of secrecy with resultant chilling effect on witness cooperation.

The Subcommittee also notes a "potential ancillary issue. Would an indigent witness summoned to the grand jury be entitled to the appointment of counsel at the obvious cost to the Treasury?"

To these concerns, the head of the Criminal Division of the Justice Department added another:

> [A]llowing defense counsel to accompany a witness before a grand jury would have adverse consequences for investigations of serious crimes by organizations, such as organized crime groups, corporations, or unions where typically a single lawyer represents all or several members of the organization. Currently, if a member of the

---

[12]   This limited opportunity to consult counsel probably reflects a practical consideration: if the witness refuses to answer, the grand jury would have to seek a contempt citation to make the witness answer; before going through that process, the grand jury may be better advised to let the witness discuss with counsel the question, because the witness may after consultation find that there is no Fifth Amendment or other privilege that is implicated.

organization wishes to cooperate with the grand jury secretly, the member may do so by appearing alone before the grand jury. But if the law allowed the member to bring the attorney, failure to do so would be a tip-off that the witness was likely cooperating, which would deter cooperation in many instances (or result in retaliation).

Letter from James K. Robinson to Subcommittee on Grand Jury Proceedings, Judicial Conference Advisory Committee on Criminal Rules, Dec. 22, 1998.

Despite these dire predictions, the evidence from the States that permit counsel in the grand jury room indicates that counsel's presence can have a positive rather than negative effect. For example, Colorado passed a law in the late 1970's permitting a witness's counsel to be present in the grand jury room. Jeffrey Bayles, a former Denver deputy district attorney, explains the salutary effect of the law as follows:

Not only does the new law speed the process by eliminating the walk outside the room on every question, but it also reduces the number of questions requiring conferences between the witness and counsel. The educational process, which of necessity accompanies having counsel in the grand jury room, promotes a better understanding of the grand jury within the bar. The more the processes are known, the less is the aura of mystery surrounding the grand jury. * * * The demand for abolition of the grand jury will decrease in direct proportion to the number of counsel who attend grand jury sessions with their clients.

Bales, Grand Jury Reform: The Colorado Experience, A.B.A.J., May, 1981, at 568. See also Hixson, Bringing Down the Curtain on the Absurd Drama of Entrances and Exits—Witness Representation in the Grand Jury Room, 15 Am.Cr.L.Rev. 307 (1978) (given that the witness is allowed to go in and out of the room to get advice of counsel, it is more efficient to permit counsel to be present in the grand jury room.).

Suggested Reforms of Grand Jury Procedures

Many commentators suggest that the abuses seen in grand jury practice can be eliminated by imposing reforms. The ABA Criminal Justice Section Committee on the Grand Jury proposed the following reforms:

1.   A witness before the grand jury shall have the right to be accompanied by counsel in his or her appearance before the grand jury. Such counsel shall be allowed to be present in the grand jury room only during the questioning of the witness and shall be allowed to advise the witness. Such counsel shall not be permitted to address the grand jurors or otherwise take part in proceedings before the grand jury.

2.   No prosecutor shall knowingly fail to disclose to the grand jury evidence which will tend substantially to negate guilt.

3.   The prosecutor shall not present to the grand jury evidence which he or she knows to be constitutionally inadmissible at trial.

4.   A target of a grand jury investigation shall be given the right to testify before the grand jury. Prosecutors shall notify such targets of their opportunity to testify unless notification may result in flight, endanger other persons, or obstruct justice, or unless the prosecutor is unable to notify said persons with reasonable diligence. A target of the grand jury may also contact the foreperson in writing to offer information or evidence to the grand jury.

5.   Witnesses should have the right to receive a transcript (at their own expense) of grand jury testimony.

6.   The grand jury shall not name a person in an indictment as an unindicted coconspirator to a criminal conspiracy.[13]

The Criminal Justice Section report, proposing the above reforms, was issued in 1977. Congress held hearings on the proposals, but did not act on them. It is easy to see why no action was taken. The reforms would overrule Supreme Court doctrine, and would create a sea-change in the historically-ingrained federal grand jury practice. The reform proposals were staunchly opposed by the Justice Department. It is unlikely that the political climate will ever warm up enough for these or similar proposals to be enacted. See, e.g., Rovella, Grand Jury Battle Begins, Nat'l L.J., May 29, 2000, p. A4 (discussing attempt by Congressman Delahunt to revive the 1977 proposals under the new title "Federal Grand Jury Bill of Rights"; no legislation resulted).

Grand Jury Nullification

Professor Laurie Levinson suggests another reform for grand jury practice: that grand jurors be told that they have the right to nullify, i.e., that they do not have to return an indictment even when they find probable cause. She notes that the history of the grand jury is laced with important cases of nullification, such as the refusal to indict John Peter Zenger on charges of sedition (as discussed in the section on the history of the grand jury, supra). She argues that there are compelling modern justifications for the nullification power:

> Federal prosecutors are not directly accountable to the community in which they serve. Rather, their appointments are made in Washington, and line prosecutors are increasingly receiving direction from Department of Justice officials who set national policy. Whether

---

[13]   See United States v. Briggs, 514 F.2d 794 (5th Cir.1975) ("the grand jury that returns an indictment naming a person as an unindicted coconspirator does not perform its shielding function but does exactly the reverse. If the charges are baseless, the named person should not be subjected to public branding, and if supported by probable cause, he should not be denied a forum.").

it is the war on drugs, the war on white-collar crime, or the war on terrorism, the national agenda may not adequately consider the needs of a particular community. A grand jury can perform this role.

* * *

The grand jury process, unlike trial jury deliberations, lends itself to a more thoughtful evaluation of community priorities and an evaluation of whether prosecutors are using the law for improper reasons, such as political grandstanding or witch-hunting of opponents.

If grand juries have the discretion to reject charges that they think are improperly motivated or unwise, prosecutors will actually benefit in the long run because there will be greater moral authority behind the charges that grand jurors do bring.

Levinson, Grand Jury Nullification, Nat'l L. J. June 14, 2004 at 14.

Yet as shown earlier in this Chapter, the model charge given to federal grand jurors does not inform them that they have the right to decline to bring charges when the prosecutor establishes probable cause. The model charge says that when probable cause is established, the grand jury "should" return an indictment; and it further states that it is not for the grand jurors to second-guess the wisdom of laws passed by Congress. These charges have withstood attack. Thus, in United States v. Navarro-Vargas, 408 F.3d 1184 (9th Cir. 2005), the court noted that the grand jury has the *power*, as a matter of practice, to nullify a law because there is no means to review a grand jury's refusal to return an indictment. But according to the court, that does not mean that grand jurors have the *right* to nullify laws—or that they should in effect be invited to nullify by an instruction of informing them of their power to do so. The court stated: "we cannot say that the grand jury's power to judge the wisdom of the laws is so firmly established that the district court must either instruct the jury on its power to nullify the laws or remain silent." The court wrote that the instructions as a whole "remind the grand jury of its independence from the federal government and leave room for it to refuse to indict." The court made clear that the word "should" does not mean "must."

Note that if the grand jury does nullify and refuses to return an indictment, all the prosecutor has to do is empanel another grand jury; it is not like petit jury nullification, which triggers double jeopardy protection. Given the fact that grand jury nullification can be so easily trumped, is there any reason to encourage it?

For a comprehensive discussion of grand jury nullification, see Fairfax, Grand Jury Discretion and Constitutional Design, 93 Cornell L. Rev. 703, 711–16 (2008).

V. THE PRELIMINARY HEARING AND ITS RELATIONSHIP TO INDICTMENTS AND INFORMATIONS

Federal Rule of Criminal Procedure 5 provides that when an arrest is made, the arrested person must be taken without unnecessary delay before the nearest available federal magistrate. You will recall that Gerstein v. Pugh, 420 U.S. 103 (1975), and County of Riverside v. McLaughlin, 500 U.S. 44(1991), discussed in Chapter 2, requires that, if there has been no previous probable cause determination, one must be made promptly. Fed.R.Crim.P. 5 provides for such a determination when the person arrested is brought before the magistrate. The rule provides that a defendant is entitled to a preliminary examination for any crime except a petty offense. Fed.R.Crim.P. 5.1 governs preliminary examinations.

Note that an indictment cuts off the right to a preliminary hearing, because probable cause is held to be validly established by the indictment itself. It is common in some federal districts for prosecutors to avoid preliminary hearings by indicting as many defendants as possible.

Virtually every state that requires felony prosecutions to commence by indictment establishes some right to a preliminary examination. In most, the filing of the indictment cuts off the right to a preliminary hearing, just as does Federal Rule 5. About half the states do not require indictments in felony cases. In these states, prosecutors can begin felony cases by filing informations. A typical information procedure is to require a magistrate's determination of probable cause following a preliminary examination. In special cases prosecutors may utilize grand jury indictments, but usually they will file the information, since it is a less burdensome way of beginning a case.

Most states that permit the filing of an information in a felony case make a magistrate's decision to bind the defendant over for trial a prerequisite to the filing of the information. A few states do allow the prosecutor to file the information directly, however. The Supreme Court has upheld the direct filing of an information in Lem Woon v. Oregon, 229 U.S. 586 (1913), and Ocampo v. United States, 234 U.S. 91 (1914). Of course, after Gerstein v. Pugh, supra, a magistrate will have to make a probable cause determination, if the accused is deprived of freedom. But the *Gerstein* opinion indicates that the limited hearing it requires is to protect against erroneous detention; it is not a screening device to check the validity of the prosecutor's charges against a defendant.

Procedural Requirements for a Preliminary Hearing

Most states have time limits in which the preliminary hearing must be held. But other aspects of the hearing are often not covered by any rule.

Even the standard to be used by the magistrate who conducts the preliminary hearing often is unclear. It is apparent that different judges sitting in the same jurisdiction have different ideas about what screening function the hearing is to serve. Some judges believe that their function is to determine probable cause, with the evidence viewed in the light most favorable to the government, ignoring credibility questions. This is the standard set forth in the federal system. See Fed.R.Crim.P. 5.1. Others take the view that there must be enough evidence for a trier of fact to find guilt beyond a reasonable doubt. Some magistrates probably consider whether a defendant should be burdened by going to trial in some cases, even if there is enough evidence to warrant a bindover.

The standard that is chosen indicates how much screening a jurisdiction wants its magistrates to do. It probably is true that if a prosecutor presents all her evidence to the magistrate and the magistrate concludes that no reasonable jury could convict, it is silly to bind the defendant over for trial, even if technically there is probable cause. But it is burdensome to require the prosecutor to present all of her evidence to the magistrate as a prerequisite to bringing charges. The more thorough the screening at the preliminary hearing, the more it resembles a trial, and the more duplicative and costly it is.

Although some jurisdictions require magistrates to follow the usual rules of evidence at preliminary hearings, most others (including the federal system, see Fed. R. Evid. 1101) provide that trial evidence rules need not be followed—which means in most cases that hearsay evidence can be used, as it can be used before grand juries. Again, the approach to the question whether evidence rules should be followed at the preliminary hearing depends on the kind of hearing that is to be held. Obviously, the more closely the evidence rules resemble the rules that will be used at trial, the more screening the magistrate is able to do. But the more screening that is done, the more time-consuming and duplicative the procedure is likely to be.

Another obvious difference among jurisdictions is in their approach to the hearing as a discovery device. If the hearing is not intended to serve a discovery purpose—as under Fed.R.Crim.P. 5.1, which does not mention discovery as a proper subject for the hearing—then questions asked for discovery reasons are unlikely to be permitted over objection.[14] If, however, a jurisdiction recognizes a discovery purpose, the scope of questioning may be quite broad.

---

[14] The preliminary hearing may be used as a device to preserve testimony, and to precipitate bargaining that will lead to a guilty plea.

Preclusive Effect of a Preliminary Determination

If the case is a felony case that will begin by a grand jury indictment, a decision by the magistrate at a preliminary hearing that there is no cause for bindover generally is not determinative for a grand jury. The grand jury still can indict, because it is an institution independent from the judiciary. See Fed.R.Crim.P. 5.1(f) ("A discharge does not preclude the government from later prosecuting the defendant for the same offense."). Likewise, a decision by the magistrate that bindover should be limited to designated offenses does not limit the grand jury in most jurisdictions. The grand jury can charge any offense for which it finds probable cause.

If the prosecution can begin by information, generally the prosecutor is limited by the bindover in the charges that can be brought. In some states only those charges designated by the magistrate can be brought. In other states the offense for which the defendant is bound over or others supported by the evidence at the preliminary hearing may be charged. Still others use a transactional test, which allows all crimes related to the same transactions and facts adduced at the examination to be charged. Under all these approaches, the defendant can challenge the information in the trial court, although it is likely that the trial court will defer to the preliminary hearing judge (and the absence of a formal record may make a challenge especially difficult). If the prosecutor is not satisfied with the bindover decision, she may drop the prosecution, file a new information and hope for a better bindover ruling from another magistrate, or take the case to a grand jury. Generally, the refusal to bind the defendant over is not appealable, although sometimes mandamus may be possible.

VI. NOTICE OF CHARGES, CONSTRUCTIVE AMENDMENT, AND VARIANCE

In Stirone v. United States, 361 U.S. 212 (1960), the Supreme Court reversed a conviction for violation of the Hobbs Act (interfering with interstate commerce) because the government's proof of the defendants' effect on interstate commerce involved shipments of steel from inside Pennsylvania to points outside the state, whereas the indictment charged that the effect was on shipments from outside the state into Pennsylvania. The Court said that it could not permit a defendant to be tried on charges not made in the indictment, because to do so would undermine the defendant's constitutional right to an indictment by grand jury, and also would deny the defendant his constitutional right to be notified of the charges against him.

An indictment, to be sufficient under the Grand Jury Clause, must sufficiently state all elements of the crime. See, e.g., United States v. Villarreal, 707 F.3d 942 (8th Cir. 2013) ("An indictment is fatally insufficient when an essential element of the crime is omitted.").

United States v. Pickett, 353 F.3d 62 (D.C. Cir. 2004), is a case involving a defective indictment. Pickett was a security guard in the Capitol building who was indicted for lying to a government official. The prosecution involved the scare that arose when several Senators received anthrax in the mail. The defendant, as part of a "bad joke," placed a white substance on a table in the Capitol, and then lied about doing it. But the statute (18 U.S.C.§ 1001) requires that the lie to the government official must be made during an "investigation or review." That element was not charged in the indictment. The court dismissed the indictment, noting that on the plain language of the statute, the conduct charged against Pickett, making false statements, "does not constitute an offense" unless it occurs during the course of and investigation or review. The court concluded that "it is a fundamental protection, which an indictment is intended to guarantee, that the indictment contain the elements of the offense intended to be charged and sufficiently apprise the defendant of what he must be prepared to meet."

In contrast, the Court in United States v. Miller, 471 U.S. 130 (1985), held that the Fifth Amendment's protection of indictment by grand jury is not violated "when a defendant is tried under an indictment that alleges a certain fraudulent scheme but is convicted based on trial proof that supports only a significantly narrower and more limited, though included, fraudulent scheme." The government had charged Miller with fraudulent acts in consenting to a burglary of his business and lying to the insurer about the value of his loss. The proof focused only on the value of the loss and Miller's lying about it. Justice Marshall wrote that "[a]s long as the crime and the elements of the offense that sustain the conviction are fully and clearly set out in the indictment, the right to a grand jury is not normally violated by the fact that the indictment alleges more crimes or other means of submitting the same crime." He distinguished *Stirone* on the ground that the offense proved at Stirone's trial was *not* fully charged in the indictment.

Constructive Amendments and Variance from Indictment at Trial

Besides an indictment that simply does not state all the elements of a crime, a situation might arise in which the indictment pleads elements that are different from the proof presented by the prosecution at trial. Courts have found two types of claims that arise when a grand jury indictment is allegedly altered during the trial. One claim is that the indictment was *constructively amended*; the other claim is that there has been a *variance* between the indictment and the proof elicited at trial. The court in Martin v. Kassulke, 970 F.2d 1539 (6th Cir.1992), discussed the difference between these two claims:

An amendment of the indictment occurs when the charging terms of the indictment are altered, either literally or in effect, by prosecutor or court after the grand jury has last passed upon them. A variance occurs when the charging terms of an indictment are left unaltered, but the evidence offered at trial proves facts materially different from those alleged in the indictment. An amendment is per se prejudicial, as it directly infringes the defendant's right to know of the charges against him by effectively allowing the jury to convict the defendant of a different crime than that for which he was charged. * * *

A variance, on the other hand, is not reversible error unless the accused has proved a prejudicial effect upon his defense, because it merely permits the prosecution to prove facts to establish the criminal charge materially different from the facts contained in the charging instrument. Although it is generally subject to the harmless error test, a variance infringes upon the apprisal function of the sixth amendment which requires that in all criminal prosecutions, the accused shall enjoy the right to be informed of the nature and cause of the accusation. If a variance infringes too strongly upon a defendant's sixth amendment rights, it is considered a constructive amendment, which is a variance that is accorded the per se prejudicial treatment of an amendment. * * * A constructive amendment occurs when the terms of an indictment are in effect altered by the presentation of evidence and jury instructions which so modify essential elements of the offense charged that there is a substantial likelihood that the defendant may have been convicted of an offense other than that charged in the indictment.

* * *

A variance is not material, or does not rise to the level of a constructive amendment, unless the variance misleads the accused in making her defense or exposes her to the danger of double jeopardy.

In *Martin*, the defendant was charged with rape by engaging in sexual intercourse "by forcible compulsion." The evidence showed, and the prosecutor argued, that the rape occurred while the victim was "physically helpless"—i.e., while unconscious. The pertinent rape statute criminalized sexual intercourse either by forcible compulsion or when the victim was physically helpless. The *Martin* court found that the difference between the proof at trial and the charging instrument constituted a variance, but did not rise to the level of a constructive amendment of the indictment. Under the statute, rape was a single crime, which could be committed by two alternative methods. The defendant was not prejudiced by the prosecution's proof of a method other than that charged, because his defense was that the victim was a willing participant in *whatever* sex occurred. This defense "clearly negates any possibility that the victim was physically helpless and that her helplessness meant that he was not guilty of the crime with which he was charged." See also United States v. Moore, 198 F.3d 793 (10th Cir. 1999) (defendant was not prejudiced by a variance where he was charged with carjacking, and the victim named in the indictment was Brent Beyers, whereas the government proved that the car was owned by his wife, Anne Byers).

A case that can be compared usefully with *Martin* is United States v. Lawton, 995 F.2d 290 (D.C.Cir.1993). Lawton was an official of a local union. He was charged with embezzling money from the Local. His defense was that he had an oral arrangement with the Local to write checks to himself to pay his salary. The federal labor embezzlement statute makes criminal only the embezzlement of the funds of a labor organization of which the defendant "is an officer, or by which he is employed, directly or indirectly." The trial court instructed the jury, however, that it could convict Lawton if it found that he embezzled the Local's funds, *or* the District Labor Council's funds, *or* the International Union's funds. It was clear that Lawton was neither an officer nor an employee of these latter two groups. The court found that the trial judge's charge constituted a constructive amendment of the indictment, which was per se reversible error:

> Under the Fifth Amendment, the infamous crimes on which a defendant must stand trial are limited by the charges contained in the grand jury's indictment. The district court's embezzlement instructions, however, allowed the petit jury to convict Lawton of additional charges. The trial court's instructions thus violated the Grand Jury Clause just as surely as if the court had written additional charges onto the grand jury's "true bill." Still worse, the instructions allowed the jury to convict on the basis of conduct that, on the face of the evidence, did not amount to a violation of [the labor embezzlement statute].

See also Lucas v. O'Dea, 169 F.3d 1028 (6th Cir.1999) (where the defendant was charged in the indictment with murder by shooting the victim with a pistol, it was a fatal variance for the jury to be instructed that the defendant could be convicted if his coconspirator fired the shot: the defendant was clearly prejudiced because his defense to the murder charge was that he was not the shooter: "Because it exposed Lucas to charges for which he had no notice and thus no opportunity to plan a defense, the variance from the indictment to the jury instruction constituted a constructive amendment that violated his Fifth Amendment rights."); Geboy v. Brigano, 489 F.3d 752 (6th Cir. 2007) (defendant was not prejudiced by variance between the indictment and the evidence as to the location of charged crimes).

Inspecific Charges

The concern of *Stirone* and its progeny is that an amendment or variance at trial will deprive the defendant of sufficient notice and so impair his ability to prepare a defense. But a notice problem can also arise when the indictment, though stating the elements of the crime, provides factual assertions so general that it is difficult or impossible to prepare a defense.[15] One remedy for inspecific factual assertions is provided by Fed.R.Crim.P. 7(f), which permits the court to direct the filing of a bill of particulars. The court in United States v. Salisbury, 983 F.2d 1369 (6th Cir.1993), described the function of a bill of particulars:

> A bill of particulars is meant to be used as a tool to minimize surprise and assist defendant in obtaining the information needed to prepare a defense and to preclude a second prosecution for the same crimes. * * * The decision to order a bill of particulars is within the sound discretion of the court. * * * A court does not abuse its discretion in light of a detailed indictment.

If the defendant moves for a bill of particulars and that motion is denied, the defendant is not entitled to relief on appeal unless he can show that he was "actually surprised at trial and suffered prejudice from the denial." United States v. Livingstone, 576 F.3d 881 (8th Cir. 2009) (no error in denying motion for bill of particulars where the defendant's strategy was to attack the credibility of government witnesses, and he could not show how a bill of particulars could have affected his defense).

Whether or not supplemented by a bill of particulars, it is at least possible for an indictment to be so vague as to provide constitutionally inadequate notice. The test for constitutional sufficiency was stated by Judge Easterbrook in Fawcett v. Bablitch, 962 F.2d 617 (7th Cir.1992): "[A] charge is sufficiently specific when it contains the elements of the crime, permits the accused to plead and prepare a defense, and allows the disposition to be used as a bar in a subsequent prosecution." The *Fawcett* court rejected the argument that an indictment is constitutionally defective whenever the prosecution could have provided more specific information in the indictment. It declared that "the prosecutor's ability to do better does not vitiate the conviction."

In *Fawcett*, the defendant was charged with two events of unlawful sexual contact with a minor "during the six months preceding December 1985." Fawcett argued that the time period was impermissibly broad, because it was impossible for him to provide an alibi for the entire six month period. The court rejected this contention, finding that sufficient notice had been given, and noting that Fawcett was free to attack the

---

[15] Fed.R.Crim.P. 7(c)(1) requires the indictment to set out the essential facts constituting the offense charged, in order to inform the defendant of the offense against which he must defend.

complainant's veracity and to deny participation. Do you agree that sufficient notice was given? Would the indictment have been sufficient if it charged one act of sexual misconduct within a ten-year period? Compare United States v. Salisbury, 983 F.2d 1369 (6th Cir.1993) (indictment insufficiently specific where it charges the defendant with "voting more than once," and that term is not defined in the criminal statute).

The Elements of the Crime: Apprendi v. New Jersey

Under *Stirone* an indictment that does not set forth all of the elements of the crime charged is constitutionally deficient. Sometimes however it is difficult to determine just what *is* an element of the crime—as distinct from a sentencing factor that can be left for the judge. This issue is discussed in detail in Chapters 10 and 11. At this juncture, it is sufficient to note that in Apprendi v. New Jersey, 530 U.S. 466 (2000), the Court held that a factual determination authorizing an increase in sentencing beyond a statutory maximum is an element of the crime, and therefore is a question for the jury that must be proved beyond a reasonable doubt—and it must accordingly be set forth in the charging instrument. So for example, if the legislature has authorized a sentencing enhancement, beyond the statutory maximum sentence, for possession of a certain amount of drugs, the jury must determine the amount that the defendant possessed, and that amount must be set forth in the indictment. The opinion in *Apprendi* is set forth in Chapter 10. In states where no indictment is required, it should be sufficient for any charging instrument to allege all of the essential elements of an offense.

CHAPTER 7

BAIL AND PREVENTIVE DETENTION

∎ ∎ ∎

I. INTRODUCTION TO THE PROBLEMS OF PRETRIAL RESTRAINT

A. THE SUSPECT'S CONCERNS

Many defendants are released or convicted and sentenced within 24 hours of their arrest.[1] The remaining defendants await disposition of their cases for days, weeks, or months, depending on prosecutors' workloads, the gravity and complexity of the cases, the condition of court calendars, and the actions of defense attorneys. The magistrate must determine which defendants may and should be released pending trial. See e.g., United States v. Briggs, 697 F.3d 98 (2nd Cir. 2012) (upholding detention without bail for two years while awaiting trial).

By the time the magistrate rules, the police have progressed sufficiently far in the investigatory process to have focused on an individual suspect. But it is possible that the suspect is innocent of all or most charges that are being considered or have been brought. The pretrial determination of probable cause, which forms the basis for arrest and detention pending trial, has the limited function of establishing only a fair probability that a suspect committed a crime. So there is a significant risk that an innocent person may be subject to detention before trial.

The suspect can certainly point to significant personal costs associated with pretrial detention. The consequences of incarceration include deprivation of contacts with friends and family, absence from employment and possibly loss of job or a house, diminished ability to support family and to hire counsel, limitations on the ability to prepare a defense, and stigmatizing effects on the prisoner's reputation and future employment prospects. If the defendant is ultimately convicted, it can be argued that any unfairness arising from pretrial incarceration serving as punishment is *de minimis* because pretrial incarceration can be treated as time served on the sentence. But this only applies to those who are incarcerated. Anyone who has charges dismissed, is acquitted, is diverted into a treatment program or is sentenced to community service or probation never

---

[1] The Challenge of Crime in a Free Society, Report of the President's Commission on Law Enforcement and the Administration of Justice (1968).

receives credit or compensation for time served, even if the length was substantial.

Moreover, studies indicate that pretrial imprisonment actually does prejudice the adjudication of guilt or innocence when it finally occurs, because a defendant who is incarcerated will find it harder to help prepare his defense.[2] In addition, prior detention erodes the rehabilitative prospects of the accused, placing him at a disadvantage both in conviction and sentencing. The defendant's demeanor, recognized as an essential element of the fact-finding determination, will reflect recent imprisonment: He is apt to be unshaven, unwashed, unkempt, and unhappy as he enters the courtroom under guard.[3] The hopelessness, the lowered self-esteem, and a decline in respect for the criminal justice system may cause detained suspects to lose their incentives to prolong the adjudication process and accordingly to plead guilty. There is evidence that a person who can't make bail is substantially more likely to plead guilty than one who can. See, e.g., Note, Detaining for Danger Under the Bail Reform Act of 1984: Paradoxes of Procedure and Proof, 35 Ariz.L. Rev. 1091, 1095 (1993) ("it is widely acknowledged that the government now commonly misuses the leverage of pretrial detention to extract premature guilty pleas and cooperation agreements in exchange for pretrial release"). Individuals sometimes challenge convictions on the ground that they only pleaded guilty because of pretrial confinement. See, e.g., Smith v. Oklahoma Co., 2013 U.S. Dist. Lexis 105754 (W. D. Okla. 2013) (habeas petitioner claims charges to which he pled were false and he only pled because of danger in pretrial confinement).

There are social costs to pretrial detention, as well. In addition to the significant costs of maintenance and support of the prisoners, society must often bear the secondary welfare costs incident to the imprisonment of a member of a household. See Colbert, Thirty-Five Years After *Gideon*: The Illusory Right to Counsel at Bail Proceedings, 1998 Univ.Ill.L.Rev. 1 (noting that pretrial incarceration imposes "a hefty price on society" in the form of job loss, family dislocation, and emotional turmoil, and that when the charges are eventually dismissed or not prosecuted, "the economic, social, and emotional consequences incurred cannot be justified or remedied.").

The individual costs of pretrial incarceration fall most heavily, of course, on the underprivileged and indigent. A very high percentage of pretrial inmates are incarcerated because they cannot even post relatively modest cash bail. The Bar Association of the City of Baltimore has reported that almost half of Baltimore's pretrial detainees had a bail of $1,000 or

---

[2] See Kinney v. Lenon, 425 F.2d 209 (9th Cir.1970), where the court held that the defendant's release was necessary so that he might track down witnesses essential to his defense.

[3] See P. Wald, Pretrial Detention and Ultimate Freedom: A Statistical Study, 39 N.Y.U.L.Rev. 631, 632 (1964).

less. See The Drug Crisis and Underfunding of the Justice System in Baltimore City 33 (1990). A 1992 study by the Department of Justice indicated that about one-third of pretrial detainees throughout the country were jailed on bail of less than $2,500. Bureau of Justice Statistics Bulletin, Pretrial Release of Felony Defendants, 1992, at 4. And a more recent NPR report stated that over 500,000 people have been incarcerated because they cannot make bail in amounts from $50–400. Talk of the Nation, January 26, 2010. The ability of a defendant to meet even a relatively small amount of bail depends on personal and family resources or the ability to post a 10% bail bond fee and the willingness of a bondsman to accept a defendant as a client.

"Pretrial" detention becomes even more of a concern if there is not even a certainty that there will ever be any trial. For example, after the 9/11 attacks, hundreds of people were rounded up on the basis of suspected ties to terrorism. Most were released after more than a year of incarceration, with no charges being filed. Obviously, these open-ended detentions, with no trial set or perhaps even planned, imposed substantial hardships on the detainees.

B. COUNTERVAILING CONCERNS

On the other hand, there are compelling societal interests that militate in favor of pretrial detention of some criminal suspects. One obvious justification for imprisonment pending trial is to guarantee the presence of the suspect in order to ensure proper judicial disposition of the case.[4]

Pretrial detention also has a *preventive* aspect. The state has an interest in protecting the community that warrants imprisonment of at least some of those accused of criminal activity. In some cases there is a legitimate concern that pretrial release will simply give the suspect an opportunity to commit more criminal acts. And this concern is obviously ratcheted up in the post-9/11 environment when the government apprehends a person with suspected ties to terrorism. See, e.g., United States v. Hir, 517 F.3d 1081 (9th Cir. 2008) (upholding pretrial detention of a defendant who was the brother of a terrorist responsible for many

---

[4] The New York Times, October 9, 1995, p.B1, col.2, reported that in New Jersey, more criminal defendants were then at large, having failed to appear in court, than were incarcerated in the state. Police departments reported a lack of resources to track down defendants who do not appear, especially if they have left the state. The article included an interview with a victim of child sexual abuse; the defendant in the case never appeared for trial, and had been at large in Florida for eight years, even though the victim had given the police his address.

The United States Department of Justice Bureau of Justice Statistics, Felony Defendants in Large Urban Counties (2004) ["BJS 2004 Large Urban County Study"], a study of the largest 75 urban counties, reported that of 21% of defendants released pretrial in 2004 for whom bench warrants were issued for violating conditions of release, 5% were still fugitives after one year.

Efforts to assist in apprehension of fugitives have given rise to multimedia efforts like http:// fugitive.com, a reality-based television and website founded in 1992 by two Bay Area police officers.

bombings in Asia, where the evidence indicating that the defendant was sending money and electronic devices to his brother).

Courts, in determining whether a person should be released pending trial, are thus essentially balancing the individual's liberty interests against the legitimate interests of the state. What mechanism will operate to release those who pose no threat to the judicial process or the community at large, while detaining criminal suspects who are dangerous or likely to flee? How can the system protect the presumption of innocence and the right to be free pending adjudication, without hampering the law enforcement process or risking public safety? These are the questions posed in this Chapter as well as in the real world of processing criminal cases.

II. BAIL: ITS HISTORY AND THE CONSTITUTION

A. THE COMMON LAW ORIGINS OF BAIL

The traditional mechanism for pretrial release, the posting of bail, originated in medieval England, where prisoners could be confined in disease-ridden and insecure prisons for years awaiting trial by traveling justices, whose visits were infrequent.

Sheriffs welcomed the opportunity to place custodial responsibility in third parties. A prisoner would seek a friend or master, usually a property owner, who accepted custody or "bailment" of the accused, and promised to surrender himself if the defendant failed to appear. Of course, the law developed to permit the surety to forfeit property or money instead of his person, but the relationship remained a personal one. Eventually Parliament specified which offenses were bailable, and the Habeas Corpus Act of 1679 provided procedures to free prisoners who were bailable by law. Some judges still circumvented these requirements by setting prohibitive levels of bail; so in 1689, Parliament responded with a provision forbidding excessive bail.

B. THE CONSTITUTIONAL PROHIBITION AGAINST EXCESSIVE BAIL: THE EIGHTH AMENDMENT

The American Constitution incorporated the right of a person in custody to seek a writ of habeas corpus in Article I § 9, and the ban on excessive bail in the Eighth Amendment ("[e]xcessive bail shall not be required"). The third aspect of British law regarding bail, that is, the actual right to bail for specific offenses, was not included in the Constitution. Thus, the Amendment prohibits excessive bail, but it does not explicitly grant a right to bail. See Fields v. Henry County, 701 F.3d 180 (6th Cir. 2012) (the Eighth Amendment does not give a right to bail but rather "mandates that when bail is granted, it may not be unreasonably high in light of the government's purpose for imposing bail."). The Supreme Court described the provenance of the Bail Clause in Carlson v. Landon, 342 U.S. 524 (1952), a civil case, in which the Court denied bail to alien communists awaiting deportation hearings:

> The bail clause was lifted with slight changes from the Bill of Rights Act. In England that clause has never been thought to accord a right to bail in all cases, but merely to provide that bail shall not be excessive in those cases where it is proper to grant bail. When this clause was carried over in our Bill of Rights, nothing was said that indicated any different concept. The Eighth Amendment has not prohibited Congress from defining the classes of cases in which bail shall be allowed in this country. * * *

Critics of the holding point out that this interpretation would subsume the Constitution to some other law. "It requires one to believe that a basic human right would be deliberately inserted in the Constitution in a form which permitted Congress to restrict it at will, or even to render the eighth amendment entirely moot by enacting legislation denying the right to bail in all cases." Foote, The Coming Constitutional Crisis in Bail, 113 U.Pa.L.Rev. 959 (1965). Some states have resolved this dilemma by adding a bail *requirement*, usually for all but capital crimes, to their state constitutions.[5]

See United States v. Salerno, infra, for a further discussion of the constitutional and policy issues surrounding bail. For a comprehensive and academic perspective, see Frase, Excessive Prison Sentences, Punishment Goals, and the Eighth Amendment: "Proportionality" Relevant to What?, 89 Minn. L. Rev. 571 (2005).

III.   THE OPERATION OF A BAIL RELEASE SYSTEM

A. THE ADMINISTRATION OF BAIL: THE PROCEDURES

The most frequently used procedure for obtaining one's pretrial release has traditionally been through *cash bail*. Having learned of the bail figure, a defendant may raise the full amount of the bond through personal savings or those of his friends and family. If he shows up for all required court appearances and complies with all conditions of release, the entire amount posted is usually refunded to him. See Fed.R.Crim.P. 46(g) (providing for release of bail when bond conditions have been satisfied). Conditions of release may include not only appearance at all court dates, but other conditions such as refraining from criminal activity, retaining

---

[5]   The Supreme Court has never held that the Eighth Amendment Bail Clause is binding on the states, though it has implied that a limitation on excessive bail is a fundamental right. Schilb v. Kuebel, 404 U.S. 357 (1971). Again, however, this does not establish a right to bail.

employment, drug treatment, avoiding association with certain individuals, etc.

A defendant who can't come up with money to post bail may seek the assistance of a bail bondsman, who has complete discretion in selecting clients. The bondsman's usual fee is 10 percent of the bond amount; this fee is non-refundable. The bondsman places the entire bond with the court and the defendant gains pretrial freedom. If the defendant fails to comply with the conditions of pretrial release the bond is forfeited. It is therefore in the bondsman's interest to assure such compliance.

Personal bond is another method of release, which may be referred to as personal surety, nominal bond, or release on own recognizance. It is used when a judge determines that the defendant is sufficiently motivated to show up for his scheduled court appearance and can be released on his own signature without bail. But, if the defendant fails to appear, a monetary penalty may be imposed.

Defendants released on personal or surety bond by a nonjudicial officer, such as a police desk sergeant, have obtained freedom only until their first court appearance, which usually occurs shortly after the initial release. At that time, unless the case is disposed of then and there, the judge reviews the bail amount and may revise it upward or downward. Similarly, bail set by a lower court for those accused of felonies may be reviewed and revised by the higher court which conducts the actual trial.

Judges might also exercise discretion to release the defendant into a third party's custody. The magistrate in such cases charges the third party with the responsibility of assuring that the defendant will appear and will not violate specified conditions of the release. Common candidates for third party responsibility include the defendant's relatives or friends, or social service agencies or pretrial release programs.

The Bureau of Justice Statistics 2004 Large Urban County Study reported that in the 75 largest urban counties, 57% of defendants charged with felonies were released pre-trial and 43% were detained. Not surprisingly, defendants charged with murder were least likely to be released (12%). More surprising is the next category of defendants least likely to be released: motor vehicle theft (39%). The other defendants least likely to be released were the following: robbery (42%), burglary (45%) and rape (52%).

The Bureau of Justice Statistics Special Report, State Court Processing Statistics, 1990–2002 Violent Felons in Large Urban Counties (July 2006) reported the following statistics: "An estimated 38% of violent felons were released from custody pending disposition of the case that resulted in their conviction. Fifty percent were held on bail, and 11% were denied bail. Among violent felons who had a bail amount set, about two-thirds were released when their bail was set at under $5,000, compared to just 4% when it was set at $100,000 or more."

B. THE BONDSMAN

Free of most political and governmental restraints, the private bail bondsman is one of the most important players in the pretrial drama. When bail is set, the accused can pay a non-refundable premium—usually 10%—to a private bondsman, who then puts up the total amount of bail. The bondsman assumes the risk of forfeiture and has traditionally been given much discretion in establishing collateral for bail, and in tracking down and retrieving a fleeing accused. The legal right of a bondsman to surrender the defendant to the court and to cancel the bond and keep the fee gives the bondsman considerable leverage, especially when bail may be set anew at different stages of a trial. The threat of being "turned in" ties the defendant to his bondsman, who may demand new premiums as the trial progresses.

Proponents of the bond system point out that without the private bondsman, numerous defendants would remain in jail for lack of available assets.[6] Also, bondsmen are often on call 24 hours a day. The profit motive provides them with the incentive to enforce a defendant's appearance in court. Thus, the system encourages private enterprise to assume part of the cost of administering the pretrial process. In theory, the bondsmen reinforce the law enforcement system by preventing flight and helping to return fugitives.

Critics, however, argue that the private bond system undercuts the purposes of bail and contravenes the ideals of the criminal justice system. Once released on a commercial bond, the defendant loses the same amount to the bondsman whether or not the defendant appears at trial. Theoretically, the court aims to set bail at a level that will ensure the appearance of the accused, but the intervening role of the bondsman supersedes the judicial determination. Thus, magistrates may fix bail with knowledge that the defendant has found a bondsman to advance funds or has been unable to secure help. Discretion in choosing clients provides one explanation for the relatively low level of risk in the bonding business. Bondsmen consider principally the type of crime for which the defendant was arrested, not necessarily the seriousness of the offense. Thus, those accused of organized crime or professional gambling are good risks, while a first time offender is considered a bad risk: unsophisticated as to the intricacies of the court system and prone to panic and jump bail. Narcotic

---

[6]   For example, the Justice Department reported that in 1992, about half of the defendants for whom bail was set had to turn to a private bondsman to get released. Bureau of Justice Statistics, Pretrial Release of Felony Defendants, 1992.

addicts are considered good risks, prostitutes are not.[7] Bondsmen are free to incorporate their own political or personal prejudices in the bonding decision. The result can be disturbing. For example, civil rights activists who were arrested in the South often were unable to obtain the services of a bondsman.[8]

On the other hand, there are numerous minor, non-dangerous offenders who simply would have to stay in jail in most states, were it not for the private bondsman. When the bondsmen in New York went on strike in 1961 and 1964, refusing to write bonds except on 100% collateral in bankbooks or real estate, the population of the city jails swelled. The strikes were in retaliation for tighter collection policies enforced on forfeitures.[9]

If the defendant flees, some bondsmen use a system of informants and "skip tracers"—modern day bounty hunters, who often carry arms and have criminal records—to locate the fugitive. Recapture has been held to be a private remedy, arising from a private action, and thus freed from the constraints of due process[10] and constitutional criminal procedure. For example, a bondsman can seize a fugitive in another jurisdiction and present him to authorities, while the state must await extradition proceedings.

Bondsmen and bounty hunters are subject to local laws, however. See, e.g., Lund v. Seneca County Sheriff's Department, 230 F.3d 196 (6th Cir. 2000), where the court dismissed a claim for illegal arrest filed by a bondsman who was arrested by police after the bondsman broke into a house to catch a woman who had skipped bail, took her away and left her two young children unattended. The bondsman took the position that he had a federal constitutional right under the Extradition Clause, Article IV section 2, to "break the law to re-arrest his fugitive." The court rejected this rather outrageous assertion and held that the Extradition Clause "does not shield a bondsman under federal law from arrest and prosecution for violating [state law] in apprehending bail jumpers."

Noting that "the methods often employed by bondsmen are hardly likely to promote respect for the administration of justice," the ABA Standards on Pretrial Release set forth a standard prohibiting, or at least severely limiting, private bonding:

---

[7] See A. Marticz, The Ups and Downs of a Bail Bondsman, L.A. Times, 8/2/76, reprinted in J. Snortum and I. Hader, Criminal Justice Allies and Adversaries (1978).

[8] R. Goldfarb, Ransom 2–3 (1965).

[9] Bail or Jail, 19 Record of the Ass'n of the N.Y. City Bar 13 (1964).

[10] Bondsmen are not public officers and therefore are not bound by the constitutional restraints that were examined in Chapters 2 and 3. Although they are not restrained by the Constitution, bondsmen rely upon it to protest forfeitures. In Wilshire Ins. Co. v. State, 94 Nev. 546, 582 P.2d 372 (1978), the court held that due process requires that the bondsmen be given notice of bail forfeiture proceedings.

§ 5.4   Prohibition of Compensated Sureties

Compensated sureties should be abolished. Pending abolition, they should be licensed and carefully registered. The amount which a compensated surety can charge for writing a bond should be set by law. No licensed surety should be permitted to reject an applicant willing to pay the statutory fee or insist upon additional collateral other than specified by law.

Similar acts have been passed in a few states, although most states have hesitated to eliminate the private bondsman for fear that fewer persons would be released, and higher bonds would result for those who are released.

Forfeiture of the Bond

A bond can be forfeited if the terms of the release are violated. See Fed.R.Crim.P. 46(f)(1) ("The court must declare the bail forfeited if a condition of the bond is breached."). Forfeiture may occur even if the defendant appears for trial; this is because the bail bond can impose numerous obligations other than attendance. For example, in United States v. Vaccaro, 51 F.3d 189 (9th Cir.1995), the defendant was charged with racketeering. His pretrial release was secured by a $100,000 bond provided by Bell Bail Bonds. As one of the conditions of his release, Vaccaro agreed that he would "not violate any local, state or federal laws or regulations." Vaccaro committed a crime while released, and the trial court ordered the bail bond forfeited. Bell argued that the forfeiture provision of Fed.R.Crim.P. 46(f)(1) was triggered only if the defendant failed to appear. But the court held that the "break no laws" provision was a material part of his release agreement, and reasoned that "a bail bond is a contract between the government and the defendant and his surety." See also United States v. Gigante, 85 F.3d 83 (2d Cir.1996) (upholding bail condition requiring forfeiture of bond if the defendant commits a federal, state or local crime while released on bail).

Bail bondsmen have (so far unsuccessfully) appealed to Congress for an amendment to Rule 46 to allow forfeiture only "if the defendant fails to appear physically before the court." (This was the language of the proposed "Bail Bond Fairness Act of 2001," H.R. 2929). The Judicial Conference opposed the legislation, having surveyed magistrate judges who reported that it is often important to impose other conditions of release as part of the bail bond—for example a condition that the defendant refrain from drug use. Magistrate judges argued that if they are not permitted to impose extra conditions, they will be less likely to grant bail in the first place. The Judicial Conference, in a letter to Congress, concluded that Rule 46 as written "provides judges with the valuable flexibility to impose added safeguards ensuring a defendant's compliance with conditions of release."

C. THE BAIL SETTING DECISION

Judges are entrusted with vast discretion in implementing the controlling statutes or court rules pertaining to bail. Bail criteria are not self-executing; it is the application of general criteria to particular cases that effectively determines which defendants are released and under what conditions. Often courts can choose among criteria in making bail decisions, and the choice often reflects a court's view of the purposes of bail.

Amount of Bail Must Support the Purposes for Setting It: Stack v. Boyle

As stated previously, the Court has never held that bail or any form of pretrial release is constitutionally required. However, the Court in Stack v. Boyle, 342 U.S. 1 (1951) recognized that, *if* bail is set, then a court must set it at an amount that appropriately furthers the purposes of bail. The Court held that bail fixed in uniform amounts of $50,000 for each of twelve defendants charged with violations of the Smith Act could not be justified in the absence of evidence relating to the particular characteristics and circumstances of each defendant. Three paragraphs from the Court's opinion follow:

> The right to release before trial is conditioned upon the accused's giving adequate assurance that he will stand trial and submit to sentence if found guilty. Like the ancient practice of securing the oaths of responsible persons to stand as sureties for the accused, the modern practice of requiring a bail bond or the deposit of a sum of money subject to forfeiture serves as additional assurance of the presence of an accused. Bail set at a figure higher than an amount reasonably calculated to fulfill this purpose is "excessive" under the Eighth Amendment.

> [T]he fixing of bail for any individual defendant must be based upon standards relevant to the purpose of assuring the presence of that defendant. * * * Upon final judgment of conviction, petitioners face imprisonment of not more than five years and a fine of not more than $10,000. It is not denied that bail for each petitioner has been fixed in a sum much higher than that usually imposed for offenses with like penalties and yet there has been no factual showing to justify such action in this case. The Government asks the courts to depart from the norm by assuming, without the introduction of evidence, that each petitioner is a pawn in a conspiracy and will, in obedience to a superior, flee the jurisdiction. To infer from the fact of indictment alone a need for bail in an unusually high amount is an arbitrary act. Such conduct would inject into our own system of government the very principles of totalitarianism which Congress was seeking to guard against in passing the statute under which petitioners have been indicted.

If bail in an amount greater than that usually fixed for serious charges of crimes is required in the case of any of the petitioners, that is a matter to which evidence should be directed in a hearing so that the constitutional rights of each petitioner may be preserved. In the absence of such a showing, we are of the opinion that the fixing of bail before trial in these cases cannot be squared with the statutory and constitutional standards for admission to bail.

Relevant Factors in Setting Bail

The most important factor in setting bail is the seriousness of the offense charged. The rationale is that the more serious the offense, the more likely that the defendant presents a risk of flight or harm to others.

A second factor in the bail-setting decision is the strength of the case against the defendant. This information is often relayed to the judge by prosecutors and police officers. Prosecutors may not be unbiased in their recommendations to judges. By suggesting a high bail amount with the expectation that the judge will lower it, prosecutors may seek to shield themselves from responsibility if the accused fails to appear in court or commits additional offenses while on release.

A third factor considered very relevant by the judiciary is the defendant's prior criminal record.

A fourth factor involves an assessment of the possibility that the defendant poses a flight risk. See, e.g., United States v. Leisure, 710 F.2d 422 (8th Cir. 1983) (finding bail of $2 million was excessive "when all of the evidence adduced before the magistrate indicated that appellants would appear at their trial").

Other factors are the defendant's background, such as his community ties, financial status, and character references.

Of course if the defendant's counsel is present at the bail hearing, she tries to supply facts in attempting to secure the client's release on the best conditions possible.[11]

Despite the Supreme Court's reasoning in *Stack*, the reality is that bond schedules are used in many places and they establish a presumption as to what bail should be required for various offenses. Such schedules may fail to account for personal differences among defendants, but they make the magistrate's job easier and increase the predictability of a bail decision. See Fields v. Henry County, 701 F.3d 180 (6th Cir. 2012) (upholding bail

---

[11] Federal Rule 44 provides that an indigent defendant has a right to counsel at the bail hearing. But the bail hearing has never been held to be a "critical stage" at which counsel must be provided as a matter of constitutional law. Twelve states do not guarantee indigents the right to counsel at bail hearings. See Colbert, Thirty-Five Years After *Gideon*: The Illusory Right to Counsel at Bail Proceedings, 1998 Univ.Ill.L.Rev. 1.

set pursuant to a bond schedule). The movement away from these bail schedules is discussed later in this Chapter.

D. FOUR SAMPLE CASES

In the following fact situations, consider what arguments you see for and against recommending bail for the accused. As judge, would you set bail? What conditions would you set, if any, in addition to a promise to appear? As a private bondsman, whose general practice is either to accept 10% of the bond as a non-refundable premium or to refuse the client, would you take the risk?

1.   The 39-year-old defendant was arrested 2 days ago for attempted murder and aggravated battery. He has a prior record of 10 armed robberies and one attempted jailbreak while awaiting an earlier trial. Yesterday, he threatened the life of a cellmate, and boasted that he always carried a loaded gun. He has an excellent record for his prior experience on parole, and a perfect attendance record while free on bond for a prior conviction. He has been working part-time, and for the past 6 months has lived with his mother. The maximum sentence is 10 years. Would your answer differ if he had no job, and no permanent address? If he were charged with burglary? With armed robbery? With vagrancy?

2.   A 36-year-old defendant is charged with breaking and entering. She is a heroin addict, and has a record of seven prior convictions for breaking and entering within the last three years, as well as two convictions for possession of narcotics in the same time period. She lives with her three young children, and works part-time in the department store where she was arrested. Should she be released on bail? How much bail should be required?

3.   A 65-year-old defendant is charged in an arson conspiracy. He owned and ran a diner in New York City for 25 years, until it burned to the ground. He has no passport and no family members who live in New York. He has a brother in Greece. This is his first offense. Should bail be set? How high? Would it make a difference if a person died in the fire? Would it make a difference if the defendant had a passport?

4.   A Muslim student is charged with lying to the grand jury about knowing some of the individuals who took part in planning terrorist attacks in Los Angeles. He is not charged with taking part in the attacks. He traveled extensively in the Middle East before settling in San Diego and becoming an American citizen. He has a brother in the United States. He has traveled back to the Middle East on several occasions, and the prosecutor submits a statement from a State Department official that the defendant has contributed to Muslim charities "known to funnel monies to Al Qaeda." Do you set bail? Are you worried about a public outcry? Would taking away his passport guarantee that he is no longer a flight risk?

IV.   BAIL REFORM

A. THE FEDERAL BAIL REFORM ACTS

Congress, concerned about the arbitrariness and unfairness of a system of pretrial release that depended heavily on bail bondsmen, enacted the Bail Reform Act of 1966, a statute emulated by many states. The purpose of the 1966 Act was to encourage federal courts to release accused persons without requiring them to deal with bail bondsmen. Apparently, courts were to consider only whether pretrial release "will reasonably assure the appearance of the person for trial." No provision was made for confinement of an accused who might pose a "danger" to the community. The Act provided for alternative methods of assuring an appearance, including in-home detention and supervision by a designated person or organization.

Congress repealed the 1966 Bail Reform Act as part of its Comprehensive Crime Control Act of 1984, 18 U.S.C.A. §§ 3141–3150. The Bail Reform Act of 1984 was an important part of the comprehensive overhaul of federal criminal law and is *much less generous* to defendants than the prior act. The most important changes are: 1) the explicit recognition that potential dangerousness to the community may be considered in pretrial release decisions; and 2) the possibility for preventive detention without bail.

The heart of the Bail Reform Act of 1984 is found in 18 U.S.C. § 3142, which proceeds in the following steps:

a. Court's Options:

The Act gives the court four options for a defendant who is bound over for trial. The court can:

(1) Release the defendant on personal recognizance or upon execution of an unsecured appearance bond;

(2) Release the defendant on a condition or combination of conditions, the violation of which will result in incarceration;

(3) If the defendant is on parole or subject to deportation, detain the defendant until he is processed; or

(4) Detain the defendant pending trial.

b. Release on personal recognizance or unsecured appearance bond:

Ostensibly this is the preferred procedure under the Bail Reform Act, and Section 3142(b) states that the court "shall order the pretrial release of the person on personal recognizance, or upon execution of an unsecured appearance bond in an amount specified by the court." But the Act contains a major exception: "unless the judicial officer determines that such release will not reasonably assure the appearance of the person as required or will endanger the safety of any other person or the community."

c. Release on conditions:

If the court determines that release on personal recognizance or on unsecured bond will not assure the defendant's appearance at trial or will endanger the safety of a person or the community, then conditions can be imposed on pretrial release. If the court decides to impose conditions, one that *must* be imposed is that the defendant "not commit a Federal, State, or local crime during the period of release." Conditions must also be set that will assure the defendant's appearance and the safety of other persons and the community. In setting conditions for appearance and safety, the court is instructed to impose the "least restrictive" conditions necessary to accomplish those objectives. The Act sets out a laundry list of possible conditions for release. The list is not intended to be exclusive or dispositive. The listed possible conditions are that the defendant:

(i) remain in the custody of a designated person, who agrees to assume supervision and to report any violation of a release condition to the court;

(ii) maintain employment, or, if unemployed, actively seek employment;

(iii) maintain or commence an educational program;

(iv) abide by specified restrictions on personal associations, place of abode, or travel;

(v) avoid all contact with an alleged victim of the crime and with any potential witness who may testify concerning the offense;

(vi) report on a regular basis to a designated law enforcement agency, pretrial services agency, or other agency;

(vii) comply with a specified curfew;

(viii) refrain from possessing a firearm, destructive device, or other dangerous weapon;

(ix) refrain from excessive use of alcohol, or any use of a narcotic drug or other controlled substance;

(x) undergo medical, psychological, or psychiatric treatment, including treatment for drug or alcohol dependency, and remain in a specified institution if required for that purpose;

(xi) execute an agreement to forfeit designated assets upon failing to appear as required;

(xii) execute a bail bond;

(xiii) return to custody for specified hours following release for employment, schooling, or the like; and

(xiv) "satisfy any other condition that is reasonably necessary to assure the appearance of the person as required and to assure the safety of any other person and the community."

The statute provides that the court "may not impose a financial condition that results in the pretrial detention of the person." That is, the court cannot impose a financial requirement for release that the defendant is not able to meet. See Wagenmann v. Adams, 829 F.2d 196 (1st Cir. 1987) (bail was unconstitutionally excessive when it was set at $500 when the court knew that he only had $480 on hand). If the defendant is going to be subject to pretrial detention, it must be upon findings, after a hearing, that he presents a flight or safety risk that no condition other than detention will reasonably alleviate (see below).

d.   Pretrial Detention:

If the court finds that "no condition or combination of conditions will reasonably assure the appearance of the person as required and the safety of any other person and the community," then it must order the pretrial detention of the defendant, without bail. Preventive detention is only available, however, if the defendant is charged with a certain kind of crime; the possible crimes include crimes of violence, drug crimes, and other crimes designated by Congress.

In addition, if the defendant is charged with or has been previously convicted of certain specified crimes (including crimes of violence) within the past five years, then there is a "rebuttable presumption" that no condition or combination of conditions will reasonably assure the safety of any other person and the community. The statute also provides that there is a rebuttable presumption of both a flight and safety risk if the defendant has ever been convicted of a federal drug crime with a maximum term of imprisonment of ten years or more. And the same rebuttable presumption applies to defendants charged with terrorism. The rebuttable presumption shifts the burden of production to the defendant to show that he does not pose a risk of flight or a safety risk. But "the burden of persuasion remains with the government." United States v. Hir, 517 F.3d 1081 (9th Cir. 2008).

The determination on pretrial detention is made after a hearing, at which the defendant has the right to counsel, including government-provided counsel if he is indigent. The defendant has the right to testify, to present witnesses, to cross-examine witnesses who appear at the hearing, and to present information by proffer or otherwise. The Federal Rules of Evidence do not apply at this hearing. Pretrial detention will be ordered if the government proves by a preponderance that the defendant is a flight risk; but if the ground of detention is that the defendant presents a safety risk, then the government must show this risk by clear and convincing evidence. 18 U.S.C. § 3142(f)(2)(B).

In determining risk of flight and risk to safety, the court is directed to consider 1) the nature and circumstances of the offense charged, including whether it is a crime of violence or a drug crime; 2) the strength of the evidence against the defendant (i.e., the stronger the evidence the greater the risks); 3) the defendant's character, including community ties and prior misconduct; and 4) specific dangers to any person that would be posed by the defendant's release.

———

There is little doubt that the 1984 legislation makes it more difficult for some defendants to obtain release pending trial. Before the 1984 Act, only about 2% of federal defendants were detained pending trial. In 1990, the figure rose to 29% of all federal defendants. The rate of detention in 1990 was 50% for those charged with violent crime, and 37% for those charged with drug crimes. Bureau of Justice Statistics, Pretrial Release of Federal Felony Defendants (1994). By 2005, 65.5% of defendants were detained pre-trial. Bureau of Justice Statistics, Federal Justice Statistics, 2005, Table 3.2.

It would be wrong to conclude, however, that the statute represents a uniformly negative attitude toward pretrial release. As noted above, no accused may be detained pending trial without findings by the judicial officer. A defendant may seek review of these findings. [§ 3145]. Most importantly, the statute explicitly provides that a financial condition may not be imposed if it results in the pretrial detention of the person. This means that, unless the judicial officer finds that no condition or conditions of release will provide that an accused will appear and will protect the community, the officer must provide for release of the accused.

Applying the Bail Reform Act of 1984

The Bail Reform Act of 1984 has raised a number of interpretive problems for the courts. One question is how a court is to assess the risk of flight. In United States v. Jessup, 757 F.2d 378 (1st Cir.1985), the court sustained the presumption in the Bail Reform Act of 1984 that a defendant charged with a serious drug offense poses a serious risk of flight. It concluded that Congress shifted only the burden of production with respect to the flight issue to the defendant and that the government continued to bear the burden of persuasion with respect to likelihood of flight. The court also concluded, however, that the presumption did not disappear when the defendant offered rebuttal evidence. Instead, it adopted a "middle ground" which requires judges and magistrates to consider Congress's finding that suspects charged with serious drug offenses pose special risks of flight and to weigh that finding when deciding whether the government has satisfied its persuasion burden. See also United States v. Xulam, 84 F.3d 441 (D.C.Cir.1996) (in non-drug cases, when the government seeks pretrial detention of a defendant on the ground that he poses a risk of flight, the standard it must satisfy is a preponderance of the evidence).

United States v. Abad, 350 F.3d 793 (8th Cir. 2003), provides a basic application of the Bail Reform Act's provisions on pretrial detention. Abad was charged with traveling in interstate commerce to have sex with a 13-year-old girl. He met the girl over the internet. This crime triggered the rebuttable presumption that the defendant presented a flight risk and presented a danger to the community (it is categorized as a crime of violence for purposes of the statutory presumption that the defendant presents a flight risk and a risk to the community). The defendant rebutted the presumption that he was a flight risk with letters from his parents and other members of the community, and with his parents' putting up their equity interest in their house as an assurance he would not flee. But this evidence served only to rebut the statutory presumption. The court found that the government had proved by a preponderance of the evidence that the defendant presented a flight risk that justified pretrial detention. The court reasoned as follows:

> Abad is not a United States citizen. Although Abad's family members are willing to pledge a $65,000 equity interest in the parents' home, such surety is insufficient to assure Abad's presence at trial. Abad faces a maximum sentence of 30 years, which reduces the significance of the surety amount and weighs strongly in favor of a finding Abad would be a flight risk. Although electronic surveillance is available, when considering all the factors at issue in the present case, there is insufficient evidence to assure Abad's appearance at trial.

> To counter the government's evidence regarding risk of flight, Abad offered five letters of support from family members and friends. However, none of the letters indicate the writers knew the nature of Abad's alleged crime. Two of the letters reference only the writers' familiarity with Abad's family rather than with Abad himself. Needless to say, these letters do not tip the scales when weighed against the government's damning evidence. Abad's family's willingness to supervise Abad while he is home is entitled to little weight, because Abad contacted the Iowa girl and engaged in web-cam sex with her while living at home with his family. Taking possession of Abad's passport has little flight deterrence considering the ease of travel to Mexico and Canada. Simply stated, we conclude Abad is a flight risk.

The *Abad* court also found that the government proved by clear and convincing evidence that the defendant presented a risk to the community that justified pretrial detention:

> Abad has no prior criminal history. However, the nature of the crime charged—sexual activity with a minor—weighs heavily against release. Strong evidence links Abad to this crime of violence. At the time of Abad's arrest, the police found a digital camera, condoms, KY Jelly, used contraceptive gels, and a dildo in Abad's hotel room. Abad admitted (1) he knew the girl was 13 years old, and he had met her in an Internet chat room for 13- and 14-year olds; (2) he engaged in telephone sex and web-cam sex with the girl before traveling to Iowa; and (3) he used a digital camera to take photos and video clips of the 13-year old girl masturbating and performing oral sex on Abad. The photos and video clips were found on the digital camera. Further, the government presented testimony Abad told the Iowa girl he previously, at the age of 22, had sex with a 15-year-old in Michigan. Based upon the evidence presented, we find the district court erred in ruling Abad is not a danger to the community. In particular, releasing Abad so he may return to his nursing position at Miami Children's Hospital is a clear abuse of discretion.

On the question of risk to the community, is the court saying that *anyone* charged with a child sex crime by definition presents a risk to the community warranting pretrial detention?

Risk to a Foreign Community?

In United States v. Hir, 517 F.3d 1081 (9th Cir. 2008), the defendant was charged with providing material support to a terrorist—his brother, who was wanted for terrorist acts in Asia. Hir had no prior record, and the government did not contend that he posed a threat to anyone in the United States. Nonetheless he was denied bail on the ground that he posed a threat to persons in Asia. The question for the court was whether the Bail Reform Act authorized pretrial detention for threats outside the country. The Act refers to threats to the "community"—but the court held that the relevant community need not be within the geographic bounds of the United States. The court reasoned that "[a]ny other interpretation would lead to an incongruous result: a court would be able to try a defendant under the laws of the United States for a crime the effects of which are felt abroad, but be unable to detain the defendant who committed the crime despite clear and convincing evidence that he continues to pose a danger to the same foreign community."

Drug Cases

The court in United States v. Rueben, 974 F.2d 580 (5th Cir.1992), set forth the standards for pretrial detention in drug cases as follows:

- probable cause of a serious drug crime creates a rebuttable presumption that no conditions of release exist which would assure the defendant's appearance and the safety of the community;

- where the defendant presents considerable evidence of longstanding ties to the community, the presumption of flight has been rebutted;

- the possibility of continued drug trafficking while on bail constitutes a safety risk to the community;

- for pretrial detention to be imposed, it is enough for the court to find either the lack of a reasonable assurance of the defendant's appearance, or a safety risk to others or the community;

- the rebuttable presumption against release shifts only the weight of producing evidence, not the burden of persuasion, but the mere production of some evidence does not completely rebut the presumption; and

- in making its ultimate determination, "the court may still consider the finding by Congress that drug offenders pose a special risk of flight and dangerousness to society."

In *Rueben*, the court held that the district court erred in releasing two drug defendants on a $100,000 unsecured bond. The court found that the defendants' "alleged family ties was hardly more than a reflection of the drug conspiracy itself." Similarly, the fact that one defendant owned a house "is not compelling as a tie to the community when its loss through forfeiture is a possibility because of its use in drug trafficking." Nor had the defendants presented any evidence to "indicate that they will not continue to engage in drug trafficking if released on bail pending trial."

Has the court in *Rueben* in effect established an irrebuttable presumption of detention in drug cases? See also United States v. Smith, 79 F.3d 1208 (D.C.Cir.1996) (indictment on drug charges creates a rebuttable presumption that no condition would reasonably assure the safety of the community; no error in ordering detention where the defendant was an "enforcer" in a drug conspiracy, and murdered a rival drug dealer in furtherance of the conspiracy); United States v. Cisneros, 328 F.3d 610 (10th Cir. 2003) (pretrial release properly denied where the defendant was charged with taking part in an international drug conspiracy, the defendant had the resources to abscond to Mexico, and the evidence suggested that the defendant was deeply involved in serious acts of violence). Compare United States v. Giampa, 755 F.Supp. 665 (W.D.Pa.1990) (presumption rebutted where drug defendant shows his long residence in the area, his close ties to his family, steady employment history, lack of resources or contacts that would enable him to flee the country with ease, and the fact that he had no record and did not appear to live the life of a serious drug dealer; court notes that the defendant was not the kind of "international narcotics trafficker" with whom Congress was most concerned when it enacted the Bail Reform Act).

Less Intrusive Alternatives

The ultimate statutory determination under the Bail Reform Act is whether "there are conditions of release that will reasonably assure the appearance of the [defendant] as required and the safety of any other person in the community." This statutory language is sometimes invoked by defendants to suggest less intrusive alternatives to pretrial detention. A typically suggested alternative is home detention and electronic monitoring. As to the effectiveness of this alternative to detention, consider the facts of United States v. Tortora, 922 F.2d 880 (1st Cir.1990):

> An alleged soldier in the Patriarca Family of the Mafia was indicted for violation of the RICO statute. His three predicate crimes in furtherance of the RICO enterprise were: extortion; violation of the Travel Act; and conspiracy to violate the Travel Act. Upon the grant of the government's motion for pretrial detention, the defendant proposed certain release conditions to assure the safety of the community. These conditions mandated, for example, that the defendant not violate the law, appear at scheduled proceedings, eschew possession of weapons and substance abuse, restrict his travel, etc. In granting the release order, the [district] court required the defendant to (1) remain at home twenty-four hours a day, except for a reasonable number of visits to doctors and lawyers, wearing an electronic bracelet; (2) refrain from communicating with any person not approved by the prosecutor and defense counsel; (3) meet with codefendants only in the presence of counsel for the purpose of preparing a defense; (4) allow only one telephone line into his residence, hooking it up to a pen register; and (5) post the residence— a house owned by his brother—as security.

The court of appeals vacated the order releasing Tortora. It first agreed with the district court that Tortora was properly classified as dangerous. The court reasoned that membership in an Organized Crime Organization was clearly relevant to dangerousness, rejecting Tortora's argument that such "associational ties" could not be considered. It concluded that as long as the defendant was judged as an individual, his devotion to the Mafia was important evidence of his dangerous character, especially where

Tortora, at a ritualistic Mafia ceremony, "threatened to kill his brother if the latter posed a danger to any member of the organization." The court also rejected Tortora's argument that devotion to his family precluded a finding of dangerousness. It responded that in light of Tortora's oath of fealty to the Mafia, "there is every reason to believe that he will prefer Family over family."

The *Tortora* court next held that the release conditions were not adequate to assure the community's safety in view of the fact that virtually all of the conditions hinged upon the defendant's good faith compliance. As such they could be too easily manipulated or circumvented. For instance, electronic monitoring "cannot be expected to prevent a defendant from committing crimes or deter him from participating in felonious activity within the monitoring radius"; and pen registers could be evaded by "the surreptitious introduction into his home of a cellular telephone." The court concluded that the "honor-dependent" nature of the restrictions took on great significance where "little about the defendant or his history suggests that good faith will be forthcoming." The court rejected the argument that the conditions of release could be amended to eliminate the risk of danger to the community:

> Given the breadth of human imagination, it will always be possible to envision some set of release conditions which might reasonably assure the safety of the community. For instance, agents could be posted by the government to watch Tortora at all times to ensure that he remains compliant; the guards could search all visitors, dog Tortora's footsteps en route to all appointments, and otherwise act as private jailers. But the Bail Reform Act, as we read it, does not require release of a dangerous defendant if the only combination of conditions that would reasonably assure societal safety consists of heroic measures beyond those which can fairly be said to have been within Congress' contemplation.

Tortora argued that the release conditions proposed by him and adopted by the lower court were sufficient because the alternative was incarceration—and if kept in prison, he would have at least as much ability to commit crimes as he would have if released. The court viewed this argument as "perverse" and stated:

> The Bail Reform Act does not ordain that dangerousness upon release is to be measured relative to dangerousness if incarcerated, and for good reason: the ability of an incarcerated person to commit crimes while in jail is a problem for the Executive Branch to solve. The idea that someone who otherwise ought not to be released should be let loose by the courts because his jailers may not prevent him from committing crimes in prison comprises a classic non sequitur * * *.

See also United States v. Gotti, 776 F.Supp. 666 (E.D.N.Y.1991) (ordering pretrial detention and rejecting home detention as an alternative: "Home detention and electronic monitoring at best elaborately replicate a detention facility without the confidence of security such a facility instills."); United States v. Hir, 517 F.3d 1081 (9th Cir. 2008) (upholding an order rejecting bail for a defendant accused of sending assistance to his brother, a wanted terrorist; proposed limitations of in-house arrest and electronic monitoring were not sufficiently effective because assistance could continue through internet monetary transfers; other limitations, such as self-imposed limitations on computer use, were insufficient as they were dependent on good-faith compliance by the defendant).

The Right to a Prompt Hearing:
United States v. Montalvo-Murillo

In United States v. Montalvo-Murillo, 495 U.S. 711 (1990), the government failed to comply with the provision in the Bail Reform Act of 1984 that a hearing to determine the propriety of pretrial release be held "immediately upon the person's first appearance before the judicial officer." The district court ultimately found that Montalvo-Murillo posed a risk of flight and a danger to the community, and that no condition of release could give reasonable assurances against these risks. The court nonetheless released Montalvo-Murillo due to the lack of a timely hearing. The government challenged the release order and argued that release was an unwarranted remedy for a violation of the prompt hearing requirement.

Justice Kennedy, writing for six Justices, agreed with the government. He acknowledged the importance of a prompt hearing, but asserted that "neither the timing requirements nor any other part of the Act can be read to require, or even suggest, that a timing error must result in release of a person who should otherwise be detained." The majority reasoned as follows:

> The safety of society does not become forfeit to the accident of noncompliance with statutory time limits where the Government is ready and able to come forward with the requisite showing to meet the burden of proof required by the statute. * * * An order of release in the face of the Government's ability to prove at once that detention is required by the law has neither causal nor proportional relation to any harm caused by the delay in holding the hearing.

Justice Kennedy concluded that release of Montalvo-Murillo was an unwarranted remedy because he had not been prejudiced by the delay:

> In this case, it is clear that the noncompliance with the timing requirement had no substantial influence on the outcome of the proceeding. Because respondent was dangerous and likely to flee, he

would have been detained if his hearing had been held upon his first appearance rather than a few days later. On these facts, the detention was harmless.

Justice Stevens, joined by Justices Brennan and Marshall, dissented and argued that the majority had undervalued the importance of a prompt hearing on the propriety of pretrial detention.

Time Served and the Bail Reform Act: Reno v. Koray

Under the Bail Reform Act, it is possible that a defendant could be released pending trial and yet remain subject to substantial restrictions on liberty, such as confinement in a treatment center or under house arrest. Is such a defendant entitled to a reduction for pre-sentence "time served" if he is ultimately sentenced? Or must he actually be incarcerated to have credit for time served? This question is controlled by statute. 18 U.S.C. § 3585(b) provides that a defendant generally must "be given credit toward the service of a term of imprisonment for any time he has spent in official detention prior to the date the sentence commences." The limits of this provision in light of the Bail Reform Act are indicated by Reno v. Koray, 515 U.S. 50 (1995). Koray was convicted of money laundering. A federal magistrate judge "released" him on bail, pending sentencing, pursuant to the Bail Reform Act. The "release" order required that Koray be confined to a community treatment center, where he stayed for 150 days. The Supreme Court, in an opinion by Chief Justice Rehnquist, held that since Koray was "released" by the magistrate judge's order under the terms of the Bail Reform Act, he could not be considered in "official detention" while confined in the treatment center so as to receive the credit provided by 18 U.S.C. § 3585(b). The Chief Justice reasoned that "under the language of the Bail Reform Act of 1984, a defendant suffers 'detention' only when committed to the custody of the Attorney General; a defendant admitted to bail on restrictive conditions, like respondent was, is 'released.'"

The Chief Justice recognized that a defendant "released" to a community treatment center "could be subject to restraints which do not materially differ from those imposed on a 'detained' defendant committed to the custody of the Attorney General, and thence assigned to a treatment center." But this did not change the result mandated by the statute. The latter defendant would be entitled to a credit while the former would not.

Justice Ginsburg wrote a concurring opinion in Koray. She agreed with the majority's statutory construction, but added that "Koray has not argued before us that he did not elect bail intelligently, i.e., with comprehension that time in the halfway house, unlike time in jail, would yield no credit against his eventual sentence." Justice Ginsburg would not foreclose the possibility that a defendant has a due process right to "notice and a comprehension check" before accepting the terms of release under the Bail Reform Act. Justice Stevens was the lone dissenter in *Koray*. Does a statutory scheme make sense where "release" and "detention" can result in similar deprivations of liberty? Does it make any sense that Koray might have been better off in jail for the time he was detained at the treatment center?

Application of the Bail Reform Act to Persons Charged with Acts of Terrorism

After the attacks of September 11, 2001, the Bail Reform Act has been used for preventive detention of a number of defendants charged with having ties to terrorism. In United States v. Goba, 240 F. Supp.2d 242 (S.D.N.Y. 2003), for example, the court denied four defendants' motions to revoke a pretrial detention order and found that the Government had demonstrated by clear and convincing evidence that defendants pose a danger to the community based on credible evidence that each defendant associated himself with al-Qaeda.

The Bail Reform Act is inapplicable to individuals detained as "enemy combatants" in Guantanamo Bay pursuant to a war powers rationale.

B. THE BAIL REFORM MOVEMENT

In recent years there has been increasing concern over the use of bail schedules that often keep individuals unable to make bail in pretrial detention despite the fact that they pose neither a danger of flight nor of harm to the community. Even in jurisdictions that purport to apply the principle that no one should be detained simply because of an inability to make bail, magistrates are prone to rely on bail schedules either because they lack sufficient information about individual defendants or they are concerned about being blamed if a person is released without bail and commits a crime.

The American Bar Association adopted the following resolution at its August 2017 annual meeting:

RESOLVED, That the American Bar Association urges federal, state, local, territorial, and tribal governments to adopt policies and procedures that:

1. favor release of defendants upon their own recognizance or unsecured bond;

2. require that a court determine that release on cash bail or secured bond is necessary to assure the defendant's appearance and no other conditions will suffice for that purpose before requiring such bail or bond;

3. prohibit a judicial officer from imposing a financial condition of release that results in the pretrial detention of a defendant solely due to the defendant's inability to pay;

4. permit a court to order a defendant to be held without bail where public safety warrants pretrial detention and no conditions of pretrial release suffice, and require that the court state on the record the reasons for detention; and

5. bar the use of "bail schedules" that consider only the nature of the charged offense, and require instead that courts make bail and release determinations based upon individualized, evidence-based assessments that use objective verifiable release criteria that do not have a discriminatory or disparate impact based on race, ethnicity, religion, socio-economic status, disability, sexual orientation, or gender identification.

http://www.americanbar.org/content/dam/aba/directories/policy/2017_am_112C.docx.

The accompanying report explained the need for the resolution:

I. Curtailing Financial Conditions of Pretrial Release

* * *

Despite the ABA's insistence that pretrial detention should occur only in exceptional situations, large-scale pretrial confinement has continued unabated in this country since adoption of the ABA Standards in 2002. In 2015, almost eleven million people were admitted into a jail. Todd D. Minton & Zhen Zeng, U.S. Dep't of Justice, *Jail Inmates in 2015* at 2 (2016). Most of the people incarcerated in jails have not been convicted of the alleged crime that led to their confinement. They are simply awaiting a decision whether they will be charged with a crime or, if charged, their trial. These unconvicted individuals comprised over 62% of the people incarcerated in jails in 2015, up from 40% in 1983. Todd D. Minton & Zhen Zeng, U.S. Dep't of Justice, *Jail Inmates in 2015* at 5, Table 4 (2016); Allen J. Beck, U.S. Dep't of Justice, *Profile of Jail Inmates, 1989*, at 2 tbl. 1 (1991).

One of the chief reasons for the extensive incarceration of presumptively innocent people is the conditioning of release from jail (or not being booked into jail) on the meeting of financial requirements, whether in the form of a cash payment, the posting of property as collateral, or a surety bond from a commercial bail bondsman. * * *

As the Vera Institute of Justice recently reported, "Money, or the lack thereof, is now the most important factor in determining whether someone is held in jail pretrial." Ram Subramanian et al., Vera Inst.

Of Justice, *Incarceration's Front Door: The Misuse of Jails in America* 29 (2015) [hereinafter Vera Report]. And therein lies the problem. Most of the people detained in jails are poor. Some manage to eventually procure the funds needed to post bail or pay a nonrefundable fee to a bail bonding company, though they have to endure days or weeks of incarceration in the meantime. Many others are unable to ever muster the financial resources needed to gain their freedom. In fact, statistics collected since the adoption of the ABA Standards have revealed that 90% of the individuals who never secure their release from jail while their criminal cases are being processed are not confined because they were denied bail due to being a flight risk or danger to the public. They are incarcerated simply because they could not muster the financial resources needed to secure their liberty. Brian A. Reaves, U.S. Dep't of Justice, *Felony Defendants in Large Urban Counties*, 2009, at 15 (2013).

Recent statistics from New York City highlight how cash bail continues to erect an insurmountable barrier to freedom for so many people. In 2013, more than half (54%) of the people who had to remain in the city's jails while their cases were being processed did not have enough money to pay bail set at $2500 or less. Vera Report 32. In fact, 31% of the non-felony defendants who were never able to secure their pretrial release were so poor that they could not even pay a bail sum as little as $500 or less. *Id.*

* * *

An abundance of research conducted and knowledge amassed since the adoption of the ABA Standards in 2002 have now made it clear that financial conditions of release fail to protect individual or public safety. At best, in rare cases, financial conditions may be used in conjunction with an individualized assessment of risk and ability to pay.

The report emphasizes that "[t]he amount of money or property a person has is not an accurate predictor of the risk of danger that person poses to others or of the risk that he or she will not show up for a scheduled court proceeding." It explains that "researchers have now developed, and jurisdictions are increasingly employing, validated risk-assessment instruments to guide pretrial-release and detention decisions," and "[t]hese empirically-tested tools are much more accurate predictors of risk than financial bail, intuition, or professional judgments unguided by such risk-assessment instruments. Conference of State Court Administrators, *2012–2013 Policy Paper: Evidence-Based Pretrial Release* 6–7 (2012)."

The report describes "[n]ew research [that] has unveiled that when low- and moderate-risk people are detained in jail for more than a day, they are significantly more likely to engage in a future crime"; "[t]he trauma and stigma that people endure from being incarcerated pretrial"; and "[n]ew research * * * reveal[ing] that pretrial detention due to an inability to post bond has a pervasive and negative impact on the outcomes of criminal cases."

The report concludes that

> where these types of schedules represent a judicial determination that defendants charged with low-risk offenses ought to be released, the appropriate mechanisms are release on recognizance or unsecured appearance bonds. Otherwise, these low bail amounts simply serve as an arrest fine or tax on those defendants who can make bail, while detaining those who can't.

The report ends with 10 key requirements for effective pretrial release and detention decision making.

The American Bar Association is not alone in urging for the reform of existing bail schemes. "Pretty much everyone who spends any time examining the American system of secured cash bail comes away with the same conclusion: It's unjust, expensive and ineffective." Editorial, Cash Bail's Lonely Defender, N.Y. Times, August 26, 2017, at A18. The bail industry has proved effective at lobbying legislatures and leaders of the industry "characterize their fight against ball reform as an all-out war." *Id.*

Concern about the unfairness of bail systems has been bipartisan. For example, Republican Senator Rand Paul and Democratic Senator Kamala Harris in 2017 proposed federal legislation (S.1593), the Pretrial Integrity and Safety Act, which would set aside $10 million in federal grant money to begin encouraging more states to drop or curtail cash bail systems and consider other factors when sorting out whether a defendant should be kept behind bars before trial. https://www.congress.gov/bill/115th-congress/senate-bill/1593/text.

For more information on efforts to reform or replace the system of cash bail, see Foderaro, New Jersey Alters its Bail System and Upends Legal Landscape, N.Y. Times, 2/7/2017, which notes that under an overhaul of New Jersey's bail system, which essentially eliminates cash bail, "judges are now considering defendant's flight risk and threat to public safety in deciding whether to detain them while they await trial. Otherwise, they are to be released, usually with certain conditions." The reform effort in New Jersey was spurred by findings that 39 percent of inmates were eligible to be released on bail but could not meet amounts as low as $2500. The bail bond industry is of course opposed, and cites public safety risks of releasing so many arrestees. But advocates of reform note that a system relying on cash bail does not guarantee safety, because those with some money—including drug dealers, etc.—can buy their freedom.

A new development intended to mitigate the adverse impact of bail decisions on the less wealthy is discussed in Jay Lambert & J. Vincent Aprile II, Bail Credit: An Innovative Way to Mitigate Oppressive Monetary Bail, 32 Criminal Justice 32 (Winter 2018). The innovation would permit pretrial detainees to earn the funds to meet their bail as they serve their pretrial confinement. An example is Kentucky Revised Statute 431.066, which was enacted in 2011, and provides that a court shall permit a defendant a credit of $100 per day as a payment toward the amount of the bail set for each day or a portion of a day that the defendant remains in jail prior to trial.

V. THE CONSTITUTIONALITY OF PREVENTIVE DETENTION

Preventive detention results in a loss of liberty, before an adjudication has been made that a person is guilty of a crime. How can this be squared with the detainee's right to due process? This question is explored in the following case.

UNITED STATES V. SALERNO

Supreme Court of the United States, 1987.
481 U.S. 739.

CHIEF JUSTICE REHNQUIST delivered the opinion of the Court.

The Bail Reform Act of 1984 allows a federal court to detain an arrestee pending trial if the government demonstrates by clear and convincing evidence after an adversary hearing that no release conditions "will reasonably assure . . . the safety of any person and the community." The United States Court of Appeals for the Second Circuit struck down this provision of the Act as facially unconstitutional, because, in that court's words, this type of pretrial detention violates "substantive due process." * * * We hold that, as against the facial attack mounted by these respondents, the Act fully comports with constitutional requirements. We therefore reverse.

* * *

Responding to "the alarming problem of crimes committed by persons on release," Congress formulated the Bail Reform Act of 1984, as the solution to a bail crisis in the federal courts. * * *

Respondents Anthony Salerno and Vincent Cafaro were arrested on March 21, 1986, after being charged in a 29-count indictment alleging various Racketeer Influenced and Corrupt Organizations Act (RICO) violations, mail and wire fraud offenses, extortion, and various criminal gambling violations. The RICO counts alleged 35 acts of racketeering activity, including fraud, extortion, gambling, and conspiracy to commit murder. At respondents' arraignment, the Government moved to have Salerno and Cafaro detained * * * on the ground that no condition of release would assure the safety of the community or any person. The District Court held a hearing at which the Government made a detailed proffer of evidence. The Government's case showed that Salerno was the "boss" of the Genovese Crime Family of La Cosa Nostra and that Cafaro was a "captain" in the Genovese Family. According to the Government's proffer, based in large part on conversations intercepted by a court-ordered wiretap, the two respondents had participated in wide-ranging conspiracies to aid their illegitimate enterprises through violent means. The Government also offered the testimony of two of its trial witnesses, who would assert that Salerno personally participated in two murder conspiracies. Salerno * * *

The District Court granted the Government's detention motion, concluding that the Government had established by clear and convincing evidence that no condition or combination of conditions of release would ensure the safety of the community or any person * * *.

Respondents appealed, contending that to the extent that the Bail Reform Act permits pretrial detention on the ground that the arrestee is likely to commit future crimes, it is unconstitutional on its face. Over a dissent, the United States Court of Appeals for the Second Circuit agreed. * * * It reasoned that our criminal law system holds persons accountable for past actions, not anticipated future actions. Although a court could detain an arrestee who threatened to flee before trial, such detention would be permissible because it would serve the basic objective of a criminal system—bringing the accused to trial. * * * The Court of Appeals also found our decision in Schall v. Martin, 467 U.S. 253 (1984), upholding postarrest pretrial detention of juveniles, inapposite because juveniles have a lesser interest in liberty than do adults. * * *

A facial challenge to a legislative Act is, of course, the most difficult challenge to mount successfully, since the challenger must establish that no set of circumstances exists under which the Act would be valid. The fact that the Bail Reform Act might operate unconstitutionally under some conceivable set of circumstances is insufficient to render it wholly invalid, since we have not recognized an "overbreadth" doctrine outside the limited context of the First Amendment. We think respondents have failed to shoulder their heavy burden to demonstrate that the Act is "facially" unconstitutional.

* * *

Respondents first argue that the Act violates substantive due process because the pretrial detention it authorizes constitutes impermissible punishment before trial. The Government, however, has never argued that pretrial detention could be upheld if it were "punishment." The Court of

Appeals assumed that pretrial detention under the Bail Reform Act is regulatory, not penal, and we agree that it is.

* * * To determine whether a restriction on liberty constitutes impermissible punishment or permissible regulation, we first look to legislative intent. Unless Congress expressly intended to impose punitive restrictions, the punitive/regulatory distinction turns on whether an alternative purpose to which the restriction] may rationally be connected is assignable for it, and whether it appears excessive in relation to the alternative purpose assigned to it.

We conclude that the detention imposed by the Act falls on the regulatory side of the dichotomy. The legislative history of the Bail Reform Act clearly indicates that Congress did not formulate the pretrial detention provisions as punishment for dangerous individuals. Congress instead perceived pretrial detention as a potential solution to a pressing societal problem. There is no doubt that preventing danger to the community is a legitimate regulatory goal.

Nor are the incidents of pretrial detention excessive in relation to the regulatory goal Congress sought to achieve. The Bail Reform Act carefully limits the circumstances under which detention may be sought to the most serious of crimes. See 18 U.S.C. § 3142(f)(detention hearings available if case involves crimes of violence, offenses for which the sentence is life imprisonment or death, serious drug offenses, or certain repeat offenders). The arrestee is entitled to a prompt detention hearing, and the maximum length of pretrial detention is limited by the stringent time limitations of the Speedy Trial Act. Moreover, as in Schall v. Martin, the conditions of confinement envisioned by the Act "appear to reflect the regulatory purposes relied upon by the government." As in *Schall* the statute at issue here requires that detainees be housed in a "facility separate, to the extent practicable, from persons awaiting or serving sentences or being held in custody pending appeal." We conclude, therefore, that the pretrial detention contemplated by the Bail Reform Act is regulatory in nature, and does not constitute punishment before trial in violation of the Due Process Clause.

The Court of Appeals nevertheless concluded that "the Due Process Clause prohibits pretrial detention on the ground of danger to the community as a regulatory measure, without regard to the duration of the detention." Respondents characterize the Due Process Clause as erecting an impenetrable "wall" in this area that "no governmental interest—rational, important, compelling or otherwise—may surmount."

We do not think the Clause lays down any such categorical imperative. We have repeatedly held that the government's regulatory interest in community safety can, in appropriate circumstances, outweigh an individual's liberty interest. For example, in times of war or insurrection, when society's interest is at its peak, the government may detain individuals whom the government believes to be dangerous. Even outside the exigencies of war, we have found that sufficiently compelling governmental interests can justify detention of dangerous persons. Thus, we have found no absolute constitutional barrier to detention of potentially dangerous resident aliens pending deportation proceedings. We have also held that the government may detain mentally unstable individuals who present a danger to the public, and dangerous defendants who become incompetent to stand trial. We have approved of postarrest regulatory detention of juveniles when they present a continuing danger to the community. Even competent adults may face substantial liberty restrictions as a result of the operation of our criminal justice system. If the police suspect an individual of a crime, they may arrest and hold him until a neutral magistrate determines whether probable cause exists. Finally, respondents concede and the Court of Appeals noted that an arrestee may be incarcerated until trial if he presents a risk of flight, or a danger to witnesses.

* * * Given the well-established authority of the government, in special circumstances, to restrain individuals' liberty prior to or even without criminal trial and conviction, we think that the present statute providing for pretrial detention on the basis of dangerousness must be evaluated in precisely the same manner that we evaluated the laws in the cases discussed above.

The government's interest in preventing crime by arrestees is both legitimate and compelling. * * * The Bail Reform Act * * * narrowly focuses on a particularly acute problem in which the government interests are overwhelming. The Act operates only on individuals who have been arrested for a specific category of extremely serious offenses. Congress specifically found that these individuals are far more likely to be responsible for dangerous acts in the community after arrest. Nor is the Act by any means a scattershot attempt to incapacitate those who are merely suspected of these serious crimes. The government must first of all demonstrate probable cause to believe that the charged crime has been committed by the arrestee, but that is not enough. In a full-blown adversary hearing, the government must convince a neutral decisionmaker by clear and convincing evidence that no conditions of release can reasonably assure the safety of the community or any person. While the government's general interest in preventing crime is compelling, even this interest is heightened when the government musters convincing proof that the arrestee, already indicted or held to answer for a serious crime, presents a demonstrable danger to the community. Under these narrow circumstances, society's interest in crime prevention is at its greatest.

On the other side of the scale, of course, is the individual's strong interest in liberty. We do not minimize the importance and fundamental nature of this right. But, as our cases hold, this right may, in circumstances where the government's interest is sufficiently weighty, be subordinated to the greater needs of society. * * * When the government proves by clear and convincing evidence that an arrestee presents an identified and articulable threat to an individual or the community, we believe that, consistent with the Due Process Clause, a court may disable the arrestee from executing that threat. * * *

Finally, we may dispose briefly of respondents' facial challenge to the procedures of the Bail Reform Act. To sustain them against such a challenge, we need only find them "adequate to authorize the pretrial detention of at least some [persons] charged with crimes," whether or not they might be insufficient in some particular circumstances. We think they pass that test. * * * Under the Bail Reform Act, the procedures by which a judicial officer evaluates the likelihood of future dangerousness are specifically designed to further the accuracy of that determination. Detainees have a right to counsel at the detention hearing. 18 U.S.C. § 3142(f). They may testify in their own behalf, present information by proffer or otherwise, and cross-examine witnesses who appear at the hearing. The judicial officer charged with the responsibility of determining the appropriateness of detention is guided by statutorily enumerated factors, which include the nature and the circumstances of the charges, the weight of the evidence, the history and characteristics of the putative offender, and the danger to the community. The government must prove its case by clear and convincing evidence. Finally, the judicial officer must include written findings of fact and a written statement of reasons for a decision to detain. The Act's review provisions provide for immediate appellate review of the detention decision.

We think these extensive safeguards suffice to repel a facial challenge. * * *

Respondents also contend that the Bail Reform Act violates the Excessive Bail Clause of the Eighth Amendment. The Court of Appeals did not address this issue because it found that the Act violates the Due Process Clause. We think that the Act survives a challenge founded upon the Eighth Amendment.

[The Court discusses both *Stack* and *Carlson* and concludes that "[w]hile we agree that a primary function of bail is to safeguard the courts' role in adjudicating the guilt or innocence of defendants, we reject the proposition that the Eighth Amendment categorically prohibits the government from pursuing other admittedly compelling interests through regulation of pretrial release."] * * * Nothing in the text of the Bail Clause limits permissible government considerations solely to questions of flight. The only arguable substantive limitation of the Bail Clause is that the government's proposed conditions of release or detention not be "excessive" in light of the perceived evil. Of course, to determine whether the government's response is excessive, we must compare that response against the interest the government seeks to protect by means of that response. Thus, when the government has admitted that its only interest is in preventing flight, bail must be set by a court at a sum designed to ensure that goal, and no more. We believe that when Congress has mandated detention on the basis of a compelling interest other than prevention of flight, as it has here, the Eighth Amendment does not require release on bail.

* * *

Reversed.

JUSTICE MARSHALL with whom JUSTICE BRENNAN joins, dissenting.

* * *

Throughout the world today there are men, women and children interned indefinitely, awaiting trials which may never come or which may be a mockery of the word, because their governments believe them to be "dangerous." Our Constitution, whose construction began two centuries ago, can shelter us forever from the evils of such unchecked power. Over two hundred years it has slowly, through our efforts, grown more durable, more expansive, and more just. But it cannot protect us if we lack the courage, and the self-restraint, to protect ourselves. Today a majority of the Court applies itself to an ominous exercise in demolition. Theirs is truly a decision which will go forth without authority, and come back without respect.

I dissent.

[The dissenting opinion of JUSTICE STEVENS is omitted.]

Unconstitutional Applications of Preventive Detention

The Court in *Salerno* left open the possibility that the federal statute might be unconstitutionally applied. But after *Salerno*, courts have upheld lengthy pretrial detentions under the circumstances, upon a showing of risk of flight (by preponderance) or a risk to safety (by clear and convincing evidence). For example, in United States v. Infelise, 934 F.2d 103 (7th Cir.1991), the court held that continued detention for two years pending trial did not violate due process. The court noted that the Government cannot delay a trial in order to use preventive detention as a surrogate for punishment. But the court found the delay to be due to the complexity of the case, the presence of multiple defendants, and pre-trial motions by the defendants. In United States v. Millan, 4 F.3d 1038 (2d Cir.1993), the court upheld a 30 month pretrial detention of a defendant who was the head of a large heroin distribution network. It noted that the prosecution was not solely responsible for the delay in the trial, and that the evidence of risk of flight and dangerousness to the community was compelling. The court stated that "the constitutional limits on a detention period based on dangerousness to the community may be looser than the limits on a detention period based solely on risk of flight. In the former case, release risks injury to others, while in the latter case, release risks only the loss of a conviction." Do cases like these give defendants detained before trial a disincentive to file pretrial motions?

Is it possible for a pretrial detention to be so prolonged that it violates due process regardless of any risk of flight or danger to the community? In *Millan,* the court stated that the length of detention "will rarely by itself offend due process" and that the prospective detention of thirty months, "while weighing in favor of release, does not, standing alone, establish that pretrial confinement has exceeded constitutional limits." Rather, the court must balance "(i) the length of the detention; (ii) the extent of the prosecution's responsibility for the delay of the trial; and (iii) the strength of the evidence upon which the detention was based." Of course, the longer the detention, the more likely it is that some of the delay is attributable to the prosecution.

Constitutionality of Other Forms of Preventive Detention— Insanity Acquittees: Foucha v. Louisiana

Salerno was distinguished by the Court in Foucha v. Louisiana, 504 U.S. 71 (1992). Foucha was tried for a violent crime and was found not guilty by reason of insanity. Under Louisiana law he was committed to a psychiatric hospital for an indefinite period. Hospital officials subsequently recommended his release on the ground that he was not currently, and probably never had been, insane. However, Louisiana law provided that commitment would continue, even in the absence of mental illness, unless the detainee could prove that he was not dangerous to himself or others; and hospital officials, noting Foucha's "anti-social" personality, refused to attest to his non-dangerousness. The State relied heavily on *Salerno* to justify Foucha's continuing commitment on grounds of dangerousness, but a five-person majority, in an opinion by Justice White, held that the Louisiana scheme violated Foucha's right to due process. Justice White rejected *Salerno's* applicability in the following passage:

> Unlike the sharply focused scheme at issue in *Salerno,* the Louisiana scheme of confinement is not carefully limited. Under the state statute, Foucha is not now entitled to an adversary hearing at which the State must prove by clear and convincing evidence that he is demonstrably dangerous to the community. Indeed, the State need

prove nothing to justify continued detention, for the statute places the burden on the detainee to prove that he is not dangerous. * * *

It was emphasized in *Salerno* that the detention we found constitutionally permissible was strictly limited in duration. Here, in contrast, the State asserts that because Foucha once committed a criminal act and now has an antisocial personality that sometimes leads to aggressive conduct, a disorder for which there is no effective treatment, he may be held indefinitely. This rationale would permit the State to hold indefinitely any other insanity acquittee not mentally ill who could be shown to have a personality disorder that may lead to criminal conduct. The same would be true of any convicted criminal, even though he has completed his prison term. It would also be only a step away from substituting confinements for dangerousness for our present system which, with only narrow exceptions and aside from permissible confinements for mental illness, incarcerates only those who are proved beyond reasonable doubt to have violated a criminal law.

Justice O'Connor wrote a concurring opinion stating that under *Salerno* it might "be permissible for Louisiana to confine an insanity acquittee who has regained sanity if, unlike the situation in this case, the nature and duration of detention were tailored to reflect pressing public safety concerns related to the acquittee's continuing dangerousness."

Justice Thomas wrote a dissenting opinion and was joined by Chief Justice Rehnquist and Justice Scalia. He agreed that *Salerno* was readily distinguishable from the instant case, but argued that the distinction cut in favor of the Louisiana commitment scheme. He noted that insanity acquittees, unlike pretrial detainees subject to the Bail Reform Act, "have had their day in court. Although they have not been convicted of crimes, neither have they been exonerated * * *." Justice Kennedy also dissented in a separate opinion in which the Chief Justice joined.

Constitutionality of Other Forms of Preventive Detention— Sexual Predators: Kansas v. Hendricks

Responding to the rising public alarm over sex crimes, many states have enacted "sexual predator" laws. These laws typically allow preventive detention of defendants who have been convicted of sex crimes and have completed their sentences. The Supreme Court considered the constitutionality of preventive detention of sexual predators in Kansas v. Hendricks, 521 U.S. 346 (1997). Kansas's Sexually Violent Predator Act establishes procedures for the civil commitment of persons who, due to a "mental abnormality" or a "personality disorder," are likely to engage in "predatory acts of sexual violence." Kansas filed a petition under the Act to commit Hendricks, who had a long history of sexually molesting children and who was scheduled for release from prison after serving time for a series of convictions for sexual assault of minors. After Hendricks testified that he agreed with the state physician's diagnosis that he suffered from pedophilia and was not cured and that he continued to harbor sexual desires for children that he could not control when he got "stressed out," the jury determined by a preponderance of the evidence that he was a sexually violent predator. Finding that pedophilia qualifies as a mental abnormality under the Act, the court ordered him committed. On appeal, the State Supreme Court invalidated the Act on the ground that the precommitment condition of a "mental abnormality" did not satisfy what it perceived to be the "substantive" due process requirement that involuntary civil commitment must be predicated on a "mental illness" finding.

The Supreme Court reversed the State Supreme Court. The Justices unanimously agreed that civil detention of sex offenders, based on a finding of "mental abnormality", did not violate any guarantee of substantive due process. Justice Thomas, writing for five members of the Court on this question, stated as follows:

> The Court has recognized that an individual's constitutionally protected interest in avoiding physical restraint may be overridden even in the civil context. * * * We have consistently upheld such involuntary commitment statutes provided the confinement takes place pursuant to proper procedures and evidentiary standards. See Addington v. Texas, 441 U.S. 418 (1979). It thus cannot be said that the involuntary civil confinement of a limited subclass of dangerous persons is contrary to our understanding of ordered liberty.

> * * * A finding of dangerousness, standing alone, is ordinarily not a sufficient ground upon which to justify indefinite involuntary commitment. We have sustained civil commitment statutes when they have coupled proof of dangerousness with the proof of some additional factor, such as a "mental illness" or "mental abnormality." * * * These added statutory requirements serve to limit involuntary civil confinement to those who suffer from a volitional impairment rendering them dangerous beyond their control. The Kansas Act is plainly of a kind with these other civil commitment statutes: It requires a finding of future dangerousness, and then links that finding to the existence of a "mental abnormality" or "personality disorder" that makes it difficult, if not impossible, for the person to control his dangerous behavior. The precommitment requirement of a "mental abnormality" or "personality disorder" is consistent with the requirements of these other statutes that we have upheld in that it narrows the class of persons eligible for confinement to those who are unable to control their dangerousness.

Focusing on the facts of the case, the Court found that Hendricks' mental abnormality justified preventive detention:

> The mental health professionals who evaluated Hendricks diagnosed him as suffering from pedophilia, a condition the psychiatric profession itself classifies as a serious mental disorder. Hendricks even conceded that, when he becomes "stressed out," he cannot "control the urge" to molest children. This admitted lack of volitional control, coupled with a prediction of future dangerousness, adequately distinguishes Hendricks from other dangerous persons who are perhaps more properly dealt with exclusively through criminal proceedings. Hendricks' diagnosis as a pedophile, which qualifies as a "mental abnormality" under the Act, thus plainly suffices for due process purposes.

Justice Kennedy wrote a short concurring opinion. Justice Breyer, joined by Justices Stevens, Souter, and Ginsburg, dissented. He argued that the statute operated as an ex post facto law on Hendricks, because the State sought to punish him retroactively for an act that had been committed before the effective date of the statute. He agreed with Justice Thomas, however, that the civil commitment of sexually dangerous persons, on the basis of a finding of mental abnormality, did not violate the Due Process Clause.

If the sexual predator law were struck down, couldn't the state respond by imposing mandatory sentences of life in prison without parole for every person convicted of an act of sexual violence? Would it be a better system to confine such an offender in prison for life rather than in a hospital for treatment? See In re Blodgett, 510 N.W.2d 910 (Minn.1994) (upholding indefinite civil commitment of sexual predators: "If the state were denied the ability to hospitalize the sexual predator, rather than let the offender out on the street, the state will counter by increasing the length of the prison sentence. * * * Arguably, then, the question is not whether the sexual predator can be confined, but where? Should it be in prison or in a security hospital?").

Constitutionality of Other Forms of Preventive Detention— Persons Subject to Deportation: Zadvydas v. Davis

In Zadvydas v. Davis, 533 U.S. 678 (2001), the Court considered the plight of an alien ordered removed from the United States but who could not be deported to a receiving country. A statute, 8 U.S.C. § 1231(a)(6), provides for detention for certain categories of aliens who have been ordered removed but who cannot be removed within 90 days of the deportation order. Those aliens subject to continued detention are: inadmissible aliens, criminal aliens, aliens who have violated their nonimmigrant status conditions, and aliens removable for certain national security or foreign relations reasons, as well as any alien "who has been determined by the Attorney General to be a risk to the community or unlikely to comply with the order of removal." The statute states that an alien who falls into one of these categories "may be detained beyond the removal period and, if released, shall be subject to [certain] terms of supervision."

The Government in *Zadvydas* argued that the statute means literally what it says and sets no limit on the length of time that an alien subject to the statute may be detained if removal is not possible within 90 days. Justice Stevens, writing for five members of the Court, refused to read the statute to provide for indefinite detention, reasoning that to so read the statute would result in a serious constitutional question under the Due Process Clause. Justice Stevens discussed the constitutional concerns in the following passage:

> The civil confinement here at issue is not limited, but potentially permanent. The provision authorizing detention does not apply narrowly to "a small segment of particularly dangerous individuals," *Hendricks,* say suspected terrorists, but broadly to aliens ordered removed for many and various reasons, including tourist visa violations. And, once the flight risk justification evaporates, the only special circumstance present is the alien's removable status itself, which bears no relation to a detainee's dangerousness. * * * The serious constitutional problem arising out of a statute that, in these circumstances, permits an indefinite, perhaps permanent, deprivation of human liberty without any such protection is obvious.

The majority in *Zadvydas* construed the statute to avoid the constitutional problem that it perceived. It held that an alien who is not removed within the 90-day period can bring a habeas corpus action to challenge his continued detention as unreasonable.

Justice Kennedy wrote a dissenting opinion joined by Chief Justice Rehnquist and joined in part by Justices Scalia and Thomas.

Constitutionality of Other Forms of Preventive Detention— Detention of Aliens During Removal Proceedings: Demore v. Kim

It might be important that *Zadvydas* was decided before the terrorist attacks of September 11, 2001. In Demore v. Kim, 538 U.S. 510 (2003), decided after those attacks, Chief Justice Rehnquist wrote for the Court as it distinguished *Zadvydas,* much to the chagrin of the dissenters. Kim, a citizen of the Republic of South Korea, entered the United States in 1984, at the age of six. After becoming a lawful permanent resident of the United States in 1986, he was convicted of first-degree burglary in state court in California in 1996 and a year later of "petty theft with priors." The

Immigration and Naturalization Service (INS) charged Kim with being deportable from the United States in light of these convictions, and detained him pending his removal hearing. The Court held "that Congress, justifiably concerned that deportable criminal aliens who are not detained continue to engage in crime and fail to appear for their removal hearings in large numbers, may require that persons such as respondent be detained for the brief period necessary for their removal proceedings." Kim challenged his detention as a violation of due process because the INS made no determination that he posed either a danger to society or a flight risk.

The Court noted that Congress adopted a mandatory detention provision "against a backdrop of wholesale failure by the INS to deal with increasing rates of criminal activity by aliens," Congress had evidence that one of the major causes of the INS' failure to remove deportable criminal aliens was the agency's failure to detain those aliens during their deportation proceedings, and more than 20% of deportable criminal aliens failed to appear for their removal hearings after their release.

Although it recognized "that the Fifth Amendment entitles aliens to due process of law in deportation proceedings," the Court reasoned that "in *Zadvydas*, the aliens challenging their detention following final orders of deportation were ones for whom removal was 'no longer practically attainable'" which meant that detention did not serve its purported immigration purpose. It found that the mandatory detention provision of "deportable criminal aliens *pending their removal proceedings* * * * necessarily serves the purpose of preventing deportable criminal aliens from fleeing prior to or during their removal proceedings, thus increasing the chance that, if ordered removed, the aliens will be successfully removed. The Court also relied on the fact that the period of detention at issue in *Zadvydas* was "indefinite" and "potentially permanent," while the detention involved in the present case is of a much shorter duration and in the majority of cases it lasts for less than the 90 days considered presumptively valid in *Zadvydas*.

Justice O'Connor, joined by Justices Scalia and Thomas, wrote a separate opinion contending that the Court had no jurisdiction over the case. She agreed, however, with the Court's resolution of the challenge on the merits. Justice Kennedy wrote a concurring opinion in which he opined that a lawful permanent resident alien like Kim "could be entitled to an individualized determination as to his risk of flight and dangerousness if the continued detention became unreasonable or unjustified.".

Justice Souter, joined by Justices Stevens and Ginsburg, dissented in relevant part and agreed with Kim's claim that "due process under the Fifth Amendment conditions a potentially lengthy detention on a hearing and an impartial decisionmaker's finding that detention is necessary to a governmental purpose." Justice Breyer also dissented in part on the ground that it was unclear whether Kim actually was deportable.

VI. SPECIAL PROBLEMS IN THE OPERATION OF BAIL

A. CAPITAL OFFENSES

The granting or denial of bail is traditionally a matter of judicial discretion where a capital offense is charged, but many states by statute prohibit bail for these offenses. A defendant charged with a capital crime may have an incentive to flee that is as great as anyone charged with a crime, and may be considered as belonging in the most dangerous category of offenders. This may explain why states have denied bail in capital cases.

B. JUVENILE OFFENDERS

In the legislative effort to afford complete treatment for juvenile offenders, many states do not provide a right to bail for juveniles charged with offenses that would be crimes if committed by an adult. The rationale is apparently that if the juvenile offender wants to be treated like an adult he has to take the bad with the good—he can only have bail if his offense is adjudicated as a crime. Some courts have noted the possibility of release into parental custody, and have held that the existence of such an option precludes bail, even in a case when the possibility is foreclosed by a judicial determination that release into parental custody would be inappropriate.

Other jurisdictions do use bail as a release mechanism for juveniles. On the same day in 2017 that the American Bar Association adopted its resolution on bail reform in criminal cases, it adopted a resolution that urged governmental entities to cease use of bail/bond in the juvenile justice system, and to utilize objective criteria that do not have a discriminatory or disparate impact and utilize the least restrictive conditions of release. The report accompanying the resolution included the following:

> The policies that have led to an over reliance on collection of bail monies, and fines and fees to fund criminal justice are paralleled in juvenile justice. The consequences of these practices are exacerbated by a child's dependence on a parent or interested adult regarding indigence determinations as well as ability or willingness to post bond or pay fees and provide transport to court. In March of 2016 the Department of Justice issued recommendations to redress practices that disproportionally affect minority populations and poor communities. Bail orders and imposition of fees that cannot be paid foster class-driven preventive detention. The D.O.J. letter was directed at court systems to ensure "court systems at every level (emphasis included) of the justice system operate fairly and effectively." The

D.O.J. letter stresses that all courts must inquire about a defendant's ability to pay in all contexts. Children, or their families, who are not able to post bond or pay fees penetrate more quickly into the juvenile and criminal justice systems, and the evidence suggests that this leads to increases in recidivism.

The D.O.J. letter is U.S. Department of Justice, Civil Rights Division. Office for Access to Justice, Dear Colleague letter (March 14, 2016).

In Schall v. Martin, 467 U.S. 253 (1984), which the Court cited in *Salerno, supra*, the Court upheld a provision in the New York Family Court Act that authorized pretrial detention of an accused juvenile delinquent based on a finding that there is a "serious risk" that the child "may before the return date commit an act which if committed by an adult would constitute a crime." Justice Rehnquist wrote for the Court that "[t]he 'legitimate and compelling state interest' in protecting the community from crime cannot be doubted."

Justice Marshall, joined by Justices Brennan and Stevens, dissented and objected to the breadth of the statute: "The provision applies to all juveniles, regardless of their prior records or the severity of the offenses of which they are accused. The provision is not limited to the prevention of dangerous crimes; a prediction that a juvenile if released may commit a minor misdemeanor is sufficient to justify his detention."

C. BAIL AFTER CONVICTION

As early as 1894, the Supreme Court held that there is no constitutional right to bail pending appeal from a conviction. McKane v. Durston, 153 U.S. 684 (1894). The courts reason that "since there is no constitutional right to appeal, there is no constitutional right to be free pending appeal." United States v. Sine, 461 F.Supp. 565 (D.S.C.1978). The fundamental rights of the convicted defendant differ in other respects, as well. "[T]he presumption of innocence and the right to participate in the preparation of a defense to ensure a fair trial—are obviously not present where the defendant has already been convicted." Gallie v. Wainwright, 362 So.2d 936, 941 (Fla.1978). At the same time, the risk of flight is arguably greater for a defendant who has already been convicted and who may have little hope of a reversal. For these reasons, the standards for postconviction release are stricter, and different criteria may be applied from those used prior to trial. After conviction, the court may consider factors such as the likelihood of reversal, the substantiality of issues on appeal, the length of the sentence imposed, future dangerousness, and the seriousness of the conviction.

The Bail Reform Act of 1984 provides that a defendant may be released pending appeal only if: 1) the court finds "by clear and convincing evidence that the person is not likely to flee or pose a danger to the safety of any other person or the community", and 2) "the appeal is not for purpose of delay and raises a substantial question of law or fact likely to result in reversal or an order for a new trial." In addition, if the defendant has been convicted of a "crime of violence" he must show, in addition to the above factors, that there are "exceptional reasons" why detention is not appropriate. 18 U.S.C. §§ 3143(b)(2) and 3145(c).

Thus, federal detention pending appeal is certainly the norm, as the definition of "crime of violence" is broad and "exceptional" circumstances are by definition rarely found. See United States v. Lea, 360 F.3d 401 (2d Cir. 2004) (bail should have been denied pending appeal because the defendant was convicted of a crime of violence—witness retaliation—and failed to show exceptional circumstances; exceptional circumstances exist where there is "a unique combination of circumstances giving rise to situations that are out of the ordinary"; there was nothing exceptional about the defendant's going to school, being employed, or being a first time offender).

The court in United States v. Koon, 6 F.3d 561 (9th Cir.1993), considered the "exceptional circumstances" language in an appeal by the two officers convicted in the beating of Rodney King (an African-American male beaten by police officers who were acquitted in a state prosecution before being convicted in a federal civil rights prosecution). Officers Koon and Powell advanced several reasons in their request for release pending appeal which they argued qualified as "exceptional," including: their offense was "highly situational"; they had been acquitted in a state court before being prosecuted and convicted for the same activity in a federal court; the victim's conduct contributed to the offense; there would be difficulty in assuring the officers' safety during detention pending appeal; and their sentences were relatively short in comparison to the relatively long process for appeal. But the court held that none of these reasons was "exceptional" because "each is an ordinary corollary of being a law enforcement officer convicted of violating another's civil rights." See also United States v. Little, 485 F.3d 1210 (8th Cir. 2007) (exceptional circumstances are those that are "clearly out of the ordinary, uncommon or rare"; bail pending appeal should have been denied because the defendant's cooperation and timely appearance at hearings, and the aggravated circumstances of his arrest, were not "exceptional circumstances").

CHAPTER 8

DISCOVERY

■ ■ ■

I. CRIMINAL DISCOVERY: UNLIKE CIVIL DISCOVERY

The Federal Rules of Civil Procedure marked an important change in the theory and practice of civil litigation. Before those Rules were adopted

> a diligent lawyer could come into court well prepared on his own case, but he was frequently in the dark as to the exact nature of his opponent's case, and consequently unprepared to meet it. Surprise was a legitimate trial tactic. A lawsuit was viewed as a game or joust in which counsel for each side strove mightily for his client, and the theory was that justice would emerge triumphant when the dust of combat settled in the judicial arena.

M. Green, The Business of the Trial Courts, in The Courts, the Public and the Law Explosion 7, 21–22 (1965).

This "sporting theory of justice" gave way to the belief that a trial should be a "quest for truth." The Federal Civil Rules, as well as the civil discovery rules in the states, provide opposing counsel and litigants with tools, such as depositions and interrogatories, for discovery of information prior to trial; they permit each party to discover much of the evidence that is in the exclusive control of the other.

In contrast, criminal discovery remains decidedly limited—despite the almost universal condemnation of the "sporting theory" of litigation. This raises obvious questions: Are the arguments in favor of broad discovery for civil litigants any less persuasive in the criminal context? Is the "quest for truth" inherently different in civil and criminal cases? If not, are there countervailing considerations in criminal cases that justify a different approach to discovery?

Within the criminal law, the wide range of possible cases makes it difficult to predict the need for discovery or its possible abuses in particular cases. Opponents of discovery tend to focus on violent criminals, citing the danger of revealing prosecutorial information to them. Proponents of more liberal discovery often point to white collar crimes in order to align the accused with the civil defendant.

Not surprisingly, there is little empirical evidence on the dangers of broader discovery in criminal cases. There is little appetite among rulemakers to experiment with exposing witnesses and evidence to pretrial discovery. There is, however, a widespread, and reasonable, belief that certain defendants—those with organized crime or terrorist connections, for example—pose the greatest threat to witnesses and evidence. When a system of discovery is established, the most important issue is whether to presume that most defendants and most defense lawyers will abuse discovery or that most will use discovery as it should be used—i.e., to prepare for trial or plea negotiations.[1] Fundamentally, though, the question is whether there is anything in criminal discovery that justifies its closed nature. As the American College of Trial Lawyers has stated:

> It is anomalous that in civil cases, where generally only money is at stake, access to information is assured while, on the contrary, in criminal cases, where liberty is in issue, the defense is provided far less information.

Proposed Codification of Disclosure of Favorable Information under Federal Rules of Criminal Procedure 11 and 16, 41 Am. Crim. L.Rev. 93 (2003).

The Role of Constitutional Law

Most of the discovery questions considered in this chapter involve nonconstitutional issues. The Supreme Court has repeatedly stated that "there is no general constitutional right to discovery in a criminal case." Weatherford v. Bursey, 429 U.S. 545, 559 (1977). On the other hand, it is clear that constitutional considerations are implicated when a jurisdiction establishes a discovery system. Some sharing of information by the government may be necessary in order to guarantee a fair trial. And an accused may have to give the government notice of certain claims, if it is to have a fair chance to meet them. It may be impossible, however, to have a truly reciprocal discovery system in view of the fact that the accused has a privilege against self-incrimination and cannot be compelled to waive it as part of a discovery regime.

---

[1] The federal discovery framework is discussed at some length herein. A number of states have used it as a model. But many states provide broader discovery for defendants than that granted in the Federal Rules of Criminal Procedure. The Department of Justice may view federal prosecutions as focused more than state counterparts on organized crime, gangs, terrorism and large-scale conspiracies, which might pose greater dangers (at least in some cases) to witnesses and evidence. But, there are a substantial number of drug, gun and immigration prosecutions that would not seem inherently more "dangerous" than many state cases. For decades the Department has opposed efforts to liberalize discovery through changes in the Federal Rules of Criminal Procedure or legislation.

II. THE BASIC ISSUES

A. ARGUMENTS AGAINST BROAD CRIMINAL DISCOVERY

Arguments against broad criminal discovery focus primarily on the risks involved in giving the accused access to prosecutorial information. Judge Learned Hand set the framework for such arguments in his oft-quoted opinion in United States v. Garsson, 291 F. 646, 649 (S.D.N.Y.1923):

> * * * Under our criminal procedure the accused has every advantage. While the prosecution is held rigidly to the charge, he need not disclose the barest outline of his defense. He is immune from question or comment on his silence; he cannot be convicted when there is the least fair doubt in the minds of any one of the twelve. Why in addition he should in advance have the whole evidence against him to pick over at his leisure, and make his defense, fairly or foully, I have never been able to see. * * * Our dangers do not lie in too little tenderness to the accused. Our procedure has been always haunted by the ghost of the innocent man convicted. It is an unreal dream.

This argument suggests that expansion of discovery for defendants would tip the balance too much on the side of the accused. Prosecutors already face a heavy burden of proof and the defendant has the benefit of a privilege against self-incrimination which allows her not to testify at all. Neither of these elements is found in a civil trial.

Opponents of discovery in criminal cases seem to argue that the accused can be treated poorly in some respects if she is treated well in other respects. But what does this say about our attitude toward constitutional rights? It is true that the defendant's right to invoke her privilege against self-incrimination makes it difficult for the prosecutor to gather evidence from a defendant in discovery. It is true that the restrictions on evidence-gathering attributable to the Fourth Amendment and the right to counsel under the Sixth Amendment sometimes impair the government's ability to gather evidence. But does this mean that defendants should not get information that might be necessary for them to prepare a defense or decide whether to enter into a plea agreement?

In a classic opinion, New Jersey Chief Justice Vanderbilt took a different tack from Judge Hand when he described the specific *dangers* that he perceived with rules providing for liberal discovery in criminal cases:

> In criminal proceedings long experience has taught the courts that often discovery will lead not to honest factfinding, but on the contrary to perjury and the suppression of evidence. Thus the criminal who is aware of the whole case against him will often procure perjured testimony in order to set up a false defense * * *. Another result of full

discovery would be that the criminal defendant who is informed of the names of all of the State's witnesses may take steps to bribe or frighten them into giving perjured testimony or into absenting themselves so that they are unavailable to testify. Moreover, many witnesses, if they know that the defendant will have knowledge of their names prior to trial, will be reluctant to come forward with information during the investigation of the crime. * * * All these dangers are more inherent in criminal proceedings where the defendant has much more at stake, often his own life, than in civil proceedings.

State v. Tune, 13 N.J. 203, 210–11, 98 A.2d 881, 884 (1953).

The danger to witnesses might be the strongest argument against extensive discovery on behalf of criminal defendants. Whether the threat to witnesses and to the administration of justice is as great as the quote suggests is subject to fair debate, but many experienced prosecutors believe the threat to be real, at least in some cases. The question is whether this danger justifies a blanket limitation on discovery in virtually all criminal cases.

Another argument against broad defense discovery is that it will result in fishing expeditions into government records. This argument probably can be addressed by providing in discovery rules that only relevant information can be requested and by indicating the classes of information that generally should be discoverable. The use of protective orders and sanctions for discovery abuse can also go far to limit excessive discovery demands—as they do in civil cases. The fact that the same prosecutors' offices appear in all criminal cases means that they should be able to learn quickly what material courts will require them to turn over to defendants.

Case-by-Case Approach?

Is it necessary to take an all-or-nothing approach to discovery issues in criminal cases? Opponents of liberal discovery claim that it poses dangers, but surely they would concede that the dangers do not exist in all cases. Advocates of discovery reform argue that the dangers are overstated in the run of the mill case, but surely they would concede that danger is real in some cases. Why should a rule be written to deny or grant discovery for all criminal cases? It is possible, for example, either to presume that discovery is to be permitted, but to allow the government to oppose it in a particular case, or to presume that it is not to be permitted absent a showing by the defendant of specialized need.

One of the problems with a case-by-case approach is that it may result in hearings when one side or the other tries to overcome the presumption. Early in a criminal case it may be hard for the side against whom the presumption operates to offer proof—for the very reason that there has been limited access to pertinent information. Also, the hearing itself may tend to produce the discovery that the government opposes. But another tack might be taken. Discovery of relevant material could be presumed proper, but the prosecutor could be empowered to deny discovery if an affidavit were submitted under seal to the trial court explaining why discovery in a particular case might threaten the fair administration of justice. See Fed.R.Crim.P. 16(d) (providing that the party opposing discovery may "show good cause by a written statement that the court will inspect ex parte"). The natural response of a defendant would be to protest against any ex parte procedure. But if the choice is to deny all defendants discovery to protect against some defendants, or to grant discovery to all except those against whom an affidavit is submitted, isn't there a good argument that the latter procedure is the better one?

B. ARGUMENTS FAVORING CRIMINAL DISCOVERY

Proponents of more liberal discovery emphasize the gravity of the liberty and reputation interests at stake in criminal cases. In a dissent in *Tune,* supra, State Supreme Court Justice (later United States Supreme Court Justice) Brennan answered Chief Justice Vanderbilt and said:

> It shocks my sense of justice that in these circumstances counsel for an accused facing a possible death sentence should be denied inspection of his confession which, were this a civil case, could not be denied.

In a later article, The Criminal Prosecution: Sporting Event or Quest for Truth? 1963 Wash.U.L.Q. 279, Justice Brennan addressed the arguments against discovery. He pointed out that the privilege against self-incrimination has not prevented prosecutors from securing confessions or incriminating non-testimonial evidence from the criminally accused; that the best protections against manipulation and perjury are early exposure of the facts and emphasis on the ethical responsibilities of defense counsel; and that the trial judge can act to protect witnesses shown to be in danger. Justice Brennan and others have pointed out that, without discovery, indigent defendants are seriously handicapped in the preparation of a defense. In addition, as Dean Pye has noted:

> Most criminal cases result in a plea of guilty. The principal role of the capable advocate in many circumstances is to advise that his client plead guilty. For this advice to be meaningful, it must be based upon knowledge of the facts and the consequences. One of these consequences is the probability of conviction if the client goes to trial. It may be impossible for counsel to make any intelligent evaluation of the alternatives if he knows only what his client has told him and what he has discovered on his own.

The Defendant's Case for More Liberal Discovery, 33 F.R.D. 82, 83 (1963).

Finally, proponents seek to dispel the arguments against discovery by pointing to jurisdictions where broad discovery works. In many states there is an "open-file" policy—either in practice or by statute—without apparent detriment to the criminal justice process. See, e.g., Langrock, Vermont's Experiment in Criminal Discovery, 53 A.B.A.J. 732 (1967); Fletcher, Pretrial Discovery in State Criminal Cases, 12 Stan.L.Rev. 293 (1960). Even in Federal practice, many U.S. Attorneys provide broader discovery than the minimum required by the Federal Rules. Seventy-six percent of U.S. Attorneys who responded to an ABA survey stated that they provided "extensive informal discovery beyond the dictates" of the Federal Rules of Criminal Procedure. Middlekauf, What Practitioners Say About Broad Criminal Discovery, Criminal Justice, Spring 1994. This broader discovery has had no apparent deleterious effect, especially because U.S. Attorneys state that they do not grant additional discovery in cases where there is a substantial risk of witness intimidation.

III. DISCOVERY ON BEHALF OF THE DEFENDANT

A. THE STATE OF THE LAW

The federal system, like many of the states, grants only very limited discovery to criminal defendants. Fed.R.Crim.P. 16 is the basic rule providing for discovery in federal criminal cases. Subdivision (a)(1) of the Rule sets forth seven categories of information that *must* be disclosed by the government "upon a defendant's request." They are:

(A) the defendant's own oral statements made in response to official interrogation, if the government intends to offer the statements at trial;

(B) the defendant's own written or recorded statements of which the government has custody;

(C) for organizational defendants, such as corporations, statements of agents that are legally attributable to the organization;

(D) the defendant's prior criminal record;

(E) documents and other tangible objects that are material to the defense, or intended for use by the government in its case in chief, or that were obtained from or belong to the defendant;

(F) reports of physical or mental examinations, as well as scientific tests, that are material to the defense or intended for use by the government in its case in chief; and

(G) a summary of testimony of expert witnesses that the government intends to call in its case in chief, including a description of the bases and reasons for the expert's opinion, and a description of the expert's qualifications.

By making discovery of certain materials a matter of right *upon request*, Rule 16 places primary responsibility on defense attorneys and prosecutors, instead of on the court.

By examining the rule's approach to various aspects of discovery and by comparing it to other approaches that have been recommended or adopted, we can outline the current state of discovery in most American criminal cases.

1.   The Defendant's Statements

The Federal Rule gives the defendant the right to discover any oral statement made by the defendant in response to interrogation by a person known by the defendant to be a government agent; the defendant also has the right to discover any relevant written or recorded statement within the custody or control of the government. The Rule provides a corresponding right to collective entities, such as corporations and labor organizations, to obtain the statements of their agents. The government must exercise due diligence in obtaining such statements upon request. Such discovery might not seem very controversial, but the fact that it has been so indicates the kind of opposition to defense discovery that has existed for some time.

The argument has been made that if the defendant's prior statements are disclosed, she can tailor her testimony at trial to eliminate any discrepancies and the prosecution will not be able to impeach her by way of prior inconsistent statements. This advantage, however, is already available for prosecution witnesses, who are "prepped" for cross-examination. Moreover, revealing prior incriminating statements may persuade the defendant to plead guilty and avoid trial—which provides an advantage not just for the defendant but for the system itself. Finally, the government will ordinarily offer the defendant's statements during its case-in-chief. So the defendant often will hear them before testifying anyway.

The importance to the defendant of discovery of her own statements is illustrated by United States v. Camargo-Vergara, 57 F.3d 993 (11th Cir.1995), where the defendant prepared a trial strategy emphasizing that he had no experience with drugs. In the middle of trial, the government called an agent who said that the defendant made a post-arrest statement to her that indicated substantial knowledge of the drug trade. This statement had not been disclosed previously to the defendant. The court found the non-disclosure a violation of Rule 16 and reversed the defendant's conviction, reasoning that the disclosure at trial "attacked the very foundation of the defense strategy." But didn't the defendant know that he had made this statement to the agent? And why is the court concerned about impairing a defense strategy that is belied by the facts? Does the defendant have the right to present a false defense?

What Is a "Statement"?

There has been some controversy over the meaning of the word "statement" in Rule 16. The difficulty arises where the defendant's words have been paraphrased or summarized in a writing. Must the writing be disclosed? The Jencks Act, discussed infra, defines statements of *government witnesses* discoverable for cross-examination purposes as:

(1) a written statement made by said witness and signed or otherwise adopted or approved by him;s

(2) a stenographic, mechanical, electrical, or other recording, or a transcription thereof, which is a substantially verbatim recital of an oral statement made by said witness and recorded contemporaneously with the making of such oral statement; or

(3) a statement, however taken or recorded, or a transcription thereof, if any, made by said witness to a grand jury.

The courts have read the Jencks Act, 18 U.S.C. § 3500 (limiting disclosure of witness statements until after direct examination) to limit discovery to statements that reproduce exact words or are substantially verbatim. The drafters of Rule 16 provided no definition; but courts construe the term "statement" under Rule 16 in accordance with the Jencks Act definition. See United States v. Malone, 49 F.3d 393 (8th Cir.1995) (holding that the definition of "statement" under Rule 16 is the same as that under the Jencks Act: agent's notes of the defendant's interview do not qualify as Rule 16 material because the notes "constitute the agent's impression of his interview with Luckett, not a statement by Luckett"). Thus, police officers can avoid disclosure by summarizing a defendant's statements rather than taking them down verbatim.

Note that oral statements to be subject to discovery must be made "in response to interrogation by a person the defendant knew was a government agent." Thus, statements made by the defendant to undercover agents are not subject to disclosure, nor are oral statements made to those who are not government agents. See United States v. Siraj, 533 F.3d 99 (2nd Cir. 2008) (statements made by defendant to an undercover informant during the course of a conspiracy are not subject to disclosure under Rule 16(a)(1)). Can you figure out why the rule is drafted as it is?

2. Codefendants' Statements

Rule 16 does not require that a defendant be given a copy of a codefendant's statements. It can be argued that the defendant needs to know what a codefendant said in advance of trial in order to move for appropriate remedies such as severance or redaction of confessions. The Court in Bruton v. United States, 391 U.S. 123 (1968), held that it is constitutional error to hold a joint trial where one non-testifying codefendant has confessed and implicated another defendant, and the confession is not admissible against that other defendant. It would make sense to require pre-trial disclosure in order to allow the defendant to implement *Bruton* rights and avoid the possibility that an inadmissible confession will find its way into evidence against him and result in a mistrial. It is true that under the Federal Rule each defendant could obtain her own statement and share it—but that depends on whether the defendants are making a common defense. In cases where the defendants are pointing fingers at each other, it would seem very helpful for a defendant to have pretrial access to inculpatory statements made by a codefendant, wouldn't it? Would any harm be done by providing for discovery directly by each defendant of all statements by all codefendants?

3.   Discovery of Prior Criminal Records

As the Advisory Committee on the Federal Rules noted in its comment to Fed.R.Crim.P. 16(a):

> A defendant may be uncertain of the precise nature of his prior record and it seems therefore in the interest of efficient and fair administration to make it possible to resolve prior to trial any disputes as to the correctness of the relevant criminal record of the defendant.

Disclosure of prior convictions should enable the defendant to seek pretrial rulings on the admissibility of such convictions to impeach her if she should choose to testify. Rules like Fed.R.Evid. 609(a)(1), which permit the trial judge some discretion in admitting and rejecting some convictions as impeachment evidence, often invite pretrial motions, and these motions often save time once trial commences.

4.   Documents and Tangible Objects

Rule 16 provides that the government must disclose upon request any material or data that it plans to use at trial, as well as any item that was obtained from or belongs to the defendant. More difficult to apply is the language in Rule 16(a)(1)(E)(i) requiring disclosure of items that are "material to preparing the defense." Consider United States v. Phillip, 948 F.2d 241 (6th Cir.1991). Phillip was on trial for murder and child abuse of one of his sons, Jamal. Jamal died after falling down a flight of stairs. The government contended that Phillip hit Jamal so hard that he fell down the steps. Phillip admitted that he had beaten Jamal for a period of weeks, but contended that Jamal had fallen down the steps accidentally while Phillip had his back turned. The government videotaped an interview with the defendant's six-year-old son, Roderick. Roderick stated that Phillip had not hit Jamal at the time of the dispute, but also stated that his mother had coached him; he also made several statements inculpating Phillip and describing acts of abuse. The court of appeals rejected Phillip's argument that the videotape was "material to preparing" his defense:

> Phillip asserts in conclusory fashion that access to the videotape * * * would have aided him in the preparation of his defense, but he does not state convincingly how the videotape would have assisted him. He does suggest that viewing the videotape would have allowed him to reach a more informed decision concerning whether or not to depose Roderick or to subpoena him as a defense witness. However, since Roderick was his son, Phillip was aware of Roderick's potential availability to testify concerning Phillip's battering of Jamal. Moreover, early access to the videotape certainly could not have enlightened Phillip with respect to the *wisdom* of deposing Roderick or calling him as a witness. * * * On the whole, the videotape is inculpatory in nature and reveals a highly impressionable young child making highly inconsistent statements within a short period of time. * * *

> [E]arly access to the videotape would have informed Phillip that if deposed or placed on the witness stand, Roderick might 1) make exculpatory statements, 2) make inculpatory statements, 3) make both exculpatory and inculpatory statements, and/or 4) have little memory of relevant events. After viewing the videotape, Phillip would have been in no better position to evaluate the wisdom of deposing Roderick or calling him as a witness. Accordingly, we conclude that the videotape was not material to the preparation of Phillip's defense * * *.

See also United States v. Stevens, 985 F.2d 1175 (2d Cir.1993) (document is not material to preparing the defense "merely because it would have persuaded the defendant from proffering easily impeached testimony"). Compare United States v. Cedano-Arellano, 332 F.3d 568 (9th Cir. 2003) (where the defendant was attacking the reliability of a drug-sniffing dog, the dog's training materials and certification records were material to preparing the defense, and should have been disclosed under Fed.R.Crim.P. 16(a)(1)(E)(i)).

Defenses Not Going to the Merits: United States v. Armstrong

In United States v. Armstrong, 517 U.S. 456 (1996), the defendants were African-Americans charged with crack cocaine offenses. They claimed that they were being prosecuted because of their race. The defendants argued that they were entitled under Rule 16(a)(1)(E) to discovery of documents relevant to their claim of selective prosecution, e.g., charging criteria, the number of unprosecuted crack violators who are white, etc. These materials were obviously not the property of the defendants. Nor did the government intend to use the documents at trial. Thus, discovery under Rule 16(a)(1)(E) hinged on whether materials supporting a claim of selective prosecution could be considered "material to preparing the defense."

The Court, in an opinion by Chief Justice Rehnquist, held that the term "material to preparing the defense" covered only those documents and objects that are responsive to the government's case-in-chief, i.e., those documents and objects that are *pertinent to the defendant's guilt or innocence.* The Chief Justice reasoned as follows:

> Respondents argue that the Rule applies because any claim that "results in nonconviction" if successful is a "defense" for the Rule's purposes, and a successful selective-prosecution claim has that effect.
>
> We reject this argument, because we conclude that in the context of Rule 16 "the defendant's defense" means the defendant's response to the Government's case-in-chief. While it might be argued that as a general matter, the concept of a "defense" includes any claim that is a "sword," challenging the prosecution's conduct of the case, the term may encompass only the narrower class of "shield" claims, which refute the Government's arguments that the defendant committed the crime charged. Rule 16 * * * tends to support the "shield-only" reading. If "defense" means an argument in response to the prosecution's case-in-chief, there is a perceptible symmetry between documents "material to the preparation of the defendant's defense," and, in the very next phrase, documents "intended for use by the government as evidence in chief at the trial."
>
> * * *
>
> We hold that Rule 16(a) * * * authorizes defendants to examine Government documents material to the preparation of their defense against the Government's case-in-chief, but not to the preparation of selective-prosecution claims.

Justices Souter and Ginsburg concurred, with the reservation that the application of Rule 16(a)(1)(E) to *other* non-merits defenses (e.g., speedy trial, or affirmative defenses unrelated to the merits) had not been decided. Justice Stevens dissented on the ground that discovery was warranted under the district court's equitable power, but he agreed with the Chief Justice's Rule 16 analysis. Justice Breyer concurred in the judgment on the ground that a sufficient preliminary showing of selective prosecution had not been made in order to justify discovery. He disagreed, however, with the Chief Justice's construction of Rule 16, and argued that the Rule authorized discovery of any document material to dismissal of the prosecution on any grounds.

The Court in *Armstrong* did not hold that defendants *never* have a right to inspect documents and other information that pertain to matters other than the government's case-in-chief. Rather, the holding was that defendants are not *entitled* to these materials under Rule 16. A defendant is free to argue, for example, that notwithstanding Rule 16, discovery of certain materials is necessary to protect a constitutional right. This constitutional argument of selective prosecution was indeed made in *Armstrong,* but the Court held that mere allegations of selective prosecution are not enough to warrant discovery. See the discussion of this aspect of *Armstrong* in Chapter 6.

Fishing Expeditions

Under Rule 16(d)(1), the judge has discretion to quash discovery requests that are vague or overbroad. The courts are properly concerned with preventing "fishing expeditions" into the government's documents; thus it has been held that a request for "anything exculpatory" is equivalent to no request at all, and the "trial judge need not accord the slightest heed to such shotgun approach." United States v. Weiner, 578 F.2d 757 (9th Cir.1978).

Because documents cannot be intimidated and cannot easily be tampered with if the government retains the original, the fear of misuse by the defendant is not great. The limits of discovery here are to protect the government from having to respond to overbroad requests. If the documents would reveal the names of witnesses or other information not discoverable, such as work product, then they need not be disclosed.

Electronic Discovery

In many cases, electronic information—given its prevalence in today's society is critical to the success of an investigation and prosecution—and critical to the defense. The use of computer technology creates significant discovery problems, however. How much electronic information is the government required to retain, search and produce?

Most courts have held that nothing about electronic information requires the government to provide more information than is already required by Rule 16 and the Constitution. See United States v. Salyer, 271 F.R.D. 148 (E.D. Cal. 2010) (finding that defendant was only entitled to discovery of electronic materials relevant to mounting a defense and rejecting the defendant's "all documents civil type discovery request" for electronic data). Specifically, courts have typically rejected the premise that the electronic discovery rules found in the Federal Rules of Civil Procedure are applicable in criminal cases. See United States v. Warshak, 631 F.3d 266 (6th Cir. 2010) (finding no discovery violation in government production of data that was in an unsearchable format; concluding that the federal civil rule requiring electronic data to be turned over in a searchable form is not applicable to criminal cases).

If data is electronic, should the government have the obligation to turn over the metadata of the documents produced? "Metadata" is the data that provides information about how a document was generated, date, time, author, etc. The courts have not generally required the government to produce metadata in a criminal case, but in some cases disclosure of metadata might be critical to a defendant challenging the documents admitted against him.

One of the problems of electronic information is that there is so much of it—and much of it is duplicative, e.g., cloned emails. There is a risk with electronic data that the defendant will be the victim of a document dump—too much information. For example, in United States v. Graham, 2008 WL 2098044 (S.D.Ohio) the court found that the sheer volume of data produced by the government—combined with its erratic and unmanageable method of turning it over, prejudiced the defendants by the delay necessary to review all the material. Consequently the court found a violation of the Speedy Trial Act and dismissed the indictment. The *Graham* court likened the government in that case to "a restless volcano" that periodically "spewed forth" masses of electronic data. But see United States v. Qadri, 2010 WL 933752 (D. Haw.), where the government produced millions of electronic documents, 30 computer harddrives and three servers. The defendants argued that it was a document dump and moved to dismiss the indictment on Speedy Trial grounds. But the court denied the motion, finding that "the delays in this case may be attributed at least in part to the nature of e-discovery, the complex nature of the alleged crimes, and the necessity of coordinating various branches of government in the investigation." Of course, the appearance of a document dump will be mitigated if the material is produced in searchable form. See, e.g., United States v. Skilling, 554 F.3d 529 (5th Cir. 2009) (no discovery violation where government turned over electronic files related to Enron; the documentation was more than 700 million pages, but it was searchable).

For more on electronic discovery in criminal and civil cases, see Scheindlin, Capra, and the Sedona Conference, Electronic Discovery and Digital Evidence (2d. ed. West 2012).

Department of Justice Principles and Guidelines on Electronic Discovery

In 2012, the Department of Justice issued recommendatinos for ESI discovery in Federal criminal cases. It is a set of principles—based on cooperation by the parties—that is now being employed as guidance in many criminal cases. The principles are as follows:

Principle 1. Lawyers have a responsibility to have an adequate understanding of electronic discovery.

Principle 2. In the process of planning, producing, and resolving disputes about ESI discovery, the parties should include individuals with sufficient technical knowledge and experience regarding ESI.

Principle 3. At the outset of a case, the parties should meet and confer about the nature, volume, and mechanics of producing ESI discovery. Where the ESI discovery is particularly complex or produced on a rolling basis, an ongoing dialogue may be helpful.

Principle 4. The parties should discuss what formats of production are possible and appropriate, and what formats can be generated. Any format selected for producing discovery should maintain the ESI's integrity, allow for reasonable usability, reasonably limit costs, and, if possible, conform to industry standards for the format.

Principle 5. When producing ESI discovery, a party should not be required to take on substantial additional processing or format conversion costs and burdens beyond what the party has alterady done or would do for its own case preparation or discovery production.

Principle 6. Following meet and confer, the parties should notify the court of ESI discovery production issues or problems that they reasonably anticipate will significantly affect the handling of the case.

Principle 7. The parties should discuss ESI discovery transmission methods and media that promote efficiency, security, and reduced costs. The producing party should provide a general description and maintain a record of what was transmitted.

Principle 8. In multi-defendant cases, the defendants should authorize one or more counsel to act as the discovery coordinator(s) or seek appointment of a Coordinating Discovery Attorney.

Principle 9. The parties should make good faith efforts to discuss and resolve disputes over ESI discovery, involving those with the requisite technical knowledge when necessary, and they should consult with a supervisor, or obtain supervisory authorization, before seeking judicial resolution of an ESI discovery dispute or alleging misconduct, abuse, or neglect concerning the production of ESI.

Principle 10. All parties should limit dissemination of ESI discovery to members of their litigation team who need and are approved for access, and they should also take reasonable and appropriate measures to secure ESI discovery against unauthorized access or disclosure.

The DOJ concludes that the Guidelines "set forth a collaborative approach to ESI discovery involving mutual and interdependent responsibilities. The goal is to benefit all parties by making ESI discovery more efficient, secure, and less costly."

The "meet and confer" guideline (Principle 3) has been incorporated into a proposed rule on electronic discovery for the Federal Rules of Criminal Procedure—a new Rule 16.1. Barring unforeseen developments, that new rule will go into effect on December 1, 2019.

5.   Experts, Examinations, and Tests

Many jurisdictions, even those with restrictive discovery rules, require the government to disclose the results of examinations and tests such as autopsy reports, reports of medical or psychiatric examinations, blood tests, handwriting or fingerprinting comparisons, ballistic tests, and so forth. Because of its factual nature, such evidence is unlikely to be misused or distorted by disclosure. There is virtually no risk of witness intimidation. And the need for such discovery is apparent—it is practically impossible for the defense to test or rebut scientific or expert evidence without opportunities to examine that evidence before the trial. Federal Rule 16(a)(1)(F) requires disclosure of all such reports that are "material to preparing the defense" or that the government intends to use in its case-in-chief at trial.

Oral reports are not discoverable under Rule 16, as the Rule requires the government to "permit a defendant to inspect and to copy or photograph the results" and this cannot be done with oral reports. Professor Giannelli, in Criminal Discovery, Scientific Evidence, and DNA, 44 Vand.L.Rev. 791 (1991), notes that when the Rule was drafted in 1966, "most scientific evidence consisted of autopsy reports and crime laboratory reports." However, "today experts have developed many new categories of scientific evidence." Examples include expert testimony on DNA identification, blood spatter testimony, rape trauma syndrome, child sexual abuse accommodation syndrome, battered woman syndrome, and bite mark comparisons. "Neither custom nor regulation requires these experts to write reports. Indeed * * * the prosecution loses the element of surprise by preparing the report."

Discovery of Expert Methodology

The ability to challenge a scientific expert's report has become especially critical after the Supreme Court's decision in Daubert v. Merrell Dow Pharmaceuticals, Inc., 509 U.S. 579 (1993). In *Daubert*, the Court held that the trial court must act as a "gatekeeper" to assure that an expert's testimony is based on "good science" and comports with the scientific method. Obviously it is difficult for the defendant to challenge a prosecution expert's scientific reasoning if he has no prior information about the expert's basis, methodology, and conclusion.[2] Accordingly, Rule 16(a)(1)(G) was added shortly after *Daubert*, to provide that at the defendant's request, the government must provide a written summary of the testimony of any expert who the government intends to call in its case-in-chief. The summary must "describe the witness's opinions, the bases and the reasons for those opinions, and the witness's qualifications."

Note that the disclosure requirement applies to any witness that the government intends to call as an expert, even if the expert is not going to testify on a scientific subject. Discovery of the opinions of non-scientific experts is made more critical after the Supreme Court's decision in Kumho Tire Co. v. Carmichael, 526 U.S. 137 (1999). The Court in *Kumho* held that the *Daubert* gatekeeping requirement applies to non-scientific experts. Thus, the trial judge must determine that non-scientific experts are using a reliable methodology and are applying that methodology properly to the facts of the case. So it is crucial for defendants to obtain discovery of reports and opinions of non-scientific experts such as experts on handwriting identification and ballistics; only with advance notice can defendants make a proper challenge to the reliability of this expert testimony.

6. Names, Addresses, and Statements of Witnesses

Most of the states require advance disclosure of the names and the written or recorded statements of witnesses that the government intends to call. See Clennon, Pre-Trial Discovery of Witness Lists: A Modest Proposal to Improve the Administration of Justice in the Superior Court of the District of Columbia, 38 Cath.U.L.Rev. 641 (1989) (noting that "twenty-eight states grant the defendant as a matter of right pre-trial disclosure of the trial witnesses the prosecutor expects to call"). Some states by statute ban disclosure of witnesses' statements.

Federal courts require disclosure of witness statements, but *not in advance of their trial testimony*. The Jencks Act, 18 U.S.C.A. § 3500 requires disclosure of "statements" by government witnesses but only after they have testified on direct examination. The Jencks Act followed the Court's opinion in Jencks v. United States, 353 U.S. 657 (1957), where the Court exercised its supervisory power to require disclosure *during the trial* of the prior statements of prosecution witnesses.

Jencks Act Timing Issue

The *Jencks* Court rejected the notion that pretrial statements should only be made available where the defense could show a probable inconsistency between the witness's pretrial statements and his in-court testimony. The Court recognized that it would be very difficult for a

---

[2] For further discussion of *Daubert* and its progeny, see Capra, The *Daubert* Puzzle, 32 Ga.L.Rev. 699 (1998).

defendant to prove that the statement was inconsistent without having access to the statement. The Jencks Act codified the *Jencks* Court's basic requirement that the government disclose pretrial statements made by its witnesses, whether or not the statements are inconsistent with trial testimony.[3] However, the *timing* of the disclosure requirement is critical. The Act *does not* provide for notification in advance of trial or even in advance of the witness's testimony. Rather, a statement covered by the Act must be disclosed, on the defendant's motion, *after* the witness testifies on direct examination. As one defense counsel has complained:

> The timing aspects of the Jencks Act [create] a dilemma for defense lawyers: either proceed without preparation or ask for a continuance in the middle of trial, which would be unfair to the jury and would understandably irritate them.

Cary, Exculpatory Evidence: A Call for Reform After the Unlawful Prosecution of Senator Ted Stevens, 36 Litigation 34 (2010).

Jencks Act Statements

"Statements" within the meaning of the Act include only 1) written statements approved by the witness; 2) stenographic or mechanical transcripts that purport to be almost verbatim accounts of oral statements; and 3) any statements, however recorded, made to a grand jury. If the information about a witness is not within those three categories, there is no obligation to disclose it at any time. See United States v. Farley, 2 F.3d 645 (6th Cir.1993) (a summary of a witness's account is not Jencks Act material unless it is a verbatim account or unless it has been adopted by the witness); United States v. Crowley, 285 F.3d 553 (7th Cir. 2002) ("The Jencks Act does not obligate the government to disclose investigative or trial preparation material; rather, it requires only the disclosure of pretrial statements a government witness signed, adopted, or otherwise approved.").

Also, a witness's prior statement need not be disclosed under the Jencks Act unless it relates to the subject matter of the witness's direct testimony. See United States v. Byrne, 83 F.3d 984 (8th Cir.1996) (where witness testifies to acts occurring during the conspiracy, there was no violation of the Jencks Act when the government failed to disclose the witness's prior statement concerning acts committed before the conspiracy—this was collateral or background information that did not relate to the subject matter of the direct testimony). The Jencks Act provides for *in camera* review for the purpose of separating portions of statements relating to the witness's trial testimony from unrelated

---

[3]   In Goldberg v. United States, 425 U.S. 94 (1976), the Court held that statements made to government lawyers otherwise producible under the Act are not barred from production by the work product doctrine.

portions. Fed.R.Crim.P. 26.2, which was promulgated after the Jencks Act, largely tracks the provisions of the Act, with the exception that the Rule requires defense production of defense witness statements as well. See the discussion after United States v. Nobles, infra.

The Objections to Advance Disclosure of Witness Names and Statements

At one time, the Supreme Court proposed an amendment to Rule 16 that would have required the government to provide advance disclosure of names, addresses and prior statements of witnesses. The reasoning behind the amendment was that disclosure of witness names and statements is necessary so that defense counsel can prepare adequately to cross-examine witnesses and test their credibility. The Department of Justice vigorously opposed the amendment and mustered the support of numerous United States Attorneys, and the amendment was never adopted. A typical complaint was expressed by the United States Attorney for the Western District of Pennsylvania at the congressional hearings on the amendment:

> It seems clear that we have a hard enough time securing the cooperation of civilian witnesses who don't want to get involved without putting them in a situation in which, months before trial, they become subject to such degradation and harassment as may occur to an ingenious defendant, who will have far more to gain under the new rules than the present post-conviction satisfaction of revenge. Indeed, we are of the view that the law should not, in the name of "enlightened" discovery procedures, expose innocent members of the public, who have had the misfortune to be victims of or witnesses to criminal conduct, to the mercy of defendants any more than the confrontation clause presently requires.[4]

Are there more direct ways to eliminate the problems of witness intimidation and harassment perceived by the U.S. Attorney? Earl Silbert testified at the hearings and suggested the following alternative:

> Alternatively, we would recommend that in the event witness disclosure is to be permitted, some burden be placed on the party seeking disclosure to show a reasonable need for the information sought, and that whatever disclosure in this regard is permitted, no party be required to disclose earlier than three days in advance of trial. Finally, it is particularly critical that in this area the trial Court retain discretion as to whether or not to grant the discovery sought.

Would this have been a preferable approach?

---

[4]   Statement of W. Vincent Rakestraw, Ass't Att'y Gen'l, in House Hearings on Federal Rules of Criminal Procedure, 93rd Cong., 2nd Sess. (1974).

Note that while there is no right to advance disclosure of a witness under Fed.R.Crim. 16, a court has discretion to order such disclosure in particular cases. See, e.g., United States v. W.R. Grace, 526 F.3d 499 (9th Cir. 2008) (en banc) (Rule 16 does not state that a court is *prohibited* from ordering advance disclosure of a witness; district court did not abuse discretion in requiring the government to provide a witness list, in light of the size and complexity of the case, which included charges reaching back 30 years, 200 proposed witnesses, and millions of pages of documents).

7. Grand Jury Minutes and Transcripts

Rule 16(a)(3) precludes defense discovery of grand jury proceedings, with two exceptions: 1) the defendant is entitled to a copy of his own grand jury testimony under Rule 16(a)(1)(B)(iii); and 2) the Jencks Act requires production of a trial witness's grand jury testimony after she has testified on direct examination. Also, of course, the prosecution is required to disclose any information obtained by the grand jury that is materially exculpatory to the defendant, as seen in the discussion of *Brady* rights, infra. But there is no right to more general disclosure of grand jury minutes and transcripts.

Once an indictment is returned, do arguments for secrecy still hold? Will secrecy protect the reputations of those accused? Will secrecy inhibit flight once a defendant is formally charged? Will secrecy protect the identity of witnesses who will appear at trial?

8. Work Product

Fed.R.Crim.P. 16(a)(2) protects against disclosure of "reports, memoranda, or other internal government documents made by an attorney for the government or other government agent in connection with investigating or prosecuting the case." What theory justifies protecting police or FBI reports under the Federal Rule? If it is true that the government has easier access to information than the defendant in many situations, why should that information not be shared with the defense?

Work product is one of those areas in which prosecutors complain that discovery would be one-sided, because the privilege against self-incrimination or the attorney-client privilege will in most cases bar the government from finding out what the defendant or her attorney has done to prepare a defense. Assume that the government could not force disclosure of much of the work product of the defense. Does that mean that one-sided disclosure of the government's work product is undesirable? Remember that the government has the power of the grand jury and the subpoena power, so there is likely to be a lot of information that will be accessible to the government but not to the defendant.

B. MECHANISMS FOR DISCOVERY BY THE DEFENDANT

The predominant means for discovery in civil cases are depositions and interrogatories. In criminal cases the defense is not permitted to discover prosecutorial information through interrogatories, and if a bill of particulars is requested as a pretext for discovery, it is likely to be denied. See United States v. Livingstone, 576 F.3d 881 (8th Cir. 2009) (bill of particulars cannot be used to obtain witness testimony).

Depositions are authorized in criminal cases, but in most jurisdictions not a means of obtaining discovery. Rather, they are allowed only where necessary to preserve testimony for trial. Federal Rule 15 illustrates the restrictions on the use of depositions in federal criminal cases.

(a) When Taken.

> **(1) In General.** A party may move that a prospective witness be deposed in order to preserve testimony for trial. The court may grant the motion because of exceptional circumstances and in the interest of justice. If the court orders the deposition to be taken, it may also require the deponent to produce at the deposition any designated material that is not privileged, including any book, paper, document, record, recording, or data.

* * *

Assume that somehow a defendant learns the names of witnesses. There is little that she can do in most jurisdictions to compel the witnesses to talk with her or with counsel. It is true that the prosecutor cannot advise the witnesses not to talk with the defendant or with defense counsel. See, e.g., Gregory v. United States, 369 F.2d 185 (D.C.Cir.1966). But many witnesses may want to have nothing to do with the defense. Should there be some mechanism for the defense to find out what the witnesses know?

Two possibilities exist. The first is that a preliminary hearing can be made a discovery hearing in part, so that witnesses can be called by the defense. The trouble with this approach is that at the time the hearing is held, the defense may not know what questions to ask. More importantly, if the defense is not careful, it will preserve the testimony of an unfavorable witness who may become unavailable, and the witness's preliminary hearing testimony will be admitted at trial under a hearsay exception (see Fed.R.Evid. 804(b)(1), exception for prior testimony), even though the defense really did not effectively examine the witness. Also, early in the case, the defense may not have discovered the identities of all the witnesses. On the other hand, the advantage of the preliminary hearing approach is that discovery is conducted in one place, at one time, and under the supervision of the court. It should be noted that when an indictment is handed down, there generally is no right to a preliminary hearing.

The other alternative is the one used in civil cases: to allow depositions to be taken for discovery. Do you believe that such a rule would threaten legitimate government interests? Can you see why witnesses in criminal cases might be more reluctant to testify at all than witnesses in civil cases? If this is true, routine availability of depositions would mean that reluctant witnesses often would have to testify twice, once in a deposition and again at trial. Would it add substantially to the cost of criminal cases? In theory, it is easy to see why a jurisdiction might fear that permitting defendants to depose witnesses routinely might not only increase the cost of processing a criminal case, but might also slow down a process that is so heavily dependent on plea bargaining. In practice, however, some states have made depositions a standard part of criminal discovery without a breakdown in the system.[5]

IV.   THE PROSECUTOR'S CONSTITUTIONAL DUTY TO DISCLOSE

A. THE *BRADY* RULE

The Supreme Court has established that, above and beyond the (minimal) obligations imposed by discovery rules, the prosecution has a *constitutional* duty to disclose certain exculpatory information to the defendant in advance of trial. The nature of the information required to be disclosed, and the scope of the prosecutor's obligation, are the subjects of this section.

Disclosure of False Evidence: Mooney v. Holohan and Its Progeny

The first case establishing a prosecutor's constitutional obligations in the discovery process was Mooney v. Holohan, 294 U.S. 103 (1935). The defendant sought habeas corpus relief, claiming "that the sole basis of his conviction was perjured testimony, which was knowingly used by the prosecuting authorities in order to obtain that conviction and also that the prosecution knowingly suppressed evidence that the defense could have used to impeach the perjured testimony." The Court said that the Due

---

[5]   Jurisdictions that have permitted depositions in criminal cases appear to be staying with it. See, e.g., Florida Rule of Criminal Procedure 3.220 (a): "(a) Notice of Discovery. After the filing of the charging document, a defendant may elect to participate in the discovery process provided by these rules, including the taking of discovery depositions, by filing with the court and serving on the prosecuting attorney a "Notice of Discovery" which shall bind both the prosecution and defendant to all discovery procedures contained in these rules." Section 3.220 (b)(1)(A) obligates the prosecutor to provide a comprehensive witness list to a defendant who elects to participate in the discovery process, and section (s)(1)(A) requires the defendant to provide the prosecutor with a list of all witnesses the defense expects to call to testify. Thereafter, either party can depose witnesses. Section (h)(1)(D) provides that there is no right to take depositions in cases in which the defendant is charged with a misdemeanor or a criminal traffic offense unless good cause is shown.

Process Clause is violated if the government engages in "a deliberate deception of court and jury by the presentation of testimony known to be perjured." Seven years later, in Pyle v. Kansas, 317 U.S. 213 (1942), a habeas petitioner charged the prosecution with knowing use of perjured testimony and the deliberate suppression of evidence favorable to the defense by threats made to witnesses. The Court cited *Mooney* and held that the "allegations * * *, if proven, would entitle petitioner to release from his present custody."

Alcorta v. Texas, 355 U.S. 28 (1957), applied and invigorated the *Mooney* principle. The defendant was convicted of first degree murder; a defense claim of "sudden passion" was rejected after a witness answered the prosecutor's questions by saying that he had not kissed the defendant's wife (the victim) on the night of the murder and that he had only a casual relationship with her. Although the witness had previously told the prosecution that he had sexual intercourse with the victim on several occasions, the prosecution did not disclose this. The Supreme Court reversed because the prosecutor knowingly allowed an important witness to create a false impression at trial.

Napue v. Illinois, 360 U.S. 264 (1959), further developed the principle that prevents the prosecutor from knowingly presenting false evidence. There, the principal government witness testified that he had received no promises of special consideration in exchange for his testimony. The prosecutor elicited the information from the witness and made no effort to correct it, although he knew the testimony was false. The Court found that the resulting conviction was invalid.

Mandatory Disclosure of Materially Exculpatory Evidence: The Brady Rule

In 1963, the Court decided one of its most important disclosure cases, Brady v. Maryland, 373 U.S. 83. Brady and a companion, Boblit, were charged with first degree murder, a capital offense. Brady was tried first; he admitted participation in the crime, but claimed that Boblit did the actual killing. Prior to trial Brady's lawyer asked the prosecutor to allow him to see Boblit's statements. Several statements were shown to counsel, but one in which Boblit admitted the homicide was not revealed. The defense did not learn about that statement until after Brady's conviction and death sentence were affirmed. The Supreme Court found that the prosecutor has an obligation to disclose all materially exculpatory evidence, and that Boblit's admission would have had a material effect on Brady's death sentence. The Court declared that "[a] prosecution that withholds evidence on demand of an accused which, if made available, would tend to exculpate him or reduce the penalty helps shape a trial that bears heavily on the defendant. That casts the prosecutor in the role of an architect of a proceeding that does not comport with standards of justice * * *."[6]

Knowledge Attributable to the Prosecutor: Giglio v. United States

In Giglio v. United States, 405 U.S. 150 (1972), the Court found a violation of due process when a key witness testified that he had not been given a deal for testifying for the government. Promises had in fact been made by a predecessor in the prosecutor's office and the trial attorney for the government did not know it. Even though the examining prosecutor was not aware that the witness's testimony was false, the Court reversed the conviction; it held that a promise by one attorney would be attributed to the government and suggested that procedures and regulations could be developed to avoid situations in which one prosecutor did not know what the other was doing.

Materiality and the Relevance of a Defense Request for Information: United States v. Agurs

The next case develops the *Brady* rule and answers important questions about the materiality of suppressed evidence and the relationship between a defense request for information and a prosecutor's suppression.

UNITED STATES V. AGURS

Supreme Court of the United States, 1976.
427 U.S. 97.

JUSTICE STEVENS delivered the opinion of the Court.

After a brief interlude in an inexpensive motel room, respondent repeatedly stabbed James Sewell, causing his death. She was convicted of second-degree murder. The question before us is whether the prosecutor's failure to provide defense counsel with certain background information about Sewell, which would have tended to support the argument that respondent acted in self-defense, deprived her of a fair trial under the rule of Brady v. Maryland.

* * *

---

[6] Aside from a constitutional duty to disclose exculpatory evidence, a prosecutor may have an ethical obligation to do so. For example, ABA Rules of Professional Conduct 3.8 (Special Responsibilities of a Prosecutor) provides in relevant part: "A prosecutor in a criminal case shall * * * (d) make timely disclosure to the defense of all evidence or information known to the prosecutor that tends to negate the guilt of the accused or mitigates the offense, and, in connection with sentencing, disclose to the defense and to the tribunal all unprivileged mitigating information known to the prosecutor, except when the prosecutor is relieved of this responsibility by a protective order of the tribunal * * *." The ethical rule is not limited to "material" evidence.

At about 4:30 p.m. on September 24, 1971, respondent, who had been there before, and Sewell, registered in a motel as man and wife. * * * Sewell was wearing a bowie knife in a sheath, and carried another knife in his pocket. Less than two hours earlier, according to the testimony of his estranged wife, he had had $360 in cash on his person.

About 15 minutes later three motel employees heard respondent screaming for help. A forced entry into their room disclosed Sewell on top of respondent struggling for possession of the bowie knife. She was holding the knife; his bleeding hand grasped the blade; according to one witness he was trying to jam the blade into her chest. The employees separated the two and summoned the authorities. Respondent departed without comment before they arrived. Sewell was dead on arrival at the hospital.

Circumstantial evidence indicated that the parties had completed an act of intercourse, that Sewell had then gone to the bathroom * * * and that the struggle occurred upon his return. The contents of his pockets were in disarray on the dresser and no money was found; the jury may have inferred that respondent took Sewell's money and that the fight started when Sewell re-entered the room and saw what she was doing.

On the following morning respondent surrendered to the police. She was given a physical examination which revealed no cuts or bruises of any kind, except needle marks on her upper arm. An autopsy of Sewell disclosed that he had several deep stab wounds in his chest and abdomen, and a number of slashes on his arms and hands, characterized by the pathologist as "defensive wounds."

Respondent offered no evidence. Her sole defense was the argument made by her attorney that Sewell had initially attacked her with the knife, and that her actions had all been directed toward saving her own life. The support for this self-defense theory was based on the fact that she had screamed for help. Sewell was on top of her when help arrived, and his possession of two knives indicated that he was a violence-prone person. It took the jury about 25 minutes to elect a foreman and return a verdict.

Three months later defense counsel filed a motion for a new trial asserting that he had discovered (1) that Sewell had a prior criminal record that would have further evidenced his violent character; (2) that the prosecutor had failed to disclose this information to the defense; and (3) that a recent opinion of the United States Court of Appeals for the District of Columbia Circuit made it clear that such evidence was admissible even if not known to the defendant. Sewell's prior record included a plea of guilty to a charge of assault and carrying a deadly weapon in 1963, and another guilty plea to a charge of carrying a deadly weapon in 1971. Apparently both weapons were knives.

The Government opposed the motion, arguing that there was no duty to tender Sewell's prior record to the defense in the absence of an appropriate request * * * and that, in all events, it was not material.

The District Court denied the motion. * * * The Court of Appeals reversed.

* * *

The rule of Brady v. Maryland arguably applies in three quite different situations. Each involves the discovery, after trial, of information which had been known to the prosecution but unknown to the defense.

In the first situation, typified by Mooney v. Holohan, the undisclosed evidence demonstrates that the prosecution's case includes perjured testimony and that the prosecution knew, or should have known, of the perjury. In a series of subsequent cases, the Court has consistently held that a conviction obtained by the knowing use of perjured testimony is fundamentally unfair, and must be set aside if there is any reasonable likelihood that the false testimony could have affected the judgment of the jury. * * * In those cases the Court has applied a strict standard of materiality, not just because they involve prosecutorial misconduct, but more importantly because they involve a corruption of the truth-seeking function of the trial process. Since this case involves no misconduct, and since there is no reason to question the veracity of any of the prosecution witnesses, the test of materiality followed in the *Mooney* line of cases is not necessarily applicable to this case.

The second situation, illustrated by the *Brady* case itself, is characterized by a pretrial request for specific evidence. In that case defense counsel had requested the extrajudicial statements made by Brady's accomplice, one Boblit. This Court held that the suppression of one of Boblit's statements deprived Brady of due process, noting specifically that the statement had been requested and that it was "material." A fair analysis of the holding in *Brady* indicates that implicit in the requirement of materiality is a concern that the suppressed evidence might have affected the outcome of the trial.

* * *

In *Brady* the request was specific. It gave the prosecutor notice of exactly what the defense desired. Although there is, of course, no duty to provide defense counsel with unlimited discovery of everything known by the prosecutor, if the subject matter of such a request is material, or indeed if a substantial basis for claiming materiality exists, it is reasonable to require the prosecutor to respond either by furnishing the information or by submitting the problem to the trial judge. When the prosecutor receives a specific and relevant request, the failure to make any response is seldom, if ever, excusable.

In many cases, however, exculpatory information in the possession of the prosecutor may be unknown to defense counsel. In such a situation he may make no request at all, or possibly ask for "all *Brady* material" or for "anything exculpatory." Such a request really gives the prosecutor no better notice than if no request is made. If there is a duty to respond to a general request of that kind, it must derive from the obviously exculpatory character of certain evidence in the hands of the prosecutor. But if the evidence is so clearly supportive of a claim of innocence that it gives the prosecution notice of a duty to produce, that duty should equally arise even if no request is made. [W]e conclude that there is no significant difference between cases in which there has been merely a general request for exculpatory matter and cases, like the one we must now decide, in which there has been no request at all. The third situation in which the *Brady* rule arguably applies, typified by this case, therefore embraces the case in which only a general request for "*Brady* material" has been made.

We now consider whether the prosecutor has any constitutional duty to volunteer exculpatory matter to the defense, and if so, what standard of materiality gives rise to that duty.

* * *

The Court of Appeals appears to have assumed that the prosecutor has a constitutional obligation to disclose any information that might affect the jury's verdict. That statement of a constitutional standard of materiality approaches the "sporting theory of justice" which the Court expressly rejected in *Brady*. For a jury's appraisal of a case "might" be affected by an improper or trivial consideration as well as by evidence giving rise to a legitimate doubt on the issue of guilt. If everything that might influence a jury must be disclosed, the only way a prosecutor could discharge his constitutional duty would be to allow complete discovery of his files as a matter of routine practice.

Whether or not procedural rules authorizing such broad discovery might be desirable, the Constitution surely does not demand that much. * * * The mere possibility that an item of undisclosed information might have helped the defense, or might have affected the outcome of the trial, does not establish "materiality" in the constitutional sense.

Nor do we believe the constitutional obligation is measured by the moral culpability, or the willfulness, of the prosecutor. If evidence highly probative of innocence is in his file, he should be presumed to recognize its significance even if he has actually overlooked it. Conversely, if evidence actually has no probative significance at all, no purpose would be served by requiring a new trial simply because an inept prosecutor incorrectly believed he was suppressing a fact that would be vital to the defense. If the suppression of evidence results in constitutional error, it is because of the character of the evidence, not the character of the prosecutor.

* * * [T]here are situations in which evidence is obviously of such substantial value to the defense that elementary fairness requires it to be disclosed even without a specific request. For though the attorney for the sovereign must prosecute the accused with earnestness and vigor, he must always be faithful to his client's overriding interest that "justice shall be done." He is the "servant of the law, the twofold aim of which is that guilt shall not escape or innocence suffer." Berger v. United States, 295 U.S. 78, 88. This description of the prosecutor's duty illuminates the standard of materiality that governs his obligation to disclose exculpatory evidence.

* * *

The proper standard of materiality must reflect our overriding concern with the justice of the finding of guilt.[a] Such a finding is permissible only if supported by evidence establishing guilt beyond a reasonable doubt. It necessarily follows that if the omitted evidence creates a reasonable doubt that did not otherwise exist, constitutional error has been committed. This means that the omission must be evaluated in the context of the entire record. If there is no reasonable doubt about guilt whether or not the additional evidence is considered, there is no justification for a new trial. On the other hand, if the verdict is already of questionable validity, additional evidence of relatively minor importance might be sufficient to create a reasonable doubt.

This statement of the standard of materiality describes the test which courts appear to have applied in actual cases although the standard has been phrased in different language. It is also the standard which the trial judge applied in this case. He evaluated the significance of Sewell's prior criminal record in the context of the full trial which he recalled in detail. Stressing in particular the incongruity of a claim that Sewell was the aggressor with the evidence of his multiple wounds and respondent's unscathed condition, the trial judge indicated his unqualified opinion that respondent was guilty. He noted that Sewell's prior record did not contradict any evidence offered by the prosecutor, and was largely cumulative of the evidence that Sewell was wearing a bowie knife in a sheath and carrying a second knife in his pocket when he registered at the motel.

---

[a] It has been argued that the standard should focus on the impact of the undisclosed evidence on the defendant's ability to prepare for trial, rather than the materiality of the evidence to the issue of guilt or innocence. See Note, The Prosecutor's Constitutional Duty to Reveal Evidence to the Defense, 74 Yale L.J. 136 (1964). Such a standard would be unacceptable for determining the materiality of what has been generally recognized as "Brady material" for two reasons. First, that standard would necessarily encompass incriminating evidence as well as exculpatory evidence, since knowledge of the prosecutor's entire case would always be useful in planning the defense. Second, such an approach would primarily involve an analysis of the adequacy of the notice given to the defendant by the State, and it has always been the Court's view that the notice component of due process refers to the charge rather than the evidentiary support for the charge.

Since the arrest record was not requested and did not even arguably give rise to any inference of perjury, since after considering it in the context of the entire record the trial judge remained convinced of respondent's guilt beyond a reasonable doubt, and since we are satisfied that his firsthand appraisal of the record was thorough and entirely reasonable, we hold that the prosecutor's failure to tender Sewell's record to the defense did not deprive respondent of a fair trial as guaranteed by the Due Process Clause of the Fifth Amendment. * * *

JUSTICE MARSHALL with whom JUSTICE BRENNAN joins, dissenting.

* * *

* * * [The majority's] rule creates little, if any, incentive for the prosecutor conscientiously to determine whether his files contain evidence helpful to the defense. Indeed, the rule reinforces the natural tendency of the prosecutor to overlook evidence favorable to the defense, and creates an incentive for the prosecutor to resolve close questions of disclosure in favor of concealment.

* * * I would hold that the defendant in this case had the burden of demonstrating that there is a significant chance that the withheld evidence, developed by skilled counsel, would have induced a reasonable doubt in the minds of enough jurors to avoid a conviction. * * *

Refining the Test of Materiality: United States v. Bagley

Justice Blackmun wrote for the Court in United States v. Bagley, 473 U.S. 667 (1985), as the Court declined to overturn a conviction because of nondisclosure of exculpatory evidence. Bagley was charged with narcotics and firearms offenses and convicted in a bench trial only on the narcotics charges. Thereafter he learned that, despite his motion to discover any deals or promises between the government and its witnesses, the government had not disclosed that its two principal witnesses had signed contracts with the Bureau of Alcohol, Tobacco and Firearms to be paid for their undercover work. Although the trial judge ruled that the contracts would not have affected the outcome because the principal witnesses testified primarily concerning the firearms charges on which Bagley was acquitted, the court of appeals disagreed. The Supreme Court agreed with the trial judge and found that nondisclosure of impeachment evidence, like nondisclosure of other exculpatory evidence, requires reversal only if the evidence was material in the sense that it might have affected the outcome of the trial. No such showing was made on the facts of this case.

Justice Blackmun's opinion set forth a single "standard of materiality" applicable to nondisclosed exculpatory evidence. Justice Blackmun borrowed from the Court's ineffective assistance of counsel cases (discussed in Chapter 10) and derived the following standard:

> [Suppressed evidence] is material only if there is a reasonable probability that, had the evidence been disclosed to the defense, the result of the proceeding would have been different. A reasonable probability is a probability sufficient to undermine confidence in the outcome.

Justice Blackmun noted that this test was "sufficiently flexible" to cover no request, general request, and specific request cases.

In a part of the opinion joined only by Justice O'Connor, Justice Blackmun reasoned that "the more specifically the defense requests certain evidence * * * the more reasonable it is for the defense to assume from the nondisclosure that the evidence does not exist and to make pretrial and trial decisions on the basis of this assumption." Thus, specific request cases present special considerations in applying the single "reasonable probability" standard of materiality. The more specific the request, the more likely the suppression will be "material" in the *Brady* sense.

Justice White, joined by Chief Justice Burger and Justice Rehnquist, concurred in the judgment in *Bagley*. Although he expressed agreement with the single materiality standard developed by Justice Blackmun, he saw "no reason to attempt to elaborate on the relevance to the inquiry of the specificity of the defense's request for disclosure."

Justice Marshall, joined by Justice Brennan, dissented and argued that "when the Government withholds from a defendant evidence that might impeach the prosecution's *only witnesses,* that failure to disclose cannot be deemed harmless error." Justice Stevens, who authored *Agurs,* also dissented. He argued that, unlike *Agurs,* the instant case involved a specific request and that *Brady* requires reversal for failure to disclose evidence favorable to an accused upon a specific request if the evidence is material either to guilt or punishment. Thus, he would have remanded for a determination of whether there was "any reasonable likelihood" that the nondisclosure could have affected the judgment of the trier of fact.

Comments on Brady-Agurs-Bagley

Professor Stacy, in The Search for the Truth in Constitutional Criminal Procedure, 91 Colum.L.Rev. 1369, 1392 (1991), has this to say about the *Bagley* standard of materiality:

> The *Bagley* standard, which focuses on the likely impact of evidence on the ultimate result in the case, suffers from two interrelated deficiencies. The first problem is that the standard will frequently be misapplied. A prosecutor's lack of information about the planned defense and partisan inclinations impede her from making an

accurate and objective assessment of the evidence's effect on the outcome. The second problem is that many misapplications of the *Bagley* standard will never be detected and remedied. Because the prosecution has exclusive possession of the evidence subject to the duty to disclose and a clear incentive to withhold it, the defense or a court will sometimes never learn of evidence wrongly withheld.

In short, the Court has interpreted the prosecution's duty to disclose exculpatory evidence more narrowly than a true concern for accurate factfinding implies. For a Court genuinely interested in the search for the truth, neither the adversarial system, prosecutorial burdens, nor the constitutional text can justify the *Bagley* standard, which will result in important exculpatory evidence not being disclosed in a significant number of cases.

Can prosecutors refuse to turn over evidence that appears to be exculpatory but not sufficiently so to require a new trial under *Brady-Agurs-Bagley?* Should prosecutors be trusted with this authority? What would be wrong with requiring the prosecutor to turn over all evidence that a defense counsel would conclude *might tend* to exculpate the defendant?

Capra, Access to Exculpatory Evidence: Avoiding the Agurs Problems of Prosecutorial Discretion and Retrospective Review, 53 Ford.L.Rev. 391 (1984), argues that a per se right to an in camera hearing, at which the court would examine a prosecutor's files for *Brady* material, would be more effective than retrospective review of claims that exculpatory evidence was suppressed.

The Relevance of a Specific Request

While the combination of the Blackmun and White opinions in *Bagley* produce a single standard of materiality for all nondisclosure cases, *Bagley* leaves ambiguity about the relevance of a specific defense request for the evidence. In *Agurs,* Justice Stevens emphasized that the specific request increased the level of prosecutorial responsibility. In *Bagley,* Justice Blackmun emphasized the greater prejudicial impact of a denied specific request due to the possibility that defense counsel will be misled. Justice White thought it appropriate to leave the precise impact of a specific request for another day. Where a case involves a specific request, lower courts after *Bagley* have continued to take account of that factor, although not always stating why it is significant. See, e.g., Jean v. Rice, 945 F.2d 82 (4th Cir.1991) (recordings and reports indicating that the prosecution's star witness had been hypnotized were *Brady* material: "We are persuaded that the audio recordings and accompanying reports—twice requested—should have been disclosed to defense counsel."). As the Fifth Circuit stated in Lindsey v. King, 769 F.2d 1034 (5th Cir.1985): "Viewing the [*Bagley*] opinions as a whole, it is fair to say that all the participating Justices agreed on one thing at least: that reversal for suppression of evidence by the government is most likely where the request for it was specific."

B. APPLYING THE *BRADY* RULE

Fact-Intensive Applications: Three Illustrative Cases

The Court reaffirmed its *Brady-Agurs-Bagley* line of cases in Kyles v. Whitley, 514 U.S. 419 (1995), and applied those cases in an intensely fact-specific manner to reverse a conviction and death sentence. Kyles was convicted (after his first trial ended in a hung jury) of murdering a woman during the course of a robbery outside Schwegmann's grocery store. There was evidence that the killer left his car in the parking lot and drove away in the victim's car. The prosecution presented four eyewitnesses who identified Kyles unequivocally both before and at the trial. Kyles argued that an acquaintance, Beanie, committed the murders and framed him by planting the murder weapon (a gun) and the victim's purse and other items at Kyles's house. Beanie had originally approached the police with information that Kyles was the killer, and received a reward for his information. Beanie was not called by either side to testify at Kyles's trial. The prosecution suppressed many pieces of evidence, including: (1) pretrial statements from two of the eyewitnesses, which were markedly inconsistent with their later identifications, and one of which appeared to point to Beanie rather than Kyles as the perpetrator; (2) a series of statements by Beanie that were inconsistent and were ignored by the investigating officer; and (3) a police report indicating that Kyles's car was not on the list of cars found at the Schwegmann's shortly after the murder.

Justice Souter, writing for five Justices, made the following general points about the Court's *Brady-Agurs-Bagley* materiality standard:

> Four aspects of materiality under *Bagley* bear emphasis. * * * *Bagley's* touchstone of materiality is a "reasonable probability" of a different result, and the adjective is important. The question is not whether the defendant would more likely than not have received a different verdict with the evidence, but whether in its absence he received a fair trial, understood as a trial resulting in a verdict worthy of confidence. A "reasonable probability" of a different result is accordingly shown when the Government's evidentiary suppression "undermines confidence in the outcome of the trial."

> The second aspect of *Bagley* materiality bearing emphasis here is that it is not a sufficiency of evidence test. * * * The possibility of an acquittal on a criminal charge does not imply an insufficient evidentiary basis to convict. One does not show a *Brady* violation by demonstrating that some of the inculpatory evidence should have been excluded, but by showing that the favorable evidence could reasonably

be taken to put the whole case in such a different light as to undermine confidence in the verdict.

Third, we note that * * * once a reviewing court applying *Bagley* has found constitutional error there is no need for further harmless-error review. Assuming arguendo that a harmless error enquiry were to apply, a *Bagley* error could not be treated as harmless, since "a reasonable probability that, had the evidence been disclosed to the defense, the result of the proceeding would have been different," necessarily entails the conclusion that the suppression must have had "substantial and injurious effect or influence in determining the jury's verdict." * * *

The fourth and final aspect of *Bagley* materiality to be stressed here is its definition in terms of suppressed evidence considered collectively, not item-by-item. * * * [T]he Constitution is not violated every time the government fails or chooses not to disclose evidence that might prove helpful to the defense. We have never held that the Constitution demands an open file policy * * *.

Justice Souter stressed that suppression of exculpatory evidence implicates *Brady* rights *even if the suppression is by police officers and the prosecutor is unaware of it.* He explained this point as follows:

* * * In the State's favor it may be said that no one doubts that police investigators sometimes fail to inform a prosecutor of all they know. But neither is there any serious doubt that procedures and regulations can be established to carry the prosecutor's burden and to insure communication of all relevant information on each case to every lawyer who deals with it. Since, then, the prosecutor has the means to discharge the government's *Brady* responsibility if he will, any argument for excusing a prosecutor from disclosing what he does not happen to know about boils down to a plea to substitute the police for the prosecutor, and even for the courts themselves, as the final arbiters of the government's obligation to ensure fair trials.

The State in *Kyles* argued that the *Brady-Bagley* standard of materiality should be made more rigorous (i.e., harder for the defendant to meet) because the current standard places a prosecutor in the uncomfortable position of having to predict the materiality of evidence before the trial. The State asked for "a certain amount of leeway in making a judgment call" as to the disclosure of any given piece of evidence. But the majority rejected the State's argument, and adhered to the *Brady-Bagley* standard of materiality, in the following analysis:

[W]ith or without more leeway, the prosecution cannot be subject to any disclosure obligation without at some point having the responsibility to determine when it must act. Indeed, even if due process were thought to be violated by every failure to disclose an item of exculpatory or impeachment evidence (leaving harmless error as the government's only fallback), the prosecutor would still be forced to make judgment calls about what would count as favorable evidence, owing to the very fact that the character of a piece of evidence as favorable will often turn on the context of the existing or potential evidentiary record. Since the prosecutor would have to exercise some judgment even if the State were subject to this most stringent disclosure obligation, it is hard to find merit in the State's complaint over the responsibility for judgment under the existing system, which does not tax the prosecutor with error for any failure to disclose, absent a further showing of materiality. * * *

This means, naturally, that a prosecutor anxious about tacking too close to the wind will disclose a favorable piece of evidence. This is as it should be. Such disclosure will serve to justify trust in the prosecutor * * * [and] will tend to preserve the criminal trial, as distinct from the prosecutor's private deliberations, as the chosen forum for ascertaining the truth about criminal accusations. The prudence of the careful prosecutor should not therefore be discouraged.

Applying all these principles to the case, Justice Souter concluded that the cumulative effect of the suppressed evidence satisfied the materiality standard of *Brady-Agurs-Bagley*. In the majority's view, the suppressed evidence would have caused the jury to doubt the statements of two eyewitnesses, due to their inconsistent prior statements, and would further have caused the jury to doubt the integrity of the lead investigator, who trusted Beanie completely and never considered him as a suspect—even though Beanie's statements were often inconsistent and implausible. The majority concluded:

[T]he question is not whether the State would have had a case to go to the jury if it had disclosed the favorable evidence, but whether we can be confident that the jury's verdict would have been the same. * * * But confidence that the verdict would have been unaffected cannot survive when suppressed evidence would have entitled a jury to find that the eyewitnesses were not consistent in describing the killer, that two out of the four eyewitnesses testifying were unreliable, that the most damning physical evidence was subject to suspicion [of having been planted], that the investigation that produced it was insufficiently probing, and that the principal police witness was insufficiently informed or candid.[7]

Justice Scalia, joined by Chief Justice Rehnquist and Justices Kennedy and Thomas, dissented in *Kyles*. The dissenters did not disagree

[7] Justice Stevens wrote a short concurring opinion, defending the Court's role in engaging in fact-intensive review of capital cases, especially where the record points to the possibility that the defendant did not commit the crime.

with the majority's restatement of the principles derived from *Brady*, *Agurs* and *Bagley*. Rather, they argued that reversal was unwarranted because the suppressed evidence, even considered cumulatively, was not materially exculpatory. Justice Scalia stated that even with the suppressed evidence, Kyles could not have overcome the implausibility of his own defense, which was that the witnesses misidentified him and that Beanie framed him. Justice Scalia explained as follows:

> [P]etitioner's theory was that he was the victim of a quadruple coincidence, in which four eyewitnesses to the crime mistakenly identified him as the murderer—three picking him out of a photo-array without hesitation, and all four affirming their identification in open court after comparing him with Beanie. The extraordinary mistake petitioner had to persuade the jury these four witnesses made was not simply to mistake the real killer, Beanie, for the very same innocent third party (hard enough to believe), but in addition to mistake him for the very man Beanie had chosen to frame—the last and most incredible level of coincidence. However small the chance that the jury would believe any one of those improbable scenarios, the likelihood that it would believe them all together is far smaller.

In Weary v. Cain, 136 S.Ct. 1002 (2016) (per curiam), the Court vacated a capital conviction because of state prosecutors' failure to disclose material evidence. Nearly two years after a murder, a state prisoner, Scott, contacted authorities and implicated Weary in the murder. Scott changed his account of the crime four different times, and each version differed from the others in material ways. The Court described Scott as the state's star witness and observed that his trial testimony bore little resemblance to his original account. The state had no physical evidence linking Weary to the murder but it had another witness, Brown (also incarcerated at the time of Weary's trial), who testified that he saw Weary on the night of the murder with someone who looked like the victim. Brown had originally made a prior inconsistent statement to the police but recanted and agreed to testify ostensibly because he knew the victim's sister. The prosecutor told the jury that Brown had "no deal on the table."

Weary's defense was alibi. He claimed he was at a wedding reception 40 miles away at the time of the murder. His girlfriend, her sister, and her aunt corroborated his claim.

Post-trial proceedings revealed that police records showed that two of Scott's fellow inmates heard Scott make statements that cast doubt on his credibility. One inmate reported hearing Scott say that he wanted to make sure that Weary "gets the needle because he jacked over me." The other inmate told investigators that he had witnessed the murder, but recanted and revealed that Scott had told him what to say.

Weary's lawyers learned post-trial that Brown had twice sought a deal to reduce his sentence in exchange for his testimony against Weary, contrary to what the prosecutors suggested to the jury. They also learned that the medical records of one of the alleged participants in the murder according to Scott revealed that he had undergone surgery that would have disabled him from doing what Scott claimed he had done.

A state post-conviction court decided against Weary, but the Supreme Court summarily reversed. The Court emphasized that Weary was not required to show that it was more likely than not that he would have been acquitted had the suppressed evidence been disclosed; he had to show that the new evidence was sufficient to "undermine confidence" in the verdict.

Justice Alito, joined by Justice Thomas, dissented. He noted that the question whether the new evidence realistically could have changed the trial's outcome was an intensely factual question, expressed concern that the Court was deciding the case on the basis of a certiorari petition and the state's brief in opposition, and suggested it was more appropriate for a lower federal court to consider Weary's post-conviction claim in a habeas corpus proceeding.

In Turner v. United States, 137 S.Ct. 1885 (2017), Justice Breyer wrote for the Court as it held that, although the government withheld evidence from seven defendants tried together for the kidnaping, armed robbery, and murder of a woman in the District of Columbia, their convictions did not have to be set aside. The government did not contest that the withheld evidence was favorable to the defendants; nor did it contest that it suppressed the evidence. The issue before the Court was materiality.

The body of the victim was found inside an alley garage just a few blocks from her home. The government's theory at trial was that she was attacked by a large group of individuals, including the seven defendants. Its key witnesses were Alston and Bennett who confessed to participating in the murders and cooperated with the government in exchange for leniency. Both witnesses described members of the group pursuing the victim, shoving her into an alley, punching and kicking her, carrying her to a garage in the alley and moving her into the garage. The government also played a videotape of a recorded statement in which one defendant described the criminal activity. A jury convicted the seven defendants who were attacking their convictions and acquitted two others.

After their convictions became final, the defendants discovered the government had withheld the following evidence: (1) the government refused to disclose the names of two men seen by the vendor who discovered the body running into the alley, stopping near the garage while the vendor awaited the police, and then running away when an officer approached— and one of them was James McMillan, who lived in a house that opened in the back to a connecting alley and was arrested in the weeks following the murder, but before the defendants' trial, for beating and robbing two women in the neighborhood; (2) Willie Luchie told police he was walking with three others through the alley around the time of the murder and heard several groans from the garage, one of the others said he heard moans, and two others heard nothing unusual; (3) Ammie Davis, who was arrested for disorderly conduct a few weeks after the murder told police that, while walking with a girlfriend, she saw another individual, James Blue, beat the victim to death in the alley and thereafter said she only saw Blue grab the victim and push her into the alley (Blue killed Davis before the defendant's trial in an unrelated drug dispute); (4) Carrie Eleby, who testified to hearing screams coming from where a "gang of boys" was beating someone near the garage was interviewed by the police along with a friend and both agreed that they heard Alston admit his involvement in robbing the victim, but the friend later recanted and said she just went along with what Eleby said; (5) Eleby told investigators she had been high on PCP; (6) a detective recorded in a note that Linda Jacobs, who was with Eleby at the time of the assault, vacillated about what she saw; and (7) a note indicated that the aunt of Maurice Thomas, a 14-year-old at the time of the murder who testified to recognizing six of the assailants, said she did not recall Maurice telling her anything like that.

The defendants argued that had they known of the identity of James McMillan and Luchie's statement about hearing groans they could have relied on the theory that the victim was killed by a single perpetrator, or two at most, rather than in a group attack. But, Justice Breyer reasoned that it was not reasonably probable that McMillan's identity and Luchie's ambiguous statement that he heard groans but saw no one could have led to a different result at trial given the testimony of Alston and Bennett, the videotaped statement, and the testimony of Thomas. He also reasoned that the undisclosed impeachment evidence was largely cumulative of evidence that the defendants had used at trial.

Justice Kagan, joined by Justice Ginsburg, dissented and pointed out that the actual trial involved 10 defendants accepting the government's theory that a gang had attacked the victim with each defendant claiming he was not part of the gang, which meant that the defendants undermined each other's arguments at every turn. She posited that had the defendants been aware of evidence suggesting that the murder was committed by someone else they might have vigorously disputed the government's gang attack theory and challenged the credibility of its investigation. She challenged the majority's "slam-dunk" description of the case and pointed out that there was no physical evidence tying any defendant to the crime, two key witnesses were testifying in exchange for favorable plea deals, two witnesses admitted they were high on PCP, and Thomas was an eighth grader whose aunt contradicted parts of his trial testimony.

Suppressed Evidence That Would Have Been Inadmissible at Trial: *Wood v. Bartholomew*

If the evidence suppressed by the prosecution would be inadmissible at the defendant's trial, could it ever be considered materially exculpatory? The Supreme Court considered this question in Wood v. Bartholomew, 516 U.S. 1 (1995), a per curiam opinion, in which exculpatory polygraph results were suppressed. Bartholomew admitted shooting a laundry attendant during a robbery, but claimed his gun accidentally discharged. This account was disputed by two prosecution witnesses, Bartholomew's brother Rodney and Rodney's girlfriend, who both claimed that Bartholomew told them that he intended to shoot the attendant. Both witnesses passed the polygraph on the questions regarding Bartholomew's intent to shoot the attendant, but Rodney was found to be deceptive when he denied all involvement in the crime. The court of appeals found that suppression of the polygraph results constituted a *Brady* violation, even though it recognized that polygraph evidence is not admissible for any purpose in Washington state courts. That court reasoned that if defense counsel had known about the polygraph results, he would have attacked Rodney's story more aggressively; that he "likely would have taken Rodney's deposition"; that in that deposition defense counsel "might well have succeeded in obtaining an admission that Rodney was lying about his participation in the crime"; and that defense counsel "would likely have uncovered a variety of conflicting statements which could have been used quite effectively in cross-examination at trial."

The Supreme Court rejected this reasoning as speculative and inconsistent with the *Brady-Agurs-Bagley* materiality requirement. The Court elaborated as follows:

> The information at issue here * * * is not "evidence" at all. Disclosure of the polygraph results, then, could have had no direct effect on the outcome of trial, because respondent could have made no mention of them either during argument or while questioning witnesses. To get around this problem, the Ninth Circuit reasoned that the information, had it been disclosed to the defense, might have led respondent's counsel to conduct additional discovery that might have led to some additional evidence that could have been utilized. Other than expressing a belief that in a deposition Rodney might have confessed to his involvement in the initial stages of the crime—a confession that itself would have been in no way inconsistent with respondent's guilt— the Court of Appeals did not specify what particular evidence it had in mind. Its judgment is based on mere speculation, in violation of the standards we have established.

The Court noted that Bartholemew's counsel, at the habeas hearing, testified that he made the strategic decision not to cross-examine Rodney aggressively at trial, for fear that Rodney would reiterate his brother's statement that he would "leave no witnesses." Thus, the lower court's judgment on what could have been done with the polygraph responses was inconsistent with the approach actually taken by Bartholemew's own trial counsel. Finally, the Court noted that the polygraph responses could not have been material in light of the overwhelming evidence of Bartholemew's guilt:

> To acquit of aggravated murder, the jury would have had to believe that respondent's single action revolver discharged accidently, not once but twice, by tragic coincidence depositing a bullet to the back of the victim's head, execution-style, as the victim lay face down on the floor. In the face of this physical evidence, as well as Rodney and Tracy's testimony * * * it should take more than supposition on the weak premises offered by respondent to undermine a court's confidence in the outcome.[8]

Does *Bartholomew* mean that inadmissible evidence can *never* be *Brady* material? See United States v. Salem, 578 F.3d 682 (7th Cir. 2009) (only admissible evidence can be "material" under *Brady*, because only admissible evidence could possibly lead to a different verdict). For a critique on limiting the *Brady* right to admissible evidence, see Ginsberg, Always Be Disclosing: The Prosecutor's Constitutional Duty to Divulge Inadmissible Evidence, 110 W.Va. L. Rev. 611 (2008).

Impeachment Evidence Found Material Under Brady: Smith v. Cain

In Smith v. Cain, 565 U.S. 73 (2012), Chief Justice Roberts wrote for an 8–1 Court, in a fact-intensive opinion, as it overturned a defendant's convictions on five first-degree murder counts due to a *Brady* violation in suppressing impeachment evidence. Boatner was the only eyewitness to the murders, and he identified the defendant as one of the perpetrators at trial. But he had told a detective on the night of the murders that he could not supply a description of the perpetrators other than that they were black males, and five days later he told the detective that he "could not ID anyone because [he] couldn't see faces" and "would not know them if [he] saw them." These statements were suppressed by the prosecution. No other witness and no physical evidence tied the defendant to the crime. The Chief Justice stated that the only question before the Court was whether the suppressed statements were "material" under *Brady*, and on that question wrote as follows:

> We have observed that evidence impeaching an eyewitness may not be material if the State's other evidence is strong enough to sustain

---

[8]   Four Justices in *Bartholomew* dissented from the summary disposition of the case.

confidence in the verdict. That is not the case here. Boatner's testimony was the only evidence linking Smith to the crime. And Boatner's undisclosed statements directly contradict his testimony: Boatner told the jury that he had "[n]o doubt" that Smith was the gunman he stood "face to face" with on the night of the crime, but Ronquillo's notes show Boatner saying that he "could not ID anyone because [he] couldn't see faces" and "would not know them if [he] saw them." Boatner's undisclosed statements were plainly material.

The State and the dissent advance various reasons why the jury might have discounted Boatner's undisclosed statements. They stress, for example, that Boatner made other remarks on the night of the murder indicating that he could identify the first gunman to enter the house, but not the others. That merely leaves us to speculate about which of Boatner's contradictory declarations the jury would have believed. The State also contends that Boatner's statements made five days after the crime can be explained by fear of retaliation. Smith responds that the record contains no evidence of any such fear. Again, the State's argument offers a reason that the jury could have disbelieved Boatner's undisclosed statements, but gives us no confidence that it would have done so.

Justice Thomas dissented.

Impeachment Evidence That Does Not Raise a Reasonable Probability of a Different Result: Strickler v. Greene

In Strickler v. Greene, 527 U.S. 263 (1999), the Court considered the effect of suppressed impeachment evidence in a prosecution for capital murder. Strickler and Henderson after abducting Whitlock at a shopping center and commandeering her car by striking a blow to her head with a 69-pound rock. There was abundant evidence connecting Strickler to the murder—among other things, he was seen driving the victim's car near the scene of the murder, he gave away some of the victim's valuables as presents, and both he and Henderson made inculpatory statements to friends. However, the only witness who testified to the abduction itself was a bystander named Stoltzfus. She gave detailed testimony indicating that Strickler took the lead in breaking into Whitlock's car and forcing her into the passenger seat, while Henderson and Strickler's girlfriend "hung back." Throughout her testimony, she referred to Strickler as "Mountain Man" and Henderson as "Shy Guy." She had no doubt about her testimony and offered that she had an excellent memory. In fact, however, Stoltzfus had been unable to identify Strickler during several meetings with a police officer, and indicated that she hadn't thought that the event she witnessed was very serious, in that it seemed like a college prank. This information about Stoltzfus' prior uncertainty was never disclosed to Strickler's defense counsel. Strickler was convicted and sentenced to death. In a separate trial, Henderson was also convicted, but did not receive a death sentence.

The District Court granted a writ of habeas corpus on Strickler's *Brady* claim. The Fourth Circuit reversed, finding no merit in the *Brady* claim on the ground that Stoltzfus' testimony related only to the abduction, and was therefore essentially irrelevant to the capital murder charges. The Supreme Court, in an opinion by Justice Stevens, agreed with the Fourth Circuit, though it found the *Brady* "prejudice" question much more difficult than had the Court of Appeals.

Justice Stevens analyzed the *Brady* "prejudice" claim in the following passage:

> The Court of Appeals' [ruling that the suppressed impeachment evidence was not "material"] rested on its conclusion that, without considering Stoltzfus' testimony, the record contained ample, independent evidence of guilt, as well as evidence sufficient to support the findings of vileness and future dangerousness that warranted the imposition of the death penalty. The standard used by that court was incorrect. As we made clear in *Kyles*, the materiality inquiry is not just a matter of determining whether, after discounting the inculpatory evidence in light of the undisclosed evidence, the remaining evidence is sufficient to support the jury's conclusions. Rather, the question is whether "the favorable evidence could reasonably be taken to put the whole case in such a different light as to undermine confidence in the verdict."

* * *

> The District Court was surely correct that there is a reasonable *possibility* that either a total, or just a substantial, discount of Stoltzfus' testimony might have produced a different result, either at the guilt or sentencing phases. Petitioner did, for example, introduce substantial mitigating evidence about abuse he had suffered as a child at the hands of his stepfather. As the District Court recognized, however, petitioner's burden is to establish a reasonable *probability* of a different result.

> Even if Stoltzfus and her testimony had been entirely discredited, the jury might still have concluded that petitioner was the leader of the criminal enterprise because he was the one seen driving the car * * * near the location of the murder and the one who kept the car for the following week. In addition, [Strickler's girlfriend] testified that petitioner threatened Henderson with a knife later in the evening.

* * *

> We recognize the importance of eyewitness testimony; Stoltzfus provided the only disinterested, narrative account of what transpired

on January 5, 1990. However, Stoltzfus' vivid description of the events at the mall was not the only evidence that the jury had before it. Two other eyewitnesses, the security guard and Henderson's friend, placed petitioner and Henderson at the Harrisonburg Valley Shopping Mall on the afternoon of Whitlock's murder. One eyewitness later saw petitioner driving Dean's car near the scene of the murder.

The record provides strong support for the conclusion that petitioner would have been convicted of capital murder and sentenced to death, even if Stoltzfus had been severely impeached. The jury was instructed on two predicates for capital murder: robbery with a deadly weapon and abduction with intent to defile. * * * [A]rmed robbery still would have supported the capital murder conviction. * * *

Petitioner also maintains that he suffered prejudice from the failure to disclose the Stoltzfus documents because her testimony impacted on the jury's decision to impose the death penalty. * * * With respect to the jury's discretionary decision to impose the death penalty, it is true that Stoltzfus described petitioner as a violent, aggressive person, but that portrayal surely was not as damaging as either the evidence that he spent the evening of the murder dancing and drinking * * * or the powerful message conveyed by the 69-pound rock that was part of the record before the jury. Notwithstanding the obvious significance of Stoltzfus' testimony, petitioner has not convinced us that there is a reasonable probability that the jury would have returned a different verdict if her testimony had been either severely impeached or excluded entirely.

Justice Souter, joined by Justice Kennedy, dissented in part in *Strickler*. He agreed with the Court that the suppressed impeachment information was not "material", in a *Brady* sense, to the defendant's guilt or innocence. But he argued that the impeachment material did create a reasonable probability that the jury would have recommended a life sentence rather than the death penalty. He explained as follows:

I could not regard Stoltzfus's colorful testimony as anything but significant on the matter of sentence. It was Stoltzfus alone who described Strickler as the initiator of the abduction, as the one who broke into Whitlock's car, who beckoned his companions to follow him, and who violently subdued the victim while 'Shy Guy' sat in the back seat. The bare content of this testimony, important enough, was enhanced by one of the inherent hallmarks of reliability, as Stoltzfus confidently recalled detail after detail. The withheld documents would have shown, however, that many of the details Stoltzfus confidently mentioned on the stand * * * had apparently escaped her memory in her initial interviews with the police. Her persuasive account did not come, indeed, until after her recollection had been aided by further conversations with the police and with the victim's boyfriend. I therefore have to assess the likely havoc that an informed cross-examiner could have wreaked upon Stoltzfus as adequate to raise a significant possibility of a different recommendation [of sentence], as sufficient to undermine confidence that the death recommendation would have been the choice. All it would have taken, after all, was one juror to hold out against death to preclude the recommendation actually given.

* * *

Professor Saltzburg, in Perjury and False Testimony: Should the Difference Matter So Much, 68 Fordham L. Rev. 1537 (2000), argues that Stoltzfus's trial testimony, which indicated confidence and certainty on her part, was amazingly inconsistent with what she told the Detective. The impression of confidence and certainty created by the prosecution appears to have been plainly false—something the Court largely ignored.

More Suppressed Impeachment Evidence: Banks v. Dretke

In Banks v. Dretke, 540 U.S. 668 (2004), the Court once again undertook a fact-intensive inquiry into whether a *Brady* violation occurred when impeachment evidence was suppressed. Banks was convicted of capital murder and sentenced to death. At the penalty phase, the jury was required to find that there was a probability that Banks would "commit criminal acts of violence that would constitute a continuing threat to society." As proof of this continuing dangerousness, the prosecution presented the testimony of Robert Farr. Farr testified that after the murder, he traveled with Banks to Dallas to retrieve Banks's gun, so that the gun could be used in a series of planned robberies. Farr testified that Banks promised to use the gun to "take care of it" if any problems arose during the robberies. On cross-examination, defense counsel asked Farr whether he had "ever taken any money from some police officers," or "given any police officers a statement." Farr answered "no" to both questions; he asserted that police officers had not promised him anything and that he had "talked to no one about this [case]" until a few days before trial. The prosecution also presented the testimony of Banks's brother-in-law, who testified that Banks had once struck him across the face with a gun and threatened to kill him.

The majority, in an opinion by Justice Ginsburg, ruled that the death penalty phase was tainted by a *Brady* error: the government had not disclosed that Farr had been paid $200 for his testimony, that Farr had instigated the adventure to retrieve the gun, and that Farr had conferred with the prosecutor in detail about the testimony. Justice Ginsburg found that the suppressed impeachment evidence was "material" for *Brady* purposes, reasoning as follows:

Our touchstone on materiality is Kyles v. Whitley, 514 U.S. 419 (1995). *Kyles* instructed that the materiality standard for *Brady* claims is met when "the favorable evidence could reasonably be taken to put the whole case in such a different light as to undermine confidence in the verdict." In short, Banks must show a "reasonable probability of a different result."

* * * Farr was paid for a critical role in the scenario that led to the indictment. * * * Farr, not Banks, initiated the proposal to obtain a gun to facilitate the commission of robberies. Had Farr not instigated, upon Deputy Sheriff Huff's request, the Dallas excursion to fetch Banks's gun, the prosecution would have had slim, if any, evidence that Banks planned to "continue" committing violent acts. Farr's admission of his instigating role, moreover, would have dampened the prosecution's zeal in urging the jury to bear in mind Banks's "planning and acquisition of a gun to commit robbery," or Banks's "planned violence."

* * *

Because Banks had no criminal record, Farr's testimony about Banks's propensity to commit violent acts was crucial to the prosecution. Without that testimony, the State could not have underscored, as it did three times in the penalty phase, that Banks would use the gun fetched in Dallas to "take care" of trouble arising during the robberies. The stress placed by the prosecution on this part of Farr's testimony, uncorroborated by any other witness, belies the State's suggestion that "Farr's testimony was adequately corroborated." The prosecution's penalty-phase summation, moreover, left no doubt about the importance the State attached to Farr's testimony. What Farr told the jury, the prosecution urged, was "of the utmost significance" to show "[Banks] is a danger to friends and strangers, alike."

* * *

At least as to the penalty phase, in sum, one can hardly be confident that Banks received a fair trial, given the jury's ignorance of Farr's true role in the investigation and trial of the case. On the record before us, one could not plausibly deny the existence of the requisite "reasonable probability of a different result" had the suppressed information been disclosed to the defense. * * *

Justice Thomas, joined by Justice Scalia, dissented on the question of *Brady* materiality. He concluded that there was no reasonable probability that the jury would have decided differently at the penalty phase if it had known about Farr's status as a paid informant and instigator.

The jury was presented with the facts of a horrible crime. Banks, after meeting the victim, Richard Whitehead, a 16-year-old boy who had the misfortune of owning a car that Banks wanted, decided "to kill the person for the hell of it" and take his car. Banks proceeded to shoot Whitehead three times, twice in the head and once in the upper back. Banks fired one of the shots only 18 to 24 inches away from Whitehead. The jury was thus presented with evidence showing that Banks, apparently on a whim, executed Whitehead simply to get his car.

* * *

The jury also heard testimony that Banks had violently pistol-whipped and threatened to kill his brother-in-law one week before the murder. * * * In sum, the jury knew that Banks had murdered a 16-year-old on a whim, had violently attacked and threatened a relative shortly before the murder, and was willing to assist another individual in committing armed robberies by providing the "means and possible death weapon" for these robberies. Even if the jury were to discredit entirely Farr's testimony that Banks was planning more robberies, in all likelihood the jury still would have found "beyond a reasonable doubt" that there "[was] a probability that [Banks] would commit criminal acts of violence that would constitute a continuing threat to society."

Brady and Guilty Pleas: United States v. Ruiz

If the prosecutor has materially exculpatory evidence, must it be disclosed before the defendant enters into a guilty plea? Or is the *Brady* right simply a trial right? The question arises in the following procedural context: the defendant pleads guilty, later learns of exculpatory evidence that was suppressed, and moves to vacate his guilty plea as insufficiently knowing and voluntary.[9]

In United States v. Ruiz, 536 U.S. 622 (2002), the Court held that during guilty plea negotiations the government is not required to disclose information that could impeach government witnesses, nor information that could be used by the defendant to prove an affirmative defense.

Justice Breyer, writing for a unanimous Court, noted that "impeachment information is special in relation to the *fairness of a trial,* not in respect to whether a plea is *voluntary.*" Justice Breyer expressed concern that requiring disclosure of impeachment information during guilty plea negotiations "could seriously interfere with the Government's interest in securing those guilty pleas that are factually justified, desired by defendants, and help to secure the efficient administration of justice."

---

[9]   See Chapter 9 for a more complete discussion of the voluntariness standards attendant to guilty pleas.

Specifically, early disclosure of impeachment evidence "could disrupt ongoing investigations and expose prospective witnesses to serious harm."

As to required disclosure of impeachment evidence, Justice Breyer concluded that it

> could force the Government to abandon its general practice of not disclosing to a defendant pleading guilty information that would reveal the identities of cooperating informants, undercover investigators, or other prospective witnesses. It could require the Government to devote substantially more resources to trial preparation prior to plea bargaining, thereby depriving the plea-bargaining process of its main resource-saving advantages. Or it could lead the Government instead to abandon its heavy reliance upon plea bargaining in a vast number—90% or more—of federal criminal cases. We cannot say that the Constitution's due process requirement demands so radical a change in the criminal justice process in order to achieve so comparatively small a constitutional benefit.

As to required disclosure of information bearing on an affirmative defense, the Court concluded as follows:

> We do not believe the Constitution here requires provision of this information to the defendant prior to plea bargaining—for most (though not all) of the reasons previously stated. That is to say, in the context of this agreement, the need for this information is more closely related to the *fairness* of a trial than to the *voluntariness* of the plea; the value in terms of the defendant's added awareness of relevant circumstances is ordinarily limited; yet the added burden imposed upon the Government by requiring its provision well in advance of trial (often before trial preparation begins) can be serious, thereby significantly interfering with the administration of the plea bargaining process.

The Court in *Ruiz* recognized the government's duty to disclose information bearing on the defendant's "factual innocence" during guilty plea negotiations, as well as a continuing duty to disclose such information throughout the plea proceedings. Indeed, the government recognized this obligation by including it in the plea agreement in *Ruiz*. See also Sanchez v. United States, 50 F.3d 1448 (9th Cir.1995) (guilty plea vacated because evidence material to innocence was suppressed, noting that otherwise "prosecutors may be tempted to deliberately withhold exculpatory information as part of an attempt to elicit guilty pleas").

What is the test of materiality in a guilty plea context? The court in *Sanchez,* supra declared that suppressed evidence is material if "there is a reasonable probability that but for the failure to disclose the *Brady* material, the defendant would have refused to plead and would have gone to trial." How is a court to determine this question? Does it rely on the defendant's assertions? On the power of the suppressed evidence? On a comparison between the deal that the defendant received and the sentence that he would have faced if convicted? See Miller v. Angliker, 848 F.2d 1312 (2d Cir.1988) (test of materiality, in the guilty plea context, is an objective one that centers on "the likely persuasiveness of the withheld information").

For a discussion of the relationship between *Brady* material and guilty pleas, see Lain, Accuracy Where It Matters: Brady v. Maryland in the Plea Bargaining Context, 80 Wash.U. L.Q. 1 (2002) (noting that *"Brady's* importance in the plea bargaining context is clear in part just because so many cases are resolved there"); Douglass, Fatal Attraction? The Uneasy Courtship of *Brady* and Plea Bargaining, 50 Emory L.J.437 (2001) ("If we are serious about better-informed guilty pleas, then we should address the problem when it matters most: before the plea.").

Disclosure of Evidence Without Indicating What Is Exculpatory

In some cases—particularly those involving electronic discovery—the government produces millions of documents to the defendant, and hidden in the haystack are some materially exculpatory documents. Has the prosecution satisfied its *Brady* obligations by such a production? In United States v. Skilling, 554 F.3d 529 (5th Cir. 2009), a prosecution of a high-ranking Enron executive, the government turned over millions of documents, and the defendant argued that the government should have identified the *Brady* material within the mountain of data. But the court rejected the defendant's argument. It stated that "[a]s a general rule, the government is under no duty to direct a defendant to exculpatory evidence within a larger mass of disclosed evidence." The court found that there would be a *Brady* violation if the prosecution was engaging in a document dump in an attempt to hide the exculpatory evidence. But in this case, all the data was electronic and provided in a searchable format. Thus, "the government was in no better position to locate any potentially exculpatory evidence than was Skilling." See also United States v. Ohle, 2011 WL 651849 (S.D.N.Y.) (where government turned over seven million pages of documents, there was no *Brady* violation because the documents were in searchable form and so "the defendants were just as likely to uncover the purportedly exculpatory evidence as was the government").

"Materially Exculpatory Evidence" or "All Favorable Evidence"?

Brady does *not* require prosecutors to turn over every piece of evidence that might be considered favorable to the defense. The duty is to turn over "materially exculpatory" evidence. But is it a problem that the determination of what is "materially exculpatory" is left to the prosecutor?

Wouldn't even a fair-minded prosecutor have a tendency to downplay the importance of evidence favorable to the defendant? For example, in Muhammad v. Kelly, 575 F.3d 359 (4th Cir. 2009), the prosecution of one of two defendants who tormented the D.C. metropolitan area by shooting innocent people from their automobile and who were referred to as "snipers," the government suppressed a number of documents favorable to the defense, such as an FBI analyst's report that the sniper committing the shootings was likely acting alone (whereas Muhammad was charged with having an accomplice). The court found that the report, while favorable, was not materially exculpatory because the language in the report was tentative and "did not definitively conclude that the killings were the work of a single shooter." Other favorable evidence that was suppressed was also found "cumulative" of evidence the defendant presented at trial and therefore not materially exculpatory. The court noted, however, that

> we by no means condone the action of the Commonwealth in this case. As a matter of practice, the prosecution should err on the side of disclosure, especially when a defendant is facing the specter of execution. When questioned at oral argument regarding why this information was withheld or why the Commonwealth did not take the step of instituting an open-file policy, the Commonwealth had no explanation. Yet, at this stage of the process, we deal only with actions that were clear violations of the Constitution. While not admirable, the Commonwealth's actions did not violate the Constitution.

Many lawyers, judges, and academics have argued for a rule requiring the prosecutor to disclose all information that a *defense counsel might consider favorable* to the defense. That is, the prosecutor reviewing the evidence in the file should put on the defense counsel's hat and, from that perspective, disclose all the information that the defense counsel would find helpful.

The push for a broader rule of disclosure—mandated by rule, beyond the constitutional minimum set by *Brady*—was spurred by revelations that prosecutors in the corruption trial of Senator Ted Stevens had suppressed evidence about the star witness in the case. Prosecutors apparently acknowledged that the evidence might have helped the defense in attacking the witness's credibility, but didn't think that the evidence was important enough to be "materially exculpatory" under *Brady*. The presiding judge was so frustrated by the prosecutors' conduct that he wrote a letter to the Judicial Conference Advisory Committee on Criminal Rules, asking the Committee to amend Rule 16 to require the government to produce all favorable information to the defense.

The Department of Justice is opposed to amending Criminal Rule 16 to require the production of all favorable evidence. Assistant Attorney General Lanny Breuer, speaking in opposition to any rule amendment, stated that, notwithstanding the Stevens case, improper suppression by the government is infrequent. He noted that an internal DOJ review uncovered only 15 cases of misconduct over a nine-year period. He argued that eliminating the materiality standard "seriously comes into conflict" with victim rights, witness security and, in some cases, national security. In response, Senator Stevens' defense counsel, Brendan Sullivan, said in a statement that the materiality limitation "allows prosecutors to play games with their constitutional duties" and that "criminal trials are supposed to be a search for the truth, and there is no justification whatsoever for concealing any exculpatory information from the defense."

One of the problems of verifying Breuer's assertion that suppression is infrequent is that he is referring only to the cases in which improper suppression was *discovered*. But the very nature of suppression is that it is hard to discover. As then-Chief Judge Wolf wrote:

> The reported cases are not, however, a true measure of the scope of the problem [of prosecutorial suppression], which it is impossible to measure precisely. The defense is, by definition, unaware of exculpatory information that has not been provided by the government. Although some information of this nature comes to light by chance from time to time, it is reasonable to assume in other similar cases such information has never come to light. There is, however, no way to determine how frequently this occurs.

United States v. Jones, 620 F.Supp.2d 163 (D.Mass.2009) (an appendix to Judge Wolf's opinion cites 70 reported Federal decisions reversing convictions for violations of *Brady*).

Ultimately the Advisory Committee chose not to propose an amendment to Rule 16 that would require the prosecutor to turn over all evidence favorable to the defendant. The Committee withdrew from the field after the Justice Department made amendments to the United States Attorney's Manual that required U.S. Attorneys to make broader disclosure of evidence favorable to the defendant. See Section 9–500, "Policy Regarding Disclosure of Exculpatory and Impeachment Information." Judge Wolf, in *Jones,* argues that an internal guideline will do little to solve the problem of suppression, because it is not enforceable by the defendant, and so the remedy, if any, is prosecutorial discipline rather than reversal of an unjust conviction.

Given the difficulties of applying *Brady* and the likelihood that suppression will never be discovered, wouldn't it make sense to require the government to simply turn over its case file to the defendant—subject to culling work product and any information that would raise a security risk? See Cary, Exculpatory Evidence: A Call for Reform After the Unlawful Prosecution of Senator Ted Stevens, 36 Litigation 34 (2010) ("Changing to an open file discovery process would lead to fairer trials and to more guilty pleas when meritorious charges are supported by credible evidence. Moreover, open file discovery should actually relieve prosecutors of the burden of sifting through information to determine whether or not it is exculpatory. Honest prosecutors would no longer required to make judgment calls regarding what defendants and their counsel might find helpful.").

C. PRESERVING AND SEEKING OUT EXCULPATORY EVIDENCE

Brady prohibits the government from *suppressing* materially exculpatory evidence. But is there a constitutional right to have such evidence *preserved*? And how do you know if it was materially exculpatory unless it is preserved in the first place?

Justice Marshall wrote for a unanimous Supreme Court in California v. Trombetta, 467 U.S. 479 (1984), declaring that law enforcement officers are not required by the Due Process Clause to preserve breath samples of suspected drunk drivers for potential use by defendants at trial. A device called an Intoxilyzer was used to test these samples. Suspects, including those challenging the police procedures in the instant case, breathed into the device and infrared light sensed their blood alcohol level. California officers purge the device after each test, thus destroying the breath samples. Although the state health department had approved a kit which officers could use to preserve breath samples, it was not standard practice for officers to use the kit.

In his opinion in *Trombetta*, Justice Marshall declared that "[w]hatever duty the Constitution imposes on the States to preserve evidence, that duty must be limited to evidence that might be expected to play a significant role in the suspect's defense." The Court found that the chances were extremely low that preserved samples would have assisted defendants. Justice Marshall observed that the state had developed procedures to protect against machine malfunctions, and that some alternative attacks were possible when a defendant raised one of the limited number of claims available to challenge the functioning of a testing machine.

Chief Justice Rehnquist wrote for the Court in Arizona v. Youngblood, 488 U.S. 51 (1988), as it expanded upon *Trombetta* and held that "unless a criminal defendant can show bad faith on the part of the police, failure to preserve potentially useful evidence does not constitute a denial of due process of law." Youngblood was convicted of sexually assaulting a young boy. Although investigative authorities attempted to analyze semen obtained from the victim's clothing, they did not refrigerate the clothing and because of this they were unable to conduct an analysis. The Supreme Court found that the failure to preserve the evidence for testing was, at worst, negligent. The Chief Justice noted that there was no evidence that the police had any reason to believe that the semen samples might have exonerated the accused when they handled the clothing at the outset of the investigation. Nor was there any indication of bad faith on the part of the police. Indeed, the evidence, had it not been destroyed, could have helped the police to find the perpetrator, who at that point was unknown.

Chief Justice Rehnquist recognized that the *Brady* cases made the good or bad faith of the police irrelevant when material exculpatory evidence is *suppressed*, but he concluded that "the Due Process Clause requires a different result when we deal with the failure of the State to preserve evidentiary material of which no more can be said than that it could have been subjected to tests, the results of which might have exonerated the defendant." With suppression, the evidence still exists, so the court and the parties can determine whether it is materially exculpatory; but such is not the case with evidence that has been destroyed. The Chief Justice reasoned "that requiring a defendant to show bad faith on the part of the police both limits the extent of the police obligation to preserve evidence to reasonable bounds and confines it to that class of cases where the interests of justice most clearly require it, i.e., those cases in which the police themselves by their conduct indicate that the evidence could form a basis for exonerating the defendant." The Court noted that if evidence is destroyed and tests are not conducted, the defendant is free to argue to the finder of fact that the test might have been exculpatory, "but the police do not have a constitutional duty to perform any particular tests."

Justice Blackmun, joined by Justices Brennan and Marshall, dissented. He suggested that the bad faith test was less than clear and might create more questions than it answers. Justice Blackmun stated his due process test as follows: "[W]here no comparable evidence is likely to be available to the defendant, police must preserve physical evidence of a type that they reasonably should know has the potential, if tested, to reveal immutable characteristics of the criminal, and hence to exculpate a defendant charged with the crime."

See also United States v. Williams, 577 F.3d 878 (8th Cir. 2009), a felon-firearm possession case, in which the firearm was destroyed by the government before trial. The court found no due process violation. The court noted that the defendant could be found guilty even if the firearm was inoperable, so the condition of the firearm could not provide exculpatory evidence.

Is There a Duty to Seek Out Exculpatory Evidence?

The Court in *Youngblood* clearly implies that while the prosecution has a duty to *disclose* exculpatory evidence, it has no duty to seek out or to investigate information that would lead to exculpatory evidence. That is, the government has no obligation to act as an investigator for the defense. If the government fails to follow leads, or to seek an alternative explanation for the crime, then the defendant is free to suggest to the trier of fact that it draw an adverse inference at trial—but he has no Due Process right to demand a certain investigation. See Fisher, "Just the Facts, Ma'am": Lying and the Omission of Exculpatory Evidence in Police Reports, 28 New Eng.L.Rev.1 (1993), for a discussion of this and other problems of police investigations that fail to develop exculpatory evidence.

D. DOES THE *BRADY* RIGHT EXTEND TO POST-TRIAL PROCEEDINGS?

DNA testing has been used in many cases to exonerate wrongfully convicted defendants. In District Attorney's Office for the Third Judicial District v. Osborne, 557 U.S. 52 (2009), a convicted defendant argued that he had a constitutional right to DNA testing that he claimed would exonerate him. The state had in fact conducted a rudimentary form of DNA testing before the trial; that test tended to include Osborne as a possible perpetrator in a sex crime, but it was not definitive. Osborne's counsel decided not to ask for a more sophisticated test to be done, fearing that it would further incriminate Osborne. Osborne was convicted and several years later brought a civil rights action against the state, alleging that he had a due process right to an even more sophisticated DNA test than was available at the time of his trial.

The lower court, in granting Osborne's demand for DNA testing, had relied on *Brady*. It reasoned that if the defendant had a constitutional right to exculpatory evidence *before* trial, he also had the right after conviction. Chief Justice Roberts, writing for a 5–4 majority, rejected this reasoning in the following passage:

> The Court of Appeals went too far * * * in concluding that the Due Process Clause requires that certain familiar preconviction trial rights be extended to protect Osborne's postconviction liberty interest. After identifying Osborne's possible liberty interests, the court concluded that the State had an obligation to comply with the principles of Brady v. Maryland. In that case, we held that due process requires a prosecutor to disclose material exculpatory evidence to the defendant before trial. * * *

> A defendant proved guilty after a fair trial does not have the same liberty interests as a free man. At trial, the defendant is presumed innocent and may demand that the government prove its case beyond reasonable doubt. But once a defendant has been afforded a fair trial and convicted of the offense for which he was charged, the presumption of innocence disappears. * * *

The State accordingly has more flexibility in deciding what procedures are needed in the context of postconviction relief. * * * Osborne's right to due process is not parallel to a trial right, but rather must be analyzed in light of the fact that he has already been found guilty at a fair trial, and has only a limited interest in postconviction relief. *Brady* is the wrong framework.

Instead, the question is whether consideration of Osborne's claim within the framework of the State's procedures for postconviction relief "offends some principle of justice so rooted in the traditions and conscience of our people as to be ranked as fundamental," or "transgresses any recognized principle of fundamental fairness in operation." Federal courts may upset a State's postconviction relief procedures only if they are fundamentally inadequate to vindicate the substantive rights provided.

Chief Justice Roberts reviewed the state post-conviction procedures and saw "nothing inadequate about the procedures Alaska has provided to vindicate its state right to postconviction relief in general, and nothing inadequate about how those procedures apply to those who seek access to DNA evidence." Accordingly, the Court denied Osborne federal relief.

Justice Alito filed a concurring opinion in which Justice Kennedy joined, and in which Justice Thomas joined in part. He argued that it would be inappropriate to allow Osborne to forego testing at trial and then to request a different test many years later. In Justice Alito's view, this would "allow prisoners to play games with the criminal justice system" because "with nothing to lose, the defendant could demand DNA testing in the hope that some happy accident—for example, degradation or contamination of the evidence—would provide the basis for postconviction relief."

Justice Stevens filed a dissenting opinion, joined by Justices Ginsburg and Breyer and by Justice Souter in part. Justice Stevens noted that no prisoner had ever obtained DNA evidence for testing in Alaska and that he had "grave doubts about the adequacy of the procedural protections" in state law. He noted that DNA testing in this case would cost the state nothing because Osborne had offered to pay for it. Justice Souter also filed a dissenting opinion, concluding that state officials had "demonstrated a combination of inattentiveness and intransigence that add up to "procedural unfairness that violates the due process clause."

Ethical Responsibilities of Prosecutors

Wholly aside from constitutional obligations to permit DNA testing or to recognize *Brady* obligations post-conviction, prosecutors may have ethical obligations when they become aware that a defendant may have been wrongly convicted. For example, in 2008, the American Bar

Association added Rules 3.8 (g) and (h) to its Model Rules of Professional Conduct.

Rule 3.8 Special Responsibilities of a Prosecutor

(g) When a prosecutor knows of new, credible and material evidence creating a reasonable likelihood that a convicted defendant did not commit an offense of which the defendant was convicted, the prosecutor shall:

(1) promptly disclose that evidence to an appropriate court or authority, and

(2) if the conviction was obtained in the prosecutor's jurisdiction,

(i) promptly disclose that evidence to the defendant unless a court authorizes delay, and

(ii) undertake further investigation, or make reasonable efforts to cause an investigation, to determine whether the defendant was convicted of an offense that the defendant did not commit.

(h) When a prosecutor knows of clear and convincing evidence establishing that a defendant in the prosecutor's jurisdiction was convicted of an offense that the defendant did not commit, the prosecutor shall seek to remedy the conviction.

V. DISCOVERY BY THE PROSECUTION

A. CONSTITUTIONAL IMPLICATIONS

Any attempt to force defendants to comply with government discovery requests runs into Fifth Amendment and due process concerns. The next case disposes of some of these.

WILLIAMS V. FLORIDA
Supreme Court of the United States, 1970.
399 U.S. 78.

JUSTICE WHITE delivered the opinion of the Court.

Prior to his trial for robbery in the State of Florida, petitioner filed a "Motion for a Protective Order," seeking to be excused from [a rule that] required a defendant, on written demand of the prosecuting attorney, to give notice in advance of trial if the defendant intends to claim an alibi, and to furnish the prosecuting attorney with information as to the place where he claims to have been and with the names and addresses of the alibi witnesses he intends to use. In his motion petitioner openly declared his intent to claim an alibi, but objected to the further disclosure requirements on the ground that the rule "compels the Defendant in a criminal case to be a witness against himself" in violation of his Fifth and Fourteenth Amendment rights. The motion was denied. * * * [The other aspect of the case involved a challenge to the six man jury provided by Florida. It also was unsuccessful. The jury issue is discussed in Chapter 10]. Petitioner was convicted as charged and was sentenced to life imprisonment. * * *

Florida's notice-of-alibi rule is in essence a requirement that a defendant submit to a limited form of pretrial discovery by the State whenever he intends to rely at trial on the defense of alibi. In exchange for the defendant's disclosure of the witnesses he proposes to use to establish that defense, the State in turn is required to notify the defendant of any witnesses it proposes to offer in rebuttal to that defense. * * * The threatened sanction for failure to comply is the exclusion at trial of the defendant's alibi evidence—except for his own testimony—or, in the case of the State, the exclusion of the State's evidence offered in rebuttal of the alibi.

In this case, following the denial of his Motion for a Protective Order, petitioner complied with the alibi rule and gave the State the name and address of one Mary Scotty. [The prosecution contacted Scotty and at trial, when she testified as an alibi witness, she was impeached with inconsistent statements she made to government investigators.]

We need not linger over the suggestion that the discovery permitted the State against petitioner in this case deprived him of "due process" or a "fair trial." Florida law provides for liberal discovery by the defendant against the State, and the notice-of-alibi rule is itself carefully hedged with reciprocal duties requiring state disclosure to the defendant. Given the ease with which an alibi can be fabricated, the State's interest in protecting itself against an eleventh-hour defense is both obvious and legitimate. * * * The adversary system of trial is hardly an end in itself; it is not yet a poker game in which players enjoy an absolute right always to conceal their cards until played. We find ample room in that system, at least as far as "due process" is concerned, for the instant Florida rule, which is designed to enhance the search for truth in the criminal trial by insuring both the defendant and the State ample opportunity to investigate certain facts crucial to the determination of guilt or innocence.

Petitioner's major contention is that he was "compelled * * * to be a witness against himself" contrary to the commands of the Fifth and Fourteenth Amendments because the notice-of-alibi rule required him to give the State the name and address of Mrs. Scotty in advance of trial and thus to furnish the State with information useful in convicting him. * * * Also, requiring him to reveal the elements of his defense is claimed to have interfered with his right to wait until after the State had presented its case to decide how to defend against it. We conclude, however, as has apparently every other court that has considered the issue, that the privilege against self-incrimination is not violated by a requirement that the defendant give notice of an alibi defense and disclose his alibi witnesses.

The defendant in a criminal trial is frequently forced to testify himself and to call other witnesses in an effort to reduce the risk of conviction. When he presents his witnesses, he must reveal their identity and submit them to cross-examination which in itself may prove incriminating or which may furnish the State with leads to incriminating rebuttal evidence. That the defendant faces such a dilemma demanding a choice between complete silence and presenting a defense has never been thought an invasion of the privilege against compelled self-incrimination. The pressures generated by the State's evidence may be severe but they do not vitiate the defendant's choice to present an alibi defense and witnesses to prove it, even though the attempted defense ends in catastrophe for the defendant. However, "testimonial" or "incriminating" the alibi defense proves to be, it cannot be considered "compelled" within the meaning of the Fifth and Fourteenth Amendments.

* * * We decline to hold that the privilege against compulsory self-incrimination guarantees the defendant the right to surprise the State with an alibi defense.

* * *

[JUSTICE BLACKMUN did not participate in the case. THE CHIEF JUSTICE filed a short concurring opinion on the alibi point. JUSTICE MARSHALL dissented on the jury issue, but concurred in the alibi ruling.]

JUSTICE BLACK, with whom JUSTICE DOUGLAS joins, concurring in part and dissenting in part.

* * *

On the surface this case involves only a notice-of-alibi provision, but in effect the decision opens the way for a profound change in one of the most important traditional safeguards of a criminal defendant. The rationale of today's decision is in no way limited to alibi defenses, or any other type or classification of evidence. The theory advanced goes at least so far as to permit the State to obtain under threat of sanction complete disclosure by the defendant in advance of trial of all evidence, testimony, and tactics he plans to use at that trial. In each case the justification will be that the rule affects only the "timing" of the disclosure, and not the substantive decision itself. * * *

Reciprocality Requirement

In Wardius v. Oregon, 412 U.S. 470 (1973), the Court struck down a notice of alibi provision that was not reciprocal—i.e., that did not require the prosecution to disclose in advance its rebuttal evidence. The Court suggested "that if there is to be any unbalance in discovery rights, it should work in the defendant's favor."

Other Notice Requirements

Besides a notice of alibi defense, the Federal Rules of Criminal Procedure also require the defendant to give advance notice of an insanity defense (Rule 12.2) and a notice of intent to assert "a defense of actual or believed exercise of public authority on behalf of a law enforcement agency or federal intelligence agency at the time of the alleged offense" (Rule 12.3). Failure to follow the notice requirements, without good cause, results in preclusion of witnesses who would testify to these defenses.

B. GENERAL DISCOVERY

The general federal discovery rule covering the defense is Rule 16(b), which provides for discovery of:

(A) documents and tangible objects within the control of the defendant and which the defendant intends to use in his case-in-chief;

(B) reports of examinations and tests within the control of the defendant and which the defendant either intends to use in his case-in-chief or which were prepared by a witness whom the defendant intends to call at trial; and

(C) a written summary of the testimony of an expert the defendant intends to call at trial, describing the opinions, bases, and qualifications of the expert. Protections are provided for privileged materials and work product. See Rule 16(b)(2).

The Federal Rule conditions government discovery of any of the above materials on a *prior request by the defendant* for discovery of similar information from the government and government compliance with that request. By conditioning the government's right to discovery on a defense request, the Federal Rule is probably intended to avoid constitutional problems—essentially, asking the government for discovery is treated as a waiver of any constitutional right to protect one's own, related information.

The Federal Rule does not require disclosure of information that the defendant expects to use to impeach government witnesses (e.g., records of prior inconsistent statements). Disclosure encompasses only information within the categories above that is going to be used in the "case-in-chief." See United States v. Medearis, 380 F.3d 1049 (8th Cir. 2004) (defendant cannot be sanctioned for failing to disclose a letter that was admissible to impeach a government witness: "the requirement of reciprocal pre-trial disclosure under Rule 16(b)(1)(A) includes only documents which the defendant intends to introduce during his own case-in-chief.").

Justice Black in *Williams* was plainly correct in foreseeing that notice requirements would not be limited to alibi defenses. Mosteller, Discovery Against the Defense: Tilting the Adversarial Balance, 74 Cal.L.Rev. 1567 (1986), describes a discovery "revolution" in the states. Mosteller found that in addition to prosecutorial discovery with respect to alibi and insanity, which is available in the great majority of states, 25 states grant the prosecution an independent (non-reciprocal) right to discover at least one of the following: "defenses, witness names, statements of witnesses, reports of experts, or documents and tangible evidence." A number of states require broad defense disclosure upon a request for discovery from the prosecution. Twelve states give the prosecution an independent right to obtain the statements of all defense witnesses, and three more permit this discovery when the defendant seeks discovery from the government. Some states require a defendant to summarize the expected testimony of defense witnesses and to create a statement summarizing oral statements of witnesses. Other states require the defense to furnish the government with statements taken from government witnesses.

C.   Sanctions for Nondisclosure

In Taylor v. Illinois, 484 U.S. 400 (1988) and Michigan v. Lucas, 500 U.S. 145 (1991), the Court considered whether it is constitutional for a trial court to preclude evidence proffered by criminal defendants who violate legitimate discovery obligations. In *Taylor,* defense counsel wilfully violated a state procedural rule by failing to identify a particular defense witness in response to a pretrial discovery request. The trial court sanctioned this violation by refusing to allow the undisclosed witness to testify. The Court rejected the argument that preclusion is never a permissible sanction for a discovery violation. The Court did not find it problematic to, in effect, sanction the defendant for his counsel's discovery violation; it reasoned that in most cases it would be quite difficult to determine whether the defense counsel or the defendant (or both) was responsible for the violation. Moreover, the Court did not consider it novel that a client would suffer due to the misstep of his counsel. Therefore, the trial court had discretion to determine whether to sanction defense counsel directly, or to use the sanction of preclusion. Justice Stevens wrote the majority opinion for six members of the Court. Justice Brennan, joined by Justices Marshall and Blackmun, dissented.

In *Lucas,* the defendant in a rape case proffered a defense of consent based in part upon the defendant's prior sexual relationship with the victim. The Michigan rape shield statute required that the defense give notice to the prosecution, within 10 days of the arraignment, of the intent to present evidence of past sexual conduct with the victim. The defendant did not comply with that notice requirement. As a discovery sanction, the trial court precluded any evidence of the sexual relationship at trial; but the State Supreme Court held that such preclusion violated the defendant's constitutional right to an effective defense. Justice O'Connor, writing for a majority of six justices, treated the case as presenting a limited question: whether the State Supreme Court had erred in adopting a per se rule that preclusion of evidence of a rape victim's prior sexual relationship with a criminal defendant violates the Constitution. The majority held that such a *per se* rule of unconstitutionality was inappropriate, because the notice requirement could serve a legitimate state purpose in some cases, and a defendant's violation of the notice requirement could be so egregious as to warrant the sanction of preclusion. The Court did not decide whether the Michigan notice period (the shortest in the nation, requiring notice to be given well before trial) was in fact "arbitrary or disproportionate" in light of the State's interests. Justice O'Connor left room for a defendant to argue that a minimal violation of a notice requirement should result in some remedy short of preclusion of the evidence, e.g., a continuance, and implied that a rigid rule of preclusion might be unconstitutional in some circumstances. The Court remanded to determine whether preclusion was appropriate under the circumstances of the case. Justice Blackmun concurred in the judgment. Justice Stevens, joined by Justice Marshall, dissented, contending that the State Supreme Court had not in fact gone so far "as to adopt the per se straw man that the Court has decided to knock down today." In their view, the State Court had simply held that preclusion was unjustified under the circumstances.

Taylor and *Lucas* do not hold that exclusion of evidence is permitted every time the defense violates a discovery obligation. Those cases do hold that the Constitution does not absolutely prohibit the sanction of exclusion of defense-proffered evidence in all cases.

C. WORK PRODUCT PROTECTION

In the following case, the Court considers the possible need for discovery at trial to assist in the examination of witnesses. And it also addresses the basis for and scope of the work product immunity as it applies to criminal cases.

UNITED STATES v. NOBLES
Supreme Court of the United States, 1975.
422 U.S. 225.

JUSTICE POWELL delivered the opinion of the Court.

In a criminal trial, defense counsel sought to impeach the credibility of key prosecution witnesses by testimony of a defense investigator regarding statements previously obtained from the witnesses by the investigator. The question presented here is whether in these circumstances a federal trial court may compel the defense to reveal the relevant portions of the investigator's report for the prosecution's use in cross-examining him. The United States Court of Appeals for the Ninth Circuit concluded that it cannot. We granted certiorari, and now reverse.

* * *

Respondent was tried and convicted on charges arising from an armed robbery of a federally insured bank. The only significant evidence linking him to the crime was the identification testimony of two witnesses, a bank teller and a salesman who was in the bank during the robbery. Respondent offered an alibi but, as the Court of Appeals recognized, his strongest defense centered around attempts to discredit these eyewitnesses. Defense efforts to impeach them gave rise to the events that led to this decision.

In the course of preparing respondent's defense, an investigator for the defense interviewed both witnesses and preserved the essence of those conversations in a written report. When the witnesses testified for the prosecution, respondent's counsel relied on the report in conducting their cross-examination. Counsel asked the bank teller whether he recalled having told the investigator that he had seen only the back of the man he identified as respondent. The witness replied that he did not remember making such a statement. He was allowed, despite defense counsel's initial objection, to refresh his recollection by referring to a portion of the investigator's report. The prosecutor also was allowed to see briefly the relevant portion of the report. The witness thereafter testified that although the report indicated that he told the investigator he had seen only respondent's back, he in fact had seen more than that and continued to insist that respondent was the bank robber.

The other witness acknowledged on cross-examination that he too had spoken to the defense investigator. Respondent's counsel twice inquired whether he told the investigator that "all blacks looked alike" to him, and in each instance the witness denied having made such a statement. The prosecution again sought inspection of the relevant portion of the investigator's report, and respondent's counsel again objected. The court declined to order disclosure at that time, but ruled that it would be required if the investigator testified as to the witnesses' alleged statements from the witness stand. * * *

After the prosecution completed its case, respondent called the investigator as a defense witness. The court [ruled] that a copy of the report, inspected and edited *in camera,* would have to be submitted to Government counsel at the completion of the investigator's impeachment testimony. When respondent's counsel stated that he did not intend to produce the report, the court ruled that the investigator would not be allowed to testify about his interviews with the witnesses. [The court of appeals found reversible error in excluding the investigator's testimony.]

* * *

* * * Decisions of this Court repeatedly have recognized the federal judiciary's inherent power to require the prosecution to produce the previously recorded statements of its witnesses so that the defense may get the full benefit of cross-examination and the truth-finding process may be enhanced. Jencks v. United States. At issue here is whether, in a proper case, the prosecution can call upon that same power for production of witness statements that facilitate "full disclosure of all the [relevant] facts."

In this case, the defense proposed to call its investigator to impeach the identification testimony of the prosecution's eyewitnesses. * * * The investigator's contemporaneous report might provide critical insight into the issues of credibility that the investigator's testimony would raise. It could assist the jury in determining the extent to which the investigator's testimony actually discredited the prosecution's witnesses. * * *

It was therefore apparent to the trial judge that the investigator's report was highly relevant to the critical issue of credibility. * * * We must determine whether compelling its production was precluded by some privilege available to the defense in the circumstances of this case.

* * *

The Court of Appeals concluded that the Fifth Amendment renders criminal discovery "basically a one-way street." Like many generalizations in constitutional law, this one is too broad. The relationship between the accused's Fifth Amendment rights and the prosecution's ability to discover materials at trial must be identified in a more discriminating manner.

* * *

In this instance disclosure of the relevant portions of the defense investigator's report would not impinge on the fundamental values protected by the Fifth Amendment. The court's order was limited to statements allegedly made by third parties who were available as witnesses to both the prosecution and the defense. Respondent did not prepare the report, and there is no suggestion that the portions subject to the disclosure order reflected any information that he conveyed to the investigator. The fact that these statements of third parties were elicited by a defense investigator on respondent's behalf does not convert them into respondent's personal communications. Requiring their production from the investigator therefore would not in any sense compel respondent to be a witness against himself or extort communications from him.

* * *

The Court of Appeals also held that Fed.Rule Crim.Proc. 16 deprived the trial court of the power to order disclosure of the relevant portions of the investigator's report. * * *

Both the language and history of Rule 16 indicate that it addresses only pretrial discovery. * * *

* * * We conclude, therefore, that Rule 16 imposes no constraint on the District Court's power to condition the impeachment testimony of respondent's witness on the production of the relevant portions of his investigative report. * * *

Respondent contends further that the work-product doctrine exempts the investigator's report from disclosure at trial. While we agree that this doctrine applies to criminal litigation as well as civil, we find its protection unavailable in this case.

The work-product doctrine, recognized by this court in Hickman v. Taylor, 329 U.S. 495 (1947), reflects the strong "public policy underlying the orderly prosecution and defense of legal claims." * * * The Court therefore recognized a qualified privilege for certain materials prepared by an attorney "acting for his client in anticipation of litigation."

Although the work-product doctrine most frequently is asserted as a bar to discovery in civil litigation, its role in assuring the proper functioning of the criminal justice system is even more vital. The interests of society and the accused in obtaining a fair and accurate resolution of the question of guilt or innocence demand that adequate safeguards assure the thorough preparation and presentation of each side of the case.

At its core, the work-product doctrine shelters the mental processes of the attorney, providing a privileged area within which he can analyze and prepare his client's case. But the doctrine is an intensely practical one, grounded in the realities of litigation in our adversary system. One of those realities is that attorneys often must rely on the assistance of investigators and other agents in the compilation of materials in preparation for trial. It is therefore necessary that the doctrine protect material prepared by agents for the attorney as well as those prepared by the attorney himself. Moreover, the concerns reflected in the work-product doctrine do not disappear once trial has begun. Disclosure of an attorney's efforts at trial, as surely as disclosure during pretrial discovery, could disrupt the orderly development and presentation of his case. We need not, however, undertake here to delineate the scope of the doctrine at trial, for in this instance it is clear that the defense waived such right as may have existed to invoke its protections.

The privilege derived from the work-product doctrine is not absolute. Like other qualified privileges, it may be waived. Here respondent sought to adduce the testimony of the investigator and contrast his recollection of the contested statements with that of the prosecution's witnesses. Respondent, by electing to present the investigator as a witness, waived the privilege with respect to matters covered in his testimony.[a] Respondent can no more advance the work-product doctrine to sustain a unilateral testimonial use of work-product materials than he could elect to testify in his own behalf and thereafter assert his Fifth Amendment privilege to resist cross-examination on matters reasonably related to those brought out in direct examination.

* * *

Finally, our examination of the record persuades us that the District Court properly exercised its discretion in this instance. The court authorized no general "fishing expedition" into the defense files or indeed even into the defense investigator's report. Rather, its considered ruling was quite limited in scope, opening to prosecution scrutiny only the portion of the report that related to the testimony the investigator would offer to discredit the witnesses' identification testimony. * * *

The court's preclusion sanction was an entirely proper method of assuring compliance with its order. Respondent's argument that this ruling deprived him of the Sixth Amendment rights to compulsory process and cross-examination misconceives the issue. The District Court did not bar the investigator's testimony. It merely prevented respondent from presenting to the jury a partial view of the credibility issue by adducing the investigator's testimony and thereafter refusing to disclose the contemporaneous report that might offer further critical insights. * * *

JUSTICE DOUGLAS **took no part in the consideration or decision of this case.**

[JUSTICE WHITE's concurring opinion, which was joined by JUSTICE REHNQUIST, is omitted.]

NOTE ON NOBLES AND THE CRIMINAL RULES

The result in *Nobles* is formalized in Fed. R. Crim. P. 26.2, which provides in relevant part as follows:

(a) MOTION TO PRODUCE. After a witness other than the defendant has testified on direct examination, the court, on motion of a party who did not call the witness, must order an attorney for the government or the defendant and the defendant's attorney to produce, for the examination and use of the moving party, any statement of the witness that is in their

---

[a] What constitutes a waiver with respect to work-product materials depends, of course, upon the circumstances. Counsel necessarily makes use throughout trial of the notes, documents, and other internal materials prepared to present adequately his client's case, and often relies on them in examining witnesses. When so used, there normally is no waiver. But where, as here, counsel attempts to make a testimonial use of these materials the normal rules of evidence come into play with respect to cross-examination and production of documents.

possession and that relates to the subject matter of the witness's testimony.

The Rule permits a trial court to inspect a statement to determine the parts that relate to the subject matter of the witness's testimony, to recess the proceedings to enable the party who receives a statement to examine it, and to strike testimony as a sanction for disobeying an order to produce. The Rule applies not only at trial, but also at a suppression hearing, a preliminary hearing, sentencing, a probation revocation proceeding, a pretrial detention proceeding, and in evidentiary hearings in collateral attack proceedings instituted by federal defendants.

CHAPTER 9

GUILTY PLEAS AND BARGAINING

■ ■ ■

I. THE GENERAL ISSUES

Once the determination to press charges is made and a case survives pre-trial motions or preliminary screening, the government becomes committed to the idea that the accused should be punished. The accused, even if innocent, must be concerned with how the case will ultimately be resolved. Questions like "Will I be convicted?" and "What kind of sentence will be imposed on me if I am convicted?" become increasingly important. Uncertainty about how these and other questions would be answered by going to trial often leads an accused to respond favorably to—or to initiate—"settlement" or "plea bargaining" discussions with the government. By agreeing to plead guilty the accused accepts punishment for some criminal activity. In exchange for this acceptance, the system—i.e., the prosecutor and the court—permits the accused to avoid some of the uncertainty endemic in any litigation system in which human beings must decide crucial questions of fact and law and often can exercise broad discretion in implementing social policy.

The extent to which negotiations actually take place, the nature of most agreements reached, the legitimacy of a bargained-for outcomes in criminal cases and the role of the various participants—i.e., the prosecutor, the trial judge, the defense counsel, the defendant, the victim, etc.—are all subjects that have been debated in the literature.

A. OVERVIEW OF THE PLEA BARGAINING SYSTEM

Although it is not possible in one chapter to capture all of the nuances of the debate, at least the surface of some of the principal issues can be scratched. This includes an overview of the system of plea bargaining, and some commentary from supporters and critics.

Prevalence (and Inevitability?) of Plea Bargaining

Almost all defendants charged with crime in the federal and state systems end up pleading guilty rather than going to trial. See O'Hear, Plea Bargaining and Procedural Justice, 42 Ga. L. Rev. 409 (2008) ("Plea bargaining now dominates the day-to-day operation of the American criminal justice system; about ninety-five percent of convictions are obtained by way of a guilty plea. Indeed, despite the strenuous objections of prominent academic commentators, plea bargaining seems to be growing only more entrenched over time."). Justice Kennedy made this point for the Court in Lafler v. Cooper, 566 U.S. 166 (2012): "criminal justice today is for the most part a system of pleas, not a system of trials." Plea bargaining rates in many jurisdictions remain remarkably consistent. For example, the United States Sentencing Commission reports that 94.6% of federal defendants pled guilty in 1999, and during the next decade the rate reached a high of 97.1 in 2002 and generally fell within the 94–97% range. From 2008 thru 2012, the cases disposed of by trial decreased each year to a low in 2012 of 3%. From 2012 thru 2016 the cases disposed of by trial declined each year to a low of 2.7% in 2016.

Plea bargaining is regulated only loosely by legal standards—it is essentially a marketplace for defendants and prosecutors, with sentencing parameters set by sentencing guidelines, statutory minimum sentences, and charging decisions, and governed by basic principles of contract. See Bibas, Regulating the Plea-Bargaining Market: From Caveat Emptor to Consumer Protection, 99 Cal. L.Rev. 1117 (2011) (noting that the Supreme Court has spent almost all its effort on regulating trials, while taking a laissez-faire attitude toward plea bargaining, resulting in "a free market that sometimes resemble[s] a Turkish bazaar.") Much of this Chapter considers whether this is any way to run a criminal justice system.

Professor Joseph Colquitt provides this overview of the plea bargaining process in Ad Hoc Plea Bargaining, 75 Tulane L.Rev. 695 (2001) (footnotes omitted):

> Plea bargaining typically is defined as an explicit or implicit exchange of concessions by the parties. Usually, the accused agrees to plead guilty and the government agrees to some form of reduction in charges or sentence. However, not all successful plea bargaining ends in a guilty plea. Some negotiations end in dismissal of the charges, perhaps after a deferral. Several types of negotiated settlements exist. First, the prosecution may agree to recommend to the court that one or more charges be dismissed in return for a plea of guilty by the defendant to another charge or other charges. The charges to which the defendant may agree to plead might include lesser offenses rather than the original charges. This approach is known as *charge bargaining*.

> Alternatively, the prosecution might agree simply to recommend a particular sentence in return for the plea. This approach frequently is called *sentence bargaining*. Sometimes the agreement includes both a reduction in the charge or a dismissal of other charges and a recommendation on the sentence. In all of these cases, in return for the prosecution's recommendation, the defendant waives the privilege

against self-incrimination and the right to a trial, including the attendant rights to confront accusers, to present witnesses on the question of guilt or innocence, and to testify in his or her own behalf.

* * *

[S]ome of plea bargaining's most resolute defenders believe that the court system needs plea bargaining in order to avoid a disastrous failure of the system as a result of the overwhelming number of cases that courts otherwise would have to try. * * * Moreover, bargaining reduces the time lag between the offense and the punishment, which potentially benefits not only the State, but also defendants, particularly those incarcerated. Reducing the time between crime and punishment also potentially enhances the deterrent effect of both conviction and punishment.

In addition to faster and more efficient case disposition, plea bargaining reduces costs, uncertainty, and risks. It allows courts and prosecutors to direct their resources more effectively, mitigates potentially severe punishment, provides flexibility, and, in the view of some, delivers justice. In sum, plea bargaining exists to a large extent because its supporters believe that the alternative, the criminal trial, is much more costly and time-consuming and no more likely to provide a just result.

Despite its widespread use and asserted benefits, the scheme is frequently criticized. * * * One of the principal arguments against plea bargaining is that those who plea bargain their cases are likely to be punished less severely than are those who insist on their constitutional right to trial. Some argue that the process abdicates control to the parties, relies too heavily on the prosecutor, or favors defense attorneys who carry favor with the prosecutor. Others fear that plea bargaining results in the conviction and punishment of innocent defendants at times. Some critics dislike the private, sometimes secret nature of the bargaining process or believe that the process causes the public to lose confidence in the criminal justice system.

* * *

In sum, many practitioners and scholars view plea bargaining as inevitable. Plea negotiation is simply too important and too ingrained in our criminal justice system to abandon it without identifying and providing a suitable replacement. That replacement has not been forthcoming, and it probably is the absence of a suitable replacement, rather than enthusiasm for plea bargaining, that supports its retention.

* * *

From time to time, the United States Department of Justice has also attempted to regulate or limit plea bargaining, but with very little success. For example, in September, 2003, Attorney General Ashcroft issued a memorandum to federal prosecutors instructing them not to charge defendants with an eye toward plea bargaining. With few exceptions, prosecutors were instructed to pursue the toughest sentences possible under the Federal Sentencing Guidelines. The memo stated that prosecutors "must charge and pursue the most serious, readily provable offenses that are supported by the facts." The purpose of the policy was to assure consistency in charging decisions across the country. The exceptions to the "highest charge" policy were limited to: 1) cases in which problems with witnesses lead to a "post-indictment reassessment"; 2) cases in which the defendant decides to provide "substantial assistance" in prosecution of other criminals; and 3) "other exceptional circumstances" where a single case might place an extraordinary burden on a local U.S. attorney's office or reduce "the total number of cases disposed of by the office."

Professor George Fisher, in an op-ed piece in the New York Times, argued that Attorney General Ashcroft's new policy was doomed to fail. Fisher, A Practice as Old as Justice Itself, N.Y. Times, Sept. 28, 2003, at WK 11. He contended that plea bargaining reaches just results and that any attempt to regulate the practice simply drives it "underground". He elaborated as follows:

> * * * [P]lea bargaining will survive Mr. Ashcroft. Most prosecutors like plea bargaining; a sound bargain means an easy victory and more time to prosecute the next serious case.

* * *

Today the entire criminal justice system depends for its survival on plea bargaining. Last year 95 percent of criminal cases adjudicated in federal courts ended with pleas of guilty or no contest. To try even one-quarter of all cases would mean five times as many trials, with a comparable increase in public expense. One wonders if Mr. Ashcroft wishes to preside over such an expansion.

It's hardly likely. His new policy claiming to clamp down on plea bargaining leaves lots of bargaining room [given the built-in exceptions.] * * *

And even if Mr. Ashcroft actually tries to limit plea bargaining, many judges will conspire with prosecutors to evade the rules. Judges know that the hundreds of new appointees needed to preside over an avalanche of new trials won't take the bench for years, if ever. * * * Defense lawyers will also help elude the policy. Private counsel often demand full payment up front and enjoy a rich payday when a case ends in an effortless plea bargain. Public defenders have limited resources and know they cannot try all or most cases.

Cooperating Witnesses

As will be seen in this Chapter, a major reason that plea bargaining is here to stay is that prosecutors find it necessary to enter into cooperation agreements with criminals in order to get the testimony necessary to convict *other* criminals. Without plea bargaining—specifically the "carrots" of reduced charges and a further reduction in sentence for "substantial cooperation"—there would be little reason for criminal associates to "flip" and become a prosecution witness. Without turncoat witnesses, many prosecutions of major criminals would become virtually impossible.

Sentencing Differential Between Guilty Plea and Trial

It has been alleged that judges induce guilty pleas by imposing more severe sentences when a defendant chooses a trial rather than pleading guilty. Some studies suggest that differential sentencing exists at both the misdemeanor and felony levels.

There is disagreement as to the propriety of differential sentencing. Proponents believe leniency is proper for those who accept responsibility for their conduct by pleading guilty and contribute to the efficient and economical administration of the law. They assert that those submitting themselves to prompt correctional measures should be granted sentence concessions, and that differential sentences for those demanding trial is not undue punishment unless it is excessive. Those opposed believe that guilty pleas have no direct relevance to the appropriate disposition of an offender and that the constitutional right to trial should not be the cause of enhanced punishment.

Pleas by Innocent Defendants

Ronald F. Wright, in Trial Distortion and the End of Innocence in Federal Criminal Justice, 154 U. Pa. L. Rev 79 (2005), analyzes the relationship between acquittals and guilty plea rates in federal criminal cases, and concludes that defendants who might have been acquitted at trial may nonetheless plead guilty because of a combination of stiff sentences imposed upon defendants who choose trial and the substantial discounts offered to defendants where the government's case is weak.

Supreme Court Support for Plea Bargaining:
Brady v. United States

The leading case in the Supreme Court on plea bargaining is Brady v. United States, 397 U.S. 742 (1970). In *Brady,* the Court rejected the defendant's argument that a guilty plea is invalid "whenever motivated by the defendant's desire to accept the certainty or probability of a lesser penalty rather than face a wider range of possibilities extending from acquittal to conviction and a higher penalty authorized by law for the crime charged." The Court provided support for the system of plea bargaining as one based on "mutuality of advantage" and elaborated as follows:

> The issue we deal with is inherent in the criminal law and its administration because guilty pleas are not constitutionally forbidden, because the criminal law characteristically extends to judge or jury a range of choice in setting the sentence in individual cases, and because both the State and the defendant often find it advantageous to preclude the possibility of the maximum penalty authorized by law. For a defendant who sees slight possibility of acquittal, the advantages of pleading guilty and limiting the probable penalty are obvious—his exposure is reduced, the correctional processes can begin immediately, and the practical burdens of a trial are eliminated. For the State there are also advantages—the more promptly imposed punishment after an admission of guilt may more effectively attain the objectives of punishment; and with the avoidance of trial, scarce judicial and prosecutorial resources are conserved for those cases in which there is a substantial issue of the defendant's guilt or in which there is substantial doubt that the State can sustain its burden of proof.

B. ARGUMENTS IN FAVOR OF PLEA BARGAINING

Judge Easterbrook, in Plea Bargaining as Compromise, 101 Yale L.J. 1969 (1992), sets forth the following defense of plea bargaining, even though he recognizes that the system of plea bargaining is not as efficient as it might be:

> On the economic side, plea bargains do not represent Pareto improvements. Instead of engaging in trades that make at least one person better off and no one worse off, the parties dicker about how much worse off one side will be. In markets persons can borrow to take advantage of good deals or withdraw from the market, wait for a better offer, and lend their assets for a price in the interim. By contrast, both sides to a plea bargain operate under strict budget constraints, and they cannot bide their time. They bargain as bilateral monopolists (defendants can't shop in competitive markets for prosecutors) in the shadow of legal rules that work suspiciously like price controls. Judges, who do not join the bargaining, set the prices, increasingly by

reference to a table of punishments that looks like something the Office of Price Administration would have promulgated. Plea bargaining is to the sentencing guidelines as black markets are to price controls.

Black markets are better than no markets. Plea bargains are preferable to mandatory litigation—not because the analogy to contract is overpowering, but because compromise is better than conflict. Settlements of civil cases make both sides better off; settlements of criminal cases do so too. Defendants have many procedural and substantive rights. By pleading guilty, they sell these rights to the prosecutor, receiving concessions they esteem more highly than the rights surrendered. Rights that may be sold are more valuable than rights that must be consumed, just as money (which may be used to buy housing, clothing, or food) is more valuable to a poor person than an opportunity to live in public housing.

Defendants can use or exchange their rights, whichever makes them better off. So plea bargaining helps defendants. Forcing them to use their rights at trial means compelling them to take the risk of conviction or acquittal; risk-averse persons prefer a certain but small punishment to a chancy but large one. Defendants also get the process over sooner, and solvent ones save the expense of trial. Compromise also benefits prosecutors and society at large. In purchasing procedural entitlements with lower sentences, prosecutors buy that most valuable commodity, Time. With time they can prosecute more criminals. * * * The ratio of prosecutions (and convictions) to crimes would be extremely low if compromises were forbidden. Sentences could not be raised high enough to maintain deterrence, especially not when both economics and principles of desert call for proportionality between crime and punishment.

* * *

Plea bargains are compromises. Autonomy and efficiency support them. "Imperfections" in bargaining reflect the imperfections of an anticipated trial. To improve plea bargaining, improve the process for deciding cases on the merits. When we deem that process adequate, there will be no reason to prevent the person most affected by the criminal process from improving his situation through compromise.

C. CRITIQUE OF PLEA BARGAINING

Professor Schulhofer, in Plea Bargaining as Disaster, 101 Yale L.J. 1979 (1992), argues that plea bargaining should be abolished because, among other things, it gives an innocent defendant a choice of pleading guilty and avoiding a trial—a choice that Professor Schulhofer argues should not be permitted:

* * * [T]he innocent defendant, facing a small possibility of conviction on a serious charge, [often] considers it in his interest to accept conviction and a small penalty. The defendant's choice to plead guilty can be rational from his private perspective, but it imposes costs on society by undermining public confidence that criminal convictions reflect guilt beyond a reasonable doubt. An "efficient" system of voluntary contracting for pleas would convict large numbers of defendants who had a high probability of acquittal at trial; indeed, to the extent that innocent defendants are likely to be more risk averse than guilty ones, the former are likely to be overrepresented in the pool of "acquittable" defendants who are attracted by prosecutorial offers to plead guilty. To deal seriously with these problems we must consider complete abolition of plea bargaining. * * * The social interest in not punishing defendants who are factually innocent justifies a bar on compromise, low-sentence settlements, even if individual defendants would prefer to have that option.

Professor Schulhofer also argues that a system of plea bargaining imposes significant disadvantages on indigent defendants, because appointed counsel are underpaid, thus giving them an incentive to plead a case at the first opportunity, whether the plea agreement is fair or not. Abolishing plea bargaining would mean that an appointed attorney's performance would be more closely monitored:

The single most serious agency problem on the defense side is that the attorney incurs a severe financial penalty if the case goes to trial. That prospect can powerfully skew his appraisal of the value of a prosecutor's plea offer and the advice he provides to his client. A prohibition on bargaining protects defendants who would accept a plea offer that was not in their interest, even if the attorney, once forced to trial, would give the same indifferent assistance that he would provide in plea negotiations.

* * *

The shift from plea bargaining to trial renders the attorney's performance highly visible to peers in the courtroom. This shift also enlarges both the attorney's formal legal obligations of effective assistance and the practical likelihood that they will be taken seriously. The institutional environment of the trial process thus limits the consequences of the agency problem in ways that are precluded when disposition occurs in a low-visibility plea. The visibility of trial also tends to generate pressure to alleviate the worst inadequacies of indigent defense funding. Indigents are far more likely to receive conscientious representation when cases are tried in open court than when the attorneys are permitted to settle on the basis of an uninformed guess about the likelihood of conviction.

Professor Schulhofer argues that one alternative for the current system of plea bargaining is a structured system in which defendants receive some automatic, non-negotiable concessions for pleading guilty.

> By abolishing bargaining but not abolishing concessions, a jurisdiction could retain control over its guilty plea rate and preserve its existing low level of resources committed to trials. * * * In such a system, the proportion of defendants pleading guilty would be similar to the present number, but the composition of the guilty plea pool presumably would change. Those who elect trial in the present system do not necessarily have the greatest chance of acquittal because such defendants are also the ones most likely to win the best sentence concessions in negotiation. Rather, those who now go to trial tend to be those who are least risk averse, a group that may include disproportionate numbers of those who are actually guilty. In contrast, in a system of nonnegotiable sentence concessions, defendants who elect trial are most likely to be those with the greatest likelihood of acquittal, a group that should include disproportionate numbers of the innocent. The normative premise of this approach is that the trial process, however infrequently used, should be reserved for cases where guilt is most in doubt.

As another alternative, Professor Schulhofer simply proposes that plea bargaining be abolished. He argues that a system without plea bargaining would provide greater protection for innocent defendants:

> Because processing each case would be more costly, and because innocents would be more difficult to convict, the prosecutor's incentives (both personal and public) to screen carefully at the charging stage would be enhanced. The total number of defendants charged might decrease if prosecutorial resources were held constant. But even if the number charged did not decline, the proportion of innocents in the pool of defendants would tend to decrease. * * * Because abolition would make it harder to convict the innocent, it would benefit defendants convicted in the plea bargaining process who would not be convicted, and perhaps would not even be charged, in a no-concessions world.

American jurisdictions that have attempted to ban or limit plea bargaining have found that it is difficult to do. This is not surprising. Prosecutors have limited resources and incentives to preserve them for cases that must be tried. See Langbein, Torture and Plea Bargaining, 46 Univ. Chi. L.Rev. 3 (1978) (arguing that the prosecutor has an incentive to coerce a guilty plea in order to avoid the panoply of rights that await the accused at a trial). Defendants have rights, as Judge Easterbrook explained, that they might find more valuable if waived than if exercised. Under-compensated defense counsel have incentives to encourage their clients to plead guilty. An over-burdened judiciary hardly yearns for more trials. So it appears that none of the participants in the criminal justice system are necessarily better off in a system that does not permit negotiations and plea bargains.

D. THE LINE BETWEEN REWARDING A GUILTY PLEA AND PUNISHING THE DECISION TO GO TO TRIAL

The trial judge in United States v. Medina-Cervantes, 690 F.2d 715 (9th Cir.1982), indicated concern that the defendant, convicted of entering the United States illegally and of reentering the United States after having been deported, was "thumbing his nose at our judicial system" by insisting on a trial and the exercise of the full panoply of trial rights. He imposed a fine that was intended to reimburse the government for the costs of the trial. The court of appeals stated that it did not doubt the good faith of the trial judge, but remanded for resentencing, observing that "[i]t is well settled that an accused may not be subjected to more severe punishment simply because he exercised his right to stand trial." It directed the trial judge to state the reasons for the sentence imposed upon remand.

Had the trial judge said nothing, and simply imposed a higher sentence after conviction within a permissible range, the court of appeals surely would have sustained the sentence. Once higher sentences are imposed, repeat players in the system know how it operates and will of course take into account a de facto higher sentence for going to trial. Do you think that a system that "encourages" pleas is likely to penalize those who insist on going to trial? Could a judge identify a lack of remorse as a basis for increasing the penalty? Should the judge do so? See Scott v. United States, 419 F.2d 264 (D.C.Cir.1969) (while a defendant may receive a longer sentence after going to trial, no part of that sentence can be attributable to punishing the defendant for having gone to trial).

Acceptance of Responsibility

These questions are not of merely theoretical interest. The United States Sentencing Guidelines [discussed in Chapter 11], which sentencing judges use as guidance, provide for a reduced sentence for defendants who accept responsibility for their criminal conduct. Section 3E1.1. Acceptance of responsibility does not require a guilty plea, but the Sentencing Commission envisioned, and the courts have held, that a defendant who goes to trial rarely will be able to qualify for the reduction.

Would the Guidelines be unconstitutional if they *conditioned* a reduction for acceptance of responsibility on a plea of guilty? See, e.g., United States v. White, 869 F.2d 822 (5th Cir.1989) (Section 3E1.1 does not impinge on defendant's Sixth Amendment right to trial: "It is not unconstitutional for the Government to bargain for a guilty plea in exchange for a reduced sentence. The fact that a more lenient sentence is imposed on a contrite defendant does not establish a corollary that those who elect to stand trial are penalized."). On questions of acceptance of responsibility and the effect on plea bargaining, see O'Hear, Remorse, Cooperation, and "Acceptance of Responsibility": The Structure, Implementation, and Reform of Section 3E1.1 of the Federal Sentencing Guidelines, 91 Nw.U.L.Rev. 1507 (1997).

E. GUILTY PLEAS, CHARGING DECISIONS, AND MANDATORY MINIMUM SENTENCES

There can be circumstances in which the pressure on a federal defendant to plead can be tremendous even without regard to the sentence reduction for acceptance of responsibility. This pressure results from two factors: (1) the existence of mandatory minimum sentencing statutes; and (2) the possibility of a reduction in sentence below a mandatory minimum for substantial assistance to the prosecution in the investigation and prosecution of other defendants.

Congress has enacted substantial mandatory minimum sentences for a number of crimes, particularly those involving drugs and firearms. The presence of a mandatory minimum penalty can produce great pressure on a defendant to plead guilty in order to escape the minimum. If a prosecutor is willing to charge under a non-mandatory or reduced-mandatory statute, the defendant may leap at a plea offer, particularly if the mandatory penalty that is avoided by the plea is five or 10 years or more. See DeBenedectis, Mandatory Minimum Sentences Hit, A.B.A.J. Dec. 1991, p. 36 (noting that "mandatory minimums give federal prosecutors wide discretion over sentencing through the crimes they charge and bargains they accept").

Should mandatory minimum penalties be permitted to go hand in hand with plea bargaining? If not, which should be abolished? For a discussion of the impact of mandatory minimum sentences on the decision to cooperate, see Richman, Cooperating Clients, 56 Ohio State L.J. 69 (1995). Professor Richman points out that clients are often caught between the pressures of severe sentencing under federal law on the one hand, and defense counsel's financial, institutional, and emotional interest in preventing the client from cooperating with the government on the other.

As discussed in Chapter 11, infra, at various times inroads are made at the federal level to reduce the use of mandatory minimums. See U.S. Orders More Steps to Curb Stiff Drug Sentences, N.Y. Times 8/20/2013, A18 ("The Obama Administration * * * expanded its effort to curtail severe penalties for low-level federal drug offenses, ordering prosecutors to refile charges against defendants in pending cases and strip out any references to specific quantities of illicit substances that would trigger mandatory minimum sentencing laws."). Such inroads should make the plea bargaining system less coercive for some defendants. But they are not guaranteed to last—as illustrated by Attorney General Jeff Sessions' May 20, 2017 Memorandum for All Prosecutors ("it is a core principle that prosecutors should charge and pursue the most serious, readily provable offense,"; "[b]y definition, the most serious offenses are those that carry the most substantial guidelines sentence, including mandatory minimum sentences").

F. EFFICIENCY AT WHAT PRICE?

Plea bargaining is almost certain to produce disturbing results in some cases. Consider, for example, the following problem:

PROBLEM

A defendant is charged with first degree murder, and he pleads self-defense. The two witnesses for the state are the daughter and wife of the deceased. Both claim that the defendant fired a gun without provocation. At a preliminary hearing the magistrate judge believes that the question of sufficiency of the evidence to hold the defendant is a close one because the eyewitnesses are less believable than the defendant, but ultimately binds the defendant over because a jury could believe the wife and daughter and return a guilty verdict. The grand jury charges first degree murder.

Assume that the prosecutor says to the defense lawyer in the course of plea bargaining, "I agree with the magistrate. The greater probability is self-defense here, but I figure that there is about a 40% chance that the defendant will be convicted of first degree murder. This surely is a case of premeditated murder or self-defense. It was one or the other, pure and simple." The prosecutor goes on to say: "If I am right, the expected minimum penalty from your client's perspective is 40% multiplied by the minimum sentence he can receive which is twenty years, or 8 years as the bottom line. In other words, your client will be found innocent and serve no time in 6 out of 10 cases, and in 4 out of 10 cases your client will serve a minimum of twenty years. The way I see it the jury either believes my witnesses or yours and that kind of case is always unpredictable. Like the magistrate judge implied, reasonable juries have leeway in determining whom to believe. Since your client has a 40% chance of serving a minimum of 20 years, a conservative, but impartial, observer would say that your client should be looking to reduce his exposure to jail. Here is what I am prepared to do: I will let your client plead to negligent homicide and recommend a two year sentence. Because your client has no prior record, the court will probably accept that recommendation, though I cannot guarantee that." The defense lawyer takes this offer back to the client, who is afraid of the possibility of a minimum twenty year sentence.

If the defense lawyer agrees on the odds and so informs the defendant, should the defendant be permitted to plead to the negligent homicide charge? Does it matter that the defendant *could not possibly have committed negligent homicide* under either side's version of the facts? If a factual basis requirement is in effect, must there be a factual basis for negligent homicide, or is it sufficient that there is a basis for the greater offense? If a basis for the lesser offense must be shown, can the prosecutor ethically permit the defendant to state to the court a distorted version of the facts? Could the prosecutor put on only part of the state's evidence in an effort to create for the court an appearance of negligent homicide? If the answer to either or both of the last two questions is "no," what incentive does the system provide for anyone to challenge an improper plea?

If the illustration uses numbers that you believe are unrealistic, change them so that there is a 60% chance of conviction. Should the defendant accept an offer to plead to second degree murder with an 8-year sentence recommendation? Could a rational lawyer advise against such a plea? If you like plea bargaining, consider whether there is any prosecutorial offer that would be so coercive as to be unreasonable.

If you don't like plea bargaining, consider whether there is any offer that you would deem proper. Do you really want to force the defendant to go to trial in the examples offered here?

Inverted Sentencing

Another disturbing phenomenon of plea bargaining is that in multi-defendant cases, those more culpable might have a chance at receiving a lighter sentence than those less culpable. That is because prosecutors often need cooperation from some criminals in order to convict others, and plea bargaining is about the only tool that the prosecutor can legitimately employ to encourage cooperation. The incentives result in what Professor Richman terms "inverted sentencing": "The more serious the defendant's crimes, the lower the sentence—because the greater his wrongs, the more information and assistance he has to offer a prosecutor." Richman, Cooperating Clients, 56 Ohio St.L.J. 69 (1995). Judge Bright, dissenting in United States v. Griffin, 17 F.3d 269 (8th Cir.1994), had this to say about the phenomenon of inverted sentencing:

> What kind of a criminal justice system rewards the drug kingpin or near-kingpin who informs on all the criminal colleagues he or she has recruited, but sends to prison for years and years the least knowledgeable or culpable conspirator, one who knows very little about the conspiracy and is without information for the prosecution?

Is inverted sentencing an indictment of the plea bargaining system? Or is it an inevitable consequence of the prosecutor's need for cooperation from criminals? If plea bargaining were abolished, what incentive would a criminal have to cooperate with the government by giving away information about his confederates?

Three Strikes

In some jurisdictions a mandatory life sentence is imposed on a conviction for a specified felony if the defendant has been twice previously convicted of certain specified felonies. How do these "three strikes and you're out" provisions affect plea bargaining for the first, second, and third offenses? Is the bargaining dynamic different at each offense? Some states structure their three strikes laws so that the prosecution must charge a "strike" felony if the facts support it. In these states, will more defendants refuse to plead guilty and go to trial on the assumption that they have nothing to lose? Or can the parties work "underground" by fudging the facts and agreeing to a charge that does not qualify as a strike?

G. PROBLEMS OF OVERCHARGING

Timing Questions: Bordenkircher v. Hayes

Not all plea bargaining involves settlements that look like a wonderful deal for the defendant. Consider, for example, Bordenkircher v. Hayes, 434 U.S. 357 (1978). Hayes was indicted by a Kentucky grand jury on a charge of uttering a forged instrument in the amount of $88.30, an offense punishable by 2–10 years imprisonment. During pretrial negotiations, the prosecutor told Hayes that if he did not plead guilty and "save the court the inconvenience and necessity of a trial," the prosecutor would seek a new indictment under the then-existing Kentucky Habitual Criminal Act, which carried a mandatory life sentence. Hayes chose not to plead guilty, was indicted under the Act and received a life sentence. The Supreme Court affirmed, holding that the decision whether to charge an offense rests with prosecutors and grand juries, and it made no difference that the indictment on a more serious crime came after the defendant refused to bargain. The Court declared that "a rigid constitutional rule that would prohibit a prosecutor from acting forthrightly in his dealings with the defense could only invite unhealthy subterfuge that would drive the practice of plea bargaining back into the shadows from which it has so recently emerged." In sum, the Court concluded that "this case would be no different if the grand jury had indicted Hayes as a recidivist from the outset, and the prosecutor had offered to drop that charge as part of the plea bargain."

Justice Blackmun, joined by Justices Brennan and Marshall, dissented. He disagreed with the Court's analysis that the timing of the indictment made no difference and suggested that prior to *Hayes* the Court "ha[d] never openly sanctioned such deliberate overcharging or taken such a cynical view of the bargaining process." He added that "[e]ven if overcharging is to be sanctioned, there are strong reasons of fairness why the charge should be presented at the beginning of the bargaining process, rather than as a filliped thread at the end." Justice Powell also dissented on the ground that the prosecutor effectively conceded that his strategy did not reflect the public interest in an appropriate sentence, but simply a desire to avoid trial even if the means of doing so was the imposition of an unreasonable sentence.[1]

II. THE REQUIREMENTS FOR A VALID GUILTY PLEA

A. DISTINGUISHING BARGAINING FROM THE PLEA PROCEDURE

Courts tend to distinguish the bargaining that takes place, which is largely unregulated as Bordenkircher v. Hayes illustrates, from the procedures surrounding the judicial acceptance of a guilty plea. These procedures have grown more formal over time. See, e.g., United States v. Livorsi, 180 F.3d 76 (2d Cir.1999) ("we examine critically even slight procedural deficiencies to ensure that the defendant's guilty plea was a voluntary and intelligent choice, and that none of the defendant's substantial rights have been compromised"). The unanswered question is whether the formality provides realistic protection for defendants or only trappings to persuade the public that justice is being done.

B. THE REQUIREMENT OF SOME KIND OF A RECORD

The Boykin Requirements

In two cases decided in 1969, McCarthy v. United States, 394 U.S. 459, and Boykin v. Alabama, 395 U.S. 238, the Supreme Court made it clear that a valid guilty plea requires "an intentional relinquishment or abandonment of a known right or privilege." This is because a defendant who pleads guilty is giving up the constitutional right to a fair trial before a jury, the right to be proven guilty of all elements of the crime beyond a reasonable doubt, the right to silence, and the right to confront adverse witnesses. The Court said that "[c]onsequently, if a defendant's guilty plea is not equally voluntary and knowing, it has been obtained in violation of due process and is therefore void."

In *McCarthy,* the Court set aside the guilty plea of a defendant who had pleaded to one count of a three count indictment charging wilful and knowing attempts to evade federal income tax payments. After discussing in dictum the constitutional requirements for a valid plea, the Court based its decision on Fed.R.Crim.P. 11, which sets forth procedural requirements for obtaining a valid guilty plea. The trial judge did not comply with the

---

[1]   In Corbitt v. New Jersey, 439 U.S. 212 (1978), the Court upheld a New Jersey statute that mandated life sentences for defendants convicted by a jury, but permitted lesser terms for those who pleaded guilty. The Court relied on Bordenkircher v. Hayes.

rule, because he failed both to ask the defendant whether he understood the nature of the charges against him and to inquire adequately into the voluntariness of the plea. The Court concluded that the defendant had to be afforded the opportunity to plead anew. Rule 11 was viewed as an attempt to avoid post-plea hearings on waiver, and the Court refused to remand the case for such a hearing into the knowing and voluntary nature of McCarthy's plea.

Boykin v. Alabama overturned death sentences imposed on a 27 year old black man who pleaded guilty to five indictments charging common-law robbery. The Supreme Court said that "[i]t was error, plain on the face of the record, for the trial judge to accept petitioner's guilty plea without an affirmative showing that it was intelligent and voluntary." The Court held that it was impermissible to presume, on the basis of a silent record, a waiver of constitutional rights as important as the privilege against self-incrimination, trial by jury, and confrontation. Thus, there must be an affirmative indication on the record that the defendant made a knowing and voluntary waiver.

Application of Boykin

Boykin's requirement of an explicit record has also been applied with some flexibility. Absence of an explicit record creates a *presumption* that the plea is invalid; but that presumption can be overcome by the government. See, e.g., United States v. Ferguson, 935 F.2d 862 (7th Cir.1991) (absence of transcript of guilty plea hearing is not fatal; the court relies on the custom, practice, and law applicable to guilty pleas in Illinois state courts, warranting a presumption that the defendant was informed of the necessary rights under *Boykin*).

Guilty Pleas Used for Enhancement of Sentence: Parke v. Raley

In Parke v. Raley, 506 U.S. 20 (1992), the Court considered the applicability of *Boykin* standards where guilty plea convictions are used to enhance punishment in subsequent cases. Raley was charged in 1986 with robbery and with being a repeat offender because he had pleaded guilty in 1979 and 1981 to two burglaries. Under Kentucky law, a presumption of regularity attaches to prior convictions resulting from guilty pleas, and an accused recidivist must produce evidence that his rights were infringed or that some other procedural irregularity occurred to render the conviction invalid. If the defendant produces such evidence, the burden shifts to the state to prove the actual validity of the prior conviction by a preponderance of the evidence. Raley argued that this procedure violated *Boykin* because it resulted in a presumption of a valid guilty plea from a silent record.

Justice O'Connor's opinion for the Court concluded that there was no tension between the Kentucky procedure and *Boykin*. She explained as follows:

> *Boykin* involved direct review of a conviction allegedly based upon an uninformed guilty plea. Respondent, however, never appealed his earlier convictions. They became final years ago, and he now seeks to revisit the question of their validity in a separate recidivism proceeding. To import *Boykin's* presumption of invalidity into this very different context would, in our view, improperly ignore another presumption deeply rooted in our jurisprudence: the "presumption of regularity" that attaches to final judgments, even when the question is waiver of constitutional rights.

Justice O'Connor also rejected Raley's policy argument that it was unfair to place on the defendant the burden of producing evidence that prior guilty pleas are invalid. Raley contended that a defendant would find it inordinately difficult to obtain information concerning a dated guilty plea hearing. Justice O'Connor responded that a rule placing the entire burden on the state to prove the validity of a conviction would force the state "to expend considerable effort and expense attempting to reconstruct records from far-flung states where procedures are unfamiliar and memories are unreliable."

C. VOLUNTARY AND KNOWING PLEAS AND THE ADVANTAGES OF A COMPLETE RECORD

1. A Voluntary Plea

To be valid, a guilty plea must be voluntary; that is, it must not be the product of improper coercion by government officials. The standard of voluntariness is similar to that employed in connection with confessions, a standard that was examined in Chapter 3, supra. As the Supreme Court said in Brady v. United States, discussed supra, "the agents of the State may not produce a plea by actual or threatened physical harm or by mental coercion overbearing the will of the defendant." Thus, it is clear that if a defendant were threatened with physical torture or actually harmed as part of an effort to get him to plead guilty, any resulting plea would be involuntary. Of course most challenges to guilty pleas do not raise those kinds of claims. Unlike the interrogation process, the procedure for accepting pleas affords opportunities for trial judges to see whether a defendant is apparently exercising free will in choosing to plead. Still, some sophisticated questions of validity of guilty pleas have arisen under the rubric of voluntariness.

Package Deals

Suppose a prosecutor in a multi-defendant case proposes a global settlement: all the defendants can plead to specified crimes, but they must plead guilty as a group; if all the defendants do not agree, the deal is off.[2] Does a "wired" plea or "package deal" present a greater risk of coercion than an individual plea? In United States v. Pollard, 959 F.2d 1011 (D.C.Cir.1992), the defendant pleaded guilty to one count of conspiracy to deliver national defense information to the Government of Israel. He later claimed that the government coerced his guilty plea by linking his wife's plea to his own, especially as his wife was seriously ill at the time. But the court rejected his argument:

> To say that a practice is "coercive" or renders a plea "involuntary" means only that it creates improper pressure that would be likely to overbear the will of some innocent persons and cause them to plead guilty. Only physical harm, threats of harassment, misrepresentation, or promises that are by their nature improper as having no proper relationship to the prosecutor's business (e.g., bribes) render a guilty plea legally involuntary. * * *

> * * * We must be mindful * * * that if the judiciary were to declare wired pleas unconstitutional, the consequences would not be altogether foreseeable and perhaps would not be beneficial to defendants. Would Pollard, for instance, have been better off had he not been able to bargain to aid his wife? Would his wife have been better off? Would the bargaining take place in any event, but with winks and nods rather than in writing?

> Nor do we believe that Mrs. Pollard's medical condition makes an otherwise acceptable linkage of their pleas unconstitutional. The appropriate dividing line between acceptable and unconstitutional plea wiring does not depend upon the physical condition or personal circumstances of the defendant; rather, it depends upon the conduct of the government. Where, as here, the government had probable cause to arrest and prosecute both defendants in a related crime, and there is no suggestion that the government conducted itself in bad faith in an effort to generate additional leverage over the defendant, we think a wired plea is constitutional.

See also United States v. Mescual-Cruz, 387 F.3d 1 (1st Cir. 2004) (package plea not involuntary simply because a defendant is taking a higher sentence to get a lower sentence for a loved one: "If a defendant elects to

---

[2] See Liebman and Snyder, Joint Guilty Pleas: "Group Justice" In Federal Plea Bargaining, N.Y.L.J., Sept.8, 1994, p.1, col.1 (noting that for the government, "group pleas dispose of cases in one fell swoop and thereby conserve scarce prosecutorial resources and, in some cases, avoid lengthy, costly or potentially embarrassing trials").

sacrifice himself, that is his choice, and he cannot reverse it after he is dissatisfied with his sentence, or with other subsequent developments.").

Pollard considered the problem of a defendant "pressured" because of feelings toward the person to whom his plea is linked. The court in United States v. Caro, 997 F.2d 657 (9th Cir.1993), considered a different problem that might be created by wired pleas—the possibility of coercion by other defendants. Caro moved to set aside his guilty plea on the ground that he was pressured by his codefendants into going along with the package deal. At the hearing in which his plea was entered, the judge was never informed that Caro's plea was part of a group settlement. Judge Kozinski analyzed the problem as follows:

> Though package deal plea agreements are not per se impermissible, they pose an additional risk of coercion not present when the defendant is dealing with the government alone. Quite possibly, one defendant will be happier with the package deal than his codefendants; looking out for his own interests, the lucky one may try to force his codefendants into going along with the deal. * * * We * * * have recognized that the trial court should make a more careful examination of the voluntariness of a plea when it might have been induced by threats or promises from a third party. We make it clear today that, in describing a plea agreement * * * the prosecutor must alert the district court to the fact that codefendants are entering into a package deal.[3]

The court held that the trial court's error—really the prosecutor's error in failing to tell the judge that the pleas were "wired"—was not harmless. It vacated Caro's guilty plea and remanded. Compare United States v. Carr, 80 F.3d 413 (10th Cir.1996) (pressures of cohorts to accept a package deal "might have been palpable" to the defendant, but they did not vitiate the voluntariness of his plea because "it was still his choice to make").

Can the Defendant Voluntarily Waive the Right to Disclosure of Information That Could Be Used to Impeach Government Witnesses or for Affirmative Defenses? United States v. Ruiz

In the following case, the Court adhered to its position that the free market principles behind plea bargaining generally permit criminal defendants to voluntarily waive rights that could be invoked at trial. We examined this case briefly in Chapter 6, but its discussion of plea bargaining warrants additional attention here.

---

[3]   Professor Green, in "Package" Plea Bargaining and the Prosecutor's Duty of Good Faith, 25 Crim.L.Bull. 507 (1989), argues that prosecutors who offer multi-defendant deals have an ethical responsibility to avoid overreaching.

UNITED STATES V. RUIZ

Supreme Court of the United States, 2002.
536 U.S. 622.

JUSTICE BREYER delivered the opinion of the Court.

In this case we primarily consider whether the Fifth and Sixth Amendments require federal prosecutors, before entering into a binding plea agreement with a criminal defendant, to disclose "impeachment information relating to any informants or other witnesses." We hold that the Constitution does not require that disclosure.

* * *

After immigration agents found 30 kilograms of marijuana in Angela Ruiz's luggage, federal prosecutors offered her what is known in the Southern District of California as a "fast track" plea bargain. That bargain—standard in that district—asks a defendant to waive indictment, trial, and an appeal. In return, the Government agrees to recommend to the sentencing judge a two-level departure downward from the otherwise applicable United States Sentencing Guidelines sentence. In Ruiz's case, a two-level departure downward would have shortened the ordinary Guidelines-specified 18-to-24-month sentencing range by 6 months, to 12-to-18 months.

The prosecutors' proposed plea agreement contains a set of detailed terms. Among other things, it specifies that "any [known] information establishing the factual innocence of the defendant" "has been turned over to the defendant," and it acknowledges the Government's "continuing duty to provide such information." At the same time it requires that the defendant "waiv[e] the right" to receive "impeachment information relating to any informants or other witnesses" as well as the right to receive information supporting any affirmative defense the defendant raises if the case goes to trial. Because Ruiz would not agree to this last-mentioned waiver, the prosecutors withdrew their bargaining offer. The Government then indicted Ruiz for unlawful drug possession. And despite the absence of any agreement, Ruiz ultimately pleaded guilty.

At sentencing, Ruiz asked the judge to grant her the same two-level downward departure that the Government would have recommended had she accepted the "fast track" agreement. The Government opposed her request, and the District Court denied it, imposing a standard Guideline sentence instead. [The Ninth Circuit vacated the sentencing decision, holding that Ruiz was entitled to disclosure of impeachment information at the guilty plea phase, and that the right could not be waived.]

* * *

In this case, the Ninth Circuit in effect held that a guilty plea is not "voluntary" (and that the defendant could not, by pleading guilty, waive his right to a fair trial) unless the prosecutors first made the same disclosure of material impeachment information that the prosecutors would have had to make had the defendant insisted upon a trial. We must decide whether the Constitution requires that preguilty plea disclosure of impeachment information. We conclude that it does not.

First, impeachment information is special in relation to the *fairness of a trial,* not in respect to whether a plea is *voluntary* ("knowing," "intelligent," and "sufficiently aware"). Of course, the more information the defendant has, the more aware he is of the likely consequences of a plea, waiver, or decision, and the wiser that decision will likely be. But the Constitution does not require the prosecutor to share all useful information with the defendant. And the law ordinarily considers a waiver knowing, intelligent, and sufficiently aware if the defendant fully understands the nature of the right and how it would likely apply *in general* in the circumstances—even though the defendant may not know the *specific detailed* consequences of invoking it. A defendant, for example, may waive his right to remain silent, his right to a jury trial, or his right to counsel even if the defendant does not know the specific questions the authorities intend to ask, who will likely serve on the jury, or the particular lawyer the State might otherwise provide.

* * *

Second, we have * * * found that the Constitution, in respect to a defendant's awareness of relevant circumstances, does not require complete knowledge of the relevant circumstances, but permits a court to accept a guilty plea, with its accompanying waiver of various constitutional rights, despite various forms of misapprehension under which a defendant might labor. See Brady v. United States (defendant "misapprehended the quality of the State's case", misapprehended "the likely penalties" and failed to "anticipate a change in the law regarding" relevant "punishments"); McMann v. Richardson, 397 U.S. 759, 770 (1970) (counsel "misjudged the admissibility" of a "confession"); United States v. Broce, 488 U.S. 563, 573 (1989) (counsel failed to point out a potential defense); Tollett v. Henderson, 411 U.S. 258, 267 (1973) (counsel failed to find a potential constitutional infirmity in grand jury proceedings). It is difficult to distinguish, in terms of importance, (1) a defendant's ignorance of grounds for impeachment of potential witnesses at a possible future trial from (2) the varying forms of ignorance at issue in these cases.

Third, due process considerations, the very considerations that led this Court to find trial-related rights to exculpatory and impeachment information, argue against the existence of the "right" that the Ninth Circuit found here. * * * [A]s the proposed plea agreement at issue here specifies, the Government will provide "any information establishing the factual innocence of the defendant" regardless. That fact, along with other guilty-plea safeguards, see Fed. Rule Crim. Proc. 11, diminishes the force of Ruiz's concern that, in the absence of impeachment information, innocent individuals, accused of crimes, will plead guilty.

At the same time, a constitutional obligation to provide impeachment information during plea bargaining, prior to entry of a guilty plea, could seriously interfere with the Government's interest in securing those guilty pleas that are factually justified, desired by defendants, and help to secure the efficient administration of justice. The Ninth Circuit's rule risks premature disclosure of Government witness information, which, the Government tells us, could "disrupt ongoing investigations" and expose prospective witnesses to serious harm. * * *

Consequently, the Ninth Circuit's requirement could force the Government to abandon its general practice of not disclosing to a defendant pleading guilty information that would reveal the identities of cooperating informants, undercover investigators, or other prospective witnesses. It could require the Government to devote substantially more resources to trial preparation prior to plea bargaining, thereby depriving the plea-bargaining process of its main resource-saving advantages. Or it could lead the Government instead to abandon its heavy reliance upon plea bargaining in a vast number—90% or more—of federal criminal cases. We cannot say that the Constitution's due process requirement demands so radical a change in the criminal justice process in order to achieve so comparatively small a constitutional benefit.

* * *

[The opinion of JUSTICE THOMAS, concurring in the judgment, is omitted.]

Fast-Track Plea Bargaining

Ruiz was presented with a "fast-track" plea bargain, as described by Professor Bibas in Regulating the Plea-Bargaining Market: From Caveat Emptor to Consumer Protection, 99 Cal. L.Rev. 1117 (2011):

Judicial districts * * * near the Mexican border have been overwhelmed with far more immigration and drug cases than they can handle. In response, federal prosecutors in many of those districts developed fast-track plea-bargaining programs. The seminal program required defendants to waive indictment, forego motions, plead guilty immediately, waive presentence reports, stipulate to a particular sentence, agree to immediate sentencing, consent to deportation, and waive all sentencing and appeals. In exchange, prosecutors stipulated to sentences substantially below what defendants would have received after trial.

In light of the steep discount that Ruiz was offered under the fast-track program, is the Court's concern about burdens on the government of having to turn over impeachment evidence understandable? Did Ruiz get a fair exchange from the government for waiving access to impeachment evidence?

2.   A Knowing Plea

Knowledge of the Elements of the Crime: Henderson v. Morgan

In Henderson v. Morgan, 426 U.S. 637 (1976), a 19 year old defendant, with substantially less than average intelligence, pleaded guilty to second degree murder after he was advised by counsel that a 25 year sentence would be imposed. The defendant had been indicted for first degree murder as a result of stabbing to death a woman who employed him while he was on release from a state school for the mentally disabled. The stabbing took place when she discovered him in her room at night trying to get his wages so that he could leave the premises unnoticed. The defendant was never informed that an intent to cause the victim's death was an element of second degree murder. The Court held the plea invalid, even though it assumed that the defendant's lawyers would have given the defendant the same advice—i.e., to plead guilty—and even if, having been informed of the elements of the crime, he would have pleaded anyway. The Court declared that a guilty plea cannot be valid unless the defendant knows the nature of the offense to which he pleads. In its footnote 18, the Court assumed that notice of a charge did not always require a description of every element of an offense, but said that "intent is such a critical element of the offense of second-degree murder that notice of that element is required."[4]

Applying Henderson v. Morgan

Defense counsel's assurance that she informed the defendant of the charges against him and the elements of those charges is enough to satisfy *Henderson*. The Supreme Court made this clear in Bradshaw v. Stumpf, 545 U.S. 175 (2005):

> While the court taking a defendant's plea is responsible for ensuring a record adequate for any review that may be later sought, we have never held that the judge must himself explain the elements of each charge to the defendant on the record. Rather, the constitutional prerequisites of a valid plea may be satisfied where the record accurately reflects that the nature of the charge and the

---

[4]   Justice White, joined by Justices Stewart, Blackmun, and Powell, concurred and emphasized that the decision whether or not to plead to a specific offense is the defendant's alone, not his lawyer's. Justice Rehnquist, joined by Chief Justice Burger, dissented.

elements of the crime were explained to the defendant by his own, competent counsel. Where a defendant is represented by competent counsel, the court usually may rely on that counsel's assurance that the defendant has been properly informed of the nature and elements of the charge to which he is pleading guilty.

Henderson establishes that a defendant must know about the "crucial" elements of the offense to which the guilty plea is addressed, such as the requisite mental state. What else must a defendant know? Generally, a defendant must know the penalty that can be imposed. See, e.g., United States v. Goins, 51 F.3d 400 (4th Cir.1995) (guilty plea invalid where defendant was not made aware that he was subjecting himself to a mandatory minimum sentence of five years). Is a general idea of the maximum penalty enough? If the defendant is to understand the potential consequences of pleading, the general rule should be that a defendant must know whether several counts or indictments will produce concurrent or consecutive sentences. See ABA Standards, Pleas of Guilty, § 11–1.4 (requiring such an understanding).

On the other hand, a guilty plea can be sufficiently knowing even though the defendant has not been informed with precision of potential punishments under sentencing guidelines and without the defendant understanding the specifics of whether a sentencing judge might impose a sentence outside applicable guidelines. This is because, at the time of the plea allocution, the court "frequently has too little information available to provide defendant with an accurate sentencing range." United States v. Andrades, 169 F.3d 131 (2d Cir.1999).

Knowledge of Immigration Consequences: Padilla v. Kentucky

In Padilla v. Kentucky, 559 U.S. 356 (2010), the Court held that a defendant who is a noncitizen has a right to be told, before pleading guilty, that he will be deported if he pleads guilty. The Court noted that "preserving the client's right to remain in the United States may be more important to the client than any potential jail sentence." The specific holding in *Padilla* was that defense counsel violated Padilla's constitutional right to effective counsel because he did not inform Padilla that the crime to which he pled guilty triggered automatic deportation under federal law. The Court in *Padilla* noted that disclosure of immigration consequences could improve bargaining from both sides:

> [I]nformed consideration of possible deportation can only benefit both the State and noncitizen defendants during the plea-bargaining process. By bringing deportation consequences into this process, the defense and prosecution may well be able to reach agreements that better satisfy the interests of both parties. As in this case, a criminal episode may provide the basis for multiple charges, of which only a

subset mandate deportation following conviction. Counsel who possess the most rudimentary understanding of the deportation consequences of a particular criminal offense may be able to plea bargain creatively with the prosecutor in order to craft a conviction and sentence that reduce the likelihood of deportation, as by avoiding a conviction for an offense that automatically triggers the removal consequence. At the same time, the threat of deportation may provide the defendant with a powerful incentive to plead guilty to an offense that does not mandate that penalty in exchange for a dismissal of a charge that does.

Padilla is discussed more fully in the Chapter 10 materials on ineffective assistance of counsel.

Pleading to Something That Is Not a Crime: Bousley v. United States

The Court in Bousley v. United States, 523 U.S. 614 (1998), considered the problem of a defendant who pled guilty to a violation of a criminal statute that was later held not to cover his conduct. Bousley pleaded guilty to drug crimes, as well as to a violation of a federal statute that prohibited "using" a firearm during the course of a drug transaction. At the time he pleaded guilty to the firearms offense, the local federal courts had construed "using" expansively to cover basically any situation in which a defendant possessed a gun during the course of a drug offense. Bousley appealed his sentence, but did not challenge his guilty plea on direct appeal. His sentence was affirmed. Thereafter, the Supreme Court determined that the term "using" in the statute meant some kind of active use, such as brandishing or shooting. Bousley sought a writ of habeas corpus challenging the factual basis for his guilty plea on the ground that neither the "evidence" nor the "plea allocution" showed a "connection between the firearms in the bedroom of the house, and the garage, where the drug trafficking occurred."

The Supreme Court, in an opinion by Chief Justice Rehnquist for six Justices, held that Bousley would be entitled to a hearing on the merits of his challenge to his guilty plea if he could make the showing necessary to relieve the procedural default resulting from his failure to directly appeal his guilty plea. (On the question of procedural default, see the discussion of this case in Chapter 13). Addressing the question of whether Bousley's guilty plea could be considered valid under the circumstances, the Chief Justice declared:

> A plea of guilty is constitutionally valid only to the extent it is voluntary and intelligent. We have long held that a plea does not qualify as intelligent unless a criminal defendant first receives real notice of the true nature of the charge against him, the first and most universally recognized requirement of due process. [It is contended]

that petitioner's plea was intelligently made because, prior to pleading guilty, he was provided with a copy of his indictment, which charged him with "using" a firearm. Such circumstances, standing alone, give rise to a presumption that the defendant was informed of the nature of the charge against him. Henderson v. Morgan. Petitioner nonetheless maintains that his guilty plea was unintelligent because the District Court subsequently misinformed him as to the elements of [the firearms] offense. In other words, petitioner contends that the record reveals that neither he, nor his counsel, nor the court correctly understood the essential elements of the crime with which he was charged. Were this contention proven, petitioner's plea would be * * * constitutionally invalid.

The Court remanded for a determination of whether Bousley could overcome his procedural default, whereupon he would receive a hearing on the merits of his invalid guilty plea claim.

Justice Stevens wrote a separate opinion concurring on the guilty plea question. He elaborated upon the Court's analysis in the following passage:

> [W]hen petitioner was advised by the trial judge, by his own lawyer, and by the prosecutor that mere possession of a firearm would support a conviction under [the firearms statute], he received critically incorrect legal advice. The fact that all of his advisers acted in good-faith reliance on existing precedent does not mitigate the impact of that erroneous advice. Its consequences for petitioner were just as severe, and just as unfair, as if the court and counsel had knowingly conspired to deceive him in order to induce him to plead guilty to a crime that he did not commit. Our cases make it perfectly clear that a guilty plea based on such misinformation is constitutionally invalid.

Justice Scalia, joined by Justice Thomas, dissented.

3. Competence to Plead Guilty

The validity of a guilty plea is also dependent on whether the defendant is *competent* to make a plea. That the "competence" factor is distinct from the "knowing and intelligent" factor was made plain by the Court in Godinez v. Moran, 509 U.S. 389 (1993). One question in *Moran* was whether the competency standard for pleading guilty is higher than the competency standard for standing trial. The competency standard for standing trial is met when the defendant is able to consult with his lawyer "with a reasonable degree of rational understanding" and has "a rational as well as factual understanding of the proceedings against him." Dusky v. United States, 362 U.S. 402 (1960). The lower court in *Moran* had held that this "rational understanding" test was insufficient to determine whether Moran was competent to plead guilty, because the decision to plead guilty required the appreciation of alternatives; that court concluded that a person cannot be competent to plead guilty unless he has the capacity to make a "reasoned choice" among the alternatives available to him.

The Supreme Court, in an opinion by Justice Thomas, rejected the lower court's position and held that the "rational understanding" test that defines competency to stand trial also defines competency to plead guilty. The Court found that the decisionmaking process attendant to standing trial was at least as complex and demanding as that required to plead guilty. Justice Thomas explained as follows:

> A defendant who stands trial is likely to be presented with choices that entail relinquishment of the same rights that are relinquished by a defendant who pleads guilty. * * * In consultation with his attorney, he may be called upon to decide, among other things, whether (and how) to put on a defense and whether to raise one or more affirmative defenses. In sum, all criminal defendants—not merely those who plead guilty—may be required to make important decisions once criminal proceedings have been initiated. And while the decision to plead guilty is undeniably a profound one, it is no more complicated than the sum total of decisions that a defendant may be called upon to make during the course of a trial. * * * This being so, we can conceive of no basis for demanding a higher level of competence for those defendants who plead guilty. If the *Dusky* standard is adequate for defendants who plead not guilty, it is necessarily adequate for those who plead guilty.

Justice Thomas stressed, however, that competence was not the only requirement for a valid guilty plea. He explained that a trial court must also "satisfy itself that the waiver of [the defendant's] constitutional rights is knowing and voluntary. In this sense there is a 'heightened' standard for pleading guilty, but it is not a heightened standard of competence."

Justice Kennedy, joined by Justice Scalia, concurred in part and in the judgment. He noted the difficulty that would result from applying different standards of competency at various stages of a criminal proceeding:

> The standard applicable at a given point in a trial could be difficult to ascertain. For instance, if a defendant decides to change his plea to guilty after a trial has commenced, one court might apply the competency standard for undergoing trial while another court might use the standard for pleading guilty. In addition, the subtle nuances among different standards are likely to be difficult to differentiate, as evidenced by the lack of any clear distinction between a "rational understanding" and a "reasoned choice" in this case.[5]

---

[5]   Justice Blackmun, joined by Justice Stevens, dissented in *Moran*.

4. Waiver of the Right to Counsel at the Plea Hearing

An accused has a constitutional right to refuse counsel at trial and represent himself. [The right to self-representation is discussed in Chapter 10 of the Casebook.] It follows that the accused has the right to represent himself at a guilty plea hearing. But as with the right to counsel at trial, a waiver of the right to assistance of counsel during guilty plea proceedings must be knowing and voluntary. The Supreme Court, in Iowa v. Tovar, 541 U.S. 77 (2004), considered what warnings an accused must receive at a guilty plea hearing before a knowing and voluntary waiver of the right to counsel can be found. Justice Ginsburg, writing for the Court, posed the question as follows:

> This case concerns the extent to which a trial judge, before accepting a guilty plea from an uncounseled defendant, must elaborate on the right to representation.

> Beyond affording the defendant the opportunity to consult with counsel prior to entry of a plea and to be assisted by counsel at the plea hearing, must the court, specifically: (1) advise the defendant that waiving the assistance of counsel in deciding whether to plead guilty entails the risk that a viable defense will be overlooked; and (2) admonish the defendant that by waiving his right to an attorney he will lose the opportunity to obtain an independent opinion on whether, under the facts and applicable law, it is wise to plead guilty?

The Court held that neither of these warnings is mandated by the Sixth Amendment. Justice Ginsburg stated that a waiver of the right to counsel is sufficiently knowing "when the trial court informs the accused of the nature of the charges against him, of his right to be counseled regarding his plea, and of the range of allowable punishments attendant upon the entry of a guilty plea." The Court reasoned that the proposed warnings might actually be counterproductive.

> [T]he admonitions at issue might confuse or mislead a defendant more than they would inform him: The warnings * * * might be misconstrued as a veiled suggestion that a meritorious defense exists or that the defendant could plead to a lesser charge, when neither prospect is a realistic one. If a defendant delays his plea in the vain hope that counsel could uncover a tenable basis for contesting or reducing the criminal charge, the prompt disposition of the case will be impeded, and the resources of either the State (if the defendant is indigent) or the defendant himself (if he is financially ineligible for appointed counsel) will be wasted.

D. REGULATING GUILTY PLEAS UNDER FEDERAL RULE 11

1. Procedural Requirements of the Rule

Fed.R.Crim.P. 11 sets forth detailed procedural requirements to assure that defendants who plead guilty are informed of their rights and that the guilty plea is fairly rendered.[6] Subdivision (b)(1) provides that the court must address the defendant personally in open court and inform the defendant of, and determine that the defendant understands, the following:

(A) the government's right, in a prosecution for perjury or false statement, to use against the defendant any statement that the defendant gives under oath;

(B) the right to plead not guilty, or having already so pleaded, to persist in that plea;

(C) the right to a jury trial;

(D) the right to be represented by counsel—and if necessary have the court appoint counsel—at trial and at every other stage of the proceeding;

(E) the right at trial to confront and cross-examine adverse witnesses, to be protected from compelled self-incrimination, to testify and present evidence, and to compel the attendance of witnesses;

(F) the defendant's waiver of these trial rights if the court accepts a plea of guilty or nolo contendere;

(G) the nature of each charge to which the defendant is pleading;

(H) any maximum possible penalty, including imprisonment, fine, and term of supervised release;

(I) any mandatory minimum penalty;

(J) any applicable forfeiture;

(K) the court's authority to order restitution;

(L) the court's obligation to impose a special assessment;

(M) in determining a sentence, the court's obligation to calculate the applicable sentencing-guideline range and to consider that range, possible departures under the Sentencing Guidelines, and other sentencing factors under 18 U.S.C. § 3553(a);

---

[6] In United States v. Timmreck, 441 U.S. 780 (1979), Justice Stevens' opinion for a unanimous court established that a conviction based on a guilty plea cannot be collaterally attacked for a Rule 11 violation, unless the violation is constitutional or jurisdictional.

(N) the terms of any plea-agreement provision waiving the right to appeal or to collaterally attack the sentence; and

(O) that, if convicted, a defendant who is not a United States citizen may be removed from the United States, denied citizenship, and denied admission to the United States in the future.

Subdivision (b)(2) of Rule 11 requires the court to "determine that the plea is voluntary and did not result from force, threats or promises (other than promises in a plea agreement)." See United States v. Smith, 184 F.3d 415 (5th Cir.1999) (Rule 11 violation found where judge did not specifically inform the defendant of the elements of the crime and did not personally ask the defendant if his plea was voluntary); United States v. Damon, 191 F.3d 561 (4th Cir. 1999) (Rule 11 violation found where the judge, after being informed that the defendant was under medication after a suicide attempt, failed to inquire into the effect that the medication may have had on the defendant's ability to make a voluntary plea and to understand the consequences: "The plea colloquy required by Rule 11 must be conducted with some flexibility. If a defendant's response to a court's question indicates the need for clarification, follow-up questions must be asked. Otherwise, the Rule 11 colloquy would be reduced to a formalistic ritual, stripped of its purpose.").

Rule 11(b)(3) provides that the court must assure itself that there is a *factual basis* for the guilty plea. See, e.g., United States v. Camacho, 233 F.3d 1308 (11th Cir. 2000) (district court satisfied its obligation of ensuring that there was an adequate factual basis for the defendant's guilty plea to a charge of possessing cocaine with intent to distribute, even though it did not explain or discuss directly the significance of the aiding and abetting theory set forth in the indictment; the court could conclude from the proffered facts that someone had knowingly possessed cocaine with intent to distribute and that the defendant had intentionally arranged for the acquisition of the cocaine, thereby committing an act that contributed to and furthered the unlawful possession.).

Rule 11(c) provides that the prosecution and the defendant can enter into any of three agreements:

(A) an agreement not to bring or to dismiss charges;

(B) a recommendation, or an agreement not to oppose the defendant's request, to the judge, "that a particular sentence or sentencing range is appropriate"—with the understanding that the recommendation or request *does not bind the court*; or

(C) an agreement between the parties "that a specific sentence or sentencing range is the appropriate disposition of the case"—which binds the court once the court accepts the plea agreement.

Rule 11(c) provides further that the court "must not participate" in the discussions leading to a plea agreement.

2.   The Role of the Court

The Judge's Power to Review the Agreement

The role of the trial judge in reviewing plea agreements is explained by the court in United States v. Bennett, 990 F.2d 998 (7th Cir.1993):

> If the plea agreement includes the dismissal of any charges (a type "A" plea agreement), or if the agreement includes a specific sentence (a type "C" plea agreement), the district court may accept or reject the plea agreement, or it may defer its decision regarding acceptance or rejection until it considers the presentence investigation report. In contrast, if the plea agreement includes sentencing recommendations or the government's promise not to oppose the defendant's sentencing requests (a type "B" plea agreement), the district court must advise the defendant of the nonbinding effect the recommendations have on the court and must also inform the defendant that he may not withdraw his guilty plea, even if the court does not adopt the recommendations. The district court does not need to make such an admonition when dealing with a type "A" or "C" plea agreement.

The court in *Bennett* found that the agreement in the case was a type "B" agreement, which did not bind the court in any respect. Thus, it refused to allow Bennett to vacate his plea when the court imposed a sentence significantly higher than that suggested in the agreement. If the agreement in *Bennett* had been a "C" agreement, the court could not have imposed a higher sentence than that agreed to between the parties. If the court objects to the terms of an "A" or "C" agreement, its only recourse is to *reject the agreement*, thus sending the prosecution and defendant back to the bargaining table.[7] See, e.g., United States v. Greener, 979 F.2d 517 (7th Cir.1992) (district court properly rejected a type "C" agreement where the sentence would not have sufficiently reflected the seriousness of the defendant's conduct); United States v. Brown, 331 F.3d 591 (8th Cir. 2003) (there is no absolute right to have a guilty plea accepted and a district court may reject a plea in the exercise of sound discretion).

Given the uncertain results, why would a defendant ever agree to a type "B" agreement? Isn't that just rolling the dice and hoping the judge is lenient? Do you think that the typical defendant really believes that the judge will not accept the recommendation? The defendant may well be

---

[7]   A trial judge's blanket policy of rejecting plea agreements that permit a defendant charged with multiple counts to plead to only one was condemned in United States v. Miller, 722 F.2d 562 (9th Cir.1983). The court of appeals reasoned that trial judges must exercise their discretion in particular cases rather than establish blanket rules regarding acceptable pleas.

informed by counsel that judges accept recommendations almost all the time. This advice, while generally accurate, may cause a defendant to underestimate the risk of a plea. It is true that the defendant is protected if the judge fails to inform her of the fact that the judge may reject the recommendation. See United States v. Livorsi, 180 F.3d 76 (2d Cir.1999) (conviction vacated where defendant and prosecution reached a "B" agreement, and the judge failed to inform the defendant that such an agreement is not binding on the court). But, there is no protection for a defendant who relies on the informed prediction of counsel regarding a judge's likely action.

Intrusion into the Negotiations

Federal Rule 11(c) prohibits the judge from taking part in plea negotiations. The reasons for this rule are set forth in United States v. Barrett, 982 F.2d 193 (6th Cir.1992):

> When a judge becomes a participant in plea bargaining he brings to bear the full force and majesty of his office. His awesome power to impose a substantially longer or even maximum sentence in excess of that proposed is present whether referred to or not. * * *

> It is not only a court's sentencing power which gives coercive potential to its participation in the plea bargaining process, but also the court's control over the conduct of a trial. The defendant must view the judge as the individual who conducts the trial and whose rulings will affect what the jury is to consider in determining guilt or innocence. The defendant may be reluctant to reject such a proposition offered by one who wields such immediate power. * * * There is also a real danger that a judge's neutrality can be compromised.

See also United States v. Daigle, 63 F.3d 346 (5th Cir.1995) (judicial participation increases the possibility of coerced guilty pleas, and may impair judicial impartiality because the judge "seems more like an advocate for the agreement than a neutral arbiter if he joins the negotiations").

If the judge rejects a plea on the ground that it is too lenient, has she participated in the negotiations? If she rejects a plea and states what terms would be acceptable to her, has she participated in the negotiations? See United States v. Miles, 10 F.3d 1135 (5th Cir.1993) (plea vacated due to judicial participation, where the trial judge rejected a plea and suggested the terms that would be acceptable to him). If she rejects the plea *without* giving an explanation, is her action subject to attack as arbitrary? If she tells the defendant at a bail hearing, "you'd better see what you can get from the prosecutor because you have no defense as far as I can see," has she participated in the negotiations? If she tells the defendant, before the agreement is filed, that she accepts the government's recommendations in most cases, has she engaged in improper participation? See United States v. Daigle, 63 F.3d 346 (5th Cir.1995) (judge who so informs the defendant has improperly participated in negotiations).

Judge Rakoff has suggested that the rules should be changed to allow more participation of judges in the plea-bargaining process. He suggests the use of plea-bargaining conferences before the judge—a sealed proceeding in which judges would examine each party's position and recommend a non-binding plea bargain. The proposal

> provides a layer of review to protect the innocent from being pressured into pleading guilty, while potentially encouraging fairer plea bargains through the oversight of a neutral party. It creates a record of plea bargaining efforts, so there can be no uncertainty as to whether an offer was requested or ignored. Finally, it might help guilty people make a more informed choice about how to resolve their cases.

Murray, A Better Way to Plead Guilty, New York Times, p. A27, 1/23/2015.

Example of Improper Intrusions and the Need for a Harmless/Plain Error Review: United States v. Davila

In United States v. Davila, 133 S.Ct. 2139 (2013), the Court unanimously found that a magistrate judge had violated Rule 11(c) by intruding into the defendant's guilty plea negotiations. The judge made the following statements to the defendant:

> "it might be a good idea for the Defendant to accept responsibility for his criminal conduct, to plead guilty, and go to sentencing with the best arguments still available without wasting the Court's time, [and] causing the Government to have to spend a bunch of money empanelling a jury to try an open and shut case."

> "[T]ry to understand, the Government, they have all of the marbles in this situation and they can file that ... motion for a downward departure from the guidelines if they want to, you know, and the rules are constructed so that nobody can force them to file that motion for you. The only thing at your disposal that is entirely up to you is the two or three level reduction for acceptance of responsibility. That means you've got to go to the cross. You've got to tell the probation officer everything you did in this case regardless of how bad it makes you appear to be because that is the way you get that three-level reduction for acceptance, and believe me, Mr. Davila, someone with your criminal history needs a three-level reduction for acceptance. [The Sentencing Guidelines range would] probably be pretty bad because your criminal history score would be so high."

The *Davila* Court however, found that the judge's error under Rule 11(c) did not necessarily mandate the relief of vacating the guilty plea.

Justice Ginsburg, writing for the Court, found that a Rule 11(c) violation did not justify automatic relief, but rather was governed by the harmless and plain error provisions of Rule 11(h) [discussed immediately below.] The Court remanded for a determination of whether the judge's violation was harmless or plain error, with the focus being on whether the defendant would have pleaded guilty in any case. Justice Scalia, joined by Justice Thomas, wrote a short opinion concurring in part and concurring in the judgment.

3.   Harmless Error and Plain Error

Fed.R.Crim.P. 11(h) provides that any error in obtaining the guilty plea under Rule 11 "that does not affect substantial rights" will be disregarded as harmless. This is the classic definition of harmless error that is also found in Fed.R.Crim.P. 52(a). But what if the defendant does not object to an error under Rule 11? Should the same harmless error standard apply as if he did? With respect to trial errors, Rule 52(b) provides that a defendant who fails to object has the burden of showing "plain error" that affected substantial rights. [See the discussion of plain error in Chapter 13]. But Rule 11(h) does not include a plain-error provision comparable to Rule 52(b).

The Court in United States v. Vonn, 535 U.S. 55 (2002), held that a defendant who does not object to an error under Rule 11 has the burden of showing "plain error." Justice Souter wrote for eight Justices. Justice Souter was not persuaded that there was any intent to differentiate by including a plain error provision in Rule 52 but not in Rule 11. He found that the lack of a plain error standard in Rule 11 would create an anomalous result, in that a defendant would be able to stand by and do nothing to correct an obvious Rule 11 error, and would lose nothing in doing so. The Court reasoned that Rule 52(b) implicitly applied to Rule 11 errors, and declared that the policy of the plain error rule is sound: "the value of finality requires defense counsel to be on his toes, not just the judge, and the defendant who just sits there when a mistake can be fixed cannot just sit there when he speaks up later on." Justice Stevens dissented from the Court's holding on plain error.

In United States v. Dominguez Benitez, 542 U.S. 74 (2004), the Court held that "a defendant who seeks reversal of his conviction after a guilty plea, on the ground that the district court committed plain error under Rule 11, must show a reasonable probability that, but for the error, he would not have entered the plea. A defendant must thus satisfy the judgment of the reviewing court, informed by the entire record, that the probability of a different result is sufficient to undermine confidence in the outcome of the proceeding."

E. GUILTY PLEA WITH A CLAIM OF INNOCENCE: *ALFORD* PLEAS

The Model Code of Pre-Arraignment Procedure § 350.4(4) provides that "[t]he court may accept the defendant's guilty plea even though the defendant does not admit that he is in fact guilty if the court finds that it is reasonable for someone in the defendant's position to plead guilty. The court shall advise the defendant that if he pleads guilty he will be treated as guilty whether he is guilty or not." This approach is consistent with North Carolina v. Alford, 400 U.S. 25 (1970).

Alford was indicted by North Carolina for the capital crime of first-degree murder. He pleaded guilty to second-degree murder, but at the plea hearing he took the stand and testified in part as follows:

> I pleaded guilty on second degree murder because they said there is too much evidence, but I ain't shot no man, but I take the fault for the other man. We never had an argument in our life and I just pleaded guilty because they said if I didn't they would gas me for it, and that is all.

Subsequently, Alford sought post-conviction relief on the ground that his plea was produced by fear and coercion. After noting that "[s]tate and lower federal courts are divided upon whether a guilty plea can be accepted when it is accompanied by protestations of innocence and hence contains only a waiver of trial but no admission of guilt," the Court concluded that "[i]n view of the strong factual basis for the plea demonstrated by the State and Alford's clearly expressed desire to enter it despite his professed belief in his innocence, we hold that the trial judge did not commit constitutional error in accepting it."[8]

One of the reasons for sustaining the plea in *Alford* was the factual basis for it. Under Rule 11 there must always be a "factual basis" for the plea to be valid, but it is not necessary under the Rule that the defendant actually admit his guilt. See Cranford v. Lockhart, 975 F.2d 1347 (8th Cir.1992) (*Alford* plea upheld where information in prosecutor's file establishes a factual basis for the guilty plea).

In the federal system, a defendant who enters an *Alford* plea is all but certain to be denied a reduction in sentence for acceptance of responsibility. See United States v. Harlan, 35 F.3d 176 (5th Cir.1994) ("A defendant's refusal to acknowledge essential elements of an offense is incongruous with the guideline's commentary that truthful admission of the conduct comprising an offense is relevant in determining whether a defendant qualifies for this reduction.").

---

[8] Justice Brennan, joined by Justices Douglas and Marshall, dissented. Justice Black concurred in "substantially all of the opinion in this case."

F. FACTUAL BASIS FOR PLEAS

The court's determination of the factual basis for a plea can help to assure that defendants who are innocent do not plead guilty. As stated above, Federal Rule 11(b)(3) requires the judge to determine that there is a factual basis for the plea. Such a factual basis can be found through statements by the defendant, factual assertions in the indictment, or information in the prosecutor's file. See generally United States v. Adams, 961 F.2d 505 (5th Cir.1992) (insufficient factual basis where the defendant did not admit facts in the plea colloquy, and no other factual information was provided; but the error was harmless because there was sufficient factual information in the presentence report filed after the plea was taken).

Lack of Factual Basis for a Forfeiture: Libretti v. United States

In Libretti v. United States, 516 U.S. 29 (1995), the defendant challenged a forfeiture order that was entered after he pleaded guilty to participating in a continuing criminal enterprise. He had stipulated to the terms of the forfeiture with the government when he entered into the plea agreement. But he argued that the stipulation was invalid because there was no factual basis for the forfeiture. In Libretti's view, Rule 11 prevented the entry of the forfeiture order because the trial judge had never determined that the forfeiture had a factual basis. But the Court, in an opinion by Justice O'Connor, rejected this argument and held that Rule 11 applies only to a "plea of guilty." She concluded that a "forfeiture provision embodied in a plea agreement is of an entirely different nature. Forfeiture is an element of the sentence imposed following conviction or, as here, a plea of guilty, and thus falls outside the scope of Rule 11." Justice Stevens dissented.

G. THE FINALITY OF GUILTY PLEAS

1. Withdrawal of a Plea

The criminal justice system abides and promotes plea bargaining because it is efficient. But in order to be efficient, plea bargains must carry some measure of finality. The system of plea bargaining could be disrupted if defendants could withdraw their pleas unilaterally and demand a trial. In effect this would create a system more inefficient than an "all trial" system. On the other hand, some safety valve must be in place to protect defendants from plea bargains that are completely unfair and unjust— especially considering that the performance of appointed counsel for indigents often leaves much to be desired, and there are a number of intricacies in the process that will be difficult for many defendants to understand, such as the rights being given up, the chances at trial, and possible sentencing ranges.

Fed.R.Crim.P. 11(d) provides that a court may allow the defendant to withdraw a guilty plea before sentence is imposed for any reason if the judge *has not yet accepted the plea*. But if the judge has accepted the plea, it may be withdrawn only if 1) the court has rejected the terms of the plea agreement, or 2) if the defendant provides the court with a "fair and just" reason for withdrawal. Courts are extremely reluctant to allow withdrawal of a guilty plea once the court accepts it, even if a sentence has not yet been imposed. See United States v. Goodson, 569 F.3d 379 (8th Cir. 2009) ("When a defendant has entered a knowing and voluntary guilty plea at a hearing at which he acknowledged the crime, the occasion for setting aside a guilty plea should seldom arise."); United States v. Hoke, 569 F.3d 718 (7th Cir. 2009) ("claims of innocence alone do not mandate permission to withdraw a plea"); United States v. Abreu, 964 F.2d 16 (D.C.Cir.1992) (pre-sentence withdrawal of plea was properly denied where motion to withdraw was based upon the defendant's "reevaluation of the strength of the government's case").

Rule 11(e) prohibits the withdrawal of a guilty plea after sentence is imposed. Of course, if a guilty plea was not knowing and voluntary, then it can be vacated under the standards discussed earlier in this Chapter.

Withdrawal of Plea Before the Agreement Is Accepted: United States v. Hyde

As stated above, Rule 11 permits withdrawal of a guilty plea after it has been accepted by the court only "if the defendant can show a fair and just reason for requesting the withdrawal." In United States v. Hyde, 520 U.S. 670 (1997), a defendant reached a plea agreement with the government. At the guilty plea hearing, the defendant pleaded guilty to four counts of an eight-count indictment. The trial judge accepted the plea, but (as is common practice) the judge *deferred* decision on whether to accept the plea *agreement*, in which the government had agreed to dismiss the remaining four charges. So at this point the court had upheld the *defendant's* part of the agreement, while deferring consideration on the government's part of the agreement (as opposed to rejecting it). The defendant then sought to withdraw his plea—he did not proffer any "fair and just reason" for doing so. The lower court permitted the withdrawal, reasoning that a defendant has an absolute right to withdraw a guilty plea until it has been accepted; the agreement and the plea itself are inextricably intertwined; and the guilty plea is not really accepted until the agreement as a whole is accepted by the trial judge.

The Supreme Court, in a unanimous opinion by Chief Justice Rehnquist, rejected this reasoning and held that when a plea is accepted and the acceptance of the plea *agreement* deferred, the defendant cannot withdraw his plea unless he satisfies the "fair and just reason" requirement of Rule 11. The Chief Justice reasoned that if the defendant were permitted an absolute right to withdraw his plea after the court had actually accepted it, it would debase the judicial proceeding at which a defendant pleads and the court accepts his plea:

> After the defendant has sworn in open court that he actually committed the crimes, after he has stated that he is pleading guilty because he is guilty, after the court has found a factual basis for the plea, and after the court has explicitly announced that it accepts the plea, the Court of Appeals would allow the defendant to withdraw his guilty plea simply on a lark. * * * We think the Court of Appeals' holding would degrade the otherwise serious act of pleading guilty into something akin to a move in a game of chess.

The Chief Justice addressed the Court of Appeals' premise that a plea and a plea agreement are inextricably intertwined:

> The guilty plea and the plea agreement are "bound up together" in the sense that a *rejection* of the agreement simultaneously frees the defendant from his commitment to plead guilty. And since the guilty plea is but one side of the plea agreement, the plea is obviously not wholly independent of the agreement.
>
> But the Rules nowhere state that the guilty plea and the plea agreement must be treated identically. Instead, they explicitly envision a situation in which the defendant performs his side of the bargain (the guilty plea) before the Government is required to perform its side (here, the motion to dismiss four counts). If the court accepts the agreement and thus the Government's promised performance, then the contemplated agreement is complete and the defendant gets the benefit of his bargain. But if the court rejects the Government's promised performance, then the agreement is terminated and the defendant has the right to back out of his promised performance (the guilty plea), just as a binding contractual duty may be extinguished by the non-occurrence of a condition subsequent.

Thus, if the agreement were to be rejected by the judge, it would be void and the defendant would not have to worry about withdrawal. But the defendant could not, during the time between the Court's accepting the guilty plea and reviewing the terms of the agreement, move to withdraw the plea without providing a fair and just reason for doing so.

Constraints on Withdrawal and Poorly Advised Defendants

Professor Cook, in All Aboard! The Supreme Court, Guilty Pleas, and the Railroading of Criminal Defendants, 55 Colo. L. Rev.863 (2004), argues that the strict limitations on withdrawal of guilty pleas, including the result in *Hyde*, lead to a system in which indigent and unschooled defendants are hoodwinked into harsh sentences and an unfair waiver of their right to a trial. He explains as follows:

> When a defendant enters a guilty plea and the court accepts that plea, the court has made a determination that the defendant has fully performed his contractual obligation. * * * [T]here is nothing more the defendant can do but wait for the promised return. Yet contrary to the law attendant to unilateral contracts, a defendant, despite having fully performed, is not entitled to demand performance under the contract. * * * To make a truly informed choice, the defendant should understand that when he enters a guilty plea prompted by the promises bandied before him in a plea agreement, that typically upon the conclusion of the Rule 11 hearing he essentially has no more of a plea deal than he did prior to the hearing. He needs to understand that * * * he is essentially binding himself to a guilt admission for a protracted period, and that he will not be entitled to any of the benefits under the contract until the court decides whether it will assent to the agreement.

> Unfortunately, few defendants are so aware. * * * [T]he bargaining system is coercive, resulting in plea dispositions that are uninformed and are of dubious contractual validity. This view is buttressed when considering the defendant populace, which is comparatively less resourceful than their prosecutorial and judicial counterparts. The Department of Justice has most recently indicated, for example, that among the federally convicted, over 70 percent had no more than a high school education, * * * and that in excess of 50 percent had appointed counsel. * * * The defendant is unaware that the contractual principles applicable in the free market are largely inapplicable in the criminal context and that his plea process will be governed by a uniquely crafted set of contractual rules designed to safeguard not his interests but those of the system's most influential participants. They are typically devoid of any knowledge that they are being asked to submit a binding guilty plea in the absence of an enforceable agreement, and that their ability to revoke and pursue other, more optimal strategies will be severely constricted.

Professor Cook suggests an amendment to Rule 11 that would allow the defendant a unilateral right to withdraw a guilty plea at any time up to the court's approval of all terms of the plea agreement. But if the judge rejects the agreement, the defendant's plea would be void in any case.

2.   Breach of a Plea Agreement

Breach by the Prosecution: Santobello v. New York

A plea agreement between the government and the defendant is treated as a contract and is enforceable under contract principles. The leading case on enforcement of plea agreements is Santobello v. New York, 404 U.S. 257 (1971). Charged with two gambling felonies, Santobello agreed to plead guilty to a lesser included offense and the prosecutor agreed to make no recommendation as to sentence. Thereafter, a second prosecutor took over the case and, ignorant of the terms of the bargain, made a sentence recommendation. In an opinion by Chief Justice Burger, the Court held that even an inadvertent breach of a plea agreement was unacceptable. The Court remanded to afford the state courts the option of allowing Santobello to withdraw the plea or to have a new sentencing proceeding before a different judge. Justice Marshall, joined by Justices Brennan and Stewart, agreed with the majority's finding of a breach, but argued that Santobello "must be permitted to withdraw his guilty plea." Justice Douglas said that "[i]n choosing a remedy, * * * a court ought to accord a defendant's preference considerable, if not controlling, weight inasmuch as the fundamental rights flouted by a prosecutor's breach of a plea bargain are those of the defendant, not of the state."

Remedies for Prosecutorial Breach

It is well-established after *Santobello* that the remedy for a breached plea agreement is for the court either to permit the plea to be withdrawn or to order specific performance of the agreement, and that the choice between these two remedies is "a discretionary one guided by the circumstances of the case." United States v. Palladino, 347 F.3d 29 (2d Cir. 2003). Thus, the choice of remedy is for *the court,* not the defendant. In *Palladino*, the prosecutor essentially promised not to ask for an enhanced sentence on the basis of certain evidence, and then did so at the sentencing hearing by introducing that evidence. The court found that the government breached the plea agreement and that under the circumstances, withdrawal of the plea was the correct remedy. It explained as follows:

> Specific performance in this case is rendered difficult by the fact that, on remand, the District Court cannot simply erase its knowledge that the Government has previously taken a position in favor of the imposition of the disputed * * * enhancement. Although remand to another judge for resentencing, pursuant to a new Presentence Report is possible, we believe that the plea agreement in this case is hopelessly tainted by the introduction of new evidence known to the Government at the time of the plea * * * that cannot be magically

erased or ignored on remand. On balance, we conclude that defendant should be permitted to withdraw his plea.

If a defendant manages to set aside a guilty plea and decides to go to trial, is the prosecutor entitled to charge a higher offense than the one to which the defendant pleaded? Most courts treat the abrogation of the plea as an erasure that allows both sides to proceed anew. See, e.g., United States ex rel. Williams v. McMann, 436 F.2d 103 (2d Cir.1970). However, the *Williams* court acknowledged that although general principles of fundamental fairness do not bar every prosecution, certain allegations such as prosecutorial vindictiveness could pose a reasonable challenge on the basis of due process. Nonetheless, "no presumption of vindictiveness arises when the prosecutor simply reinstates the indictment that was in effect before the plea agreement was entered." Taylor v. Kincheloe, 920 F.2d 599 (9th Cir.1990), citing Blackledge v. Perry, 417 U.S. 21 (1974). See Chapter 12 for a discussion of vindictive prosecution.

Is There a Breach?

Sometimes it is difficult to determine whether a plea agreement has been breached. For example, if a prosecutor agrees to drop two counts of a three count indictment in exchange for a plea to the remaining count, and the sentencing judge relies on the fact that three offenses were committed, has the bargain been breached? In deciding how to answer, would you view an objective or subjective test of the bargain as more appropriate?

The courts have held that any ambiguity in the terms of the agreement is to be construed against the government. See United States v. Palladino, 347 F.3d 29 (2d Cir. 2003) ("because the government ordinarily has certain awesome advantages in bargaining power, any ambiguities in the agreement must be resolved in favor of the defendant."). See also United States v. Hayes, 946 F.2d 230 (3d Cir.1991) (where government promised to "make no recommendation as to the specific sentence to be imposed" and then emphasized the seriousness of the offense at the sentencing hearing, the government breached the terms of the plea agreement; principles of contract control whether plea agreement has been breached); United States v. Johnson, 187 F.3d 1129 (9th Cir.1999) (where the plea agreement required the prosecution to recommend a certain sentence, the prosecutor violated the agreement by recommending the sentence and then introducing a victim impact statement: "We see no way to view the introduction of McDonald's statement other than as an attempt by the prosecutor to influence the court to give a higher sentence than the prosecutor's recommendation.").

Government Agreement to Recommend a Sentence

Questions of breach often arise when the government, as part of a plea agreement, agrees to recommend a certain sentence. Defendants often object that the government at the sentencing hearing might have recommended the agreed-upon sentence, but made clear to the judge that it was doing so only reluctantly, and wouldn't mind at all if the judge were to impose a higher sentence. Under such circumstances the Court in United States v. Benchimol, 471 U.S. 453 (1985), found no breach. The Court reasoned that the agreement called only for the prosecutor to *recommend* a certain sentence, and the prosecutor did make the recommendation—there was nothing in the agreement specifically requiring the prosecutor to make an *enthusiastic* recommendation. See also United States v. Johnson, 187 F.3d 1129 (9th Cir.1999) ("unless specifically required in the agreement, the government need not make the agreed-upon recommendation enthusiastically"). If you are defense counsel, do you insist on having the word "enthusiastic" added to the plea agreement before "recommendation"? How would a reviewing court decide whether the government's recommendation was enthusiastic?

Oral Promises

If the government is to be held to an obligation, it must be in the plea agreement. Thus, in United States v. Austin, 255 F.3d 593 (8th Cir. 2001), the defendant argued that the government breached its agreement when it sought a sentencing enhancement based on the defendant's leadership role in the offense. The defendant argued that the prosecutor had promised during negotiations not to seek such an enhancement. But the agreement itself was silent on the issue of enhancement, and a clause in the agreement provided that the agreement reflected "all promises, agreements, and conditions between the parties." The court therefore found that the government did not breach the agreement by arguing for enhancement at sentencing.

Cooperation Agreements

The question of prosecutorial breach becomes particularly difficult when the agreement imposes cooperation obligations on the defendant in exchange for the government's agreement to recommend a lesser sentence. Generally the prosecution prefers that its obligations under such an agreement remain vague, and contingent on its own view of the *quality* of the defendant's cooperation. When the defendant claims that the prosecution breached the agreement by failing to recommend a certain sentence or a sentence reduction, the prosecution often responds that its duty was contingent on the defendant's cooperation, and in its opinion the defendant failed to comply with his contractual obligations. Professor

Richman, in Cooperating Clients, 56 Ohio St.L.J. 69 (1995), describes this phenomenon:

> Typically, the defendant will broadly promise to testify truthfully, and to truthfully disclose all information concerning matters covered by the government's inquiries. Any effort to bind a cooperator to a particular "story" would be unseemly, and probably illegal. The government will reserve for itself the right to determine, prior to sentencing, whether the defendant has in fact cooperated fully and told the truth. * * * If the government determines that a cooperator has not lived up to his obligations, it will * * * generally be able to prevent the sentencing judge from showing the defendant any significant leniency based on his cooperation.

Professor Richman notes that while a government's obligations under a cooperation agreement are thus difficult to enforce in court, there is some discipline that is imposed by the marketplace. "The prosecutor who mistreats snitches risks not being able to attract such assets in the future."

One defense attorney became so frustrated at what he perceived as a failure of a United States Attorney's office to live up to its obligations under a cooperation agreement, that he was moved to publish an open letter in a full-page advertisement in the National Law Journal:

> [Despite the client's cooperation], your office broke two written promises to make a 5K.1 motion [for reduction in sentence due to cooperation]. The reasons given by your office were pure bovine do-do. Even the district judge was appalled.

> During the sentence proceedings I stated that I was going to tell every defense lawyer in our nation not to enter any plea agreement with your office. Your office cannot be trusted. Your office cares nothing about promises and agreements. I am surprised that the eagle in the Great Seal of the United States didn't fly from the wall in horror. * * * Like some sleazy insurance company who refuses to pay the widow because it wants the premiums but doesn't want to honor its obligations, your office will go to any length to renege on its solemn promises.

Michael Metzger, Advertisement, Nat'l L.J., May 24, 1993, at 26. Metzger was complaining about the U.S. Attorney's office in the Southern District of Florida. If you were a defense attorney practicing in Miami, would this advertisement affect the advice that you would give to a client who seeks a benefit from cooperation? Can you write a cooperation agreement that would bind the prosecution to its promises?

For a case in which a breach was found when the government failed to move for a sentence reduction in a cooperation agreement, see United States v. Lukse, 286 F.3d 906 (6th Cir. 2002), where the government was required in the agreement to file a downward departure motion if the defendant provided the government with substantial assistance. At the sentencing hearing, the government conceded that the defendant *had* provided substantial assistance, but argued that the defendant had breached the agreement because he was caught smoking marijuana in jail after providing the assistance. Because the defendant made no promises in the agreement that were breached by this conduct, the agreement was found fully enforceable against the government. The court remanded and ordered the government to file a downward departure motion at a new sentencing proceeding.

Breach by the Defendant: Ricketts v. Adamson

In Ricketts v. Adamson, 483 U.S. 1 (1987), the Court held that the Double Jeopardy Clause did not bar a state from filing capital charges against a defendant who had entered a guilty plea in return for a specific prison term and subsequently violated the terms of the plea agreement. Adamson was one of three individuals charged with first-degree murder in the dynamiting of a reporter's car. He agreed to plead guilty to second-degree murder and to testify against the other defendants in exchange for a designated prison sentence. Although Adamson testified as promised and the other defendants were convicted, the State Supreme Court reversed the convictions and remanded their cases for new trials. Adamson's lawyer informed the prosecutor that Adamson would only testify at second trials if certain conditions were met, including his release from prison following his testimony. The state took the position that Adamson's refusal to testify would put him in breach of the agreement. Adamson nevertheless invoked his privilege against self-incrimination when called to testify at a pretrial proceeding. Thereafter, the state filed a new information and convicted Adamson of first-degree murder. He was sentenced to death. An en banc court of appeals found that Adamson was placed in jeopardy twice, but the Supreme Court disagreed.

Justice White wrote for the Court. The Court assumed that jeopardy attached when Adamson was sentenced pursuant to his guilty plea and that absent special circumstances, Adamson could not have been retried for first-degree murder. Justice White agreed with the state that special circumstances arose from the plea agreement which specifically provided that the entire agreement would be null and void if Adamson refused to testify. He was unimpressed with the court of appeals' reasoning that Adamson acted in good faith. Justice White concluded that Adamson knew that if he breached the agreement he could be retried, "it is incredible to believe that he did not anticipate that the extent of his obligation would be decided by a court," and the end "result was that respondent was returned to the position that he occupied prior to execution of the plea bargain; he stood charged with first-degree murder."

Justice White reasoned that it was "of no moment" that Adamson offered to comply with the agreement after the state supreme court decision interpreting it, since "[t]he parties did not agree that respondent would be relieved of the consequences of his refusal to testify if he were able to advance a colorable argument that a testimonial obligation was not owing." Justice White ended his opinion with the observation that "[t]he parties could have struck a different bargain, but permitting the State to enforce the agreement the parties actually made does not violate the Double Jeopardy Clause."

Justice Brennan, joined by Justices Marshall, Blackmun, and Stevens, dissented. He disagreed that Adamson ever breached the plea agreement and argued that, assuming such a breach occurred, Adamson never made a conscious decision to violate the agreement. Justice Brennan focused on the provision of the agreement stating that Adamson was to be sentenced at the conclusion of his promised testimony, and noted that Adamson was sentenced after he had provided extensive testimony. Thus, Justice Brennan found that Adamson reasonably could have concluded that he had met his contractual obligations.

3.   Appeal and Collateral Attack

Jurisdictions that do not like to see guilty pleas withdrawn or vacated also do not like to see them challenged on appeal or collaterally attacked.[9] Thus, they generally establish a regime in which a voluntary and intelligent guilty plea is a waiver of all claims that the pleader has. The Supreme Court has promoted this approach in four cases: the *Brady* trilogy—Brady v. United States, 397 U.S. 742 (1970); McMann v. Richardson, 397 U.S. 759 (1970); Parker v. North Carolina, 397 U.S. 790 (1970)—and Tollett v. Henderson, 411 U.S. 258 (1973). We first examine the specific claims that are waived when a defendant pleads guilty.

The defendant in *Brady* was charged with kidnaping under a federal statute that authorized the death penalty if a jury recommended it but not in a bench trial. Brady pleaded guilty when it appeared that the trial judge would not try the case without a jury, but Brady sought to challenge his guilty plea via habeas corpus on the ground that the statute unconstitutionally infringed his right to jury trial. The Supreme Court held that even if Brady would not have pleaded guilty but for the death penalty provision, he pleaded voluntarily and intelligently with the advice of counsel. Thus, he was not entitled to withdraw his plea collaterally, even if a Supreme Court decision rendered after his plea was entered suggested

---

[9]   For a discussion of the defendant's right to appeal a guilty plea conviction see United States v. Melancon, 972 F.2d 566 (5th Cir.1992) (defendant may, as part of his plea agreement, waive the right to appeal his sentence; finding a knowing and intelligent waiver under the circumstances). Compare United States v. Padilla-Colon, 578 F.3d 23 (1st Cir. 2009) (statements by the court about appeal from the guilty plea were so misleading that they abrogated any waiver of the right to appeal).

that the kidnaping statute was invalid in burdening the right to jury trial (i.e., even if the statute violated the Sixth Amendment). In *Parker,* the Court reached a similar result with respect to a state court defendant who was charged with first-degree burglary and who pleaded guilty to avoid a possible jury-imposed death sentence.

The Court also said in *Parker* and in *McMann* that a defendant who pleaded guilty could not attack the plea in a subsequent collateral proceeding on the ground that it was motivated by a prior coerced confession (i.e., the plea resulted from a violation of the 5th or 14th Amendment).

Following this trilogy, the Court held in *Tollett* that a defendant who pleaded guilty to first-degree murder could not challenge in subsequent habeas corpus proceedings the racial composition of the grand jury that indicted him (i.e., the grand jury was selected in violation of Equal Protection).

The four cases appeared to hold that a guilty plea represents acceptance by a defendant of his conviction and that the conviction is valid unless the defendant was not adequately represented by counsel. But, the Court soon muddied the waters in Blackledge v. Perry, 417 U.S. 21 (1974), as it held that a prison inmate who pleaded guilty to a felony charge in a North Carolina court after seeking a trial de novo following a conviction on a misdemeanor charge could attack his plea on the ground that the prosecutor acted improperly in retaliating against the defendant by raising the charge to a felony from a misdemeanor (a vindictiveness claim discussed in Chapter 12, infra). Thereafter, the Court held in Menna v. New York, 423 U.S. 61 (1975), that a defendant who pleaded guilty did not lose the right to challenge the plea as a violation of double jeopardy rights. So, prosecutorial vindictiveness and double jeopardy claims are treated as unwaived.

The Court held in United States v. Broce, 488 U.S. 563 (1989), that defendants, who pleaded guilty to two separate counts charging bidrigging conspiracies, could not successfully move to vacate their sentences on the ground that they actually were involved in a single, large conspiracy. Justice Kennedy reasoned for the Court that the indictments charged two conspiracies and that the defendants conceded by their pleas that they committed two separate crimes. He observed that *Blackledge* and *Menna* were resolved on the basis of the existing record and did not require an inquiry into evidence outside the record; in contrast, the instant case involved indictments which on their face charged separate offenses—the only way to determine whether it was a single conspiracy would be to conduct a detailed inquiry into the facts. Does the distinction work? Does it explain the difference between waived and unwaived claims?

It is clear that the Supreme Court has attempted to promote plea bargaining. Yet, the Court has identified a narrow range of cases in which guilty pleas cannot bar a subsequent collateral attack. Can you draw from *Broce* or from your own analysis of these cases any rule that would rationalize the cases?[10]

4.   Conditional Pleas

Plea bargaining can be promoted if defendants who plead guilty are permitted to raise some particular kinds of post-plea claims. For example, Fed.R.Crim. P. 11(a)(2) provides that with the approval of the court and with the consent of the government, "a defendant may enter a conditional plea of guilty * * * reserving in writing the right to have an appellate court review an adverse determination of a specified pretrial motion." If the defendant prevails on appeal, he has the right to withdraw the plea. A typical example of the use of a conditional plea is where the defendant moves to suppress evidence on the ground that it was obtained as a result of an illegal search and seizure, and the court denies the motion to suppress. At that point, the defendant could go to trial to preserve the right to appeal the suppression motion, but this might make little sense to a defendant who is actually guilty. So the defendant pleads guilty on condition that he can appeal the judge's suppression ruling. Thus, a defendant need not go to trial just to preserve a search and seizure or confession challenge.[11] If the defendant prevails on appeal, he then withdraws the plea and it is up to the government to determine whether to proceed in the absence of the evidence.[12]

---

[10] For two attempts at stating such a rule, see Saltzburg, Pleas of Guilty and the Loss of Constitutional Rights: The Current Price of Pleading Guilty, 76 Mich.L.Rev. 1265 (1978); Westen, Away from Waiver: A Rationale for the Forfeiture of Constitutional Rights in Criminal Procedure, 75 Mich.L.Rev. 1214 (1977). See also Alschuler, The Supreme Court, the Defense Attorney, and the Guilty Plea, 47 U.Colo.L.Rev. 1 (1975); Dix, Waiver in Criminal Procedure: A Brief for More Careful Analysis, 55 Tex.L.Rev. 193 (1977).

[11] United States v. Burns, 684 F.2d 1066 (2d Cir.1982), urges trial courts to consent to the reservation of issues only where they can be reviewed without a full trial and are likely to be dispositive of the case.

[12] Note, Conditional Guilty Pleas, 93 Harv.L.Rev. (1980), argues that a defendant has a constitutional right to enter a conditional guilty plea.

CHAPTER 10

TRIAL AND TRIAL-RELATED RIGHTS

■ ■ ■

In the previous Chapter we found that almost all criminal prosecutions in the United States end in a guilty plea. Why, then, is it worth it to spend much time studying criminal trials? The answer is that trials and trial rights remain important because the decision to plead guilty or not is dependent on the parties' view of how a trial would unfold. Moreover, prosecutions of extremely serious or high profile crimes usually do go to trial. Finally, the explication and development of constitutional rights at trial indicates our attitude toward civil rights in this country. So we proceed to an in-depth discussion of trial rights in America.

I. THE RIGHT TO A SPEEDY TRIAL

A. THE BACKGROUND OF AND POLICIES SUPPORTING THE RIGHT

The Sixth Amendment provides that "[i]n all criminal prosecutions, the accused shall enjoy the right to a speedy and public trial * * *" It is a guarantee of deliberate speed in the prosecution of a case and a protection against several evils associated with delayed litigation. The Supreme Court has long recognized that "[t]he right of a speedy trial is necessarily relative. It is consistent with delays and depends upon circumstances." Beavers v. Haubert, 198 U.S. 77 (1905). Careful analysis of the facts of each case, rather than bright line tests, has been, and is still, the preferred approach of the Court to constitutionally-based speedy trial claims.

Fundamental Right: Klopfer v. North Carolina

Klopfer v. North Carolina, 386 U.S. 213 (1967), established that the right to a speedy trial is fundamental and thus binding upon the states through the Due Process Clause of the Fourteenth Amendment. In *Klopfer*, the Court found a speedy trial violation when a Duke University professor, who was indicted for criminal trespass for participation in a sit-in at a restaurant, saw the prosecutor obtain a "nolle prosequi with leave" following a trial that ended in a hung jury. The nolle prosequi permitted the prosecutor to reinstate the case without further order. Because the procedure indefinitely prolonged the anxiety and concern accompanying public accusation, the Court found that it violated the defendant's right to a speedy trial.

Interests Protected by the Speedy Trial Right

There are three interests protected by the right to a speedy trial:

1. The interest of an accused person in avoiding prolonged detention prior to trial. Innocent persons are never compensated for the losses that result from such detention. Those who are convicted following trial may have been confined for long periods in inadequate jails. Some who receive probation would never have spent time incarcerated except for pretrial delay.

2. The interest of the accused in avoiding prolonged anxiety concerning the charges made and public suspicion while charges are pending.

3. The accused's interest in litigating a case before evidence disappears and memories fade.

Not all of these concerns are present in all cases, but they can be. See generally Godbold, Speedy Trial—Major Surgery for a National Ill, 24 Ala.L.Rev. 265 (1972).

Imprisonment on Other Offenses:
Smith v. Hooey and Dickey v. Florida

In Smith v. Hooey, 393 U.S. 374 (1969), the Court held that speedy trial rights extend to people imprisoned on other offenses. The Court reasoned as follows:

> At first blush it might appear that a man already in prison under a lawful sentence is hardly in a position to suffer from "undue and oppressive incarceration prior to trial." But the fact is that delay in bringing such a person to trial on a pending charge may ultimately result in as much oppression as is suffered by one who is jailed without bail upon an untried charge. First, the possibility that the defendant already in prison might receive a sentence at least partially concurrent with the one he is serving may be forever lost if trial of the pending charge is postponed. Secondly, under procedures now widely practiced, the duration of his present imprisonment may be increased, and the conditions under which he must serve his sentence greatly worsened, by the pendency of another criminal charge outstanding against him.

> And while it might be argued that a person already in prison would be less likely than others to be affected by "anxiety and concern accompanying public accusation," there is reason to believe that an outstanding untried charge (of which even a convict may, of course, be

innocent) can have fully as depressive an effect upon a prisoner as upon a person who is at large.

* * *

Finally, * * * while "evidence and witnesses disappear, memories fade, and events lose their perspective," a man isolated in prison is powerless to exert his own investigative efforts to mitigate these erosive effects of the passage of time.

One year later, in Dickey v. Florida, 398 U.S. 30 (1970), the Court ordered a prosecution dismissed when a federal prisoner made persistent requests for a speedy trial on an armed robbery charge, and for seven years Florida took no action to bring him to trial. In the interim, potential defense witnesses had died or disappeared. Chief Justice Burger wrote the opinion for a unanimous court, stating that "[a]lthough a great many accused persons seek to put off the confrontation as long as possible, the right to a prompt inquiry into criminal charges is fundamental and the duty of the charging authority is to provide a prompt trial."

B. DELAY IN ARRESTING OR CHARGING THE DEFENDANT

Klopfer, *Smith*, and *Dickey* all wanted the charges brought against them disposed of promptly. But what if no formal charge or arrest is made against a person, and yet it is clear that one might be forthcoming at some future time? Presumably the suspect is concerned about the prosecution that is looming, but what protection, if any, can be claimed? That is the issue in the next two principal cases.

1. Speedy Trial Clause Analysis

UNITED STATES V. MARION
Supreme Court of the United States, 1971.
404 U.S. 307.

JUSTICE WHITE delivered the opinion of the Court.

This appeal requires us to decide whether dismissal of a federal indictment was constitutionally required by reason of a period of three years between the occurrence of the alleged criminal acts and the filing of the indictment.

* * *

Appellees * * * claim that their rights to a speedy trial were violated by the period of approximately three years between the end of the criminal scheme charged and the return of the indictment * * *. In our view, however, the Sixth Amendment speedy trial provision has no application until the putative defendant in some way becomes an "accused," an event that occurred in this case only when the appellees were indicted on April 21, 1970.

The Sixth Amendment provides that "[i]n all criminal prosecutions, the accused shall enjoy the right to a speedy and public trial * * *." On its face, the protection of the Amendment is activated only when a criminal prosecution has begun and extends only to those persons who have been "accused" in the course of that prosecution. * * *

It is apparent also that very little support for appellees' position emerges from a consideration of the purposes of the Sixth Amendment's speedy trial provision, a guarantee that this Court has termed "an important safeguard to prevent undue and oppressive incarceration prior to trial, to minimize anxiety and concern accompanying public accusation and to limit the possibilities that long delay will impair the ability of an accused to defend himself." Inordinate delay between arrest, indictment, and trial may impair a defendant's ability to present an effective defense. But the major evils protected against by the speedy trial guarantee exist quite apart from actual or possible prejudice to an accused's defense. * * * Arrest is a public act that may seriously interfere with the defendant's liberty, whether he is free on bail or not, and that may disrupt his employment, drain his financial resources, curtail his associations, subject him to public obloquy, and create anxiety in him, his family and his friends. * * * So viewed, it is readily understandable that it is either a formal indictment or information or else the actual restraints imposed by arrest and holding to answer a criminal charge that engage the particular protections of the speedy trial provision of the Sixth Amendment.

Invocation of the speedy trial provision thus need not await indictment, information, or other formal charge. But we decline to extend the reach of the amendment to the period prior to arrest. Until this event occurs, a citizen suffers no restraints on his liberty and is not the subject of public accusation; his situation does not compare with that of a defendant who has been arrested and held to answer. * * *

* * * [T]he applicable statute of limitations is the primary guarantee against bringing overly stale criminal charges. * * * These statutes provide predictability by specifying a limit beyond which there is an irrebuttable presumption that a defendant's right to a fair trial would be prejudiced. * * * There is thus no need to press the Sixth Amendment into service to guard against the mere possibility that pre-accusation delays will prejudice the defense in a criminal case since statutes of limitation already perform that function.

* * *

[JUSTICE DOUGLAS, joined by JUSTICES BRENNAN and MARSHALL concurred in the result on the ground that the case against the defendants was complex and required extensive investigation, so that the government's three-year delay in bringing the prosecution was permissible under the circumstances.]

Second Indictment: United States v. MacDonald

In United States v. MacDonald, 456 U.S. 1 (1982), charges were brought against the defendant for murdering his wife and children. Those charges were dismissed without prejudice. Four years later the defendant was indicted on the same murder charges. MacDonald alleged a speedy trial violation—arguing that the speedy trial clock started ticking upon the initial indictment. MacDonald contended that the long delay allowed the prosecution to refresh the memory of its witnesses, and the defense could not adequately probe the recollection of the witnesses whose memories were refreshed. But the Supreme Court rejected these concerns as irrelevant and held that the time between the dropping of charges and a later indictment does not count toward the speedy trial determination.

The *MacDonald* Court reasoned that the speedy trial guarantee is designed to "minimize the possibility of lengthy incarceration prior to trial" and that after charges are dismissed, the citizen, as in *Marion,* suffers no restraints on his liberty. Chief Justice Burger, writing for the majority, concluded that once charges are dismissed, "the formerly accused is, at most, in the same position as any other subject of a criminal investigation." Justice Marshall, joined by Justices Brennan and Blackmun dissented, arguing that MacDonald suffered continuous anxiety, disruption of employment, financial strain, and public obloquy while the same government that arrested him continued to investigate him from the time that formal charges were dropped in 1970 until he was indicted in 1975. Justice Stevens concurred in the judgment. He agreed with the dissenters that the Speedy Trial Clause applied, but he found no violation because the government had a need "to proceed cautiously and deliberately before making a final decision to prosecute for such a serious offense."

Inconsistent Attachment of Sixth Amendment Rights?

The Sixth Amendment begins "In all criminal prosecutions" and then lists the rights protected, including the right to speedy trial and the right to counsel. United States v. Gouveia (Chapter 5, supra), and Kirby v. Illinois (Chapter 4, supra) construe the term "criminal prosecutions" and conclude that the right to counsel does not begin until a formal charge has been filed. In contrast, *Marion* construes the term "criminal prosecutions" and holds that the right to speedy trial attaches at *arrest.* How can the same term mean something different depending on the right invoked?

2. Due Process Clause Analysis

UNITED STATES V. LOVASCO

Supreme Court of the United States, 1977.

431 U.S. 783.

JUSTICE MARSHALL delivered the opinion of the Court.

* * *

On March 6, 1975, respondent was indicted for possessing eight firearms stolen from the United States mails, and for dealing in firearms without a license. The offenses were alleged to have occurred between July 25 and August 31, 1973, more than 18 months before the indictment was filed. Respondent moved to dismiss the indictment due to the delay.

The District Court conducted a hearing on respondent's motion at which the respondent sought to prove that the delay was unnecessary and that it had prejudiced his defense. In an effort to establish the former proposition, respondent presented a Postal Inspector's report on his investigation that was prepared one month after the crimes were committed, and a stipulation concerning the post-report progress of the probe. The report stated, in brief, that within the first month of the investigation respondent had admitted to Government agents that he had possessed and then sold five of the stolen guns, and that the agents had developed strong evidence linking respondent to the remaining three weapons. The report also stated, however, that the agents had been unable to confirm or refute respondent's claim that he had found the guns in his car when he returned to it after visiting his son, a mail handler, at work. The stipulation into which the Assistant United States Attorney entered indicated that little additional information concerning the crimes was uncovered in the 17 months following the preparation of the Inspector's report.

To establish prejudice to the defense, respondent testified that he had lost the testimony of two material witnesses due to the delay. The first witness, Tom Stewart, died more than a year after the alleged crimes occurred. At the hearing respondent claimed that Stewart had been his source for two or three of the guns. The second witness, respondent's brother, died in April 1974, eight months after the crimes were completed. Respondent testified that his brother was present when respondent called Stewart to secure the guns, and witnessed all of respondent's sales. Respondent did not state how the witnesses would have aided the defense had they been willing to testify.

* * * [P]roof of prejudice is generally a necessary but not sufficient element of a due process claim, and * * * the due process inquiry must consider the reasons for the delay as well as the prejudice to the accused.

The Court of Appeals found that the sole reason for the delay here was a hope on the part of the Government that others might be discovered who may have participated in the theft. It concluded that this hope did not justify the delay, and therefore affirmed the dismissal of the indictment. But the Due Process Clause does not permit courts to abort criminal prosecutions simply because they disagree with a prosecutor's judgment as to when to seek an indictment. * * *

[P]rosecutors are under no duty to file charges as soon as probable cause exists but before they are satisfied they will be able to establish the suspect's guilt beyond a reasonable doubt. To impose such a duty would have a deleterious effect both upon the rights of the accused and upon the ability of society to protect itself. From the perspective of potential defendants, requiring prosecutions to commence when probable cause is established is undesirable because it would increase the likelihood of unwarranted charges being filed, and would add to the time during which defendants stand accused but untried. * * * From the perspective of law enforcement officials, a requirement of immediate prosecution upon probable cause is equally unacceptable because it could make obtaining proof of guilt beyond a reasonable doubt impossible by causing potentially fruitful sources of information to evaporate before they are fully exploited. And from the standpoint of the courts, such a requirement is unwise because it would cause scarce resources to be consumed on cases that prove to be insubstantial, or that involve only some of the responsible parties or some of the criminal acts. Thus, no one's interests would be well served by compelling prosecutors to initiate prosecutions as soon as they are legally entitled to do so.

It might be argued that once the Government has assembled sufficient evidence to prove guilt beyond a reasonable doubt, it should be constitutionally required to file charges promptly, even if its investigation of the entire criminal transaction is not complete. Adopting such a rule, however, would have many of the same consequences as adopting a rule requiring immediate prosecution upon probable cause.

First, compelling a prosecutor to file public charges as soon as the requisite proof has been developed against one participant on one charge would cause numerous problems in those cases in which a criminal transaction involves more than one person or more than one illegal act. In some instances, an immediate arrest or indictment would impair the prosecutor's ability to continue his investigation, thereby preventing society from bringing lawbreakers to justice. In other cases, the prosecutor would be able to obtain additional indictments despite an early prosecution, but the necessary result would be multiple trials involving a single set of facts. Such trials place needless burdens on defendants, law enforcement officials, and courts.

Second, insisting on immediate prosecution once sufficient evidence is developed to obtain a conviction would pressure prosecutors into resolving doubtful cases in favor of early—and possibly unwarranted—prosecutions. * * * In the instant case, for example, since respondent admitted possessing at least five of the firearms, the primary factual issue in dispute was whether respondent knew the guns were stolen * * *. Not surprisingly, the Postal Inspector's report contained no direct evidence bearing on this issue. The decision whether to prosecute, therefore, required a necessarily subjective evaluation of the strength of the circumstantial evidence available and the credibility of respondent's denial. * * * To avoid the risk that a subsequent indictment would be dismissed for preindictment delay, the prosecutor might feel constrained to file premature charges, with all the disadvantages that would entail.

Finally, requiring the Government to make charging decisions immediately upon assembling evidence sufficient to establish guilt would preclude the Government from giving full consideration to the desirability of not prosecuting in particular cases. The decision to file criminal charges, with the awesome consequences it entails, requires consideration of a wide range of factors in addition to the strength of the Government's case, in order to determine whether prosecution would be in the public interest. * * * [T]he instant case provides a useful illustration. Although proof of the identity of the mail thieves was not necessary to convict respondent of the possessory crimes with which he was charged, it might have been crucial in assessing respondent's culpability, as distinguished from his legal guilt. If, for example, further investigation were to show that respondent had no role in or advance knowledge of the theft and simply agreed, out of paternal loyalty, to help his son dispose of the guns once respondent discovered his son had stolen them, the United States Attorney might have decided not to prosecute, especially since at the time of the crime respondent was over 60 years old and had no prior criminal record. Requiring prosecution once the evidence of guilt is clear, however, could prevent a prosecutor from awaiting the information necessary for such a decision.

We would be most reluctant to adopt a rule which would have these consequences absent a clear constitutional command to do so. We can find no such command in the Due Process Clause of the Fifth Amendment. In our view, investigative delay is fundamentally unlike delay undertaken by the Government solely "to gain tactical advantage over the accused," precisely because investigative delay is not so one-sided. Rather than deviating from elementary standards of "fair play and decency," a prosecutor abides by them if he refuses to seek indictments until he is completely satisfied that he should prosecute and will be able promptly to establish guilt beyond a reasonable doubt. Penalizing prosecutors who defer action for these reasons would subordinate the goal of "orderly expedition" to that of "mere speed." * * * We therefore hold that to prosecute a defendant following investigative delay does not deprive him of due process, even if his defense might have been somewhat prejudiced by the lapse of time.

* * *

[The dissenting opinion of JUSTICE STEVENS is omitted.]

COMMENT ON LOVASCO

If *Lovasco* had come out the other way, consider the oddity of the arguments that the parties would have to make. The defendant would have to argue that his case was indictment-worthy—he would point to the strength of the evidence against him. Then he would have to turn around and argue, to prove prejudice, that his important witnesses had been lost, thus impairing his strong defense. The government would have to argue that its case was weak, justifying delay for more investigation. This all seems reason enough to reject the idea that pre-accusation delay is actionable in the absence of bad faith on the part of the government.

Dismissal of indictments for pre-accusation delay, in the absence of bad faith, would also raise separation of powers problems. For example, in United States v. Crouch, 84 F.3d 1497 (5th Cir.1996) (en banc), the defendants, who were charged with bank fraud, argued that their indictments should be dismissed due to pre-accusation delay of seven years. They attributed the delay in their case to "lack of manpower and the low priority which this investigation was assigned." This resulted from "the failure of the Executive Branch and the Department of Justice to request sufficient funding and to assign appropriate priorities." The court responded to these contentions as follows:

> What are we to make of all this? Are we to say that there would be no due process violation if the President had vigorously and timely requested additional funds to investigate and prosecute these cases, but Congress had refused? Or, that even so we will find a due process violation because Congress shouldn't have refused? Of course, funds must come from somewhere. Are we to say that such additional funding is better than increasing taxes or the deficit or decreasing funding for some other programs? Are we to judge whether financial institution fraud should be assigned a higher priority than drug or other offenses? It seems to us that all those decisions are quintessentially the business of either the legislative or the executive branch, or both, rather than the judiciary. * * *

> Accordingly, we * * * hold that for preindictment delay to violate the due process clause it must not only cause the accused substantial, actual prejudice, but the delay must also have been intentionally undertaken by the government for the purpose of gaining some tactical advantage over the accused in the contemplated prosecution or for some other impermissible, bad faith purpose.

It must be remembered that the limits of Due Process protection for pre-indictment delay are set within the premise that "[t]he primary safeguard against unreasonable prosecutorial delay is the statute of limitations, not the Constitution." United States v. Hagler, 700 F.3d 1091 (7th Cir. 2012). So for example, the defendant does not establish prejudice under the Due Process Clause simply because memories may have faded. That is so because "statutes of limitations reflect a legislative judgment that so long as prosecutions are brought within the designated timeframe, then, notwithstanding the possible loss of crucial evidence or failure of memory, a defendant will be able to adequately defend himself." Id. Moreover, faded recollection affects both prosecution and defense witnesses.

C. ASSESSING SPEEDY TRIAL CLAIMS

BARKER V. WINGO
Supreme Court of the United States, 1972.
407 U.S. 514.

JUSTICE POWELL delivered the opinion of the Court.

* * *

On July 20, 1958, in Christian County, Kentucky, an elderly couple was beaten to death by intruders wielding an iron tire tool. Two suspects, Silas Manning and Willie Barker, the petitioner, were arrested shortly thereafter. The grand jury indicted them on September 15. Counsel was appointed on September 17, and Barker's trial was set for October 21. The Commonwealth had a stronger case against Manning, and it believed that Barker could not be convicted unless Manning testified against him. Manning was naturally unwilling to incriminate himself. Accordingly, on October 23, the day Silas Manning was brought to trial, the Commonwealth sought and obtained the first of what was to be a series of 16 continuances of Barker's trial. Barker made no objection. By first convicting Manning, the Commonwealth would remove possible problems of self-incrimination and would be able to assure his testimony against Barker.

The Commonwealth encountered more than a few difficulties in its prosecution of Manning. The first trial ended in a hung jury. A second trial resulted in a conviction, but the Kentucky Court of Appeals reversed because of the admission of evidence obtained by an illegal search. At his third trial, Manning was again convicted, and the Court of Appeals again reversed because the trial court had not granted a change of venue. A fourth trial resulted in a hung jury. Finally, after five trials, Manning was convicted, in March 1962, of murdering one victim, and after a sixth trial, in December 1962, he was convicted of murdering the other.

The Christian County Circuit Court holds three terms each year—in February, June, and September. Barker's initial trial was to take place in the September term of 1958. The first continuance postponed it until the

February 1959 term. The second continuance was granted for one month only. Every term thereafter for as long as the Manning prosecutions were in process, the Commonwealth routinely moved to continue Barker's case to the next term. When the case was continued from the June 1959 term until the following September, Barker, having spent 10 months in jail, obtained his release by posting a $5,000 bond. He thereafter remained free in the community until his trial. Barker made no objection, through his counsel, to the first 11 continuances.

When on February 12, 1962, the Commonwealth moved for the twelfth time to continue the case until the following term, Barker's counsel filed a motion to dismiss the indictment. The motion to dismiss was denied two weeks later, and the Commonwealth's motion for a continuance was granted. The Commonwealth was granted further continuances in June 1962 and September 1962, to which Barker did not object.

In February 1963, the first term of court following Manning's final conviction, the Commonwealth moved to set Barker's trial for March 19. But on the day scheduled for trial, it again moved for a continuance until the June term. It gave as its reason the illness of the ex-sheriff who was the chief investigating officer in the case. To this continuance, Barker objected unsuccessfully.

The witness was still unable to testify in June, and the trial, which had been set for June 19, was continued again until the September term over Barker's objection. This time the court announced that the case would be dismissed for lack of prosecution if it were not tried during the next term. The final trial date was set for October 9, 1963. On that date, Barker again moved to dismiss the indictment, and this time specified that his right to a speedy trial had been violated. The motion was denied; the trial commenced with Manning as the chief prosecution witness; Barker was convicted and given a life sentence.

* * *

The right to a speedy trial is generically different from any of the other rights enshrined in the Constitution for the protection of the accused. * * * [T]here is a societal interest in providing a speedy trial which exists separate from, and at times in opposition to, the interests of the accused. The inability of courts to provide a prompt trial has contributed to a large backlog of cases in urban courts which, among other things, enables defendants to negotiate more effectively for pleas of guilty to lesser offenses and otherwise manipulate the system. In addition, persons released on bond for lengthy periods awaiting trial have an opportunity to commit other crimes. * * * Moreover, the longer an accused is free awaiting trial, the more tempting becomes his opportunity to jump bail and escape. Finally, delay between arrest and punishment may have a detrimental effect on rehabilitation.

If an accused cannot make bail, he is generally confined, as was Barker for 10 months, in a local jail. This contributes to the overcrowding and generally deplorable state of those institutions. Lengthy exposure to these conditions has a destructive effect on human character and makes the rehabilitation of the individual offender much more difficult. * * * Finally, lengthy pretrial detention is costly. * * * In addition, society loses wages which might have been earned, and it must often support families of incarcerated breadwinners.

A second difference between the right to speedy trial and the accused's other constitutional rights is that deprivation of the right may work to the accused's advantage. Delay is not an uncommon defense tactic. As the time between the commission of the crime and trial lengthens, witnesses may become unavailable or their memories may fade. If the witnesses support the prosecution, its case will be weakened, sometimes seriously so. And it is the prosecution which carries the burden of proof. Thus, unlike the right to counsel or the right to be free from compelled self-incrimination, deprivation of the right to speedy trial does not *per se* prejudice the accused's ability to defend himself.

Finally, and perhaps most importantly, the right to speedy trial is a more vague concept than other procedural rights. It is, for example, impossible to determine with precision when the right has been denied. * * * As a consequence, there is no fixed point in the criminal process when the State can put the defendant to the choice of either exercising or waiving the right to a speedy trial. * * *

The amorphous quality of the right also leads to the unsatisfactorily severe remedy of dismissal of the indictment when the right has been deprived. This is indeed a serious consequence because it means that a defendant who may be guilty of a serious crime will go free, without having been tried. Such a remedy is more serious than an exclusionary rule or a reversal for a new trial, but it is the only possible remedy.

* * *

Perhaps because the speedy trial right is so slippery, two rigid approaches are urged upon us as ways of eliminating some of the uncertainty which courts experience in protecting the right. The first suggestion is that we hold that the Constitution requires a criminal defendant to be offered a trial within a specified time period. * * *

But such a result would require this Court to engage in legislative or rulemaking activity, rather than in the adjudicative process to which we should confine our efforts. * * * We find no constitutional basis for holding that the speedy trial right can be quantified into a specified number of days or months. * * *

The second suggested alternative would restrict consideration of the right to those cases in which the accused has demanded a speedy trial. * * *

Such an approach, by presuming waiver of a fundamental right from inaction, is inconsistent with this Court's pronouncements on waiver of constitutional rights. * * *

The nature of the speedy trial right does make it impossible to pinpoint a precise time in the process when the right must be asserted or waived, but that fact does not argue for placing the burden of protecting the right solely on defendants. A defendant has no duty to bring himself to trial; the State has that duty as well as the duty of insuring that the trial is consistent with due process. Moreover, for the reasons earlier expressed, society has a particular interest in bringing swift prosecutions, and society's representatives are the ones who should protect that interest.

* * *

We reject, therefore, the rule that a defendant who fails to demand a speedy trial forever waives his right. This does not mean, however, that the defendant has no responsibility to assert his right. We think the better rule is that the defendant's assertion of or failure to assert his right to a speedy trial is one of the factors to be considered in an inquiry into the deprivation of the right. Such a formulation * * * allows the trial court to exercise a judicial discretion based on the circumstances * * *. It would permit, for example, a court to attach a different weight to a situation in which the defendant knowingly fails to object from a situation in which his attorney acquiesces in long delay without adequately informing his client, or from a situation in which no counsel is appointed. It would also allow a court to weigh the frequency and force of the objections as opposed to attaching significant weight to a purely *pro forma* objection.

* * * We have shown above that the right to a speedy trial is unique in its uncertainty as to when and under what circumstances it must be asserted or may be deemed waived. But the rule we announce today, which comports with constitutional principles, places the primary burden on the courts and the prosecutors to assure that cases are brought to trial. We hardly need add that if delay is attributable to the defendant, then his waiver may be given effect under standard waiver doctrine, the demand rule aside.

* * *

A balancing test necessarily compels courts to approach speedy trial cases on an *ad hoc* basis. We can do little more than identify some of the factors which courts should assess in determining whether a particular defendant has been deprived of his right. Though some might express them in different ways, we identify four such factors: Length of delay, the reason for the delay, the defendant's assertion of his right, and prejudice to the defendant.

The length of the delay is to some extent a triggering mechanism. Until there is some delay which is presumptively prejudicial, there is no necessity for inquiry into the other factors that go into the balance. Nevertheless, because of the imprecision of the right to speedy trial, the length of delay that will provoke such an inquiry is necessarily dependent upon the peculiar circumstances of the case. To take but one example, the delay that can be tolerated for an ordinary street crime is considerably less than for a serious, complex conspiracy charge.

Closely related to length of delay is the reason the government assigns to justify the delay. Here, too, different weights should be assigned to different reasons. A deliberate attempt to delay the trial in order to hamper the defense should be weighted heavily against the government. A more neutral reason such as negligence or overcrowded courts should be weighted less heavily but nevertheless should be considered since the ultimate responsibility for such circumstances must rest with the government rather than with the defendant. Finally, a valid reason, such as a missing witness, should serve to justify appropriate delay.

We have already discussed the third factor, the defendant's responsibility to assert his right. Whether and how a defendant asserts his right is closely related to the other factors we have mentioned. * * * The more serious the deprivation, the more likely a defendant is to complain. The defendant's assertion of his speedy trial right, then, is entitled to strong evidentiary weight in determining whether the defendant is being deprived of the right. We emphasize that failure to assert the right will make it difficult for a defendant to prove that he was denied a speedy trial.

A fourth factor is prejudice to the defendant. Prejudice, of course, should be assessed in the light of the interests of defendants which the speedy trial right was designed to protect. This Court has identified three such interests: (i) to prevent oppressive pretrial incarceration; (ii) to minimize anxiety and concern of the accused; and (iii) to limit the possibility that the defense will be impaired. Of these, the most serious is the last, because the inability of a defendant adequately to prepare his case skews the fairness of the entire system. If witnesses die or disappear during a delay, the prejudice is obvious. * * *

We have discussed previously the societal disadvantages of lengthy pretrial incarceration, but obviously the disadvantages for the accused who cannot obtain his release are even more serious. The time spent in jail awaiting trial has a detrimental impact on the individual. It often means loss of a job; it disrupts family life; and it enforces idleness. * * * Moreover, if a defendant is locked up, he is hindered in his ability to gather evidence, contact witnesses, or otherwise prepare his defense. * * * Finally, even if an accused is not incarcerated prior to trial, he is still disadvantaged by restraints on his liberty and by living under a cloud of anxiety, suspicion, and often hostility.

We regard none of the four factors identified above as either a necessary or sufficient condition to the finding of a deprivation of the right of speedy trial. Rather, they are related factors and must be considered together with such other circumstances as may be relevant.

* * *

The difficulty of the task of balancing these factors is illustrated by this case, which we consider to be close. It is clear that the length of delay between arrest and trial—well over five years—was extraordinary. Only seven months of that period can be attributed to a strong excuse, the illness of the ex-sheriff who was in charge of the investigation. Perhaps some delay would have been permissible under ordinary circumstances, so that Manning could be utilized as a witness in Barker's trial, but more than four years was too long a period, particularly since a good part of that period was attributable to the Commonwealth's failure or inability to try Manning under circumstances that comported with due process.

Two counterbalancing factors, however, outweigh these deficiencies. The first is that prejudice was minimal. Of course, Barker was prejudiced to some extent by living for over four years under a cloud of suspicion and anxiety. Moreover, although he was released on bond for most of the period, he did spend 10 months in jail before trial. But there is no claim that any of Barker's witnesses died or otherwise became unavailable owing to the delay. The trial transcript indicates only two very minor lapses of memory—one on the part of a prosecution witness—which were in no way significant to the outcome.

More important than the absence of serious prejudice, is the fact that Barker did not want a speedy trial. * * * Instead the record strongly suggests that while he hoped to take advantage of the delay in which he had acquiesced, and thereby obtain a dismissal of the charges, he definitely did not want to be tried.

* * *

The probable reason for Barker's attitude was that he was gambling on Manning's acquittal. The evidence was not very strong against Manning, as the reversals and hung juries suggest, and Barker undoubtedly thought that if Manning were acquitted, he would never be tried.

* * *

We do not hold that there may never be a situation in which an indictment may be dismissed on speedy trial grounds where the defendant has failed to object to continuances. There may be a situation in which the defendant was represented by incompetent counsel, was severely prejudiced, or even cases in which the continuances were granted *ex parte*. But barring extraordinary circumstances, we would be reluctant indeed to rule that a defendant was denied this constitutional right on a record that strongly indicates as does this one, that the defendant did not want a speedy trial. We hold, therefore, that Barker was not deprived of his due process right to a speedy trial.

The judgment of the Court of Appeals is affirmed.

JUSTICE WHITE, with whom JUSTICE BRENNAN joins, concurring.

Although the Court rejects petitioner's speedy trial claim * * *, it is apparent that had Barker not so clearly acquiesced in the major delays * * * the result would have been otherwise. * * *

Application of the Barker Test: Doggett v. United States

In Doggett v. United States, 505 U.S. 647 (1992), the Court applied and elaborated upon the *Barker* factors. It found that an 8 1/2 year-delay between Doggett's indictment and trial violated his Sixth Amendment right to a speedy trial, even though Doggett knew nothing about the indictment during that delay. Doggett was indicted on federal drug charges, but he left the country before he could be informed of the indictment. Two years after leaving, he returned to the United States, passed unhindered through Customs, married, went to college, found a job, lived openly under his own name, and engaged in no further criminal misconduct. Six years after his return, the Marshal's Service ran a credit check on several thousand people subject to outstanding arrest warrants and, within minutes, found where Doggett lived and worked. He was arrested within days of the credit check. Up to the time of his arrest, Doggett was never aware of the fact that he had been indicted more than eight years earlier.

Justice Souter wrote the majority opinion for five Justices. He addressed the first *Barker* factor—whether delay before trial was "uncommonly long"—as a "double enquiry." He explained as follows:

> Simply to trigger a speedy trial analysis, an accused must allege that the interval between accusation and trial has crossed the threshold dividing ordinary from "presumptively prejudicial" delay, * * *. If the accused makes this showing, the court must then consider, as one factor among several, the extent to which the delay stretches beyond the bare minimum needed to trigger judicial examination of the claim. This latter enquiry is significant to the speedy trial analysis

because * * * the presumption that pretrial delay has prejudiced the accused intensifies over time.

So to trigger a *Barker* enquiry, the defendant must show that the delay was presumptively prejudicial. The *Doggett* majority stated that lower courts have generally undertaken the *Barker* enquiry when the period of postaccusation delay "approaches one year."[1] The Court therefore had no trouble finding that the "extraordinary" delay in Doggett's case was sufficient "to trigger the speedy trial enquiry."

As to the second *Barker* factor, concerning responsibility for the delay, Justice Souter relied on the findings of the lower court that the delay occurring after Doggett returned to the United States was attributable to the government. He concluded that "while the Government's lethargy may have reflected no more than Doggett's relative unimportance in the world of drug trafficking, it was still findable negligence, and the finding stands."

As to the third *Barker* factor, concerning the defendant's diligence in asserting his speedy trial rights, Justice Souter again relied on the findings of the lower court that Doggett was unaware of his indictment until he was arrested. Had that not been the case, the third factor would have been "weighed heavily against him." Thus, Justice Souter implied that a person who knows he is indicted, and who is at large, will lose his speedy trial claim because of his failure to timely assert it, even if he is not being diligently pursued by the authorities.

The fourth *Barker* factor, that of prejudice due to the delay, presented the most difficult problem for the majority, because Doggett was neither incarcerated nor aware of his indictment during the delay. Justice Souter noted that there was more to the "prejudice" factor than incarceration and anxiety over the indictment:

> We have observed in prior cases that unreasonable delay between formal accusation and trial threatens to produce more than one sort of harm, including * * * the possibility that the accused's defense will be impaired by dimming memories and loss of exculpatory evidence. * * * [T]he inability of a defendant adequately to prepare his case skews the fairness of the entire system.

After holding that the defendant could be prejudiced by the delay even though he was not incarcerated or under any anxiety during that time, the majority addressed the Government's argument that Doggett's claim should fail because he had "failed to make any affirmative showing that the delay weakened his ability to raise specific defenses, elicit specific testimony, or produce specific items of evidence." Justice Souter responded

---

[1] See also Joseph, Speedy Trial Rights in Application, 48 Fordham L.Rev. 611 (1980) (quoted in *Doggett*, noting a general consensus that a delay is presumptively prejudicial if it is longer than eight months, and that there is general agreement that a delay of less than five months is not presumptively prejudicial).

to this argument by stating that "consideration of prejudice is not limited to the specifically demonstrable" and that "affirmative proof of particularized prejudice is not essential to every speedy trial claim." He elaborated as follows:

> Our speedy trial standards recognize that pretrial delay is often both inevitable and wholly justifiable. The government may need time to collect witnesses against the accused, oppose his pretrial motions, or, if he goes into hiding, track him down. We attach great weight to such considerations when balancing them against the costs of going forward with a trial whose probative accuracy the passage of time has begun by degrees to throw into question. Thus, in this case, if the Government had pursued Doggett with reasonable diligence from his indictment to his arrest, his speedy trial claim would fail. * * *

> * * * [O]n the other hand, Doggett would prevail if he could show that the Government had intentionally held back in its prosecution of him to gain some impermissible advantage at trial. * * *

> Between diligent prosecution and bad-faith delay, official negligence in bringing an accused to trial occupies the middle ground. While not compelling relief in every case where bad-faith delay would make relief virtually automatic, neither is negligence automatically tolerable simply because the accused cannot demonstrate exactly how it has prejudiced him. * * *

> Although negligence is obviously to be weighed more lightly than a deliberate intent to harm the accused's defense, it still falls on the wrong side of the divide between acceptable and unacceptable reasons for delaying a criminal prosecution once it has begun. And such is the nature of the prejudice presumed that the weight we assign to official negligence compounds over time as the presumption of evidentiary prejudice grows. Thus, our toleration of such negligence varies inversely with its protractedness, and its consequent threat to the fairness of the accused's trial. * * *

> To be sure, to warrant granting relief, negligence unaccompanied by particularized trial prejudice must have lasted longer than negligence demonstrably causing such prejudice. But even so, the Government's egregious persistence in failing to prosecute Doggett is clearly sufficient.

Applying these factors, Justice Souter concluded that Doggett was entitled to dismissal of the indictment because the Government's negligence caused a delay "six times as long as that generally sufficient to trigger judicial review" and the presumption of prejudice was "neither extenuated, as by the defendant's acquiescence, nor persuasively rebutted."

Justice O'Connor wrote a short dissenting opinion in *Doggett*. She would have required a showing of actual prejudice. She also noted that "delay is a two-edged sword" because the Government bears the burden of proof beyond a reasonable doubt, and "the passage of time may make it difficult or impossible for the Government to carry this burden."

Justice Thomas, joined by Chief Justice Rehnquist and Justice Scalia, wrote a lengthy dissent in which he argued that the Speedy Trial Clause provides direct protection against only two "evils": 1) "oppressive and undue incarceration;" and 2) the "anxiety and concern accompanying public accusation." Because Doggett suffered neither of these burdens during the delay, Justice Thomas would have dismissed the speedy trial claim even if Doggett had proven that the passage of time had prejudiced his defense. In Justice Thomas's view, any possibility that a defendant may not be able to defend himself due to a pretrial delay was adequately protected by the Due Process Clause and by statutes of limitations.

Justice Thomas argued that the Speedy Trial Clause could not logically be concerned with prejudice to the defense resulting from pretrial delay. He explained as follows:

> [P]rejudice to the defense stems from the interval between crime and trial, which is quite distinct from the interval between accusation and trial. * * * A defendant prosecuted 10 years after a crime is just as hampered in his ability to defend himself whether he was indicted the week after the crime or the week before the trial—but no one would suggest that the Clause protects him in the latter situation, where the delay did not substantially impair his liberty, either through oppressive incarceration or the anxiety of known criminal charges. * * * The initiation of a formal criminal prosecution is simply irrelevant to whether the defense has been prejudiced by delay.

QUESTIONS AFTER DOGGETT

Who suffers more from a pretrial delay: a person who knows he is being investigated but has not been arrested, or a person like Doggett who has been indicted but knows nothing about it? If you think that a person who knows he is being investigated suffers more than a person like Doggett, does that mean that Justice Thomas is correct in concluding that *Barker's* fuzzy prejudice analysis is flawed? Or does it mean that the Court in *Marion* was wrong when it denied the protection of the Speedy Trial Clause to persons who have not yet been arrested or charged?

Justice O'Connor's point about the government's ability to prove its case being hampered by delay is made in Green, "Hare and Hounds": The Fugitive Defendant's Constitutional Right to be Pursued, 56 Brooklyn L.Rev. 439, 507 (1990) ("the passage of time is more likely to hurt the prosecution than the defense which, after all, has no obligation to call witnesses or present evidence, but need only, and in many cases does only, put the government to its proof").

Excusable Delay

Doggett holds that when the government has a good reason for a post-charge delay, the defendant's burden of showing prejudice is substantially increased. What constitutes excusable delay? In United States v. Vassell, 970 F.2d 1162 (2nd Cir.1992), the court held that a seven-month delay did not amount to a Speedy Trial Clause violation where the government spent most of that time trying to get Vassell's co-defendant to take a deal and testify against Vassell. The court stated:

> A guilty plea takes time to negotiate. A defendant may initially reject the plea offered by the government. Because prosecutors must obtain approval of a plea from their superiors, negotiations may drag on almost interminably. At some point the process may become so extreme as to prejudice co-defendants who are either not offered a plea, or who reject the plea offer. However, we are not called upon to establish a rigid time table prescribing how long the government may take to procure a guilty plea. Rather, consistent with the ad hoc balancing required by *Barker*, we hold only that a seven-month delay in a complex case is not transformed into a Sixth Amendment violation just because the government sought the delay to encourage a co-defendant to testify against a remaining defendant at trial.

In United States v. Loud Hawk, 474 U.S. 302 (1986), a majority of the Supreme Court concluded that "an interlocutory appeal by the Government [an appeal on a judge's ruling before a verdict has been rendered] ordinarily is a valid reason that justifies delay." Justice Powell's opinion observed that in assessing whether the delay is justifiable, the factors that might be examined "include the strength of the Government's position on the appealed issue, the importance of the issue in the posture of the case, and— in some cases—the seriousness of the crime." The opinion also stated that defendants ordinarily cannot use the delay caused by their *own* interlocutory appeals to support a speedy trial claim. Justice Marshall's dissenting opinion, joined by Justices Brennan, Blackmun, and Stevens, argued that the court of appeals, which took over five years to decide two interlocutory appeals, one of which was expedited, delayed a "patently unreasonable" amount of time and that the prosecutor's good faith could not discharge the responsibility of a court to decide an appeal within a reasonable period of time.

Defendant's Diligence

Under *Barker* and *Doggett*, a defendant's diligence in asserting his speedy trial right is a critical factor. Exemplary is United States v. Aguirre,

994 F.2d 1454 (9th Cir.1993). Aguirre knew about his indictment during the five-year period before he was arrested. While the five-year delay was presumptively prejudicial under *Doggett*, the court noted that the government had diligently pursued the defendant during that period. Because the delay was not attributable to the government but to Aguirre's evasive actions, Aguirre was required to show prejudice, and this he could not do. But the court said that even if Aguirre had shown prejudice, his speedy trial claim would have been denied:

> Where, as here, the government diligently pursues the defendant and the defendant is aware that the government is trying to find him, even severe prejudice would still not be enough to tip the balance in his favor. Here Aguirre knew his charges were pending, but [chose not to appear]; the government, on the other hand, conducted a reasonably diligent investigation to find him. It's true that prejudice can arise with time, but it's equally true in situations like Aguirre's that the defendant, not the government, is in the best position to stop the clock and avoid the damage.

It goes without saying that to the extent the trial is delayed because the defendant is making pre-trial motions that are being considered and disposed of, this will not count against the government in the *Barker/Doggett* calculus. See United States v. Munoz-Amado, 182 F.3d 57 (1st Cir.1999) (rejecting a speedy trial claim and noting that the defendant "ignores the role his many pretrial motions played in causing the nineteen month delay between his indictment and the jury trial").

Delay and Prejudice

The Court in *Doggett* stated that, at some point, delay attributable to the government will be so extended that prejudice will be presumed— meaning that the defendant will not have to show, specifically, how he was prejudiced by the delay. The need to find prejudice thus diminishes as the delay mounts. The eight-year delay in *Doggett* went beyond the point of presumptive prejudice; but where is that point exactly? In United States v. Beamon, 992 F.2d 1009 (9th Cir.1993), the government was responsible for a 17 month delay. While this was long enough to trigger a *Barker-Doggett* inquiry, the court held that it was not long enough "to relieve the defendant of the burden of coming forward with any showing of actual prejudice." Thus forced to show prejudice, the defendant argued that the delay impaired his ability to negotiate a deal with the government. But the court held that "a diminished plea bargaining position does not amount to impairment of defense."[2] Because the defendant could not show that he

---

[2] For another case on the meaning of "prejudice" under *Barker* and *Doggett*, see United States v. Mundt, 29 F.3d 233 (6th Cir.1994) (in a tax prosecution, the defendant suffered no prejudice from a long delay where his "position was and continues to be that he is not subject to the federal tax laws"; that defense is not dependent on witnesses or fresh recollections).

suffered any form of prejudice in trial presentation, his appeal was dismissed.

Thus, under *Doggett*, the term "presumptive prejudice" has two distinct meanings. First, the delay must be so long as to trigger the *Barker-Doggett* inquiry in the first place. In this sense, the delay is presumptively prejudicial when it approaches one year. Second, if the delay is attributable to the government, it might be so long as to be presumptively prejudicial—meaning in this context that the defendant does not need to show specifically how the delay prejudiced him. In *Beamon*, the 17 month delay was presumptively prejudicial in the first (threshold, triggering) sense, but not in the second (balancing) sense. In *Doggett*, the delay was presumptively prejudicial as to both the threshold and the balancing inquiries. See also United States v. Brown, 169 F.3d 344 (6th Cir.1999) ("Given the extraordinary [five-year] delay in this case combined with the fact that the delay was attributable to the government's negligence in pursuing Brown, we conclude that the government did not sufficiently rebut the presumption that its delay did not prejudice Brown's case."); United States v. Graham, 128 F.3d 372 (6th Cir.1997) (eight year delay, much of it due to the trial court's failure to move discovery along and to appoint new counsel for one of the co-defendants; prejudice in *Barker-Doggett* balancing inquiry was presumed due to the length of the delay).

Delay Caused by Appointed Counsel Is Not Attributable to the State: Vermont v. Brillon

The *Barker* test for assessing whether the right to speedy trial is violated focuses in part on "the reason for delay." A speedy trial violation cannot be found unless the delay can be attributed to the state. What happens if the delay is attributable to defense counsel who was *appointed* by the state? In Vermont v. Brillon, 556 U.S. 81 (2009), the lower court found a speedy trial violation by attributing to the state the delays caused by the failure of Brillon's appointed counsel "to move his case forward." But the Supreme Court, in an opinion by Justice Ginsburg, held that "an assigned counsel's failure to move the case forward does not warrant attribution of delay to the state." While the Vermont Defender's office is funded by the State, Justice Ginsburg declared that "the individual counsel here acted only on behalf of Brillon, not the State." Justice Ginsburg noted the problems that would arise if delay by appointed counsel could be considered delay by the state:

A contrary conclusion could encourage appointed counsel to delay proceedings by seeking unreasonable continuances, hoping thereby to obtain a dismissal of the indictment on speedy-trial grounds. Trial courts might well respond by viewing continuance requests made by appointed counsel with skepticism, concerned that even an apparently genuine need for more time is in reality a delay tactic.

Justice Ginsburg noted however that "the general rule attributing to the defendant delay caused by assigned counsel is not absolute." Specifically, delay resulting from a "systemic breakdown in the public defender system" could be charged to the State. But Justice Ginsburg found "nothing in the record suggests, that institutional problems caused any part of the delay in Brillon's case."[3]

D. REMEDIES FOR SPEEDY TRIAL VIOLATIONS

In Strunk v. United States, 412 U.S. 434 (1973), the Court considered what remedies are available when the defendant's right to a speedy trial has been violated. The court of appeals had found a speedy trial violation, but declared that the "extreme" remedy of dismissal of the charges with prejudice was unwarranted. The court of appeals thought that a more appropriate remedy would be reduction in Strunk's sentence to compensate for the period of unnecessary delay. But Chief Justice Burger's opinion for a unanimous Court rejected this alternative. The Chief Justice wrote that "[i]n light of the policies which underlie the right to a speedy trial, dismissal must remain, as *Barker* noted, the only possible remedy."

Can you imagine situations in which you might find a speedy trial violation but *not* require dismissal? For example, if the only form of prejudice suffered by delay was incarceration, would it make sense to simply reduce the sentence of a defendant who was convicted after a delayed trial? Why is dismissal necessary in such a case?

If *Strunk* really means that there is only one remedy for all speedy trial violations and that remedy is the drastic one of dismissal, how likely is it that the courts will find speedy trial violations in the first place? Professor Arkin, in Speedy Criminal Appeal: A Right Without a Remedy, 74 Minn.L.Rev. 437, 482 (1990), argues that because of the extreme, exclusive remedy provided by *Barker* and *Strunk,* courts have "refused to find speedy trial violations except in the most outlandish cases" and that the *Barker-Strunk* remedy "effectively gutted the right."

E. THE RIGHT TO SPEEDY SENTENCING

In Betterman v. Montana, 136 S.Ct. 1609 (2016), Justice Ginsburg wrote for the Court as it held that the Speedy Trial Clause does not apply to delayed sentencing. Betterman failed to appear in court on domestic relation charges. He pled guilty to bail-jumping and was jailed for over 14 months prior to sentencing due to delay in preparation of the pre-sentence report, the trial court's ruling on motions, and the trial court's setting a

---

[3]   Justice Breyer, joined by Justice Stevens, wrote a short dissent, arguing that the writ of certiorari should have been dismissed as improvidently granted.

sentencing hearing. The Montana Supreme Court rejected Betterman's claim that his speedy trial right had been denied and the U.S. Supreme Court agreed.

Justice Ginsburg described the three phases of criminal proceedings: the investigation and decision to charge a suspect, the disposition by trial or plea, and sentencing. She identified statutes of limitations as providing the primary protection against delay, with the Due Process Clause protecting against fundamentally unfair prosecutorial conduct; and the Speedy Trial Clause as providing the primary protection against delay in the second stage during which a defendant is presumed innocent until final disposition. She found that the Speedy Trial Clause was concerned with presumptively innocent individuals and that the Clause loses force upon conviction.

Because dismissal of charges is the remedy for a speedy trial violation, Justice Ginsburg found that such a remedy would be an unwarranted windfall for a convicted defendant whose sentence is delayed. She rejected Betterman's argument that because guilty pleas are so prevalent, sentencing is the real forum for dispute resolution and the Clause should require speedy sentences. She observed that a central feature of contemporary sentences is preparation of pre-sentence reports that often will delay sentencing.

Justice Ginsburg pointed out that the inapplicability of the Speedy Trial Clause to sentencing did not mean that a defendant has no protection against undue delay. She pointed to court rules like Fed. Rule Crim. Proc. 32(b)(1), which directs the court to "impose sentence without unnecessary delay," and noted that a defendant "retains an interest in a sentencing proceeding that is fundamentally fair" and comports with due process.

Justice Thomas, joined by Justice Alito, concurred and agreed "with the Court that the Sixth Amendment's Speedy Trial Clause does not apply to sentencing proceedings, except perhaps to bifurcated sentencing proceedings where sentencing enhancements operate as functional elements of a greater offense" and with the Court's judgment not to elaborate on the role of the Due Process Clause in a case in which no due process claim was raised.

Justice Sotomayor also concurred and, after observing that the Court left open what a defendant might have to show to make out a Due Process Clause violation based on a delay in sentencing, suggested that "the *Barker* factors capture many of the concerns posed in the sentencing delay context and that because the *Barker* test is flexible, it will allow courts to take account of any differences between trial and sentencing delays."

Justice Thomas's concurrence responded to Justice Sotomayor's suggestion by saying he would not prejudge the matter and that the *Barker* factors "may not necessarily translate to the delayed sentencing context."

F. BEYOND THE CONSTITUTION: STATUTORY AND JUDICIAL TIME LIMITS

Although not required by the Sixth Amendment, a large number of jurisdictions have, by statute or court rule, set time limits for bringing cases to trial. The statutes and rules that have been adopted differ greatly, as each jurisdiction is free to set up any protective system that it wishes. Because of these statutes and rules, there has been a shift from constitutional litigation to statutory interpretation.

The Federal Speedy Trial Act

One important statute is the Speedy Trial Act of 1974. 18 U.S.C.A. §§ 3161–74. The Act provides definite time periods for bringing an accused to trial. The operation of the Speedy Trial Act was described by the Court in Zedner v. United States, 547 U.S. 489 (2006):

> [T]he Speedy Trial Act generally requires a trial to begin within 70 days of the filing of an information or indictment or the defendant's initial appearance, 18 U.S.C. § 3161(c)(1), but the Act recognizes that criminal cases vary widely and that there are valid reasons for greater delay in particular cases. To provide the necessary flexibility, the Act includes a long and detailed list of periods of delay that are excluded in computing the time within which trial must start. See § 3161(h). For example, the Act excludes "delay resulting from other proceedings concerning the defendant," § 3161(h)(1), "delay resulting from the absence or unavailability of the defendant or an essential witness," § 3161(h)(3), "delay resulting from the fact that the defendant is mentally incompetent or physically unable to stand trial," § 3161(h)(4), and "[a] reasonable period of delay when the defendant is joined for trial with a codefendant as to whom the time for trial has not run and no motion for severance has been granted," § 3161(h)(7).

> Much of the Act's flexibility is furnished by § 3161(h)(8), which governs ends-of-justice continuances * * *. This provision permits a district court to grant a continuance and to exclude the resulting delay if the court, after considering certain factors, makes on-the-record findings that the ends of justice served by granting the continuance outweigh the public's and defendant's interests in a speedy trial. This provision gives the district court discretion—within limits and subject to specific procedures—to accommodate limited delays for case-specific needs.

Dismissal with or Without Prejudice

If the applicable time limits of the Speedy Trial Act are not adhered to, charges against the defendant may be dismissed *either with or without prejudice.*[4] See 18 U.S.C.A. § 3162(a)(1)(2). The Court in *Zedner* described how the appropriate remedy is determined:

> In making that choice [between dismissal with or without prejudice], the court must take into account, among other things, "the seriousness of the offense; the facts and circumstances of the case which led to the dismissal; and the impact of a reprosecution on the administration of [the Act] and on the administration of justice." § 3162(a)(2).

> This scheme is designed to promote compliance with the Act without needlessly subverting important criminal prosecutions. The more severe sanction (dismissal with prejudice) is available for use where appropriate, and the knowledge that a violation could potentially result in the imposition of this sanction gives the prosecution a powerful incentive to be careful about compliance. The less severe sanction (dismissal without prejudice) lets the court avoid unduly impairing the enforcement of federal criminal laws—though even this sanction imposes some costs on the prosecution and the court, which further encourages compliance. When an indictment is dismissed without prejudice, the prosecutor may of course seek—and in the great majority of cases will be able to obtain—a new indictment, for even if "the period prescribed by the applicable statute of limitations has expired, a new indictment may be returned . . . within six calendar months of the date of the dismissal." § 3288.

In United States v. Taylor, 487 U.S. 326 (1988), the Supreme Court held that an indictment should have been dismissed *without* prejudice where the defendant failed to appear for his trial on federal narcotics charges, which was scheduled one day prior to expiration of the statutory period, and subsequently the government exceeded by 15 days the period permitted between the defendant's arrest and the filing of a superseding indictment. Justice Blackmun wrote for the court and reasoned that the statute provides no preference for whether a dismissal should be with or without prejudice; it permits district courts to exercise sound discretion. The Court noted that the statute sets forth specific factors—seriousness of the offense, facts and circumstances leading to dismissal, and the impact of a reprosecution on the speedy trial process and the administration of justice—as being "among others" that the Court may consider in ruling on a motion to dismiss. The Court determined that prejudice to the defendant was also a factor. It observed that the district court did not explain why these factors justified a dismissal with prejudice and that it had ignored the "brevity of the delay" as well as Taylor's own "illicit contribution to the delay" (i.e., his failure to appear).

---

[4]   Some states require dismissals to be with prejudice. See, e.g., Alaska Crim.R. 45(g); Wash. CrRLJ 3.3(h).

Where the defendant has already served a good part of his sentence by the time of appeal, the preferred remedy for a Speedy Trial Act violation is a dismissal of the indictment. The court applied this preference in United States v. Blackwell, 12 F.3d 44 (5th Cir.1994):

> [W]hile the maximum time of incarceration Blackwell could receive for committing the offense of impersonating a federal officer is three years, he has already been incarcerated for over two years. * * * [A] reprosecution would work a manifest injustice upon Blackwell, given the time he has already effectively "served" for this conviction which we reverse today due to the Speedy Trial Act violation in this case.

Time Limits of the Speedy Trial Act Cannot Be Waived Prospectively: Zedner v. United States

The Court in Zedner v. United States, 547 U.S. 489 (2006), considered the validity and relevance of the defendant's waiver of rights under the Speedy Trial Act. The defendant had asked for a long adjournment (which of course was excludible delay), but the trial court was concerned that the defendant might waive the right "only for so long as it is convenient for you to waive." So the trial judge said "if I am going to give you that long an adjournment, I will have to take a waiver for all time." After conferring with counsel, the defendant signed a waiver of speedy trial rights. After a variety of delays—including withdrawal of counsel, a competency determination, and a motion to dismiss for violation of the Speedy Trial Act—the trial finally began, six years after the defendant was indicted. Justice Alito, writing for the Court, declared that the protections of the Act are not prospectively waivable, most importantly because the Act protects more than the rights of the defendant:

> If the Act were designed solely to protect a defendant's right to a speedy trial, it would make sense to allow a defendant to waive the application of the Act. But the Act was designed with the public interest firmly in mind. That public interest cannot be served, the Act recognizes, if defendants may opt out of the Act entirely. * * * Because defendants may be content to remain on pretrial release, and indeed may welcome delay, it is unsurprising that Congress refrained from empowering defendants to make prospective waivers of the Act's application.

The Court distinguished waivers of a completed violation of the Act (for example, by simply not objecting), which are permitted by the Act, from prospective waivers, which are not:

> It is significant that § 3162(a)(2) makes no mention of prospective waivers, and there is no reason to think that Congress wanted to treat prospective and retrospective waivers similarly. Allowing prospective waivers would seriously undermine the Act because there are many

cases—like the case at hand—in which the prosecution, the defense, and the court would all be happy to opt out of the Act, to the detriment of the public interest. The sort of retrospective waiver allowed by § 3161(a)(2) does not pose a comparable danger because the prosecution and the court cannot know until the trial actually starts or the guilty plea is actually entered whether the defendant will forgo moving to dismiss. As a consequence, the prosecution and the court retain a strong incentive to make sure that the trial begins on time.

II. JOINDER AND SEVERANCE

A. SOME GENERAL RULES AND PROBLEMS

The outcome of a criminal case can be affected by the number and nature of charges and defendants joined together. There was a time when the government could only charge one offense in an indictment and was greatly restricted in trying defendants jointly over objection. But that time is long past, largely because of the perceived economies of joinder in an era of scarce resources. In Richardson v. Marsh, 481 U.S. 200 (1987), Justice Scalia, writing for the Court, had this to say about the advantages of joining defendants:

> Joint trials play a vital role in the criminal justice system, accounting for almost one third of federal criminal trials in the past five years. Many joint trials—for example, those involving large conspiracies to import and distribute illegal drugs—involve a dozen or more codefendants. * * * It would impair both the efficiency and the fairness of the criminal justice system to require * * * that prosecutors bring separate proceedings, presenting the same evidence again and again, requiring victims and witnesses to repeat the inconvenience (and sometimes trauma) of testifying, and randomly favoring the last-tried defendants who have the advantage of knowing the prosecution's case beforehand. Joint trials generally serve the interests of justice by avoiding inconsistent verdicts and enabling more accurate assessment of relative culpability—advantages which sometimes operate to the defendant's benefit. Even apart from these tactical considerations, joint trials generally serve the interests of justice by avoiding the scandal and inequity of inconsistent verdicts.

Similar benefits—especially from the government's point of view—can flow from joining multiple counts against a single defendant. But there also are dangers when joinder is effected—most obviously, that defendants will suffer prejudice from the jury's possible tendency to merge defendants and charges into one big guilty verdict.

The Federal Rules of Criminal Procedure attempt to strike a balance of efficiency and fairness through three separate but related rules:

- Rule 8 governs the charges and defendants that can be joined. The Rule provides that charges against a single defendant can be joined if the offenses "are of the same or similar character or are based on the same act or transaction, or are connected with or constitute parts of a common scheme or plan." The Rule further provides that defendants can be joined "if they are alleged to have participated in the same act or transaction, or in the same series of acts or transactions, constituting an offense or offenses."

- Rule 13 permits the court to consolidate separate actions if they could have been joined under Rule 8.

- Rule 14 gives the court discretion to sever or to provide other relief if prejudice would result from joinder.

The principal arguments respecting joinder center around two competing assertions: (1) The defense contends that the government is seeking an unfair advantage by having charges combined in order to brand the defendant as a bad person, to show that "birds of a feather flock together," to reduce a jury's regret at convicting the defendant in a world of imperfect proof, or to establish a "where there's smoke, there's fire" attitude in the trier of fact.[5] (2) The government contends that the defense is trying to separate out issues to wear down the government, to compartmentalize a case in order to weaken it, to increase the odds that witnesses and evidence will become unavailable, or to increase the odds of winning at least one case.[6]

The competing policy considerations—efficiency in the presentation of evidence versus a fair trial on each charge made against a defendant—are best understood in the context of actual cases.

B. JOINDER OF CLAIMS

United States v. Holloway, 1 F.3d 307 (5th Cir.1993), illustrates a simple problem of joinder of claims. Holloway was identified as a culprit in two armed bank robberies. When he was arrested for these robberies, he was found to be carrying a firearm. Holloway had been convicted previously of a felony. The government joined the bank robbery counts with an additional count for felon firearm possession. The government never contended that the gun found on Holloway when he was arrested was the same gun used in the bank robberies. Holloway requested a severance of the felon firearm possession count from the other counts, but this was denied. The court of appeals, however, found that the firearms count was improperly joined under Rule 8(a), and therefore that the trial court abused

---

[5] Conversely, the defendant sometimes may want weak charges combined with strong ones in the hope that reasonable doubts as to the weak ones will carry over to the others.

[6] Usually the government wants to win at least one case. But defendants may believe that their best strategy is "divide and conquer."

its discretion in failing to sever it. The court analyzed the severance question in light of the standards of Rule 8(a):

> * * * Plainly speaking, we can see no basis for the United States Attorney to have included this weapons charge in the indictment in the first place unless he was seeking to get before the jury evidence that likely would be otherwise inadmissible, i.e., that Holloway was a convicted felon and that he had a weapon on his person when arrested. * * *
>
> We thus conclude that this remote weapons charge should never have been joined with the other counts of Holloway's indictment in the first place. [By joining] the weapons charge with the robbery charges, the jury emphatically was told that Holloway was a bad and dangerous person "by his very nature" and that a felon who carried a gun was just the sort of character who was most likely to have committed the robberies charged in the indictment. In short, Holloway was unjustifiably tried, at least in part, on the basis of who he was, and not on the basis of the material evidence presented against him.

The *Holloway* court noted, however, that if evidence of the gun possession had been admissible as proof on the robbery charges, or if the gun had been used in the robbery, it would have been a different case and joinder would have been permitted.

Under Rule 404(b) of the Federal Rules of Evidence, evidence of the defendant's uncharged bad acts cannot be admitted to show he is a bad person, but they can be admitted where relevant to prove intent, knowledge, identity, or any other "non-character" issue.[7] Thus, if evidence of a criminal act would be admissible to prove a different crime, there is no prejudice in joining charges for both crimes in a single trial. See United States v. Windom, 19 F.3d 1190 (7th Cir.1994) (gun charge was properly joined with a narcotics charge, "for the same reasons that allow the government to introduce weapons into evidence at narcotics trials"); United States v. Johnson, 462 F.3d 815 (8th Cir. 2006) (firearms charge was sufficiently related to narcotics charge, even though drug activity occurred on the streets and the gun was found in the defendant's girlfriend's apartment: "Johnson's firearms possession could be linked to his need to protect his ongoing distribution of illegal drugs" and so the charged were "part of a common scheme or plan."). Compare United States v. Randazzo, 80 F.3d 623 (1st Cir.1996) (charges of filing false tax returns could not be joined with charges for introducing misbranded or adulterated food into interstate commerce; crimes were completely unrelated and evidence as to one could not be admitted to prove the other).

---

[7] Complete coverage of Rule 404(b) is left for a course in evidence. For an extensive discussion of that Rule, see Saltzburg, Martin and Capra, Federal Rules of Evidence Manual § 404.02 (11th ed. 2015).

It is notable that the trial court in *Holloway* failed to instruct the jury to refrain from using evidence concerning the firearms charge as proof on the robbery charge. Where the judge makes an effort to protect the defendant from prejudicial misjoinder, the risks of reversal are substantially diminished. See Leach v. Kolb, 911 F.2d 1249 (7th Cir.1990) (improper joinder of attempted murder, armed robbery, and attempted armed robbery charges arising from separate incidents did not deprive defendant of a fair trial, where evidence of the defendant's guilt on each charge was overwhelming, and the trial court gave explicit limiting instructions requiring the jury to determine guilt or innocence on each count without reference to guilt or innocence on other charged counts).

C. JOINDER OF DEFENDANTS

It is common to find joinder of defendants in several classes of cases, especially conspiracy cases. Generally, courts express sympathy for the plight of defendants joined in conspiracy cases, but find the Government interest in efficiency to be paramount. The general rule of thumb is that "persons who are indicted together should be tried together." United States v. O'Bryant, 998 F.2d 21 (1st Cir.1993). For example, in Schaffer v. United States, 362 U.S. 511 (1960), defendants were joined on the basis of a conspiracy charge, though the substantive counts charged each defendant with different acts of theft. At the close of the government's case, the trial court dismissed the conspiracy count for lack of proof. But the substantive counts were submitted to the jury and the defendants were convicted. The defendants argued that the only joinder "hook" was the conspiracy charge and once that was dismissed the cases should have been severed. The Supreme Court found, however, that the defendants had not suffered any prejudice warranting severance, because the proof at trial was "carefully compartmentalized" as to each defendant. It noted that, as of the beginning of the trial, the joinder was authorized by Rule 8(b), and it refused to adopt "a hard-and-fast formula that, when a conspiracy count fails, joinder [becomes] error as a matter of law." Justice Douglas, joined by Chief Justice Warren and Justices Black and Brennan, in dissent, found "implicit prejudice" in trying separate offenses in a joint trial, because "a subtle bond is likely to be created between the several defendants even though they have never met nor acted in unison."

Exculpatory Testimony from a Codefendant

Joinder of defendants may be improper where one or more of the defendants would, if separately tried, offer testimony that would exculpate the defendant who complains about joinder. The complaint is that the witness/codefendant will not testify if he is joined, for fear that he will injure his own defense. But in order to trigger severance on this ground, a defendant "must establish a bona fide need for the codefendant's testimony, the substance of the testimony, the exculpatory nature and effect of the testimony, and that the codefendant would in fact testify." United States v. Neal, 27 F.3d 1035 (5th Cir.1994) (severance should have been granted where codefendant would have taken the stand in a separate trial to exculpate the complaining defendants); United States v. Cobb, 185 F.3d 1193 (11th Cir.1999) (finding a "rare case" in which severance should have been granted, because the codefendant's testimony would have been critical to the defendant's defense, and the codefendant stated unequivocally that he would testify at the defendant's trial if his case were severed). Compare United States v. Pursley, 577 F.3d 1204 (10th Cir.2009) (joint trial permissible where codefendant would only have made a conclusory statement that both defendants were innocent, and the codefendant would have been extensively impeached).

Disparity in the Evidence

Another, limited exception to the general rule of joinder is where there is a gross disparity in the evidence against the joined defendants. In these cases, "the danger is that the bit players may not be able to differentiate themselves in the jurors' minds from the stars." United States v. Zafiro, 945 F.2d 881 (7th Cir.1991), aff'd 506 U.S. 534 (1993). In order to obtain a severance on this ground, the defendant will have to show a disparity in the evidence so great that the jury will not be able to follow limiting instructions. See, e.g., United States v. Gonzalez, 933 F.2d 417 (7th Cir.1991) (some disparity between defendants is permissible if it is within the jury's capacity to follow the court's limiting instructions). Given the institutional interest in trying all participants in a crime together, the gross disparity argument is rarely successful. And it is particularly unlikely to be successful on appeal if the jury returned acquittals as to some defendants and/or some charges. See United States v. Neal, 27 F.3d 1035 (5th Cir.1994) ("the jury's not guilty verdicts as to some defendants demonstrate that the jurors followed the district court's instructions and considered the evidence separately as to each defendant").

It should be noted that not all defendants prefer to be tried separately. A gross disparity in evidence might result in lesser defendants being acquitted altogether when the cases against them suffer in comparison to other defendants. When a defense counsel concludes that a defendant might benefit from having counsel for other defendants make arguments or present evidence, defense counsel might make the reasonable choice to "lay low."

Finger-Pointing: Zafiro v. United States

Is severance required if defendants are "pointing fingers" at each other, such that if one defense is believed the other cannot be? This was the question in Zafiro v. United States, 506 U.S. 534 (1993), a case in which four defendants were tried for a narcotics conspiracy. Officers discovered a large amount of cocaine at a residence to which all four defendants were connected. Soto and Garcia argued lack of knowledge and that Martinez and Zafiro were the drug dealers. Martinez and Zafiro argued lack of knowledge and that Soto and Garcia were the drug dealers. Justice O'Connor, writing for eight members of the Court, held that all of the defendants were properly tried together. She declared that "[t]here is a preference in the federal system for joint trials of defendants who are indicted together" and rejected the defendants' proposed bright line test that severance is required whenever defendants have mutually antagonistic defenses. She concluded that severance might be required in only a few exceptional circumstances:

> Mutually antagonistic defenses are not prejudicial *per se*. Moreover, Rule 14 does not require severance even if prejudice is shown; rather, it leaves the tailoring of the relief to be granted, if any, to the district court's sound discretion.

> We believe that, when defendants properly have been joined under Rule 8(b), a district court should grant a severance under Rule 14 only if there is a serious risk that a joint trial would compromise a specific trial right of one of the defendants, or prevent the jury from making a reliable judgment about guilt or innocence. Such a risk might occur when evidence that the jury should not consider against a defendant and that would not be admissible if a defendant were tried alone is admitted against a codefendant. For example, evidence of a codefendant's wrongdoing in some circumstances erroneously could lead a jury to conclude that a defendant was guilty. When many defendants are tried together in a complex case and they have markedly different degrees of culpability, this risk of prejudice is heightened. Evidence that is probative of a defendant's guilt but technically admissible only against a codefendant also might present a risk of prejudice. Conversely, a defendant might suffer prejudice if essential exculpatory evidence that would be available to a defendant tried alone were unavailable in a joint trial.

Justice O'Connor noted that the defendants in *Zafiro* did not articulate any specific instances of prejudice, but merely argued that "the very nature of their defenses, without more, prejudiced them." She responded that "it is well settled that defendants are not entitled to severance merely because they may have a better chance of acquittal in separate trials."

The defendants in *Zafiro* argued that they suffered a risk of prejudice from the possibility that the jury could conclude, in light of the finger-pointing defenses, that *some* defendant must be guilty without regard to whether the evidence proved so beyond a reasonable doubt. But Justice

O'Connor responded that "the short answer is that petitioners' scenario did not occur here" because the "Government argued that all four petitioners were guilty and offered sufficient evidence as to all four petitioners; the jury in turn found all four petitioners guilty of various offenses." She further stated that "even if there were some risk of prejudice, here it is of the type that can be cured with proper instructions." Justice O'Connor noted that the trial court instructed the jury to give separate consideration to each defendant, and also warned the jury that each defendant was entitled to have his or her case judged only on the basis of the evidence applicable to the individual defendant. She concluded that these instructions "sufficed to cure any possibility of prejudice."

Justice Stevens concurred in the judgment, observing that he did not share the majority's preference for joint trials. He pointed out two ways in which joinder is problematic in cases involving mutually antagonistic defenses:

> First, joinder may introduce what is in effect a second prosecutor into a case, by turning each codefendant into the other's most forceful adversary. Second, joinder may invite a jury confronted with two defendants, at least one of whom is almost certainly guilty, to convict the defendant who appears the more guilty of the two regardless of whether the prosecutor has proven guilt beyond a reasonable doubt as to that particular defendant.

D. MISJOINDER

Violation of Rule 8: United States v. Lane

The Supreme Court held in United States v. Lane, 474 U.S. 438 (1986), that misjoinder of counts in violation of Fed.R.Crim.P. 8(b) does not automatically compel reversal of convictions. A father and son were charged with various offenses arising out of an arson conspiracy. They persuaded a court of appeals that one count, brought solely against the father, was improperly joined with four counts naming them both and another count charging the son with perjury. The court of appeals concluded that misjoinder is prejudicial per se. Chief Justice Burger's opinion for the Court disagreed, reasoning that misjoinder surely can be harmless in light of decisions holding that even constitutional errors do not inevitably require reversal of convictions. The question in cases of misjoinder, then, is whether under Fed.R.Crim.P. 52(a) the error affected the "substantial rights" of a defendant.

The Bruton Problem

While the misjoinder in *Lane* was not of constitutional dimension, constitutional error can occur in a joint trial that would not arise if the defendants were tried separately. The predominant example is Bruton v. United States, 391 U.S. 123 (1968). The *Bruton* Court found constitutional error when Bruton's nontestifying codefendant made a post-custodial confession implicating both himself and Bruton, and this confession was admitted into evidence at the joint trial. The confession was admissible against the codefendant as a party admission, but it was inadmissible hearsay as to Bruton. The trial judge gave a limiting instruction that the statement could only be used against the codefendant. But the Court held that, in light of the "powerfully incriminating" nature of the confession, the instruction was insufficient to protect Bruton's constitutional right to confront his accuser.

The Court suggested separate trials to avoid a *"Bruton"* problem, but courts after *Bruton* have often used means short of separate trials to protect against the use of the confession of one codefendant against another. The Supreme Court has approved redaction of a confession as a permissible substitute for severance, so long as all reference to the existence of the non-confessing defendant is excised from the confession. See Richardson v. Marsh, 481 U.S. 200 (1987). In *Marsh,* the confession was redacted to refer only to the confessing codefendant and another perpetrator who had absconded. In contrast, in Gray v. Maryland, 523 U.S. 185 (1998), redaction was held insufficient to protect the defendant where the confession was changed, in essence, from "Gray and I did it" to "deleted and I did it." The *Gray* Court held that the redaction provided no protection, because the jury would know that "deleted" would have to be the other defendant sitting there at the trial.

Bruton has been held inapplicable to a bench trial of joined defendants, because the problem that the Court was concerned about in *Bruton* was the jury's inability to follow the judge's instruction not to use one codefendant's confession against another. Rogers v. McMackin, 884 F.2d 252 (6th Cir.1989). A *Bruton* violation can be harmless. Cruz v. New York, 481 U.S. 186 (1987).

III. CONSTITUTIONALLY BASED PROOF REQUIREMENTS

A. PROOF BEYOND A REASONABLE DOUBT GENERALLY

Constitutional Requirement: In re Winship

The Court in In re Winship, 397 U.S. 358 (1970), decided that the Due Process Clause requires the government in a criminal case to prove *every element* of the charged crime beyond a reasonable doubt. Samuel Winship, a 12-year-old boy, was brought before a juvenile court and charged with delinquency for taking $112 from a woman's pocketbook in a locker. The judge acknowledged that the conduct might not have been proved beyond a reasonable doubt, but determined that Winship could be adjudged a delinquent by a preponderance of the evidence. The Court in *Winship* held that the requirement of proof beyond a reasonable doubt is one of the "essentials of due process and fair treatment" required during the adjudicatory stage when a juvenile is charged with an act that would constitute a crime if committed by an adult. Justice Brennan's majority opinion traced the history of proof in American criminal trials and found "virtually unanimous" authority supporting the reasonable doubt standard for all elements of the crime. He concluded that the criminal defendant has a transcendent liberty interest in criminal trials that requires the narrowest margin for error.

> * * * [U]se of the reasonable-doubt standard is indispensable to command the respect and confidence of the community in applications of the criminal law. It is critical that the moral force of the criminal law not be diluted by a standard of proof that leaves people in doubt whether innocent men are being condemned. It is also important in our free society that every individual going about his ordinary affairs have confidence that his government cannot adjudge him guilty of a criminal offense without convincing a proper factfinder of his guilt with utmost certainty.

> Lest there remain any doubt about the constitutional stature of the reasonable-doubt standard, we explicitly hold that the Due Process Clause protects the accused against conviction except upon proof beyond a reasonable doubt of every fact necessary to constitute the crime with which he is charged.

Justice Harlan wrote an influential concurring opinion, stressing the policy arguments that support the reasonable doubt standard.

> [T]he choice of the standard for a particular variety of adjudication does, I think, reflect a very fundamental assessment of the comparative social costs of erroneous factual determinations. * * * [A] standard of proof represents an attempt to instruct the factfinder concerning the degree of confidence our society thinks he should have in the correctness of factual conclusions for a particular type of adjudication. Although the phrases "preponderance of the evidence" and "proof beyond a reasonable doubt" are quantitatively imprecise, they do communicate to the finder of fact different notions concerning the degree of confidence he is expected to have in the correctness of his factual conclusions.

> * * * If * * * the standard of proof for a criminal trial were a preponderance of the evidence rather than proof beyond a reasonable doubt, there would be a smaller risk of factual errors that result in

freeing guilty persons, but a far greater risk of factual errors that result in convicting the innocent. Because the standard of proof affects the comparative frequency of these two types of erroneous outcomes, the choice of the standard to be applied in a particular kind of litigation should, in a rational world, reflect an assessment of the comparative social disutility of each.

When one makes such an assessment, the reason for different standards of proof in civil as opposed to criminal litigation becomes apparent. In a civil suit between two private parties for money damages, for example, we view it as no more serious in general for there to be an erroneous verdict in the defendant's favor than for there to be an erroneous verdict in the plaintiff's favor. * * *

In a criminal case, on the other hand, we do not view the social disutility of convicting an innocent man as equivalent to the disutility of acquitting someone who is guilty. * * *

In this context, I view the requirement of proof beyond a reasonable doubt in a criminal case as bottomed on a fundamental value determination of our society that it is far worse to convict an innocent man than to let a guilty man go free.

B. REASONABLE DOUBT AND JURY INSTRUCTIONS

"Presumed Innocent" Instructions

In Taylor v. Kentucky, 436 U.S. 478 (1978), the Court reversed a conviction where the judge refused to give a requested instruction that the defendant was presumed innocent. Later, however, in Kentucky v. Whorton, 441 U.S. 786 (1979), the Court held that a presumption of innocence instruction was not constitutionally required in every case. It stressed the facts of *Taylor,* where the trial judge's instructions were "spartan," the prosecutor made improper remarks, and the evidence against the defendant was weak. The Court concluded that the failure to give a requested instruction on the presumption of innocence "must be evaluated in light of the totality of the circumstances—including all the instructions to the jury, the arguments of counsel, whether the weight of the evidence was overwhelming, and other relevant factors—to determine whether the defendant received a constitutionally fair trial." See also United States v. Payne, 944 F.2d 1458 (9th Cir.1991) (underlying purposes of a presumption of innocence instruction were "served adequately by other instructions which squarely placed the burden on the government of proving its case beyond a reasonable doubt, defined beyond a reasonable doubt, and clearly confined the scope of the evidence properly before the jury").

Reasonable Doubt Instructions

What should the judge say to the jury about the meaning of reasonable doubt? The instruction in Cage v. Louisiana, 498 U.S. 39 (1990), defined reasonable doubt as one creating "a grave uncertainty" and "an actual substantial doubt." The trial court elaborated that a "moral certainty" was required to convict. The Supreme Court in a per curiam opinion held that the words "grave" and "substantial" "suggest a higher degree of doubt than is required for acquittal under the reasonable doubt standard." The Court concluded that the instruction was constitutionally defective; the references to the juries needing a grave and substantial doubt to acquit, combined with the reference to moral certainty, as opposed to evidentiary certainty, could have led a reasonable juror to find guilt on a lesser standard than that required by *Winship.*

In Sullivan v. Louisiana, 508 U.S. 275 (1993), the Court unanimously held that a constitutionally-defective reasonable doubt instruction cannot be harmless error. At Sullivan's trial, the judge gave a reasonable doubt instruction substantially identical to the instruction found defective in *Cage.* Justice Scalia, writing for the Court, stated that because of the instruction, Sullivan was deprived of his Sixth Amendment right to a jury verdict of guilt beyond a reasonable doubt. Under these circumstances, an appellate court cannot determine that the error was harmless, because "the wrong entity" would be judging the defendant guilty. *Sullivan* is discussed in more detail, infra, in the Chapter 13 discussion of harmless error.

In the consolidated cases of Sandoval v. California and Victor v. Nebraska, 511 U.S. 1 (1994), the Court considered the constitutionality of two reasonable doubt instructions in light of *Cage.* In *Sandoval,* the trial court defined reasonable doubt as follows:

> It is not a mere possible doubt; because everything relating to human affairs, and depending on *moral evidence*, is open to some possible or imaginary doubt. It is that state of the case which, after the entire comparison and consideration of all the evidence, leaves the minds of the jurors in that condition that they cannot say they feel *an abiding conviction, to a moral certainty*, of the truth of the charge. [Emphasis added.]

Justice O'Connor, writing for the Court, found that while the instruction lacked clarity, there was no "reasonable likelihood" that the jury understood it to allow conviction to be based on proof less than the *Winship* standard. She rejected Sandoval's argument that the trial judge's reference to "moral certainty" would be understood by modern jurors to mean a standard of proof less stringent than that of reasonable doubt. She recognized that while the reference to moral certainty was "ambiguous in the abstract," the rest of the instruction sufficiently corrected any ambiguity by requiring "an abiding conviction" as to guilt. She stated that "we are satisfied that the reference to moral certainty, in conjunction with the abiding conviction language, impressed upon the factfinder the need to reach a subjective state of near certitude of the guilt of the accused."

While the Court found that the "moral certainty" language was not fatal, it stressed that it did not "condone the use of the phrase" and noted that the pattern jury instructions for federal courts do not refer to moral certainty.

The instruction defining reasonable doubt given by the trial court in *Victor* was as follows:

> Reasonable doubt is such a doubt as would cause a reasonable and prudent person, in one of the graver and more important transactions of life, to *pause and hesitate* before taking the represented facts as true and relying and acting thereon. It is such a doubt as will not permit you, after full, fair, and impartial consideration of all the evidence, to have an *abiding conviction, to a moral certainty*, of the guilt of the accused. At the same time, absolute or mathematical certainty is not required. You may be convinced of the truth of a fact beyond a reasonable doubt and yet be fully aware that possibly you may be mistaken. You may find an accused guilty upon the strong probabilities of the case, provided such probabilities are strong enough to exclude any doubt of his guilt that is reasonable. A reasonable doubt is an *actual and substantial doubt* arising from the evidence, or from the lack of evidence on the part of the state, *as distinguished from a doubt arising from mere possibility, from bare imagination, or from fanciful conjecture*. [Emphasis added.]

As with the instruction in *Sandoval*, Justice O'Connor found that the instruction in *Victor* adequately conveyed the concept of reasonable doubt to the jury. Justice O'Connor rejected Victor's argument that the reference to "substantial doubt" overstated the degree of doubt necessary for acquittal. She noted that the trial court had distinguished "substantial doubt" from "a doubt rising from mere possibility, from bare imagination, or from fanciful conjecture." This was enough to distinguish the instruction in *Victor* from that in *Cage,* where the "substantial doubt" language was also used. According to Justice O'Connor:

> This explicit distinction between a substantial doubt and a fanciful conjecture was not present in the *Cage* instruction. * * * [In *Cage*] we were concerned that the jury would interpret the term "substantial doubt" in parallel with the preceding reference to "grave uncertainty," leading to an overstatement of the doubt necessary to acquit. In the instruction given in Victor's case, the context makes clear that "substantial" is used in the sense of existence rather than magnitude of the doubt, so the same concern is not present.

Justice O'Connor noted in the alternative that the trial court's "hesitate to act" instruction cured whatever defect might have existed in the reference to substantial doubt. She concluded that "to the extent the word 'substantial' denotes the quantum of doubt necessary for acquittal, the hesitate to act standard gives a common-sense benchmark for just how substantial such a doubt must be."

Justice Kennedy wrote a short concurring opinion, in which he stated that a reference to moral certainty might once have made sense to jurors, but that it has "long since become archaic."

Justice Ginsburg wrote a concurring opinion, agreeing with the Court's suggestion that the term "moral certainty," "while not in itself so misleading as to render the instructions unconstitutional, should be avoided as an unhelpful way of explaining what reasonable doubt means." Unlike the Court, however, she also criticized the "hesitate to act" instruction as providing a "misplaced analogy." She reasoned that important decisions in one's life "generally involve a very heavy element of uncertainty and risk-taking" and thus are "wholly unlike the decisions jurors ought to make in criminal cases."[8]

Justice Ginsburg took issue with the statements of some federal circuit courts that a reasonable doubt instruction should *never* be given. See, e.g., United States v. Adkins, 937 F.2d 947 (4th Cir.1991) (arguing that such instructions "tend to impermissibly lessen the burden of proof"); Seventh Circuit Committee on Federal Jury Instructions ("The phrase 'reasonable doubt' is self-explanatory and is its own best definition. Further elaboration tends to misleading refinements which weaken and make imprecise the existing phrase."). See also Newman, Beyond Reasonable Doubt, 68 N.Y.U.L.Rev. 979 (1994) (arguing that the concept of reasonable doubt "will become less clear the more we explain it").

Justice Ginsburg noted studies indicating that "jurors are often confused about the meaning of reasonable doubt when that term is left undefined."

Justice Ginsburg approved of the reasonable doubt instruction proposed by the Federal Judicial Center. That instruction reads as follows:

> Proof beyond a reasonable doubt is proof that leaves you *firmly convinced* of the defendant's guilt. There are very few things in this world that we know with absolute certainty, and in criminal cases the law does not require proof that overcomes every possible doubt. If,

---

[8] See also Vargas v. Keane, 86 F.3d 1273 (2d Cir.1996) (Weinstein, J., concurring) (criticizing a "hesitate to act" instruction: "It could be misunderstood since many of us recognize that in the most important affairs of our lives—such as choice of mate, careers and conception—we tend to be largely emotional. Were we to require proof beyond a reasonable doubt that our important decisions are correct, few of us would marry, choose law as a career or have children. Most of us are probably comfortable with more risk-taking when making important personal decisions than we would be in declaring as criminals people who may be innocent.").

based on your consideration of the evidence, you are firmly convinced that the defendant is guilty of the crime charged, you must find him guilty. If on the other hand, you think there is a *real possibility* that he is not guilty, you must give him the benefit of the doubt and find him not guilty. [Emphasis added.]

Justice Ginsburg concluded that the FJC instruction is "clear, straightforward and accurate" and that it avoids a choice between two potential sources of jury confusion: "on one hand, the confusions that may be caused by leaving reasonable doubt undefined, and on the other, the confusion that might be induced by the anachronism of 'moral certainty,' the misplaced analogy of 'hesitation to act,' or the circularity of 'doubt that is reasonable.'"

C. THE SCOPE OF THE REASONABLE DOUBT REQUIREMENT: WHAT IS AN ELEMENT OF THE CRIME?

Winship requires the government to prove all *elements* of the crime beyond a reasonable doubt. But does this leave the government with an unfettered discretion to determine just what the elements of a crime are? What if the government changes what was once an element of the crime into an affirmative defense—thus shifting the burden of proof? What if the government shifts what might be considered an element of the crime into a sentencing consideration, thus lessening the burden of proof? Does any of this violate *Winship*? These questions have been the subject of much Supreme Court and lower court case law.

1. Element of the Crime or Affirmative Defense?

Impermissible Burden-Shifting: Mullaney v. Wilbur

The Court's first attempt to identify *Winship's* scope came in Mullaney v. Wilbur, 421 U.S. 684 (1975). Maine required a defendant charged with murder to prove that he acted "in the heat of passion on sudden provocation" in order to reduce the homicide to manslaughter. Under the Maine system, the prosecutor had to show beyond a reasonable doubt that a homicide was both intentional and unlawful. Unless the defendant proved heat of passion or sudden provocation by a preponderance of the evidence, the defendant was convicted of murder. Justice Powell's majority opinion declared that "the Due Process Clause requires the prosecution to prove beyond a reasonable doubt the absence of the heat of passion or sudden provocation when the issue is properly presented in a homicide case."[9] In other words, the absence of heat of passion or provocation was an

---

[9] In contrast to the burden of persuasion is the burden of production. Many jurisdictions put the burden on a defendant to raise sufficient evidence to bring a defense into a case, at which time

element of the crime, and could not be shifted to an affirmative defense. The Court reasoned as follows:

> [T]he criminal law of Maine, like that of other jurisdictions, is concerned not only with guilt or innocence in the abstract but also with the degree of criminal culpability. Maine has chosen to distinguish those who kill in the heat of passion from those who kill in the absence of this factor. * * * By drawing this distinction, while refusing to require the prosecution to establish beyond a reasonable doubt the fact upon which it turns, Maine denigrates the interests found critical in *Winship.*

* * *

> Moreover, if *Winship* were limited to those facts that constitute a crime as defined by state law, a State could undermine many of the interests that decision sought to protect without effecting any substantive change in its law. It would only be necessary to redefine the elements that constitute different crimes, characterizing them as factors that bear solely on the extent of punishment.

Justice Rehnquist, joined by Chief Justice Burger, concurred and noted that he saw no inconsistency between *Mullaney* and Leland v. Oregon, 343 U.S. 790 (1952) (upholding placement upon defendant of burden of persuasion beyond a reasonable doubt on issue of insanity).[10]

Flexibility to Determine Affirmative Defenses: Patterson v. New York

In Patterson v. New York, 432 U.S. 197 (1977), Justice White wrote for the majority as it upheld a New York statute that placed the burden on the defendant to prove extreme emotional disturbance by a preponderance of the evidence—after the prosecutor proved an intentional homicide beyond a reasonable doubt—in order to reduce second degree murder to manslaughter. After citing Leland v. Oregon, the majority reasoned as follows:

> Here, in revising its criminal code, New York provided the affirmative defense of extreme emotional disturbance, a substantially

---

the prosecutor must disprove the defense beyond a reasonable doubt. Even if the Constitution permits a jurisdiction to impose the persuasion burden on a defendant, a jurisdiction may be satisfied with imposing the production burden instead. Whenever it is constitutional to put a burden of persuasion on a defendant, it will be constitutional to impose the lesser burden of production. *Mullaney* establishes that in some cases only a production burden may be imposed.

[10] Nor did the majority of the Court. In Rivera v. Delaware, 429 U.S. 877 (1976), over the dissent of Justice Brennan joined by Justice Marshall, the Court dismissed, for want of a substantial federal question, an appeal from the Delaware Supreme Court's holding that it was constitutional to put the burden of persuasion on insanity on the defendant. The federal Insanity Defense Reform Act—passed after the prosecution of John Hinckley for the attempted assassination of President Reagan—imposes the burden of persuasion of proving insanity on the defendant by clear and convincing evidence.

expanded version of the older heat-of-passion concept; but it was willing to do so only if the facts making out the defense were established by the defendant with sufficient certainty. The State was itself unwilling to undertake to establish the absence of those facts beyond a reasonable doubt, perhaps fearing that proof would be too difficult and that too many persons deserving treatment as murderers would escape that punishment if the evidence need merely raise a reasonable doubt about the defendant's emotional state. It has been said that the new criminal code of New York contains some 25 affirmative defenses which exculpate or mitigate but which must be established by the defendant to be operative. The Due Process Clause, as we see it, does not put New York to the choice of abandoning those defenses or undertaking to disprove their existence in order to convict of a crime which otherwise is within its constitutional powers to sanction by substantial punishment.

* * *

We thus decline to adopt as a constitutional imperative, operative countrywide, that a State must disprove beyond a reasonable doubt every fact constituting any and all affirmative defenses related to the culpability of an accused. * * *

Justice White noted that there are limits to shifting the burden of proof to the defendant—the state could not transmute what has *traditionally been an element of the crime* into an affirmative defense:

It is not within the province of a legislature to declare an individual guilty or presumptively guilty of a crime. The legislature cannot validly command that the finding of an indictment, or mere proof of the identity of the accused, should create a presumption of the existence of all the facts essential to guilt.

In a footnote, Justice White quoted extensively from Chief Judge Breitel's concurring opinion in the New York Court of Appeals:

Absent the affirmative defense, the crime of murder or manslaughter could legislatively be defined simply to require an intent to kill, unaffected by the spontaneity with which that intent is formed or the provocative or mitigating circumstances which should legally or morally lower the grade of crime. The placing of the burden of proof on the defense, with a lower threshold, however, is fair because of defendant's knowledge or access to the evidence other than his own on the issue. * * *

In sum, the appropriate use of affirmative defenses enlarges the ameliorative aspects of a statutory scheme for the punishment of crime, rather than the other way around—a shift from primitive mechanical classifications based on the bare antisocial act and its consequences, rather than on the nature of the offender and the conditions which produce some degree of excuse for his conduct, the mark of an advanced criminology.

Thus, the Court reasoned that the state should be allowed to provide for affirmative defenses, because otherwise the state would simply legislate a single crime, making no attempt to differentiate levels of culpability. That would not be doing defendants any favors.

Justice Powell's dissent in *Patterson* was joined by Justices Brennan and Marshall. He argued that the distinction between the Maine law invalidated in *Mullaney* and the New York law upheld in *Patterson* was "formalistic rather than substantive."

After *Patterson*, can the state define murder as causing a death, and shift the burden of persuasion to the defendant to prove lack of intent? If not, why not? See also Mason v. Gramley, 9 F.3d 1345 (7th Cir.1993) (upholding Illinois murder statute, which requires the state to prove first degree murder, then permits the defendant to establish, by a preponderance, mitigating evidence to reduce the crime to second degree murder).[11]

For other Supreme Court cases involving the *Mullaney/Patterson* divide, see Martin v. Ohio, 480 U.S. 228 (1987) (upholding an Ohio rule placing the burden of persuasion on self-defense on the defendant); Montana v. Egelhoff, 518 U.S. 37 (1996) (upholding a state statute that prohibited the defendant from offering evidence of intoxication as a defense to the mental state necessary to commit homicide). In both *Martin* and *Egelhoff*, the Court relied on *Patterson* for the proposition that states are generally free to construct the elements of a crime.

Withdrawal from a Conspiracy as an Affirmative Defense: Smith v. United States

In Smith v. United States, 568 U.S. 106 (2013), the defendant was charged with conspiracy and claimed that he had withdrawn from it, and further that the date of his withdrawal meant that the statute of limitations had expired. The trial court instructed the jury that it had to find the defendant guilty of conspiracy beyond a reasonable doubt, but that the defendant had the burden of showing that he had withdrawn from the conspiracy. The defendant argued that this allocation of the burden of showing withdrawal violated his due process rights under *In re Winship*

---

[11] The Court relied heavily on *Patterson* in Medina v. California, 505 U.S. 437 (1992), as it upheld a state statute that established a presumption of competency to stand trial, and required the defendant to prove his incompetency by a preponderance of the evidence. Justice Kennedy wrote the opinion for the Court. He stated that under *Patterson*, it is appropriate to give "substantial deference to legislative judgments" allocating the burden of proof, because "the States have considerable expertise in matters of criminal procedure and the criminal process is grounded in centuries of common-law tradition."

But the Court disagreed in a unanimous opinion by Justice Scalia. Justice Scalia relied on Patterson v. New York and declared as follows:

> The State is foreclosed from shifting the burden of proof to the defendant only when an affirmative defense does negate an element of the crime. Where instead it excuses conduct that would otherwise be punishable, but does not controvert any of the elements of the offense itself, the Government has no constitutional duty to overcome the defense beyond a reasonable doubt.

> Withdrawal does not negate an element of the conspiracy crimes charged here. * * * To convict a defendant of narcotics or RICO conspiracy, the Government must prove beyond a reasonable doubt that two or more people agreed to commit a crime covered by the specific conspiracy statute (that a conspiracy existed) and that the defendant knowingly and willfully participated in the agreement (that he was a member of the conspiracy). Far from contradicting an element of the offense, withdrawal presupposes that the defendant committed the offense. * * * Withdrawal terminates the defendant's liability for postwithdrawal acts of his co-conspirators, but he remains guilty of conspiracy.

* * *

> Having joined forces to achieve collectively more evil than he could accomplish alone, Smith tied his fate to that of the group. His individual change of heart (assuming it occurred) could not put the conspiracy genie back in the bottle. We punish him for the havoc wreaked by the unlawful scheme, whether or not he remained actively involved. It is his withdrawal that must be active, and it was his burden to show that.

2. Element of the Crime or Sentencing Factor?

While the government has the burden of proving an element of the crime beyond a reasonable doubt, facts determined at sentencing have traditionally been subject to the preponderance of the evidence standard. For example, the defendant's criminal history is a sentencing factor, and the government need not prove that the defendant committed a prior crime beyond a reasonable doubt. The preponderance of the evidence standard is sufficient. [See Chapter 11 for a discussion of the standard of proof at sentencing].

Given the difference between the standard of proof at trial and sentencing, it is possible that a legislature might try to allocate certain facts to sentencing factors rather than to an element of the crime. Such a shift to sentencing factors implicates not only the reasonable doubt requirement of *Winship*, but also the defendant's constitutional right to a trial by jury on all elements of the crime. This is because sentencing factors are tried to the judge, not the jury.

In a series of important cases, the Court has sought to distinguish between what is a permissible sentencing factor and what must be an element of a crime. It is fair to state that the Court's journey down this path has been a winding one.

Preponderance of the Evidence at Sentencing: McMillan v. Pennsylvania

At issue in McMillan v. Pennsylvania, 477 U.S. 79 (1986), was a state statute providing that anyone convicted of certain enumerated felonies is subject to a mandatory minimum sentence of five years' imprisonment if the sentencing judge finds by a preponderance of the evidence that the defendant "visibly possessed a firearm" during the commission of the offense. If the aggravating factor of possessing a firearm were an element of the crime, it would of course have to be proven beyond a reasonable doubt—but the state chose instead to make it a sentencing factor.

The Court upheld the statute against a due process challenge. Justice Rehnquist wrote for the Court and argued that the state statute did not create a new offense, nor did it change the maximum punishment that could be imposed for an offense. Instead, it limited judicial discretion in sentencing. The Court found no problem with permitting a higher sentence to be based on proof of a fact by preponderance of the evidence, noting that the beyond the reasonable doubt standard had never been applied to sentencing factors. Justice Rehnquist stated that "*Patterson* stressed that in determining what facts must be proved beyond a reasonable doubt the state legislature's definition of the elements of the offense is usually dispositive," and that the Pennsylvania statute did not go beyond the minimal limitations set by *Patterson*: it did not create a presumption of guilt, and did not relieve the prosecution of its burden of proving guilt of the underlying crime.

Justice Stevens dissented, arguing that "the Due Process Clause requires proof beyond a reasonable doubt of conduct which exposes a criminal defendant to greater stigma or punishment * * *." Justice Marshall, joined by Justices Brennan and Blackmun, also dissented. He agreed with Justice Stevens that the Pennsylvania statute operated to create a special stigma and a special punishment upon a finding of specific conduct, and this was enough to mandate that the prosecution prove the conduct beyond a reasonable doubt.

Recidivism as a Sentencing Factor
or as an Element of the Crime?

In Almendarez-Torres v. United States, 523 U.S. 224 (1998), the Court considered whether the defendant's prior conviction was an element of the crime or a sentencing factor. Almendarez-Torres was convicted under a statute with two provisions. The first provision prohibits a deported alien from returning to the United States, and authorizes a maximum prison term of two years. The second provision authorizes a maximum prison term of 20 years if the initial "deportation was subsequent to a conviction for commission of an aggravated felony." The defendant was convicted under the second provision and was sentenced to 85 months' imprisonment. The defendant argued that he could not be subject to such a serious sentence, as his indictment did not mention his aggravated felony convictions. Because an indictment must recite all elements of the crime charged [see Chapter 6], the defendant argued that he could not be convicted under the statute's second provision. The government argued that the second provision of the statute did not set forth a separate crime, but was rather a provision mandating an enhanced sentence for recidivism; thus, the first provision of the statute defined the elements of the crime, and the second provision established a *sentencing enhancement* for felons who committed the crime.

In a 5–4 decision written by Justice Breyer, the Court held that the legislature had the constitutional authority to treat recidivism as a sentencing factor rather than as an element of the crime. Therefore it was not necessary to include the defendant's prior felony record in the indictment. Justice Breyer concluded that "the sentencing factor at issue here—recidivism—is a traditional, if not the most traditional, basis for a sentencing court's increasing an offender's sentence. * * * [T]o hold that the Constitution requires that recidivism be deemed an element of petitioner's offense would mark an abrupt departure from a longstanding tradition of treating recidivism as going to the punishment only."

Justice Scalia, joined by Justices Stevens, Souter and Ginsburg, dissented. He contended that it would violate the defendant's right to jury trial to take from the jury factual issues that affect the penalty to which a defendant is exposed.

Facts That, if Found, Extend the Sentence Beyond the
Statutory Maximum Penalty, Are Elements of
the Crime: Apprendi v. New Jersey

In the following case, the Court limited *McMillan* to its facts, and established a broad principle that prohibits the state and federal governments from using sentencing enhancements to increase a sentence beyond the statutory maximum provided for the crime by the legislature. Where the fact supporting a sentencing enhancement is used in that way, it is an element of the crime that must be set forth in the indictment, and the defendant has the right to have the fact proved beyond a reasonable doubt to a jury. In reaching this ruling, the Court relies on a case decided between *Almendarez-Torres* and this one—Jones v. United States, 526 U.S. 227 (1999), which questioned whether serious bodily injury could be considered a sentencing factor when it raised the sentence for the crime of car-jacking beyond the statutory maximum imposed for the simple offense.

APPRENDI V. NEW JERSEY

Supreme Court of the United States, 2000.
530 U.S. 466.

JUSTICE STEVENS delivered the opinion of the Court.

A New Jersey statute classifies the possession of a firearm for an unlawful purpose as a "second-degree" offense. Such an offense is punishable by imprisonment for between five years and 10 years. A separate statute, described by that State's Supreme Court as a "hate crime" law, provides for an "extended term" of imprisonment if the trial judge finds, by a preponderance of the evidence, that "[t]he defendant in committing the crime acted with a purpose to intimidate an individual or group of individuals because of race, color, gender, handicap, religion, sexual orientation or ethnicity." The extended term authorized by the hate crime law for second-degree offenses is imprisonment for between 10 and 20 years.

The question presented is whether the Due Process Clause of the Fourteenth Amendment requires that a factual determination authorizing an increase in the maximum prison sentence for an offense from 10 to 20 years be made by a jury on the basis of proof beyond a reasonable doubt.

[Apprendi pleaded guilty to a shooting, and at sentencing the government proffered evidence that the shooting was racially motivated. The sentencing court found evidence of racial bias by a preponderance of the evidence, and imposed an enhanced sentence on the basis of the hate crime law. That sentence was two years longer than the statutory maximum that Apprendi could have received for the crime to which he pled guilty. The sentence was upheld by the New Jersey court, which concluded that the state had the authority to define racial motivation as a sentencing factor rather than as an element of the crime.]

* * * The constitutional question * * * is whether the 12-year sentence imposed on count 18 was permissible, given that it was above the 10-year maximum for the offense charged in that count. The finding is legally significant because it increased—indeed, it doubled—the maximum range within which the judge could exercise his discretion, converting what

otherwise was a maximum 10-year sentence on that count into a minimum sentence. * * * The question whether Apprendi had a constitutional right to have a jury find such bias on the basis of proof beyond a reasonable doubt is starkly presented.

* * *

[Justice Stevens reviewed the historical basis of the right to jury trial and the right to a beyond a reasonable doubt standard of proof as to all elements of the crime. He noted specifically that the right to jury trial was needed "to guard against a spirit of oppression and tyranny on the part of rulers, and as the great bulwark of our civil and political liberties."]

Any possible distinction between an "element" of a felony offense and a "sentencing factor" was unknown to the practice of criminal indictment, trial by jury, and judgment by court as it existed during the years surrounding our Nation's founding.

* * *

We do not suggest that trial practices cannot change in the course of centuries and still remain true to the principles that emerged from the Framers' fears "that the jury right could be lost not only by gross denial, but by erosion." But practice must at least adhere to the basic principles undergirding the requirements of trying to a jury all facts necessary to constitute a statutory offense, and proving those facts beyond reasonable doubt. * * *

Since *Winship*, we have made clear beyond peradventure that *Winship's* due process and associated jury protections extend, to some degree, "to determinations that [go] not to a defendant's guilt or innocence, but simply to the length of his sentence."

* * *

It was in McMillan v. Pennsylvania that this Court, for the first time, coined the term "sentencing factor" to refer to a fact that was not found by a jury but that could affect the sentence imposed by the judge. * * * We did not, however, there budge from the position that (1) constitutional limits exist to States' authority to define away facts necessary to constitute a criminal offense, and (2) that a state scheme that keeps from the jury facts that expose defendants to greater or additional punishment, may raise serious constitutional concern. As we explained:

> Section 9712 neither alters the maximum penalty for the crime committed nor creates a separate offense calling for a separate penalty; * * *. The statute gives no impression of having been tailored

to permit the visible possession finding to be a tail which wags the dog of the substantive offense. * * *a

Finally, * * * Almendarez-Torres v. United States represents at best an exceptional departure from the historic practice that we have described. * * * [O]ur conclusion in *Almendarez-Torres* turned heavily upon the fact that the additional sentence to which the defendant was subject was "the prior commission of a serious crime." (explaining that "recidivism . . . is a traditional, if not the most traditional, basis for a sentencing Court's increasing an offender's sentence"). * * *

Even though it is arguable that *Almendarez-Torres* was incorrectly decided, and that a logical application of our reasoning today should apply if the recidivist issue were contested, Apprendi does not contest the decision's validity and we need not revisit it for purposes of our decision today to treat the case as a narrow exception to the general rule we recalled at the outset. * * *

In sum, our reexamination of our cases in this area, and of the history upon which they rely, confirms the opinion that we expressed in *Jones*. Other than the fact of a prior conviction, any fact that increases the penalty for a crime beyond the prescribed statutory maximum must be submitted to a jury, and proved beyond a reasonable doubt. * * *b

The New Jersey statutory scheme that Apprendi asks us to invalidate allows a jury to convict a defendant of a second-degree offense based on its finding beyond a reasonable doubt that he unlawfully possessed a prohibited weapon; after a subsequent and separate proceeding, it then allows a judge to impose punishment identical to that New Jersey provides for crimes of the first degree, based upon the judge's finding, by a preponderance of the evidence, that the defendant's "purpose" for unlawfully possessing the weapon was "to intimidate" his victim on the basis of a particular characteristic the victim possessed. In light of the

---

a   The principal dissent accuses us of today "overruling *McMillan*." We do not overrule *McMillan*. We limit its holding to cases that do not involve the imposition of a sentence more severe than the statutory maximum for the offense established by the jury's verdict—a limitation identified in the *McMillan* opinion itself. * * *

b   The principal dissent would reject the Court's rule as a "meaningless formalism," because it can conceive of hypothetical statutes that would comply with the rule and achieve the same result as the New Jersey statute. While a State could, hypothetically, undertake to revise its entire criminal code in the manner the dissent suggests—extending all statutory maximum sentences to, for example, 50 years and giving judges guided discretion as to a few specially selected factors within that range—this possibility seems remote. Among other reasons, structural democratic constraints exist to discourage legislatures from enacting penal statutes that expose every defendant convicted of, for example, weapons possession, to a maximum sentence exceeding that which is, in the legislature's judgment, generally proportional to the crime. * * * Our rule ensures that a State is obliged to make its choices concerning the substantive content of its criminal laws with full awareness of the consequence, unable to mask substantive policy choices of exposing all who are convicted to the maximum sentence it provides. So exposed, the political check on potentially harsh legislative action is then more likely to operate.

* * *

constitutional rule explained above, and all of the cases supporting it, this practice cannot stand. * * * Just because the state legislature placed its hate crime sentence "enhancer" within the sentencing provisions of the criminal code does not mean that the finding of a biased purpose to intimidate is not an essential element of the offense. * * *

* * *

The New Jersey procedure challenged in this case is an unacceptable departure from the jury tradition that is an indispensable part of our criminal justice system. * * *

JUSTICE SCALIA, concurring.

I feel the need to say a few words in response to Justice Breyer's dissent. It sketches an admirably fair and efficient scheme of criminal justice designed for a society that is prepared to leave criminal justice to the State. * * * The founders of the American Republic were not prepared to leave it to the State, which is why the jury-trial guarantee was one of the least controversial provisions of the Bill of Rights. It has never been efficient; but it has always been free.

As for fairness, which Justice Breyer believes "[i]n modern times," the jury cannot provide: I think it not unfair to tell a prospective felon that if he commits his contemplated crime he is exposing himself to a jail sentence of 30 years—and that if, upon conviction, he gets anything less than that he may thank the mercy of a tenderhearted judge * * *. Will there be disparities? Of course. But the criminal will never get more punishment than he bargained for when he did the crime, and his guilt of the crime (and hence the length of the sentence to which he is exposed) will be determined beyond a reasonable doubt by the unanimous vote of 12 of his fellow citizens.

In Justice Breyer's bureaucratic realm of perfect equity, by contrast, the facts that determine the length of sentence to which the defendant is exposed will be determined to exist (on a more-likely-than-not basis) by a single employee of the State. It is certainly arguable (Justice Breyer argues it) that this sacrifice of prior protections is worth it. But it is not arguable that, just because one thinks it is a better system, it must be, or is even more likely to be, the system envisioned by a Constitution that guarantees trial by jury. * * *

> **JUSTICE THOMAS, with whom JUSTICE SCALIA joins [in pertinent part] concurring.**
>
> * * *
>
> [A] "crime" includes every fact that is by law a basis for imposing or increasing punishment (in contrast with a fact that mitigates punishment). Thus, if the legislature defines some core crime and then provides for increasing the punishment of that crime upon a finding of some aggravating fact—of whatever sort, including the fact of a prior conviction—the core crime and the aggravating fact together constitute an aggravated crime, just as much as grand larceny is an aggravated form of petit larceny. The aggravating fact is an element of the aggravated crime. * * *
>
> [O]ne of the chief errors of *Almendarez-Torres*—an error to which I succumbed—was to attempt to discern whether a particular fact is traditionally (or typically) a basis for a sentencing court to increase an offender's sentence. * * * What matters is the way by which a fact enters into the sentence. If a fact is by law the basis for imposing or increasing punishment—for establishing or increasing the prosecution's entitlement—it is an element. * * *
>
> * * *

> **JUSTICE O'CONNOR, with whom THE CHIEF JUSTICE, JUSTICE KENNEDY, and JUSTICE BREYER join, dissenting.**
>
> * * *
>
> [Justice O'Connor accuses the majority of ignoring *Patterson,* which gave the states flexibility to define the elements of the crime.]
>
> * * *
>
> Any discussion of either the constitutional necessity or the likely effect of the Court's rule must begin, of course, with an understanding of what exactly that rule is. * * * In fact, there appear to be several plausible interpretations of the constitutional principle on which the Court's decision rests.
>
> For example, under one reading, the Court appears to hold that the Constitution requires that a fact be submitted to a jury and proved beyond a reasonable doubt only if that fact, as a formal matter, extends the range of punishment beyond the prescribed statutory maximum. A State could, however, remove from the jury (and subject to a standard of proof below "beyond a reasonable doubt") the assessment of those facts that define narrower ranges of punishment, within the overall statutory range, to which the defendant may be sentenced. Thus, apparently New Jersey could cure its sentencing scheme, and achieve virtually the same results, by

drafting its weapons possession statute in the following manner: First, New Jersey could prescribe, in the weapons possession statute itself, a range of 5 to 20 years' imprisonment for one who commits that criminal offense. Second, New Jersey could provide that only those defendants convicted under the statute who are found by a judge, by a preponderance of the evidence, to have acted with a purpose to intimidate an individual on the basis of race may receive a sentence greater than 10 years' imprisonment. * * * It is difficult to understand, and the Court does not explain, why the Constitution would require a state legislature to follow such a meaningless and formalistic difference in drafting its criminal statutes.

Under another reading of the Court's decision, it may mean only that the Constitution requires that a fact be submitted to a jury and proved beyond a reasonable doubt if it, as a formal matter, increases the range of punishment beyond that which could legally be imposed absent that fact. A State could, however, remove from the jury (and subject to a standard of proof below "beyond a reasonable doubt") the assessment of those facts that, as a formal matter, decrease the range of punishment below that which could legally be imposed absent that fact. Thus, consistent with our decision in *Patterson*, New Jersey could cure its sentencing scheme, and achieve virtually the same results, by drafting its weapons possession statute in the following manner: First, New Jersey could prescribe, in the weapons possession statute itself, a range of 5 to 20 years' imprisonment for one who commits that criminal offense. Second, New Jersey could provide that a defendant convicted under the statute whom a judge finds, by a preponderance of the evidence, not to have acted with a purpose to intimidate an individual on the basis of race may receive a sentence no greater than 10 years' imprisonment. * * * Again, it is difficult to understand * * * why the Constitution would require a state legislature to follow such a meaningless and formalistic difference in drafting its criminal statutes.

If either of the above readings is all that the Court's decision means, the Court's principle amounts to nothing more than chastising the New Jersey Legislature for failing to use the approved phrasing in expressing its intent as to how unlawful weapons possession should be punished.

* * *

[Justice O'Connor expresses concern that the majority's decision could result in invalidating the Federal Sentencing Guidelines, under which sentences can be enhanced on the basis of judicial findings by a preponderance of the evidence. The Court takes up this point in United States v. Booker, infra.]

JUSTICE BREYER, with whom CHIEF JUSTICE REHNQUIST joins, dissenting.

The majority holds that the Constitution contains the following requirement: "any fact [other than recidivism] that increases the penalty for a crime beyond the prescribed statutory maximum must be submitted to a jury, and proved beyond a reasonable doubt." This rule would seem to promote a procedural ideal—that of juries, not judges, determining the existence of those facts upon which increased punishment turns. But the real world of criminal justice cannot hope to meet any such ideal. * * * There are, to put it simply, far too many potentially relevant sentencing factors to permit submission of all (or even many) of them to a jury. As the Sentencing Guidelines state the matter, "[a] bank robber with (or without) a gun, which the robber kept hidden (or brandished), might have frightened (or merely warned), injured seriously (or less seriously), tied up (or simply pushed) a guard, a teller or a customer, at night (or at noon), for a bad (or arguably less bad) motive, in an effort to obtain money for other crimes (or for other purposes), in the company of a few (or many) other robbers, for the first (or fourth) time that day, while sober (or under the influence of drugs or alcohol), and so forth." The Guidelines note that "a sentencing system tailored to fit every conceivable wrinkle of each case can become unworkable and seriously compromise the certainty of punishment and its deterrent effect." To ask a jury to consider all, or many, such matters would do the same.

At the same time, to require jury consideration of all such factors— say, during trial where the issue is guilt or innocence—could easily place the defendant in the awkward (and conceivably unfair) position of having to deny he committed the crime yet offer proof about how he committed it, e.g., "I did not sell drugs, but I sold no more than 500 grams." And while special postverdict sentencing juries could cure this problem, they have seemed (but for capital cases) not worth their administrative costs. * * *

* * * The majority raises no objection to traditional pre-Guidelines sentencing procedures under which judges, not juries, made the factual findings that would lead to an increase in an individual offender's sentence. How does a legislative determination differ in any significant way? For example, if a judge may on his or her own decide that victim injury or bad motive should increase a bank robber's sentence from 5 years to 10, why does it matter that a legislature instead enacts a statute that increases a bank robber's sentence from 5 years to 10 based on this same judicial finding?

* * *

I certainly do not believe that the present sentencing system is one of "perfect equity," and I am willing, consequently, to assume that the majority's rule would provide a degree of increased procedural protection in respect to those particular sentencing factors currently embodied in statutes. I nonetheless believe that any such increased protection provides little practical help and comes at too high a price.

* * *

NOTE ON APPRENDI

Professor Jacqueline Ross points out that the Court's ruling in *Apprendi* does not do defendants any favors. In fact, defendants may be put to added disadvantages after *Apprendi*, as Justice Breyer intimates in his dissent. Professor Ross elaborates as follows:

> Turning sentencing factors into offense elements to be tried to a jury will put defendants under pressure to produce evidence on an increasing range of issues. If the government must prove racial animus, drug amounts, relative culpability of different participants, or similar aggravating factors that may increase the maximum penalty for certain crimes, the government's presentation of evidence on these issues will put pressure on defendants to rebut the government's prima facie case by presenting their own evidence. Reallocating factual determinations from the sentencing judge to the jury in effect shifts the burden of production onto defendants, while the burden of proof remains formally on the government. * * * If he wishes to rebut the government's evidence on the disputed aggravating circumstances, a defendant may have to forego the benefits of the presumption of innocence (a) by presenting evidence and (b) by admitting some level of guilt or criminal involvement as the price of disagreeing with the degree of imputed culpability.

> For example, if the government were required to prove to the jury the amount of drugs sold by co-conspirators in furtherance of a narcotics conspiracy, government evidence that the conspirators sold at least 100 grams of heroin would potentially raise the maximum prison term from twenty to forty years' imprisonment. Defendants wanting to deny their identification as members of the conspiracy, or their presence at a drug transaction, may have to choose between presenting no evidence on the issue of drug amounts, in effect solidifying the often circumstantial inferences raised by the government's evidence, or producing evidence [of smaller than 100 gram drug amounts, which is] inconsistent with putting the government to its proof on the issues of defendant's identity and presence at the drug deal.

Ross, Unanticipated Consequences of Turning Sentencing Factors Into Offense Elements: The *Apprendi* Debate, 12 Federal Sentencing Reporter 197 (2000). As a juror, how would you react to the defendant's argument that "I wasn't there at the drug deal, but if I was there, the deal involved a lot less than 100 grams."?

Apprendi and Sentencing Factors That Do Not Increase the Minimum Penalty: Harris v. United States and Alleyne v. United States

Harris v. United States, 536 U.S. 545 (2002), involved a mandatory minimum sentencing provision—like that in *McMillan*. Harris was convicted of a narcotics violation. The statute called for a mandatory minimum of a five year sentence for drug trafficking, but if the defendant brandished a gun during the drug trafficking, the mandatory minimum was raised to seven years. The question of whether Harris brandished a gun was not addressed in the indictment and was not presented to the jury. Rather, the sentencing judge found by a preponderance of the evidence that Harris brandished a gun, and so employed the seven year mandatory minimum sentence. Harris's actual sentence was not more than he could have received just for drug trafficking—it did not go higher than the maximum sentence for drug trafficking. But a higher *floor* to the sentence was guaranteed by the judge's finding.

The Court found that the triggering of the mandatory minimum on the basis of a finding by the sentencing judge did not run afoul of *Apprendi*. Justice Kennedy, writing for the Court, declared as follows.

> *Apprendi* said that any fact extending the defendant's sentence beyond the maximum authorized by the jury's verdict would have been considered an element of an aggravated crime—and thus the domain of the jury—by those who framed the Bill of Rights. The same cannot be said of a fact increasing the mandatory minimum (but not extending the sentence beyond the statutory maximum), for the jury's verdict has authorized the judge to impose the minimum with or without the finding. As *McMillan* recognized, a statute may reserve this type of factual finding for the judge without violating the Constitution.

In Alleyne v. United States, 570 U.S. 99 (2013), the Court overruled Harris v. United States. Justice Thomas delivered an opinion which commanded five votes in part and four votes in part. Alleyne was subject to a mandatory minimum sentence if he "brandished" a firearm during his crime. The trial court treated the "brandishment" question as a sentencing factor and found by a preponderance of evidence that Alleyne had brandished a weapon. Alleyne received a 7-year sentence which comported with the mandatory minimum, but it was a sentence less than the maximum sentence that the defendant could have received for the crime. The core of the Court's holding is the following:

> *Harris* drew a distinction between facts that increase the statutory maximum and facts that increase only the mandatory minimum. We conclude that this distinction is inconsistent with our decision in Apprendi v. New Jersey, and with the original meaning of the Sixth Amendment. Any fact that, by law, increases the penalty for

a crime is an "element" that must be submitted to the jury and found beyond a reasonable doubt. Mandatory minimum sentences increase the penalty for a crime. It follows, then, that any fact that increases the mandatory minimum is an "element" that must be submitted to the jury. Accordingly, *Harris* is overruled.

Justice Thomas discussed *McMillan* and *Apprendi* and, in a part of the opinion commanding five votes, he wrote that

> "[i]t is indisputable that a fact triggering a mandatory minimum alters the prescribed range of sentences to which a criminal defendant is exposed";

> "[i]t is impossible to dissociate the floor of a sentencing range from the penalty affixed to the crime";

> "[a] fact that increases a sentencing floor, thus, forms an essential ingredient of the offense";

> "it is impossible to dispute that facts increasing the legally prescribed floor *aggravate* the punishment"; and

> "because the fact of brandishing aggravates the legally prescribed range of allowable sentences, it constitutes an element of a separate, aggravated offense that must be found by the jury, regardless of what sentence the defendant *might* have received if a different range had been applicable."

Justice Sotomayor, joined by Justices Ginsburg and Kagan, agreed that both *Harris* and *McMillan* "were wrongly decided," and argued that *Apprendi* and other cases like Cunningham v. California and Blakely v. Washington, discussed infra, made *Harris* "even more of an outlier" and made it "appropriate for the Court to overrule *Harris* and to apply *Apprendi*'s basic jury-determination rule to mandatory minimum sentences in order to erase this anomaly in our case law."

Justice Breyer concurred in part and in the judgment. He had written in *Harris* that he could not distinguish it from *Apprendi* in terms of logic, expressed his continuing disagreement with *Apprendi*, and concluded that "[w]hile *Harris* has been the law for 11 years, *Apprendi* has been the law for even longer; and I think the time has come to end this anomaly in *Apprendi*'s application."

Chief Justice Roberts, joined by Justices Scalia and Kennedy, dissented and argued that

> "the jury's verdict fully authorized the judge to impose a sentence of anywhere from five years to life in prison";

> "[n]o additional finding of fact was 'essential' to any punishment within the range";

"[a]fter rendering the verdict, the jury's role was completed, it was discharged, and the judge began the process of determining where within that range to set Alleyne's sentence";

"[e]veryone agrees that in making that determination, the judge was free to consider any relevant facts about the offense and offender, including facts not found by the jury beyond a reasonable doubt";

Apprendi did not make it impermissible for judges to consider various factors relating to offense and offender;

"under the majority's rule, in the absence of a statutory mandatory minimum, there would have been no constitutional problem had the judge, exercising the discretion given him by the jury's verdict, decided that seven years in prison was the appropriate penalty for the crime *because of* his finding that the firearm had been brandished during the offense"; and

"[i]n my view, that is enough to resolve this case."

Justice Alito also dissented, arguing that if the Court were to reconsider existing precedent it should reconsider *Apprendi*, critiqued the historical analysis of the *Apprendi* majority, and concluded that "[t]he Court's decision creates a precedent about precedent that may have greater precedential effect than the dubious decisions on which it relies."

Apprendi and the Death Penalty: Ring v. Arizona

In Ring v. Arizona, 536 U.S. 584 (2002), the Court held that the Arizona capital sentencing statute was constitutionally infirm after *Apprendi*. Arizona provided that the judge would determine whether sufficient aggravating factors existed to justify the death penalty. Thus, if the judge found the factors to exist, she would impose a sentence—death—greater than that which could be authorized by the jury, because the jury's verdict could only justify a sentence of life imprisonment. Justice Ginsburg, writing for the Court, held that such a system could not be squared with *Apprendi*. She declared that "[c]apital defendants, no less than non-capital defendants * * * are entitled to a jury determination of any fact on which the legislature conditions an increase in their maximum punishment." Justice Ginsburg concluded as follows:

The right to trial by jury guaranteed by the Sixth Amendment would be senselessly diminished if it encompassed the factfinding necessary to increase a defendant's sentence by two years, but not the factfinding necessary to put him to death. We hold that the Sixth Amendment applies to both.

The Court in *Ring* overruled its prior holding in Walton v. Arizona, 497 U.S. 639 (1990), which held that it was permissible for a judge to sentence the defendant to death on the basis of judicial findings of aggravating circumstances. The holding in *Walton* could not be squared with *Apprendi*.

Justice Scalia wrote a concurring opinion joined by Justice Thomas, in which he declared that "the accelerating propensity of both state and federal legislatures to adopt 'sentencing factors' determined by judges that increase punishment beyond what is authorized by the jury's verdict * * * cause me to believe that our people's traditional belief in the right of trial by jury is in perilous decline. That decline is bound to be confirmed, and indeed accelerated, by the repeated spectacle of a man's going to his death because *a judge* found that an aggravating factor existed. We cannot preserve our veneration for the protection of the jury in criminal cases if we render ourselves callous to the need for that protection by regularly imposing the death penalty without it."

Justice Kennedy wrote a short concurring opinion in *Ring* noting that while he disagreed with *Apprendi,* that case "is now the law, and its holding must be implemented in a principled way. * * * Justice Breyer concurred in the judgment, continuing to reject *Apprendi*, but concluding that jury sentencing in capital cases is mandated by the Eighth Amendment. Justice O'Connor wrote a dissenting opinion joined by Chief Justice Rehnquist. She agreed that *Walton* could not be squared with *Apprendi*. But forced to choose one case or the other to overrule, she would overrule *Apprendi*.

Application of Ring v. Arizona: Hurst v. Florida

In Hurst v. Florida, 136 S.Ct. 616 (2016), the Court reviewed a capital proceeding under Florida law, where state law provided that the death penalty was imposed by the judge, and the role of the jury was to provide an "advisory sentence" that the judge must accord great weight when imposing a sentence. To impose the death penalty, the judge was required to find facts that support the aggravating circumstances that warrant that punishment. The Court in *Hurst* found that this system ran afoul of the Sixth Amendment, according to the principles set forth in *Apprendi* and its progeny, including most importantly Ring v. Arizona. Justice Sotomayor, writing for the majority, declared as follows:

> The analysis the *Ring* Court applied to Arizona's sentencing scheme applies equally to Florida's. Like Arizona at the time of *Ring,* Florida does not require the jury to make the critical findings necessary to impose the death penalty. Rather, Florida requires a judge to find these facts. Although Florida incorporates an advisory jury verdict that Arizona lacked, we have previously made clear that this distinction is immaterial: "It is true that in Florida the jury recommends a sentence, but it does not make specific factual findings with regard to the existence of mitigating or aggravating

circumstances and its recommendation is not binding on the trial judge. A Florida trial court no more has the assistance of a jury's findings of fact with respect to sentencing issues than does a trial judge in Arizona." Walton v. Arizona, 497 U.S. 639, 648 (1990).

As with Timothy Ring, the maximum punishment Timothy Hurst could have received without any judge-made findings was life in prison without parole. As with Ring, a judge increased Hurst's authorized punishment based on her own factfinding. In light of *Ring,* we hold that Hurst's sentence violates the Sixth Amendment.

Justice Breyer concurred in the judgment.

Justice Alito dissented. He argued, as he had in previous cases, that *Apprendi* is inconsistent with the original understanding of the jury trial right. He also argued that the Arizona system gave the jury no fact finding role, whereas Florida permits a jury to recommend a death sentence only if it finds that the state has proved one or more aggravating factors beyond a reasonable doubt and has weighed aggravating and mitigating factors. He found this sufficient to distinguish *Ring.*

Facts That Trigger Enhancement of a Sentence Under Mandatory Sentencing Guidelines Must Be Proved to a Jury: Blakely v. Washington

In Blakely v. Washington, 542 U.S. 296 (2004), the Court considered how *Apprendi* applied to a state sentencing scheme that allowed sentences to be enhanced on the basis of judicial findings pursuant to *mandatory sentencing guidelines.* Blakely entered a guilty plea admitting the elements of second-degree kidnaping and domestic-violence and firearm allegations, but no other relevant facts. The crimes to which he pleaded guilty called for a standard sentencing range, under the state's sentencing guidelines, of 49 to 53 months. The guidelines provided that a judge may impose a sentence above the standard range if the judge finds "substantial and compelling reasons justifying an exceptional sentence." The sentencing judge found, after a hearing, that the defendant had acted with deliberate cruelty, a statutorily enumerated ground for upward departure in domestic-violence cases. This finding resulted in the judge imposing an exceptional sentence of 90 months—37 months beyond the standard maximum. Blakely argued that this sentencing procedure deprived him of his constitutional right to have a jury determine beyond a reasonable doubt all facts legally essential to his sentence.

The State argued that *Apprendi* was inapplicable because the statute under which Blakely was convicted called for a sentence of up to 10 years, and he received a sentence within that range. Blakely argued that the effective sentencing range, for *Apprendi* purposes, was the sentencing *guideline* applicable to the crime, which topped out at 53 months. The Court sided with Blakely. Justice Scalia reasoned as follows:

> Our precedents make clear * * * that the "statutory maximum" for *Apprendi* purposes is the maximum sentence a judge may impose *solely on the basis of the facts reflected in the jury verdict or admitted by the defendant.* In other words, the relevant "statutory maximum" is not the maximum sentence a judge may impose after finding additional facts, but the maximum he may impose *without* any additional findings. When a judge inflicts punishment that the jury's verdict alone does not allow, the jury has not found all the facts which the law makes essential to the punishment, and the judge exceeds his proper authority.
>
> The judge in this case could not have imposed the exceptional 90-month sentence solely on the basis of the facts admitted in the guilty plea. Had the judge imposed the 90-month sentence solely on the basis of the plea, he would have been reversed. The "maximum sentence" is no more 10 years here than it was 20 years in *Apprendi* (because that is what the judge could have imposed upon finding a hate crime) * * *.

Justice Scalia spent some time explaining and defending the rationale of *Apprendi:*

> Our commitment to *Apprendi* in this context reflects not just respect for longstanding precedent, but the need to give intelligible content to the right of jury trial. That right is no mere procedural formality, but a fundamental reservation of power in our constitutional structure. Just as suffrage ensures the people's ultimate control in the legislative and executive branches, jury trial is meant to ensure their control in the judiciary. * * * *Apprendi* carries out this design by ensuring that the judge's authority to sentence derives wholly from the jury's verdict. Without that restriction, the jury would not exercise the control that the Framers intended.
>
> Those who would reject *Apprendi* are resigned to one of two alternatives. The first is that the jury need only find whatever facts the legislature chooses to label elements of the crime, and that those it labels sentencing factors—no matter how much they may increase the punishment—may be found by the judge. This would mean, for example, that a judge could sentence a man for committing murder even if the jury convicted him only of illegally possessing the firearm used to commit it—or of making an illegal lane change while fleeing the death scene. Not even *Apprendi*'s critics would advocate this absurd result. The jury could not function as circuitbreaker in the State's machinery of justice if it were relegated to making a determination that the defendant at some point did something wrong,

a mere preliminary to a judicial inquisition into the facts of the crime the State *actually* seeks to punish.

The second alternative is that legislatures may establish legally essential sentencing factors *within limits*—limits crossed when, perhaps, the sentencing factor is a "tail which wags the dog of the substantive offense." *McMillan.* What this means in operation is that the law must not go *too far*—it must not exceed the judicial estimation of the proper role of the judge.

* * * With *too far* as the yardstick, it is always possible to disagree with such judgments and never to refute them.

Whether the Sixth Amendment incorporates this manipulable standard rather than *Apprendi*'s bright-line rule depends on the plausibility of the claim that the Framers would have left definition of the scope of jury power up to judges' intuitive sense of how far is *too far*. We think that claim not plausible at all, because the very reason the Framers put a jury-trial guarantee in the Constitution is that they were unwilling to trust government to mark out the role of the jury.

Justice O'Connor dissented in *Blakely,* in an opinion joined in whole by Justice Breyer and in pertinent part by Chief Justice Rehnquist and Justice Kennedy. She argued much as Justice Breyer had in *Apprendi* that requiring the jury to decide the many facts that go into sentencing decisions under guidelines regimes will probably make guidelines sentencing unworkable.

Justice Kennedy wrote a separate dissenting opinion, noting that while the majority struck down sentencing under a state system, its rationale was equally applicable to the Federal Sentencing Guidelines (discussed in Chapter 11).

Justice Breyer also wrote a dissenting opinion in *Blakely* that was joined by Justice O'Connor. Justice Breyer addressed the rationale for permitting legislatures the leeway in identifying elements of the crime on the one hand and sentencing facts on the other:

Why does the Sixth Amendment permit a jury trial right (in respect to a particular fact) to depend upon a legislative labeling decision, namely, the legislative decision to label the fact a *sentencing fact*, instead of an *element of the crime?* The answer is that the fairness and effectiveness of a sentencing system, and the related fairness and effectiveness of the criminal justice system itself, depends upon the legislature's possessing the constitutional authority (within due process limits) to make that labeling decision. To restrict radically the legislature's power in this respect, as the majority interprets the Sixth Amendment to do, prevents the legislature from seeking sentencing systems that are consistent with, and indeed may help to advance, the Constitution's greater fairness goals.

To say this is not simply to express concerns about fairness to defendants. It is also to express concerns about the serious practical (or impractical) changes that the Court's decision seems likely to impose upon the criminal process; about the tendency of the Court's decision to embed further plea bargaining processes that lack transparency and too often mean nonuniform, sometimes arbitrary, sentencing practices; about the obstacles the Court's decision poses to legislative efforts to bring about greater uniformity between real criminal conduct and real punishment; and ultimately about the limitations that the Court imposes upon legislatures' ability to make democratic legislative decisions. Whatever the faults of guidelines systems—and there are many—they are more likely to find their cure in legislation emerging from the experience of, and discussion among, all elements of the criminal justice community, than in a virtually unchangeable constitutional decision of this Court.

Applying Apprendi-Blakely to the Federal Sentencing Guidelines: United States v. Booker

Federal courts struggled to determine the precise impact of *Blakely* on the Federal Sentencing Guidelines, discussed fully in Chapter 11. In United States v. Booker, 543 U.S. 220 (2005), the Court in an opinion by Justice Stevens, held that the Federal Sentencing Guidelines are not distinguishable from the state guidelines found invalid in *Blakely*. That is, to the extent that the Federal Guidelines *require* the sentencing court to enhance a sentence beyond the guideline for the basic crime for which the defendant was convicted, on the basis of facts (other than prior convictions) found by the sentencing judge, then they violate the defendant's right to jury trial and the right to have the government prove all elements of the crime beyond a reasonable doubt.

But the most important part of Booker is the remedial opinion by Justice Breyer. There, a different majority of the Court found that the problem with the Guidelines is not that judges sentence on the basis of facts not found by the jury. Rather the problem is that those findings trigger *mandatory* enhancements, because the Guidelines had been construed up to then to bind district judges in their sentencing decisions. Under the remedial opinion, the Sentencing Guidelines become guidelines in the real sense. They are advisory only.

The remedial opinion, and the dissents to that opinion, are set forth in Chapter 11, as the matters discussed in those opinions delve deeply into the mechanics of the Sentencing Guidelines. This section describes the opinions discussing the applicability of *Apprendi* and *Blakely* to the Federal Sentencing Guidelines.

Justice Stevens found no relevant distinction between the State guidelines struck down in *Blakely* and the Federal Guidelines, as both require judges to impose a higher sentence than is applicable to the crime for which the defendant was convicted, on the basis of facts found by the district judge at sentencing. He noted that it was the mandatory aspect of the Guidelines that led to the constitutional problem. He explained as follows:

> If the Guidelines as currently written could be read as merely advisory provisions that recommended, rather than required, the selection of particular sentences in response to differing sets of facts, their use would not implicate the Sixth Amendment. We have never doubted the authority of a judge to exercise broad discretion in imposing a sentence within a statutory range. Indeed, everyone agrees that the constitutional issues presented by these cases would have been avoided entirely if Congress had omitted * * * the provisions that make the Guidelines binding on district judges * * *. For when a trial judge exercises his discretion to select a specific sentence within a defined range, the defendant has no right to a jury determination of the facts that the judge deems relevant.

> * * *

> Booker's case illustrates the mandatory nature of the Guidelines. The jury convicted him of possessing at least 50 grams of crack based on evidence that he had 92.5 grams of crack in his duffel bag. * * * Booker's actual sentence, however, was 360 months, almost 10 years longer than the Guidelines range supported by the jury verdict alone. To reach this sentence, the judge found facts beyond those found by the jury: namely, that Booker possessed 566 grams of crack in addition to the 92.5 grams in his duffel bag. The jury never heard any evidence of the additional drug quantity, and the judge found it true by a preponderance of the evidence. Thus, just as in *Blakely*, "the jury's verdict alone does not authorize the sentence. The judge acquires that authority only upon finding some additional fact." There is no relevant distinction between the sentence imposed pursuant to the Washington statutes in *Blakely* and the sentences imposed pursuant to the Federal Sentencing Guidelines in these cases.

Justice Breyer (who played a major role in writing the Sentencing Guidelines), joined by the Chief Justice, Justice O'Connor, and Justice Kennedy, dissented. He reiterated the objections he made in both *Apprendi* and *Blakely*:

> * * * [T]he Court's Sixth Amendment decision would risk unwieldy trials, a two-tier jury system, a return to judicial sentencing

discretion, or the replacement of sentencing ranges with specific mandatory sentences. The decision would pose a serious obstacle to congressional efforts to create a sentencing law that would mandate more similar treatment of like offenders, that would thereby diminish sentencing disparity, and that would consequently help to overcome irrational discrimination (including racial discrimination) in sentencing. These consequences would seem perverse when viewed through the lens of a Constitution that seeks a fair criminal process.

The upshot is that the Court's Sixth Amendment decisions— *Apprendi, Blakely,* and today's—deprive Congress and state legislatures of authority that is constitutionally theirs. Congress' share of this joint responsibility has long included not only the power to define crimes (by enacting statutes setting forth their factual elements) but also the power to specify sentences, whether by setting forth a range of individual-crime-related sentences (say, 0 to 10 years' imprisonment for bank robbery) or by identifying sentencing factors that permit or require a judge to impose higher or lower sentences in particular circumstances.

This last mentioned power is not absolute. * * * But the power does give Congress a degree of freedom (within constraints of fairness) to choose to characterize a fact as a "sentencing factor," relevant only to punishment, or as an element of a crime, relevant to guilt or innocence. The Court has rejected this approach apparently because it finds too difficult the judicial job of managing the "fairness" constraint, *i.e.*, of determining when Congress has overreached. But the Court has nowhere asked, "compared to what?" Had it done so, it could not have found the practical difficulty it has mentioned, sufficient to justify the severe limits that its approach imposes upon Congress' legislative authority.

Justice Breyer also argued that the Federal Sentencing Guidelines were distinguishable from the Guidelines struck down in *Blakely*. This part of his argument presented a detailed analysis of the Federal Guidelines.

Ultimately, a majority of the Court, in an opinion on remedies for the Guidelines' unconstitutionality, found that the solution was not to strike down the Guidelines *in toto*, but rather to strike down those aspects of the Guidelines that made them *mandatory* on district judges. That remedial opinion, in an ironic twist, was authored by Justice Breyer.

State Sentencing Scheme Found Mandatory, Not Advisory: Cunningham v. California

In Cunningham v. California, 549 U.S. 270 (2007), Justice Ginsburg wrote for the Court as it found that California's determinate sentencing law (DSL) violated the *Apprendi* line of cases. Cunningham was tried and convicted of continuous sexual abuse of a child under the age of 14. The DSL provided that his offense was punishable by imprisonment for a lower term sentence of 6 years, a middle term sentence of 12 years, or an upper term sentence of 16 years, and that the trial judge was required to sentence Cunningham to the 12-year middle term unless the judge found one or more additional facts in aggravation. The judge conducted a post-trial hearing and found six aggravating circumstances and one mitigating factor. The judge found that the aggravators outweighed the mitigating factor and sentenced Cunningham to the upper term of 16 years.

The key provision of the California law for Justice Ginsburg was Penal Code § 1170(b), which provided that "the court shall order imposition of the middle term, unless there are circumstances in aggravation or mitigation of the crime."

Relying on *Blakely*, Justice Ginsburg wrote as follows:

> Under California's DSL, an upper term sentence may be imposed only when the trial judge finds an aggravating circumstance. An element of the charged offense, essential to a jury's determination of guilt, or admitted in a defendant's guilty plea, does not qualify as such a circumstance. Instead, aggravating circumstances depend on facts found discretely and solely by the judge. In accord with *Blakely*, therefore, the middle term prescribed in California's statutes, not the upper term, is the relevant statutory maximum. Because circumstances in aggravation are found by the judge, not the jury, and need only be established by a preponderance of the evidence, not beyond a reasonable doubt, the DSL violates *Apprendi*'s bright-line rule: Except for a prior conviction, "any fact that increases the penalty for a crime beyond the prescribed statutory maximum must be submitted to a jury, and proved beyond a reasonable doubt."

Justice Ginsburg concluded that "California's DSL does not resemble the advisory system the *Booker* Court had in view," because under California's system, judges are not free to exercise their "discretion to select a specific sentence within a defined range."

Justice Kennedy, joined by Justice Breyer, dissented and continued to attack the *Apprendi* reasoning.

Justice Alito, joined by the same two Justices, also dissented and argued as follows:

> The California sentencing law that the Court strikes down today is indistinguishable in any constitutionally significant respect from the advisory Guidelines scheme that the Court approved in United States v. Booker. Both sentencing schemes grant trial judges considerable discretion in sentencing; both subject the exercise of that discretion to appellate review for "reasonableness"; and both—the California law

explicitly, and the federal scheme implicitly—require a sentencing judge to find some factor to justify a sentence above the minimum that could be imposed based solely on the jury's verdict. Because this Court has held unequivocally that the post-*Booker* federal sentencing system satisfies the requirements of the Sixth Amendment, the same should be true with regard to the California system. * * *

Apprendi and the Determination of Facts Necessary to Impose a Consecutive Sentence: Oregon v. Ice

Justice Ginsburg wrote for the Court in Oregon v. Ice, 555 U.S. 160 (2009), as it addressed this question: "When a defendant has been tried and convicted of multiple offenses, each involving discrete sentencing prescriptions, does the Sixth Amendment mandate jury determination of any fact declared necessary to the imposition of consecutive, in lieu of concurrent, sentences?" She answered the question by reference to historical practice and deference to state procedure:

> Most States continue the common-law tradition: They entrust to judges' unfettered discretion the decision whether sentences for discrete offenses shall be served consecutively or concurrently. In some States, sentences for multiple offenses are presumed to run consecutively, but sentencing judges may order concurrent sentences upon finding cause therefor. Other States, including Oregon, constrain judges' discretion by requiring them to find certain facts before imposing consecutive, rather than concurrent, sentences. It is undisputed that States may proceed on the first two tracks without transgressing the Sixth Amendment. The sole issue in dispute, then, is whether the Sixth Amendment, as construed in *Apprendi* and *Blakely*, precludes the mode of proceeding chosen by Oregon and several of her sister States. We hold, in light of historical practice and the authority of States over administration of their criminal justice systems, that the Sixth Amendment does not exclude Oregon's choice.

Justice Ginsburg looked to the historical role of the jury in sentencing, found that it differed greatly from the jury's role in determining guilt or innocence, and concluded that the concerns of *Apprendi* were not present:

> The historical record demonstrates that the jury played no role in the decision to impose sentences consecutively or concurrently. Rather, the choice rested exclusively with the judge. * * * The historical record further indicates that a judge's imposition of consecutive, rather than concurrent, sentences was the prevailing practice.

> In light of this history, legislative reforms regarding the imposition of multiple sentences do not implicate the core concerns that prompted our decision in *Apprendi*. * * *

Justice Scalia, joined by Chief Justice Roberts and Justices Souter and Thomas, dissented and argued that *Apprendi* clearly controlled the outcome:

> The rule of Apprendi v. New Jersey is clear: Any fact—other than that of a prior conviction—that increases the maximum punishment to which a defendant may be sentenced must be admitted by the defendant or proved beyond a reasonable doubt to a jury. Oregon's sentencing scheme allows judges rather than juries to find the facts necessary to commit defendants to longer prison sentences, and thus directly contradicts what we held eight years ago and have reaffirmed several times since.

Application of Apprendi to Criminal Fines: Southern Union Co. v. United States

A 6–3 majority of the Supreme Court held that *Apprendi* and its progeny apply to criminal fines in Southern Union Co. v. United States, 567 U.S. 343 (2012). A jury convicted Southern Union Company on one count of violating the Resource Conservation and Recovery Act of 1976 by knowingly storing liquid mercury at a subsidiary's facility "on or about September 19, 2002 to October 19, 2004." The statute makes violations punishable by a fine of not more than $50,000 for each day of violation. The probation office calculated a maximum fine of $38.1 million, on the basis that Southern Union violated the statute for *each* of the 762 days from September 19, 2002, through October 19, 2004. Southern Union contended that, based on the jury verdict and the district court's instructions, the jury necessarily found a violation for only one day within the period covered by the indictment. The district court held that *Apprendi* applied but concluded from the "content and context of the verdict all together" that the jury found a 762-day violation. It imposed a fine of $6 million and a "community service obligation" of $12 million. The First Circuit did not agree with the district court's analysis of the jury's verdict but affirmed the sentence on the ground that *Apprendi* did not apply to criminal fines—so the Government could, and did, prove by a preponderance of the evidence at sentencing that the storage occurred on each of the 762 days. The Supreme Court reversed.

Justice Sotomayor writing for the majority, discussed the *Apprendi* line of cases, and reasoned as follows:

> While the punishments at stake in those cases were imprisonment or a death sentence, we see no principled basis under *Apprendi* for treating criminal fines differently. *Apprendi*'s "core concern" is to reserve to the jury "the determination of facts that warrant punishment for a specific statutory offense." That concern applies whether the sentence is a criminal fine or imprisonment or death.

Criminal fines, like these other forms of punishment, are penalties inflicted by the sovereign for the commission of offenses. Fines * * * are frequently imposed today, especially upon organizational defendants who cannot be imprisoned. And the amount of a fine, like the maximum term of imprisonment or eligibility for the death penalty, is often calculated by reference to particular facts. Sometimes, as here, the fact is the duration of a statutory violation; under other statutes it is the amount of the defendant's gain or the victim's loss, or some other factor. In all such cases, requiring juries to find beyond a reasonable doubt facts that determine the fine's maximum amount is necessary to implement *Apprendi*'s "animating principle": the "preservation of the jury's historic role as a bulwark between the State and the accused at the trial for an alleged offense."

Justice Breyer, joined by Justices Kennedy and Alito, dissented. He reiterated previous arguments made in dissent in *Apprendi* cases and argued that applying *Apprendi* to fines would do no favors for criminal defendants:

The consequence of the majority's holding, insisting that juries make such determinations, is likely to diminish the fairness of the criminal trial process. A defendant will not find it easy to show the jury at trial that (1) he committed no environmental crime, but (2) in any event, he committed the crime only on 20 days, not 30.

D. PROOF OF ALTERNATIVE MEANS OF COMMITTING A SINGLE CRIME

The requirement of proof beyond a reasonable doubt of all elements of a crime raises another question: whether it is constitutionally acceptable to define a "crime" so broadly as to permit jurors to reach one verdict based on any combination of alternative findings of fact. The Court considered this question in Schad v. Arizona, 501 U.S. 624 (1991). Schad was charged with first-degree murder. In Arizona, the crime of first-degree murder encompasses both premeditated murder and felony murder. At trial, the prosecutor advanced both premeditated and felony murder theories, and offered proof under both theories. The jury returned a general verdict of guilty of first degree murder. Schad complained that this procedure was invalid, because it excused the state from having to prove all of the elements of one specific crime beyond a reasonable doubt.

Justice Souter, writing for a plurality of four Justices, stated that it was constitutionally permissible to define first-degree murder in such a way that it could be committed by alternative means, so long as those means "reasonably reflect notions of equivalent blameworthiness or culpability." Justice Souter recognized that the Due Process Clause would not permit a state "to convict anyone under a charge of 'Crime' so generic that any combination of jury findings of embezzlement, reckless driving, murder, burglary, tax evasion, or littering, for example, would suffice for conviction." However, the Arizona statute did not create such a disparate collection of alternative means to commit first degree murder. Justice Souter concluded that felony murder and premeditated murder were of sufficient "moral equivalence" to be grouped together as two ways of committing the same crime, and that therefore the general verdict of guilt was constitutionally permissible.

Justice Souter found it highly relevant that many states have traditionally considered felony murder and premeditated murder as alternative means of committing first degree murder. He stated that the "historical and contemporary acceptance of Arizona's definition of the offense and verdict practice is a strong indication" that it did not violate due process, because "legal definitions, and the practices comporting with them, are unlikely to endure for long, or to retain wide acceptance, if they are at odds with notions of fairness and rationality sufficiently fundamental to be comprehended in due process."

Justice Scalia concurred in the judgment. In his view, the fact that the Arizona statutory definition of first-degree murder is traditionally and currently accepted in most states was dispositive of the due process issue. He concluded as follows:

> Submitting killing in the course of a robbery and premeditated killing to the jury under a single charge is not some novel composite that can be subjected to the indignity of fundamental fairness review. It was the norm when this country was founded, * * * and remains the norm today. Unless we are here to invent a Constitution rather than enforce one, it is impossible that a practice as old as the common law and still in existence in the vast majority of States does not provide that process which is due.

Justice White, joined by Justices Marshall, Blackmun, and Stevens, dissented. He noted that felony murder and premeditated murder contain separate elements of conduct and state of mind and argued that these elements could not "be mixed and matched at will." He asserted that "it is particularly fanciful to equate an intent to do no more than rob with a premeditated intent to murder."

The prosecution in *Schad* was required to prove all elements beyond a reasonable doubt, and the defendant was not required to prove anything. So how does the *Schad* issue relate to the *Mullaney-Patterson-Apprendi* line of cases, which deals with the state's power to define the elements of a crime? The answer lies in the possibility that by combining alternative theories of guilt, a prosecutor may manage to convict a defendant without proving beyond a reasonable doubt all of the elements of any one theory to a constitutionally adequate number of jurors. At the logical limit of the analysis, a prosecutor could argue twelve alternatives to a twelve-person jury and persuade only one juror beyond a reasonable doubt of each theory. Were the theories set forth in separate counts, a defendant would never be convicted. In fact, the vote would be 11–1 for acquittal on each count. But, by combining the theories, all twelve jurors would agree that the defendant is "guilty" of a "crime." All members of the Court in *Schad* agreed that at some point this tactic would be impermissible under the Due Process Clause. They disagreed, however, on where that point lies. Four Justices gave traditional and current acceptance significant weight, and one found traditional and current acceptance dispositive.

For a cogent criticism of *Schad,* see Howe, Jury Fact-Finding in Criminal Cases: Constitutional Limits on Factual Disagreements Among Convicting Jurors, 58 Missouri L.Rev.1 (1993).

Distinction Between Means and Elements:
Richardson v. United States

Under *Schad,* the means by which a defendant commits a crime need not be proven beyond a reasonable doubt, if there are alternative means to commit the crime. Under *Winship,* the elements of the crime must be proven beyond a reasonable doubt. The distinction between means and elements is sometimes unclear. The Supreme Court encountered a problem of delineation between means and elements in Richardson v. United States, 526 U.S. 813 (1999). Richardson was convicted under the Continuing Criminal Enterprise statute. The statute defines "continuing criminal enterprise" (CCE) as involving a "violat[ion]" of the drug statutes where "such violation is a part of a continuing series of violations." The definitional problem arising under the statute was set forth in the majority opinion by Justice Breyer:

> The question before us arises out of the trial court's instruction about the statute's "series of violations" requirement. The judge rejected Richardson's proposal to instruct the jury that it must "unanimously agree on which three acts constituted [the] series of violations." Instead, the judge instructed the jurors that they "must unanimously agree that the defendant committed at least three federal narcotics offenses," while adding, "[y]ou do not . . . have to agree as to the particular three or more federal narcotics offenses committed by the defendant." * * *

> The question before us arises because a federal jury need not always decide unanimously which of several possible sets of underlying brute facts make up a particular element, say, which of several possible means the defendant used to commit an element of the crime. Schad v. Arizona. Where, for example, an element of robbery is force or the threat of force, some jurors might conclude that the

defendant used a knife to create the threat; others might conclude he used a gun. But that disagreement—a disagreement about means— would not matter as long as all 12 jurors unanimously concluded that the Government had proved the necessary related element, namely that the defendant had threatened force.

In this case, we must decide whether the statute's phrase "series of violations" refers to one element, namely a "series," in respect to which the "violations" constitute the underlying brute facts or means, or whether those words create several elements, namely the several "violations," in respect to each of which the jury must agree unanimously and separately. * * * If the statute creates a single element, a "series," in respect to which individual violations are but the means, then the jury need only agree that the defendant committed at least three of all the underlying crimes the Government has tried to prove. The jury need not agree about which three. On the other hand, if the statute makes each "violation" a separate element, then the jury must agree unanimously about which three crimes the defendant committed.

The majority held that the underlying illegal activity constituted an element of the crime, and not the means. Thus, the jury in order to convict the defendant would have to agree unanimously that the defendant committed at least three underlying drug transactions—*and* they would have to agree on the specific transactions in order for them to count toward the "series." Justice Breyer explained the majority's decision in the following passage:

The CCE statute's breadth * * * argues against treating each individual violation as a means, for that breadth aggravates the dangers of unfairness that doing so would risk. Cf. Schad v. Arizona. The statute's word "violations" covers many different kinds of behavior of varying degrees of seriousness. * * * At the same time, the Government in a CCE case may well seek to prove that a defendant, charged as a drug kingpin, has been involved in numerous underlying violations. The first of these considerations increases the likelihood that treating violations simply as alternative means, by permitting a jury to avoid discussion of the specific factual details of each violation, will cover-up wide disagreement among the jurors about just what the defendant did, or did not, do. The second consideration significantly aggravates the risk (present at least to a small degree whenever multiple means are at issue) that jurors, unless required to focus upon specific factual detail, will fail to do so, simply concluding from testimony, say, of bad reputation, that where there is smoke there must be fire.

Finally, this Court has indicated that the Constitution itself limits a State's power to define crimes in ways that would permit juries to convict while disagreeing about means, at least where that definition risks serious unfairness and lacks support in history or tradition. Schad v. Arizona, 501 U.S., at 632–633 (plurality opinion); id., at 651 (SCALIA, J., concurring) ("We would not permit . . . an indictment charging that the defendant assaulted either X on Tuesday or Y on Wednesday . . ."). We have no reason to believe that Congress intended to come close to, or to test, those constitutional limits when it wrote this statute.

Justice Kennedy, joined by Justices O'Connor and Ginsburg, dissented in *Richardson.* He argued that "[t]he CCE statute does not in any way implicate the suggestion in *Schad* that an irrational single crime consisting of, for instance, either robbery or failure to file a tax return would offend due process."

E. PRESUMPTIONS

An alternative to placing a burden of persuasion on a defendant in order to reduce the burden on the government of presenting evidence is to utilize a presumption or a judicially recognized inference.[12] Few aspects of procedural law can be more confusing than presumptions, as the word "presumption" is used to mean several different things in different contexts.

The following case illustrates how the Supreme Court has approached many criminal presumptions, and indicates the importance of jury instructions in assessing the permissibility of presumptions. The extensive footnotes provided by the Court are particularly helpful.

COUNTY COURT V. ALLEN
Supreme Court of the United States, 1979.
442 U.S. 140.

JUSTICE STEVENS delivered the opinion of the Court.

A New York statute provides that, with certain exceptions, the presence of a firearm in an automobile is presumptive evidence of its illegal possession by all persons then occupying the vehicle. The United States Court of Appeals for the Second Circuit held that respondents may challenge the constitutionality of this statute in a federal habeas corpus proceeding and that the statute is "unconstitutional on its face." * * *

---

[12] In this section, the word "presumption" is used to cover situations in which the court instructs a jury that proof of one fact entitles the jury to infer, assume, or presume the existence of another fact.

Four persons, three adult males (respondents) and a 16-year-old girl (Jane Doe, who is not a respondent here), were jointly tried on charges that they possessed two loaded handguns, a loaded machinegun, and over a pound of heroin found in a Chevrolet in which they were riding when it was stopped for speeding * * *. The two large-caliber handguns, which together with their ammunition weighed approximately six pounds, were seen through the window of the car by the investigating police officer. They were positioned crosswise in an open handbag on either the front floor or the front seat of the car on the passenger side where Jane Doe was sitting. Jane Doe admitted that the handbag was hers. The machinegun and the heroin were discovered in the trunk after the police pried it open. The car had been borrowed from the driver's brother earlier that day; the key to the trunk could not be found in the car or on the person of any of its occupants, although there was testimony that two of the occupants had placed something in the trunk before embarking in the borrowed car. The jury convicted all four of possession of the handguns and acquitted them of possession of the contents of the trunk.

Counsel for all four defendants objected to the introduction into evidence of the two handguns, the machinegun, and the drugs, arguing that the State had not adequately demonstrated a connection between their clients and the contraband. The trial court overruled the objection, relying on the presumption of possession created by the New York statute. Because that presumption does not apply if a weapon is found "upon the person" of one of the occupants of the car, the three male defendants also moved to dismiss the charges relating to the handguns on the ground that the guns were found on the person of Jane Doe. * * *

At the close of the trial, the judge instructed the jurors that they were entitled to infer possession from the defendants' presence in the car. He did not make any reference to the "on the person" exception in his explanation of the statutory presumption, nor did any of the defendants object to this omission or request alternative or additional instructions on the subject.

* * *

Inferences and presumptions are a staple of our adversary system of factfinding. It is often necessary for the trier of fact to determine the existence of an element of the crime—that is, an "ultimate" or "elemental" fact—from the existence of one or more "evidentiary" or "basic" facts. The value of these evidentiary devices, and their validity under the Due Process Clause, vary from case to case, however, depending on the strength of the connection between the particular basic and elemental facts involved and on the degree to which the device curtails the factfinder's freedom to assess the evidence independently. Nonetheless, in criminal cases, the ultimate test of any device's constitutional validity in a given case remains constant; the device must not undermine the factfinder's responsibility at trial, based on evidence adduced by the State, to find the ultimate facts beyond a reasonable doubt.

The most common evidentiary device is the entirely permissive inference or presumption, which allows—but does not require—the trier of fact to infer the elemental fact from proof by the prosecutor of the basic one and that places no burden of any kind on the defendant. In that situation the basic fact may constitute prima facie evidence of the elemental fact. When reviewing this type of device, the Court has required the party challenging it to demonstrate its invalidity as applied to him. Because this permissive presumption leaves the trier of fact free to credit or reject the inference and does not shift the burden of proof, it affects the application of the "beyond a reasonable doubt" standard only if, under the facts of the case, there is no rational way the trier could make the connection permitted by the inference. For only in that situation is there any risk that an explanation of the permissible inference to a jury, or its use by a jury, has caused the presumptively rational factfinder to make an erroneous factual determination.

A mandatory presumption is a far more troublesome evidentiary device. For it may affect not only the strength of the "no reasonable doubt" burden but also the placement of that burden; it tells the trier that he or they must find the elemental fact upon proof of the basic fact, at least unless the defendant has come forward with some evidence to rebut the presumed connection between the two facts.[a] In this situation, the Court

---

[a] This class of more or less mandatory presumptions can be subdivided into two parts; presumptions that merely shift the burden of production to the defendant, following the satisfaction of which the ultimate burden of persuasion returns to the prosecution; and presumptions that entirely shift the burden of proof to the defendant. The mandatory presumptions examined by our cases have almost uniformly fit into the former subclass, in that they never totally removed the ultimate burden of proof beyond a reasonable doubt from the prosecution. E.g., Tot v. United States, 319 U.S. 463 (1943) [requiring a "rational connection between the fact proved and the ultimate fact presumed"].

To the extent that a presumption imposes an extremely low burden of production—e.g., being satisfied by "any" evidence—it may well be that its impact is no greater than that of a permissive inference, and it may be proper to analyze it as such.

In deciding what type of inference or presumption is involved in a case, the jury instructions will generally be controlling, although their interpretation may require recourse to the statute involved and the cases decided under it. * * *

The importance of focusing attention on the precise presentation of the presumption to the jury and the scope of that presumption is illustrated by a comparison of United States v. Gainey, 380 U.S. 63 (1965), with United States v. Romano, 382 U.S. 136 (1965). Both cases involved statutory presumptions based on proof that the defendant was present at the site of an illegal still. In Gainey the Court sustained a conviction "for carrying on" the business of the distillery in violation of 26 U.S.C. § 5601(a)(4), whereas in Romano, the Court set aside a conviction for being in "possession, or custody, or * * * control" of such a distillery in violation of § 5601(a)(1). The difference in outcome was attributable to two important differences between the cases. Because the statute involved in Gainey was a sweeping prohibition of almost any activity associated with the still, whereas the Romano statute involved only one narrow aspect of the total undertaking, there was a much higher probability that mere presence could support an inference of guilt in the former case than in the latter.

Of perhaps greater importance, however, was the difference between the trial judge's instructions to the jury in the two cases. In Gainey, the judge had explained that the presumption

has generally examined the presumption on its face to determine the extent to which the basic and elemental facts coincide. To the extent that the trier of fact is forced to abide by the presumption, and may not reject it based on an independent evaluation of the particular facts presented by the State, the analysis of the presumption's constitutional validity is logically divorced from those facts and based on the presumption's accuracy in the run of cases.[b] It is for this reason that the Court has held it irrelevant in analyzing a mandatory presumption, but not in analyzing a purely permissive one, that there is ample evidence in the record other than the presumption to support a conviction.

* * *

The trial judge's instructions [in this case] make it clear that the presumption * * * gave rise to a permissive inference available only in certain circumstances, rather than a mandatory conclusion of possession, and that it could be ignored by the jury even if there was no affirmative proof offered by defendants in rebuttal. The judge explained that possession could be actual or constructive, but that constructive possession could not exist without the intent and ability to exercise control or dominion over the weapons. He also carefully instructed the jury that there is a mandatory presumption of innocence in favor of the defendants that controls unless it, as the exclusive trier of fact, is satisfied beyond a reasonable doubt that the defendants possessed the handguns in the manner described by the judge. In short, the instructions plainly directed

---

was permissive; it did not require the jury to convict the defendant even if it was convinced that he was present at the site. * * * In *Romano*, the trial judge told the jury that the defendant's presence at the still "shall be deemed sufficient evidence to authorize conviction." Although there was other evidence of guilt, that instruction authorized conviction even if the jury disbelieved all of the testimony except the proof of presence at the site. This Court's holding that the statutory presumption could not support the *Romano* conviction was thus dependent, in part, on the specific instructions given by the trial judge. Under those instructions it was necessary to decide whether, regardless of the specific circumstances of the particular case, the statutory presumption adequately supported the guilty verdict.

    b   * * * [T]his point is illustrated by Leary v. United States, 395 U.S. 6 (1969). In that case, Dr. Timothy Leary, a professor at Harvard University, was stopped by customs inspectors in Laredo, Tex., as he was returning from the Mexican side of the international border. Marihuana seeds and a silver snuffbox filled with semirefined marihuana and three partially smoked marihuana cigarettes were discovered in his car. He was convicted of having knowingly transported marihuana which he knew had been illegally imported into this country in violation of 21 U.S.C. § 176a (1964 ed.) That statute included a mandatory presumption: "possession shall be deemed sufficient evidence to authorize conviction [for importation] unless the defendant explains his possession to the satisfaction of the jury." Leary admitted possession of the marihuana and claimed that he had carried it from New York to Mexico and then back.

* * *

    Despite the fact that the defendant was well educated and had recently traveled to a country that is a major exporter of marihuana to this country, the Court found the presumption of knowledge of importation from possession irrational. It did so, not because Dr. Leary was unlikely to know the source of the marihuana, but instead because "a majority of possessors" were unlikely to have such knowledge. Because the jury had been instructed to rely on the presumption even if it did not believe the Government's direct evidence of knowledge of importation (unless, of course, the defendant met his burden of "satisfying" the jury to the contrary), the Court reversed the conviction.

the jury to consider all the circumstances tending to support or contradict the inference that all four occupants of the car had possession of the two loaded handguns and to decide the matter for itself without regard to how much evidence the defendants introduced.

* * *

As applied to the facts of this case, the presumption of possession is entirely rational. * * * [R]espondents were not hitch-hikers or other casual passengers, and the guns were neither a few inches in length nor out of respondents' sight. The argument against possession by any of the respondents was predicated solely on the fact that the guns were in Jane Doe's pocketbook. But several circumstances * * * made it highly improbable that she was the sole custodian of those weapons.

Even if it was reasonable to conclude that she had placed the guns in her purse before the car was stopped by police, the facts strongly suggest that Jane Doe was not the only person able to exercise dominion over them. The two guns were too large to be concealed in her handbag. The bag was consequently open, and part of one of the guns was in plain view, within easy access of the driver of the car and even, perhaps, of the other two respondents who were riding in the rear seat.

Moreover, it is highly improbable that the loaded guns belonged to Jane Doe or that she was solely responsible for their being in her purse. As a 16-year-old girl in the company of three adult men she was the least likely of the four to be carrying one, let alone two, heavy handguns. It is far more probable that she relied on the pocketknife found in her brassiere for any necessary self-protection. Under these circumstances, it was not unreasonable for her counsel to argue and for the jury to infer that when the car was halted for speeding, the other passengers in the car anticipated the risk of a search and attempted to conceal their weapons in a pocketbook in the front seat. The inference is surely more likely than the notion that these weapons were the sole property of the 16-year-old girl.

Under these circumstances, the jury would have been entirely reasonable in rejecting the suggestion * * * that the handguns were in the sole possession of Jane Doe. Assuming that the jury did reject it, the case is tantamount to one in which the guns were lying on the floor or the seat of the car in plain view of the three other occupants of the automobile. In such a case, it is surely rational to infer that each of the respondents was fully aware of the presence of the guns and had both the ability and the intent to exercise dominion and control over the weapons.

JUSTICE POWELL, with whom JUSTICE BRENNAN, JUSTICE STEWART, and JUSTICE MARSHALL join, dissenting.

* * *

Undeniably, the presumption charged in this case encouraged the jury to draw a particular factual inference regardless of any other evidence presented: to infer that respondents possessed the weapons found in the automobile "upon proof of the presence of the machine gun and the hand weapon" and proof that respondents "occupied the automobile at the time such instruments were found." I believe that the presumption thus charged was unconstitutional because it did not fairly reflect what common sense and experience tell us about passengers in automobiles and the possession of handguns. People present in automobiles where there are weapons simply are not "more likely than not" the possessors of those weapons.

* * *

COMMENT ON PRESUMPTION CASES

The presumption cases establish three rules:

The first rule is that where the prosecution bears the burden of persuasion, a trial judge may not encourage the jury to make logical jumps not supported by the evidence. Otherwise the persuasion burden would be compromised.

The second rule, which would apply only where a persuasion burden could be shifted to a defendant, is that any "instruction must be a fair statement about evidence actually produced in the case." Saltzburg, Burdens of Persuasion in Criminal Cases: Harmonizing the Views of the Justices, 20 Am.Cr.L.Rev. 393 (1983).

The third rule is that any presumption that shifts to the defendant the burden of proof on an element of the crime is unconstitutional under *Winship*. That rule is applied in the cases immediately below.

Shifting the Burden on Intent: Sandstrom v. Montana and Francis v. Franklin

After deciding *Allen*, the Court held in Sandstrom v. Montana, 442 U.S. 510 (1979), that an instruction to the jury in a homicide case that "the law presumes that a person intends the ordinary consequences of his voluntary acts" violated the Constitution, because it may have removed from the prosecution some of its burden to prove beyond a reasonable doubt all elements of the crime charged. The Court observed that unlike in *Allen*, a reasonable jury could have interpreted the instruction as a legal command that was not rebuttable. Alternatively, the jury may have interpreted the instruction as a direction to find intent once voluntary action was proven unless the defendant proved the lack of intent. Finally, the jury could have read the instruction as authorizing it to draw a permissive inference. Because the first two interpretations would have shifted a constitutionally required burden from the prosecutor, and since the Court could not be sure how the jury treated the instruction, the Court found that reversal of the conviction was required.

Justice Brennan, who authored *Sandstrom*, wrote for five members of the Court in Francis v. Franklin, 471 U.S. 307 (1985), as it held invalid the following jury instruction:

> A crime is a violation of a statute of this State in which there shall be a union of joint operation of act or omission to act, and intention or criminal negligence. A person shall not be found guilty of any crime committed by misfortune or accident where it satisfactorily appears there was no criminal scheme or undertaking or intention or criminal negligence. *The acts of a person of sound mind and discretion are presumed to be the product of the person's will, but the presumption may be rebutted. A person of sound mind and discretion is presumed to intend the natural and probable consequences of his acts but the presumption may be rebutted.* A person will not be presumed to act with criminal intention but the trier of facts, that is, the jury, may find criminal intention upon a consideration of the words, conduct, demeanor, motive and all other circumstances connected with the act for which the accused is prosecuted. [Emphasis added.]

The defendant escaped from custody and attempted to obtain a car to speed his flight. He pounded on the door of a house until a 72-year-old resident opened the door. When the defendant pointed a gun and demanded the keys to the resident's car, the resident slammed the door and the gun fired and killed him. The defendant claimed that he did not intend to kill and that the firing was accidental. The jury found him guilty.

Justice Brennan began his analysis by restating the principles the Court had laid down for determining the constitutionality of presumptions:

> The court must determine whether the challenged portion of the instruction creates a mandatory presumption or merely a permissive inference. A mandatory presumption instructs the jury that it must infer the presumed fact if the State proves certain predicate facts. A permissive inference suggests to the jury a possible conclusion to be drawn if the State proves predicate facts, but does not require the jury to draw the conclusion.

Justice Brennan concluded that the challenged instruction created a mandatory presumption, because it was "cast in the language of command." The fact that the judge said the presumption "may be rebutted" did not affect the mandatory nature of the presumption itself. According to Justice Brennan, a mandatory rebuttable presumption can be just as constitutionally infirm as a mandatory irrebuttable presumption.

A mandatory rebuttable presumption does not remove the presumed element from the case if the State proves the predicate facts, but it nonetheless relieves the State of the affirmative burden of persuasion on the presumed element by instructing the jury that it must find the presumed element unless the defendant persuades the jury not to make such a finding. A mandatory rebuttable presumption is perhaps less onerous from the defendant's perspective, but it is no less unconstitutional.

Justice Brennan reasoned that a reasonable jury could have concluded that it had to find an intent to kill unless the defendant persuaded it that intent should not be inferred.

Justice Powell dissented and argued that the combination of the trial court's instructions on reasonable doubt, the presumption of innocence, and interpretation of circumstantial evidence, and the portion of the challenged instructions stating that "criminal intention" cannot be presumed sufficiently removed any danger that a reasonable jury would have imposed a persuasion burden on the defendant. Justice Rehnquist also dissented, joined by the Chief Justice and Justice O'Connor. He suggested that instead of focusing on what a reasonable jury *might* have interpreted the instructions to mean, the Court should find it *likely* that a juror so understood the charge before finding constitutional error.[13]

Observations About Sandstrom and Francis

Sandstrom and *Francis* are cases in which the trial court impermissibly shifted a burden of persuasion through a jury instruction imposing a mandatory presumption. Remember, however, that such an impermissible shift can occur by way of statute as well. See Government of Virgin Islands v. Parrilla, 7 F.3d 1097 (3d Cir.1993) (statute criminalizing maiming, which provides that the infliction of injury is presumptive evidence of intent, constitutes an impermissible mandatory presumption, invalid on its face).

After *Sandstrom, Francis,* and *Allen,* why would a trial court choose to instruct the jury with a presumption, unless the defendant stipulated to it? If the presumption is mandatory, it runs the risk of violating *Winship* and *Mullaney.* If the instruction is permissive, it must be in accord with reason and common sense and as such it would seem to be superfluous to a jury of reasonable people.

---

[13] See also United States v. Johnson, 71 F.3d 139 (4th Cir.1995) (defendant charged with armed robbery of a credit union; trial judge instructs jury that the institution was a credit union within the meaning of the statute; reversal required because the instruction was a mandatory, irrebuttable presumption, and the status of the victim institution as a credit union was an element of the crime).

The cases do leave a trial judge free, however, to instruct the jury that a given inference is permissible. Moreover, the prosecutor is entitled to mention to the jury during argument that the judge has informed the jury of a permissible inference, thereby seeking to take advantage of the judicial imprimatur placed upon the inference. Because a permissible inference instruction could have significant impact on a jury, most trial judges wisely avoid the use of the word "presumption" in criminal cases other than to refer to the presumption of innocence; the use of the word "presumption" is always risky, while a permissive instruction may have almost as much practical impact with almost no risk.

IV. TRIAL BY JURY

A. THE FUNDAMENTAL RIGHT

Article III, Section 2, clause 3 of the Constitution provides that "[t]he trial of all Crimes, except in Cases of Impeachment, shall be by Jury; and such Trial shall be held in the State where the said Crimes shall have been committed; but when not committed within any State, the Trial shall be at such Place or Places as the Congress may by Law have directed." The Sixth Amendment is, in part, redundant; it provides that "[i]n all criminal prosecutions, the accused shall enjoy the right to a speedy and public trial, by an impartial jury of the State and district wherein the crime shall have been committed, which district shall have been previously ascertained by law * * *." Certainly, a right found in two places in the Constitution is likely to be regarded as fundamental. And that is just how the Supreme Court viewed it when it incorporated the Sixth Amendment through the Fourteenth and made it binding on the states.

Note that we have already discussed the right to a jury trial in one context—its interrelationship with the right to require the state to prove every element of the crime beyond a reasonable doubt. Thus, in *Apprendi, supra*, the Court held that the state violated both *Winship* and the constitutional right to a jury trial when it treated an element of a crime as a sentencing factor. The Court in *Apprendi* and its progeny emphasizes that the jury is a bulwark against government overreaching.

The importance of jury determination of all elements of the crime was set out forcefully in the following case.

DUNCAN V. LOUISIANA
Supreme Court of the United States, 1968.
391 U.S. 145.

JUSTICE WHITE delivered the opinion of the Court.

Appellant, Gary Duncan, was convicted of simple battery in the Twenty-fifth Judicial District Court of Louisiana. Under Louisiana law simple battery is a misdemeanor, punishable by a maximum of two years' imprisonment and a $300 fine. Appellant sought trial by jury, but because the Louisiana Constitution grants jury trials only in cases in which capital punishment or imprisonment at hard labor may be imposed, the trial judge denied the request. Appellant was convicted and sentenced to serve 60 days in the parish prison and pay a fine of $150. * * *

Appellant was 19 years of age when tried. While driving on Highway 23 in Plaquemines Parish on October 18, 1966, he saw two younger cousins engaged in a conversation by the side of the road with four white boys. Knowing his cousins, Negroes who had recently transferred to a formerly all-white high school, had reported the occurrence of racial incidents at the school, Duncan stopped the car, got out, and approached the six boys. At trial the white boys and a white onlooker testified, as did appellant and his cousins. The testimony was in dispute on many points, but the witnesses agreed that appellant and the white boys spoke to each other, that appellant encouraged his cousins to break off the encounter and enter his car, and that appellant was about to enter the car himself for the purpose of driving away with his cousins. The whites testified that just before getting in the car appellant slapped Herman Landry, one of the white boys, on the elbow. The Negroes testified that appellant had not slapped Landry, but had merely touched him. The trial judge concluded that the State had proved beyond a reasonable doubt that Duncan had committed simple battery, and found him guilty.

[The Court discusses its prior incorporation cases.]

* * * The claim before us is that the right to trial by jury guaranteed by the Sixth Amendment meets these tests. The position of Louisiana, on the other hand, is that the Constitution imposes upon the State no duty to give a jury trial in any criminal case, regardless of the seriousness of the crime or the size of the punishment which may be imposed. Because we believe that trial by jury in criminal cases is fundamental to the American scheme of justice, we hold that the Fourteenth Amendment guarantees a right of jury trial in all criminal cases which—were they to be tried in a federal court—would come within the Sixth Amendment's guarantee.

* * *

The guarantees of jury trial in the Federal and State Constitutions reflect a profound judgment about the way in which law should be enforced and justice administered. A right to a jury trial is granted to criminal defendants in order to prevent oppression by the Government. Those who wrote our constitutions knew from history and experience that it was necessary to protect against unfounded criminal charges brought to eliminate enemies and against judges too responsive to the voice of higher authority. * * * Providing an accused with the right to be tried by a jury of his peers gave him an inestimable safeguard against the corrupt or overzealous prosecutor and against the compliant, biased, or eccentric judge. If the defendant preferred the common-sense judgment of a jury to the more tutored but perhaps less sympathetic reaction of the single judge, he was to have it. Beyond this, the jury trial provisions in the Federal and State Constitutions reflect a fundamental decision about the exercise of official power—a reluctance to entrust plenary powers over the life and liberty of the citizen to one judge or to a group of judges. Fear of unchecked power, so typical of our State and Federal Governments in other respects, found expression in the criminal law in this insistence upon community participation in the determination of guilt or innocence. The deep commitment of the Nation to the right of jury trial in serious criminal cases as a defense against arbitrary law enforcement qualifies for protection under the Due Process Clause of the Fourteenth Amendment, and must therefore be respected by the States.

Of course jury trial has its weaknesses and the potential for misuse. We are aware of the long debate, especially in this century, among those who write about the administration of justice, as to the wisdom of permitting untrained laymen to determine the facts in civil and criminal proceedings. * * *

The State of Louisiana urges that holding that the Fourteenth Amendment assures a right to jury trial will cast doubt on the integrity of every trial conducted without a jury. Plainly, this is not the import of our holding. Our conclusion is that in the American States, as in the federal judicial system, a general grant of jury trial for serious offenses is a fundamental right, essential for preventing miscarriages of justice and for assuring that fair trials are provided for all defendants. We would not assert, however, that every criminal trial—or any particular trial—held before a judge alone is unfair or that a defendant may never be as fairly treated by a judge as he would be by a jury. Thus we hold no constitutional doubts about the practices common in both federal and state courts, of accepting waivers of jury trial and prosecuting petty crimes without extending a right to jury trial.

* * *

Louisiana's final contention is that even if it must grant jury trials in serious criminal cases, the conviction before us is valid and constitutional because here the petitioner was tried for simple battery and was sentenced to only 60 days in the parish prison. We are not persuaded. It is doubtless true that there is a category of petty crimes or offenses which is not subject to the Sixth Amendment jury trial provision and should not be subject to the Fourteenth Amendment jury trial requirement here applied to the States. Crimes carrying possible penalties up to six months do not require a jury trial if they otherwise qualify as petty offenses, Cheff v. Schnackenberg, 384 U.S. 373 (1966). But the penalty authorized for a particular crime is of major relevance in determining whether it is serious or not and may in itself, if severe enough, subject the trial to the mandates of the Sixth Amendment. * * * In the case before us the Legislature of Louisiana has made simple battery a criminal offense punishable by imprisonment for up to two years and a fine. The question, then, is whether a crime carrying such a penalty is an offense which Louisiana may insist on trying without a jury.

We think not. * * * Of course the boundaries of the petty offense category have always been ill-defined, if not ambulatory. * * * [I]t is necessary to draw a line in the spectrum of crime, separating petty from serious infractions. This process, although essential, cannot be wholly satisfactory, for it requires attaching different consequences to events which, when they lie near the line, actually differ very little.

* * * We need not, however, settle in this case the exact location of the line between petty offenses and serious crimes. It is sufficient for our purposes to hold that a crime punishable by two years in prison is, based on past and contemporary standards in this country, a serious crime and not a petty offense. Consequently, appellant was entitled to a jury trial and it was error to deny it.

* * *

[The concurring opinions of Justice Fortas, and Justice Black (who was joined by Justice Douglas), and the dissenting opinion by Justice Harlan, joined by Justice Stewart, are all omitted.]

NOTE ON THE DEFINITION OF PETTY OFFENSES

The Court clarified its definition of a "petty" offense—to which the right to jury trial does not extend—in Baldwin v. New York, 399 U.S. 66 (1970). In Baldwin the Court defined "petty" by considering the severity of the maximum penalty authorized by the legislature, and concluded that "no offense can be deemed petty for purposes of the right to trial by jury where imprisonment for more than six months is authorized."

Recall Scott v. Illinois, Chapter 5, supra, where the Court held that Scott was not entitled to appointed counsel because he was not imprisoned after his conviction. The offense for which Scott was convicted *authorized* imprisonment for up to a year. Apparently Scott had the right to a jury trial under *Baldwin*. Does it make sense to have a right to jury trial but no right to appointed counsel?

Joinder of Multiple Petty Offenses: Lewis v. United States

In Lewis v. United States, 518 U.S. 322 (1996), the defendant was charged with two misdemeanor counts of obstructing the mails. Each count carried a maximum prison term of six months, and thus each was a "petty offense" within the meaning of the Supreme Court's jury trial jurisprudence. However, the defendant could have been subject to consecutive sentences if convicted of both counts. The lower court denied the defendant's motion for a jury trial and also stated for the record that it would not impose a sentence of more than six months, even if the defendant were convicted of both counts.

Lewis appealed the denial of jury trial, arguing that petty offenses, when they are joined in a single trial, must be aggregated to determine the seriousness of the charges for purposes of the jury trial right. But the Supreme Court rejected this aggregation argument in an opinion by Justice O'Connor. Justice O'Connor analyzed the problem as follows:

> The Sixth Amendment reserves the jury-trial right to defendants accused of serious crimes. * * * [W]e determine whether an offense is serious by looking to the judgment of the legislature, primarily as expressed in the maximum authorized term of imprisonment. Here, by setting the maximum authorized prison term at six months, the legislature categorized the offense of obstructing the mail as petty. The fact that the petitioner was charged with two counts of a petty offense does not revise the legislative judgment as to the gravity of that particular offense, nor does it transform the petty offense into a serious one, to which the jury-trial right would apply.
>
> * * *
>
> * * * As petitioner acknowledges, even if he were to prevail, the Government could properly circumvent the jury-trial right by charging the counts in separate informations and trying them separately.

Justice Kennedy, joined by Justice Breyer, concurred only in the judgment. He agreed that Lewis had no right to jury trial, but only because the lower court had stated that it would not sentence Lewis to more than six months even if he were convicted of both counts. In the absence of this self-imposed limitation, Justice Kennedy would have found a violation of the jury trial right. Justice Kennedy attacked the majority's analysis in the following passage:

> Providing a defendant with the right to be tried by a jury gives "him an inestimable safeguard against the corrupt or overzealous prosecutor and against the compliant, biased, or eccentric judge." These considerations all are present when a judge in a single case sends a defendant to prison for years, whether the sentence is the result of one serious offense or several petty offenses.
>
> On the Court's view of the case, however, there is no limit to the length of the sentence a judge can impose on a defendant without entitling him to a jury, so long as the prosecutor carves up the charges into segments punishable by no more than six months apiece.

Prosecutors have broad discretion in framing charges, for criminal conduct often does not arrange itself in neat categories. In many cases, a prosecutor can choose to charge a defendant with multiple petty offenses rather than a single serious offense, and so prevent him under today's holding from obtaining a trial by jury while still obtaining the same punishment.[14]

Penalties Other than Incarceration

Justice Marshall wrote for a unanimous Court in Blanton v. City of North Las Vegas, 489 U.S. 538 (1989), rejecting the jury trial claim of a defendant charged under Nevada law with driving under the influence (DUI). Under the Nevada law, a convicted defendant is subject to a minimum term of two days' imprisonment and a maximum term of six months' imprisonment. Alternatively, a trial court may order the defendant to perform 48 hours of community work while wearing distinctive garb identifying him as a DUI offender. A convicted defendant may also be fined from $200 to $1,000, he automatically loses his license for 90 days, and he must attend an alcohol abuse education class at his own expense. Blanton argued that all of these non-incarceration penalties made the crime sufficiently serious to require a jury trial.

Justice Marshall relied upon prior cases for the proposition that the primary emphasis in assessing the right to jury trial is on the maximum authorized term of incarceration. Although he recognized that a legislature's view of the seriousness of an offense might also be reflected in other penalties, he reasoned that incarceration is intrinsically different from other penalties and is the most powerful indication of whether an offense is "serious." Justice Marshall stated that penalties other than imprisonment were relevant to the jury trial right only if the defendant can demonstrate that "any additional statutory penalties, viewed in conjunction with the maximum authorized period of incarceration, are so severe that they clearly reflect a legislative determination that the offense in question is a 'serious' one." The Nevada penalties other than incarceration were not onerous enough to overcome the presumption that the offense was "petty."

The Court relied on its decision in *Blanton* in deciding United States v. Nachtigal, 507 U.S. 1 (1993) (per curiam). Nachtigal was charged with operating a motor vehicle in a national park while under the influence of alcohol. The maximum punishment was six months imprisonment and a $5,000 fine, and the sentencing court had the authority to impose a five year probationary sentence as an alternative to incarceration. A unanimous Supreme Court held that *Blanton* was controlling. The Court noted that "it is a rare case where a legislature packs an offense it deems

---

[14]   Justice Stevens wrote a short dissenting opinion in *Lewis*.

serious with onerous penalties that nonetheless do not puncture the 6-month incarceration line." The Court reasoned that Congress limited penalties to six months and thereby made a legislative judgment as to the non-seriousness of such offenses, and that the possibility of a probationary sentence or a fine of $5,000 were not sufficiently severe to overcome the *Blanton* presumption.

B. WHAT THE JURY DECIDES

Are there any questions of fact that should or can be decided by the court rather than the jury? This question underlies much of the law concerning the use of presumptions, supra. Another important question, also previously discussed in this Chapter, under the *Apprendi* line of cases, is whether factual issues can be allocated to the judge rather than the jury as part of a sentencing determination.

We have seen that all elements of a crime must be left for the jury and must be proved beyond a reasonable doubt. When courts occasionally forget this principle, they are reminded by the Supreme Court. Thus, in United States v. Gaudin, 515 U.S. 506 (1995), the defendant was charged with violating 18 U.S.C. § 1001, which prohibits the making of false "material" statements to government agencies. The trial judge instructed the jury that the defendant's statements were material within the meaning of the statute. The Court, in a unanimous opinion by Justice Scalia, held that the question of materiality was for the jury. Therefore, the defendant's rights to jury trial and due process were violated when the judge rather than the jury decided whether the statements were material. Justice Scalia declared:

> The Constitution gives a criminal defendant the right to demand that a jury find him guilty of all the elements of the crime with which he is charged; one of the elements in the present case is materiality; respondent therefore had a right to have the jury decide materiality.

Justice Scalia rejected the government's argument that the Sixth Amendment permits judges to decide whether elements of the crime have been proved when those elements present mixed questions of law and fact. He noted that juries typically decide mixed questions of law and fact—including the ultimate question of whether the defendant is guilty of the crime charged.

If, however, an issue is collateral to the resolution of an element of the crime, it is generally resolved by the judge rather than the jury. For example, it is the judge who decides whether evidence was illegally obtained and should be excluded. Also, the admissibility of evidence is generally a question for the judge, while the jury decides the weight to be given to evidence that is admitted. See Federal Rule of Evidence 104.

C. REQUISITE FEATURES OF THE JURY

1. Size

WILLIAMS V. FLORIDA
Supreme Court of the United States, 1970.
399 U.S. 78.

JUSTICE WHITE delivered the opinion of the court.

[Williams filed a pretrial motion for a 12-person jury instead of the six-person jury provided by Florida law in all but capital cases. The motion was denied and Williams was convicted of robbery by a jury of six persons and sentenced to life imprisonment. In Part I of the opinion, the Court rejected Williams's attack on a state rule requiring the defendant to give notice of an alibi defense. See Chapter 8 for a discussion of that point.]

* * * The question in this case then is whether the constitutional guarantee of a trial by "jury" necessarily requires trial by exactly 12 persons, rather than some lesser number—in this case six. We hold that the 12-man panel is not a necessary ingredient of "trial by jury," and that respondent's refusal to impanel more than the six members provided for by Florida law did not violate petitioner's Sixth Amendment rights as applied to the States through the Fourteenth.

We had occasion in Duncan v. Louisiana to review briefly the oft-told history of the development of trial by jury in criminal cases. That history revealed a long tradition attaching great importance to the concept of relying on a body of one's peers to determine guilt or innocence as a safeguard against arbitrary law enforcement. That same history, however, affords little insight into the considerations that gradually led the size of that body to be generally fixed at 12. Some have suggested that the number 12 was fixed upon simply because that was the number of the presentment jury from the hundred, from which the petit jury developed. Other, less circular but more fanciful reasons for the number 12 have been given, "but they were all brought forward after the number was fixed," and rest on little more than mystical or superstitious insights into the significance of "12." Lord Coke's explanation that the *number of twelve* is much respected *in holy writ,* as 12 *apostles,* 12 *stones,* 12 *tribes, etc.,*" is typical. In short, while sometime in the 14th century the size of the jury at common law came to be fixed generally at 12, that particular feature of the jury system appears to have been a historical accident, unrelated to the great purposes which gave rise to the jury in the first place. The question before us is whether this accidental feature of the jury has been immutably codified into our Constitution.

* * *

While "the intent of the Framers" is often an elusive quarry, the relevant constitutional history casts considerable doubt on the easy assumption in our past decisions that if a given feature existed in a jury at common law in 1789, then it was necessarily preserved in the Constitution. Provisions for jury trial were first placed in the Constitution in Article III's provision that "[t]he Trial of all Crimes * * * shall be by Jury; and such Trial shall be held in the State where the said Crimes shall have been committed." The "very scanty history [of this provision] in the records of the Constitutional Convention" sheds little light either way on the intended correlation between Article III's "jury" and the features of the jury at common law. Indeed, pending and after the adoption of the Constitution, fears were expressed that Article III's provision failed to preserve the common-law right to be tried by a "jury of the vicinage." That concern, as well as the concern to preserve the right to jury in civil as well as criminal cases, furnished part of the impetus for introducing amendments to the Constitution that ultimately resulted in the jury trial provisions of the Sixth and Seventh Amendments. As introduced by James Madison in the House, the Amendment relating to jury trial in criminal cases would have provided that:

> "The trial of all crimes * * * shall be by an impartial jury of free-holders of the vicinage, with the requisite of unanimity for conviction, of the right of challenge, and other accustomed requisites * * *."

The Amendment passed the House in substantially this form, but after more than a week of debate in the Senate it returned to the House considerably altered. * * * [The Court discusses more history, including appointment of a Conference committee.] The version that finally emerged from the Committee was the version that ultimately became the Sixth Amendment, ensuring an accused:

> "the right to a speedy and public trial, by an impartial jury of the State and district wherein the crime shall have been committed, which district shall have been previously ascertained by law * * *."

Gone were the provisions spelling out such common-law features of the jury as "unanimity," or "the accustomed requisites." And the "vicinage" requirement itself had been replaced by wording that reflected a compromise between broad and narrow definitions of that term, and that left Congress the power to determine the actual size of the "vicinage" by its creation of judicial districts.

Three significant features may be observed in this sketch of the background of the Constitution's jury trial provisions. First, even though the vicinage requirement was as much a feature of the common-law jury as was the 12-man requirement, the mere reference to "trial by jury" in Article III was not interpreted to include that feature. * * * Second, provisions that would have explicitly tied the "jury" concept to the "accustomed requisites" of the time were eliminated. * * * Finally, contemporary legislative and constitutional provisions indicate that where Congress wanted to leave no doubt that it was incorporating existing common-law features of the jury system, it knew how to use express language to that effect. * * *

* * * Nothing in this history suggests, then, that we do violence to the letter of the Constitution by turning to other than purely historical considerations to determine which features of the jury system, as it existed at common law, were preserved in the Constitution. The relevant inquiry, as we see it, must be the function that the particular feature performs and its relation to the purposes of the jury trial. Measured by this standard, the 12-man requirement cannot be regarded as an indispensable component of the Sixth Amendment.

The purpose of the jury trial, as we noted in *Duncan,* is to prevent oppression by the Government. * * * Given this purpose, the essential feature of a jury obviously lies in the interposition between the accused and his accuser of the commonsense judgment of a group of laymen, and in the community participation and shared responsibility that results from that group's determination of guilt or innocence. The performance of this role is not a function of the particular number of the body that makes up the jury. To be sure, the number should probably be large enough to promote group deliberation, free from outside attempts at intimidation, and to provide a fair possibility for obtaining a representative cross-section of the community. But we find little reason to think that these goals are in any meaningful sense less likely to be achieved when the jury numbers six, than when it numbers 12—particularly if the requirement of unanimity is retained. * * *

It might be suggested that the 12-man jury gives a defendant a greater advantage since he has more "chances" of finding a juror who will insist on acquittal and thus prevent conviction. But the advantage might just as easily belong to the State which also needs only one juror out of twelve insisting on guilt to prevent acquittal. What few experiments have occurred—usually in the civil area—indicate that there is no discernible difference between the results reached by the two different-sized juries. In short, neither currently available evidence nor theory suggests that the 12-man jury is necessarily more advantageous to the defendant than a jury composed of fewer members.

Similarly, while in theory the number of viewpoints represented on a randomly selected jury ought to increase as the size of the jury increases, in practice the difference between the 12-man and the six-man jury in terms of the cross-section of the community represented seems likely to be negligible. Even the 12-man jury cannot insure representation of every distinct voice in the community, particularly given the use of the peremptory challenge. * * *

* * *

[Justice Harlan, concurring in the result, reiterated his concern expressed in *Duncan*, that incorporation of the Sixth Amendment dilutes federal guarantees in order to reconcile the logic of "incorporation" with the reality of federalism.]

[The Chief Justice concurred. Justice Black and Justice Douglas concurred in part and dissented in part. Justice Marshall dissented in part. Justice Stewart concurred in the result. Justice Blackmun took no part in the decision of the case.]

BALLEW V. GEORGIA

Supreme Court of the United States, 1978.
435 U.S. 223.

JUSTICE BLACKMUN announced the judgment of the court and delivered an opinion in which JUSTICE STEVENS joined.

[Ballew was convicted on two misdemeanor counts of distributing obscene material by a five-person jury impaneled according to Georgia law. The opinion recites the facts and describes *Williams*].

When the Court in *Williams* permitted the reduction in jury size * * * it expressly reserved ruling on the issue whether a number smaller than six passed constitutional scrutiny. The Court refused to speculate when this so-called "slippery slope" would become too steep. We face now, however, the two-fold question whether a further reduction in the size of the state criminal trial jury does make the grade too dangerous, that is, whether it inhibits the functioning of the jury as an institution to a significant degree, and, if so, whether any state interest counterbalances and justifies the disruption so as to preserve its constitutionality.

Williams v. Florida * * * generated a quantity of scholarly work on jury size. These writings do not draw or identify a bright line below which the number of jurors would not be able to function as required by the standards enunciated in *Williams*. On the other hand, they raise significant questions about the wisdom and constitutionality of a reduction below six. We examine these concerns:

First, recent empirical data suggest that progressively smaller juries are less likely to foster effective group deliberation. At some point, this decline leads to inaccurate fact-finding and incorrect application of the common sense of the community to the facts. Generally, a positive correlation exists between group size and the quality of both group performance and group productivity. A variety of explanations have been offered for this conclusion. Several are particularly applicable in the jury setting. The smaller the group, the less likely are members to make critical contributions necessary for the solution of a given problem. Because most juries are not permitted to take notes, memory is important for accurate jury deliberations. As juries decrease in size, then, they are less likely to have members who remember each of the important pieces of evidence or argument. Furthermore, the smaller the group, the less likely it is to overcome the biases of its members to obtain an accurate result. When individual and group decisionmaking were compared, it was seen that groups performed better because prejudices of individuals were frequently counterbalanced, and objectivity resulted. Groups also exhibited increased motivation and self-criticism. All of these advantages, except, perhaps, self-motivation, tend to diminish as the size of the group diminishes. * * *

Second, the data now raise doubts about the accuracy of the results achieved by smaller and smaller panels. Statistical studies suggest that the risk of convicting an innocent person rises as the size of the jury diminishes * * *. [The studies posit that by considering the risk of not convicting a guilty party, an optimal jury size between six and eight is identified.] As the size diminished to five and below, the weighted sum of errors increased because of the enlarging risk of the conviction of innocent defendants.

Another doubt about progressively smaller juries arises from the increasing inconsistency that results from the decreases. [Several studies suggest that 12-person panels considering the same case will reach the same result, or compromise to the same result, with greater consistency than a six-person panel.]

Third, the data suggest that the verdicts of jury deliberation in criminal cases will vary as juries become smaller, and that the variance amounts to an imbalance to the detriment of one side, the defense. [The Court noted that hung juries will diminish because a person in the minority is less likely to have an ally on the six-person panel, and thus is less likely to speak up.]

Fourth, what has just been said about the presence of minority viewpoint as juries decrease in size foretells problems not only for jury decisionmaking, but also for the representation of minority groups in the community. * * * Further reduction in size will erect additional barriers to representation.

Fifth, several authors have identified in jury research methodological problems tending to mask differences in the operation of smaller and larger juries. Nationwide, however, these small percentages will represent a large number of cases. And it is with respect to those cases that the jury trial right has its greatest value. When the case is close, and the guilt or innocence of the defendant is not readily apparent, a properly functioning jury system will insure evaluation by the sense of the community and will also tend to insure accurate factfinding. * * *

* * *

While we adhere to, and reaffirm our holding in Williams v. Florida, these studies, most of which have been made since *Williams* was decided in 1970, lead us to conclude that the purpose and functioning of the jury in a criminal trial is seriously impaired, and to a constitutional degree, by a reduction in size to below six members. We readily admit that we do not pretend to discern a clear line between six members and five. But the assembled data raise substantial doubt about the reliability and appropriate representation of panels smaller than six. Because of the fundamental importance of the jury trial to the American system of criminal justice, any further reduction that promotes inaccurate and possibly biased decisionmaking, that causes untoward differences in verdicts, and that prevents juries from truly representing their communities, attains constitutional significance.

* * *

* * * We find no significant state advantage in reducing the number of jurors from six to five. * * *

[The concurring opinion of Justice Stevens is omitted.]

JUSTICE WHITE concurring in the judgment.

Agreeing that a jury of fewer than six persons would fail to represent the sense of the community and hence not satisfy the fair cross-section requirement of the Sixth and Fourteenth Amendments, I concur in the judgment of reversal.

JUSTICE POWELL, with whom THE CHIEF JUSTICE and MR. JUSTICE REHNQUIST join, concurring in the judgment.

I concur in the judgment, as I agree that use of a jury as small as five members, with authority to convict for serious offenses, involves grave questions of fairness. As the opinion of Mr. Justice Blackmun indicates, the line between five-and six-member juries is difficult to justify, but a line has to be drawn somewhere if the substance of jury trial is to be preserved.

* * * I have reservations as to the wisdom—as well as the necessity—of Mr. Justice Blackmun's heavy reliance on numerology derived from statistical studies. Moreover, neither the validity nor the methodology employed by the studies cited was subjected to the traditional testing mechanisms of the adversary process. The studies relied on merely represent unexamined findings of persons interested in the jury system.

For these reasons I concur only in the judgment.

JUSTICE BRENNAN, with whom JUSTICE STEWART and JUSTICE MARSHALL join.

I join Mr. Justice Blackmun's opinion insofar as it holds that the Sixth and Fourteenth Amendments require juries in criminal trials to contain more than five persons. * * *

2. Unanimity

APODACA V. OREGON

Supreme Court of the United States, 1972.
406 U.S. 404.

JUSTICE WHITE announced the judgment of the Court and an opinion in which THE CHIEF JUSTICE, JUSTICE BLACKMUN and JUSTICE REHNQUIST joined.

[The three petitioners were convicted of various criminal charges by three separate, less than unanimous Oregon juries. Two juries returned 11–1 votes, the third returned the minimum (under state law) 10–2 verdict. The court decided this case together with Johnson v. Louisiana, 406 U.S.356 (1972), upholding a 9 vote requirement for conviction or acquittal by a 12 person jury. Justice White wrote that opinion also. Justice Powell's opinion concurred in *Johnson* and concurred in the judgment in *Apodaca*. Justice Blackmun's concurring opinion, Justice Douglas's dissent, Justice Stewart's dissent and Justice Brennan's dissent applied to both cases.]

* * *

Our inquiry must focus upon the function served by the jury in contemporary society. As we said in *Duncan,* the purpose of trial by jury is to prevent oppression by the Government by providing a "safeguard against the corrupt or overzealous prosecutor and against the compliant, biased, or eccentric judge." "Given this purpose, the essential feature of a jury obviously lies in the interposition between the accused and his accuser of the commonsense judgment of a group of laymen * * *." A requirement of unanimity, however, does not materially contribute to the exercise of this commonsense judgment. As we said in *Williams,* a jury will come to such a judgment as long as it consists of a group of laymen representative of a cross section of the community who have the duty and the opportunity to deliberate, free from outside attempts at intimidation, on the question of a defendant's guilt. In terms of this function we perceive no difference between juries required to act unanimously and those permitted to convict or acquit by votes of 10 to two or 11 to one. Requiring unanimity would obviously produce hung juries in some situations where nonunanimous juries will convict or acquit. But in either case, the interest of the defendant in having the judgment of his peers interposed between himself and the officers of the State who prosecute and judge him is equally well served.

* * *

Petitioners also cite quite accurately a long line of decisions of this Court upholding the principle that the Fourteenth Amendment requires jury panels to reflect a cross section of the community. They then contend that unanimity is a necessary precondition for effective application of the cross-section requirement, because a rule permitting less than unanimous verdicts will make it possible for convictions to occur without the acquiescence of minority elements within the community.

There are two flaws in this argument. One is petitioners' assumption that every distinct voice in the community has a right to be represented on every jury and a right to prevent conviction of a defendant in any case. All that the Constitution forbids, however, is systematic exclusion of identifiable segments of the community from jury panels * * *.

We also cannot accept petitioners' second assumption—that minority groups, even when they are represented on a jury, will not adequately represent the viewpoint of those groups simply because they may be outvoted in the final result. They will be present during all deliberations, and their views will be heard. We cannot assume that the majority of the jury will refuse to weigh the evidence and reach a decision upon rational grounds, just as it must now do in order to obtain unanimous verdicts, or that a majority will deprive a man of his liberty on the basis of prejudice when a minority is presenting a reasonable argument in favor of acquittal. We simply find no proof for the notion that a majority will disregard its instructions and cast its votes for guilt or innocence based on prejudice rather than the evidence.

* * *

JUSTICE POWELL, concurring in the judgment.

[Justice Powell—subscribing to the views of Justice Harlan set forth in Chapter 1, supra—rejected the theory that all elements of the jury trial within the meaning of the Sixth Amendment are incorporated into the Due Process Clause of the Fourteenth Amendment and applied against the states. Using a due process analysis, he agreed with the plurality that unanimity is not required in state trials, even though he believed that the Sixth Amendment requires unanimity in federal trials.]

JUSTICE DOUGLAS, with whom JUSTICE BRENNAN and JUSTICE MARSHALL concur, dissenting.

* * *

The plurality approves a procedure which diminishes the reliability of a jury. * * *

The diminution of verdict reliability flows from the fact that nonunanimous juries need not debate and deliberate as fully as must unanimous juries. As soon as the requisite majority is attained, further consideration is not required * * * even though the dissident jurors might, if given the chance, be able to convince the majority. * * * The Court now extracts from the jury room this automatic check against hasty factfinding by relieving jurors of the duty to hear out fully the dissenters.

* * *

[Justice Blackmun filed a concurring opinion. Justices Brennan, Stewart, and Marshall filed dissenting opinions.]

QUESTIONS ON SIZE AND UNANIMITY

Go back to *Duncan* and examine the reasons that the Court gave for holding that the right to jury trial is fundamental and binding on the states. If protection against eccentric or biased judges and vindictive prosecutions underlies the right, what would common sense tell you about the likelihood that a six-person, as opposed to a twelve-person jury, would provide such protection? If a 10–2 verdict is acceptable, can you think of any good reason why a 7–5 verdict would not be acceptable? Do you think that conviction or acquittal by a divided jury is consistent with the values that make the jury trial right fundamental? If a state provided a five-person jury but required unanimity, are you as sure as the *Ballew* Court that this would have been worse than a 10–2 verdict?

One of the arguments against unanimous verdicts is that it forces compromises. For example, if ten jurors decide a defendant is guilty of first degree murder and two believe that the defendant is innocent, the jury if required to be unanimous might compromise on second degree murder as an alternative to continued deliberation. But is a compromise by a jury that follows the instructions of a court (requiring each juror to support the verdict) an evil? Is it arguable that any compromise by a unanimous jury is a final agreement by all jurors on a just verdict?

Remember that *Apodaca* dealt only with state jury verdicts. Fed.R.Crim.P. 31(a) requires jury verdicts in federal criminal cases to be unanimous, as Justice Powell would have required. Almost all states still require unanimous verdicts as well. When mistrials due to hung juries in high profile prosecutions occur, there may be a call for consideration of non-unanimous verdicts to limit the risk of the deadweight cost of a hung jury. But, there is clearly no trend toward adopting rules permitting non-unanimous verdicts.

Waiver

In unanimity jurisdictions, should the prosecution and defense be able to stipulate in advance that they agree to be bound by a non-unanimous verdict? The court in United States v. Ullah, 976 F.2d 509 (9th Cir.1992), declared that "the right to a unanimous verdict is so important that it is one of the few rights of a criminal defendant that cannot, under any circumstances, be waived." But if the parties can agree to opt for a bench trial and dispense with the jury entirely, why can't they agree to a non-unanimous verdict? See Sanchez v. United States, 782 F.2d 928 (11th Cir.1986) (permitting waiver of unanimity, but only in situations where the jury has been deliberating and is unable to come to an agreement).

3.   The Interplay Between Size and Unanimity

The Court analyzed the interplay between the constitutionally sufficient six-person jury, and the issue of unanimity, in Burch v. Louisiana, 441 U.S. 130 (1979). In an opinion by Justice Rehnquist, the Court held that "conviction by a nonunanimous six-person jury in a state criminal trial for a nonpetty offense deprives an accused of his constitutional right to trial by jury." The Court conceded that drawing lines was difficult, but found it essential to draw the line somewhere. It concluded that use of nonunanimous six-person juries violated the right to jury trial. There were no dissents.

In *Burch,* Justice Rehnquist stated that the "near-uniform judgment of the Nation"—as reflected by the fact that only two states permitted non-unanimous verdicts by a six-person jury—"provides a useful guide in delimiting the line between those jury practices that are constitutionally permissible and those that are not." But when *Apodaca* was decided, the vast majority of states required unanimous verdicts, and still do. How, then, did *Apodaca* get decided the way it did?

D. JURY SELECTION AND COMPOSITION

1. The Jury Pool

The Sixth Amendment assures the defendant "an impartial jury of the State and district wherein the crime shall have been committed." This language, with its emphasis on both the impartial and community character of the jury, has served as a touchstone in the regulation of the pool from which the petit jury is drawn. (The body of candidates from which the petit jury is drawn is also known as the "venire"). Another constitutional regulation on selection of the jury pool is the Equal

Protection Clause, which prohibits exclusion from the jury pool on the basis of suspect classifications such as race.

In Glasser v. United States, 315 U.S. 60, 85–86 (1942), the Court observed as follows:

> [The jury selection process] must always accord with the fact that the proper functioning of the jury system, and, indeed, our democracy itself, requires that the jury be a "body truly representative of the community," and not the organ of any special group or class. If that requirement is observed, the officials charged with choosing federal jurors may exercise some discretion to the end that competent jurors may be called. But they must not allow the desire for competent jurors to lead them into selections which do not comport with the concept of the jury as a cross-section of the community.

Thus, the selection of the jury pool must be unbiased; it must generate a panel representing a cross-section of the community. Selection of jurors cannot violate principles of equal protection. And finally, each individual juror must be impartial, unbiased and free from outside influences.

2. The Fair Cross-Section Requirement and the Equal Protection Clause

Two Separate Rights

As stated above, there are two separate constitutional provisions that can impact the selection of the pool from which a jury is drawn. The Equal Protection Clause prohibits the selection or rejection of jurors on the basis of race, sex, or any other suspect classification. Application of equal protection standards to jury selection is similar to the equal protection law applied in other contexts. See, e.g., Castaneda v. Partida, 430 U.S. 482 (1977) (in order to establish a prima facie equal protection violation, the defendant "must show that the procedure employed resulted in substantial underrepresentation of his race or of the identifiable group to which he belongs"; the burden then shifts to the state to rebut the inference of discrimination by showing neutral selection criteria); United States v. Esquivel, 75 F.3d 545 (9th Cir.1996) (rejecting a challenge that selection of jury panel violated equal protection due to underrepresentation of Hispanics; defendant failed to show statistical disparity or intent to discriminate).[15] The Sixth Amendment independently requires that the jury be chosen from a fair cross-section of the community. The Supreme Court has used both constitutional protections to attempt to assure fair and representative jury selection procedures.

---

[15] Equal protection standards also regulate the use of peremptory challenges to prospective jurors. See the discussion of Batson v. Kentucky and its progeny, infra in this Chapter.

The goals of the two constitutional guarantees are somewhat different, though overlapping, in the context of selection of the jury pool. The goal of the Equal Protection Clause is of course to prevent government discrimination on the basis of race, sex, or other suspect classification. The goal of the fair cross-section requirement is to assure that the defendant get the benefit of a jury that is representative of the community. As one court put it, the purposes of the fair cross-section requirement include "ensuring that the common sense judgment of the community will act as a hedge against overzealous prosecutions; preserving public confidence in the criminal justice system; and furthering the notion that participation in the administration of justice is a part of one's civic responsibility." United States v. Raszkiewicz, 169 F.3d 459 (7th Cir.1999).

Early Cases Establishing the Rights

The first challenges to the selection of the jury developed under the rubric of the Equal Protection Clause, in response to race-related exclusions. In Strauder v. West Virginia, 100 U.S. 303 (1879), the Court struck down a state statute that excluded African-Americans from grand and petit jury service as violative of the Fourteenth Amendment's Equal Protection Clause.

The Court first recognized the impact of the exclusion of a non-race-related group in a civil case, Thiel v. Southern Pacific Co., 328 U.S. 217 (1946). The Court held that the systematic exclusion of daily wage earners from a federal court jury panel violated the fair cross-section requirement—no violation of equal protection could be found in the exclusion of daily wage earners as they were not a suspect class. See, e.g., United States v. Esquivel, 75 F.3d 545 (9th Cir.1996) (in contrast to an equal protection violation, "a prima facie case for establishing a Sixth Amendment, fair cross section violation does not require the appellant to prove discriminatory intent or require that the appellant be a member of the distinct, excluded group").

In *Thiel,* the jury commissioner and clerk used a city directory to identify and exclude daily wage earners from a federal court jury panel. The Court ruled that although a judge may exclude a person from jury service when participation entails a financial hardship, complete exclusion in the absence of such a finding is forbidden.

In Ballard v. United States, 329 U.S. 187 (1946), the Court held that the purposeful and systematic exclusion of women from both grand and petit juries in the district where an indictment was returned required its dismissal. The court exercised its supervisory power after concluding that the selection scheme departed from that which Congress adopted.

Fair Cross-Section Requirement Does Not Apply to Petit Jury

In recognizing the existence of cognizable classes other than race under the Fair Cross-Section Clause, the Court has been careful to delineate the scope of the defendant's challenge. Both *Thiel* and *Ballard* emphasized that a defendant has no right to challenge a particular jury as failing to represent all social, economic, and political groups. Rather, the defendant is restricted to challenging the selection *procedure* as systematically excluding a cognizable group. That is, the fair cross-section requirement is applicable to the jury *pool*, but not to the ultimate petit jury that hears the defendant's case. This was confirmed in Holland v. Illinois, 493 U.S. 474 (1990), where a five-person majority explicitly held that the fair cross-section requirement does not allow a defendant to attack the composition of the petit jury. Consequently, the Sixth Amendment did not protect the defendant, who was white, from the prosecutor's discriminatory use of peremptory challenges to exclude African-Americans from the petit jury. Justice Scalia, writing for the Court, stressed that it would be all but impossible to form a petit jury that mirrored a cross-section of the community. The impact of *Holland* has been severely curtailed, however, by the Court's use of the Equal Protection Clause to limit the exercise of peremptory challenges. Thus, the Equal Protection Clause, and not the Fair Cross-Section Clause, imposes restrictions on the composition of the petit jury. See the discussion of Batson v. Kentucky, infra.

Standing to Object to a Fair Cross-Section Violation

TAYLOR v. LOUISIANA
Supreme Court of the United States, 1975.
419 U.S. 522.

JUSTICE WHITE delivered the opinion of the Court.

[The Louisiana Code provided that a woman should not be selected for jury service unless she had previously filed a written declaration of her desire to be subject to jury service. Appellant, a male, alleged that the statute violated his Sixth and Fourteenth Amendment right to a jury drawn from a fair cross-section of the community.]

The Louisiana jury-selection system does not disqualify women from jury service, but in operation its conceded systematic impact is that only a very few women, grossly disproportionate to the number of eligible women in the community, are called for jury service. In this case, no women were on the venire from which the petit jury was drawn. * * *

The State first insists that Taylor, a male, has no standing to object to the exclusion of women from his jury. But Taylor's claim is that he was constitutionally entitled to a jury drawn from a venire constituting a fair cross section of the community and that the jury that tried him was not such a jury by reason of the exclusion of women. Taylor was not a member of the excluded class; but there is no rule that claims such as Taylor presents may be made only by those defendants who are members of the group excluded from jury service. Taylor, in the case before us, was similarly entitled to tender and have adjudicated the claim that the exclusion of women from jury service deprived him of the kind of factfinder to which he was constitutionally entitled.

* * *

We accept the fair-cross-section requirement as fundamental to the jury trial guaranteed by the Sixth Amendment and are convinced that the requirement has solid foundation. The purpose of a jury is to guard against the exercise of arbitrary power—to make available the commonsense judgment of the community as a hedge against the overzealous or mistaken prosecutor and in preference to the professional or perhaps over-conditioned or biased response of a judge. This prophylactic vehicle is not provided if the jury pool is made up of only special segments of the populace or if large, distinctive groups are excluded from the pool. Community participation in the administration of the criminal law, moreover, is not only consistent with our democratic heritage but is also critical to public confidence in the fairness of the criminal justice system. * * *

We are also persuaded that the fair-cross-section requirement is violated by the systematic exclusion of women, who in the judicial district involved here amounted to 53% of the citizens eligible for jury service. This conclusion necessarily entails the judgment that women are sufficiently numerous and distinct from men and that if they are systematically eliminated from jury panels, the Sixth Amendment's fair-cross-section requirement cannot be satisfied. * * *

There remains the argument that women as a class serve a distinctive role in society and that jury service would so substantially interfere with that function that the state has ample justification for excluding women from service unless they volunteer, even though the result is that almost all jurors are men. * * *

The States are free to grant exemptions from jury service to individuals in case of special hardship or incapacity and to those engaged in particular occupations the uninterrupted performance of which is critical to the community's welfare. * * * A system excluding all women, however, is a wholly different matter. It is untenable to suggest these days that it would be a special hardship for each and every woman to perform jury service or that society cannot spare *any* women from their present duties. This may be the case with many, and it may be burdensome to sort out those who should be exempted from those who should serve. But that task is performed in the case of men, and the administrative convenience in dealing with women as a class is insufficient justification for diluting the quality of community judgment represented by the jury in criminal trials.

* * *

Standards for Prima Facie Violation of the Fair Cross-Section Requirement: Duren v. Missouri

In Duren v. Missouri, 439 U.S. 357 (1979), the Court held that in order to establish a prima facie violation of the fair cross-section requirement, a defendant must show three things:

- the group excluded from the jury array is a distinctive group within the community;

- the representation of the group in the venire from which jurors are selected is not fair and reasonable in relation to the number of such persons in the community; and

- this underrepresentation is the result of a systematic exclusion of the group in the jury selection process.

If the defendant establishes these three factors, the burden shifts to the state to show that the inclusion of the underrepresented group would be "incompatible with a significant state interest."

The Court found that Duren had made out a prima facie case by showing that 54% of the adult inhabitants of the county were women, while only 15% of the persons placed on venires were women, and a woman could decline jury service by simply not reporting for jury duty while a man did not have the same option. Justice White, writing for the Court, stated that an exemption tailored to women who could not leave their children might effectuate a state interest sufficient to satisfy the fair cross-section requirement, but that no such limited exemption was operative in this case.

Distinctive Groups for Fair Cross-Section Purposes

What groups are distinctive under the fair cross-section requirement? After *Duren,* is a constitutional challenge alleging, for example, that blue collar workers are excluded from state juries likely to succeed? What about young adults? See Anaya v. Hansen, 781 F.2d 1 (1st Cir.1986) (neither young adults nor blue collar workers constituted a cognizable group for cross-section analysis).

The court in United States v. Fletcher, 965 F.2d 781 (9th Cir.1992), set forth a test, followed by many courts, for determining whether a group is "distinctive" under *Duren:*

[A] defendant must show (1) that the group is defined and limited by some factor (i.e., that the group has a definite composition such as by race or sex); (2) that a common thread or basic similarity in attitude, ideas, or experience runs through the group; and (3) that there is a community of interests among members of the group such that the group's interest cannot be adequately represented if the group is excluded from the jury selection process.

Applying this three-factor test, the *Fletcher* court held that college students are not a distinctive group for fair cross-section purposes:

The group of individuals we call "college students" is no more capable of fitting into a pigeon hole than the group we call "young adults." The group is not defined by any "limiting factor"—anyone may be a college student. Nor is there a common thread of "attitude" or "experience" that runs through the group, beyond the fact that every member spends a certain percentage of his or her time in a classroom. It is true that the privilege of a college education continues to be enjoyed only by a minority of our citizens. Nevertheless, the variety of groups that are represented in college classrooms is vast and growing, so that the economic, geographic, racial, sexual, political, and religious demographics of that minority are nearly as diverse as those of the nation itself. It is farfetched to suggest that the college experience could coalesce the diverse points of view that are the necessary product of such divergent experiences into a single "community of interest" that will go unrepresented on a jury if there are no "college students" among its members.

While college students do not have a sufficient community of interest to be distinctive, what about Grateful Dead fans? Liberal arts majors?

For other cases analyzing the distinctiveness of certain groups, see Brewer v. Nix, 963 F.2d 1111 (8th Cir.1992) (people over 65 are not a distinctive group for cross-section purposes); United States v. Raszkiewicz, 169 F.3d 459 (7th Cir.1999) (exclusion from jury venires of Native Americans who live on reservations did not violate the fair-cross section requirement because they are not a distinctive group); United States v. Barry, 71 F.3d 1269 (7th Cir.1995) (upholding exclusion from jury service of persons who have felony charges pending against them: "We are not convinced that alleged felons comprise a distinctive group. They have in common that they may have run afoul of the criminal justice system. However, there are many and varied ways to do that.").

Proper Sources for the Jury Pool

If a state can show a truly random selection process, and if the state uses a source (or sources) of jury names—e.g., driver's license lists as well as voting lists—that is likely to include most members of a community, most challenges to selection of the jury pool will be rejected.[16]

Contentions have been made that certain groups are especially likely not to register to vote and therefore that voter lists do not produce a cross-section of the community. However, as long as voter lists do not have racial identifications and are used as part of some non-discriminatory selection scheme, their use is likely to be sustained. See United States v. Lewis, 10 F.3d 1086 (4th Cir.1993) (use of voter lists is presumptively proper). In fact, underrepresentation should be rare if voting lists are used. But if a state refuses to follow clear, visible selection procedures, invalidation on fair cross-section grounds becomes more likely.[17]

3.   Voir Dire and Court Control

Establishing a jury venire representing a fair cross-section of the community, and selected without violating principles of equal protection, is only the first stage in the jury selection procedure. The second stage, also regulated by these constitutional guarantees, is to assure that the actual trial jury is impartial and fairly chosen. Because preconceived notions about the case at issue threaten impartiality, each juror must be free of bias. Accordingly, in a process called voir dire—meaning "to speak the truth"—prospective jurors are subject to two kinds of challenges:

- An unlimited number of challenges based on a "narrowly specified, provable and legally cognizable basis of partiality"—i.e., challenges "for cause"; and

- A specified (by statute or rule) number of *peremptory* challenges, which at one time were exercised for any reason or no reason— though as we will see the use of peremptory challenges has been limited by Batson v. Kentucky and its progeny, infra.

Voir dire may be conducted in any of several methods: 1) by addressing all questions to the panel at one time, or by addressing each juror individually; 2) by having the judge put questions to the jurors or by allowing counsel to ask the questions; and 3) by allowing a broad inquiry into juror attitudes or by limiting the number and scope of questions that

---

[16]   The Federal Jury Selection and Service Act of 1968, 28 U.S.C.A. §§ 1861–69, provides that Federal district courts must devise a plan for random selection of grand and petit jurors, and sets forth procedures for drawing names from a master wheel and summoning, qualifying, and impaneling jurors for service. The Act calls for the use of voter registration lists or lists of actual voters and "some other source or sources of names in addition to voter lists where necessary to foster the policy and protect the rights" set forth in the Act. The Act permits criminal defendants to move to dismiss the indictment or stay proceedings "on the ground of substantial failure to comply" with the provisions of the Act.

[17]   Jurisdictions vary on whether a defendant has a right to inspect and copy jury lists. In Test v. United States, 420 U.S. 28 (1975), the Court held that a federal criminal defendant has the right to inspect in order to prepare challenges to petit and grand jury selection procedures. In some cases—e.g., treason or capital cases—statutes may require that the defendant be served with a list. See 18 U.S.C.A. § 3432.

may be asked to the narrow issues presented in a specific case. Voir dire vests broad authority in the trial judge.

The general practice in the federal system is for the judge to conduct the voir dire questioning of prospective jurors. See Fed.R.Crim.P. 24(a)(court *may* allow attorneys to question jurors). Some jurisdictions give parties or their counsel a right to conduct voir dire.

Court control over voir dire questioning became the usual practice in federal and some state courts after perceived abuses by counsel, including waste of time and inquiry into improper areas during voir dire examination. Some courts have questioned the practice of court control. For example, the court in United States v. Ible, 630 F.2d 389 (5th Cir.1980), stated that "the federal practice of almost exclusive voir dire examination by the court does not take into account the fact that it is parties, rather than the court, who have a full grasp of the nuances and the strength and weaknesses of the case." But the practice of court-controlled voir dire questioning remains the federal norm, with counsel left to making requests as to what questions to ask. See McMillion, Advocating Voir Dire Reform, 77 A.B.A.J., Nov. 1991, p. 114 (discussing legislation proposed in the Senate (but never enacted) to give attorneys a limited right to conduct questioning of jurors in the federal courts).

The judge has discretion to permit questions suggested by counsel for voir dire, and has the right to refuse to allow and to strike questions deemed irrelevant or inappropriate. The judge's determinations are fact-specific; they frequently turn on the particular aspects of the case to be tried. In most instances the appellate court will defer to the trial court, believing that the trial judge has a better feel than an appellate court for the need to put questions to prospective jurors. But the Constitution requires that some inquiries be made at the request of a defendant if necessary to assure an effective voir dire.

QUESTIONS CONCERNING RACIAL PREJUDICE: HAM V. SOUTH CAROLINA

In Ham v. South Carolina, 409 U.S. 524 (1973), a young, bearded African-American, active in the civil rights movement, was charged with possession of marijuana. He alleged, in defense, that police officials had framed him because of his civil rights activities. During voir dire, he requested that the trial judge ask four questions relating to potential juror prejudice: two related to prejudice against African-Americans, the third related to prejudice against individuals with beards, and the fourth related to pretrial publicity. The trial judge refused to ask any of the questions. The Supreme Court granted review to consider whether the refusal violated Ham's constitutional rights.

Justice Rehnquist, writing for the Court, declared as follows:

[W]e think that the Fourteenth Amendment required the judge in this case to interrogate the jurors upon the subject of racial prejudice. South Carolina law permits challenges for cause, and authorizes the trial judge to conduct *voir dire* examination of potential jurors. The State having created this statutory framework for the selection of juries, the essential fairness required by the Due Process Clause of the Fourteenth Amendment requires that under the facts shown by this record the petitioner be permitted to have the jurors interrogated on the issue of racial bias.

* * * [T]he trial judge was not required to put the question in any particular form, or to ask any particular number of questions on the subject, simply because requested to do so by petitioner. * * * In this context, either of the brief, general questions urged by the petitioner would appear sufficient to focus the attention of prospective jurors on any racial prejudice they might entertain.

The third of petitioner's proposed questions was addressed to the fact that he wore a beard. While we cannot say that prejudice against people with beards might not have been harbored by one or more of the potential jurors in this case, this is the beginning and not the end of the inquiry as to whether the Fourteenth Amendment required the trial judge to interrogate the prospective jurors about such possible prejudice. Given the traditionally broad discretion accorded to the trial judge in conducting *voir dire,* and our inability to constitutionally distinguish possible prejudice against beards from a host of other possible similar prejudices, we do not believe the petitioner's constitutional rights were violated when the trial judge refused to put this question.

Inquiry into Racial Prejudice Not Automatically Required: Ristaino v. Ross

Ham's holding, that due process required the judge to inquire into the prospective jurors' possible racial prejudice, was distinguished in Ristaino v. Ross, 424 U.S. 589 (1976).

An African-American, charged in a state court with violent crimes against a white security guard, requested the trial court to ask during voir dire a question specifically directed to possible racial prejudice on the part of any prospective jurors. The trial court refused and was affirmed on appeal. The Supreme Court was reviewing a federal court of appeals' decision granting habeas relief on the basis of *Ham.* Justice Powell's opinion for the Court stated that:

The Constitution does not always entitle a defendant to have questions posed during *voir dire* specifically directed to matters that conceivably might prejudice veniremen against him. *Voir dire* is conducted under the supervision of the court, and a great deal must, of necessity, be left to its sound discretion. This is so because the determination of impartiality, in which demeanor plays such an important part, is particularly within the province of the trial judge. Thus, the State's obligation to the defendant to impanel an impartial jury generally can be satisfied by less than an inquiry into a specific prejudice feared by the defendant.

* * *

Justice Powell distinguished *Ham* as a case in which Ham's civil rights record and his claim to have been framed as a result of it meant that racial issues "were inextricably bound up with the conduct of the trial" and the defense he raised was "likely to intensify any prejudice that individual members of the jury might harbor."

Justice White concurred in the judgment. Justice Marshall, joined by justice Brennan, dissented and argued that "the Court emphatically confirms that the promises inherent in *Ham* * * * will not be fulfilled." Justice Stevens took no part in the case.

Limits on Mandatory Inquiry into Race: *Rosales-Lopez v. United States*

A divided Supreme Court held that there was no reversible error in a district court's refusal to voir dire prospective jurors on their racial prejudices in Rosales-Lopez v. United States, 451 U.S. 182 (1981). The defendant was a Mexican National charged with smuggling aliens into the United States. The trial judge asked jurors about attitudes toward "the alien problem" and aliens, but not about racial or ethnic prejudices. Justice White, writing for a plurality (Justices Stewart, Blackmun, and Powell) concluded that "it is usually best to allow the defendant * * * to have the inquiry into racial or ethnic prejudice pursued," but refused to require such an inquiry in all cases involving a defendant of a racial minority, reasoning that an inquiry into racial matters may create an impression that justice turns on race. The plurality said that prior federal cases invoking the Supreme Court's supervisory authority "fairly imply that federal trial courts must make such an inquiry when requested by a defendant accused of a violent crime and where the defendant and the victim are members of different racial or ethnic groups."

Justice Rehnquist, joined by Chief Justice Burger, concurred in the judgment, noting that the scope of voir dire was necessarily dependent on the discretion of trial judges. Justice Stevens, joined by Justices Brennan and Marshall, dissented and argued that "[m]uch as we wish it were otherwise, we should acknowledge the fact that there are many potential jurors who harbor strong prejudices against all members of certain racial, religious or ethnic groups for no reason other than hostility to the group as a whole."

Capital Defendants and Interracial Crime: Turner v. Murray

The Supreme Court departed from *Ristaino* in capital cases as it held in Turner v. Murray, 476 U.S. 28 (1986), that a death sentence was invalid where a trial judge refused an African-American defendant's request to question prospective jurors on racial prejudice in a prosecution charging him with murdering a white man. Justice White wrote for the Court as it held that "a capital defendant accused of an interracial crime is entitled to have prospective jurors informed of the race of the victim and questioned on the issue of racial bias." He noted that the trial judge retains discretion as to the form and number of questions, including whether to question jurors individually or collectively, and that a defendant cannot complain unless he has specifically asked for voir dire questions concerning race.

Voir Dire and the Need to Screen for Prejudicial Pretrial Publicity: Mu'Min v. Virginia

Chief Justice Rehnquist relied on *Ristaino* in his opinion for the Court in Mu'Min v. Virginia, 500 U.S. 415 (1991), holding that a state trial judge is not obliged to question prospective jurors individually about the contents of pretrial publicity to which they may have been exposed. Mu'Min was a state prisoner serving time for first-degree murder when he was charged with capital murder while on a work detail. The case was widely publicized, as it arose during the 1988 presidential campaign in which another case of a murder by a prisoner on furlough became an issue of national debate. Articles in the newspapers revealed details of the prior murder for which Mu'Min was incarcerated; the fact that the death penalty was unavailable at the time he committed the first murder; the denial of parole six times to Mu'Min; his confession to the crime charged; and criticism of the supervision of work gangs in Virginia.

Prior to trial, the defendant submitted proposed voir dire questions and asked for individual voir dire concerning the content of the publicity to which each prospective juror had been exposed. The trial judge rejected this request. The judge instead asked jurors whether they had heard or read anything about the case and whether they could be fair. Jurors who indicated that they had received information about the case were examined in panels of four; they were asked to respond if they had an opinion about the case, and if they could not enter the jury box with an open mind. Prospective jurors who remained silent were considered to have asserted that they could remain fair.

As the Court had done in *Ristaino,* Chief Justice Rehnquist distinguished the requirements of the Due Process Clause concerning voir dire in state trials from the more extensive supervisory power of federal courts over federal trials. He reasoned that the need to weed out prejudicial pretrial publicity through voir dire was certainly no greater than the need to protect against racial or ethnic prejudice. He observed that if the effect of pretrial publicity must be the subject of inquiry, each juror would have to be voir dired individually, in order to prevent jurors from infecting each other with the publicity giving rise to the inquiry. In the Chief Justice's view, such a substantial burden on the system was not justified. He rejected the less burdensome alternative of written questions concerning the content of publicity to which each juror had been exposed, reasoning that written answers would not give counsel or the court access to the demeanor of jurors. Thus, because efforts to fully protect the defendant from jurors infected by pretrial publicity were too onerous, the constitution did not require the court to take less effective efforts.

Justice O'Connor wrote a concurring opinion. She concluded that a trial judge could realistically assess whether jurors could be fair without knowing what each juror had heard about a case. Justice O'Connor agreed with Justice Marshall's dissenting view that the trial judge in this case could have done more, but ultimately concluded that "content" questions are not so indispensable to a fair trial that it violates the Constitution for a trial court to evaluate jurors without asking them.

Justice Marshall's dissenting opinion was joined by Justice Blackmun and Justice Stevens. His basic principle was that "[w]hen a prospective juror has been exposed to prejudicial pretrial publicity, a trial court cannot realistically assess the juror's impartiality without first establishing what the juror already has learned about the case."

Justice Kennedy also dissented. He contended that "the trial judge should have substantial discretion in conducting the voir dire, but, in my judgment, findings of impartiality must be based on something more than the mere silence of the individual in response to questions asked *en masse*."

Voir Dire and Jurors' Feelings About the Death Penalty: Morgan v. Illinois

The Court in Morgan v. Illinois, 504 U.S. 719 (1992), departed from its deferential analysis in *Mu'Min* when considering voir dire of jurors' views of the death penalty. Morgan was sentenced to death under an Illinois procedure that first required the jury unanimously to find at least one aggravating circumstance. After the jury determined that the defendant was death-eligible, it was instructed that it "should consider" all mitigating circumstances, and that it should impose the death sentence if "there are no mitigating factors sufficient to preclude" the death penalty in light of the aggravating factors.

During jury selection, Morgan requested that the judge ask prospective jurors whether they would automatically—regardless of any mitigating circumstances—impose the death penalty upon a finding that the defendant was death-eligible. The trial judge refused Morgan's request on the ground that each prospective juror had already been asked whether they would be able to follow the instructions on the law, and they were also asked whether they would be fair and impartial. Justice White, writing for the majority, found that this general questioning was insufficient under the Due Process Clause. He first noted the defendant's stake in voir dire:

> We deal here with petitioner's ability to exercise his * * * challenge for cause against those biased persons on the venire who as jurors would unwaveringly impose death after a finding of guilt. Were voir dire not available to lay bare the foundation of petitioner's challenge for cause against those prospective jurors who would always impose death following conviction, his right not to be tried by such jurors would be rendered * * * nugatory and meaningless * * *.

Justice White rejected the State's argument that general "fairness" and "follow the law" questions were sufficient to satisfy Morgan's right to inquire about a prospective juror's bias in favor of the death penalty:

> As to general questions of fairness and impartiality, such jurors could in all truth and candor respond affirmatively, personally confident that such dogmatic views are fair and impartial, while leaving the specific concern unprobed. * * * It may be that a juror could, in good conscience, swear to uphold that law and yet be unaware that maintaining such dogmatic beliefs about the death penalty would prevent him or her from doing so. A defendant on trial for his life must be permitted on voir dire to ascertain whether his prospective jurors function under such misconception. The risk that such jurors may have been empaneled in this case and infected petitioner's capital sentencing is unacceptable in light of the ease with which that risk could have been minimized.

Justice Scalia, joined by Chief Justice Rehnquist and Justice Thomas, dissented, accusing the majority of ignoring the deferential standard of review of voir dire in state courts, established in cases such as *Mu'Min*. He concluded that "[t]aking appropriate account of the opportunity for the trial court to observe and evaluate the demeanor of the veniremen, I see no basis for concluding that its finding that the 12 jurors were impartial was manifestly erroneous."

Voir Dire and the Federal Supervisory Power

As indicated in *Mu'Min*, the regulation of voir dire under the federal supervisory power is more rigorous than that required by the Constitution. Generally speaking, individual voir dire of jurors has been required in three situations in the Federal courts—although trial judges have significant discretion as to how to frame the questions. These three situations are:

- where a case has racial overtones;

- where the case involves matters concerning which the local community is known to harbor strong feelings, that may stop short of a need for a change of venue but may nonetheless affect the trial—such as child abuse or narcotics distribution; and

- where testimony from law enforcement agents is important in the case and might be overvalued.

See generally United States v. Contreras-Castro, 825 F.2d 185 (9th Cir.1987), where the trial court's failure to inquire about a bias in favor of law enforcement officers was held reversible error because the government's entire case rested on the testimony of government agents.

4. Challenges for Cause

The scope of voir dire, discussed above, is intricately related to the possibility of challenging prospective jurors for cause. The argument for expansive voir dire is that counsel needs information in order to make challenges for cause possible and meaningful.

The cognizable, specific biases that permit a challenge for cause are defined by statute. The typical statute permits such a challenge where the juror is of unsound mind or lacks the qualifications required by law; is related to a party; has served in a related case or on the indicting grand jury; or "is unable or unwilling to hear the case at issue fairly or impartially." ABA Standards for Criminal Justice, Trial by Jury 15–2.5 (1993). See 28 U.S.C. § 1866 (district court may exclude any person summoned for jury service "on the ground that such person may be unable to render impartial jury service").

a. *Jurors Who Cannot Be Excused for Cause*

Willingness and Ability to Follow Instructions as to the Death Penalty: Witherspoon v. Illinois and Adams v. Texas

Usually the question is whether a person *must* be excused for cause. However, one line of cases focuses on when persons may not be so excused. In Witherspoon v. Illinois, 391 U.S. 510 (1968), a statute provided that the prosecutor could challenge a juror for cause if the prospective juror stated "that he has conscientious scruples against capital punishment, or that he is opposed to the same." At Witherspoon's trial 47 veniremen, referred to by the trial court as "conscientious objectors," were successfully challenged on the basis of their negative attitude toward the death penalty. These jurors were not asked whether their scruples would invariably compel them to vote against capital punishment. Justice Stewart, writing for the Court, found that Witherspoon's death sentence was invalid because "in its role as arbiter of the punishment to be imposed, this jury fell woefully short of that impartiality to which the petitioner was entitled under the Sixth and Fourteenth Amendments." Justice Stewart reasoned as follows:

> A man who opposes the death penalty, no less than one who favors it, can make the discretionary judgment entrusted to him by the State and can thus obey the oath he takes as a juror. But a jury from which all such men have been excluded cannot perform the task demanded of it. * * *

> If the State had excluded only those prospective jurors who stated in advance of trial that they would not even consider returning a verdict of death, it could argue the resulting jury was simply neutral with respect to the penalty. But when it swept from the jury all who expressed conscientious or religious scruples against capital punishment and all who opposed it in principle, the State crossed the line of neutrality. In its quest for a jury capable of imposing the death penalty, the State produced a jury uncommonly willing to condemn a man to die. * * *

> [W]e hold that a sentence of death cannot be carried out if the jury that imposed or recommended it was chosen by excluding veniremen for cause simply because they voiced general objections to the death penalty or expressed conscientious or religious scruples against its infliction.

The Court in *Witherspoon* emphasized the narrowness of its holding. It did not prohibit the State from impanelling a "death-qualified" jury. It simply prohibited the exclusion for cause of a juror who expresses reservations about the death penalty but states that these reservations would not preclude a vote for the death penalty in the proper case.

In *Adams v. Texas*, 448 U.S. 38 (1980), the Court addressed a bifurcated Texas procedure in capital cases, in which the jury first considered the question of the defendant's guilt or innocence, and after a finding of guilt, heard evidence about mitigation or aggravation. The jury was required by statute to answer three specific questions concerning (1) whether the defendant's conduct causing the death at issue was deliberate, (2) whether the defendant's conduct in the future would constitute a continuing threat to society, and (3) whether his conduct in killing the victim was unreasonable in response to the victim's provocation, if any. A "Yes" answer to all three questions required the court to impose a death sentence, while "No" to a single one of the questions would have resulted in a life sentence. The trial judge had excluded from the jury a number of prospective jurors who were unwilling or unable to take an oath that the mandatory penalty of death or life imprisonment would not "affect [their] deliberations on any issue of fact." The resulting jury answered "Yes" to all three questions, and the court imposed a death sentence.

Justice White's opinion for the Court found that the Texas procedure violated *Witherspoon*. He explained as follows: "[T]he touchstone of the inquiry * * * was not whether putative jurors could and would follow their instructions and answer the posited questions in the affirmative if they honestly believed the evidence warranted it beyond reasonable doubt. Rather, the touchstone was whether the fact that the imposition of the death penalty would follow automatically from affirmative answers to the questions would have any effect at all on the jurors' performance of their duties. Such a test could, and did, exclude jurors who stated that they would be 'affected' by the possibility of the death penalty, but who apparently meant only that the potentially lethal consequences of their decision would invest their deliberations with greater seriousness and gravity or would involve them emotionally."

Death-Qualified Juries and Guilty Verdicts: Lockhart v. McCree and Buchanan v. Kentucky

In *Witherspoon*, the Court invalidated the defendant's death sentence, but it did not reverse the guilty verdict. The Court rejected the defendant's argument that a "death-qualified" jury would be biased in favor of the prosecution and therefore more likely to convict the defendant at the guilt phase. The basis for this rejection was that Witherspoon's empirical evidence was tentative and sketchy. The defendant in Lockhart v. McCree, 476 U.S. 162 (1986), made a similar argument with updated empirical evidence, and met a similar fate. The Court held that the Constitution does not prohibit the removal for cause, prior to the guilt phase of a bifurcated trial, of prospective jurors whose opposition to the death penalty is so strong that it would prevent or substantially impair the performance of their duties as jurors at the sentencing phase of the trial.

Writing for the Court, Justice Rehnquist refused to find that a jury is biased as to guilt when it is "death qualified." Justice Rehnquist reasoned that an impartial jury is one that will conscientiously apply the law and find the facts, and there was no showing that any of the twelve jurors in the case under review was partial. Justice Rehnquist stated that the removal of "*Witherspoon*-excludables"—those whose views against the death penalty would cause them to disregard the judge's instructions and refuse to return a capital sentence—serves the proper interest of attaining a jury that could impartially decide all of the issues in a case.

Justice Marshall, joined by Justices Brennan and Stevens, dissented. He argued that "the Court upholds a practice that allows a State a special advantage in those prosecutions where the charges are the most serious and the possible punishments, the most severe." The advantage is that "[t]he State's mere announcement that it intends to seek the death penalty if the defendant is found guilty of a capital offense will give the prosecution a license to empanel a jury especially likely to return that very verdict." Justice Blackmun concurred in the judgment without opinion.

Relying on *McCree,* the Supreme Court held, in Buchanan v. Kentucky, 483 U.S. 402 (1987), that a defendant as to whom the capital portion of an indictment was dismissed was not denied an impartial jury when he was tried together with another defendant facing a capital charge, by a jury from which prospective jurors unalterably opposed to the death penalty were excluded. Justice Blackmun's opinion for the Court reasoned that *"McCree* requires rejection of petitioner's claim that 'death qualification' violated his right to a jury selected from a representative cross-section of the community." He added that the state had not excluded the jurors opposed to the death penalty for arbitrary reasons unrelated to their ability to serve as jurors. Finally, he concluded that the state's interest in a joint trial is as compelling an interest as that recognized in *McCree* as sufficient to justify exclusion of jurors.

Justice Marshall, joined by Justices Brennan and Stevens, argued in dissent that the additional costs to a state of implementing a system of separate juries, or of providing alternate jurors who would replace those who opposed the death penalty after the guilt determination had been made, are minimal in comparison to a defendant's interest in an impartial jury at the guilt determination stage.

Limitation on Witherspoon: Wainwright v. Witt

The Court limited the impact of *Witherspoon* in Wainwright v. Witt, 469 U.S. 412 (1985). One of the prospective jurors in Witt's capital murder trial indicated that personal beliefs concerning the death penalty would "interfere" with her judging the guilt or innocence of the defendant. That juror was excluded for cause and Witt argued that *Witherspoon* was violated because the juror did not state that she would *automatically* vote against the death penalty, nor that she would be prevented from making an impartial decision as to guilt. Justice Rehnquist, writing for the Court, stated that *Witherspoon* did not require a "ritualistic adherence" to a requirement that a prospective juror make it "unmistakably clear that he would automatically vote against the death penalty." Justice Rehnquist set forth the following standard for determining whether a juror could be excluded for cause due to a negative attitude about the death penalty:

> [The] standard is whether the juror's views would prevent or substantially impair the performance of his duties as a juror in accordance with his instructions and his oath. * * * What common sense should have realized experience has proved: many veniremen

simply cannot be asked enough questions to reach the point where their bias has been made "unmistakably clear"; these veniremen may not know how they will react when faced with imposing the death sentence, or may be unable to articulate, or may wish to hide their true feelings. Despite this lack of clarity in the printed record, however, there will be situations where the trial judge is left with the definite impression that a prospective juror would be unable to faithfully and impartially apply the law. * * * [T]his is why deference must be paid to the trial judge who sees and hears the juror.

Justice Rehnquist concluded that, giving proper deference to the trial judge, the juror in Witt's case was properly excused for cause.

Justice Stevens concurred in the judgment. Justice Brennan, joined by Justice Marshall, dissented and argued that "the inevitable result of the quest for such purity in the jury room in a capital case is not a neutral jury drawn from a fair cross-section of the community but a jury biased against the defendant, at least with respect to penalty, and a jury from which an identifiable segment of the community has been excluded."

Trial Court Discretion to Strike Jurors to Maintain a Death-Qualified Jury: Uttecht v. Brown

In Uttecht v. Brown, 551 U.S. 1 (2007), a 5–4 majority of the Court held that a trial judge did not violate *Witherspoon* and its progeny by excusing a juror for cause. The majority emphasized the deference owed to a trial judge who is called upon to screen jurors to determine whether they will give fair consideration to the state's argument in favor of the death penalty. Justice Kennedy's majority opinion found that the Court's decisions established four relevant principles:

First, a criminal defendant has the right to an impartial jury drawn from a venire that has not been tilted in favor of capital punishment by selective prosecutorial challenges for cause. * * * Second, the State has a strong interest in having jurors who are able to apply capital punishment within the framework state law prescribes. * * * Third, to balance these interests, a juror who is substantially impaired in his or her ability to impose the death penalty under the state-law framework can be excused for cause; but if the juror is not substantially impaired, removal for cause is impermissible. * * * Fourth, in determining whether the removal of a potential juror would vindicate the State's interest without violating the defendant's right, the trial court makes a judgment based in part on the demeanor of the juror, a judgment owed deference by reviewing courts.

Justice Kennedy summarized the problems with the one juror that the defendant thought was erroneously struck for cause:

Juror Z was examined on the seventh day of the voir dire and the fifth day of the death-qualification phase. The State argues that Juror Z was impaired not by his general outlook on the death penalty, but rather by his position regarding the specific circumstances in which the death penalty would be appropriate. The transcript of Juror Z's questioning reveals that, despite the preceding instructions and information, he had both serious misunderstandings about his responsibility as a juror and an attitude toward capital punishment that could have prevented him from returning a death sentence under the facts of this case.

Justice Stevens, joined by Justices Souter, Ginsburg and Breyer, dissented and contended that the majority mischaracterized Juror Z's stated attitude toward the death penalty.

Justice Breyer, joined by Justice Souter, wrote a separate, short dissent.

Effect of a Witherspoon Violation: Gray v. Mississippi

The Court found a *Witherspoon* violation in Gray v. Mississippi, 481 U.S. 648 (1987), and rejected the argument that exclusion of the juror was harmless error. In *Gray*, the prosecutor essentially argued that a *Witherspoon* violation was harmless because he would have exercised a peremptory strike on the juror if she had not been (improperly) excused for cause. But Justice Blackmun concluded that "[t]he nature of the jury selection process defies any attempt to establish that an erroneous *Witherspoon-Witt* exclusion of a juror is harmless."

Justice Blackmun was concerned with the practical implications of the prosecutor's argument that a *Witherspoon* violation should be deemed harmless whenever the prosecutor has an unexercised peremptory challenge that she said she would have exercised on the juror improperly excused for cause:

> The practical result of this unexercised peremptory argument would be to insulate jury-selection error from meaningful appellate review. By simply stating during voir dire that the State is prepared to exercise a peremptory challenge if the court denies its motion for cause, a prosecutor would ensure that a reviewing court would consider any erroneous exclusion harmless.

Justice Scalia, joined by Chief Justice Rehnquist and Justices White and O'Connor, dissented in *Gray*.

b. Jurors Who Must Be Excused for Cause

Courts often face the question of whether a juror *must* be excused for cause. It is fair to state that judges vary in aggressiveness in striking jurors for cause. Generally, the judge has considerable discretion in these matters, because it is the judge who sees and hears the suspect juror, and who knows the impact that any problems with the juror will have on the case.

The most frequently invoked grounds for excusal for cause are: 1) bias; 2) taint from trial publicity; 3) preconceived notions inconsistent with a presumption of innocence; 4) inability or refusal to follow instructions from the court. But with respect to these and other grounds, the question is not only whether some disability exists but whether the prospective juror, despite the disability, can fairly assess the evidence.

The following cases illustrate the kinds of challenges for cause that are attempted.

a.   The defendant was convicted on two counts of aggravated bank robbery and attempted bank robbery. The government's case indicated that the defendant participated in three bank robberies and engaged in a shootout with police at a residence. During the voir dire, one venireman stated he was "not interested in convicting anybody," and when asked if he would be prejudiced against conviction, he said there was a "reasonable doubt in my mind, [and] it would take an awful lot." He was removed for cause, over the defendant's objection. The trial court thereafter denied the defendant's two motions to strike for cause. One was directed at a juror who was a senior vice-president of another bank and had previously served on a grand jury. The other was directed at a juror whose daughter had been robbed and raped. Both jurors said they believed they could give the defendant a fair trial.[18] The appellate court sustained the trial court's rulings as to all three prospective jurors. United States v. Young, 553 F.2d 1132 (8th Cir.1977).

b.   The defendant was convicted for robbery and sentenced to twelve years' imprisonment. During the trial court voir dire, the following exchange took place.

Mr. Pickard (Defense Counsel): Has anybody been robbed? Due to the fact that you have recently been robbed do you think you might be a little bit more inclined to convict regardless of the evidence?

Juror Spencer: Yes sir, I probably would.

Mr. Pickard: You think you may be a little biased?

Juror Spencer: Yes sir.

---

[18]   One commentator has suggested that "[c]ourts, feeling helpless before questions of human psychology, are unable to decide whether a person can be fair in spite of having an opinion on the matter at issue—thus the technique of 'just asking her.' Once having asked, however, the court cannot easily impugn the credibility of a citizen who has professed her impartiality." B. Babcock, Voir Dire: Preserving "Its Wonderful Power", 27 Stan.L.Rev. 545, 550 (1975).

Mr. Pickard: You're saying in all probability you wouldn't be able to give him a fair trial and view the evidence objectively?

Juror Spencer: Yes sir.

Mr. Pickard: We challenge for cause.

The Court: In spite of your experience a couple of weeks ago, could you still listen to the evidence that comes from this witness stand, and this evidence alone, and render a fair and impartial decision concerning the defendant, Beauford Harold Johnson?

Juror Spencer: Yes sir, I believe I could.

The Court: You wouldn't let that experience that you had affect you?

Juror Spencer: No sir.

The Court: Challenge denied.

Juror Spencer became the foreman of the jury. (Emphasis added.)

The appellate court sustained the trial court's denial of challenge. Johnson v. State, 356 So.2d 769 (Ala.Cr.App.1978).

c. Is a juror who is a county commissioner and also a part-time deputy sheriff subject to a challenge for cause? See State v. Radi, 176 Mont. 451, 578 P.2d 1169 (1978) (statute does not permit challenge). How does a decision like this affect the impartial appearance of the jury? In Dennis v. United States, 339 U.S. 162 (1950), the Court held that where the government was a party in a litigation, jurors could not be excused for cause merely because they were government employees. The Court stated that actual bias must be shown. Should the result in *Dennis* have been affected by the fact that the defendant was charged with failure to comply with a subpoena issued by the House Un-American Activities Committee? Would jurors who are government employees be less impartial in cases where the substantive offense is a wrong done to the government itself?

d. The defendant was charged with cocaine distribution. During jury selection, the court asked the prospective jurors whether they or anyone to whom they were close had any experience with illegal drugs. Juror Camacho responded affirmatively. She said that her ex-husband, the father of her five-year-old daughter, had both used and dealt cocaine during their marriage. His involvement in cocaine was one of the reasons for their divorce. Upon questioning by the court, Camacho admitted that the experience was painful. The court, apparently concerned by her answers, asked Camacho three times whether she could put her personal experience aside and serve impartially. Each time, she responded "I'll try."

The trial judge denied the defendant's motion to strike Camacho for cause. But the Court of Appeals reversed. It reasoned as follows:

Camacho was asked three times whether she could be fair, and each time she responded equivocally. Not *once* did she affirmatively state that she could or would serve fairly or impartially. * * *

* * * When a juror is unable to state that she will serve fairly and impartially despite being asked repeatedly for such assurances, we can have no confidence that the juror will put aside her biases or her prejudicial personal experiences and render a fair and impartial verdict. Given Camacho's responses to the court's questions and the similarity between her traumatic familial experience and the defendant's alleged conduct, we conclude that the failure to excuse her for cause * * * requires reversal.

United States v. Gonzalez, 214 F.3d 1109 (9th Cir. 2000). What if Camacho responded to the court's inquiries by saying "I am pretty sure I can" rather than "I'll try"? Must she be excused for cause?

e.   Is the trial judge permitted to disqualify a juror for cause during the *deliberations*? Fed.R.Crim.P. 23(b) provides: "After a jury has retired to deliberate, the court may permit a jury of 11 persons to return a verdict, even without a stipulation by the parties, if the court finds good cause to excuse a juror." See United States v. Ruggiero, 928 F.2d 1289 (2d Cir.1991) (proper to excuse juror during deliberations when it was disclosed that the juror had been threatened by associates of the defendant). If the juror seems to have no grasp of the facts during deliberations, should or must he be struck for cause? See also United States v. Geffrard, 87 F.3d 448 (11th Cir.1996) (trial judge acted properly in excusing a juror for cause during the deliberations and proceeding to verdict with 11 jurors; the juror wrote a note to the judge which stated that she could not convict the defendants because of her beliefs in Swedenborgianism). Shouldn't jurors presenting these problems during deliberations have been rooted out during the voir dire process? Does this tell you anything about the voir dire process?

Jurors Who Will Never Consider Mitigating Evidence in a Capital Case: Morgan v. Illinois

Under *Witherspoon* and its progeny, the State is not permitted to exclude jurors for cause merely because they are reluctant to impose the death penalty, but the State is permitted to exclude jurors whose views against the death penalty would lead them to disregard the judge's instructions in the capital phase. The question in Morgan v. Illinois, 504 U.S. 719 (1992), was the reverse of *Witherspoon:* whether a juror *must* be excluded for cause if he would automatically *impose* the death penalty without regard to mitigating circumstances. Justice White, writing for the majority, held that the defendant had a due process right to have a prospective juror excused for cause if the juror would impose death regardless of the mitigating circumstances. He concluded that while the prosecutor has the right to seek a "death-qualified" jury, the defendant has the right to seek a "life-qualified" jury to assure that all jurors are actually impartial.

Justice Scalia, joined by Chief Justice Rehnquist and Justice Thomas, dissented. Justice Scalia distinguished *Witherspoon* on the ground that under Illinois law, a finding of aggravating circumstances must be considered by the jury, whereas the consideration of mitigating evidence "is left up to the judgment of each juror." He therefore concluded that a *Witherspoon*-excludible—one who says he will never vote for the death penalty and thus that he will never consider aggravating factors—is "saying that he will not apply the law" whereas the juror who says he will not consider mitigating evidence "is not promising to be lawless, since there is no case in which he is by law *compelled* to find a mitigating fact sufficiently mitigating." Is this persuasive, or is there a difference between saying an impartial juror must be willing to consider all evidence and not automatically reject a mitigating fact and saying that a juror is not compelled to find a mitigating fact?

Error by Failure to Excuse for Cause, Corrected by a Peremptory Challenge: Ross v. Oklahoma and Martinez-Salazar v. United States

In *Ross v. Oklahoma*, 487 U.S. 81 (1988), the defendant in a capital case challenged a juror who stated that he would automatically vote for capital punishment. Under *Morgan,* supra, that juror had to be excluded for cause—but the trial judge refused to disqualify the juror. The defendant then exercised a peremptory challenge to get the juror off the panel. On appeal, the state conceded that the juror should have been disqualified, but argued that the defendant's use of one of his nine peremptory challenges rectified the trial court's error. The defendant responded that he ultimately exhausted all of his peremptories, and would have used the one that he expended due to the trial court's error to excuse another juror who ultimately sat on his panel.

Chief Justice Rehnquist, writing for the Court, concluded that Ross had not been denied an impartial jury because the juror who would have automatically imposed the death penalty was "removed from the jury as effectively as if the trial court excused him for cause." The Chief Justice rejected the argument that the loss of a peremptory challenge constitutes a violation of the right to be tried by an impartial jury, reasoning that "peremptory challenges are not of constitutional dimension." He declared that the state may deny peremptory challenges altogether, and that Oklahoma had properly qualified its grant of such challenges "by the requirement that the defendant must use those challenges to cure erroneous refusal by the trial court to excuse jurors for cause." He concluded that Ross made no claim that any of the jurors who convicted him and sentenced him to death was biased or partial, and that an error with respect to a juror who did not sit did not mandate reversal.

Justice Marshall, joined by Justices Brennan, Blackmun, and Stevens, wrote that "[a] man's life is at stake," and "[w]e should not be playing games."

In United States v. Martinez-Salazar, 528 U.S. 304 (2000), a prospective juror indicated that he would favor the prosecution; he assumed "people are on trial because they did something wrong", though he understood the presumption of innocence "in theory". The defendant moved to strike the juror for cause, but the trial judge refused. So the defendant exercised a peremptory challenge to strike the juror. Eventually he expended all his peremptories. On appeal, the parties agreed that the juror should have been struck for cause. The defendant claimed a violation of Fed.R.Crim.P. 24(b), under which the defense was entitled to 10 peremptory challenges. He argued that he did not receive his full complement of peremptories, because he was forced to expend a challenge on a juror who should have been struck for cause.

The Supreme Court, in an opinion by Justice Ginsburg, held that Rule 24(b) was not violated. She reasoned that the trial court's mistake did not force the defendant to expend a peremptory challenge. She stated that a "hard choice is not the same as no choice" and concluded as follows:

> After objecting to the District Court's denial of his for-cause challenge, Martinez-Salazar had the option of letting Gilbert sit on the petit jury and, upon conviction, pursuing a Sixth Amendment challenge on appeal. Instead, Martinez-Salazar elected to use a challenge to remove Gilbert because he did not want Gilbert to sit on his jury. This was Martinez-Salazar's choice. * * * In choosing to remove Gilbert rather than taking his chances on appeal, Martinez-Salazar did not lose a peremptory challenge. Rather, he used the challenge in line with a principal reason for peremptories: to help secure the constitutional guarantee of trial by an impartial jury.

Justice Ginsburg observed that it would have been a different matter if the trial court's ruling resulted in the seating of any juror who should have been dismissed for cause. Justice Souter wrote a short concurring opinion. Justice Scalia, joined by Justice Kennedy, wrote a short opinion concurring in the judgment.

5. The Use of Peremptory Challenges

a. *The Purpose and Function of the Peremptory Challenge*

The Supreme Court has described the peremptory challenge as follows:

> The essential nature of the peremptory challenge is that it is one exercised without a reason stated, without inquiry, and without being subject to the court's control. While challenges for cause permit rejection of jurors on a narrowly specified, provable and legally cognizable basis of partiality, the peremptory permits rejection for a real or imagined partiality that is less easily designated or demonstrable.

Swain v. Alabama, 380 U.S. 202 (1965). The Court in *Swain* stated that the peremptory challenge serves salutary purposes in the adversary system:

> The function of the challenge is not only to eliminate extremes of partiality on both sides, but to assure the parties that the jurors before whom they try the case will decide on the basis of the evidence placed before them, and not otherwise. * * * Indeed the very availability of peremptories allows counsel to ascertain the possibility of bias through probing questions on the *voir dire* and facilitates the exercise of challenges for cause by removing the fear of incurring a juror's hostility through examination and challenge for cause.

Another purpose for the peremptory is to encourage a litigant to accept the jury and its decision because it belongs to him in a vivid sense: he picked it and was able to exclude those he feared. See Babcock, Voir Dire: Preserving "Its Wonderful Power," 27 Stan.L.Rev. 545, 552 (1975). Finally, as Ross v. Oklahoma, supra, points out, the peremptory challenge serves as a "safety valve" when the trial judge erroneously refuses to excuse a juror for cause. But as the Court also noted in *Ross*, there is no constitutional right to a peremptory challenge.

Voir Dire and the Peremptory Challenge

The relationship between peremptory challenges and voir dire should be apparent. In cases like Mu'Min v. Virginia, supra, the defendant argues that extensive voir dire is essential not only to determine whether a juror should be excluded for cause, but also to give defense counsel the information necessary to decide whether to expend a peremptory. As you go through the materials on peremptory challenges, see if the Court has been consistent in protecting peremptories at the same time as it has, in cases like *Mu'Min,* accepted trial court limitations of voir dire. Can limitations on voir dire be justified by the fact that there is no constitutional right to a peremptory challenge given that there is a right to challenge jurors for cause (especially partiality)?

Number of Peremptories

In felony cases, Fed.R.Crim.P. 24(b) gives all of the defendants together ten peremptory challenges (20 in capital cases) and the prosecution six. Most states allocate equal numbers of challenges to prosecutors and defendants. In multiple defendant cases, the court will allocate challenges to defendants if they cannot agree on how to use them. Fed.R.Crim.P. 24(b) states that in multiple defendant cases the court may allow the parties additional peremptory challenges and may allow the defendants to exercise those challenges "separately or jointly."

Procedure for Exercising Peremptories

There are several different procedural approaches to the exercise of peremptory challenges. Some jurisdictions use the strike system, in which the parties get to see the entire panel and to strike the least desirable (from their viewpoints) jurors first. Some use the challenge system, where a party will not be sure who will take the seat of a challenged juror. In some courts, once a juror is "passed" (that is, not struck) the juror remains. Other courts permit challenges to any member of the panel until challenges are exhausted.

b. Constitutional Limits on Peremptory Challenges

While the peremptory challenge ostensibly allows the litigant to exclude a prospective juror on any grounds, the Equal Protection Clause imposes some limits on this choice. In Swain v. Alabama, supra, the defendant argued that the prosecutor exercised peremptories to exclude African-Americans from serving on petit juries. The Court held that if this allegation could be proven, the prosecutor's action would violate the Equal Protection Clause. However, in the Court's view, such a violation could not be proven by the discriminatory use of peremptory challenges in a single case. Rather, the defendant would have to show that the prosecutor "in case after case, whatever the circumstances" was responsible for the removal of prospective jurors who survived challenges for cause "with the result that no Negroes ever serve on petit juries."

It should be apparent that the proof requirement set forth in *Swain* is all but impossible to meet. See People v. Wheeler, 22 Cal.3d 258, 148 Cal.Rptr. 890, 583 P.2d 748 (1978) (noting that data on such practices is inaccessible, and that at the time a peremptory is exercised, trial judges would be reluctant to allow a continuance for an investigation into a pattern of discrimination in other cases). Moreover, *Swain* did nothing to protect the first several victims of discrimination in the use of peremptories. As the court in *Wheeler* stated, "each and every defendant, not merely the last in this artificial sequence," ought to be entitled to the same constitutional protection.

The following case reconsiders *Swain* and finds that its proof requirements are too stringent. Consider whom the Court is trying to protect and the costs involved in this protection?

BATSON V. KENTUCKY
Supreme Court of the United States, 1986.
476 U.S. 79.

JUSTICE POWELL delivered the opinion of the Court.

This case requires us to reexamine that portion of Swain v. Alabama, 380 U.S. 202 (1965), concerning the evidentiary burden placed on a criminal defendant who claims that he has been denied equal protection through the State's use of peremptory challenges to exclude members of his race from the petit jury.

* * *

Petitioner, a black man, was indicted in Kentucky on charges of second-degree burglary and receipt of stolen goods. * * * The prosecutor used his peremptory challenges to strike all four black persons on the venire, and a jury composed only of white persons was selected. Defense counsel moved to discharge the jury before it was sworn on the ground that the prosecutor's removal of the black veniremen violated petitioner's rights under the * * * Fourteenth Amendment to equal protection of the laws. * * * The judge then denied petitioner's motion * * *.

The jury convicted petitioner on both counts. * * * The Supreme Court of Kentucky affirmed. * * * We granted certiorari, and now reverse.

* * *

In Swain v. Alabama, this Court recognized that a "State's purposeful or deliberate denial to Negroes on account of race of participation as jurors in the administration of justice violates the Equal Protection Clause." * * * We reaffirm the principle today.

* * *

Purposeful racial discrimination in selection of the venire violates a defendant's right to equal protection because it denies him the protection that a trial by jury is intended to secure. * * * The petit jury has occupied a central position in our system of justice by safeguarding a person accused of crime against the arbitrary exercise of power by prosecutor or judge. Duncan v. Louisiana. Those on the venire must be "indifferently chosen," to secure the defendant's right under the Fourteenth Amendment to "protection of life and liberty against race or color prejudice."

Racial discrimination in selection of jurors harms not only the accused whose life or liberty they are summoned to try. Competence to serve as a juror ultimately depends on an assessment of individual qualifications and ability impartially to consider evidence presented at a trial. A person's race simply "is unrelated to his fitness as a juror." * * * [B]y denying a person participation in jury service on account of his race, the State unconstitutionally discriminated against the excluded juror.

The harm from discriminatory jury selection extends beyond that inflicted on the defendant and the excluded juror to touch the entire community. Selection procedures that purposefully exclude black persons from juries undermine public confidence in the fairness of our system of justice. * * *

* * * While decisions of this Court have been concerned largely with discrimination during selection of the venire, the principles announced there also forbid discrimination on account of race in selection of the petit jury. Since the Fourteenth Amendment protects an accused throughout the proceedings bringing him to justice, the State may not draw up its jury lists pursuant to neutral procedures but then resort to discrimination at "other stages in the selection process."

Accordingly, the component of the jury selection process at issue here, the State's privilege to strike individual jurors through peremptory challenges, is subject to the commands of the Equal Protection Clause. Although a prosecutor ordinarily is entitled to exercise permitted peremptory challenges "for any reason at all, as long as that reason is related to his view concerning the outcome" of the case to be tried, the Equal Protection Clause forbids the prosecutor to challenge potential jurors solely on account of their race or on the assumption that black jurors as a group will be unable impartially to consider the State's case against a black defendant.

* * *

A number of lower courts following the teaching of *Swain* reasoned that proof of repeated striking of blacks over a number of cases was necessary to establish a violation of the Equal Protection Clause. Since this interpretation of *Swain* has placed on defendants a crippling burden of proof, prosecutors' peremptory challenges are now largely immune from constitutional scrutiny. For reasons that follow, we reject this evidentiary formulation as inconsistent with standards that have been developed since *Swain* for assessing a prima facie case under the Equal Protection Clause.

[Justice Powell discusses and relies on general equal protection cases outside the peremptory challenge context].

[S]ince *Swain*, we have recognized that a black defendant alleging that members of his race have been impermissibly excluded from the venire may make out a prima facie case of purposeful discrimination by showing that the totality of the relevant facts gives rise to an inference of discriminatory purpose. Once the defendant makes the requisite showing, the burden shifts to the State to explain adequately the racial exclusion. The State cannot meet this burden on mere general assertions that its officials did not discriminate or that they properly performed their official duties. Rather, the State must demonstrate that "permissible racially neutral selection criteria and procedures have produced the monochromatic result."[a]

* * *

[T]his Court has recognized that a defendant may make a prima facie showing of purposeful racial discrimination in selection of the venire by relying solely on the facts concerning its selection *in his case.* * * * "A single invidiously discriminatory governmental act" is not "immunized by the absence of such discrimination in the making of other comparable decisions." For evidentiary requirements to dictate that "several must suffer discrimination" before one could object, would be inconsistent with the promise of equal protection to all.

* * *

The standards for assessing a prima facie case in the context of discriminatory selection of the venire * * * support our conclusion that a defendant may establish a prima facie case of purposeful discrimination in selection of the petit jury solely on evidence concerning the prosecutor's exercise of peremptory challenges at the defendant's trial. To establish such a case, the defendant first must show that he is a member of a cognizable racial group, and that the prosecutor has exercised peremptory challenges to remove from the venire members of the defendant's race. Second, the defendant is entitled to rely on the fact, as to which there can be no dispute, that peremptory challenges constitute a jury selection practice that permits "those to discriminate who are of a mind to discriminate." Finally, the defendant must show that these facts and any other relevant circumstances raise an inference that the prosecutor used that practice to exclude the veniremen from the petit jury on account of their race. This combination of factors in the empaneling of the petit jury, as in the selection of the venire, raises the necessary inference of purposeful discrimination.

In deciding whether the defendant has made the requisite showing, the trial court should consider all relevant circumstances. For example, a "pattern" of strikes against black jurors included in the particular venire might give rise to an inference of discrimination. Similarly, the prosecutor's questions and statements during *voir dire* examination and in exercising

---

[a] Our decisions concerning "disparate treatment" under Title VII of the Civil Rights Act of 1964 have explained the operation of prima facie burden of proof rules. See McDonnell Douglas Corp. v. Green, 411 U.S. 792 (1973); Texas Dept. of Community Affairs v. Burdine, 450 U.S. 248 (1981); United States Postal Service Board of Governors v. Aikens, 460 U.S. 711 (1983). The party alleging that he has been the victim of intentional discrimination carries the ultimate burden of persuasion.

his challenges may support or refute an inference of discriminatory purpose. These examples are merely illustrative. We have confidence that trial judges, experienced in supervising *voir dire,* will be able to decide if the circumstances concerning the prosecutor's use of peremptory challenges creates a prima facie case of discrimination against black jurors.

Once the defendant makes a prima facie showing, the burden shifts to the State to come forward with a neutral explanation for challenging black jurors. Though this requirement imposes a limitation in some cases on the full peremptory character of the historic challenge, we emphasize that the prosecutor's explanation need not rise to the level justifying exercise of a challenge for cause. But the prosecutor may not rebut the defendant's prima facie case of discrimination by stating merely that he challenged jurors of the defendant's race on the assumption—or his intuitive judgment—that they would be partial to the defendant because of their shared race. * * * The core guarantee of equal protection, ensuring citizens that their State will not discriminate on account of race, would be meaningless were we to approve the exclusion of jurors on the basis of such assumptions, which arise solely from the jurors' race. Nor may the prosecutor rebut the defendant's case merely by denying that he had a discriminatory motive * * *. If these general assertions were accepted as rebutting a defendant's prima facie case, the Equal Protection Clause would be but a vain and illusory requirement. The prosecutor therefore must articulate a neutral explanation related to the particular case to be tried. The trial court then will have the duty to determine if the defendant has established purposeful discrimination.

* * *

In this case, petitioner made a timely objection to the prosecutor's removal of all black persons on the venire. Because the trial court flatly rejected the objection without requiring the prosecutor to give an explanation for his action, we remand this case for further proceedings. If the trial court decides that the facts establish, prima facie, purposeful discrimination and the prosecutor does not come forward with a neutral explanation for his action, our precedents require that petitioner's conviction be reversed.

[Justice White's concurring opinion is omitted].

JUSTICE MARSHALL, concurring.

I join JUSTICE POWELL'S eloquent opinion for the Court, which takes a historic step toward eliminating the shameful practice of racial discrimination in the selection of juries. The Court's opinion cogently explains the pernicious nature of the racially discriminatory use of peremptory challenges, and the repugnancy of such discrimination to the

Equal Protection Clause. * * * I nonetheless write separately to express my views. The decision today will not end the racial discrimination that peremptories inject into the jury-selection process. That goal can be accomplished only by eliminating peremptory challenges entirely.

* * *

* * * Merely allowing defendants the opportunity to challenge the racially discriminatory use of peremptory challenges in individual cases will not end the illegitimate use of the peremptory challenge.

* * * First, defendants cannot attack the discriminatory use of peremptory challenges at all unless the challenges are so flagrant as to establish a prima facie case. * * * [W]here only one or two black jurors survive the challenges for cause, the prosecutor need have no compunction about striking them from the jury because of their race. Prosecutors are left free to discriminate against blacks in jury selection provided that they hold that discrimination to an "acceptable" level.

Second, when a defendant can establish a prima facie case, trial courts face the difficult burden of assessing prosecutors' motives. Any prosecutor can easily assert facially neutral reasons for striking a juror, and trial courts are ill equipped to second-guess those reasons. How is the court to treat a prosecutor's statement that he struck a juror because the juror had a son about the same age as defendant, or seemed "uncommunicative," or "never cracked a smile" and, therefore "did not possess the sensitivities necessary to realistically look at the issues and decide the facts in this case"? If such easily generated explanations are sufficient to discharge the prosecutor's obligation to justify his strikes on nonracial grounds, then the protection erected by the Court today may be illusory.

Nor is outright prevarication by prosecutors the only danger here. * * * A prosecutor's own conscious or unconscious racism may lead him easily to the conclusion that a prospective black juror is "sullen," or "distant," a characterization that would not have come to his mind if a white juror had acted identically. A judge's own conscious or unconscious racism may lead him to accept such an explanation as well supported. * * * Even if all parties approach the Court's mandate with the best of conscious intentions, that mandate requires them to confront and overcome their own racism on all levels—a challenge I doubt all of them can meet. * * *

The inherent potential of peremptory challenges to distort the jury process by permitting the exclusion of jurors on racial grounds should ideally lead the Court to ban them entirely from the criminal justice system. * * *

Some authors have suggested that the courts should ban prosecutors' peremptories entirely, but should zealously guard the defendant's peremptory as "essential to the fairness of trial by jury," and "one of the most important of the rights secured to the accused." I would not find that an acceptable solution. Our criminal justice system requires not only freedom from any bias against the accused, but also from any prejudice against his prosecution. Between him and the state the scales are to be evenly held. We can maintain that balance, not by permitting both prosecutor and defendant to engage in racial discrimination in jury selection, but by banning the use of peremptory challenges by prosecutors and by allowing the States to eliminate the defendant's peremptories as well.

* * *

[The concurring opinion of Justice Stevens, joined by Justice Brennan, and the concurring opinion of Justice O'Connor, are omitted.]

CHIEF JUSTICE BURGER, joined by JUSTICE REHNQUIST, dissenting.

* * *

Our system permits two types of challenges: challenges for cause and peremptory challenges. Challenges for cause obviously have to be explained; by definition, peremptory challenges do not. * * * Analytically, there is no middle ground: A challenge either has to be explained or it does not. It is readily apparent, then, that to permit inquiry into the basis for a peremptory challenge would force the peremptory challenge to collapse into the challenge for cause. * * *

* * *

Today we mark the return of racial differentiation as the Court accepts a positive evil for a perceived one. Prosecutors and defense attorneys alike will build records in support of their claims that peremptory challenges have been exercised in a racially discriminatory fashion by asking jurors to state their racial background and national origin for the record, despite the fact that such questions may be offensive to some jurors and thus are not ordinarily asked on voir dire. This process is sure to tax even the most capable counsel and judges since determining whether a prima facie case has been established will require a continued monitoring and recording of the "group" composition of the panel present and prospective.

* * *

JUSTICE Rehnquist, with whom THE CHIEF JUSTICE joins, dissenting.

* * *

In my view, there is simply nothing "unequal" about the State's using its peremptory challenges to strike blacks from the jury in cases involving black defendants, so long as such challenges are also used to exclude whites in cases involving white defendants, Hispanics in cases involving Hispanic defendants, Asians in cases involving Asian defendants, and so on. This case-specific use of peremptory challenges by the State does not single out blacks, or members of any other race for that matter, for discriminatory treatment. Such use of peremptories is at best based upon seat-of-the-pants instincts, which are undoubtedly crudely stereotypical and may in many cases be hopelessly mistaken. But as long as they are applied across-the-board to jurors of all races and nationalities, I do not see—and the Court most certainly has not explained—how their use violates the Equal Protection Clause.

* * *

OPEN QUESTIONS LEFT BY BATSON

Batson left a number of open questions, including:

- Is *Batson* applicable only to exclusion of African-Americans?

- Does *Batson* apply to discriminatory use of peremptories by parties other than the prosecutor?

- Must the defendant be a member of the excluded group?

- How does a party establish a prima facie case of racial discrimination in the exercise of peremptories?

- What kind of neutral explanation, short of a challenge for cause, will suffice?

The Court has decided several cases in an attempt to answer some of these questions.

Standing to Assert a Batson Violation: Powers v. Ohio

In Powers v. Ohio, 499 U.S. 400 (1991), the defendant, a white man, alleged that the prosecutor exercised peremptory challenges to exclude African-American jurors on the basis of race. Powers was not asserting that his own equal protection rights were violated. Rather, he asserted that the equal protection rights of the jurors excluded on racial grounds were violated. The question boiled down to one of standing. In a 7–2 decision, the Court held that Powers had standing to bring an equal protection claim on behalf of the excluded African-American jurors. The case was remanded to determine whether the prosecutor had in fact excluded African-Americans on the basis of race.

The majority opinion, written by Justice Kennedy, downplayed the numerous references in *Batson* to the racial identity between the defendant and the excused prospective juror. Justice Kennedy asserted that *"Batson* was designed to serve multiple ends, only one of which was to protect individual defendants from discrimination in the selection of jurors. * * * *Batson* recognized that a prosecutor's discriminatory use of peremptory challenges harms the excluded jurors and the community at large."[19]

Justice Kennedy noted three requirements for third party standing, based on the Court's previous cases: (1) the litigant must have suffered an "injury in fact;" (2) the litigant must have a "close relation to the third party;" and (3) there must exist some hindrance to the third party's ability to protect his or her own interests.

As to the first requirement of injury in fact, Justice Kennedy argued that a criminal defendant suffers from exclusion of jurors of a different race because "racial discrimination in the selection of jurors casts doubt on the integrity of the judicial process * * * and places the fairness of a criminal proceeding in doubt."

As to the second requirement of a close relationship between the litigant and the third party, the Court stated that "the excluded juror and the criminal defendant have a common interest in eliminating racial discrimination from the courtroom. * * * The rejected juror may lose confidence in the court and its verdicts, as may the defendant if his or her objections cannot be heard." Justice Kennedy also asserted that *"voir dire* permits a party to establish a relation, if not a bond of trust, with the jurors."

Concerning the third requirement for third party standing, the majority found that it was very unlikely that the excluded prospective juror would assert his or her own equal protection rights. Justice Kennedy noted that the barriers to bringing an individual action are "daunting," and concluded that "the reality is that a juror dismissed because of his race probably will leave the courtroom possessing little incentive to set in motion the arduous process needed to vindicate his own rights."

Justice Scalia, joined by Chief Justice Rehnquist, filed a stinging dissent. Justice Scalia contended that the majority had misapplied the holding and reasoning of *Batson* and stated that:

> This case * * * involves not a clarification of *Batson,* but the creation of an additional, *ultra-Batson* departure from established law.

---

[19] Does this mean that the community at large has a cause of action when prospective jurors are excluded on account of race? What if a defendant intentionally decides not to object to race-based strikes? Does the defendant waive the community's right to challenge exclusion?

* * * Notwithstanding history, precedent, and the significant benefits of the peremptory challenge system, it is intolerably offensive for the State to imprison a person on the basis of a conviction rendered by a jury from which members of that person's minority race were carefully excluded. I am unmoved, however, and I think most Americans would be, by this white defendant's complaint that he was sought to be tried by an all-white jury * * *."

Recall that in Holland v. Illinois, supra, the Court held that a white defendant could not challenge the exclusion of African-Americans from the petit jury under the fair cross-section requirement of the Sixth Amendment. After *Powers,* does *Holland* have any practical effect?

Peremptory Strikes by Private Litigants: Edmonson v. Leesville Concrete Co.

After *Powers,* the fact that the objecting party is not of the same race as the excluded juror is irrelevant. However, in *Powers,* the party exercising the peremptory challenge was a government actor. If the party exercising the peremptory is a *private* actor, the issue is whether the challenge, even if racially discriminatory, constitutes state action. In Edmonson v. Leesville Concrete Co., 500 U.S. 614 (1991), the Court held that a private litigant in a civil case may not use peremptory challenges to exclude jurors on account of race. Justice Kennedy, writing for six members of the Court, found the necessary state action in the trial judge's excusing of the juror once a peremptory challenge is exercised: "By enforcing a discriminatory peremptory challenge, the court has not only made itself a party to the biased act, but has elected to place its power, property and prestige behind the alleged discrimination."

Justice O'Connor, joined by Chief Justice Rehnquist and Justice Scalia, dissented. She asserted that "not everything that happens in a courtroom is state action" and that "the peremptory is, by design, an enclave of private action in a government-managed proceeding." She concluded that "it is antithetical to the nature of our adversarial process * * * to say that a private attorney acting on behalf of a private client represents the government for constitutional purposes."

Peremptory Challenges by Criminal Defense Counsel: Georgia v. McCollum

In Georgia v. McCollum, 505 U.S. 42 (1992), two white defendants were charged with assault and battery of two African-Americans. The incident had sparked racial conflict in the community. The prosecution moved to prohibit the defendants from using their peremptory strikes in a racially discriminatory manner. This motion was denied by the Georgia trial and appellate courts.

Justice Blackmun wrote for the majority and relied heavily on *Edmonson.* He first found that "a criminal defendant's exercise of peremptory challenges in a racially discriminatory manner inflicts the harms addressed by *Batson.*" He noted that regardless of who exercises the challenge, the harm to the excluded juror is the same, in that the juror is "subjected to open and public racial discrimination." He also noted that the need for public confidence in the judicial system, addressed by *Batson* and *Edmonson,* is at stake when a criminal defendant exercises a peremptory challenge on racial grounds, and especially so in cases involving race-related crimes. On this point, he concluded as follows:

> Be it at the hands of the State or the defense, if a court allows jurors to be excluded because of group bias, it is a willing participant in a scheme that could only undermine the very foundation of our system of justice—our citizens' confidence in it.

On the question of state action, Justice Blackmun concluded that no matter who exercises the peremptory, "the perception and the reality in a criminal trial will be that the court has excused jurors based on race, an outcome that will be attributed to the State."

Justice Blackmun further relied on *Edmonson* and *Powers* to conclude that the prosecution had third-party standing to assert the equal protection rights of jurors excluded on racial grounds. On this point he concluded that "the State's relation to potential jurors in this case is closer than the relationships approved in *Powers* and *Edmonson*" because "[a]s the representative of all its citizens, the State is the logical and proper party to assert the invasion of the constitutional rights of the excluded jurors in a criminal trial."

Finally, Justice Blackmun concluded that prohibiting a defendant from exercising race-based peremptory challenges does not violate any constitutional or other right afforded to criminal defendants.

Chief Justice Rehnquist wrote a short concurring opinion, stating that while he disagreed with *Edmonson,* it "controls the disposition of this case."

Justice Thomas concurred in the judgment. Like the Chief Justice, he agreed that *Edmonson* logically prohibited the exercise of race-based challenges by a criminal defendant. Having not been on the Court when the previous cases were decided, however, he took the opportunity to express his "general dissatisfaction with our continuing attempts to use the Constitution to regulate peremptory challenges." He asserted that "black criminal defendants will rue the day that this Court ventured down this road that inexorably will lead to the elimination of peremptory strikes." In his view, the Court had inverted its priorities and had "exalted the right of citizens to sit on juries over the rights of the criminal defendant, even though it is the defendant, not the jurors, who faces imprisonment or even death."

Justice O'Connor dissented from what she termed "the remarkable conclusion that criminal defendants being prosecuted by the State act on behalf of their adversary when they exercise peremptory challenges during jury selection."

Justice Scalia dissented in a separate opinion. He agreed with the Chief Justice and Justice Thomas that *Edmonson* logically applied to the exercise of race-based peremptory challenges by a criminal defendant. However, he asserted that "a bad decision should not be followed logically to its illogical conclusion." He argued that the Court should not, in the interest of promoting race relations, "use the Constitution to destroy the ages-old right of criminal defendants to exercise peremptory challenges as they wish, to secure a jury that they consider fair."

QUESTIONS AFTER MCCOLLUM

Would the result in *McCollum* have been different if the defendant had been African-American, and had exercised race-based peremptory challenges against prospective white jurors? The NAACP filed an amicus brief in *McCollum,* which argued that "whether white defendants can use peremptory challenges to purge minority jurors presents quite different issues from whether a minority defendant can strike majority group jurors." In his separate opinion, Justice Thomas commented that while this issue "technically remains open, it is difficult to see how the result could be different if the defendants here were black." The courts have read *McCollum* to prohibit minority defendants from challenging majority jurors on racial grounds. See, e.g., State v. Knox, 609 So.2d 803 (La.1992) (relying on *McCollum*, the court holds that the State "may properly object to a minority criminal defendant's racially discriminatory exercise of peremptory challenges" and "require the defendant to assert a racially neutral explanation for the peremptory challenge").

Applying Batson Beyond Racial Exclusions: J.E.B. v. Alabama

The Court in Hernandez v. New York, 500 U.S. 352 (1991), held, not surprisingly, that Hispanics also have a right under the Equal Protection Clause to be free from discrimination in jury selection. In J.E.B. v. Alabama, 511 U.S. 127 (1994), the Court extended *Batson* and held that the Equal Protection Clause prohibits the exercise of a peremptory challenge on the basis of the gender of a prospective juror. The case involved a child support action brought by the State against a father. The State used 9 of its 10 strikes to remove male jurors; as a result, all the selected jurors were female. Justice Blackmun, writing for five members of the Court, applied the "heightened scrutiny" test that the Court ordinarily applies to gender-based classifications in other contexts. Justice Blackmun stated that under that test, the question was whether gender-based peremptory challenges "substantially further the State's legitimate interest in achieving a fair and impartial trial." He found that gender-based challenges could not meet this strict test, because there was no correlation between sex and impartiality.

Justice Blackmun rejected the State's argument that the Equal Protection Clause was not violated in this case because it was men, and not women, who were excluded in the action. He reasoned as follows:

> All persons, when granted the opportunity to serve on a jury, have the right not to be excluded summarily because of discriminatory and stereotypical presumptions that reflect and reinforce patterns of historical discrimination. Striking individuals on the assumption that they hold particular views simply because of their gender is practically a brand upon them, affixed by law, an assertion of their inferiority.

Justice Blackmun also found it irrelevant that women and men, unlike racial minorities, are found in such numbers in the jury pool that they are likely to be represented on the jury even if each side uses all of its peremptory challenges on one gender or another. He explained as follows:

> Because the right to nondiscriminatory jury selection procedures belongs to the potential jurors, as well as to the litigants, the possibility that members of both genders will get on the jury despite the intentional discrimination is beside the point. The exclusion of even one juror for impermissible reasons harms that juror and undermines public confidence in the fairness of the system.

Justice Blackmun concluded the majority opinion by contending that it was of limited scope:

> Our conclusion that litigants may not strike potential jurors solely on the basis of gender does not imply the elimination of all peremptory challenges. * * * Parties still may remove jurors whom they feel might be less acceptable than others on the panel; gender simply may not serve as a proxy for bias. * * * Even strikes based on characteristics that are disproportionately associated with one gender could be appropriate, absent a showing of pretext.

As an explanation of the last sentence in the above quote, Justice Blackmun wrote the following footnote:

> For example, challenging all persons who have had military experience would disproportionately affect men at this time, while challenging all persons employed as nurses would disproportionately affect women. Without a showing of pretext, however, these challenges may well not be unconstitutional, since they are not gender or race-based.

Justice O'Connor wrote a reluctant concurring opinion, reasoning that the Court's *Batson* jurisprudence led to a conclusion that gender-biased peremptory challenges are unconstitutional. But she emphasized that "[i]n extending *Batson* to gender we have added an additional burden to the state and federal trial process, taken a step closer to eliminating the peremptory challenge, and diminished the ability of litigants to act on sometimes accurate gender-based assumptions about juror attitudes."

Chief Justice Rehnquist wrote a dissenting opinion in *J.E.B.*, arguing that "there are sufficient differences between race and gender discrimination such that the principle of *Batson* should not be extended to peremptory challenges to potential jurors based on sex." He declared that the "two sexes differ, both biologically and, to a diminishing extent, in experience. It is not merely stereotyping to say that these differences may produce a difference in outlook which is brought to the jury room."

Justice Scalia also dissented in an opinion joined by the Chief Justice and Justice Thomas. He declared as follows:

> In order, it seems to me, not to eliminate any real denial of equal protection, but simply to pay conspicuous obeisance to the equality of the sexes, the Court imperils a practice [the peremptory challenge] that has been considered an essential part of fair jury trial since the dawn of the common law. The Constitution of the United States neither requires nor permits this vandalizing of our people's traditions.

Prima Facie Case of Discrimination

What exactly constitutes a prima facie case of discrimination under *Batson?* What if a litigant strikes three of six prospective African-American jurors? What if five of six are struck, but the litigant still has a peremptory to use and does not use it against the sixth African-American? Is it relevant that the litigant exercised peremptory challenges against non-minorities? How important are the questions asked or suggested by counsel on voir dire? See generally United States v. Esparsen, 930 F.2d 1461 (10th Cir.1991) (courts have looked to questions asked on voir dire; the answers given by those jurors who were struck as compared to those who were not struck; the number of challenges used on a certain group; whether members of the group actually sat on the jury; whether the litigant had unexpended peremptories; the rate at which members of the group were struck compared to the rate at which non-members were struck; and other factors particular to the case).

While no single factor is usually dispositive, a prima facie case of discrimination will ordinarily be found if the litigant strikes *all* prospective jurors belonging to a protected group. As the court in *Esparsen* put it, "the striking of a single juror will not always constitute a prima facie case, but when no members of a racial group remain because of that strike, it does."

For other examples of a prima facie case of discrimination in the use of peremptories, see Morse v. Hanks, 172 F.3d 983 (7th Cir.1999) (prima facie case of discrimination found where the prosecutor struck the only African-American vireman on the panel, and the voir dire was perfunctory, giving no indication of any other reason to exercise a peremptory challenge: "It might be different, we think, if the excused black juror had given an answer that would expose a clear basis for the state to want to remove him from the pool."); United States v. Hughes, 864 F.2d 78 (8th Cir.1988) (questioning on voir dire did not reveal sufficient independent reasons, other than race, for the striking of two African-Americans). The court in *Hughes* also found it relevant that there had been frequent charges of systematic exclusion of African-Americans from juries in the judicial district.

More Likely than Not Is Too Stringent a Standard for a Prima Facie Case: Johnson v. California

In Johnson v. California, 545 U.S. 162 (2005), the Court struck down a state procedure because it imposed too strict an evidentiary requirement on a party seeking to establish a *Batson* violation. The case involved a prosecutor who was accused of violating the Equal Protection Clause by striking African-Americans from the venire. The California rule required the defendant to show at the stage where a prima facie case must be shown that it was more likely than not that the prosecutor's peremptory challenges, if unexplained, were based on impermissible group bias. Justice Kennedy, writing for the Court, explained why this standard was too stringent.

The issue in this case * * * concerns the scope of the first of three steps this Court enumerated in *Batson*, which together guide trial courts' constitutional review of peremptory strikes. Those three *Batson* steps should by now be familiar. First, the defendant must make out a prima facie case by showing that the totality of the relevant facts gives rise to an inference of discriminatory purpose. Second, once the defendant has made out a prima facie case, the burden shifts to the State to explain adequately the racial exclusion by offering permissible race-neutral justifications for the strikes. Third, if a race-neutral explanation is tendered, the trial court must then decide whether the opponent of the strike has proved purposeful racial discrimination.

The question before us is whether *Batson* permits California to require at step one that "the objector must show that it is more likely than not the other party's peremptory challenges, if unexplained, were based on impermissible group bias." [W]e conclude that California's "more likely than not" standard is an inappropriate yardstick by which to measure the sufficiency of a prima facie case.

We begin with *Batson* itself, which on its own terms provides no support for California's rule. There, we held that a prima facie case of discrimination can be made out by offering a wide variety of evidence, so long as the sum of the proffered facts gives "rise to an inference of discriminatory purpose." * * *

Thus, in describing the burden-shifting framework, we assumed in *Batson* that the trial judge would have the benefit of all relevant circumstances, including the prosecutor's explanation, before deciding whether it was more likely than not that the challenge was improperly motivated. We did not intend the first step to be so onerous that a defendant would have to persuade the judge—on the basis of all the facts, some of which are impossible for the defendant to know with certainty—that the challenge was more likely than not the product of purposeful discrimination. Instead, a defendant satisfies the requirements of *Batson's* first step by producing evidence sufficient to permit the trial judge to draw an inference that discrimination has occurred.

Justice Breyer wrote a short concurring opinion in *Johnson*. Justice Thomas wrote a short dissenting opinion.

Neutral Explanations: Purkett v. Elem

A *Batson* violation is not found every time that prima facie proof of a discriminatory peremptory challenge is established. A prima facie case of discrimination merely requires the party exercising the peremptory to provide a neutral explanation. The Court emphasized the minimal nature of the neutral explanation requirement in Purkett v. Elem, 514 U.S. 765 (1995), a per curiam opinion joined by seven Justices.

The prosecutor in Elem's trial excluded two African-American jurors, and offered as an explanation that they had long unkempt hair, a mustache, and a goatee-type beard. The Court of Appeals, on review of the denial of Elem's habeas petition, ordered that the writ be granted because of a *Batson* violation. The Court of Appeals reasoned that a prosecutor must give some explanation for exclusion that might be related to the prospective juror's performance in the case. It found that the prosecutor's explanations had nothing to do with juror performance and therefore were pretextual.

But the Supreme Court reversed, reasoning that the Court of Appeals had not properly applied the three-step analysis required by *Batson*. The Court explained that after a prima facie case is made and the prosecutor offers a race-neutral justification for a challenge, the trial court must decide in the final step whether the opponent of the strike has proven racial discrimination. The Court found that the Court of Appeals had conflated the second and third steps, reasoned that "to say that a trial judge may choose to disbelieve a silly or superstitious reason at step 3 is quite different from saying that a trial judge must terminate the inquiry at step 2 when the race-neutral reason is silly or superstitious," and explained that "[t]he latter violates the principle that the ultimate burden of persuasion regarding racial motivation rests with, and never shifts from, the opponent of the strike."

Because the prosecutor's explanation in *Purkett* was neutral—in that long, unkempt hair and mustaches and goatees are not indicative of a particular race—the Court held that the state had met its obligation under the second step of *Batson*. The state court had concluded that Elem failed to prove purposeful racial discrimination, and the Court remanded to allow the lower federal court to determine, on habeas review, whether the state court's conclusion was fairly supported by the record.[20]

Justice Stevens, joined by Justice Breyer, dissented. He contended that the Court had watered down the race-neutral explanation requirement of *Batson* to the point where it had no meaning at all. He elaborated as follows:

> In my opinion, preoccupation with the niceties of a three-step analysis should not foreclose meaningful judicial review of prosecutorial explanations that are entirely unrelated to the case to be tried. * * * The Court's unnecessary tolerance of silly, fantastic, and implausible explanations, together with its assumption that there is a difference of constitutional magnitude between a statement that "I had a hunch about this juror based on his appearance," and "I challenged this juror because he had a mustache," demeans the importance of the values vindicated by our decision in *Batson*.

Neutral Explanations and Bilingual Jurors:
 Hernandez v. New York

In Hernandez v. New York, 500 U.S. 352 (1991), the defendant claimed that the prosecutor struck Latino jurors on account of race. The prosecutor did not wait for the trial court's ruling on whether a prima facie case of discrimination had been established. Rather, the prosecutor defended his strikes on the ground that the prospective jurors were bilingual and many witnesses would be Spanish-speaking; therefore he "was very uncertain that they would be able to listen and follow the interpreter." The prosecutor based his assertion on the answers given by the prospective jurors to

---

[20] On remand, the court of appeals found no *Batson* violation, reasoning that the prosecutor proffered reasons for striking the juror that were facially race-neutral, and the defendant made no attempt to persuade the state trial court that the prosecutor's reasons for striking the juror were pretextual. Elem v. Purkett, 64 F.3d 1195 (8th Cir.1995).

whether they could accept the interpreter as the final arbiter of what was said by the Spanish-speaking witnesses. According to the prosecutor, the excluded prospective jurors "looked away from me and said with some hesitancy that they would try * * * to follow the interpreter." The trial court and the State appellate courts found that this explanation was race-neutral and sufficient to rebut the defendant's prima facie case. The Supreme Court agreed, but there was no majority opinion.

Justice Kennedy wrote an opinion joined by Chief Justice Rehnquist, Justice White, and Justice Souter. Justice Kennedy found that the prosecutor's explanation "rested neither on the intention to exclude Latino or bilingual jurors, nor on stereotypical assumptions about Latinos or bilinguals." According to Justice Kennedy, the prosecutor properly divided jurors into two potential classes: "those whose conduct during *voir dire* would persuade him they might have difficulty in accepting the translator's rendition of Spanish-language testimony and those potential jurors who gave no reason for such doubt. Each category would include both Latinos and non-Latinos."

Justice Kennedy recognized that the prosecutor's criterion for exclusion would have a disparate impact on prospective Latino jurors, because they were more likely to be fluent in Spanish than non-Latino jurors. He responded, however, that while disparate impact was relevant in determining whether the prosecutor acted with discriminatory intent, "it will not be conclusive in the preliminary race-neutrality step of the *Batson* inquiry. * * * Unless the government actor adopted a criterion with the intent of causing the impact asserted, that impact itself does not violate the principle of race-neutrality. Nothing in the prosecutor's explanation shows that he chose to exclude jurors * * * *because* he wanted to prevent bilingual Latinos from serving on the jury."[21]

Justice Kennedy cautioned that his opinion did not imply that the prosecutor had untrammeled discretion to exclude bilingual jurors. He noted that the case would be different if the prosecutor had merely stated that he did not want Spanish-speaking jurors.

Justice O'Connor, joined by Justice Scalia, concurred in the judgment. She agreed with much of Justice Kennedy's opinion, but felt that the plurality went "farther than it needs to in assessing the constitutionality of the prosecutor's asserted justification for his peremptory strikes." According to Justice O'Connor, "if the trial court believes the prosecutor's nonracial justification, and that finding is not clearly erroneous, that is the

---

[21] See also United States v. Uwaezhoke, 995 F.2d 388 (3d Cir.1993) (in a drug prosecution, the prosecutor gave a neutral explanation when he excluded an African-American juror on the ground that she lived in public housing in Newark, an area known for drugs and crime; exclusion was permissible even though the prosecutor's justification resulted in a disparate impact on African-Americans).

end of the matter." Justice O'Connor stressed that disparate impact was no substitute for a finding of intentional discrimination.

Justice Stevens, joined by Justices Marshall and Blackmun, dissented in *Hernandez.* He argued that the prosecutor's explanation was insufficient to overcome the prima facie case of discrimination because, among other things, "the justification would inevitably result in a disproportionate disqualification of Spanish-speaking venirepersons." According to Justice Stevens "an explanation that is race-neutral on its face is nonetheless unacceptable if it is merely a proxy for a discriminatory practice."

What limitations are placed on a prosecutor's explanation for exercising peremptory challenges after *Hernandez* and *Purkett?* Will a prosecutor who is intentionally discriminating on the basis of race always be able to assert some credible race-neutral explanation? For examples of explanations found race-neutral, see Jordan v. Lefevre, 293 F.3d 587 (2d Cir. 2002) (race-neutral explanation found where African-American juror did not know the occupations or whereabouts of her children, and prosecutor explained that she lacked the common sense he was looking for in a juror; it was also permissible to exclude an African-American juror who lived with her mother, worked only part-time, and spent the rest of her time watching television; the prosecutor explained that she seemed to lack both maturity and experience in making important decisions); Stubbs v. Gomez, 189 F.3d 1099 (9th Cir. 1999) (prosecutor's reasons for striking African-American juror were race-neutral under *Batson*: the prosecutor felt that the juror's demeanor and lack of eye contact showed disinterest in being a juror, and she had no employment record); United States v. Nichols, 937 F.2d 1257 (7th Cir.1991) (neutral explanation found where the prospective juror was young and living with a man to whom she was not married); United States v. Biaggi, 853 F.2d 89 (2d Cir.1988) (*Batson* limits exclusion of Italian-Americans, but prosecutor gave neutral explanation for exclusion; prospective jurors had displayed angry, arrogant, or flippant demeanors).

Commentators have argued that the Court has rendered *Batson* a nullity, because any prosecutor can come up with a facially neutral explanation for what is really a race-based challenge. See Cavise, The *Batson* Doctrine: The Supreme Court's Utter Failure to Meet the Challenge of Discrimination in Jury Selection, 1999 Wis.L.Rev. 501; Charlow, Tolerating Deception and Discrimination After *Batson*, 50 Stan.L.Rev. 9 (1997).

Fact-Intensive Reviews of Peremptory Challenges: Snyder v. Louisiana and Foster v. Chapman

In Snyder v. Louisiana, 552 U.S. 472 (2008), the Supreme Court engaged in an extensive review of the facts surrounding jury selection in a case in which Snyder was convicted of first-degree murder and sentenced to death. Justice Alito wrote the opinion of the Court and found "the trial court committed clear error in its ruling on a *Batson* objection."

Justice Alito found the prosecutor's explanation for challenging an African-American juror to be unpersuasive. The prosecutor claimed that he struck a college senior who was attempting to fulfill his student-teaching obligation because he looked nervous and as a student teacher he might not want to miss class and therefore might vote for a lesser verdict to avoid a penalty phase. Justice Alito noted that the trial judge never made a determination as to demeanor and found that the nervousness explanation warranted no deference. He found that the explanation that the juror might want to go home early was belied by the fact that the trial was expected to be short and the prosecutor accepted white jurors who disclosed conflicting obligations as serious as the challenged juror. Justice Thomas, joined by Justice Scalia dissented and objected to the Court's second-guessing the state courts.

In Foster v. Chatman, 136 S.Ct. 1737 (2016), Chief Justice Roberts wrote for the Court as it reversed lower federal courts who denied habeas relief to an African-American defendant convicted and sentenced to death in Georgia for the sexual assault and murder of a 79-year-old woman. The prosecutor had stricken all four qualified African-American jurors. During post-conviction proceedings the defendant had obtained documents pursuant to the state Open Records Act. They revealed, among other things, that the prosecutors had highlighted the names of the Black jurors on the jury venire list; a prosecutor had indicated in a note that one of the Black jurors might be okay if they were forced to pick a Black juror; a typed list of the qualified jurors who remained after voir dire had an N next to all qualified Black jurors; and a handwritten document titled "definite NO's" listed all Black jurors and only one other. The Court examined in detail the prosecutors' "neutral" explanation for the strikes and found as to two of the stricken jurors that the strikes "were motivated in substantial part by discriminatory intent" and "the focus on race in the prosecution's file plainly demonstrates a concerted effort to keep black jurors off the jury." Justice Alito filed an opinion concurring in the judgment. Justice Thomas dissented and argued that the Supreme Court of Georgia had properly analyzed the strikes and found them to have been race-neutral.

c. The Future of Peremptory Challenges

Justice Breyer has argued, as had Justice Marshall in *Batson,* that peremptory challenges should be abolished. See Miller-El v. Dretke, 545 U.S. 231 (2005) (concurring opinion). Justice Breyer contends that *Batson's* legal test is fraught with difficulty:

> At *Batson*'s first step, litigants remain free to misuse peremptory challenges as long as the strikes fall *below* the prima facie threshold

level. At *Batson*'s second step, prosecutors need only tender a neutral reason, not a "persuasive, or even plausible" one. And most importantly, at step three, *Batson* asks judges to engage in the awkward, sometime hopeless, task of second-guessing a prosecutor's instinctive judgment—the underlying basis for which may be invisible even to the prosecutor exercising the challenge. * * * In such circumstances, it may be impossible for trial courts to discern if a "seat-of-the-pants" peremptory challenge reflects a "seat-of-the-pants" racial stereotype.

Justice Breyer notes the extensive literature concluding that *Batson* has been ineffective in eradicating discrimination in peremptory challenges:

> Given the inevitably clumsy fit between any objectively measurable standard and the subjective decisionmaking at issue, I am not surprised to find studies and anecdotal reports suggesting that, despite *Batson*, the discriminatory use of peremptory challenges remains a problem. See, *e.g.*, Baldus, Woodworth, Zuckerman, Weiner, & Broffitt, The Use of Peremptory Challenges in Capital Murder Trials: A Legal and Empirical Analysis, 3 U. Pa. J. Const. L. 3, 52–53, 73, n. 197 (2001) (in 317 capital trials in Philadelphia between 1981 and 1997, prosecutors struck 51% of black jurors and 26% of nonblack jurors; defense counsel struck 26% of black jurors and 54% of nonblack jurors; and race-based uses of prosecutorial peremptories declined by only 2% after *Batson*); Rose, The Peremptory Challenge Accused of Race or Gender Discrimination? Some Data from One County, 23 Law and Human Behavior 695, 698–699 (1999) (in one North Carolina county, 71% of excused black jurors were removed by the prosecution; 81% of excused white jurors were removed by the defense).

Justice Breyer further contends that *Batson's* promise will never be implemented so long as lawyers are trained and encouraged to rely on stereotypes in exercising peremptory challenges. He described examples of this stereotyping:

> [Despite *Batson*] the use of race-and gender-based stereotypes in the jury-selection process seems better organized and more systematized than ever before. For example, one jury-selection guide counsels attorneys to perform a "demographic analysis" that assigns numerical points to characteristics such as age, occupation, and marital status—in addition to race as well as gender. See V. Starr & A. McCormick, Jury Selection 193–200 (3d ed. 2001). Thus, in a hypothetical dispute between a white landlord and an African-American tenant, the authors suggest awarding two points to an African-American venire member while subtracting one point from her white counterpart. * * * [A] bar journal article counsels lawyers to "rate" potential jurors "demographically (age, gender, marital status,

etc.) and mark who would be under stereotypical circumstances [their] natural *enemies* and *allies*." Drake, The Art of Litigating: Deselecting Jurors Like the Pros, 34 Md. Bar J. 18, 22 (Mar.–Apr. 2001). * * * These examples reflect a professional effort to fulfill the lawyer's obligation to help his or her client. Nevertheless, the outcome in terms of jury selection is the same as it would be were the motive less benign. And as long as that is so, the law's antidiscrimination command and a peremptory jury-selection system that permits or encourages the use of stereotypes work at cross-purposes.

Justice Breyer concludes as follows:

> I recognize that peremptory challenges have a long historical pedigree. They may help to reassure a party of the fairness of the jury. But [i]f used to express stereotypical judgments about race, gender, religion, or national origin, peremptory challenges betray the jury's democratic origins and undermine its representative function. The "scientific" use of peremptory challenges may also contribute to public cynicism about the fairness of the jury system and its role in American government. And, of course, the right to a jury free of discriminatory taint is constitutionally protected—the right to use peremptory challenges is not. * * * In light of the considerations I have mentioned, I believe it necessary to reconsider *Batson*'s test and the peremptory challenge system as a whole.

Consider also Judge Gee's comments about *Batson,* which were made in dissent in the court of appeals decision in *Edmonson,* 860 F.2d 1308 (5th Cir.1988), the case in which the Court ultimately extended *Batson* to civil cases:

> What remains after [*Batson*] is not the peremptory challenge which our procedure has known for decades—or not one which can be freely exercised against all jurors in all cases, at any rate. Justice Marshall would dispense with strikes entirely, and perhaps this will be the final outcome. In this much at least he is surely correct, that we must go on or backward; to stay here is to rest content with a strange procedural creature indeed: a challenge for semi-cause, * * * a skewed and curious device, exercisable without giving reasons in some cases but not in others, all depending on race.

For a view in favor of peremptory challenges, at least when exercised by criminal defendants, see Goldwasser, Limiting the Criminal Defendant's Use of Peremptory Challenges: On Symmetry and the Jury in a Criminal Trial, 102 Harv.L.Rev. 808 (1989).

E. PRESERVING THE INTEGRITY OF JURY DELIBERATIONS

Many devices are employed to assure that the jury process works as smoothly and as fairly as possible. Sometimes, however, efforts to protect the jury's deliberation process are in tension with the rights of the defendant or the interest in judicial efficiency.

1. Anonymous Juries

Ordinarily, the names of jurors are made known to counsel and the defendant during the voir dire process. However, in some cases prosecutors make the argument that juror anonymity is required to preserve the integrity of deliberations. For example, in United States v. Barnes, 604 F.2d 121 (2d Cir.1979), a divided court approved the trial judge's decision to keep the names and addresses of jurors secret from counsel and to bar defense counsel from inquiring into the jurors' ethnic and religious backgrounds. The defendant was charged with being a drug kingpin and the government made a preliminary showing that the defendant engaged in acts of violence and intimidation. The trial judge permitted an inquiry of prospective jurors only as to their county and length of residence and certain family history. The limitations on voir dire were intended to protect the jurors from harassment and threats to themselves and their families. In United States v. Tutino, 883 F.2d 1125 (2d Cir.1989), the judge ordered that the jury would remain anonymous in a trial alleging a heroin distribution conspiracy, when presented with the following submission from the government:

> The government requested an anonymous jury for five reasons: (1) the defendants faced serious penalties, including substantial prison terms and a possible parole revocation, and, according to the government, were therefore likely to bribe or threaten the jury; (2) [defendant] Tutino had attempted to tamper with a jury in a prior trial; (3) [defendants] Tutino and Guarino were known associates of organized crime figures; (4) Tutino had a prior extortion conviction and Guarino and [defendant] Larca had prior narcotics convictions; and (5) the jury had to be protected from the media.

In affirming the decision to use an anonymous jury, the court of appeals noted that the trial court issued instructions regarding the presumption of innocence more than once. The court believed that "these instructions were carefully framed to avoid any risk that the anonymous procedures would appear extraordinary or reflect adversely on the defendants." Do you believe that *any* instructions would suffice to protect the presumption of innocence when a jury is anonymous? Isn't the jury bound to think that there is a good reason why their names are not going to be made public?

There are limits, however, to ordering juror anonymity. For example, in United States v. Sanchez, 74 F.3d 562 (5th Cir.1996), the defendant, a police officer, was charged with coercing prostitutes to engage in sex acts with him. The trial judge ordered that the jury remain anonymous, reasoning that "I don't think there's anything more frightening to the populace than having a rogue cop on their hands." The court of appeals reversed the conviction. It noted that 1) the defendant was not involved in organized crime; 2) there was no evidence that the defendant had ever attempted to interfere with the judicial process; and 3) there was no indication that the case would receive extensive publicity that would enhance the possibility that the jurors' names would become public and expose them to intimidation or harassment. The court emphasized that anonymous juries are an extraordinary remedy that could only be used as a device of last resort. See also United States v. Wecht, 537 F.3d 222 (3rd Cir. 2008) (withholding names of jurors was error where the only unusual factor about the case was the local prominence of the defendant).

The *Sanchez* court held that the impermissible use of an anonymous jury can never be harmless and explained as follows:

> The defendant has a right to a jury of known individuals not just because information such as was redacted here yields valuable clues for purposes of jury selection, but also because the verdict is both personalized and personified when rendered by 12 known fellow citizens. [Unless strong factors supporting anonymity exist, the defendant] should receive a verdict not from anonymous decisionmakers, but from people he can name as responsible for their actions.

2. Protecting Against Judicial Influence on Jury Deliberations

Once the jury retires to deliberate, there is good reason to be concerned about any further contact with the judge.

Breaking a Deadlock: The Allen Charge

Assume that a jury has been deliberating for a day when it reports back that it is deadlocked. One possibility for the judge at this point is to consider granting a mistrial; but either or both parties might object to a mistrial for their own strategic reasons, and the judge is likely to be concerned about the substantial cost of a retrial. Therefore, the trial judge may want to encourage the jury to deliberate further in the hope of reaching a verdict. But just what should the judge tell the jury at this point? One jury charge was considered in Allen v. United States, 164 U.S. 492 (1896), and is commonly referred to as the "Allen charge" or the "dynamite" charge. The instruction provides as follows:

In a large proportion of cases absolute certainty cannot be expected. Although your verdict must be the verdict of each of you individually and not a mere acquiescence in the conclusion of your fellows, yet you should examine the question submitted with candor and with a proper regard for and deference to the opinions of each other. It is your duty to decide the case if you can conscientiously do so. You should listen, with a disposition to be convinced, to each other's arguments. If much the larger number are for conviction, a dissenting juror should consider whether his doubts are reasonable ones when they make no impression upon the minds of so many others, equally honest and equally intelligent. If, upon the other hand, the majority is for acquittal, the minority ought to ask themselves whether they might not reasonably doubt the correctness of a judgment which was not concurred in by the majority.

The concern with an *Allen*-type charge is that it will *coerce* the minority into agreeing with the majority, simply to reach a verdict. See, e.g., United States v. Robinson, 953 F.2d 433 (8th Cir.1992) (impermissible coercion where judge implied that deadlock would be wasteful and unpatriotic, and instructed the minority to give special consideration to the majority's position).

To limit the possibility of coercion, courts have generally required an *Allen* charge to include the following:

1)   a recognition that a majority of jurors may favor acquittal;

2)   a reminder that the government has the burden of proof beyond a reasonable doubt;

3)   a statement that both the majority and the minority should reexamine their views;

4)   a statement that no juror should abandon his or her conscientiously held view; and

5)   a statement that the jury is free to deliberate as long as necessary.

These propositions go beyond the charge given in *Allen* itself, reproduced above. An instruction containing these five propositions is referred to as a "modified *Allen* charge." See United States v. Webb, 816 F.2d 1263 (8th Cir.1987) (finding reversible error where an *Allen* charge did not contain these five elements).

Courts have cautioned against an instruction that refers to the costs of a retrial, as this might pressure jurors to dispense with honestly-held views. United States v. Clinton, 338 F.3d 483 (6th Cir. 2003) (cautioning against such a statement, but noting that it didn't render the charge "coercive per se"). But courts have permitted an instruction stating that if the case is tried again "there is no reason to believe that any new evidence will be presented, or that the next twelve jurors will be any more conscientious or impartial than you are." See, e.g., Sixth Circuit Pattern Jury Instruction 9.04. Courts have generally not required the trial judge to instruct the jury that it is free to hang, i.e., that a deadlock is an acceptable resolution. United States v. Arpan, 887 F.2d 873 (8th Cir.1989) (en banc).

Even if a coercive deadlock charge is given, it does not necessarily mean that the verdict is tainted. Whether a coercive charge actually affected the jury depends on the circumstances. Thus, in United States v. Ajiboye, 961 F.2d 892 (9th Cir.1992), the judge gave a deadlock instruction that did not include all the protective elements of a modified *Allen* charge. The defendant was tried on two counts, and the jury was deadlocked 9–3 for acquittal on one count and 9–3 for conviction on the other. After receiving the charge, the jury deliberated for two more days, and asked to review some of the evidence. The jury then returned a guilty verdict on both counts. The court found that the *Allen* charge did not coerce the jury into rendering guilty verdicts. Does the fact that the jury deliberated for two days after hearing the charge signify that it was not coercive?

Successive Allen Charges

Some courts have found reversible error when the trial judge gives successive *Allen* charges—i.e., the jury reports a deadlock, a deadlock charge is given, the jury comes back deadlocked again, and the judge gives another deadlock charge. The concern is that the dissenting jurors are being worn down, and are getting the message that they will never be able to leave so long as they are deadlocked. This concern exists even if the charge contains the ameliorative language of a modified *Allen* charge. See United States v. Seawell, 550 F.2d 1159 (9th Cir.1977) (reversible error when successive *Allen* charges are given). However, even multiple *Allen* charges may be permissible, depending on the circumstances. Thus, in United States v. Nickell, 883 F.2d 824 (9th Cir.1989), the judge gave one modified *Allen* charge on Friday immediately before the jurors recessed for the weekend, and another when they resumed deliberations on Monday. The court found no error given that there were no deliberations between the two charges. See also United States v. Ruggiero, 928 F.2d 1289 (2d Cir.1991) ("we do not regard a repeated *Allen* charge as inevitably coercive").

Capital Punishment and the Allen Charge

The Supreme Court held, 5–3, in Lowenfield v. Phelps, 484 U.S. 231 (1988), that the trial judge did not act improperly in a capital case in giving a modified *Allen* charge during the sentencing phase of the case. When the jury indicated to the trial judge that it was unable to reach a decision on sentence, the judge gave each juror a piece of paper and asked each to indicate whether further deliberations would be helpful in obtaining a verdict. Eight jurors initially answered affirmatively, and three others subsequently indicated that they had misunderstood the question. The judge then asked each to indicate whether further deliberations would enable the jury to reach a verdict, and eleven jurors responded affirmatively. At this point, the judge told the jurors that they should consider each other's views with the objective of reaching a verdict without surrendering their honest beliefs in doing so, and that the court would impose a sentence of life imprisonment without possibility of probation, parole, or suspension of sentence if the jury failed to agree on a sanction. Shortly thereafter, the jury voted for the death penalty.

Chief Justice Rehnquist's majority opinion reasoned that the trial judge had not coerced the jury into reaching a decision and distinguished Brasfield v. United States, 272 U.S. 448 (1926), in which the Court had invoked its supervisory powers to condemn judicial inquiry into the numerical division of jurors. The Court also distinguished Jenkins v. United States, 380 U.S. 445 (1965), where the trial judge told the jury that "you have got to reach a decision in this case." Justice Marshall, joined by Justices Brennan and Stevens, dissented and argued that the two polls of the jury whittled the minority jurors from four to one. He condemned the fact that in the instant case, as in *Brasfield,* the jurors were asked to identify themselves by name in the polls. He also expressed doubts as to the wisdom of the *Allen* charge, especially in a case in which a hung jury would produce a life sentence rather than a new proceeding, and therefore the costs of a deadlock were not so substantial.

3.   Protecting Against Jury Misconduct and Outside Influence

The conduct of individual jurors during the trial proceedings and deliberations must comport with the requirement of impartiality. The trial judge must deal with any particular action that could undermine a juror's impartiality. So for example, when jurors are exposed to highly inflammatory information that will not be brought out in evidence, and they can no longer remain impartial, they should be disqualified. See, e.g., United States v. Martinez, 14 F.3d 543 (11th Cir.1994) (juror saw newscast); People v. Honeycutt, 20 Cal.3d 150, 141 Cal.Rptr. 698, 570 P.2d 1050 (1977) (information and advice from an attorney friend of the foreman was prejudicial.) Even if the juror is adversely affected by events outside her control, she may have to be excused. See, e.g., United States v. Angulo, 4 F.3d 843 (9th Cir.1993) (juror excused after receiving threatening phone call).

Additionally, a juror must remain able and qualified to perform his duty. See United States v. Smith, 550 F.2d 277 (5th Cir.1977) (sleeping juror and juror whose conduct suggests that tampering has occurred are disqualified). Of course, the trial judge must be careful not to excuse a juror too quickly, and to excuse jurors in a way that does not prejudice either of the parties. See, e.g., United States v. Hernandez, 862 F.2d 17 (2d Cir.1988) (finding error in the trial court's decision to dismiss a juror where "the record seemed to reflect that the cause of the removal was as much to avoid a mistrial because of a hung jury as to excuse an incompetent juror").

The trial court has discretion in determining whether some development that might affect a juror is so substantial that a juror can no longer remain impartial. Thus, in Smith v. Phillips, 455 U.S. 209 (1982), the prosecutor learned during the trial that one juror's employment application was pending in his office, and the prosecutor did not disclose this fact to the court or the defense until after the jury returned its guilty verdict. The Supreme Court held that this development did not require a new trial under the circumstances. The Court observed that due process does not require a new trial every time a juror is placed in a potentially compromising situation The trial judge conducted a post-trial hearing and found that the juror was not actually biased, and this finding was entitled to deference, especially on habeas review.

Sequestration

During the course of trial, the judge has discretion to sequester the jury, i.e., to confine them, regulate access to media, prevent them from going home, etc. Some jurisdictions require sequestration, unless it is waived by the parties. See N.Y.C.P.L. § 310.10.

One famous trial lawyer believes that sequestration is usually prejudicial to the defendant:

> Every trial lawyer knows that a sequestered jury behaves radically differently from one whose members can go home at night. The jurors react to confinement with resentment. Sometimes they resent their captors. More often, they come to identify with the cops who are guarding them. And as the trial wears on, and the defense case threatens to lengthen their confinement, jurors begin to look at defense counsel with baleful eyes.

Tigar, Television and the Jury, Nat'l L.J., Aug. 21, 1995, p. A19.

Sequestration is ordinarily a response to the risk of prejudicial trial publicity. Is there a less onerous means of protecting the jurors from hearing about extrajudicial information? Would court orders preventing the jurors from reading newspapers, watching television, and accessing the internet be sufficient? Can we trust the jurors to close their eyes and ears and laptops if they are not sequestered?

Sequestration During Deliberations

It is more likely that a judge will exercise her discretion to sequester the jury once deliberations begin. The court in Hunley v. Godinez, 975 F.2d 316 (7th Cir.1992), considered a unique problem that arose with a jury that was sequestered during deliberations. The defendant was charged with murder and burglary, the prosecution contending that the murder occurred when the defendant was discovered by the victim while burgling her apartment. After the first day of deliberations, the jury stood 8 to 4 in favor of conviction. The jurors were then sequestered overnight in a hotel. That night, a burglar made an unforced entry into the rooms of four jurors, and stole several items. The jurors talked about the burglary among themselves the next day. The jury reached a guilty verdict after one hour of deliberation that day. Two of the four jurors who changed their minds from the previous day had been victims of the burglary. The trial judge held an in camera hearing, and each of the jurors said that the burglary had not affected their verdict. Nonetheless, the court of appeals reversed the conviction. It reasoned that "[t]he burglary placed the jurors in the shoes of the victim just before she was murdered." Obviously, the trial judge could not have prevented the burglary. Once it occurred, was there anything the judge could have done to assure fair deliberations? For example, would it have been sufficient if the judge permitted the jurors to take a day or two off and go home before returning to resume deliberations?

Ex Parte Communications with the Jury

In Rushen v. Spain, 464 U.S. 114 (1983), the Court denied relief to a petitioner who complained about ex parte communications between a trial judge and a juror. The juror had indicated to the judge that she was an acquaintance of a woman who had been murdered by one of the defense witnesses, although she expressed the view that she could be fair to the defendants. The lower courts had reasoned that the contact between judge and juror could not be deemed harmless, because no contemporaneous record had been made. But the Supreme Court ruled that the lower federal courts should have deferred to the "presumptively correct" state court finding that the jury's deliberations had not been affected by the ex parte contact. See also United States v. Strickland, 935 F.2d 822 (7th Cir.1991) (a juror acted improperly when he asked a question of a government witness outside of court; but this was not prejudicial because the witness did not answer, curative instructions were given, and the trial judge determined after questioning that the juror could remain impartial).

Evidentiary Limitations on Proof of Jury
Misconduct: *Tanner v. United States*

The Supreme Court held, 5–4, in Tanner v. United States, 483 U.S. 107 (1987), that two defendants were properly denied a hearing concerning juror misconduct. The defendants called to the trial judge's attention one juror's statement that several jurors had consumed alcohol at lunch throughout the trial, causing them to sleep during the afternoons. The only other evidence offered in the trial court in support of a hearing was defense counsel's testimony that he had observed one of the jurors "in a sort of giggly mood" during the trial, something not called to the judge's attention. While the case was pending on appeal, the defendants presented a second juror's affidavit indicating that numerous members of the jury, including the affiant, consumed alcohol during the trial and some jurors used illegal drugs.

Writing for the majority in *Tanner*, Justice O'Connor relied upon Rule 606(b) of the Federal Rules of Evidence, which generally prohibits an inquiry into the course of the jury's deliberations. Rule 606(b) does permit proof of "extraneous prejudicial information" that was brought to the jury's attention, and it also permits proof that an "outside influence was improperly brought to bear upon any juror." But Justice O'Connor declared that these exceptions did not apply to allegations of substance abuse by the jurors—rather, these exceptions covered matters such as threats or bribes to jurors from *outside sources*, or exposure to prejudicial trial publicity. Justice O'Connor also rejected the argument that the failure to inquire into juror intoxication denies a defendant a fair trial before an impartial and competent jury, reasoning that other aspects of the trial process—voir dire of jurors, observations by the trial judge and courtroom participants, and observations and reports by fellow jurors—are adequate to assure defendants fair trials.

Justice O'Connor expressed concern that routine impeachment of jury verdicts, by inquiring into what went on in the deliberations, would have a negative effect on finality and on the free flow of communications between jurors during deliberations.

Justice Marshall, joined by Justices Brennan, Blackmun, and Stevens, dissented. He concluded that "[e]very criminal defendant has a constitutional right to be tried by competent jurors," and that "[i]f, as charged, members of petitioners' jury were intoxicated as a result of their use of drugs and alcohol to the point of sleeping through material portions of the trial, the verdict in this case must be set aside." He concluded that voir dire of jurors prior to trial cannot disclose whether they will use drugs during the trial, and the type of misconduct alleged would not have been verified easily by courtroom personnel.

Examples of alleged jury misconduct that have been held immune from inquiry under Rule 606(b) after *Tanner* include:

- intimidation of one juror by another (United States v. Stansfield, 101 F.3d 909 (3d Cir.1996));

- unfair inferences drawn from the evidence (United States v. DiSalvo, 34 F.3d 1204 (3d Cir.1994));

- assumptions that if the defendant failed to take the stand, he must be guilty (United States v. Voigt, 877 F.2d 1465 (10th Cir.1989));

- a vote for conviction because extended deliberation would cut into the juror's vacation (United States v. Murphy, 836 F.2d 248 (6th Cir.1988)).

The court in United States v. Ruggiero, 56 F.3d 647, 652 (5th Cir.1995), summed it up by stating that Rule 606(b) bars juror testimony on "at least four topics: (1) the methods or arguments of the jury's deliberations, (2) the effect of any particular thing upon an outcome in the deliberations, (3) the mindset or emotions of any juror during deliberations, and (4) the testifying juror's own mental process during deliberations." See also United States v. Benally, 546 F.3d 1230 (10th Cir. 2008) (statements made by jurors during deliberations, indicating racial bias against the defendant, may not be introduced into evidence under the terms of Rule 606(b)).

But in Pena-Rodriguez v. Colorado, 137 S.Ct. 855 (2017), the Court found that an exception to the bar imposed by Rule 606(b) was required by the Sixth Amendment. The case involved racist statements made by a juror during deliberations: a juror stated that the defendant, a Hispanic, was likely to be guilty of the crime charged (accosting two women) because that was how Hispanic men acted. The Court held that applying Rule 606(b) to exclude a juror's statement about these racist comments violated the defendant's Sixth Amendment right to a fair trial. Justice Kennedy, writing for the Court, ruled as follows:

> [W]here a juror makes a clear statement that indicates he or she relied on racial stereotypes or animus to convict a criminal defendant, the Sixth Amendment requires that the no-impeachment rule give way in order to permit the trial court to consider the evidence of the juror's statement and any resulting denial of the jury trial guarantee.

Justice Kennedy emphasized, however, that "[n]ot every offhand comment indicating racial bias or hostility will justify setting aside the no-impeachment bar to allow further judicial inquiry. For the inquiry to proceed, there must be a showing that one or more jurors made statements exhibiting overt racial bias that cast serious doubt on the fairness and impartiality of the jury's deliberations and resulting verdict. To qualify, the statement must tend to show that racial animus was a significant motivating factor in the juror's vote to convict."

Justice Alito, joined by Chief Justice Roberts and Justice Thomas, dissented in *Pena-Rodriguez*. He argued that the majority's rule would undermine the finality of verdicts, that the rule could be expanded to allow proof of other forms of bias, and that the question of exceptions to Rule 606(b) is better left to rulemakers.

Lies on Voir Dire

Tanner states that the voir dire process is preferable to post-conviction review for determining whether jurors are competent and impartial. But what if the witness lies at the voir dire? In United States v. Colombo, 869 F.2d 149 (2d Cir.1989), the defendant submitted a post-conviction affidavit from an alternate juror, averring that a juror deliberately failed to reveal on voir dire that her brother-in-law was an attorney for the government. Her motivation for concealment was that she thought it would hurt her chances to sit on the case. The court held that if it could be shown that the juror's brother-in-law was a government attorney, "the conviction cannot stand, because such conduct obstructed the voir dire and indicated an impermissible partiality on the juror's part." The court rejected as irrelevant the argument that merely having a government attorney as a brother-in-law would not have been enough to challenge the juror for cause.

> The point is not that her relationship with her brother-in-law tainted the proceedings but that her willingness to lie about it exhibited an interest strongly suggesting partiality. * * * [C]ourts cannot administer justice in circumstances in which a juror can commit a federal crime in order to serve as a juror in a criminal case and do so with no fear of sanction so long as a conviction results.

See also Dyer v. Calderon, 151 F.3d 970 (9th Cir.1998) (en banc) (conviction must be reversed where juror lies in answering voir dire question as to whether a family member had ever been a victim of a crime: "[T]here is a fine line between being willing to serve and being anxious, between accepting the grave responsibility for passing judgment on a human life and being so eager that you court perjury to avoid being struck. The individual who lies in order to improve his chances of serving has too much of a stake in the matter to be considered indifferent.").

Should a conviction be automatically reversed whenever it is discovered that the juror told a lie on voir dire? See United States v. Langford, 990 F.2d 65 (2d Cir.1993), where a juror failed to admit that she had been arrested three times for prostitution fifteen years earlier. At the time of voir dire, the juror worked as a mental health assistant, had just taken a test to be a nurse, had a six-year-old daughter, and taught Sunday School. The court found that the juror had deliberately lied, but that her motivation was embarrassment. Unlike the juror in *Colombo*, she "had no interest in being on that particular jury." Accordingly, the defendant suffered no prejudice.

In Warger v. Shauers, 135 S.Ct. 521 (2014), the Court held that the fact that a juror lied during voir dire cannot be proved by comparing what she said during deliberations with what she said during voir dire. Rule 606(b), discussed *supra,* barred evidence of juror deliberations for this purpose. The case involved a crash involving a motorcycle and a truck after which the motorcycle rider sued the driver of the truck. During an extensive voir dire, all of the jurors, including the juror who became foreperson, claimed that they could be fair and impartial. After the jury found for the truck driver, one of the jurors submitted an affidavit saying that the foreperson said during deliberations that her daughter was at fault in an automobile accident in which a man died, and if her daughter had been sued it would have ruined her life. The Court held that statements made during jury deliberations were not a proper subject of post-verdict inquiry, but recognized that there were permissible other ways to prove that a juror was dishonest on voir dire (e.g., by relying on non-juror witnesses or documentary evidence that contradicts the juror's statements on voir dire).

4.   The Use and Function of Alternate Jurors

Federal Rule of Criminal Procedure 24(c) provides that the court may empanel up to six alternate jurors, to provide for the possibility that one or more of the regular jurors may become unable or unqualified to serve as the trial progresses. The Federal Rule further provides that alternate jurors may be retained after the jury retires to consider its verdict; but the court must ensure that a retained alternate does not discuss the case with anyone until that alternate replaces a juror or is discharged. Thus, the alternate who is retained, but does not replace a juror, is not permitted to take part in the jury deliberations. The Federal Rule further provides that if "an alternate replaces a juror after deliberations have begun, the court must instruct the jury to begin its deliberations anew."

Some judges impanel a jury without telling the jurors who is an actual juror and who is an alternate. The theory is that this keeps the alternates as focused on the evidence as the actual jurors, which is important in any case in which a juror is excused and replaced by an alternate.

F.   THE TRIAL JUDGE AND THE RIGHT TO JURY TRIAL

1.   The Role of the Judge Generally

If the right to jury trial is to work as intended—i.e., to provide protection against eccentric, biased, overreaching or bureaucratic judges and public officials—it is necessary that the judge not take action that unduly invades the independence of the jury.

There is no doubt that judges have enormous powers reserved to them, powers that are exercised more or less independently of juries. For example, trial judges decide whether or not to accept guilty pleas and plea bargains; there is no right to jury trial on the advisability of any contract between the prosecutor and the defendant. Earlier in this Chapter, we saw that judges rule on questions of joinder and severance, that judges rule on speedy trial questions and that judges even control the selection process of the jury. Moreover, judges rule on the admissibility of evidence—the jury does not even hear evidence if one party objects and the judge finds it inadmissible. And judges of course have the power and duty to instruct the jury. It is not difficult, then, to demonstrate that the meaningfulness of the jury trial right will depend in large part on the role played by the trial judge.

2. Selection of Judges

Who are these trial judges and how are they selected? Federal trial judges are, of course, nominated by the President and confirmed by the Senate, with life tenure as long as there is good behavior. State judges are selected by a variety of different methods; often they must win elections to continue in office. Proposals are often made to make judicial selection and retention decisions less political. But, in many states, political officials resist any attempt to limit the use of judicial positions as patronage or to remove the political constraints on the day-to-day actions of trial judges.

3. Challenges Against the Judge

Some jurisdictions recognize the potential impact that a judge can have on the ultimate disposition of any case, even one tried to a jury, by providing for a right of either the prosecution or defense to challenge one judge peremptorily—i.e., as a matter of right. See, e.g., Alaska Stat. 22.20.022. And all allow judges to be challenged for cause, although the standards by which such challenges are measured differ.

Where peremptory challenges of judges are permitted, can a judge be struck for discriminatory reasons? In People v. Williams, 8 Cal.App.4th 688, 10 Cal.Rptr.2d 873 (1992), the court held that the principles set forth in *Batson*, prohibiting discrimination in peremptory challenges of jurors, were applicable by analogy to peremptory challenges of judges. Is there a difference between excluding a juror and excluding a judge?

Biased Judge: Bracy v. Gramley

A judge that is biased is subject to a challenge for cause. And if the bias is not discovered until after the verdict, the verdict is subject to reversal. See Ward v. Village of Monroeville, 409 U.S. 57 (1972) (traffic offense; judge not impartial where he is also the Mayor who is responsible for village finances); Tumey v. Ohio, 273 U.S. 510 (1927) (judge was paid only if the defendant was convicted).

In Bracy v. Gramley, 520 U.S. 899 (1997), Chief Justice Rehnquist wrote for the Court as it held that Bracy, who was convicted in state court of participation in an execution-style triple murder and sentenced to death, was entitled to discovery in his habeas corpus action challenging his conviction and sentence. The judge who had presided over Bracy's trial had been convicted of corruption and had been shown to have paid bribes to judges while a defense lawyer and to have received bribes as a judge. Bracy claimed that the judge might have been pro-prosecution in some cases, including his, to throw off suspicion that he was taking bribes from defense counsel and favoring their defendants. The lower courts found the claim speculative and denied discovery. The Chief Justice disagreed, stating that "the Due Process Clause clearly requires a fair trial in a fair tribunal, before a judge with no actual bias against the defendant or interest in the outcome of his particular case," and found that Bracy's trial judge "was shown to be thoroughly steeped in corruption through his public trial and conviction." The Chief Justice also observed that Bracy made specific allegations that his trial attorney, "a former associate of the corrupt judge in a law practice that was familiar and comfortable with corruption, may have agreed to take this capital case to trial quickly so that petitioner's conviction would deflect any suspicion the rigged * * * cases might attract."

NOTE ON BRACY

On remand, the Court of Appeals found that Bracy, after getting discovery, did not show that the judge was biased against him and that Bracy's claim was "hopelessly speculative."

> For all that appears, Maloney was a prosecution-minded judge for reasons unrelated to his taking bribes. That he would accept payment to acquit criminals does not imply any affection for criminal defendants or their lawyers such that he *must* have been acting against character when he ruled in favor of the prosecution in cases in which he was not bribed. That is a possibility, but no more than a possibility. Maloney's conduct was appalling, his character depraved, but the bridge to the trial of Bracy * * * is missing. He was certainly capable of dreaming up and acting on compensatory bias, but there is no evidence that he did.

Bracy v. Shomig, 248 F.3d 604 (7th Cir. 2001). See also Mann v. Thalacker, 246 F.3d 1092 (8th Cir. 2001) (due process did not require state trial judge to recuse himself in a bench trial on charges involving sexual abuse of a child, even though the judge had been sexually abused by his father when he was a child; the record did not reveal any statements or actions by the judge that indicated actual bias; and the judge's personal history did not make bias so likely that it should be presumed).

Judge with a Conflict of Interest Due to Previous Role as Prosecutor: *Williams v. Pennsylvania*

In Williams v. Pennsylvania, 136 S.Ct. 1899 (2016), the Court held that the due process rights of a capital defendant were violated, when one of the Justices of the State Supreme Court who denied his *Brady* claim had previously served as the district attorney who made the decision on behalf of the state to seek the death penalty. The Court determined that the Due Process Clause required recusal of the State Supreme Court justice under these circumstances. Justice Kennedy, writing for five members of the Court, wrote that "[d]ue process guarantees an absence of actual bias on the part of a judge" and "[t]he due process guarantee that 'no man can be a judge in his own case' would have little substance if it did not disqualify a former prosecutor from sitting in judgment of a prosecution in which he or she had made a critical decision." Justice Kennedy found the conflict of interest to be particularly potent in this case because the *Brady* claim accused a prosecutor whom the state justice had previously supervised of suppressing materially exculpatory evidence.

Chief Justice Roberts, joined by Justice Alito, dissented. He argued the Due Process Clause was not violated because the state justice's decision— to seek the death penalty—was not related to the decision to reject the *Brady* claim. Justice Thomas wrote a separate dissent in which he argued that "the due process rights of the already convicted * * * do not include policing alleged violations of state codes of judicial ethics in postconviction proceedings."

Showing of Actual Bias Not Required: *Rippo v. Baker*

In the per curiam decision in Rippo v. Baker, 137 S.Ct. 905 (2017) the Court considered the defendant's claim of a due process violation because his trial judge was the target of a criminal investigation in which the District Attorney was taking part. The state courts ruled against the defendant on the ground that his allegations "did not support the assertion that the trial judge was actually biased [against him] in this case."

The Supreme Court remanded because the Nevada courts' requirement of showing "actual bias" was too strict. The Court explained as follows:

> Under our precedents, the Due Process Clause may sometimes demand recusal even when a judge has no actual bias. Recusal is required when, objectively speaking, the probability of actual bias on the part of the judge or decisionmaker is too high to be constitutionally

tolerable. Our decision in *Bracy* is not to the contrary: Although we explained that the petitioner there had pointed to facts suggesting actual, subjective bias, we did not hold that a litigant must show as a matter of course that a judge was actually biased in the litigant's case—much less that he must do so when, as here, he does not allege a theory of "camouflaging bias." The Nevada Supreme Court did not ask the question our precedents require: whether, considering all the circumstances alleged, the risk of bias was too high to be constitutionally tolerable.

4. Limitations on Judicial Powers

Although it is clear that the trial judge can influence the outcome of a jury trial, the constitutional right to a jury trial means that there are some things that are beyond the power of trial judges.

No Directed Verdict of Guilt

One constitutionally-based rule is that the trial judge may not direct a verdict of guilty in a criminal jury trial, even if the defendant admits every material element of an offense. This is because a directed verdict deprives the defendant of the right to a jury trial. See Sullivan v. Louisiana, 508 U.S. 275 (1993) (recognizing that trial judges are constitutionally prohibited from directing a verdict against the defendant). Of course a trial judge has the power, and duty, to direct a verdict for the *defendant* if the evidence is insufficient to sustain a conviction. See Fed.R. Crim.P.29.

Jury Nullification

Because a trial judge cannot direct a verdict against the defendant, and because the prosecution cannot appeal a not guilty verdict, the jury is essentially given the power to nullify the prosecution by refusing to convict even if there is evidence beyond a reasonable doubt that the defendant committed the crime with which he is charged. Examples of cases in which jury nullification might be a possibility include cases where abused wives have been charged with murdering their abusive husbands, as well as cases alleging drug possession or distribution of minor amounts of narcotics.

Jurors have the power to nullify, because the court cannot overturn a verdict of not guilty any more than the judge can direct a guilty verdict— to do so would violate the defendant's right to jury trial. But while jurors have the power to nullify, should they be informed of that power? Aren't jurors expected to follow the instructions of the trial judge, which tell them to convict if they find that the defendant has committed the charged crime beyond a reasonable doubt? Does nullification create chaos, or is the nullification power necessary to enforce the jury's role as the conscience of the community and the shield against abuse of power? See Weinstein,

Considering Jury Nullification: When May and Should a Jury Reject the Law and Do Justice?, 30 Am.Crim.L.Rev. 239 (1993). For a history of jury nullification, see Clay S. Conrad, Jury Nullification: the Evolution of a Doctrine (2014).

The Second Circuit discussed the checkered history of jury nullification in United States v. Thomas, 116 F.3d 606 (2d Cir.1997):

> We are mindful that the term "nullification" can cover a number of distinct, though related, phenomena, encompassing in one word conduct that takes place for a variety of different reasons; jurors may nullify, for example, because of the identity of a party, a disapprobation of the particular prosecution at issue, or a more general opposition to the applicable criminal law or laws. We recognize, too, that nullification may at times manifest itself as a form of civil disobedience that some may regard as tolerable. The case of John Peter Zenger, the publisher of the New York Weekly Journal acquitted of criminal libel in 1735, and the nineteenth-century acquittals in prosecutions under the fugitive slave laws, are perhaps our country's most renowned examples of "benevolent" nullification. * * *

> [M]ore recent history presents numerous and notorious examples of jurors nullifying—cases that reveal the destructive potential of a practice Professor Randall Kennedy of the Harvard Law School has rightly termed a "sabotage of justice." Consider, for example, the two hung juries in the 1964 trials of Byron De La Beckwith in Mississippi for the murder of NAACP field secretary Medgar Evers, or the 1955 acquittal of J.W. Millam and Roy Bryant for the murder of fourteen-year-old Emmett Till—shameful examples of how nullification has been used to sanction murder and lynching.

The *Thomas* court emphasized that the trial judge must try to limit the possibility of jury nullification:

> * * * [T]he power of juries to "nullify" or exercise a power of lenity is just that—a power; it is by no means a right or something that a judge should encourage or permit if it is within his authority to prevent. * * * A jury has no more "right" to find a "guilty" defendant "not guilty" than it has to find a "not guilty" defendant guilty, and the fact that the former cannot be corrected by a court, while the latter can be, does not create a right out of the power to misapply the law. Such verdicts are lawless, a denial of due process and constitute an exercise of erroneously seized power. * * *

> Inasmuch as no juror has a right to engage in nullification—and, on the contrary, it is a violation of a juror's sworn duty to follow the law as instructed by the court—trial courts have the duty to forestall or prevent such conduct, whether by firm instruction or admonition or, where it does not interfere with guaranteed rights or the need to

protect the secrecy of jury deliberations, by dismissal of an offending juror from the venire or the jury. * * * Accordingly, every day in courtrooms across the length and breadth of this country, jurors are dismissed from the venire "for cause" precisely because they are unwilling or unable to follow the applicable law. * * *

So also, a presiding judge possesses both the responsibility and the authority to dismiss a juror whose refusal or unwillingness to follow the applicable law becomes known to the judge during the course of trial.

But how, exactly, is the judge to control the possibility of jury nullification once the jury has been empaneled? The facts of *Thomas* indicate the difficulty of the problem. After the jury retired to deliberate, the trial judge was informed by many of the jurors that Juror No. 5 was adamant in his opposition to a guilty verdict, rude to other jurors, and essentially refused to deliberate. There was a difference of views, however, on whether Juror No. 5 was basing his view on the evidence, or rather upon some moral objection to convicting the defendant. The trial court interviewed all the jurors in camera, and concluded that Juror No. 5 was purposely refusing to apply the law given in the judge's instructions, i.e., he was engaged in a personal act of nullification. So the juror was excused for cause, and the remainder of the jury found the defendant guilty.

The Second Circuit reversed in *Thomas*, despite its attack on jury nullification excerpted above. It noted that inquiries into jury nullification during deliberations were especially sensitive, and necessarily truncated, because of the need to protect jury secrecy, and to avoid intimidation of the jury. The court held that the trial court essentially did not have enough information to conclude, without any doubt, that Juror No. 5 was refusing to follow instructions or to consider the evidence. The court recognized, however, that the trial judge could not have obtained any more information without treading upon the secrecy of the jury deliberations. So essentially, the court held that a trial judge has a duty to inquire into allegations of juror nullification, but not to inquire so deeply that the judge would be able to find, without doubt, that a juror was actually engaged in nullification. The power to control jury nullification during deliberations was essentially limited to situations, undoubtedly rare, where the trial court asks jurors a few preliminary questions and a juror blurts out that he is engaged in nullification. The *Thomas* court summed up this way.

Where the duty and authority to prevent defiant disregard of the law or evidence comes into conflict with the principle of secret jury deliberations, we are compelled to err in favor of the lesser of two evils—protecting the secrecy of jury deliberations at the expense of possibly allowing irresponsible juror activity. * * *

We are required to vacate these judgments because the court dismissed Juror No. 5 largely on the ground that the juror was acting in purposeful disregard of the court's instructions on the law, when the record evidence raises a possibility that the juror was simply unpersuaded by the Government's case against the defendants.

So the bottom line is that a juror bent on nullification might not have a right to nullify, but basically has an unreviewable power to do so.

Is it a crime for a person to tell a prospective juror about the power to nullify? Julian Heicklen, a jury nullification advocate in the Southern District of New York, was prosecuted under 18 U.S.C. § 1504, which makes it a crime to "influence the action or decision" of a juror. He handed out pamphlets to prospective jurors telling them they could acquit a guilty defendant if they believed that "the government is just trying to flex its muscle by making an example out of the defendant." District Judge Kimba Wood dismissed the indictment, concluding that a person violates the jury tampering statute only when he knowingly tried to influence a juror's decision through a written communication "made in relation to a specific case pending before that juror." Benjamin Weiser, Jury Statute Not Violated by Protester, Judge Rules, N.Y.Times, April 19, 2012).

Racially-Based Jury Nullification

Marion Barry, the former Mayor of Washington, D.C., was caught on tape by federal agents while smoking crack cocaine. However, the African-American jury convicted Barry of only one minor count in a fourteen count indictment, despite the trial judge's post-verdict comment that he had "never seen a stronger government case." Was this an example of jury nullification? If so, should jury nullification by minority jurors be treated or considered differently from jury nullification in general? Professor Paul Butler, in Racially Based Jury Nullification: Black Power in the Criminal Justice System, 105 Yale L.J. 677 (1995), provides an argument in favor of race-based jury nullification:

> My thesis is that, for pragmatic and political purposes, the black community is better off when some nonviolent lawbreakers remain in the community rather than go to prison. The decision as to what kind of conduct by African-Americans ought to be punished is better made by African-Americans themselves, based on the costs and benefits to their community, than by the traditional criminal justice process, which is controlled by white lawmakers and white law enforcers. * * *

Applying this thesis to specific crimes, Professor Butler makes the following conclusions:

> In cases involving violent *malum in se* crimes like murder, rape, and assault, jurors should consider the case strictly on the evidence

presented, and, if they have no reasonable doubt that the defendant is guilty, they should convict. For nonviolent *malum in se* crimes such as theft or perjury, nullification is an option that the juror should consider, although there should be no presumption in favor of it. A juror might vote for acquittal, for example, when a poor woman steals from Tiffany's, but not when the same woman steals from her next door neighbor. Finally, in cases involving nonviolent, *malum prohibitum* offenses, including "victimless" crimes like narcotics offenses, there should be a presumption in favor of nullification.

Professor Nancy Marder, in The Myth of the Nullifying Jury, 93 Nw.U.L.Rev. 877 (1999), states that nullification can provide important benefits to the judicial system by operating as a device to curb overzealous prosecution or the application of bad laws. She takes issue, however, with Professor Butler's proposal for race-based nullification.

Under Butler's proposal, the jury would become a mini-legislature in which jurors represent constituencies based on race and try to change social policy through their vote of not guilty. * * * Not only does Butler's plan for the jury compromise a basic tenet of due process—the need for an impartial decisionmaker—but it does so in a particularly cynical and divisive way. Butler's proposal is cynical because it seeks to replicate in the jury the politics of the legislature, in which politicians vote according to the interests of their constituents and because it reduces all African-American jurors to one view based upon their race. Butler's plan is divisive because it pits African-American jurors against jurors of all other races and backgrounds. * * *

Finally, Butler's plan contains the seeds of its own undoing. If African-American jurors take Butler's advice seriously and vote to acquit in all cases of nonviolent African-American defendants as a way of protesting social conditions, then African-American jurors will no longer be seated on juries. Judges could excuse such jurors with for cause challenges on the theory that these jurors could not be impartial. * * *

Instructions on the Power to Nullify

United States v. Dougherty, 473 F.2d 1113 (D.C.Cir.1972), was a prosecution brought against Vietnam War protesters, who broke into property owned by Dow Chemical, the manufacturer of napalm. The defendants argued that the trial judge erred in refusing to instruct the jury that it had the power to nullify. Judge Leventhal responded that the jury should not be told that it may refuse to apply the law given it by the court. See also United States v. Trujillo, 714 F.2d 102 (11th Cir.1983) (defense counsel is not permitted to argue that the jury should nullify); United States v. Edwards, 101 F.3d 17 (2d Cir.1996) (defendant has no right to a jury instruction alerting jurors of the power to nullify, because this power is in contravention of their duty to follow jury instructions).

Commenting on the Evidence and Questioning Witnesses

Most states will not allow a trial judge to comment on the weight of the evidence or on the credibility of witnesses, although some of these states will allow the judge to sum up the evidence presented by both sides.

The federal courts and a minority of the states give much more power to the trial judge and allow comment and summation. But, they do not allow unlimited comment so that it is difficult to demarcate when the limits of permissible comment are exceeded and how much leeway the trial judge actually has. It appears that the practice is less expansive than the theory.

Virtually all jurisdictions allow the trial judge to call and to question witnesses, but none provides unlimited authority to the judge. See Federal Rule of Evidence 614. Again, drawing lines is difficult. See Saltzburg, Martin and Capra, Federal Rule of Evidence Manual § 614.02 (11th ed. 2015), for a discussion of the dangers of trial court questioning of witnesses, and the limitations imposed on the practice. The cases cited there indicate that trial judges are allowed to question witnesses to *clarify* matters, but must take care not to give the impression that they are taking sides in the case. See generally Saltzburg, The Unnecessarily Expanding Role of the American Trial Judge, 64 Va.L.Rev. 1 (1978).

Instructing the Jury

The most important aspect of judicial control may be the judge's instructions to the jury and responses to their inquiries after instructions are given. Since in most jurisdictions the judge instructs the jury on the law and binds them to follow the instructions, what the judge says is critical to the disposition of the case by the jurors. It is common to find provisions like Fed.R.Crim.P. 30, which requires the court to accept or reject proposed instructions by counsel before closing argument, and before the instructions as a whole are given.[22] The judge's choice of what to include in instructions might reflect to some extent the judge's views about certain witnesses and evidence, although the instructions will generally not name particular witnesses.

---

[22] Aside from instructing the jurors on the law, the trial judge controls the jury in many ways. For example, some judges do not allow note-taking by jurors, while others do. See United States v. Maclean, 578 F.2d 64 (3d Cir.1978). Trial judges differ in their attitude toward questions by the jurors to witnesses during the trial. For a discussion of the case law, see Saltzburg, Martin & Capra, Federal Rules of Evidence Manual at § 611.02[4]. For a suggested procedure, see Saltzburg, The Unnecessarily Expanding Role of the American Trial Judge, 64 Va.L.Rev. 1, 63–65 (1978).

G. THE JURY VERDICT

Generally the verdict that the jury returns must be in writing. It must be returned by the jury in open court. See Fed.R.Crim.P. 31(a). "If there are multiple defendants, the jury may return a verdict at any time during its deliberations as to any defendant about whom it has agreed." Fed.R.Crim.P. 31(b). Some jurisdictions provide that unless the parties waive the right to a poll, the clerk will ask each juror individually whether the verdict announced is his or her verdict. Fed.R.Crim.P. 31(d) provides that after a verdict is returned and before it is excused, "the court must on a party's request, or may on its own, poll the jurors individually." See also United States v. Randle, 966 F.2d 1209 (7th Cir.1992) (reversible error to deny the defendant the opportunity to poll the jury). Verdicts are usually general verdicts of guilty or not guilty on each count. In rare instances a special interrogatory is used.

Inconsistent Verdicts

Generally speaking, jury verdicts are valid even if they are inherently inconsistent. The idea is that the inconsistent jury may be attempting to mitigate the force of its verdicts—the jury may be engaging in a form of nullification, as they have the power to do. Of course, if a verdict is not supported by sufficient evidence, it is subject to attack on post-trial review; but sufficiency and inconsistency are not identical concepts.

Justice Rehnquist, writing for a unanimous Court in United States v. Powell, 469 U.S. 57 (1984), applied the general rule that a defendant convicted on one count of an indictment cannot attack the verdict as being inconsistent with acquittal on another count. Powell was charged on 15 federal counts involving narcotics offenses and was convicted of only three for using the telephone in connection with a cocaine conspiracy and possession charges. She was acquitted of the conspiracy itself and of possession with intent to distribute. The Court recognized that the verdict could not be reconciled, but reasoned that it is always uncertain why the jury returns such a verdict and that it is unclear "whose ox has been gored." Because the government may not appeal an inconsistent acquittal, the Court declined to give the defendant a new trial on the inconsistent conviction as a matter of course. Moreover, the Court expressed the view that inconsistent verdicts are often a matter of lenity and rejected as unworkable a rule that would permit criminal defendants to challenge verdicts by arguing that in particular cases they are not the product of lenity. The Court noted that the defendant received sufficient protection against jury irrationality "by the independent review of the sufficiency of the evidence undertaken by the trial and appellate courts." See also Dunn v. United States, 284 U.S. 390, 393 (1932) ("[c]onsistency in the verdict is not necessary").

In a footnote in *Powell,* Justice Rehnquist stated that "[n]othing in this opinion is intended to decide the proper resolution of a situation where a defendant is convicted of two crimes, where a guilty verdict on one count logically excludes a finding of guilt on the other." See State v. Moore, 458 N.W.2d 90 (Minn.1990) (vacating convictions for first degree murder and manslaughter because, as instructed, the jury necessarily found that the defendant's act was both intentional and reckless, mental states that are mutually exclusive).

Applying *Powell,* courts have held that a defendant can be properly convicted of conspiracy even if all of the other named co-conspirators are acquitted. See United States v. Zuniga-Salinas, 952 F.2d 876 (5th Cir.1992).

Although *Powell* holds that a defendant cannot set aside a conviction on the ground that a verdict is inconsistent, it does not address a situation in which a trial judge explicitly instructs a jury that its verdict need not be consistent. United States v. Moran-Toala, 726 F.3d 334 (2d Cir. 2013), addresses this and makes clear that inconsistent verdicts are tolerated because they often result from partial nullification that is unreviewable, but courts will not knowingly encourage nullification. If they do the encouragement is reviewable and may, as in the case of Moran-Toala, result in the setting aside of a conviction when it is too difficult to ascertain what the jury would have done absent the improper judicial encouragement.

Inconsistent Defenses

While verdicts can be inconsistent, does it follow that defendants ought to be allowed to assert inconsistent defenses, such as "I wasn't there and if I was, it was self-defense"? Or, "I didn't do it but if I did, I was entrapped"? In Mathews v. United States, 485 U.S. 58 (1988), Chief Justice Rehnquist wrote for the Court as it held that "even if the defendant denies one or more elements of the crime, he is entitled to an entrapment instruction whenever there is sufficient evidence from which a reasonable jury could find entrapment." The Court rejected the government's argument "that allowing a defendant to rely on inconsistent defenses will encourage perjury" and confuse a jury. Justice White, joined by Justice Blackmun, dissented.

Although a defendant is legally permitted to offer inconsistent defenses, as a matter of trial strategy defense counsel rarely want to be in the position of arguing inconsistent defenses because they are arguing against themselves—something that rarely is effective.

Use of Interrogatories

The question whether special interrogatories can and should be used in a criminal case is touched upon in United States v. Ruggiero, 726 F.2d 913 (2d Cir.1984). In a complicated prosecution for racketeering and other offenses, the government alleged various predicate acts to support its racketeering charges. (A minimum number of predicate acts must be proved to support a conviction.) The court found that one of the predicate acts alleged was improper as it could not support the charge. Because it was impossible to determine whether the jury relied upon this particular act in returning its guilty verdict on the racketeering charges, the court found that reversal was required. The majority opinion stated that "in a complex RICO [racketeering] trial such as this one, it can be extremely useful for a trial judge to request the jury to record their specific dispositions of the separate predicate acts charged, in addition to their verdict of guilt or innocence on the RICO charge."

Judge Newman wrote a separate opinion analyzing the subject of special interrogatories at greater length. He explained the reasons for judicial reluctance to use interrogatories in criminal cases:

> There is apprehension that eliciting "yes" or "no" answers to questions concerning the elements of an offense may propel a jury toward a logical conclusion of guilt, whereas a more generalized assessment might have yielded an acquittal. The possibility also exists that fragmenting a single count into the various ways an offense may be committed affords a divided jury an opportunity to resolve its differences to the defendant's disadvantage by saying "yes" to some means and "no" to others, although unified consideration of the count might have produced an acquittal or at least a hung jury.

Judge Newman noted that "[i]nterrogatories are especially objectionable when they make resolution of a single fact issue determinative of guilt or innocence, without regard to the elements of an offense, * * * or when their wording shifts the burden of proof to the defendant." On balance, he concluded that a trial judge "should have the discretion to use a jury interrogatory in cases where risk of prejudice to the defendant is slight and the advantage of securing particularized factfinding is substantial."

Lesser Included Offenses

The jury may find the defendant guilty of the crime charged or of any lesser included offense. The issue at trial is usually whether the defendant is entitled to a jury instruction on a lesser included offense.

In Schmuck v. United States, 489 U.S. 705 (1989), the Court adopted the "elements" test for determining whether a trial court must give a lesser included offense instruction under Fed.R.Crim.P. 31(c). Under this test, a lesser included offense is one in which each statutory element is also present in the more serious offense. For example, the elements required to prove involuntary manslaughter in most states are also required to prove the more serious offense of murder. Murder, of course, has additional elements, which is why manslaughter is referred to as "lesser included." The Court in *Schmuck* rejected the broader "inherent relationship" test, under which an offense is included within another when the facts proven at trial support the inference that the defendant committed the less serious offense, and an inherent relationship exists between the two offenses. Under this "inherent relationship" test, the lower court held that Schmuck was entitled to an instruction concerning odometer tampering, when he was charged with mail fraud arising from a scheme to sell cars with turned-back odometers. However, under the elements test, an instruction on odometer tampering was not required, because Schmuck could have been convicted of mail fraud without a showing that he actually turned back any odometers; thus, the elements of odometer tampering were not a "subset" of the elements of mail fraud.

In adopting the elements approach to Rule 31(c), the *Schmuck* Court noted that it was "grounded in the language and history of the Rule and provides greater certainty in its application." The Court also reasoned that the inherent relationship test may create notice problems where the prosecutor asks for a jury charge on an offense whose elements were not charged in the indictment. In contrast, the elements approach, which "involves a textual comparison of criminal statutes and does not depend on inferences that may be drawn from evidence introduced at trial * * * permits both sides to know in advance what jury instructions will be available and to plan their trial strategy accordingly." The Court found the inherent relationship approach to be "rife with the potential for confusion."

For an application of *Schmuck*, see Carter v. United States, 530 U.S. 255 (2000). Carter entered a bank, confronted an exiting customer, and pushed her back inside. She screamed, startling others in the bank. Undeterred, Carter ran inside and leaped over a counter and through one of the teller windows. A teller rushed into the manager's office. Meanwhile, Carter opened several teller drawers and emptied the money into a bag. After removing almost $16,000, he jumped back over the counter and fled. He was charged with violating 18 U.S.C. § 2113(a), which punishes "[w]hoever, by force and violence, or by intimidation, takes . . . any . . . thing of value [from a] bank." While not contesting the basic facts, Carter pleaded not guilty on the theory that he had not taken the bank's money "by force and violence, or by intimidation," as § 2113(a) requires. Before trial, he moved for a jury instruction on the offense described by § 2113(b) as a lesser included offense of the offense described by § 2113(a). Section 2113(b) entails less severe penalties than § 2113(a), punishing "[w]hoever takes and carries away, with intent to steal or purloin, any . . . thing of value exceeding $1,000 [from a] . . . bank." The District Court denied the motion. The jury, instructed on § 2113(a) alone, returned a guilty verdict.

The Supreme Court, in an opinion by Justice Thomas for five members of the Court, held that subsection (b) was not a lesser included offense of subsection (a), because it contains three elements that are not required by subsection (a). Justice Thomas applied a "textual comparison" of the elements of the two offenses and concluded as follows:

> First, whereas subsection (b) requires that the defendant act "with intent to steal or purloin," subsection (a) contains no similar requirement. Second, whereas subsection (b) requires that the defendant "tak[e] and carr[y] away" the property, subsection (a) only requires that the defendant "tak[e]" the property. Third, whereas the first paragraph of subsection (b) requires that the property have a "value exceeding $1,000," subsection (a) contains no valuation requirement. These extra clauses in subsection (b) cannot be regarded as mere surplusage; they mean something.

Justice Ginsburg, joined by Justices Stevens, Souter and Breyer, dissented in *Carter*. She relied on common law traditions rather than strict textual comparison. She explained as follows:

> At common law, robbery meant larceny plus force, violence, or putting in fear. Because robbery was an aggravated form of larceny at common law, larceny was a lesser included offense of robbery. Congress, I conclude, did not depart from that traditional understanding when it rendered "Bank robbery and incidental crimes" federal offenses. Accordingly, I would hold that petitioner Carter is not prohibited as a matter of law from obtaining an instruction on bank larceny as a lesser included offense.[23]

H. WAIVER OF JURY TRIAL; TRIAL BY THE COURT

A defendant with a right to a jury trial might desire to be tried by a judge. Certain crimes—e.g., child abuse—may be difficult for lay jurors to view dispassionately. Defendants with prior records may believe that in reaching a decision on the merits of a case, a judge can discount prior convictions offered for impeachment purposes somewhat better than a jury can.

Jurisdictions differ on whether the defendant can waive a jury trial at all, on whether the prosecutor can force a jury trial when the defendant prefers a judge trial, and on whether the court can try a case with a jury when neither side wants one.

---

[23] The concept of lesser included offense is also discussed in Chapter 12, in connection with double jeopardy rules.

In Singer v. United States, 380 U.S. 24 (1965), the Supreme Court rebuffed a constitutional attack on Fed.R.Crim.P. 23(a), which permits the defendant to waive a jury trial only with the consent of both the government and the court. The Court rejected the argument that the Sixth Amendment's right to jury trial implies a correlative, unilateral right to waive a jury trial. The Court did say that it would not "assume that federal prosecutors would demand a jury trial for an ignoble purpose." And it left open the possibility that in some circumstances the defendant's reasons for wanting to avoid a jury would be so compelling that the government would deny "an impartial trial" if it insisted on a jury.[24] See also United States v. Clark, 943 F.2d 775 (7th Cir.1991) (no violation of the Constitution where "the result is simply that the defendant is subject to an impartial trial by jury—the very thing that the Constitution guarantees him"; in dictum, the court states that a defendant may have a right to a bench trial in a case involving "very complex facts").

Why would the prosecution ever object to the defendant's request for a bench trial?[25] Take the case of United States v. District Court for the Eastern District of California, 464 F.3d 1065 (9th Cir. 2006), where the defendants were charged with multiple counts arising out of the transport of young children in interstate commerce for the purpose of engaging in unlawful sexual acts. The facts involved ritualistic sexual abuse of children as young as seven. Defendants moved for a bench trial and the government opposed the motion. The trial judge granted the motion on the ground that "the heinous and repugnant conduct of the defendants * * * which will be vividly apparent to the jury from the evidence to be presented, would render it impossible that ordinary jurors would be able to dispassionately listen to and consider defendants' more technical arguments having to do with interstate commerce in defense to some of the charges." The government was so intent on a jury trial that it took an immediate appeal of the order and sought a writ of mandamus. The court of appeals granted the writ. The court noted that language in *Singer* implied that defendants might have a unilateral right to a bench trial in extreme circumstances, but found that "no United States Court of Appeals appears to have ever approved a defendant's waiver of a jury over the government's objection." The court concluded that while trying this case before a jury "is not without its challenges, we are confident that the able and experienced trial judge is fully capable of ensuring these defendants an impartial trial." The court

---

[24] For a discussion of the proper procedure for a court to use in accepting a waiver of jury trial in federal court, see Marone v. United States, 10 F.3d 65 (2d Cir.1993) ("This court urges that at a minimum the district courts inform each defendant that a jury is composed of twelve members of the community, that the defendant may participate in the selection of the jurors, that the jury's verdict must be unanimous, and that a judge alone will decide guilt or innocence if the defendant waives the right to a jury trial.").

[25] For a critical view of the Federal Rule, see Kurland, Providing a Defendant With a Unilateral Right to a Bench Trial: A Renewed Call to Amend Federal Rule of Criminal Procedure 23(a), 26 U.C.D.L.Rev. 309 (1993).

noted that the trial judge could control prejudice in a number of ways, including extensive voir dire, exclusion of evidence as unduly prejudicial, exclusion of cumulative evidence, and instructions to the jury.

V. THE IMPARTIALITY OF THE TRIBUNAL AND THE INFLUENCE OF THE MEDIA

We have already seen one way of protecting against a biased jury— i.e., voir dire of prospective jurors in order to eliminate those whose partiality would threaten the integrity of the jury as factfinder. Another way of preventing or inhibiting jury bias is to control the flow of information to the potential pool of jurors in a community and, even more importantly, to control the flow of information to those selected as jurors.

Whenever any government agency wants to control the flow of information to the public, it is likely to be resisted by the media and the public. Efforts to afford all parties a fair trial can threaten some of the interests served by a free press. How to accommodate the competing interests has become known as the "fair trial—free press" issue and is the subject of this section of the Chapter.

A. THE IMPACT OF MEDIA COVERAGE ON LITIGATION

1. Prejudicial Pretrial Publicity

Pervasive Prejudice: Irvin v. Dowd

In Irvin v. Dowd, 366 U.S. 717 (1961), a unanimous Supreme Court for the first time struck down a state conviction because pretrial publicity violated the defendant's right to a fair trial.[26] Irvin was convicted of murder and sentenced to death. The charge arose after six murders were committed in the vicinity of Evansville, Indiana. Police issued press releases saying that Irvin had confessed to murder. Although one change of venue was granted, it was from Evansville to an adjoining rural county that had received some of the publicity concerning the crimes and Irvin's arrest. A second change of venue was denied. Justice Clark's opinion for the Court stressed that the Constitution does not require a jury that is completely untouched by pretrial publicity:

> It is not required * * * that jurors be totally ignorant of the facts and issues involved. In these days of swift, widespread and diverse methods of communication, an important case can be expected to arouse the interest of the public in the vicinity, and scarcely any of

---

[26] Prior to *Irvin*, the Court set aside a conviction in Marshall v. United States, 360 U.S. 310 (1959), under its supervisory powers because of news articles the jurors had read.

those best qualified to serve as jurors will not have formed some impression or opinion as to the merits of the case. * * * To hold that the mere existence of any preconceived notion as to the guilt or innocence of the accused, without more, is sufficient to rebut the presumption of a prospective juror's impartiality would be to establish an impossible standard. It is sufficient if the juror can lay aside his impression or opinion and render a verdict based on the evidence presented in court.

The Court described the publicity that accompanied the case, and evaluated its effect on Irvin's trial, in the following passage:

> Here the build-up of prejudice is clear and convincing. * * * [A] barrage of newspaper headlines, articles, cartoons and pictures was unleashed against him during the six or seven months preceding his trial. * * * [T]he newspapers in which the stories appeared were delivered regularly to approximately 95% of the dwellings in Gibson County and * * * in addition, the Evansville radio and TV stations, which likewise blanketed that county, also carried extensive newscasts covering the same incidents. These stories revealed the details of his background, including a reference to crimes committed when a juvenile, his convictions for arson almost 20 years previously, for burglary and by a court-martial on AWOL charges during the war. He was accused of being a parole violator. The headlines announced his police line-up identification, that he faced a lie detector test, had been placed at the scene of the crime and that the six murders were solved but petitioner refused to confess. Finally, they announced his confession to the six murders and the fact of his indictment for four of them in Indiana. * * * One story * * * characterized petitioner as remorseless and without conscience but also as having been found sane by a court-appointed panel of doctors. In many of the stories petitioner was described as the "confessed slayer of six," a parole violator and fraudulent-check artist.

> * * *

> Here the "pattern of deep and bitter prejudice" shown to be present throughout the community, was clearly reflected in the sum total of the voir dire examination of a majority of the jurors finally placed in the jury box. Eight out of the 12 thought petitioner was guilty. With such an opinion permeating their minds, it would be difficult to say that each could exclude this preconception of guilt from his deliberations. * * * With his life at stake, it is not requiring too much that petitioner be tried in an atmosphere undisturbed by so huge a wave of public passion and by a jury other than one in which two-thirds of the members admit, before hearing any testimony, to possessing a belief in his guilt.

Thus, the Court set aside the conviction. Justice Frankfurter's concurring opinion suggested both that the problem of undue publicity was not isolated in Evansville, and that its impact on the *Irvin* case was not atypical.

Televised Confession: Rideau v. Louisiana

The Court overturned another state conviction in Rideau v. Louisiana, 373 U.S. 723 (1963), a murder case in which Rideau's confession to police officers was heavily televised in the locality. His lawyers filed a motion for a change of venue, on the ground that he would be deprived of a fair trial because of the extensive airing of his confession. The motion was denied and Rideau was convicted and sentenced to death on the murder charge in the local trial court. Three members of the jury had stated on voir dire that they had seen and heard Rideau's confession at least once. Two members of the jury were deputy sheriffs of the locality. Rideau's counsel had requested that these jurors be excused for cause, having exhausted all peremptory challenges, but these challenges for cause had been denied by the trial judge.

The *Rideau* Court held that "it was a denial of due process of law to refuse the request for a change of venue, after the people of Calcasieu Parish had been exposed repeatedly and in depth to the spectacle of Rideau personally confessing in detail to the crimes with which he was later to be charged." The Court stated that the televised confession "in a very real sense *was* Rideau's trial—at which he pleaded guilty to murder," and that a later trial in a community so pervasively exposed to the confession "could be but a hollow formality." Justice Clark, joined by Justice Harlan, dissented, complaining that the defendant had not established any "substantial nexus" between the televised confession and any prejudice suffered at the trial.

QUESTIONS ABOUT RIDEAU

In *Rideau,* there was no indication that the confession was coerced, and therefore it was undoubtedly admissible against Rideau at trial. If the jurors would hear the confession at trial, what prejudice could Rideau have suffered from the pretrial publicity? Isn't the case really about the failure to strike the two law enforcement officers for cause?

If the facts of *Rideau* suffice to establish constitutional error, how many trials are tainted in these days of extensive media coverage of high profile trials—not to speak of widespread and real-time communications on Facebook and Twitter? Compare Fetterly v. Paskett, 163 F.3d 1144 (9th Cir.1998) (pretrial publicity not prejudicial where it focuses on facts and evidence that was ultimately presented at trial).

Questions about the impact of social media and other forms of communication about trials caused the American Bar Association to change the title of its Fair Trial-Free Press Standards to Fair Trial and Public Discourse when it adopted the 4th Edition of the Standards in 2013.

Extended Period of Time Between Publicity and the Trial: Patton v. Yount

Irvin and *Rideau* seem to indicate that the Court would find prejudicial pretrial publicity in a large number of cases. But the Court cut back in Patton v. Yount, 467 U.S. 1025 (1984), where it reinstated a state defendant's murder conviction that had been overturned due to prejudicial trial publicity. Justice Powell's opinion for the Court emphasized that the court of appeals' reliance on *Irvin* was misplaced because the trial in *Irvin* took place six or seven months after extensive publicity began, whereas Yount was convicted in a second trial *four years* after most of the publicity occurred in connection with his first trial. That most jurors remembered the murder and surrounding publicity was not decisive. The Court stated that "[t]he relevant question is not whether the community remembered the case, but whether the jurors at Yount's trial had such fixed opinions that they could not judge impartially the guilt of the defendant." Justice Powell reasoned as follows:

> It is not unusual that one's recollection of the fact that a notorious crime was committed lingers long after the feelings of revulsion that create prejudice have passed. It would be fruitless to attempt to identify any particular lapse of time that in itself would distinguish the situation that existed in *Irvin*. But it is clear that the passage of time between a first and a second trial can be a highly relevant fact. In the circumstances of this case, we hold that it clearly rebuts any presumption of partiality or prejudice that existed at the time of the initial trial.

Justice Stevens, joined by Justice Brennan, dissented. Justice Marshall did not participate.

Deference to Trial Courts: Mu'Min v. Virginia

In Mu'Min v. Virginia, 500 U.S. 415 (1991), (discussed supra in the section on voir dire) the defendant was a state prisoner serving time for first-degree murder when he was charged with capital murder while on a work detail. The case was widely publicized. Articles in the newspapers revealed details of the prior murder for which Mu'Min was incarcerated, the fact that the death penalty was unavailable at the time of his earlier murder trial, the denial of parole six times to Mu'Min, his confession to the crime charged, and criticism of the supervision of work gangs in Virginia. Mu'Min claimed that the jurors could not be impartial in such a setting, despite the judge's finding on voir dire that the jurors had not been substantially affected by the publicity.

Chief Justice Rehnquist, writing for the Court, held that a trial court's finding of juror impartiality may be overturned only for manifest error. He stated that "particularly with respect to pretrial publicity, we think this primary reliance on the judgment of the trial court makes good sense. The judge of that court sits in the locale where the publicity is said to have had its effect, and brings to his evaluation of any such claim his own perception of the depth and extent of news stories that might influence a juror." This was so even though the judge in this case had not questioned jurors individually to determine whether they had been affected by pre-trial publicity.

The majority rejected Mu'Min's reliance on Irvin v. Dowd on the ground that the pretrial publicity in the instant case was not of the same kind or extent as in *Irvin*.

Justice O'Connor wrote a concurring opinion. She cited Patton v. Yount for the proposition that even jurors who had read about inadmissible confessions are not disqualified as a matter of law, and concluded that a trial judge could realistically assess whether jurors could be fair without knowing what each juror had heard about a case. Justices Marshall, Blackmun, Stevens, and Kennedy dissented.

Lower Court Cases

Generally speaking, the lower courts have been reluctant to find that prejudicial pretrial publicity has tainted a trial. See, e.g., Swindler v. Lockhart, 885 F.2d 1342 (8th Cir.1989) (substantial publicity, 98 out of 120 prospective jurors had heard about the case, no reversal); Simmons v. Lockhart, 814 F.2d 504 (8th Cir.1987) (55 of 56 members of the venire had heard about the case, but "[t]he accused is not entitled to an ignorant jury, just a fair one"); United States v. Lehder-Rivas, 955 F.2d 1510 (11th Cir.1992) (extensive media coverage describing the defendant as a "drug kingpin" and a "narco-terrorist"; but the trial judge conducted extensive voir dire and the jurors credibly asserted that they could remain impartial); United States v. Campa, 459 F.3d 1121 (11th Cir. 2006) (defendants charged with spying for Cuba, trial held in Miami; prejudicial publicity was not so great as to require change of venue, given the court's extensive voir dire and limiting instructions).

2. Television in the Courtroom

Televising criminal trials is controversial. Those who denigrate the practice argue among other things that television simply encourages the lawyers, and maybe the judge as well, to play to the cameras. Those who support cameras in the courtroom argue that television provides the public a crucial viewpoint into the workings of the criminal justice system. The Supreme Court has evaluated the effect of cameras in the courtroom on the right to fair trial in a number of cases.

Media Invades the Courtroom: Estes v. Texas

Billy Sol Estes was one of the first "subjects" of a high profile, televised trial. In Estes v. Texas, 381 U.S. 532 (1965), the Court held that Estes was denied a fair trial due to the pervasive and disruptive media presence in the courtroom. Justice Clark, writing for the Court, described the effect that the media had on the courtroom during both pre-trial hearings and at the trial:

> [A]t least 12 cameramen were engaged in the courtroom throughout the hearing taking motion and still pictures and televising the proceedings. * * * The trial witnesses present at the hearing, as well as the original jury panel, were undoubtedly made aware of the peculiar public importance of the case by the press and television coverage being provided, and by the fact that they themselves were televised live and their pictures rebroadcast on the evening show. * * *

The Court held that the First Amendment did not extend a right to the news media to televise from the courtroom, and that the disruption of the proceedings in this case created by television coverage required a new trial—even though Estes had not made a showing of actual prejudice. Justice Clark concluded with these critical comments about televised coverage of courtroom proceedings:

> [T]he chief function of our judicial machinery is to ascertain the truth. The use of television, however, cannot be said to contribute materially to this objective. Rather its use amounts to the injection of an irrelevant factor into court proceedings. In addition experience teaches that there are numerous situations in which it might cause actual unfairness—some so subtle as to defy detection by the accused or control by the judge. We enumerate some in summary:
>
> 1.   The potential impact of television on the jurors is perhaps of the greatest significance. * * *
>
> 2.   The quality of the testimony in criminal trials will often be impaired. * * * Embarrassment may impede the search for the truth, as may a natural tendency toward overdramatization. * * *
>
> * * *
>
> 3.   A major aspect of the problem is the additional responsibilities the presence of television places on the trial judge. His job is to make certain that the accused receives a fair trial. This most

difficult task requires his undivided attention. Still when television comes into the courtroom he must also supervise it. * * *

* * *

4. Finally, we cannot ignore the impact of courtroom television on the defendant. * * * The inevitable close-ups of his gestures and expressions during the ordeal of his trial might well transgress his personal sensibilities, his dignity, and his ability to concentrate on the proceedings before him * * *. A defendant on trial for a specific crime is entitled to his day in court, not in a stadium, or a city or nationwide arena. * * *. Furthermore, telecasting may also deprive an accused of effective counsel. The distractions, intrusions into confidential attorney-client relationships and the temptation offered by television to play to the public audience might often have a direct effect not only upon the lawyers, but the judge, the jury and the witnesses.

Chief Justice Warren, joined by Justices Douglas and Goldberg, wrote a concurring opinion concluding that "televising of criminal proceedings is inherently a denial of due process."

Justice Harlan wrote a separate opinion, agreeing with the Court that the First Amendment does not require that television be allowed in the courtroom, but disagreeing with the Court that televised proceedings were per se prohibited by the constitution. He suggested a case-by-case approach. Justice Stewart's dissent, joined by Justices Black, Brennan, and White concluded that "in the present state of the art" televised judicial proceedings were unwise, but found no denial of Estes' constitutional rights. Justice White's short dissent noted that advances in technology might make televised judicial proceedings more acceptable. Justice Brennan's separate statement noted that because of Justice Harlan's vote, *Estes* could not be read as an absolute bar to televised trials.

In the following case, the Court clearly agreed with Justice Brennan's view that there is no bar on televised trials—thus allowing us all to watch the trials of George Zimmerman, Jody Arias, Casey Anthony, and other "important" trials of the day.

CHANDLER V. FLORIDA

Supreme Court of the United States, 1981.
449 U.S. 560.

CHIEF JUSTICE BURGER delivered the opinion of the Court.

The question presented on this appeal is whether, consistent with constitutional guarantees, a state may provide for radio, television, and still photographic coverage of a criminal trial for public broadcast, notwithstanding the objection of the accused.

[The Florida Supreme Court established a pilot program permitting electronic media to cover all judicial proceedings, without reference to the consent of the participants. After the pilot program ended, the Florida Supreme Court sought comments and reviewed camera-in-the-courts projects in other states. The court concluded that "on balance there [was] more to be gained than lost by permitting electronic media coverage of judicial proceedings subject to standards for such coverage."]

The Florida court was of the view that because of the significant effect of the courts on the day-to-day lives of the citizenry, it was essential that the people have confidence in the process. It felt that broadcast coverage of trials would contribute to wider public acceptance and understanding of decisions. Consequently, * * * the Florida Supreme Court promulgated a revised Canon 3A(7). The canon provides:

"Subject at all times to the authority of the presiding judge to (i) control the conduct of proceedings before the court, (ii) ensure decorum and prevent distractions, and (iii) ensure fair administration of justice in the pending cause, electronic media and still photography coverage of public judicial proceedings in the appellate and trial courts of this state shall be allowed in accordance with standards of conduct and technology promulgated by the Supreme Court of Florida."

* * *

[The defendants were Miami policemen charged with burglary. The case received extensive publicity.]

* * *

After several * * * fruitless attempts by the appellants to prevent electronic coverage of the trial, the jury was selected. At *voir dire*, the appellants' counsel asked each prospective juror whether he or she would be able to be "fair and impartial" despite the presence of a television camera during some, or all, of the trial. Each juror selected responded that such coverage would not affect his or her consideration in any way. A television camera recorded the *voir dire*.

A defense motion to sequester the jury because of the television coverage was denied by the trial judge. However, the court instructed the jury not to watch or read anything about the case in the media and suggested that jurors "avoid the local news and watch only the national news on television." * * *

A television camera was in place for one entire afternoon, during which the state presented the testimony of Sion, its chief witness. No camera was present for the presentation of any part of the case for the defense. The camera returned to cover closing arguments. Only two minutes and fifty-five seconds of the trial below were broadcast—and those depicted only the prosecution's side of the case.

The jury returned a guilty verdict on all counts. [The conviction was upheld on appeal.]

Appellants * * * argue that the televising of criminal trials is inherently a denial of due process, and they read *Estes* as announcing a *per se* constitutional rule to that effect.

* * *

An absolute constitutional ban on broadcast coverage of trials cannot be justified simply because there is a danger that, in some cases, prejudicial broadcast accounts of pretrial and trial events may impair the ability of jurors to decide the issue of guilt or innocence uninfluenced by extraneous matter. The risk of juror prejudice in some cases does not justify an absolute ban on news coverage of trials by the printed media; so also the risk of such prejudice does not warrant an absolute constitutional ban on all broadcast coverage. * * *

Not unimportant to the position asserted by Florida and other states is the change in television technology since 1962, when Estes was tried. It is urged, and some empirical data are presented, that many of the negative factors found in *Estes*—cumbersome equipment, cables, distracting lighting, numerous camera technicians—are less substantial factors today than they were at that time.

It is also significant that safeguards have been built into the experimental programs in state courts, and into the Florida program, to avoid some of the most egregious problems envisioned by the six opinions in the *Estes* case. Florida admonishes its courts to take special pains to protect certain witnesses—for example, children, victims of sex crimes, some informants, and even the very timid witness or party—from the glare of publicity and the tensions of being "on camera."

* * *

[A]t present no one has been able to present empirical data sufficient to establish that the mere presence of the broadcast media inherently has an adverse effect on that process. The appellants have offered nothing to demonstrate that their trial was subtly tainted by broadcast coverage—let alone that all broadcast trials would be so tainted.

* * *

To demonstrate prejudice in a specific case a defendant must show something more than juror awareness that the trial is such as to attract the attention of broadcasters.

* * *

[The Court affirmed the convictions.]

3.   Protecting the Integrity of Judicial Proceedings

Circus Atmosphere: Sheppard v. Maxwell

The Supreme Court considered the effect of media coverage of a high-profile trial in Sheppard v. Maxwell, 384 U.S. 333 (1966). Sheppard was tried and convicted for murdering his wife. He claimed that she was killed by an intruder. Apparently because Sheppard was a well-to-do doctor, the case received substantial media coverage. (Yes, the case may well have been the model for the television series "The Fugitive" in which David Janssen played Dr. Richard Kimble, and the movie "The Fugitive" in which Harrison Ford played the same role.)

In his opinion for the Court, Justice Clark noted the pervasive pre-trial publicity and the circus-type media coverage during the trial. Pretrial publicity included media coverage indicating that other suspects had been cleared and that the defendant had been having an affair. Newspapers called for Sheppard's arrest. The media invaded the courtroom. Pictures of the jury were published. During the nine week murder trial the courtroom "remained crowded to capacity with representatives of news media. Their movement in and out of the courtroom often caused so much confusion that, despite the loud-speaker system installed in the courtroom, it was difficult for the witnesses and counsel to be heard." Sheppard and counsel found it almost impossible to confer confidentially.

The *Sheppard* Court held that the trial judge's failure to control the media coverage of the judicial proceedings deprived Sheppard of his right to a fair trial, requiring a reversal of his conviction. Justice Clark reasoned as follows:

> The fact is that bedlam reigned at the courthouse during the trial and newsmen took over practically the entire courtroom, hounding most of the participants in the trial, especially Sheppard. * * * The erection of a press table for reporters inside the bar is unprecedented. The bar of the court is reserved for counsel, providing them a safe place in which to keep papers and exhibits, and to confer privately with client and co-counsel. It is designed to protect the witness and the jury from any distractions, intrusions or influences, and to permit bench discussions of the judge's rulings away from the hearing of the public and the jury. Having assigned almost all of the available seats in the courtroom to the news media, the judge lost his ability to supervise that environment. * * *

Justice Clark emphasized that the trial court had substantial authority to control media coverage in order to protect the defendant's right to a fair trial, and that the trial court in *Sheppard* should have exercised this authority. The Court gave the following suggestions as to what could and should have been done:

Bearing in mind the massive pretrial publicity, the judge should have adopted stricter rules governing the use of the courtroom by newsmen, as Sheppard's counsel requested. The number of reporters in the courtroom itself could have been limited at the first sign that their presence would disrupt the trial. They certainly should not have been placed inside the bar. Furthermore, the judge should have more closely regulated the conduct of newsmen in the courtroom. For instance, the judge belatedly asked them not to handle and photograph trial exhibits lying on the counsel table during recesses.

Secondly, the court should have insulated the witnesses. All of the newspapers and radio stations apparently interviewed prospective witnesses at will, and in many instances disclosed their testimony. * * * Although the witnesses were barred from the courtroom during the trial the full verbatim testimony was available to them in the press. This completely nullified the judge's imposition of the rule [sequestering witnesses].

Thirdly, the court should have made some effort to control the release of leads, information, and gossip to the press by police officers, witnesses, and the counsel for both sides. * * *

Justice Clark concluded that "where there is a reasonable likelihood that prejudicial news prior to trial will prevent a fair trial, the judge should continue the case until the threat abates, or transfer it to another county not so permeated with publicity." With respect to publicity during the proceedings, he concluded that "courts must take such steps by rule and regulation that will protect their processes from prejudicial outside interferences."

Gag Orders

Following the suggestion of the *Sheppard* Court, many judges in high profile cases have barred lawyers, their employees, law enforcement and court personnel, and witnesses from making extrajudicial statements prior to the entry of a verdict. An example arose in United States v. Cutler, 58 F.3d 825 (2d Cir.1995), where the lawyer for Mafia boss John Gotti was convicted of criminal contempt for violating a gag order entered in Gotti's murder prosecution. The order incorporated a local rule of court prohibiting statements from counsel that would create a reasonable likelihood of interfering with a fair trial. Despite the order, Cutler gave numerous interviews to the press and television. In these interviews, he claimed, among other things, that: the government was persecuting John Gotti; John Gotti was "anti-drugs" and a legitimate businessman; government witnesses were liars; and the Mafia does not exist. Cutler also mischaracterized important parts of the government's evidence.

Cutler argued that he did not violate the gag order because his statements were not reasonably likely to interfere with a fair trial. He contended that he was simply responding to the "veritable firestorm of anti-Gotti publicity." The court was not persuaded, however, by Cutler's "Uriah Heep pose." It stated that Cutler could be found in contempt for statements *likely* to impair a fair trial, even if the statements in fact had no effect. (Indeed, Cutler's p.r. campaign had no effect; almost all members of the venire panel had heard about Gotti, but apparently none had heard about Cutler's statements).

Cutler argued, finally, that he had not *willfully* violated the gag order. But the court found what it termed a "smoking gun" in a statement Cutler had made, while speaking at a seminar at Brooklyn Law School, about contacts with the press. At the seminar, Cutler said:

> I have honest reasons why I don't want to alienate [the press], that I want the prospective veniremen out there to feel that I mean what I say and say what I mean, and if that can spill over and help my client, then I feel it's important for me to do that.

The court upheld Cutler's sentence of 90 days' house arrest, three years' probation, and a six month suspension from the practice of law. It concluded as follows:

> In some quarters, doubtless, this affirmance will elicit thunderbolts that we are chilling effective advocacy. Obviously, that is neither our intention nor our result. The advocate is still entitled—indeed encouraged—to strike hard blows, but not unfair blows. Trial practice, whether civil or criminal, is not a contact sport. And its tactics do not include eye-gouging or shin-kicking.

> In this case, a conscientious trial judge tried mightily to limit the lawyers to press statements that were accurate and fair. The defendant's statements were dipped in venom and were deliberately couched to poison the well from which the jury would be selected. Such conduct goes beyond the pale, by any reasonable standard, and cannot be condoned under the rubric of "effective advocacy."

What kind of "fair blows" could Cutler have struck, given the anti-Gotti publicity that pervaded New York when the prosecution began? What's wrong with Cutler's desire to shape the opinions of the jury venire? It should be noted that the prosecutor gave an interview shortly after the indictment against Gotti was handed down. In the interview, he said that Gotti was "a murderer, not a folk hero," and expressed pleasure that the evidence he had was much stronger than the evidence in prior prosecutions in which Gotti had been acquitted. These statements were made before the trial judge imposed the gag order. Are they relevant to Cutler's contempt prosecution? Do you think the prosecutor would have been found guilty of criminal contempt if he had made those statements after the trial judge imposed a gag order?

Overbroad Gag Orders

United States v. Salameh, 992 F.2d 445 (2d Cir.1993), was a prosecution of defendants accused of bombing the World Trade Center. It was obviously a high profile case, and the judge was concerned about trial publicity in general and extrajudicial statements by lawyers in particular. So he imposed the following gag order:

> There will be no more statements in the press, on TV, in radio, or in any other electronic media, issued by either side or their agents. The next time I pick up a paper and see a quotation from any of you, you had best be prepared to have some money. The first fine will be $200. Thereafter, the fines will be squared.

After the order was entered, defense counsel had some questions for the judge about the scope of the order, such as, could counsel make a statement that his client had been tortured in Egypt? Could the lawyer talk to reporters about the client's background and family? The trial judge responded that the gag order applied to "what we are dealing with here."

The court of appeals vacated the gag order, on the ground that it violated the first amendment principle that an order limiting speech "should be no broader than necessary to protect the integrity of the judicial system and the defendant's right to a fair trial." The court concluded as follows:

> The order imposed by the district court in the present case does not meet these standards. The restraint on the attorneys' speech is not narrowly tailored; rather, it is a blanket prohibition that extends to any statements that * * * may have something to do with the case. The court did not make a finding that alternatives to this blanket prohibition would be inadequate to protect defendants' rights to a fair trial before an impartial jury. * * * The record does not support a conclusion that no reasonable alternatives to a blanket prohibition exist.

Why was the order in *Salameh* any more problematic than the order at issue in *Cutler*, which prohibited counsel from making a statement that had a "reasonable likelihood of impairing a fair trial"? At least the order in *Salameh* had the virtue of clarity, did it not?

Ethical Proscriptions: Gentile v. State Bar of Nevada

To the extent that prejudicial trial publicity is caused by lawyers, codes of ethics impose limitations even if no gag order is in place. Rule 3.6 of the

Model Rules of Professional Conduct makes disclosure of information by lawyers involved in a trial an ethical violation under some circumstances. These rules generally prohibit statements that create a reasonable likelihood of materially prejudicing the proceeding. See, e.g., United States v. Bingham, 769 F.Supp. 1039 (N.D.Ill.1991) (defense attorneys' conduct was referred to disciplinary committee, where attorneys criticized the empanelment of an anonymous jury in televised interviews the night before jury selection).

Like gag orders, lawyer disciplinary rules limiting speech raise first amendment issues. In Gentile v. State Bar of Nevada, 501 U.S. 1030 (1991), the Supreme Court rebuffed a first amendment challenge to a state disciplinary rule proscribing "an extrajudicial statement that a reasonable person would expect to be disseminated by means of media communication if the lawyer knows or reasonably should know that it will have a substantial likelihood of materially prejudicing an adjudicative proceeding." Chief Justice Rehnquist's opinion upholding this standard was joined by Justices White, O'Connor, Scalia, and Souter.

The case arose after cocaine and traveler's checks used in an undercover police operation were found missing from a vault, and an investigation led to the indictment of Gentile's client. Gentile held a press conference in which he suggested that the thief was a police officer, not his client, and that his client was not guilty. Gentile's main purpose in holding the press conference was to counter the adverse publicity that had been aired concerning his client. Gentile's client was ultimately acquitted.

Chief Justice Rehnquist's opinion for the Court on the relevant standard held that lawyers are entitled to less First Amendment protection than the press. The Chief Justice reasoned that "lawyers representing clients in pending cases are key participants in the criminal justice system, and the State may demand some adherence to the precepts of that system in regulating their speech as well as their conduct." He noted that a lawyer's extrajudicial statements can have significant impact on the trial "since lawyers' statements are likely to be received as especially authoritative." He concluded that the "substantial likelihood of material prejudice" test was an appropriate balance of the interests of the lawyer and the state, since it imposes "only narrow and necessary limitations on lawyers' speech," and "it merely postpones the attorney's comments until after the trial." A more rigorous "clear and present danger" standard was therefore not required.

Despite the Court's upholding the standard, Justice Kennedy wrote for the Court, joined by Justices Marshall, Blackmun, Stevens, and O'Connor, as it held that one aspect of the particular Nevada rule was void for vagueness. Consequently, the Court held that the rule could not support a reprimand of counsel for remarks made at a press conference following the indictment of his client.

Justice Kennedy found it unnecessary to address the constitutionality of the "substantial likelihood of material prejudice" standard, or to determine whether the First Amendment provides less protection for lawyers than for the press. He reasoned instead that the Nevada rule was vague because of its safe harbor provision, which set forth examples of some statements that would not violate the rule. He stated that a lawyer seeking to avail himself of the Nevada safe harbor provision "must guess at its contours." The safe harbor provision gave defense counsel the right to "explain the general nature of the defense" but "without elaboration." Justice Kennedy concluded that this provision was unconstitutionally vague because "general and elaboration are both classic terms of degree" with "no settled usage or tradition of interpretation in law." According to Justice Kennedy, Gentile was given "no principle for determining when his remarks pass from the safe harbor of the general to the forbidden sea of the elaborated." Justice Kennedy noted that Gentile had spent several hours researching the requirements of the Nevada rule, and that at his press conference his remarks were guarded and general. Still the Nevada courts had found that he violated the disciplinary rule. Justice Kennedy asserted that "the fact Gentile was found in violation of the Rules after studying them and making a conscious effort at compliance demonstrates that [the Nevada Rule] creates a trap for the wary as well as the unwary."

Justice O'Connor, who wrote a brief concurring opinion, agreed with Justice Kennedy's void for vagueness analysis. She also agreed, however, with Chief Justice Rehnquist's opinion that the "substantial likelihood of prejudice" standard set forth in the Nevada rule was indeed constitutional, even though it provided less protection to lawyers than the "clear and present danger" standard applicable to the press.

In the end, the Court invalidated the sanction imposed upon Gentile, indicated that state rules providing ambiguous examples may be invalidated as a result of vagueness, and yet upheld the standard that lawyers in pending cases may not make public comments when they know or should know that such comments will have a substantial likelihood of materially prejudicing an adjudicative proceeding.

B. CONTROLLING THE MEDIA'S IMPACT

Many participants in and observers of the criminal justice system have argued that undue or unfair media coverage can be remedied by limiting the information disseminated to the public. This can be accomplished in two ways: by controlling media access to information and by restricting what the media reports. The Supreme Court and lower courts have often been confronted with whether and under what circumstances media access to trials can be controlled consistently with the First Amendment and the defendant's Sixth Amendment right to a public trial.

1.   Controlling Media Access to Criminal Proceedings

Pretrial Proceedings: Gannett Co., Inc. v. DePasquale

In Gannett Co., Inc. v. DePasquale, 443 U.S. 368 (1979), a state trial judge had granted two defendants' motions to exclude the press and public from a pretrial hearing on a motion to suppress confessions and physical evidence. The media challenged the judge's decision, which was upheld in the Supreme Court. The Court stated that the Framers of the Sixth Amendment did not intend "to create a constitutional right in strangers to attend a pretrial proceeding, when all that they actually did was to confer upon the accused an explicit right to demand a public trial." The Court also noted that, assuming the First Amendment granted a right of access to pretrial proceedings, the trial court had appropriately balanced the First Amendment interests with the defendant's right to be free from prejudicial pretrial publicity. Justice Powell's concurring opinion suggested that he would recognize some such right, but Justice Rehnquist's concurring opinion indicated that he thought the Court's prior decisions had rejected the idea that the First Amendment guaranteed access to government facilities. Chief Justice Burger also concurred, noting that a pretrial hearing was not a "trial" within the meaning of the Sixth Amendment. Justice Blackmun's dissenting opinion was joined by Justices Brennan, White and Marshall.

The result in *Gannett* was muddled. The Court had before it a pretrial proceeding, but the reasoning of the majority opinion restricting press access was not necessarily confined to such proceedings. Did *Gannett* mean to allow any and all exclusions of the media from any and all parts of trials? Subsequent case law has attempted to clarify the permissible limits on public access to criminal proceedings.

Limited Right of Access to Criminal Trials: Richmond Newspapers, Inc. v. Virginia

In Richmond Newspapers, Inc. v. Virginia, 448 U.S. 555 (1980), the Court held that the First Amendment does give the public and the media a limited right of access to criminal trials. Chief Justice Burger's plurality opinion commanded the most votes in the case. Only Justices White and Stevens joined the opinion, however. Justice Stevens also added a separate concurrence, and Justice White added a concurring statement. The Chief Justice distinguished *Gannett* as dealing with pretrial proceedings, looked to the history of American criminal trials, and found that they had long been conducted in public places in which the public and the media were welcome. He observed that the presence of the public added something of importance to the proceedings.

The Chief Justice concluded that the right of the public and the press to be present was not absolute and would give way to overriding governmental interests articulated in findings of a court. He suggested, however that alternatives must be explored before closure is ordered. Justice Brennan, joined by Justice Marshall, concurred in the judgment and would have held the underlying Virginia statute unconstitutional for giving trial judges too much discretion. Justice Brennan was reluctant to specify the countervailing government interests that might justify overriding the presumption of open trials. Justices Stewart and Blackmun wrote separate opinions concurring in the result. Justice Stewart distinguished the trial setting from places like jails not generally open to the public. Justice Rehnquist dissented. Justice Powell did not participate in the decision.

For cases applying *Richmond Newspapers*, see, e.g., People v. Martinez, 82 N.Y.2d 436, 604 N.Y.S.2d 932 (1993) (holding that the public may be excluded from testimony by an undercover informant, but only if a factual showing is made that continued confidentiality is necessary for the informant's safety or to preserve the integrity of an ongoing investigation); People v. Kin Kan, 78 N.Y.2d 54, 571 N.Y.S.2d 436 (1991) (error to exclude the public, including the defendant's family, during the testimony of the key cooperating witness-accomplice to the defendant's crime; the witness stated that he feared retaliation from testifying in open court, but not from the defendant's family, who knew him already anyway: "the expulsion of everyone during this accomplice's testimony was broader than constitutionally tolerable and constituted a violation of Kan's overriding right to a public trial").

One court has read *Richmond Newspapers* to articulate six societal interests advanced by open court proceedings. They are:

- promotion of informed discussion of governmental affairs by providing the public with the more complete understanding of the judicial system;

- promotion of the public perception of fairness which can be achieved only by permitting full public view of the proceedings;

- providing a significant community therapeutic value as an outlet for community concern, hostility and emotion;

- serving as a check on corrupt practices by exposing the judicial process to public scrutiny;

- enhancement of the performance of all involved; and

- discouragement of perjury.

United States v. Simone, 14 F.3d 833 (3d Cir.1994).

Closure to Protect Witnesses:
Globe Newspaper Co. v. Superior Court

The Court relied on *Richmond Newspapers* in Globe Newspaper Co. v. Superior Court, 457 U.S. 596 (1982), to invalidate a state statute that required exclusion of the media and general public from the courtroom during the testimony of a sex offense victim under the age of 18. Justice Brennan's opinion for the Court observed that where "the State attempts to deny the right of access in order to inhibit the disclosure of sensitive information, it must be shown that the denial is necessitated by a compelling governmental interest, and is narrowly tailored to serve that interest." Although the Court agreed that safeguarding the physical and psychological well-being of a minor is a compelling state interest, it found that this could be accomplished on a case-by-case basis with the trial judge weighing "the minor victim's age, psychological maturity and understanding, the nature of the crime, the desires of the victim, and the interests of parents and relatives."[27] It rejected the assertion that the statute was necessary to encourage minor victims to come forward and to provide accurate testimony, saying that "[n]ot only is the claim speculative in empirical terms, but it is also open to serious question as a matter of logic and common sense."

Chief Justice Burger, joined by Justice Rehnquist, dissented in *Globe Newspapers*. He argued that there was historical support for exclusion of the public from trials involving sexual assaults, particularly those against minors; that the law was a rational response to the undisputed problem of the underreporting of rapes and other sexual offenses; and that the states should have room to experiment before a court demands empirical data to justify a law permitting closure. Justice O'Connor concurred in the judgment, emphasizing that *Richmond Newspapers* applies only to criminal trials. Justice Stevens dissented on procedural grounds.

Globe Newspaper Co. answered some of the questions raised by *Richmond Newspapers*, but did not decide whether the First Amendment right of access applied in pretrial proceedings.

Closure of Voir Dire: Press Enterprise I

Richmond Newspapers was the authority that Chief Justice Burger cited in his opinion for the Court in Press-Enterprise Co. v. Superior Court,

---

[27] United States v. Sherlock, 962 F.2d 1349 (9th Cir.1989), upheld a trial court order excluding the defendant's family in a rape case. The victim, a child, became upset when the defendant's family began giggling and making faces at her during her testimony. The court held that a partial closure (excluding only certain people) was easier to justify than a total closure of a criminal proceeding.

464 U.S. 501 (1984) ("Press-Enterprise I"). The important facts were as follows: Jury selection in a capital prosecution for rape and murder took six weeks. Only three days of the voir dire of the jury was open to the public, because the trial judge was concerned about the privacy of the jurors. After the jury was selected, the trial judge denied a request by Press-Enterprise to release a transcript of the voir dire. A state appellate court sustained the trial judge and the state supreme court denied review.

Citing neither the First nor the Sixth Amendment, the Supreme Court stated that "how we allocate the 'right' to openness as between the accused and the public, or whether we view it as a component inherent in the system benefitting both, is not crucial. No right ranks higher than the right of the accused to a fair trial. But the primacy of the accused's right is difficult to separate from the right of everyone in the community to attend the voir dire which promotes fairness." It reasoned that openness has "a community therapeutic value" and that secret proceedings would deny an outlet for community reaction to serious crime.

Openness, while prized, was not absolutely required, however:

> The presumption of openness may be overcome only by an overriding interest based on findings that closure is essential to preserve higher values and is narrowly tailored to serve that interest. The interest is to be articulated along with findings specific enough that a reviewing court can determine whether the closure order was properly entered.

As an example of proper closure, the Court suggested that in a rape prosecution a prospective juror might privately inform the judge that she or a member of her family had been raped, but had declined to seek prosecution because of the associated emotional trauma. It also suggested that "[b]y requiring the prospective juror to make an affirmative request, the trial judge can ensure that there is in fact a valid basis for a belief that disclosure infringes a significant interest in privacy," and that "[w]hen limited closure is ordered, the constitutional values sought to be protected by holding open proceedings may be satisfied later by making a transcript of the closed proceedings available within a reasonable time, if the judge determines that disclosure can be accomplished while safeguarding the juror's valid privacy interests."

On the facts presented, the Court found that the closure order and the sealing of the transcript were unwarranted. It observed that there were less onerous alternatives than a total preclusion of media access to the voir dire transcript. For example, parts of the transcript might have been sealed and other parts disclosed; also, the judge could have considered revealing the substance of answers without disclosing the identity of jurors.

Justice Blackmun concurred, stating that he saw no need to decide whether privacy interests of jurors might outweigh a defendant's need for information about jurors. Justice Marshall, who concurred in the judgment, also expressed concern about denying the public and the press private information about jurors. Justice Stevens also concurred. He explicitly relied upon a First Amendment right of access.

Closure of Voir Dire Proceedings in a High Profile Trial—Martha Stewart

In ABC, Inc. v. Stewart, 360 F.3d 90 (2d Cir. 2004)—involving the prosecution of the television personality Martha Stewart—the trial judge barred the media from attending voir dire examinations of jurors, but provided that the voir dire transcripts would be released to the media with the names of the prospective jurors redacted. The trial judge was concerned that members of the media, in this high profile prosecution, would attempt to interview prospective jurors during jury selection. But the court of appeals found that the trial judge had erred under *Press Enterprise* because it had not made factual findings that its limitations on media access were "essential" to protect against juror interviews. There was no showing, for example, that any member of the media had ever attempted to interview a prospective juror. The court stated that "[t]he mere fact that the suit has been the subject of intense media coverage is not, however, sufficient to justify closure. To hold otherwise would render the First Amendment right of access meaningless; the very demand for openness would paradoxically defeat its availability."

Procedural Requirements for Determining the Propriety of Closure: Waller v. Georgia

In Waller v. Georgia, 467 U.S. 39 (1984), the Court considered the propriety of closure of a suppression hearing. An indictment charged a number of people with racketeering and other offenses. Prior to the trial of one group of defendants, a motion was made to suppress evidence obtained through wiretaps and searches of homes. The prosecution moved to have the suppression hearing closed to all persons other than those involved in the prosecution on the ground that the taps would "involve" some persons who were indicted but not on trial in this case and other persons not indicted at all. Over the objection of some defendants, the trial judge granted the motion. The suppression hearing lasted seven days, although only two and a half hours were devoted to playing tapes of intercepted conversations. The trial judge suppressed some, but not all, evidence. At trial the defendants were acquitted of racketeering and convicted on gambling charges. Thereafter, but before other persons named in the indictment were tried, a transcript of the suppression hearing was released. The Georgia Supreme Court found that the trial judge had properly balanced the defendants' right to a public hearing against the privacy rights of other persons. The United States Supreme Court disagreed.

Justice Powell, writing for the Court, stated that "there can be little doubt that the explicit Sixth Amendment right of the accused is no less protective than the implicit First Amendment right of the press and public." He also observed that "suppression hearings often are as important as the trial itself. In *Gannett*, as in many cases, the suppression hearing was the *only* trial, because the defendants thereafter pleaded guilty pursuant to a plea bargain." And he concluded that a suppression hearing often resembles a bench trial in which witnesses are sworn and testify, making the need for an open proceeding especially strong. Thus, the Court held "that under the Sixth Amendment any closure of a suppression hearing over the objections of the accused must meet the tests set out in *Press-Enterprise* and its predecessors."

The Court found that the trial judge erred in not considering alternatives to closing the entire hearing and in not requiring the government to provide more details about its need for closure. One option the Court cited was to close only the part of the hearing—e.g., the playing of the tapes—that jeopardized the interests articulated by the government. Rather than reverse the convictions, the Court remanded the case for a new suppression hearing to be conducted in accordance with the constitutional standards articulated in this and prior cases.

Lower courts have read *Waller* as articulating a four-prong test by which to assess the propriety of closure:

(1) The party seeking to close the hearing must advance an overriding interest that is likely to be prejudiced; (2) the closure must be no broader than necessary to protect that interest; (3) the trial court must consider reasonable alternatives to closing the proceeding; and (4) the trial court must make findings adequate to support the closure.

People v. Kin Kan, 78 N.Y.2d 54, 571 N.Y.S.2d 436 (1991).

Sixth Amendment Limitation on Excluding the Public from Juror Voir Dire: Presley v. Georgia

In Presley v. Georgia, 558 U.S. 209 (2010) (per curiam), the defendant's uncle sought to sit in the courtroom during the voir dire of jurors, but the trial court determined that there were no seats available given the number of prospective jurors, and so excluded him from the courtroom. The defendant argued that his Sixth Amendment right to a public trial was violated, because the trial court failed to consider any alternatives that might accommodate the uncle. The Court observed that it held in *Press-Enterprise I* that the First Amendment right to a public trial in criminal cases extended to voir dire of prospective jurors and in *Waller* it held that the Sixth Amendment public trial right extended to a pretrial suppression hearing. The Court observed that "[t]he extent to which the First and Sixth Amendment public trial rights are coextensive is an open question, and it is not necessary here to speculate whether or in what circumstances the reach or protections of one might be greater than the other," but concluded that "there is no legitimate reason, at least in the context of juror selection proceedings, to give one who asserts a First Amendment privilege greater rights to insist on public proceedings than the accused has." The Court also concluded that "[t]rial courts are obligated to take every reasonable measure to accommodate public attendance at criminal trials," and "[n]othing in the record shows that the trial court could not have accommodated the public at Presley's trial." Justice Thomas, joined by Justice Scalia, dissented.

Preliminary Hearings: Press-Enterprise II

In Press-Enterprise Co. v. Superior Court, 478 U.S. 1 (1986) ("*Press-Enterprise II*"), Chief Justice Burger wrote for the majority as it concluded "that the qualified First Amendment right of access to criminal proceedings applies to preliminary hearings as they are conducted in California." He reasoned that preliminary hearings have usually been open, and that preliminary hearings are sufficiently like trials in California to justify the conclusion that public access is essential. Thus, the Chief Justice focused on two factors in determining the applicability of the First Amendment right of access to proceedings other than trials: 1) whether there has been a tradition of openness at such proceedings, and 2) whether the proceeding is "trial-like." Chief Justice Burger concluded that preliminary hearings may only be closed "if specific findings are made demonstrating that, first, there is a substantial probability that the defendant's right to a fair trial will be prejudiced by publicity that closure would prevent and, second, reasonable alternatives to closure cannot adequately protect the defendant's free trial rights."

Justice Stevens, joined in part by Justice Rehnquist, dissented. He challenged the reliance on the value of openness as proving too much, because the same argument could be made with respect to grand jury proceedings, even though these proceedings have historically been secret.[28]

---

[28] *Press-Enterprise II* was found controlling in El Vocero de Puerto Rico v. Puerto Rico, 508 U.S. 147 (1993) (per curiam). Under Puerto Rican law, an accused felon is entitled to a hearing to determine if he shall be held for trial. Both sides may introduce evidence and cross-examine witnesses, and the defendant has the right to counsel. Puerto Rican law provided that the hearing is private unless the defendant requests otherwise. The Supreme Court held that the privacy provision of the Puerto Rican law was unconstitutional. As in *Press-Enterprise II,* the Court found that the Puerto Rican hearing was "sufficiently like a trial" to require public access. The Court rejected the notion that the unique history and traditions of Puerto Rican culture were at all relevant to whether the press and public could have access to the hearing. The Court concluded that any concerns that the defendant might not receive a fair trial must be addressed on a case-by-case basis.

See also United States v. Simone, 14 F.3d 833 (3d Cir.1994) (relying on *Press-Enterprise II* and holding that the First Amendment qualified right of access applies to a post-trial investigation of juror misconduct).

2. Change of Venue and Continuance

Media coverage of a crime is often the most intense and pervasive in the place where the crime occurred. And coverage often is greater immediately after a crime is committed or an arrest takes place than later. By transferring a case, or by continuing a trial until passions cool, some of the ill effects of pretrial publicity might be avoided.

Transfer of Venue

Fed.R.Crim.P. 21(a) provides that the court must transfer proceedings to another district upon the defendant's motion if the judge is "satisfied that so great a prejudice against the defendant exists in the transferring district that the defendant cannot obtain a fair and impartial trial there." In *Sheppard* the Court said that "where there is a *reasonable likelihood* that the prejudicial news prior to trial will prevent a fair trial, the judge should continue the case until the threat abates, or transfer it to another county not so permeated with publicity." (Emphasis added.) But most courts require much more than a reasonable likelihood of prejudice from pretrial publicity before transfer of venue is mandated. A defendant must ordinarily make a showing of *actual and substantial prejudice* before change of venue is required.

An application of the actual and substantial prejudice standard is shown in United States v. Angiulo, 897 F.2d 1169 (1st Cir.1990), a widely publicized Mafia/RICO case, in which the court denied the defendant's motion for change of venue. The court, relying on Patton v. Yount, supra, held that the mere fact that a majority of the empaneled jurors had been exposed to the Patriarca-Angiulo names, or that some linked the Angiulo name with the Mafia, was not sufficient to support a finding of actual prejudice requiring a change of venue. The court deferred to the trial court's conclusion that the jurors could lay aside their impressions and render a verdict based on the evidence in court.

Because courts focus more on actual prejudice than on the likelihood of prejudice, it is common for the ruling on a change of venue motion to be reserved until jury selection, because it is then that the effect of trial publicity on potential jurors can be best assessed. But what happens then is predictable. Courts invest resources in voir dire of potential jurors, and the more they invest the more they want to get a return—to go ahead and try the case. It is the rare case in which a change of venue is granted once the jury is empaneled. The "solution" then becomes a set of stern jury instructions.

The hostility of some courts to change of venue motions can be attributed to feelings that trial at a distant location will burden witnesses, that the community in which the crime was committed has a substantial interest in seeing the law enforced against wrongdoers by means of the criminal justice system, and that a change of prosecutors may be required, which might be disruptive of legitimate interests of the government.[29] Courts may also be concerned that the selection of the transferee jurisdiction may be viewed as unfair to one side or the other. These interests in not changing venue are usually found to outweigh the benefits to the defendant of a venue change; less onerous alternatives such as careful voir dire and strong jury instructions are usually held sufficient to protect the defendant's interests, whether that is actually true or not.

Continuance

A continuance may be less disruptive than a change of venue, because it does not change the place where trial is held. In Patton v. Yount, supra, the Supreme Court emphasized that the passage of time would go far to dissipate the taint of prejudicial pretrial publicity. 18 U.S.C.A. § 316(b)(8)(A) indicates that a continuance can be granted if the judge determines that "the ends of justice served by taking such action outweigh the best interest of the public and the defendant in a speedy trial." What this apparently means is that the defendant's right to a speedy trial must be balanced against his right to a fair trial free of prejudicial publicity. Does that make any sense? Is a continuance a proper solution if the defendant is subject to pretrial incarceration?

VI.   THE DEFENDANT'S RIGHT TO PARTICIPATE IN THE TRIAL

A.   THE RIGHT OF THE DEFENDANT TO BE PRESENT

One aspect of the Sixth Amendment's right to a fair trial involves the defendant's right to be present during the trial. This right and its limits are discussed in the next case.

---

[29] Sometimes the government wants a change of venue despite the burden it may place on prosecutors. Because the defendant generally has a right to be tried in the jurisdiction where the crime was committed, courts are most reluctant to recognize change of venue requests by the government. See State v. Mendoza, 80 Wis.2d 122, 258 N.W.2d 260 (1977). Some states have upheld the prosecutor's right to seek a venue change. Others have limited the right to defendants.

ILLINOIS V. ALLEN

Supreme Court of the United States, 1970.
397 U.S. 337.

JUSTICE BLACK delivered the opinion of the Court.

The Confrontation Clause of the Sixth Amendment to the United States Constitution provides that: "In all criminal prosecutions, the accused shall enjoy the right * * * to be confronted with the witnesses against him * * *." * * * One of the most basic of the rights guaranteed by the Confrontation Clause is the accused's right to be present in the courtroom at every stage of his trial. The question presented in this case is whether an accused can claim the benefit of this constitutional right to remain in the courtroom while at the same time he engages in speech and conduct which is so noisy, disorderly, and disruptive that it is exceedingly difficult or wholly impossible to carry on the trial.

[Allen was charged with armed robbery. He insisted on representing himself, but the trial judge assigned counsel to "sit in and protect the record" for Allen. During his voir dire of the first juror, Allen asked so many questions that the judge instructed him to limit himself to the juror's qualifications. Allen argued so much that the judge asked the assigned counsel to take over voir dire. The federal court of appeals, which held that Allen's rights were violated when he was removed from the courtroom following disruptive behavior described some of that behavior, beginning with Allen's threat to the judge: "When I go out for lunchtime, you're [the judge] going to be a corpse here." At that point he tore the file which his attorney had and threw the papers on the floor. The trial judge thereupon stated to the petitioner, "One more outbreak of that sort and I'll remove you from the courtroom." This warning had no effect on the petitioner. He continued to talk back to the judge, saying, "There's not going to be no trial, either. I'm going to sit here and you're going to talk and you can bring your shackles out and straight jacket and put them on me and tape my mouth, but it will do no good because there's not going to be no trial." After more abusive remarks by Allen, the trial judge ordered the trial to proceed in Allen's absence.]

It is essential to the proper administration of criminal justice that dignity, order, and decorum be the hallmarks of all court proceedings in our country. The flagrant disregard in the courtroom of elementary standards of proper conduct should not and cannot be tolerated. We believe trial judges confronted with disruptive, contumacious, stubbornly defiant defendants must be given sufficient discretion to meet the circumstances of each case. * * * We think there are at least three constitutionally permissible ways for a trial judge to handle an obstreperous defendant like Allen: (1) bind and gag him, thereby keeping him present; (2) cite him for contempt; (3) take him out of the courtroom until he promises to conduct himself properly.

* * *

Trying a defendant for a crime while he sits bound and gagged before the judge and jury would to an extent comply with that part of the Sixth Amendment's purposes that accords the defendant an opportunity to confront the witnesses at the trial. But even to contemplate such a technique, much less see it, arouses a feeling that no person should be tried while shackled and gagged except as a last resort. Not only is it possible that the sight of shackles and gags might have a significant effect on the jury's feelings about the defendant, but the use of this technique is itself something of an affront to the very dignity and decorum of judicial proceedings that the judge is seeking to uphold. Moreover, one of the defendant's primary advantages of being present at the trial, his ability to communicate with his counsel, is greatly reduced when the defendant is in a condition of total physical restraint. * * * However, in some situations which we need not attempt to foresee, binding and gagging might possibly be the fairest and most reasonable way to handle a defendant * * *.

* * *

Allen's behavior was clearly of such an extreme and aggravated nature as to justify either his removal from the courtroom or his total physical restraint. Prior to his removal he was repeatedly warned by the trial judge that he would be removed from the courtroom if he persisted in his unruly conduct, and * * * the record demonstrates that Allen would not have been at all dissuaded by the trial judge's use of his criminal contempt powers. Allen was constantly informed that he could return to the trial when he would agree to conduct himself in an orderly manner. Under these circumstances we hold that Allen lost his right guaranteed by the Sixth and Fourteenth Amendments to be present throughout his trial.

* * *

Shackling, Courtroom Security, and Prejudice to the Defendant

The Supreme Court held in Holbrook v. Flynn, 475 U.S. 560 (1986), that deployment of uniformed law enforcement officers in a courtroom during a trial for security reasons is not inherently prejudicial to a defendant. It found no denial of due process or equal protection when four uniformed state troopers sat in the spectator section of the courtroom behind the defense table. Justice Marshall's unanimous opinion for the Court stated that it would never be possible "to eliminate from trial procedures every reminder that the State has chosen to marshal its resources against a defendant to punish him for allegedly criminal conduct." According to Justice Marshall, the Due Process Clause prohibits only such procedures so inherently prejudicial that they "brand the defendant with an unmistakable mark of guilt." The use of security officers was not considered inherently prejudicial because "the presence of guards at a defendant's trial need not be interpreted as a sign that he is particularly dangerous or culpable." Justice Marshall concluded that four troopers, sitting in the first row of the spectator's section, "are unlikely to have been taken as a sign of anything other than a normal official concern for the safety and order of the proceedings." The Court distinguished Estelle v. Williams, 425 U.S. 501 (1976), where it had found a due process violation when the defendant was forced to wear prison garb at trial. Justice Marshall concluded that even if the presence of the guards was somewhat prejudicial, "sufficient cause for this level of security could be found in the State's need to maintain custody over defendants who had been denied bail after an individualized determination that their presence at trial could not otherwise be ensured." In contrast, there was no justifiable need in *Williams* to dress the defendant in prison garb for trial.

What about forcing the defendant to wear an electronic "stun belt" during trial proceedings? This can be hidden under the defendant's clothes, so it wouldn't seem to be the badge of guilt that the Court was concerned about in *Holbrook*. But the courts have been—understandably—wary, because of the possible psychological effects on the defendant. See Gonzalez v. Pliler, 341 F.3d 897 (9th Cir. 2003) (forcing defendant to wear an electronic "stun belt" during trial proceedings was improper where the only justification was that the court heard from the bailiff that the defendant had a "bit of an attitude"); United States v. Durham, 287 F.3d 1297 (11th Cir. 2002) (use of stun belt improper where court did not inquire into the possibility that the belt might be activated accidentally, and the defendant was already shackled during the trial).

Shackling at the Penalty Phase of a Capital Case: Deck v. Missouri

In Deck v. Missouri, 544 U.S. 622 (2005), Justice Breyer wrote for the Court as it considered the applicability of *Holbrook* and *Allen* to the practice of shackling capital defendants during the sentencing phase and held "that the Constitution forbids the use of visible shackles during the penalty phase, as it forbids their use during the guilt phase, *unless* that use is justified by an essential state interest—such as the interest in courtroom security—specific to the defendant on trial." The Court found that freedom from shackling in the absence of substantial government interests was grounded in three important considerations: 1) protecting the presumption of innocence; 2) protecting the right to confer with counsel; and 3) maintaining the dignity of the courtroom. But, the Court also recognized that "[t]here will be cases, of course, where these perils of shackling are unavoidable," and made clear that it did "not underestimate the need to restrain dangerous defendants to prevent courtroom attacks, or the need to give trial courts latitude in making individualized security determinations."

Justice Thomas, joined by Justice Scalia, dissented. He engaged in an extensive discussion of English common law and noted that the irons of that period were "heavy and painful" and thus raised concerns about torture. Justice Thomas argued that "[t]reating shackling at sentencing as inherently prejudicial ignores the commonsense distinction between a defendant who stands accused and a defendant who stands convicted," and "[c]apital sentencing jurors know that the defendant has been convicted of a dangerous crime" so that jurors are hardly "surprised at the sight of restraints." Is this persuasive? If a defendant is not shackled when guilt is determined but appears in shackles at sentencing, might the jury assume, incorrectly, that the defendant engaged in dangerous conduct after being convicted? If so, what impact is this likely to have on a sentencing recommendation?

Commenting on the Defendant's Presence at Trial: Portuondo v. Agard

Witnesses are often sequestered before they testify in a criminal trial. See Federal Rule of Evidence 615. Sequestration addresses the concern that if a witness knows the evidence already presented, he might tailor his testimony to fit that evidence. But a criminal defendant who chooses to testify cannot be sequestered, because he has a constitutional right to attend the trial. In Portuondo v. Agard, 529 U.S. 61 (2000), the prosecutor in summation sought to draw this fact to the jury's attention. The case required the jury to make a credibility judgment regarding both the defendant Agard and the victims. Although the more typical practice in federal court is to have the prosecution make the first closing argument and to make a rebuttal argument after the defense closes, apparently in this case each side had only one closing opportunity with the defense going first and the prosecutor (with the burden of persuasion) going last. The prosecutor argued as follows:

> You know, ladies and gentlemen, unlike all the other witnesses in this case the defendant has a benefit and the benefit that he has, unlike all the other witnesses, is he gets to sit here and listen to the testimony of all the other witnesses before he testifies. * * * That gives you a big advantage, doesn't it. You get to sit here and think what am I going to say and how am I going to say it? How am I going to fit it into the evidence? * * * He's a smart man. I never said he was stupid. . . . He used everything to his advantage.

Agard contended that the prosecutor's argument placed an impermissible burden on his right to be present at trial. The trial court rejected this claim, reasoning that Agard's status as the last witness in the case was simply a matter of fact. The Supreme Court, in an opinion by Justice Scalia for five Justices, agreed with the trial court. Justice Scalia concluded as follows:

> In sum, we see no reason to depart from the practice of treating testifying defendants the same as other witnesses. A witness's ability to hear prior testimony and to tailor his account accordingly, and the threat that ability presents to the integrity of the trial, are no different when it is the defendant doing the listening. Allowing comment upon the fact that a defendant's presence in the courtroom provides him a unique opportunity to tailor his testimony is appropriate—and indeed, given the inability to sequester the defendant, sometimes essential—to the central function of the trial, which is to discover the truth.

Justice Stevens, joined by Justice Breyer, concurred in the judgment in *Agard*. Justice Stevens found no constitutional violation in the prosecutor's tailoring argument. He wrote, however, to express his "disagreement with the Court's implicit endorsement of her summation" and concluded that such arguments should be discouraged as a matter of fair trial practice.

Justice Ginsburg, joined by Justice Souter, dissented in *Agard*. She focused on the fact that the prosecutor's tailoring argument was "generic", i.e., it could be applied in any case in which the defendant testified. Such an "automatic burden" on the defendant's credibility resulted, in her view, in an unfair penalty for the defendant's exercise of his constitutional right to be present.

For a discussion of the some of the implications of *Agard* on the admissibility of evidence and the possible use of the case to the benefit of the defense, see Saltzburg and Capra, The Unrecognized Right of Criminal Defendants to Admit Their Own Pretrial Statements, 49 William & Mary L.Rev. 1991 (2008).

B. THE REQUIREMENT OF COMPETENCE TO STAND TRIAL

The premise of the constitutional right to be present is that the defendant has the right to participate in his own defense. Indeed, participation by the defendant is ordinarily essential to assure that witnesses are fully cross-examined, exculpatory facts are presented, and jurors are challenged when necessary, etc. But if the defendant is mentally incapable of participating in his defense, the right to be present is a nullity. Not surprisingly, then, the Supreme Court has often held that the Due Process Clause prohibits the criminal prosecution of a defendant who is not competent to stand trial. Drope v. Missouri, 420 U.S. 162 (1975); Pate v. Robinson, 383 U.S. 375 (1966).

In Dusky v. United States, 362 U.S. 402 (1960), the Court held that a defendant is competent to stand trial when he has "sufficient present ability to consult with his lawyer with a reasonable degree of rational understanding" and has a "rational as well as factual understanding of the proceedings against him." See also Drope v. Missouri, supra (a person "whose mental condition is such that he lacks the capacity to understand the nature and object of the proceedings against him, to consult with counsel, and to assist in preparing his defense may not be subjected to a trial").

A criminal prosecution must be delayed during the time that a defendant is incompetent, and a verdict rendered against an incompetent defendant is voidable. As a practical matter, it is often in the state's interest to press for a trial of a defendant whose claim of incompetency is questionable, and it is often in the defendant's interest to seek to delay such a trial in the hope that witnesses will become unavailable. Predictably, disputes arise on whether a defendant is actually incompetent, and whether the state can use certain methods to assure that the defendant is competent to stand trial.

Forced Medication to Assure Competence: Riggins v. Nevada

What should the state do if a defendant is only competent when taking medication and he refuses to take it? In Riggins v. Nevada, 504 U.S. 127 (1992), the defendant moved to terminate use of Mellaril, an anti-psychotic drug. His proposed defense at trial was insanity, and he argued that continued administration of the drug would deprive him of the right to show the jury his true mental state. The trial court held a hearing at which experts disagreed about whether Riggins would be competent to stand trial in the absence of medication. The experts also disagreed about the effects of the medication upon Riggins's demeanor at trial and upon his ability to participate in his defense. The trial court denied Riggins' motion. At the trial, Riggins testified while under medication. He was eventually convicted and sentenced to death.

The Supreme Court, in an opinion by Justice O'Connor, reversed the conviction. Justice O'Connor noted that a person has a liberty interest in being free from unwanted medication, citing Washington v. Harper, 494 U.S. 210 (1990). She recognized that the state could compel medication in certain circumstances—such as when the person presented a risk of harm to himself or to others—but concluded that the trial court had erred when it "allowed the administration of Mellaril to continue without making *any* determination of the need for this course or *any* findings about reasonable alternatives." She also noted that the trial court had not specifically acknowledged Riggins's liberty interest in freedom from unwanted anti-psychotic drugs. Relying on scientific literature, Justice O'Connor asserted that the side effects of Mellaril may have affected Riggins's demeanor, his testimony at trial, his ability to follow the proceedings, and his ability to communicate with counsel. She concluded that the forced medication created "a strong possibility that Riggins's defense was impaired due to the administration of Mellaril."

Justice O'Connor recognized that under *Holbrook* and *Allen,* "trial prejudice can sometimes be justified by an essential state interest." But because the record contained no finding that forced medication was necessary to accomplish an essential state policy, the majority held that there was no basis "for saying that the substantial probability of trial prejudice in this case was justified."

Justice Kennedy concurred in the judgment and argued that by forcing medication at trial, the state was "manipulating the evidence." He concluded that "if the State cannot render the defendant competent without involuntary medication, then it must resort to civil commitment, if appropriate, unless the defendant becomes competent through other means."

Justice Thomas, joined by Justice Scalia, dissented. He noted that the trial court had allowed defense experts to testify as to the effects of Mellaril on Riggins's demeanor, and that insofar as his ability to participate in his defense was concerned, "the record indicates that Riggins's mental capacity was *enhanced* by his administration of Mellaril." Accordingly, Justice Thomas concluded that Riggins had suffered no trial prejudice from the forced medication.

In Sell v. United States, 539 U.S. 166 (2003), the Court held that the Due Process Clause permits the Government to administer antipsychotic drugs to a mentally ill defendant facing serious criminal charges in order to render that defendant competent to stand trial—but only if the treatment is 1) medically appropriate; 2) substantially unlikely to have side effects that may undermine the fairness of the trial; and 3) necessary to further important governmental trial-related interests. The Court held that the defendant could not be ordered to take antipsychotic drugs solely to render him competent to stand trial without consideration of other factors.

Burden of Proof as to Competency: Medina v. California

The Court held in Medina v. California, 505 U.S. 437 (1992), that the Due Process Clause permits a state to allocate to the defendant the burden of proving that he is not competent to stand trial. On the basis of conflicting psychiatric testimony, Medina was found competent to stand trial under a state rule requiring that he show incompetence by a preponderance of the evidence. Medina was ultimately sentenced to death. Justice Kennedy wrote the majority opinion for five Justices. He asserted that the Due

Process Clause does not "require a state to adopt one procedure over another on the basis that it may produce results more favorable to the accused." He concluded that "it is enough that the State affords the criminal defendant on whose behalf a plea of incompetence is asserted a reasonable opportunity to demonstrate that he is not competent to stand trial."

Justice Kennedy rejected the argument that the defendant's impairment may itself make it all but impossible to satisfy a burden of proof at the incompetency hearing. He explained that "although an impaired defendant might be limited in his ability to assist counsel in demonstrating incompetence, the defendant's inability to assist counsel can, in and of itself, constitute probative evidence of incompetence, and defense counsel will often have the best-informed view of the defendant's ability to participate in his defense."

Justice O'Connor, joined by Justice Souter, concurred in the judgment. Justice Blackmun dissented in an opinion joined by Justice Stevens. He concluded that the constitutional prohibition against convicting incompetent defendants is severely diminished "if the State is at liberty to go forward with a trial when the evidence of competency is inconclusive."

Does it really make much difference who has the burden of persuasion if the standard of proof is a preponderance of the evidence and the decision-maker is the trial judge? What is is the likelihood that the judge will be in equipoise, which is the only time the burden is really meaningful?

Requiring the Defendant to Prove Competency by Clear and Convincing Evidence: Cooper v. Oklahoma

The State of Oklahoma sought to extend *Medina* in Cooper v. Oklahoma, 517 U.S. 348 (1996). The Oklahoma competency statute established a presumption that the defendant was competent to stand trial, and required the defendant to prove his incompetence by *clear and convincing evidence*. The trial court found it more likely than not that Cooper was incompetent, but nonetheless proceeded with the trial on the ground that Cooper had not shown incompetence by clear and convincing evidence. Cooper was convicted and sentenced to death, but his conviction was reversed in a unanimous opinion written by Justice Stevens.

Justice Stevens declared that the result in *Medina* (permitting the state to require the defendant to prove incompetence by a *preponderance* of the evidence) rested in part on the fact that the preponderance standard "affects the outcome only in a narrow class of cases where the evidence is in equipoise." In contrast, Oklahoma's practice of requiring the defendant to prove incompetence by clear and convincing evidence "poses a significant risk of an erroneous determination that the defendant is competent" and "affects a class of cases in which the defendant has already demonstrated that he is more likely than not incompetent."

Justice Stevens reasoned that a heightened standard of proof "does not decrease the risk of error, but simply reallocates that risk between the parties." Given the balance of interests at stake in the risk of a mistaken determination of a defendant's competence to stand trial, the Court found it unjust to allocate such a heavy burden to the defendant. The risk to the defendant of an erroneous determination of competence is that he will be unable to participate in his defense, thus impairing "the basic fairness of the trial itself." In contrast, the risk to the state of an erroneous determination of incompetence is "modest." While the state's interest in swift justice is implicated, the defendant can still be detained while incompetent, and a trial at a later date is possible if the defendant becomes competent.

C. THE RIGHT TO BE PRESENT AT ALL STAGES OF THE PROCEEDINGS

Fed.R.Crim.P. 43 provides that the defendant has the right to be present at the arraignment, at the plea, at every trial stage—including jury impanelment and the return of the verdict—and at sentencing. Rogers v. United States, 422 U.S. 35 (1975), indicates the importance of the words "every trial stage" in the Federal Rule. Rogers's conviction for threatening the President was overturned because the jury sent a note to the trial judge inquiring whether the court would "accept the Verdict—'Guilty as charged with extreme mercy of the Court,'" and the judge answered in the affirmative without notifying Rogers or his counsel. Despite the fact that Rogers did not know of the judge's action until after certiorari was granted and therefore never questioned it, the Court, in a unanimous opinion by Chief Justice Burger, concluded that Rule 43 was violated and that the error was not harmless.[30] The Court reasoned that the response that the judge gave the jury could have been improved considerably and might have induced unanimity among jury members.

Exclusion from Hearing on Competency of Witnesses: Kentucky v. Stincer

The Supreme Court held in Kentucky v. Stincer, 482 U.S. 730 (1987), that a defendant was not denied his right of confrontation when he was

---

[30] The Supreme Court reversed a court of appeals summarily in United States v. Gagnon, 470 U.S. 522 (1985), and found that four defendants waived a right to be present when a trial judge questioned a juror in chambers concerning his statement of concern to a bailiff about one defendant's drawing pictures of the jury. The Court held that the presence of counsel and the defendants was not necessary to ensure fundamental fairness and that the defendants waived any right to be present under Fed.R.Crim.P. 43 by not objecting to the procedure used by the trial judge.

barred from an in-chambers hearing to determine the competency to testify of two minors who allegedly were sodomized by the defendant. Justice Blackmun reasoned in his majority opinion that there was no indication that the defendant's presence at the hearing would have promoted a more reliable competency determination. The defendant was represented at the hearing by counsel, who was permitted to question the victims on competency issues. After the judge found the victims to be competent, they testified in open court in the presence of the defendant and were asked by defense counsel questions about their memory and understanding of the difference between the truth and a lie.

Justice Blackmun declined to decide whether a competency hearing is a trial or pretrial proceeding and stated that "it is more useful to consider whether excluding the defendant from the hearing interferes with his opportunity for effective cross-examination." He emphasized that state law permitted the defendant to cross-examine the victims completely at trial and to address their competency, even to the point of repeating questions asked at the competency hearing.

Justice Blackmun placed great weight on the fact that at the competency hearing "[n]o question regarding the substantive testimony that the two girls would have given during trial was asked," and stated that "although a competency hearing in which a witness is asked to discuss upcoming substantive testimony might bear a substantial relationship to a defendant's opportunity better to defend himself at trial, that kind of inquiry is not before us in this case."

Justice Marshall, joined by Justices Brennan and Stevens, dissented. Justice Marshall reasoned that "[p]hysical presence of the defendant enhances the reliability of the fact-finding process" and that "[i]t is both functionally inefficient and fundamentally unfair to attribute to the defendant's attorney complete knowledge of the facts which the trial judge, in the defendant's involuntary absence, deems relevant to the competency determination."

D. TRIAL IN ABSENTIA

Federal Rule 43(c) provides that a defendant loses his right to be present by disruptive conduct or by voluntarily absenting himself *after the trial starts*. In Crosby v. United States, 506 U.S. 255 (1993), Justice Blackmun wrote for a unanimous Court as it held that Rule 43 does not permit the trial *in absentia* of a defendant who absconds *prior* to trial and is absent at its beginning. Crosby, charged with mail fraud, was released on bond pending his trial. He failed to appear for trial while three codefendants and a pool of 54 jurors waited for him. The trial judge found that his absence was deliberate and that the trial should commence. The Supreme Court recognized that Rule 43 permits a trial to continue if a defendant absconds *after* it begins, but held that the Rule means what it says and that it does not permit a trial to be started when a defendant is absent.

Justice Blackmun stated that the distinction in the Rule between pretrial and mid-trial flight was not "so farfetched as to convince us that Rule 43 cannot mean what it says." He noted the following reasons for making such a distinction: 1) "the costs of suspending a proceeding already under way will be greater than the cost of postponing a trial not yet begun;" 2) "the defendant's initial presence assures that any waiver is indeed knowing," whereas it could not as easily be assumed that a defendant not yet at trial would know that a trial could occur in his absence; and 3) "a rule that allows an ongoing trial to continue when a defendant disappears deprives the defendant of the option of gambling on an acquittal knowing that he can terminate the trial if it seems that the verdict will go against him—an option that might otherwise appear preferable to the costly, perhaps unnecessary, path of becoming a fugitive from the outset." The Court did not decide whether trying Crosby *in absentia* violated his constitutional right to be present, as well as Rule 43.

VII.   THE RIGHT TO EFFECTIVE ASSISTANCE OF COUNSEL

In Chapter 5 we saw that the accused is guaranteed the right to counsel. Here we examine the kind of counsel that the accused has a right to expect during the trial process.

A. INEFFECTIVENESS AND PREJUDICE

Although counsel is constitutionally required at trial and at many pre- and post-trial stages of a criminal prosecution, the quality of representation afforded defendants is uneven. A defendant who is acquitted has little reason to complain, even if her lawyer made serious errors at trial. But a defendant who is convicted may believe that her lawyer did not provide sufficiently competent representation. If so, she may challenge her conviction on the theory that she was denied "effective" assistance of counsel.

The notion that counsel must provide at least some minimal level of representation first appeared in Powell v. Alabama, 287 U.S. 45 (1932). Justice Sutherland's opinion concluded that the trial judge's failure to make an effective appointment of counsel resulted in the "denial of effective and substantial aid. * * * [D]efendants were not accorded the right of counsel in any substantial sense." The Court in *Powell* concluded that the right to counsel means the right to a reasonably effective counsel.

1.   The *Strickland* Two-Pronged Test

In the following case, the Court set forth the standards that a defendant must meet to justify the reversal of a conviction or sentence for ineffective assistance of counsel.

STRICKLAND V. WASHINGTON
Supreme Court of the United States, 1984.
466 U.S. 668.

JUSTICE O'CONNOR delivered the opinion of the Court.

This case requires us to consider the proper standards for judging a criminal defendant's contention that the Constitution requires a conviction or death sentence to be set aside because counsel's assistance at the trial or sentencing was ineffective.

* * *

During a ten-day period in September 1976, respondent planned and committed three groups of crimes, which included three brutal stabbing murders, torture, kidnaping, severe assaults, attempted murders, attempted extortion, and theft. After his two accomplices were arrested, respondent surrendered to police and voluntarily gave a lengthy statement confessing to the third of the criminal episodes. The State of Florida indicted respondent for kidnaping and murder and appointed an experienced criminal lawyer to represent him.

Counsel actively pursued pretrial motions and discovery. He cut his efforts short, however, and he experienced a sense of hopelessness about the case, when he learned that, against his specific advice, respondent had also confessed to the first two murders. By the date set for trial, respondent was subject to indictment for three counts of first degree murder and multiple counts of robbery, kidnapping for ransom, breaking and entering and assault, attempted murder, and conspiracy to commit robbery. Respondent waived his right to a jury trial, again acting against counsel's advice, and pleaded guilty to all charges, including the three capital murder charges.

In the plea colloquy, respondent told the trial judge that, although he had committed a string of burglaries, he had no significant prior criminal record and that at the time of his criminal spree he was under extreme stress caused by his inability to support his family. He also stated, however, that he accepted responsibility for the crimes. The trial judge told respondent that he had "a great deal of respect for people who are willing to step forward and admit their responsibility" but that he was making no statement at all about his likely sentencing decision.

Counsel advised respondent to invoke his right under Florida law to an advisory jury at his capital sentencing hearing. Respondent rejected the advice and waived the right. He chose instead to be sentenced by the trial judge without a jury recommendation.

In preparing for the sentencing hearing, counsel spoke with respondent about his background. He also spoke on the telephone with respondent's wife and mother, though he did not follow up on the one unsuccessful effort to meet with them. He did not otherwise seek out character witnesses for respondent. Nor did he request a psychiatric examination, since his conversations with his client gave no indication that respondent had psychological problems.

Counsel decided not to present and hence not to look further for evidence concerning respondent's character and emotional state. That decision reflected trial counsel's sense of hopelessness about overcoming the evidentiary effect of respondent's confessions to the gruesome crimes. It also reflected the judgment that it was advisable to rely on the plea colloquy for evidence about respondent's background and about his claim of emotional stress: the plea colloquy communicated sufficient information about these subjects, and by foregoing the opportunity to present new evidence on these subjects, counsel prevented the State from cross-examining respondent on his claim and from putting on psychiatric evidence of its own.

Counsel also excluded from the sentencing hearing other evidence he thought was potentially damaging. He successfully moved to exclude respondent's "rap sheet." Because he judged that a presentence report might prove more detrimental than helpful, as it would have included respondent's criminal history and thereby undermined the claim of no significant history of criminal activity, he did not request that one be prepared.

At the sentencing hearing, counsel's strategy was based primarily on the trial judge's remarks at the plea colloquy as well as on his reputation as a sentencing judge who thought it important for a convicted defendant to own up to his crime. Counsel argued that respondent's remorse and acceptance of responsibility justified sparing him from the death penalty. Counsel also argued that respondent had no history of criminal activity and that respondent committed the crimes under extreme mental or emotional disturbance, thus coming within the statutory list of mitigating circumstances. He further argued that respondent should be spared death because he had surrendered, confessed, and offered to testify against a co-defendant and because respondent was fundamentally a good person who had briefly gone badly wrong in extremely stressful circumstances. The State put on evidence and witnesses largely for the purpose of describing the details of the crimes. Counsel did not cross-examine the medical experts who testified about the manner of death of respondent's victims.

The trial judge found several aggravating circumstances with respect to each of the three murders. He found that all three murders were especially heinous, atrocious, and cruel, all involving repeated stabbings. All three murders were committed in the course of at least one other dangerous and violent felony, and since all involved robbery, the murders were for pecuniary gain. * * *

With respect to mitigating circumstances, the trial judge made the same findings for all three capital murders. First, although there was no admitted evidence of prior convictions, respondent had stated that he had engaged in a course of stealing. In any case, even if respondent had no significant history of criminal activity, the aggravating circumstances "would still clearly far outweigh" that mitigating factor. Second, the judge found that, during all three crimes, respondent was not suffering from extreme mental or emotional disturbance and could appreciate the criminality of his acts. Third, none of the victims was a participant in, or consented to, respondent's conduct. Fourth, respondent's participation in the crimes was neither minor nor the result of duress or domination by an accomplice. Finally, respondent's age (26) could not be considered a factor in mitigation, especially when viewed in light of respondent's planning of the crimes and disposition of the proceeds of the various accompanying thefts.

In short, the trial judge found numerous aggravating circumstances and no (or a single comparatively insignificant) mitigating circumstance. * * * He therefore sentenced respondent to death on each of the three counts of murder and to prison terms for the other crimes. The Florida Supreme Court upheld the convictions and sentences on direct appeal.

* * *

Respondent subsequently sought collateral relief in state court on numerous grounds, among them that counsel had rendered ineffective assistance at the sentencing proceeding. Respondent challenged counsel's assistance in six respects. He asserted that counsel was ineffective because he failed to move for a continuance to prepare for sentencing, to request a psychiatric report, to investigate and present character witnesses, to seek a presentence investigation report, to present meaningful arguments to the sentencing judge, and to investigate the medical examiner's reports or cross-examine the medical experts. In support of the claim, respondent submitted fourteen affidavits from friends, neighbors, and relatives stating that they would have testified if asked to do so. He also submitted one psychiatric report and one psychological report stating that respondent, though not under the influence of extreme mental or emotional disturbance, was "chronically frustrated and depressed because of his economic dilemma" at the time of his crimes.

The trial court denied relief without an evidentiary hearing, finding that the record evidence conclusively showed that the ineffectiveness claim was meritless. Four of the assertedly prejudicial errors required little discussion. First, there were no grounds to request a continuance, so there was no error in not requesting one when respondent pleaded guilty. Second, failure to request a presentence investigation was not a serious error because the trial judge had discretion not to grant such a request and because any presentence investigation would have resulted in admission of respondent's rap sheet and thus undermined his assertion of no significant history of criminal activity. Third, the argument and memorandum given to the sentencing judge were "admirable" in light of the overwhelming aggravating circumstances and absence of mitigating circumstances. Fourth, there was no error in failure to examine the medical examiner's reports or to cross-examine the medical witnesses testifying on the manner of death of respondent's victims, since respondent admitted that the victims died in the ways shown by the unchallenged medical evidence.

The trial court dealt at greater length with the two other bases for the ineffectiveness claim. The court pointed out that a psychiatric examination of respondent was conducted by state order soon after respondent's initial arraignment. That report states that there was no indication of major mental illness at the time of the crimes. Moreover, both the reports submitted in the collateral proceeding state that, although respondent was "chronically frustrated and depressed because of his economic dilemma," he was not under the influence of extreme mental or emotional disturbance. * * * Accordingly, counsel could reasonably decide not to seek psychiatric reports; indeed, by relying solely on the plea colloquy to support the emotional disturbance contention, counsel denied the State an opportunity to rebut his claim with psychiatric testimony. In any event, the aggravating circumstances were so overwhelming that no substantial prejudice resulted from the absence at sentencing of the psychiatric evidence offered in the collateral attack.

The court rejected the challenge to counsel's failure to develop and to present character evidence for much the same reasons. The affidavits submitted in the collateral proceeding showed nothing more than that certain persons would have testified that respondent was basically a good person who was worried about his family's financial problems. Respondent himself had already testified along those lines at the plea colloquy. Moreover, respondent's admission of a course of stealing rebutted many of the factual allegations in the affidavits. For those reasons, and because the sentencing judge had stated that the death sentence would be appropriate even if respondent had no significant prior criminal history, no substantial prejudice resulted from the absence at sentencing of the character evidence offered in the collateral attack.

* * *

The Florida Supreme Court affirmed the denial of relief.

Respondent next filed a petition for a writ of habeas corpus in the United States District Court for the Southern District of Florida. * * *

The District Court disputed none of the state court factual findings concerning trial counsel's assistance and made findings of its own that are consistent with the state court findings. * * * On the legal issue of ineffectiveness, the District Court concluded that, although trial counsel made errors in judgment in failing to investigate nonstatutory mitigating evidence further than he did, no prejudice to respondent's sentence resulted from any such error in judgment. * * *

[The Court of Appeals, en banc, reversed the judgment of the District Court and remanded].

* * *

The Sixth Amendment recognizes the right to the assistance of counsel because it envisions counsel's playing a role that is critical to the ability of the adversarial system to produce just results. An accused is entitled to be assisted by an attorney, whether retained or appointed, who plays the role necessary to ensure that the trial is fair.

For that reason, the Court has recognized that "the right to counsel is the right to the effective assistance of counsel." Government violates the right to effective assistance when it interferes in certain ways with the ability of counsel to make independent decisions about how to conduct the defense. See, e.g., Geders v. United States, 425 U.S. 80 (1976) (bar on attorney-client consultation during overnight recess); Herring v. New York, 422 U.S. 853 (1975) (bar on summation at bench trial); Brooks v. Tennessee, 406 U.S. 605 (1972) (requirement that defendant be first defense witness); Ferguson v. Georgia, 365 U.S. 570 (1961) (bar on direct examination of defendant). Counsel, however, can also deprive a defendant of the right to effective assistance, simply by failing to render adequate legal assistance.

The Court has not elaborated on the meaning of the constitutional requirement of effective assistance in the latter class of cases—that is, those presenting claims of "actual ineffectiveness." In giving meaning to the requirement, however, we must take its purpose—to ensure a fair trial—as the guide. The benchmark for judging any claim of ineffectiveness must be whether counsel's conduct so undermined the proper functioning of the adversarial process that the trial cannot be relied on as having produced a just result.

The same principle applies to a capital sentencing proceeding such as that provided by Florida law. * * *

A convicted defendant's claim that counsel's assistance was so defective as to require reversal of a conviction or death sentence has two components. First, the defendant must show that counsel's performance was deficient. This requires showing that counsel made errors so serious that counsel was not functioning as the "counsel" guaranteed the defendant by the Sixth Amendment. Second, the defendant must show that the deficient performance prejudiced the defense. This requires showing that counsel's errors were so serious as to deprive the defendant of a fair trial, a trial whose result is reliable. Unless a defendant makes both showings, it cannot be said that the conviction or death sentence resulted from a breakdown in the adversary process that renders the result unreliable.

* * * When a convicted defendant complains of the ineffectiveness of counsel's assistance, the defendant must show that counsel's representation fell below an objective standard of reasonableness.

* * *

In any case presenting an ineffectiveness claim, the performance inquiry must be whether counsel's assistance was reasonable considering all the circumstances. * * * No particular set of detailed rules for counsel's conduct can satisfactorily take account of the variety of circumstances faced by defense counsel or the range of legitimate decisions regarding how best to represent a criminal defendant. Any such set of rules would interfere with the constitutionally protected independence of counsel and restrict the wide latitude counsel must have in making tactical decisions. Indeed, the existence of detailed guidelines for representation could distract counsel from the overriding mission of vigorous advocacy of the defendant's cause. * * *

Judicial scrutiny of counsel's performance must be highly deferential. It is all too tempting for a defendant to second-guess counsel's assistance after conviction or adverse sentence, and it is all too easy for a court, examining counsel's defense after it has proved unsuccessful, to conclude that a particular act or omission of counsel was unreasonable. A fair assessment of attorney performance requires that every effort be made to eliminate the distorting effects of hindsight, to reconstruct the circumstances of counsel's challenged conduct, and to evaluate the conduct from counsel's perspective at the time. Because of the difficulties inherent in making the evaluation, a court must indulge a strong presumption that counsel's conduct falls within the wide range of reasonable professional assistance; that is, the defendant must overcome the presumption that, under the circumstances, the challenged action might be considered sound trial strategy. There are countless ways to provide effective assistance in any given case. Even the best criminal defense attorneys would not defend a particular client in the same way.

* * *

These standards require no special amplification in order to define counsel's duty to investigate, the duty at issue in this case. As the Court of Appeals concluded, strategic choices made after thorough investigation of law and facts relevant to plausible options are virtually unchallengeable; and strategic choices made after less than complete investigation are reasonable precisely to the extent that reasonable professional judgments support the limitations on investigation. * * *

The reasonableness of counsel's actions may be determined or substantially influenced by the defendant's own statements or actions. Counsel's actions are usually based, quite properly, on informed strategic choices made by the defendant and on information supplied by the defendant. In particular, what investigation decisions are reasonable depends critically on such information. For example, when the facts that support a certain potential line of defense are generally known to counsel because of what the defendant has said, the need for further investigation may be considerably diminished or eliminated altogether. And when a defendant has given counsel reason to believe that pursuing certain investigations would be fruitless or even harmful, counsel's failure to pursue those investigations may not later be challenged as unreasonable.

* * *

An error by counsel, even if professionally unreasonable, does not warrant setting aside the judgment of a criminal proceeding if the error had no effect on the judgment. * * * Accordingly, any deficiencies in counsel's performance must be prejudicial to the defense in order to constitute ineffective assistance under the Constitution.

In certain Sixth Amendment contexts, prejudice is presumed. Actual or constructive denial of the assistance of counsel altogether is legally presumed to result in prejudice. So are various kinds of state interference with counsel's assistance. Prejudice in these circumstances is so likely that case by case inquiry into prejudice is not worth the cost. Moreover, such circumstances involve impairments of the Sixth Amendment right that are easy to identify and, for that reason and because the prosecution is directly responsible, easy for the government to prevent.

One type of actual ineffectiveness claim warrants a similar, though more limited, presumption of prejudice. In Cuyler v. Sullivan [discussed infra], the Court held that prejudice is presumed when counsel is burdened by an actual conflict of interest. In those circumstances, counsel breaches the duty of loyalty, perhaps the most basic of counsel's duties. Moreover, it is difficult to measure the precise effect on the defense of representation corrupted by conflicting interests. Given the obligation of counsel to avoid conflicts of interest and the ability of trial courts to make early inquiry in certain situations likely to give rise to conflicts, it is reasonable for the criminal justice system to maintain a fairly rigid rule of presumed prejudice for conflicts of interest. Even so, the rule is not quite the *per se* rule of prejudice that exists for the Sixth Amendment claims mentioned above. Prejudice is presumed only if the defendant demonstrates that counsel "actively represented conflicting interests" and "that an actual conflict of interest adversely affected his lawyer's performance."

Conflict of interest claims aside, actual ineffectiveness claims alleging a deficiency in attorney performance are subject to a general requirement that the defendant affirmatively prove prejudice. The government is not responsible for, and hence not able to prevent, attorney errors that will result in reversal of a conviction or sentence. Attorney errors come in an infinite variety and are as likely to be utterly harmless in a particular case as they are to be prejudicial. * * * Representation is an art, and an act or omission that is unprofessional in one case may be sound or even brilliant in another. * * *

It is not enough for the defendant to show that the errors had some conceivable effect on the outcome of the proceeding. Virtually every act or omission of counsel would meet that test, and not every error that conceivably could have influenced the outcome undermines the reliability of the result of the proceeding. Respondent suggests requiring a showing that the errors "impaired the presentation of the defense." That standard, however, provides no workable principle. * * *

On the other hand, we believe that a defendant need not show that counsel's deficient conduct more likely than not altered the outcome in the case. This outcome-determinative standard has several strengths. It defines the relevant inquiry in a way familiar to courts, though the inquiry, as is inevitable, is anything but precise. The standard also reflects the profound importance of finality in criminal proceedings. Moreover, it comports with the widely used standard for assessing motions for new trial based on newly discovered evidence. Nevertheless, the standard is not quite appropriate.

Even when the specified attorney error results in the omission of certain evidence, the newly discovered evidence standard is not an apt source from which to draw a prejudice standard for ineffectiveness claims. The high standard for newly discovered evidence claims presupposes that all the essential elements of a presumptively accurate and fair proceeding were present in the proceeding whose result is challenged. An ineffective assistance claim asserts the absence of one of the crucial assurances that the result of the proceeding is reliable, so finality concerns are somewhat weaker and the appropriate standard of prejudice should be somewhat lower. * * *

Accordingly, the appropriate test for prejudice finds its roots in the test for materiality of exculpatory information not disclosed to the defense by the prosecution * * *. The defendant must show that there is a reasonable probability that, but for counsel's unprofessional errors, the result of the proceeding would have been different. A reasonable probability is a probability sufficient to undermine confidence in the outcome.

* * *

When a defendant challenges a conviction, the question is whether there is a reasonable probability that, absent the errors, the factfinder would have had a reasonable doubt respecting guilt. When a defendant challenges a death sentence such as the one at issue in this case, the question is whether there is a reasonable probability that, absent the errors, the sentencer—including an appellate court, to the extent it independently reweighs the evidence—would have concluded that the balance of aggravating and mitigating circumstances did not warrant death.

* * *

Although we have discussed the performance component of an ineffectiveness claim prior to the prejudice component, there is no reason for a court deciding an ineffective assistance claim to approach the inquiry in the same order or even to address both components of the inquiry if the defendant makes an insufficient showing on one. * * *

* * *

Application of the governing principles is not difficult in this case. The facts as described above make clear that the conduct of respondent's counsel at and before respondent's sentencing proceeding cannot be found unreasonable. They also make clear that, even assuming the challenged conduct of counsel was unreasonable, respondent suffered insufficient prejudice to warrant setting aside his death sentence.

* * *

JUSTICE MARSHALL, dissenting.

* * *

My objection to the performance standard adopted by the Court is that it is so malleable that, in practice, it will either have no grip at all or will yield excessive variation in the manner in which the Sixth Amendment is interpreted and applied by different courts. * * *

* * * I agree that counsel must be afforded "wide latitude" when making "tactical decisions" regarding trial strategy, but many aspects of the job of a criminal defense attorney are more amenable to judicial oversight. For example, much of the work involved in preparing for a trial, applying for bail, conferring with one's client, making timely objections to significant, arguably erroneous rulings of the trial judge, and filing a notice of appeal if there are colorable grounds therefor could profitably be made the subject of uniform standards.

* * *

I object to the prejudice standard adopted by the Court for two independent reasons. First, it is often very difficult to tell whether a defendant convicted after a trial in which he was ineffectively represented would have fared better if his lawyer had been competent. Seemingly impregnable cases can sometimes be dismantled by good defense counsel. On the basis of a cold record, it may be impossible for a reviewing court confidently to ascertain how the government's evidence and arguments would have stood up against rebuttal and cross-examination by a shrewd, well prepared lawyer. The difficulties of estimating prejudice after the fact are exacerbated by the possibility that evidence of injury to the defendant may be missing from the record precisely because of the incompetence of defense counsel. * * *

Second and more fundamentally, the assumption on which the Court's holding rests is that the only purpose of the constitutional guarantee of effective assistance of counsel is to reduce the chance that innocent persons will be convicted. In my view, the guarantee also functions to ensure that convictions are obtained only through fundamentally fair procedures. * * *

* * *

[The separate opinion of Justice Brennan, concurring in Part and dissenting in part, is omitted.]

2. Scope of the Right to Effective Assistance of Counsel

Questions have arisen on the extent of a defendant's right to effective assistance. Does it apply to retained counsel? Does it apply to later stages such as appeal and collateral attack?

Retained Counsel

In Cuyler v. Sullivan, 446 U.S. 335 (1980), the Court held that persons who retain counsel are entitled to the same standards of effectiveness as persons for whom the State appoints counsel. The Court reasoned that "[s]ince the State's conduct of a criminal trial itself implicates the State in the defendant's conviction, we see no basis for drawing a distinction between retained and appointed counsel that would deny equal justice to defendants who must choose their own lawyers."

First Appeal of Right: Evitts v. Lucey and Roe v. Flores-Ortega

Justice Brennan wrote for the majority in Evitts v. Lucey, 469 U.S. 387 (1985), which holds that criminal defendants have the right to effective assistance of counsel on their first appeal of right. Lucey had been convicted of drug trafficking. He appealed, but his counsel failed to file a "statement of appeal," as required by state law, along with the appellate brief. For this reason, the state appellate courts refused to review the conviction. Justice Brennan reasoned that cases holding that a defendant has a right to counsel on a first appeal as of right dispositively established that a defendant also has a right to *effective* counsel on a first appeal as of right. The Court recognized that it had held that there is no constitutional right to appeal from a criminal conviction; however, the Court reasoned that "when a State opts to act in a field where its action has significant discretionary elements, it must nonetheless act in accord with the dictates of the Constitution—and, in particular, in accord with the Due Process Clause." Thus, because the state had instituted an appeal of right, it was required to comport with the constitutional standards for effective assistance of counsel. The Court affirmed lower court rulings requiring the state to release the defendant unless it either reinstated his appeal or granted him a new trial. Justice Rehnquist, joined by Chief Justice Burger, dissented. The Chief Justice added two short dissenting paragraphs of his own.

In Roe v. Flores-Ortega, 528 U.S. 470 (2000), the Court considered whether it was automatically ineffective assistance for counsel to fail to file a notice of appeal. The Court set forth the following standard:

> [C]ounsel has a constitutionally-imposed duty to consult with the defendant about an appeal when there is reason to think either (1) that a rational defendant would want to appeal (for example, because there are non-frivolous grounds for appeal), or (2) that this particular defendant reasonably demonstrated to counsel that he was interested in appealing.

If counsel fails to comply with this standard, then the Court determined that prejudice would be found if the defendant can show that he would have filed an appeal if not for counsel's failure to file a notice. This standard does not require the defendant to show that his appeal would have been successful.

Appeals Without Merit: Anders v. California

The Court in Anders v. California, 386 U.S. 738 (1967), determined how appointed counsel should proceed if she believes that an appeal lacks merit. The Court held that if, after a "conscientious examination" of the case, counsel finds an appeal to be "wholly frivolous," counsel should advise the court and request permission to withdraw. However, that request must be accompanied by a brief (now called an "*Anders* brief") "referring to anything in the record that might arguably support the appeal." If the court thereafter finds that there are non-frivolous arguments to be made, counsel must be appointed to bring the appeal. In McCoy v. Court of Appeals of Wisconsin, 486 U.S. 429 (1988), the Court upheld a state rule that required an *Anders* brief to include a discussion of why the appeal lacks merit. The Court noted that the point of an *Anders* brief is to inform the court that the defendant's right to counsel has been satisfied, and a requirement of stated reasons would further that goal. The Court rejected the argument that it would be unethical for counsel to explain why she thought the appeal was frivolous. It stated that "if an attorney can advise the court of his or her conclusion that an appeal is frivolous without impairment of the client's fundamental rights, it must follow that no constitutional deprivation occurs when the attorney explains the basis for that conclusion."[31]

Other Methods to Determine Whether an Appeal Is Frivolous: Smith v. Robbins

The Court in *Anders* required counsel who thought his client's appeal frivolous to file a brief with the court, directing the court to anything in the record "that might arguably support the appeal." After *Anders*, California instituted a different procedure for dealing with appeals that a lawyer believes to be without merit. In California, a lawyer who believes the client's appeal to be frivolous must file a brief with the court that summarizes the procedural and factual history of the case, with citations to the record. The lawyer also must attest that he has reviewed the record, explained his evaluation of the case to his client, provided the client with a copy of the brief, and informed the client of his right to file a pro se supplemental brief. The lawyer further requests that the court independently examine the record for arguable issues. Unlike under the *Anders* procedure, counsel neither explicitly states that his review has led him to conclude that an appeal would be frivolous nor requests leave to withdraw. Instead, he is silent on the merits of the case and expresses his availability to brief any issues on which the court might desire briefing.

---

[31] In Penson v. Ohio, 488 U.S. 75 (1988), the Court held that no showing of prejudice is required by a defendant whose counsel fails to file an *Anders* brief. The Court concluded that judicial scrutiny of the record is not an adequate substitute for a complete lack of counsel. It noted that "the denial of counsel in this case left petitioner completely without representation during the appellate court's actual decisional process."

The appellate court, upon receiving the brief, must conduct a review of the entire record. If the appellate court after its review of the record also finds the appeal to be frivolous, it may affirm. If, however, it finds an arguable (i.e., nonfrivolous) issue, it orders briefing on that issue.

In Smith v. Robbins, 528 U.S. 259 (2000), the majority in a 5–4 decision by Justice Thomas held that the California procedure provided sufficient protection of the defendant's constitutional right to effective assistance of counsel on the first appeal of right. While the procedure differed from that set forth in *Anders* (most importantly in the fact that a lawyer in California is not required to direct the court to matters that might arguably support the appeal), Justice Thomas stated that the *Anders* procedure is only one method of satisfying the Constitution's requirement for indigent criminal appeals; the States are free to adopt different procedures, so long as those procedures adequately safeguard a defendant's right to effective counsel on the first appeal. In Justice Thomas' view, the California procedure adequately assured that non-frivolous issues would be discovered and considered by counsel and the reviewing court.

Justice Souter, joined by Justice Stevens, Ginsburg, and Breyer, dissented. The dissenters complained that arguably non-frivolous issues on appeal would be unlikely to be discovered by the court, if counsel is not required to direct the court to those issues.

Subsequent Appeals and Collateral Attack

The right to effective assistance of counsel on appeal, of which *Anders* is a part, extends only to the first appeal of right. It is not applicable to any subsequent attacks on the judgment. This is because, as seen in Chapter 5, there is no constitutional right to counsel at these later stages. The Court has held that where there is no constitutional right to counsel, there can be no right to effective assistance of counsel. See Pennsylvania v. Finley, 481 U.S. 551 (1987) (no right to *Anders* brief in postconviction proceedings, therefore no claim of ineffective assistance of counsel is cognizable); Wainwright v. Torna, 455 U.S. 586 (1982) (no right to counsel at certiorari stage, therefore no claim of ineffective assistance can be asserted, even though defendant had retained counsel); Murray v. Giarratano, 492 U.S. 1 (1989) (no right to effective assistance of counsel in collateral attack of conviction of capital offense); Coleman v. Thompson, 501 U.S. 722 (1991) (no right to effective assistance of counsel on collateral attack even though the issues presented could not be addressed on direct review).

Strickland Procedures

Ordinarily, ineffectiveness claims are not considered on direct appeal, because the trial record and the appellate briefs rarely provide sufficient information with which to evaluate counsel's performance and its impact on the trial. For example, it is hard to determine whether counsel made a strategic decision to forego cross-examination of a witness simply by looking at the record; ordinarily it would be necessary to take testimony from counsel as to trial strategy. Thus, *Strickland* claims are almost always deferred to a collateral attack in which an evidentiary hearing is conducted—at which the defense counsel is a prime witness. See United States v. Bounds, 943 F.2d 541 (5th Cir.1991) (declining to address ineffectiveness claim on appeal, where the only information in the record is the defendant's own assertions in his brief).

3. Assessing Counsel's Effectiveness

In *Strickland*, the Court found that counsel was not constitutionally ineffective, because he undertook sufficient investigation, made reasonable strategic choices, and generally made the best out of a bad situation. *Strickland* was a fairly easy case, however, especially in light of the stringent standards imposed for proving counsel's ineffectiveness. Since *Strickland*, hundreds of dissatisfied defendants have charged that their counsel acted ineffectively. Federal and state courts have been required to apply the intentionally demanding *Strickland* standards to a wide variety of ineffectiveness claims.

Concerns About Prosecutorial Rebuttal: Darden v. Wainright

In Darden v. Wainwright, 477 U.S. 168 (1986), the Court held that a defendant convicted of murder and sentenced to death failed to demonstrate that his trial lawyers' performance fell below an objective standard of reasonableness. At the sentencing hearing, defense counsel failed to introduce any evidence in mitigation and relied solely on a simple plea for mercy from Darden himself. The Court, emphasizing the deference to defense counsel required by *Strickland,* noted several reasons why counsel may have made this strategic decision. If Darden's non-violence were introduced in mitigation, it would have opened the door to Darden's prior convictions. Any evidence of psychological impairment could have been rebutted by a state psychiatric report in which the expert concluded that Darden was a sociopath. Evidence that Darden was a family man could have been rebutted by his extramarital affairs. The Court concluded that Darden had failed to "overcome the presumption that, under the circumstances, the challenged action might be considered sound trial strategy." See also Stewart v. Dugger, 847 F.2d 1486 (11th Cir.1988) (counsel's decision to reargue innocence at capital sentencing hearing, rather than to present mitigating evidence, held reasonable strategy under *Strickland:* "Trial counsel cannot be faulted for attempting to make the best of a bad situation."). Compare Caro v. Calderon, 165 F.3d 1223 (9th Cir.1999) (failure to notify evaluating psychiatrist that defendant suffered organic brain damage from exposure to toxic chemicals was ineffective;

information was critical to a psychiatric analysis, and disclosure did not present a risk of prosecutorial rebuttal).

Ignorance of the Law: *Kimmelman v. Morrison and Hinton v. Alabama*

The Court found that a lawyer who didn't know the law had acted ineffectively in Kimmelman v. Morrison, 477 U.S. 365 (1986). Justice Brennan's opinion for the Court noted that the defendant's trial counsel "failed to file a timely suppression motion, not due to strategic considerations, but because, until the day of trial, he was unaware of the search and of the State's intention to introduce the * * * evidence * * * because he had conducted no pretrial discovery." Counsel mistakenly believed that the State was required to turn over all inculpatory evidence to the defense.

Although the Court indicated that generally a reviewing court should assess counsel's overall performance in order to determine whether identified acts or omissions overcome the presumption that reasonable professional assistance was provided, it found that the total failure to conduct pretrial discovery was sufficient to justify the conclusion that the lawyer had not acted in accordance with standards of reasonable competence. Justice Brennan noted that "the justifications Morrison's attorney offered for his omission betray a startling ignorance of the law— or a weak attempt to shift blame for inadequate preparation," and that "such a complete lack of pre-trial preparation puts at risk both the defendant's right to meet the case of the prosecution and the reliability of the adversarial testing process." The Court remanded for an examination of possible prejudice. It noted that if the error alleged is counsel's failure to move to suppress evidence, the defendant must show both a reasonable probability of a successful suppression motion and a reasonable probability that without the suppressed evidence, the fact finder would have had a reasonable doubt as to guilt.

Justice Powell, joined by Chief Justice Burger and Justice Rehnquist, concurred in the judgment. He noted that a strong argument could be made that the admission of illegally seized but reliable evidence could not constitute prejudice—this is because the admission of illegally obtained evidence does not impeach the integrity of a guilty verdict.

In Hinton v. Alabama, 134 S.Ct. 1081 (2014) (per curiam), the Court reversed a decision denying habeas corpus relief to a defendant convicted of two murders and sentenced to death. At trial, the prosecutor relied virtually exclusively on ballistics evidence to tie the defendant's gun to bullets used in the murders. Defense counsel (and the trial judge) mistakenly believed that the defense was only entitled to $500 per case (or $1,000 in total given that there were two homicide charges) to hire a defense expert. The defense could find only one expert who would testify for $1,000, his credentials were not strong, and cross-examination at trial cast doubt on whether his opinion that the bullets were not fired from the defendant's gun was reliable. Defense counsel was wrong about the limit on state-provided funds, because the law had changed and the defense was permitted to seek sufficient funds to hire an adequate expert. The state courts agreed that defense counsel failed the first prong of the *Strickland* test by being unfamiliar with and wrong on the law and thus failing to ask for sufficient funds to support the defense. The state court of appeals held that the defendant failed to show prejudice because the three experts who tested for the defendant during habeas proceedings testified to the same conclusion as the defense expert at trial. The Supreme Court found that this was an incorrect analysis because the jury might not have believed the expert at trial and said that "if there is a reasonable possibility that Hinton's attorney would have hired an expert who would have instilled in the jury a reasonable doubt as to Hinton's guilt had the attorney known that the statutory funding limit had been lifted, then Hinton was prejudiced by his lawyer's deficient performance and is entitled to a new trial."

Strategy or Not?

Strickland indicated that the performance prong will be satisfied if, using appropriate deference, counsel's actions fall within the realm of *reasonable trial strategy*. Most courts appear to bend over backwards to justify defense counsel's actions as proper strategy. See, e.g., Stringer v. Jackson, 862 F.2d 1108 (5th Cir.1988) (failure to present mitigating evidence was not ineffective); People v. Russell, 71 N.Y.2d 1016, 530 N.Y.S.2d 101 (1988) (failure to move to suppress evidence was a strategic decision); Brown v. Dixon, 891 F.2d 490 (4th Cir.1989) (not ineffective to argue inconsistent defenses); Rogers-Bey v. Lane, 896 F.2d 279 (7th Cir.1990) (proper strategy to inculpate the defendant in order to impeach a prosecution witness); United States v. Guerrero, 938 F.2d 725 (7th Cir.1991) (in light of overwhelming evidence of the defendant's involvement with narcotics, it was not ineffective to argue that the defendant was involved in a drug conspiracy different from that which was charged).

Consider the following cases. Has counsel been ineffective, or has counsel used a reasonable, albeit unsuccessful, strategy?

1.   Martin was charged with sexual abuse of his two stepdaughters. He denied the charges, and claimed that he had a witness who would testify that the children had been encouraged to falsify their charges. Martin's counsel, appointed shortly before trial, filed a motion for a continuance, alleging that he was unprepared to try the case. This motion was denied.

Counsel was convinced that the denial of a continuance was error. So he decided to "rely on his motion"; by design, he did not put on any proof in defense, and did not cross-examine or participate in the trial, other than to make an opening statement to the jury. This opening statement indicated that the defense was relying on its motion for continuance, and that the jury should not think "that my lack of participation is, uh, that I'm a dummy over here, and I don't know what's going on." The court of appeals stated that "even deliberate trial tactics may constitute ineffective assistance of counsel if they fall outside the wide range of professionally competent assistance." The court asserted that by calling the defendant and his witness to testify, the attorney could have presented a strong defense "without compromising" the motion for continuance. The court concluded that "the decision of Martin's attorney not to participate cannot be considered sound trial strategy," and that the failure of counsel to put on a defense was prejudicial as well. Martin v. Leech, 744 F.2d 1245 (6th Cir. 1984). Is the court second-guessing defense counsel? Is that permissible after *Strickland?*

See also United States v. Wolf, 787 F.2d 1094 (7th Cir.1986), where the court criticized defense counsel's "tactic of no objections" and held it ineffective:

> It is true that lawyers will frequently not object to objectionable questions, believing either that the witness will give an answer helpful to the defense (or at least not harmful to it) or that too-frequent objecting will irritate the jury or make it think the defendant is trying to hide the truth. But to have a *policy* of never objecting to improper questions is forensic suicide. It shifts the main responsibility for the defense from defense counsel to the judge.

Compare Warner v. Ford, 752 F.2d 622 (11th Cir.1985) (strategy of silence not ineffective in multi-defendant trial, where other defendants were defending aggressively and evidence against counsel's client was overwhelming; under these circumstances, it was reasonable to keep a "low profile").

2. Willis was charged with murdering his son. At trial, the victim's wife testified that Willis came to his son's home to get a deer rifle. She then saw Willis shoot his son with a handgun. Willis denied this claim. No handgun was ever found or linked with the killing. No autopsy was ever performed. No bullet or bullet fragments were ever found. The medical examiner was unable to identify the caliber or type of gun used. Upon his arrest, Willis had stated with respect to his son "it was either him or me," and that statement was introduced at trial. The prosecution also introduced a trace metal test which showed that Willis had fired a gun on the day of his son's death. Willis' first trial ended in a deadlocked jury. He was convicted at the second trial. He claimed ineffective assistance because

counsel failed to have an autopsy performed on the victim, which would have determined whether the victim was shot with a handgun. The court held that the failure to obtain an autopsy was a "reasonable tactical decision" because counsel "decided that it was better for there to be uncertainty concerning the weapon used than to chance that an autopsy would reveal that a handgun was the murder weapon, thereby confirming the daughter-in-law's testimony." Willis v. Newsome, 771 F.2d 1445 (11th Cir.1985). Consider that defense counsel's explanation for making a certain decision is given at a hearing long after the trial, and that counsel has been charged at that point with ineffectiveness. Is there a risk that counsel will "color" his or her testimony under these circumstances, by providing a post hoc "strategy" that was never actually thought about at the time of trial?

3. John Wayne Gacy was a notorious mass murderer. At the penalty phase of his capital murder trial, defense counsel argued to the jury that Gacy should not be executed. The argument was not based on an appeal for mercy, nor on proof of mitigating circumstances. Rather, defense counsel argued "that Gacy should be sentenced to life imprisonment so that he could be studied to find out why he committed the murders." Is this "spare him for science" argument ineffective, or is it proper strategy? See Gacy v. Welborn, 994 F.2d 305 (7th Cir.1993) ("spare him for science" argument does not violate *Strickland* performance prong). See also Waters v. Thomas, 46 F.3d 1506 (11th Cir.1995), upholding a death sentence where a "spare him for science" argument was made. The court stated: "It was not unreasonable for counsel to have thought at least one juror in this case might have been persuaded that, given all the harm Waters had done it was time to get some good out of him, and that the way to do that was to keep him alive for study." The dissent in *Waters* stated that defense counsel "concluded the case for his client—not with a plea for mercy for a human being, but with a dehumanizing request to allow a specimen to be studied."

No Strategy at All

In some cases, counsel cannot even come up with a reason for acting (or not acting) as they did at trial. And in those cases courts have not been hesitant to find ineffectiveness. See, e.g., Jones v. Thigpen, 788 F.2d 1101 (5th Cir.1986) (no explanation for failure to argue mental retardation in mitigation at a capital sentencing hearing; defendant had an I.Q. of 41); Harding v. Davis, 878 F.2d 1341 (11th Cir.1989) (failure to object to judge's entry of directed guilty verdict—which deprived the defendant of his right to jury trial—is ineffective and per se prejudicial); Ouber v. Guarino, 293 F.3d 19 (2002) (no strategic reason for emphasizing in opening argument that the defendant would take the stand and tell her side of the story, and then not calling the defendant as a witness at trial).

Closing Argument: Yarborough v. Gentry

In *Yarborough v.* Gentry, 540 U.S. 1 (2003) (per curiam), the Court gave deference to defense counsel's strategy in making a closing argument. It is interesting to describe the facts to seasoned trial lawyers and ask their opinion about the effectiveness of counsel, which often results in a strong judgment of ineffectiveness. This is a reminder that the judges who rule on ineffectiveness claims are not all seasoned trial lawyers.

Gentry was convicted in a California state court of assault with a deadly weapon for stabbing his girlfriend. He claimed he stabbed her accidentally during a dispute with a drug dealer. The girlfriend testified at trial that she could not remember what happened, so the prosecution relied on her damaging preliminary hearing testimony. In her closing argument, the prosecutor expressed sympathy for the girlfriend's plight as a pregnant, drug-addicted mother of three and accused Gentry of telling the jury a "pack of lies."

Defense counsel responded with a closing argument that included the following statements:

> I don't know what happened. I can't tell you. And if I sit here and try to tell you what happened, I'm lying to you.

> I don't care that Tanaysha is pregnant. I don't care that she has three children. I don't know why that had to be brought out in closing. What does that have to do with this case?

> She was stabbed. The question is, did he intend to stab her? He said he did it by accident. If he's lying and you think he's lying then you have to convict him. If you don't think he's lying, bad person, lousy drug addict, stinking thief, jail bird, all that to the contrary, he's not guilty. It's as simple as that. I don't care if he's been in prison.

> I don't know if thievery and stabbing your girlfriend are all in the same pot. I don't know if just because of the fact that you stole some things in the past that means you must have stabbed your girlfriend. That sounds like a jump to me, but that's just [me]. * * *

After deliberating for about six hours, the jury convicted.

California appellate courts denied relief on direct appeal, as did a federal district court on habeas. But the Ninth Circuit held that Gentry was deprived of effective assistance of counsel. The Supreme Court disagreed and observed that there was double deference in this case: deference to the strategic judgment of defense counsel and deference on habeas to the judgment of the state courts. It reasoned that defense counsel made several key points during closing argument: the girlfriend's personal circumstances were irrelevant, Gentry's criminal history was irrelevant to guilt; and the jury, like the prosecutor and defense counsel had no personal knowledge of what happened and could only speculate. The Court recognized that defense counsel omitted facts that might have been favorable to the defense but opined that some of the omitted facts were ambiguous and it was not unreasonable to focus on a small number of key points.

The Court reasoned that, although the Ninth Circuit was concerned that defense counsel mentioned "a host of details that hurt his client's position, none of which mattered as a matter of law," defense counsel's tactic was not unreasonable because he "mentioned those details * * * precisely to remind the jury that they *were* legally irrelevant." The Court also reasoned that "there is nothing wrong with a rhetorical device that personalizes the doubts anyone but an eyewitness must necessarily have."

In the end, the Court concluded that "Gentry's lawyer was no Aristotle or even Clarence Darrow," but he was not ineffective.

Conceding Guilt in a Capital Prosecution: Florida v. Nixon

In Florida v. Nixon, 543 U.S. 175 (2004), Justice Ginsburg wrote for the Court as it refused to establish a per se rule prohibiting defense counsel from conceding the defendant's guilt in a capital prosecution in order "to concentrate the defense on establishing, at the penalty phase, cause for sparing the defendant's life." The Florida Supreme Court held that regardless of how gruesome a crime is and how strong the prosecution's case might be, any concession of guilt was prejudicial ineffective assistance of counsel unless made with the defendant's express consent. Justice Ginsburg rejected this rule and wrote that "[d]efense counsel undoubtedly has a duty to discuss potential strategies with the defendant," but counsel is not automatically barred from conceding guilt after explaining to the defendant that strategy and finding that the defendant neither consents nor objects to it. She reasoned that "[t]he reasonableness of counsel's performance, after consultation with the defendant yields no response, must be judged in accord with the inquiry generally applicable to ineffective-assistance-of-counsel claims: Did counsel's representation 'fall below an objective standard of reasonableness'?" She concluded that "[t]he Florida Supreme Court erred in applying, instead, a presumption of deficient performance, as well as a presumption of prejudice." The state gathered overwhelming evidence that Nixon had kidnaped Jeanne Bickner and then burned her alive. Nixon confessed to the crime in graphic detail. Public Defender Corin sought to negotiate a guilty plea but the prosecutors were unwilling to recommend a sentence other than death.

Justice Ginsburg emphasized that Nixon persistently resisted anwering questions from his counsel and the Court, and she concluded that although a concession of guilt "in a run-of-the-mine trial might present a closer question, the gravity of the potential sentence in a capital trial and the proceeding's two-phase structure vitally affect counsel's strategic calculus.

Ineffectiveness Charge Against a Lawyer Who Refuses to Bring a Defense That Is Likely to Fail: Knowles v. Mirzayance

In Knowles v. Mirzayance, 556 U.S. 111 (2009), the Court considered an ineffectiveness challenge to a defense lawyer's decision not to bring a claim at one phase of a trial, when that claim had already been rejected by the jury in an earlier phase. Justice Thomas, writing for the Court, recounted the facts:

> Mirzayance confessed that he stabbed his 19-year-old cousin nine times with a hunting knife and then shot her four times. At trial, he entered pleas of not guilty and not guilty by reason of insanity (NGI). Under California law, when both of these pleas are entered, the court must hold a bifurcated trial, with guilt determined during the first phase and the viability of the defendant's NGI plea during the second. During the guilt phase of Mirzayance's trial, he sought to avoid a conviction for first-degree murder by obtaining a verdict on the lesser included offense of second-degree murder. To that end, he presented medical testimony that he was insane at the time of the crime and was, therefore, incapable of the premeditation or deliberation necessary for a first-degree murder conviction. The jury nevertheless convicted Mirzayance of first-degree murder.

> The trial judge set the NGI phase to begin the day after the conviction was entered but, on the advice of counsel, Mirzayance abandoned his NGI plea before it commenced. He would have borne the burden of proving his insanity during the NGI phase to the same jury that had just convicted him of first-degree murder.

Justice Thomas explained that "[b]ecause the jury rejected similar evidence at the guilt phase (where the State bore the burden of proof), counsel believed a defense verdict at the NGI phase (where the burden was on the defendant) was unlikely." Although defense counsel planned to have Mirzayance's parents testify in order to provide an emotional account of Mirzayance's struggles with mental illness to supplement the medical evidence of insanity previously presented, the parents refused to testify and Mirzayance accepted counsel's advice to withdraw the NGI plea.

Justice Thomas found that defense counsel was not unreasonable in recommending the withdrawal of a doomed defense even if it were the only available defense. He found "no prevailing professional norms that prevent counsel from recommending that a plea be withdrawn when it is almost certain to lose." He also found that, even if ineffectiveness could be shown, Mirzayance had not been prejudiced by the decision not to pursue the NGI defense.

Failure to Challenge a Widely Accepted Analysis That Is Later Discredited: Maryland v. Kulbicki

In Maryland v. Kulbicki, 136 S.Ct. 2 (2015) (per curiam), the Court summarily reversed the Maryland Court of Appeals' grant of habeas corpus relief from a state murder conviction. Kulbicki argued that his lawyers were ineffective for failing to challenge expert testimony that the bullet fragment found in the victim's brain matched a bullet fragment found in Kulbicki's truck. The expert employed the "comparative bullet lead analysis" (CBLA) that was widely used at the time of trial. Eleven years later, that process had fallen out of favor and was found by the courts to be not generally accepted by the scientific community. The Court held that "[c]ounsel did not perform deficiently by dedicating their time and focus to elements of the defense that did not involve poking methodological holes in a then-uncontroversial mode of ballistics analysis." The Court added that it was highly unlikely that due diligence would have uncovered an obscure report—prepared four years before the defendant's trial by the same FBI agent who testified for the State—suggesting that CBLA was an invalid way to compare bullet fragments. It concluded that the lower court had "demanded something close to 'perfect advocacy'—far more than the 'reasonable competence' the right to counsel guarantees."

Insufficient Deference Given by Reviewing Court to Counsel's Decision Not to Object: Woods v. Etherton

In Woods v. Etherton, 136 S.Ct. 1149 (2016) (per curiam), the defendant was convicted of drug offenses. At his trial the court admitted evidence of an anonymous tip to law enforcement that led to his arrest. The defendant had been arrested while driving a car with a passenger, and a search of the car uncovered cocaine. The officers made the arrest after receiving an anonymous tip that two men were traveling in a car carrying cocaine. The defendant was convicted and argued that his trial counsel was ineffective for failing to object to admission of the tip on the ground that it violated his right to confrontation. The court of appeals, on habeas review, agreed with the defendant—but the Supreme Court unanimously reversed and held that the court of appeals gave insufficient deference to the state court's determination that the anonymous tip was properly admitted for the non-hearsay purpose of explaining the context of the police investigation. Moreover, the Court concluded that "it would not be objectively unreasonable for a fair-minded judge to conclude" that the failure to raise the Confrontation claim "was not due to incompetence but because the facts of the tip were uncontested and in any event consistent with Etherton's defense"—that the drugs belonged to the passenger.

4. The Duty to Investigate

According to *Strickland,* reasonable pre-trial investigation is one component of effective assistance. Courts have found that a complete failure to investigate cannot be considered strategic, because a counsel who has done no investigation will lack the information necessary to make a strategic decision. See Frierson v. Woodford, 463 F.3d 982 (9th Cir. 2006) ("Counsel can hardly be said to have made a strategic choice when he has not obtained the facts on which such a decision could be made."); Foster v. Lockhart, 9 F.3d 722 (8th Cir.1993) (defense counsel in a rape case was ineffective for failing to discover, and develop at trial, the fact that the defendant was impotent).

In Wiggins v. Smith, 539 U.S. 510 (2003), Justice O'Connor wrote for the Court as it addressed both the duty to investigate in the context of a capital sentencing proceeding and the "prejudice" prong of *Strickland.*

Wiggins was convicted of murder and other offenses after police discovered 77-year-old Florence Lacs drowned in the bathtub of her ransacked apartment. Two Baltimore County public defenders represented him at trial and in the sentencing stage of his capital trial which resulted in conviction and a death sentence.

During post-conviction proceedings with new counsel, Wiggins alleged that his trial counsel were ineffective because they failed to investigate and present mitigating evidence of his dysfunctional background. He offered expert testimony from a licensed social worker certified as an expert by the court. The expert described Wiggins' severe physical and sexual abuse inflicted by his mother and various foster parents. The social worker relied on interviews with Wiggins and family members and reviewed state social services, medical, and school records.

During the postconviction proceedings, one of the trial counsel testified that, although the State made funds available to hire a social worker to prepare a social history, he did not recall retaining one. He explained that the trial strategy was to try to the factual case and dispute whether Wiggins was directly responsible for the murder.

The state courts found no ineffectiveness, a federal district court granted a writ of habeas corpus, and the Fourth Circuit reversed and agreed with the state courts. The Supreme Court reversed the Fourth Circuit.

Justice O'Connor wrote that the question "is not whether counsel should have presented a mitigation case. Rather, we focus on whether the investigation supporting counsel's decision not to introduce mitigating evidence of Wiggins' background was itself reasonable."

She concluded that the investigation was not reasonable. Noting that trial counsel had available to them the written pre-sentence report in which Wiggins noted his "misery as a youth" and records kept by the Baltimore City Department of Social Services (DSS) documenting petitioner's various placements in the State's foster care system, Justice O'Connor found that "[c]ounsel's decision not to expand their investigation beyond the PSI and the DSS records fell short of the professional standards that prevailed in Maryland in 1989." She noted that the "acknowledged, standard practice in Maryland in capital cases at the time of Wiggins' trial included the preparation of a social history report" and funds were available to have such a report prepared.

Justice O'Connor also found that the scope of the investigation was also unreasonable in light of what counsel actually discovered in the DSS records, which included the following: "Petitioner's mother was a chronic alcoholic; Wiggins was shuttled from foster home to foster home and displayed some emotional difficulties while there; he had frequent, lengthy absences from school; and, on at least one occasion, his mother left him and his siblings alone for days without food." This led Justice O'Connor to conclude that "any reasonably competent attorney would have realized that pursuing these leads was necessary to making an informed choice among possible defenses, particularly given the apparent absence of any aggravating factors in petitioner's background," especially in view of the fact that "counsel uncovered no evidence in their investigation to suggest that a mitigation case, in its own right, would have been counterproductive, or that further investigation would have been fruitless."

The opinion emphasized that "*Strickland* does not require counsel to investigate every conceivable line of mitigating evidence no matter how unlikely the effort would be to assist the defendant at sentencing. Nor does *Strickland* require defense counsel to present mitigating evidence at sentencing in every case." But, in this case the Court found no reasonable explanation for not investigating mitigation and that there is "a reasonable probability that a competent attorney, aware of this history, would have introduced it at sentencing in an admissible form"; "given the strength of the available evidence, a reasonable attorney may well have chosen to prioritize the mitigation case over the direct responsibility challenge"; and "had the jury been confronted with this considerable mitigating evidence, there is a reasonable probability that it would have returned with a different sentence."

Justice Scalia, joined by Justice Thomas, dissented and argued that the court improperly chose to disbelieve Wiggins' trial counsel who testified under oath that he was aware of the basic features of Wiggins' troubled childhood that the Court claims he overlooked, and "even if this disbelief could plausibly be entertained, that would certainly not establish (as 28 U.S.C. § 2254(d) requires) that the Maryland Court of Appeals was unreasonable in believing it, and in therefore concluding that counsel adequately investigated Wiggins' background."

Complete Failure to Investigate the Defendant's Background in a Capital Case: Porter v. McCollum

The Court relied on *Wiggins* in Porter v. McCollum, 558 U.S. 30 (2009) (per curiam). Porter was sentenced to death after a sentencing phase in which defense counsel failed to present any evidence of Porter's background—even though Porter was abused as a child, was shot at by his father, and suffered trauma from horrific battles in the Korean War. The Court had no trouble finding that defense counsel had conducted an insufficient investigation of Porter's background and consequently rendered ineffective assistance:

> At the postconviction hearing, [the lawyer] testified that he had only one short meeting with Porter regarding the penalty phase. He did not obtain any of Porter's school, medical, or military service records or interview any members of Porter's family. * * * Here, counsel did not even take the first step of interviewing witnesses or requesting records. Beyond that, like the counsel in *Wiggins*, he ignored pertinent avenues for investigation of which he should have been aware. The court-ordered competency evaluations, for example, collectively reported Porter's very few years of regular school, his military service and wounds sustained in combat, and his father's "over-disciplin[e]." As an explanation, counsel described Porter as fatalistic and uncooperative. But he acknowledged that although Porter instructed him not to speak with Porter's ex-wife or son, Porter did not give him any other instructions limiting the witnesses he could interview.

> Counsel thus failed to uncover and present any evidence of Porter's mental health or mental impairment, his family background, or his military service. The decision not to investigate did not reflect reasonable professional judgment. Porter may have been fatalistic or uncooperative, but that does not obviate the need for defense counsel to conduct some sort of mitigation investigation.

The Duty to Investigate the Case File of the Defendant's Prior Criminal Trial: Rompilla v. Beard

In Rompilla v. Beard, 545 U.S. 374 (2005), the Court came close to saying that defense counsel has an obligation to engage in a detailed review of the case file for every conviction that the prosecution will seek to introduce, at least if the conviction is to be used in the penalty phase of a capital proceeding. Rompilla's counsel prepared for the capital phase, but did not review the case file of a prior criminal trial in which the defendant was convicted of a violent crime. That case file happened to have information concerning Rompilla's horrific childhood, mental illness and alcoholism, all of which would have been relevant to mitigation in the capital phase of the instant case. Most of this information was found in a transfer petition prepared by the Department of Corrections after Rompilla had been convicted. The mitigation evidence that counsel presented at trial was pretty thin: five of Rompilla's family members asked the jury for mercy, saying that they believed Rompilla was innocent and a good man; and Rompilla's son testified that he loved his father and would visit him in prison. The jury found that the aggravating factors (including prior violent felonies) outweighed the mitigating factors and sentenced Rompilla to death.

Justice Souter, writing for the Court, first noted that this was not a case in which defense counsel completely defaulted on their duty to investigate. The lawyers interviewed family members and reviewed reports by three mental health experts who gave opinions at the guilt phase. The Court held, however, that "the lawyers were deficient in failing to examine the court file on Rompilla's prior conviction." Justice Souter explained as follows:

> There is an obvious reason that the failure to examine Rompilla's prior conviction file fell below the level of reasonable performance. Counsel knew that the Commonwealth intended to seek the death penalty by proving Rompilla had a significant history of felony convictions indicating the use or threat of violence, an aggravator under state law. Counsel further knew that the Commonwealth would attempt to establish this history by proving Rompilla's prior conviction for rape and assault, and would emphasize his violent character by introducing a transcript of the rape victim's testimony given in that earlier trial. * * * It is also undisputed that the prior conviction file was a public document, readily available for the asking at the very courthouse where Rompilla was to be tried.

Justice Souter stated that the Court was not establishing a per se rule that defense counsel must always review the case file of all of a defendant's prior convictions, but in this case the Court found that it was unreasonable for counsel not to review the file "despite knowing that the prosecution intended to introduce Rompilla's prior conviction not merely by entering a notice of conviction into evidence but by quoting damaging testimony of the rape victim in that case." So the Court concluded that the case file for the prior conviction was the key to a mass of mitigating evidence; but the Court did not say that defense counsel should have looked at the case file for *mitigating* evidence. Rather, defense counsel should have looked at the case file in order to prepare for the prosecution's *aggravating* evidence, and in doing so, it would have found a treasure trove of mitigating evidence.

Finally, Justice Souter found that the failure to investigate the case file was prejudicial, because it happened to contain information that would have been very useful in mitigation.

Justice O'Connor wrote a concurring opinion emphasizing that the Court was not establishing a bright line rule that defense counsel must always investigate the case files for all of the defendant's prior convictions. She noted three factors that made defense counsel's failure to investigate unreasonable: 1) "Rompilla's attorneys knew that their client's prior conviction would be at the very heart of the prosecution's case"; 2) "In announcing an intention to introduce testimony about Rompilla's similar prior offense, the prosecutor put Rompilla's attorneys on notice that the prospective defense on mitigation [i.e., residual doubt] likely would be ineffective and counterproductive"; and 3) "the attorneys' * * * failure to obtain the crucial file was the result of inattention, not reasoned strategic judgment."

Justice Kennedy, joined by Chief Justice Rehnquist and Justices Scalia and Thomas, dissented in *Rompilla*. He noted that defense counsel had no reason to think there was mitigating evidence in the case file:

> Today the Court brands two committed criminal defense attorneys as ineffective * * * because they did not look in an old case file and stumble upon something they had not set out to find. * * * To reach this result, the majority imposes on defense counsel a rigid requirement to review all documents in what it calls the "case file" of any prior conviction that the prosecution might rely on at trial.

Justice Kennedy argued that reviewing a case file is not always as easy as the majority implied and that the Court's decision might cause defense counsel in capital cases to divert resources from other tasks in order to examine case files:

> Case files often comprise numerous boxes. The file may contain, among other things, witness statements, forensic evidence, arrest reports, grand jury transcripts, testimony and exhibits relating to any pretrial suppression hearings, trial transcripts, trial exhibits, post-trial motions and presentence reports. Full review of even a single prior conviction case file could be time consuming, and many of the documents in a file are duplicative or irrelevant.

Fact-Intensive Review Under AEDPA of Claim of Ineffectiveness for Failure to Investigate and Present Mitigating Evidence at the Penalty Phase: Cullen v. Pinholster

In Cullen v. Pinholster, 563 U.S. 170 (2011), the Court considered whether defense counsel at the penalty phase of a capital trial failed to conduct a sufficient investigation into possible mitigating evidence. Pinholster and others robbed and murdered a drug dealer. He was convicted of murder in the guilt phase. He was represented by appointed attorneys Brainard and Dettmar.

At the penalty phase the prosecution produced eight witnesses, who testified about Pinholster's history of threatening and violent behavior, including resisting arrest and assaulting police officers and involvement with juvenile gangs. The prosecution also offered evidence of a substantial prison disciplinary record. Defense counsel called only Pinholster's mother, who gave an account of Pinholster's troubled childhood and adolescent years, discussed Pinholster's siblings, and described Pinholster as "a perfect gentleman at home." Defense counsel did not call a psychiatrist, though they had consulted Dr. John Stalberg at least six weeks earlier. Dr. Stalberg noted Pinholster's "psychopathic personality traits," diagnosed him with antisocial personality disorder, and concluded that he "was not under the influence of extreme mental or emotional disturbance" at the time of the murders.

In his habeas case, Pinholster argued that Brainard and Dettmar had failed to adequately investigate and present mitigating evidence, including evidence of mental disorders. Pinholster contended that they should have pursued and presented additional evidence about: his family members and their criminal, mental, and substance abuse problems; his schooling; and his medical and mental health history, including his epileptic disorder. To support his allegation that his trial counsel had "no reasonable tactical basis" for the approach they took, Pinholster relied on statements his counsel made at trial. Counsel had moved to exclude the government's aggravating evidence, arguing that the government had failed to provide pretrial notice under the state statute. Dettmar stated on the record that because the State did not provide notice, he was "not presently prepared to offer anything by way of mitigation." In response to the trial court's inquiry as to whether a continuance might be helpful, Dettmar noted that the only mitigation witness he could think of was Pinholster's mother. Additional time, Dettmar stated, would not "make a great deal of difference."

The state courts rejected Pinholster's ineffectiveness claim, but Pinholster was successful in the Ninth Circuit in his habeas claim. The Supreme Court, in an opinion by Justice Thomas, reversed. In evaluating the ineffective investigation claim, Justice Thomas first emphasized the extremely deferential standard of review to be applied to state court decisions concerning ineffectiveness on habeas review. Justice Thomas concluded that defense counsel made a reasoned professional judgment that the best way to serve their client would be to rely on the fact that they never got the required notice and hope the judge would bar the state from putting on their aggravation witnesses; defense counsel were prepared, if their motion was denied, to present only Pinholster's mother in the penalty phase in an effort to create sympathy and utilize the "family sympathy" mitigation defense that had been used by other California attorneys. Justice Thomas added that "[t]he record also shows that Pinholster's counsel confronted a challenging penalty phase with an unsympathetic client, which limited their feasible mitigation strategies." He concluded as follows:

> Given these impediments, it would have been a reasonable penalty-phase strategy to focus on evoking sympathy for Pinholster's mother. In fact, such a family sympathy defense is precisely how the State understood defense counsel's strategy. The prosecutor carefully opened her cross-examination of Pinholster's mother with, "I hope you understand I don't enjoy cross-examining a mother of anybody." And in her closing argument, the prosecutor attempted to undercut defense counsel's strategy by pointing out, "Even the most heinous person born, even Adolph Hitler[,] probably had a mother who loved him."

In short opinions, Justice Alito concurred in part and in the judgment, and Justice Breyer, concurred in part and dissented in part. Justice Sotomayor dissented in a lengthy opinion joined by Justices Ginsburg and Kagan. She stated as follows:

> The majority surmises that counsel decided on a strategy "to get the prosecution's aggravation witnesses excluded for lack of notice, and if that failed, to put on Pinholster's mother." This is the sort of post hoc rationalization for counsel's decisionmaking that contradicts the available evidence of counsel's actions that courts cannot indulge. The majority's explanation for counsel's conduct contradicts the best available evidence of counsel's actions: Dettmar's frank, contemporaneous statement to the trial judge that he "had not prepared any evidence by way of mitigation." The majority's conjecture that counsel had in fact prepared a mitigation defense, based primarily on isolated entries in counsel's billing records, requires it to assume that Dettmar was lying to the trial judge.

Application of Strickland—and AEDPA Standards of Deference—To Trial Counsel's Failure to Retain and Present a Forensic Expert: Harrington v. Richter

In Harrington v. Richter, 562 U.S. 86 (2011), the Court considered whether defense counsel had been ineffective for failure to investigate the possibility of presenting forensic expert testimony. The case was on habeas review from a state court decision finding no violation of the right to effective assistance of counsel.

Four men—Johnson, Richter, Branscombe and Klein—were smoking marijuana together. Klein and Johnson ended up each being shot twice. Johnson recovered; Klein died of his wounds. Johnson told investigators that he fell asleep and when he awoke he found Richter and Branscombe in his bedroom, at which point Branscombe shot him. Johnson heard more gunfire in the living room and the sound of his assailants leaving. He got up, found Klein bleeding on the living room couch, and called 911. A gun safe, a pistol, and $6,000 cash, all of which had been in the bedroom, were missing. Blood was found in the living room and the bedroom doorway, but investigators took only a few samples. Richter was tried for murder and related offenses. He contended that Branscombe was the shooter and that he was outside Johnson's house when he heard screams and gunshots and entered the house. A jury found him guilty.

In the state courts, Richter claimed his counsel was deficient for failing to present expert testimony on serology, pathology, and blood spatter patterns—testimony that, he argued, would disclose the source of the blood pool in the bedroom doorway. This, he contended, would bolster his theory of defense. The state courts denied relief but Harrington was successful in his habeas petition before the Ninth Circuit.

Justice Kennedy, writing for the Court, found that the Ninth Circuit erred by failing to give sufficient deference to the state court's determination that counsel was not ineffective for failing to pursue expert testimony on the blood found at the scene. As Justice Thomas had in *Pinholster*, Justice Kennedy noted that there was double deference at work: deference to the state court findings (reviewing whether "the state court's ruling on the claim being presented in federal court was so lacking in justification that there was an error well understood and comprehended in existing law beyond any possibility for fairminded disagreement") and also deference to counsel's strategic judgments.

Justice Kennedy found that defense counsel's decision not to consult blood evidence experts was well within the deferential standard of reasonableness. He noted that *Strickland* "permits counsel to make a reasonable decision that makes particular investigations unnecessary. It was at least arguable that a reasonable attorney could decide to forgo inquiry into the blood evidence in the circumstances here." Justice Kennedy concluded that "[f]rom the perspective of Richter's defense counsel when he was preparing Richter's defense, there were any number of hypothetical experts—specialists in psychiatry, psychology, ballistics, fingerprints, tire treads, physiology, or numerous other disciplines and subdisciplines—whose insight might possibly have been useful." He added that the court of appeals' view that blood evidence that might have shown the location of Klein was relevant to "the single most critical issue in the case" was not necessarily correct given that "[t]here were many factual differences between prosecution and defense versions of the events on the night of the shootings" and it was only "because forensic evidence has emerged concerning the source of the blood pool that the issue could with any plausibility be said to stand apart." Justice Kennedy wrote that "[r]eliance on 'the harsh light of hindsight' to cast doubt on a trial that took place now more than 15 years ago is precisely what *Strickland* and AEDPA seek to prevent."

He added that "[e]ven if it had been apparent that expert blood testimony could support Richter's defense, it would be reasonable to conclude that a competent attorney might elect not to use it out of concern that if it was inconsistent with Richter's version, it might undercut the defense. Justice Kennedy noted that defense counsel had reason to question the credibility of Richter's version of events.

Justice Kagan took no part in the decision. Justice Ginsburg wrote a short opinion concurring in the judgment.

The Duty to Investigate Mitigating Evidence in a Capital Case—The Relevance of ABA Standards: Bobby v. Van Hook

In Bobby v. Van Hook, 558 U.S. 4 (2009) (per curiam), the Court rejected the contention that counsel's duty to investigate under *Strickland* could be determined by ABA Guidelines for the Appointment and Performance of Defense Counsel in Death Penalty Cases (rev. ed. 2003). The Court described the ABA Guidelines on investigation of mitigating evidence as follows:

> [T]he Guidelines discuss the duty to investigate mitigating evidence in exhaustive detail, specifying what attorneys should look for, where to look, and when to begin. They include, for example, the requirement that counsel's investigation cover every period of the defendant's life from "the moment of conception," and that counsel contact "virtually everyone . . . who knew [the defendant] and his family" and obtain records "concerning not only the client, but also his parents, grandparents, siblings, and children."

The Court held that the Guidelines could not be read or applied to establish the minimum standard required by *Strickland*. It noted that *Strickland* stressed that

> American Bar Association standards and the like are only guides to what reasonableness means, not its definition. We have since regarded them as such. What we have said of state requirements is a fortiori true of standards set by private organizations: While States are free to impose whatever specific rules they see fit to ensure that criminal defendants are well represented, we have held that the Federal Constitution imposes one general requirement: that counsel make objectively reasonable choices.

On the question of whether Van Hook's lawyers in fact did an adequate job of investigation, the Court found that the lawyers presented witnesses, close family members, who related compelling evidence of Van Hook's horrible upbringing, his alcohol and drug abuse, and his five attempts to commit suicide. The Court faulted the Sixth Circuit for criticizing counsel for not interviewing more family members. It stated that "there comes a point at which evidence from more distant relatives can reasonably be expected to be only cumulative, and the search for it distractive from more important duties. * * * And given all the evidence they unearthed from those closest to Van Hook's upbringing and the experts who reviewed his history, it was not unreasonable for his counsel not to identify and interview every other living family member or every therapist who once treated his parents." Accordingly, the Court found that the Sixth Circuit erred in finding counsel's investigation to be inadequate.

Justice Alito wrote a short concurring opinion, stating that "[i]t is the responsibility of the courts to determine the nature of the work that a defense attorney must do in a capital case in order to meet the obligations imposed by the Constitution, and I see no reason why the ABA Guidelines should be given a privileged position in making that determination."

5. Assessing Prejudice

In *Strickland,* the Court held that lower courts may proceed directly to the prejudice prong if that would dispose of the case, and thereby avoid having to evaluate defense counsel's performance. Many lower courts have done so. See, e.g., United States ex rel. Cross v. DeRobertis, 811 F.2d 1008 (7th Cir.1987) (performance issue requires "a particularly subtle assessment," so court proceeds directly to prejudice prong and rejects the defendant's claim). If it is important for courts to provide guidance on effectiveness standards, is it acceptable for a court to proceed directly to the prejudice prong of *Strickland?*

The Strength of the Case Against the Defendant

Concerning the prejudice prong of *Strickland,* it is obvious that the defendant is more likely to prove prejudice if the prosecution's evidence is weak. For example, in Atkins v. Attorney General of Alabama, 932 F.2d 1430 (11th Cir.1991), counsel failed to object to the introduction of a fingerprint card offered to make a comparison between Atkins's fingerprints and those found at the scene of the crime. The card included a printed notation of a prior arrest that would not have been admissible. The court found that the failure to object constituted ineffectiveness, and that without the error there was a reasonable probability that the outcome of the trial would have been different. Atkins's fingerprints had been found at the scene, but the victim testified that Atkins had worked for him at the house two days prior to the crime; no other physical evidence tied Atkins to the crime. The court asserted that "the introduction of a previous arrest can have an almost irreversible impact on the minds of the jurors" and that the evidence against Atkins was "not overwhelming." See also Hart v. Gomez, 174 F.3d 1067 (9th Cir.1999) (where trial was basically a credibility determination between the defendant's witness and the complainant, defense counsel's failure to introduce record evidence corroborating the defense witness' account was ineffective and prejudicial); Ouber v. Guarino, 293 F.3d 19 (1st Cir. 2002) (error in stating that defendant would testify and then not calling defendant was prejudicial; case had been tried twice previously and resulted in hung jury each time, when defendant testified in those trials).

The Strength of Evidence Not Presented

Where the error is in *not* presenting evidence, the prejudice inquiry will focus on the strength and persuasiveness of that evidence, as well as the strength and persuasiveness of other evidence on the point that was offered by the defendant. Thus, in Rompilla v. Beard, supra, the evidence of the defendant's horrific childhood was found by the Court to be very strong proof of mitigation, especially as compared to the relatively weak evidence on mitigation that was actually presented.

Prejudice Assessed at Time of Review: Lockhart v. Fretwell

In Lockhart v. Fretwell, 506 U.S. 364 (1993), the Court made it clear that prejudice under *Strickland* is not always found simply because effective assistance would have changed the outcome. Fretwell was tried for capital murder in an Arkansas state court. His trial counsel at the sentencing phase failed to object to the use of an aggravating factor that was unconstitutional under then-existing precedent of the United States Court of Appeals for the Eighth Circuit. The jury relied solely on this aggravating factor and sentenced Fretwell to death. Subsequent to Fretwell's trial, and in a different case, the Eighth Circuit Court of Appeals overruled its precedent and held that it was constitutional to use the Arkansas aggravating factor that had been relied upon by the jury in Fretwell's trial. Fretwell argued on habeas that trial counsel had acted ineffectively in failing to object to the use of the aggravating factor that the Court of Appeals had originally (and as of the time of his trial) declared unconstitutional. He argued further that counsel's ineffectiveness prejudiced him, because if counsel had made the objection, the jury could not have used the aggravating factor at that time, and Fretwell could not have been sentenced to death.

Chief Justice Rehnquist wrote for seven Justices as the Court held that "counsel's failure to make an objection in a state criminal sentencing proceeding—an objection that would have been supported by a decision which subsequently was overruled—" could not constitute prejudice, because "the result of the sentencing proceeding * * * was rendered neither unreliable nor fundamentally unfair as a result of counsel's failure to make the objection." The Chief Justice reasoned that the right to effective assistance of counsel is intended to provide a fair trial. "Thus, an analysis focusing solely on mere outcome determination, without attention to whether the result of the proceeding was fundamentally unfair or unreliable, is defective. To set aside a conviction or sentence solely because the outcome would have been different but for counsel's error may grant the defendant a windfall to which the law does not entitle him."

The Chief Justice relied heavily on Nix v. Whiteside, 475 U.S. 157 (1986), where the Court held that the defendant was not prejudiced under *Strickland* when counsel refused to cooperate in presenting perjured testimony. Even though Whiteside might have swayed the jury with perjurious testimony, the Court in *Whiteside* held that "in judging prejudice and the likelihood of a different outcome, a defendant has no right to the luck of a lawless decisionmaker." The Chief Justice interpreted *Whiteside* as establishing that "sheer outcome determination" is not sufficient to make out a claim of prejudice under *Strickland*.

Fretwell argued that a finding of prejudice on the basis of case law arising after a defendant's trial would result in "hindsight" determination, and that this was inappropriate in light of *Strickland*, where the Court specifically precluded a hindsight-oriented review of counsel's conduct. But Chief Justice Rehnquist responded that the preclusion of hindsight-oriented review in *Strickland* was limited to the *performance prong* of the two-pronged test. He explained as follows:

> [F]rom the perspective of hindsight there is a natural tendency to speculate as to whether a different trial strategy might have been more successful. We adopted the rule of contemporary assessment of counsel's conduct [in *Strickland*] because a more rigid requirement "could dampen the ardor and impair the independence of defense counsel, discourage the acceptance of assigned cases, and undermine the trust between attorney and client." But the "prejudice" component of the *Strickland* test does not implicate these concerns. It focuses on the question whether counsel's deficient performance renders the result of the trial unreliable or the proceeding fundamentally unfair.

Justice O'Connor wrote a concurring opinion, describing the Court's holding as follows: "the court making the prejudice determination may not consider the effect of an objection it knows to be wholly meritless under current governing law, even if the objection might have been considered meritorious at the time of its omission." Justice Thomas also wrote a brief concurring opinion.

Justice Stevens, joined by Justice Blackmun, dissented and argued that "the Court today reaches the astonishing conclusion that deficient performance by counsel does not prejudice a defendant even when it results in the erroneous imposition of a death sentence," and "[t]he Court's aversion to windfalls seems to disappear * * * when the State is the favored recipient."

Prejudice Must Be Assessed by What Evidence—Including Damaging Evidence—Would Have Been Admitted Had Defense Counsel Acted Effectively: Wong v. Belmontes

In Wong v. Belmontes, 558 U.S. 15 (2009) (per curiam), the Court assumed that Belmontes's defense counsel had been ineffective at the capital phase of a state trial by failing to introduce some available mitigating evidence. But the Court held that in assessing prejudice, a reviewing court has to consider not only the evidence that counsel might have presented, but also the evidence that the government would introduce in response. Belmontes bludgeoned Steacy McConnell to death, striking her in the head 15 to 20 times with a steel dumbbell bar. At his capital trial the judge excluded evidence that Belmontes had murdered Jerry Howard execution-style, and had bragged about it. Evidence of the Howard murder was found not admissible, but the parties recognized that it might be admissible if Belmontes opened the door to it.

The Court found that some of the evidence that Belmontes argued should have been presented at the penalty phase might have been helpful for mitigation purposes but "would have triggered admission of the powerful Howard evidence in rebuttal. This evidence would have made a difference, but in the wrong direction for Belmontes." The Court gave the following example:

> [Belmontes] argues that the jury should have been told that he suffered an "extended bout with rheumatic fever," which led to "emotional instability, impulsivity, and impairment of the neurophysiological mechanisms for planning and reasoning." But the cold, calculated nature of the Howard murder and Belmontes' subsequent bragging about it would have served as a powerful counterpoint.

> The type of "more-evidence-is-better" approach advocated by Belmontes * * * might seem appealing—after all, what is there to lose? But here there was a lot to lose. A heavyhanded case to portray Belmontes in a positive light * * * would have invited the strongest possible evidence in rebuttal—the evidence that Belmontes was responsible for not one but two murders.

The Court criticized the Ninth Circuit, which found prejudice, for describing the aggravating evidence the State had as "scant." The Court observed this this description "misses *Strickland's* point that the reviewing court must consider all the evidence—the good and the bad—when evaluating prejudice. Here, the worst kind of bad evidence would have come in with the good."

Justice Stevens wrote a short concurring opinion.

Defense Counsel's Argument at the Penalty Phase of a Capital Trial, Stressing the Severity of the Crimes, Did Not Prejudice the Defendant: Smith v. Spisak

Justice Breyer wrote for the Court in Smith v. Spisak, 558 U.S. 139 (2010), as it reversed a grant of habeas corpus relief to a state defendant convicted of three murders and two attempted murders. The court of appeals had found ineffective assistance of counsel in the closing argument of Spisak's lawyer. Justice Breyer described that argument as follows:

> In his closing argument at the penalty phase, Spisak's counsel described Spisak's killings in some detail. He acknowledged that Spisak's admiration for Hitler inspired his crimes. He portrayed Spisak as "sick," "twisted," and "demented." And he said that Spisak was "never going to be any different." He then pointed out that all the experts had testified that Spisak suffered from some degree of mental illness. And, after a fairly lengthy and rambling disquisition about his own decisions about calling expert witnesses and preparing them, counsel argued that, even if Spisak was not legally insane so as to warrant a verdict of not guilty by reason of insanity, he nonetheless was sufficiently mentally ill to lessen his culpability to the point where he should not be executed. Counsel also told the jury that, when weighing Spisak's mental illness against the "substantial" aggravating factors present in the case, the jurors should draw on their own sense of "pride" for living in "a humane society" made up of "a humane people." That humanity, he said, required the jury to weigh the evidence "fairly" and to be "loyal to that oath" the jurors had taken to uphold the law.

Spisak argued that the closing argument was defective because: (1) It overly emphasized the gruesome nature of the killings; (2) it overly emphasized Spisak's threats to continue his crimes; (3) it understated the facts upon which the experts based their mental illness conclusions; (4) it said little or nothing about any other possible mitigating circumstance; and (5) it made no explicit request that the jury return a verdict against death. Justice Breyer responded that the Court would assume that the closing argument was inadequate, but that "[w]e nevertheless find no reasonable probability that a better closing argument without these defects would have made a significant difference." He went into detail about the evidence against Spisak and the testimony that he gave during the trial when called by defense counsel who was seeking to establish an insanity defense. Spisak described his crimes and testified that he would continue to commit such crimes if he could.

Justice Breyer gave three reasons why a better closing argument would not have mattered:

First, since the sentencing phase took place immediately following the conclusion of the guilt phase, the jurors had fresh in their minds the government's evidence regarding the killings—which included photographs of the dead bodies, images that formed the basis of defense counsel's vivid descriptions of the crimes—as well as Spisak's boastful and unrepentant confessions and his threats to commit further acts of violence. * * * Similarly fresh in the jurors' minds was the three defense experts' testimony that Spisak suffered from mental illness. The jury had heard the experts explain the specific facts upon which they had based their conclusions, as well as what they had learned of his family background and his struggles with gender identity. And the jury had heard the experts draw connections between his mental illness and the crimes. * * * Finally, in light of counsel's several appeals to the jurors' sense of humanity—he used the words "humane people" and "humane society" 10 times at various points in the argument—we cannot find that a more explicit or more elaborate appeal for mercy could have changed the result, either alone or together with the other circumstances just discussed. * * *

Justice Stevens, concurring in part and concurring in the judgment, wrote that "[i]t is difficult to convey how thoroughly egregious counsel's closing argument was without reproducing it in its entirety." He concluded that "counsel's argument grossly transgressed the bounds of what constitutionally competent counsel would have done in a similar situation," but "[i]n my judgment even the most skillful of closing arguments—even one befitting Clarence Darrow—would not have created a reasonable probability of a different outcome in this case."

Calling an Expert Who Testifies at the Capital Phase That the Defendant is Dangerous Because He Is Black: Buck v. Davis

In Buck v. Davis, 137 S.Ct. 759 (2017), the future dangerousness of the defendant was contested by the parties in the penalty phase of Buck's trial for capital murder. The defense counsel called a psychologist, who testified that Buck was unlikely to act violently in the future, because his violent acts were triggered by romantic relationships with women, which presumably he wouldn't have when imprisoned for life. But defense counsel also asked the expert about the assertion in his report regarding "statistical factors"—including an assertion that a black person (like Buck) is more likely to be dangerous than a white person. The expert then testified to this belief on both direct and cross-examination. Buck was sentenced to death.

The Supreme Court vacated the death sentence in an opinion by Chief Justice Roberts, on the ground that defense counsel's decision to invite the defense expert to testify about a supposed statistical connection between race and future dangerousness was ineffective and prejudicial. The Chief

Justice easily found that the racial reference was objectively unreasonable and, as to the more difficult issue of prejudice, he observed that the state had to prove future dangerousness beyond a reasonable doubt, the brutality of the crime and lack of remorse did not necessarily prove that Buck would be dangerous in the future, and the most important evidence about future dangerousness came improperly from the defendant's expert.

Justice Thomas dissented, arguing that evidence of the heinousness of the crime and the defendant's clear lack of remorse were sufficient to support the jury's finding of future dangerousness.

"Significant" Prejudice Requirement Rejected: Glover v. United States

In Glover v. United States, 531 U.S. 198 (2001), Glover argued that his trial counsel was ineffective for failing to challenge a sentence that was allegedly set in violation of the Federal Sentencing Guidelines. The Court of Appeals assumed that counsel was ineffective, but denied relief on the ground that any ineffectiveness did not prejudice Glover within the meaning of *Strickland*. The Court of Appeals read the Supreme Court cases on prejudice to require a finding of "significant" prejudice. In this case, counsel's ineffectiveness resulted in an increased sentence somewhere between 6 and 21 months; the Court of Appeals did not view this increase as "significant".

The Supreme Court unanimously reversed in an opinion by Justice Kennedy. The Court assumed, as did the lower court, that counsel had been ineffective. Justice Kennedy criticized the lower court's analysis of prejudice in the following passage:

> Authority does not suggest that a minimal amount of additional time in prison cannot constitute prejudice. Quite to the contrary, our jurisprudence suggests that any amount of actual jail time has Sixth Amendment significance.
>
> The Seventh Circuit's rule is not well considered in any event, because there is no obvious dividing line by which to measure how much longer a sentence must be for the increase to constitute substantial prejudice.

Prejudice Due to Ineffectiveness on Appeal

How does the prejudice prong of *Strickland* apply to claims of ineffective assistance of counsel on appeal? In Lozada v. Deeds, 498 U.S. 430 (1991), the defendant alleged that his counsel failed to inform him of his right to appeal or of the procedures and time limitations for an appeal, and that counsel had misled him into thinking that his case had been forwarded to the public defender's office. The district court dismissed

Lozada's habeas corpus petition on the ground that Lozada had not indicated what issues he would have raised on appeal and had not demonstrated that the appeal might have succeeded. Both the district court and the court of appeals denied a certificate of probable cause to appeal the denial of habeas relief under 28 U.S.C. § 2253. The Supreme Court in a per curiam opinion held that the certificate of probable cause should have been granted. The standard for granting such a certificate is that a court "could resolve the issues" in petitioner's favor. The Court held that Lozada had met that standard, because the issue of prejudice "could be resolved in a different manner than the one followed by the District Court."

Subsequently, in Roe v. Flores-Ortega, 528 U.S. 470 (2000), the Court considered the circumstances under which defense counsel's failure to file a notice of appeal would be prejudicial within the meaning of *Strickland*. The Court declared that "to show prejudice in these circumstances, a defendant must demonstrate that there is a reasonable probability that, but for counsel's deficient failure to consult with him about an appeal, he would have timely appealed." The defendant did not have to show that the appeal would be likely to result in a reversal of the conviction—though obviously the merits of an appeal bear somewhat on whether the defendant would have pursued it.

6.   Per Se Ineffectiveness and Prejudice

In United States v. Cronic, 466 U.S. 648 (1984), the Court recognized that there might be some unusual, egregious, situations in which counsel's ineffectiveness and prejudice could be presumed and therefore reversal would be automatic. But the Court did not find such an extreme situation presented under the facts. Justice Stevens, writing for the Court, set forth the facts as follows:

> Respondent and two associates were indicted on mail fraud charges involving the transfer of over $9,400,000 in checks between banks in Tampa, Florida, and Norman, Oklahoma * * *. Shortly before the scheduled trial date, respondent's retained counsel withdrew. The court appointed a young lawyer with a real estate practice to represent respondent, but allowed him only 25 days for pretrial preparation, even though it had taken the Government over four and one-half years to investigate the case and it had reviewed thousands of documents during that investigation. The two codefendants agreed to testify for the Government; respondent was convicted on 11 of the 13 counts in the indictment and received a 25-year sentence.

Cronic argued that under these circumstances there was no way that counsel could have been effective, and therefore ineffectiveness and prejudice should be presumed without having to look at the record. Justice Stevens considered the possibility of automatic reversal:

[B]ecause we presume that the lawyer is competent to provide the guiding hand that the defendant needs, the burden rests on the accused to demonstrate a constitutional violation. There are, however, circumstances that are so likely to prejudice the accused that the cost of litigating their effect in a particular case is unjustified.

Most obvious, of course, is the complete denial of counsel. The presumption that counsel's assistance is essential requires us to conclude that a trial is unfair if the accused is denied counsel at a critical stage of his trial. Similarly, if counsel entirely fails to subject the prosecution's case to meaningful adversarial testing, then there has been a denial of Sixth Amendment rights that makes the adversary process itself presumptively unreliable. * * *

Circumstances of that magnitude may be present on some occasions when although counsel is available to assist the accused during trial, the likelihood that any lawyer, even a fully competent one, could provide effective assistance is so small that a presumption of prejudice is appropriate without inquiry into the actual conduct of the trial. Powell v. Alabama, 287 U.S. 45 (1932), [set forth in Chapter 5] was such a case.

* * *

But every refusal to postpone a criminal trial will not give rise to such a presumption. * * *

Justice Stevens found nothing so extreme in *Cronic* that would justify an automatic rule that counsel could not have been effective.

Neither the period of time that the Government spent investigating the case, nor the number of documents that its agents reviewed during that investigation, is necessarily relevant to the question whether a competent lawyer could prepare to defend the case in 25 days. * * * In this case, the time devoted by the Government to the assembly, organization, and summarization of the thousands of written records * * * simplified the work of defense counsel in identifying and understanding the basic character of the defendants' scheme. * * *

* * * [T]he only *bona fide* jury issue open to competent defense counsel on these facts was whether respondent acted with intent to defraud. When there is no reason to dispute the underlying historical facts, the period of 25 days to consider the question whether those facts justify an inference of criminal intent is not so short that it even arguably justifies a presumption that no lawyer could provide the respondent with the effective assistance of counsel required by the Constitution.

That conclusion is not undermined by the fact that respondent's lawyer was young, that his principal practice was in real estate, or that this was his first jury trial. Every experienced criminal defense attorney once tried his first criminal case. Moreover, a lawyer's experience with real estate transactions might be more useful in preparing to try a criminal case involving financial transactions than would prior experience in handling, for example, armed robbery prosecutions. * * *

The Court in *Cronic* remanded for a determination of whether defense counsel's performance was in fact ineffective and prejudicial under the *Strickland* standards. Justice Marshall concurred in the judgment.

Note that the Court in *Cronic* did not hold that Cronic had received effective assistance of counsel. Rather, it rejected the per se rule of reversal applied by the lower court. On remand in *Cronic,* the court of appeals reviewed counsel's actual performance and held that it was ineffective and that Cronic was prejudiced. United States v. Cronic, 839 F.2d 1401 (10th Cir.1988). The court found that defense counsel ignored the issues of the defendant's intent and good faith, which were, as the Supreme Court had recognized, the only issues of dispute in the case. Cronic's attorney testified at the hearing on ineffectiveness that the defense he used was one seeking to "cloud the issues." The court held that "this cannot be a satisfactory explanation under *Strickland* or any other authority for a selection of a defense." The court also noted that defense counsel failed to object to evidence due to a misunderstanding of the statute under which Cronic was tried.

Denial of "Counsel" Within the Meaning of the Sixth Amendment

Cronic holds that in some limited cases, ineffectiveness and prejudice will be presumed without having to investigate counsel's performance. But it is clear that this rule of per se reversal is very narrow. If it did not apply under the facts of *Cronic,* where could it apply? Consider Solina v. United States, 709 F.2d 160 (2d Cir.1983), where the court concluded that per se reversal was required because defendant's trial counsel had held himself out as an attorney, but had never passed a bar exam. The evidence against Solina was overwhelming, and Solina could point to no error of judgment on the part of his counsel at trial. Yet the court reasoned as follows:

The problem of representation by [one not admitted to the bar] is not simply one of competence * * * but that he was engaging in a crime. Such a person cannot be wholly free from fear of what might happen if a vigorous defense should lead the prosecutor or the trial judge to inquire into his background and discover his lack of credentials.

The court found that Solina had been denied "counsel," as that term is used in the Sixth Amendment, and that this total denial of counsel was per se prejudicial, as it was in Gideon v. Wainwright.

Solina preceded *Cronic,* but it has been followed by lower courts even after *Cronic.* See, e.g., United States v. Novak, 903 F.2d 883 (2d Cir.1990) (per se reversal where defense counsel had obtained admission to the bar by fraud). Compare Reese v. Peters, 926 F.2d 668 (7th Cir.1991) (*Solina* distinguished; no per se reversal where attorney's license had been suspended for failure to pay dues: "persons who obtain credentials by fraud, are classes apart from persons who satisfied the court of their legal skills but later ran afoul of some technical legal rule."). See also Pilchak v. Camper, 935 F.2d 145 (8th Cir.1991) (per se reversal where defense counsel was suffering from Alzheimer's disease at the time of trial).

Sleeping Defense Counsel

In Tippins v. Walker, 77 F.3d 682 (2d Cir.1996), Tippins argued for per se reversal of his conviction on the ground that his trial counsel slept through major portions of the trial. Testimony at the ineffectiveness hearing from the trial judge, court reporter, prosecutor, jurors and other defendants and defense counsel corroborated Tippins' account. Tippins' counsel slept every day of the trial; he could often be heard snoring; he slept through the testimony of several critical witnesses; and he was admonished by the trial judge for sleeping throughout the trial. The court held that this was a sufficient showing to trigger per se reversal under *Cronic.* It was careful to state, however, that not every instance of apparent sleeping on the part of defense counsel would be ineffective or cause for reversal. But the facts of this case were special:

> [T]he appearance of "sleeping" may cover a range of behavior. Lawyers may sometimes affect a drowsy or bored look to downplay an adversary's presentation of evidence. We are also mindful * * * that a per se rule would give unscrupulous attorneys a delayed-trigger weapon to be sprung at some later strategic phase of the proceeding if events developed very badly for a defendant. However, [the government] has not contended that Tirelli's sleeping was a charade or a tactical device. And it would be difficult for [the government] to make that claim, given the testimony that the trial prosecutor acknowledged his adversary's snoring by exchanging knowing looks with the court reporter. In any event, trial judges are well-positioned to detect, guard against, and penalize such a tactical abuse of the right to counsel.

Absence of Counsel for Ten Minutes During Presentation of Evidence Unrelated to the Defendant Is Not Clearly Per Se Prejudicial Under Cronic: Woods v. Donald

In Woods v. Donald, 135 S.Ct. 1372 (2015) (per curiam), lower federal courts on habeas held that Donald was denied his right to effective assistance of counsel when his attorney was absent for approximately ten minutes during Donald's joint trial with two other defendants. The Supreme Court disagreed. Donald's defense counsel absented himself from the government's presentation of a chart chronicling phone calls that did not include Donald. Donald's attorney indicated before a recess that he had no "dog in this race" when the defense counsel for the other defendants objected to the government's introduction of the chart. Donald's lawyer returned after the trial was underway for approximately 10 minutes and the trial judge informed him that the focus had been on the chart. Donald's lawyer reiterated that he had no interest in that subject.

The Supreme Court stated it had "never addressed whether the rule announced in Cronic applies to testimony regarding codefendants' actions." It also concluded that "[w]ithin the contours of Cronic, a fair-minded jurist could conclude that a presumption of prejudice is not warranted by counsel's short absence during testimony about other defendants where that testimony was irrelevant to the defendant's theory of the case." The Court emphasized that its ruling was "only in the narrow context of federal habeas review" and expressed no view on the underlying Sixth Amendment question.

Counsel Present Only by Speakerphone: Wright v. Van Patten

In Wright v. Van Patten, 552 U.S. 120 (2008) (per curiam), a habeas petitioner argued that he was per se prejudiced when his counsel participated at his plea hearing only through a speakerphone. He contended that this amounted to a virtual absence of counsel and therefore counsel was automatically ineffective under Cronic. The government argued that counsel's effectiveness should be evaluated under the Strickland standard—and under that standard all parties agreed that the defendant could not prove ineffectiveness and prejudice. The state court had held that Strickland and not Cronic was applicable.

The Supreme Court held that "[n]o decision of this Court, * * * squarely addresses the issue in this case, or clearly establishes that Cronic should replace Strickland in this novel factual context," and it could not be said that the state court unreasonably applied clearly established Federal law—which is the standard for relief in habeas cases. Justice Stevens, the author of Cronic, reluctantly concurred in the judgment. He rued the fact that his opinion for the Court in Cronic did not make it clear that the physical presence of counsel at trial or a guilty plea hearing was critical.

Application of Per Se Prejudice Standard
Not Warranted: Bell v. Cone

In Bell v. Cone, 535 U.S. 685 (2002), the Court found that defense counsel in a capital case did not perform so poorly as to justify a ruling of *per se* ineffectiveness and prejudice under *Cronic*. Chief Justice Rehnquist wrote the opinion for the Court. Cone was sentenced to death for murdering a couple after a two-day "crime rampage." He claimed, and the Court of Appeals found, that defense counsel was per se ineffective during the capital phase of the trial. The Chief Justice noted that the defense during the guilt phase was insanity and that defense counsel presented testimony from experts to support the defense, as well as testimony from witnesses that the defendant had suffered from drug use, trauma from his service in Vietnam, and depression from the deaths of his father and fiancée. The Chief Justice then observed that during the capital phase defense counsel called the jury's attention to the mitigating evidence already presented at the guilt phase of the trial and suggested that Cone was under the influence of extreme mental disturbance or duress, that he was an addict whose drug and other problems stemmed from the stress of his military service, and that he felt remorse.

The Supreme Court found no justification for per se reversal for ineffectiveness. Chief Justice Rehnquist stated that *Strickland*, and not *Cronic*, was the relevant case for assessing counsel's performance in this case and that in this habeas case there was no showing of a clear case of ineffectiveness. The Chief Justice observed that defense counsel had offered substantial mitigating evidence in the guilt phase of the case and, once the junior prosecutor gave a low key closing argument, defense counsel might well have decided not to risk repeating the opening statement and giving the lead prosecutor, who was very effective, the chance to brand the defendant as a cold-blooded killer immediately before jury deliberations.

Justice Stevens dissented in *Cone*. He noted that counsel, subsequent to trial, was diagnosed with a mental illness that rendered him unfit to practice law and that apparently led to his suicide. Justice Stevens argued that counsel completely failed to present a defense at the capital phase, and therefore *Cronic's* per se reversal rule applied.

7. The Right to Effective Assistance of Counsel at the Guilty Plea Stage

More than 90% of criminal prosecutions end up in guilty pleas, so it is not surprising that the right to effective assistance of counsel has been applied to the guilty plea phase. See Hill v. Lockhart, 474 U.S. 52 (1985) (claims of ineffectiveness at the guilty plea stage governed by the *Strickland* two-pronged test). In the following case, the Court finds that counsel can be ineffective by failing to provide information that would be critical to a defendant's decision to accept or reject a plea offer.

The Duty to Inform the Defendant About Immigration Consequences of a Guilty Plea: Padilla v. Kentucky

PADILLA V. KENTUCKY

Supreme Court of the United States, 2010.
559 U.S. 356.

JUSTICE STEVENS delivered the opinion of the Court.

Petitioner Jose Padilla, a native of Honduras, has been a lawful permanent resident of the United States for more than 40 years. Padilla served this Nation with honor as a member of the U.S. Armed Forces during the Vietnam War. He now faces deportation after pleading guilty to the transportation of a large amount of marijuana in his tractor-trailer in the Commonwealth of Kentucky.

In this postconviction proceeding, Padilla claims that his counsel not only failed to advise him of this consequence prior to his entering the plea, but also told him that he "did not have to worry about immigration status since he had been in the country so long." Padilla relied on his counsel's erroneous advice when he pleaded guilty to the drug charges that made his deportation virtually mandatory. He alleges that he would have insisted on going to trial if he had not received incorrect advice from his attorney.

Assuming the truth of his allegations, the Supreme Court of Kentucky denied Padilla postconviction relief without the benefit of an evidentiary hearing. The court held that the Sixth Amendment's guarantee of effective assistance of counsel does not protect a criminal defendant from erroneous advice about deportation because it is merely a "collateral" consequence of his conviction. * * *

We granted certiorari to decide whether, as a matter of federal law, Padilla's counsel had an obligation to advise him that the offense to which he was pleading guilty would result in his removal from this country. We agree with Padilla that constitutionally competent counsel would have advised him that his conviction for drug distribution made him subject to automatic deportation. Whether he is entitled to relief depends on whether he has been prejudiced, a matter that we do not address.

* * *

The landscape of federal immigration law has changed dramatically over the last 90 years. While once there was only a narrow class of deportable offenses and judges wielded broad discretionary authority to prevent deportation, immigration reforms over time have expanded the class of deportable offenses and limited the authority of judges to alleviate the harsh consequences of deportation. The drastic measure of deportation or removal, is now virtually inevitable for a vast number of noncitizens convicted of crimes.

* * *

* * * Under contemporary law, if a noncitizen has committed a removable offense * * * his removal is practically inevitable * * * .

* * * These changes confirm our view that, as a matter of federal law, deportation is an integral part—indeed, sometimes the most important part—of the penalty that may be imposed on noncitizen defendants who plead guilty to specified crimes.

* * * The Supreme Court of Kentucky rejected Padilla's ineffectiveness claim on the ground that the advice he sought about the risk of deportation concerned only collateral matters, i.e., those matters not within the sentencing authority of the state trial court. * * * We, however, have never applied a distinction between direct and collateral consequences to define the scope of constitutionally "reasonable professional assistance" required under *Strickland.*

* * *

Deportation as a consequence of a criminal conviction is, because of its close connection to the criminal process, uniquely difficult to classify as either a direct or a collateral consequence. The collateral versus direct distinction is thus ill-suited to evaluating a *Strickland* claim concerning the specific risk of deportation. We conclude that advice regarding deportation is not categorically removed from the ambit of the Sixth Amendment right to counsel. *Strickland* applies to Padilla's claim.

* * *

In the instant case, the terms of the relevant immigration statute are succinct, clear, and explicit in defining the removal consequence for Padilla's conviction. Padilla's counsel could have easily determined that his plea would make him eligible for deportation simply from reading the text of the statute, which addresses not some broad classification of crimes but specifically commands removal for all controlled substances convictions except for the most trivial of marijuana possession offenses. Instead, Padilla's counsel provided him false assurance that his conviction would not result in his removal from this country. This is not a hard case in which to find deficiency * * *.

Immigration law can be complex, and it is a legal specialty of its own. * * * When the law is not succinct and straightforward * * * a criminal defense attorney need do no more than advise a noncitizen client that pending criminal charges may carry a risk of adverse immigration consequences. But when the deportation consequence is truly clear, as it was in this case, the duty to give correct advice is equally clear.

Accepting his allegations as true, Padilla has sufficiently alleged constitutional deficiency to satisfy the first prong of *Strickland*. * * *

We have given serious consideration to the concerns that the Solicitor General, respondent, and amici have stressed regarding the importance of protecting the finality of convictions obtained through guilty pleas. * * *

* * *

[A]lthough we must be especially careful about recognizing new grounds for attacking the validity of guilty pleas, in the 25 years since we first applied *Strickland* to claims of ineffective assistance at the plea stage, practice has shown that pleas are less frequently the subject of collateral challenges than convictions obtained after a trial. Pleas account for nearly 95% of all criminal convictions. But they account for only approximately 30% of the habeas petitions filed. The nature of relief secured by a successful collateral challenge to a guilty plea—an opportunity to withdraw the plea and proceed to trial—imposes its own significant limiting principle: Those who collaterally attack their guilty pleas lose the benefit of the bargain obtained as a result of the plea. Thus, a different calculus informs whether it is wise to challenge a guilty plea in a habeas proceeding because, ultimately, the challenge may result in a less favorable outcome for the defendant, whereas a collateral challenge to a conviction obtained after a jury trial has no similar downside potential.

Finally, informed consideration of possible deportation can only benefit both the State and noncitizen defendants during the plea-bargaining process. By bringing deportation consequences into this process, the defense and prosecution may well be able to reach agreements that better satisfy the interests of both parties. * * * Counsel who possess the most rudimentary understanding of the deportation consequences of a particular criminal offense may be able to plea bargain creatively with the prosecutor in order to craft a conviction and sentence that reduce the likelihood of deportation, as by avoiding a conviction for an offense that automatically triggers the removal consequence. At the same time, the threat of deportation may provide the defendant with a powerful incentive to plead guilty to an offense that does not mandate that penalty in exchange for a dismissal of a charge that does.

* * *

JUSTICE ALITO, with whom THE CHIEF JUSTICE joins, concurring in the judgment.

I concur in the judgment because a criminal defense attorney fails to provide effective assistance * * * if the attorney misleads a noncitizen client regarding the removal consequences of a conviction. In my view, such an attorney must (1) refrain from unreasonably providing incorrect advice and (2) advise the defendant that a criminal conviction may have adverse immigration consequences and that, if the alien wants advice on this issue, the alien should consult an immigration attorney.

* * *

[A] criminal defense attorney should not be required to provide advice on immigration law, a complex specialty that generally lies outside the scope of a criminal defense attorney's expertise. * * * [A]n alien defendant's Sixth Amendment right to counsel is satisfied if defense counsel advises the client that a conviction may have immigration consequences, that immigration law is a specialized field, that the attorney is not an immigration lawyer, and that the client should consult an immigration specialist if the client wants advice on that subject.

JUSTICE SCALIA, with whom JUSTICE THOMAS joins, dissenting.

* * *

There is no basis in text or in principle to extend the constitutionally required advice regarding guilty pleas beyond those matters germane to the criminal prosecution at hand—to wit, the sentence that the plea will produce, the higher sentence that conviction after trial might entail, and the chances of such a conviction. * * * Because the subject of the misadvice here was not the prosecution for which Jose Padilla was entitled to effective assistance of counsel, the Sixth Amendment has no application.

* * *

The Court's holding prevents legislation that could solve the problems addressed by today's opinions in a more precise and targeted fashion. * * *

Application of Strickland and AEDPA Review Standards to Counsel's Conduct When a Guilty Plea Is Entered Early in the Proceedings: Premo v. Moore

Justice Kennedy wrote for the Court in Premo v. Moore, 562 U.S. 115 (2011), as it considered the adequacy of representation in providing an assessment of a plea bargain without first seeking suppression of a confession assumed to have been improperly obtained. Moore and two others essentially kidnapped and murdered a man. Moore and one accomplice told Moore's brother and the accomplice's girlfriend about the crimes and later repeated their accounts during police interrogation. On the advice of counsel Moore agreed to plead no contest to felony murder in exchange for a sentence of 300 months, the minimum sentence allowed by law for the offense.

Moore later filed for postconviction relief in an Oregon state court, alleging that he had been denied his right to effective assistance of counsel because his lawyer had not filed a motion to suppress his confession to police in advance of the lawyer's advice that Moore considered before accepting the plea offer. The Oregon court held a hearing and concluded that a "motion to suppress would have been fruitless" in light of the other admissible confession by Moore, to which two witnesses could testify.

Counsel added at the hearing that he had made Moore aware of the possibility of being charged with aggravated murder, which carried a potential death sentence, as well as the possibility of a sentence of life imprisonment without parole. The intense and serious abuse to the victim before the shooting might well have led the State to insist on a strong response. In light of these facts the Oregon court concluded Moore had not established ineffective assistance of counsel under *Strickland*.

A federal district court denied habeas relief but the Ninth Circuit found that the state court's conclusion that counsel's action did not constitute ineffective assistance was an unreasonable application of clearly established law in light of *Strickland*. Justice Kennedy's opinion for the Court disagreed with the Ninth Circuit. He concluded that the Court of Appeals "was wrong to accord scant deference to counsel's judgment, and doubly wrong to conclude it would have been unreasonable to find that the defense attorney qualified as counsel for Sixth Amendment purposes."

Justice Kennedy noted that "[i]n the case of an early plea, neither the prosecution nor the defense may know with much certainty what course the case may take" so that "each side, of necessity, risks consequences that may arise from contingencies or circumstances yet unperceived." He reasoned that the prosecutors faced the cost of litigation and the risk of trying their case without Moore's confession to the police, which meant that Moore's counsel could reasonably believe that a swift plea bargain would allow Moore to take advantage of the State's aversion to these hazards." In the final analysis, he concluded that "Moore's counsel made a reasonable choice to opt for a quick plea bargain," and "[a]t the very least, the state court would not have been unreasonable to so conclude." With respect to prejudice, Justice Kennedy found that "[d]eference to the state court's prejudice determination is all the more significant in light of the uncertainty inherent in plea negotiations * * *." He explained that "[h]indsight and second guesses are also inappropriate, and often more so, where a plea has been entered without a full trial or, as in this case, even before the prosecution decided on the charges."

Justice Ginsburg concurred in the judgment on the ground that "[a]s Moore's counsel confirmed at oral argument, Moore never declared that, better informed, he would have resisted the plea bargain and opted for trial."

Justice Kagan took no part in the consideration or decision of this case.

Assessing Prejudice Where the Defendant, Through Counsel's Ineffectiveness, Is Not Informed of a Plea Bargain and Accepts a Less Favorable One: Missouri v. Frye

In the 2011 Term the Court decided two companion cases to determine whether and how a defendant could establish *Strickland* prejudice for bad (or no) advice given by his lawyer at the plea bargaining stage. The cases cover two fact situations: one where the defendant took a bad plea bargain (because he didn't know a better one was out there) and the other where the defendant rejected a good plea bargain on counsel's bad advice and was convicted at trial.

MISSOURI V. FRYE

Supreme Court of the United States, 2012.
566 U.S. 134.

JUSTICE KENNEDY delivered the opinion of the Court.

* * * This case arises in the context of claimed ineffective assistance that led to the lapse of a prosecution offer of a plea bargain, a proposal that offered terms more lenient than the terms of the guilty plea entered later. The initial question is whether the constitutional right to counsel extends to the negotiation and consideration of plea offers that lapse or are rejected. If there is a right to effective assistance with respect to those offers, a further question is what a defendant must demonstrate in order to show that prejudice resulted from counsel's deficient performance. * * *

In August 2007, Respondent Galin Frye was charged with driving with a revoked license. Frye had been convicted for that offense on three other occasions, so the State of Missouri charged him with a class D felony, which carries a maximum term of imprisonment of four years.

On November 15, 2007, the prosecutor sent a letter to Frye's counsel offering a choice of two plea bargains. The prosecutor first offered to recommend a 3-year sentence if there was a guilty plea to the felony charge, without a recommendation regarding probation but with a recommendation that Frye serve 10 days in jail as so-called "shock" time. The second offer was to reduce the charge to a misdemeanor and, if Frye pleaded guilty to it, to recommend a 90-day sentence. The misdemeanor charge of driving with a revoked license carries a maximum term of imprisonment of one year. The letter stated both offers would expire on December 28. Frye's attorney did not advise Frye that the offers had been made.

Frye's preliminary hearing was scheduled for January 4, 2008. On December 30, 2007, less than a week before the hearing, Frye was again arrested for driving with a revoked license. [Frye pleaded guilty to the August charge.] There was no underlying plea agreement. The state trial court accepted Frye's guilty plea. The prosecutor recommended a 3-year sentence, made no recommendation regarding probation, and requested 10 days shock time in jail. The trial judge sentenced Frye to three years in prison.

Frye filed for postconviction relief in state court. He alleged his counsel's failure to inform him of the prosecution's plea offer denied him the effective assistance of counsel. At an evidentiary hearing, Frye testified he would have entered a guilty plea to the misdemeanor had he known about the offer.

[The Missouri appellate court found that Frye had established ineffectiveness and prejudice. To implement a remedy, the Missouri court held that Frye's guilty plea would be withdrawn, and gave Frye the option to either insist on a trial or to plead guilty to any offense the prosecutor deemed appropriate to charge.]

* * *

With respect to the right to effective counsel in plea negotiations, a proper beginning point is to discuss two cases from this Court considering the role of counsel in advising a client about a plea offer and an ensuing guilty plea: Hill v. Lockhart, 474 U.S. 52 (1985), and Padilla v. Kentucky.

* * * In the case now before the Court the State * * * points out that the legal question presented is different from that in *Hill* and *Padilla*. In those cases the claim was that the prisoner's plea of guilty was invalid because counsel had provided incorrect advice pertinent to the plea. In the instant case, by contrast, the guilty plea that was accepted, and the plea proceedings concerning it in court, were all based on accurate advice and information from counsel. * * *

To give further support to its contention that the instant case is in a category different from what the Court considered in *Hill* and *Padilla*, the State urges that there is no right to a plea offer or a plea bargain in any event. It claims Frye therefore was not deprived of any legal benefit to which he was entitled. Under this view, any wrongful or mistaken action of counsel with respect to earlier plea offers is beside the point.

* * * The State's contentions are neither illogical nor without some persuasive force, yet they do not suffice to overcome a simple reality. Ninety-seven percent of federal convictions and ninety-four percent of state convictions are the result of guilty pleas. The reality is that plea bargains have become so central to the administration of the criminal justice system that defense counsel have responsibilities in the plea bargain process, responsibilities that must be met to render the adequate assistance of counsel that the Sixth Amendment requires in the criminal process at critical stages. Because ours is for the most part a system of pleas, not a system of trials, it is insufficient simply to point to the guarantee of a fair trial as a backstop that inoculates any errors in the pretrial process. * * * In today's criminal justice system, therefore, the negotiation of a plea bargain, rather than the unfolding of a trial, is almost always the critical point for a defendant.

* * *

The inquiry then becomes how to define the duty and responsibilities of defense counsel in the plea bargain process. This is a difficult question. The art of negotiation is at least as nuanced as the art of trial advocacy and it presents questions farther removed from immediate judicial supervision. * * * The alternative courses and tactics in negotiation are so individual that it may be neither prudent nor practicable to try to elaborate or define detailed standards for the proper discharge of defense counsel's participation in the process.

This case presents neither the necessity nor the occasion to define the duties of defense counsel in those respects, however. Here the question is whether defense counsel has the duty to communicate the terms of a formal offer to accept a plea on terms and conditions that may result in a lesser sentence, a conviction on lesser charges, or both.

This Court now holds that, as a general rule, defense counsel has the duty to communicate formal offers from the prosecution to accept a plea on terms and conditions that may be favorable to the accused. Any exceptions to that rule need not be explored here, for the offer was a formal one with a fixed expiration date. When defense counsel allowed the offer to expire without advising the defendant or allowing him to consider it, defense counsel did not render the effective assistance the Constitution requires.

* * *

Here defense counsel did not communicate the formal offers to the defendant. As a result of that deficient performance, the offers lapsed. Under *Strickland*, the question then becomes what, if any, prejudice resulted from the breach of duty.

* * *

* * * In cases where a defendant complains that ineffective assistance led him to accept a plea offer as opposed to proceeding to trial, the defendant will have to show "a reasonable probability that, but for counsel's errors, he would not have pleaded guilty and would have insisted on going to trial." * * * In a case, such as this, where a defendant pleads guilty to less favorable terms and claims that ineffective assistance of counsel caused him to miss out on a more favorable earlier plea offer, *Strickland*'s inquiry into whether "the result of the proceeding would have been different" requires looking not at whether the defendant would have proceeded to trial absent ineffective assistance but whether he would have accepted the offer to plead pursuant to the terms earlier proposed.

In order to complete a showing of *Strickland* prejudice, defendants who have shown a reasonable probability they would have accepted the earlier plea offer must also show that, if the prosecution had the discretion to cancel it or if the trial court had the discretion to refuse to accept it, there is a reasonable probability that neither the prosecution nor the trial court would have prevented the offer from being accepted or implemented. This further showing is of particular importance because a defendant has no right to be offered a plea, nor a federal right that the judge accept it. * * *

These standards must be applied to the instant case. * * * On this record, it is evident that Frye's attorney did not make a meaningful attempt to inform the defendant of a written plea offer before the offer expired. The Missouri Court of Appeals was correct that "counsel's representation fell below an objective standard of reasonableness."

* * *

There appears to be a reasonable probability Frye would have accepted the prosecutor's original offer of a plea bargain if the offer had been communicated to him, because he pleaded guilty to a more serious charge, with no promise of a sentencing recommendation from the prosecutor. It may be that in some cases defendants must show more than just a guilty plea to a charge or sentence harsher than the original offer. For example, revelations between plea offers about the strength of the prosecution's case may make a late decision to plead guilty insufficient to demonstrate, without further evidence, that the defendant would have pleaded guilty to an earlier, more generous plea offer if his counsel had reported it to him. Here, however, that is not the case. * * *

The Court of Appeals failed, however, to require Frye to show that the first plea offer, if accepted by Frye, would have been adhered to by the prosecution and accepted by the trial court. Whether the prosecution and trial court are required to do so is a matter of state law, and it is not the place of this Court to settle those matters. * * * In Missouri, it appears "a plea offer once accepted by the defendant can be withdrawn without recourse" by the prosecution. The extent of the trial court's discretion in Missouri to reject a plea agreement appears to be in some doubt.

* * * If * * * the prosecutor could have canceled the plea agreement, and if Frye fails to show a reasonable probability the prosecutor would have adhered to the agreement, there is no *Strickland* prejudice. Likewise, if the trial court could have refused to accept the plea agreement, and if Frye fails to show a reasonable probability the trial court would have accepted the plea, there is no *Strickland* prejudice. In this case, given Frye's new offense for driving without a license on December 30, 2007, there is reason to doubt that the prosecution would have adhered to the agreement or that the trial court would have accepted it at the January 4, 2008, hearing, unless they were required by state law to do so.

It is appropriate to allow the Missouri Court of Appeals to address this question in the first instance. * * *

JUSTICE SCALIA, with whom THE CHIEF JUSTICE, JUSTICE THOMAS, and JUSTICE ALITO join, dissenting.

* * *

Galin Frye's attorney failed to inform him about a plea offer, and Frye ultimately pleaded guilty without the benefit of a deal. Counsel's mistake did not deprive Frye of any substantive or procedural right; only of the opportunity to accept a plea bargain to which he had no entitlement in the first place. So little entitlement that, had he known of and accepted the bargain, the prosecution would have been able to withdraw it right up to the point that his guilty plea pursuant to the bargain was accepted.

* * *

While the inadequacy of counsel's performance in this case is clear enough, whether it was prejudicial (in the sense that the Court's new version of *Strickland* requires) is not. The Court's description of how that question is to be answered on remand is alone enough to show how unwise it is to constitutionalize the plea-bargaining process. Prejudice is to be determined, the Court tells us, by a process of retrospective crystal-ball gazing posing as legal analysis.

* * *

Assessing Prejudice When the Defendant, on Bad Advice, Rejects a Plea Bargain and Goes to Trial: Lafler v. Cooper

LAFLER V. COOPER

Supreme Court of the United States, 2012.
566 U.S. 156.

JUSTICE KENNEDY delivered the opinion of the Court.

In this case, as in Missouri v. Frye also decided today, a criminal defendant seeks a remedy when inadequate assistance of counsel caused nonacceptance of a plea offer and further proceedings led to a less favorable outcome. Here, the favorable plea offer was reported to the client but, on advice of counsel, was rejected. In *Frye* there was a later guilty plea. Here, after the plea offer had been rejected, there was a full and fair trial before a jury. After a guilty verdict, the defendant received a sentence harsher than that offered in the rejected plea bargain. [In the Supreme Court the state conceded that counsel had acted ineffectively, so the only question was prejudice.]

On the evening of March 25, 2003, respondent pointed a gun toward Kali Mundy's head and fired. From the record, it is unclear why respondent did this, and at trial it was suggested that he might have acted either in self-defense or in defense of another person. In any event the shot missed and Mundy fled. Respondent followed in pursuit, firing repeatedly. Mundy was shot in her buttock, hip, and abdomen but survived the assault.

Respondent was charged under Michigan law with assault with intent to murder, possession of a firearm by a felon, possession of a firearm in the commission of a felony, misdemeanor possession of marijuana, and for being a habitual offender. On two occasions, the prosecution offered to dismiss two of the charges and to recommend a sentence of 51 to 85 months for the other two, in exchange for a guilty plea. In a communication with the court respondent admitted guilt and expressed a willingness to accept the offer. Respondent, however, later rejected the offer on both occasions, allegedly after his attorney convinced him that the prosecution would be unable to establish his intent to murder Mundy because she had been shot below the waist. On the first day of trial the prosecution offered a significantly less favorable plea deal, which respondent again rejected. After trial, respondent was convicted on all counts and received a mandatory minimum sentence of 185 to 360 months' imprisonment. [The defendant's claims of ineffective assistance were rejected in the state courts but the lower federal court granted habeas relief.]

The question for this Court is how to apply *Strickland's* prejudice test where ineffective assistance results in a rejection of the plea offer and the defendant is convicted at the ensuing trial.

* * *

In Hill v. Lockhart, when evaluating the petitioner's claim that ineffective assistance led to the improvident acceptance of a guilty plea, the Court required the petitioner to show "that there is a reasonable probability that, but for counsel's errors, [the defendant] would not have pleaded guilty and would have insisted on going to trial."

In contrast to *Hill*, here the ineffective advice led not to an offer's acceptance but to its rejection. Having to stand trial, not choosing to waive it, is the prejudice alleged. In these circumstances a defendant must show that but for the ineffective advice of counsel there is a reasonable probability that the plea offer would have been presented to the court (i.e., that the defendant would have accepted the plea and the prosecution would not have withdrawn it in light of intervening circumstances), that the court would have accepted its terms, and that the conviction or sentence, or both, under the offer's terms would have been less severe than under the judgment and sentence that in fact were imposed. * * *

In the instant case respondent went to trial rather than accept a plea deal, and it is conceded this was the result of ineffective assistance during the plea negotiation process. Respondent received a more severe sentence at trial, one 3 ½ times more severe than he likely would have received by pleading guilty. Far from curing the error, the trial caused the injury from the error. Even if the trial itself is free from constitutional flaw, the defendant who goes to trial instead of taking a more favorable plea may be prejudiced from either a conviction on more serious counts or the imposition of a more severe sentence.

* * *

Even if a defendant shows ineffective assistance of counsel has caused the rejection of a plea leading to a trial and a more severe sentence, there is the question of what constitutes an appropriate remedy. That question must now be addressed.

* * *

The specific injury suffered by defendants who decline a plea offer as a result of ineffective assistance of counsel and then receive a greater sentence as a result of trial can come in at least one of two forms. In some cases, the sole advantage a defendant would have received under the plea is a lesser sentence. This is typically the case when the charges that would have been admitted as part of the plea bargain are the same as the charges the defendant was convicted of after trial. In this situation the court may conduct an evidentiary hearing to determine whether the defendant has shown a reasonable probability that but for counsel's errors he would have accepted the plea. If the showing is made, the court may exercise discretion in determining whether the defendant should receive the term of imprisonment the government offered in the plea, the sentence he received at trial, or something in between.

In some situations it may be that resentencing alone will not be full redress for the constitutional injury. If, for example, an offer was for a guilty plea to a count or counts less serious than the ones for which a defendant was convicted after trial, or if a mandatory sentence confines a judge's sentencing discretion after trial, a resentencing based on the conviction at trial may not suffice. In these circumstances, the proper exercise of discretion to remedy the constitutional injury may be to require the prosecution to reoffer the plea proposal. Once this has occurred, the judge can then exercise discretion in deciding whether to vacate the conviction from trial and accept the plea or leave the conviction undisturbed.

In implementing a remedy in both of these situations, the trial court must weigh various factors; and the boundaries of proper discretion need not be defined here. Principles elaborated over time in decisions of state and federal courts, and in statutes and rules, will serve to give more complete guidance as to the factors that should bear upon the exercise of the judge's discretion. At this point, however, it suffices to note two considerations that are of relevance.

First, a court may take account of a defendant's earlier expressed willingness, or unwillingness, to accept responsibility for his or her actions. Second, it is not necessary here to decide as a constitutional rule that a judge is required to prescind (that is to say disregard) any information concerning the crime that was discovered after the plea offer was made. The time continuum makes it difficult to restore the defendant and the prosecution to the precise positions they occupied prior to the rejection of the plea offer, but that baseline can be consulted in finding a remedy that does not require the prosecution to incur the expense of conducting a new trial.

[Justice Kennedy applied the AEDPA standard to the decision of the Michigan Court of Appeals and found that it was "contrary to, or involved an unreasonable application of, clearly established Federal law, as determined by the Supreme Court of the United States." The state court failed to apply *Strickland* to the ineffective assistance of counsel claim.]

As to prejudice, respondent has shown that but for counsel's deficient performance there is a reasonable probability he and the trial court would have accepted the guilty plea. In addition, as a result of not accepting the plea and being convicted at trial, respondent received a minimum sentence 3 1/2 times greater than he would have received under the plea. The standard for ineffective assistance under *Strickland* has thus been satisfied.

As a remedy, the District Court ordered specific performance of the original plea agreement. The correct remedy in these circumstances, however, is to order the State to reoffer the plea agreement. Presuming respondent accepts the offer, the state trial court can then exercise its discretion in determining whether to vacate the convictions and resentence respondent pursuant to the plea agreement, to vacate only some of the convictions and resentence respondent accordingly, or to leave the convictions and sentence from trial undisturbed. Today's decision leaves open to the trial court how best to exercise that discretion in all the circumstances of the case.

The judgment of the Court of Appeals for the Sixth Circuit is vacated, and the case is remanded for further proceedings consistent with this opinion.

JUSTICE SCALIA, with whom JUSTICE THOMAS joins, and with whom THE CHIEF JUSTICE joins in relevant part, dissenting.

* * * [T]he Court today opens a whole new field of constitutionalized criminal procedure: plea-bargaining law. The ordinary criminal process has become too long, too expensive, and unpredictable, in no small part as a consequence of an intricate federal Code of Criminal Procedure imposed on the States by this Court in pursuit of perfect justice. The Court now moves to bring perfection to the alternative in which prosecutors and defendants have sought relief. * * *

In many—perhaps most—countries of the world, American-style plea bargaining is forbidden in cases as serious as this one, even for the purpose of obtaining testimony that enables conviction of a greater malefactor, much less for the purpose of sparing the expense of trial. * * *

In the United States, we have plea bargaining a-plenty, but until today it has been regarded as a necessary evil. It presents grave risks of prosecutorial overcharging that effectively compels an innocent defendant to avoid massive risk by pleading guilty to a lesser offense; and for guilty defendants it often—perhaps usually—results in a sentence well below what the law prescribes for the actual crime. But even so, we accept plea bargaining because many believe that without it our long and expensive process of criminal trial could not sustain the burden imposed on it, and our system of criminal justice would grind to a halt.

Today, however, the Supreme Court of the United States elevates plea bargaining from a necessary evil to a constitutional entitlement. It is no longer a somewhat embarrassing adjunct to our criminal justice system; rather, as the Court announces in the companion case to this one, "it is the criminal justice system." Thus, even though there is no doubt that the respondent here is guilty of the offense with which he was charged; even though he has received the exorbitant gold standard of American justice—a full-dress criminal trial with its innumerable constitutional and statutory limitations upon the evidence that the prosecution can bring forward, and (in Michigan as in most States) the requirement of a unanimous guilty verdict by impartial jurors; the Court says that his conviction is invalid because he was deprived of his constitutional entitlement to plea-bargain.

* * *

Today's decision * * * opens a whole new boutique of constitutional jurisprudence ("plea-bargaining law") without even specifying the remedies the boutique offers. The result in the present case is the undoing of an adjudicatory process that worked exactly as it is supposed to. Released felon Anthony Cooper, who shot repeatedly and gravely injured a woman named Kali Mundy, was tried and convicted for his crimes by a jury of his peers, and given a punishment that Michigan's elected representatives have deemed appropriate. Nothing about that result is unfair or unconstitutional. To the contrary, it is wonderfully just, and infinitely superior to the trial-by-bargain that today's opinion affords constitutional status. I respectfully dissent.

[The dissenting opinion of Justice Alito is omitted.]

Counseling Client to Withdraw a Cooperation Agreement on the Basis of the Client's Protestation of Innocence: Burt v. Titlow

Justice Alito delivered the opinion of the Court in Burt v. Titlow, 134 S.Ct. 10 (2014), as the Court again emphasized the double deference due a state court holding that a defense lawyer was not ineffective. Titlow and her aunt murdered the aunt's husband by pouring vodka down his throat and smothering him with a pillow. Titlow, with the help of his lawyer, reached an agreement with state prosecutors to testify against the aunt, plead guilty to manslaughter, and receive a 7- to 15-year sentence. At a plea hearing, counsel confirmed that he had spen much time with Tidlow and that Tidlow understood that the evidence against her could support a conviction for first-degree murder. The trial court approved the plea bargain, but three days before the aunt's trial was to begin, Tidlow obtained a new lawyer who helped him demand a three year rather than a seven year minimum sentence. The prosecutor refused the demand, Titlow withdrew his plea, and she acknowledged in open court that a first degree murder charge could be reinstated. She was tried, a jury found her guilty of second-degree murder, and the judge imposed a 20–40 year sentence.

On direct appeal, Titlow argued that her new trial lawyer was ineffective because he had not taken time to learn the case and realize the strength of the state's evidence. The state appellate court found no ineffectiveness. Nor did a federal district court in habeas proceedings, but the Sixth Circuit reversed and found that "the factual predicate for the state court's decision—that the withdrawal of the plea was based on respondent's assertion of innocence—was an unreasonable interpretation of the factual record, given [the new trial lawyer's] explanation at the withdrawal hearing that 'the decision to withdraw Titlow's plea was based on the fact that the State's plea offer was substantially higher than the Michigan guidelines for second-degree murder.' "

On remand with instructions from the Sixth Circuit, the prosecution offered its original plea agreement despite the fact that the aunt had died and Titlow no longer could assist the state in prosecuting her. Incredibly, at the plea hearing Titlow balked and refused to provide a factual basis for the plea. With the assistance of habeas counsel, Titlow finally admitted placing the uncle in danger, and the trial court took the plea under advisement. The Supreme Court granted review and concluded that "the record readily supports the [State court's] factual finding that Toca advised withdrawal of the guilty plea only after respondent's proclamation of innocence."

Justice Sotomayor concurred on the ground that Titlow failed to overcome the presumptions that the new trial counsel performed effectively and that the state court ruled correctly. Justice Ginsburg concurred in the result, although she found "dubious the [State court's] conclusion that Toca acted reasonably in light of Titlow's protestations of innocence."

Reasonable Probability of Going Trial Even Without a Strong Defense: Lee v. United States

Chief Justice Roberts wrote for the Court in Lee v. United States, 137 S.Ct. 1958 (2017), as it addressed a situation in which Lee, a non-citizen, was indicted on one count of possessing ecstasy with intent to distribute. He had lived for most of his life in the United States and feared that a criminal conviction might affect his status as a lawful permanent resident. Because his attorney assured him that the Government would not deport him if he pleaded guilty and because he had no real defense to the charge, he accepted a plea that carried a lesser prison sentence than he would have faced at trial. The advice was wrong, and Lee was subject to mandatory deportation from this country. He sought to vacate his conviction on the ground that he accepted the plea because he received ineffective assistance of counsel in violation of the Sixth Amendment.

Chief Justice Roberts stated that everyone agreed that that Lee received objectively unreasonable representation and the question was whether he could show prejudice. Lower federal courts denied relief on the ground that, without a defense at trial, Lee could not show prejudice. The Supreme Court disagreed.

The Chief Justice explained that "[w]hen a defendant alleges his counsel's deficient performance led him to accept a guilty plea rather than go to trial, we do not ask whether, had he gone to trial, the result of that trial 'would have been different' than the result of the plea bargain * * * because, while we ordinarily apply a strong presumption of reliability to judicial proceedings, we cannot accord any such presumption to judicial proceedings that never took place." He cited Hill v. Lockhart and further explained that "[w]e instead consider whether the defendant was prejudiced by the denial of the entire judicial proceeding to which he had a right."

Although the Chief Justice agreed with dissenters that a defendant must also show that he would have been better off going to trial when the defendant's decision about going to trial turns on his prospects of success and those are affected by the attorney's error, he reasoned that there are different types of errors. In Lee's case, the error had nothing to do with his trial chances; counsel's error affected Lee's understanding of the consequences of pleading guilty.

Chief Justice Roberts illustrated why a defendant with little chance of winning at trial might still choose trial over plea.

> [C]ommon sense (not to mention our precedent) recognizes that there is more to consider than simply the likelihood of success at trial. The decision whether to plead guilty also involves assessing the respective consequences of a conviction after trial and by plea. When those consequences are, from the defendant's perspective, similarly dire, even the smallest chance of success at trial may look attractive. For example, a defendant with no realistic defense to a charge carrying a 20-year sentence may nevertheless choose trial, if the prosecution's plea offer is 18 years. Here Lee alleges that avoiding deportation was *the* determinative factor for him; deportation after some time in prison was not meaningfully different from deportation after somewhat less time. He says he accordingly would have rejected any plea leading to deportation—even if it shaved off prison time—in favor of throwing a "Hail Mary" at trial.

The Chief Justice concluded that "[i]n the unusual circumstances of this case, we conclude that Lee has adequately demonstrated a reasonable probability that he would have rejected the plea had he known that it would lead to mandatory deportation," and "[w]e cannot agree that it would be irrational for a defendant in Lee's position to reject the plea offer in favor of trial."

The Court remanded for further proceedings.

Justice Thomas, joined in large part by Justice Alito, dissented and maintained his view that "the Sixth Amendment to the Constitution does not require counsel to provide accurate advice concerning the potential removal consequences of a guilty plea." He also challenged the prejudice standard adopted by the Court. Justice Alito did not participate in the decision.

8. Waiver of the Right to Effective Assistance

In Schriro v. Landrigan, 550 U.S. 465 (2007), Justice Thomas wrote for the Court as it held, in a habeas case, that a state court was not objectively unreasonably in finding that a criminal defendant had waived his right to challenge counsel's ineffectiveness by refusing to pursue the strategy urged by counsel.

Landrigan was convicted of murder and other offenses and sentenced to death. At his sentencing hearing, his counsel planned to call his ex-wife and birth mother as witnesses but both refused to testify and indicated that they did so at Landrigan's request. The trial judge inquired of both witnesses and Landrigan to confirm that he did not want them to testify. At the conclusion of the hearing, the trial judge asked Landrigan whether he had anything to say and he responded with a statement that concluded "I think if you want to give me the death penalty, just bring it right on. I'm ready for it." After his conviction and sentence were affirmed on direct appeal, Landrigan sought state habeas corpus relief and claimed ineffective assistance of counsel for failure to present mitigating evidence.

The same judge who presided at trial rejected Landrigan's habeas claim, finding that "[Landrigan] instructed his attorney not to present any evidence at the sentencing hearing, [so] it is difficult to comprehend how [Landrigan] can claim counsel should have presented other evidence at sentencing." Although Landrigan contended that he would have cooperated had mitigating evidence other than the testimony of the ex-wife and birth mother been presented, the judge concluded that Landrigan's "statements at sentencing belie his new-found sense of cooperation."

In rejecting the claim of ineffectiveness, Justice Thomas distinguished prior cases, including *Rompilla*, found that the Court had "never addressed a situation like this," and concluded "[i]n short, at the time of the Arizona postconviction court's decision, it was not objectively unreasonable for that court to conclude that a defendant who refused to allow the presentation of any mitigating evidence could not establish *Strickland* prejudice based on his counsel's failure to investigate further possible mitigating evidence."

Justice Stevens, joined by Justices Souter, Ginsburg and Breyer, dissented.

B. THE RIGHT TO CONFLICT-FREE REPRESENTATION

The right to effective assistance of counsel may be denied if defense counsel is operating under a conflict of interest, and as a result cannot or does not properly protect her client's interests. One situation of potential conflict arises when counsel represents multiple defendants. Codefendants may have divergent interests at all stages of a prosecution. A plea bargain advantageous to one defendant may produce testimony adverse to another defendant. Defendants may have inconsistent defenses, or wish to testify in ways that incriminate codefendants. See, e.g., United States v. Hall, 200 F.3d 962 (6th Cir. 2000) (conflict of interest where defense counsel represents two brothers, and one has a public authority defense while the other does not). Evidence inculpating one defendant might exculpate another, forcing counsel to make unsatisfactory choices in response to offered testimony. Separate counsel also might choose differing approaches to closing argument that one lawyer for multiple defendants might not be able to choose.

Conflicts also might arise because defense counsel has a personal interest that could be negatively affected by aggressive representation of the defendant. For example, in one notorious case, a defense counsel was representing the defendant in a felony prosecution and simultaneously having a sexual relationship with the defendant's wife. Counsel's ardor for the wife may well have dampened his ardor to have the defendant set free. See Hernandez v. State, 750 So.2d 50 (Fla.App. 1999).

Another possibility is that the interests of the defendant may be in conflict with the interests of defense counsel's client in another matter, or with the interests of a former client. For example, if counsel represents two defendants charged with the same crime in separate matters, the decision whether to call one defendant to testify in the other's trial may be impacted by counsel's conflicting loyalties. See, e.g., United States v. Elliot, 463 F.3d 858 (9th Cir. 2006) (conflict where two clients are separately tried for the same crime and their best defense is to shift blame to each other: "To represent Elliot adequately, Gordon needed to interview, aggressively examine, and possibly place blame on Hevia, all of which clashed with his attorney-client relationship with Hevia."). And the lawyer's duty to preserve the confidences and secrets of a former client may impair a current client's representation if the former client is called as a witness for the prosecution.

The rules adopted by the Supreme Court for assessing claims of defense counsel conflict of interest have been usefully summarized by the court in United States v. Kliti, 156 F.3d 150 (2d Cir.1998):

A defendant's right to counsel under the Sixth Amendment includes the right to be represented by an attorney who is free from conflicts of interest. When the trial court knows or reasonably should know of the possibility of a conflict of interest, it has a threshold obligation to determine whether the attorney has an actual conflict, a potential conflict, or no conflict. In fulfilling this initial obligation to inquire into the existence of a conflict of interest, the trial court may rely on counsel's representations. If a district court ignores a possible conflict and does not conduct this initial inquiry, reversal of a defendant's conviction is automatic. If, through this inquiry, the court determines that the attorney suffers from an actual or potential conflict of interest, the court has a "disqualification/waiver" obligation.

* * *

If the conflict is so severe that no rational defendant would waive it, the court must disqualify the attorney. If it is a lesser conflict, the court must conduct a * * * hearing to determine whether the defendant will knowingly and intelligently waive his right to conflict-free representation. (Before a defendant can knowingly and intelligently waive a conflict, the court must: (1) advise the defendant about potential conflicts; (2) determine whether the defendant understands the risks of those conflicts; and (3) give the defendant time to digest and contemplate the risks, with the aid of independent counsel if desired.)

1. The Duty of Court Inquiry

Per Se Reversal for Failure to Inquire into Joint Representation: Holloway v. Arkansas

In Holloway v. Arkansas, 435 U.S. 475 (1978), the Court made it clear that joint representation of codefendants by a single attorney is not a *per se* violation of the right to effective assistance of counsel. The Court noted that a common defense often gives strength against a common attack. Under some circumstances, however, joint representation may create a conflict that can deny a defendant effective assistance of counsel. In *Holloway,* the defense counsel made pretrial motions for appointment of separate counsel for each defendant because of possible conflicts of interest. The trial court denied the motion, and refused defense counsel's renewed request during the trial for separate counsel when the three codefendants each wished to testify. Counsel felt that he would be unable to examine or cross-examine any defendant to protect the interests of the others.

Without ever reaching the issue of whether there was an actual conflict of interest, the Supreme Court reversed the defendants' convictions. Reversal was required because the judge, after timely motions, erred in failing to "either appoint separate counsel, or to take adequate steps to ascertain whether the risk was too remote to warrant separate counsel." The Court held that in these circumstances, prejudice to the defendants must be presumed:

> Joint representation of conflicting interests is suspect because of what it tends to prevent the attorney from doing. For example, in this case it may well have precluded defense counsel for [one of the

codefendants] from exploring possible plea negotiations and the possibility of an agreement to testify for the prosecution, provided a lesser charge or a favorable sentencing recommendation would be acceptable. Generally speaking a conflict may also prevent an attorney from challenging the admission of evidence prejudicial to one client but perhaps favorable to another, or from arguing at the sentencing hearing the relative involvement and culpability of his clients in order to minimize the culpability of one by emphasizing that of another. Examples can be readily multiplied. * * *

[A] rule requiring a defendant to show that a conflict of interests— which he and his counsel tried to avoid by timely objections to the joint representation—prejudiced him in some specific fashion would not be susceptible to intelligent, evenhanded application. In the normal case where a harmless error rule is applied, the error occurs at trial and its scope is readily identifiable. * * * But in a case of joint representation of conflicting interests the evil * * * is in what the advocate finds himself compelled to *refrain* from doing, not only at trial but also as to possible pretrial plea negotiations and in the sentencing process. * * * Thus, an inquiry into a claim of harmless error here would require, unlike most cases, unguided speculation.

QUESTION ABOUT HOLLOWAY

Holloway was decided before *Strickland*. How does *Holloway*'s rule of per se reversal square with *Strickland*'s holding that a defendant must show that counsel was ineffective and that the ineffectiveness was prejudicial? In Selsor v. Kaiser, 22 F.3d 1029 (10th Cir.1994), the court concluded that the per se reversal rule of *Holloway* was unaffected by the Court's later requirement of a showing of prejudice in *Strickland*. It reasoned as follows:

> *Strickland*'s requirement of a showing of actual conflict presupposes that trial courts conduct an appropriate inquiry when the defendant properly raises the issue. *Holloway*, however, addresses the situation where the trial court *fails* to make such inquiry in the face of the defendant's timely objection. As a result, the *Strickland* rule requiring a defendant to demonstrate an actual conflict of interest in order to obtain a presumption of prejudice is inapplicable in a *Holloway*-type case.

So *Holloway* is a limited exception to the *Strickland* case-by-case approach. Automatic reversal is required where 1) joint defendants are being represented by a single counsel; 2) defense counsel or the defendant raises the conflict issue with the court; and 3) the court fails even to conduct a hearing on the matter.

Federal Rule 44

Fed.R.Crim.P. 44 attempts to address the problem of joint representation, and the need for a hearing, that the Court was concerned with in *Holloway*:

Rule 44. Right to and Appointment of Counsel

* * *

(c)(2) Court's Responsibilities in Cases of Joint Representation. The court must promptly inquire about the propriety of joint representation and must personally advise each defendant of the right to the effective assistance of counsel, including separate representation. Unless there is good cause to believe that no conflict of interest is likely to arise, the court must take appropriate measures to protect each defendant's right to counsel.

It should be apparent that Rule 44 does not address all the conflict situations that can arise in a criminal case. Rule 44 addresses only questions of multiple representation in the same criminal proceeding. So, for example, the Rule does not apply if defense counsel has previously represented a person who is now a government witness in the case against the defendant. It does not apply if the lawyer has a personal conflict. It does not apply if the lawyer is representing two related defendants in *separate* proceedings.

But these less obvious conflicts are in fact reviewed by the court at a hearing if they are raised with the court. Usually it is the government that raises such conflicts for the court to consider. Why would the prosecution raise these conflicts?

2. Active Conflict Impairing the Representation

A Different Kind of Prejudice Test: Cuyler v. Sullivan

In Cuyler v. Sullivan, 446 U.S. 335 (1980), the Court considered the propriety of relief where defense counsel operated under a conflict of interest that was not brought to the attention of the trial judge. Justice Powell's opinion for the Court rejected the petitioner's claim that *Holloway* requires a trial judge to inquire in every case into the propriety of joint representation, even in the absence of the defense's timely motion. He reasoned as follows:

> Defense counsel have an ethical obligation to avoid conflicting representations and to advise the court promptly when a conflict of interest arises during the course of a trial. Absent special circumstances, therefore, trial courts may assume that multiple

representation entails no conflict or that the lawyer and his clients knowingly accept such risk of conflict as may exist.

The Court recognized that multiple representation does give rise to a possibility of an improper conflict of interest and Justice Powell stated that a defendant "must have the opportunity to show that potential conflicts impermissibly imperil his right to a fair trial." But, "a defendant who raised no objection at trial must demonstrate that an actual conflict of interest adversely affected his lawyer's performance." Thus, the Court created a limited presumption of prejudice in cases where a defendant fails to make a timely objection to conflicted simultaneous representation: prejudice is presumed, but only if the defendant demonstrates that counsel "actively represented conflicting interests" and that "an actual conflict of interest adversely affected his lawyer's performance."[32]

The *Cuyler* prejudice standard applies when a defendant fails to bring a potential conflict to the trial court's attention. But it also applies when the defendant notifies the trial court of a potential conflict and the trial court, after a full hearing, finds that there is no actual or potential conflict and orders the multiple representation to continue. See Freund v. Butterworth, 165 F.3d 839 (11th Cir.1999) (en banc). *Holloway's* rule of per se reversal applies only when the court *refuses to hold a hearing* after the defense counsel brings a potential conflict to its attention.

Application of the Cuyler Standard: Burger v. Kemp

The Supreme Court found no ineffective assistance of counsel under the *Cuyler* standards in Burger v. Kemp, 483 U.S. 776 (1987), a capital case in which Burger and a codefendant were represented by law partners. The defendants were soldiers charged with the murder of a fellow soldier who worked part-time driving a taxi. Each defendant confessed, and Burger took military police to the place where the victim had been drowned. Leaphart, an experienced lawyer, was appointed to represent Burger, and he insisted that his law partner represent the codefendant. The two defendants were tried separately, and at their trials each defendant sought to avoid the death penalty by emphasizing the other's culpability. Burger was sentenced to death, and attacked his representation in a habeas corpus proceeding on the ground that Leaphart's partnership relationship created a conflict of interest for him.

Justice Stevens wrote for the Court and found that Burger was not entitled to relief. He conceded that "[t]here is certainly much substance to petitioner's argument that the appointment of two partners to represent

---

[32] When the Supreme Court remanded *Cuyler*, the court of appeals found that there was an actual conflict of interest that required reversal of Sullivan's conviction. Sullivan v. Cuyler, 723 F.2d 1077 (3d Cir.1983). Counsel, representing both a prospective witness and Sullivan, admitted at an evidentiary hearing that he did not call the witness on Sullivan's behalf because he had to take the witness's interests into account as well as those of Sullivan.

coindictees in their respective trials creates a possible conflict of interest that could prejudice either or both clients," and that "the risk of prejudice is increased when the two lawyers cooperate with one another in planning and conduct of trial strategy." He observed, however, that the Court's decisions do not presume prejudice in all cases, and he concluded that "the overlap of counsel, if any, did not so infect Leaphart's representation as to constitute an active representation of competing interests." Justice Stevens added that "[p]articularly in smaller communities where the supply of qualified lawyers willing to accept the demanding and unrewarding work of representing capital prisoners is extremely limited, the two defendants may actually benefit from the joint efforts of two partners who supplement one another in their preparation." Justice Stevens also emphasized that each defendant was tried separately, and that separate trials significantly reduce the risk of a conflict of interest. The Court declined to disturb the lower courts' findings that there was no actual conflict of interest.

Justice Stevens added that, even if an actual conflict had been established, counsel's advocacy was unaffected by it. He concluded that there was no evidence that the prosecutor would have been receptive to a plea bargain and no doubt that Leaphart sought to negotiate for a life sentence; there was no reason to believe that Leaphart attempted to protect the other defendant who was not on trial with Burger; and the decision not to offer mitigating evidence and open the door to cross-examination about Burger's background was not unreasonable even if it was erroneous.[33]

Relationship Between the Holloway Automatic Reversal Rule and the Cuyler Rule Regulating Active Representation of Conflicting Interests: Mickens v. Taylor

In Mickens v. Taylor, 535 U.S. 162 (2002), Justice Scalia wrote for the Court as it held that the *Holloway* rule—requiring automatic reversal when the trial court fails to inquire into a multiple representation conflict raised by defense counsel—does not apply when "the trial court fails to inquire into a potential conflict of interest about which it knew or reasonably should have known" but is not raised by defense counsel. The trial judge appointed Bryan Saunders counsel for a juvenile on assault and concealed weapons charges. Saunders met with the juvenile just once after being appointed and within days of that meeting, the juvenile was killed and Mickens was charged. The same judge appointed Saunders to represent Mickens approximately two weeks after appointing Saunders to represent the juvenile.

---

[33] Justice Blackmun filed a dissenting opinion, in which Justices Brennan and Marshall joined, and in which Justice Powell joined in part. Justice Powell filed a separate dissenting opinion, in which Justice Brennan joined.

Justice Scalia discussed *Cronic, Holloway,* and *Sullivan,* reminded that "*Holloway* * * * creates an automatic reversal rule only where defense counsel is forced to represent codefendants over his timely objection, unless the trial court has determined that there is no conflict," and contrasted the latter two cases: "* * * *Sullivan* addressed separately a trial court's duty to inquire into the propriety of a multiple representation, construing *Holloway* to require inquiry only when 'the trial court knows or reasonably should know that a particular conflict exists'—which is not to be confused with when the trial court is aware of a vague, unspecified possibility of conflict, such as that which 'inheres in almost every instance of multiple representation.'"

Justice Scalia rejected Mickens' argument for automatic reversal in a case in which a conflict existed but did not affect counsel's performance:

> Petitioner's proposed rule of automatic reversal when there existed a conflict that did not affect counsel's performance, but the trial judge failed to make the *Sullivan*-mandated inquiry, makes little policy sense. * * * The trial court's awareness of a potential conflict neither renders it more likely that counsel's performance was significantly affected nor in any other way renders the verdict unreliable. Nor does the trial judge's failure to make the *Sullivan*-mandated inquiry often make it harder for reviewing courts to determine conflict and effect, particularly since those courts may rely on evidence and testimony whose importance only becomes established at the trial.

Justice Scalia also rejected the argument that automatic reversal is an appropriate means of enforcing *Sullivan's* mandate of inquiry and suggested that "the *Sullivan* standard, which requires proof of effect upon representation but (once such effect is shown) presumes prejudice, already creates an 'incentive' to inquire into a potential conflict.

The Court affirmed the court of appeals' decision denying habeas corpus relief on the ground that Mickens was required and failed to establish that the conflict of interest adversely affected his counsel's performance.

Justice Kennedy, joined by Justice O'Connor wrote a concurring opinion in which he observed that

> the District Court conducted an evidentiary hearing on the conflict claim and issued a thorough opinion, which found that counsel's brief representation of the victim had no effect whatsoever on the course of petitioner's trial. * * * This conclusion is a good example of why a case-by-case inquiry is required, rather than simply adopting an automatic rule of reversal.

Justice Stevens dissented, arguing that Saunders had a duty to disclose to both Mickens and the trial court his prior representation of the juvenile, and that, having failed to do so, "[s]etting aside Mickens' conviction is the only remedy that can maintain public confidence in the fairness of the procedures employed in capital cases." Justice Breyer's dissent, joined by Justice Ginsburg, argued similarly that "the Commonwealth seeks to execute a defendant, having provided that defendant with a lawyer who, only yesterday, represented the victim," and "to carry out a death sentence so obtained would invariably diminish faith in the fairness and integrity of our criminal justice system."

Justice Souter also dissented and argued that "[s]ince the District Court in this case found that the state judge was on notice of a prospective potential conflict, this case calls for nothing more than the application of the prospective notice rule announced and exemplified by *Holloway* * * *."

COMMENT ON MICKENS

The Cuyler v. Sullivan standard requires the defendant to show that counsel made one decision that was due to a conflict of interest, i.e., one decision that was made because counsel was furthering another interest at the expense of the defendant. At that point, prejudice is presumed. It is a standard that is easier for defendant to meet than that employed in *Strickland*, which requires the court to look at the entire record to determine whether there is a reasonable probability that, if not for counsel's ineffectiveness, the outcome of the proceeding would have been different.

In *Mickens*, Justice Scalia avoids deciding whether the *Strickland* standard of prejudice governs conflict of interest challenges arising from some conflict other than multiple simultaneous representation. Other conflicts could include conflicts between the defendant's interests and the lawyer's personal interests, and conflicts arising from successive, rather than concurrent, representations (although the opinion explicitly takes no position on successive representations).

After *Mickens*, lower courts appear to be taking Justice Scalia's opinion as an indication that *Strickland,* and not *Cuyler*, governs conflict claims arising out of something other than multiple concurrent representation. For example, in Whiting v. Burt, 395 F.3d 602 (6th Cir. 2005), the defendant argued ineffective assistance of counsel on appeal, because his appellate counsel was also his trial counsel, and so could not be expected to raise any claims on appeal about his own ineffectiveness at trial. This conflict was not based on multiple representation, but rather on the lawyer's personal interest in not subjecting his own trial performance to a public self-critique. The court held that, after *Mickens*, every lower court has refused to apply the *Cuyler* standard outside the "concurrent joint representation context." The court reviewed for prejudice under *Strickland* and found none under the circumstances.

Conflict with the Attorney's Personal Interests

As noted above, in some cases counsel's personal interests may be in conflict with the duty of loyalty owed the client. United States v. Cancilla, 725 F.2d 867 (2d Cir.1984), is an example. Cancilla's counsel, while defending him, was engaged in criminal conduct with the defendant's coconspirators. The court reasoned that "with the similarity of counsel's criminal activities to Cancilla's schemes and the link between them, it must have occurred to counsel that a vigorous defense might uncover evidence or prompt testimony revealing his own crimes." See also United States ex rel. Duncan v. O'Leary, 806 F.2d 1307 (7th Cir.1986) (reversal where defense counsel is the prosecutor's campaign manager and the prosecutor is running on a "law and order" ticket).

In Winkler v. Keane, 7 F.3d 304 (2d Cir.1993), the court found an actual conflict of interest where counsel represented a criminal defendant on a contingent fee basis; under the agreement, defense counsel would receive a fee of $25,000, but only if the defendant was found not guilty. The court reasoned that counsel had "a disincentive to seek a plea agreement, or to put forth mitigating defenses that would result in conviction of a lesser included offense." But the court held that the conflict of interest did not adversely affect the defense, because the defendant steadfastly maintained his innocence throughout, rejected all attempts to plea bargain, and vetoed any attempt of defense counsel to argue the partial defense of intoxication. Thus, there was no reason to believe that defense counsel's representation would have been any different "if a proper fee arrangement had been utilized."

These cases strongly suggest that while operating under a conflict with personal interests is an act of ineffectiveness, the defendant must establish prejudice under *Strickland*. The more generous Cuyler v. Sullivan standard appears applicable, after *Mickens*, only to cases of multiple concurrent representation.

3.   Waiver of the Right to Conflict-Free Counsel

The premise of Federal Rule 44 is that if the defendant is properly warned of the possible conflicts that could arise, then he can knowingly and voluntarily waive the right to conflict-free representation. Generally speaking, a knowing and voluntary waiver of conflict-free representation can be found if the trial court informs the defendant about the ways in which conflicted counsel can impair the representation—for example, that one client could shift blame to another, or testify against another, and defense counsel would be impaired in representing the multiple interests.

The trial court must assure itself that the defendant understands the consequences, and has made a rational decision to proceed with counsel despite the conflict. An example of a typical colloquy is found in United

States v. Flores, 5 F.3d 1070 (7th Cir.1993). In *Flores*, three defendants charged with major narcotics transactions had used a group of lawyers in previous brushes with the law. According to the court,

> like sick patients who call up longtime family doctors, they contacted attorneys who represented them before. Potential conflicts of interest arose, however, as the three defendants and their attorneys played a virtual musical chairs game of attorney-client relationships. The lawyers chosen to represent Flores and Fontanez, respectively Michael Green and Roberta Samotny, represented Rodriguez in prior, unrelated criminal proceedings. Further, Rodriguez's counsel, Glenn Seiden, initially represented Fontanez in the current case then switched to Rodriguez.

The government in *Flores* moved to disqualify all counsel, and the trial court held a Rule 44 hearing, at which the court asked the defendants and their respective attorneys about the alleged conflicts. The court questioned each attorney to make sure he or she had explained the problem to their respective clients. The court then asked each defendant if he wanted to continue with his current counsel and explained the possible conflicts. Each defendant on the record said they wanted to continue to retain their attorney.

The trial court in *Flores* respected the expressed preferences of each defendant and declined the government's invitation to intrude into the defendants' counsel of choice. Each defendant subsequently appealed on the ground that they had not *knowingly* waived their right to conflict-free counsel. They argued that the district court failed to make a detailed inquiry into how the conflict of interest might relate to the individual defendants and noted that the defendants' answers were usually only one or two words. The court of appeals rejected these arguments and found that the colloquies were sufficient to establish a knowing waiver of conflict-free counsel. The court provided the following analysis:

> First of all there is no requirement that the district court follow some pre-ordained, detailed script when eliciting a criminal defendant's waiver of the Sixth Amendment right to conflict-free counsel. We do not ask whether a defendant's decision to waive is foolish. Rather, we ask only whether the defendant made an informed decision. * * * The district court need not conduct a long-winded dialogue with counsel and defendants when inquiring about a waiver. It is enough that the district court inform each defendant of the nature and importance of the right to conflict-free counsel and ensure that the defendant understands something of the consequences of a conflict.

> The defendants' other argument—that their waivers are not valid because most of their answers at the Rule 44(c) hearing consisted of only one or two words—is also without merit. * * * The defendants

answers at the Rule 44(c) hearing adequately expressed their preferences. We respect the defendants' choice of trial counsel and hold that the defendants waived their Sixth Amendment right to conflict-free counsel.

It should be noted as a matter of practice that some judges require the defendant to articulate, in his own words, what counsel's conflict is, and how it could impair his representation. While the court in *Flores* found that this is not required, such a practice does help to assure that the defendant is making a knowing and intelligent waiver, or, to the contrary, could indicate that the defendant doesn't really know what he is giving up.

C. INEFFECTIVE ASSISTANCE WITHOUT FAULT ON THE PART OF DEFENSE COUNSEL

Impairing Defense Strategy

Governmental or prosecutorial action can deprive a defendant of effective assistance of counsel, by impairing the performance of even the best counsel. For example in Brooks v. Tennessee, 406 U.S. 605 (1972), a Tennessee rule required the defendant to testify as the first witness in the case or not at all. (This was an attempt to prevent the defendant from altering his testimony in the light of testimony provided by prosecution witnesses). The Court held that the rule violated the defendant's right to remain silent, and also deprived him of the aid of counsel in planning his defense, particularly in the decision to testify or remain silent.

> By requiring the accused and his lawyer to make that choice without an opportunity to evaluate the actual worth of their evidence, the state restricts the defense—particularly counsel—in the planning of its case. Furthermore, the penalty for not testifying first is to keep the defendant off the stand entirely, even though as a matter of professional judgment his lawyer might want to call him later in the trial. The accused is thereby deprived of the "guiding hand of counsel" in the timing of this critical element of his defense.

Similarly, in Herring v. New York, 422 U.S. 853 (1975), a New York statute giving a judge in a nonjury criminal trial the power to deny absolutely the opportunity for defense counsel to make a closing argument was held to be unconstitutional. New York denied Herring the effective assistance of counsel by permitting the judge to dispense with his counsel's summation.

Limiting Consultation Between Defendant and Counsel

In Geders v. United States, 425 U.S. 80 (1976), the defendant was prohibited from consulting with counsel during a 17-hour overnight recess between the direct and cross-examination of the defendant. Although recognizing the problem of "coached" witnesses, the Court decided that this method of preventing coaching violated the defendant's right to the effective assistance of counsel.

Justice Stevens wrote for a majority in Perry v. Leeke, 488 U.S. 272 (1989), as it distinguished *Geders* and held that a state trial judge did not commit constitutional error in declaring a 15 minute recess after the defendant's direct testimony in his murder trial and in ordering that the defendant talk to no one, including his lawyer, during the recess. Although Justice Stevens recognized that "[t]here is merit in petitioner's argument that a showing of prejudice is not an essential component of a violation of the rule announced in *Geders*," he reasoned that "when a defendant becomes a witness, he has no constitutional right to consult with his lawyer while he is testifying." Justice Stevens recognized that nondiscussion orders can prevent coaching of witnesses that might interfere with the search for truth. He described *Geders* as a case involving an overnight recess in which matters that go beyond a defendant's own testimony would be discussed with counsel and stated that "in a short recess in which it is appropriate to presume that nothing but the testimony will be discussed, the testifying defendant does not have a constitutional right to advice."

Justice Marshall, joined by Justices Brennan and Blackmun, dissented. He argued that a defendant cannot be prevented from consulting with counsel during a recess and that the defendant was not arguing for a right to interrupt cross-examination in order to consult with his lawyer.

Interference with the Attorney-Client Relationship

State intrusion into attorney-client consultations can be a problem outside the trial context as well. The Supreme Court addressed one such problem in Weatherford v. Bursey, 429 U.S. 545 (1977). The defendant claimed a Sixth Amendment violation when an undercover agent and informant attended two meetings between the defendant and counsel; the undercover informant was ostensibly a codefendant. The Court concluded that despite this intrusion, the defendant received effective assistance of counsel. Those meetings resulted in no tainted evidence, and no communication of defense strategy to the government. Thus, there was indication of prejudice that would require reversal. Justices Marshall and Brennan dissented, because they believed that when the prosecution acquires information about the defense, the fairness and integrity of the adversary system are impaired, so the intrusion cannot be harmless.

In United States v. Morrison, 449 U.S. 361 (1981), the Supreme Court unanimously concluded that "absent demonstrable prejudice, or substantial threat thereof, dismissal of the indictment is plainly inappropriate, even though the [Sixth Amendment] violation may have been deliberate." See also United States v. Noriega, 752 F.Supp. 1045

(S.D.Fla.1990), which held that despite outrageous, unconscionable conduct of law enforcement officers in eavesdropping on two conversations between the defendant and his counsel, dismissal of the prosecution was not warranted where there was no showing that trial strategy was revealed or that the defendant's ability to work in confidence with his attorney was impaired.

In Glebe v. Frost, 135 S.Ct. 1429 (2014) (per curiam), a habeas petitioner relied on *Herring* to argue that per se reversible error occurred when the state trial court restricted defense counsel from making a particular argument in closing. Trial counsel wanted to argue to the jury in the alternative: 1) that the prosecution failed to prove that the defendant was an accomplice to robberies; and 2) that in committing the crime, the defendant was acting under duress. The trial judge insisted that defense counsel choose one argument or the other for closing, as the arguments were inconsistent. Defense counsel limited his closing argument to duress, and the defendant was convicted. On habeas review, Frost argued that the trial judge's restriction violated his right to effective counsel and that this violation was a "structural" error that could not be assessed for harmlessness. (See Chapter 13 for a discussion of structural errors).

Because the case was on habeas review, Frost was required to show not just that an error occurred but that the state court violated clearly established law as determined by the Supreme Court. 22 U.S.C. § 2254(d). The Court found that *Herring* did *not* clearly establish that a trial court was prohibited from requiring defense counsel to choose between inconsistent arguments.

D. THE PERJURY PROBLEM

When a defense attorney believes that her client is about to commit perjury, she faces a particularly difficult dilemma that bears on the right to effective assistance of counsel.

Applying Strickland to Client Perjury: Nix v. Whiteside

In Nix v. Whiteside, 475 U.S. 157 (1986), the defendant pleaded self-defense, but in his initial statement to defense counsel, he did not mention that the victim had a gun. In a later interview, the defendant stated that he now remembered that he saw the victim with "something metallic" in his hand. When challenged about the discrepancy by defense counsel, the defendant referred to a case in which an acquaintance was acquitted after testifying that his victim wielded a gun. In apparent comparison with that case, the defendant concluded: "If I don't say I saw a gun, I'm dead." The defense counsel told the client that any statement about a gun would be perjury; that if the defendant testified about a gun at trial, the lawyer would advise the court of the perjury, would probably be permitted to impeach the testimony, and would seek to withdraw. The client succumbed to the threats. He testified at trial that he believed the victim was reaching for a gun, but he had not seen one. The client challenged his second degree murder conviction on an ineffective assistance of counsel ground. Although the state courts commended the lawyer's integrity, a federal court of appeals granted habeas corpus relief.

The Supreme Court unanimously reversed in an opinion by Chief Justice Burger. He reasoned that no defendant has a right to commit perjury, therefore no defendant has a right to rely upon counsel to assist in the development of false testimony. The Court noted that under *Strickland,* the defendant must prove prejudice, and Whiteside "has no valid claim that confidence in the result of his trial has been diminished by his desisting from the contemplated perjury." Even if the jury would have been persuaded by the perjury, the Court concluded that under *Strickland,* "a defendant has no entitlement to the luck of a lawless decisionmaker."

Although lack of cognizable prejudice was enough to decide the case, the Chief Justice went further and held that Whiteside's counsel had not been ineffective in discouraging his client from committing perjury. He concluded that for the purposes of this case, effectiveness could be determined by reference to the prevailing rules of professional responsibility governing the conduct of lawyers. He noted that Disciplinary Rule 7–102(A)(4) of the ABA Code of Professional Responsibility (in effect in Iowa at that time) provided that a lawyer shall not "knowingly use perjured testimony or false evidence;" and that Rule 3.3 of the more recent Model Rules of Professional Conduct (in effect in almost all of the states, with some state-to-state variations) requires disclosure of client perjury to the tribunal as a last resort. The Chief Justice found that the prevailing ethical standards "confirm that the legal profession has accepted that an attorney's ethical duty to advance the interests of his client is limited by an equally solemn duty to comply with the law and standards of professional conduct." He concluded as follows:

> [U]nder no circumstances may a lawyer either advocate or passively tolerate a client's giving false testimony. * * * The rule adopted by the Court of Appeals, which seemingly would require an attorney to remain silent while his client committed perjury, is wholly incompatible with the established standards of ethical conduct and the laws of Iowa and contrary to professional standards promulgated by that State. The position advanced by the [Government], on the contrary, is wholly consistent with the Iowa standards of professional conduct and law, with the overwhelming majority of courts, and with codes of professional ethics. Since there has been no breach of any recognized professional duty, it follows that there can be no deprivation of the right to assistance of counsel under the *Strickland* standard.

Justice Brennan wrote an opinion concurring in the judgment. He agreed with the majority's analysis on the prejudice prong of *Strickland*. As to the performance prong, however, he argued that the Court "has no constitutional authority to establish rules of ethical conduct for lawyers practicing in the state courts," and that "the Court's essay regarding what constitutes the correct response to a criminal client's suggestion that he will perjure himself is pure discourse without force of law." Justice Blackmun wrote an opinion concurring in the judgment, joined by Justices Brennan, Marshall, and Stevens. He agreed that Whiteside had not shown prejudice from his lawyer's conduct, and saw no need to "grade counsel's performance." He argued, however, that the client perjury problem could not be solved by a simple reference to lawyers' ethics codes:

> Whether an attorney's response to what he sees as a client's command to commit perjury violates a defendant's Sixth Amendment rights may depend on many factors: how certain the attorney is that the proposed testimony is false, the stage of the proceedings at which the attorney discovers the plan, or the ways in which the attorney may be able to dissuade his client, to name just three. The complex interaction of factors, which is likely to vary from case to case, makes inappropriate a blanket rule that defense attorneys must reveal, or threaten to reveal, a client's anticipated perjury to the court. Except in the rarest of cases, attorneys who adopt the role of the judge or jury to determine the facts, pose a danger of depriving their clients of the zealous and loyal advocacy required by the Sixth Amendment.

Justice Stevens also wrote an opinion concurring in the judgment, emphasizing that it is often difficult to determine whether the client's proposed testimony is perjurious.

> A lawyer's certainty that a change in his client's recollection is a harbinger of intended perjury—as well as judicial review of such apparent certainty—should be tempered by the realization that, after reflection, the most honest witness may recall (or sincerely believe he recalls) details that he previously overlooked.

Whiteside Was Too Easy

Assuming there was a real risk of perjury, *Whiteside* is an easy case. Most lawyers would think it entirely appropriate to try to discourage the client from a planned course of perjury. Indeed, discouragement of perjury is effective advocacy, because the jury may disbelieve the lie, the prosecutor may easily tear it apart on cross-examination, and the client may subject himself to a perjury charge. Moreover, if the trial judge believes that a defendant lied on the stand, this will be taken into account at sentencing. See United States v. Dunnigan, 507 U.S. 87 (1993) (discussing enhancement of sentences under the Federal Sentencing Guidelines if the court finds that the defendant lied while testifying). So it certainly makes sense to do everything reasonable to discourage a client from committing perjury on the witness stand.

HARDER QUESTIONS

The difficult questions, not presented by *Whiteside,* are three. First, what if the client refuses to be dissuaded from a course of perjury and demands to testify? Second, what if the client appears to have been dissuaded from testifying falsely, but then commits perjury after taking the stand? Third, what if the lawyer discovers *after* the testimony that the client has perjured himself? See Freedman, Client Confidences and Client Perjury: Some Unanswered Questions, 136 U.Pa.L.Rev. 1939 (1988) (arguing that all of these problems should be left to the adversary system and to cross-examination by the prosecutor). After *Whiteside,* the A.B.A. Standing Committee on Ethics issued Formal Opinion 87–353 (1987). That opinion provides that if the lawyer is convinced that a witness is going to commit perjury, and all discussions with the client fail, *then the lawyer must inform the court.* And if the lawyer discovers perjury after the fact but before the proceedings are terminated, the lawyer must inform the court as well. The opinion justifies this result as follows:

> [The] ethical rules clearly recognize that a lawyer representing a client who admits guilt in fact, but wants to plead not guilty and put the state to its proof, may assist the client in entering such a plea and vigorously challenge the state's case at trial through cross-examination, legal motions and argument to the jury. However, neither the adversary system nor the ethical rules permit the lawyer to participate in the corruption of the judicial process by assisting the client in the introduction of evidence the lawyer knows is false. * * *

> On the contrary, the lawyer, as an officer of the court, has a duty to prevent the perjury, and if the perjury has already been committed, to prevent its playing any part in the judgment of the court. This duty the lawyer owes the court is not inconsistent with any duty owed to the client. More particularly, it is not inconsistent with the lawyer's duty to preserve the client's confidences. For that duty is based on the lawyer's need for information from the client to obtain for the client all that the law and lawful process provide. Implicit in the promise of confidentiality is its nonapplicability where the client seeks the unlawful end of corrupting the judicial process by false evidence.

The ABA opinion emphasizes, however (as did the concurring opinions in *Whiteside*), that it is not for defense counsel to judge the client, and that the lawyer should not presume that the client is going to present perjured testimony simply because it is inconsistent with a previous statement.

> It must be emphasized that this opinion does not change the professional relationship the lawyer has with the client and require the lawyer now to judge, rather than represent, the client. The lawyer's

obligation to disclose client perjury to the tribunal * * * is strictly limited by [Model] Rule 3.3 to the situation where the lawyer *knows* that the client has committed perjury, ordinarily based on admissions the client has made to the lawyer. (The Committee notes that some trial lawyers report that they have avoided the ethical dilemma posed by Rule 3.3 because they follow a practice of not questioning the client about the facts in the case and, therefore, never "know" that a client has given false testimony. Lawyers who engage in such practice may be violating their duties under Rule 3.3 and their obligation to provide competent representation under Rule 1.1.) * * *.

Can you think of anything more destructive to the attorney-client relationship than the lawyer ratting out her client? Why can't the perjury problem instead be handled through cross-examination by the prosecutor? When a District Attorney was asked what the defense lawyer should do when a client intends to commit perjury, he responded "Do me a favor. Let him try it." (Quoted in Freedman, Client Confidences and Client Perjury: Some Unanswered Questions, 136 U.Pa.L.Rev.1939 (1988)). Would most prosecutors respond the same way? See Saltzburg, Lawyers, Clients, and the Adversary System, 37 Mercer L.Rev. 674 (1986).

One problem with the ABA solution is that criminal defendants have a constitutional right to testify. They don't of course have a constitutional right to commit perjury; but perjury occurs only when the defendant actually testifies. What happens when defense counsel believes that the client is adamant about committing perjury, even after counsel gives the defendant *Whiteside* warnings. According to the ABA, counsel must now inform the trial judge that her client intends to commit perjury. But the trial judge cannot at this point, on defense counsel's word alone, prevent the defendant from testifying. To do so would risk almost certain reversal for violating the defendant's constitutional right to testify (because perjury has not been shown to a reviewing court's satisfaction). So the trial judge would have to hold some kind of hearing. At that hearing, the defendant will not admit that he is going to commit perjury if he is permitted to testify. The trial judge will be most reluctant to get into a quagmire of confidential communications between client and counsel in determining who is right about whether perjury is planned. It is very likely in most cases that a trial judge will be uncertain as to whether the defendant is going to commit perjury. The judge will not in these circumstances risk violating the constitutional right to testify by keeping the defendant off the stand. So in the vast majority of cases, defense counsel will have accomplished nothing by informing the tribunal of the client's planned perjury—the defendant will be permitted to testify anyway. The only thing accomplished is the destruction of the attorney-client relationship.

Compare the solution proposed by the A.B.A. Ethics Committee with that proposed by Professor Monroe Freedman, who addressed the perjury problem in Lawyer's Ethics in an Adversary System 31–37 (1985).

In my opinion, the attorney's obligation in such a situation would be to advise the client that the proposed testimony is unlawful, but to proceed in the normal fashion in presenting the testimony and arguing the case to the jury if the client makes the decision to go forward. Any other course would be a betrayal of the assurances of confidentiality given by the attorney in order to induce the client to reveal everything, however damaging it might appear.

Professor Friedman argues that none of the other alternatives are workable. For example, the lawyer cannot effectively withdraw from the representation because

[t]he client will then go to the nearest law office, realizing that the obligation of confidentiality is not what it has been represented to be, and withhold incriminating information or the fact of guilt from the new attorney. In terms of professional ethics, the practice of withdrawing from a case under such circumstances is difficult to defend, since the identical perjured testimony will ultimately be presented. Moreover, the new attorney will be ignorant of the perjury and therefore will be in no position to attempt to discourage the client from presenting it. Only the original attorney, who knows the truth, has that opportunity, but loses it in the very act of evading the ethical problem.

Professor Freedman describes the "Free Narrative" alternative, in which defense counsel lets the defendant tell his story on the stand, without asking questions and without referring to the statement in closing argument. He finds the free narrative solution unworkable:

[E]xperienced trial attorneys have often noted that jurors assume that the defendant's lawyer knows the truth about the case, and that the jury will frequently judge the defendant by drawing inferences from the attorney's conduct in the case. There is, of course, only one inference that can be drawn if the defendant's own attorney turns his or her back on the defendant at the most critical point in the trial, and then, in closing argument, sums up the case with no reference to the fact that the defendant has given exculpatory testimony.

Despite the rejection of the "free narrative" solution by the A.B.A., the Court in *Whiteside,* and Professor Freedman, the narrative "continues to be a commonly accepted method of dealing with client perjury." Shockley v. State, 565 A.2d 1373 (Del.1989) (holding that use of free narrative was ethically permissible and did not constitute ineffective assistance of counsel). See also Florida Bar v. Rubin, 549 So.2d 1000 (Fla.1989) (lawyer jailed for thirty days for refusing to defend client who intended to commit perjury; proper solution would have been to use a free narrative).

E. INEFFECTIVENESS AND SYSTEMS OF APPOINTED COUNSEL

Inadequate Funding

The overall quality and effectiveness of court-appointed attorneys may be limited by low compensation for services. For example, in South Carolina, a statute provided the following payment for appointed counsel in capital cases: $15/hour for in-court work, $10 for out-of-court time, with a $5,000 cap for trial work and a $2,500 cap for investigative and expert services. The South Carolina Supreme Court, in Bailey v. State, 309 S.C. 455, 424 S.E.2d 503 (1992), found that these statutory limits imposed a "gross and fundamental unfairness" on defense attorneys, and "do not provide compensation adequate to ensure effective assistance of counsel." The court remanded to determine what compensation would be reasonable. See also Smith v. New Hampshire, 118 N.H. 764, 394 A.2d 834 (1978) (invalidating similar statutory limits).

Cases like *Bailey* raise the question whether there are systemic flaws in the process of appointing counsel for indigents. Public defenders often have enormous caseloads and limited resources and might feel no choice but to choose to dispose of cases in ways that maximize the overall output of the agency, rather than the welfare of any one client. See Miranda v. Clark County, Nevada, 319 F.3d 465 (9th Cir. 2003) (invalidating a rule adopted by the public defender that sharply curtailed the quality of appointed counsel if the defendant fails a polygraph examination—the policy was designed to give priority in allocation of scarce resources to innocent defendants, but this would violate the right to effective assistance of counsel for other defendants) Private appointed attorneys are often so poorly compensated that talented counsel are discouraged from taking on a representation; and even the best counsel become so financially strapped that it becomes impossible to put on a defense.

Systematic Inadequacy in Capital Cases

Justice Blackmun, in his last term on the Court, took the occasion of the Court's denial of certiorari in a death penalty case to express concern about the system of appointed counsel in capital cases. Dissenting from denial of certiorari in McFarland v. Scott, 512 U.S. 1256 (1994), Justice Blackmun declared as follows:

> Without question, the principal failings of the capital punishment review process today are the inadequacy and inadequate compensation of counsel at trial and the unavailability of counsel in state post-conviction proceedings. The unique, bifurcated nature of capital trials and the special investigation into a defendant's personal history and

background that may be required, the complexity and fluidity of the law, and the high, emotional stakes involved all make capital cases more costly and difficult to litigate than ordinary criminal trials. Yet, the attorneys assigned to represent indigent capital defendants at times are less qualified than those appointed in ordinary criminal cases. See Green, Lethal Fiction: The Meaning of "Counsel" in the Sixth Amendment, 78 Iowa L.Rev. 433, 434 (1993); Coyle, et al., Fatal Defense, 12 Nat'l L.J. 30, 44 (June 11, 1990) (Capital-defense attorneys in eight States were disbarred, suspended, or disciplined at rates 3 to 46 times higher than the general attorney-discipline rates).

* * * [C]ompensation for attorneys representing indigent capital defendants often is perversely low. Although a properly conducted capital trial can involve hundreds of hours of investigation, preparation, and lengthy trial proceedings, many States severely limit the compensation paid for capital defense. * * * See generally Klein, The Eleventh Commandment: Thou Shalt Not be Compelled to Render the Ineffective Assistance of Counsel, 68 Ind.L.J. 363, 364–375 (1993).

Court-awarded funds for the appointment of investigators and experts often are either unavailable, severely limited, or not provided by state courts. As a result, attorneys appointed to represent capital defendants at the trial level frequently are unable to recoup even their overhead costs and out-of-pocket expenses, and effectively may be required to work at minimum wage or below while funding from their own pockets their client's defense. * * * The prospect that hours spent in trial preparation or funds expended hiring psychiatrists or ballistics experts will be uncompensated unquestionably chills even a qualified attorney's zealous representation of his client.

The practical costs of such ad hoc systems of attorney selection and compensation are well documented. Capital defendants have been sentenced to death when represented by counsel who never bothered to read the state death penalty statute, e.g., Smith v. State, 581 So.2d 497 (Ala.Crim.App.1990), slept through or otherwise were not present during trial, or failed to investigate or present any mitigating evidence at the penalty phase, Mitchell v. Kemp, 483 U.S. 1026 (1987) (Marshall, J., dissenting from denial of certiorari). * * * One Louisiana defendant was convicted of capital murder following a one-day trial and 20-minute penalty phase proceeding, in which his counsel stipulated to the defendant's age at the time of the crime and rested. State v. Messiah, 538 So.2d 175, 187 (La.1988). When asked to cite the criminal cases he knew, one defense attorney who failed to challenge his client's racially unrepresentative jury pool, could name only two cases: *Miranda* and *Dred Scott*. See Bright, Counsel for the Poor: The Death Sentence Not for the Worst Crime but for the Worst Lawyer, 103 Yale L.J. 1835, 1839.

Justice Blackmun contended that the *Strickland* test for reviewing the effectiveness of counsel provides insufficient protection for capital defendants, in light of the systemic underfunding and underregulation of appointed counsel in capital cases. He elaborated as follows:

> The impotence of the *Strickland* standard is perhaps best evidenced in the cases in which ineffective assistance claims have been denied. John Young, for example, was represented in his capital trial by an attorney who was addicted to drugs and who a few weeks later was incarcerated on federal drug charges. The Court of Appeals for the Eleventh Circuit rejected Young's ineffective assistance of counsel claim on federal habeas, Young v. Zant, 727 F.2d 1489 (11th Cir.1984), and this Court denied review. * * *

> Jesus Romero's attorney failed to present any evidence at the penalty phase and delivered a closing argument totaling 29 words. Although the attorney later was suspended on unrelated grounds, Romero's ineffective assistance claim was rejected by the Court of Appeals for the Fifth Circuit, Romero v. Lynaugh, 884 F.2d 871, 875 (1989), and this Court denied certiorari. Romero was executed in 1992. Larry Heath was represented on direct appeal by counsel who filed a 6-page brief before the Alabama Court of Criminal Appeals. The attorney failed to appear for oral argument before the Alabama Supreme Court and filed a brief in that court containing a 1-page argument and citing a single case. The Eleventh Circuit found no prejudice, Heath v. Jones, 941 F.2d 1126, 1131 (11th Cir.1991), and this Court denied review. Heath was executed in Alabama in 1992.

> James Messer, a mentally impaired capital defendant, was represented by an attorney who at the trial's guilt phase presented no defense, made no objections, and emphasized the horror of the capital crime in his closing statement. At the penalty phase, the attorney presented no evidence of mental impairment, failed to introduce other substantial mitigating evidence, and again repeatedly suggested in closing that death was the appropriate punishment. The Eleventh Circuit refused to grant relief, Messer v. Kemp, 760 F.2d 1080 (11th Cir.1985), and this Court denied certiorari. Messer was executed in 1988. * * *

Justice Blackmun concluded with the hope that the system of appointed counsel in capital cases would be improved:

> Our system of justice is adversarial and depends for its legitimacy on the fair and adequate representation of all parties at all levels of the judicial process. * * * My 24 years of overseeing the imposition of the death penalty from this Court have left me in grave doubt whether this reliance is justified and whether the constitutional requirement of competent legal counsel for capital defendants is being fulfilled. * * *

[W]e must have the courage to recognize the failings of our present system of capital representation and the conviction to do what is necessary to improve it.

Justice Blackmun's opinion was written before the Court's decisions in Wiggins v. Smith and Rompilla v. Beard, supra; in each of those cases, the Court vacated the death penalty because counsel had not been effective in the penalty phase. Does this mean that Justice Blackmun's concerns are now beginning to be addressed?

F. THE RIGHT TO COUNSEL OF CHOICE

Gideon guarantees an absolute right to counsel for all serious crimes. The Sixth Amendment also provides a right to counsel of one's own choosing. But that right is not absolute. Its most important limitation is that it is dependent on the ability to pay chosen counsel. The Supreme Court has held that so long as an indigent receives effective representation, he has no right to choose a particular counsel. In Morris v. Slappy, 461 U.S. 1 (1983), Slappy was appointed counsel whom he trusted, but that counsel became ill before trial, and another was substituted. Slappy argued that a continuance should have been granted until trusted counsel could return. He did not contend that substitute counsel was ineffective. Chief Justice Burger, writing for the Court, interpreted Slappy's request, and the lower court's holding, as assuming that the indigent had the right to a "meaningful attorney-client relationship." He rejected this argument in no uncertain terms.

> No authority was cited for this novel ingredient of the Sixth Amendment guarantee, and of course none could be. No court could possibly guarantee that a defendant will develop the kind of rapport with his attorney * * * that the Court of Appeals thought part of the Sixth Amendment guarantee of counsel.

See also United States v. Pina, 844 F.2d 1 (1st Cir.1988) (court has no obligation to appoint a lawyer outside the public defender's office, simply because the defendant believes that all lawyers from that office are incompetent).

For a proposal that the current indigent defense system should be replaced by a voucher program in which an indigent could select his own attorney, see Schulhofer and Friedman, Reforming Indigent Defense: How Free Market Principles Can Help to Fix a Broken System, Cato Institute Policy Analysis No. 666, September 1, 2010. The authors conclude as follows:

> [B]y denying freedom of choice to the indigent defendant in what will often be the most important matter of his lifetime, the current system presents a glaring breach of our ideas of personal autonomy and freedom from unwarranted government control. We conclude that

present institutions for criminal defense ought to be replaced with a voucher system, in order to provide indigent defendants with freedom of choice and to provide attorneys with the same incentive to serve their clients that attorneys have always had when they represent clients other than the poor.

Violation of Right to Chosen Counsel Can Never Be Harmless: United States v. Gonzalez-Lopez

The right to pay for a particular counsel is grounded in personal autonomy: a defendant, whose liberty is at stake, should generally have the right to pick whom he wants to assist him. In United States v. Gonzalez-Lopez, 548 U.S. 140 (2006), the Court considered whether the violation of the constitutional right to counsel of choice was subject to harmless error review. The trial court had denied the defendant the right to hire a lawyer from outside the state; the defendant then hired a different lawyer to defend him. The Court of Appeals found the denial to be a violation of the right to the defendant's constitutional right to counsel of choice; that ruling was not contested in the Supreme Court. The government did argue, however, that the defendant was required to show "prejudice" from the denial of his right to counsel of choice. The government relied on the cases requiring the defendant to show "prejudice" for a violation of the right to *effective* assistance of counsel, most notably Strickland v. Washington.

The Court, in an opinion by Justice Scalia for five Justices, held that a violation of the right to counsel of choice required automatic reversal; no showing of prejudice was necessary. Justice Scalia addressed the government's argument that a violation of the right to counsel of choice was not "complete" unless the defendant could show that substitute counsel prejudiced his defense; this argument was based on an analysis that the right to counsel of choice protects the right to a fair trial. Justice Scalia responded as follows:

> [The Sixth Amendment] commands, not that a trial be fair, but that a particular guarantee of fairness be provided—to wit, that the accused be defended by the counsel he believes to be best. * * * In sum, the right at stake here is the right to counsel of choice, not the right to a fair trial; and that right was violated because the deprivation of counsel was erroneous. No additional showing of prejudice is required to make the violation "complete."

Justice Scalia then distinguished the cases on effective assistance of counsel, requiring a showing of "prejudice" before reversal:

> [T]he requirement of showing prejudice in ineffectiveness claims stems from the very definition of the right at issue; it is not a matter of showing that the violation was harmless, but of showing that a violation of the right to effective representation *occurred*. A choice-of-

counsel violation occurs *whenever* the defendant's choice is wrongfully denied. Moreover, if and when counsel's ineffectiveness "pervades" a trial, it does so * * * through identifiable mistakes. We can assess how those mistakes affected the outcome. To determine the effect of wrongful denial of choice of counsel, however, we would not be looking for mistakes committed by the actual counsel, but for differences in the defense that would have been made by the rejected counsel—in matters ranging from questions asked on *voir dire* and cross-examination to such intangibles as argument style and relationship with the prosecutors. * * * The difficulties of conducting the two assessments of prejudice are not remotely comparable.

Justice Alito, joined by Chief Justice Roberts, Justice Kennedy, and Justice Thomas, dissented. He argued that the majority's rule of automatic reversal created some "anomalous and unjustifiable consequences." He elaborated as follows:

Suppose, for example, that a defendant is initially represented by an attorney who previously represented the defendant in civil matters and who has little criminal experience. Suppose that this attorney is erroneously disqualified and that the defendant is then able to secure the services of a nationally acclaimed and highly experienced criminal defense attorney who secures a surprisingly favorable result at trial—for instance, acquittal on most but not all counts. Under the majority's holding, the trial court's erroneous ruling automatically means that the Sixth Amendment was violated—even if the defendant makes no attempt to argue that the disqualified attorney would have done a better job.

1. Disqualification of Defendant's Counsel of Choice

If the defendant can afford to pay, there is a *qualified* right to retain counsel of choice. In Wheat v. United States, 386 U.S. 153 (1988), Chief Justice Rehnquist wrote for the Court as it evaluated a district court's denial of Wheat's waiver of his right to conflict-free counsel and the court's refusal to permit a proposed substitution of attorneys.

Wheat was charged along with numerous others with participating in a farflung drug distribution conspiracy. One codefendant, Gomez-Barajas, was represented along with another, Bravo, by the same attorney, Iredale. Gomez-Barajas was tried first and acquitted on drug charges overlapping Wheat's. Gomez-Barajas sought to avoid a second trial on other charges and offered to plead guilty to tax evasion and illegal importation of merchandise. His plea was pending before the district court when Wheat's trial was to commence. Bravo, who apparently was a less significant defendant, pled guilty to one count of transporting approximately 2,400 pounds of marijuana.

Iredale, who had represented both of these defendants, notified the court that Wheat asked Iredale to try his case. The government raised with the court two possible conflicts: the court had not yet accepted the plea and sentencing arrangement negotiated between Gomez-Barajas and the Government, which meant that he could withdraw his plea and would be facing a trial represented by Iredale in which Wheat might be called as a government witness and Iredale would have already tried Wheat's case; and Iredale's representation of Bravo would directly affect Iredale's ability to represent Wheat because the government believed that the marijuana transported by Bravo was transferred to Wheat and the government asked Iredale to make Bravo available as a witness against Wheat in exchange for a change in the government's position as to Bravo's sentence.

Wheat responded to the government's concerns by emphasizing his right to have the counsel of his choice and noting that he, Gomez-Barajas, and Bravo all were willing to waive the right to conflict-free counsel. Wheat argued that, if called to testify against him, Bravo would simply say he did not know Wheat and had no dealings with him, and that in the unlikely event that Gomez-Barajas went to trial on tax evasion and illegal importation charges, Wheat would unlikely be a witness because he was not involved in those alleged crimes.

The trial court found for the Government and refused to permit Iredale to substitute in as Wheat's counsel. Wheat was convicted, the court of appeals affirmed the conviction, and the Supreme Court also affirmed. Chief Justice Rehnquist observed that the right to choose one's counsel is not absolute, noting as examples that a client who cannot afford a lawyer cannot insist on representation by that lawyer, and a client cannot generally compel a lawyer to accept a case.

The Chief Justice rejected Wheat's argument that he had the right waive any conflict and observed that "[f]ederal courts have an independent interest in ensuring that criminal trials are conducted within the ethical standards of the profession and that legal proceedings appear fair to all who observe them," and "[n]ot only the interest of a criminal defendant but the institutional interest in the rendition of just verdicts in criminal cases may be jeopardized by unregulated multiple representation." He concluded that "[w]here a court justifiably finds an actual conflict of interest, there can be no doubt that it may decline a proffer of waiver, and insist that defendants be separately represented."

The Chief Justice recognized the difficulty that trial courts have in dealing with conflict waivers because "[u]nfortunately for all concerned, a district court must pass on the issue of whether or not to allow a waiver of a conflict of interest by a criminal defendant not with the wisdom of hindsight after the trial has taken place, but in the murkier pre-trial context when relationships between parties are seen through a glass, darkly"; and accordingly "the district court must be allowed substantial latitude in refusing waivers of conflicts of interest not only in those rare cases where an actual conflict may be demonstrated before trial, but in the more common cases where a potential for conflict exists which may or may not burgeon into an actual conflict as the trial progresses." He concluded that "[i]n the circumstances of this case, with the motion for substitution of counsel made so close to the time of trial the District Court relied on instinct and judgment based on experience in making its decision," and "[w]e do not think it can be said that the court exceeded the broad latitude which must be accorded it in making this decision."

Justice Marshall, joined by Justice Brennan, dissented, and argued that the conflict arguments were too speculative to deny Wheat the benefit of Iredale as his lawyer. He found the likelihood that Gomez-Barajas's plea agreement would be rejected to be small, and that even if he went to trial there was no indication that Wheat was a percipient witness to the remaining charges. He also found it unlikely that Bravo could identify Wheat so that Iredale's prior representation of Bravo was not a problem. Justice Stevens, joined by Justice Blackmun, also dissented.

Analysis of Wheat

Wheat is criticized in Green, "Through a Glass, Darkly": How the Court Sees Motions to Disqualify Criminal Defense Lawyers, 89 Colum.L.Rev. 1201 (1989). Among other criticisms, Professor Green notes that "the Court relied on an unwarranted assumption that if the defendant is willing to waive potential conflict of interest claims his attorney probably has not complied with the ethical standards governing the investigation and disclosure of potential conflicts."

Wheat is defended in Stuntz, Waiving Rights in Criminal Procedure, 75 Va.L.Rev. 761 (1989). Professor Stuntz argues that clients jointly represented by a single counsel may or may not have improper motives. It may be that joint counsel is retained to deter conspirators from cutting an individual deal and cooperating with the government. Thus, some defendants may be coerced into accepting a joint counsel relationship. On the other hand, it may be that the clients have proper motives—they all want the same lawyer because that lawyer is excellent. Stuntz argues that the capability of the lawyer is likely to be known by the trial judge; if the lawyer is known to be merely average, bad motives for the multiple representation can be inferred, and disqualification should be ordered because the client's waiver of conflict-free counsel is not really voluntary. Therefore a broad grant of discretion to the trial judge is necessary to allow the judge to separate good from bad motives in joint representation. Professor Stuntz's arguments are not borne out by the facts in *Wheat*, however, where it appeared that a number of the defendants came to

Iredale fairly far along in the proceedings, because he had been so successful in defending other defendants. The trial judge specifically noted that Iredale was an excellent and highly successful defense attorney, and disqualified him nonetheless.

Another concern that might have animated the result in *Wheat* is that it is trial judges who see the defendant who is purporting to waive the right to conflict-free counsel. Conflicts of interest are complicated. How is the court to be sure that the defendant really understands what he is giving up? Especially with unsophisticated defendants, a trial judge might conclude that the defendant who says he wants to waive is in fact not making a truly knowing waiver. And because it is the trial judge who sees what is going on, appellate courts should be deferent to the trial judge's assessment and decision to override the defendant's "waiver." Otherwise the trial court will be whipsawed by granting the defendant's wish to proceed with counsel and then, on appeal, having the defendant argue that he did not really know what he was doing when he elected to go with conflicted counsel.

Cases Applying Wheat

After *Wheat*, appellate courts have usually upheld trial court disqualifications of defense counsel. For example, in United States v. Stites, 56 F.3d 1020 (9th Cir.1995), Stites and his sister Cheryl Dark were charged with RICO violations resulting from a scheme of insurance fraud. Stites fled the state, and Cheryl was represented by Juanita Brooks. Cheryl pleaded guilty and at the sentencing hearing, Brooks argued that Cheryl was a pawn of Stites; that Stites was "the mastermind," "a thief and a fraud," and a "cheap con artist." She added for good measure that "as an officer of the court and attorney myself, it makes me angry to see that people are able to so pervert our system of justice." Brooks won a light sentence for Dark. Two years later, Stites finally turned up for trial—and retained Brooks. When the prosecution objected, both Stites and Dark waived any conflict. But the trial judge—who happened to be the same judge who sentenced Dark—disqualified Brooks. The court of appeals upheld the disqualification. The court found that Brooks was properly disqualified because "[s]he could not, in the very same criminal prosecution, tell the court that Stites was a liar, a thief, and the mastermind of the massive fraud charged by the government and then represent the same person contending that he was innocent of the crimes charged." The court concluded as follows:

> Students of the classics may recall Cicero's comment that speeches at trials are for "the case and the occasion," they do not disclose "the man himself." But even if a certain insincerity may accompany the filling of an advocate's role, nothing in our professional ethics permits an

advocate to tell a court one set of facts today and a contradictory set of facts tomorrow.

One of the more notable disqualifications of counsel occurred in the prosecution of former Mafia boss John Gotti. United States v. Locascio, 6 F.3d 924 (2d Cir.1993). The trial court disqualified Gotti's long-time counsel, Bruce Cutler, on two grounds: (1) The government had proof that Cutler served as house counsel to the Mafia, representing various conspirators who had not personally retained him—thus his representation would actually be proof of conspiratorial activity at trial; and (2) The government had tapes of conversations in which Cutler was present while criminal activity was being discussed—thus, in challenging the government's interpretation of the tapes, Cutler would be acting as an unsworn witness. The court of appeals upheld the disqualification, even though Gotti had waived his right to conflict-free counsel. The court noted in particular with respect to Cutler's status as an unsworn witness, that Gotti's waiver of conflict was irrelevant:

> When an attorney is an unsworn witness * * * the detriment is to the government, since the defendant gains an unfair advantage, and to the court, since the factfinding process is impaired. Waiver by the defendant is ineffective in such situations, since he is not the party prejudiced.

> * * * The government was legitimately concerned that, when Cutler argued before the jury for a particular interpretation of the tapes, his interpretation would be given added credibility due to his presence in the room when the statements were made. This would have given Gotti an unfair advantage, since Cutler would not have had to take an oath in presenting his interpretation, but could merely frame it in the form of legal argument.

See also United States v. Register, 182 F.3d 820 (11th Cir.1999) (no error in disqualifying counsel over the defendant's objections, where a government informant might testify that the defendant paid the attorney with drugs from the conspiracy: "It would have been virtually impossible for the attorney to question the informant without being concerned to a significant degree about his own interests rather than those of his client").

2. Rendering the Defendant Unable to Pay for Counsel of Choice

CAPLIN & DRYSDALE V. UNITED STATES

Supreme Court of the United States, 1989.
491 U.S. 617.

JUSTICE WHITE delivered the opinion of the Court.

We are called on to determine whether the federal drug forfeiture statute includes an exemption for assets that a defendant wishes to use to pay an attorney who conducted his defense in the criminal case where forfeiture was sought. Because we determine that no such exemption exists, we must decide whether that statute, so interpreted, is consistent with the Fifth and Sixth Amendments. We hold that it is.

[The defendant Reckmeyer was charged with running a massive drug importation and distribution scheme that was a continuing criminal enterprise (CCE), in violation of 21 U.S.C. § 848. The district cout relied on the CCE statute and entered a restraining order forbidding the defendant to transfer any of the listed assets that were potentially forfeitable. The defendant had retained Caplin & Drysdale as counsel to represent him in grand jury investigations that resulted in the charges. The defendant moved to modify the restraining order to permit him to pay the law firm's fees and to exempt from any postconviction forfeiture order the assets that he intended to use to pay the firm. One week later, before the court ruled on the motion, the defendant pled guilty and agreed to forfeit all of the specified assets listed in the indictment. The district court entered an order forfeiting virtually all of the assets in the defendant's possession.

The law firm then filed a petition under a provision that permits third parties with an interest in forfeited property to ask the sentencing court for an adjudication of their rights to that property. The firm argued that a third party had a right to make claims against forfeited property if it was without cause to believe the property was subject to forfeiture at the time of a transaction and, alternatively, assets used to pay an attorney were exempt from forfeiture. The district court granted the firm's claim, and the court of appeals reversed in an en banc decision. The Supreme Court agreed with the court of appeals as to the firm's statutory argument in reliance on its decision in the companion case of United States v. Monsanto, 491 U.S. 600 (1989) (holding that the Comprehensive Forfeiture Act of 1984 (CFA), 21 U.S.C.S. § 853(a), clearly established that all of the assets of an accused are to be forfeited upon a finding of probable cause that they were the fruits of criminal activity and that the CFA made no allowances whatsoever for any discretionary release of funds by the courts to pay for an accused's attorney's fees).]

We therefore address petitioner's constitutional challenges to the forfeiture law. Petitioner contends that the statute infringes on criminal defendants' Sixth Amendment right to counsel of choice, and upsets the "balance of power" between the Government and the accused in a manner contrary to the Due Process Clause of the Fifth Amendment. We consider these contentions in turn.

* * *

Petitioner's first claim is that the forfeiture law makes impossible, or at least impermissibly burdens, a defendant's right "to select and be represented by one's preferred attorney." Petitioner does not, nor could it defensibly do so, assert that impecunious defendants have a Sixth Amendment right to choose their counsel. The Amendment guarantees defendants in criminal cases the right to adequate representation, but those who do not have the means to hire their own lawyers have no cognizable complaint so long as they are adequately represented by attorneys appointed by the courts. * * * The forfeiture statute does not prevent a defendant who has nonforfeitable assets from retaining any attorney of his choosing. Nor is it necessarily the case that a defendant who possesses nothing but assets the Government seeks to have forfeited will be prevented from retaining counsel of choice. Defendants like Reckmeyer may be able to find lawyers willing to represent them, hoping that their fees will be paid in the event of acquittal, or via some other means that a defendant might come by in the future. The burden placed on defendants by the forfeiture law is therefore a limited one.

Nonetheless, there will be cases where a defendant will be unable to retain the attorney of his choice, when that defendant would have been able to hire that lawyer if he had access to forfeitable assets * * *. It is in these cases, petitioner argues, that the Sixth Amendment puts limits on the forfeiture statute.

This submission is untenable. Whatever the full extent of the Sixth Amendment's protection of one's right to retain counsel of his choosing, that protection does not go beyond the individual's right to spend his own money to obtain the advice and assistance of counsel. A defendant has no Sixth Amendment right to spend another person's money for services rendered by an attorney, even if those funds are the only way that that defendant will be able to retain the attorney of his choice. A robbery suspect, for example, has no Sixth Amendment right to use funds he has stolen from a bank to retain an attorney to defend him if he is apprehended. The money, though in his possession, is not rightfully his; the Government does not violate the Sixth Amendment if it seizes the robbery proceeds and refuses to permit the defendant to use them to pay for his defense. * * *

* * *

There is no constitutional principle that gives one person the right to give another's property to a third party, even where the person seeking to complete the exchange wishes to do so in order to exercise a constitutionally protected right. * * *

Petitioner's "balancing analysis" to the contrary rests substantially on the view that the Government has only a modest interest in forfeitable assets that may be used to retain an attorney. Petitioner takes the position that, in large part, once assets have been paid over from client to attorney, the principal ends of forfeiture have been achieved: dispossessing a drug dealer or racketeer of the proceeds of his wrongdoing. We think that this view misses the mark for three reasons.

First, the Government has a pecuniary interest in forfeiture that goes beyond merely separating a criminal from his ill-gotten gains; that legitimate interest extends to recovering all forfeitable assets, for such assets are deposited in a Fund that supports law-enforcement efforts in a variety of important and useful ways. The sums of money that can be raised for law-enforcement activities this way are substantial,[a] and the Government's interest in using the profits of crime to fund these activities should not be discounted.

Second, the statute permits "rightful owners" of forfeited assets to make claims for forfeited assets before they are retained by the Government. The Government's interest in winning undiminished forfeiture thus includes the objective of returning property, in full, to those wrongfully deprived or defrauded of it. * * *

Finally * * * a major purpose motivating congressional adoption and continued refinement of the racketeer influenced and corrupt organizations (RICO) and CCE forfeiture provisions has been the desire to lessen the economic power of organized crime and drug enterprises. This includes the use of such economic power to retain private counsel. * * * The notion that the Government has a legitimate interest in depriving criminals of economic power, even insofar as that power is used to retain counsel of choice, may be somewhat unsettling. But when a defendant claims that he has suffered some substantial impairment of his Sixth Amendment rights by virtue of the seizure or forfeiture of assets in his possession, such a complaint is no more than the reflection of the harsh reality that the quality of a criminal defendant's representation frequently may turn on his ability to retain the best counsel money can buy. * * * [T]he Court of Appeals put it aptly: "The modern day Jean Valjean must be satisfied with appointed counsel. Yet the drug merchant claims that his possession of huge sums of money . . . entitles him to something more. We reject this

---

[a]   For example, just one of the assets which Reckmeyer agreed to forfeit, a parcel of land known as "Shelburne Glebe," was recently sold by federal authorities for $5.3 million. The proceeds of the sale will fund federal, state, and local law-enforcement activities.

contention, and any notion of a constitutional right to use the proceeds of crime to finance an expensive defense."[b]

It is our view that there is a strong governmental interest in obtaining full recovery of all forfeitable assets, an interest that overrides any Sixth Amendment interest in permitting criminals to use assets adjudged forfeitable to pay for their defense. * * *

We therefore reject petitioner's claim of a Sixth Amendment right of criminal defendants to use assets that are the Government's—assets adjudged forfeitable, as Reckmeyer's were—to pay attorney's fees, merely because those assets are in their possession.[c] See also *Monsanto,* which rejects a similar claim with respect to pretrial orders and assets not yet judged forfeitable.

* * *

---

[b] We also reject the contention, advanced by amici, see, e.g., Brief for American Bar Association as Amicus Curiae 20–22, * * * that a type of "per se" ineffective assistance of counsel results—due to the particular complexity of RICO or drug-enterprise cases—when a defendant is not permitted to use assets in his possession to retain counsel of choice, and instead must rely on appointed counsel. If such an argument were accepted, it would bar the trial of indigents charged with such offenses, because those persons would have to rely on appointed counsel—which this view considers per se ineffective. * * *

[c] Petitioner advances * * * possible ethical conflicts created for lawyers defending persons facing forfeiture of assets in their possession.

Petitioner first notes the statute's exemption from forfeiture of property transferred to a bona fide purchaser who was "reasonably without cause to believe that the property was subject to forfeiture." This provision, it is said, might give an attorney an incentive not to investigate a defendant's case as fully as possible, so that the lawyer can invoke it to protect from forfeiture any fees he has received. Yet given the requirement that any assets which the Government wishes to have forfeited must be specified in the indictment, see Fed.Rule Crim.Proc. 7(c)(2), the only way a lawyer could be a beneficiary * * * would be to fail to read the indictment of his client. In this light, the prospect that a lawyer might find himself in conflict with his client, by seeking to take advantage of § 853(n)(6)(B), amounts to very little. * * *

The second possible conflict arises in plea bargaining: petitioner posits that a lawyer may advise a client to accept an agreement entailing a more harsh prison sentence but no forfeiture—even where contrary to the client's interests—in an effort to preserve the lawyer's fee. Following such a strategy, however, would surely constitute ineffective assistance of counsel. We see no reason why our cases such as Strickland v. Washington are inadequate to deal with any such ineffectiveness where it arises. * * *

Finally, petitioner argues that the forfeiture statute, in operation, will create a system akin to "contingency fees" for defense lawyers: only a defense lawyer who wins acquittal for his client will be able to collect his fees, and contingent fees in criminal cases are generally considered unethical. See ABA Model Rule of Professional Conduct 1.5(d)(2)(1983). But there is no indication here that petitioner, or any other firm, has actually sought to charge a defendant on a contingency basis; rather the claim is that a law firm's prospect of collecting its fee may turn on the outcome at trial. This, however, may often be the case in criminal defense work. Nor is it clear why permitting contingent fees in criminal cases—if that is what the forfeiture statute does—violates a criminal defendant's Sixth Amendment rights. The fact that a federal statutory scheme authorizing contingency fees—again, if that is what Congress has created in § 853 (a premise we doubt)—is at odds with model disciplinary rules or state disciplinary codes hardly renders the federal statute invalid.

JUSTICE BLACKMUN, with whom JUSTICES BRENNAN, MARSHALL and STEVENS join, dissenting.

* * *

Had it been Congress' express aim to undermine the adversary system as we know it, it could hardly have found a better engine of destruction than attorney's-fee forfeiture. The main effect of forfeitures under the Act, of course, will be to deny the defendant the right to retain counsel, and therefore the right to have his defense designed and presented by an attorney he has chosen and trusts. If the Government restrains the defendant's assets before trial, private counsel will be unwilling to continue, or to take on, the defense. Even if no restraining order is entered, the possibility of forfeiture after conviction will itself substantially diminish the likelihood that private counsel will agree to take the case.

* * *

Perhaps most troubling is the fact that forfeiture statutes place the Government in the position to exercise an intolerable degree of power over any private attorney who takes on the task of representing a defendant in a forfeiture case. * * * The Government will be ever tempted to use the forfeiture weapon against a defense attorney who is particularly talented or aggressive on the client's behalf—the attorney who is better than what, in the Government's view, the defendant deserves. * * *

The long-term effects of the fee-forfeiture practice will be to decimate the private criminal-defense bar. As the use of the forfeiture mechanism expands to new categories of federal crimes and spreads to the States, only one class of defendants will be free routinely to retain private counsel: the affluent defendant accused of a crime that generates no economic gain. As the number of private clients diminishes, only the most idealistic and the least skilled of young lawyers will be attracted to the field, while the remainder seek greener pastures elsewhere.

* * *

QUESTIONS ON CAPLIN

Hasn't the majority—by presuming the assets are ill-gotten and thus not the defendant's—begged the question? Maybe not, because according to the dissenters, it is the risk that assets will later be adjudicated forfeitable at trial that prevents the defendant from being able to retain an attorney, i.e., an attorney will not take the case given the risk that all of the assets will be forfeited at the end. Thus, even if the government only relied on *post-trial* forfeitures, defense counsel would be deterred from the representation due to the relation-back provision in the statute, which takes forfeited assets out of the hands of third parties.

Forfeiture Hearings Not Required After Indictment: Kaley v. United States

In Kaley v. United States, 134 S.Ct. 1090 (2014), Justice Kagan wrote for the Court as it held that criminal defendants are not entitled to a hearing to contest a grand jury's finding of probable cause to believe they committed the crimes charged when they desire to challenge a pre-trial restraint on their property in order to use that property to hire counsel to defend them. Relying on the probable cause standard the Court established in *Monsanto*, the majority noted that pretrial restraint is permissible "based upon a finding of probable cause to believe that the property will ultimately be forfeitable." The finding has two parts: (1) that the defendant has committed a crime permitting forfeiture, and (2) the property at issue has the requisite connection to that crime. Justice Kagan noted that lower courts have generally permitted a hearing on the second part and have disagreed as to whether a hearing is permitted on the first part. Noting that a grand jury indictment "may do more than commence a criminal proceeding (with all the economic, reputational, and personal harm that entails)," she added that the indictment may also result in immediate deprivation of a defendant's freedom. The bottom line was that "[i]f judicial review of the grand jury's determination is not warranted (as we have so often held) to put a defendant on trial or place her in custody, then neither is it needed to freeze her property." The majority concluded that a judge's determination that there was no probable cause could create "legal dissonance" with the grand jury's indictment.

The defendants argued that the Court should apply the balancing test of Mathews v. Eldridge, 424 U.S. 319 (1976), to determine whether they should get a hearing. Justice Kagan responded that "[e]ven if *Mathews* applied here—even if, that is, its balancing inquiry were capable of trumping this Court's repeated admonitions that the grand jury's word is conclusive—the Kaleys still would not be entitled to the hearing they seek." She emphasized that "the Government has a substantial interest in freezing potentially forfeitable assists without an evidentiary hearing about the probable cause underlying criminal charges."

Chief Justice Roberts, joined by Justices Breyer and Sotomayor, dissented and began his opinion with these words: "An individual facing serious criminal charges brought by the United States has little but the Constitution and his attorney standing between him and prison. He might readily give all he owns to defend himself." The Chief Justice observed that *Monsanto* had left open the question whether the accused was entitled to a hearing before his property was restrained so that it could not be used to hire counsel and wrote that "[t]he possibility that a prosecutor could elect to hamstring his target by preventing him from paying his counsel of choice raises substantial concerns about the fairness of the entire proceeding."

The Chief Justice responded to the majority's analysis of *Mathews* by citing the important interests of defendants in a criminal proceeding, including the presumption of innocence and the choice of counsel "to vindicate that presumption by choosing the advocate that they believe will best defend them" which is "at the very core of the Sixth Amendment."

Freezing Untainted Assets That Would Be Used to Pay for Counsel: Luis v. United States

LUIS V. UNITED STATES
Supreme Court of the United States, 2016.
136 S.Ct. 1083.

JUSTICE BREYER announced the judgment of the Court and delivered an opinion in which THE CHIEF JUSTICE, JUSTICE GINSBURG, and JUSTICE SOTOMAYOR join.

A federal statute provides that a court may freeze before trial certain assets belonging to a criminal defendant accused of violations of federal health care or banking laws. See 18 U.S.C. § 1345. Those assets include: (1) property "obtained as a result of" the crime, (2) property "traceable" to the crime, and (3) other "property of equivalent value." § 1345(a)(2). In this case, the Government has obtained a court order that freezes assets belonging to the third category of property, namely, property that is untainted by the crime, and that belongs fully to the defendant. That order, the defendant says, prevents her from paying her lawyer. She claims that insofar as it does so, it violates her Sixth Amendment "right . . . to have the Assistance of Counsel for [her] defence." We agree.

* * * In October 2012, a federal grand jury charged the petitioner, Sila Luis, with paying kickbacks, conspiring to commit fraud, and engaging in other crimes all related to health care. The Government claimed that Luis had fraudulently obtained close to $45 million, almost all of which she had already spent. Believing it would convict Luis of the crimes charged, and hoping to preserve the $2 million remaining in Luis' possession for payment of restitution and other criminal penalties (often referred to as criminal forfeitures, which can include innocent—not just tainted—assets, a point of critical importance here), the Government sought a pretrial order prohibiting Luis from dissipating her assets. And the District Court ultimately issued an order prohibiting her from "dissipating, or otherwise disposing of . . . assets, real or personal . . . up to the equivalent value of the proceeds of the Federal health care fraud ($45 million)."

The Government and Luis agree that this court order will prevent Luis from using her own untainted funds, *i.e.*, funds not connected with the crime, to hire counsel to defend her in her criminal case. * * * Although the District Court recognized that the order might prevent Luis from obtaining counsel of her choice, it held "that there is no Sixth Amendment right to use untainted, substitute assets to hire counsel."

The Eleventh Circuit upheld the District Court. We granted Luis' petition for certiorari.

* * *

No one doubts the fundamental character of a criminal defendant's Sixth Amendment right to the "Assistance of Counsel." [Justice Breyer cites and quotes from *Gideon v. Wainright.*]

Given the necessarily close working relationship between lawyer and client, the need for confidence, and the critical importance of trust, * * * the Court has held that the Sixth Amendment grants a defendant "a fair opportunity to secure counsel of his own choice." This "fair opportunity" for the defendant to secure counsel of choice has limits. A defendant has no right, for example, to an attorney who is not a member of the bar, or who has a conflict of interest due to a relationship with an opposing party. And an indigent defendant, while entitled to adequate representation, has no right to have the Government pay for his preferred representational choice.

We nonetheless emphasize that the constitutional right at issue here is fundamental: The Sixth Amendment guarantees a defendant the right to be represented by an otherwise qualified attorney whom that defendant can afford to hire.

The Government cannot, and does not, deny Luis' right to be represented by a qualified attorney whom she chooses and can afford. But the Government would undermine the value of that right by taking from Luis the ability to use the funds she needs to pay for her chosen attorney. The Government points out that, while freezing the funds may have this consequence, there are important interests on the other side of the legal equation: It wishes to guarantee that those funds will be available later to help pay for statutory penalties (including forfeiture of untainted assets) and restitution, should it secure convictions. And it points to two cases from this Court, *Caplin & Drysdale*, and [*United States v.*] *Monsanto*, which, in the Government's view, hold that the Sixth Amendment does not pose an obstacle to its doing so here. In our view, however, the nature of the assets at issue here differs from the assets at issue in those earlier cases. And that distinction makes a difference.

* * * The relevant difference consists of the fact that the property here is untainted; *i.e.*, it belongs to the defendant, pure and simple. In this respect it differs from a robber's loot, a drug seller's cocaine, a burglar's tools, or other property associated with the planning, implementing, or concealing of a crime. * * * The robber's loot belongs to the victim, not to the defendant. * * * The cocaine is contraband, long considered forfeitable to the Government wherever found. * * * And title to property used to commit a crime (or otherwise "traceable" to a crime) often passes to the Government at the instant the crime is planned or committed. * * *

The property at issue here, however, is not loot, contraband, or otherwise "tainted." It belongs to the defendant. That fact undermines the Government's reliance upon precedent, for both *Caplin & Drysdale* and *Monsanto* relied critically upon the fact that the property at issue was "tainted," and that title to the property therefore had passed from the defendant to the Government before the court issued its order freezing (or otherwise disposing of) the assets.

* * *

The Court in those cases * * * acknowledged that whether property is "forfeitable" or subject to pretrial restraint under Congress' scheme is a nuanced inquiry that very much depends on who has the superior interest in the property at issue. * * *

The distinction * * * is thus an important one, not a technicality. It is the difference between what is yours and what is mine. In *Caplin & Drysdale* and *Monsanto*, the Government wanted to impose restrictions upon (or seize) property that the Government had probable cause to believe was the proceeds of, or traceable to, a crime. The relevant statute said that the Government took title to those tainted assets as of the time of the crime. And the defendants in those cases consequently had to concede that the disputed property was in an important sense the Government's at the time the court imposed the restrictions.

This is not to say that the Government "owned" the tainted property outright (in the sense that it could take possession of the property even before obtaining a conviction). Rather, it is to say that the Government even before trial had a "substantial" interest in the tainted property sufficient to justify the property's pretrial restraint. * * *

If we analogize to bankruptcy law, the Government [in *Caplin & Drysdale* and *Monsanto*] became something like a secured creditor with a lien on the defendant's tainted assets superior to that of most any other party. * * *

Here, by contrast, the Government seeks to impose restrictions upon Luis' *untainted* property without any showing of any equivalent governmental interest in that property. Again, if this were a bankruptcy case, the Government would be at most an unsecured creditor. Although such creditors someday might collect from a debtor's general assets, they cannot be said to have any present claim to, or interest in, the debtor's property. * * * At least regarding her untainted assets, Luis can at this point reasonably claim that the property is still "mine," free and clear.

* * *

This distinction between (1) what is primarily "mine" (the defendant's) and (2) what is primarily "yours" (the Government's) does not by itself answer the constitutional question posed, for the law of property sometimes allows a person without a present interest in a piece of property to impose restrictions upon a current owner, say, to prevent waste. A holder of a reversionary interest, for example, can prevent the owner of a life estate from wasting the property. * * * The Government here seeks a somewhat analogous order, *i.e.*, an order that will preserve Luis' untainted assets so that they will be available to cover the costs of forfeiture and restitution if she is convicted, and if the court later determines that her tainted assets are insufficient or otherwise unavailable.

The Government finds statutory authority for its request in language authorizing a court to enjoin a criminal defendant from, for example, disposing of innocent "property of equivalent value" to that of tainted property. 18 U.S.C. § 1345(a)(2)(B)(i). * * *

[But] the nature of the competing interests argues against this kind of court order. On the one side we find, as we have previously explained, a Sixth Amendment right to assistance of counsel that is a fundamental constituent of due process of law. * * * The order at issue in this case would seriously undermine that constitutional right.

On the other side we find interests that include the Government's contingent interest in securing its punishment of choice (namely, criminal forfeiture) as well as the victims' interest in securing restitution (notably, from funds belonging to the defendant, not the victims). While these interests are important, to deny the Government the order it requests will not inevitably undermine them, for, at least sometimes, the defendant may possess other assets—say, "tainted" property—that might be used for forfeitures and restitution. Nor do the interests in obtaining payment of a criminal forfeiture or restitution order enjoy constitutional protection. Rather, despite their importance, compared to the right to counsel of choice, these interests would seem to lie somewhat further from the heart of a fair, effective criminal justice system.

* * *

[A]s a practical matter, to accept the Government's position could well erode the right to counsel to a considerably greater extent than we have so far indicated. To permit the Government to freeze Luis' untainted assets would unleash a principle of constitutional law that would have no obvious stopping place. The statutory provision before us authorizing the present restraining order refers only to "banking law violation[s]" and "Federal health care offense[s]." 18 U.S.C. § 1345(a)(2). But, in the Government's view, Congress could write more statutes authorizing pretrial restraints in cases involving other illegal behavior—after all, a broad range of such behavior can lead to postconviction forfeiture of untainted assets.

* * *

These defendants, rendered indigent, would fall back upon publicly paid counsel, including overworked and underpaid public defenders. As the Department of Justice explains, only 27 percent of county-based public defender offices have sufficient attorneys to meet nationally recommended caseload standards. And as one *amicus* points out, "[m]any federal public defender organizations and lawyers appointed under the Criminal Justice Act serve numerous clients and have only limited resources." The upshot is a substantial risk that accepting the Government's views would—by increasing the government-paid-defender workload—render less effective the basic right the Sixth Amendment seeks to protect.

* * * We add that the constitutional line we have drawn should prove workable. That line distinguishes between a criminal defendant's (1) tainted funds and (2) innocent funds needed to pay for counsel. We concede, as JUSTICE KENNEDY points out, that money is fungible; and sometimes it will be difficult to say whether a particular bank account contains tainted or untainted funds. But the law has tracing rules that help courts implement the kind of distinction we require in this case. * * * And those rules will likely also prevent Luis from benefiting from many of the money transfers and purchases JUSTICE KENNEDY describes.

Courts use tracing rules in cases involving fraud, pension rights, bankruptcy, trusts, etc. They consequently have experience separating tainted assets from untainted assets, just as they have experience determining how much money is needed to cover the costs of a lawyer.

* * *

For the reasons stated, we conclude that the defendant in this case has a Sixth Amendment right to use her own "innocent" property to pay a reasonable fee for the assistance of counsel. On the assumptions made here, the District Court's order prevents Luis from exercising that right. * * *

JUSTICE THOMAS, concurring in the judgment.

I agree with the plurality that a pretrial freeze of untainted assets violates a criminal defendant's Sixth Amendment right to counsel of choice. But * * * my reasoning rests strictly on the Sixth Amendment's text and common-law backdrop.

The Sixth Amendment provides important limits on the Government's power to freeze a criminal defendant's forfeitable assets before trial. And, constitutional rights necessarily protect the prerequisites for their exercise. The right "to have the Assistance of Counsel," U.S. Const., Amdt. 6, thus implies the right to use lawfully owned property to pay for an attorney. Otherwise the right to counsel—originally understood to protect only the right to hire counsel of choice—would be meaningless. History confirms this textual understanding. The common law limited pretrial asset restraints to tainted assets. Both this textual understanding and history establish that the Sixth Amendment prevents the Government from freezing untainted assets in order to secure a potential forfeiture. The freeze here accordingly violates the Constitution.

* * *

JUSTICE KENNEDY, with whom JUSTICE ALITO joins, dissenting.

The plurality and JUSTICE THOMAS find in the Sixth Amendment a right of criminal defendants to pay for an attorney with funds that are forfeitable upon conviction so long as those funds are not derived from the crime alleged. That unprecedented holding rewards criminals who hurry to spend, conceal, or launder stolen property by assuring them that they may use their own funds to pay for an attorney after they have dissipated the proceeds of their crime. * * * By granting a defendant a constitutional right to hire an attorney with assets needed to make a property-crime victim whole, the plurality and JUSTICE THOMAS ignore this Court's precedents and distort the Sixth Amendment right to counsel.

The result reached today makes little sense in cases that involve fungible assets preceded by fraud, embezzlement, or other theft. An example illustrates the point. Assume a thief steals $1 million and then wins another $1 million in a lottery. After putting the sums in separate accounts, he or she spends $1 million. If the thief spends his or her lottery winnings, the Government can restrain the stolen funds in their entirety. The thief has no right to use those funds to pay for an attorney. Yet if the thief heeds today's decision, he or she will spend the stolen money first; for if the thief is apprehended, the $1 million won in the lottery can be used for an attorney. This result is not required by the Constitution.

* * *

The true winners today are sophisticated criminals who know how to make criminal proceeds look untainted. They do so every day. * * * They structure their transactions to avoid triggering recordkeeping and reporting requirements. And they open bank accounts in other people's names and through shell companies, all to disguise the origins of their funds.

* * *

JUSTICE KAGAN, dissenting.

I find *United States* v. *Monsanto* a troubling decision. It is one thing to hold, as this Court did in *Caplin & Drysdale* that a convicted felon has no Sixth Amendment right to pay his lawyer with funds adjudged forfeitable. Following conviction, such assets belong to the Government, and "[t]here is no constitutional principle that gives one person the right to give another's property to a third party." But it is quite another thing to say that the Government may, prior to trial, freeze assets that a defendant needs to hire an attorney, based on nothing more than "probable cause to believe that the property will ultimately be proved forfeitable." At that time, the presumption of innocence still applies, and the Government's interest in the assets is wholly contingent on future judgments of conviction and forfeiture. * * *

But the correctness of *Monsanto* is not at issue today. Petitioner Sila Luis has not asked this Court either to overrule or to modify that decision; she argues only that it does not answer the question presented here. And because Luis takes *Monsanto* as a given, the Court must do so as well.

On that basis, I agree with the principal dissent that *Monsanto* controls this case. Because the Government has established probable cause to believe that it will eventually recover Luis's assets, she has no right to use them to pay an attorney. * * *

The plurality reaches a contrary result only by differentiating between the direct fruits of criminal activity and substitute assets that become subject to forfeiture when the defendant has run through those proceeds. But * * * the Government's and the defendant's respective legal interests in those two kinds of property, prior to a judgment of guilt, are exactly the same: The defendant maintains ownership of either type, with the Government holding only a contingent interest. * * *

3. Other Limitations on the Right to Counsel of Choice

There are other situations in which the right to chosen counsel has been trumped by a state interest. For example, if the defendant's chosen counsel is from out-of-state, counsel must apply for *pro hac vice* admission and be admitted by the court. In Leis v. Flynt, 439 U.S. 438 (1979), the Court held that the attorney had no due process right to be admitted *pro hac vice*. But the Court in *Leis* did not consider whether a criminal defendant's right to chosen counsel would be violated if out-of-state counsel is denied *pro hac vice* admission. Generally, courts have found that the state has a legitimate interest in regulating the practice of out-of-state lawyers who want to try cases in local courts, and that *pro hac vice* admission can be denied so long as the exclusion is not arbitrary. See Panzardi-Alvarez v. United States, 879 F.2d 975 (1st Cir.1989) (denial of *pro hac vice* admission does not violate right to chosen counsel where

SEC. VIII   SELF-REPRESENTATION   1499

counsel had previously represented joint clients with conflicting interests). Compare Fuller v. Diesslin, 868 F.2d 604 (3d Cir.1989), where the trial court denied *pro hac vice* admission of the defendant's chosen counsel on the following grounds: 1) that local lawyers were always better prepared on local practice rules; 2) that out-of-state attorneys created delays due to traveling; and 3) that there were many local attorneys who could effectively represent the defendant. The court of appeals found that the right to chosen counsel had been violated:

> [T]he trial court's wooden approach and its failure to make record-supported findings balancing the right to [chosen] counsel with the demands of the administration of justice resulted in an arbitrary denial [that] constituted per se constitutional error * * *. We conclude that [the argument that if there is adequate local counsel, then *pro hac vice* admission can be denied] is without merit, because it collapses the right to counsel of choice into the right to effective assistance of counsel. * * * [A]lthough the core value in the sixth amendment is effective assistance of counsel, the amendment also comprehends other related rights, such as the right to select and be represented by one's preferred attorney.

VIII. SELF-REPRESENTATION

A. THE CONSTITUTIONAL RIGHT

Although a defendant has a right to the assistance of counsel in all criminal prosecutions, sometimes she may prefer to defend herself. Beginning with the Judiciary Act of 1789, the right of self-representation in federal courts has been protected by statute. But California, where Anthony Faretta was convicted of grand theft, did not grant that right. It allowed a judge to appoint counsel over Faretta's objection and despite his knowing and voluntary waiver of his right to counsel.

FARETTA V. CALIFORNIA
Supreme Court of the United States, 1975.
422 U.S. 806.

JUSTICE STEWART delivered the opinion of the Court.

* * *

Anthony Faretta was charged with grand theft in an information filed in the Superior Court of Los Angeles County, Cal. At the arraignment, the Superior Court Judge assigned to preside at the trial appointed the public defender to represent Faretta. Well before the date of trial, however, Faretta requested that he be permitted to represent himself. Questioning by the judge revealed that Faretta had once represented himself in a criminal prosecution, that he had a high school education, and that he did not want to be represented by the public defender because he believed that that office was "very loaded down with * * * a heavy case load." The judge responded that he believed Faretta was "making a mistake" and emphasized that in further proceedings Faretta would receive no special favors. Nevertheless, after establishing that Faretta wanted to represent himself and did not want a lawyer, the judge, in a "preliminary ruling," accepted Faretta's waiver of the assistance of counsel. The judge indicated, however, that he might reverse this ruling if it later appeared that Faretta was unable adequately to represent himself.

Several weeks thereafter, but still prior to trial, the judge *sua sponte* held a hearing to inquire into Faretta's ability to conduct his own defense, and questioned him specifically about both the hearsay rule and the state law governing the challenge of potential jurors. After consideration of Faretta's answers, and observation of his demeanor, the judge ruled that Faretta had not made an intelligent and knowing waiver of his right to the assistance of counsel, and also ruled that Faretta had no constitutional right to conduct his own defense. The judge, accordingly, reversed his earlier ruling permitting self-representation and again appointed the public defender to represent Faretta. * * * Throughout the subsequent trial, the judge required that Faretta's defense be conducted only through the appointed lawyer from the public defender's office. At the conclusion of the trial, the jury found Faretta guilty as charged, and the judge sentenced him to prison.

[The appellate court affirmed Faretta's conviction.]

[The Court reviewed federal and state statutes according the right of self-representation, and decisions supporting such a right.]

* * * We confront here a nearly universal conviction, on the part of our people as well as our courts, that forcing a lawyer upon an unwilling defendant is contrary to his basic right to defend himself if he truly wants to do so.

This consensus is soundly premised. The right of self-representation finds support in the structure of the Sixth Amendment, as well as in the English and colonial jurisprudence from which the Amendment emerged.

* * *

The Sixth Amendment does not provide merely that a defense shall be made for the accused; it grants to the accused personally the right to make his defense. It is the accused, not counsel, who must be "informed of the nature and cause of the accusation," who must be "confronted with the witnesses against him," and who must be accorded "compulsory process for obtaining witnesses in his favor." Although not stated in the Amendment in so many words, the right to self-representation—to make one's own defense personally—is thus necessarily implied by the structure of the

Amendment. The right to defend is given directly to the accused; for it is he who suffers the consequences if the defense fails.

The counsel provision supplements this design. It speaks of the "assistance" of counsel, and an assistant, however expert, is still an assistant. The language and spirit of the Sixth Amendment contemplate that counsel, like the other defense tools guaranteed by the Amendment, shall be an aid to a willing defendant—not an organ of the State interposed between an unwilling defendant and his right to defend himself personally. To thrust counsel upon the accused, against his considered wish, thus violates the logic of the Amendment. In such a case, counsel is not an assistant, but a master; and the right to make a defense is stripped of the personal character upon which the Amendment insists. It is true that when a defendant chooses to have a lawyer manage and present his case, law and tradition may allocate to the counsel the power to make binding decisions of trial strategy in many areas. This allocation can only be justified, however, by the defendant's consent, at the outset, to accept counsel as his representative. An unwanted counsel "represents" the defendant only through a tenuous and unacceptable legal fiction. Unless the accused has acquiesced in such representation, the defense presented is not the defense guaranteed him by the Constitution, for, in a very real sense, it is not *his* defense.

* * *

[The Court explored in detail the historical development of the right to counsel in England and in the United States. It found that both English and colonial legal history support interpreting the Sixth Amendment to imply a right of self-representation].

There can be no blinking the fact that the right of an accused to conduct his own defense seems to cut against the grain of this Court's decisions holding that the Constitution requires that no accused can be convicted and imprisoned unless he has been accorded the right to the assistance of counsel. For it is surely true that the basic thesis of those decisions is that the help of a lawyer is essential to assure the defendant a fair trial. And a strong argument can surely be made that the whole thrust of those decisions must inevitably lead to the conclusion that a State may constitutionally impose a lawyer upon even an unwilling defendant.

But it is one thing to hold that every defendant, rich or poor, has the right to the assistance of counsel, and quite another to say that a State may compel a defendant to accept a lawyer he does not want. The value of state-appointed counsel was not unappreciated by the Founders, yet the notion of compulsory counsel was utterly foreign to them. And whatever else may be said of those who wrote the Bill of Rights, surely there can be no doubt that they understood the inestimable worth of free choice.

It is undeniable that in most criminal prosecutions defendants could better defend with counsel's guidance than by their own unskilled efforts. But where the defendant will not voluntarily accept representation by counsel, the potential advantage of a lawyer's training and experience can be realized, if at all, only imperfectly. To force a lawyer on a defendant can only lead him to believe that the law contrives against him. Moreover, it is not inconceivable that in some rare instances, the defendant might in fact present his case more effectively by conducting his own defense. Personal liberties are not rooted in the law of averages. The right to defend is personal. The defendant, and not his lawyer or the State, will bear the personal consequences of a conviction. It is the defendant, therefore, who must be free personally to decide whether in his particular case counsel is to his advantage. And although he may conduct his own defense ultimately to his own detriment, his choice must be honored out of "that respect for the individual which is the lifeblood of the law."[a]

* * *

When an accused manages his own defense, he relinquishes, as a purely factual matter, many of the traditional benefits associated with the right to counsel. For this reason, in order to represent himself, the accused must "knowingly and intelligently" forego those relinquished benefits. Although a defendant need not himself have the skill and experience of a lawyer in order competently and intelligently to choose self-representation, he should be made aware of the dangers and disadvantages of self-representation, so that the record will establish that he knows what he is doing and his choice is made with eyes open.

Here, weeks before trial, Faretta clearly and unequivocally declared to the trial judge that he wanted to represent himself and did not want counsel. The record affirmatively shows that Faretta was literate, competent, and understanding, and that he was voluntarily exercising his informed free will. The trial judge had warned Faretta that he thought it was a mistake not to accept the assistance of counsel, and that Faretta would be required to follow all the "ground rules" of trial procedure. We need make no assessment of how well or poorly Faretta had mastered the intricacies of the hearsay rule and the California code provisions that govern challenges of potential jurors on *voir dire*. For his technical legal knowledge, as such, was not relevant to an assessment of his knowing exercise of the right to defend himself.

---

[a]   Of course, a State may—even over objection by the accused—appoint a "standby counsel" to aid the accused if and when the accused requests help, and to be available to represent the accused in the event that termination of the defendant's self-representation is necessary.

The right of self-representation is not a license to abuse the dignity of the courtroom. Neither is it a license not to comply with relevant rules of procedural and substantive law. Thus, whatever else may or may not be open to him on appeal, a defendant who elects to represent himself cannot thereafter complain that the quality of his own defense amounted to a denial of "effective assistance of counsel."

In forcing Faretta, under these circumstances, to accept against his will a state-appointed public defender, the California courts deprived him of his constitutional right to conduct his own defense. Accordingly, the judgment before us is vacated, and the case is remanded for further proceedings not inconsistent with this opinion.

CHIEF JUSTICE BURGER, with whom JUSTICE BLACKMUN and JUSTICE REHNQUIST join, dissenting.

* * *

This case * * * is an example of the judicial tendency to constitutionalize what is thought "good." That effort fails on its own terms here, because there is nothing desirable or useful in permitting every accused person, even the most uneducated and inexperienced, to insist upon conducting his own defense to criminal charges. Moreover, there is no constitutional basis for the Court's holding, and it can only add to the problems of an already malfunctioning criminal justice system. I therefore dissent.

The most striking feature of the Court's opinion is that it devotes so little discussion to the matter which it concedes is the core of the decision, that is, discerning an independent basis in the Constitution for the supposed right to represent oneself in a criminal trial. Its ultimate assertion that such a right is tucked between the lines of the Sixth Amendment is contradicted by the Amendment's language and its consistent judicial interpretation.

* * *

[Justice Blackmun also wrote a dissenting opinion in which the Chief Justice and Justice Rehnquist joined. He argued that the procedural problems spawned by the case "will far outweigh whatever tactical advantage the defendant may feel he has gained by electing to represent himself." Referring to the old proverb that "one who is his own lawyer has a fool for a client," Justice Blackmun opined that "the Court * * * now bestows a *constitutional* right on one to make a fool of himself."]

Defendant May Be Prohibited from Pro Se Representation if Not Competent to Conduct a Trial: Indiana v. Edwards

In Indiana v. Edwards, 554 U.S. 164 (2008), Justice Breyer wrote for the Court as it held that neither the Sixth Amendment nor *Faretta* barred a state from insisting that a defendant who is mentally competent to stand trial with counsel—but not mentally competent to conduct a trial himself—proceed to trial with counsel.

After Edwards was charged, issues as to his mental competency were ever-present. In extended proceedings, the trial judge found that the defendant was competent to stand trial under the *Dusky* standard, but that he suffered from schizophrenia. The trial judge concluded that "[w]ith these findings, he's competent to stand trial but I'm not going to find he's competent to defend himself." Counsel represented Edwards who was convicted.

Justice Breyer concluded that the Court's precedents did not provide a clear answer to Edwards' self-representation claim but that three factors supported permitting a state to compel a defendant who is competent to stand trial but not to represent himself to be tried with counsel.

> First, the Court's precedent, while not answering the question, points slightly in the direction of our affirmative answer. [T]he Court's "mental competency" cases set forth a standard that focuses directly upon a defendant's "present ability to consult with his lawyer." These standards assume representation by counsel and emphasize the importance of counsel. They thus suggest (though do not hold) that an instance in which a defendant who would choose to forgo counsel at trial presents a very different set of circumstances, which in our view, calls for a different standard.

* * *

> Second, the nature of the problem before us cautions against the use of a single mental competency standard for deciding both (1) whether a defendant who is represented by counsel can proceed to trial and (2) whether a defendant who goes to trial must be permitted to represent himself. Mental illness itself is not a unitary concept. It varies in degree. It can vary over time. It interferes with an individual's functioning at different times in different ways. * * * In certain instances an individual may well be able to satisfy *Dusky*'s mental competence standard, for he will be able to work with counsel at trial, yet at the same time he may be unable to carry out the basic tasks needed to present his own defense without the help of counsel.

* * *

> Third, in our view, a right of self-representation at trial will not "affirm the dignity" of a defendant who lacks the mental capacity to conduct his defense without the assistance of counsel. To the contrary, given that defendant's uncertain mental state, the spectacle that could well result from his self-representation at trial is at least as likely to prove humiliating as ennobling. Moreover, insofar as a defendant's lack of capacity threatens an improper conviction or sentence, self-representation in that exceptional context undercuts the most basic of the Constitution's criminal law objectives, providing a fair trial. * * *

Indiana also argued a step further—it asked the Court overrule *Faretta*. The Court responded:

> * * * We decline to do so. We recognize that judges have sometimes expressed concern that *Faretta,* contrary to its intent, has led to trials that are unfair. But recent empirical research suggests that such instances are not common. See, *e.g.*, Hashimoto, Defending the Right of Self-Representation: An Empirical Look at the Pro Se Felony Defendant, 85 N. C. L. Rev. 423, 427, 447, 428 (2007) (noting that of the small number of defendants who chose to proceed *pro se*—"roughly 0.3% to 0.5%" of the total, state felony defendants in particular "appear to have achieved higher felony acquittal rates than their represented counterparts in that they were less likely to have been convicted of felonies"). At the same time, instances in which the trial's fairness is in doubt may well be concentrated in the 20 percent or so of self-representation cases where the mental competence of the defendant is also at issue. If so, today's opinion, assuring trial judges the authority to deal appropriately with cases in the latter category, may well alleviate those fair trial concerns.

Justice Scalia, joined by Justice Thomas, dissented and stated that "[i]n my view the Constitution does not permit a State to substitute its own perception of fairness for the defendant's right to make his own case before the jury—a specific right long understood as essential to a fair trial."

Knowing and Intelligent Waiver

In order to exercise the right of self-representation, a defendant must not only be competent; he must know and understand the consequences of waiving the assistance of counsel. See Godinez v. Moran, 509 U.S. 389 (1993) (besides finding competence, the trial court must also "satisfy itself that the waiver of his constitutional rights is knowing and voluntary."). A criminal defendant usually is untrained and unskilled in law and trial procedures. Studies indicate that representation by an attorney substantially improves an accused's chances of receiving a preliminary hearing and release on bail. A defendant represented by an attorney more frequently receives a jury trial, dismissal, or acquittal and, if convicted, more frequently receives a suspended sentence, a relatively short sentence, or probation. Should a defendant be advised of these and other dangers of self-representation before he waives the assistance of counsel? See United States v. Robinson, 913 F.2d 712 (9th Cir.1990) (for a knowing and intelligent waiver, "a criminal defendant must be aware of the nature of the charges against him, the possible penalties, and the dangers and disadvantages of self-representation").

A model inquiry for Federal District Judges to use with defendants who wish to proceed *pro se* is contained in 1 Bench Book for United States District Judges 1.02–2 to –5:

When a defendant states that he wishes to represent himself, you should ask questions similar to the following:

(a) Have you ever studied law?

(b) Have you ever represented yourself or any other defendant in a criminal action?

(c) You realize, do you not, that you are charged with these crimes: (Here state the crimes with which the defendant is charged.)

(d) You realize, do you not, that if you are found guilty of the crime charged in Count I the court must impose an assessment of at least _____ and could sentence you to as much as _____ years in prison and fine you as much as $_____?

(Then ask him a similar question with respect to each other crime with which he may be charged in the indictment or information.)

(e) You realize, do you not, that if you are found guilty of more than one of those crimes this court can order that the sentences be served consecutively, that is, one after another?

(f) You realize, do you not, that if you represent yourself, you are on your own? I cannot tell you how you should try your case or even advise you as to how to try your case.

(g) Are you familiar with the Federal Rules of Evidence?

(h) You realize, do you not, that the Federal Rules of Evidence govern what evidence may or may not be introduced at trial and, in representing yourself, you must abide by those rules?

(i) Are you familiar with the Federal Rules of Criminal Procedure?

(j) You realize, do you not, that those rules govern the way in which a criminal action is tried in federal court?

(k) You realize, do you not, that if you decide to take the witness stand, you must present your testimony by asking questions of yourself? You cannot just take the stand and tell your story. You must proceed question by question through your testimony.

(*l*) (Then say to the defendant something to this effect):

I must advise you that in my opinion you would be far better defended by a trained lawyer than you can be by yourself. I think it is unwise of you to try to represent yourself. You are not familiar with the law. You are not familiar with court procedure. You are not familiar with the rules of evidence. I would strongly urge you not to try to represent yourself.

(m) Now, in light of the penalty that you might suffer if you are found guilty and in light of all of the difficulties of representing yourself, is it still your desire to represent yourself and to give up your right to be represented by a lawyer?

(n) Is your decision entirely voluntary on your part?

(o) If the answers to the two preceding questions are in the affirmative, [and in your opinion the waiver of counsel *is* knowing and voluntary,] you should then say something to the following effect:

> "I find that the defendant has knowingly and voluntarily waived his right to counsel. I will therefore permit him to represent himself."

(p) You should consider the appointment of standby counsel to assist the defendant and to replace him if the court should determine during trial that the defendant can no longer be permitted to represent himself.

Failure to conduct a waiver inquiry at least similar to that suggested in the Bench Book has been held reversible error. See United States v. McDowell, 814 F.2d 245 (6th Cir.1987); United States v. Balough, 820 F.2d 1485 (9th Cir.1987) (noting "limited exception" to per se reversal where the record on the whole reveals a knowing and intelligent waiver of counsel). See also Overton v. Mathes, 425 F.3d 518 (8th Cir. 2005) (no requirement to inform defendant that if he proceeds pro se, he will remain in leg restraints during the trial as a security measure).

Faretta Warning?

A defendant who invokes the right to self-representation is at the same time waiving the right to counsel. Conversely, invoking the right to counsel is at the same time waiving the right to self-representation. The defendant must receive detailed warnings, as discussed above, before a waiver of the right to counsel will be found. Is the defendant who invokes a right to counsel entitled to be notified of his right to proceed *pro se* before a waiver of *that* right can be found? In United States v. Martin, 25 F.3d 293 (6th Cir.1994), the court answered this question in the negative:

> While the right to self-representation is related to the right to counsel, [it] is grounded more in considerations of free choice than in fair trial concerns. Thus, the right to self-representation does not implicate constitutional fair trial concerns to the same extent as does an accused's right to counsel. As the constitutional basis of the right to self-representation does not require a knowing and intelligent waiver

of that right, the district court need not advise a defendant of her right to proceed pro se prior to assertion of such a right.

Accord Munkus v. Furlong, 170 F.3d 980 (10th Cir.1999) (right to counsel is absolute while right to self-representation is subject to many conditions; given the constraints on the right to self-representation, a criminal defendant does not have to be informed of this right).

Requirement of Unequivocal Invocation

Courts have held that a defendant's waiver of the right to assistance of counsel must be "unequivocal." Courts are justifiably concerned that if the *Faretta* right is not clearly invoked, a defendant who ends up representing himself and losing will appeal on the ground that he never really waived his right to counsel. See United States v. Singleton, 107 F.3d 1091 (4th Cir.1997) (noting that a trial court evaluating a defendant's request to represent himself must "traverse a thin line between improperly allowing the defendant to proceed pro se, thereby violating his right to counsel, and improperly having the defendant proceed with counsel, thereby violating his right to self-representation"; noting also that "a skillful defendant could manipulate this dilemma to create reversible error.").

Courts have divided, however, about whether an unequivocal waiver is found when the defendant says that he wants to represent himself because he is in disagreement with defense counsel. Thus, in United States v. Mendez-Sanchez, 563 F.3d 935 (9th Cir. 2009), the court found that the defendant did not unequivocally waive his right to counsel and assert his right to self-representation when he stated that he wished to go to trial, but not with his appointed counsel, and when asked if he wished to represent himself, responded "that would be better than having one of these guys." Compare United States v. Volpontesta, 727 F.3d 666 (7th Cir. 2013), where the court found that

> the record shows that Volpontesta disagreed with his attorneys over trial strategy: specifically, their refusal to file certain motions they deemed frivolous, interview the large number of witnesses Volpontesta requested, and immediately provide Volpontesta with printed copies of discovery materials. The record indicates that Volpontesta's waiver of his right to counsel was a strategic decision he made so that he could pursue the case as he desired. We have held that a defendant's tactical decision to proceed pro se supports a finding of a knowing waiver. We find nothing in the context of Volpontesta's decision to represent himself that indicates that his waiver was anything but knowing and informed."

Of course, when the defendant's only choice is between self-representation and *incompetent* counsel, choice of *pro se* status does not indicate a voluntary waiver of the right to counsel, and reversal is required. Therefore, if the defendant states that he wishes to defend himself because he believes appointed counsel to be incompetent, the trial court must conduct a thorough inquiry into the allegations, and must appoint substitute counsel if the counsel has, up to that point, given ineffective representation under the standards of Strickland v. Washington. See United States v. Silkwood, 893 F.2d 245 (10th Cir.1989) (trial court erred when it failed to conduct inquiry to ensure that the defendant was not forced to make the "Hobson's choice * * * between incompetent or unprepared counsel and appearing *pro se*"); Crandell v. Bunnell, 144 F.3d 1213 (9th Cir.1998) (where counsel did nothing to prepare a defense for two months, his representation fell below an objective standard of reasonableness; the defendant's choice to represent himself, after the court refused to appoint substitute counsel, was therefore involuntary).

Remedy for a Faretta Violation

What is the remedy for the denial of the right to self-representation? Is reversal required even where counsel did a better job at trial than the defendant would have done? In McKaskle v. Wiggins, 465 U.S. 168 (1984), the Court held that the denial of the right to proceed *pro se* was a violation of the defendant's right to personal autonomy. It had nothing to do with the likelihood of a successful outcome at trial. The Court therefore concluded that "the right is either respected or denied; its deprivation cannot be harmless."

Thus, per se reversal is required for a violation of *Gideon,* and for the opposite violation of *Faretta.* Suppose that the defendant's *Faretta* rights are violated by the trial court's appointment of counsel over the defendant's explicit invocation of the right to represent himself. The conviction is therefore reversed. On re-trial, the defendant changes his mind and *demands* counsel. Can the trial judge refuse this demand and require the defendant to represent himself, because that is what he wanted to do in the first place? Why should the state have to give him what he so strongly objected to in the first trial? In Johnstone v. Kelly, 812 F.2d 821 (2d Cir.1987), the court stated that counsel must be provided on retrial unless the defendant makes an unequivocal invocation of the right of self-representation. The court explained as follows:

> If Johnstone elects to be represented by counsel at a retrial, it is not quite true, as the State contends, that he will again receive what the State once provided him. Though the State previously provided him with counsel, it denied him the choice whether to have counsel or proceed *pro se*. It is that choice that must be accorded at a retrial * * *.

Right to Self-Representation in Death Penalty Proceedings

In United States v. Davis, 285 F.3d 378 (5th Cir. 2002), the defendant stated that he wanted to represent himself in the penalty phase of the capital trial. He stated that he didn't want to present mitigating evidence. The trial court found that his waiver of the right to counsel was unequivocal and was knowing and intelligent; but it concluded that the *Faretta* right to self-representation did not extend to the penalty phase, and that the defendant's interest in self-representation at that stage was outweighed by the Eighth Amendment requirement that the death penalty not be imposed arbitrarily and capriciously. Counsel was appointed over the defendant's wishes. But the Court of Appeals found this to be error. The court concluded as follows:

> *Faretta* teaches us that a right to self-representation is a personal right. It cannot be impinged upon merely because society, or a judge, may have a different opinion with the accused as to what type of evidence, if any, should be presented in a penalty trial.

The court noted information in the record that Davis was inviting the death penalty, but nonetheless concluded "that Davis has the right to conduct his penalty defense in the manner of his choosing for it is he who suffers the consequences if the defense fails." Does this mean that if the defendant simply wants to give up and be executed, he has the absolute right to do so? Does the right to self-representation justify a state-sponsored suicide?

B. LIMITS ON THE RIGHT OF SELF-REPRESENTATION

The Court in *Faretta* was careful to note that the right to self-representation is not absolute. It is fair to state that courts after *Faretta* have not given the right to self-representation preferred status. Many qualifications on the right have been found reasonable.

1. Timeliness

If the defendant waits until trial, or just before it, to invoke his right to self-representation, then the trial court has the discretion to deny it. See Horton v. Dugger, 895 F.2d 714 (11th Cir.1990) (request to proceed *pro se,* made on first day of trial, held untimely).

2. Disruption of the Court

The majority in *Faretta* recognized that "the right to self-representation is not a license to abuse the dignity of the courtroom." What type of acts can be considered so "obstructionist" that the right to self-representation is lost? In United States v. Flewitt, 874 F.2d 669 (9th Cir.1989), the trial court appointed counsel, against the Flewitts' wishes, because the Flewitts were unprepared at the time of trial, had made excessive and "poorly formulated" discovery motions, and had refused to cooperate with the government in utilizing discovery opportunities. On appeal, they argued that their right to self-representation had been violated, and the government argued that the Flewitts had lost their right due to their "obstructionist" tactics. The court found that the reference in *Faretta* to obstructionist tactics spoke of "disruption in the courtroom." The court noted that the Flewitts' pretrial activity may have been ill-advised and detrimental to them, but "that was their choice to make." Compare Savage v. Estelle, 924 F.2d 1459 (9th Cir.1990) (defendant with a severe speech impediment is found unable to "abide by rules of procedure and courtroom protocol"; therefore, the right to self-representation was properly denied); Overton v. Mathes, 425 F.3d 518 (8th Cir. 2005) (defendant who represents himself can still be shackled if that is a reasonable security measure).

Is the defendant "disruptive" when he makes ridiculous arguments in court, tries to introduce clearly irrelevant evidence, concocts outlandish defenses, and proffers long-winded questions on cross-examination? If such conduct at the trial is enough to be considered "disruptive" under *Faretta*, how many defendants will be permitted to invoke the right to self-representation?

3. Protection of Witnesses

In many cases, the defendant's self-representation is especially unsettling to prosecution witnesses. For example, in a case on Long Island where the defendant Colin Ferguson was tried for shooting commuters on a Long Island Railroad train, Ferguson demanded to represent himself. The shooting victims who survived were therefore subjected to the ordeal of having to be questioned directly in court by the very person who shot them. Can the interests of witnesses ever outweigh the defendant's qualified right to self-representation?

The Fourth Circuit, in Fields v. Murray, 49 F.3d 1024 (4th Cir.1995) (en banc), explored the limitations on a defendant's *Faretta* right to personally question witnesses in the context of a sex crimes prosecution. Fields sought to act, in his words, as "co-counsel" in order to question the alleged sex abuse victims himself, because he "firmly believed these kids cannot look me in the eye and lie to me." The state trial court did not permit Fields to personally cross-examine the young girls who were witnesses against him, but did permit him to write out his questions and give them to his appointed lawyer. Fields was convicted. His *Faretta* claim was rejected by the state appellate courts, on the ground that since he only wanted to cross-examine the prosecution witnesses, and not to represent himself in any other respect, he had failed to unequivocally invoke his right to self-representation.

On habeas review, the court of appeals agreed with the state courts that Field had not unequivocally invoked his right to self-representation. But the court held further that even if Fields had represented himself, he would have had no right under the circumstances to cross-examine the witnesses personally. The court relied on Maryland v. Craig, 497 U.S. 836 (1990), where the Supreme Court held that a defendant's right to face-to-face confrontation could be restricted where such confrontation would traumatize a child-witness. The court of appeals reasoned as follows:

> If a defendant's Confrontation Clause right can be limited in the manner provided in *Craig,* we have little doubt that a defendant's self-representation right can be similarly limited. While the Confrontation Clause right is guaranteed explicitly in the Sixth Amendment, * * * the self-representation right is only implicit in that Amendment. The self-representation right was only firmly established in 1975 in *Faretta,* and then only over the dissent of three justices. Moreover, it is universally recognized that the self-representation right is not absolute.

> The State's interest here in protecting child sexual abuse victims from the emotional trauma of being cross-examined by their alleged abuser is at least as great as, and likely greater than, the State's interest in *Craig* of protecting children from the emotional harm of merely having to testify in their alleged abuser's presence. We have little trouble determining, therefore, that the State's interest here was sufficiently important to outweigh Fields' right to cross-examine personally witnesses against him if denial of this cross-examination was necessary to protect the young girls from emotional trauma.

4. Standby Counsel

Faretta indicates that a court may appoint standby counsel, even over the defendant's objection, to aid the defendant and to be available to represent him if self-representation is for some reason terminated. The limits of standby counsel's role were explored in McKaskle v. Wiggins, 465 U.S. 168 (1984), where the Court found that advisory counsel's conduct did not unconstitutionally interfere with Wiggins' right to self-representation. Wiggins first waived his right to counsel, then requested counsel, and finally decided to represent himself. The trial court appointed two attorneys to advise him. Disagreements between counsel and Wiggins occurred and at times counsel quarreled openly with Wiggins. From time-to-time throughout the trial, Wiggins would give in and let standby counsel take over the defense.

Justice O'Connor wrote for the majority and stated that *Faretta* requires that a defendant be given more than just the chance to be heard along with others: he must be given control over the defense. *Faretta* held that the right to self-representation was based on two factors: first, the defendant has the right grounded in personal autonomy to choose to control his own defense; second, self-representation may in some cases be an effective strategy, because it would allow the jury to sympathize with a defendant matched up against overwhelming prosecutorial forces. So while the court has the power to appoint standby counsel against the defendant's wishes, that counsel cannot seize actual control over the defendant's case, or else the first, "core" aspect of the right to self-representation would be violated. And standby counsel cannot without the defendant's consent "destroy the jury's perception that the defendant is representing himself," or else the strategy aspect of the right to self-representation would be undermined. The Court stated that "participation by standby counsel outside the presence of the jury engages only the first of these two limitations." It further noted that "*Faretta* rights are adequately vindicated in proceedings outside the presence of the jury if the *pro se* defendant is allowed to address the court freely" and if "all disagreements between counsel and the *pro se* defendant are resolved in the defendant's favor whenever the matter is one that would normally be left to the discretion of counsel." It found that most of the incidents of which Wiggins complained occurred outside the jury's presence. And it emphasized that all conflicts between Wiggins and his counsel were resolved in Wiggins's favor, although it opined that several incidents in which counsel engaged in acrimonious exchanges with their client were "regrettable."

In dissent, Justice White, joined by Justices Brennan and Marshall, argued that the court of appeals correctly found that standby counsel continuously participated in the trial, disrupted the proceedings, and turned the trial into an ordeal for the jury. He expressed concern about the subtle influences that squabbles between counsel and client can have on the outcome of a case and about the defendant's (not the jury's) perception of fairness, observing that *Faretta* is premised on the importance of the appearance of justice to the accused.

It is worth noting that in later proceedings, Wiggins maintained that he was impermissibly *denied* his right to counsel at his trial, because he had not unequivocally invoked his right to self-representation. The court in Wiggins v. Procunier, 753 F.2d 1318 (5th Cir.1985), rejected his claim. This may give one some perspective on why courts require the right of self-representation to be unequivocally invoked?

Is standby counsel part of the right to effective assistance of counsel under the Sixth Amendment? In United States v. Pollani, 146 F.3d 269 (5th Cir.1998), the Court held that the trial court erred in allowing the defendant to proceed pro se, because the defendant had not unequivocally waived his right to counsel. The government responded that there was no error, because the trial court provided counsel—specifically, standby counsel to assist Pollani at the trial. But the court rejected the government's argument, stating that the appointment of standby counsel "is a tactic for assisting a pro se litigant in vindicating his Sixth Amendment right of self-representation, not a substitute for representation by counsel for a defendant who seeks to exercise his right to counsel."

For a discussion on standby counsel's proper role and how standby counsel can be most effective, see Poulin, The Role of Standby Counsel in Criminal Cases: In the Twilight Zone of the Criminal Justice System, 75 N.Y.U. L.Rev. 676 (2000).

5. Hybrid Counsel and Control of the Defense

Frequently a defendant wants to appear as "co-counsel" or to defend partially *pro se* and partially by counsel. The Court in *Wiggins* held that there is no constitutional right to "hybrid representation"; either the defendant could represent himself or cede control of the defense to counsel, but there is no constitutionally-required middle ground. But the *Wiggins* Court did state that a court could *permit* a hybrid relationship in the exercise of its discretion.

Only a few courts have exercised their discretion and permitted hybrid representation. See, e.g., State v. McCleary, 149 N.J.Super. 77, 373 A.2d 400 (1977). See also United States v. Turnbull, 888 F.2d 636 (9th Cir.1989) ("if the defendant assumes any of the 'core functions' of the lawyer, the hybrid scheme is acceptable only if the defendant has voluntarily waived counsel"). If the costs of the representation do not increase, what purpose, other than to discourage the exercise of *Faretta* rights, is served by denying hybrid representation? See generally Note, The Accused as Co-Counsel: The Case for the Hybrid Defense, 12 Valparaiso L.Rev. 329 (1978).

Ceding Control over the Defense

Unless hybrid representation is granted, a defendant who chooses the right to counsel over the right to self-representation gives up substantial control over the defense. Strategic choices are left to the lawyer; the lawyer can veto the client's wishes as to what defenses can be raised, what arguments will be made, how to cross-examine a witness, etc. See, e.g., United States v. Padilla, 819 F.2d 952 (10th Cir.1987), where the court found no constitutional violation even though counsel refused to structure a defense as the defendant directed. The court stated that "the Sixth Amendment provides no right to counsel blindly following a defendant's instructions."

There are three notable exceptions to counsel's control over the defense. It is ultimately the defendant's decision (1) whether to waive a jury trial, (2) whether to testify, and (3) whether to plead guilty. See, e.g., Stano v. Dugger, 921 F.2d 1125 (11th Cir.1991) (counsel cannot be deemed ineffective where defendant pleads guilty against counsel's advice). See also Rule 1.2 of the Model Rules of Professional Conduct (lawyer shall abide by client's decision "after consultation with the lawyer" as to these three matters).

In Jones v. Barnes, 463 U.S. 745 (1983), the Court held that the Sixth Amendment does not require appointed appellate counsel to raise all nonfrivolous claims on appeal. The Court reasoned that a contrary rule would seriously undermine "the ability of counsel to present the client's case in accord with counsel's professional evaluation." The Court stated that the right of personal autonomy recognized in *Faretta* did not extend to strategic choices once the right to counsel has been invoked. Justice Brennan, joined by Justice Marshall, dissented and argued that the defendant's right to "the assistance of counsel" requires that counsel raise all issues of arguable merit that his client insists upon raising. Justice Blackmun concurred in the result, reasoning that an attorney should, as an ethical, not a constitutional, requirement, raise all nonfrivolous claims upon which his client insists.

Retained Hybrid Counsel?

Does the defendant have the right to hybrid representation if he *retains* counsel? The Court in United States v. Singleton, 107 F.3d 1091 (4th Cir.1997), stated that there was no such right—if the defendant is asking for a constitutional right to control the "lawyer" aspects of the defense, then he must represent himself. The court reasoned as follows:

> A trial judge has broad supervisory power over his courtroom and may within that discretion insist that a trial before him, if orchestrated or guided by an attorney, be presented in accordance with the ethical, professional, and prudential rules of trial conduct. And in order to be so satisfied, the judge has discretion to insist that in the courtroom counsel, not the client, take over completely and act as the spokesperson of the defense's case. Thus, the district court, having properly recognized no constitutional right to have advisory counsel support Singleton in the courtroom during trial, had discretion, should Singleton have retained counsel, to insist that Singleton's case be presented in court either by his attorney or by himself, but not by a combination of the two.

6. Non-Lawyer Representation

A non-lawyer has the constitutional right to represent himself; but he has no constitutional right to have another person represent him if that person is not a lawyer. See, e.g., United States v. Turnbull, 888 F.2d 636 (9th Cir.1989) (" 'Counsel' means 'attorney' "). The reasoning of the court in United States v. Kelley, 539 F.2d 1199 (9th Cir.1976), is typical. Kelley wanted his friend Hurd, a roofer, to serve as trial counsel, but the district court denied that request. The court of appeals held that a defendant has no Sixth Amendment right to delegate his power of self-representation to a non-lawyer.

> The personal autonomy protected by the right of self-representation does not require that a delegation of this right to a non-lawyer be respected. It is true that autonomy is to some extent vindicated by allowing a right to be exercised by a designated proxy. However, such an interpretation of autonomy is at odds with the whole tenor of the *Faretta* opinion and runs counter to the competing institutional interest in seeing that justice is administered fairly and efficiently with the assistance of competent lawyers.

A judge may, in her discretion, permit hybrid representation, but may she allow representation by a layperson?[34] Some courts would say "no," out of concern about unauthorized practice of law. Should what some regard as monopolistic bar practices stand in the way of a defendant's choice of counsel?

7. Self-Representation on Appeal

Does a defendant have the right to proceed pro se on appeal? The Court answered "no" in Martinez v. Court of Appeal of California, 528 U.S. 152 (2000). Justice Stevens, writing for the Court, first distinguished the *Faretta* right to self-representation as grounded in the structure of the Sixth Amendment; he reasoned that Sixth Amendment rights are trial rights, and that the Amendment "does not include any right to appeal." Because the right to appeal is "a creature of statute," it followed that the Sixth Amendment "does not provide any basis for finding a right to self-representation on appeal."

Justice Stevens also noted that even at trial, the right to self-representation is not absolute. The autonomy-based right of self-representation is sometimes outweighed by "the government's interest in ensuring the integrity and efficiency of the trial." Justice Stevens applied this balancing of interests to the appellate context in the following passage:

> In the appellate context, the balance between the two competing interests surely tips in favor of the State. The status of the accused defendant, who retains a presumption of innocence throughout the trial process, changes dramatically when a jury returns a guilty verdict. * * * Considering the change in position from defendant to appellant, the autonomy interests that survive a felony conviction are less compelling than those motivating the decision in *Faretta*. Yet the overriding state interest in the fair and efficient administration of

---

[34] For an argument in favor of a defendant's right to elect lay representation, see Comment, The Criminal Defendant's Sixth Amendment Right to Lay Representation, 52 U.Chi.L.Rev. 460 (1985).

justice remains as strong as at the trial level. Thus, the States are clearly within their discretion to conclude that the government's interests outweigh an invasion of the appellant's interest in self-representation.

Justice Stevens seemed to go out of his way to cast doubt on the wisdom of the *Faretta* decision, even as applied to trials. He criticized the *Faretta* Court's reliance on the historical grounding of the right to self-representation; he contended that self-representation was an absolute necessity in Colonial times, given the scarcity and widespread incompetence of counsel. But the original reasons for protecting the right to self-representation "do not have the same force when the availability of competent counsel for every indigent defendant has displaced the need—though not always the desire—for self-representation." Justice Stevens also stated that "[n]o one * * * attempts to argue as a rule pro se representation is wise, desirable or efficient" and that "it is representation by counsel that is the standard, not the exception."

Justice Kennedy wrote a short concurring opinion. Justice Breyer also concurred in a short opinion, noting that judges "have sometimes expressed dismay about the practical consequences" of *Faretta*. He cited United States v. Farhad, 190 F.3d 1097 (9th Cir. 1999), in which Judge Reinhardt stated that the right to self-representation frequently "conflicts squarely and inherently with the right to a fair trial." Justice Breyer stated, however, that he had "found no empirical research * * * that might help determine whether, in general, the right to represent oneself furthers, or inhibits, the Constitution's basic guarantee of fairness. And without some strong factual basis for believing that *Faretta's* holding has proved counterproductive in practice, we are not in a position to reconsider the constitutional assumptions that underlie that case."

Subsequently, in his opinion in Indiana v. Edwards, 554 U.S. 164 (2008), Justice Breyer wrote for the Court and explicitly declined to overrule *Faretta*. He expressed some hope that *Edwards*, discussed earlier in this Chapter, might ameliorate some of the practical problems courts have had in dealing with self-representation.

Justice Scalia concurred in the judgment. He objected to what he viewed as an inference in the majority opinion that *Faretta* itself was wrongly decided:

> I have no doubt that the Framers of our Constitution, who were suspicious enough of governmental power—including judicial power—that they insisted upon a citizen's right to be judged by an independent jury of private citizens, would not have found acceptable the compulsory assignment of counsel by the Government to plead a criminal defendant's case. * * *

> That asserting the right of self-representation may often, or even usually, work to the defendant's disadvantage is no more

remarkable—and no more a basis for withdrawing the right—than is the fact that proceeding without counsel in custodial interrogation, or confessing to the crime, usually works to the defendant's disadvantage. Our system of laws generally presumes that the criminal defendant, after being fully informed, knows his own best interests and does not need them dictated by the State. Any other approach is unworthy of a free people.

CHAPTER 11

SENTENCING

■ ■ ■

I. INTRODUCTION

A. THE IMPORTANCE OF SENTENCING

Before and during trial, the constitutional and other protections afforded one accused of crime are various and important. The most striking thing about the criminal process *following* a conviction is the relative absence of constitutional safeguards to assure evenhanded, fair, and accurate decisionmaking. Yet, the consequences of a sentence are obviously of critical importance. If too short or of the wrong type, it can deprive the law of its effectiveness and result in the premature release of a dangerous criminal. If too severe or improperly conceived, it can lead to injustice, sometimes grave injustice.

B. THE RESPONSIBILITY FOR SENTENCING

Who does sentencing in American courts? The usual answer is that in the federal courts and in most states, judges sentence convicted defendants, while in a small minority of jurisdictions the jury sentences those who are convicted.

But this is a most misleading answer, because the sentencing function hardly is confined to judges and juries. The prosecutor plainly has the power to affect the sentence that will be imposed on an offender through sentence and charge bargaining. Although the prosecutor never will pronounce the sentence in the sense of making it official, the power of the prosecutor to choose the charge upon which to proceed before a judge or jury and to press for either harsh or lenient treatment is substantial. And, of course, because most prosecutions end in a guilty plea, the sentencing power is in effect shifted to some extent to prosecutors (and defendants and their counsel) through plea bargaining.

Of course another source of responsibility for sentencing is the legislature. Because the legislature prescribes punishments and sentencing ranges, it can narrow the choices available to judges and juries. In theory, it can abolish plea bargaining, although it is unclear that the legislature ever could totally eliminate prosecutorial discretion. The legislature can expand, contract or abolish parole schemes, and it can raise or lower overall punishment levels.

The United States Congress has acted in this area by imposing mandatory minimum sentences for a number of crimes (especially drug and firearms crimes). These mandatory minimums limit judicial discretion because they set a floor under which the judge cannot go. Correspondingly, they increase the opportunity of the prosecutor to exercise discretion and bargaining power—a prosecutor can assure that a defendant will avoid a mandatory minimum through charge bargaining.

C. THE DETERMINATION OF SENTENCES

How are sentences determined? For much of the 20th Century, American jurisdictions selected the penalty for any particular crime that the legislature, acting at the time a statute was enacted, thought appropriate. Little effort was made to make the punishments for different crimes consistent with one another or to explain how minimum and maximum punishments were chosen, and the range between the minimum and maximum often was considerable. In 1962, the Model Penal Code endeavored to fashion a more orderly system. It divided felonies into three degrees and specified two kinds of sentencing ranges for each degree—one for ordinary felony offenders, and one for persistent, professional, multiple, or especially dangerous offenders. Numerous states followed the lead of the Code and classified their crimes, although they may have used a different classification scheme than that proposed in the Code. But many jurisdictions have a variety of statutes enacted at different times that define crimes and prescribe punishment levels.

Indeterminate Sentencing

Whether a classification or a more ad hoc system is used to prescribe punishments, many state legislatures have left the sentencing judge (and in a minority of states the sentencing jury) with enormous flexibility in setting a sentence. Sentencing ranges for offenses are often wide, e.g., first degree murder might be punishable by 20 years to life, and arson by 5 to 20 years. If no plea bargain has been made or accepted, a judge doing the sentencing in these states has uncontrolled discretion to choose a sentence within the prescribed range.

The term *"indeterminate sentencing"* describes a scheme in many jurisdictions, in which a prison sentence is subject to reconsideration by a parole or pardon board. Thus, a sentence of incarceration is not determinate because no one may know how much of a sentence a defendant will actually serve. Even in the most indeterminate system, however, there is an element of determinacy, because statutes usually prescribe when an offender becomes eligible for parole—e.g., after serving a quarter or a third of the imposed sentence. It should be noted that agencies like parole boards can protect a defendant to some extent from sentences that are too high, but they have no control over sentences that are too lenient.

Federal Rejection of Indeterminate Sentencing

The Sentencing Reform Act of 1984 established the U.S. Sentencing Commission. The Act and the Commission's Guidelines are discussed later in the Chapter. An important goal of the Guidelines is to limit disparity in sentencing. As will be discussed more fully below, the Guidelines limit the range of sentences based on a list of prescribed factors and considerations. But as we will see, today the Guidelines are advisory only, so judges retain some measure of discretion in setting the sentence. Still, the federal system remains a determinate sentencing system because the sentence imposed upon a defendant is the sentence the defendant actually will serve (although the defendant may get a minor reduction for "good time" or good behavior). There is no parole for those convicted and sentenced under the federal Guideline system.

For an analysis of the developments in American sentencing policy over more than four decades and some perspective on the future, see Michael Tonry, Sentencing in America, 1975–2025, 42 Crime and Justice 141 (2013).

D. CONSTITUTIONAL LIMITATIONS ON PUNISHMENT

The Constitution places a number of limitations on sentencing. The applicable rights include the Sixth Amendment right to jury trial and the Fifth and Fourteenth Amendment right to due process. These guarantees together prohibit the government from shifting elements of the crime (determined at trial beyond a reasonable doubt) to sentencing factors (determined by the sentencing judge by a preponderance of the evidence). These constitutional guarantees were discussed and applied in Apprendi v. New Jersey and subsequent cases that are discussed in detail in Chapter 10. But they are further developed here, with the focus on the impact of *Apprendi* on the Federal Sentencing Guidelines and on state guideline systems.

Other constitutional protections potentially applicable to sentencing are: 1) the Eighth Amendment; 2) the First Amendment; and 3) the Equal Protection Clause. Each will be discussed below after the discussion of the Sixth Amendment and Due Process Clause impact on sentencing.

1. **Sentencing Enhancements, the Right to Jury Trial, and the Right to Due Process**

Apprendi v. New Jersey and Blakely v. Washington

In Apprendi v. New Jersey, 530 U.S. 466 (2000), the Court held that the defendant's rights to jury trial and due process were violated when he received a sentence that was higher than the maximum sentence provided by the legislature for the crime of which he was convicted. The legislature authorized the enhancement on the basis of a finding by the sentencing judge. The Court stated that "other than the fact of a prior conviction, any fact that increases the penalty for a crime beyond the prescribed statutory maximum must be submitted to a jury, and proved beyond a reasonable doubt." The Court did not, however, challenge the traditional premise that sentencing courts were free to decide facts—and set a sentence on the basis of those facts—so long as the sentence is within the prescribed sentencing range set forth by the legislature for the crime of which the defendant was convicted. The problem in *Apprendi* was that the sentencing judge was *required* by the legislature to sentence beyond the prescribed range, on the basis of facts not determined by the jury.

Subsequently, in Blakely v. Washington, 542 U.S. 296 (2004), the Court struck down a sentencing guidelines system that required judges to enhance a sentence beyond the basic *guideline* applicable to the crime of which the defendant was convicted, on the basis of facts determined by the judge at sentencing and not the jury at trial. The sentence was within a broad statutory range, but the state had imposed mandatory sentencing guidelines to limit judicial discretion within that broad range. So the *Blakely* Court determined that it was the mandatory guidelines range, and not the broader sentencing range, that was relevant for *Apprendi* purposes. *Apprendi* and *Blakely* are discussed more fully in Chapter 10, in the section on constitutionally-based proof requirements.

Apprendi and the Federal Sentencing Guidelines: United States v. Booker

In United States v. Booker, 543 U.S. 220 (2005), the Court, in an opinion by Justice Stevens, held that the Federal Sentencing Guidelines were not distinguishable from the state guidelines found invalid in *Blakely*. That is, to the extent that the Federal Guidelines require the sentencing court to enhance a sentence beyond the guideline for the basic crime for which the defendant was convicted, on the basis of facts (other than prior convictions) found by the sentencing judge, they violate the defendant's right to jury trial and the right to have the government prove all elements of the crime beyond a reasonable doubt. This part of the *Booker* opinion is discussed after *Apprendi* in Chapter 10.

But the most important part of Booker is the remedial opinion by Justice Breyer, i.e., the determination of the appropriate remedy for the unconstitutionality of the Guidelines. Justice Breyer, who dissented from the decision finding the Guidelines unconstitutional, cobbled together a different majority of the Court, and found that the problem with the Guidelines is not that judges sentence on the basis of facts at sentencing. Rather the problem is that those findings trigger *mandatory enhancements,* because the Guidelines had been construed up to then to bind district judges in their sentencing decisions. The *Booker* "remedial" majority found that the proper remedy was not to strike down the Guidelines as a whole, but only those parts of the Guidelines that made enhancements mandatory on the basis of judicially-determined facts. Under the remedial opinion, the Sentencing Guidelines become guidelines in the real sense. They are advisory only.

Justice Breyer's opinion for the remedial majority, and portions of the dissenting opinions, are set forth in the section on the Sentencing Guidelines, later in this Chapter.

2.   Eighth Amendment Limitations on Sentencing

The Eighth Amendment provides that "[e]xcessive bail shall not be required, nor excessive fines imposed, nor cruel and unusual punishments inflicted." Thus it has two clauses that are potentially relevant to sentencing. The application of the Excessive Fines Clause is considered later in this Chapter in the section on fines as an alternative or supplement to imprisonment. This section considers the limitations established by the Cruel and Unusual Punishment Clause.

Rummell v. Estelle

In Rummel v. Estelle, 445 U.S. 263 (1980), the defendant received a life sentence for obtaining $120.75 by false pretenses. That conviction was his third felony (the other two were fraudulent use of a credit card to obtain $80, and passing a forged check in the amount of $28.36). Justice Rehnquist's majority opinion concluded that it was unnecessary to decide whether a life sentence for a false pretenses conviction was itself cruel and unusual. He noted that the fact it was a third offense, and the possibility of parole after 12 years, made the punishment justifiable and not necessarily as severe as it might first appear. Justice Powell dissented and was joined by Justices Brennan, Marshall, and Stevens. He argued that the possibility of parole should not be considered in deciding the cruel and unusual punishment question because it was not guaranteed, and that the penalty for the offense was unconstitutionally disproportionate in view of the nonviolent nature of the offenses.

Three-Pronged Test for Disproportionality: Solem v. Helm

The Court departed somewhat from *Rummel* in Solem v. Helm, 463 U.S. 277 (1983), as it struck down a life sentence without parole for a seventh nonviolent felony. Helm's crimes were relatively petty and nonviolent (e.g., burglary and driving under the influence). His seventh crime was uttering a "no account" check for $100. Because of his criminal record, Helm was subject to South Dakota's recidivist statute, resulting in a life sentence without parole.

Justice Powell, writing for the Court, rejected the state's argument that the Eighth Amendment proportionality principle was completely inapplicable to felony prison sentences. He explained as follows:

> The constitutional language itself suggests no exception for imprisonment. We have recognized that the Eighth Amendment imposes "parallel limitations" on bail, fines, and other punishments, and the text is explicit that bail and fines may not be excessive. It would be anomalous indeed if the lesser punishment of a fine and the greater punishment of death were both subject to proportionality analysis, but the intermediate punishment of imprisonment were not. * * *
>
> In sum, we hold as a matter of principle that a criminal sentence must be proportionate to the crime for which the defendant has been convicted. Reviewing courts, of course, should grant substantial deference to the broad authority that legislatures necessarily possess in determining the types and limits of punishments for crimes, as well as to the discretion that trial courts possess in sentencing convicted criminals. But no penalty is *per se* constitutional.

Justice Powell declared that proportionality review should be guided by three "objective" factors:

> First, we look to the gravity of the offense and the harshness of the penalty. * * * Of course, a court must consider the severity of the penalty in deciding whether it is disproportionate.
>
> Second, it may be helpful to compare the sentences imposed on other criminals in the same jurisdiction. If more serious crimes are subject to the same penalty, or to less serious penalties, that is some indication that the punishment at issue may be excessive. * * *
>
> Third, courts may find it useful to compare the sentences imposed for commission of the same crime in other jurisdictions. * * *

Applying the three-pronged test to Helm's life sentence without parole, the Court found it constitutionally disproportionate:

> Helm's crime was "one of the most passive felonies a person could commit." It involved neither violence nor threat of violence to any

person. * * * His prior offenses, although classified as felonies, were all relatively minor. All were nonviolent and none was a crime against a person. * * * Barring executive clemency, Helm will spend the rest of his life in the state penitentiary. This sentence is far more severe than the life sentence we considered in Rummel v. Estelle. Rummel was likely to have been eligible for parole within 12 years of his initial confinement, a fact on which the Court relied heavily. * * * Helm has been treated in the same manner as, or more severely than, criminals who have committed far more serious crimes. * * * Helm could not have received such a severe sentence in 48 of the 50 States.

Chief Justice Burger, joined by Justices White, Rehnquist, and O'Connor, dissented in *Solem*. The dissenters objected to the majority's three-pronged test. The Chief Justice viewed the test as unduly intrusive into legislative judgments, and impermissibly subjective:

> * * * Today's conclusion by five Justices that they are able to say that one offense has less "gravity" than another is nothing other than a bald substitution of individual subjective moral values for those of the legislature.

* * *

By asserting the power to review sentences of imprisonment for excessiveness the Court launches into uncharted and unchartable waters. Today it holds that a sentence of life imprisonment, without the possibility of parole, is excessive punishment for a seventh allegedly "nonviolent" felony. How about the eighth "nonviolent" felony? The ninth? The twelfth? Suppose one offense was a simple assault? Or selling liquor to a minor? Or statutory rape? Or price-fixing? The permutations are endless and the Court's opinion is bankrupt of realistic guiding principles. * * * I can see no limiting principle in the Court's holding.[1]

Limiting Proportionality Review: Harmelin v. Michigan

The Court substantially limited the application of the *Solem* three-factor test of disproportionality in Harmelin v. Michigan, 501 U.S. 957 (1991), although there was no majority opinion for the Court. Harmelin received a life sentence without parole for possession of 672 grams of cocaine. The Michigan statute was unique in the United States in the severity of punishment for possession of large amounts of cocaine. Moreover, the statute prescribed the same penalty, life without parole, for possession as well as for distribution of a large amount of cocaine.

---

[1]   On remand, Helm received a 20 year sentence. Is it constitutionally valid? Would 25 years have been too much?

Harmelin argued that under the *Solem* three-factor test, his sentence was constitutionally disproportionate.

The Scalia Opinion in Harmelin

Justice Scalia, joined by Chief Justice Rehnquist, engaged in an extensive historical analysis and concluded that "there is no proportionality requirement in the Eighth Amendment." Justice Scalia noted that the proportionality principle in the Eighth Amendment is derived from the term "excessive"; but the term "excessive" is used in the Amendment in reference to bail and to fines, and is pointedly not used to modify the term "punishment."

Justice Scalia concluded that *Solem* should be overruled. He argued that the *Solem* factors were indeterminate and led to judicial subjectivity.

Justice Scalia recognized that the Court had previously invalidated death sentences because of disproportionality. He stated, however, that proportionality review "is one of several respects in which we have held that death is different, and have imposed protections that the Constitution nowhere else provides."

The Kennedy Opinion in Harmelin

Justice Kennedy, joined by Justices O'Connor and Souter, stated that "stare decisis counsels our adherence to the narrow proportionality principle that has existed in our Eighth Amendment jurisprudence for 80 years." Justice Kennedy concluded that the Eighth Amendment "forbids only extreme sentences that are grossly disproportionate to the crime." He stated that the second and third factors of *Solem*—which mandate an intra- and inter-jurisdictional comparative analysis—are appropriate "only in the rare case in which a threshold comparison of the crime committed and the sentence imposed leads to an inference of gross disproportionality."

In Justice Kennedy's view, a comparative analysis was not required for Harmelin's sentence, because life imprisonment without parole was not grossly disproportionate to the crime. Justice Kennedy emphasized the pernicious effects of the drug epidemic, and stated that "the Michigan Legislature could with reason conclude that the threat imposed to the individual and society by possession of this large an amount of cocaine—in terms of violence, crime, and social displacement—is momentous enough to warrant the deterrence and retribution of a life sentence without parole."

The White Dissent in Harmelin

Justice White, joined by Justices Marshall, Blackmun, and Stevens, dissented. Justice White reasoned that the Framers would not have included an excessive fines clause in the Eighth Amendment (which specifically refers to proportionality) without also intending to prevent excessive sentences that could be imposed in lieu of fines. He argued that Justice Scalia's view failed to explain why the words "cruel and unusual punishment" would impose a proportionality requirement in capital cases but not in noncapital cases. He contended that the *Solem* analysis "has worked well in practice" and stated that "Justice Kennedy's abandonment of the second and third factors set forth in *Solem* makes any attempt at an objective proportionality analysis futile."

Applying the *Solem* analysis to Harmelin's sentence, Justice White found it to be disproportionate. On the first factor—the gravity of the offense and the severity of the punishment—he found that mere possession of drugs, even in a large quantity, "is not so serious an offense that it will always warrant, much less mandate, life imprisonment without possibility of parole." He noted that the statute was undifferentiated in that it applied to first-time offenders as well as to recidivists. Justice White was also concerned that Michigan imposed the same sentence for possession and distribution of large amounts of cocaine. He stated that "the State succeeded in punishing Harmelin as if he had been convicted of the more serious crime without being put to the test of proving his guilt on those charges."

On the second *Solem* factor of intra-jurisdictional comparison, Justice White noted that Michigan imposed a life sentence without parole for three crimes: first-degree murder, possession or manufacture with intent to distribute 650 grams or more of narcotics, and the possession offense for which Harmelin was convicted. Justice White concluded that Harmelin had been treated the same as "criminals who have committed far more serious crimes."

On the third factor of inter-jurisdictional comparison, Justice White emphasized that "no other jurisdiction imposes a punishment nearly as severe as Michigan's for possession of the amount of drugs at issue here." Justice White pointed out that under the Federal Sentencing Guidelines, Harmelin would have received a ten-year sentence.

The Mandatory Sentencing Issue in Harmelin

Harmelin also attacked the constitutionality of his sentence on the ground that, even if it was not disproportionate, it was cruel and unusual to impose a mandatory life sentence without any consideration of mitigating factors. Justice Scalia, writing for five members of the Court on this question, held that if a sentence is not otherwise cruel and unusual, it cannot become so simply because it is mandatory. Justice Scalia recognized that in capital cases, the Eighth Amendment requires individualized sentencing and consideration of all relevant mitigating evidence. He stated, however, that "we have drawn the line of required individualized sentencing at capital cases, and see no basis for extending it further." Justices White, Marshall, Blackmun, and Stevens did not find it necessary to consider Harmelin's mandatory sentencing issue in light of their view that the sentence was constitutionally disproportionate.

Three Strikes Legislation: California v. Ewing

In the following case, the Court applies its *Rummel-Harmelin* line of Eighth Amendment jurisprudence to the California "Three Strikes" law.

EWING V. CALIFORNIA
Supreme Court of the United States, 2003.
538 U.S. 11.

JUSTICE O'CONNOR announced the judgment of the Court and delivered an opinion in which THE CHIEF JUSTICE and JUSTICE KENNEDY join.

In this case, we decide whether the Eighth Amendment prohibits the State of California from sentencing a repeat felon to a prison term of 25 years to life under the State's "Three Strikes and You're Out" law.

* * *

California's three strikes law reflects a shift in the State's sentencing policies toward incapacitating and deterring repeat offenders who threaten the public safety. * * * Between 1993 and 1995, 24 States and the Federal Government enacted three strikes laws. Though the three strikes laws vary from State to State, they share a common goal of protecting the public safety by providing lengthy prison terms for habitual felons.

* * * If the defendant has two or more prior "serious" or "violent" felony convictions, he must receive "an indeterminate term of life imprisonment." Defendants sentenced to life under the three strikes law become eligible for parole on a date calculated by reference to a "minimum term" * * *.

[Ewing was convicted of stealing three golf clubs from a pro shop. He had previously convicted of three burglaries and a robbery. His prior record made him subject to the three strikes law and he was given a sentence from 25 years to life for the stealing conviction.]

* * *

The Eighth Amendment, which forbids cruel and unusual punishments, contains a narrow proportionality principle that applies to noncapital sentences. We have most recently addressed the proportionality principle as applied to terms of years in a series of cases beginning with Rummel v. Estelle.

[Justice O'Connor discusses the facts and analyses in Rummel v. Estelle and Solem v. Helm. She noted that Justice Kennedy's opinion in *Harmelin* was the controlling opinion for determining whether a sentence is disproportionate under the Eighth Amendment—as it was the most limited opinion on which the majority of justices could agree.]

* * * Though three strikes laws may be relatively new, our tradition of deferring to state legislatures in making and implementing such important policy decisions is longstanding.

* * *

When the California Legislature enacted the three strikes law, it made a judgment that protecting the public safety requires incapacitating criminals who have already been convicted of at least one serious or violent crime. Nothing in the Eighth Amendment prohibits California from making that choice. * * * Recidivism has long been recognized as a legitimate basis for increased punishment.

California's justification is no pretext. Recidivism is a serious public safety concern in California and throughout the Nation. * * *

The State's interest in deterring crime also lends some support to the three strikes law. We have long viewed both incapacitation and deterrence as rationales for recidivism statutes. Four years after the passage of California's three strikes law, the recidivism rate of parolees returned to prison for the commission of a new crime dropped by nearly 25 percent.

[Justice O'Connor also cites statistics indicating that the three strikes law has led parolees to leave California, which was a "positive development."]

To be sure, California's three strikes law has sparked controversy. Critics have doubted the law's wisdom, cost-efficiency, and effectiveness in reaching its goals. This criticism is appropriately directed at the legislature, which has primary responsibility for making the difficult policy choices that underlie any criminal sentencing scheme. We do not sit as a "superlegislature" to second-guess these policy choices. * * *

* * *

Against this backdrop, we consider Ewing's claim that his three strikes sentence of 25 years to life is unconstitutionally disproportionate to his offense * * *. We first address the gravity of the offense compared to the harshness of the penalty. At the threshold, we note that Ewing incorrectly frames the issue. * * * Even standing alone, Ewing's theft should not be taken lightly. His crime was certainly not one of the most passive felonies a person could commit. * * * Theft of $1,200 in property is a felony under federal law, and in the vast majority of States. * * *

In weighing the gravity of Ewing's offense, we must place on the scales not only his current felony, but also his long history of felony recidivism. Any other approach would fail to accord proper deference to the policy judgments that find expression in the legislature's choice of sanctions. * * * His prior "strikes" were serious felonies including robbery and three residential burglaries. To be sure, Ewing's sentence is a long one. But it reflects a rational legislative judgment, entitled to deference, that offenders who have committed serious or violent felonies and who continue to commit felonies must be incapacitated. * * * Ewing's is not "the rare case in which a threshold comparison of the crime committed and the sentence imposed leads to an inference of gross disproportionality." *Harmelin* (Kennedy, J., concurring in part and concurring in judgment).

We hold that Ewing's sentence of 25 years to life in prison, imposed for the offense of felony grand theft under the three strikes law, is not grossly disproportionate and therefore does not violate the Eighth Amendment's prohibition on cruel and unusual punishments. * * *

JUSTICE SCALIA, concurring in the judgment.

In my concurring opinion in Harmelin v. Michigan, I concluded that the Eighth Amendment's prohibition of "cruel and unusual punishments" was aimed at excluding only certain *modes* of punishment, and was not a "guarantee against disproportionate sentences." Out of respect for the principle of *stare decisis*, I might nonetheless accept the contrary holding of Solem v. Helm—that the Eighth Amendment contains a narrow proportionality principle—if I felt I could intelligently apply it. This case demonstrates why I cannot.

Proportionality—the notion that the punishment should fit the crime—is inherently a concept tied to the penological goal of retribution. It becomes difficult even to speak intelligently of "proportionality," once deterrence and rehabilitation are given significant weight—not to mention giving weight to the purpose of California's three strikes law: incapacitation. * * * Perhaps the plurality should revise its terminology, so that what it reads into the Eighth Amendment is not the unstated proposition that all punishment should be reasonably proportionate to the gravity of the offense, but rather the unstated proposition that all punishment should reasonably pursue the multiple purposes of the criminal law. That formulation would make it clearer than ever, of course, that the plurality is not applying law but evaluating policy.

Because I agree that petitioner's sentence does not violate the Eighth Amendment's prohibition against cruel and unusual punishments, I concur in the judgment.

JUSTICE THOMAS, concurring in the judgment.

I agree with JUSTICE SCALIA'S view that the proportionality test announced in Solem v. Helm, is incapable of judicial application. Even were *Solem's* test perfectly clear, however, I would not feel compelled by *stare decisis* to apply it. In my view, the Cruel and Unusual Punishments Clause of the Eighth Amendment contains no proportionality principle.

Because the plurality concludes that petitioner's sentence does not violate the Eighth Amendment's prohibition on cruel and unusual punishments, I concur in the judgment.

JUSTICE STEVENS, with whom JUSTICE SOUTER, JUSTICE GINSBURG and JUSTICE BREYER join, dissenting.

* * * It would be anomalous indeed to suggest that the Eighth Amendment makes proportionality review applicable in the context of bail and fines but not in the context of other forms of punishment, such as imprisonment. Rather, by broadly prohibiting excessive sanctions, the Eighth Amendment directs judges to exercise their wise judgment in assessing the proportionality of all forms of punishment.

* * *

* * * I think it clear that the Eighth Amendment's prohibition of "cruel and unusual punishments" expresses a broad and basic proportionality principle that takes into account all of the justifications for penal sanctions. It is this broad proportionality principle that would preclude reliance on any of the justifications for punishment to support, for example, a life sentence for overtime parking.

JUSTICE BREYER, with whom JUSTICE STEVENS, JUSTICE SOUTER, and JUSTICE GINSBURG join, dissenting.

* * *

Ewing's sentence on its face imposes one of the most severe punishments available upon a recidivist who subsequently engaged in one of the less serious forms of criminal conduct. I do not deny the seriousness of shoplifting, which an *amicus curiae* tells us costs retailers in the range of $30 billion annually. But consider that conduct in terms of the factors that this Court mentioned in *Solem*—the "harm caused or threatened to the victim or society," the "absolute magnitude of the crime," and the offender's "culpability." In respect to all three criteria, the sentence-triggering behavior here ranks well toward the bottom of the criminal conduct scale. * * *[2]

Life Without Parole Sentence Imposed on a Person Who Was Less than 18 at the Time of the Crime: Graham v. Florida and Miller v. Alabama

In the cases of Graham v. Florida, 560 U.S. 48 (2010), and Miller v. Alabama, 567 U.S. 460 (2012), the Court held that the Eighth Amendment imposed limitations on life without parole sentences for defendants who were under 18 years old when they committed the crime charged. *Graham* involved a defendant who, when 16 years old, committed a violent robbery of a restaurant—and while on probation for that crime, committed an armed robbery of a private home. He was sentenced to life without parole. Justice Kennedy, writing for the Court, applied his own "controlling" opinion in *Harmelin,* and stated categorically that the Eighth Amendment "prohibits the imposition of a life without parole sentence on a juvenile offender who did not commit homicide." Justice Kennedy relied on the following principles for this conclusion:

- while many jurisdictions statutorily permit sentences like that in this case, "an examination of *actual* sentencing practices * * * discloses a consensus" against the use of life without parole sentences for juveniles who did not commit homicide.

- "parts of the brain involved in behavior control continue to mature through late adolescence" and "because juveniles have lessened culpability they are less deserving of the most sever punishments."

- "defendants who do not kill, intend to kill, or foresee that life will be taken are categorically less deserving of the most serious forms of punishment than are murderers."

- "life without parole sentences share some characteristics with death sentences that are shared by no other sentences" as the sentence "deprives the convict of the most basic liberties without giving hope of restoration, except perhaps by executive clemency—the remote possibility of which does not mitigate the harshness of the sentence."

---

[2] See also the companion case of Lockyer v. Andrade, 538 U.S. 63 (2003), rejecting an Eighth Amendment challenge to a sentence of two consecutive terms of 25 years to life for stealing videotapes worth about $150 from two stores. Andrade had been convicted previously of three counts of residential burglary. The Supreme Court, in an opinion by Justice O'Connor for five members of the Court, held that the state court's interpretation of the Eighth amendment was neither "contrary to" nor "an unreasonable application of clearly established federal law"—which are the relevant standards for reviewing state court determinations on habeas corpus review.

- "Life without parole is an especially harsh punishment for a juvenile" because "a juvenile offender will on average serve more years and a greater percentage of his life in prison than an adult offender."

- "retribution does not justify imposing the second most severe penalty on the less culpable juvenile nonhomicide offender."

- "Deterrence does not justify the sentence either" because "juveniles' lack of maturity and underdeveloped sense of responsibility often result in impetuous and ill-considered actions and decisions" so "they are less likely to take a possible punishment into consideration when making decisions."

- "incapacitation may be a legitimate penological goal sufficient to justify life without parole in other contexts" but it is dependent on an assumption that the defendant is incorrigible, and "incorrigibility is inconsistent with youth. * * * A life without parole sentence improperly denies the juvenile offender a chance to demonstrate growth and maturity."

- "A sentence of life imprisonment without parole * * * cannot be justified by the goal of rehabilitation. The penalty forswears altogether the rehabilitative ideal."

Justice Kennedy clarified that the Court was not precluding the possibility that a person who committed a nonhomicide crime as a juvenile might spend his life in prison.

> A state is not required to guarantee eventual freedom to a juvenile convicted of a nonhomicide crime. What the State must do, however, is give defendants like Graham some meaningful opportunity to obtain release based on demonstrated maturity and rehabilitiation.

Chief Justice Roberts wrote a lengthy opinion concurring in the judgment in *Graham*. He agreed that Graham's sentence was cruel and unusual, because it failed under the *Harmelin* factors: Graham was less culpable and his crime less serious than other adult defendants who received sentences of life without parole, in both Florida and other jurisdictions. But the Chief Justice objected to the Court's bright-line rule, because it "ignores the fact that some nonhomicide crimes * * * are especially heinous and grotesque, and thus may be deserving of more severe punishment."

Justice Thomas dissented in *Graham* in an opinion joined in full by Justice Scalia and in part by Justice Alito. Justices Thomas and Scalia reiterated their position that the Cruel and Unusual Punishments clause was not originally understood to provide proportionality in sentencing. The three dissenters contended that the majority of states permit life without parole sentences for nonhomicide convictions of juveniles. They concluded as follows:

> The fact that the Court categorically prohibits life without parole sentences for juvenile nonhomicide offenders in the face of an overwhelming legislative majority in favor of leaving that sentencing option available under certain cases simply illustrates how far beyond any cognizable constitutional principle the Court has reached to ensure that its own sense of morality and retributive justice pre-empts that of the people and their representatives.

Justice Alito wrote a short dissenting opinion in *Graham*.

In Miller v. Alabama, the Court considered the constitutionality of *mandatory* life without parole sentences for juveniles convicted of homicide. The Court was reviewing two cases in which 14-year-olds were convicted of murder and sentenced to a mandatory term of life without parole. The Court, in an opinion by Justice Kagan for five Justices, held that the Eighth Amendment forbids a sentencing scheme that *mandates* life without parole sentences for juvenile homicide offenders. Justice Kagan essentially found that the analysis in *Graham*—particularly its reliance on the fact that juveniles were less culpable than adults and a life without parole sentence is more serious because of its comparative length—applied equally to juvenile homicide offenders. She explained as follows:

> Mandatory life without parole for a juvenile precludes consideration of his chronological age and its hallmark features— among them, immaturity, impetuosity, and failure to appreciate risks and consequences. It prevents taking into account the family and home environment that surrounds him—and from which he cannot usually extricate himself—no matter how brutal or dysfunctional. It neglects the circumstances of the homicide offense, including the extent of his participation in the conduct and the way familial and peer pressures may have affected him. Indeed, it ignores that he might have been charged and convicted of a lesser offense if not for incompetencies associated with youth—for example, his inability to deal with police officers or prosecutors (including on a plea agreement) or his incapacity to assist his own attorneys.

Justice Kagan summed up and noted that the Court had not held that life without parole could *never* be imposed on a juvenile who committed a homicide:

> We therefore hold that the Eighth Amendment forbids a sentencing scheme that mandates life in prison without possibility of parole for juvenile offenders. By making youth (and all that accompanies it) irrelevant to imposition of that harshest prison sentence, such a scheme poses too great a risk of disproportionate punishment. Because that holding is sufficient to decide these cases,

we do not consider [the] alternative argument that the Eighth Amendment requires a categorical bar on life without parole for juveniles, or at least for those 14 and younger. But given all we have said * * * about children's diminished culpability and heightened capacity for change, we think appropriate occasions for sentencing juveniles to this harshest possible penalty will be uncommon. * * * Although we do not foreclose a sentencer's ability to make that judgment in homicide cases, we require it to take into account how children are different, and how those differences counsel against irrevocably sentencing them to a lifetime in prison.

Chief Justice Roberts dissented in *Miller,* in an opinion joined by Justices Scalia, Thomas, and Alito. His major argument was that the punishment could not be cruel and unusual under the Eighth Amendment because it was not unusual:

The parties agree that nearly 2,500 prisoners are presently serving life sentences without the possibility of parole for murders they committed before the age of 18. The Court accepts that over 2,000 of those prisoners received that sentence because it was mandated by a legislature. And it recognizes that the Federal Government and most States impose such mandatory sentences. Put simply, if a 17-year-old is convicted of deliberately murdering an innocent victim, it is not "unusual" for the murderer to receive a mandatory sentence of life without parole. That reality should preclude finding that mandatory life imprisonment for juvenile killers violates the Eighth Amendment.

Justice Thomas wrote a separate dissenting opinion joined by Justice Scalia, and Justice Alito wrote a dissent joined by Justice Scalia.

NOTE ON THE DEATH PENALTY

As the Court recognized in *Harmelin*, the Eighth Amendment does impose proportionality limitations on the use of the death penalty. The complexities of the death penalty are often considered in a separate law school course. A full treatment of the Supreme Court's complicated jurisprudence on the subject is beyond the scope of this Book. What follows is a short summary of the framework that the Court has established for regulating the death penalty under the Eighth Amendment.

1. A death sentence cannot be imposed arbitrarily. Furman v. Georgia, 408 U.S. 238 (1972). The Eighth Amendment requires each defendant to be considered individually, and that the death penalty be "narrowed" to apply only to those who truly merit such severe and final punishment. Gregg v. Georgia, 428 U.S. 153 (1976) (statute upheld where it provided that the sentencer could not impose a death sentence without stating in writing that it found an aggravating circumstance beyond a reasonable doubt).

2.   A death sentence cannot be imposed on the basis of aggravating circumstances that are vague, overbroad, or ill-defined. See Maynard v. Cartwright, 486 U.S. 356 (1988), where the Court struck down death sentences based on a finding that the defendant had committed a murder in an "especially heinous, atrocious or cruel" manner. The Court held that this aggravating circumstance was impermissibly broad and vague. It did not sufficiently channel the sentencer's discretion, and thus presented the risk of arbitrary enforcement of the death penalty. Overbroad statutory aggravators can be "narrowed", however, by judicial construction that provides more definition.

3.   Another line of cases concerns a different "narrowing" principle—that the death penalty should only be applied to the most egregious types of crime. See, e.g., Enmund v. Florida, 458 U.S. 782 (1982) (capital sanction for aiding and abetting a murder without regard to the intent of the defendant was cruel and unusual punishment); Coker v. Georgia, 433 U.S. 584 (1977) (rape not resulting in death could not be punished by death).

4.   The *Furman-Gregg* line of cases deals with arbitrary imposition of the death penalty. The concern is that the sentencer will have too much discretion to choose among similarly situated defendants. The solution to the *Gregg* problem is to control the sentencer by guiding discretion through particularized aggravating circumstances that control the sentencing determination. In Lockett v. Ohio, 438 U.S. 586 (1978), the Court expressed a different concern about the death penalty—that the sentencer would not consider the individual *mitigating* characteristics of each defendant. *Lockett* requires that a defendant in a capital sentencing proceeding must have reasonably free reign to introduce, *and to require the sentencer to consider*, relevant evidence in mitigation of a death sentence. The Court declared that the sentencer "in all but the rarest kind of capital case, [must] not be precluded from considering *as a mitigating factor*, any aspect of a defendant's character or record and any of the circumstances of the offense that the defendant proffers as a basis for a sentence less than death." However, the state is permitted to structure the sentencer's consideration of mitigating evidence in reasonable ways. Compare Saffle v. Parks, 494 U.S. 484 (1990) (no Eighth Amendment violation in permitting judge to instruct jury to caution against giving undue sympathy to the defendant), with McKoy v. North Carolina, 494 U.S. 433 (1990) (Eighth Amendment prohibits a state from requiring mitigating circumstances to be found unanimously).

———

Justice Stevens provides a useful summary of the Court's death penalty jurisprudence in his opinion in Graham v. Collins, 506 U.S. 461 (1993):

[T]he Court's capital punishment cases have erected four important safeguards against arbitrary imposition of the death penalty. First, * * * we have concluded that death is an impermissible punishment for certain offenses. Specifically, neither the crime of rape nor the crime of unintentional homicide * * * may now support a death sentence. See Enmund v. Florida; Coker v. Georgia.

Second, as a corollary to the proportionality requirement, the Court has demanded that the States narrow the class of individuals eligible for the death penalty, either through statutory definitions of capital murder, or through statutory specification of aggravating circumstances. This narrowing requirement, like the categorical exclusion of the offense of rape, has significantly minimized the risk of racial bias in the sentencing process. * * *

Third, the Court has condemned the use of aggravating factors so vague that they actually enhance the risk that unguided discretion will control the sentencing determination. See, e.g., Maynard v. Cartwright (invalidating "especially heinous, atrocious, or cruel" aggravating circumstance); Godfrey v. Georgia (invalidating "outrageously or wantonly vile, horrible or inhuman" aggravating circumstance). An aggravating factor that invites a judgment as to whether a murder committed by a member of another race is especially "heinous" or "inhuman" may increase, rather than decrease, the chance of arbitrary decisionmaking, by creating room for the influence of personal prejudices. * * *

Finally, at the end of the process, when dealing with the narrow class of offenders deemed death-eligible, we insist that the sentencer be permitted to give effect to all relevant mitigating evidence offered by the defendant, in making the final sentencing determination. See, e.g., Lockett v. Ohio. * * * [O]nce the class of death-eligible offenders is sufficiently narrowed, consideration of relevant, individual mitigating circumstances in no way compromises the rationalizing principle of Furman v. Georgia. To the contrary, the requirement that sentencing decisions be guided by consideration of relevant mitigating evidence reduces still further the chance that the decision will be based on irrelevant factors such as race. *Lockett* itself illustrates this point. A young black woman, Lockett was sentenced to death because the Ohio statute "did not permit the sentencing judge to consider, as mitigating factors, her character, prior record, age, lack of specific intent to cause death, and her relatively minor part in the crime." When such relevant facts are excluded from the sentencing determination, there is more, not less, reason to believe that the sentencer will be left to rely on irrational considerations like racial animus.

There is much more to the Court's death penalty jurisprudence than this thumbnail sketch can provide. For more on this difficult subject, see the Symposium on the death penalty, 83 Cornell L.Rev. 1431–1820 (1998); Steiker and Steiker, Sober Second Thoughts: Reflections on Two Decades of Constitutional Regulation of Capital Punishment, 109 Harv.L.Rev. 355 (1995); Sundby, The *Lockett* Paradox: Reconciling Guided Discretion and Unguided Mitigation in Capital Sentencing, 38 UCLA L.Rev. 1147 (1991).

For other developments in death penalty jurisprudence, *see, e.g.,* Atkins v. Virginia, 536 U.S. 304 (2002) (execution of a mentally retarded defendant is a cruel and unusual punishment prohibited by the Eighth Amendment); Ring v. Arizona, 536 U.S. 584 (2002) (Sixth Amendment right to jury trial requires that statutory aggravating factors must be determined by the jury, not the judge); Roper v. Simmons, 534 U.S. 551 (2005) (Eighth Amendment prohibits execution of a person who was under 18 years old at the time of the crime).

3. The First Amendment

Enhancement for Hate Crimes: Wisconsin v. Mitchell

In Wisconsin v. Mitchell, 508 U.S. 476 (1993), the Court explored the extent of First Amendment limitations on punishment. Mitchell, an African-American, was convicted of aggravated battery for his part in the beating of a young white boy. The maximum sentence for aggravated battery was two years' imprisonment. However, the jury found that Mitchell intentionally selected his victim on account of the victim's race. Under a Wisconsin "hate crime" law, this finding resulted in an enhanced sentence of up to seven years' imprisonment; Mitchell received a four-year prison term for the aggravated battery. Mitchell argued that the enhancement statute violated his First Amendment rights because it resulted in punishment for his bigoted beliefs. But his argument was rejected by a unanimous Court in an opinion by Chief Justice Rehnquist.

The Chief Justice noted that "[t]raditionally, sentencing judges have considered a wide variety of factors in addition to evidence bearing on guilt in determining what sentence to impose," and that the defendant's "motive for committing the offense is one important factor." He observed that the First Amendment would prohibit a sentencer from taking a defendant's "abstract beliefs" into consideration in imposing a sentence. However, he declared that the enhancement of Mitchell's sentence was not based merely on his abstract beliefs. Rather, Mitchell received an enhanced sentence because Wisconsin had made an assessment that *conduct* motivated by racial animus was more harmful than conduct that was not. Citing Rummel v. Estelle, the Chief Justice declared that "the primary responsibility for fixing criminal penalties lies with the legislature."

Mitchell also argued that the enhancement statute was unconstitutional because it chilled free speech. His argument proceeded as follows: the prosecution may use statements made by the defendant on occasions unrelated to the crime charged (e.g., at meetings), in order to prove a racial animus in committing the charged crime; therefore, a person concerned about the possibility of an enhanced sentence, should they commit a crime in the future, would have to refrain from expressing ideas reflecting a racial bias. The Court rejected Mitchell's argument, concluding that the "chill" he envisioned was "attenuated and unlikely." The Chief

Justice also declared that the First Amendment "does not prohibit the evidentiary use of speech to establish the elements of a crime or to prove motive or intent."

4. The Equal Protection Clause

Individual sentencing determinations are rarely the subject of equal protection claims—if for no other reason than they would be virtually impossible to prove. Some broad attacks have been launched at certain statutes or guidelines that are perceived to have a disproportionate effect on racial minorities. One target of attack was the federal statute and accompanying Sentencing Guideline providing for a far higher sentence for crack distribution than for distribution of a similar amount of powder cocaine. The equal protection arguments were addressed in United States v. Thurmond, 7 F.3d 947 (10th Cir.1993), a case in which the defendants were sentenced to 87 months and 97 months of imprisonment respectively, for distributing six grams of crack cocaine:

> Defendants argue that their national statistics, which indicate that 95% of federal cocaine base prosecutions are brought against African-Americans while 40% of federal cocaine powder prosecutions are brought against whites, are so stark, that this case is one of those rare cases * * * wherein statistical evidence alone is enough to prove that Congress had a racially discriminatory purpose in enacting the provisions, as well as in leaving them intact. * * *

> * * *

> However, * * * there is ample evidence of Congress's reasons, other than race, for providing harsher penalties for offenses involving cocaine base. * * * [T]he government offered evidence that Congress provided for enhanced penalties for cocaine base offenses because cocaine base (1) has a more rapid onset of action, (2) is more potent, (3) is more highly addictive, (4) is less expensive than cocaine powder, and (5) has widespread availability. [Citing to legislative history]. * * * Finally, cocaine base is simply a different drug than cocaine powder, with a different chemical composition; as a result, Congress can justifiably provide for different penalties for each. Therefore, because reasons exist, other than race, for enhanced penalties for cocaine base offenses, we conclude that Defendants' statistics of disproportionate impact are not sufficient * * * to demonstrate that Congress or the Sentencing Commission had a discriminatory purpose * * *.

After the Court's decision in United States v. Booker, supra, the Sentencing Guidelines are advisory and not mandatory. So a sentencing court is not *required* to sentence more severely for crack than powder. The Supreme Court has made it clear that sentencing judges may depart from the crack guideline. Kimbrough v. United States, 552 U.S. 85 (2007).

Moreover, the disparity has been lessened by subsequent amendments to the Guidelines, and by the Fair Sentencing Act of 2010 (Public Law 111–220), signed into law by President Obama on August 3, 2010 (reducing the disparity between the amount of crack cocaine and powder cocaine needed to trigger certain United States federal criminal penalties from a 100:1 weight ratio to an 18:1 weight ratio and eliminating the five-year mandatory minimum sentence for simple possession of crack cocaine).

E. SENTENCING ALTERNATIVES OTHER THAN INCARCERATION

What sentencing options other than traditional imprisonment are available? The answer is that a number of options exist; some are substitutes for imprisonment, and others amount to punishment in addition to imprisonment.

1. Fines and Forfeitures

Problems in Using a Fine as a Sanction

One of the most familiar alternatives is the fine. But there are several problems with the fine as a sanction. One problem is that it works better for middle-class or wealthier defendants than poorer defendants. Should ability to pay dictate the choice between jail and an alternative such as a fine? Should a fine be added to a prison sentence as punishment simply because the defendant can afford to pay it?

Another problem is that judges often are not well enough informed about a defendant's ability to pay or to earn money to arrive at a realistic fine. Many defendants find that they are unable to pay the fine that the judge sets. A related problem is what to do with the defendant who attempts to pay the fine, but is unable to do so. A further problem is designating the kinds of offenses that are appropriately punished by fines. Is it ever appropriate to respond to violent crime with a fine? Are fines more appropriate for nonviolent theft crimes? Another issue is that the proceeds of a fine go to the government, usually to defray the expenses of law enforcement. Is there a concern that the government may have an economic incentive to seek an unduly harsh fine? Finally, there is the question whether corporations should be penalized by fine in a different and harsher manner than natural persons, on the ground that corporations cannot be incarcerated. See 18 U.S.C. § 3571(c) and (d), providing that an organizational defendant that has been found guilty of a felony may be sentenced to pay a maximum statutory fine of not more than the greater of $500,000, twice the gross gain, or twice the gross loss.

Indigents and Fines

Williams v. Illinois, 399 U.S. 235 (1970), and Tate v. Short, 401 U.S. 395 (1971), protect indigents against oppressive fine systems. In *Williams,* the Court held that an indigent defendant was denied equal protection when he was imprisoned beyond the maximum term authorized by statute because of an inability to pay a fine and court costs. Tate v. Short held that an indigent defendant could not be imprisoned for failure to pay a fine when the state statute made traffic offenses punishable by fine only. Thus, imposing a fine is not the problem—imprisonment for inability to pay the fine is the problem.

The Supreme Court again considered the permissible treatment of indigents unable to pay fines in Bearden v. Georgia, 461 U.S. 660 (1983). Bearden was convicted of burglary and theft. Under the state's first offender statute, the trial judge did not enter a judgment of guilt, but deferred further proceedings and sentenced Bearden to three years on probation for the burglary charge and a concurrent one year on probation for the theft charge. As a condition of probation he ordered Bearden to pay a $500 fine and $250 restitution. Bearden borrowed $200 to make the initial payments required by the order, but was unable to make further payments. Subsequently, the court revoked Bearden's probation for failure to pay the balance of the fine and restitution, entered a judgment of conviction, and sentenced him to serve the remaining portion of the probationary period (more than two years) in prison.

Justice O'Connor's opinion for the Court observed that "[a] defendant's poverty in no way immunizes him from punishment." Thus, a state court may consider a defendant's entire background including employment and financial resources in arriving at a sentence. She reasoned further that a state could imprison a probationer who wilfully refused to pay a fine or restitution or to make bona fide efforts to seek employment or borrow money to pay a fine; but that "if the probationer has made all reasonable efforts to pay the fine or restitution, and yet cannot do so through no fault of his own, it is fundamentally unfair to revoke probation automatically without considering whether adequate alternative methods of punishing the defendant are available." Alternatives might include an extension of time to make payments, a reduction of the fine, or a requirement of some form of public service.

Justice White, joined by Chief Justice Burger and Justices Powell and Rehnquist, concurred in the judgment. He argued that nothing in the Constitution prohibited a state from making "a good-faith effort to impose a jail sentence that in terms of the state's sentencing objectives will be roughly equivalent to the fine and restitution that the defendant failed to pay." He found no such effort by the trial court in this case.

Forfeiture of the Proceeds of Crime

A variation on the fine is forfeiture of property used in or the proceeds of criminal activity. Many federal and state laws provide for forfeiture upon conviction and other statutes provide for civil forfeiture, which does not require a conviction. Congress has provided that a court must order forfeiture where appropriate in addition to imposing other sanctions upon a defendant. 18 U.S.C. § 3554. As part of its Comprehensive Crime Control Act of 1984, Congress enacted the Comprehensive Forfeiture Act of 1984, which expands the forfeiture provisions in racketeering and drug cases. See 28 U.S.C. § 881. For a discussion of how these forfeiture provisions operate, see Caplin & Drysdale v. United States, discussed in Chapter 10.

The government's economic interest in forfeiture is undeniable. At the federal level, all assets seized by the Department of Justice go into its Asset Forfeiture Fund, which the Attorney General is authorized to use for law enforcement purposes. 28 U.S.C. § 524(c). This has led Attorneys General in recent years to urge United States attorneys to increase the volume of forfeitures in order to meet the Department of Justice's annual budget target. As one court put it: "Forfeitures, in effect, impose an impressive levy on wrongdoers to finance, in part, the law enforcement efforts of both the state and national governments." United States v. Real Property Located in El Dorado, 59 F.3d 974 (9th Cir.1995).

Constitutional Limitations on Forfeiture: *Alexander v. United States*

In Alexander v. United States, 509 U.S. 544 (1993), the Court considered some constitutional questions arising from an application of the RICO forfeiture statute, 18 U.S.C. § 1963. Alexander was found guilty of 17 counts of obscenity and three counts of violating RICO, arising from the sale of obscene magazines and tapes. Alexander owned more than a dozen stores and theaters dealing in sexually explicit materials; the jury found that four magazines and three videotapes sold through Alexander's retail stores were obscene. Alexander was sentenced to six years in prison, fined $100,000, and ordered to pay the costs of prosecution, incarceration, and supervised release. The District Court then reconvened the same jury and conducted a forfeiture proceeding pursuant to 18 U.S.C. § 1963(a)(2). At this proceeding, the government sought forfeiture of the entirety of Alexander's interest in the stores and theaters. The jury found that Alexander had an interest in 10 pieces of commercial real estate and 31 current or former businesses, all of which had been used to conduct his racketeering enterprise. The District Court ultimately ordered Alexander to forfeit his wholesale and retail businesses, and all the assets thereof, as well as almost $9 million dollars acquired through racketeering activity.

Alexander argued that the forfeiture order, considered together with his six-year prison term and $100,000 fine, was disproportionate to the gravity of his offenses and thus violated the Eighth Amendment. The lower court dismissed this claim by reasoning that the Eighth Amendment does not require any proportionality review of a sentence less than life imprisonment without the possibility of parole. But the Chief Justice rejected the lower court's analysis as misdirected to the Cruel and Unusual Punishments Clause of the Eighth Amendment, whereas Alexander's claim was more properly based in the Excessive Fines Clause. The Chief Justice explained as follows:

> Unlike the Cruel and Unusual Punishments Clause, which is concerned with matters such as the duration or conditions of confinement, the Excessive Fines Clause limits the Government's power to extract payments, whether in cash or kind, as punishment for some offense. The in personam criminal forfeiture at issue here is clearly a form of monetary punishment no different, for Eighth Amendment purposes, from a traditional "fine."

The Court remanded for a determination of whether the forfeiture in combination with the other penalties was constitutionally disproportionate under the Excessive Fines Clause. On remand, the court of appeals found no constitutional infirmity in the forfeiture. It distinguished forfeiture of the proceeds of a crime from property that is used for criminal activity. The forfeiture of proceeds from an illegal enterprise "is not considered punishment subject to the excessive fines analysis because the forfeiture of proceeds simply deprives the owner of the fruits of his criminal activity." The court found that the amount of proceeds from Alexander's racketeering activity amounted to almost $9 million; that amount was excluded from the proportionality analysis. The remainder of the property forfeited was found to be not disproportionate in light of Alexander's racketeering crimes. United States v. Alexander, 108 F.3d 853 (8th Cir.1997).

Excessive Forfeiture: United States v. Bajakajian

In United States v. Bajakajian, 524 U.S. 321 (1998), the Court struck down a criminal forfeiture of assets as excessive under the Eighth Amendment. Justice Thomas wrote the majority opinion for five members of the Court. Bajakajian was found trying to leave the country with more than $350,000. He was charged with, and pled guilty to, failure to report the currency. The government sought forfeiture of all the currency, under a statute permitting forfeiture of property "involved" in a criminal offense. The majority found that forfeiture of the entire amount was disproportionate to Bajakajian's offense. Justice Thomas analyzed the proportionality question in the following passage:

Respondent's crime was solely a reporting offense. It was permissible to transport the currency out of the country so long as he reported it. * * * Furthermore, as the District Court found, respondent's violation was unrelated to any other illegal activities. The money was the proceeds of legal activity and was to be used to repay a lawful debt. Whatever his other vices, respondent does not fit into the class of persons for whom the statute was principally designed: He is not a money launderer, a drug trafficker, or a tax evader. And under the Sentencing Guidelines, the maximum sentence that could have been imposed on respondent was six months, while the maximum fine was $5,000. Such penalties confirm a minimal level of culpability.

The harm that respondent caused was also minimal. Failure to report his currency affected only one party, the Government, and in a relatively minor way. There was no fraud on the United States, and respondent caused no loss to the public fisc. Had his crime gone undetected, the Government would have been deprived only of the information that $357,144 had left the country. * * * There is no inherent proportionality in such a forfeiture. * * *

Justice Kennedy, joined by Chief Justice Rehnquist and Justices O'Connor and Scalia, dissented. He argued that the forfeiture of the entire sum of smuggled cash was a reasonable means of deterring criminals such as money launderers and drug dealers.

Proportionality Limitations on in Rem Forfeitures: Austin v. United States

Austin v. United States, 509 U.S. 602 (1993), dealt with a type of forfeiture known as *in rem*, i.e., a forfeiture proceeding brought against the property rather than against the owner. After a state court sentenced Austin on his guilty plea to one count of possessing cocaine with intent to distribute, the United States filed an in rem civil forfeiture action against his mobile home and auto body shop under 21 U.S.C. § 881, which provides for the forfeiture of property used, or intended to be used, to facilitate the commission of certain drug-related crimes. The government presented evidence that Austin had brought two ounces of cocaine from his mobile home to his body shop in order to consummate a pre-arranged sale there. The lower court ordered the properties to be forfeited to the government. Austin objected that forfeiture of the properties, in light of the relatively minor offense, constituted a violation of the Eighth Amendment's Excessive Fines Clause. The lower court rejected this argument and agreed with the government that when it is proceeding in rem—against the property rather than its owner—the guilt or innocence of the owner is "constitutionally irrelevant" and therefore such a forfeiture could not be considered excessive in relationship to any offense.

The Supreme Court, in an opinion by Justice Blackmun, rejected the lower court's reasoning and held that the forfeiture *was* subject to review for proportionality under the Excessive Fines Clause. Justice Blackmun noted that the text of the Eighth Amendment contained no specific limitation to criminal cases—unlike the Sixth Amendment, for example. Justice Blackmun elaborated as follows:

> The Excessive Fines Clause limits the Government's power to extract payments, whether in cash or kind, as punishment for some offense. The notion of punishment, as we commonly understand it, cuts across the division between the civil and the criminal law. It is commonly understood that civil proceedings may advance punitive and remedial goals, and, conversely, that both punitive and remedial goals may be served by criminal penalties. Thus, the question is not, as the United States would have it, whether forfeiture under [the provisions for in rem forfeiture] is civil or criminal, but rather whether it is punishment.

Justice Blackmun further stressed that—whatever the status of in rem forfeiture under the common-law—the statutory forfeiture provisions applicable to drug cases provide an "innocent owner" defense. He reasoned that these exemptions "serve to focus the provisions on the culpability of the owner in a way that makes them look more like punishment, not less" and concluded that the inclusion of innocent owner defenses revealed a "congressional intent to punish only those involved in drug trafficking." In other words, the statutory "in rem" forfeiture at issue in *Austin* was operating against the owner, not just against the property.

The Court remanded to determine whether the forfeiture was constitutionally excessive in light of the offense. It refused to set forth a particular test for determining proportionality in forfeiture actions. Justice Kennedy, joined by Chief Justice Rehnquist and Justice Thomas, wrote an opinion concurring in part and in the judgment.[3]

2. Probation

Another alternative to incarceration is probation—called "supervised release" in the federal system. Probation means that a prison sentence is held in abeyance in whole or in part, and the defendant is released subject to terms and conditions. If the defendant fails to meet those conditions, then the sentence can be reinstated upon proof by a preponderance of evidence at a probation revocation hearing. Familiar conditions for probation are that the probationer meet his family obligations, pay a fine if possible, keep a job, undergo medical (including psychiatric) treatment, submit to drug testing, follow a prescribed course of study or training,

---

[3]   See Bennis v. Michigan, 516 U.S. 442 (1996) (forfeiture of automobile was permissible even though the owner was unaware of illegal activity occurring in the automobile).

report regularly to a probation officer, remain within a specified geographical area and, most importantly, refrain from further criminal conduct. Community service requirements may also be imposed. See generally United States v. Smith, 332 F.3d 455 (7th Cir. 2003) ("A district court may impose special conditions of supervised release that it deems appropriate so long as the conditions are reasonably related to 1) the nature and circumstances of the offense and the history and characteristics of the defendant; 2) the need for the sentence imposed to afford adequate deterrence to criminal conduct; 3) the need to protect the public from further crimes of the defendant; and 4) the need to provide the defendant with needed educational or vocational training, medical care or other correctional treatment in the most effective manner.").

More controversial conditions are those that call upon probationers to forego personal liberties that the unconvicted citizen may claim under the Bill of Rights. For example, in United States v. Smith, 972 F.2d 960 (8th Cir.1992), the court imposed as a condition of supervised release that "the defendant shall not cause the conception of another child other than to his wife, unless he can demonstrate he is fully providing support to the three children presently in existence, and the two en ventre sa mere." The sentencing judge was concerned that the defendant if released would father children who would not be supported and sustained. But the court of appeals held that the sentencing court had no authority to impose that condition. Under the Federal Probation Act, 18 U.S.C. § 3563, conditions imposed on liberty or property must be reasonably necessary to foster rehabilitation of the defendant or the protection of the public. The court held that restricting Smith's right to have offspring did not meet this test, and also noted that the right to have children is a "sensitive and important area of human rights." What conditions should the court have imposed to allay its concerns? Compare United States v. Zobel, 696 F.3d 558 (6th Cir. 2012) (blanket prohibition on pornography use was valid where there was evidence that the defendant's self-professed addiction to pornography caused an increased risk of recidivism for the crime for which he was convicted—coercing and enticing a minor to engage in sexual activity); United States v. Tome, 611 F.3d 1371 (11th Cir. 2010) (ban on internet access as a condition for supervised release of defendant convicted of possession of child pornography was valid where the defendant had violated the terms of his prior supervised release by using the internet to communicate with sex offenders).

If the judge cannot impose what she feels to be effective conditions, she can presumably deny probation and incarcerate the defendant. Is this a better result for the defendant?

Whatever conditions may be imposed, they must be sufficiently clear so that the person on supervised release will know when he violates them. Thus, in United States v. Reeves, 591 F.3d 77 (2d Cir. 2010), the defendant pled guilty to child pornography charges, and received a term of imprisonment and supervised release. The judge imposed a condition on supervised release requiring Reeves to "Notify the Probation Department when he establishes a significant romantic relationship and inform the other party of his prior criminal history concerning his sentencing offenses." The court of appeals found that the condition, triggered by a "significant romantic relationship," was void for vagueness under the Due Process Clause:

> What makes a relationship "romantic," let alone "significant" in its romantic depth, can be the subject of endless debate * * *. for some, it would involve the exchange of gifts, such as flowers or chocolates; for others, it would depend on acts of physical intimacy; and for still others, all of these elements could be present yet the relationship, without a promise of exclusivity, would not be "significant." The history of romance is replete with precisely these blurred lines and misunderstandings. See, e.g. Wolfgang Amadeus Mozart, *The Marriage of Figaro* (1786); Jane Austen, *Mansfield Park* (1814); *When Harry Met Sally* (Columbia Pictures, 1989); *He's Just Not That Into You* (Flower Films 2009).

The trial judge usually has broad discretion to select a probation period. In United States v. Thomas, 934 F.2d 840 (7th Cir.1991), the defendant thought the conditions and length of the imposed probation to be onerous and argued that he had an absolute right to reject probation and opt for a prison sentence—which would not have been as long as the probation period. The court of appeals held that the defendant had no such option. It reasoned that it is the court, not the defendant, who is given the task of determining the sentence for a crime.

3. Restitution

A third alternative to incarceration (or a penalty in addition to incarceration) is restitution. There is increasing concern in the United States with the plight of victims of crime. So it is not surprising that courts are ordering more defendants to make financial restitution to victims. The Victim and Witness Protection Act of 1982 ("VWPA") provided two new sections on restitution, 18 U.S.C.A. §§ 3663 and 3664, which authorize restitution for victims of certain offenses and require a court to justify a sentence that does not include restitution. 18 U.S.C.A. § 3664(c) requires that the defendant and the government be informed of provisions of the presentence report relating to restitution. The prosecution must bear the burden of persuasion as to the victim's loss, while the defendant has the burden of persuasion as to his financial resources.

Congress again demonstrated its concern for crime victims and its interest in promoting restitution in the Sentencing Reform Act of 1984. The Act recognizes that restitution may be a condition of probation, 18 U.S.C.

§ 3563, provides that a defendant may have to give notice to victims of fraud or deception in connection with sentencing, 18 U.S.C. § 3555, provides that a court may order portions of a fine remitted if a defendant makes restitution, 18 U.S.C. § 3572, and states that restitution may be imposed in addition to other sanctions, 18 U.S.C. § 3556. As part of the Comprehensive Crime Control Act of 1984, Congress also enacted the Victims of Crime Act of 1984, which creates a crime victims fund and provides for crime victim compensation.

In 1996 Congress enacted the Mandatory Victim's Restitution Act (MVRA). The MVRA further amended 18 U.S.C. §§ 3663 and 3664, and added new section 3663A, all with the view to fortifying the remedy of restitution for victims of crime. The VWPA provided a presumption in favor of restitution. The MVRA goes much further by providing that restitution is *mandatory* for crimes of violence, offenses against property, and for the crime of tampering with consumer products. With respect to these crimes, an order of restitution is mandatory even if the defendant has no ability to pay. See, e.g., United States v. Nichols, 169 F.3d 1255 (10th Cir.1999) (upholding order requiring defendant, convicted of conspiracy to bomb the Federal building Oklahoma City, to pay restitution in the amount of $14.5 million: "The district court was not required to consider Mr. Nichols' financial condition under 18 U.S.C. 3664(f)(1)(A)."). The Act does provide, however, that an indigent defendant cannot be incarcerated "solely on the basis of inability" to make restitution payments. And for the crimes not covered by the MVRA amendments, a restitution order must be structured within the defendant's ability to pay. See United States v. Dunigan, 163 F.3d 979 (6th Cir.1999) (defendant convicted of defrauding the United States; restitution order in the amount of $311,000 was vacated because defendant was indigent).

The MVRA specifically provides for restitution to victims who suffer bodily injury, essentially applying tort damages principles. See, e.g., United States v. Cienfuegos, 462 F.3d 1160 (9th Cir. 2006) (manslaughter victim's estate is entitled to a restitution award for future lost income). Another innovation of the MVRA is to provide restitution for drug crimes. The money is allocated 65% to the government's crime assistance fund, and 35% to a fund for substance abuse block grants. The Act also contains special provisions for compensation of victims of terrorism. The MVRA requires restitution even where counts involving injured victims are dismissed at trial, so long as the defendant has been convicted of a crime triggering restitution, and the trial judge finds causation. See United States v. Edwards, 728 F.3d 1286 (11th Cir. 2013) ("While a conviction is required to trigger restitution under the MVRA, once the defendant is convicted, a court may order restitution for acts of related conduct for which the defendant was not convicted * * * so long as the injury is related to an offense of which the defendant was convicted.").

Restitution for Victims of Child Pornography:
Paroline v. United States

Congress enacted the Mandatory Restitution for Sexual Exploitation of Children Act—18 U.S.C. § 2259—as a special provision to protect and compensate children who are the subjects of sexual abuse, including the abuse of appearing in child pornography. The Act provides that a defendant convicted of an offense of sexual exploitation of a child must provide restitution of "the full amount of the victim's losses."

In Paroline v. United States, 134 S.Ct. 1710 (2014), the Court considered whether restitution to victims of child pornography requires proof that the defendant proximately caused the victim's injury. Paroline pleaded guilty to possessing child pornography, including two images of "Amy" being sexually abused by her uncle when she was a child. Amy sought restitution for the psychological harm she suffered from knowing that the pictures of her were being seen by thousands of people over the Internet. The Court, in an opinion by Justice Kennedy for five Justices, read the restitution statute to require a showing by the government that the defendant proximately caused the victim's injuries. The Court rejected the victim's argument that every possessor should be responsible for the entirety of her damages as too extreme a position, especially in light of the purposes of imposing restitution as a part of a criminal punishment. Justice Kennedy elaborated as follows:

> The striking outcome of this reasoning—that each possessor of the victim's images would bear the consequences of the acts of the many thousands who possessed those images—illustrates why the Court has been reluctant to adopt aggregate causation logic in an incautious manner, especially in interpreting criminal statutes where there is no language expressly suggesting Congress intended that approach. * * *

> Contrary to the victim's suggestion, this is not akin to a case in which a "gang of ruffians" collectively beats a person, or in which a woman is "gang raped by five men on one night or by five men on five sequential nights." First, this case does not involve a set of wrongdoers acting in concert; for Paroline had no contact with the overwhelming majority of the offenders for whose actions the victim would hold him accountable. Second, adopting the victim's approach would make an individual possessor liable for the combined consequences of the acts of not just 2, 5, or even 100 independently acting offenders; but instead, a number that may reach into the tens of thousands.

> It is unclear whether it could ever be sensible to embrace the fiction that this victim's entire losses were the "proximate result," of a single possessor's offense. Paroline's contribution to the causal process underlying the victim's losses was very minor, both compared to the combined acts of all other relevant offenders, and in comparison to the

contributions of other individual offenders, particularly distributors (who may have caused hundreds or thousands of further viewings) and the initial producer of the child pornography. Congress gave no indication that it intended its statute to be applied in the expansive manner the victim suggests, a manner contrary to the bedrock principle that restitution should reflect the consequences of the defendant's own conduct, not the conduct of thousands of geographically and temporally distant offenders acting independently, and with whom the defendant had no contact.

The reality is that the victim's suggested approach would amount to holding each possessor of her images liable for the conduct of thousands of other independently acting possessors and distributors, with no legal or practical avenue for seeking contribution. That approach is so severe it might raise questions under the Excessive Fines Clause of the Eighth Amendment.

The victim (and the government) in *Paroline* argued that under a strict requirement of proximate cause, the victim would never be able to recover *anything* from an individual wrongdoer, because the victim's damages stemmed from the fact that there was an entire market of individuals accessing the offensive pictures over the Internet. Justice Kennedy was sympathetic to this argument, and essentially crafted a compromise approach—between the victim's position that each user should be liable for all of her injuries and the defendant's position that the victim could not recover anything from a single user because the harm was coming from the market. Justice Kennedy set forth the Court's position in the following passage:

> In this special context, where it can be shown both that a defendant possessed a victim's images and that a victim has outstanding losses caused by the continuing traffic in those images but where it is impossible to trace a particular amount of those losses to the individual defendant by recourse to a more traditional causal inquiry, a court applying 18 U.S.C. § 2259 should order restitution in an amount that comports with the defendant's relative role in the causal process that underlies the victim's general losses. The amount would not be severe in a case like this, given the nature of the causal connection between the conduct of a possessor like Paroline and the entirety of the victim's general losses from the trade in her images, which are the product of the acts of thousands of offenders. It would not, however, be a token or nominal amount. The required restitution would be a reasonable and circumscribed award imposed in recognition of the indisputable role of the offender in the causal process underlying the victim's losses and suited to the relative size of that causal role. This would serve the twin goals of helping the victim achieve eventual restitution for all her child-pornography losses and

impressing upon offenders the fact that child-pornography crimes, even simple possession, affect real victims.

Chief Justice Roberts, joined by Justices Scalia and Thomas, "regretfully" dissented in *Paroline*. The Chief Justice contended that Congress had not authorized the majority's compromise approach to assessing restitution for victims of child pornography. In his view, "the restitution statute that Congress wrote for child pornography offenses makes it impossible to award relief" for damages caused by viewing the pictures of the victim over the Internet—because the statute requires proof of damage by a preponderance of the evidence. The Chief Justice concluded that it could not be possible to show that Paroline caused Amy any damage by a preponderance, because even without his viewing, Amy would have suffered the same damages from viewing by thousands of others. The Chief Justice concluded as follows:

> The Court's decision today means that Amy will not go home with nothing. But it would be a mistake for that salutary outcome to lead readers to conclude that Amy has prevailed or that Congress has done justice for victims of child pornography. The statute as written allows no recovery; we ought to say so, and give Congress a chance to fix it.

Justice Sotomayor wrote a separate dissent in *Paroline*. She argued that the statute should be read to allow apportionment of a victim's damages, and that each convicted defendant should have a payment schedule imposed in light of that defendant's financial circumstances.

4. Youth Offenders

Special detention provisions are often made for juvenile offenders. One statutory scheme was the Federal Youth Corrections Act, which provided the trial judge with special sentencing options for offenders under 22 years of age. Although the result of sentencing under the Act could have been a longer sentence than would be served by an adult, there was greater emphasis on treatment under the Act. More treatment facilities were made available to youth offenders; more individualized treatment for youth offenders was expected; and special release provisions (in lieu of parole) applied to youth offenders. In the Comprehensive Crime Control Act of 1984, Congress decided to replace the Youth Corrections Act with its general guideline approach to sentencing. In United States v. R.L.C., 503 U.S. 291 (1992), the Court held that the maximum permissible sentence in federal juvenile-delinquency proceedings must be limited to that which could have been imposed upon an adult under the Sentencing Guidelines.

What is often a crucial question for a juvenile charged with a crime is whether he will be treated as a "child" or as an adult. Perhaps no advantage is more significant than the limit on incarceration to a designated age. If a person is transferred to the typical criminal court, the potential range of prison sentences may increase, so the transfer decision is of critical importance. 18 U.S.C. § 5032 provides that if a person between 15 and 18 commits a federal crime, he can be tried as an adult "in the interest of justice." In determining whether trying the defendant as an adult is in the interest of justice, the judge must consider the defendant's age and social background, the nature of the offense, any prior acts of delinquency, the juvenile's intellectual development and emotional maturity, the nature of past treatment efforts, if any, and the juvenile's response to such treatment, and the availability of juvenile programs. See United States v. Nelson, 68 F.3d 583 (2d Cir.1995) (trial court erred in refusing to try the defendant as an adult, where he was 19 at the time of trial, charged with murder, and had committed previous acts of delinquency).

5. Insanity Acquittees and Civil Commitment

In the Insanity Defense Reform Act of 1984 ("IDRA"), Congress made insanity an affirmative defense, created a special verdict of "not guilty only by reason of insanity" ("NGI"), and established a comprehensive civil commitment procedure. See 18 U.S.C. §§ 17, 4241–4247. Under that procedure, a defendant found NGI is held in custody pending a court hearing, which must occur within 40 days of the verdict. At the conclusion of the hearing, the court determines whether the defendant should be hospitalized or released. Provisions similar to IDRA exist in many states.

One question arising under IDRA is whether the defendant has the right to have the jury instructed that an NGI verdict will result in his involuntary commitment. In Shannon v. United States, 512 U.S. 573 (1994), Shannon argued that such an instruction was necessary to prevent a possible misconception among the jurors that he would be quickly set free after an NGI verdict. But the trial court refused to give the instruction and Shannon was found guilty.

The Supreme Court, in an opinion written by Justice Thomas for seven members of the Court, held that Shannon had no right to an instruction concerning the consequences of an NGI verdict. Justice Thomas relied on the "well established" principle that "when a jury has no sentencing function, it should be admonished to reach its verdict without regard to what sentence might be imposed." He argued that "providing jurors sentencing information invites them to ponder matters that are not within their province, distracts them from their factfinding responsibilities, and creates a strong possibility of confusion."

Justice Thomas noted, however, that a clarifying instruction about an NGI verdict might be required if "a witness or prosecutor states in the presence of the jury that a particular defendant would 'go free' if found NGI." Justice Stevens, joined by Justice Blackmun, dissented in *Shannon*. He contended that "[t]here is no reason to keep this information from the jurors and every reason to make them aware of it."

II. GUIDELINES SENTENCING

A. THE PERCEIVED NEED FOR CONSISTENCY IN SENTENCING

Judge Marvin Frankel conducted a study of sentencing and published his results in 1972. See Frankel, Criminal Sentences: Law Without Order. In that influential study, Judge Frankel found significant disparities in federal sentencing decisions. He attributed the disparities to "the almost wholly unchecked and sweeping powers we give to judges in the fashioning of sentences"—powers that Judge Frankel himself had exercised and found "terrifying and intolerable for a society that professes devotion to the rule of law." The solution, for Judge Frankel, was "concrete agreement on concrete factors capable of being stated, discussed and thought about in the style of a legal system for rational people rather than a lottery." He posited the possibility of "scientific sentencing." Judge Frankel's views eventually bore fruit in Congress, with a statute sponsored by Senators Kennedy and Thurmond, designed to replace "our haphazard approach to sentencing." It should not be surprising that a statutory scheme that appealed to both liberals and conservatives and to both Democrats and Republicans had several rationales. One was the importance of avoiding unwarranted disparities in sentencing. Another was the desire to promote "truth in sentencing" (meaning that a 15-year sentence should really mean 15 years rather than release on parole after 5).

Professor Robinson provides the following perspective about the move away from discretionary sentencing and toward guidelines sentencing:

> Although almost ubiquitous in state and federal systems by the 1960's, the indeterminate sentence became the subject of intense criticism. Prisoners complained of the uncertainty of their situation and disparate sentences proposed by judges. Law and order advocates worried about the possibility of quick parole. Libertarians expressed concern with the length of time inmates spent prior to parole. Social scientists complained about the lack of empirical support for the proposition that prisons were rehabilitative institutions. Other critics pointed out that prison behavior correlated poorly with post-release recidivism and that the best predictors were factors known at the time of the original sentences. Thus, if guidelines could be directed at the courts, rather than the parole boards, the uncertainty and potential deceptiveness of indeterminate sentences could be avoided.

Robinson, The Decline and Potential Collapse of Federal Guideline Sentencing, 74 Wash.U.L.Q 881 (1996).

The Sentencing Reform Act of 1984 made a number of important changes in Federal sentencing. Among other changes, the Act 1) classifies federal criminal offenses and designates the sentencing range for the new classes; 2) states the purposes to be served by any sentence; 3) establishes a Sentencing Commission to promulgate guidelines binding on sentencing courts; 4) and requires judges to give reasons for sentencing.[4]

The Reform Act abolishes parole in the Federal system. The rationale for abolishing parole is that the discretion exercised by parole boards was one of the major causes of disparity in sentencing. As Professor Robinson, supra, puts it:

> To achieve the goal of minimizing judge-created disparities, the danger of merely shifting discretion from the district court judges to other actors in the criminal justice process had to be faced. One such actor was the United States Parole Commission, which had authority to release inmates prior to completion of their maximum terms of confinement. The Sentencing Reform Act addressed this problem by abolishing parole for persons sentenced under the guidelines to be established by the Sentencing Commission.

The Goals of the Sentencing Commission

The U.S. Sentencing Commission found that adoption of guidelines satisfactory to legislators, prosecutors, defense lawyers, and judges was no simple task. After the circulation of various drafts and extensive debate within the Commission, the Commission finally agreed to the following principles:

(1) Similar offense categories—e.g., for various kinds of fraud—would be grouped together under a single generic heading.

(2) The base sentence for each offense would be determined by a discussion process, *"anchored, but not bound by,"* estimates of the average time served in past years by offenders convicted of that offense and the percentage of offenders given a non-incarceration sentence.

(3) For articulated policy reasons—e.g., to increase deterrence—sentences could be raised or lowered with respect to past practice.

(4) Base offense sentences would be modified by a set of specific offense characteristics that would be determined by looking to past sentencing practices, statutory aggravating or mitigating factors, factors that are taken into consideration in similar offenses, the vulnerability of victims, the offender's role in an offense, acceptance of responsibility, and the criminal history of the offender.

Thus, the Commission began with past practice, emphasized the importance of rationalizing sentences, and adopted an approach that

---

[4] In Mistretta v. United States, 488 U.S. 361 (1989), the defendant argued that Congress, in the Sentencing Reform Act, had delegated excessive power to the Sentencing Commission to establish Guidelines. But the Court rejected this argument in an 8–1 decision, with Justice Scalia dissenting.

focuses on the charges actually brought and the real offense behavior of the offender. It decided that conspiracies and attempts would generally be treated the same as the object offense, with a modest downward adjustment.

B. HOW THE FEDERAL SENTENCING GUIDELINES WORK

The process of sentencing under the Federal Guidelines has been described succinctly as follows:

> Under the federal guidelines, sentences are based on a mathematical equation that begins with an offense level depending on its seriousness. Murder, for instance, is at level 43, while robbery is at 20, altering or removing a motor vehicle identification number is at level 8 and obscenity is at 6.

> That offense level is then reduced or increased depending on factors such as a defendant's criminal history, level of cooperation, use of a deadly weapon and role in the offense. Other key factors are the quantities of drugs or money involved, injury to a victim and vulnerability of the victim.

> The sum of factors leads to a box on a grid that suggests a sentencing range such as 0 to 6 months at the low end or 292 to 365 months at the high end.

Pines, After Five Years, No One Loves Federal Sentencing Guidelines, N.Y.L.J., November 4, 1992, p. 3.

It is critical to note, as you proceed through these materials, that the Guidelines are only *advisory*. While sentencing courts are required to calculate the Guidelines sentence, they are not bound by the Guidelines. They can diverge from the Guidelines to adjust for various factors to be discussed below. See United States v. Booker, infra (holding that Sentencing Guidelines are advisory, not mandatory).

Base Offense Level

To understand how the Guidelines work as an advisory source for the sentence imposed by the court, it is useful to consider a hypothetical case.[5] Suppose that a defendant is convicted of obstruction of justice. The Guidelines describe offenses generically and contain an index indicating which Guidelines cover various code sections. Obstruction of justice is

---

[5] Citations to and quotations of particular Guidelines in the following discussion may not be definitive at the time you read this. The Sentencing Commission has amended the Guidelines hundreds of times since 1984. The discussion that follows is therefore intended merely to give you a general impression of how the Guidelines work.

governed by Guideline § 2J1.2. The base offense level is 14 (raised from 12 after the Enron scandal); but the level increases to 16 if the obstruction involved destruction or alteration of either a substantial number of records or an especially probative record. (Similarly, with drug crimes, the base offense level increases as the quantity increases, and with financial crimes the base level increases as the amount of loss to victims increases.)

Relevant Conduct

Section 1B1.3 of the Guidelines provides that the sentencing range is based not only on evidence with which the defendant was convicted, but also on evidence that is *related* to the conduct forming the basis of the conviction. See, e.g., United States v. Santiago, 906 F.2d 867 (2d Cir.1990) (in a drug distribution case, quantities and types of drugs not specified in the count of conviction are to be included in determining the base offense level if they were part of the same course of conduct or part of a common scheme or plan as the count of conviction; the sentencing court properly considered previous, uncharged sales to the same buyer). "Relevant conduct" is to be proven to the sentencing judge by a preponderance of the evidence—*not* beyond a reasonable doubt. United States v. Mourning, 914 F.2d 699 (5th Cir.1990) (trial court properly considered uncharged acts of money laundering, proven by a preponderance of the evidence). Thus, in our obstruction of justice hypothetical, if the government could show by a preponderance that the defendant engaged in related acts of fraud or perjury, these acts would be considered in setting the base offense level. And they would *count as much for sentencing purposes as the acts for which the defendant was convicted.*

Adjustments

The Guidelines call for certain adjustments of a sentence from the base offense level. There are victim-related adjustments—e.g., a two-level increase when the victim is especially vulnerable, § 3A1.1, or a three-level increase when the victim is a government official or employee. § 3A1.2. See, e.g., United States v. Wright, 160 F.3d 905 (2d Cir.1998) (two-step upward adjustment upheld under vulnerable victim provision, based on defendant's embezzlement of funds from mentally disabled individuals). Adjustments are provided when the defendant had an aggravating role (two to four-level upward adjustment) or mitigating role (two to four-level decrease) in an offense. §§ 3B1.1, 3B1.2. The offense level is increased by two levels if the defendant is found to have "abused a position of public or private trust * * * in a manner that significantly facilitated the commission or concealment of the offense." § 3B1.3. That same Guideline provides a two-level increase if the defendant committed the crime by exploiting a "special skill." See, e.g., United States v. Smith, 332 F.3d 455 (7th Cir.

2003) (conviction for theft of interstate freight raised by two levels because the defendant exploited his "special skills" in operating a tractor-trailer). Another adjustment increases punishment by two levels for obstruction of justice with respect to the investigation or prosecution of the offense charged. § 3C1.1. See United States v. Thompson, 944 F.2d 1331 (7th Cir.1991) (enhancement for obstruction of justice not permitted under the Guidelines where the defendant merely denies wrongdoing); United States v. Dunnigan, 507 U.S. 87 (1993) (upward adjustment where the court finds that the defendant committed perjury while testifying at trial).

If the defendant is convicted on several counts, the calculation is usually made separately for each count, and a set of rules is applied to the totality. But there are special rules that aggregate some conduct. §§ 3D1.1– 3D1.5. Assume, for example, that a securities fraud defendant was convicted of defrauding three victims whose estimated losses were $250,000, $100,000, and $500,000. For crimes in which offense level is determined primarily on the basis of the amount of the loss, the three estimated losses are added together for a total of $850,000, increasing the punishment above the base offense level.

Acceptance of Responsibility

The final determinant of the offense level is the defendant's acceptance of responsibility. § 3E1.1. A defendant who clearly demonstrates recognition and affirmative acceptance of personal responsibility for his crime may receive a reduction of two levels. The defendant receives a further one level reduction if his offense level is 16 or above and his acceptance of responsibility includes assistance to the government in the investigation or prosecution of his own misconduct. Thus, if the obstruction of justice defendant cooperates with the government and promises to institute corrective measures, his level might drop from 14 to 12. It could not drop to 11, however, even if he supplies the government complete information concerning his involvement in the crime, or promptly notifies the government of his intent to plead guilty (because the offense level started below 16). See, e.g., United States v. Phillip, 948 F.2d 241 (6th Cir.1991) (defendant not entitled to reduction for acceptance of responsibility where he gave a false alibi to the investigating officers); United States v. Burns, 925 F.2d 18 (1st Cir.1991) (defendant who enters *Alford* plea—pleading guilty while protesting his innocence—is not entitled to reduction for acceptance of responsibility under the Guidelines); United States v. Boos, 329 F.3d 907 (7th Cir. 2003) (defendant who pleaded guilty to drug activity was not entitled to reduction for acceptance of responsibility under the Guidelines, where the sentencing judge enhanced the sentence for obstruction of justice).

Criminal History Category

Once the offense level is fixed, the sentencing judge, with the assistance of the probation officer, must determine the defendant's criminal history. §§ 4A1.1–4A1.3. Criminal history points are determined by a defendant's prior convictions. Three points are allocated, for example, for each prior sentence of imprisonment exceeding one year and one month, and two points are added for each sentence of imprisonment of at least 60 days but less than one year and one month. Some offenses are excluded, and time periods are designated to exclude stale convictions. Special provision is made for "career offenders"—i.e., defendants who were at least 18 at the time they commit the crime of conviction, which is a crime of violence or trafficking in a controlled substance, and who had at least two prior felony convictions for violent crimes or trafficking in controlled substances. § 4B1.1.

Using this formula, an obstruction of justice defendant with no prior criminal record would have a criminal history of 0. A prior conviction for a non-violent crime would put him in category I.

Using the 258-Box Sentencing Grid

Using the sentencing table, and assuming no prior criminal history, an obstruction of justice defendant convicted of one count involving extensive destruction of documents, but who was able to obtain all possible credit for acceptance of responsibility, would fall within a guideline for offense level 13 calling for a sentence of 12–18 months.

If instead of no criminal record, a defendant had a category III criminal record, the sentence for a level 13 offense increases to 18–24 months and for a level 16 offense to 30–37 months. Defendants in the worst criminal category (VI) would face a Guideline of 33–41 months at level 13 and 51–63 months at level 16.

Each row of the sentencing table contains levels that overlap with the levels in the preceding and succeeding rows. By overlapping the levels, the Commission intended to discourage unnecessary litigation. Both the prosecutor and the defendant are expected to realize that the difference between one level and another will not necessarily make a difference in sentencing.

Authorized Departures

The Guidelines contain a section on "departures." They authorize departures from the Guidelines when a defendant has provided substantial assistance to authorities (downward departure), death or serious injury has resulted from conduct (upward departure), the defendant's conduct was unusually extreme or cruel (upward departure), and in unusual circumstances not otherwise covered by the Guidelines. §§ 5K1, 5K2. See, e.g., United States v. Orchard, 332 F.3d 1133 (8th Cir. 2003) (the defendant was convicted of knowingly distributing a controlled substance analogue to a person under 21; the seriousness of the psychological harm to victim, the defendant's abuse of a relationship of trust, and his facilitation of a sex crime on the victim justified an upward departure); United States v. Phillip, 948 F.2d 241 (6th Cir.1991) (three-level upward departure under § 5K2.8 for extreme cruelty inflicted by the defendant on his four-year-old son); United States v. Williams, 937 F.2d 979 (5th Cir.1991) (defendant's advantageous social background does not justify an upward departure).

The Guidelines departure system was intended to be limited. But those limitations are no longer binding on sentencing courts after *Booker*, because the Guidelines are now advisory, not mandatory.

The Effect of Mandatory Minimum Sentences on Guidelines Sentencing

The Sentencing Guidelines establish sentencing ranges to be considered by judges. But Congress has set mandatory minimum sentences for certain crimes—especially drug and firearms offenses—and has required that these sentences be incorporated into the Guidelines structure. What this means is that if the Guidelines calculation is lower than the minimum sentence statutorily provided, the mandatory minimum controls. In these circumstances, mandatory minimum sentences operate to limit judicial discretion in favor of an across-the-board result.

In 1991, the Sentencing Commission released a report concluding that mandatory minimum sentences clash with the concept of sentencing guidelines, lead to unduly harsh sentences, and are responsible for increased racial disparities in sentencing. See McMillion, Hard Time, A.B.A.J., March, 1993, p. 100. See also Hansen, Mandatories Going, Going, Gone, ABAJ, April, 1999, p. 14 ("More and more people who once supported mandatory minimums have realized that they have done nothing to reduce crime or put big-time drug dealers out of business. What they have done, critics say, is fill prisons with young, nonviolent, low-level drug offenders serving long sentences at enormous and growing cost to taxpayers.").

The Sentencing Commission issued a 2011 report on federal mandatory minimums, and its most recent report on mandatory minimums, Overview of Mandatory Minimum Penalties in the Federal Criminal Justice System (2017), revealed that more than one-fifth of federal offenders sentenced in fical year 2016 were convicted of an offense carrying a mandatory minimum penalty; their average sentence was nearly four times the average sentence for offenders whose offense did not carry a mandatory minimum; and 55.7% of of federal inmates in federal custody were convicted of an offense carrying a mandatory minimum penalty.

Justice Kennedy, in a speech before the American Bar Association in 2003, made a point of criticizing mandatory minimums as 1) often leading to harsh results that have no relation to the actual facts of a particular case; and 2) allowing prosecutors, by charging decisions, to control the sentencing system. Justice Breyer added to the chorus in his concurring opinion in Harris v. United States, 536 U.S. 545 (2002):

> Mandatory minimum statutes are fundamentally inconsistent with Congress' simultaneous effort to create a fair, honest, and rational sentencing system through the use of Sentencing Guidelines. Unlike Guideline sentences, statutory mandatory minimums generally deny the judge the legal power to depart downward, no matter how unusual the special circumstances that call for leniency. They rarely reflect an effort to achieve sentencing proportionality—a key element of sentencing fairness that demands that the law punish a drug "kingpin" and a "mule" differently. They transfer sentencing power to prosecutors, who can determine sentences through the charges they decide to bring, and who thereby have reintroduced much of the sentencing disparity that Congress created Guidelines to eliminate. They rarely are based upon empirical study. And there is evidence that they encourage subterfuge, leading to more frequent downward departures (on a random basis), thereby making them a comparatively ineffective means of guaranteeing tough sentences.

The chorus of criticism of mandatory minimum sentences, especially in drug cases, led the Obama administration to prohibit the practice of prosecutors charging drug crimes calling for mandatory minimum sentences when the defendant is a low-level drug offender. The policy applied to defendants who meet four criteria: 1) their offense did not involve violence, the use of a weapon, or selling drugs to minors; 2) they are not leaders of a criminal organization; 3) they have no significant ties to large-scale gangs or drug trafficking organizations; and 4) they have no significant criminal histories. As reported by the New York Times, 9/23/13 at page A8:

> The Justice Department Policy follows efforts pioneered in conservative-leaning Texas and South Carolina to control soaring taxpayer money that is spent to incarcerate huge numbers of nonviolent offenders. * * * Mr. Holder [the Attorney General] has repeatedly criticized the moral impact of the nation's high incarceration rate, emphasizing that while the United States has only 5 percent of the world's population, it has 25 percent of its prisoners.

Attorney General Eric Holder set forth the Obama Administration's policy in a May 19, 2010 Memorandum to All Federal Prosecutors. But Attorney

General Jeff Sessions abandoned the Obama administration's policy in a May 10, 2016 Memorandum For All Federal Prosecutors.

C. CRITICISM OF MANDATORY FEDERAL SENTENCING GUIDELINES

As promulgated in the Sentencing Reform Act, 18 U.S.C. § 3553(b) provided that courts "shall" impose a sentence under the Guidelines. For 20 years, the "Guidelines" were a misnomer. They were in fact mandatory rules that substantially limited judicial discretion in sentencing. Many judges and commentators viewed the mandatory Guidelines as a failure. Some of the major criticisms were:

- In the desire to bring mathematical precision to sentencing, the Guidelines turned judges into accountants, and turned sentencing proceedings into highly technical and burdensome ordeals for all concerned.

- The Guidelines when mandatory replaced the discretion of an unbiased judge with the charging discretion of a prosecutor who is, obviously, an advocate for the government.

- The Guidelines were (and remain, though only in an advisory capacity) unduly harsh, especially in drug cases.[6]

- The Guidelines punish equally for charged conduct and uncharged "relevant conduct" even though the latter need only be proven by a preponderance of the evidence.

- In drug cases, the Guidelines use weight of the drug as a surrogate for culpability, when that may not always be the case.

- In monetary cases, the Guidelines use amount of loss as a surrogate for culpability, when that may not always be the case.

The following is a small sampling of some of the criticism of the Guidelines during the time that they were mandatory:

Judge Edwards, concurring in United States v. Harrington, 947 F.2d 956 (D.C.Cir.1991):

> [T]he Guidelines do not, by any stretch of the imagination, ensure uniformity in sentencing. Assistant U.S. Attorneys have been heard to say, with open candor, that there are many "games to be played," both in charging defendants and in plea bargaining, to circumvent the Guidelines. Because of this reality, sentences under the Guidelines

---

6   See Richman, Cooperating Clients, 56 Ohio St.L.J. 69 (1995) (citing federal statistics showing a significant increase in both incarceration and in the average length of prison sentences since 1984, and an increase in mean prison terms for drug offenses from 27 months to 67 months).

often bear no relationship to what the Sentencing Commission may have envisioned as appropriate to any given case.

The first "game" to be played under the Guidelines occurs in connection with the charging decision. The confluence of the Guidelines' restriction of judicial discretion and the enactment of mandatory minimum sentences for many drug crimes has placed enormous power in the hands of the AUSA, effectively replacing judicial discretion over sentencing with prosecutorial discretion. Consider the case of a defendant who is charged with possessing ten grams of crack cocaine with intent to distribute—an offense carrying a Guideline sentence of 63–78 months for a defendant with no criminal record, and a mandatory minimum sentence of five years. If the prosecutor elects to add a weapons charge in connection with the drug offense, the Guideline range goes to 78–97 months and the mandatory minimum rises to ten years. * * *

The second disparity-creating game to be played—this one by prosecutors and defense attorneys in collaboration—is the plea bargaining process. By offering a plea, defense counsel may be able to cut a deal with the prosecutor to "bend the rules." However, whether the rules actually get bent may depend upon the luck of the draw in judicial assignment: if the trial judge is willing to look the other way, the facts can be manipulated and the Guidelines ignored because no appeal will be taken by the prosecutor.

* * *

Perhaps most importantly, the Probation Officer determines and evaluates the defendant's "relevant conduct"—that is, conduct (often uncharged) that is related to, but not part of, the offense for which conviction has been sought. This determination can have a substantial impact on the applicable sentencing range.

* * *

Judge Bright, concurring in United States v. Baker, 961 F.2d 1390 (8th Cir.1992), a case in which the court upheld a sentence of almost 20 years for a "career offender" convicted of cocaine distribution and money laundering:

> This sentence demonstrates yet again the vagaries of Guideline sentencing. A similar offender, who would have been under age eighteen when the prior offenses occurred, would not be a career offender, and would not have received this lengthy sentence but one no longer than eleven years and five months. This sort of gross disparity in sentencing often occurs under the Guidelines. * * * This

case is another example of rigid guidelines sentencing producing inequity and injustice in sentencing, and demonstrates a need for the reformation, if not the abolishment, of Guideline sentencing.

Professor Raeder, Gender and Sentencing: Single Moms, Battered Women, and Other Sex-Based Anomalies in the Gender-Free World of the Federal Sentencing Guidelines, 20 Pepp.L.Rev. 905 (1993):

> [T]he Guidelines explicitly mandate that sex is not relevant in the determination of a sentence. However, such legislated equality poses difficulties for many women whose criminal behavior and history, as well as family responsibilities, cannot easily be shoehorned into a punitive pro-prison model for sentencing males assumed to be violent and/or major drug dealers. For example, female offenders are often mothers who have sole or primary responsibility for the care of their children, a consideration virtually ignored by the current Guidelines. Many women * * * may find themselves involved in criminal activity because of social and cultural pressures or occasionally as a result of more obvious means of coercion such as battering. Harsh mandatory minimums combined with the inflexible Guidelines regime result in lengthy incarceration of such women whose actual role in drug cases is often quite limited.

For more judicial commentary on the mandatory Guidelines, see United States v. Concepcion, 983 F.2d 369 (2d Cir.1992) (Newman, J., concurring) (complaining that because the Guidelines treat relevant conduct equally with conduct that is the subject of the conviction, the defendant who was charged with two crimes, and acquitted of one, received the same sentence as if he were convicted of both!); Bonin v. Calderon, 59 F.3d 815 (9th Cir.1995) (Kozinski, J., concurring) (criticizing the fact that the Guidelines often provide harsher sentences for small-time drug offenders than for murderers and rapists).

D. SUPREME COURT CONSTRUCTION OF THE FEDERAL SENTENCING GUIDELINES

1. Guidelines as Advisory, Not Mandatory: United States v. Booker

The *Booker* opinion comes in two parts, with different majorities for each part. In the first part—which might be called the *Apprendi* part—the majority opinion, written by Justice Stevens, holds that the Sentencing Guidelines violate the defendant's rights to jury trial and due process to the extent they require the sentencing judge to increase the sentence beyond that applicable to the crime for which the defendant was convicted, on the basis of facts found by the judge, not the jury. The Guidelines therefore violated the defendant's right to a jury trial on the facts used by the judge to increase the sentence; and they violated the due process right to a determination of all elements of the crime beyond a reasonable doubt, because sentencing facts are determined by the lesser standard of proof by preponderance of the evidence. United States v. Booker, 543 U.S. 220 (2005).

Justice Stevens focused on the fact that the Guidelines as written *required* an enhancement of the sentence, beyond that applicable to the crime found by the jury, on the basis of facts found by the judge by a preponderance of the evidence at sentencing. He explained as follows:

> If the Guidelines as currently written could be read as merely advisory provisions that recommended, rather than required, the selection of particular sentences in response to differing sets of facts, their use would not implicate the Sixth Amendment. We have never doubted the authority of a judge to exercise broad discretion in imposing a sentence within a statutory range. Indeed, everyone agrees that the constitutional issues presented by these cases would have been avoided entirely if Congress had omitted * * * provisions that make the Guidelines binding on district judges; it is that circumstance that makes the Court's answer to the second question presented possible. For when a trial judge exercises his discretion to select a specific sentence within a defined range, the defendant has no right to a jury determination of the facts that the judge deems relevant.

> The Guidelines as written, however, are not advisory; they are mandatory and binding on all judges. While subsection (a) of § 3553 of the sentencing statute lists the Sentencing Guidelines as one factor to be considered in imposing a sentence, subsection (b) directs that the court "*shall* impose a sentence of the kind, and within the range" established by the Guidelines, subject to departures in specific, limited cases.

How to Solve the Constitutional Infirmity in the Guidelines?

After a majority in *Booker* held that the Guidelines can operate to deprive the accused of the right to jury trial and the right to a determination of all elements of the crime beyond a reasonable doubt, the question was, what to do about it? Five members of the Court, in an opinion by Justice Breyer, held that the proper solution—the one most in accord with Congress's intent when it set up the system of Sentencing Guidelines—was to **invalidate the statutory provisions that made the Guidelines mandatory.** If the Guidelines are only advisory, then, as Justice Stevens recognized in the excerpt above, they could not violate

Apprendi—because then sentencing would be based on judicial discretion, and the Court has always accepted the premise that the exercise of judicial discretion to set a sentence does not violate the defendant's constitutional rights to jury trial or due process. The problem with the Guidelines was that Congress *required* sentencing courts to increase the sentence beyond the sentencing range for the crime found by the jury, on the basis of facts found at sentencing by a preponderance of the evidence.

Both Justice Stevens and Justice Breyer recognize a constitutional distinction between (1) finding facts that increase a sentencing range set by a legislature or sentencing commission (a task for juries), and (2) exercising judgment based on the consideration of relevant sentencing factors (a task for judges). See generally Berman, Conceptualizing *Booker*, 38 Ariz. St. L.J. 387, 406–14 (2006), for a discussion of this distinction.

In order to understand Justice Breyer's opinion for the "remedial" majority, you need to review the statute that establishes the system of Federal Sentencing Guidelines. That statute is 18 U.S.C. § 3553. Subdivision (a) provides as follows:

(a) Factors to be considered in imposing a sentence.—The court shall impose a sentence sufficient, but not greater than necessary, to comply with the purposes set forth in paragraph (2) of this subsection. The court, in determining the particular sentence to be imposed, shall consider—

(1) the nature and circumstances of the offense and the history and characteristics of the defendant;

(2) the need for the sentence imposed—

(A) to reflect the seriousness of the offense, to promote respect for the law, and to provide just punishment for the offense;

(B) to afford adequate deterrence to criminal conduct;

(C) to protect the public from further crimes of the defendant; and

(D) to provide the defendant with needed educational or vocational training, medical care, or other correctional treatment in the most effective manner;

(3) the kinds of sentences available;

(4) the kinds of sentence and the sentencing range established for—

(A) the applicable category of offense committed by the applicable category of defendant as set forth in the guidelines—

(i) issued by the Sentencing Commission * * * subject to any amendments made to such guidelines by act of Congress; and

(ii) that * * * are in effect on the date the defendant is sentenced; or

(B) in the case of a violation of probation or supervised release, the applicable guidelines or policy statements issued by the Sentencing Commission * * * taking into account any amendments made to such guidelines or policy statements by act of Congress * * *;

(5) any pertinent policy statement—

(A) issued by the Sentencing Commission * * * subject to any amendments made to such policy statement by act of Congress * * *; and

(B) that * * * is in effect on the date the defendant is sentenced.

(6) the need to avoid unwarranted sentence disparities among defendants with similar records who have been found guilty of similar conduct; and

(7) the need to provide restitution to any victims of the offense.

So section 3553(a) sets forth a grab bag of factors—including a reference to the Guidelines—that the court is to take into account. Looking only to this subdivision, it would appear that judges have a lot of discretion to set a sentence, after considering broad factors, and that the Guidelines are only one source for setting a reasonable sentence.

But subdivision (b)(1) of section 3553 required that the sentencing court adhere to the Guidelines.

(b) Application of guidelines in imposing a sentence.—(1) In general.—* * * the court *shall* impose a sentence of the kind, and within the range, referred to in subsection (a)(4) unless the court finds that there exists an aggravating or mitigating circumstance of a kind, or to a degree, not adequately taken into consideration by the Sentencing Commission in formulating the guidelines that should result in a sentence different from that described. In determining whether a circumstance was adequately taken into consideration, the court shall consider only the sentencing guidelines, policy statements, and official commentary of the Sentencing Commission. * * *

The *Booker* Court was essentially left with two alternatives: 1) it could require that the Guidelines system of judicial factfinding be scrapped, replacing it with a system requiring juries to find all of the facts that are relevant to sentencing enhancements; or 2) it could invalidate the provisions that require mandatory adherence to the Guidelines, thus returning to judicial discretion in sentencing that all members of the Court had found acceptable. The remedial majority chose the latter option. The dissenters opted for the former.

The Remedial Majority Opinion in Booker

Justice Breyer started with a concise statement of the remedial holding:

> We answer the question of remedy by finding the provision of the federal sentencing statute that makes the Guidelines mandatory, 18 USC § 3553(b)(1), incompatible with today's constitutional holding. We conclude that this provision must be severed and excised, as must one other statutory section, § 3742(e), which depends upon the Guidelines' mandatory nature. [Section 3742 covers appeal, and will be discussed below.] So modified, the Federal Sentencing Act makes the Guidelines effectively advisory. It requires a sentencing court to consider Guidelines ranges, see 18 USC § 3553(a)(4), but it permits the court to tailor the sentence in light of other statutory concerns as well, see § 3553(a).

Justice Breyer described the task at hand:

> We answer the remedial question by looking to legislative intent. We seek to determine what Congress would have intended in light of the Court's constitutional holding. In this instance, we must determine which of the two following remedial approaches is the more compatible with the legislature's intent as embodied in the 1984 Sentencing Act.

Justice Breyer found that making the Guidelines Advisory was more consistent with congressional intent in establishing the Guidelines system than a system depending on jury determination of sentencing factors. He argued that a system based on jury determination of all the facts that could increase a sentence beyond a base offense level would increase sentencing disparity—a result that Congress (which passed the Sentencing Reform Act to *cure* sentencing disparities) would not have accepted. He explained as follows:

> Congress' basic statutory goal—a system that diminishes sentencing disparity—depends for its success upon judicial efforts to determine, and to base punishment upon, the *real conduct* that underlies the crime of conviction. * * * Judges have long looked to real conduct when sentencing. Federal judges have long relied upon a presentence report, prepared by a probation officer, for information (often unavailable until *after* the trial) relevant to the manner in which the convicted offender committed the crime of conviction.

Congress expected this system to continue. * * *

To engraft the Court's constitutional requirement onto the sentencing statutes, however, would destroy the system. It would prevent a judge from relying upon a presentence report for factual information, relevant to sentencing, uncovered after the trial. In doing so, it would, even compared to pre-Guidelines sentencing, weaken the tie between a sentence and an offender's real conduct. It would thereby undermine the sentencing statute's basic aim of ensuring similar sentences for those who have committed similar crimes in similar ways.

* * *

Congress' basic goal in passing the Sentencing Act was to move the sentencing system in the direction of increased uniformity. That uniformity does not consist simply of similar sentences for those convicted of violations of the same statute * * *. It consists, more importantly, of similar relationships between sentences and real conduct, relationships that Congress' sentencing statutes helped to advance * * *.

Justice Breyer also argued that a system requiring jury determination of all facts pertinent to sentencing enhancements would be unworkable—and Congress obviously wanted a workable system of sentencing.

How would courts and counsel work with an indictment and a jury trial that involved not just whether a defendant robbed a bank but also how? Would the indictment have to allege, in addition to the elements of robbery, whether the defendant possessed a firearm, whether he brandished or discharged it, whether he threatened death, whether he caused bodily injury, whether any such injury was ordinary, serious, permanent or life threatening, whether he abducted or physically restrained anyone, whether any victim was unusually vulnerable, how much money was taken, and whether he was an organizer, leader, manager, or supervisor in a robbery gang? If so, how could a defendant mount a defense against some or all such specific claims should he also try simultaneously to maintain that the Government's evidence failed to place him at the scene of the crime? * * * How could a judge expect a jury to work with the Guidelines' definitions of, say, "relevant conduct" * * * ? How would a jury measure "loss" in a securities fraud case—a matter so complex as to lead the Commission to instruct judges to make "only . . . a reasonable estimate"? § 2B1.1, comment., n. 3(C). How would the court take account, for punishment purposes, of a defendant's contemptuous behavior at trial—a matter that the Government could not have charged in the indictment? § 3C1.1.

Justice Breyer also argued that a jury-based sentencing system would transfer too much discretion to prosecutors, who could affect sentencing dramatically by their charging decisions.

In respondent Booker's case, for example, the jury heard evidence that the crime had involved 92.5 grams of crack cocaine, and convicted Booker of possessing more than 50 grams. But the judge, at sentencing, found that the crime had involved an additional 566 grams, for a total of 658.5 grams. A system that would require the jury, not the judge, to make the additional "566 grams" finding is a system in which the prosecutor, not the judge, would control the sentence. That is because it is the prosecutor who would have to decide what drug amount to charge.

Justice Breyer then turned to what had to be done to make the Guidelines advisory rather than mandatory:

Most of the statute is perfectly valid. See, e.g., 18 USC § 3551 (describing authorized sentences as probation, fine, or imprisonment); § 3552 (presentence reports); § 3554 (forfeiture); § 3555 (notification to the victims); § 3583 (supervised release). And we must refrain from invalidating more of the statute than is necessary. Indeed, we must retain those portions of the Act that are (1) constitutionally valid, (2) capable of functioning independently, and (3) consistent with Congress' basic objectives in enacting the statute.

Application of these criteria indicates that we must sever and excise two specific statutory provisions: the provision that requires sentencing courts to impose a sentence within the applicable Guidelines range (in the absence of circumstances that justify a departure), see 18 USC § 3553(b)(1), and the provision that sets forth standards of review on appeal, including *de novo* review of departures from the applicable Guidelines range, see § 3742(e) [which provides that the court of appeals must reverse a sentencing decision that was "imposed as a result of an incorrect application of the sentencing guidelines."] With these two sections excised (and statutory cross-references to the two sections consequently invalidated), the remainder of the Act satisfies the Court's constitutional requirements.

Justice Breyer described how sentencing would work in the absence of these mandatory provisions.

The remainder of the Act functions independently. Without the "mandatory" provision, the Act nonetheless requires judges to take account of the Guidelines together with other sentencing goals. See 18 USC § 3553(a). The Act nonetheless requires judges to consider the Guidelines "sentencing range established for . . . the applicable category of offense committed by the applicable category of defendant," § 3553(a)(4), the pertinent Sentencing Commission policy statements, the need to avoid unwarranted sentencing disparities, and the need to provide restitution to victims, §§ 3553(a)(1), (3), (5)–(7). And the Act nonetheless requires judges to impose sentences that reflect the seriousness of the offense, promote respect for the law, provide just punishment, afford adequate deterrence, protect the public, and effectively provide the defendant with needed educational or vocational training and medical care. § 3553(a)(2).

Moreover, despite the absence of § 3553(b)(1), the Act continues to provide for appeals from sentencing decisions (irrespective of whether the trial judge sentences within or outside the Guidelines range in the exercise of his discretionary power under § 3553(a)). See § 3742(a) (appeal by defendant); § 3742(b) (appeal by Government). We concede that the excision of § 3553(b)(1) requires the excision of a different, appeals-related section, namely § 3742(e), which sets forth standards of review on appeal. That section contains critical cross-references to the (now-excised) § 3553(b)(1) and consequently must be severed and excised for similar reasons

Having struck the standard for appellate review, Justice Breyer recognized that it was necessary to determine what standard would apply. He reached the following conclusion:

Excision of § 3742(e), however, does not pose a critical problem for the handling of appeals. That is because, as we have previously held, a statute that does not *explicitly* set forth a standard of review may nonetheless do so *implicitly*. We infer appropriate review standards from related statutory language, the structure of the statute, and the "sound administration of justice." And in this instance those factors, in addition to the past two decades of appellate practice in cases involving departures, imply a practical standard of review already familiar to appellate courts: review for "unreasonable[ness]." 18 USC § 3742(e)(3).

Justice Breyer concluded as follows on the future of sentencing after *Booker:*

[T]he Sentencing Commission remains in place, writing Guidelines, collecting information about actual district court sentencing decisions, undertaking research, and revising the Guidelines accordingly. The district courts, while not bound to apply the Guidelines, must consult those Guidelines and take them into account when sentencing. The courts of appeals review sentencing decisions for unreasonableness. These features of the remaining system, while not the system Congress enacted, nonetheless continue to move sentencing in Congress' preferred direction, helping to avoid excessive sentencing disparities while maintaining flexibility sufficient to individualize sentences where necessary. We can find no feature of the remaining system that tends to hinder, rather than to further, these basic objectives.

Dissents from the Booker Remedial Opinion

Justice Stevens, joined by Justices Souter and Scalia, took issue with the majority's contention that jury determination of sentencing facts would be unworkable. He elaborated as follows:

> * * * [T]he majority argues that my remedy would make sentencing proceedings far too complex. But of the very small number of cases in which a Guidelines sentence would implicate the Sixth Amendment * * * most involve drug quantity determinations, firearm enhancements, and other factual findings that can readily be made by juries. I am not blind to the fact that some cases, such as fraud prosecutions, would pose new problems for prosecutors and trial judges. In such cases, I am confident that federal trial judges, assisted by capable prosecutors and defense attorneys, could have devised appropriate procedures to impose the sentences the Guidelines envision in a manner that is consistent with the Sixth Amendment. We have always trusted juries to sort through complex facts in various areas of law. This may not be the most efficient system imaginable, but the Constitution does not permit efficiency to be our primary concern.

Justice Scalia dissented and argued that the system of appellate review left by the majority's opinion would lead to uncertainty and to disparity in sentencing—results clearly contrary to Congress's intent in the Sentencing Reform Act.

> What I anticipate will happen is that "unreasonableness" review will produce a discordant symphony of different standards, varying from court to court and judge to judge, giving the lie to the remedial majority's sanguine claim that no feature of its avant-garde Guidelines system will tend to hinder the avoidance of excessive sentencing disparities.

Justice Thomas wrote a separate dissent, arguing that the mandatory application of the Guidelines was constitutional in a number of situations (e.g., where the sentence stayed within the Guideline for the base offense level, or where the Guideline controlled a *downward* adjustment of a sentence). He concluded that "the majority, by facially invalidating the statute, also invalidates these unobjectionable applications of the statute and thereby ignores the longstanding distinction between as-applied and facial challenges."

2.   Application of Advisory Guidelines After *Booker*

The remedial opinion in *Booker* emphasizes that the Guidelines remain critical to sentencing determinations. The Guidelines *must still be considered* in setting a reasonable sentence. The circuit courts after *Booker* have clearly stated that sentencing courts must determine what the Guideline sentence is, in the same way as they did before *Booker*. See generally United States v. Crosby, 397 F.3d 103 (2d Cir. 2005). A sentencing court that does not compute the Guidelines sentence will be reversed for unreasonableness, without regard to the length of the sentence. See United States v. McVay, 447 F.3d 1348 (11th Cir. 2006) ("Before we conduct a reasonableness review of the ultimate sentence imposed, we must first determine whether the district court correctly interpreted and applied the Guidelines to calculate the appropriate advisory Guidelines range. It is only after a district court correctly calculates the Guidelines range, which it still must do after *Booker*, that it may consider imposing a more severe or lenient sentence."); United States v. Johnson, 467 F.3d 559 (6th Cir. 2006) ("Although no longer bound by the Guidelines, district courts are still required to consider the applicable Guideline range along with the other statutory factors.").

It is also important to note that factfinding by the sentencing court has not been altered by *Booker*. The Second Circuit in *Crosby* held that judicial factfinding should proceed as previously; now that the Guidelines are advisory only, there can be no Sixth Amendment objection to judicial factfinding, even where it is used to increase a sentence. And there can be no complaint that the district judge, in making sentencing decisions, is deciding facts by a *preponderance of the evidence* rather than beyond a reasonable doubt. The problem with the Guidelines was that judicial factfinding occurred within the context of a mandatory sentencing scheme. As the Third Circuit explained in United States v. Grier, 449 F.3d 558 (3d Cir. 2006):

There can be no question, in light of the holding of *Booker*, and the reasoning of *Apprendi*, that the right to proof beyond a reasonable doubt does not apply to facts relevant to enhancements under an advisory Guidelines regime. Like the right to jury trial, the right to proof beyond a reasonable doubt attaches only when the facts at issue have the effect of increasing the maximum punishment to which the defendant is exposed. The advisory Guidelines do not have this effect. They require the district judge to make findings of fact, but none of these alters the judge's final sentencing authority. They merely inform the judge's broad discretion.

Guidelines Entitled to "Great Weight" After Booker?

How much weight should be given to the advisory Guidelines after *Booker*? In United States v. Wilson, 355 F.Supp.2d 1269 (D.Utah 2005),

Judge Cassell concluded that "considerable weight should be given to the Guidelines in determining what sentence to impose."

Judge Cassell argued that the Guidelines are the best expression of Congress's intent in setting an appropriate sentence under Section 3553. He further argued—relying on opinion polls and social science data—that the Guidelines generally achieve the goals of "just punishment" and "deterrence" that still bind the federal courts after *Booker*. Judge Cassell concluded that the most important reason for applying the Guidelines was to assure uniformity of sentencing after *Booker*. He elaborated as follows:

> The only way of avoiding gross disparities in sentencing from judge-to judge and district-to-district is for sentencing courts to apply some uniform measure in all cases. The only standard currently available is the Sentencing Guidelines. If each district judge follows his or her own views of "just punishment" and "adequate deterrence," the result will be a system in which prison terms will depend on "what the judge ate for breakfast" on the day of sentencing and other irrelevant factors. * * * It would, in short, be a return to the pre-Guidelines days, which produced astounding disparities among the sentences that were imposed on defendants convicted of the same offense with similar backgrounds with different judicial districts across the country—and even among different judges in the same district.

Other courts have argued that to give the Guidelines heavy weight would be improper after *Booker*, because it would essentially make the Guidelines mandatory, which is prohibited by the *Booker* merits opinion. One leading proponent of this view is Judge Adelman in United States v. Ranum, 353 F.Supp.2d 984 (E.D.Wis.2005). The court in *Ranum* stated that after *Booker*, sentencing courts are required to *consult* the Guidelines, but they are also required to consider the factors set forth in 18 U.S.C. 3553(a) as well. The court contended that some of those statutory factors actually conflict with the Guidelines. For example, section 3553(a) states that the court must consider the characteristics and history of the defendant; but under the Guidelines, the defendant's character and background are generally irrelevant, and the only history that can be considered is criminal history. "Thus, in cases in which a defendant's history and character are positive, consideration of all of the § 3553(a) factors might call for a sentence outside the guideline range." The court declared that "in every case, courts must now consider all of the § 3553(a) factors, not just the guidelines. And where the guidelines conflict with other factors set forth in § 3553(a), courts will have to resolve the conflicts."

The defendant in *Ranum* was a bank official who made unauthorized loans to a start-up corporation, GLC, and lied to the bank about it. His actions were not motivated by personal profit. The court found that the

Guidelines called for a sentence of 37–46 months. The defendant argued for a period of home confinement. The court decided that the appropriate sentence was imprisonment for a year and a day.

Judge Adelman argued that a strict application of the Guidelines might lead to an inappropriate sentence because the Guidelines for monetary crimes are driven almost exclusively by the amount of loss.

> One of the primary limitations of the guidelines, particularly in white-collar cases, is their mechanical correlation between loss and offense level. For example, the guidelines treat a person who steals $100,000 to finance a lavish lifestyle the same as someone who steals the same amount to pay for an operation for a sick child. It is true that * * * from the victim's perspective the loss is the same no matter why it occurred. But from the standpoint of personal culpability, there is a significant difference. In the present case, defendant did not act for personal gain. He made loans outside his authority and was reckless with his employer's money. But that is not the same as stealing it. Thus, due to the nature of the case, I found the guideline range, which depended so heavily on the loss amount, greater than necessary.

Ultimately, Judge Adelman found that "in order to promote respect for the law and in recognition of the significant loss to the bank, * * * defendant had to be confined for a significant period of time" but that "the sentence called for by the guidelines, 37–46 months, was much greater than necessary to satisfy the purposes of sentencing set forth in § 3553(a)" because that range "does not properly account for defendant's absence of interest in personal gain, * * * for defendant's otherwise outstanding character and for the significant benefits to family members resulting from his presence." He concluded that a sentence of twelve months and one day, followed by five years of supervised release, "was sufficient to promote respect for the law and account for defendant's serious abuse of trust over an extended period of time."

So after *Booker*, federal sentencing courts must tread the line between *excessive* reliance on the Guidelines (which will in effect make them mandatory and thus in violation of the *Booker* merits opinion) and *insufficient* reliance on the Guidelines (which could lead to unbridled discretion and disparity in sentencing). See, e.g., United States v. Zavala, 443 F.3d 1165 (9th Cir. 2006) (district court erred by treating the Guidelines sentence as the "presumptive" sentence after *Booker,* from which it would depart only if the defendant provided satisfactory reasons: "The court's approach brings us perilously close to the mandatory Guidelines regime squarely rejected by the Supreme Court in *Booker.*").

Sentencing Disparity After Booker?

Professor Ryan Scott evaluated post-*Booker* sentencing decisions in the District of Massachusetts and came to the following conclusions:

> Analysis of those sentences reveals a clear increase in inter-judge disparity * * *. In cases not governed by a mandatory minimum, the court's three most lenient judges have imposed average sentences of 25.5 months or less, while its two most severe judges have imposed average sentences of 51.4 months or more.
>
> Similarly, the * * * data reveal that some judges have taken advantage of their enhanced discretion to depart from the Guidelines to a far greater extent than others. Two judges * * * continue to impose below-Guidelines sentences at essentially the same rate as before *Booker*, as little as 16% of the time. But four other judges * * * now sentence below the guideline range at triple or quadruple their pre-*Booker* rates, as much as 53% of the time.

Scott, Inter-Judge Sentencing Disparity After *Booker*: A First Look, 63 Stan. L.Rev. 1 (2010). See also Memorandum of Department of Justice to the Sentencing Commission, 6/28/2010 ("More and more, we are receiving reports from our prosecutors that in many federal courts, a defendant's sentence will largely be determined by the judicial assignment of the case.").

Disagreement with Guidelines Policy: Kimbrough v. United States

In the following case, the Court emphasizes that sentencing courts have discretion, under the *Booker* regime of advisory guidelines, to disagree with a policy decision upon which a guideline is based.

KIMBROUGH V. UNITED STATES

Supreme Court of the United States, 2007.
552 U.S. 85.

JUSTICE GINSBURG delivered the opinion of the Court.

This Court's remedial opinion in United States v. Booker instructed district courts to read the United States Sentencing Guidelines as "effectively advisory." In accord with 18 U.S.C. § 3553(a), the Guidelines, formerly mandatory, now serve as one factor among several courts must consider in determining an appropriate sentence. *Booker* further instructed that "reasonableness" is the standard controlling appellate review of the sentences district courts impose.

Under the statute criminalizing the manufacture and distribution of crack cocaine, 21 U.S.C. § 841, and the relevant Guidelines prescription,

§ 2D1.1, a drug trafficker dealing in crack cocaine is subject to the same sentence as one dealing in 100 times more powder cocaine. [This disparity was subsequently reduced to 18:1 by the Fair Sentencing Act of 2010]. The question here presented is whether, as the Court of Appeals held in this case, "a sentence . . . outside the guidelines range is per se unreasonable when it is based on a disagreement with the sentencing disparity for crack and powder cocaine offenses." We hold that, under *Booker*, the cocaine Guidelines, like all other Guidelines, are advisory only, and that the Court of Appeals erred in holding the crack/powder disparity effectively mandatory. A district judge must include the Guidelines range in the array of factors warranting consideration. The judge may determine, however, that, in the particular case, a within-Guidelines sentence is "greater than necessary" to serve the objectives of sentencing. 18 U.S.C. § 3553(a). In making that determination, the judge may consider the disparity between the Guidelines' treatment of crack and powder cocaine offenses.

* * *

[P]etitioner Derrick Kimbrough was indicted * * * and charged with four offenses: conspiracy to distribute crack and powder cocaine; possession with intent to distribute more than 50 grams of crack cocaine; possession with intent to distribute powder cocaine; and possession of a firearm in furtherance of a drug-trafficking offense. Kimbrough pleaded guilty to all four charges.

Under the relevant statutes, Kimbrough's plea subjected him to an aggregate sentence of 15 years to life in prison: 10 years to life for the three drug offenses, plus a consecutive term of 5 years to life for the firearm offense. In order to determine the appropriate sentence within this statutory range, the District Court first calculated Kimbrough's sentence under the advisory Sentencing Guidelines. Kimbrough's guilty plea acknowledged that he was accountable for 56 grams of crack cocaine and 92.1 grams of powder cocaine. This quantity of drugs yielded a base offense level of 32 for the three drug charges. See United States Sentencing Commission, Guidelines Manual § 2D1.1(c). Finding that Kimbrough, by asserting sole culpability for the crime, had testified falsely at his codefendant's trial, the District Court increased his offense level to 34. See § 3C1.1. In accord with the presentence report, the court determined that Kimbrough's criminal history category was II. An offense level of 34 and a criminal history category of II yielded a Guidelines range of 168 to 210 months for the three drug charges. The Guidelines sentence for the firearm offense was the statutory minimum, 60 months. See USSG § 2K2.4(b). Kimbrough's final advisory Guidelines range was thus 228 to 270 months, or 19 to 22.5 years.

A sentence in this range, in the District Court's judgment, would have been "greater than necessary" to accomplish the purposes of sentencing set forth in 18 U.S.C. § 3553(a). As required by § 3553(a), the court took into account the "nature and circumstances" of the offense and Kimbrough's "history and characteristics." The court also commented that the case exemplified the "disproportionate and unjust effect that crack cocaine guidelines have in sentencing." In this regard, the court contrasted Kimbrough's Guidelines range of 228 to 270 months with the range that would have applied had he been accountable for an equivalent amount of powder cocaine: 97 to 106 months, inclusive of the 5-year mandatory minimum for the firearm charge, see USSG § 2D1.1(c). Concluding that the statutory minimum sentence was "clearly long enough" to accomplish the objectives listed in § 3553(a), the court sentenced Kimbrough to 15 years, or 180 months, in prison plus 5 years of supervised release. [The Fourth Circuit reversed.]

Although chemically similar, crack and powder cocaine are handled very differently for sentencing purposes. The 100-to-1 ratio [under the Guidelines applicable at the time of Kimbrough's sentencing] yields sentences for crack offenses three to six times longer than those for powder offenses involving equal amounts of drugs. This disparity means that a major supplier of powder cocaine may receive a shorter sentence than a low-level dealer who buys powder from the supplier but then converts it to crack.

* * *

[T]he Government argues that if district courts are * * * permitted to vary from the Guidelines based on their disagreement with the crack/powder disparity, "defendants with identical real conduct will receive markedly different sentences, depending on nothing more than the particular judge drawn for sentencing." * * * [I]t is unquestioned that uniformity remains an important goal of sentencing. As we explained in *Booker*, however, advisory Guidelines combined with appellate review for reasonableness and ongoing revision of the Guidelines in response to sentencing practices will help to "avoid excessive sentencing disparities." These measures will not eliminate variations between district courts, but our opinion in *Booker* recognized that some departures from uniformity were a necessary cost of the remedy we adopted. * * *

Moreover, to the extent that the Government correctly identifies risks of "unwarranted sentence disparities" within the meaning of 18 U.S.C. § 3553(a)(6), the proper solution is not to treat the crack/powder ratio as mandatory. Section 3553(a)(6) directs district courts to consider the need to avoid unwarranted disparities—along with other § 3553(a) factors—when imposing sentences. * * * To reach an appropriate sentence, these disparities must be weighed against the other § 3553(a) factors and any unwarranted disparity created by the crack/powder ratio itself.

* * *

While rendering the Sentencing Guidelines advisory, we have nevertheless preserved a key role for the Sentencing Commission. * * * [D]istrict courts must treat the Guidelines as the starting point and the initial benchmark. * * *

We have accordingly recognized that, in the ordinary case, the Commission's recommendation of a sentencing range will reflect a rough approximation of sentences that might achieve § 3553(a)'s objectives. The sentencing judge, on the other hand, has greater familiarity with the individual case and the individual defendant before him than the Commission or the appeals court. He is therefore in a superior position to find facts and judge their import under § 3553(a) in each particular case. In light of these discrete institutional strengths, a district court's decision to vary from the advisory Guidelines may attract greatest respect when the sentencing judge finds a particular case outside the "heartland" to which the Commission intends individual Guidelines to apply. On the other hand, while the Guidelines are no longer binding, closer review may be in order when the sentencing judge varies from the Guidelines based solely on the judge's view that the Guidelines range fails properly to reflect § 3553(a) considerations even in a mine-run case.

The crack cocaine Guidelines, however, present no occasion for elaborative discussion of this matter because those Guidelines do not exemplify the Commission's exercise of its characteristic institutional role. In formulating Guidelines ranges for crack cocaine offenses, * * * the Commission looked to the mandatory minimum sentences set [by Congress], and did not take account of empirical data and national experience. Indeed, the Commission itself has reported that the crack/powder disparity produces disproportionately harsh sanctions * * *. Given all this, it would not be an abuse of discretion for a district court to conclude when sentencing a particular defendant that the crack/powder disparity yields a sentence greater than necessary to achieve § 3553(a)'s purposes, even in a mine-run case.

* * *

Taking account of the foregoing discussion in appraising the District Court's disposition in this case, we conclude that the 180-month sentence imposed on Kimbrough should survive appellate inspection. The District Court began by properly calculating and considering the advisory Guidelines range. It then addressed the relevant § 3553(a) factors. First, the court considered "the nature and circumstances" of the crime, see 18 U.S.C. § 3553(a)(1), which was an unremarkable drug-trafficking offense. * * * Second, the court considered Kimbrough's "history and characteristics." § 3553(a)(1). The court noted that Kimbrough had no prior felony convictions, that he had served in combat during Operation Desert

Storm and received an honorable discharge from the Marine Corps, and that he had a steady history of employment.

Furthermore, the court alluded to the Sentencing Commission's reports criticizing the 100-to-1 ratio, noting that the Commission "recognizes that crack cocaine has not caused the damage that the Justice Department alleges it has." Comparing the Guidelines range to the range that would have applied if Kimbrough had possessed an equal amount of powder, the court suggested that the 100-to-1 ratio itself created an unwarranted disparity within the meaning of § 3553(a). Finally, the court did not purport to establish a ratio of its own. Rather, it appropriately framed its final determination in line with § 3553(a)'s overarching instruction to "impose a sentence sufficient, but not greater than necessary" to accomplish the sentencing goals advanced in § 3553(a)(2). * * *

The ultimate question in Kimbrough's case is whether the sentence was reasonable—*i.e.*, whether the District Judge abused his discretion in determining that the § 3553(a) factors supported a sentence of [15 years] and justified a substantial deviation from the Guidelines range. The sentence the District Court imposed on Kimbrough was 4.5 years below the bottom of the Guidelines range. But in determining that 15 years was the appropriate prison term, the District Court properly homed in on the particular circumstances of Kimbrough's case and accorded weight to the Sentencing Commission's consistent and emphatic position that the crack/powder disparity is at odds with § 3553(a). * * *

[The concurring opinion of Justice Scalia is omitted.]

JUSTICE THOMAS, dissenting.

I continue to disagree with the remedy fashioned in *United States* v. *Booker*. The Court's post-*Booker* sentencing cases illustrate why the remedial majority in *Booker* was mistaken to craft a remedy far broader than necessary to correct constitutional error. The Court is now confronted with a host of questions about how to administer a sentencing scheme that has no basis in the statute. Because the Court's decisions in this area are necessarily grounded in policy considerations rather than law, I respectfully dissent.

* * *

[The dissenting opinion of Justice Alito is omitted.]

Rehabilitation and Guidelines Sentencing:
Tapia v. United States

In Tapia v. United States, 564 U.S. 319 (2011), Justice Kagan wrote for a unanimous court as it held that 18 U.S.C. 3582(a), a part of the Sentencing Reform Act, does not permit a sentencing court to impose or lengthen a prison term in order to foster a defendant's rehabilitation. The statute provides as follows:

> The court, in determining whether to impose a term of imprisonment, and, if a term of imprisonment is to be imposed, in determining the length of the term, shall consider the factors set forth in section 3553(a) to the extent that they are applicable, recognizing that imprisonment is not an appropriate means of promoting correction and rehabilitation.

The Court found that the language of the statute clearly supported its holding, but added the following: "A court commits no error by discussing the opportunities for rehabilitation within prison or the benefits of specific treatment or training programs. To the contrary, a court properly may address a person who is about to begin a prison term about these important matters. And * * * a court may urge the BOP [Bureau of Prisons] to place an offender in a prison treatment program."

Appellate Review of Advisory Guidelines Sentences

After *Booker*, appellate courts are to review sentences for "reasonableness" as opposed to strict adherence to the Guidelines. One question for the appellate courts was whether a sentence within the Guidelines range is "presumptively" reasonable. The Supreme Court answered that question in the next case.

RITA V. UNITED STATES
Supreme Court of the United States, 2007.
551 U.S. 338.

JUSTICE BREYER delivered the opinion of the Court.

The federal courts of appeals review federal sentences and set aside those they find "unreasonable." Several Circuits have held that, when doing so, they will presume that a sentence imposed within a properly calculated United States Sentencing Guidelines range is a reasonable sentence. The most important question before us is whether the law permits the courts of appeals to use this presumption. We hold that it does.

* * *

The basic crime in this case concerns two false statements which Victor Rita, the petitioner, made under oath to a federal grand jury. * * *

Rita [was charged] with perjury, making false statements, and obstructing justice, and, after a jury trial, obtained convictions on all counts.

* * *

The parties subsequently proceeded to sentencing. Initially, a probation officer, with the help of the parties, and after investigating the background both of the offenses and of the offender, prepared a presentence report. * * * Ultimately, the report calculates the Guidelines sentencing range. The Guidelines specify for base level 20, criminal history category I, a sentence of 33-to-41 months' imprisonment. The report adds that there "appears to be no circumstance or combination of circumstances that warrant a departure from the prescribed sentencing guidelines."

* * *

At the sentencing hearing, both Rita and the Government presented their sentencing arguments. * * * Rita argued for a sentence outside (and lower than) the recommended Guidelines 33-to-41 month range.

The judge made clear that Rita's argument for a lower sentence could take either of two forms. First, Rita might argue *within the Guidelines' framework,* for a departure from the applicable Guidelines range on the ground that his circumstances present an "atypical case" that falls outside the "heartland" to which the United States Sentencing Commission intends each individual Guideline to apply. USSG § 5K2.0(a)(2). Second, Rita might argue that, independent of the Guidelines, application of the sentencing factors set forth in 18 U.S.C. § 3553(a) warrants a lower sentence. See *Booker.*

Thus, the judge asked Rita's counsel, "Are you going to put on evidence to show that [Rita] should be getting a downward departure, or under 3553, your client would be entitled to a different sentence than he should get under sentencing guidelines?" And the judge later summarized:

"You're asking for a departure from the guidelines or a sentence under 3553 that is lower than the guidelines, and here are the reasons:

"One, he is a vulnerable defendant because he's been involved in [government criminal justice] work which has caused people to become convicted criminals who are in prison and there may be retribution against him.

"Two, his military experience. . . ."

Counsel agreed, while adding that Rita's poor physical condition constituted a third reason. And counsel said that he rested his claim for a lower sentence on "just [those] three" special circumstances, "physical condition, vulnerability in prison and the military service." * * *

After hearing * * * arguments, the judge concluded that he was "unable to find that the [report's recommended] sentencing guideline range

... is an inappropriate guideline range for that, and under 3553 ... the public needs to be protected if it is true, and I must accept as true the jury verdict." The court concluded: "So the Court finds that it is appropriate to enter" a sentence at the bottom of the Guidelines range, namely a sentence of imprisonment "for a period of 33 months."

* * *

On appeal, Rita argued that his 33-month sentence was "unreasonable" because (1) it did not adequately take account of "the defendant's history and characteristics," and (2) it "is greater than necessary to comply with the purposes of sentencing set forth in 18 U.S.C. § 3553(a)(2)." The Fourth Circuit * * * stated that "a sentence imposed within the properly calculated Guidelines range ... is presumptively reasonable." * * * The Fourth Circuit then rejected Rita's arguments and upheld the sentence.

* * *

The first question is whether a court of appeals may apply a presumption of reasonableness to a district court sentence that reflects a proper application of the Sentencing Guidelines. We conclude that it can.

* * *

For one thing, the presumption is not binding. * * * Rather, the presumption reflects the fact that, by the time an appeals court is considering a within-Guidelines sentence on review, *both* the sentencing judge and the Sentencing Commission will have reached the *same* conclusion as to the proper sentence in the particular case. That double determination significantly increases the likelihood that the sentence is a reasonable one.

Further, the presumption reflects the nature of the Guidelines-writing task that Congress set for the Commission and the manner in which the Commission carried out that task. * * * The upshot is that the sentencing statutes envision both the sentencing judge and the Commission as carrying out the same basic § 3553(a) objectives, the one, at retail, the other at wholesale.

* * * The Commission, in describing its Guidelines-writing efforts, * * * says that it has tried to embody in the Guidelines the factors and considerations set forth in § 3553(a). * * * Rather than choose among differing practical and philosophical objectives, the Commission took an "empirical approach," beginning with an empirical examination of 10,000 presentence reports setting forth what judges had done in the past and then modifying and adjusting past practice in the interests of greater rationality, avoiding inconsistency, complying with congressional instructions, and the like.

* * *

The result is a set of Guidelines that seek to embody the § 3553(a) considerations, both in principle and in practice. * * * [I]t is fair to assume that the Guidelines, insofar as practicable, reflect a rough approximation of sentences that might achieve § 3553(a)'s objectives.

[T]he courts of appeals' "reasonableness" presumption, rather than having independent legal effect, simply recognizes the real-world circumstance that when the judge's discretionary decision accords with the Commission's view of the appropriate application of § 3553(a) in the mine run of cases, it is probable that the sentence is reasonable. * * *

We repeat that the presumption before us is an *appellate* court presumption. * * * The sentencing judge, as a matter of process, will normally begin by considering the presentence report and its interpretation of the Guidelines. He may hear arguments by prosecution or defense that the Guidelines sentence should not apply, perhaps because (as the Guidelines themselves foresee) the case at hand falls outside the "heartland" to which the Commission intends individual Guidelines to apply, perhaps because the Guidelines sentence itself fails properly to reflect § 3553(a) considerations, or perhaps because the case warrants a different sentence regardless. * * * In determining the merits of these arguments, the sentencing court does not enjoy the benefit of a legal presumption that the Guidelines sentence should apply.

* * *

A nonbinding appellate presumption that a Guidelines sentence is reasonable does not *require* the sentencing judge to impose that sentence. Still less does it *forbid* the sentencing judge from imposing a sentence higher than the Guidelines provide for the jury-determined facts standing alone. * * *

In the present case the sentencing judge's statement of reasons was brief but legally sufficient. * * * The record makes clear that the sentencing judge listened to each argument. The judge considered the supporting evidence. The judge was fully aware of defendant's various physical ailments and imposed a sentence that takes them into account. The judge understood that Rita had previously worked in the immigration service where he had been involved in detecting criminal offenses. And he considered Rita's lengthy military service, including over 25 years of service, both on active duty and in the Reserve, and Rita's receipt of 35 medals, awards, and nominations.

The judge then simply found these circumstances insufficient to warrant a sentence lower than the Guidelines range of 33 to 45 months. * * * He immediately added that he found that the 33-month sentence at the bottom of the Guidelines range was "appropriate." He must have believed that there was not much more to say.

* * *

We turn to the final question: Was the Court of Appeals, after applying its presumption, legally correct in holding that Rita's sentence (a sentence that applied, and did not depart from, the relevant sentencing Guideline) was not "unreasonable"? In our view, the Court of Appeals' conclusion was lawful.

As we previously said, the crimes at issue are perjury and obstruction of justice. In essence those offenses involved the making of knowingly false, material statements under oath before a grand jury, thereby impeding its criminal investigation. The Guidelines provide for a typical such offense a base offense level of 20, 6 levels below the level provided for a simple violation of the crime being investigated (here the unlawful importation of machineguns). The offender, Rita, has no countable prior offenses and consequently falls within criminal history category I. The intersection of base offense level 20 and criminal history category I sets forth a sentencing range of imprisonment of 33 to 45 months.

Rita argued at sentencing that his circumstances are special. He based this argument upon his health, his fear of retaliation, and his prior military record. His sentence explicitly takes health into account by seeking assurance that the Bureau of Prisons will provide appropriate treatment. The record makes out no special fear of retaliation, asserting only that the threat is one that any former law enforcement official might suffer. Similarly, though Rita has a lengthy and distinguished military record, he did not claim at sentencing that military service should ordinarily lead to a sentence more lenient than the sentence the Guidelines impose. Like the District Court and the Court of Appeals, we simply cannot say that Rita's special circumstances are special enough that, in light of § 3553(a), they require a sentence lower than the sentence the Guidelines provide.

* * * [The concurring opinion of Justice Stevens, joined in part by Justice Ginsburg, is omitted.]

JUSTICE SCALIA, with whom JUSTICE THOMAS joins, concurring in part and concurring in the judgment.

* * * Nothing in the Court's opinion explains why, under the advisory Guidelines scheme, judge-found facts are *never* legally necessary to justify the sentence. By this I mean the Court has failed to establish that every sentence which will be imposed under the advisory Guidelines scheme could equally have been imposed had the judge relied upon no facts other than those found by the jury or admitted by the defendant. In fact, the Court implicitly, but quite plainly, acknowledges that this will not be the

case, by treating as a permissible post-*Booker* claim petitioner's challenge of his within-Guidelines sentence as substantively excessive. Under the scheme promulgated today, some sentences reversed as excessive will be legally authorized in later cases only because additional judge-found facts are present; and, * * * some lengthy sentences will be affirmed (*i.e.,* held lawful) only because of the presence of aggravating facts, not found by the jury, that distinguish the case from the mine-run. The Court does not even attempt to explain how this is consistent with the Sixth Amendment.

* * *

To be clear, I am not suggesting that the Sixth Amendment prohibits judges from ever finding any facts. We have repeatedly affirmed the proposition that judges can find facts that help guide their discretion *within* the sentencing range that is authorized by the facts found by the jury or admitted by the defendant. But there is a fundamental difference, one underpinning our entire *Apprendi* jurisprudence, between facts that *must* be found in order for a sentence to be lawful, and facts that individual judges *choose* to make relevant to the exercise of their discretion. * * *

I am also not contending that there is a Sixth Amendment problem with the Court's affirmation of a presumption of reasonableness for within-Guidelines sentences. * * *

Rather, my position is that there will inevitably be *some* constitutional violations under a system of substantive reasonableness review, because there will be some sentences that will be upheld as reasonable only because of the existence of judge-found facts.* * *

Abandoning substantive reasonableness review does not require a return to the pre-SRA regime that the *Booker* remedial opinion sought to avoid. * * * I believe it is possible to give some effect to the *Booker* remedial opinion and the purposes that it sought to serve while still avoiding the constitutional defect identified in the *Booker* merits opinion. Specifically, I would limit reasonableness review to the sentencing *procedures* mandated by statute.

* * *

JUSTICE SOUTER, dissenting.

[Justice Souter conducts a lengthy description of the *Apprendi* line of cases.]

If district judges treated the now-discretionary Guidelines simply as worthy of consideration but open to rejection in any given case, the *Booker* remedy would threaten a return to the old sentencing regime and would presumably produce the apparent disuniformity that convinced Congress to adopt Guidelines sentencing in the first place. But if sentencing judges attributed substantial gravitational pull to the now-discretionary Guidelines, if they treated the Guidelines result as persuasive or presumptively appropriate, the *Booker* remedy would in practical terms preserve the very feature of the Guidelines that threatened to trivialize the jury right. For a presumption of Guidelines reasonableness would tend to produce Guidelines sentences almost as regularly as mandatory Guidelines had done, with judges finding the facts needed for a sentence in an upper subrange. This would open the door to undermining *Apprendi* itself, and this is what has happened today. * * * [I]t seems fair to ask just what has been accomplished in real terms by all the judicial labor imposed by *Apprendi* and its associated cases.

* * *

Review of Outside-Guidelines Sentences for Reasonableness: Gall v. United States

In Gall v. United States, 552 U.S. 38 (2007), Justice Stevens wrote for the Court as it addressed an issue left open in *Rita*: whether sentences *outside* the Guidelines are presumptively *un*reasonable.

Gall was found guilty of conspiracy to distribute the drug "ecstasy." The probation officer calculated the Guideline sentencing range as 30 to 37 months of imprisonment. The District Judge sentenced Gall to probation for a term of 36 months and, in doing so, made a lengthy statement on the record and filed a detailed sentencing memorandum explaining his decision—noting that Gall had quit his criminal conduct, and citing a number of personal factors in his favor. The Court of Appeals held that a sentence outside of the Guidelines range must be supported by a justification that "is proportional to the extent of the difference between the advisory range and the sentence imposed." That court characterized the difference between a sentence of probation and the bottom of Gall's advisory Guidelines range of 30 months as "extraordinary" because it amounted to "a 100% downward variance," and held that such a variance must be supported by extraordinary circumstances not present in the case.

Justice Stevens found that the Court of Appeals' rule was inappropriately rigid and it had erred in essentially establishing a presumption of unreasonableness for outside-Guidelines sentences. He elaborated as follows:

> In reviewing the reasonableness of a sentence outside the Guidelines range, appellate courts may * * * take the degree of variance into account and consider the extent of a deviation from the Guidelines. We reject, however, an appellate rule that requires "extraordinary" circumstances to justify a sentence outside the Guidelines range. We also reject the use of a rigid mathematical formula that uses the percentage of a departure as the standard for

determining the strength of the justifications required for a specific sentence.

As an initial matter, the approaches we reject come too close to creating an impermissible presumption of unreasonableness for sentences outside the Guidelines range. Even the Government has acknowledged that such a presumption would not be consistent with *Booker.*

* * *

Most importantly, both the exceptional circumstances requirement and the rigid mathematical formulation reflect a practice—common among courts that have adopted "proportional review"—of applying a heightened standard of review to sentences outside the Guidelines range. This is inconsistent with the rule that the abuse-of-discretion standard of review applies to appellate review of all sentencing decisions—whether inside or outside the Guidelines range.

Justice Stevens then explained the proper operation of sentencing by the trial court, and reasonableness review, after *Booker:*

As we explained in *Rita,* a district court should begin all sentencing proceedings by correctly calculating the applicable Guidelines range. As a matter of administration and to secure nationwide consistency, the Guidelines should be the starting point and the initial benchmark. The Guidelines are not the only consideration, however. Accordingly, * * * the district judge should then consider all of the § 3553(a) factors to determine whether they support the sentence requested by a party. In so doing, he may not presume that the Guidelines range is reasonable. He must make an individualized assessment based on the facts presented. If he decides that an outside-Guidelines sentence is warranted, he must consider the extent of the deviation and ensure that the justification is sufficiently compelling to support the degree of the variance. We find it uncontroversial that a major departure should be supported by a more significant justification than a minor one. After settling on the appropriate sentence, he must adequately explain the chosen sentence to allow for meaningful appellate review and to promote the perception of fair sentencing.

Regardless of whether the sentence imposed is inside or outside the Guidelines range, the appellate court must review the sentence under an abuse-of-discretion standard. It must first ensure that the district court committed no significant procedural error, such as failing to calculate (or improperly calculating) the Guidelines range, treating the Guidelines as mandatory, failing to consider the § 3553(a) factors, selecting a sentence based on clearly erroneous facts, or failing to adequately explain the chosen sentence—including an explanation for any deviation from the Guidelines range. Assuming that the district court's sentencing decision is procedurally sound, the appellate court should then consider the substantive reasonableness of the sentence imposed under an abuse-of-discretion standard. * * * If the sentence is within the Guidelines range, the appellate court may, but is not required to, apply a presumption of reasonableness. But if the sentence is outside the Guidelines range, the court may not apply a presumption of unreasonableness. It may consider the extent of the deviation, but must give due deference to the district court's decision that the § 3553(a) factors, on a whole, justify the extent of the variance. The fact that the appellate court might reasonably have concluded that a different sentence was appropriate is insufficient to justify reversal of the district court.

Justice Stevens concluded that although the court of appeals "believed that the circumstances presented here were insufficient to sustain such a marked deviation from the Guidelines range," it was "not for the Court of Appeals to decide *de novo* whether the justification for a variance is sufficient or the sentence reasonable," and "[o]n abuse-of-discretion review, the Court of Appeals should have given due deference to the District Court's reasoned and reasonable decision that the § 3553(a) factors, on the whole, justified the sentence."

Justice Scalia wrote a concurring opinion in which he repeated his argument "that substantive-reasonableness review is inherently flawed" but recognized the *stare decisis* effect of the statutory holding of *Rita*. He observed that "[t]he highly deferential standard adopted by the Court today will result in far fewer unconstitutional sentences than the proportionality standard employed by the Eighth Circuit."

Justice Souter also concurred and wrote that "I continue to think that the best resolution of the tension between substantial consistency throughout the system and the right of jury trial would be a new Act of Congress: reestablishing a statutory system of mandatory sentencing guidelines (though not identical to the original in all points of detail), but providing for jury findings of all facts necessary to set the upper range of sentencing discretion."

Justice Thomas dissented and "would affirm the judgment of the Court of Appeals because the District Court committed statutory error when it departed below the applicable Guidelines range."

Justice Alito also dissented and argued that "a district court must give the policy decisions that are embodied in the Sentencing Guidelines at least some significant weight in making a sentencing decision" because if those policies are rejected there will, over time, be significant disparity in sentencing—contrary to the intent of Congress, which the remedial opinion in *Booker* purported to implement.

Appellate Court May Not Increase a Sentence in the Absence of a Government Appeal: Greenlaw v. United States

In Greenlaw v. United States, 554 U.S. 237 (2008), the defendant appealed from his sentence, and the government filed no cross-appeal. The court of appeals rejected the defendant's challenge to his sentence and then proceeded *sua sponte* to determine whether the defendant's sentence was too low. Relying on the doctrine of plain error, the court of appeals entered an order increasing the defendant's sentence by 15 years. The Supreme Court, in an opinion by Justice Ginsburg for six Justices, held that the court of appeals could not use the plain error doctrine to increase a sentence from which the government had not appealed.

Justice Ginsburg relied on 18 U. S. C. § 3742(b), which provides that the government may not appeal a sentence "without the personal approval of the Attorney General, the Solicitor General, or a deputy solicitor general designated by the Solicitor General." She declared that "Congress, in § 3742(b), has accorded to the top representatives of the United States in litigation the prerogative to seek or forgo appellate correction of sentencing errors, however plain they may be. That measure should garner the Judiciary's full respect."

Justice Alito, joined by Justices Breyer and Stevens, dissented. He argued that § 3742(b) "does not apportion authority over sentencing appeals between the Executive and Judicial Branches. By its terms, § 3742(b) simply apportions that authority *within* an executive department." According to Justice Alito, the rule that conditions increase of a sentence on an appeal from the government was one of "trial practice" that did not prevent an appellate court from increasing the sentences under the narrow circumstances permitted by the plain error rule.

Sentencing Under a Guideline That Advises a Greater Sentence than the Guideline Existing When the Crime Was Committed: Peugh v. United States

In Peugh v. United States, 569 U.S. 530 (2013), the defendant committed a crime in 1999 but he was not caught, convicted and sentenced until 2009. The Sentencing Guideline applicable to his crime has changed in the interim—it has become more severe. Peugh argued that sentencing him under the later Guideline would violate the Ex Post Facto Clause, which prohibits application of a law in a criminal case that "changes the punishment, and inflicts a greater punishment, than the law annexed to the crime, when committed." Calder v. Bull, 1 L.Ed. 648 (1798). The Supreme Court, in an opinion by Justice Sotomayor, agreed.

The government's major contention against the Ex Post Facto claim was that after *Booker,* the Sentencing Guidelines are merely advisory—therefore there was no "law" that required a harsher sentence to be imposed. But Justice Sotomayor disagreed. She reasoned that while the Guidelines are advisory, they impose constraints that were sufficient to constitute a real risk that Peugh's sentence would be harsher than that imposed under the then-mandatory but less harsh Guideline in 1999. She noted that the Guidelines after *Booker* "impose a series of requirements on sentencing courts that cabin the exercise of [judicial] discretion. Common sense indicates that in general, this system will steer district courts to more within-Guidelines sentences." Justice Sotomayor noted that as a matter of fact, most sentences after *Booker* have fallen within the Guidelines.

Justice Sotomayor concluded that "[t]he federal system adopts procedural measures intended to make the Guidelines the lodestone of sentencing. A retrospective increase in the Guidelines range applicable to a defendant creates a sufficient risk of a higher sentence to constitute an ex post facto violation."

Justice Thomas dissented in an opinion joined by the Chief Justice and Justice Scalia, and in part by Justice Alito.

Incorrect Sentencing That Ends Up to Be in the Correct Guidelines Range: Molina-Martinez v. United States

In Molina-Martinez v. United States, 136 S.Ct. 1338 (2016), the Court considered a situation in which the trial court applied an incorrect Guidelines range—higher than the applicable one. But the sentence actually fell within the range for the right Guideline. The government argued that the defendant was not entitled to relief, but the Court in an opinion by Justice Kennedy, found that "in most cases, when a district court adopts an incorrect Guidelines range, there is a reasonable probability that the defendant's sentence would be different absent the error." Justice Kennedy declared that "[f]rom the centrality of the Guidelines in the sentencing process it must follow that, when the defendant shows that the district court used an incorrect range, he should not be barred from relief on appeal simply because there is no other evidence that the sentencing outcome would have been different had the correct range been used." Justice Kennedy found it notable that the sentencing judge in this case had expressed an interest in sentencing at the lower end of the (incorrect) Guideline that the court applied, while if the correct Guideline had been applied, the lower end of sentencing would have resulted in a sentence several months shorter than the one that the defendant received.

Justice Kennedy observed that "[t]here may be instances when, despite application of an erroneous Guidelines range, a reasonable probability of prejudice does not exist." He elaborated as follows:

> The record in a case may show, for example, that the district court thought the sentence it chose was appropriate irrespective of the Guidelines range. Judges may find that some cases merit a detailed explanation of the reasons the selected sentence is appropriate. And that explanation could make it clear that the judge based the sentence he or she selected on factors independent of the Guidelines. The Government remains free to point to parts of the record—including relevant statements by the judge—to counter any ostensible showing of prejudice the defendant may make. Where, however, the record is silent as to what the district court might have done had it considered the correct Guidelines range, the court's reliance on an incorrect range in most instances will suffice to show an effect on the defendant's substantial rights.

Justice Alito, joined by Justice Thomas, concurred in the judgment in *Molina-Martinez.*

Considering Post-Sentence Rehabilitation When a Sentence Is Vacated on Appeal: Pepper v. United States

In Pepper v. United States, 562 U.S. 476 (2011), the Court considered whether the Sentencing Guidelines allow a district court, when called on to resentence a defendant, to further reduce the sentence on the basis of post-sentence rehabilitation. The Court, in an opinion by Justice Sotomayor, held that when a defendant's sentence has been set aside on appeal, a district court at resentencing may consider evidence of the defendant's postsentencing rehabilitation, and such evidence may, in appropriate cases, support a downward variance from the now-advisory Guidelines range. She explained as follows:

> This Court has long recognized that sentencing judges "exercise a wide discretion" in the types of evidence they may consider when imposing sentence and that "[h]ighly relevant-if not essential-to [the] selection of an appropriate sentence is the possession of the fullest information possible concerning the defendant's life and characteristics." Williams v. New York, 337 U.S. 241 (1949). Congress codified this principle at 18 U.S.C. § 3661, which provides that "[n]o limitation shall be placed on the information" a sentencing court may consider "concerning the [defendant's] background, character, and conduct," and at § 3553(a), which sets forth certain factors that sentencing courts must consider, including "the history and characteristics of the defendant," § 3553(a)(1). * * * Although a separate statutory provision, § 3742(g)(2), prohibits a district court at

resentencing from imposing a sentence outside the Federal Sentencing Guidelines range except upon a ground it relied upon at the prior sentencing—thus effectively precluding the court from considering postsentencing rehabilitation for purposes of imposing a non-Guidelines sentence—that provision did not survive our holding in United States v. Booker, 543 U.S. 220 (2005), and we expressly invalidate it today.

Justice Sotomayor noted that "evidence of postsentencing rehabilitation may be highly relevant to several of the § 3553(a) factors that Congress has expressly instructed district courts to consider at sentencing."

Justice Sotomayor emphasized that Pepper's post-sentencing rehabilitation was plainly relevant to the § 3553 sentencing factors:

> Most fundamentally, evidence of Pepper's conduct since his release from custody in June 2005 provides the most up-to-date picture of Pepper's "history and characteristics." § 3553(a)(1). At the time of his initial sentencing in 2004, Pepper was a 25-year-old drug addict who was unemployed, estranged from his family, and had recently sold drugs as part of a methamphetamine conspiracy. By the time of his second resentencing in 2009, Pepper had been drug-free for nearly five years, had attended college and achieved high grades, was a top employee at his job slated for a promotion, had re-established a relationship with his father, and was married and supporting his wife's daughter. There is no question that this evidence of Pepper's conduct since his initial sentencing constitutes a critical part of the "history and characteristics" of a defendant that Congress intended sentencing courts to consider. § 3553(a).

> Pepper's postsentencing conduct also sheds light on the likelihood that he will engage in future criminal conduct, a central factor that district courts must assess when imposing sentence. See §§ 3553(a)(2)(B)–(C). As recognized by Pepper's probation officer, Pepper's steady employment, as well as his successful completion of a 500-hour drug treatment program and his drug-free condition, also suggest a diminished need for "educational or vocational training . . . or other correctional treatment." § 3553(a)(2)(D). Finally, Pepper's exemplary postsentencing conduct may be taken as the most accurate indicator of his present purposes and tendencies and significantly to suggest the period of restraint and the kind of discipline that ought to be imposed upon him.

Justice Breyer wrote a separate opinion concurring in part and in the judgment.

Justice Alito also wrote a separate opinion, concurring in part, concurring in the judgment in part, and dissenting in part. Justice Alito criticized the majority's reliance on *Williams* as a justification for considering post-sentencing rehabilitation.

> Anyone familiar with the history of criminal sentencing in this country cannot fail to see the irony in the Court's praise for the sentencing scheme exemplified by Williams v. New York, 337 U.S. 241 (1949). By the time of the enactment of the Sentencing Reform Act in 1984, this scheme had fallen into widespread disrepute. Under this system, each federal district judge was free to implement his or her individual sentencing philosophy, and therefore the sentence imposed in a particular case often depended heavily on the spin of the wheel that determined the judge to whom the case was assigned.
>
> Some language in today's opinion reads like a paean to that old regime, and I fear that it may be interpreted as sanctioning a move back toward the system that prevailed prior to 1984. If that occurs, I suspect that the day will come when the irrationality of that system is once again seen, and perhaps then the entire *Booker* line of cases will be reexamined.

Justice Thomas dissented, basically continuing his objection to the Court's remedial opinion in *Booker*. Justice Kagan took no part in the decision in *Pepper*.

Sentencing Guidelines Cannot Be Subject to Void-for-Vagueness Challenges: Beckles v. United States

In Beckles v. United States, 137 S.Ct. 886 (2017), the defendant was found eligible for a sentencing enhancement under the Guidelines because he was a career offender and his offense qualified as a "crime of violence." The Guidelines definition of "crime of violence" tracked a federal penal statute that the Supreme Court had previously found to be void-for-vagueness under the Due Process Clause. The defendant relied on the Supreme Court's striking down the penal statute as a basis for attack under the Sentencing Guidelines. But the Supreme Court held that Sentencing Guidelines (unlike penal statutes) cannot be subject to void-for-vagueness challenges. Justice Thomas, writing for seven Justices, reasoned that allowing a void for vagueness challenge was inconsistent with Supreme Court precedent upholding essentially unlimited sentencing discretion. He explained as follows:

> The limited scope of the void-for-vagueness doctrine in this context is rooted in the history of federal sentencing. Instead of enacting specific sentences for particular federal crimes, Congress historically permitted district courts wide discretion to decide whether the offender should be incarcerated and for how long. * * *

Yet in the long history of discretionary sentencing, this Court has "never doubted the authority of a judge to exercise broad discretion in imposing a sentence within a statutory range." United States v. Booker; see also, e.g., *Apprendi* ("[N]othing in this history suggests that it is impermissible for judges to exercise discretion . . . in imposing a judgment within the range prescribed by statute").

More specifically, our cases have never suggested that a defendant can successfully challenge as vague a sentencing statute conferring discretion to select an appropriate sentence from within a statutory range, even when that discretion is unfettered. * * * Indeed, no party to this case suggests that a system of purely discretionary sentencing could be subject to a vagueness challenge.

Turning specifically to the Guidelines, Justice Thomas concluded that a void-for-vagueness challenge was inapt because the Guidelines are, after *Booker,* discretionary and not binding.

Because they merely guide the district courts' discretion, the Guidelines are not amenable to a vagueness challenge. As discussed above, the system of purely discretionary sentencing that predated the Guidelines was constitutionally permissible. If a system of unfettered discretion is not unconstitutionally vague, then it is difficult to see how the present system of guided discretion could be.

Justice Thomas closed by emphasizing that the Guidelines are not free from all constitutional concerns. He noted some limitations:

Our holding today does not render the advisory Guidelines immune from constitutional scrutiny. This Court held in *Peugh*, for example, that a "retrospective increase in the Guidelines range applicable to a defendant" violates the Ex Post Facto Clause." But the void-for-vagueness and ex post facto inquiries are analytically distinct. Our ex post facto cases have focused on whether a change in law creates a significant risk of a higher sentence. A retroactive change in the Guidelines creates such a risk because sentencing decisions are anchored by the Guidelines, which establish the framework for sentencing. In contrast, the void-for-vagueness doctrine requires a different inquiry. The question is whether a law regulating private conduct by fixing permissible sentences provides notice and avoids arbitrary enforcement by clearly specifying the range of penalties available.

* * *

Finally, our holding today also does not render sentencing procedures entirely immune from scrutiny under the due process clause. See, e.g., Townsend v. Burke, 334 U.S. 736, 741 (1948) (holding that due process is violated when a court relies on "extensively and materially false" evidence to impose a sentence on an uncounseled defendant).

Justices Ginsburg and Sotomayor concurred only in the judgment. They argued that the Guideline under which Beckles was sentenced was not in fact constitutionally vague, so it was unnecessary to reach the broad holding that the majority did. Justice Sotomayor wrote separately to argue that the Guidelines should be subject to scrutiny as void-for-vagueness. She concluded that "[i]t violates the Due Process Clause to condemn someone to prison on the basis of a sentencing rule so shapeless as to resist interpretation. But the Court's decision today permits exactly that result."

3. The Principle of Relevant Conduct

Relevant Conduct and Subsequent Convictions: Witte v. United States

As discussed above, the Sentencing Guidelines assess the now-advisory sentence on the basis not only of the charge for which the defendant is convicted, but also on the basis of relevant uncharged conduct. If a defendant ends up with a longer sentence because the judge relies on uncharged "relevant conduct," what happens if the defendant is subsequently convicted of that uncharged conduct? Does he, in effect, get sentenced twice for the same conduct? This question arose in Witte v. United States, 515 U.S. 389 (1995), where Witte pleaded guilty to a marijuana offense. His uncharged cocaine transactions were considered as relevant conduct, and he received a longer sentence for the marijuana offense than he would otherwise have received. He was then charged with the cocaine transactions. He moved to dismiss the charges on double jeopardy grounds. The Court, in an opinion by Justice O'Connor, rejected Witte's double jeopardy attack, reasoning that he had not been punished previously for the cocaine transactions. Those transactions were simply a basis for "a stiffened penalty for the [marijuana] crime, which is considered to be an aggravated offense because a repetitive one."

4. Reductions for Substantial Assistance to the Government

Substantial Assistance Motions: Wade v. United States

Sentencing Guideline 5K1.1 provides for a possible reduction in sentence if the government files a motion to reduce the sentence on the basis of the defendant's substantial assistance in the prosecution of other defendants. In Wade v. United States, 504 U.S. 181 (1992), the Court held that a reduction for substantial assistance was, by the terms of the Guideline, contingent on a Government motion. Thus, at least under the Guidelines, the district court has no discretion to reduce the sentence for the defendant's assistance in other cases, unless the prosecution moves for such a reduction. The Court stated that the Government's decision not to make a substantial-assistance motion was reviewable only under two limited conditions: 1) if the prosecutor was acting pursuant to an unconstitutional motive such as to discriminate on the basis of race or religion; or 2) if the prosecutor's decision was totally arbitrary.

After *Booker,* however, district courts are not bound by the Guidelines—they are only advisory. So can a judge take account of the defendant's cooperation, even in the absence of a government motion, in reaching a sentence below the Guidelines? A fair reading of *Booker* would indicate that the sentencing judge can consider cooperation and sentence below the Guidelines range, without having to wait for a government motion, and can also reduce the sentence below the recommendation of the government if it does make a 5K1.1 motion. Of course, the ultimate sentence reached would have to be reasonable under Section 3553(a). See United States v. Saenz, 428 F.3d 1159 (8th Cir. 2005) (sentencing court can depart below government's recommended reduction, but in this case the reduction was unreasonable because the court was operating under a presumption that timely and truthful cooperation always warrants a reduction of more than 50 percent).

Substantial Assistance Motions and Mandatory Minimums: Melendez v. United States

In Melendez v. United States, 518 U.S. 120 (1996), the defendant entered into a plea agreement in which the government agreed to make a substantial assistance motion for reduction of the applicable Guideline sentence. As discussed above, such a motion is provided for under § 5K1.1 of the Guidelines. However, the defendant pleaded guilty to a drug crime that was also subject to a mandatory minimum sentence of 10 years. The government moved, in accordance with the agreement, for a reduction of the applicable sentence under the Guidelines, which would have resulted in a sentence of less than 10 years. The government did not move, as it could have done, for a departure from the statutory minimum—there was no requirement in the agreement that the government make such a motion. The sentencing court held itself bound by the statutory minimum, and sentenced the defendant to 10 years.

Justice Thomas, writing for the Court, held that the trial court acted appropriately. Justice Thomas relied on 18 U.S.C. § 3553(e), which requires a specific government motion to depart from an applicable mandatory minimum sentence on the basis of the defendant's substantial assistance. Justice Thomas referred to this system as "binary." Thus, if the defendant is to receive a reduction from an applicable statutory minimum as well as from the Sentencing Guideline, the government must specifically move for reduction from both—and defense counsel must seek an agreement from the government for two substantial assistance motions rather than being content with one.

As a result of 18 U.S.C. § 3553(e), mandatory minimum statutes increase the prosecutor's bargaining power. Because a sentencing judge can apply the 18 U.S.C. § 3553(a) factors to reach an appropriate sentence in every case in which no mandatory minimum statute applies, the threat to charge an offense governed by a mandatory minimum statute can be a powerful incentive for a defendant to plead guilty to a charge the prosecutor will accept that is not governed by such a statute.

E. SENTENCING DEVELOPMENTS IN THE STATES

Both before and after the adoption of federal sentencing guidelines, there has been a move in many states toward some form of determinate sentencing. This move often reflected cynicism toward the concept of parole and doubts about the ability of prisons to rehabilitate inmates. Truth in sentencing is frequently the mantra of sentencing advocates who believe that offenders and the public should know how long the offender will serve at the time the sentence is imposed.

Not all truth in sentencing states are alike. Most states use between 75% and 85% of a pre-determined "benchmark" as their standard to implement a truth in sentencing program, but the states differ in how they implement the program. For example, Virginia requires a mandatory 85% of an offender's effective sentence (which is the imposed sentence minus any suspended portion) to be served. Thus, judges in Virginia retain some freedom to individualize sentences at the time of sentencing. Other states—Utah, for example—have guideline sentencing and require an offender to serve 85% of a guideline sentence before any release is considered.

Some states—Florida and North Carolina, for example—have abolished parole completely. Other states retain some form of parole system. It may be misleading, however, to view the abolition of parole as meaning that offenders will serve their entire sentences in prison. In Virginia, for example, it is very common for judges to suspend large parts of a sentence of incarceration, which results in an offender serving a determinate time in prison and then being under supervision for the suspended portion of incarceration. The difference between this and parole is that the *judge* makes the decision to suspend a sentence at the time of sentencing, rather than having a parole board make a decision after sentence is imposed. But, the resulting punishment may be a shorter period of incarceration followed by a longer period of supervision, which may resemble a parole system and may be quite similar to a probationary system.

All states with guidelines appear to have the same basic goals: to reduce sentencing disparity and provide guidance to judges as to appropriate sentences for particular crimes and types of offenders. As in the federal system, most state jurisdictions with guidelines have made some effort to examine the pre-guideline sentences imposed by all judges in a state and to tailor the guidelines to the average or typical sentence previously imposed.

In drafting guidelines some sentencing commissions have considered the effect of sentences on prison populations. This may be viewed as consistent with the basic goal of reducing disparity. It may also be necessary for a state to consider adjusting some guidelines downward if the state desires to raise sentences for some violent offenders without creating additional prison space.

Of course, after *Apprendi* and *Blakely,* if Guidelines are mandatory, they run afoul of the Sixth Amendment and due process if they require a court to enhance a sentence on the basis of facts found by a judge at sentencing, and the enhancement takes it above the maximum provided for the base offense. For a discussion of how advisory guidelines can and do work in the states, see Pfaff, The Continued Vitality of Structured Sentencing After *Blakely*: The Effectiveness of Voluntary Guidelines, 54 U.C.L.A. L. Rev. 235 (2006).

In Cunningham v. California, 549 U.S. 270 (2007), the Court held that the California Determinative Sentencing Law violated *Apprendi* because it required a trial judge to impose a sentence in a higher sentencing category, upon the basis of certain aggravating facts found by the judge. Justice Ginsburg, writing for the six-person majority, declared as follows:

> Under California's DSL, an upper term sentence may be imposed only when the trial judge finds an aggravating circumstance. An element of the charged offense, essential to a jury's determination of guilt, or admitted in a defendant's guilty plea, does not qualify as such a circumstance. Instead, aggravating circumstances depend on facts found discretely and solely by the judge. In accord with *Blakely*, therefore, the middle term prescribed in California's statutes [for the crime charged and proved to the jury], not the upper term, is the relevant statutory maximum. Because circumstances in aggravation are found by the judge, not the jury, and need only be established by a preponderance of the evidence, not beyond a reasonable doubt, the DSL violates *Apprendi*'s bright-line rule: Except for a prior conviction, "any fact that increases the penalty for a crime beyond the prescribed statutory maximum must be submitted to a jury, and proved beyond a reasonable doubt."

Justice Kennedy (joined by Justice Breyer) and Justice Alito (joined by Justices Kennedy and Breyer) dissented.

In Oregon v. Ice, 555 U.S. 160 (2009), the Court upheld a state law allowing the judge to impose consecutive, rather than concurrent, sentences after finding certain facts. The Court distinguished *Apprendi* as a case involving "sentencing for a discrete crime, not—as here—for multiple offenses different in character or committed at different times."

III. SENTENCING PROCEDURES

A. GENERAL PROCEDURES

One might suppose that a part of the criminal justice system as important as sentencing would carry with it extensive procedural protections to guard against abuse of authority. But that supposition would be largely unfounded. Due process rights in sentencing have been hard to establish since 1949 when the Supreme Court decided the next case, the one to which Justice Alito referred in his separate opinion in *Pepper*.

WILLIAMS V. NEW YORK

Supreme Court of the United States, 1949.
337 U.S. 241.

JUSTICE BLACK delivered the opinion of the court.

A jury in a New York state court found appellant guilty of murder in the first degree. The jury recommended life imprisonment, but the trial judge imposed sentence of death. In giving his reason for imposing the death sentence the judge discussed in open court the evidence upon which the jury had convicted stating that this evidence had been considered in the light of additional information obtained through the court's "Probation Department, and through other sources." * * *

The Court of Appeals of New York affirmed the conviction and sentence over the contention that * * * "the sentence of death was based upon information supplied by witnesses with whom the accused had not been confronted and as to whom he had no opportunity for cross-examination or rebuttal" [and accordingly was in violation of due process].

* * * The record shows a carefully conducted trial lasting more than two weeks in which appellant was represented by three appointed lawyers who conducted his defense with fidelity and zeal. The evidence proved a wholly indefensible murder committed by a person engaged in a burglary. * * *

The case presents a serious and difficult question. The question relates to the rules of evidence applicable to the manner in which a judge may obtain information to guide him in the imposition of sentence upon an already convicted defendant. * * * To aid a judge in exercising * * * discretion intelligently the New York procedural policy encourages him to consider information about the convicted person's past life, health, habits, conduct, and mental and moral propensities. The sentencing judge may consider such information even though obtained outside the courtroom from persons whom a defendant has not been permitted to confront or cross-examine. It is the consideration of information obtained by a sentencing judge in this manner that is the basis for appellant's broad constitutional challenge * * *.

Tribunals passing on the guilt of a defendant always have been hedged in by strict evidentiary procedural limitations. But both before and since the American colonies became a nation, courts in this country and in England practiced a policy under which a sentencing judge could exercise a wide discretion in the sources and types of evidence used to assist him in determining the kind and extent of punishment to be imposed within limits fixed by law. Out-of-court affidavits have been used frequently, and of course in the smaller communities sentencing judges naturally have in mind their knowledge of the personalities and backgrounds of convicted offenders. * * *

In addition to the historical basis for different evidentiary rules governing trial and sentencing procedures there are sound practical reasons for the distinction. In a trial before verdict the issue is whether a defendant is guilty of having engaged in certain criminal conduct of which he has been specifically accused. Rules of evidence have been fashioned for criminal trials which narrowly confine the trial contest to evidence that is strictly relevant to the particular offense charged. * * * A sentencing judge, however, is not confined to the narrow issue of guilt. * * * Highly relevant—if not essential—to his selection of an appropriate sentence is the possession of the fullest information possible concerning the defendant's life and characteristics. And modern concepts individualizing punishment have made it all the more necessary that a sentencing judge not be denied an opportunity to obtain pertinent information by a requirement of rigid adherence to restrictive rules of evidence properly applicable to the trial.

* * * We must recognize that most of the information now relied upon by judges to guide them in the intelligent imposition of sentences would be unavailable if information were restricted to that given in open court by witnesses subject to cross-examination. And the modern probation report draws on information concerning every aspect of a defendant's life. The type and extent of this information make totally impractical if not impossible open court testimony with cross-examination. * * *

* * * New York criminal statutes set wide limits for maximum and minimum sentences. Under New York statutes a state judge cannot escape his grave responsibility of fixing sentence. In determining whether a defendant shall receive a one-year minimum or a twenty-year maximum

sentence, we do not think the Federal Constitution restricts the view of the sentencing judge to the information received in open court.

* * *

[The dissenting opinion of JUSTICE MURPHY is omitted.]

Pre-Sentence Reports and the Sentencing Guidelines

Fed.R.Cr.P. 32 requires that a presentence report inform the defendant of the guidelines that govern his case and of pertinent policy statements by the Sentencing Commission. Ordinarily the presentence report is prepared by a probation officer. The goal of Rule 32 is to focus "on preparation of the presentence report as a means of identifying and narrowing the issues to be decided at the sentencing hearing." Advisory Committee's Note to 1994 amendment to Rule 32. Some of the procedural requirements in the Rule are:

(1) defense counsel is entitled to notice and a reasonable opportunity to be present at any interview of the defendant conducted by the probation officer who is preparing the presentence report;

(2) the probation officer must present the presentence report to the parties not later than 35 days before the sentencing hearing, in order to provide additional time for the parties and the probation officer to attempt to resolve any objections to the report;

(3) parties must provide the probation officer with a written list of objections to the presentence report within 14 days of receiving it;

(4) the probation officer must meet with the defendant, defense counsel, and an attorney for the Government, in order to go over objections to the report and to arrange for additional investigation and revisions to the report if necessary; and

(5) the sentencing court may treat the presentencing report as its findings of fact, except for material subject to the parties' unresolved objections.

The Court's opinion in United States v. Booker, which held that the Sentencing Guidelines are advisory and not mandatory, did not render presentence reports irrelevant or unhelpful. After *Booker,* sentencing courts still must determine the Guidelines sentence and must consider it as a factor among others listed in Section 3553(a). So sentencing courts still rely on presentence reports in determining the Guidelines sentence. Moreover, presentence reports have been expanded to assist the court in considering Section 3553(a) factors that had not previously been considered relevant to Guidelines sentencing, e.g., rehabilitation, personal circumstances of the defendant, etc.

Rule 32 Notice Requirement Does Not Apply to Court's Decision to Consider a Sentence Outside the Guidelines: Irizzary v. United States

Federal Rule 32(h) states that "[b]efore the court may depart from the applicable sentencing range on a ground not identified for departure either in the presentence report or in a party's prehearing submission, the court must give the parties reasonable notice that it is contemplating such a departure." In Irizarry v. United States, 553 U.S. 708 (2008), the Court held that this notice requirement does not apply to the sentencing court's consideration of whether to impose a sentence *outside the Guidelines*, which were made advisory in United States v. Booker. Justice Stevens, writing for the Court, found that the notice requirement was not appropriate as applied to the consideration of sentences outside the Guidelines after *Booker*. He explained that when the Guidelines were mandatory, the defendant needed notice of an anticipated departure in order to be able to have meaningful input into the sentencing decision. But "faced with advisory Guidelines, neither the Government nor the defendant may place the same degree of reliance on the type of expectancy that gave rise to a special need for notice."

Justice Stevens concluded as follows:

> Sound practice dictates that judges in all cases should make sure that the information provided to the parties in advance of the hearing, and in the hearing itself, has given them an adequate opportunity to confront and debate the relevant issues. We recognize that there will be some cases in which the factual basis for a particular sentence will come as a surprise to a defendant or the Government. The more appropriate response to such a problem is not to extend the reach of Rule 32(h)'s notice requirement categorically, but rather for a district judge to consider granting a continuance when a party has a legitimate basis for claiming that the surprise was prejudicial.

Justice Thomas concurred. Justice Breyer, joined by Justices Kennedy, Souter and Ginsburg dissented. The dissenters argued that a notice requirement would provide an important procedural safeguard and would help to assure the effective advocacy made all the more important after the Court's decision in *Booker*.

Preponderance of the Evidence

Factual determinations in sentencing are by a preponderance of the evidence rather than beyond a reasonable doubt. The Court in United States v. Watts, 519 U.S. 148 (1997), held that defendants can be sentenced under the Guidelines on the basis of relevant conduct for which they have been acquitted, so long as the conduct is shown at sentencing by a preponderance of the evidence. Courts after *Booker* have held that *Watts* is still the rule for assessing relevant conduct as part of an advisory Guidelines sentence. The court in United States v. Magallanez, 408 F.3d 672 (10th Cir. 2005) explains *Watts* and its applicability post-*Booker*, as follows:

> The decision in *Watts* was predicated on the rationale that "different standards of proof . . . govern at trial and sentencing." An acquittal by the jury proves only that the defendant was not guilty beyond a reasonable doubt. Both before and under the Guidelines, facts relevant to sentencing have generally been found by a preponderance of the evidence. A jury verdict of acquittal on related conduct, therefore, "does not prevent the sentencing court from considering conduct underlying the acquitted charge, so long as that conduct has been proved by a preponderance of the evidence."

> * * * Applying the logic of *Watts* to the Guidelines system as modified by *Booker*, we conclude that when a district court makes a determination of sentencing facts by a preponderance test under the now-advisory Guidelines, it is not bound by jury determinations reached through application of the more onerous reasonable doubt standard. In this respect, the prior Guidelines scheme is unchanged by the seeming revolution of *Booker*.

Consideration of Prior Convictions at the Sentencing Proceeding

In many cases, the prosecution offers evidence of the defendant's prior convictions at the sentencing proceeding. Under the Federal Sentencing Guidelines, a defendant's prior convictions, both state and federal, are relevant to the criminal history category that is part of the sentencing matrix. Moreover, many specific sentencing statutes provide for enhancement if the defendant has been convicted of certain specified state or federal crimes—such as the "Three Strikes and You're Out" provisions that exist in a number of states and are called into question in some as states seek to reduce the costs associated with their penal systems.

One question that arises with the use of these prior convictions for sentencing purposes is whether the defendant has a right to challenge their validity at the sentencing proceeding. This is a particular problem in federal sentencing proceedings where the defendant wishes to attack prior state convictions. For example, in Custis v. United States, 511 U.S. 485 (1994), the defendant was given an enhanced sentence under the Armed Career Criminal Act (18 U.S.C. § 924(e)) on the basis of having three previous state convictions "for a violent felony or a serious drug offense." At the sentencing hearing, Custis sought to attack his prior state convictions collaterally on the ground that one was based on an invalid guilty plea and another was tainted by ineffective assistance of counsel.

The Court, in an opinion by Chief Justice Rehnquist, held that Custis had no statutory or constitutional right to collaterally attack a prior state conviction at his federal sentencing hearing. The only exception would be if the state conviction was obtained in the complete absence of counsel in violation of Gideon v. Wainwright. The Chief Justice distinguished a collateral attack for absence of counsel from a collateral attack for an invalid guilty plea or ineffective assistance of counsel, on the basis that a *Gideon* defect is "jurisdictional" while the other defects are not. He expressed concern about upsetting the finality of convictions, and about the costliness of having to investigate the effectiveness of counsel or the voluntariness of a guilty plea in a long-completed state proceeding. Justice Souter, joined by Justices Blackmun and Stevens, dissented in *Custis*. He saw no constitutional distinction between a collateral attack based on the absence of counsel and a collateral attack based on ineffective assistance of counsel or an invalid guilty plea.

Use of Hearsay at Sentencing Under the Guidelines

Williams permitted the use of hearsay by a sentencing judge. Should the rationale of *Williams* apply to guidelines sentencing? In United States v. Silverman, 976 F.2d 1502 (6th Cir.1992), the court held that the right to confrontation was not applicable to sentencing proceedings involving disputed facts under the Federal Sentencing Guidelines. Thus, the sentencing court is permitted to use hearsay in assessing a sentence under the Guidelines. The court rejected the contention that sentencing under the Guidelines is substantially different from the discretionary sentencing procedures reviewed in *Williams*. The court asserted that procedural requirements for establishing the "factual basis of sentencing, akin to the real offense aspects of pre-guideline sentencing, continue from former sentencing practices." It concluded that "[s]o long as the evidence in the presentence report bears some minimal indicia of reliability in respect of defendant's right to due process, the district court may still continue to consider and rely on hearsay evidence without any confrontation requirement." See also United States v. Petty, 982 F.2d 1365 (9th Cir.1993) (joining all other circuits in holding that the Confrontation Clause does not apply to Guidelines sentencing and declaring that "the procedural protections afforded a convicted defendant at sentencing are traditionally less stringent than the protections afforded a presumptively innocent defendant at trial").

Courts have held that *Booker* has not changed the traditional rule that a sentencing court can rely on hearsay in assessing facts, and that the defendant still has no right to confrontation at a sentencing proceeding.

The rationale is that *Booker* simply made the Guidelines advisory; there was no intent and no reason to alter the accepted rules of factual determinations by sentencing courts. See United States v. Umana, 750 F.3d 320 (4th Cir. 2014) ("We conclude that *Williams* squarely disposes of Umana's argument that the Sixth Amendment right to confrontation should apply to capital sentencing."); United States v. Brown, 430 F.3d 942 (8th Cir. 2005) (sentencing court can rely on hearsay in determining sentence after *Booker:* "In determining the appropriate guidelines sentencing range to be considered as a factor under § 3553(a), we see nothing in *Booker* that would require the court to determine the sentence in any manner other than the way the sentence would have been determined pre-*Booker*."); United States v. Luciano, 414 F.3d 174 (1st Cir. 2005) (*Booker* did not alter the view that there is no Sixth Amendment right to confront witnesses during the sentencing phase.). See also Fed.R.Evid. 1101 (Evidence Rules, other than privilege, are not applicable to sentencing proceedings).

B. PAROLE AND PROBATION PROCEDURES

1. Probation and Parole Denials; Classification Decisions

When a trial judge considers whether to impose a sentence of probation—either in addition to or in lieu of a sentence of incarceration—the *Williams* attitude toward procedural rights prevails. In People v. Edwards, 18 Cal.3d 796, 135 Cal.Rptr. 411, 557 P.2d 995 (1976), for example, the court held that a trial judge need not state reasons for denying probation. But parole is a different concept altogether. The parole board makes a determination whether someone who has been sentenced should be released before the sentence is fully served (though as we have seen, this is no longer the case in the federal system and in those states that have abolished parole). For some time courts differed over the question of what, if any, procedural protections are constitutionally required in parole-release decisionmaking. The threshold question was whether a constitutionally protected liberty interest was at stake; if so, then certain procedural protections would be constitutionally mandated under the Due Process Clause. The Supreme Court considered the due process questions in a series of cases.

In Greenholtz v. Inmates, 442 U.S. 1 (1979), Chief Justice Burger wrote for the Court as it held that the possibility of parole does not by itself create an entitlement to due process protections, but that some parole systems, including Nebraska's which was at issue in the case, create legitimate expectations of release that require some procedural protections. The decision required some opportunity for the parole applicant to be heard and some indication of the reasons why parole is not granted. Justice Marshall's dissenting opinion was joined by Justices

Brennan and Stevens. Justice Powell agreed with these dissenters that parole decisionmaking triggered due process safeguards, but was unwilling to provide as many safeguards as the others would have. However, he concluded that Nebraska provided an inadequate opportunity for prisoners to present information to parole authorities. The Court relied upon *Greenholtz* in Board of Pardons v. Allen, 482 U.S. 369 (1987), which held, 6–3, that Montana parole law created a liberty interest. Justice O'Connor, joined Chief Justice Rehnquist and Justice Scalia, dissented.

No constitutionally protected expectancy interest was found in an explicitly discretionary pardon system despite the frequency with which pardons were granted. Connecticut Bd. of Pardons v. Dumschat, 452 U.S. 458 (1981). See also Jago v. Van Curen, 454 U.S. 14 (1981) (inmate told that he was being paroled had no protected interest that was violated when parole was rescinded before release from custody).

2. Probation and Parole Revocations

MORRISSEY V. BREWER
Supreme Court of the United States, 1972.
408 U.S. 471.

CHIEF JUSTICE BURGER delivered the opinion of the Court.

[Morrisey and Booher both were paroled from Iowa state prisons. Each subsequently had his parole revoked because of violations of parole conditions, and each sued, challenging the revocation procedures. One principal line of attack was that the absence of a revocation hearing violated due process.]

To accomplish the purpose of parole, those who are allowed to leave prison early are subjected to specified conditions for the duration of their terms. These conditions restrict their activities substantially beyond the ordinary restrictions imposed by law on an individual citizen. * * *

It has been estimated that 35–45% of all parolees are subjected to revocation and return to prison. Sometimes revocation occurs when the parolee is accused of another crime; it is often preferred to a new prosecution because of the procedural ease of recommitting the individual on the basis of a lesser showing by the State.

Implicit in the system's concern with parole violations is the notion that the parolee is entitled to retain his liberty as long as he substantially abides by the conditions of his parole. The first step in a revocation decision thus involves a wholly retrospective factual question: whether the parolee has in fact acted in violation of one or more conditions of his parole. Only if it is determined that the parolee did violate the conditions does the second question arise: should the parolee be recommitted to prison or should other steps be taken to protect society and improve chances of rehabilitation? The first step is relatively simple; the second is more complex. The second question involves the application of expertise by the parole authority in making a prediction as to the ability of the individual to live in society without committing antisocial acts. This part of the decision, too, depends on facts, and therefore it is important for the Board to know not only that some violation was committed but also to know accurately how many and how serious the violations were. Yet this second step, deciding what to do about the violation once it is identified, is not purely factual but also predictive and discretionary.

If a parolee is returned to prison, he often receives no credit for the time "served" on parole. Thus the returnee may face a potential of substantial imprisonment.

* * *

We begin with the proposition that the revocation of parole is not part of a criminal prosecution and thus the full panoply of rights due a defendant in such a proceeding does not apply to parole revocations. * * * Revocation deprives an individual not of the absolute liberty to which every citizen is entitled, but only of the conditional liberty properly dependent on observance of special parole restrictions.

We turn therefore to the question whether the requirements of due process in general apply to parole revocations. * * *

* * * The liberty of a parolee enables him to do a wide range of things open to persons who have never been convicted of any crime. * * * Though the State properly subjects him to many restrictions not applicable to other citizens, his condition is very different from that of confinement in a prison. * * * The parolee has relied on at least an implicit promise that parole will be revoked only if he fails to live up to the parole conditions. * * *

We see, therefore, that the liberty of a parolee, although indeterminate, includes many of the core values of unqualified liberty and its termination inflicts a "grievous loss" on the parolee and often on others. * * * Its termination calls for some orderly process, however informal.

Turning to the question what process is due, we find that the State's interests are several. The State has found the parolee guilty of a crime against the people. * * * Given the previous conviction and the proper imposition of conditions, the State has an overwhelming interest in being able to return the individual to imprisonment without the burden of a new adversary criminal trial if in fact he has failed to abide by the conditions of his parole.

Yet the State has no interest in revoking parole without some informal procedural guarantees. Although the parolee is often formally described as being "in custody," the argument cannot even be made here that summary treatment is necessary as it may be with respect to controlling a large group of potentially disruptive prisoners in actual custody. Nor are we persuaded by the argument that revocation is so totally a discretionary matter that some form of hearing would be administratively intolerable. A simple factual hearing will not interfere with the exercise of discretion. * * *

* * * What is needed is an informal hearing structured to assure that the finding of a parole violation will be based on verified facts and that the exercise of discretion will be informed by an accurate knowledge of the parolee's behavior.

* * *

We now turn to the nature of the process that is due, bearing in mind that the interest of both State and parolee will be furthered by an effective but informal hearing. In analyzing what is due, we see two important stages in the typical process of parole revocation.

(a) Arrest of Parolee and Preliminary Hearing. * * *

In our view due process requires that after the arrest, the determination that reasonable grounds exist for revocation of parole should be made by someone not directly involved in the case. * * * The officer directly involved in making recommendations cannot always have complete objectivity in evaluating them. * * *

This independent officer need not be a judicial officer. The granting and revocation of parole are matters traditionally handled by administrative officers. * * * It will be sufficient, therefore, in the parole revocation context, if an evaluation of whether reasonable cause exists to believe that conditions of parole have been violated is made by someone such as a parole officer other than the one who has made the report of parole violations or has recommended revocation. * * *

With respect to the preliminary hearing before this officer, the parolee should be given notice that the hearing will take place and that its purpose is to determine whether there is probable cause to believe he has committed a parole violation. The notice should state what parole violations have been alleged. At the hearing the parolee may appear and speak in his own behalf; he may bring letters, documents, or individuals who can give relevant information to the hearing officer. On request of the parolee, persons who have given adverse information on which parole revocation is to be based are to be made available for questioning in his presence. However, if the hearing officer determines that the informant would be subjected to risk of harm if his identity were disclosed, he need not be subjected to confrontation and cross-examination.

The hearing officer * * * should determine whether there is probable cause to hold the parolee for the final decision of the parole board on revocation. Such a determination would be sufficient to warrant the parolee's continued detention and return to the state correctional institution pending the final decision. * * *

(b) The Revocation Hearing. There must also be an opportunity for a hearing, if it is desired by the parolee, prior to the final decision on revocation by the parole authority. This hearing must be the basis for more than determining probable cause; it must lead to a final evaluation of any contested relevant facts and consideration of whether the facts as determined warrant revocation. The parolee must have an opportunity to be heard and to show, if he can, that he did not violate the conditions, or, if he did, that circumstances in mitigation suggest the violation does not warrant revocation. The revocation hearing must be tendered within a reasonable time after the parolee is taken into custody. A lapse of two months, as the State suggests occurs in some cases, would not appear to be unreasonable.

* * * Our task is limited to deciding the minimum requirements of due process. They include (a) written notice of the claimed violations of parole; (b) disclosure to the parolee of evidence against him; (c) opportunity to be heard in person and to present witnesses and documentary evidence; (d) the right to confront and cross-examine adverse witnesses (unless the hearing officer specifically finds good cause for not allowing confrontation); (e) a "neutral and detached" hearing body such as a traditional parole board, members of which need not be judicial officers or lawyers; and (f) a written statement by the factfinders as to the evidence relied on and reasons for revoking parole. We emphasize that there is no thought to equate this second stage of parole revocation to a criminal prosecution in any sense; it is a narrow inquiry; the process should be flexible enough to consider evidence including letters, affidavits, and other material that would not be admissible in an adversary criminal trial.

We do not reach or decide the question whether the parolee is entitled to the assistance of retained counsel or to appointed counsel if he is indigent.

We have no thought to create an inflexible structure for parole revocation procedures. The few basic requirements set out above, which are applicable to future revocations of parole, should not impose a great burden on any State's parole system. * * *

[JUSTICE BRENNAN, joined by JUSTICE MARSHALL, concurred in the result. He expressed his view that prisoners who can afford to retain and wish to retain counsel must be permitted to do so. He left open the question of whether counsel must be appointed for indigents. JUSTICE DOUGLAS dissented in part; although his view was not very different from the majority's, he would not as readily allow revocation upon a preliminary showing.]

Procedural Protections as a Probation Revocation Proceeding: Gagnon v. Scarpelli

In Gagnon v. Scarpelli, 411 U.S. 778 (1973), decided the year after Morrisey v. Brewer, Justice Powell wrote for the Court as it addressed what protections an individual was entitled to in a probation revocation proceeding. Gagnon pleaded guilty to a state charge of armed robbery, the trial judge sentenced him to 15 years' imprisonment, and the judge then suspended the sentence, placed Gagnon on probation for 7 years. After he was arrested for burglary, the state revoked his probation because of the burglary arrest without affording him either a hearing or counsel. Gagnon began serving his 15 year sentence and sought federal habeas corpus relief on the ground that the revocation of his probation without affording him a hearing or counsel was a denial of due process. The district court and the court of appeals agreed with him.

The Court affirmed in part, reversed in part, and remanded the case. Justice Powell's opinion for a unanimous Court held that Gagnon was entitled to both a preliminary hearing to determine whether there was probable cause to believe that he had violated his probation and a final hearing prior to the ultimate decision whether his probation should be revoked. Justice Powell wrote for eight Justices as the Court held that the state was not under a constitutional duty to provide counsel for indigents in all probation revocation cases, but that the state authority charged with responsibility for administering the probation system must use sound discretion to decide on the need for counsel on a case-by-case basis, and certain general guidelines as to whether the assistance of counsel was constitutionally necessary should be applied in the first instance by those charged with conducting the revocation hearing.

Justice Douglas dissented in part on the ground that since Gagnon claimed that his confession of the burglary had been made under coercion, due process required the appointment of counsel.

Consideration of Alternatives: Black v. Romano

A unanimous Supreme Court held in Black v. Romano, 471 U.S. 606 (1985), that the Due Process Clause does not require a sentencing court to indicate that it has considered alternatives to incarceration before revoking probation. Romano pleaded guilty to two counts of transferring and selling a controlled substance. The trial judge imposed two concurrent twenty-year sentences, suspended execution of the sentences, and placed Romano on probation for five years. Two months later Romano was arrested for leaving the scene of an accident after he had run over a pedestrian. The trial judge held a probation revocation hearing during which no suggestion was made by Romano or his two lawyers that an alternative to incarceration be considered. Instead, Romano's argument was that he had not violated his probation conditions.

Justice O'Connor's opinion for the Court analyzed *Morrissey* and *Gagnon* and concluded that although the Court did "not question the desirability of considering possible alternatives to imprisonment before probation is revoked," the "decision to revoke probation is generally predictive and subjective in nature" and "incarceration for violation of a probation condition is not constitutionally limited to circumstances where that sanction represents the only means of promoting the State's interest in punishment and deterrence." A statement of reasons for revocation is not required because "[t]he written statement required by *Gagnon* and *Morrissey* helps to insure accurate factfinding with respect to any alleged violation and provides an adequate basis for review to determine if the decision rests on permissible grounds supported by the evidence."

3. The Relationship Between Supervised Release and Imprisonment

In Johnson v. United States, 529 U.S. 694 (2000), the defendant was convicted on a number of narcotics and firearm counts. He was sentenced to a lengthy prison term on all these sentences, as well as a mandatory 3-year term of supervised release on the narcotics offenses. But because the firearms offenses were based on an incorrect interpretation of the law, they were vacated, and the court reduced the prison sentence. By the time this happened, Johnson had already served 30 months longer than the valid sentence. He was immediately released, and filed a motion to have his term of supervised release reduced by the amount of extra prison time he had served. The district court's refusal to grant this motion was upheld in a unanimous opinion written by Justice Kennedy. The Court held that a period of supervised release is not altered by the fact that a defendant serves excess prison time.

Justice Kennedy parsed 18 U.S.C. § 3624(e), the statutory provision governing the time at which a period of supervised release can begin. That statute provides explicitly that the term of supervised release "commences on the day the person is released from imprisonment." Justice Kennedy reasoned that "released" means what it says, and to say that Johnson "was released while still imprisoned diminishes the concept the word intends to convey."

Justice Kennedy also noted that beginning the period of supervised release upon actual release from imprisonment is consistent with Congress's purpose in establishing a system of supervised release. He observed that "Congress intended supervised release to assist individuals in their transition to community life. Supervised release fulfills rehabilitative ends, distinct from those served by incarceration." Therefore, it would be error to treat time in prison as interchangeable with a period of supervised release.

4. Probation and Parole Officers

Chief Justice Burger mentioned the number of parole revocations in *Morrisey*. In many jurisdictions, probation and parole revocations are common, in part because supervising officers are often rated on the basis of how many revocations they make. These officers operate on a "trail 'em and jail 'em" system. In 2004, the ABA Justice Kennedy Commission, appointed by to address large questions about the criminal justice system raised by Justice Kennedy in an August 9, 2003 speech at the ABA annual meeting, recommended a different approach to parole and probation revocation that was approved by the ABA House of Delegates:

> The Commission makes one recommendation concerning probation and parole: i.e., develop graduated sanctions for probation and parole violations that result in incarceration only when a probation or parole violator has committed a new crime or poses a serious danger to the community.

> * * * Hundreds of thousands of individuals on parole or probation are incarcerated each year for some type of violation of parole or probation. Many of these violations are "technical"—i.e., they do not reflect commission of a new crime or a threat to the community. The revolving door in which inmates are released to the community, returned to prison, released to the community, etc. is most evident in California, but it is also a problem in other jurisdictions. * * *

* * *

> The [California] Little Hoover Commission concludes that a number of alternatives would be cost-effective and protect public safety:

> - Establish clear, transparent and binding guidelines for parole revocation

> - Work with police chiefs and sheriffs to develop a range of sanctions for violations

> - Include as sanctions community-based alternatives for "technical violations" (e.g., drug treatment, home monitoring, curfews)

> - Identify the serious violations justifying a return to prison;

> - Lower the revocation sentences based on offender risk assessments; and

> - Provide short term incarceration in community correctional facilities as an alternative.

One way for jurisdictions to improve their parole and probation revocation decision-making is to utilize risk assessment tools. Washington and Oregon are two states that have taken the lead in using risk assessments in their criminal justice systems. Under its Offender Accountability Act, Washington classifies offenders according to the risk they pose of re-offending in the future and the amount of harm they have caused in the past. By classifying offenders by risk, Washington can devote more resources on higher-risk offenders and spend less on lower-risk offenders. * * * Jurisdictions may find that risk assessments offer useful data in deciding whether to incarcerate a parole or probation violator.

A successor to the ABA Justice Kennedy Commission, the ABA Commission on Effective Criminal Sanctions, developed another resolution to reform parole and probation revocation decisions that was approved by the ABA House of Delegates: "That the American Bar Association urges federal, state, territorial and local governments, to create standards for the performance of probation or parole officers that will consider, in addition to other appropriate factors, the number of individuals under an officer's supervision who successfully complete supervision, as well as those whose probation or parole is appropriately revoked, taking into account the nature of the officer's caseload." The report accompanying the resolution explains the goal:

> If parole and probation officers are empowered and encouraged to utilize sanctions other than outright revocation when offenders violate the conditions of supervision, if they are permitted to focus their energy on offenders who need the most help, and if an important factor in assessing the performance of officers is their success in helping offenders reintegrate, there is a greater opportunity to enhance public safety by enabling offenders to overcome addictions, find housing, receive job training and placement assistance, and other services. Public safety must remain the central responsibility of parole and probation agencies, but it is not enhanced by taking offenders whose behavior could be modified and recycling them in and out of prison without providing them the tools they need to change.

CHAPTER 12

DOUBLE JEOPARDY

■ ■ ■

I. INTRODUCTION

The Double Jeopardy Clause of the Fifth Amendment provides: "[N]or shall any person be subject for the same offense to be twice put in jeopardy of life or limb." Made applicable to the states in Benton v. Maryland, 395 U.S. 784 (1969), the clause provides three basic related protections:

> It protects against a second prosecution for the same offense after acquittal. It protects against a second prosecution for the same offense after conviction. And it protects against multiple punishments for the same offense.

North Carolina v. Pearce, 395 U.S. 711, 717 (1969). As you will see, the case law on the Double Jeopardy Clause seeks to balance the defendant's interest in finality and the government's interest in having one fair opportunity to prosecute and convict.

The Double Jeopardy Clause is not easily understood. Although its history suggests some answers to a few questions, most hard questions were not debated, perhaps not even contemplated, during the drafting and discussion of the Bill of Rights and the Fourteenth Amendment. And when the words of the Double Jeopardy Clause are parsed, it appears that the language offers few clues to the intent of its drafters.

II. THE EFFECT OF AN ACQUITTAL

If the defendant is "acquitted" the government cannot bring a second prosecution on the theory that the acquittal was mistaken. And the government may not appeal from an acquittal or legal rulings that produced the acquittal, even if there was error. In Sanabria v. United States, 437 U.S. 54 (1978), for example, the trial court erroneously excluded evidence of the alleged crime and then granted an acquittal based on the insufficiency of the remaining evidence. The Double Jeopardy Clause barred retrial.

It follows that if a jury acquits a defendant, the trial judge cannot grant the government a second trial, even if the judge believes the jury erred badly or was engaged in nullifying the court's instructions.

Given the preclusive effect of an acquittal, it is important to know what constitutes an acquittal—that is, to know when the government can appeal an adverse ruling or dismissal of a case on the ground that the trial court did something other than acquit the defendant. The Supreme Court considered these questions in United States v. Scott.

UNITED STATES V. SCOTT
Supreme Court of the United States, 1978.
437 U.S. 82.

JUSTICE REHNQUIST delivered the opinion of the Court.

[The defendant moved to dismiss a count against him on grounds of preindictment delay. The trial court granted the motion. The government sought to appeal the dismissal, but the Court of Appeals, relying on United States v. Jenkins, 420 U.S. 358 (1975), concluded that any further prosecution was barred by the Double Jeopardy Clause, due to the trial court's dismissal.] We now reverse.

* * * The Court has long taken the view that the United States has no right of appeal in a criminal case, absent explicit statutory authority. [Under the Criminal Appeals Act the government may appeal] "except that no appeal shall lie where the Double Jeopardy Clause of the United States Constitution prohibits further prosecution." 18 U.S.C.A. § 3731. * * *

* * * "Congress [in the Criminal Appeals Act] intended to remove all statutory barriers to Government appeals and to allow appeals whenever the Constitution would permit." United States v. Wilson, 420 U.S. 332, 337 (1975). * * * A detailed canvass of the history of the double jeopardy principles in English and American law led us to conclude that the Double Jeopardy Clause was primarily "directed at the threat of multiple prosecutions," and posed no bar to Government appeals "where those appeals would not require a new trial." We accordingly held in *Jenkins*, that, whether or not a dismissal of an indictment after jeopardy had attached amounted to an acquittal on the merits, the Government had no right to appeal, because "further proceedings of some sort, devoted to the resolution of factual issues going to the elements of the offense charged, would have been required upon reversal and remand."[a]

---

[a]   The rule established in *Wilson* and *Jenkins* was later described in the following terms:

"[D]ismissals (as opposed to mistrials) if they occurred at a stage of the proceeding after which jeopardy had attached, but prior to the factfinder's conclusion as to guilt or innocence, were final so far as the accused defendant was concerned and could not be appealed by the Government because retrial was barred by double jeopardy. This made the issue of double jeopardy turn very largely on temporal considerations—if the Court granted an order of dismissal during the factfinding stage of the proceedings, the defendant could not be reprosecuted, but if the dismissal came later, he could." Lee v. United States, 432 U.S. 23, 36 (1977) (Rehnquist, J., concurring).

[Editor's Note: In *Lee*, a defendant, after the prosecutor's opening statement, moved to dismiss an information because it failed to allege specific intent. Following a two hour trial, the court noted

If *Jenkins* is a correct statement of the law, the judgment of the Court of Appeals relying on that decision, as it was bound to do, would in all likelihood have to be affirmed. Yet, though our assessment of the history and meaning of the Double Jeopardy Clause in *Wilson, Jenkins,* and Serfass v. United States, 420 U.S. 377 (1975),[b] occurred only three Terms ago, our vastly increased exposure to the various facets of the Double Jeopardy Clause has now convinced us that *Jenkins* was wrongly decided. It placed an unwarrantedly great emphasis on the defendant's right to have his guilt decided by the first jury empaneled to try him so as to include those cases where the defendant himself seeks to terminate the trial before verdict on grounds unrelated to factual guilt or innocence. We have therefore decided to overrule *Jenkins*, and thus to reverse the judgment of the Court of Appeals in this case.[c]

The origin and history of the Double Jeopardy Clause are hardly a matter of dispute. The constitutional provision had its origin in the three common-law pleas of *autrefois acquit, autrefois convict,* and pardon. These three pleas prevented the retrial of a person who had previously been acquitted, convicted, or pardoned for the same offense. As this Court has described the purpose underlying the prohibition against double jeopardy:

"The underlying idea, one that is deeply ingrained in at least the Anglo-American system of jurisprudence, is that the State with all its resources and power should not be allowed to make repeated attempts to convict an individual for an alleged offense, thereby subjecting him to embarrassment, expense and ordeal and compelling him to live in a continuing state of anxiety and insecurity, as well as enhancing the possibility that even though innocent he may be found guilty." *Green* [v. United States, 355 U.S. 184] at 187–188.

These historical purposes are necessarily general in nature, and their application has come to abound in often subtle distinctions which cannot

---

that the defendant had been proved guilty beyond a reasonable doubt, but granted the motion to dismiss the information. Subsequently, the defendant was charged again with the same crime and convicted. The Court held that retrial was not barred by the double jeopardy clause. The Court reasoned that the trial court granted the motion to dismiss in contemplation of a second prosecution, and that it was permissible under the circumstances to delay a ruling on the motion to dismiss until the trial was completed.]

b [Editor's Note: In *Serfass*, the Court held that the government could appeal a *pre-trial* dismissal of an indictment, because the defendant, having never been subjected to factfinding on the guilt and innocence question, could be tried if the trial judge erred in dismissing the indictment.]

c [Editor's Note: The appellate scheme in the federal courts is described in this opinion. Note that there can be no appeal in circumstances where new trial court proceedings would be necessary for there to be a valid conviction and those proceedings are barred by the Double Jeopardy Clause. For purposes of this chapter, it is not critical to master the federal statute governing appeals; it is sufficient to remember that when the Supreme Court holds that there can be no appeal because of the double jeopardy clause, the Supreme Court is saying that there can be no further trial proceedings. The Court would say the same thing if the government tried to bring a second action instead of appealing, and the defendant complained.]

by any means all be traced to the original three common-law pleas referred to above.

* * *

[In] United States v. Ball, 163 U.S. 662 (1896), the Court established principles that have been adhered to ever since. Three persons had been tried together for murder; two were convicted, the other acquitted. This Court reversed the convictions, finding the indictment fatally defective, whereupon all three defendants were tried again. This time all three were convicted and they again sought review here. This Court held that the Double Jeopardy Clause precluded further prosecution of the defendant who had been *acquitted* at the original trial but that it posed no such bar to the prosecution of those defendants who had been *convicted* in the earlier proceeding. The Court disposed of their objection almost peremptorily:

> "Their plea of former conviction cannot be sustained, because upon a writ of error sued out by themselves the judgment and sentence against them were reversed, and the indictment ordered to be dismissed. * * * [I]t is quite clear that a defendant, who procures a judgment against him upon an indictment to be set aside, may be tried anew upon the same indictment, or upon another indictment, for the same offence of which he had been convicted."

Although *Ball* firmly established that a successful appeal of a conviction precludes a subsequent plea of double jeopardy, the opinion shed no light on whether a judgment of acquittal could be reversed on appeal consistently with the Double Jeopardy Clause. * * *

* * * [I]n Fong Foo v. United States, 369 U.S. 141 (1962), this Court reviewed the issuance of a writ of mandamus by the Court of Appeals for the First Circuit instructing a District Court to vacate certain judgments of acquittal. Although indicating its agreement with the Court of Appeals that the judgments had been entered erroneously, this Court nonetheless held that a second trial was barred by the Double Jeopardy Clause. Only last Term, this Court relied upon these precedents in United States v. Martin Linen Supply Co., 430 U.S. 564 (1977), and held that the Government could not appeal the granting of a motion to acquit pursuant to Fed.Rule Crim.Proc. 29 where a second trial would be required upon remand.[d] The Court * * * stated: "Perhaps the most fundamental rule in the history of double jeopardy jurisprudence has been that a verdict of acquittal * * * could not be reviewed, on error or otherwise, without putting [a defendant] twice in jeopardy, and thereby violating the Constitution."

These, then, at least, are two venerable principles of double jeopardy jurisprudence. The successful appeal of a judgment of conviction, on any

---

[d] [Editor's Note: In *Martin* the jury was hopelessly deadlocked and was discharged. Subsequently, the trial judge entered a judgment of acquittal. The Court held that any retrial would violate the Double Jeopardy Clause.]

ground other than the insufficiency of the evidence to support the verdict, poses no bar to further prosecution on the same charge. A judgment of acquittal, whether based on a jury verdict of not guilty or on a ruling by the court that the evidence is insufficient to convict, may not be appealed and terminates the prosecution when a second trial would be necessitated by a reversal.

* * * [T]he law attaches particular significance to an acquittal. To permit a second trial after an acquittal, however mistaken the acquittal may have been, would present an unacceptably high risk that the Government, with its vastly superior resources, might wear down the defendant so that even though innocent he may be found guilty. On the other hand, to require a criminal defendant to stand trial again after he has successfully invoked a statutory right of appeal to upset his first conviction is not an act of governmental oppression of the sort against which the Double Jeopardy Clause was intended to protect.

* * *

Although the primary purpose of the Double Jeopardy Clause was to protect the integrity of a final judgment, this Court has also developed a body of law guarding the separate but related interest of a defendant in avoiding multiple prosecutions even where no final determination of guilt or innocence has been made. Such interests may be involved in two different situations: the first, in which the trial judge declares a mistrial; the second, in which the trial judge terminates the proceedings favorably to the defendant on a basis not related to factual guilt or innocence.

* * *

When a trial court declares a mistrial, it all but invariably contemplates that the prosecutor will be permitted to proceed anew notwithstanding the defendant's plea of double jeopardy. Such a motion may be granted upon the initiative of either party or upon the court's own initiative. The fact that the trial judge contemplates that there will be a new trial is not conclusive on the issue of double jeopardy; in passing on the propriety of a declaration of mistrial granted at the behest of the prosecutor or on the court's own motion, this Court has balanced "the valued right of a defendant to have his trial completed by the particular tribunal summoned to sit in judgment on him," Downum v. United States, 372 U.S. 734, 736 (1963), against the public interest in insuring that justice is meted out to offenders.

Our very first encounter with this situation came in United States v. Perez, 9 Wheat. 579 (1824), in which the trial judge had on his own motion declared a mistrial because of the jury's inability to reach a verdict. The Court said that trial judges might declare mistrials "whenever, in their opinion, taking all the circumstances into consideration, there is a manifest necessity for the act, or the ends of public justice would otherwise be defeated." In our recent decision in Arizona v. Washington, 434 U.S. 497 (1978), we reviewed this Court's attempts to give content to the term "manifest necessity." That case, like *Downum,* supra, arose from a motion of the prosecution for a mistrial, and we noted that the trial court's discretion must be exercised with a careful regard for the interests first described in United States v. Perez.

Where, on the other hand, a *defendant* successfully seeks to avoid his trial prior to its conclusion by a motion for mistrial, the Double Jeopardy Clause is not offended by a second prosecution. * * * Such a motion by the defendant is deemed to be a deliberate election on his part to forego his valued right to have his guilt or innocence determined before the first trier of fact. * * *e

* * *

We turn now to the relationship between the Double Jeopardy Clause and reprosecution of a defendant who has successfully obtained not a mistrial but a termination of the trial in his favor before any determination of factual guilt or innocence. * * *

In the present case, the District Court's dismissal of the first count of the indictment was based upon a claim of preindictment delay and not on the court's conclusion that the Government had not produced sufficient evidence to establish the guilt of the defendant. Respondent Scott points out quite correctly that he had moved to dismiss the indictment on this ground prior to trial, and that had the District Court chosen to grant it at that time the Government could have appealed the ruling under our holding in Serfass v. United States, 420 U.S. 377 (1975). He also quite correctly points out that jeopardy had undeniably "attached" at the time the District Court terminated the trial in his favor; since a successful Government appeal would require further proceedings in the District Court leading to a factual resolution of the issue of guilt or innocence, *Jenkins* bars the Government's appeal. However, our growing experience with Government appeals convinces us that we must re-examine the rationale of *Jenkins* in light of *Lee, Martin Linen,* and other recent expositions of the Double Jeopardy Clause.

* * * It is quite true that the Government with all its resources and power should not be allowed to make repeated attempts to convict an individual for an alleged offense. * * * As we have recognized * * * a defendant once acquitted may not be again subjected to trial without violating the Double Jeopardy Clause.

But that situation is obviously a far cry from the present case, where the Government was quite willing to continue with its production of

---

e   [Editor's Note: But see the limited exception to this principle, established in the later case of Oregon v. Kennedy, discussed infra.]

evidence to show the defendant guilty before the jury first empaneled to try him, but the defendant elected to seek termination of the trial on grounds unrelated to guilt or innocence. This is scarcely a picture of an all-powerful state relentlessly pursuing a defendant who had either been found not guilty or who had at least insisted on having the issue of guilt submitted to the first trier of fact. It is instead a picture of a defendant who chooses to avoid conviction and imprisonment, not because of his assertion that the Government has failed to make out a case against him, but because of a legal claim that the Government's case against him must fail even though it might satisfy the trier of fact that he was guilty beyond a reasonable doubt.

We have previously noted that "the trial judge's characterization of his own action cannot control the classification of the action." Despite respondent's contentions, an appeal is not barred simply because a ruling in favor of a defendant "is based upon facts outside the face of the indictment," or because it "is granted on the ground * * * that the defendant simply cannot be convicted of the offense charged." Rather, a defendant is acquitted only when "the ruling of the judge, whatever its label, actually represents a resolution [in the defendant's favor], correct or not, of some or all of the factual elements of the offense charged." Where the court, before the jury returns a verdict, enters a judgment of acquittal pursuant to Fed.Rule Crim.Proc. 29, appeal will be barred only when "it is plain that the District Court * * * evaluated the Government's evidence and determined that it was legally insufficient to sustain a conviction."

* * *

We think that in a case such as this the defendant, by deliberately choosing to seek termination of the proceedings against him on a basis unrelated to factual guilt or innocence of the offense of which he is accused, suffers no injury cognizable under the Double Jeopardy Clause if the Government is permitted to appeal from such a ruling of the trial court in favor of the defendant. * * * [I]n the present case, respondent successfully avoided * * * a submission of the first count of the indictment [to the jury] by persuading the trial court to dismiss it on a basis which did not depend on guilt or innocence. He was thus neither acquitted nor convicted, because he himself successfully undertook to persuade the trial court not to submit the issue of guilt or innocence to the jury which had been empaneled to try him.

* * * [W]here the defendant, instead of obtaining a reversal of his conviction on appeal, obtains the termination of the proceedings against him in the trial court without any finding by a court or jury as to his guilt or innocence [h]e has not been "deprived" of his valued right to go to the first jury; only the public has been deprived of its valued right to one complete opportunity to convict those who have violated its laws. No

interest protected by the Double Jeopardy Clause is invaded when the Government is allowed to appeal and seek reversal of such a midtrial termination of the proceedings in a manner favorable to the defendant.[f]

* * *

JUSTICE BRENNAN, with whom JUSTICE WHITE, JUSTICE MARSHALL, and JUSTICE STEVENS join, dissenting.

* * *

It is manifest that the reasons that bar a retrial following an acquittal are equally applicable to a final judgment entered on a ground "unrelated to factual innocence." The heavy personal strain of the second trial is the same in either case. So too is the risk that, though innocent, the defendant may be found guilty at a second trial. If the appeal is allowed in either situation, the Government will, following any reversal, not only obtain the benefit of the favorable appellate ruling but also be permitted to shore up any other weak points of its case and obtain all the other advantages at the second trial that the Double Jeopardy Clause was designed to forbid.

[The dissenters also objected to the difficulties in applying the Court's approach. They questioned the difference between a dismissal based on the defenses of insanity and entrapment and a dismissal for pre-indictment delay. The decision, in their view, needlessly complicates an area of law which was "crystal clear."]

Entry of a Judgment of Acquittal

If a trial judge enters a judgment of acquittal, before the jury reaches a verdict, that determination is final. United States v. Martin Linen Supply, 430 U.S. 564 (1977), so indicates. In fact, it holds that a judgment of acquittal following a mistrial is as final as a directed verdict.[g]

---

[f] We should point out that it is entirely possible for a trial court to reconcile the public interest in the Government's right to appeal from an erroneous conclusion of law with the defendant's interest in avoiding a second prosecution. In *Wilson*, supra, the court permitted the case to go to the jury, which returned a verdict of guilty, but it subsequently dismissed the indictment for preindictment delay on the basis of evidence adduced at trial. More recently in United States v. Ceccolini, 435 U.S. 268 (1978), we described similar action with approval: "The District Court had sensibly first made its finding on the factual question of guilt or innocence, and then ruled on the motion to suppress; a reversal of these rulings would require no further proceedings in the District Court, but merely a reinstatement of the finding of guilt."

We, of course, do not suggest that a midtrial dismissal of a prosecution, in response to a defense motion on grounds unrelated to guilt or innocence, is necessarily improper. Such rulings may be necessary to terminate proceedings marred by fundamental error. But where a defendant prevails on such a motion, he takes the risk that an appellate court will reverse the trial court.

[g] Compare *Martin Linen Supply* with United States v. Sanford, 429 U.S. 14 (1976) (no double jeopardy problem where trial court dismissed indictment after mistrial was declared, even though the court's determination was based on evidence presented at trial). See also United States v. Maddox, 944 F.2d 1223 (6th Cir.1991) (no double jeopardy violation where the trial judge

In Smalis v. Pennsylvania, 476 U.S. 140 (1986), Justice White wrote for a unanimous Court as it found that a husband and wife, charged with various crimes in connection with a fire in a building they owned that killed two tenants, were acquitted for double jeopardy purposes when a state trial judge sustained a motion to dismiss at the close of the prosecution's case in a bench trial. The state trial judge in so ruling determined that the state's evidence was insufficient to establish factual guilt, so the Double Jeopardy Clause barred a post-judgment appeal by the government. Even if the state trial court was incorrect about the sufficiency of the evidence, jeopardy had attached and was terminated by the acquittal. The Court held that an acquittal would be found not only where the judge assessed the evidence as a matter of credibility and found it insufficient, but also where the judge determined that evidence was insufficient "as a matter of law." For a discussion of *Smalis* and other cases concerning government appeals, see Strazzella, The Relationship of Double Jeopardy to Prosecution Appeals, 73 Notre Dame L.Rev. 1 (1997).

In Price v. Vincent, 538 U.S. 634 (2003), the Court distinguished *Smalis* and *Martin Linen* and held that a trial judge's ruling was not sufficiently final to terminate jeopardy. The defendant was charged with murder. At the close of the government's case, defense counsel moved for a directed verdict of acquittal as to first degree murder, arguing that there was insufficient evidence of deliberation and premeditation. The trial judge stated:

> "My impression at this time is that there's not been shown premeditation or planning in the, in the alleged slaying. That what we have at the very best is Second Degree Murder. . . . I think that Second Degree Murder is an appropriate charge as to the defendants. Okay."

The prosecutor asked to make a brief statement regarding first-degree murder, but the defendant objected, arguing that his motion for directed verdict had been granted, and that further consideration of that charge would violate the Double Jeopardy Clause. The trial judge responded that he had "granted a motion" but had not directed a verdict. The judge noted that the jury had not been informed of his statements, and that his language indicated that he was going to reserve a ruling on the matter. Subsequently, the trial judge submitted the charge of first-degree murder to the jury and the defendant was convicted on that charge. The state courts, on review, concluded that the trial judge's comments on the directed verdict motion were not sufficiently final to constitute a judgment of acquittal terminating jeopardy.

---

granted a post-trial motion for acquittal, then changed his mind and reinstated the conviction; *Martin Linen* distinguished as a case in which the jury never reached a verdict, and therefore further proceedings would have been necessary).

The defendant sought habeas corpus relief, arguing that his rights under the Double Jeopardy Clause had been violated. Chief Justice Rehnquist, in an opinion for a unanimous Court, noted first that to obtain habeas relief the petitioner must show that the state court's adjudication of his claim was "contrary to, or involved an unreasonable application of, clearly established Federal law, as determined by the Supreme Court of the United States." [See the discussion of the standard of review of a state conviction on a collateral attack in Chapter 13]. Thus, if reasonable minds could differ about whether the state courts were correct in finding insufficient finality to the trial court's ruling in this case, habeas relief must be denied. On the question of finality, the Court noted that in *Smalis* and *Martin Linen*, unlike in the present case, "the trial courts not only rendered statements of clarity and finality but also entered formal orders from which appeals were taken." No such order was entered in the instant case. Under these circumstances, the Michigan courts were not unreasonable in concluding that the trial judge's oral ruling was insufficiently final to terminate jeopardy.

Acquittal for Failure to Prove an Element That the Government Never Had to Prove: Evans v. Michigan

In Evans v. Michigan, 568 U.S. 313 (2013), Justice Sotomayor wrote for the Court as it held that double jeopardy barred retrial of a defendant where the trial court entered a directed verdict of acquittal, based upon its view that the State had not provided sufficient evidence of a particular element of the offense—but that element was not actually required. Evans was charged with burning "other real property." The State's evidence at trial suggested that Evans had burned down an unoccupied house. At the close of the State's case Evans moved for a directed verdict of acquittal, citing pattern jury instructions which indicated that an element of the crime for which he was charged is that the real property had to be a dwelling house. The trial court granted the directed verdict on that ground. On appeal by the government, all parties agreed that the trial court was wrong on the law—no proof that the property was a dwelling house was required. The appellate court rejected the defendant's argument that a retrial was barred by the Double Jeopardy Clause.

Justice Sotomayor relied on Arizona v. Rumsey, 467 U.S. 203 (1984), in which the trial court, sitting as sentencer in a capital case involving a murder committed during a robbery, mistakenly held that Arizona's statutory aggravating factor describing killings for pecuniary gain was limited to murders for hire. In *Rumsey,* the Court had held that a judicial acquittal premised upon a "misconstruction" of a criminal statute is an "acquittal on the merits . . . [that] bars retrial." Justice Sotomayor concluded that there was "no meaningful constitutional distinction between a trial court's 'misconstruction' of a statute and its erroneous addition of a statutory element."

Justice Sotomayor reasoned that "[t]he law attaches particular significance to an acquittal, so a merits-related ruling concludes proceedings absolutely." In this case, she found that the judge, albeit erroneously, had made a merits-based ruling. She rejected alternative arguments made by the State:

> [T]he State suggests that because Evans induced the trial court's error, he should not be heard to complain when that error is corrected and the State wishes to retry him. But we have recognized that "most judgments of acquittal result from defense motions," so "to hold that a defendant waives his double jeopardy protection whenever a trial court error in his favor on a midtrial motion leads to an acquittal would undercut the adversary assumption on which our system of criminal justice rests, and would vitiate one of the fundamental rights established by the Fifth Amendment." *Sanabria*, 437 U.S., at 78. It is true that when a defendant persuades the court to declare a mistrial, jeopardy continues and retrial is generally allowed. But in such circumstances the defendant consents to a disposition that contemplates reprosecution, whereas when a defendant moves for acquittal he does not.

* * *

Justice Sotomayor rejected the government's argument to reconsider its double jeopardy cases involving judicial acquittals, including *Scott, supra*. She made clear that states do not have to permit certain types of trial court rulings:

> First, we have no reason to believe the existing rules have become so unworkable as to justify overruling precedent. The distinction drawn in *Scott* has stood the test of time, and we expect courts will continue to have little difficulty in distinguishing between those rulings which relate to the ultimate question of guilt or innocence and those which serve other purposes.

* * *

Finally, the State and the United States object that this rule denies the prosecution a full and fair opportunity to present its evidence to the jury, while the defendant reaps a "windfall" from the trial court's unreviewable error. But sovereigns are hardly powerless to prevent this sort of situation * * *. Nothing obligates a jurisdiction to afford its trial courts the power to grant a midtrial acquittal, and at least two States disallow the practice. Many jurisdictions, including the federal system, allow or encourage their courts to defer consideration of a motion to acquit until after the jury returns a verdict, which mitigates double jeopardy concerns [because appellate reversal of the trial court's dismissal simply allows the jury verdict to be reinstated]. See Fed. Rule Crim. Proc. 29(b). * * * But having chosen to vest its courts with the power to grant midtrial acquittals, the State must bear the corresponding risk that some acquittals will be granted in error.

Justice Alito dissented, arguing that "[f]or no good reason, the Court deprives the State of Michigan of its right to have one fair opportunity to convict petitioner, " and would have held "that double jeopardy protection is not triggered by a judge's erroneous preverdict ruling that creates an 'element' out of thin air and then holds that the element is not satisfied."

Is the Jury's Announcement That It Is Unanimous Against Guilt on One Count—But Deadlocked on Others—an Acquittal on That Count?: Blueford v. Arkansas

In Blueford v. Arkansas, 566 U.S. 599 (2012), the Court reviewed a capital case in which the jury reported to the judge that it 1) was unanimous against guilt on charges of capital murder and first degree murder, 2) was deadlocked on manslaughter, and 3) had not voted on negligent homicide. The court declared a mistrial. Before the Supreme Court, all agreed that the defendant could be retried on charges of manslaughter and negligent homicide. But Blueford argued that the Double Jeopardy Clause prohibited retrial on capital and first degree murder, as he had been "acquitted" on those charges.

Chief Justice Roberts, writing for the Court, held that Blueford had not been acquitted of the most serious charges for Double Jeopardy purposes. He reasoned as follows:

> When the foreperson told the court how the jury had voted on each offense, the jury's deliberations had not yet concluded. The jurors in fact went back to the jury room to deliberate further, even after the foreperson had delivered her report. When they emerged a half hour later, the foreperson stated only that they were unable to reach a verdict. She gave no indication whether it was still the case that all 12 jurors believed Blueford was not guilty of capital or first-degree murder, that 9 of them believed he was guilty of manslaughter, or that a vote had not been taken on negligent homicide. The fact that deliberations continued after the report deprives that report of the finality necessary to constitute an acquittal on the murder offenses.

Justice Sotomayor, joined by Justices Ginsburg and Kagan, dissented in *Blueford*. She stated as follows:

> Here, the trial judge instructed Blueford's jury to consider the offenses in order, from the charged offense of capital murder to the

lesser included offenses of first-degree murder, manslaughter, and negligent homicide. The judge told the jury to proceed past capital murder only upon a unanimous finding of a "reasonable doubt" as to that offense—that is, upon an acquittal. * * *

In this context, the forewoman's announcement in open court that the jury was "unanimous against" conviction on capital and first-degree murder was an acquittal for double jeopardy purposes. * * * That acquittal cannot be reconsidered without putting Blueford twice in jeopardy.

Reversal of a Judgment of Acquittal During the Trial: Smith v. Massachusetts

In Smith v. Massachusetts, 554 U.S. 442 (2005), the trial court, midway through a jury trial, granted Smith's motion for acquittal on one of the three offenses with which he was charged. The judge found that the government presented insufficient evidence on that count. Later in the trial, after Smith rested his case, the judge reconsidered and changed his mind about the acquittal. The jury was never informed of the acquittal and Smith was eventually convicted of all three charges.

The Court, in an opinion by Justice Scalia, found that the Double Jeopardy Clause prevented the trial judge from reversing his order of acquittal during the trial. He reasoned as follows:

[W]hen, as here, the trial has proceeded to the defendant's presentation of his case, the possibility of prejudice arises. The seeming dismissal may induce a defendant to present a defense to the undismissed charges when he would be better advised to stand silent. Many jurisdictions still follow the traditional rule that after trial or on appeal, sufficiency-of-the-evidence challenges are reviewed on the basis of the *entire* trial record, even if the defendant moved for acquittal when the prosecution rested and the court erroneously denied that motion. In these jurisdictions, the defendant who puts on a case runs the risk that he will bolster the Government case enough for it to support a verdict of guilty. The defendant's evidence may lay the foundation for otherwise inadmissible evidence in the Government's initial presentation or provide corroboration for essential elements of the Government's case. In all jurisdictions, moreover, false assurance of acquittal on one count may induce the defendant to present defenses to the remaining counts that are inadvisable—for example, a defense that entails admission of guilt on the acquitted count.

The Double Jeopardy Clause's guarantee cannot be allowed to become a potential snare for those who reasonably rely upon it. If, after a facially unqualified midtrial dismissal of one count, the trial has proceeded to the defendant's introduction of evidence, the acquittal must be treated as final, unless the availability of reconsideration has been plainly established by pre-existing rule or case authority expressly applicable to midtrial rulings on the sufficiency of the evidence. That requirement was not met here. * * *

Justice Ginsburg, joined by Chief Justice Roberts and Justices Kennedy and Breyer, dissented in *Smith*. She stated that "Smith was subjected to a single, unbroken trial proceeding in which he was denied no opportunity to air his defense before presentation of the case to the jury. I would not deny prosecutors in such circumstances, based on a trial judge's temporary error, *one* full and fair opportunity to present the State's case."

Acquittal After a Jury Convicts

If a judge waits until after a jury convicts to enter a judgment of acquittal, may the government appeal that ruling? A footnote in *Scott* suggests that an appeal in those circumstances is permissible. The lower courts have agreed, reasoning that if the government is successful on appeal, the verdict can simply be reinstated and further proceedings are unnecessary. See United States v. Maddox, 944 F.2d 1223 (6th Cir.1991). You can see in the Supreme Court decisions suggestions that this approach avoids some double jeopardy problems.

Dismissal When the Government Refuses to Participate in the Trial After the Jury Has Been Empanelled: Martinez v. Illinois

In Martinez v. Illinois, 134 S.Ct. 2070 (2014), the defendant was charged with aggravated battery and mob action against two individuals whom the prosecution had difficulty in getting to trial. On the morning of trial, the victims were nowhere to be found. The trial judge offered to delay swearing in the jurors until a complete jury had been empaneled and to give the prosecution the opportunity to have the jury sworn or to dismiss its case. The state filed a written motion for a continuance on the ground it could not proceed without the victims. The judge denied it and offered to delay the trial for several more hours if that would help the prosecution. After the prosecution made clear that the whereabouts of the victims were "unknown," the judge swore in the jury and invited the prosecution to call its first witness. The prosecution declined to present any evidence. The defendant moved for a directed not-guilty verdict, which the judge granted. The state appealed and the Illinois Supreme Court held that Martinez was never at risk of conviction and jeopardy never attached.

The Court reversed in a per curiam opinion in which it said that "[t]here are few if any rules of criminal procedure clearer than the rule that jeopardy attaches when the jury is empaneled and sworn." The Court held that there was no doubt that Martinez's jeopardy ended in a manner that barred his retrial, as the trial judge granted the motion for a directed finding of not guilty and "[t]hat is a textbook acquittal." It stated that it had "never suggested that jeopardy may not have attached where, under the circumstances of a particular case, the defendant was not genuinely at risk of conviction."

III. ABORTED PROCEEDINGS

A. THE RIGHT TO A DETERMINATION FROM THE FIRST JURY IMPANELED

As noted earlier, the Double Jeopardy Clause is derived from English law, which provided that a defendant was put in jeopardy only after a conviction or an acquittal. The protection was afforded to a defendant only after a complete trial. The notion that a defendant may be put in jeopardy in a prosecution that does not terminate in a conviction or acquittal was incorporated gradually into the Double Jeopardy Clause. The Court determined that the defendant's interest in finality could be undermined if the prosecution could terminate a trial before the verdict, and institute a new proceeding. This protection, like other double jeopardy guarantees, becomes operative when jeopardy "attaches."

In Crist v. Bretz, 437 U.S. 28 (1978), the Court held that jeopardy attaches when the jury is impaneled and sworn. The Court reasoned that the impaneled-and-sworn rule of attachment reflects and protects the defendant's interest in retaining a chosen jury, which the Court found to be one of the core principles of double jeopardy protection. See United States v. Juarez-Fierro, 935 F.2d 672 (5th Cir.1991) (pre-voir dire oath to the venire does not constitute attachment of jeopardy; a jury is not empaneled until all parties have exercised their challenges, and jurors have been selected to serve on the petit jury). In a non-jury trial, jeopardy attaches when the court begins to hear evidence.

B. MISTRIAL DECLARED OVER THE DEFENDANT'S OBJECTION

The following cases consider when a retrial is permissible following a mistrial. The next case discusses the major prior cases on the subject.

1. The Requirement of Manifest Necessity for a Mistrial Granted over the Defendant's Objection

ILLINOIS V. SOMERVILLE

Supreme Court of the United States, 1973.
410 U.S. 458.

JUSTICE REHNQUIST delivered the opinion of the Court.

We must here decide whether declaration of a mistrial over the defendant's objection, because the trial court concluded that the indictment was insufficient to charge a crime, necessarily prevents a State from subsequently trying the defendant under a valid indictment. We hold that the mistrial met the "manifest necessity" requirement of our cases, since the trial court could reasonably have concluded that the "ends of public justice" would be defeated by having allowed the trial to continue. Therefore, the Double Jeopardy Clause of the Fifth Amendment, made applicable to the States through the Due Process Clause of the Fourteenth Amendment, did not bar retrial under a valid indictment.

[The defendant was indicted for theft. After the jury was sworn, but before any evidence was presented, the trial court granted the State's motion for a mistrial despite the defendant's objection, because the indictment was fatally defective for failure to allege the requisite intent. After a new trial and conviction, the defendant sought a writ of habeas corpus. He alleged that the new trial violated his rights under the Double Jeopardy Clause.]

The fountainhead decision construing the Double Jeopardy Clause in the context of a declaration of a mistrial over a defendant's objection is United States v. Perez, 9 Wheat. 579 (1824). Mr. Justice Story, writing for a unanimous Court, set forth the standards for determining whether a retrial, following a declaration of a mistrial over a defendant's objection, constitutes double jeopardy within the meaning of the Fifth Amendment. In holding that the failure of the jury to agree on a verdict of either acquittal or conviction did not bar retrial of the defendant, Mr. Justice Story wrote:

> We think that in all cases of this nature, the law has invested Courts of justice with the authority to discharge a jury from giving any verdict, whenever, in their opinion, taking all the circumstances into consideration, there is a manifest necessity for the act, or the ends of public justice would otherwise be defeated. They are to exercise a sound discretion on the subject; and it is impossible to define all the circumstances, which would render it proper to interfere. To be sure, the power ought to be used with the greatest caution, under urgent circumstances, and for very plain and obvious causes * * *.

This formulation, consistently adhered to by this Court in subsequent decisions, abjures the application of any mechanical formula by which to judge the propriety of declaring a mistrial in the varying and often unique situations arising during the course of a criminal trial. The broad discretion reserved to the trial judge in such circumstances has been consistently reiterated in decisions of this Court. * * *

While virtually all of the cases turn on the particular facts and thus escape meaningful categorization, it is possible to distill from them a general approach, premised on the "public justice" policy enunciated in United States v. Perez, to situations such as that presented by this case. A trial judge properly exercises his discretion to declare a mistrial if an impartial verdict cannot be reached, or if a verdict of conviction could be reached but would have to be reversed on appeal due to an obvious procedural error in the trial. If an error would make reversal on appeal a certainty, it would not serve "the ends of public justice" to require that the Government proceed with its proof when, if it succeeded before the jury, it would automatically be stripped of that success by an appellate court. * * * While the declaration of a mistrial on the basis of a rule or a defective procedure that would lend itself to prosecutorial manipulation would involve an entirely different question, such was not the situation * * * in the instant case.

In Downum v. United States [372 U.S. 734 (1963)], the defendant was charged with six counts of mail theft, and forging and uttering stolen checks. A jury was selected and sworn in the morning, and instructed to return that afternoon. When the jury returned, the Government moved for the discharge of the jury on the ground that a key prosecution witness, for two of the six counts against defendant, was not present. The prosecution knew, prior to the selection and swearing of the jury, that this witness could not be found and had not been served with a subpoena. The trial judge discharged the jury over the defendant's motions to dismiss two counts for failure to prosecute and to continue the other four. This Court, in reversing the convictions on the ground of double jeopardy * * * held that the second prosecution constituted double jeopardy, because the absence of the witness and the reason therefore did not there justify, in terms of "manifest necessity," the declaration of a mistrial.

In United States v. Jorn [400 U.S. 470 (1971)], the Government called a taxpayer witness in a prosecution for wilfully assisting in the preparation of fraudulent income tax returns. Prior to his testimony, defense counsel suggested he be warned of his constitutional right against compulsory self-incrimination. The trial judge warned him of his rights, and the witness stated that he was willing to testify and that the Internal Revenue Service agent who first contacted him warned him of his rights. The trial judge, however, did not believe the witness' declaration that the IRS had so warned him, and refused to allow him to testify until after he had consulted with an attorney. After learning from the Government that the remaining four witnesses were "similarly situated," and after surmising that they, too, had not been properly informed of their rights, the trial judge declared a mistrial to give the witnesses the opportunity to consult with attorneys. In sustaining a plea in bar of double jeopardy to an attempted second trial of the defendant, the plurality opinion of the Court, emphasizing the importance to the defendant of proceeding before the first jury sworn, concluded:

> It is apparent from the record that no consideration was given to the possibility of a trial continuance; indeed, the trial judge acted so abruptly in discharging the jury that, had the prosecutor been disposed to suggest a continuance, or the defendant to object to the discharge of the jury, there would have been no opportunity to do so. When one examines the circumstances surrounding the discharge of this jury, it seems abundantly apparent that the trial judge made no effort to exercise a sound discretion to assure that, taking all the circumstances into account, there was a manifest necessity for the *sua sponte* declaration of this mistrial.

* * *

[The Court rejected Somerville's argument that any trial on a defective indictment precludes retrial, and then considered whether the circumstances of the case justified the mistrial.]

In the instant case, the trial judge terminated the proceeding because a defect was found to exist in the indictment that was, as a matter of Illinois law, not curable by amendment. The Illinois courts have held that even after a judgment of conviction has become final, the defendant may be released on habeas corpus, because the defect in the indictment deprives the trial court of "jurisdiction." * * * The trial judge was faced with a situation * * * in which a procedural defect might or would preclude the public from either obtaining an impartial verdict or keeping a verdict of conviction if its evidence persuaded the jury. If a mistrial were constitutionally unavailable in situations such as this, the State's policy could only be implemented by conducting a second trial after verdict and reversal on appeal, thus wasting time, energy, and money for all concerned. Here, the trial judge's action was a rational determination designed to implement a legitimate state policy, with no suggestion that the implementation of that policy in this manner could be manipulated so as to prejudice the defendant. * * * Given the established standard of discretion * * *, we cannot say that the declaration of a mistrial was not required by "manifest necessity" or the "ends of public justice."

Our decision in *Jorn*, relied upon by the court below and respondent, does not support the opposite conclusion. * * * That opinion dealt with action by a trial judge that can fairly be described as erratic. The Court held that the lack of apparent harm to the defendant from the declaration of a mistrial did not itself justify the mistrial, and concluded that there was no "manifest necessity" for the mistrial, as opposed to less drastic alternatives. The Court emphasized that the absence of any manifest need for the mistrial had deprived the defendant of his right to proceed before the first jury, but it did not hold that that right may never be forced to yield, as in this case, to "the public's interest in fair trials designed to end in just judgments." * * *.

The determination by the trial court to abort a criminal proceeding where jeopardy has attached is not one to be lightly undertaken, since the interest of the defendant in having his fate determined by the jury first impaneled is itself a weighty one. Nor will the lack of demonstrable additional prejudice preclude the defendant's invocation of the double jeopardy bar in the absence of some important countervailing interest of proper judicial administration. But where the declaration of a mistrial implements a reasonable state policy and aborts a proceeding that at best would have produced a verdict that could have been upset at will by one of the parties, the defendant's interest in proceeding to verdict is outweighed by the competing and equally legitimate demand for public justice.

[Justice White, joined by Justices Douglas and Brennan, dissented. Relying on *Downum* and *Jorn,* Justice White argued that even when prosecutorial misconduct consists of a mistake or oversight, the defendant's interest in having the trial completed by the first tribunal prevails. This should be true even when no specific prejudice to the defendant is shown. In this case, the reason for the mistrial was the state's error.

Justice Marshall dissented separately. Also relying on *Downum* and *Jorn*, he argued that the court's "balancing" approach underemphasized the defendant's interest in continuing with the trial. Continuation, under the circumstances of the case, was a viable alternative to a mistrial in his view.]

NOTE ON THE IMPACT OF SOMERVILLE

Somerville generally has been considered a retreat from the heightened scrutiny of mistrials granted without the defendant's consent in *Downum* and *Jorn*. It is clear that after *Somerville*, the term "manifest necessity" is no longer an accurate description of what constitutes a proper ground for a mistrial sufficient to allow a new trial. It is more like "reasonable cause." See United States v. Toribio-Lugo, 376 F.3d 33 (1st Cir. 2004) (In assessing "manifest necessity," an appellate court's inquiry "inevitably reduces to whether the district judge's declaration of a mistrial was reasonably necessary under all the circumstances."). Is there really ever a "manifest necessity" to abort a trial because of a defective indictment when the defect could have been noticed by the prosecutor or the court and corrected before jeopardy attached?

Trial Court's Declaring Mistrial Was Not an Unreasonable Application of Manifest Necessity Standard: Renico v. Lett

In Renico v. Lett, 559 U.S. 766 (2010), the Court reviewed a habeas claim in which the petitioner argued that the trial court declared a mistrial without "manifest necessity" and therefore his retrial violated Double Jeopardy. Because the case was on habeas, the standard of review for trial court's decision was extremely deferential. The question was not whether the trial court erred but whether its ruling was an unreasonable application of clearly established Supreme Court law. The trial judge granted a mistrial in a murder case in which the foreperson of the jury told the judge, in response to a question after the jury sent seven notes to the judge, that the jury would not be unanimous. Chief Justice Roberts noted that "the jury only deliberated for four hours, its notes were arguably ambiguous, the trial judge's initial question to the foreperson was imprecise, and the judge neither asked for elaboration of the foreperson's answers nor took any other measures to confirm the foreperson's prediction that a unanimous verdict would not be reached."

Nonetheless, the Chief Justice found that the trial court's grant of a mistrial was not an unreasonable application of the Supreme Court cases (the standard for review on habeas). The Chief Justice reasoned as follows:

> Since *Perez*, we have clarified that the "manifest necessity" standard "cannot be interpreted literally," and that a mistrial is appropriate when there is a "high degree" of necessity. * * * In particular, the trial judge's decision to declare a mistrial when he considers the jury deadlocked is accorded great deference by a reviewing court. * * *

> The reasons for allowing the trial judge to exercise broad discretion are especially compelling in cases involving a potentially deadlocked jury. There, the justification for deference is that the trial court is in the best position to assess all the factors which must be considered in making a necessarily discretionary determination whether the jury will be able to reach a just verdict if it continues to deliberate. In the absence of such deference, trial judges might otherwise employ coercive means to break the apparent deadlock, thereby creating a significant risk that a verdict may result from pressures inherent in the situation rather than the considered judgment of all the jurors.

Justice Stevens, joined by Justices Sotomayor and Breyer, dissented in *Renico*. She failed to see how the trial court's "abrupt" action could be considered "sound discretion" under any standard of review.

2.　Manifest Necessity as a Flexible Test

ARIZONA V. WASHINGTON
Supreme Court of the United States, 1978.
434 U.S. 497.

JUSTICE STEVENS delivered the opinion of the Court.

An Arizona trial judge granted the prosecutor's motion for a mistrial predicated on improper and prejudicial comment during defense counsel's opening statement. * * *. The questions presented are whether the record reflects the kind of "necessity" for the mistrial ruling that will avoid a valid plea of double jeopardy, and if so, whether the plea must nevertheless be allowed because the Arizona trial judge did not fully explain the reasons for his mistrial ruling.

* * *

In 1971 respondent was found guilty of murdering a hotel night clerk. In 1973, the Superior Court of Pima County, Ariz., ordered a new trial because the prosecutor had withheld exculpatory evidence from the defense. * * *

Respondent's second trial began in January 1975. During the *voir dire* examination of prospective jurors, the prosecutor made reference to the fact that some of the witnesses whose testimony the jurors would hear had testified in proceedings four years earlier. Defense counsel told the prospective jurors "that there was evidence hidden from [respondent] at the last trial." In his opening statement, he made this point more forcefully:

> "You will hear testimony that notwithstanding the fact that we had a trial in May of 1971 in this matter, that the prosecutor hid those statements and didn't give those to the lawyer for George saying the man was Spanish speaking, didn't give those statements at all, hid them.

> "You will hear that that evidence was suppressed and hidden by the prosecutor in that case. You will hear that that evidence was purposely withheld. You will hear that because of the misconduct of the County Attorney at that time and because he withheld evidence, that the Supreme Court of Arizona granted a new trial in this case."

[The prosecutor moved for a mistrial, because there was no theory on which the prior suppression of evidence and granting of a new trial could be admissible, and the prejudice to the jury could not be repaired by any cautionary instruction. The judge granted the motion, but did not expressly find that there was "manifest necessity" for a mistrial, and did not expressly state that he had considered and found alternative solutions to be inadequate.]

Because jeopardy attaches before the judgment becomes final, the constitutional protection * * * embraces the defendant's "valued right to have his trial completed by a particular tribunal." The reasons why this "valued right" merits constitutional protection are worthy of repetition. Even if the first trial is not completed, a second prosecution may be grossly unfair. It increases the financial and emotional burden on the accused, prolongs the period in which he is stigmatized by an unresolved accusation of wrongdoing, and may even enhance the risk that an innocent defendant may be convicted. * * *

Unlike the situation in which the trial has ended in an acquittal or conviction, retrial is not automatically barred when a criminal proceeding is terminated without finally resolving the merits of the charges against the accused. Because of the variety of circumstances that may make it necessary to discharge a jury before a trial is concluded, and because those circumstances do not invariably create unfairness to the accused, his valued right to have the trial concluded by a particular tribunal is sometimes subordinate to the public interest in affording the prosecutor one full and fair opportunity to present his evidence to an impartial jury. Yet in view of the importance of the right, and the fact that it is frustrated by any mistrial, the prosecutor must shoulder the burden of justifying the mistrial if he is to avoid the double jeopardy bar. * * * The prosecutor must demonstrate "manifest necessity" for any mistrial declared over the objection of the defendant.

The words "manifest necessity" * * * do not describe a standard that can be applied mechanically or without attention to the particular problem confronting the trial judge. Indeed, it is manifest that the key word "necessity" cannot be interpreted literally; instead, contrary to the teaching of Webster, we assume that there are degrees of necessity and we require a "high degree" before concluding that a mistrial is appropriate.

The question whether that "high degree" has been reached is answered more easily in some kinds of cases than in others. At one extreme are cases in which a prosecutor requests a mistrial in order to buttress weaknesses in his evidence. * * * Thus, the strictest scrutiny is appropriate when the basis for the mistrial is the unavailability of critical prosecution evidence,[a] or when there is reason to believe that the prosecutor is using the superior resources of the State to harass or to achieve a tactical advantage over the accused.[b]

---

[a] If, for example, a prosecutor proceeds to trial aware that key witnesses are not available to give testimony and a mistrial is later granted for that reason, a second prosecution is barred. Downum v. United States, 372 U.S. 734. The prohibition against double jeopardy unquestionably "forbids the prosecutor to use the first proceeding as a trial run of his case." Note, Twice in Jeopardy, 75 Yale L.J. 262, 287–288 (1965).

[b] * * * The "particular tribunal" principle is implicated whenever a mistrial is declared over the defendant's objection and without regard to the presence or absence of governmental overreaching. If the "right to go to a particular tribunal is valued, it is because, independent of the

At the other extreme is the mistrial premised upon the trial judge's belief that the jury is unable to reach a verdict, long considered the classic basis for a proper mistrial. * * * This rule accords recognition to society's interest in giving the prosecution one complete opportunity to convict those who have violated its laws.

Moreover, in this situation there are especially compelling reasons for allowing the trial judge to exercise broad discretion in deciding whether or not "manifest necessity" justifies a discharge of the jury. * * * If retrial of the defendant were barred whenever an appellate court views the "necessity" for a mistrial differently from the trial judge, there would be a danger that the latter, cognizant of the serious societal consequences of an erroneous ruling, would employ coercive means to break the apparent deadlock. * * *

We are persuaded that, along the spectrum of trial problems which may warrant a mistrial and which vary in their amenability to appellate scrutiny, the difficulty which led to the mistrial in this case also falls in an area where the trial judge's determination is entitled to special respect.

In this case the trial judge ordered a mistrial because the defendant's lawyer made improper and prejudicial remarks during his opening statement to the jury. * * * We therefore start from the premise that defense counsel's comment was improper and may have affected the impartiality of the jury.

We recognize that the extent of the possible bias cannot be measured, and that the District Court was quite correct in believing that some trial judges might have proceeded with the trial after giving the jury appropriate cautionary instructions. In a strict, literal sense, the mistrial was not "necessary." Nevertheless, the overriding interest in the evenhanded administration of justice requires that we accord the highest degree of respect to the trial judge's evaluation of the likelihood that the impartiality of one or more jurors may have been affected by the improper comment.

* * * We are * * * persuaded by the record that the trial judge acted responsibly and deliberately, and accorded careful consideration to respondent's interest in having the trial concluded in a single proceeding. * * * Neither party has a right to have his case decided by a jury which may be tainted by bias; in these circumstances, "the public's interest in fair trials designed to end in just judgments" must prevail over the defendant's "valued right" to have his trial concluded before the first jury impaneled.

* * *

---

threat of bad-faith conduct by judge or prosecutor, the defendant has a significant interest in the decision whether or not to take the case from the jury." United States v. Jorn, 400 U.S., at 485.

One final matter requires consideration. The absence of an explicit finding of "manifest necessity" appears to have been determinative for the District Court and may have been so for the Court of Appeals. If those courts regarded that omission as critical, they required too much. Since the record provides sufficient justification for the state-court ruling, the failure to explain that ruling more completely does not render it constitutionally defective.

* * *

[Justice White argued in dissent that the case should have been remanded to the district court for a new determination of manifest necessity for the mistrial. Justice Marshall, joined by Justice Brennan, dissented on the ground that a finding of manifest necessity must be explicit, rather than implied from the record.]

Applying the Manifest Necessity Test

One court has set forth helpful standards for determining whether a mistrial was granted out of manifest necessity:

> The Supreme Court and appellate courts have relied on four indicators in determining whether the trial court abused its discretion. Has the trial judge (1) heard the opinions of the parties about the propriety of the mistrial, (2) considered the alternatives to a mistrial and chosen the alternative least harmful to a defendant's rights, (3) acted deliberately instead of abruptly, and (4) properly determined that the defendant would benefit from the declaration of mistrial? If a district court engages in this type of effort, it is much more likely to have exercised sound discretion in concluding that manifest necessity for a mistrial existed.

United States v. Elliot, 463 F.3d 858 (9th Cir.2006).

Deadlocked Juries: Blueford v. Arkansas

In Arizona v. Washington, the Court indicated that great deference should be given to a judge's determination to declare a mistrial when the jury appears deadlocked. The subsequent decision in Renico v. Lett supra, reaffirms that requirement of extreme deference. Similarly, in Blueford v. Arkansas, supra, the Court rejected the defendant's argument that the trial judge abused discretion in granting a mistrial on all counts when the jury reported that it had agreed to acquit on some counts but disagreed on others. Chief Justice Roberts analyzed Blueford's "manifest necessity" attack in the following passage:

> Blueford * * * accepts that a second trial on manslaughter and negligent homicide would pose no double jeopardy problem. He

contends, however, that there was no necessity for a mistrial on capital and first-degree murder, given the foreperson's report that the jury had voted unanimously against guilt on those charges. According to Blueford, the court at that time should have taken "some action," whether through partial verdict forms or other means, to allow the jury to give effect to those votes, and then considered a mistrial only as to the remaining charges.

We reject that suggestion. We have never required a trial court, before declaring a mistrial because of a hung jury, to consider any particular means of breaking the impasse—let alone to consider giving the jury new options for a verdict. As permitted under Arkansas law, the jury's options in this case were limited to two: either convict on one of the offenses, or acquit on all. The instructions explained those options in plain terms, and the verdict forms likewise contemplated no other outcome. * * * When the foreperson disclosed the jury's votes on capital and first-degree murder, the trial court did not abuse its discretion by refusing to add another option—that of acquitting on some offenses but not others. That, however, is precisely the relief Blueford seeks—relief the Double Jeopardy Clause does not afford him.

C. MISTRIAL DECLARED UPON DEFENDANT'S MOTION

Goading the Defendant into Moving for a Mistrial: Oregon v. Kennedy

Under what circumstances, if any, can the defendant who *moves* for a mistrial invoke double jeopardy protections against a retrial? This question was considered in Oregon v. Kennedy, 456 U.S. 667 (1982). After defense counsel had brought out during cross-examination of the state's expert witness that the expert had previously filed a criminal complaint against the defendant, the prosecutor suggested on redirect examination that the reason for the filing was that the defendant was "a crook." Kennedy moved for a mistrial, and the trial court granted Kennedy's motion. When the state sought to retry Kennedy, he moved to dismiss the charges because of double jeopardy. Justice Rehnquist, writing for the Court, concluded that a retrial was not barred. He reasoned as follows:

> Where the trial is terminated over the objection of the defendant, the classical test for lifting the double jeopardy bar to a second trial is the "manifest necessity" standard * * *. But in the case of a mistrial declared at the behest of the defendant, quite different principles come into play. Here the defendant himself has elected to terminate the

proceedings against him, and the manifest necessity standard has no place in the application of the Double Jeopardy Clause. * * *

Our cases, however, have indicated that even where the defendant moves for a mistrial, there is a narrow exception to the rule that the Double Jeopardy Clause is no bar to retrial. * * *

Since one of the principal threads making up the protection embodied in the Double Jeopardy Clause is the right of the defendant to have his trial completed before the first jury empaneled to try him, it may be wondered as a matter of original inquiry why the defendant's election to terminate the first trial by his own motion should not be deemed a renunciation of that right for all purposes. We have recognized, however, that there would be great difficulty in applying such a rule where the prosecutor's actions giving rise to the mistrial were done in order to goad the defendant into requesting a mistrial. In such a case, the defendant's valued right to complete his trial before the first jury would be a hollow shell if the inevitable motion for mistrial were held to prevent a later invocation of the bar of double jeopardy in all circumstances. But the precise phrasing of the circumstances which *will* allow a defendant to interpose the defense of double jeopardy * * * have been stated with less than crystal clarity * * *.

Justice Rehnquist rejected the argument that double jeopardy should apply whenever the prosecutor's conduct at the first trial indicated "overreaching." He argued that such a test offered "virtually no standards" for application. He opted for an approach that examined the intent of the prosecutor:

[A] standard that examines the intent of the prosecutor, though certainly not entirely free from practical difficulties, is a manageable standard to apply. It merely calls for the court to make a finding of fact. Inferring the existence or nonexistence of intent from objective facts and circumstances is a familiar process in our criminal justice system. * * *

* * * Only where the governmental conduct in question is intended to "goad" the defendant into moving for a mistrial may a defendant raise the bar of double jeopardy. * * *

Justice Powell's concurring opinion emphasized that a court determining the intent of the prosecutor "should rely primarily upon the objective facts and circumstances of the particular case." He noted that in the instant case, the prosecutor had made only a single comment, and that the prosecutor was surprised by and resisted the defendant's motion for a mistrial. Justice Stevens, joined by Justices Brennan, Marshall, and Blackmun, concurred in the judgment. He argued that "[i]t is almost inconceivable that a defendant could prove that the prosecutor's deliberate misconduct was motivated by an intent to provoke a mistrial," and asserted that an "overreaching" standard was preferable even though it would be a "rare and compelling case" in which retrial would be barred.[1]

For an application of *Kennedy*, see United States v. Curry, 328 F.3d 970 (8th Cir. 2003) (mistrial granted on defendant's motion because the prosecutor suppressed impeachment evidence and made improper comments during closing argument; but retrial was not barred because the prosecutor did not engage in this conduct with the intent to goad the defendant into declaring a mistrial).

The Rationale of Oregon v. Kennedy

Judge Easterbrook, writing for the court in United States v. Jozwiak, 954 F.2d 458 (7th Cir.1992), provides an excellent explanation and application of Oregon v. Kennedy. Judge Easterbrook set forth the facts of the case as follows:

> Nine of the twenty-six defendants in this case charging a conspiracy to distribute cocaine went to trial on November 4, 1991. A prosecutor—whose first trial this was—told the jury during his opening statement that five of the original defendants were cooperating with the government and would appear as witnesses and that four others had also pleaded guilty. The mention that some of the defendants had entered pleas of guilty led the defendants to seek a mistrial. A senior prosecutor from the United States Attorney's office confessed error and apologized. As everyone wanted a mistrial, the district judge sent the jury home. There was no point conducting a long trial with a built-in error.
>
> All nine defendants then insisted that the double jeopardy clause bars further prosecution. The district court denied the motion, observing that the defendants had requested the mistrial.

The defendants requested a hearing to probe the prosecutor's intent, but the trial judge denied the request. Judge Easterbrook analyzed the double jeopardy question and the applicability of Oregon v. Kennedy while distinguishing between an intent to goad and an intent to win:

> Any search for steps intended to goad defendants into seeking mistrials encounters a problem. Because intent is a matter of characterization, you cannot even know what indicia to look for unless you know the direction toward which the (forbidden) intent would be bent. Prosecutors intend to secure convictions, intend to secure all

---

[1]   When Oregon v. Kennedy returned to state court, the state supreme court relied upon the state constitution to find that Kennedy's rights were violated. State v. Kennedy, 295 Or. 260, 666 P.2d 1316 (1983). It reasoned that retrial should be barred when the prosecution "either intends or is indifferent to the resulting mistrial or reversal."

advantages the adversary system allows. An overstep (sometimes even a correct step) may lead to howls from the defense, and next to an argument that the overstep was intended to goad the adversary into howling. Yet a search for intent that leads only to a conclusion that the prosecutor wanted to win is pointless. We must be looking for intent to do something that undercuts the interests protected by the double jeopardy clause. *Kennedy* distinguishes intent to improve the chance that the trier of fact will return a favorable decision from the forbidden intent to avoid decision by the trier of fact.

Judge Easterbrook provided a rule of thumb for determining prosecutorial intent in these murky circumstances:

> A defendant's interest in preserving the benefits of a trial that has been going well enables us to distinguish these two characterizations of prosecutorial intent. Only a prosecutor who thinks the trial is going sour—or who seeks to get just far enough into the trial to preview the defense—would want to precipitate a mistrial. Otherwise the mistrial means a waste for both sides, injuring the prosecutor along with the defense. (Trying one defendant twice means, for a prosecutor with limited resources, letting some other defendant go.) Unless there is reason to believe that the prosecutor set out to rescue a case on the path to acquittal or filch a road map of the defense, a court may cut off the inquiry; whatever may have been in the prosecutor's head was not the kind of intent with which the Double Jeopardy Clause is concerned.

Applying these standards to the facts, Judge Easterbrook concluded that the prosecutor had no intent to goad the defendant into asking for a mistrial when he referred, in opening argument, to the fact that some of the conspirators had entered guilty pleas.

> The prosecutor's case against these nine defendants was not going downhill; it was not going, period. It ended within minutes after the prosecutor rose to speak. * * * Defense counsel did not tip their hands; they barely had time to tip their hats. Scuttling a trial at dockside poses few if any risks to the defendant's legitimate interests.

Why Should the Defendant's Motion Make a Difference?

As we have seen, if the prosecution moves for a mistrial, double jeopardy bars a new trial unless the "manifest necessity" standard is met. However, if the defendant moves for a mistrial, double jeopardy only bars a new trial in the very rare case in which the prosecutor has intentionally goaded the defendant into moving for a mistrial. Why should it matter, for double jeopardy purposes, whether it is the prosecutor or the defendant who moves for the mistrial? Judge Easterbrook, in Miller v. Indiana Dept. of Corrections, 75 F.3d 330 (7th Cir.1996), posits that if double jeopardy would routinely bar a retrial whenever the defendant moved for a mistrial in good faith, such a rule would in the long run harm defendants. He reasoned that the threat of double jeopardy in such circumstances would mean that "judges would be even more reluctant to grant mistrials than they are already."

IV.   THE CONVICTED DEFENDANT APPEALS

May a defendant who successfully appeals a conviction be retried? Ball v. United States, 163 U.S. 662 (1896), mentioned in *Scott* and discussed in the following case, established that a retrial following a reversal of a conviction is generally permissible. In the next case, the Court considered whether a defendant may be retried when the appellate reversal is based on insufficiency of the evidence rather than on trial error.

A.   INSUFFICIENT EVIDENCE TO CONVICT

BURKS V. UNITED STATES
Supreme Court of the United States, 1978.
437 U.S. 1.

CHIEF JUSTICE BURGER delivered the opinion of the Court.

We granted certiorari to resolve the question of whether an accused may be subjected to a second trial when conviction in a prior trial was reversed by an appellate court solely for lack of sufficient evidence to sustain the jury's verdict.

* * *

Petitioner Burks was tried in the United States District Court for the crime of robbing a federally insured bank by use of a dangerous weapon * * *. Burks' principal defense was insanity.

[The defendant moved for acquittal at trial, on grounds that the government had not shown a culpable mental state. The trial court denied the motion. But the court of appeals found that there was insufficient evidence of the necessary mental state, and reversed the conviction. The Court of Appeals, rather than terminating the case, remanded to the District Court for a determination of whether a directed verdict of acquittal should be entered or a new trial ordered.]

[By way of introduction, the Court examined several prior decisions—Bryan v. United States, 338 U.S. 552 (1950); Sapir v. United States, 348 U.S. 373 (1955); Yates v. United States, 354 U.S. 298 (1957); Forman v. United States, 361 U.S. 416 (1960)—which had held that a defendant who requests a new trial, as did Burks, may be required to stand trial even when his conviction is reversed for failure of proof.]

It is unquestionably true that the Court of Appeals' decision "represented a resolution, correct or not, of some or all of the factual elements of the offense charged." United States v. Martin Linen Supply Co., 430 U.S. 564, 571 (1977). By deciding that the Government had failed to come forward with sufficient proof of petitioner's capacity to be responsible for criminal acts, that court was clearly saying that Burks' criminal culpability had not been established. If the District Court had so held in the first instance, as the reviewing court said it should have done, a judgment of acquittal would have been entered and, of course, petitioner could not be retried for the same offense. Consequently * * * it should make no difference that the *reviewing* court, rather than the trial court, determined the evidence to be insufficient. The appellate decision unmistakably meant that the District Court had erred in failing to grant a judgment of acquittal. To hold otherwise would create a purely arbitrary distinction between those in petitioner's position and others who would enjoy the benefit of a correct decision by the District Court.

* * *

Nonetheless, * * * our past holdings do not appear consistent with what we believe the Double Jeopardy Clause commands. A close reexamination of those precedents, however, persuades us that they have not properly construed the Clause, and accordingly should no longer be followed.

[Reconsideration of the prior cases involved an examination of Ball v. United States, 163 U.S. 662 (1896), which permitted a new trial when the accused successfully sought review of a conviction.]

Ball came before the Court twice, the first occasion being on writ of error from federal convictions for murder. On this initial review, those defendants who had been found guilty obtained a reversal of their convictions due to a fatally defective indictment. On remand after appeal, the trial court dismissed the flawed indictment and proceeded to retry the defendants on a new indictment. They were again convicted and the defendants came once more to this Court, arguing that their second trial was barred because of former jeopardy. The Court rejected this plea in a brief statement * * *. The reversal in *Ball* was therefore based not on insufficiency of evidence but rather on trial error, i.e., failure to dismiss a faulty indictment. * * * We have no doubt that *Ball* was correct in allowing a new trial to rectify *trial error* * * *.

* * * In short, reversal for trial error, as distinguished from evidentiary insufficiency, does not constitute a decision to the effect that the government has failed to prove its case. As such, it implies nothing with respect to the guilt or innocence of the defendant. Rather, it is a determination that a defendant has been convicted through a judicial process which is defective in some fundamental respect, e.g., incorrect

receipt or rejection of evidence, incorrect instructions, or prosecutorial misconduct. When this occurs, the accused has a strong interest in obtaining a fair readjudication of his guilt free from error, just as society maintains a valid concern for insuring that the guilty are punished. * * *

The same cannot be said when a defendant's conviction has been overturned due to a failure of proof at trial, in which case the prosecution cannot complain of prejudice, for it has been given one fair opportunity to offer whatever proof it could assemble. Moreover, such an appellate reversal means that the government's case was so lacking that it should not have even been *submitted* to the jury. Since we necessarily afford absolute finality to a jury's *verdict* of acquittal—no matter how erroneous its decision—it is difficult to conceive how society has any greater interest in retrying a defendant when, on review, it is decided as a matter of law that the jury could not properly have returned a verdict of guilty.

* * *

In our view it makes no difference that a defendant has sought a new trial as one of his remedies, or even as the sole remedy. It cannot be meaningfully said that a person "waives" his right to a judgment of acquittal by moving for a new trial. * * * Since we hold today that the Double Jeopardy Clause precludes a second trial once the reviewing court has found the evidence legally insufficient, the only "just" remedy available for that court is the direction of a judgment of acquittal. To the extent that our prior decisions suggest that by moving for a new trial, a defendant waives his right to a judgment of acquittal on the basis of evidentiary insufficiency, those cases are overruled.

* * *

MR. JUSTICE BLACKMUN took no part in the consideration or decision of this case.

Burks Applied: Hudson v. Louisiana

Hudson v. Louisiana, 450 U.S. 40 (1981), held that *Burks* applied when a second trial was held after the trial judge at the first trial granted a motion for a new trial on the ground that the evidence was insufficient to support the jury's guilty verdict. The basis for the trial judge's ruling was insufficiency of the evidence, and under *Burks,* that ruling terminates the proceedings.

B. INSUFFICIENT EVIDENCE AND TRIAL COURT ERROR

Erroneously Admitted Evidence: Lockhart v. Nelson

Does *Burks* apply when the evidence actually introduced at trial is sufficient to sustain the convictions, but the legally competent evidence—excluding from consideration evidence erroneously admitted by the trial court—is insufficient? The Court in Lockhart v. Nelson, 488 U.S. 33 (1988), answered that *Burks* does not apply and that the defendant can be retried after a successful appeal. The prosecutor used Nelson's prior convictions at a sentencing hearing, to prove that Nelson should receive an enhanced sentence as a habitual offender. This was error under state law as to one of the convictions, for which Nelson had been pardoned. On habeas review, the district court found the sentence invalid. The State announced its intention to resentence Nelson as a habitual offender, by using a prior conviction not offered or admitted at the initial sentencing hearing. Nelson interposed a claim of double jeopardy. Chief Justice Rehnquist, writing for the Court, concluded that the *Burks* exception was inapplicable and that Nelson's resentencing would not implicate Double Jeopardy concerns.

> *Burks* was based on the view that an appellate court's reversal for insufficiency of the evidence is in effect a determination that the government's case against the defendant was so lacking that the trial court should have entered a judgment of acquittal, rather than submitting the case to the jury. * * *

> *Burks* was careful to point out that a reversal based solely on evidentiary insufficiency has fundamentally different implications * * * than a reversal based on such ordinary "trial errors" as the incorrect receipt or rejection of evidence. While the former is in effect a finding that the government has failed to prove its case against the defendant, the latter implies nothing with respect to the guilt or innocence of the defendant, but is simply a determination that he has been convicted through a judicial *process* which is defective in some fundamental respect.

Justice Marshall, joined by Justices Brennan and Blackmun, dissented. Justice Marshall argued that if the State had produced a "blank piece of paper" at the sentencing hearing "no one would doubt that Arkansas had produced insufficient evidence and that the Double Jeopardy Clause barred retrial." He concluded that "there is no constitutionally significant difference between that hypothetical and this case."

Charged with the Wrong Crime: Montana v. Hall

In Montana v. Hall, 481 U.S. 400 (1987), the Court summarily reversed a state supreme court decision that a defendant whose conviction was overturned could not be retried on another charge. Hall was originally charged with sexual assault of the daughter of his ex-wife. He successfully moved to dismiss the charge, persuading the trial court that he could only be prosecuted for incest. After his conviction for incest, he persuaded the state supreme court that the incest statute did not apply on the facts of the case because the statute had not been in effect on the date of the charged criminal act. That court concluded that Hall could not be retried on the original charge because sexual assault and incest were the same offense, so that a retrial after a conviction for committing a nonexistent crime (incest under these circumstances) would violate double jeopardy. The Supreme Court disagreed, finding no constitutional bar to Hall's reprosecution for sexual assault, because a reversal of a conviction on grounds other than insufficiency of the evidence—such as, in this case, a "defect in the charging instrument"—does not bar a retrial. Justice Marshall dissented from the summary handling of the case, and Justice Stevens filed a separate dissent suggesting that the state supreme court may have rested its decision on state law. See also United States v. Dalton, 990 F.2d 1166 (10th Cir.1993) (new trial permitted where defendant's conviction was reversed because the statute under which he was charged had been implicitly repealed; reversal was due to a "defect in the charging instrument," not insufficiency of evidence).

Reversal of Convictions Rendered Against the Weight of the Evidence: Tibbs v. Florida

In Tibbs v. Florida, 457 U.S. 31 (1982), the Supreme Court held 5–4 that a defendant could be retried after an appellate court overturned an initial conviction on the ground that it was *against the weight* of the evidence. Writing for the majority, Justice O'Connor reasoned that "[a] reversal based on the weight of the evidence * * * can occur only after the State both has presented sufficient evidence to support conviction and has persuaded the jury to convict. The reversal simply affords the defendant a second opportunity to seek a favorable judgment." That is, there is a distinction between a reversal based on *insufficiency* of the evidence and a reversal of a guilty verdict against the weight of the evidence—under applicable legal standards, the prosecution's case is stronger in the latter instance, indeed it is legally sufficient to support a conviction.

Justice White's dissent in *Tibbs*, joined by Justices Brennan, Marshall, and Blackmun, argued that whether a reversal is based on insufficiency or weight of the evidence, a retrial gives the prosecution a second chance to do what it was unable to do in the first trial—i.e., put on stronger evidence.

The dissenters suggested that appellate judges, when deciding that a conviction should be reversed, might use weight-of-the-evidence reasoning to permit retrial where it ought to be prohibited under *Burks*. In response, the majority observed that "trial and appellate judges commonly distinguish between the weight and the sufficiency of the evidence. We have no reason to believe that today's decision will erode the demonstrated ability of judges to distinguish legally insufficient evidence from evidence that rationally supports a verdict."

C. TRIAL DE NOVO AND CONTINUING JEOPARDY

Two-Tiered System: Justices v. Lydon

The Court distinguished *Burks* in Justices v. Lydon, 466 U.S. 294 (1984). Lydon was arrested after breaking into an automobile in Boston. Under state procedure, Lydon had a right to choose a jury trial or an initial trial to the bench. An acquittal before either a judge or a jury would have been final; but a guilty verdict was final only if rendered by a jury; a defendant who elected a bench trial had an absolute right to a trial de novo if convicted.

Lydon, like most Massachusetts defendants, opted for the bench trial. (Why not?). He was convicted. He then requested a trial de novo to a jury, but he attempted in state court, and then in federal court, to bar the second trial on the ground that there had been insufficient evidence to warrant a conviction in the bench trial. He claimed that *Burks* barred retrial. The Court disagreed.

Justice White wrote for the Court and recognized that *Burks* prohibited a second trial after a court found that a conviction was based on insufficient evidence. However, under the Massachusetts system, no such determination had been made. The policies underlying *Burks* did not apply, he said, because this was not a case in which the prosecution had an incentive to offer a weak case first, in order to discover the defendant's evidence and theories, since an acquittal would be a final victory for the defendant; and the prosecutor received no education as to how to present a better case from reviewing judges, since there had been no review. Justice White explained that the two-tiered option granted to a defendant offered benefits not generally available in a single-tiered system. He noted that if the defendant were convicted on insufficient evidence at the trial de novo, *Burks* would apply at that point.

Event Necessary to Terminate Jeopardy:
Richardson v. United States

Justice Rehnquist relied on the Court's reasoning in *Lydon* in his majority opinion in Richardson v. United States, 468 U.S. 317 (1984). The

Court held that a defendant was not placed in jeopardy twice when a mistrial was declared due to a genuine jury deadlock, Richardson's motion for judgment of acquittal was denied, and the trial judge scheduled a second trial. The Court held that the defendant had never been acquitted. Therefore he had no valid double jeopardy claim that a second trial was barred because of the failure to introduce legally sufficient evidence to go to the jury, regardless of the actual sufficiency of evidence at first trial.

As it had in *Lydon,* the Court read *Burks* as holding only that "once a defendant obtained an unreversed * * * ruling that the Government had failed to introduce sufficient evidence to convict him at trial, a second trial was barred by the Double Jeopardy Clause." Examining Richardson's claim, the Court said that "[w]here, as here, there has been only a mistrial resulting from a hung jury, *Burks* simply does not require that an appellate court rule on the sufficiency of the evidence because retrial might be barred by the Double Jeopardy Clause." The Court found that the declaration of a mistrial was not the equivalent of an acquittal, it did not terminate jeopardy, and that "[r]egardless of the sufficiency of the evidence at petitioner's first trial, he has no valid double jeopardy claim to prevent his retrial." Justice Brennan, joined by Justice Marshall, dissented. He agreed with the majority that a new trial is not barred simply because a jury could not reach a verdict, but urged that "[w]hen the prosecution has failed to present constitutionally sufficient evidence, it cannot complain of unfairness in being denied a second chance, and the interests in finality, shared by the defendant and society, strongly outweigh the reasons for a retrial."

Does *Lydon* really provide support for the result in *Richardson?* Isn't there a difference between a two-tiered system in which a defendant gets a free shot at acquittal without running the risk of a conviction that sticks (*Lydon*) and a case in which both sides would be bound by the result, the prosecution has failed to produce sufficient evidence to convict, and the trial judge erroneously fails to enter a judgment of acquittal (*Richardson*)? After all, the declaration of a mistrial ends the first trial, and if the prosecution failed to offer sufficient proof to convict, why should it be permitted to make a second attempt to convict?

V. MULTIPLE PROSECUTIONS OF CONVICTED DEFENDANTS

A. THE SAME OFFENSE

Double jeopardy bars not only the retrial of a defendant who is acquitted; it also bars the reprosecution of a defendant who has already been convicted of the same offense. Here the policies are obvious. The defendant may be forced to defend, but not repetitively. Once the government gets the conviction it originally sought or loses at trial on a charge, further proceedings might well be vexatious, and the proceedings will certainly subject the defendant to the inconvenience, anxiety and expense of having to defend again. Thus, there is no doubt that after a valid conviction or acquittal, the *same offense* cannot be prosecuted again. But what constitutes the same offense?

Lesser Included Offenses: Brown v. Ohio and the Blockburger Test

In Brown v. Ohio, 432 U.S. 161 (1977), the defendant stole a car in East Cleveland, Ohio. Nine days later, he was arrested in another city and charged with joyriding. He pled guilty and served his sentence. After his release, he was returned to East Cleveland and charged with auto theft and joyriding. He pled guilty to auto theft, but reserved his double jeopardy claim for a motion to withdraw his plea. The court overruled his double jeopardy objection and sentenced him. The Supreme Court concluded that the conviction violated the Double Jeopardy Clause, because joyriding is a lesser included offense of auto theft under Ohio law. The Court applied the test of different offenses that was established in Blockburger v. United States, 284 U.S. 299 (1932), for the purpose of determining whether it is permissible to cumulate punishment. It found no reason to apply different tests to multiple trials and multiple punishments. The Court noted that "[w]here the judge is forbidden to impose cumulative punishment for two crimes at the end of a single proceeding, the prosecutor is forbidden to strive for the same result in successive proceedings." Under *Blockburger,* the test for the same offense is whether *each statutory provision contains an element that the other does not.* Because the Ohio statute under which Brown was convicted defined auto theft as joyriding with the intent to permanently deprive the owner of possession, the only difference in proof between the two crimes was the intent. (i.e., only one crime—auto theft—required something that the other—joy riding—did not).

The government argued that Brown could be tried twice because the second charge covered a different *part* of the joy ride than that considered in the first trial. But the Court disagreed. The nine-day joyride could not be divided into a series of temporal or spatial units, because Ohio law did not create separate offenses for each day someone was joyriding. Justices Blackmun, Burger, and Rehnquist argued in dissent that Brown committed a separate offense when he operated the car nine days after stealing it.

It is important under *Blockburger* that *each* statutory crime must require an element that the other does not for there to be separate offenses. In Illinois v. Vitale, 447 U.S. 410 (1980), the Court considered whether a driver of an automobile that struck and killed two children could be prosecuted for involuntary manslaughter, following his conviction for failing to reduce speed to avoid the collision. The Court remanded the case for further development of state law, observing that "if manslaughter by automobile does not always entail proof of a failure to slow, then the two offenses are not the 'same' under the *Blockburger* test," but cautioning also that if the state would "find it necessary to prove a failure to slow or to rely on conduct necessarily involving such failure" Vitale's double jeopardy claim "would be substantial." Four dissenters argued that no further proceedings were appropriate. The decisions in *Grady* and *Dixon*, discussed below, deal with the Court's cautionary statement.

The Grady v. Corbin "Same Conduct" Test

The Court held that the *Blockburger* test of "same offense" was not sufficient to protect double jeopardy rights in Grady v. Corbin, 495 U.S. 508 (1990)—though the holding proved to be short-lived, as demonstrated in *Dixon*, infra. Justice Brennan, writing for a five-Justice majority in *Grady*, stated that "the Double Jeopardy Clause bars a subsequent prosecution if, to establish an essential element of an offense charged in that prosecution, the government will prove *conduct* that constitutes an offense for which the defendant has already been prosecuted."(Emphasis added). The case involved Corbin, who was at fault in a car accident resulting in fatal injuries, and was also intoxicated. He was served with traffic tickets charging him with the misdemeanor of driving while intoxicated and with failing to keep right of the median. He pleaded guilty to the two traffic tickets, with the presiding judge being unaware of the fatality stemming from the accident. Thereafter he was indicted for reckless manslaughter, second-degree vehicular manslaughter, and criminally negligent homicide, third-degree reckless assault, and driving while intoxicated.

Justice Brennan held that a trial on manslaughter and homicide charges was barred by the Double Jeopardy Clause, if the government sought to prove the crimes through evidence of drunk driving or failure to keep to the right of the median. He recognized that the prosecution for these crimes would not be barred under the *Blockburger* test, because each of the minor crimes to which Corbin pled guilty contained elements that the more serious crimes did not, and vice versa. (For example, reckless manslaughter does not include an element of driving, or driving while intoxicated, and driving while intoxicated does not contain an element of reckless disregard for human life). Justice Brennan argued, however, that the *Blockburger* test was insufficient to protect against the risk of multiple prosecutions:

> If *Blockburger* constituted the entire double jeopardy inquiry in the context of successive prosecutions, the State could try Corbin in four consecutive trials: for failure to keep right of the median, for driving while intoxicated, for assault, and for homicide. The State

could improve its presentation of proof with each trial, assessing which witnesses gave the most persuasive testimony, which documents had the greatest impact, which opening and closing arguments most persuaded the jurors. Corbin would be forced either to contest each of these trials or to plead guilty to avoid the harassment and expense.

Justice Brennan applied the "same conduct" test to Corbin's situation, and held that prosecution on the serious charges was barred, because the state had admitted that it would use the conduct for which he was convicted (i.e., driving carelessly and while drunk) to prove the more serious charges.

Justice O'Connor wrote a dissent. Justice Scalia also wrote a dissent, in which Chief Justice Rehnquist and Justice Kennedy joined. Justice Scalia "would adhere to the *Blockburger* rule that successive prosecutions under two different statutes do not constitute double jeopardy if each statutory crime contains an element that the other does not, regardless of the overlap between the proof required for each prosecution in the particular case." He argued that the "same conduct" test was an impermissible expansion from the common-law jurisprudence that spawned the Double Jeopardy Clause, and that it was inconsistent with precedent, which had relied solely on the *Blockburger* test.

Return to the Blockburger Test

The expansive *Grady* test was not the law for long. Only three years later, the Court, in the following case, overruled *Grady* and returned to the *Blockburger* test as the sole benchmark for determining the permissibility of successive prosecutions. However, there was dispute among the Justices as to how to apply *Blockburger*.

UNITED STATES V. DIXON
Supreme Court of the United States, 1993.
509 U.S. 688.

JUSTICE SCALIA announced the judgment of the Court and delivered the opinion of the Court with respect to Parts I, II, and IV, and an opinion with respect to Parts III and V, in which JUSTICE KENNEDY joins.

In both of these cases, respondents were tried for criminal contempt of court for violating court orders that prohibited them from engaging in conduct that was later the subject of a criminal prosecution. We consider whether the subsequent criminal prosecutions are barred by the Double Jeopardy Clause.

I

Respondent Alvin Dixon was arrested for second-degree murder and was released on bond. * * * Dixon's release form specified that he was not to commit "any criminal offense," and warned that any violation of the conditions of release would subject him "to revocation of release, an order of detention, and prosecution for contempt of court."

While awaiting trial, Dixon was arrested and indicted for possession of cocaine with intent to distribute. The court issued an order requiring Dixon to show cause why he should not be held in contempt or have the terms of his pretrial release modified. At the show-cause hearing, four police officers testified to facts surrounding the alleged drug offense; Dixon's counsel cross-examined these witnesses and introduced other evidence. The court concluded that the Government had established "beyond a reasonable doubt that [Dixon] was in possession of drugs and that those drugs were possessed with the intent to distribute." The court therefore found Dixon guilty of criminal contempt under D.C.Code Ann. § 23–1329(c) * * *. Dixon was sentenced to 180 days in jail. He later moved to dismiss the cocaine indictment on double jeopardy grounds; the trial court granted the motion.

Respondent Michael Foster's route to this Court is similar. Based on Foster's alleged physical attacks upon her in the past, Foster's estranged wife Ana obtained a civil protection order (CPO) in Superior Court of the District of Columbia. The order, to which Foster consented, required that he not "molest, assault, or in any manner threaten or physically abuse" Ana Foster * * *.

Over the course of eight months, Ana Foster filed three separate motions to have her husband held in contempt for numerous violations of the CPO. Of the 16 alleged episodes, the only charges relevant here are three separate instances of threats (on November 12, 1987, and March 26 and May 17, 1988) and two assaults (on November 6, 1987, and May 21, 1988), in the most serious of which Foster "threw [his wife] down basement stairs, kicking her body[,] * * * pushed her head into the floor causing head injuries, [and Ana Foster] lost consciousness."

After issuing a notice of hearing and ordering Foster to appear, the court held a 3-day bench trial. Counsel for Ana Foster * * * prosecuted the action * * *. As to the assault charges, the court stated that Ana Foster would have "to prove as an element, first that there was a Civil Protection Order, and then [that] . . . the assault as defined by the criminal code, in fact occurred." * * * The court found Foster guilty beyond a reasonable doubt of four counts of criminal contempt including the November 6, 1987 and May 21, 1988 assaults, but acquitted him on other counts, including the March 26 alleged threats. He was sentenced to an aggregate 600 days' imprisonment.

The United States Attorney's Office later obtained an indictment charging Foster with simple assault on or about November 6, 1987 (Count I, violation of § 22–504); threatening to injure another on or about

November 12, 1987, and March 26 and May 17, 1988 (Counts II–IV, violation of § 22–2307); and assault with intent to kill on or about May 21, 1988 (Count V, violation of § 22–501). Ana Foster was the complainant in all counts; the first and last counts were based on the events for which Foster had been held in contempt, and the other three were based on the alleged events for which Foster was acquitted of contempt. Like Dixon, Foster filed a motion to dismiss, claiming a double jeopardy bar to all counts, and also collateral estoppel as to Counts II–IV. The trial court denied the double-jeopardy claim and did not rule on the collateral-estoppel assertion.

The Government appealed the double jeopardy ruling in *Dixon,* and Foster appealed the trial court's denial of his motion. The District of Columbia Court of Appeals * * * relying on our recent decision in Grady v. Corbin, ruled that both subsequent prosecutions were barred by the Double Jeopardy Clause. In its petition for certiorari, the Government presented the sole question "[w]hether the Double Jeopardy Clause bars prosecution of a defendant on substantive criminal charges based upon the same conduct for which he previously has been held in criminal contempt of court."

II

* * *

We recently held in *Grady* that in addition to passing the *Blockburger* test, a subsequent prosecution must satisfy a "same-conduct" test to avoid the double jeopardy bar. The *Grady* test provides that, "if, to establish an essential element of an offense charged in that prosecution, the government will prove conduct that constitutes an offense for which the defendant has already been prosecuted," a second prosecution may not be had.

III

* * *

The first question before us today is whether *Blockburger* analysis permits subsequent prosecution in [the] criminal contempt context, where judicial order has prohibited criminal act. If it does, we must then proceed to consider whether *Grady* also permits it.

We begin with *Dixon.* The statute applicable in Dixon's contempt prosecution provides that "[a] person who has been conditionally released . . . and who has violated a condition of release shall be subject to . . . prosecution for contempt of court." * * *

In this situation, in which the contempt sanction is imposed for violating the order through commission of the incorporated drug offense, the later attempt to prosecute Dixon for the drug offense resembles the situation that produced our judgment of double jeopardy in Harris v. Oklahoma, 433 U.S. 682 (1977) (*per curiam*). There we held that a subsequent prosecution for robbery with a firearm was barred by the Double Jeopardy Clause, because the defendant had already been tried for felony-murder based on the same underlying felony. We have described our terse *per curiam* in *Harris* as standing for the proposition that, for double jeopardy purposes, "the crime generally described as felony murder" is not "a separate offense distinct from its various elements." Illinois v. Vitale, 447 U.S. 410, 420–421 (1980). So too here, the "crime" of violating a condition of release cannot be abstracted from the "element" of the violated condition. The *Dixon* court order incorporated the entire governing criminal code in the same manner as the *Harris* felony-murder statute incorporated the several enumerated felonies. Here, as in *Harris,* the underlying substantive criminal offense is "a species of lesser-included offense."

* * * Because Dixon's drug offense did not include any element not contained in his previous contempt offense, his subsequent prosecution violates the Double Jeopardy Clause.

The foregoing analysis obviously applies as well to Count I of the indictment against Foster, charging assault in violation of § 22–504, based on the same event that was the subject of his prior contempt conviction for violating the provision of the CPO forbidding him to commit simple assault under § 22–504. The subsequent prosecution for assault fails the *Blockburger* test, and is barred.

* * *

The remaining four counts in *Foster,* assault with intent to kill (Count V; § 22–501) and threats to injure or kidnap (Counts II–IV; § 22–2307), are not barred under *Blockburger.* As to Count V: Foster's conduct on May 21, 1988 was found to violate the Family Division's order that he not "molest, assault, or in any manner threaten or physically abuse" his wife. At the contempt hearing, the court stated that Ana Foster's attorney, who prosecuted the contempt, would have to prove first, knowledge of a CPO, and second, a willful violation of one of its conditions, here simple assault as defined by the criminal code. On the basis of the same episode, Foster was then indicted for violation of § 22–501, which proscribes assault with intent to kill. Under governing law, that offense requires proof of specific intent to kill; simple assault does not. Similarly, the contempt offense required proof of knowledge of the CPO, which assault with intent to kill does not. Applying the *Blockburger* elements test, the result is clear: These crimes were different offenses and the subsequent prosecution did not violate the Double Jeopardy Clause.

Counts II, III, and IV of Foster's indictment are likewise not barred. These charged Foster under § 22–2307 (forbidding anyone to "threate[n]

* * * to kidnap any person or to injure the person of another or physically damage the property of any person") for his alleged threats on three separate dates. Foster's contempt prosecution included charges that, on the same dates, he violated the CPO provision ordering that he not "in any manner threaten" Ana Foster. Conviction of the contempt required willful violation of the CPO—which conviction under § 22–2307 did not; and conviction under § 22–2307 required that the threat be a threat to kidnap, to inflict bodily injury, or to damage property—which conviction of the contempt (for violating the CPO provision that Foster not "in any manner threaten") did not. Each offense therefore contained a separate element, and the *Blockburger* test for double jeopardy was not met.

IV

Having found that at least some of the counts at issue here are not barred by the *Blockburger* test, we must consider whether they are barred by the new, additional double jeopardy test we announced three Terms ago in Grady v. Corbin. They undoubtedly are * * *.

We have concluded, however, that *Grady* must be overruled. Unlike *Blockburger* analysis, whose definition of what prevents two crimes from being the "same offence," U.S. Const., Amdt. 5, has deep historical roots and has been accepted in numerous precedents of this Court, *Grady* lacks constitutional roots. The "same-conduct" rule it announced is wholly inconsistent with earlier Supreme Court precedent and with the clear common-law understanding of double jeopardy. See, e.g., Gavieres v. United States, 220 U.S., at 345 (in subsequent prosecution, "[w]hile it is true that the conduct of the accused was one and the same, two offenses resulted, each of which had an element not embraced in the other"). We need not discuss the many proofs of these statements, which were set forth at length in the *Grady* dissent. See 495 U.S., at 526 (Scalia, J., dissenting). * * *

* * * *Grady* * * * has already proved unstable in application. Less than two years after it came down, in United States v. Felix, 503 U.S. 378 (1992), we were forced to recognize a large exception to it. There we concluded that a subsequent prosecution for conspiracy to manufacture, possess, and distribute methamphetamine was not barred by a previous conviction for attempt to manufacture the same substance. We offered as a justification for avoiding a "literal" (i.e., faithful) reading of *Grady* "longstanding authority" to the effect that prosecution for conspiracy is not precluded by prior prosecution for the substantive offense. Of course the very existence of such a large and longstanding "exception" to the *Grady* rule gave cause for concern that the rule was not an accurate expression of the law. This "past practice" excuse is not available to support the ignoring of *Grady* in the present case, since there is no Supreme Court precedent even discussing this fairly new breed of successive prosecution (criminal contempt for violation of a court order prohibiting a crime, followed by prosecution for the crime itself).

A hypothetical based on the facts in *Harris* reinforces the conclusion that *Grady* is a continuing source of confusion and must be overruled. Suppose the State first tries the defendant for felony-murder, based on robbery, and then indicts the defendant for robbery with a firearm in the same incident. Absent *Grady,* our cases provide a clear answer to the double-jeopardy claim in this situation. Under *Blockburger,* the second prosecution is not barred—as it clearly was not barred at common law * * *.ᵃ

Having encountered today yet another situation in which the pre-*Grady* understanding of the Double Jeopardy Clause allows a second trial, though the "same-conduct" test would not, we think it time to acknowledge what is now, three years after *Grady,* compellingly clear: the case was a mistake. We do not lightly reconsider a precedent, but, because *Grady* contradicted an "unbroken line of decisions," contained "less than accurate" historical analysis, and has produced "confusion,"ᵇ we do so here. Although stare decisis is the "preferred course" in constitutional adjudication, "when governing decisions are unworkable or are badly reasoned, this Court has never felt constrained to follow precedent." We would mock stare decisis and only add chaos to our double jeopardy jurisprudence by pretending that *Grady* survives when it does not.

CHIEF JUSTICE REHNQUIST, with whom JUSTICE O'CONNOR and JUSTICE THOMAS join, concurring in part and dissenting in part.

* * * I do not join Part III of Justice Scalia's opinion because I think that none of the criminal prosecutions in this case were barred under *Blockburger.* I must then confront the expanded version of double jeopardy embodied in *Grady.* For the reasons set forth in the *Grady* dissent, and in Part IV of the Court's opinion, I, too, think that *Grady* must be overruled.

ᵃ * * * Justice Souter's concern that prosecutors will bring separate prosecutions in order to perfect their case seems unjustified. They have little to gain and much to lose from such a strategy. Under Ashe v. Swenson, 397 U.S. 436 (1970), an acquittal in the first prosecution might well bar litigation of certain facts essential to the second one—though a conviction in the first prosecution would not excuse the Government from proving the same facts the second time. Surely, moreover, the Government must be deterred from abusive, repeated prosecutions of a single offender for similar offenses by the sheer press of other demands upon prosecutorial and judicial resources. Finally, even if Justice Souter's fear were well founded, no double-jeopardy bar short of a same-transaction analysis will eliminate this problem; but that interpretation of the Double Jeopardy Clause has been soundly rejected, and would require overruling numerous precedents, the latest of which is barely a year old * * *.

ᵇ See, e.g., Sharpton v. Turner, 964 F.2d 1284, 1287 (CA2) (*Grady* formulation "has proven difficult to apply" and "whatever difficulties we have previously encountered in grappling with the *Grady* language have not been eased by" *Felix*); Ladner v. Smith, 941 F.2d 356, 362, 364 (C.A.5 1991) (a divided court adopts a four-part test for application of *Grady* and notes that *Grady,* "even if carefully analyzed and painstakingly administered, is not easy to apply"). * * *

I therefore join Parts I, II, and IV of the Court's opinion, and write separately to express my disagreement with Justice Scalia's application of *Blockburger* in Part III.

In my view, *Blockburger*'s same-elements test requires us to focus not on the terms of the particular court orders involved, but on the elements of contempt of court in the ordinary sense. Relying on *Harris*, a three-paragraph *per curiam* in an unargued case, Justice Scalia concludes otherwise today, and thus incorrectly finds * * * that the subsequent prosecutions of Dixon for drug distribution and of Foster for assault violated the Double Jeopardy Clause. * * * Because the generic crime of contempt of court has different elements than the substantive criminal charges in this case, I believe that they are separate offenses under *Blockburger*. I would therefore limit *Harris* to the context in which it arose: where the crimes in question are analogous to greater and lesser included offenses. The crimes at issue here bear no such resemblance.

[In *Blockburger*] we stated that two offenses are different for purposes of double jeopardy if "each *provision* requires proof of a fact which the other does not." Applying this test to the offenses at bar, it is clear that the elements of the governing contempt *provision* are entirely different from the elements of the substantive crimes. Contempt of court comprises two elements: (i) a court order made known to the defendant, followed by (ii) willful violation of that order. Neither of those elements is necessarily satisfied by proof that a defendant has committed the substantive offenses of assault or drug distribution. Likewise, no element of either of those substantive offenses is necessarily satisfied by proof that a defendant has been found guilty of contempt of court.

* * * Justice Scalia * * * concludes that *Harris* somehow requires us to look to the facts that must be proven under the particular court orders in question (rather than under the general law of criminal contempt) in determining whether contempt and the related substantive offenses are the same for double jeopardy purposes. This interpretation of *Harris* is both unprecedented and mistaken.

* * * By focusing on the facts needed to show a violation of the specific court orders involved in this case, and not on the generic elements of the crime of contempt of court, Justice Scalia's double-jeopardy analysis bears a striking resemblance to that found in *Grady*—not what one would expect in an opinion that overrules *Grady*.

* * *

The following analogy * * * helps illustrate the absurd results that Justice Scalia's *Harris/Blockburger* analysis could in theory produce. Suppose that the offense in question is failure to comply with a lawful order of a police officer, and that the police officer's order was, "Don't shoot that man." Under Justice Scalia's flawed reading of *Harris*, the elements of the offense of failure to obey a police officer's lawful order would include, for purposes of *Blockburger*'s same-elements test, the elements of, perhaps, murder or manslaughter, in effect converting those felonies into a lesser included offense of the crime of failure to comply with a lawful order of a police officer.

* * *

[The short opinion by Justice White joined by Justices Stevens and Souter, concurring in the judgment and dissenting in part, is omitted. Justice White disagreed with the Court's overruling of *Grady*.]

JUSTICE SOUTER, with whom JUSTICE STEVENS joins, concurring in the judgment in part and dissenting in part.

* * *

If a separate prosecution were permitted for every offense arising out of the same conduct, the government could manipulate the definitions of offenses, creating fine distinctions among them and permitting a zealous prosecutor to try a person again and again for essentially the same criminal conduct. * * *

* * * Whatever may have been the merits of the debate in *Grady,* the decision deserves more respect than it receives from the Court today. Although adherence to precedent is not rigidly required in constitutional cases, any departure from the doctrine of *stare decisis* demands special justification.

The search for any justification fails to reveal that *Grady*'s conclusion was either "unsound in principle," or "unworkable in practice." *Grady*'s rule is straightforward, and a departure from it is not justified by the fact that two Court of Appeals decisions have described it as difficult to apply. * * * The protection of the Double Jeopardy Clause against successive prosecutions is not so fragile that it can be avoided by finely drafted statutes and carefully planned prosecutions.

* * *

[Justice Blackmun's opinion, concurring in the judgment in part and dissenting in part, is omitted.]

QUESTION AFTER DIXON

In civil cases, the plaintiff is required by the doctrine of res judicata to join in one case all claims against a single defendant arising from the same transaction. See Restatement, Second of Judgments, § 24 (1980). Why should we demand any less of a prosecutor?

Dispute About the Blockburger Test

The Justices in *Dixon*, especially Justice Scalia and Chief Justice Rehnquist, disagree on how to apply the *Blockburger* test. In determining the elements of two crimes, do you look at the statute itself (the Rehnquist view) or to the factual allegations in the indictment, at least when the crime covers a wide range of conduct (the Scalia view)? The different approaches are discussed by the court in United States v. Liller, 999 F.2d 61 (2d Cir.1993). Liller was charged with interstate transportation of a stolen firearm, and was acquitted, apparently on the basis of his testimony that he had taken the gun from its owner in order to prevent her from committing suicide. The government then discovered that Liller had been convicted of felonies under a different name. Liller was then charged with being a felon in possession of a firearm—the same firearm that was the subject of the first prosecution. The district court dismissed the indictment, relying on *Grady*; but by the time the case reached the Second Circuit, *Dixon* had been decided. The court analyzed the double jeopardy question as follows:

> While the District Court's application of *Grady* to the facts of the pending case would present several interesting questions, the analysis after *Dixon* is straightforward. Normally we would apply *Blockburger* by examining the facts required to be proved for conviction under the provisions supporting Liller's prior and pending charges. However, in certain circumstances, including where one of the statute covers a broad range of conduct, it is appropriate under *Blockburger* to examine the allegations of the indictment rather than only the terms of the statutes. * * * [I]n *Dixon*, at least four Justices, see (Scalia, J., joined by Kennedy, J.) (White, J., joined by Stevens, J.), and perhaps five, see (Souter, J., joined by Stevens, J.), examined the content of the particular Court order violated by the defendants rather than the more general statutory elements of the criminal contempt provision under which they were charged. But see (Rehnquist, C.J., joined by O'Connor, J., and Thomas, J.).

The *Liller* court found that it did not have to decide whether the more narrow "elements" test or the broader "facts in the indictment" test of *Blockburger* was controlling:

> In this case, whether we examine only the statutes or broaden the inquiry to include the facts alleged in the indictments, Liller's offenses are separate. Only the new charge under [the felon-firearm-possession statute] requires proof that the possessor is a felon, and only the old charge * * * requires proof that the firearm was stolen and was transported interstate. Thus, each charge requires proof of a fact not required for the other. Therefore, the Double Jeopardy Clause does not bar the Government from prosecuting Liller for possession of a firearm

by a felon despite his prior prosecution for transporting the same weapon in interstate commerce knowing it was stolen.

See also United States v. Bennett, 44 F.3d 1364 (8th Cir.1995) ("[W]e note that courts are split on whether the test is to be applied by looking solely to the statutory elements of the offense, or by going beyond the statute and looking at the underlying facts or averments in the indictment" and that there is "disagreement on this issue among members of the Supreme Court").

Chief Justice Rehnquist accuses Justice Scalia of resurrecting *Grady* by employing a "facts of the indictment" approach to the *Blockburger* test. Is this a fair criticism? What is the difference between a "facts of the indictment" approach and the *Grady* "same conduct" test? Should the Court be concerned that a "statutory elements" test might allow the government to charge a defendant with violation of a broad statute in one prosecution, and violations of more narrow statutes in successive prosecutions, even though the conduct at issue is identical in all cases?

Application of Blockburger to Criminal Enterprises: Rutledge v. United States

The Court applied the *Blockburger* test to a case of conspiracy and continuing criminal enterprise in Rutledge v. United States, 517 U.S. 292 (1996). The defendant was convicted of a conspiracy to distribute controlled substances in violation of 21 U.S.C. § 846, and one count of conducting a continuing criminal enterprise (CCE) "in concert" with others in violation of 21 U.S.C. § 848. Rutledge contended that the conspiracy count was a lesser included offense of the CCE count, and that therefore he had been punished twice for the same offense. The Supreme Court agreed. Justice Stevens, writing for a unanimous Court, reasoned that the elements of conspiracy were precisely the same as the "in concert" element of CCE. Thus, proof of the CCE offense requires proof of a conspiracy that would also violate 21 U.S.C. § 846. While the CCE offense required proof of several elements other than conspiracy (such as the derivation of substantial income), the *Blockburger* test requires that *each* crime contain an element that the other does not. Accordingly, one of the defendant's convictions was unauthorized punishment, and had to be vacated.

Guilty Plea Problems Under the Blockburger Test

However the *Blockburger* test is conceived, it obviously gives the prosecution a good deal of discretion in bringing successive prosecutions on related conduct. There are a lot of criminal statutes out there, with different elements, that could cover some aspect of a defendant's pattern of criminal conduct. Professor Richman, in Bargaining About Future Jeopardy, 49 Vand. L.Rev. 1181 (1996), notes the problems created by the

Blockburger test that must be encountered by defendants who are engaged in bargaining with prosecutors.

Consider the plight of a savings and loan executive who finds herself facing a federal indictment in one district, charging her with several offenses relating to a fraudulent loan scheme. She would like to dispose of the pending charges but worries that whatever sentencing concessions she gains in exchange for her guilty plea would be effectively nullified if she were prosecuted for the other loan scams she engineered, some of which involved real estate in other federal districts. The pending indictment—and her limited knowledge of the investigation—give her no reason to think that the government knows of these other crimes. Yet she cannot be sure of what the future will hold. Should she bring the uncharged crimes to the government's attention and seek to reach a global settlement, or should she discount the value of the sentencing concessions offered on the pending indictment? If she fails to volunteer this information, to what extent would a plea agreement reached with respect to the charged counts bar the government from prosecuting on the uncharged counts?

This dilemma is not confined to the white-collar context. Consider the drug defendant charged with a single count of narcotics distribution who, upon arrest, confesses to having sold cocaine on thirty other occasions at the same street corner.

In neither case will the Double Jeopardy Clause, as currently interpreted [in *Blockburger*], be of much help.

Professor Richman concludes that because *Blockburger* provides so little in the way of protection against multiple prosecutions, defendants in the plea bargaining process may be forced to disclose information to the prosecution that they would not otherwise wish to without some corresponding concessions. He criticizes a system "that frequently works to extract private information from defendants as the price of repose."

Remedy for Multiple Prosecutions in Violation of the Double Jeopardy Clause: Morris v. Mathews

In Morris v. Mathews, 475 U.S. 237 (1986), the Court found that the defendant was not prejudiced by a double jeopardy violation in a second prosecution. The defendant pleaded guilty to aggravated robbery of a bank. Subsequently, he was charged with and convicted of aggravated murder, which was defined as causing the death of another while fleeing immediately after committing aggravated robbery. A state appellate court concluded that the Double Jeopardy Clause barred the conviction for aggravated murder under the *Vitale* decision. But the court held that the jury had properly found the defendant guilty of murder (a crime not barred by the Double Jeopardy Clause), and it reduced his sentence accordingly.

Justice White's opinion for the Court reasoned that "when a jeopardy-barred conviction is reduced to a conviction for a lesser included offense which is not jeopardy-barred, the burden shifts to the defendant to demonstrate a reasonable probability that he would not have been convicted of the non-jeopardy-barred offense absent the presence of the jeopardy-barred offense."[2] He added that "[t]o prevail in a case like this, the defendant must show that, but for the improper inclusion of the jeopardy-barred charge, the result of the proceeding would have been different." The Court remanded the case for a determination of whether the result would have been different if the defendant had been tried only on the lesser offense.

Justice Blackmun, joined by Justice Powell, concurred in the judgment. He argued that the usual harmless error test should apply and that reversal should be required unless the error was harmless beyond a reasonable doubt.

Justice Brennan dissented. He agreed with Justice Blackmun's argument that the harmless error test should apply, but found the error not harmless beyond a reasonable doubt. Justice Marshall also agreed that the harmless error test should apply, and argued that the court of appeals properly found the error to be prejudicial.

B. DEFENSE RESPONSIBILITY FOR MULTIPLE TRIALS

Opposing Joinder of Charges: Jeffers v. United States

The constitutional limitation on multiple prosecutions does not apply if the defendant is responsible for the multiplicity. In Jeffers v. United States, 432 U.S. 137 (1977), the defendant was charged with conspiracy to distribute drugs and with engaging in a continuing criminal enterprise to violate the drug laws. Jeffers opposed a government motion to consolidate the indictments. He moved for a severance, arguing that he would be prejudiced by joinder because much of the evidence that would be admitted against him on the conspiracy charge would be inadmissible in his trial for conducting a continuing criminal enterprise. The trial court granted a severance and he was tried on the conspiracy charge. Jenkins maintained that his subsequent prosecution for engaging in a continuing criminal enterprise violated the Double Jeopardy Clause because the conspiracy charge was a lesser included offense. The Supreme Court rejected the claim (prior to the Court's decision in *Rutledge, supra*).

---

[2]   He cited *Strickland v. Washington,* an ineffective assistance of counsel case, discussed in connection with Chapter 10. Justice White explained that a reasonable probability is one that is "sufficient to undermine confidence in the outcome."

In this case, trial together of the conspiracy and continuing criminal enterprise charges could have taken place without undue prejudice to petitioner's Sixth Amendment right to a fair trial. * * * Nevertheless, petitioner did not adopt that course. Instead, he was solely responsible for the successive prosecutions for the conspiracy offense and the continuing-criminal-enterprise offense. Under the circumstances, we hold that his action deprived him of any right that he might have had against consecutive trials.

Guilty Plea to a Lesser Offense over Government Objection: Ohio v. Johnson

If a trial judge accepts a guilty plea to a lesser offense over the objection of a prosecutor who seeks to convict on a greater offense, the fact that the trial judge dismisses the greater charges does not bar reprosecution on those charges. So the Supreme Court held in Ohio v. Johnson, 467 U.S. 493 (1984).

Johnson was charged with four offenses, including murder. He offered to plead guilty to involuntary manslaughter and grand theft, but not to murder and aggravated robbery. The trial judge accepted his offer and dismissed the remaining charges on the ground that to prosecute him on these charges would place him in jeopardy twice. The prosecutor objected to this procedure and appealed from the dismissals. The Supreme Court, in an opinion by Justice Rehnquist, rejected the claim that the Constitution barred a trial on the more serious charges. It was the defendant who made the choice, over government objection, to split the offenses. For an analysis of the problems created by Ohio v. Johnson, see Ohio v. Johnson: Prohibiting the Offensive Use of Guilty Pleas to Invoke Double Jeopardy Protection, 19 Ga.L.Rev. 159 (1984).

C. SUBSEQUENT DEVELOPMENTS AND JEOPARDY

Continuing Violations: Garrett v. United States

In Garrett v. United States, 471 U.S. 773 (1985), the Court held that a defendant who had pleaded guilty to importing marijuana could be prosecuted thereafter and punished for engaging in a "continuing criminal enterprise," even though the marijuana importation to which he had pleaded was used as evidence of the enterprise. The enterprise charged had not been completed when the defendant was indicted for importing marijuana. The Court stated that "one who insists that the music stop and the piper be paid at a particular point must at least have stopped dancing himself before he may seek such an accounting." See also United States v. Paternostro, 966 F.2d 907 (5th Cir.1992) (permissible to bring multiple prosecutions for violating the terms of a Corps of Engineers use permit, because the defendant continued to violate the terms after his conviction, and thus the violation was a continuing one; citing *Garrett*, the court stated that "[i]n this case, Paternostro has not stopped dancing").

Post-Charge Changes of Fact

In Diaz v. United States, 223 U.S. 442 (1912), the defendant was convicted of assault and battery. Then his victim died. He was then tried for homicide, and moved to dismiss the charges on double jeopardy grounds. But the Court held that the homicide prosecution was permissible, because the government could not possibly have brought homicide charges in the original prosecution.

D. SENTENCING ENHANCEMENTS AND SUBSEQUENT PROSECUTION

If criminal conduct is used to enhance a sentence, can that same conduct be charged in a subsequent prosecution? This question was addressed by the Court in Witte v. United States, 515 U.S. 389 (1995). After Witte pleaded guilty to a federal marijuana charge, a presentence report calculated the base offense level under the Sentencing Guidelines by aggregating the total quantity of drugs involved not only in Witte's offense of conviction but also in uncharged cocaine transactions in which he had engaged with several coconspirators. Under the Sentencing Guidelines, the sentencing range for a particular offense is determined on the basis of all "relevant conduct" in which the defendant was engaged, not just the conduct underlying the offense of conviction. See Sentencing Guidelines, § 1B1.3; see also the discussion in Chapter 11. Witte's resulting sentencing range on the marijuana offense was higher than it would have been if only the drugs involved in his conviction had been considered, but it still fell within the scope of the legislatively authorized penalty. The district court accepted the presentence report's calculation in sentencing Witte, concluding that the other offenses were part of a continuing conspiracy that should be taken into account under the Guidelines as "relevant conduct." When Witte was subsequently indicted for conspiring and attempting to import cocaine, he moved to dismiss the charges, arguing that he had already been punished for those offenses because that cocaine had been considered as "relevant conduct" at his marijuana sentencing.

The Supreme Court, in an opinion by Justice O'Connor, held that the Double Jeopardy Clause would not prevent prosecution of Witte for the subsequently charged cocaine offenses, because he had not been *prosecuted* for those offenses previously. The prior sentence was imposed only for the marijuana offense for which Witte was convicted. Consideration of uncharged relevant conduct was not prosecution for that conduct, but rather a basis for "a stiffened penalty for the [charged] crime, which is considered to be an aggravated offense because a repetitive one."

Justice Stevens dissented in *Witte*. He argued that from the defendant's point of view, it was clear that he was being punished twice for the relevant conduct used to enhance his sentence on the marijuana conviction.

VI. MULTIPLE PUNISHMENTS IN A SINGLE CASE

A. PROHIBITION ON TWO PUNISHMENTS WHEN ONLY ONE IS AUTHORIZED

So far we have considered the application of the Double Jeopardy Clause to multiple actions brought against the defendant for the "same offence." Another line of cases indicates that the Double Jeopardy Clause has some relevance when the defendant is subject to multiple *punishments* for the same offense *in a single case*. However, if there is no multiple prosecution, only multiple punishment, the reach of the Double Jeopardy Clause is limited—the Clause does not *prohibit* the legislature from imposing multiple punishments in a single case. Rather, it prohibits the prosecution from charging and the *court* from sentencing a defendant to multiple punishments in the absence of statutory authorization.

The limitations on multiple punishments in a single case were first explored by the Court in Ex parte Lange, 85 U.S. (18 Wall.) 163 (1873). Lange was sentenced to both a fine and imprisonment for the same conduct. After Lange fully paid the fine, the judge realized that the statute allowed only a fine *or* imprisonment. He vacated the sentence and imposed a new sentence of imprisonment. But since the defendant had suffered complete punishment for the crime by paying the fine, the Supreme Court held that no further punishment could be imposed. To do so would be outside the punishment authorized by the legislature. Thus the Double Jeopardy Clause in this context works as a means of keeping sentencing courts within the range authorized by the legislature.

The Court distinguished *Lange* in Jones v. Thomas, 491 U.S. 376 (1989). Thomas had been convicted of attempted robbery and of first-degree felony murder for a killing during the commission of a felony and was sentenced to 15 years and life respectively, with the 15 years to be served first. He sought state postconviction relief, arguing that the legislature did not authorize separate punishment for the enhanced murder and the underlying felony. After the state supreme court accepted this argument in another case, the Governor commuted Thomas's sentence, and he remained in custody pursuant to the murder conviction with credit for the time served on the underlying felony. The Supreme Court held that the Double

Jeopardy Clause did not require that Thomas be released simply because he had completed his sentence on the underlying felony offense.

Justice Kennedy wrote for the Court and acknowledged that the Double Jeopardy Clause protects against "additions to a sentence in a subsequent proceeding that upset a defendant's legitimate expectation of finality." He nonetheless concluded that the state had properly cured the double jeopardy problem, because the defendant was, in effect, being subject to a single prison sentence (for the murder) that was authorized by the legislature. He distinguished *Lange* as involving more punishment than the legislature authorized. Justice Scalia, joined by Justices Stevens, Brennan and Marshall, dissented.

B. LEGISLATIVE INTENT TO IMPOSE MULTIPLE PUNISHMENTS FOR THE SAME OFFENSE

The protection against multiple punishments in a single case is directed against prosecutors and trial courts, not against legislators. If a legislature decides that it wants a robber or burglar to serve twice as much time for an offense, it can increase the maximum sentence (and raise the minimum also, if necessary)—subject to the Eighth Amendment's almost-nonexistent proportionality requirements. But a prosecutor who wants someone to serve more time than the legislature has prescribed may try to join multiple charges for the same offense.

Generally, a legislature that establishes a hierarchy of lesser and greater offenses increases the punishment for each greater offense. The increased punishment represents punishment for the additional elements that distinguish the greater from the lesser offense. For example, if the legislature imposes a five year sentence for robbery and a ten year sentence for armed robbery, it can reasonably be assumed that the armed robbery penalty includes the robbery penalty, and adds on five years for the use of a weapon. Courts properly assume that prosecutors and trial courts cannot add together sentences for greater and lesser offenses, because to do so would constitute double-counting.

While there is a presumption that the legislature did not intend multiple punishment for the same conduct, the Supreme Court has emphasized that a legislature may provide separate, cumulative penalties for the same offense if it wishes to do so. It is a matter of legislative intent.

Felony Murder and the Underlying Felony: Whalen v. United States

In Whalen v. United States, 445 U.S. 684 (1980), Justice Stewart's opinion for the Court held that the federal defendant was improperly sentenced when he was given one sentence for felony (first-degree) murder and another for the underlying offense of rape. Justice Stewart found that

Congress had not authorized multiple sentences for these crimes. He stated that "[t]he Double Jeopardy Clause at the very least precludes federal courts from imposing consecutive sentences unless authorized by Congress to do so. * * * If a federal court exceeds its own authority by imposing multiple punishments not authorized by Congress, it violates not only the specific guarantee against double jeopardy, but also the constitutional principle of separation of powers in a manner that trenches particularly harshly on individual liberty." Separate opinions by Justice Blackmun and Justice White emphasized that their votes turned solely on the intent of Congress, not on double jeopardy principles—though that is really the same thing in this branch of Double Jeopardy law. Justice Rehnquist dissented and was joined by Chief Justice Burger.

Conspiracy to Import and Conspiracy to Distribute: Albernaz v. United States

In Albernaz v. United States, 450 U.S. 333 (1981), the defendants received consecutive sentences for conspiracy to import and conspiracy to distribute marijuana. Both convictions were under the Comprehensive Drug Abuse and Control Act of 1970. The lower court focused on Congressional intent and found no double jeopardy problem, reasoning that "the Double Jeopardy Clause imposes no limits on Congress' power to define the allowable unit of prosecution and punishment, at least so long as all charges are brought in a single proceeding." The Supreme Court affirmed this analysis, saying that "the question of what punishments are constitutionally permissible is not different from the question of what punishment the Legislative Branch intended to be imposed." Justice Stewart, joined by Justices Marshall and Stevens, concurred in the judgment.

Overcoming the Presumption That Multiple Punishments for the Same Offense Are Not Intended: Missouri v. Hunter

In the context of multiple punishments in a single prosecution (as opposed to multiple prosecutions in cases like *Dixon*), the *Blockburger* test has been used by the Court as a tool to divine legislative intent. As discussed above, the *Blockburger* test provides that offenses are separate if each contains an element that the other does not. If two offenses not the same under this test, the Court indulges a *presumption* that the legislature did not intend for multiple punishments to be imposed. However, the Court in Missouri v. Hunter, 459 U.S. 359 (1983), held that *Blockburger* is, in this context, merely a rule of statutory construction—the presumption can be overcome by a clear showing that the legislature in fact intended multiple punishments. The Court stated that where "a legislature specifically authorizes cumulative punishments under two statutes, regardless of whether those two statutes proscribe the same conduct under *Blockburger,* a court's task of statutory construction is at an end" and cumulative punishments can be imposed so long as it is done in a single trial.

Hunter was convicted of first degree robbery of a grocery store (which meant that he used a deadly weapon in the robbery) and also of armed criminal action (which meant that he committed a felony with a deadly weapon). The lower court held that the state legislature intended to provide two punishments for what it found to be the same offense. Writing for the majority, Chief Justice Burger observed that Hunter had not been subjected to two trials, only to two punishments. He reasoned that there is nothing in the Double Jeopardy Clause to prohibit a state from punishing conduct by means of cumulative statutes, and that it was clear that the legislature intended to do so in this case. Justice Marshall, joined by Justice Stevens, dissented. The dissent argued that where multiple charges for the same conduct are brought, the prosecution obtains an unfair advantage because a jury is more likely to convict on one count, even as a compromise; that several convictions, rather than one, mean greater collateral consequences for the defendant; and that the stigma resulting from more than one conviction for the same conduct would be excessive.

Charged with Two, Sentenced for One: Ball v. United States

Chief Justice Burger wrote for the Court in Ball v. United States, 470 U.S. 856 (1985), as it found that Congress did not intend that a felon could be convicted and concurrently sentenced for both receiving a firearm and possessing it in violation of federal law. The Court concluded, however, that a defendant could be *charged* with two of the same offenses in a single prosecution. Should the defendant be found guilty of both, the trial judge could solve the double jeopardy problem by entering a judgment as to only one offense. Justice Stevens concurred in the judgment. He suggested that the Court correctly held that the defendant's conduct supported a conviction under either statute but not both, but it was unnecessary for the Court to decide whether a defendant could be charged with the two offenses as long as he was convicted of only one. He added that "I see no reason why this Court should go out of its way to encourage prosecutors to tilt the scales of justice against the defendant by employing such tactics." Justice Stevens relied upon Justice Marshall's dissent in *Hunter.*

VII.   DOUBLE JEOPARDY AND SENTENCING

A. GOVERNMENT APPEALS OF SENTENCES

Seeking a Harsher Sentence: United States v. DiFrancesco

Justice Blackmun wrote for the majority in United States v. DiFrancesco, 449 U.S. 117 (1980), upholding the government's right to appeal the *sentence* imposed upon a "dangerous special offender." The majority said that the prohibition against multiple *trials* is the controlling constitutional principle in double jeopardy cases and that the prohibition on appellate review of acquittals is based on the fact that a second trial is necessary if relief is granted. In contrast, appellate review of sentencing need not require a second trial. Moreover, the majority noted that "the pronouncement of sentence has never carried the finality that attaches to an acquittal." The Court also observed that the defendant is not subjected to multiple sentences when resentenced following an appeal, because the defendant understands that an initial sentence is not final. Justice Brennan, joined by Justices White, Marshall, and Stevens, dissented and argued that "most defendants are more concerned with how much time they must spend in prison than with whether their record shows a conviction" and that the anxiety associated with multiple trials is equally present when the government can take an appeal from sentencing. Justice Stevens also filed a separate dissent.

B. CAPITAL SENTENCES

Death Is Different: Bullington v. Missouri

The Supreme Court distinguished *DiFrancesco* in Bullington v. Missouri, 451 U.S. 430 (1981), and held that it would violate the Double Jeopardy Clause to impose a death penalty at a second trial when the jury in the first trial in which the prosecution had the burden in the separate sentencing proceeding of proving certain elements beyond a reasonable doubt returned a verdict of life imprisonment. The Court noted that the capital sentencing procedure was more like a trial on guilt or innocence than are most sentencing proceedings and that the prior jury determination was tantamount to an acquittal on the death sentence. Four dissenters argued that the purpose of double jeopardy protection is to protect the innocent from wrongful conviction and that sentencing procedures present no danger of convicting the innocent.

Trial Court Error in Favor of the Defendant:
Arizona v. Rumsey

Bullington proved to be controlling in Arizona v. Rumsey, 467 U.S. 203 (1984), as the Supreme Court held that a state judge's erroneous finding that there were no aggravating factors warranting capital punishment had the same effect as an "acquittal"—so the state supreme court violated the Double Jeopardy Clause when it remanded a defendant's case back for resentencing and a death sentence was then imposed. Like Missouri, Arizona placed on the prosecution the burden of proving aggravating circumstances beyond a reasonable doubt. The Court declined to distinguish the jury findings in Bullington's case from the Arizona judge's findings in *Rumsey*. Even though the state supreme court held that the trial judge had erred as a matter of law in construing one of the statutory aggravating circumstances and thus prejudiced the government, the Supreme Court held that "[r]eliance on an error of law * * * does not change the double jeopardy effects of a judgment that amounts to an acquittal on the merits." Justice O'Connor wrote for the Court. Justice Rehnquist dissented and was joined by Justice White.

Review of Individual Issues After a Death Sentence
Is Imposed: Poland v. Arizona

The Supreme Court distinguished *Bullington* and *Rumsey* in Poland v. Arizona, 476 U.S. 147 (1986). The defendants were convicted of robbing a bank van and killing its guards. The trial court, making the same error as in *Rumsey*, found that the offense was not committed for "pecuniary gain," because the statutory aggravating circumstance applied only to contract killings. But, the court found that the crime was committed in "an especially heinous" manner, which was a specified aggravating circumstance, and imposed death sentences. On appeal, the state supreme court, reversing and remanding on another ground, held both that there was insufficient evidence of heinousness and that the trial judge erred in ruling that the crime was not for pecuniary gain under the statute.

Justice White's majority opinion found that both *Bullington* and *Rumsey* involved the equivalent of acquittals during sentencing, while there was no finding in the instant case that the prosecution failed to prove its case. The Court rejected the argument that a capital sentencer's failure to find a particular aggravating circumstance constitutes an acquittal of that circumstance for double jeopardy purposes and held instead that the proper inquiry is whether the sentencer or reviewing court has decided that the prosecution has failed to prove that death is an appropriate sentence. Thus, the Court ruled that the state supreme court acted properly in reviewing the "pecuniary gain" ruling by the trial judge and in permitting the judge to consider this aggravating circumstance once again upon retrial.

Justice Marshall, joined by Justices Brennan and Blackmun, dissented and argued that the only difference between this case and *Rumsey* was that the sentencing judge made two errors of state law while the *Rumsey* judge made only one. The dissent reasoned that the state supreme court effectively held that the defendants were entitled to acquittals on the only aggravating circumstance that the trial court found to have been validly proved.

Capital Sentencing Proceeding Is Not a Successive Prosecution: Schiro v. Farley

The Court once again distinguished *Bullington* in Schiro v. Farley, 510 U.S. 222 (1994). Schiro admitted to raping and killing a woman and was subsequently charged in separate counts with intentional murder and felony murder. The State sought the death penalty for the felony murder count. The State of Indiana, where Schiro was tried, does not require a showing of intent to kill for felony murder. The jury was given verdict forms for both charges and found Schiro guilty of felony murder, but not intentional murder. The trial judge at the capital phase nonetheless sentenced Schiro to death on the basis of the aggravating circumstance that Schiro had "intentionally" murdered his victim. In the Supreme Court, Schiro argued that imposing the death sentence, on the basis of the intentional murder aggravating circumstance, violated the Double Jeopardy Clause. He reasoned that the sentencing proceeding became a successive prosecution for intentional murder, in light of the jury's failure to find an intent to kill at trial.

Justice O'Connor, writing for seven members of the Court, rejected Schiro's argument and concluded that an initial sentencing proceeding cannot constitute a successive prosecution for purposes of the Double Jeopardy Clause. She distinguished *Bullington* as follows:

> In *Bullington* we recognized the general rule that "the Double Jeopardy Clause imposes no absolute prohibition against the imposition of a harsher sentence at retrial." Nonetheless, we recognized a narrow exception to this general principle because the capital sentencing scheme at issue "differed significantly from those employed in any of the Court's cases where the Double Jeopardy Clause has been held inapplicable to sentencing." Because the capital sentencing proceeding "was itself a trial on the issue of punishment," requiring a defendant to submit to a second, identical proceeding was tantamount to permitting a second prosecution of an acquitted defendant.

This case is manifestly different. Neither the prohibition against a successive trial on the issue of guilt, nor the *Bullington* prohibition against a second capital sentencing proceeding, is implicated here— the State did not reprosecute Schiro for intentional murder, nor did it force him to submit to a second death penalty hearing. It simply conducted a single sentencing hearing in the course of a single prosecution. The state is entitled to "one fair opportunity" to prosecute a defendant, and that opportunity extends not only to prosecution at the guilt phase, but also to present evidence at an ensuing sentencing proceeding.

Justice Blackmun, in dissent, argued that the "sentencing proceeding at issue here is indistinguishable from that confronted in *Bullington*." Justice Stevens wrote a separate dissent in which Justice Blackmun joined.

Jury Deadlock on the Death Penalty and Death Penalty Imposed on a Retrial: Sattazahn v. Pennsylvania

The Court applied its *Bullington-Rumsey* line of cases in Sattazahn v. Pennsylvania, 537 U.S. 101 (2003), and found that the state could permissibly impose the death penalty on a retrial, after the defendant appealed a conviction in which life imprisonment was imposed. The jury at Sattazahn's first trial convicted him of first degree murder but then deadlocked on the death penalty. Under Pennsylvania law, if the jury deadlocks on a penalty of death, the judge must sentence the defendant to life imprisonment. Sattazahn appealed his conviction, alleging that the jury in the guilt phase had received improper instructions on certain matters. The state court agreed with Sattazahn, reversing his conviction and remanding. On retrial, the defendant was found guilty; the state again sought the death penalty, and this time (in part based on facts not presented previously) the jury unanimously agreed on a death sentence.

Justice Scalia, joined by Chief Justice Rehnquist and Justice Thomas, and in most respects by Justice O'Connor and Justice Kennedy, reasoned that Satterzahn's double jeopardy rights were not violated because he had never been "acquitted" of a death sentence. Justice Scalia addressed the defendant's argument that a jury deadlock should trigger double jeopardy protection in the death penalty context:

> Under the *Bullington* line of cases * * *, the touchstone for double-jeopardy protection in capital-sentencing proceedings is whether there has been an "acquittal." Petitioner here cannot establish that the jury or the court "acquitted" him during his first capital-sentencing proceeding. As to the jury: The verdict form returned by the foreman stated that the jury deadlocked 9-to-3 on whether to impose the death penalty; it made no findings with respect to the alleged aggravating circumstance. That result—or more appropriately, that non-result—

cannot fairly be called an acquittal "based on findings sufficient to establish legal entitlement to the life sentence." *Rumsey.*

The entry of a life sentence by the judge was not "acquittal," either. Justice Scalia noted that under the Pennsylvania's sentencing scheme, the court has no discretion once it finds that the jury is deadlocked. The court makes no factual findings, it must enter a life sentence. Justice Scalia concluded that a "default judgment does not trigger a double jeopardy bar to the death penalty upon retrial."

Justice Ginsburg, joined by Justices Stevens, Souter and Breyer, dissented. She argued that the policies of the Double Jeopardy Clause are at stake when the defendant is sentenced to life imprisonment rather than death and is then subject to the death penalty on retrial. She explained as follows:

> I would decide the double jeopardy issue in Sattazahn's favor [because the] Court's holding confronts defendants with a perilous choice * * *. Under the Court's decision, if a defendant sentenced to life after a jury deadlock chooses to appeal her underlying conviction, she faces the possibility of death if she is successful on appeal but convicted on retrial. If, on the other hand, the defendant loses her appeal, or chooses to forgo an appeal, the final judgment for life stands. In other words, a defendant in Sattazahn's position must relinquish either her right to file a potentially meritorious appeal, or her state-granted entitlement to avoid the death penalty.

C. RESENTENCING FOLLOWING PARTIAL REVERSAL

The Supreme Court cited *DiFrancesco* in its per curiam opinion in Pennsylvania v. Goldhammer, 474 U.S. 28 (1985), which held that the Double Jeopardy Clause did not prevent a state court from resentencing a defendant after some of his convictions had been overturned on appeal. Goldhammer had been convicted on 56 counts of forgery and 56 counts of theft, but he was sentenced to 2–5 years on a single theft count and five years of probation on a single forgery count with sentence on all other counts suspended. The state supreme court overturned 34 of the theft convictions, including the one count on which Goldhammer had been sentenced to prison, because the statute of limitations had run. The Supreme Court remanded the case for a determination of whether state law permitted resentencing.

VIII. COLLATERAL ESTOPPEL

Closely related to the double jeopardy prohibition against retrial after an acquittal is the bar to relitigation of any ultimate fact determined in favor of the defendant in a prior prosecution. In the following case—which holds that the rule of collateral estoppel is a constitutional requirement of the Double Jeopardy Clause—note what the prosecutor was trying to do.

ASHE V. SWENSON

Supreme Court of the United States, 1970.
397 U.S. 436.

JUSTICE STEWART delivered the opinion of the Court.

* * *

Sometime in the early hours of the morning of January 10, 1960, six men were engaged in a poker game in the basement of the home of John Gladson at Lee's Summit, Missouri. Suddenly three or four masked men, armed with a shotgun and pistols, broke into the basement and robbed each of the poker players of money and various articles of personal property. The robbers—and it has never been clear whether there were three or four of them—then fled in a car belonging to one of the victims of the robbery. Shortly thereafter the stolen car was discovered in a field, and later that morning three men were arrested by a state trooper while they were walking on a highway not far from where the abandoned car had been found. The petitioner was arrested by another officer some distance away.

The four were subsequently charged with seven separate offenses—the armed robbery of each of the six poker players and the theft of the car. In May 1960 the petitioner went to trial on the charge of robbing Donald Knight, one of the participants in the poker game. At the trial the State called Knight and three of his fellow poker players as prosecution witnesses. Each of them described the circumstances of the holdup and itemized his own individual losses. The proof that an armed robbery had occurred and that personal property had been taken from Knight as well as from each of the others was unassailable. * * * But the State's evidence that the petitioner had been one of the robbers was weak. Two of the witnesses thought that there had been only three robbers altogether, and could not identify the petitioner as one of them. Another of the victims, who was the petitioner's uncle by marriage, said that at the "patrol station" he had positively identified each of the other three men accused of the holdup, but could say only that the petitioner's voice "sounded very much like" that of one of the robbers. The fourth participant in the poker game did identify the petitioner, but only by his "size and height, and his actions."

The cross-examination of these witnesses was brief, and it was aimed primarily at exposing the weakness of their identification testimony. Defense counsel made no attempt to question their testimony regarding the holdup itself or their claims as to their losses. * * *

The trial judge instructed the jury that if it found that the petitioner was one of the participants in the armed robbery, the theft of "any money" from Knight would sustain a conviction. He also instructed the jury that if the petitioner was one of the robbers, he was guilty under the law even if he had not personally robbed Knight. The jury—though not instructed to elaborate upon its verdict—found the petitioner "not guilty due to insufficient evidence."

Six weeks later the petitioner was brought to trial again, this time for the robbery of another participant in the poker game, a man named Roberts. The petitioner filed a motion to dismiss, based on his previous acquittal. The motion was overruled, and the second trial began. The witnesses were for the most part the same, though this time their testimony was substantially stronger on the issue of the petitioner's identity. For example, two witnesses who at the first trial had been wholly unable to identify the petitioner as one of the robbers, now testified that his features, size, and mannerisms matched those of one of their assailants. Another witness who before had identified the petitioner only by his size and actions now also remembered him by the unusual sound of his voice. The State further refined its case at the second trial by declining to call one of the participants in the poker game whose identification testimony at the first trial had been conspicuously negative. The case went to the jury on instructions virtually identical to those given at the first trial. This time the jury found the petitioner guilty, and he was sentenced to a 35-year term in the state penitentiary.

* * *

"Collateral estoppel" is an awkward phrase, but it stands for an extremely important principle in our adversary system of justice. It means simply that when an issue of ultimate fact has once been determined by a valid and final judgment, that issue cannot again be litigated between the same parties in any future lawsuit. * * *

The federal decisions have made clear that the rule of collateral estoppel in criminal cases is not to be applied with the hypertechnical and archaic approach of a 19th century pleading book, but with realism and rationality. Where a previous judgment of acquittal was based upon a general verdict, as is usually the case, this approach requires a court to "examine the record of a prior proceeding, taking into account the pleadings, evidence, charge, and other relevant matter, and conclude whether a rational jury could have grounded its verdict upon an issue other than that which the defendant seeks to foreclose from consideration." * * * Any test more technically restrictive would, of course, simply amount to a rejection of the rule of collateral estoppel in criminal proceedings, at least in every case where the first judgment was based upon a general verdict of acquittal.

Straightforward application of the federal rule to the present case can lead to but one conclusion. For the record is utterly devoid of any indication that the first jury could rationally have found that an armed robbery had not occurred, or that Knight had not been a victim of that robbery. The single rationally conceivable issue in dispute before the jury was whether the petitioner had been one of the robbers. And the jury by its verdict found that he had not. The federal rule of law, therefore, would make a second prosecution for the robbery of Roberts wholly impermissible.

The ultimate question to be determined, then, is whether this established rule of federal law is embodied in the Fifth Amendment guarantee against double jeopardy. We do not hesitate to hold that it is. For whatever else that constitutional guarantee may embrace, it surely protects a man who has been acquitted from having to "run the gantlet" a second time.

The question is not whether Missouri could validly charge the petitioner with six separate offenses for the robbery of the six poker players. It is not whether he could have received a total of six punishments if he had been convicted in a single trial of robbing the six victims. It is simply whether, after a jury determined by its verdict that the petitioner was not one of the robbers, the State could constitutionally hale him before a new jury to litigate that issue again.

After the first jury had acquitted the petitioner of robbing Knight, Missouri could certainly not have brought him to trial again upon that charge. * * * The situation is constitutionally no different here, even though the second trial related to another victim of the same robbery. For the name of the victim, in the circumstances of this case, had no bearing whatever upon the issue of whether the petitioner was one of the robbers.

In this case the State in its brief has frankly conceded that following the petitioner's acquittal, it treated the first trial as no more than a dry run for the second prosecution: "No doubt the prosecutor felt the state had a provable case on the first charge and, when he lost, he did what every good attorney would do—he refined his presentation in light of the turn of events at the first trial." But this is precisely what the constitutional guarantee forbids.

[The concurring opinions by Justice Black (joined by Justice Harlan), and by Justice Brennan (joined by Justices Douglas and Marshall), are omitted, as is the dissenting opinion by Chief Justice Burger.]

The Problem of General Verdicts

Ashe provides some protection for a defendant who is acquitted and then subject to prosecution on a crime that is related, but not the "same offence." However, collateral estoppel (or, more descriptively, issue preclusion) applies only to facts that were actually and necessarily decided by the jury in the defendant's favor. Juries usually return general verdicts in criminal cases. The defense of collateral estoppel may not be available because any number of issues might have been the basis for the acquittal; what issues the jury necessarily decided often cannot be determined.

The Court in *Ashe* suggests a functional approach to determine what the jury decided. An example of that approach is found in Wright v. Whitley, 11 F.3d 542 (5th Cir.1994). Wright was charged with a firearm offense based on an alleged gunfight in which he participated in March 1986. He testified that he was unarmed, and presented corroborating witnesses. The jury acquitted. Subsequently, Wright was indicted for a triple murder by firearm, occurring in May 1986. The court held that the first acquittal had no preclusive effect on any issue in the second prosecution. The fact that Wright was unarmed in one conflagration was not determinative of whether he possessed a firearm two months later. Compare United States v. Seley, 957 F.2d 717 (9th Cir.1992), where the defendant was acquitted of knowingly importing marijuana across the border. The court held that the government was precluded from proving in a subsequent prosecution that the defendant was involved in a conspiracy to import that same marijuana.

Application of Ashe When There Is an Acquittal on Some Counts and a Deadlock on Others: Yeager v. United States

In Yeager v. United States, 557 U.S. 10 (2009), the defendant, a former Enron executive, was charged with a number of counts of fraud and a number of counts of insider trading. The theory of prosecution was that Yeager had deceived the public about an Enron project in order to inflate the value of Enron stock, and then sold his own stock on the basis of inside information. At his trial, the jury acquitted him of the fraud counts but hung on the insider trading counts. The government sought to reprosecute him on the insider trading counts and the defendant, citing *Ashe,* argued that the government was collaterally estopped due to the acquittal on the fraud counts. He argued that the jury by acquitting him of fraud had necessarily decided that he did not possess material inside information. The Court of Appeals disagreed. It reasoned that if the jury had actually found that he had no inside information, then it would not have hung on the insider trading counts. Since the jury hung, it could not be concluded that they necessarily found that the defendant had no inside information.

The question for the Supreme Court was whether a hung verdict is relevant to a court's determination of what was actually decided when the defendant was acquitted on other charges. The Court, in an opinion by Justice Stevens, found that a juror deadlock on a count could not be considered in the collateral estoppel analysis. Justice Stevens reasoned as follows:

A hung count is not a relevant part of the record of the prior proceeding. Because a jury speaks only through its verdict, its failure to reach a verdict cannot—by negative implication—yield a piece of information that helps put together the trial puzzle. * * * A host of reasons—sharp disagreement, confusion about the issues, exhaustion after a long trial, to name but a few—could work alone or in tandem to cause a jury to hang. To ascribe meaning to a hung count would presume an ability to identify which factor was at play in the jury room. But that is not reasoned analysis; it is guesswork. Such conjecture about possible reasons for a jury's failure to reach a decision should play no part in assessing the legal consequences of a unanimous verdict that the jurors did return.

A contrary conclusion would require speculation into what transpired in the jury room. Courts properly avoid such explorations into the jury's sovereign space, and for good reason. The jury's deliberations are secret and not subject to outside examination. If there is to be an inquiry into what the jury decided, the evidence should be confined to the points in controversy on the former trial, to the testimony given by the parties, and to the questions submitted to the jury for their consideration.

Accordingly, we hold that the consideration of hung counts has no place in the issue-preclusion analysis. Indeed, if it were relevant, the fact that petitioner has already survived one trial should be a factor cutting in favor of, rather than against, applying a double jeopardy bar. * * * Thus, if the possession of insider information was a critical issue of ultimate fact in all of the charges against petitioner, a jury verdict that necessarily decided that issue in his favor protects him from prosecution for any charge for which that is an essential element.

The Court remanded for a determination of whether the acquittal on the fraud charges was preclusive on the factual issues contested on the insider trading charges.

Justice Scalia, joined by Justices Thomas and Alito, dissented. He first criticized *Ashe* as improperly extending Double Jeopardy protection beyond its historic origins:

This case would be easy indeed if our cases had adhered to the Clause's original meaning. The English common-law pleas of auterfoits acquit and auterfoits convict, on which the Clause was based, barred only repeated "prosecution for the same identical act and crime." As described by Sir Matthew Hale, "a man acquitted for stealing [a] horse" could be later "arraigned and convict[ed] for stealing the saddle, tho both were done at the same time." Under the common-law pleas, the jury's acquittal of Yeager on the fraud counts would have posed no bar to further prosecution for the distinct crimes of insider trading and money laundering.

* * * In *Ashe* the Court departed from the original meaning of the Double Jeopardy Clause, holding that it precludes successive prosecutions on distinct crimes when facts essential to conviction of the second crime have necessarily been resolved in the defendant's favor by a verdict of acquittal of the first crime.

Justice Scalia argued that even under *Ashe,* there was no clear determination that precluded retrial on the insider trading counts:

> There is no clear, unanimous jury finding here. In the unusual situation in which a factual finding upon which an acquittal must have been based would also logically require an acquittal on the hung count, all that can be said for certain is that the conflicting dispositions are irrational—the result of mistake, compromise, or lenity. It is at least as likely that the irrationality consisted of failing to make the factual finding necessary to support the acquittal as it is that the irrationality consisted of failing to adhere to that factual finding with respect to the hung count.

Justice Alito wrote a separate dissenting opinion joined by Justices Scalia and Thomas.

Identity of Party Requirement

Only a party to the prior criminal proceeding may take advantage of the issue preclusion rule against the government in criminal cases. A unanimous Court in Standefer v. United States, 447 U.S. 10 (1980), held that a defendant accused of aiding and abetting the commission of a federal offense may be convicted after the named principal has been acquitted of that offense. Chief Justice Burger's opinion rejected the attempt to extend the concept of "nonmutual collateral estoppel," developed in civil cases, into constitutional criminal procedure. Among the special attributes of criminal cases relied upon were the following: the government's limited discovery rights; the impossibility of a directed verdict for the government; the limitations on the government's right to appeal; the existence of exclusionary rules that may exclude evidence as to one defendant but not another; and the government's interest in enforcement of the criminal law.

Non-parties cannot be bound by a prior adjudication of facts. See Vestal, Issue Preclusion and Criminal Prosecutions, 65 Iowa L.Rev. 281 (1980). So, for example, the suppression of evidence in a state prosecution does not automatically prevent the United States from using that evidence in a federal proceeding against the same defendant. "Since the United States was not a party to the state action, and had no way of making its views on the issue known to the state judge, it cannot be fairly considered to have had its day in court." United States v. Davis, 906 F.2d 829 (2d Cir.1990). The same principles would apply to a subsequent prosecution in a different state.

Issue Preclusion Applied Against the Accused?

Courts have held that issue preclusion cannot be used by the government to preclude an accused from relitigating a fact found against him in a prior criminal proceeding. See, e.g., United States v. Harnage, 976 F.2d 633 (11th Cir.1992). The reasoning is that the use of issue preclusion against the accused would violate his constitutional right to a jury trial in the later prosecution. United States v. Pelullo, 14 F.3d 881 (3d Cir.1994) ("applying collateral estoppel against the defendant in a criminal case interferes with the power of the jury to determine every element of the crime, impinging upon the accused's right to a jury trial").

Relitigation of Facts Offered as Uncharged Misconduct: Dowling v. United States

In Dowling v. United States, 493 U.S. 342 (1990), the Court refused to apply the collateral estoppel doctrine when facts underlying an acquittal were used as evidence of uncharged misconduct in a subsequent prosecution. Dowling was charged with bank robbery. On the issue of identification, the prosecution offered evidence that the defendant had participated in a different robbery—one that was conducted similarly to the robbery with which Dowling was charged. Evidence of the prior robbery was admitted under Federal Rule of Evidence 404(b), which permits proof of the defendant's uncharged misconduct when offered to show intent, knowledge, identity, or any purpose other than to show that the defendant is a bad person. Dowling had been acquitted of the prior robbery. He argued that admitting evidence of the robbery at the later trial was prohibited by *Ashe*. Justice White's majority opinion distinguished *Ashe* on the ground that Dowling's prior acquittal "did not determine the ultimate issue in the present case." The Court further noted that, to introduce evidence of an unrelated crime, the prosecution was not required to show that the defendant committed that crime beyond a reasonable doubt. Under the Federal Rules of Evidence, similar act evidence is admissible if the jury could reasonably conclude by a preponderance of the evidence that the act occurred and the defendant was the actor.

Justice Brennan, joined by Justices Marshall and Stevens, dissented. Justice Brennan argued that the majority took insufficient account of the burdens imposed upon a defendant if facts are relitigated in a subsequent criminal prosecution.

Use of Acquitted Conduct for Sentencing Purposes

Under the "relevant conduct" provisions of the Federal Sentencing Guidelines the district court considers all of the defendant's criminal acts that were part of the offense of conviction, whether those acts were the basis of the conviction or not. All that is required is that the government prove that the relevant conduct occurred by a preponderance of the evidence. Suppose the defendant is charged in a multiple count indictment. He is acquitted on some counts and convicted on others. Assume further that while the government could not prove the acquitted counts beyond a reasonable doubt, it can prove them by a preponderance of the evidence. Under these circumstances, the advisory Guidelines sentence includes consideration of the acquitted conduct; and indeed the Guidelines provide that the acquitted conduct is given *the same weight in sentencing* as the conduct for which the defendant was convicted. See United States v. Concepcion, 983 F.2d 369 (2d Cir.1992) (defendant acquitted on one count and convicted on another receives the same sentence as if he had been convicted of both).

In the per curiam opinion in United States v. Watts, 519 U.S. 148 (1997), the Court relied on *Dowling* and *Ashe* and held that it was permissible for defendants to be sentenced in part on the basis of conduct for which they had been acquitted. Watts was charged with drug and firearms offenses. He was convicted of the former and acquitted of the latter. But the trial judge, using the preponderance of the evidence standard mandated by the Federal Sentencing Guidelines, found by a preponderance that Watts had possessed guns in connection with the drug offenses, and added two points to his base offense level for the Guidelines sentence. The Court found that this did not violate the Double Jeopardy Clause, because "sentencing enhancements do not punish a defendant for crimes of which he was not convicted, but rather increase his sentence because of the manner in which he committed the crime of conviction." The Court also noted that an acquittal could have no preclusive effect on a sentencing determination, because of the lesser standard of proof involved in sentencing. Justice Stevens dissented.

IX. DUAL SOVEREIGNS

The Double Jeopardy Clause prohibits successive prosecutions only if brought by the same "sovereign." The dual sovereignty doctrine is well-explained by the court in United States v. Davis, 906 F.2d 829 (2d Cir.1990):

> The states and the national government are distinct political communities, drawing their separate sovereign power from different sources, each from the organic law that established it. Each has the power, inherent in any sovereign, independently to determine what

shall be an offense against its authority and to punish such offenses. When a single act violates the laws of two sovereigns, the wrongdoer has committed two distinct offenses. See generally United States v. Wheeler, 435 U.S. 313 (1978).

In practice, successive prosecutions for the same conduct remain rarities. In the normal exercise of prosecutorial discretion, one sovereign usually defers to the other. * * * However, this is no limitation on the government's sovereign right to vindicate its interests and values, and nothing prevents a federal prosecution whenever the state proceeding has not adequately protected the federal interest.

The only legally binding exception to the dual sovereignty doctrine is a narrow one carved out by the Supreme Court in Bartkus v. Illinois, 359 U.S. 121 (1959). Successive prosecutions will be barred where one prosecuting sovereign can be said to be acting as a "tool" of the other, or where one prosecution is merely a "sham and a cover" for another. Except for this extraordinary type of case, successive state and federal prosecutions may, in fact as well as form, be brought by different sovereigns and the outcome in a state proceeding is not binding upon the later prosecution.

As implied by the discussion in *Davis,* the dual sovereignty principle also allows two different states to prosecute the defendant for the same conduct. Heath v. Alabama, 474 U.S. 82 (1985) (discussed below). Also, it does not matter that the defendant is acquitted by one sovereign, because another sovereign is not bound by the prior adjudication. See Bartkus v. Illinois, 359 U.S. 121 (1959) (upholding state conviction for robbery where defendant had been acquitted of federal charges stemming from the same robbery); United States v. Farmer, 924 F.2d 647 (7th Cir.1991) (previous acquittal on predicate acts in state court does not prohibit subsequent RICO prosecution in federal court).

The Petite Policy

In Abbate v. United States, 359 U.S. 187 (1959), the Court upheld a federal prosecution following a state conviction based upon the same criminal act. The Court expressed concern that without the dual sovereignty doctrine, one sovereign, acting quickly, could hinder the law enforcement efforts of another.

Shortly after the decision in *Abbate,* the Justice Department established the "Petite Policy" of not prosecuting an individual after a state prosecution for the same act, unless there are "compelling interests of federal law enforcement" at stake. The policy is set forth in the United States Attorneys' Manual, § 9–2.031, which provides, among other things:

This policy precludes the initiation or continuation of a federal prosecution, following a prior state or federal prosecution based on substantially the same act(s) or transaction(s) unless three substantive prerequisites are satisfied: first, the matter must involve a substantial federal interest; second, the prior prosecution must have left that interest demonstrably unvindicated; and third, applying the same test that is applicable to all federal prosecutions, the government must believe that the defendant's conduct constitutes a federal offense, and that the admissible evidence probably will be sufficient to obtain and sustain a conviction by an unbiased trier of fact. In addition, there is a procedural prerequisite to be satisfied, that is, the prosecution must be approved by the appropriate Assistant Attorney General.[3]

One of the most famous examples of the "substantial unvindicated interests" exception in the Petite Policy arose in the federal prosecution of the Los Angeles police officers who beat Rodney King, an African-American arrestee. Two officers were convicted of federal civil rights violations, after an all-white state jury had acquitted them of most charges of excessive force, and deadlocked on one charge. While many applauded the federal prosecution, others argued that the Justice Department's decision to prosecute was essentially a political one. See Ricker, Double Exposure, A.B.A.J., August, 1993, p. 66.[4] Interestingly, the district court set a sentence that was below the Federal Sentencing Guidelines. The court departed downward, in part on the ground that the defendants had unfairly (though not unlawfully) suffered from having been twice placed in jeopardy. In Koon v. United States, 518 U.S. 81 (1996), the Court held that the District Court did not abuse its discretion in departing downward in part on the basis of the hardships suffered by the defendants due to successive prosecutions.

Note that the dual sovereignty doctrine can work in reverse as well—the Double Jeopardy Clause does not prevent a state from prosecuting the defendant for a crime after the Federal government has prosecuted him on the same crime. An example is the prosecution of Terry Nichols by the State of Oklahoma for his involvement in the bombing of the Murrah Building in Oklahoma City. That prosecution was brought after he had been convicted

---

[3] The court held in United States v. Renfro, 620 F.2d 569 (6th Cir.1980), that the decision whether or not to prosecute after a state prosecution was left to the United States Attorney, and a defendant could not challenge the government's failure to comply with its Petite policy. See also United States v. Lester, 992 F.2d 174 (8th Cir.1993) (Petite policy does not grant substantive rights to the defendant).

[4] The federal prosecution in the Rodney King case receives support in Amar and Marcus, Double Jeopardy After Rodney King, 95 Colum.L.Rev. 1 (1995). The authors argue that the dual sovereignty doctrine is generally insupportable in light of the incorporation of the Bill of Rights protections under the Fourteenth Amendment. However, the doctrine "still has a narrow but crucial role to play in enforcing the Reconstruction values [i.e., protecting against abuses of power by state actors] of that same Amendment against state officials."

under Federal law but received a life sentence rather than the death penalty.

Municipality Is Not a Separate Sovereign: Waller v. Florida

In Waller v. Florida, 397 U.S. 387 (1970), the Court held that, for double jeopardy purposes, a municipality was not a separate sovereign from the state of which it is a part. The defendant, who removed a mural from a wall in the St. Petersburg city hall, was convicted in municipal court of violating a city ordinance prohibiting destruction of city property and of disorderly breach of the peace. The State of Florida subsequently charged him with grand larceny. The Court refused to permit successive municipality-state prosecutions, and analogized the relationship to that of the federal government and a federal territory.[5]

The States as Dual Sovereigns: Heath v. Alabama

In Heath v. Alabama, 474 U.S. 82 (1985), the Supreme Court affirmed an Alabama capital murder conviction of a man who had pleaded guilty in Georgia to murder based on the same homicide. Heath hired two men to kill his wife. The men kidnapped her in Alabama and apparently killed her in Georgia. Heath pleaded guilty in Georgia and received a life sentence. Thereafter, Alabama indicted him and convicted him of a murder during a kidnaping.

Justice O'Connor wrote for the Court and stated that "in applying the dual sovereignty doctrine * * * the crucial determination is whether the two entities that seek successively to prosecute a defendant for the same course of conduct can be termed separate sovereigns. This determination turns on whether the two entities draw their authority to punish the offender from distinct sources of power." She cited *Waller* as confirmation that "it is the presence of independent authority to prosecute, not the relation between the States and the Federal Government in our federalist system, that constitutes the basis for the dual sovereignty doctrine." She concluded that "[t]he States are no less sovereign with respect to each other than they are with respect to the Federal Government."

Justice O'Connor asserted that "to deny a State its power to enforce its criminal laws because another state won the race to the courthouse would be a shocking and untoward deprivation of the historic right and obligation of the States to maintain peace and order within their confines." She stated that "a State's interest in vindicating its sovereign authority through

---

[5]　In United States v. Wheeler, 435 U.S. 313 (1978), federal prosecution of a Native American for statutory rape was permitted even though he had been convicted of a lesser offense by a tribal court.

enforcement of its laws by definition can never be satisfied by another State's enforcement of its own laws."

Justice Marshall, joined by Justice Brennan, dissented and argued that the fact that the federal government and the states have differing interests in criminal prosecutions does not necessarily mean that two states have differing interests in prosecuting the same crime. He argued that "in contrast to the federal-state context, barring the second prosecution would still permit one government to act upon the broad range of sovereign concerns that have been reserved to the States by the Constitution."

Heath's Supreme Court lawyer has criticized the reasoning of the Supreme Court. See Allen & Ratnaswamy, Heath v. Alabama: A Case Study of Doctrine and Rationality in the Supreme Court, 76 J.Crim.L. & Crim. 801 (1985). The article predicts that ambitious prosecutors will abuse the authority conferred upon them in noteworthy cases in order to further their political advancement.

The United States and Puerto Rico: Dual Sovereigns?

In Commonwealth of Puerto Rico v. Sanchez Valle, 136 S.Ct. 1863 (2016), Justice Kagan wrote for the Court as it held that Puerto Rico and the United States are not separate sovereigns for purposes of the Double Jeopardy Clause. Therefore the defendant could not be prosecuted by Puerto Rico and the Federal government for the same offense. Justice Kagan explained how the Court determines whether jurisdictions are separate sovereigns:

> To determine whether two prosecuting authorities are different sovereigns for double jeopardy purposes, this Court asks a narrow, historically focused question. The inquiry does not turn, as the term "sovereignty" sometimes suggests, on the degree to which the second entity is autonomous from the first or sets its own political course. Rather, the issue is only whether the prosecutorial powers of the two jurisdictions have independent origins—or, said conversely, whether those powers derive from the same "ultimate source." United States v. Wheeler, 435 U.S. 313, 320 (1978).

* * *

> Whether two prosecuting entities are dual sovereigns in the double jeopardy context * * * depends on whether they draw their authority to punish the offender from distinct sources of power. The inquiry is thus historical, not functional—looking at the deepest wellsprings, not the current exercise, of prosecutorial authority. If two entities derive their power to punish from wholly independent sources (imagine here a pair of parallel lines), then they may bring successive prosecutions. Conversely, if those entities draw their power from the

same ultimate source (imagine now two lines emerging from a common point, even if later diverging), then they may not.

Justice Kagan concluded that Puerto Rico's authority to establish and enforce criminal laws came from Congress. Justice Ginsburg, joined by Justice Thomas, concurred and suggested that the Court should at some point examine whether parts of the United States should be considered separate sovereigns. Justice Thomas concurred in part and in the judgment, indicating his disagreement with the Court's analysis of successive prosecutions involving Indian tribes. Justice Breyer, joined by Justice Sotomayor, dissented, and argued that Congress was not the source of prosecutorial power for Puerto Rico.

Joint Efforts in the War on Drugs

State and Federal law enforcement often act jointly in combating the drug trade, for example through the auspices of a joint task force. Apparently this cooperation has not resulted in any limitation on the power of both sovereigns to prosecute the same defendant for the same drug activity. Professor Sandra Guerra, in The Myth of Dual Sovereignty: Multijurisdictional Drug Law Enforcement and Double Jeopardy, 73 No.Car.L.Rev. 1159 (1995), found over 100 federal drug prosecutions in the previous 20 years that took place after a state prosecution on the same conduct. She draws the following conclusions:

> [T]he dual sovereignty doctrine rests on a federalist theory that envisions two separate and independent sovereigns, each of which has its respective laws that reflect its unique priorities and interests. The doctrine shows respect for each sovereign's right to vindicate its own interests without interference from another sovereign. The irony lies in the fact that it is precisely in drug cases where this theory least reflects reality. In drug cases, multijurisdictional drug task forces bring the sovereigns together in a united effort against a common foe. * * * To insist that the cooperating governments make a choice of forum for criminal prosecutions resulting from their joint efforts would neither infringe the sovereign rights of the participating governments, nor create incentives for defendants to race to the courthouse of the jurisdiction offering the best plea bargain.

X. CONTROLS ON JUDICIAL AND PROSECUTORIAL VINDICTIVENESS

In the cases that follow, the Court holds that the Double Jeopardy Clause is not applicable to control judicial vindictiveness in sentencing or prosecutorial vindictiveness in charging. However, the Due Process Clause is held to impose some limitations on those practices.

A. JUDICIAL VINDICTIVENESS

NORTH CAROLINA V. PEARCE

Supreme Court of the United States, 1969.
395 U.S. 711.

JUSTICE STEWART delivered the opinion of the Court.

When at the behest of the defendant a criminal conviction has been set aside and a new trial ordered, to what extent does the Constitution limit the imposition of a harsher sentence after conviction upon retrial? That is the question presented by these two cases.

In No. 413 the respondent Pearce was convicted in a North Carolina court upon a charge of assault with intent to commit rape. The trial judge sentenced him to prison for a term of 12 to 15 years. Several years later he initiated a state post-conviction proceeding which culminated in the reversal of his conviction by the Supreme Court of North Carolina, upon the ground that an involuntary confession had unconstitutionally been admitted in evidence against him. He was retried, convicted, and sentenced by the trial judge to an eight-year prison term, which, when added to the time Pearce had already spent in prison, the parties agree amounted to a longer total sentence than that originally imposed. * * *

In No. 418 the respondent Rice pleaded guilty in an Alabama trial court to four separate charges of second-degree burglary. He was sentenced to prison terms aggregating 10 years. Two and one-half years later the judgments were set aside in a state * * * proceeding, upon the ground that Rice had not been accorded his constitutional right to counsel. He was retried upon three of the charges, convicted, and sentenced to prison on terms aggregating 25 years. No credit was given for the time he had spent in prison on the original judgments.

* * *

The problem before us involves * * * the constitutional limitations upon the imposition of a more severe punishment after conviction for the same offense upon retrial. * * *

* * *

Long-established constitutional doctrine makes clear that * * * the guarantee against double jeopardy imposes no restrictions upon the length of a sentence imposed upon reconviction. * * * [I]t has been settled that this constitutional guarantee imposes no limitations whatever upon the power to *retry* a defendant who has succeeded in getting his first conviction set aside. * * * And * * * it has been settled that a corollary of the power to retry a defendant is the power, upon the defendant's reconviction, to impose whatever sentence may be legally authorized, whether or not it is greater than the sentence imposed after the first conviction. * * *

Although the rationale for this well-established part of our constitutional jurisprudence has been variously verbalized, it rests ultimately upon the premise that the original conviction has, at the defendant's behest, been wholly nullified and the slate wiped clean. As to whatever punishment has actually been suffered under the first conviction, that premise is, of course, an unmitigated fiction * * *. But, so far as the conviction itself goes, and that part of the sentence that has not yet been served, it is no more than a simple statement of fact to say that the slate *has* been wiped clean. The conviction *has* been set aside, and the unexpired portion of the original sentence will never be served. A new trial may result in an acquittal. But if it does result in a conviction, we cannot say that the constitutional guarantee against double jeopardy of its own weight restricts the imposition of an otherwise lawful single punishment for the offense in question. * * *

[The Court rejected an argument that the Equal Protection Clause forbids the imposition of a more severe sentence upon retrial.]

To say that there exists no absolute constitutional bar to the imposition of a more severe sentence upon retrial is not, however, to end the inquiry. There remains for consideration the impact of the Due Process Clause of the Fourteenth Amendment.

It can hardly be doubted that it would be a flagrant violation of the Fourteenth Amendment for a state trial court to follow an announced practice of imposing a heavier sentence upon every reconvicted defendant for the explicit purpose of punishing the defendant for his having succeeded in getting his original conviction set aside. Where, as in each of the cases before us, the original conviction has been set aside because of a constitutional error, the imposition of such a punishment, penalizing those who choose to exercise constitutional rights, would be patently unconstitutional. And the very threat inherent in the existence of such a punitive policy would, with respect to those still in prison, serve to chill the exercise of basic constitutional rights. But even if the first conviction has been set aside for nonconstitutional error, the imposition of a penalty upon the defendant for having successfully pursued a statutory right of appeal or collateral remedy would be no less a violation of due process of law. * * *

Due process of law, then, requires that vindictiveness against a defendant for having successfully attacked his first conviction must play no part in the sentence he receives after a new trial. And since the fear of such vindictiveness may unconstitutionally deter a defendant's exercise of the right to appeal or collaterally attack his first conviction, due process also requires that a defendant be freed of apprehension of such a retaliatory motivation on the part of the sentencing judge.

In order to assure the absence of such a motivation, we have concluded that whenever a judge imposes a more severe sentence upon a defendant after a new trial, the reasons for his doing so must affirmatively appear. Those reasons must be based upon objective information concerning identifiable conduct on the part of the defendant occurring after the time of the original sentencing proceeding. And the factual data upon which the increased sentence is based must be made part of the record, so that the constitutional legitimacy of the increased sentence may be fully reviewed on appeal.

We dispose of the two cases before us in the light of these conclusions. In No. 418 Judge Johnson noted that "the State of Alabama offers no evidence attempting to justify the increase in Rice's original sentences * * *." He found it "shocking that the State of Alabama has not attempted to explain or justify the increase in Rice's punishment—in these three cases, over threefold." And he found that "the conclusion is inescapable that the State of Alabama is punishing petitioner Rice for his having exercised his post-conviction right of review * * *." In No. 413 the situation is not so dramatically clear. Nonetheless, the fact remains that neither at the time the increased sentence was imposed upon Pearce, nor at any stage in this habeas corpus proceeding, has the State offered any reason or justification for that sentence beyond the naked power to impose it.

[The Court upheld the relief granted to Pearce and Rice by the lower courts. Justices Douglas and Marshall concurred, but would have held that the Double Jeopardy Clause bars a higher penalty upon reconviction in every case. Justice Harlan's separate opinion largely agreed with the view of Justices Douglas and Marshall.

Justice Black wrote a concurring and dissenting opinion. He concluded that due process prohibited a higher sentence imposed on appeal for the purpose of punishing a defendant for appealing, but that the detailed procedure mandated by the Court was not required. Justice White wrote an opinion concurring in part.]

Determining Vindictiveness After Pearce

That *Pearce* was decided as a due process and not a double jeopardy case is of great importance. As we will see, the more flexible due process approach produced subsequent rulings that narrowed the potential reach of *Pearce*, rulings that would have been more difficult had *Pearce* rested on the more absolutist double jeopardy language of the Fifth Amendment.

More Convictions in the Interim: Wasman v. United States

The Supreme Court explained in Wasman v. United States, 468 U.S. 559 (1984), that *Pearce* did not prevent imposing a higher sentence upon reconviction of a defendant who had been convicted of additional offenses between the first and second trials. The trial judge who sentenced Wasman carefully explained that he gave him a greater sentence after the second trial than he had after the first because of these additional defenses. The Court found this explanation sufficient to rebut the presumption of vindictiveness established by *Pearce*.

Trial After a Guilty Plea: Alabama v. Smith

In Alabama v. Smith, 490 U.S. 794 (1989), the defendant pleaded guilty and was sentenced; he appealed to have his guilty plea vacated and was successful. He was then tried on the original charges before the judge who had sentenced him under the vacated guilty plea. He was found guilty after trial, and the judge imposed a sentence more severe than the one he rendered after the guilty plea. Chief Justice Rehnquist, writing for eight Justices, held that the *Pearce* presumption of vindictiveness does not apply when a sentence imposed after a trial is greater than that previously imposed after a guilty plea that was subsequently found invalid.

The Court asserted that the *Pearce* presumption should apply only to circumstances where there is "a reasonable likelihood that the increase in sentence is the product of actual vindictiveness." The Chief Justice stated that "when a greater penalty is imposed after trial than was imposed after a prior guilty plea, the increase in sentence is not more likely than not attributable to the vindictiveness on the part of the sentencing judge." He reasoned that "[e]ven when the same judge imposes both sentences, the relevant sentencing information available to the judge after the plea will usually be considerably less than that available after a trial," and "after trial, the factors that may have indicated leniency as consideration for the guilty plea are no longer present." The Court distinguished *Pearce* as a situation in which the sentencing judge, who presided at both trials, could be "expected to operate in the context of roughly the same sentencing considerations after the second trial as he does after the first; any unexplained change in the sentence is therefore subject to a presumption of vindictiveness." Justice Marshall dissented.

B. PROSECUTORIAL VINDICTIVENESS

Prosecutor's Conduct After the Defendant Exercises the Right to Appeal: Blackledge v. Perry

The court found prosecutorial vindictiveness and, accordingly, a due process violation in Blackledge v. Perry, 417 U.S. 21 (1974). Perry, an inmate in a North Carolina prison, was involved in a fight with another inmate and was charged with misdemeanor assault with a deadly weapon. After he was convicted in the lower trial court, he appealed as of right to the higher trial court where he was entitled to a trial de novo. After the filing of the notice of appeal, the prosecutor obtained an indictment from a grand jury, charging Perry with felonious assault with intent to kill or inflict serious bodily injury. Perry pleaded guilty to the felony charge and received a sentence that was less favorable than that imposed by the lower trial court on the misdemeanor conviction. The Supreme Court held that a person who is convicted of an offense and who has an opportunity for a trial de novo has a right to avail himself of the opportunity without apprehension that the prosecutor will substitute a more serious charge for the one brought in the lower court. The Court found that where a prosecutor brings more serious charges after a trial has been completed, a presumption of vindictiveness arises. The Court reasoned as follows:

> A prosecutor clearly has a considerable stake in discouraging [appeals which] will clearly require increased expenditures of prosecutorial resources before the defendant's conviction becomes final, and may even result in a formerly convicted defendant going free. And, if the prosecutor has the means readily at hand to discourage such appeals—by "upping the ante" through a felony indictment * * * the state can insure that only the most hardy defendants will brave the hazards of a de novo trial.

> There is, of course, no evidence that the prosecutor in this case acted in bad faith or maliciously in seeking a felony indictment against Perry. The rationale of [Pearce], however, was not grounded upon the proposition that actual retaliatory motivation must inevitably exist. Rather, we emphasized that since the fear of such vindictiveness may unconstitutionally deter a defendant's exercise of the right to appeal * * * due process also requires that a defendant be freed of apprehension of such a retaliatory motivation on the part of the sentencing judge. We think it clear that the same considerations apply here.

The Court noted that the presumption of vindictiveness would be overcome if the State could show "that it was impossible to proceed on the more serious charge at the outset" and cited Diaz v. United States, 223 U.S. 442 (1912), discussed supra. In *Diaz,* the Double Jeopardy Clause was held not to bar a later murder trial where the victim did not die until after the defendant's trial for assault and battery. See also United States v. York, 933 F.2d 1343 (7th Cir.1991), where the defendant was subjected to an additional charge of obstruction of justice after a successful appeal of his murder conviction. The court found that the testimony required to support the obstruction charge came from the defendant's son, who had expressed an unwillingness to testify against his father at the first trial. When the son changed his mind and approached the authorities two years later, the prosecution could not be presumed vindictive when it added the obstruction charge.[6]

Prosecutor's Conduct After the Defendant Invokes a Trial Right: United States v. Goodwin

In United States v. Goodwin, 454 U.S. 1138 (1982), the Court distinguished *Blackledge* and refused to apply a presumption of vindictiveness to a prosecutor's decisions in the pretrial setting. Goodwin was charged with several misdemeanors, including assault, following an incident in which a police officer stopped his car for speeding. After he invoked his right to a jury trial, an Assistant United States Attorney obtained a four count indictment against Goodwin that included a felony charge of forcibly assaulting a federal officer. Goodwin was convicted on the felony count and one misdemeanor count. The Supreme Court, in an opinion by Justice Stevens, held that the Due Process Clause does not prohibit the government from bringing more serious charges against a defendant after he has exercised his right to jury trial. Distinguishing *Pearce* and *Blackledge* as decisions reflecting "a recognition by the Court of the institutional bias inherent in the judicial system against the retrial of issues that have already been decided," Justice Stevens's opinion reasoned as follows:

> There is good reason to be cautious before adopting an inflexible presumption of prosecutorial vindictiveness in a pre-trial setting. In the course of preparing for trial, the prosecutor may uncover additional information that suggests a basis for further prosecution or he simply may come to realize that information possessed by the State has a broader significance. At this stage of the proceedings, the prosecutor's assessment of the proper extent of prosecution may not have crystallized. In contrast, once a trial begins—and certainly by the time a conviction has been obtained—it is much more likely that the State has discovered and assessed all of the information against an accused and has made a determination, on the basis of that information, of the extent to which he should be prosecuted. Thus, a change in the charging decision made after an initial trial is completed is much more likely to be improperly motivated than is a pretrial decision.

Although Justice Stevens declined to adopt a presumption of vindictiveness in the circumstances presented, he stated that "we of course do not

---

[6] The Court found that *Blackledge* clearly controlled in Thigpen v. Roberts, 468 U.S. 27 (1984). The defendant was convicted in a lower level court of several misdemeanors, he sought a de novo trial in a higher level court, and he was indicted for a felony offense arising out of the same conduct. Finding that the same prosecutor was involved in both prosecutions, the Court stated that it "need not determine the correct rule when two independent prosecutors are involved." It observed that the *Blackledge* presumption of vindictiveness is rebuttable, but that no attempt at rebuttal had been made in the lower courts.

foreclose the possibility that a defendant in an appropriate case might prove objectively that the prosecutor's decision was motivated by a desire to punish him for doing something that the law plainly allowed him to do." Justice Blackmun would have presumed vindictiveness but found that the prosecutor's reasons for seeking a felony indictment adequately rebutted the presumption. Justice Brennan, joined by Justice Marshall, dissented.

Applications of Goodwin

The lower courts have rarely found prosecutorial vindictiveness. For example, in United States v. Sinigaglio, 942 F.2d 581 (9th Cir.1991), the court stated that "when increased charges are filed in the routine course of prosecutorial review or as a result of continuing investigation, there is no realistic likelihood of prosecutorial abuse, and therefore no appearance of vindictive prosecution arises merely because the prosecutor's action was taken after a defense right was exercised." It has also been held that the increase in charges due to the prosecutor's discovery of a new law does not warrant a presumption of vindictiveness. United States v. Austin, 902 F.2d 743 (9th Cir.1990). In United States v. Muldoon, 931 F.2d 282 (4th Cir.1991), the court held that a presumption of vindictiveness "does not arise from plea negotiations when the prosecutor threatens to bring additional charges if the accused refuses to plead guilty to pending charges. The Due Process Clause does not bar the prosecutor from carrying out his threat." See also United States v. Williams, 47 F.3d 658 (4th Cir.1995) (no presumption of vindictiveness where prosecutor increases the charges when the defendant refuses to become a cooperating witness and undercover informant).

XI. CIVIL PENALTIES AS PUNISHMENT

In several cases, the Court has considered whether civil sanctions may constitute "punishment" under the Double Jeopardy Clause. If a civil sanction triggers the Double Jeopardy Clause, the state cannot bring multiple actions to enforce both the civil sanction and a criminal sanction for the same conduct.

Does the Double Jeopardy Clause Regulate Civil Penalties? United States v. Halper

The first in the line of cases was United States v. Halper, 490 U.S. 435 (1989). The facts involved a manager of a medical service company who was convicted of submitting 65 false claims for government reimbursement and fined $5,000. Thereafter, the government sought summary judgment under the False Claims Act, which provided for a civil penalty of $2,000 on each claim, as well as a penalty for twice the amount of the government's actual damages of $585 and the costs of the action. Thus, the government sought a sanction of $130,000 for a $585 fraud.

Justice Blackmun wrote as follows:

What we announce now is a rule for the rare case, the case such as the one before us, where a fixed-penalty provision subjects a prolific but small-gauge offender to a sanction overwhelmingly disproportionate to the damages he has caused. The rule is one of reason: Where a defendant previously has sustained a criminal penalty and the civil penalty sought in the subsequent proceeding bears no rational relation to the goal of compensating the Government for its loss, but rather appears to qualify as "punishment" in the plain meaning of the word, then the defendant is entitled to an accounting of the Government's damages and costs to determine if the penalty sought in fact constitutes a second punishment. * * *

The scope of *Halper* was potentially broad. Criminal law violators often suffer substantial civil sanctions for the same conduct. For example, a defendant convicted of drunk driving will often lose his license; a lawyer convicted of stealing from clients will usually be disbarred; and a defendant convicted of a drug crime may also face civil charges for failure to pay taxes. Are all of these civil consequences barred by the Double Jeopardy Clause after the criminal conviction? In subsequent cases, the Court has taken pains to shy away from the implication in *Halper* that the Double Jeopardy Clause imposes some significant limitation on civil penalties. Indeed, less than a decade after deciding *Halper*, the Court would decide that the decision was a mistake, as explained below.

Civil in Rem Forfeiture: United States v. Ursery

In United States v. Ursery, 518 U.S. 267 (1996), the Court held that civil in rem forfeitures generally do not constitute punishment within the meaning of the Double Jeopardy Clause. *Ursery* involved an attempt to forfeit property in two cases, after the respective property owners had been convicted of criminal offenses. In one case, the government sought forfeiture of the proceeds of drug and money-laundering activity that was the subject of the criminal prosecution. In the other case, the government sought forfeiture of the house of a person convicted of marijuana offenses. In this latter case, the government argued that the house was used as an instrumentality of the crime for which the defendant had been convicted.

Chief Justice Rehnquist, writing for the Court, relied heavily on previous cases involving civil in rem forfeitures and noted the precedent indicating "a sharp distinction between in rem civil forfeitures and in personam civil penalties such as fines: Though the latter could, in some circumstances, be punitive, the former could not."

Applying the "non-punitive" presumption to the in rem forfeitures at issue, the Chief Justice found no violation of the Double Jeopardy Clause. The claimants had not come close to establishing the "clearest proof" that the forfeitures were punitive rather than civil in nature. While "perhaps having punitive aspects" the forfeiture statutes at issue served significant nonpunitive goals, such as: encouraging property owners to use their property legally; abating a nuisance; and preventing drug dealers and money launderers from profiting. The Court also noted that the procedural requirements for establishing forfeitability in the relevant statutes tracked civil rather than criminal law. For example, the government was not required to establish scienter for purposes of civil in rem forfeiture. The Court also disregarded the fact that forfeiture statutes serve a deterrent purpose, reasoning that deterrence is a proper motive of both civil and criminal laws.

Justice Kennedy wrote a concurring opinion in *Ursery*. Justice Scalia, joined by Justice Thomas, concurred in the judgment. Justice Stevens concurred in part and dissented in part.

Repudiating Halper: Hudson v. United States

The Court repudiated the *Halper* analysis in Hudson v. United States, 522 U.S. 93 (1997). The Office of the Comptroller of the Currency (OCC) imposed monetary penalties and occupational debarment on Hudson, a bank official, for violating Federal banking laws by making improper loans. When the Government later indicted Hudson for essentially the same conduct, he moved to dismiss under the Double Jeopardy Clause. The Court of Appeals rejected the double jeopardy claims; it applied *Halper* and concluded that the monetary and other penalties were not disproportionate to the harm caused by Hudson and so was not punishment. The Supreme Court, in an opinion by Chief Justice Rehnquist, affirmed the result reached by the Court of Appeals but rejected the *Halper* analysis.

The Chief Justice's analysis of the relationship between ostensibly civil penalties and the Double Jeopardy Clause proceeded as follows:

> Whether a particular punishment is criminal or civil is, at least initially, a matter of statutory construction. A court must first ask whether the legislature, "in establishing the penalizing mechanism, indicated either expressly or impliedly a preference for one label or the other." [United States v.] Ward, 448 U.S. at 248. Even in those cases where the legislature "has indicated an intention to establish a civil penalty, we have inquired further whether the statutory scheme was so punitive either in purpose or effect," as to "transform what was clearly intended as a civil remedy into a criminal penalty,"
>
> In making this latter determination, the factors listed in Kennedy v. Mendoza-Martinez, 372 U.S. 144 (1963), provide useful guideposts,

including: (1) "whether the sanction involves an affirmative disability or restraint"; (2) "whether it has historically been regarded as a punishment"; (3) "whether it comes into play only on a finding of scienter"; (4) "whether its operation will promote the traditional aims of punishment—retribution and deterrence"; (5) "whether the behavior to which it applies is already a crime"; (6) "whether an alternative purpose to which it may rationally be connected is assignable for it"; and (7) "whether it appears excessive in relation to the alternative purpose assigned." It is important to note, however, that "these factors must be considered in relation to the statute on its face," and "only the clearest proof" will suffice to override legislative intent and transform what has been denominated a civil remedy into a criminal penalty.

Our opinion in United States v. Halper marked the first time we applied the Double Jeopardy Clause to a sanction without first determining that it was criminal in nature. * * *

The analysis applied by the *Halper* Court deviated from our traditional double jeopardy doctrine in two key respects. First, the *Halper* Court bypassed the threshold question: whether the successive punishment at issue is a "criminal" punishment. Instead, it focused on whether the sanction, regardless of whether it was civil or criminal, was so grossly disproportionate to the harm caused as to constitute "punishment." In so doing, the Court elevated a single *Kennedy* factor—whether the sanction appeared excessive in relation to its nonpunitive purposes—to dispositive status. But as we emphasized in *Kennedy* itself, no one factor should be considered controlling as they "may often point in differing directions." The second significant departure in *Halper* was the Court's decision to "assess the character of the actual sanctions imposed," rather than, as *Kennedy* demanded, evaluating the "statute on its face" to determine whether it provided for what amounted to a criminal sanction.

We believe that *Halper's* deviation from longstanding double jeopardy principles was ill considered. As subsequent cases have demonstrated, *Halper's* test for determining whether a particular sanction is "punitive," and thus subject to the strictures of the Double Jeopardy Clause, has proved unworkable. We have since recognized that all civil penalties have some deterrent effect. See United States v. Ursery. If a sanction must be "solely" remedial (i.e., entirely nondeterrent) to avoid implicating the Double Jeopardy Clause, then no civil penalties are beyond the scope of the Clause. Under *Halper's* method of analysis, a court must also look at the "sanction actually imposed" to determine whether the Double Jeopardy Clause is implicated. Thus, it will not be possible to determine whether the Double Jeopardy Clause is violated until a defendant has proceeded through a trial to judgment. But in those cases where the civil proceeding follows the criminal proceeding, this approach flies in the face of the notion that the Double Jeopardy Clause forbids the government from even attempting a second time to punish criminally.

Applying "traditional double jeopardy principles" to the facts, the Chief Justice found that the OCC penalties and debarment sanctions were clearly civil rather than criminal, and therefore the subsequent prosecution of Hudson did not violate the Double Jeopardy Clause. The monetary penalties were explicitly designated as civil, and the fact that debarment proceedings were conducted administratively was a strong indication that they were civil rather than criminal. The Chief Justice also noted "that there is little evidence, much less the clearest proof that we require, suggesting that either OCC money penalties or debarment sanctions are so punitive in form and effect as to render them criminal despite Congress' intent to the contrary." Neither money penalties nor debarment have historically been viewed as punishment. Nor did the sanctions involve an "affirmative disability or restraint," as that term is normally understood. While Hudson was prohibited from further participating in the banking industry, this is "certainly nothing approaching the 'infamous punishment' of imprisonment." Furthermore, neither sanction came into play only on a finding of scienter. The regulatory provisions under which the monetary penalties were imposed allow for the assessment of a penalty against any person "who violates" any of the underlying banking statutes, without regard to the violator's state of mind.

The Chief Justice recognized that imposing monetary penalties and debarment sanctions will deter others from engaging in similar conduct, a traditional goal of criminal punishment. "But the mere presence of this purpose is insufficient to render a sanction criminal, as deterrence may serve civil as well as criminal goals." The Chief Justice noted that the monetary and debarment sanctions, "while intended to deter future wrongdoing, also serve to promote the stability of the banking industry. To hold that the mere presence of a deterrent purpose renders such sanctions criminal for double jeopardy purposes would severely undermine the Government's ability to engage in effective regulation of institutions such as banks."

Justice Stevens concurred in the judgment. He found it unnecessary to consider the viability of *Halper,* because even if the civil sanctions were punishment, the statute under which they were imposed did not constitute the "same offense" as the criminal charges. Justices Souter, and Justice Breyer joined by Justice Ginsburg, also wrote separate opinions concurring in the judgment.

CHAPTER 13

POST-CONVICTION CHALLENGES

■ ■ ■

I. INTRODUCTION

Because of the Double Jeopardy Clause and the constitutional right to a jury trial, the prosecutor generally will be unable to seek review of an acquittal.[1] The criminal defendant who is convicted has greater opportunities to challenge the trial court's judgment.[2] This Chapter addresses the opportunities most likely to be made available in the typical criminal case.

Three types of post-conviction proceedings will be examined in this Chapter: 1) motions made in the trial court after a conviction, 2) direct appellate review of convictions, and 3) collateral attacks on convictions. We assume that everyone has a basic familiarity with the following facts: criminal cases are tried in both federal and state courts; an appeal of one sort or another generally is provided a convicted defendant; the defendant may raise claims concerning almost any trial errors, defects in trial procedure, problems with the substantive law or the overall fairness of the results on appeal; but crowded appellate courts may screen some appeals and decide them on the basis of written briefs, reserving oral argument for special cases. Questions concerning the right to counsel and to the effective assistance of counsel in post-conviction proceedings are addressed in Chapters 5 and 10. Appellate review of sentences is examined in Chapter 11 and also touched upon in Chapter 12.

---

[1] This Chapter does not examine the issue of when a decision becomes final for purposes of appeal. See, e.g., United States v. Nixon, 418 U.S. 683, 690–92 (1974). Nor are special techniques of avoiding review examined—e.g., the concurrent sentence doctrine, see, e.g., Benton v. Maryland, 395 U.S. 784 (1969) (discretion to avoid review of one of concurrent judgments); the mootness doctrine, see, e.g., Sibron v. New York, 392 U.S. 40 (1968) (case not moot on direct appeal where adverse collateral consequences are possible); Dove v. United States, 423 U.S. 325 (1976) (certiorari petition dismissed when petitioner dies). The examination of appeals, as opposed to collateral attack, focuses on defendants who have been convicted at trial as opposed to those who have pled guilty, although a few cases do address defendants who pled guilty.

[2] As noted in the previous chapter on double jeopardy, not all government appeals are constitutionally barred. Generally, if the prosecutor is not challenging an acquittal or seeking a second adjudication on the guilt-innocence question, the Constitution will not stand in the way of an appeal. While Congress has acted to open the doors to government appeals virtually to the limits of the Constitution in 18 U.S.C.A. § 3731, not all states permit the government such review.

II. GROUNDS FOR DIRECT ATTACKS ON A CONVICTION

If the defendant has been convicted, there are two procedural avenues by which he can attack the judgment "directly": through motions to the trial judge or by way of direct appeal. This section considers some possible grounds for a direct attack, and some defenses that the government might have against a remedy that would vacate the judgment.

A. INSUFFICIENT EVIDENCE

1. The General Standard

A defendant may move during trial or after a verdict is returned for an acquittal on the ground that the evidence is insufficient to sustain a conviction. Federal Rule of Criminal Procedure 29 indicates the opportunities available to a defendant to make and repeat such a motion. The same legal standard is used in judging post-verdict as mid-trial motions. The general rule is that a guilty verdict can only stand if there is sufficient evidence to convince a reasonable jury of guilt beyond a reasonable doubt of all necessary elements of the government's case.[3] See United States v. Ramirez, 362 F.3d 521 (8th Cir. 2004) ("While the evidence need not preclude every outcome other than guilty, we consider whether it would be sufficient to convince a reasonable jury beyond a reasonable doubt."). After In re Winship, discussed in Chapter 10, this standard of review is probably required by the Constitution. When the burden of persuasion as to a defense is placed upon the defendant, a guilty verdict will be set aside if no reasonable jury could have rejected the defendant's evidence, when measured under the appropriate standard of proof. For example, if a defendant bears the burden of proving insanity by a preponderance of the evidence, a jury verdict of guilty will be set aside if the defendant's evidence is so strong that any *reasonable* jury would have found the proof of insanity to be preponderant.

Review by Trial Judge for Insufficiency

The standard for review by a trial judge upon a motion for acquittal is well-stated by the court in United States v. Mariani, 725 F.2d 862 (2d Cir.1984):

> When a defendant moves for a judgment of acquittal, the court must determine whether upon the evidence, giving full play to the right of the jury to determine credibility, weigh the evidence, and draw

---

[3] In conspiracy cases, an ill-defined and objectionable "slight evidence" standard has been utilized by some courts, but it never has been justified. See, e.g., United States v. Shoffner, 71 F.3d 1429 (8th Cir.1995) ("Once the existence of a conspiracy is established, even slight evidence connecting a defendant to the conspiracy may be sufficient to prove the defendant's involvement.").

justifiable inferences of fact, a reasonable mind might fairly conclude guilt beyond a reasonable doubt. If it concludes that upon the evidence there must be such a doubt in a reasonable mind, it must grant the motion; or, to state it another way, if there is no evidence upon which a reasonable mind might fairly conclude guilt beyond a reasonable doubt, the motion must be granted. If it concludes that either of the two results, a reasonable doubt or no reasonable doubt, is fairly possible, it must let the jury decide the matter.

Timing of a Motion for Acquittal

Fed.R.Crim.P. 29 provides, as does the law of most states, that a motion for judgment of acquittal must be granted after the evidence of either side is concluded if the evidence against the defendant is insufficient to warrant conviction. If the defendant makes a motion for acquittal at the close of the government's case, the trial court may reserve a ruling on the motion until the end of the case. If the defendant, after making the motion, puts on evidence, the trial court in subsequently ruling on the motion for acquittal is to consider only the evidence presented as of the time "the ruling was reserved." Rule 29(b). Therefore, the defendant who puts on evidence after the judge reserves a ruling on the motion avoids the risk that the evidence and the government's rebuttal will be considered as favorable to the government for purposes of the dismissal motion. That is, the defendant does not waive the right to have the acquittal motion judged solely on the basis of the government's evidence, without reference to the evidence offered after the government rests. While Rule 29 specifically limits only the trial court and not the appellate court, the Advisory Committee's comment to the Rule states that "in reviewing a trial court's ruling, the appellate court would be similarly limited" to the evidence presented as of the time the motion was made.

Fed.R.Crim.P. 29(c) provides that a motion for judgment of acquittal can be made after the jury returns a verdict, but it sets a time limit for such a motion—it must be made "within 7 days after a guilty verdict or after the court discharges the jury, whichever is later." In Carlisle v. United States, 517 U.S. 416 (1996), the defendant's motion for acquittal was made 8 days after the jury was discharged. The Court, in an opinion by Justice Scalia, held that the district court has no jurisdiction to entertain a motion for acquittal made outside the time limit of Rule 29(c)—even if the defendant is innocent. Justice Scalia declared that the Rule is "plain and unambiguous" and that there is "simply no room in the text * * * for the granting of an untimely post-verdict motion for judgment of acquittal, regardless of whether the motion is accompanied by a claim of legal innocence, is filed before sentencing, or was filed late because of attorney error." Justice Souter wrote a short concurring opinion, as did Justice Ginsburg, joined by Justices Souter and Breyer. Justice Ginsburg argued that the Rule 29 time bar might be lifted if defense counsel were somehow misled by the trial court. But Carlisle's counsel was not misled; rather, he neglected to follow plain instructions as set forth in the Rule. She also observed that Carlisle was not bereft of protection at this point, because he could still challenge his conviction on appeal, and could also bring a collateral attack on grounds of ineffective assistance of counsel.

Justice Stevens, joined by Justice Kennedy, dissented in *Carlisle*. He contended that there was nothing in Rule 29(c) that "withdraws the court's pre-existing authority to refrain from entering judgment of conviction against a defendant whom it knows to be legally innocent."

2. The Standard of Appellate Review of Sufficiency of the Evidence

Rational Trier of Fact Test: Jackson v. Virginia

At one time, there was a tendency among appellate courts to uphold verdicts supported by *any* evidence. Only "no evidence" cases produced reversals. But in Jackson v. Virginia, 443 U.S. 307 (1979), the Supreme Court rejected the "no evidence" test. Writing for the Court, Justice Stewart opined that the "no evidence" rule was inadequate to protect against misapplication of the proof beyond a reasonable doubt requirement, and that the critical question on review of a criminal conviction is whether the record evidence could reasonably support a finding of guilt beyond a reasonable doubt. He also wrote that the standard should be utilized by federal courts hearing habeas corpus attacks on state convictions. Justice Stewart elaborated on the appropriate test for review of sufficiency claims:

> After *Winship* the critical inquiry on review of the sufficiency of the evidence to support a criminal conviction must be not simply to determine whether the jury was properly instructed, but to determine whether the record evidence could reasonably support a finding of guilt beyond a reasonable doubt. But this inquiry does not require a court to ask itself whether *it* believes that the evidence at the trial established guilt beyond a reasonable doubt. Instead, the relevant question is whether, after viewing the evidence in the light most favorable to the prosecution, *any* rational trier of fact could have found the essential elements of the crime beyond a reasonable doubt. This familiar standard gives full play to the responsibility of the trier of fact fairly to resolve conflicts in the testimony, to weigh the evidence, and to draw reasonable inferences from basic facts to ultimate facts. * * * The criterion thus impinges upon jury discretion only to the extent

necessary to guarantee the fundamental protection of due process of law.[4]

Thus, the standard for appellate review of sufficiency of the evidence under *Jackson* is the same as the standard used by the trial court in ruling on a motion for acquittal.

Ironically, Jackson, who was convicted of first degree murder, did not benefit from his victory on the legal standard of sufficiency. Jackson was convicted of premeditated murder and claimed that he shot the victim by accident. The Court found that because Jackson, among other things, admitted firing several shots into the ground and reloading his gun before killing the deceased, a rational trier of fact could have found beyond a reasonable doubt that the killing was premeditated.

Jackson was a habeas corpus case, but the standards set forth in *Jackson* apply to direct appeals as well. See, e.g., United States v. Aina-Marshall, 336 F.3d 167 (2d Cir. 2003) ("A defendant challenging a conviction based on insufficient evidence bears a heavy burden. * * * A conviction will be affirmed so long as any rational trier of fact could have found the essential elements of the crime beyond a reasonable doubt.").

As discussed later in this Chapter, changes in federal habeas corpus law have made it especially difficult to win a *Jackson* challenge in a federal habeas proceeding. See Coleman v. Johnson, *infra*.

Application of Jackson: Wright v. West

In Wright v. West, 505 U.S. 277 (1992), West was convicted of grand larceny on the basis of possession of stolen goods. The theft occurred several weeks before the items were found in West's house; only a few of the stolen items were found there; West had made no attempt to conceal the items; and West testified that he had bought the items at a flea market. West challenged his conviction on sufficiency grounds, arguing that his was a "mere possession" case, and that a rational trier of fact could not conclude that West had the intent to commit grand larceny. The court of appeals held in favor of West, but the Supreme Court concluded that the lower court had misapplied the standards of *Jackson* in reversing West's conviction.

Justice Thomas, in a plurality opinion joined by Chief Justice Rehnquist and Justice Scalia, concluded that "the case against West was strong." He stressed the following points: 1) over 15 of the stolen items were recovered from West's home; 2) West had failed to offer specific information about how he came to possess the stolen items, saying only that he frequently bought and sold items at various flea markets; 3) West contradicted himself repeatedly on the witness stand as to where he had

---

[4] Justice Stevens dissented and was joined by Chief Justice Burger and Justice Rehnquist. Justice Powell did not participate.

bought the stolen goods; 4) West had no explanation whatsoever for the presence of some of the stolen goods in his home; 5) West failed to produce any other supporting evidence, such as testimony of the person from whom he claimed to have purchased some of the goods, even though he stated that he had known this person for years; and 6) the jury was entitled to disbelieve West's "uncorroborated and confused" testimony, and "was further entitled to consider whatever it concluded to be perjured testimony as affirmative evidence of guilt."

Justice Thomas concluded as follows:

> In *Jackson,* we emphasized repeatedly the deference owed to the trier of fact and, correspondingly, the sharply limited nature of constitutional sufficiency review. We said that "all of the evidence is to be considered in the light most favorable to the prosecution"; that the prosecution need not affirmatively "rule out every hypothesis except that of guilt"; and that a reviewing court "faced with a record of historical facts that supports conflicting inferences must presume— even if it does not appear affirmatively in the record—that the trier of fact resolved any such conflicts in favor of the prosecution, and must defer to that resolution." Under these standards, we think it clear that the trial record contained sufficient evidence to support West's conviction.[5]

For other examples of appellate review of sufficiency challenges, see United States v. Jackson, 368 F.3d 59 (2d Cir. 2004) (defendant convicted of felon-firearm-possession; conviction reversed because of insufficient evidence that the defendant was a felon; the government offered a conviction entered against "Aaron Jackson", but there are many Aaron Jacksons, and the government "offered no evidence that the two Aaron Jacksons were of the same race, or of similar height, coloring, fingerprint configuration, or even general physical description."); United States v. Ramirez, 362 F.3d 521 (8th Cir. 2004) (driver of car contended he did not know that drugs were in the car; appellate court finds sufficient evidence: "The circumstances surrounding the traffic stop and Ramirez's trip, including documents found inside the truck and his inconsistent and improbable explanations for his trip; his lies regarding his plans to meet his uncle; * * * his implausible trial testimony; and expert testimony concerning the methods used by drug traffickers, when considered together" provided sufficient evidence of the defendant's knowing participation in drug trafficking).

---

[5] Justices White, O'Connor, Blackmun, Stevens, and Kennedy all concurred in the judgment, in three separate opinions. They all agreed that under *Jackson,* there was sufficient evidence to convince a rational factfinder of West's guilt beyond a reasonable doubt. Justice Souter also concurred in the judgment, but did not reach the sufficiency issue.

More on Deference to Jury Determinations: Cavazos v. Smith

The Court repeated its emphasis in Wright v. West on deference to jury verdicts in a per curiam summary disposition in Cavazos v. Smith, 565 U.S. 1 (2011), where it reversed a Ninth Circuit opinion granting habeas relief to a state defendant convicted in a case involving "shaken baby syndrome." The Court noted that the fact that the government's evidence and theory might be disputed is no reason to overturn a jury verdict, in a case in which expert testimony was in dispute and there were affirmative indications of trauma that supported the government's experts' opinion that the death occurred from sudden tearing of the brainstem caused by shaking, even though the experts were unable to identify the precise point of the tearing. Three dissenters protested the summary disposition.

Two Layers of Deference to Jury Determinations on Habeas Review: Coleman v. Johnson and Parker v. Matthews

In Coleman v. Johnson, 566 U.S. 650 (2012) (per curiam), the Court once again considered and applied the standard for reviewing habeas claims challenging the sufficiency of evidence at a state trial. Johnson was convicted of being an accomplice and conspirator in the murder of a victim killed by a shotgun blast to the chest. Johnson's convictions were affirmed in state court, and a federal district court denied relief before the Third Circuit held that the evidence at trial was insufficient to support Johnson's conviction under the standard set forth in Jackson v. Virginia.

The Supreme Court observed that *Jackson* claims "face a high bar in federal habeas proceedings because they are subject to two layers of judicial deference." As to the first layer, the Court noted its instruction from Cavazos v. Smith, supra: "it is the responsibility of the jury—not the court—to decide what conclusions should be drawn from evidence admitted at trial. A reviewing court may set aside the jury's verdict on the ground of insufficient evidence only if no rational trier of fact could have agreed with the jury." Thus, the first layer of deference is appellate deference to jury findings. The second level is federal habeas deference to state court decisions. A federal court may not overturn a state court's finding of sufficient evidence merely because the federal court disagrees with the finding; a federal court may only overturn a state court finding if it is "objectively unreasonable."

The trial evidence left little doubt that Johnson, along with the shooter, intended to confront the victim, but the Third Circuit (contrary to the state courts) found insufficient evidence that Johnson shared the shooter's intent to kill the victim. Reviewing the record, the Supreme Court concluded that the state appellate court's ruling finding sufficient evidence was entitled to greater deference than the Third Circuit gave it.

Court Reviewing Sufficiency of the Evidence Must Consider All Evidence Admitted at Trial, Even if Erroneously: McDaniel v. Brown

In McDaniel v. Brown, 558 U.S.120 (2010), the Court considered whether, in reviewing a conviction for sufficiency of evidence, the reviewing court must consider evidence that was admitted in error. Brown was convicted of sexual assault, and challenged the verdict for sufficiency, but also argued that DNA evidence was unreliable and therefore erroneously admitted. Brown did not, however, dispute the fact that the evidence presented at trial was sufficient. Under these circumstances, the Court in a per curiam opinion ruled that there could be no relief under *Jackson* for insufficiency. The Court explained as follows:

> An appellate court's reversal for insufficiency of the evidence is in effect a determination that the government's case against the defendant was so lacking that the trial court should have entered a judgment of acquittal. Because reversal for insufficiency of the evidence is equivalent to a judgment of acquittal, such a reversal bars a retrial. To make the analogy complete between a reversal for insufficiency of the evidence and the trial court's granting a judgment of acquittal, a reviewing court must consider all of the evidence admitted by the trial court, regardless whether that evidence was admitted erroneously.

Assessment of Sufficiency Where the Jury Instructions Add an Extra Element to the Crime: Musacchio v. United States

In Musacchio v. United States, 136 S.Ct. 709 (2016), the trial judge misinstructed the jury that it had to find two facts rather than one: the instruction was that the jury had to find that the defendant intentionally accessed a computer without authorization *and* exceeded authorized use, whereas the statute under which Musacchio was charged makes it a crime if a person "intentionally accesses a computer without authorization *or* exceeds authorized use." The Government failed to object to the trial court's jury instruction that, in essence, erroneously added an element that it had to prove. The defendant was nonetheless convicted, and appealed on grounds of insufficient evidence. One question for the Supreme Court was whether the sufficiency review would have to evaluate the evidence in light of the elements of the crime, or instead in light of all the elements provided in the jury instruction. The Court, in a unanimous opinion written by Justice Thomas, ruled that a sufficiency challenge must be assessed against the elements of the charged crime, not against the elements set forth in an erroneously heightened jury instruction. He reasoned as follows:

When a jury finds guilt after being instructed on all elements of the charged crime plus one more element, the jury has made all the findings that due process requires. If a jury instruction requires the jury to find guilt on the elements of the charged crime, a defendant will have had a meaningful opportunity to defend against the charge. And if the jury instruction requires the jury to find those elements "beyond a reasonable doubt," the defendant has been accorded the procedure that this Court has required to protect the presumption of innocence. The Government's failure to introduce evidence of an additional element does not implicate the principles that sufficiency review protects.

General Verdict with Insufficient Evidence on One Ground: Griffin v. United States

Is reversal required when a defendant is charged with multiple acts or means of committing a crime in a single count, and the evidence is insufficient as to one of the acts or means? In Griffin v. United States, 502 U.S. 46 (1991), the Court relied on the common-law rule that a general verdict is valid so long as it is legally supportable on any one of the submitted grounds—"even though that gave no assurance that a valid ground, rather than an invalid one, was actually the basis for the jury's action."

Griffin was charged, with others, in a conspiracy that was alleged to have two objects: (1) impairing the efforts of the Internal Revenue Service to ascertain income taxes (the "IRS object"); and (2) impairing the efforts of the Drug Enforcement Administration to ascertain forfeitable assets (the "DEA object"). The evidence introduced at trial implicated Griffin's codefendants in both conspiratorial objects, but it did not sufficiently connect Griffin with the DEA object. The trial court over objection instructed the jury that it could return a guilty verdict if it found Griffin to have participated in either one of the two objects of the conspiracy. The jury returned a general verdict of guilty. The court of appeals found the evidence tying Griffin to the DEA object insufficient, but nonetheless affirmed Griffin's conviction on the ground that sufficient evidence existed to tie her to the IRS object. Griffin argued that this result violated her right to due process, because the jury might not actually have found her guilty of the IRS crime. But the Supreme Court disagreed in an opinion by Justice Scalia.

Justice Scalia recognized that despite the general common-law rule upholding an ambiguous general verdict, the Court had held in Stromberg v. California, 283 U.S. 359 (1931), that "where a provision of the Constitution forbids conviction on a particular ground, the constitutional guarantee is violated by a general verdict that may have rested on that ground." He also recognized that in Yates v. United States, 354 U.S. 298 (1957), the Court used a similar principle to void a conviction in which one means alleged in a single count was insufficient in law because barred by the statute of limitations. But Justice Scalia found these precedents to be exceptions to the general rule, and inapposite to a case where one of the objects in a single count was void not because of a legal error but rather due to factual insufficiency. He explained the *Stromberg-Yates* exception, and distinguished it from the general rule, as follows:

> Jurors are not generally equipped to determine whether a particular theory of conviction submitted to them is contrary to law— whether, for example, the action in question is protected by the Constitution, is time barred, or fails to come within the statutory definition of the crime. When, therefore, jurors have been left the option of relying upon a legally inadequate theory, there is no reason to think that their own intelligence and expertise will save them from that error. Quite the opposite is true, however, when they have been left the option of relying upon a factually inadequate theory, since jurors *are* well equipped to analyze the evidence. * * *

Thus, the Court found it fair to presume from the general verdict that the jury convicted on the factually sufficient ground.[6] Compare United States v. Garcia, 992 F.2d 409 (2d Cir.1993) (*Griffin* distinguished where three legal theories were submitted to the jury, and two of them were legally erroneous: "If the challenge is evidentiary, as long as there was sufficient evidence to support one of the theories presented, then the verdict should be affirmed. However, if the challenge is legal and any of the theories was legally insufficient, then the verdict must be reversed.").

B. MOTION FOR NEW TRIAL

Federal Rule of Criminal Procedure 33, providing for a new trial on motion "if the interest of justice so requires," affords another avenue for direct attack on a conviction. Note that, as was true of motions for acquittal, post-verdict new trial motions are defendants' remedies.

One might expect that the same trial judge who erred once is unlikely to be quick to change her mind, but it sometimes happens. The trial judge knows that it is likely that a convicted defendant will appeal, and the post-trial motion enables the trial judge to correct any error that an appellate court would correct. In close cases, the trial judge has authority to grant a new trial even if an appellate court, acting on the basis of a cold record, would not, because the trial judge is well situated to see or feel the prejudicial impact of an error that on paper does not appear to be significant.

---

[6]   Justice Blackmun concurred in the judgment. Justice Thomas did not participate.

One ground on which a motion for a new trial might be granted is that the trial judge is convinced that a verdict is against the weight of the evidence. "Against the weight of the evidence" is not the same as "insufficient evidence." The standards governing a trial judge's ruling on a motion for a new trial on "weight of the evidence" grounds are well-stated by the court in United States v. Martinez, 763 F.2d 1297 (11th Cir.1985):

> On a motion for judgment of acquittal, the court must view the evidence in the light most favorable to the verdict, and, under that light, determine whether the evidence is sufficient to support the verdict. Thus * * * the court assumes the truth of the evidence offered by the prosecution. On a motion for a new trial based on the weight of the evidence, the court need not view the evidence in the light most favorable to the verdict. It may weigh the evidence and consider the credibility of the witnesses. If the court concludes that despite the abstract sufficiency of the evidence to sustain the verdict, the evidence preponderates sufficiently heavily against the verdict that a serious miscarriage of justice may have occurred, it may set aside the verdict, grant a new trial, and submit the issues for determination by another jury.

> * * * While the district court's discretion is quite broad, there are limits to it. The court may not reweigh the evidence and set aside the verdict simply because it feels some other result would be more reasonable. The evidence must preponderate heavily against the verdict, such that it would be a miscarriage of justice to let the verdict stand. Motions for new trials based on weight of the evidence are not favored. Courts are to grant them sparingly and with caution, doing so only in those really exceptional cases.

> Applying these principles trial courts, generally speaking, have granted new trial motions on weight of the evidence only where the credibility of the government's witnesses has been impeached and the government's case has been marked by uncertainties and discrepancies.

C. NEWLY DISCOVERED EVIDENCE CLAIMS

Judges are understandably reluctant to overturn verdicts supported by sufficient evidence to prove guilt beyond a reasonable doubt. If courts readily accepted newly discovered evidence claims, litigants who discovered that a tactical judgment made in one trial did not work would ask for another chance to litigate, and litigation finality interests would be undermined. The line between discovery of new evidence and discovery of new theories of how to use evidence is fuzzy, but rarely must it be sharpened in light of the reluctance of courts to take seriously either claim.

Requirements for a Newly Discovered Evidence Claim

A defendant must meet a four prong test before a court will grant him a retrial based on any newly discovered evidence. As stated in United States v. Lenz, 577 F.3d 377 (1st Cir.2009), the defendant must establish the following:

(1)   the evidence was unknown or unavailable at the time of the trial;

(2)   the evidence could not have been discovered earlier with due diligence;

(3)   the evidence is material and not merely cumulative or impeaching; and

(4)   the evidence would probably result in an acquittal upon retrial.

In *Lenz*, the court concluded that a witness's newfound willingness to corroborate the defendant's story was not newly discovered evidence: "Whether or not a witness will testify truthfully is simply not 'evidence' that can be used as a basis to invoke Rule 33 of the Federal Rules of Criminal Procedure." See also United States v. Gonzalez, 933 F.2d 417 (7th Cir.1991) (defendants were not entitled to a new trial on the basis of newly discovered evidence where the evidence would merely impeach a government witness's testimony that he had never had anything to do with cocaine, and evidence of the defendants' guilt was overwhelming).

Newly Discovered vs. Newly Available

There is a distinction between newly *discovered* and newly *available* evidence. Evidence is not "new" merely because it has been generated after the conviction. For example, in Harris v. Vasquez, 913 F.2d 606 (9th Cir.1990), a death penalty case, the court concluded that the defendant's new psychiatric reports did not justify another penalty hearing. Because defense counsel possessed evidence of the defendant's brain damage at the original hearing, and no new psychiatric techniques or theories were alleged to have arisen in the interim, the court concluded that the new reports were not new evidence but merely new opinions from new psychiatrists.

New Forensic Techniques: District Attorney's Office v. Osborne

Advances in forensic testing techniques have occasionally given rise to new evidence claims—e.g., exculpatory DNA tests. But they are not always successful. When the forensic testing is conducted long after the crime, it will sometimes be insufficiently conclusive to show that the defendant would probably be acquitted on retrial. See Dumond v. Lockhart, 911 F.2d 104 (8th Cir.1990), where the court held that evidence of a genetic marker test done on a semen sample, showing that the sample was unlikely to be the defendant's, was newly discovered evidence. Yet the defendant's motion for a new trial was found properly denied because it was not likely that the evidence would produce an acquittal on retrial.

In District Attorney's Office for the Third Judicial District v. Osborne, 557 U.S. 52 (2009), a convicted defendant argued that he had a constitutional right to DNA testing that he claimed would provide newly discovered evidence to exonerate him. The state had in fact conducted a rudimentary form of DNA testing before the trial; that test tended to include Osborne as a possible perpetrator in a sex crime, but it was not definitive. Osborne's counsel decided not to ask for a more sophisticated test to be done, fearing that it would further incriminate Osborne. Osborne was convicted and several years later brought a civil rights action against the state, alleging that he had a due process right to an even more sophisticated DNA test than was available at the time of his trial.

In a 5–4 opinion, the Court held that convicted defendants have no freestanding due process right to DNA testing. Chief Justice Roberts, writing for the majority, declared as follows:

> DNA testing has an unparalleled ability both to exonerate the wrongly convicted and to identify the guilty. It has the potential to significantly improve both the criminal justice system and police investigative practices. The Federal Government and the States have recognized this, and have developed special approaches to ensure that this evidentiary tool can be effectively incorporated into established criminal procedure—usually but not always through legislation.

> Against this prompt and considered response, the respondent, William Osborne, proposes a different approach: the recognition of a freestanding and far-reaching constitutional right of access to this new type of evidence. The nature of what he seeks is confirmed by his decision to file this lawsuit in federal court under 42 U. S. C. § 1983, not within the state criminal justice system. This approach would take the development of rules and procedures in this area out of the hands of legislatures and state courts shaping policy in a focused manner and turn it over to federal courts applying the broad parameters of the Due Process Clause. There is no reason to constitutionalize the issue in this way. Because the decision below would do just that, we reverse.

Chief Justice Roberts noted that the defendant's right to obtain evidence after trial is more circumscribed than the right to exculpatory evidence before or during trial:

> Osborne's right to due process is not parallel to a trial right, but rather must be analyzed in light of the fact that he has already been found guilty at a fair trial, and has only a limited interest in postconviction relief. *Brady* is the wrong framework.

Instead, the question is whether consideration of Osborne's claim within the framework of the State's procedures for postconviction relief "offends some principle of justice so rooted in the traditions and conscience of our people as to be ranked as fundamental," or "transgresses any recognized principle of fundamental fairness in operation." Federal courts may upset a State's postconviction relief procedures only if they are fundamentally inadequate to vindicate the substantive rights provided.

We see nothing inadequate about the procedures Alaska has provided to vindicate its state right to postconviction relief in general, and nothing inadequate about how those procedures apply to those who seek access to DNA evidence. Alaska provides a substantive right to be released on a sufficiently compelling showing of new evidence that establishes innocence. It exempts such claims from otherwise applicable time limits. The State provides for discovery in postconviction proceedings, and has—through judicial decision—specified that this discovery procedure is available to those seeking access to DNA evidence. These procedures are not without limits. The evidence must indeed be newly available to qualify under Alaska's statute, must have been diligently pursued, and must also be sufficiently material. These procedures are similar to those provided for DNA evidence by federal law and the law of other States, see, e.g., 18 U. S. C. § 3600(a), and they are not inconsistent with the "traditions and conscience of our people" or with "any recognized principle of fundamental fairness."

Justice Alito filed a concurring opinion in which Justice Kennedy, joined, and in which Justice Thomas joined in part. He argued that it would be inappropriate to allow Osborne to forego testing at trial and then to request a different test many years later. In Justice Alito's view, this would "allow prisoners to play games with the criminal justice system" because "with nothing to lose, the defendant could demand DNA testing in the hope that some happy accident—for example, degradation or contamination of the evidence—would provide the basis for postconviction relief."

Justice Stevens filed a dissenting opinion, joined by Justices Ginsburg and Breyer and by Justice Souter in part. Justice Stevens argued that the state had no legitimate interest in denying the test, because Osborne had agreed to pay for it; and the state's interest in finality could not outweigh a plausible claim of innocence.

Justice Souter also filed a dissenting opinion, concluding that state officials had "demonstrated a combination of inattentiveness and intransigence that add up to procedural unfairness that violates the due process clause."

Second Thoughts of Witnesses and Jurors

Once a verdict is rendered and judgment is imposed, experienced judges know that the participants in the trial process might have second thoughts after sending a person to prison, or even to death. Most second thoughts, when raised as grounds for reversal due to newly discovered evidence, are treated as routine and ignored. See, e.g., Mastrian v. McManus, 554 F.2d 813 (8th Cir.1977) (recantation by star witness does not warrant new trial). For example, jurors generally cannot attack their verdicts by raising questions about the quality of the deliberations or the firmness of their votes. See Fed.R.Evid. 606(b). Similarly, witnesses who recant their trial testimony and change stories are viewed with utmost suspicion, not only because of the commonness of feelings of remorse, but also because of a judicial fear that improper post-trial influence may be encouraged by ready judicial acceptance of recantations. Third party confessions exculpating the defendant, which are viewed with suspicion even if offered during a trial, see, e.g., Fed.R.Evid. 804(b)(3), are scrutinized with great care. See, e.g., United States v. Kamel, 965 F.2d 484 (7th Cir.1992) (third party "repeatedly and firmly denied involvement in the crime for a period of three years. [The third party's] purported confession, coming after his conviction and shortly before sentencing, when he has relatively little to lose by accepting sole responsibility * * * is far less credible.").

Time Limits

The Advisory Committee on Criminal Rules had suggested that newly discovered evidence motions could be made "at any time before or after final judgment," but the Federal Rule (Rule 33(b)(1)) imposes a three-year time limit. See Herrera v. Collins, 506 U.S. 390 (1993), upholding, against a constitutional attack, a Texas procedure that requires a new trial motion based on newly discovered evidence to be made within 30 days of judgment.

D. THE EFFECT OF AN ERROR ON THE VERDICT

1. Harmless Error

If constitutional error has occurred at a trial (e.g., introduction of a confession in violation of the Sixth Amendment), should reversal be automatic? The next case considers this question.

CHAPMAN V. CALIFORNIA
Supreme Court of the United States, 1967.
386 U.S. 18.

JUSTICE BLACK delivered the opinion of the Court.

[At a murder trial the prosecutor commented on Chapman's failure to testify and the trial court told the jury it could draw adverse inferences from their silence. The comment and the instruction violated Chapman's privilege against self-incrimination under Griffin v. California, 380 U.S. 609 (1965). Although it recognized this, the California Supreme Court held that the error was harmless. Justice Black indicated at the outset of his opinion that two questions were presented: (1) whether a *Griffin* error could ever be harmless, and (2) if so, was the error harmless in this case? Justice Black also stated as an introductory point that the effect of a constitutional error on a state proceeding is a question of federal law.]

We are urged by petitioners to hold that all federal constitutional errors, regardless of the facts and circumstances, must always be deemed harmful. Such a holding, as petitioners correctly point out, would require an automatic reversal of their convictions and make further discussion unnecessary. We decline to adopt any such rule. All 50 States have harmless-error statutes or rules, and the United States long ago through its Congress established for its courts the rule that judgments shall not be reversed for "errors or defects which do not affect the substantial rights of the parties." 28 U.S.C.A. § 2111. * * * All of these rules, state or federal, serve a very useful purpose insofar as they block setting aside convictions for small errors or defects that have little, if any, likelihood of having changed the result of the trial. We conclude that there may be some constitutional errors which in the setting of a particular case are so unimportant and insignificant that they may, consistent with the Federal Constitution, be deemed harmless, not requiring the automatic reversal of the conviction.

* * *

In fashioning a harmless-constitutional-error rule, we must recognize that harmless-error rules can work very unfair and mischievous results when, for example, highly important and persuasive evidence, or argument, though legally forbidden, finds its way into a trial in which the question of guilt or innocence is a close one. What harmless-error rules all aim at is a rule that will save the good in harmless-error practices while avoiding the bad, so far as possible.

[Justice Black refers to Fahy v. Connecticut, 375 U.S. 85, where the Court, construing the harmless error statute, said: "The question is whether there is a reasonable possibility that the evidence complained of might have contributed to the conviction."] Although our prior cases have indicated that there are some constitutional rights so basic to a fair trial that their infraction can never be treated as harmless error,[a] this statement in *Fahy* itself belies any belief that all trial errors which violate the Constitution automatically call for reversal. At the same time, however, like the federal harmless-error statute, it emphasizes an intention not to treat as harmless those constitutional errors that "affect substantial rights" of a party. An error in admitting plainly relevant evidence which possibly influenced the jury adversely to a litigant cannot, under *Fahy,* be conceived of as harmless. Certainly error, constitutional error, in illegally admitting highly prejudicial evidence or comments, casts on someone other than the person prejudiced by it a burden to show that it was harmless. * * * We, therefore, do no more than adhere to the meaning of our *Fahy* case when we hold, as we now do, that before a federal constitutional error can be held harmless, the court must be able to declare a belief that it was harmless beyond a reasonable doubt. While appellate courts do not ordinarily have the original task of applying such a test, it is a familiar standard to all courts, and we believe its adoption will provide a more workable standard, although achieving the same result as that aimed at in our *Fahy* case.

* * *

[The Court went on to hold that the error was not harmless. Justice Stewart concurred in the result and opted for automatic reversal for *Griffin* violations. Justice Harlan dissented on the ground that application of a state harmless error rule was an independent state ground barring Supreme Court review.]

Errors Subject to the Chapman Analysis

The Court has invoked *Chapman* in several cases to hold errors harmless. See Harrington v. California, 395 U.S. 250 (1969) (holding harmless the improper introduction of confessions of non-testifying codefendants); Milton v. Wainwright, 407 U.S. 371 (1972) (declaring that any error in obtaining statements of accused in violation of right to counsel was harmless). The harmless error rule applies to all Fourth Amendment violations as well; see the discussion of the exclusionary rule in Chapter 2.[7]

Harmless Error Review as a Way to Avoid Ruling on the Merits of the Constitutional Challenge

Note that a court may refuse to consider the merits of a constitutional claim on the ground that, even if error, it would be harmless in any event.

---

[a]   See, e.g., Payne v. Arkansas, 356 U.S. 560 (coerced confession); Gideon v. Wainwright, 372 U.S. 335 (right to counsel); Tumey v. Ohio, 273 U.S. 510 (impartial judge).

[7]   The harmless error rule employed in habeas corpus cases is stricter (i.e., reversal less likely) than the *Chapman* standard that is applied to constitutional errors on direct review. See the discussion of habeas corpus later in this Chapter.

This use of harmless error as merits-avoidance is taken to task by Professor Kamin in Harmless Error and the Rights/Remedies Split, 88 Va. L.Rev. 1 (2002). Professor Kamin argues that excessive use of the harmless error rule will fail to deter official misconduct. He therefore suggests that the "harmlessness of an alleged error should never be used as a threshold question; that is, courts should determine whether or not the conduct alleged was error, and should turn to the impact of that error only after determining that it occurred." Professor Kamins also suggests that "where a state official should have known that her conduct was error, the state should be denied the benefit of the harmless error rule." He concludes that "it is only by applying the harmless error rule in these ways * * * that the rule can be kept from stifling the development of constitutional law and can become a tool for changing the behaviors of prosecutors and law enforcement."

Constitutional Errors Not Subject to Harmless Error Review

The Supreme Court has held that most constitutional violations are subject to the harmless error rule, but, as it recognized in the footnote in *Chapman,* some errors can never be harmless. The question is how to determine which errors can be harmless and which cannot.

The errors that the Court has held can never be harmless include: (1) total deprivation of the right to counsel (*Gideon,* cited in the footnote in *Chapman*); (2) a biased judge (Tumey v. Ohio, cited in the footnote in *Chapman*); (3) unlawful exclusion of members of the defendant's race from the grand jury (Vasquez v. Hillery, 474 U.S. 254 (1986)); (4) violation of the right to a public trial (Waller v. Georgia, 467 U.S. 39 (1984)); (5) violation of the right of self-representation (McKaskle v. Wiggins, discussed in Chapter 10); (6) improper exclusion of a juror who is reluctant to impose the death penalty (Gray v. Mississippi, discussed in Chapter 10); (7) improper instruction on the prosecution's burden of proof (Sullivan v. Louisiana, discussed infra); and (8) improper denial of the defendant's right to chosen counsel (United States v. Gonzalez-Lopez, infra).

In addition, harmless error analysis cannot apply if a new trial would in itself be the harm. Thus, violations of the right to speedy trial and a multiple prosecution in violation of the Double Jeopardy Clause will never be harmless error. Finally, some errors require a showing of prejudice before a constitutional violation can even be found. This is so, for example, under the *Strickland* standard for ineffective assistance of counsel and under the *Brady* standard for disclosure of exculpatory evidence by the prosecution. In these two areas, a court that finds a constitutional violation has by definition determined that the error is harmful, and the *Chapman* standard becomes superfluous. See Capra, Access to Exculpatory Evidence: Resolving the *Agurs* Problems of Prosecutorial Discretion and

Retrospective Review, 53 Ford.L.Rev. 391 (1984); Kyles v. Whitley, discussed in Chapter 8 (harmless error analysis redundant after *Brady* violation has been found).

Involuntary Confessions: Arizona v. Fulminante

In Arizona v. Fulminante, 499 U.S. 279 (1991), the Court retreated from the *Chapman* footnote insofar as it implied that admission of an involuntary confession could never be harmless error. Chief Justice Rehnquist, writing for five members of the Court, explained the *Chapman* footnote as a "historical reference."

The Chief Justice distinguished a trial error—"error which occurred during the presentation of the case to the jury, and which may therefore be quantitatively assessed in the context of other evidence presented in order to determine whether its admission was harmless beyond a reasonable doubt"—from an error that is not subject to such an assessment, "a structural defect affecting the framework in which the trial proceeds." A structural defect can never be harmless, because by definition the error infects the entirety of the trial. In contrast, a trial error can be harmless, because it is a more discrete violation and its harm can be more easily pinpointed. According to the majority, admission of an involuntary confession falls into the category of trial error, while total deprivation of counsel as in *Gideon,* or a biased judge as in *Tumey,* falls into the category of structural defect.

For purposes of harmless error analysis, the Chief Justice saw no reason to distinguish admission of coerced confessions from admissions of confessions obtained in violation of the defendant's Sixth Amendment rights or in violation of *Miranda.* As the Court had already found that these violations could be harmless, the Chief Justice concluded that admission of a coerced confession could also be harmless. The Chief Justice noted, however, that due to the substantial impact that a confession has on the trial, it would be the rare case in which admission of a coerced confession would be harmless on the facts. On the merits, the Court found that the admission of Fulminante's involuntary confession was not harmless error.

QUESTIONS ABOUT FULMINANTE

Chief Justice Rehnquist's reference to "structural" error requires a determination of which errors affect an entire trial. In some instances, there is structural error even if a trial was arguably "fair." Consider the defendant who is deprived of the right to proceed *pro se.* It is no answer to say that at his trial, his counsel performed very well and the evidence against him was overwhelming. The right to self-representation is not based upon an effective defense and a correct verdict, but rather upon personal autonomy. Whether or not a violation of this right can be labeled a structural defect, the harmless error rule cannot apply because harmlessness as to the verdict is irrelevant to the wrong suffered. A similar example is the denial of the accused's right to counsel of choice, discussed infra.

Is it possible that the application of the harmless error standard to coerced confessions will make a reviewing court more likely to find certain police tactics impermissible? Is anyone better off when a court holds that a confession was coerced but that its introduction at trial is harmless, where if automatic reversal were required, a court concerned about the cost of retrial might hold the confession voluntary?

Error in a Burden of Proof Instruction: *Sullivan v. Louisiana*

In Sullivan v. Louisiana, 508 U.S. 275 (1993), the Court unanimously held that a constitutionally deficient beyond-a-reasonable-doubt instruction can never be harmless error. At Sullivan's trial, the judge gave an instruction as to reasonable doubt that was virtually identical to the instruction held constitutionally defective in Cage v. Louisiana, 498 U.S. 39 (1990) (instruction defining reasonable doubt in terms of grave and substantial doubt suggests "a higher degree of doubt than is required for acquittal under the reasonable doubt standard"). The state appellate court determined that the evidence against Sullivan was overwhelming and that therefore the erroneous instruction was harmless beyond a reasonable doubt.

Justice Scalia, writing for the Court, noted that the Sixth Amendment right to jury trial means an entitlement to a jury verdict; so, for example, the trial judge may not direct a verdict for the State, no matter how overwhelming the evidence. Justice Scalia explained why, under *Chapman,* an erroneous reasonable doubt instruction could not be harmless:

> Harmless-error review looks, we have said, to the basis on which "the jury actually rested its verdict." The inquiry, in other words, is not whether, in a trial that occurred without the error, a guilty verdict would surely have been rendered, but whether the guilty verdict actually rendered in *this* trial was surely unattributable to the error. This must be so, because to hypothesize a guilty verdict that was never in fact rendered—no matter how inescapable the findings to support that verdict might be—would violate the jury trial guarantee.

> Once the proper role of an appellate court engaged in the *Chapman* inquiry is understood, the illogic of harmless-error review in the present case becomes evident. Since there has been no jury verdict within the meaning of the Sixth Amendment, the entire premise of *Chapman* review is simply absent. * * * There is no *object,* so to speak, upon which harmless-error scrutiny can operate. * * * The Sixth

Amendment requires more than appellate speculation about a hypothetical jury's action, or else directed verdicts for the State would be sustainable on appeal; it requires an actual jury verdict of guilty.

Justice Scalia distinguished cases where the trial court gives an erroneous instruction that erects a presumption regarding an element of the offense that might affect the jury's finding of a predicate fact (e.g., that malice can be presumed if the jury finds that the defendant possessed a deadly weapon). See Yates v. Evatt, 500 U.S. 391 (1991) (erroneous burden-shifting presumption can be assessed for harmlessness). While such an instruction may impermissibly ease the State's burden of having to prove all elements of the offense, the jury is still instructed that it must find the existence of the predicate facts supporting the presumption beyond a reasonable doubt. In contrast, where the instructional error consists of a misdescription of the burden of proof, this "vitiates *all* of the jury's findings," and a reviewing court can only engage in "pure speculation," which would mean that "the wrong entity judges the defendant guilty."

Erroneous Instructions on the Elements of a Crime: Neder v. United States

The trial judge in Neder v. United States, 527 U.S. 1 (1999) erroneously instructed the jury that it would not have to decide whether Neder's false statements on tax forms were "material." In the trial judge's view, the question of materiality was for the judge, not the jury. Neder was convicted. The instruction was error because materiality is an element of the crime of tax fraud, and therefore the question of materiality was for the jury. On appeal, the government agreed with the defendant that the erroneous instruction was error, but argued that the error was harmless. Neder argued that depriving the jury of the power to decide an element of the crime can never be harmless. The Supreme Court, in an opinion by Chief Justice Rehnquist, held that such an error was subject to harmless error review. He analyzed the harmless error question in the following passage:

> Unlike such defects as the complete deprivation of counsel or trial before a biased judge, an instruction that omits an element of the offense does not necessarily render a criminal trial fundamentally unfair or an unreliable vehicle for determining guilt or innocence. * * * In fact, as this case shows, quite the opposite is true: Neder was tried before an impartial judge, under the correct standard of proof and with the assistance of counsel; a fairly selected, impartial jury was instructed to consider all of the evidence and argument in respect to Neder's defense against the tax charges. Of course, the court erroneously failed to charge the jury on the element of materiality, but

that error did not render Neder's trial "fundamentally unfair," as that term is used in our cases.

The Chief Justice distinguished *Sullivan* on the ground that a defective instruction as to one element of a crime did not vitiate *all* of the jury's findings. He also relied on prior case law finding defective instructions on issues other than reasonable doubt to be harmless error. On the applicability of *Sullivan*, the Chief Justice concluded as follows:

> It would not be illogical to extend the reasoning of *Sullivan* from a defective "reasonable doubt" instruction to a failure to instruct on an element of the crime. But * * * the matter is not res nova under our case law. And if the life of the law has not been logic but experience, we are entitled to stand back and see what would be accomplished by such an extension in this case. The omitted element was materiality. Petitioner underreported $5 million on his tax returns, and did not contest the element of materiality at trial. Petitioner does not suggest that he would introduce any evidence bearing upon the issue of materiality if so allowed. Reversal without any consideration of the effect of the error upon the verdict would send the case back for retrial—a retrial not focused at all on the issue of materiality, but on contested issues on which the jury was properly instructed. We do not think the Sixth Amendment requires us to veer away from settled precedent to reach such a result.

Justice Stevens concurred in the judgment in *Neder*. Justice Scalia, joined by Justices Souter and Ginsburg, dissented. He noted that cases such as *Sullivan* indicate that if the entire case is taken away from the jury, this cannot be harmless error. If that is so, how could it be harmless error to take an element of the case away from the jury? Justice Scalia stated that

> we do not know, when the Court's opinion is done, how many elements can be taken away from the jury with impunity, so long as appellate judges are persuaded that the defendant is surely guilty. What if, in the present case, besides keeping the materiality issue for itself, the District Court had also refused to instruct the jury to decide whether the defendant signed his tax return? If Neder had never contested that element of the offense, and the record contained a copy of his signed return, would his conviction be automatically reversed in that situation but not in this one, even though he would be just as obviously guilty? We do not know. We know that all elements cannot be taken from the jury, and that one can. How many is too many (or perhaps what proportion is too high) remains to be determined by future improvisation.

Apprendi Violations Can Be Harmless: Washington v. Recuenco

In Apprendi v. New Jersey, discussed in Chapters 10 and 11, the Court held that the Sixth Amendment was violated when the defendant received a sentence beyond the statutory maximum on the basis of facts proven to the judge at sentencing, but not to the jury. In Washington v. Recuenco, 548 U.S. 212 (2006), the Court held that *Apprendi* violations are not "structural" and are subject to harmless error review. Justice Thomas, writing for six members of the Court, relied heavily on Neder v. United States; as in *Neder* an issue was taken from the jury and given to the judge (the difference in *Apprendi* being that the issue was decided by the judge at sentencing rather than at trial). Justice Thomas reasoned as follows:

> The only difference between this case and *Neder* is that in *Neder*, the prosecution failed to prove the element of materiality to the jury beyond a reasonable doubt, while here the prosecution failed to prove the sentencing factor of "armed with a firearm" to the jury beyond a reasonable doubt. Assigning this distinction constitutional significance cannot be reconciled with our recognition in *Apprendi* that elements and sentencing factors must be treated the same for Sixth Amendment purposes.

The Court remanded for a determination of whether the error was harmless. Justice Kennedy wrote a short concurring opinion emphasizing that the Court was not revisiting the merits of its *Apprendi* jurisprudence. Justice Stevens wrote a short dissent, contending that the Court should never have taken the case because the state court's decision could have been based on its own constitution. Justice Ginsburg wrote a separate dissenting opinion joined by Justice Stevens.

Restricting Closing Argument Is Not Clearly Structural Error: Glebe v. Frost

In Glebe v. Frost, 135 S.Ct. 1429 (2014) (per curiam), a habeas petitioner argued that a structural error occurred when the state trial court restricted defense counsel from making a particular argument in closing. Trial counsel wanted to argue to the jury in closing 1) that the prosecution failed to prove that the defendant was an accomplice to robberies; and 2) that in committing the crime, the defendant was acting under duress. The trial judge insisted that defense counsel choose one argument or the other to close, as the arguments were inconsistent. Defense counsel limited his closing argument to duress, and the defendant was convicted. On direct review, the state court found the trial court's restriction to be a due process violation, but also found the error to be harmless. On habeas review, Frost argued that the state court erred in finding harmless error, because the restriction of counsel's argument was a "structural" error that could not be assessed for harmlessness.

Because the case was on habeas review, Frost was required to show not just that an error occurred but that the state court violated clearly established law as determined by the Supreme Court. 22 U.S.C. § 2254(d). The Court concluded that assuming an error occurred, it was not clearly established that the error was structural. It declared that "[o]nly the rare type of error—in general, one that infects the entire trial process and necessarily renders it fundamentally unfair—requires automatic reversal. None of our cases clearly requires placing improper restriction of closing argument in this narrow category."

Frost argued that the Court's decision in Herring v. New York, 442 U.S. 853 (1975), clearly established that structural error occurred in his case. In *Herring,* [discussed in Chapter Ten) the Court found a violation of due process when the trial court prevented defense counsel from making a closing argument. But the Court in *Frost* held that *Herring* did *not* clearly establish that a trial court was prohibited from requiring defense counsel to choose between inconsistent arguments. The Court reasoned as follows:

> *Herring* held that complete denial of summation violates the Assistance of Counsel Clause. According to the Ninth Circuit, *Herring* further held that this denial amounts to structural error. We need not opine on the accuracy of that interpretation. For even assuming that *Herring* established that *complete denial* of summation amounts to structural error, it did not clearly establish that the *restriction* of summation also amounts to structural error. A court could reasonably conclude, after all, that prohibiting all argument differs from prohibiting argument in the alternative.

Automatic Reversal for Violation of the Right to Counsel of Choice: United States v. Gonzalez-Lopez

In United States v. Gonzalez-Lopez, 548 U.S. 140 (2006), the Court held that the violation of the constitutional right to counsel of choice can never be harmless. The trial court had denied the defendant the right to hire a lawyer from outside the state; the defendant then hired a different lawyer to defend him. The Court of Appeals found the denial to be a violation of the right to the defendant's constitutional right to counsel of choice; that ruling was not contested in the Supreme Court. The government did contend, however, that the defendant was required to show "prejudice" from the denial of his right to counsel of choice. But the Court, in an opinion by Justice Scalia for five Justices, held that no showing of prejudice was required. He noted that any prejudice inquiry would be "speculative" because "[d]ifferent attorneys will pursue different strategies with regard to investigation and discovery, development of the theory of defense, selection of the jury, presentation of the witnesses, and style of witness examination and jury argument. And the choice of attorney will affect whether and on what terms the defendant cooperates with the prosecution, plea bargains, or decides instead to go to trial."

Justice Alito, joined by Chief Justice Roberts, Justice Kennedy, and Justice Thomas, dissented. He argued that the majority's rule of automatic reversal was anomalous because "a defendant who is erroneously required to go to trial with a second-choice attorney is automatically entitled to a new trial even if this attorney performed brilliantly."

Breach of Plea Agreement Is Not a Structural Error Justifying Automatic Relief: Puckett v. United States

In Puckett v. United States, 556 U.S. 129 (2009), Puckett entered into a plea agreement in which the government agreed to support a reduction of Puckett's sentence for acceptance of responsibility. But at the sentencing proceeding the government opposed a sentence reduction on those grounds. Yet Puckett's counsel did not object to, or even mention, the government's breach of its plea agreement. On appeal Puckett raised the issue of breach, but the reviewing court found that he had forfeited his claim of error. It reviewed for plain error and found none—specifically finding that the error did not affect Puckett's substantial rights because the sentencing court indicated that it would not reduce his sentence in any case.

In the Supreme Court, Puckett argued that the plain error standard was inappropriate because a breach of a plea agreement amounts to a "structural error"—rendering it unnecessary to show prejudice and mandating automatic relief. But the Supreme Court, in an opinion by Justice Scalia, rejected this argument. Justice Scalia declared as follows:

> [B]reach of a plea deal is not a "structural" error as we have used that term. * * * A plea breach does not "necessarily render a criminal trial fundamentally unfair or an unreliable vehicle for determining guilt or innocence," Neder v. United States; it does not "defy analysis by harmless-error standards" by affecting the entire adjudicatory framework; and the "difficulty of assessing the effect of the error," United States v. Gonzalez-Lopez, is no greater with respect to plea breaches at sentencing than with respect to other procedural errors at sentencing, which are routinely subject to harmlessness review.

Justice Souter, joined by Justice Stevens, dissented.

Improper Denial of a Peremptory Challenge Is Not Automatically Reversible: Rivera v. Illinois

The defendant in Rivera v. Illinois, 556 U.S. 148 (2009), exercised a peremptory challenge at trial. The trial judge denied the challenge and seated the juror (who ended up serving as foreperson). The trial judge concluded that the defendant struck the juror on impermissible grounds under *Batson*. Rivera was convicted and appealed on the ground that he had a proper reason for striking the juror. The appellate court agreed, but nonetheless affirmed the conviction, on the ground that the trial court's error in seating the juror was harmless: Rivera conceded that the jury (including the juror he sought to strike) was unbiased. Rivera argued, however, that automatic reversal was necessary because it was impossible to tell whether the outcome would have been different had the juror been struck.

The Court, in a unanimous opinion by Justice Ginsburg, held that an improper denial of a peremptory strike did not warrant an automatic reversal. Justice Ginsburg emphasized that the defendant has no constitutional right to a peremptory challenge, and concluded as follows:

> If a defendant is tried before a qualified jury composed of individuals not challengeable for cause, the loss of a peremptory challenge due to a state court's good-faith error is not a matter of federal constitutional concern. Rather, it is a matter for the State to address under its own laws.

Overview on Structural Error: Weaver v. Massachusetts

The Court in Weaver v. Massachusetts, 137 S.Ct. 1899 (2017) (per curiam) considered whether a structural error must result in automatic reversal when the error was not raised until the defendant complained about it on collateral attack in the form of an ineffective assistance of counsel claim. The ineffective assistance claim was that defense counsel failed to object to the exclusion of the public during two days of jury selection.

Justice Kennedy, writing for six members of the Court, held that when a structural error is raised collaterally as a ground for ineffective assistance, the defendant must show prejudice under *Strickland*. He first laid out an overview of the Court's case law on structural error; he noted that the Court had found three different types of errors that it has defined as structural:

> First, an error has been deemed structural in some instances if the right at issue is not designed to protect the defendant from erroneous conviction but instead protects some other interest. This is true of the defendant's right to conduct his own defense, which, when exercised, "usually increases the likelihood of a trial outcome unfavorable to the defendant." McKaskle v. Wiggins, 465 U.S. 168, 177, n. 8 (1984). * * *

> Second, an error has been deemed structural if the effects of the error are simply too hard to measure. For example, when a defendant

is denied the right to select his or her own attorney, the precise effect of the violation cannot be ascertained. * * *

Third, an error has been deemed structural if the error always results in fundamental unfairness. For example, if an indigent defendant is denied an attorney or if the judge fails to give a reasonable-doubt instruction, the resulting trial is always a fundamentally unfair one. See Gideon v. Wainwright, 372 U.S. 335, 343–345 (1963) (right to an attorney); Sullivan v. Louisiana, 508 U.S. 275, 279 (1993) (right to a reasonable-doubt instruction). It therefore would be futile for the government to try to show harmlessness.

These categories are not rigid. In a particular case, more than one of these rationales may be part of the explanation for why an error is deemed to be structural. For these purposes, however, one point is critical: An error can count as structural even if the error does not lead to fundamental unfairness in every case.

Next, Justice Kennedy evaluated the right to a public trial [discussed in Chapter Ten] and why the deprivation of that right is a structural error; but also why it is not the type of structural error that always leads to fundamental unfairness:

[A] violation of the right to a public trial is a structural error. It is relevant to determine why that is so. In particular, the question is whether a public-trial violation counts as structural because it always leads to fundamental unfairness or for some other reason.

Justice Kennedy concluded that its public trial jurisprudence [discussed in Chapter Ten] provide "that courtroom closure is to be avoided, but that there are some circumstances when it is justified"; "although the public-trial right is structural, it is subject to exceptions"; and "in some cases an unlawful closure might take place and yet the trial still will be fundamentally fair from the defendant's standpoint."

Justice Kennedy found a critical difference between structural errors raised at the time of trial or direct review, and those raised in the course of an ineffective counsel claim:

[W]hen a defendant objects to a courtroom closure, the trial court can either order the courtroom opened or explain the reasons for keeping it closed. When a defendant first raises the closure in an ineffective-assistance claim, however, the trial court is deprived of the chance to cure the violation either by opening the courtroom or by explaining the reasons for closure.

Furthermore, when state or federal courts adjudicate errors objected to during trial and then raised on direct review, the systemic costs of remedying the error are diminished to some extent. That is because, if a new trial is ordered on direct review, there may be a reasonable chance that not too much time will have elapsed for witness memories still to be accurate and physical evidence not to be lost. * * *

When an ineffective-assistance-of-counsel claim is raised in postconviction proceedings, the costs and uncertainties of a new trial are greater because more time will have elapsed in most cases. The finality interest is more at risk, * * * and direct review often has given at least one opportunity for an appellate review of trial proceedings. * * *

Justice Kennedy found that Weaver "offered no evidence or legal argument establishing prejudice in the sense of a reasonable probability of a different outcome but for counsel's failure to object," and further that he had not "shown that counsel's failure to object rendered the trial fundamentally unfair."

Justice Thomas, joined by Justice Gorsuch, wrote a short concurring opinion, stating that there were open questions as to two of the Court's assumptions: that the right to a public trial extends to jury selection, and that *Strickland* prejudice can be found by errors that lead to fundamental unfairness.

Justice Alito, joined by Justice Thomas, concurred in the judgment, seeing the case as presenting a straightforward application of *Strickland* prejudice requirements. He concluded that "in order to obtain relief under *Strickland,* Weaver must show that the result of his trial was unreliable. He could do so by demonstrating a reasonable likelihood that his counsel's error affected the verdict. Alternatively, he could establish that the error falls within the very short list of errors for which prejudice [under *Strickland*] is presumed. Weaver has not attempted to make either argument, so his claim must be rejected."

Justice Breyer, joined by Justice Kagan, dissented in *Weaver*. He argued that all structural errors require automatic reversal and therefore could not be evaluated under *Strickland* prejudice standards.

Harmlessness Standard for Non-Constitutional Error: The Kotteakos-Lane Rule

In Kotteakos v. United States, 328 U.S. 750 (1946), the Court established a test of harmlessness for trial errors of a *nonconstitutional* dimension: reversal is not required if the federal appellate court "is sure that the error did not influence the jury or had but very slight effect." Put the other way, reversal is required for a non-constitutional error if it "had substantial and injurious effect or influence in determining the jury's verdict." United States v. Lane, 474 U.S. 438 (1986) (applying the *Kotteakos* standard to a misjoinder under Fed.R.Crim.P. 8(b)). See also Fed.R.Crim.P.

52(a) (an error that does not affect "substantial rights must be disregarded.").

The *Kotteakos-Lane* standard is clearly less protective of defendants than the harmless error rule applied to constitutional errors under *Chapman*. See United States v. Owens, 789 F.2d 750 (9th Cir.1986) (if admission of prior identification was merely a violation of the hearsay rule, it was harmless under the *Kotteakos-Lane* standard; but if admission also violated the defendant's constitutional right to confrontation, the error was harmful under the *Chapman* standard and reversal was required).

If you read federal cases from different circuits, you undoubtedly will find varying statements of the standard for harmless nonconstitutional error. Some examples are found in Saltzburg, Capra & Martin, 1 Federal Rules of Evidence manual § 103.03[1][d] (11th ed. 2015). State courts, although bound to apply *Chapman* to constitutional errors, are free to adopt their own harmless error standards for nonconstitutional errors.

2. Plain Error

The harmless error standards discussed above are applied when the defendant makes a timely and specific objection at trial. A more stringent standard for reversal is applied when the defendant fails to make an objection at trial, and then argues on appeal that the trial court was in error. The appellate court in such a situation reviews for "plain error." The rationale for the more stringent standard is that if a defendant does not properly object at trial, he deprives the trial judge of the opportunity to focus on the problem and perhaps correct the error at that point. The distinction between harmful error and plain error is set forth in Federal Rule of Criminal Procedure 52, which states as follows:

> **(a) Harmless Error.** Any error, defect, irregularity or variance that does not affect substantial rights must be disregarded.

> **(b) Plain Error.** A plain error that affects substantial rights may be considered even though it was not brought to the court's attention.

Thus, Rule 52(a), by negative implication, states that reversal is required if the error affected substantial rights.[8] However, if the defendant did not bring the error to the attention of the court, then a reversal *may* be granted under Rule 52(b) if the error affected substantial rights.

---

[8] This is the harmless error standard applied for non-constitutional errors. For constitutional errors on direct review, the more defendant-friendly *Chapman* standard requires reversal unless the error was harmless beyond a reasonable doubt.

Application of the Plain Error Standard:
United States v. Olano

The Supreme Court had occasion to review the concept of "plain error," and its distinction from harmful error, in United States v. Olano, 507 U.S. 725 (1993). The Court held that the presence of alternate jurors during deliberations was not, under the circumstances of the case, an error that the court of appeals was authorized to correct under Fed.R.Crim.P. 52(b). The defendants had not objected to the presence of the alternate jurors during the deliberations, even though this practice at the time violated the plain terms of Fed.R.Crim.P. 24(c). [The current Rule 24 allows the court to retain alternate jurors even after the jury retires to deliberate although the alternates cannot participate in deliberations unless they actually replace regular jurors].

Writing for the Court, Justice O'Connor reasoned that Rule 52(b) "defines a single category of forfeited-but-reversible error." She identified *three conditions* on a court's power to reverse because of errors that were not properly preserved for review in the trial court:

1.   There must be an error, i.e., a deviation from a legal rule *absent a waiver* by a defendant. Justice O'Connor distinguished waiver of a right from forfeiture of a right, stating that "[w]hereas forfeiture is the failure to make the timely assertion of a right, waiver is the intentional relinquishment of a known right." Thus, if the defendant knowingly and voluntarily waives a right—such as the right to a jury trial—there is no error in the proceedings and the plain error rule is inapplicable. If, on the other hand, the defendant fails to object to an erroneous ruling by the trial court, then the plain error standard is applicable.

2.   The error must be plain, which means it must be clear or obvious—so obvious that the judge should have seen it even though it was not flagged by defense counsel.

3.   The plain error must affect substantial rights, which means that it must have been prejudicial in the sense of affecting the outcome of the case.

Justice O'Connor emphasized that the language of Rule 52(b) is permissive, not mandatory. She stated that "the Court of Appeals should correct a plain forfeited error affecting substantial rights if the error seriously affects the fairness, integrity or public reputation of judicial proceedings." However, a "plain error affecting substantial rights, does not, without more" mandate reversal, "for otherwise the discretion afforded by Rule 52(b) would be rendered illusory."

So in essence there is a fourth requirement for plain error reversal—the error if uncorrected would seriously affect the fairness, integrity or public reputation of judicial proceedings.

Justice O'Connor compared Rule 52(a), which defines harmless error, with Rule 52(b). She concluded that the rules were different in the manner in which they allocated the burden of persuasion in showing prejudice. She analyzed the difference between the rules as follows:

> When the defendant has made a timely objection to an error and Rule 52(a) applies, the Court of Appeals normally engages in a specific analysis of the District Court record—a so-called "harmless error" inquiry—to determine whether the error was prejudicial. Rule 52(b) normally requires the same kind of inquiry, with one important difference: It is the defendant rather than the Government who bears the burden of persuasion with respect to prejudice. In most cases, the Court of Appeals cannot correct the forfeited error unless the defendant shows that the error was prejudicial. This burden-shifting is dictated by a subtle but important difference in language between the two parts of Rule 52: while Rule 52(a) precludes error-correction only if the error "does *not* affect substantial rights" (emphasis added), Rule 52(b) authorizes no remedy unless the error *does* "affec[t] substantial rights."

Justice O'Connor left open the possibility that "[t]here may be a special category of forfeited errors that can be corrected regardless of their effect on the outcome," and declined to address the errors that should be presumed prejudicial. She concluded that normally, the defendant must make a "specific showing of prejudice" under Rule 52(b).

In *Olano,* the Court held that the defendants had failed to show that their substantial rights had been affected by any error. Justice O'Connor noted that the trial judge instructed the alternates that they were not to participate in deliberations, and that the defendants had made no showing that the presence of the alternates affected deliberations in any way.[9]

Error "Plain" at the Time of Appellate Review: *Johnson v. United States*

Can an error be "plain" when the trial court rules correctly at the time of trial, but then the law changes while the case is on direct appeal? This was one of the questions in Johnson v. United States, 520 U.S. 461 (1997). At Johnson's trial for perjury, the trial judge rather than the jury decided the question of whether Johnson's false statement to a grand jury was "material." This practice was in accord with circuit precedent at the time. However, in United States v. Gaudin, 515 U.S. 506 (1995), the Court held that the jury and not the judge must decide whether a false statement is material in cases such as Johnson's. *Gaudin* was decided after Johnson's trial, but while Johnson's case was on direct appeal—therefore *Gaudin* was

---

[9] Justice Kennedy wrote a short concurring opinion. Justice Stevens, joined by Justices White and Blackmun, dissented.

applicable retroactively to Johnson's case. (See the discussion on retroactivity in Chapter 1). However, Johnson had not objected at trial to the trial judge taking the materiality question away from the jury. Indeed, Johnson complained at trial about the prosecution's proffer of evidence of materiality; he argued that the evidence was irrelevant, on the ground that materiality was a question for the judge rather than the jury.

Chief Justice Rehnquist, writing for a unanimous Court, noted that because of *Gaudin*, an "error" had occurred at Johnson's trial. He also noted, however, that because *Gaudin* was decided after Johnson's trial, it was difficult to determine whether the error complained of was "plain" within the meaning of *Olano*:

> In the case with which we are faced today, the error is certainly clear under "current law," but it was by no means clear at the time of trial.
>
> The Government contends that for an error to be "plain," it must have been so both at the time of trial and at the time of appellate consideration. In this case, it says, petitioner should have objected to the court's deciding the issue of materiality, even though near-uniform precedent both from this Court and from the Courts of Appeals held that course proper. Petitioner, on the other hand, urges that such a rule would result in counsel's inevitably making a long and virtually useless laundry list of objections to rulings that were plainly supported by existing precedent. We agree with petitioner on this point, and hold that in a case such as this—where the law at the time of trial was settled and clearly contrary to the law at the time of appeal—it is enough that an error be "plain" at the time of appellate consideration. * * * The second part of the *Olano* test is therefore satisfied.

It must be remembered, though, that under *Olano* plain error does not give rise to relief unless the error affected "substantial rights" and "seriously affects the fairness, integrity or public reputation of judicial proceedings." The Chief Justice concluded that it was not necessary to decide whether the error at Johnson's trial affected substantial rights, because it was clear that the error did not affect the fairness or integrity of the proceedings. He found that the evidence indicating that statements were material was "overwhelming," and that the question of materiality was "essentially uncontroverted at trial and remains so on appeal." Therefore, "no miscarriage of justice will occur if we do not notice the error."

Plain Error Review of an Apprendi Violation: United States v. Cotton

In Apprendi v. New Jersey, 530 U.S. 466 (2000), the Court held that "[o]ther than the fact of a prior conviction, any fact that increases the penalty for a crime beyond the prescribed statutory maximum must be submitted to a jury, and proved beyond a reasonable doubt." [*Apprendi* is set forth in full in the Chapter 10 discussion of constitutionally-based proof requirements]. In federal prosecutions, such facts must also be charged in the indictment. In United States v. Cotton, 535 U.S. 625 (2002), the Court reviewed an *Apprendi* violation for plain error. The defendants in *Cotton* received a sentence beyond the statutory maximum, after the trial judge (rather than the jury) found that the drug offenses involved more than 50 grams of cocaine base. The indictment made no allegation as to any amount of drugs. The government conceded that the defendants' enhanced sentence was erroneous under *Apprendi*, but pointed out that the defendants had failed to raise the *Apprendi* argument before the district court.

The Supreme Court, in an opinion by Chief Justice Rehnquist, held that the defendants were not entitled to relief because they could not meet their burden of showing plain error under the circumstances. Chief Justice Rehnquist concluded that the error did not seriously affect the fairness, integrity, or public reputation of judicial proceedings. He explained as follows:

> The evidence that the conspiracy involved at least 50 grams of cocaine base was overwhelming and essentially uncontroverted. Much of the evidence implicating respondents in the drug conspiracy revealed the conspiracy's involvement with far more than 50 grams of cocaine base. Baltimore police officers made numerous state arrests and seizures between February 1996 and April 1997 that resulted in the seizure of 795 ziplock bags and clear bags containing approximately 380 grams of cocaine base. A federal search of respondent Jovan Powell's residence resulted in the seizure of 51.3 grams of cocaine base. A cooperating co-conspirator testified at trial that he witnessed respondent Hall cook one-quarter of a kilogram of cocaine powder into cocaine base. Another cooperating co-conspirator testified at trial that she was present in a hotel room where the drug operation bagged one kilogram of cocaine base into ziplock bags. Surely the grand jury, having found that the conspiracy existed, would have also found that the conspiracy involved at least 50 grams of cocaine base.

Plain Error Review of Failure to Obtain a Knowing and Intelligent Guilty Plea: United States v. Dominguez-Benitez

As discussed in Chapter 9, Fed.R.Crim.P. 11 sets forth procedural requirements that the court must follow to obtain a valid guilty plea. These requirements are to ensure that the defendant knows the rights he is giving up by pleading guilty and foregoing a trial. In United States v. Dominguez-Benitez, 542 U.S. 74 (2004), the Court considered how a violation of the Rule 11 requirements are to be reviewed for plain error. The parties in *Dominguez-Benitez* entered into the kind of plea in which the government agrees to make a sentencing recommendation, but the court is not bound to accept it. Fed.R.Crim. P. 11(c)(3)(B). Under Rule 11, the defendant entering into such an agreement must be warned that he cannot withdraw his guilty plea if the court refuses to go along with the Government's recommendations. Dominguez-Benitez was not so warned, and he received a sentence much higher than he expected under the agreement. But he never made a timely objection. On appeal, he argued that he should be allowed to withdraw his plea because of plain error.

Justice Souter, writing for the Court, analyzed the function of plain error review for an alleged error in following the procedural requirements of Rule 11.

> [T]he burden of establishing entitlement to relief for plain error is on the defendant claiming it, and for several reasons, we think that burden should not be too easy for defendants in Dominguez's position. First, the standard should enforce the policies that underpin Rule 52(b) generally, to encourage timely objections and reduce wasteful reversals by demanding strenuous exertion to get relief for unpreserved error. Second, it should respect the particular importance of the finality of guilty pleas, which usually rest, after all, on a defendant's profession of guilt in open court, and are indispensable in the operation of the modern criminal justice system. And, in this case, these reasons are complemented by the fact, worth repeating, that the violation claimed was of Rule 11, not of due process.

> We hold, therefore, that a defendant who seeks reversal of his conviction after a guilty plea, on the ground that the district court committed plain error under Rule 11, must show a reasonable probability that, but for the error, he would not have entered the plea. A defendant must thus satisfy the judgment of the reviewing court, informed by the entire record, that the probability of a different result is "sufficient to undermine confidence in the outcome" of the proceeding.

The Court remanded for a determination of whether the defendant could prove plain error. It noted that relevant factors would include the difference between the sentence the defendant received and the sentence he anticipated under the agreement; the strength of the evidence that could have been presented at trial; and "any record evidence tending to show that a misunderstanding was inconsequential to a defendant's decision, or evidence indicating the relative significance of other facts that may have borne on his choice regardless of any Rule 11 error."

Plain Error Standard Applies to Forfeited Objection on Breach of Plea Agreement: Puckett v. United States

In Puckett v. United States, 556 U.S. 129 (2009), Puckett argued that the plain error standard was inappropriate when the error was the breach of a plea agreement. But the Court, in an opinion by Justice Scalia, disagreed. Justice Scalia reviewed the plain error doctrine, and in the following passage found it applicable:

> If an error is not properly preserved, appellate-court authority to remedy the error (by reversing the judgment, for example, or ordering a new trial) is strictly circumscribed. There is good reason for this; anyone familiar with the work of courts understands that errors are a constant in the trial process, that most do not much matter, and that a reflexive inclination by appellate courts to reverse because of unpreserved error would be fatal.

> This limitation on appellate-court authority serves to induce the timely raising of claims and objections, which gives the district court the opportunity to consider and resolve them. That court is ordinarily in the best position to determine the relevant facts and adjudicate the dispute. In the case of an actual or invited procedural error, the district court can often correct or avoid the mistake so that it cannot possibly affect the ultimate outcome. And of course the contemporaneous-objection rule prevents a litigant from "sandbagging" the court—remaining silent about his objection and belatedly raising the error only if the case does not conclude in his favor.

* * *

> We have repeatedly cautioned that any unwarranted extension of the authority granted by Rule 52(b) would disturb the careful balance it strikes between judicial efficiency and the redress of injustice; and that the creation of an unjustified exception to the Rule would be even less appropriate. The real question in this case is not whether plain-error review applies when a defendant fails to preserve a claim that the Government defaulted on its plea-agreement obligations, but rather what conceivable reason exists for disregarding its evident application. Such a breach is undoubtedly a violation of the defendant's rights, but the defendant has the opportunity to seek vindication of those rights in district court; if he fails to do so, Rule 52(b) as clearly sets forth the consequences for that forfeiture as it does for all others.

Justice Souter, joined by Justice Stevens, dissented.

"Any Possibility" Test Is Too Permissive for Plain Error Review: United States v. Marcus

In United States v. Marcus, 560 U.S. 258 (2010), the Court was reviewing a Second Circuit decision conducting plain error review of a claim that Marcus did not raise at trial. Marcus was convicted of sex trafficking. On appeal, for the first time, he argued that some of his conduct preceded the statute under which he was convicted, and therefore his conviction violated the Ex Post Facto Clause of the Constitution. The Government argued that because some of the conduct was conceded to be after the statute went into effect, there was no error that affected Marcus's substantial rights. Justice Breyer, writing for the Court, rejected the Second Circuit's ruling that it must recognize a "plain error" if there is "any possibility," however remote, that a jury convicted a defendant exclusively on the basis of actions taken before enactment of the statute that made those actions criminal. He concluded that a "plain error" must affect substantial rights and therefore be prejudicial and "seriously affect[ ] the fairness, integrity, or public reputation of judicial proceedings.". Justice Breyer noted that there is an exception permitting plain error review for "structural" errors, but concluded that the Ex Post Facto error was not structural.

Justice Stevens dissented in *Marcus*. He contended that the Court's plain error jurisprudence was too formalistic:

> In our attempt to clarify Rule 52(b), we have, I fear, both muddied the waters and lost sight of the wisdom embodied in the Rule's spare text. Errors come in an endless variety of shapes and sizes. Because error-free trials are so rare, appellate courts must repeatedly confront the question whether a trial judge's mistake was harmless or warrants reversal. * * * This Court's ever more intensive efforts to rationalize plain-error review may have been born of a worthy instinct. But they have trapped the appellate courts in an analytic maze that, I have increasingly come to believe, is more liable to frustrate than to facilitate sound decisionmaking.

Justice Sotomayor did not participate in the decision in *Marcus*.

Appellate Court May Not Invoke Plain Error to Increase a Sentence in the Absence of a Government Appeal: Greenlaw v. United States

In Greenlaw v. United States, 554 U.S. 237 (2008), the defendant appealed from his sentence, and the government filed no cross-appeal. The court of appeals rejected the defendant's challenge to his sentence and then proceeded *sua sponte* to determine whether the defendant's sentence was too low. Relying on the doctrine of plain error, the court of appeals entered an order increasing the defendant's sentence by 15 years. The Supreme Court, in an opinion by Justice Ginsburg for six Justices, held that the court of appeals could not use the plain error doctrine to increase a sentence from which the government had not appealed.

Justice Ginsburg relied on 18 U. S. C. § 3742(b), which provides that the government may not appeal a sentence "without the personal approval of the Attorney General, the Solicitor General, or a deputy solicitor general designated by the Solicitor General." She declared that "Congress, in § 3742(b), has accorded to the top representatives of the United States in litigation the prerogative to seek or forgo appellate correction of sentencing errors, however plain they may be. That measure should garner the Judiciary's full respect." Justice Alito, joined by Justices Breyer and Stevens, dissented.

E. DISENTITLEMENT FROM THE RIGHT TO APPEAL

The Fugitive Dismissal Rule:
Ortega-Rodriguez v. United States

If a defendant flees during the pendency of his appeal, the appellate court has the authority to dismiss the appeal. See Molinaro v. New Jersey, 396 U.S. 365 (1970). This "fugitive dismissal" rule is based upon two justifications: 1) the appellate court should not render a judgment that may prove unenforceable; and 2) a defendant who takes flight disentitles himself from the right to call upon the resources of the appellate court.

In Ortega-Rodriguez v. United States, 507 U.S. 234 (1993), the Court considered whether the justifications behind the fugitive dismissal rule apply when a defendant flees the jurisdiction of a district court and is recaptured *before* he invokes the jurisdiction of the appellate court. The Court, in a 5–4 decision, held that "when a defendant's flight and recapture occur before appeal, the defendant's former fugitive status may well lack the kind of connection to the appellate process that would justify an appellate sanction of dismissal."

Justice Stevens pointed out that the enforceability concerns behind the fugitive dismissal rule are not applicable to a defendant who has been returned before the appellate process has begun. He further claimed that flight while the case is pending in the district court was a sign of disrespect for the authority of that court, not of the appellate court; therefore the disentitlement justification of the fugitive dismissal rule would ordinarily not apply to pre-appeal flight, and the defendant's act of flight "is best sanctioned by the district court itself."

The Court refused, however, to adopt a bright-line rule that pre-appeal flight could never result in dismissal of an appeal. Justice Stevens noted that "some actions by a defendant, though they occur while his case is before the district court, might have an impact on the appellate process sufficient to warrant an appellate sanction." For example, the government may be prejudiced in locating witnesses for retrial if the appeal is significantly delayed; or the appellate court may be inconvenienced due to the inability to consolidate the fugitive defendant's appeal with other related appeals. The Court ruled that if such circumstances existed, "a dismissal rule could properly be applied." The Court remanded the case to determine whether the defendant's pre-appeal flight imposed consequences on the appellate system sufficient to justify dismissal of his appeal.

Chief Justice Rehnquist, joined by Justices White, O'Connor, and Thomas, dissented. He stated that "there is as much of a chance that flight will disrupt the proper functioning of the appellate process if it occurs before the court of appeals obtains jurisdiction as there is if it occurs after the court of appeals obtains jurisdiction."

III.   COLLATERAL ATTACK

A.   REMEDIES GENERALLY

1.   Collateral Attacks

After new trial motions have been rejected and all appeals are exhausted—or lost, perhaps for failure to comply with an appellate rule, such as a time limit on filing a notice of appeal—a defendant has a natural incentive to attempt additional attacks on the conviction.

Post-conviction remedies, of which habeas corpus is the most common, have always been regarded as *collateral* remedies, "providing an avenue for upsetting judgments that have become otherwise final." Mackey v. United States, 401 U.S. 667 (1971) (Harlan, J., separate opinion). They are not designed to substitute for direct review of convictions, nor can all the questions properly subject to appeal be raised collaterally. Because collateral attacks collide with principles of finality, there are substantial limitations imposed on persons who want to bring such attacks.

2.   Coram Nobis

One rarely used form of collateral attack is for the petitioner to obtain a writ of coram nobis. This is a remedy of last resort, available only to one otherwise remediless. Given the availability of a habeas corpus petition for those in custody, the coram nobis remedy has only very limited applicability. See Lowery v. United States, 956 F.2d 227 (11th Cir.1992) (coram nobis relief is not available where the defendant is still in custody and can petition for habeas relief). As the court in Telink, Inc. v. United States, 24 F.3d 42 (9th Cir.1994), put it:

> The writ of error coram nobis affords a remedy to attack an unconstitutional or unlawful conviction in cases when the petitioner has already served a sentence. The petition fills a very precise gap in federal criminal procedure. A convicted defendant in federal custody may petition to have a sentence or conviction vacated, set aside or corrected under the federal habeas statute, 28 U.S.C. § 2255. However, if the sentence has been served, there is no statutory basis to remedy the lingering collateral consequences of the unlawful conviction.

Recognizing this statutory gap, the Supreme Court has held that the common law petition for writ of error coram nobis is available in such situations * * *.

Availability of the Writ of Coram Nobis in Federal Courts: United States v. Morgan and Korematsu v. United States

The Supreme Court held in United States v. Morgan, 346 U.S. 502 (1954) that the writ of coram nobis is available in federal courts. After Morgan was convicted in federal court and served his sentence, he was convicted in a state court and sentenced to a longer term as a second offender on the basis of the federal conviction. Collateral attack on the federal conviction under 28 U.S.C.A. § 2255, discussed infra, was not possible because Morgan was not in federal custody. But the Court held that an attack in the nature of coram nobis—in *Morgan* the challenge was that he had not been represented by counsel—was available. The burden of proving a right to relief was placed upon the convicted person. The Court stated that the grant of relief "should be allowed through this extraordinary remedy only under circumstances compelling such action to achieve justice."

Subsequently the Court recognized "the obvious fact of life that most criminal convictions do in fact entail adverse collateral legal consequences." Sibron v. New York, 392 U.S. 40, 55 (1968). Coram nobis, in the absence of other remedies, will allow a convicted person to attempt to avoid these consequences—for example, disentitlement from the right to vote.

One of the most celebrated uses of the writ of coram nobis is Korematsu v. United States, 584 F.Supp. 1406 (N.D.Cal.1984), in which the court vacated the notorious conviction of an American citizen of Japanese ancestry for being in a place where all persons of Japanese ancestry had been excluded following the declaration of war by the United States against Japan in 1941. The conviction had been sustained by the Supreme Court in 1944. 323 U.S. 214 (1944). The district court relied upon a Report of the Commission on Wartime Relocation and Internment of Civilians (1982), which concluded that military necessity did not warrant the exclusion and detention of ethnic Japanese. It also relied upon internal government documents that demonstrated that the government knowingly withheld information from the courts when they were considering the critical question of military necessity in this case.

3. Habeas Corpus

Habeas corpus is a remedy for those who are in custody; the petitioner seeks a writ to be served against the official holding him in custody—

usually the warden. The justification for the writ is that some error occurred that makes the custody illegal.

History of the Great Writ

"The early function of the writ of habeas corpus, say from 1150, was simply to get an unwilling party into court regardless of the kind of case involved." R. Sokol, Federal Habeas Corpus § B, at 4. It did not begin a proceeding; rather, it assured that once a proceeding was otherwise begun, it would not be futile because of the absence of a party. In the fourteenth century, the writ, in addition to its earlier function, also became an independent action to test the cause of a detention. With the development of this aspect of the writ, it took its place in the struggle between the common-law and the chancery courts. "Time and again * * * the common-law judges through habeas corpus released from custody persons committed by other courts," and thus undercut the authority of the Chancellor. D. Meador, Habeas Corpus and Magna Carta: Dualism of Power and Liberty 12 (1966).

Darnel's Case, 3 St.Trials 1, arose in 1627 and probably accounts significantly for the development of the writ. Darnel and four other knights were sent to prison for refusing to "loan" money to a demanding monarch. They sought habeas corpus to inquire into the power of the monarch to imprison them. Unsuccessful though they were, they invoked the concept of "due process of law," and they relied on Magna Carta in a way that led parliament to modify the decision by providing in its Petition of Right that no person should be imprisoned without being charged in some way that allowed an opportunity for an answer. The writ of habeas corpus became the established vehicle for challenging confinement as denying due process of law. In the famous decision in Bushell's Case, 124 Eng.Rep. 1006, 6 St.Trials 999 (1670), the court utilized habeas corpus to order the release of a juror committed for contempt for returning a not guilty verdict in the trial of William Penn and others. A century later Blackstone would call the writ "the most celebrated in the English law."

But the writ was far from a perfect remedy for all illegal detentions. It developed that one court would not order the release of a person held by order of another court if the latter had proper jurisdiction. And, with respect to detentions ordered by the King, it was generally sufficient that the King asserted a right to detain a person despite the Petition of Right.

Following English common-law, the writ of habeas corpus became a part of American law. See generally Oaks, Habeas Corpus in the States—1776–1865, 32 U.Chi.L.Rev. 243 (1965). At the time of the constitutional convention, 4 of the 12 states with written constitutions had provisions regarding habeas corpus. In Article I of the Constitution, which sets forth the powers of Congress and restrictions upon those powers, clause 2 of section 9 provides that "[t]he Privilege of the Writ of Habeas Corpus shall not be suspended, unless when in Cases of Rebellion or Invasion the public Safety may require it."

Congressional Power to Restrict Habeas Corpus

It is unclear how far Congress could go in restricting the habeas corpus power of federal courts. If, for example, Congress did not authorize lower federal courts to hear any habeas corpus cases, would the anti-suspension clause be violated? Under the Constitution, Congress need not create federal courts at all. This might suggest that no habeas power necessarily must be placed in lower courts. See generally Developments in the Law—Federal Habeas Corpus, 83 Harv.L.Rev. 1038, 1049–50, 1263–66 (1970). Some suggestions have been made that even without statutory authority federal courts could grant writs of habeas corpus. See, e.g., Chafee, The Most Important Human Right in the Constitution, 32 B.U.L.Rev. 143 (1952).

Until 2006, no serious effort had been made by Congress to deprive federal courts of habeas corpus jurisdiction. Indeed, as will be seen below, Congress has passed statutes that authorize collateral attack by a petition for habeas corpus. But in the Military Commissions Act of 2006, Congress did purport to deny habeas jurisdiction over a certain set of claims of detained persons who were alleged to be enemy combatants after 9/11. The Military Commissions Act expressly provided that "[n]o court, justice, or judge shall have jurisdiction to hear or consider an application for a writ of habeas corpus filed by or on behalf of an alien detained by the United States who has been determined by the United States to have been properly detained as an enemy combatant or is awaiting such determination" and that "no court, justice, or judge shall have jurisdiction to hear or consider any other action against the United States or its agents relating to any aspect of the detention, transfer, treatment, trial, or conditions of confinement of an alien who is or was detained by the United States and has been determined by the United States to have been properly detained as an enemy combatant or is awaiting such determination."

In Boumediene v. Bush, 553 U.S. 723 (2008), a five-Justice majority invalidated the provision of the Military Commissions Act that purported to deprive the federal courts of habeas jurisdiction over the proceedings against alleged enemy combatants. The Court held that this provision of the Military Commissions Act operated as a suspension of the writ of habeas corpus. The Court rejected the government's argument that the alternative procedures provided by the Act were the functional equivalent of the habeas remedy.

State Habeas Provisions

At one time the Supreme Court granted certiorari to decide whether states are obliged under the Federal Constitution to provide persons convicted in state court with some post-conviction process to correct judgments of conviction obtained in violation of federal law. But the Court remanded the case to the Nebraska Supreme Court when the state legislature passed a post-conviction statute. Case v. Nebraska, 381 U.S. 336 (1965). Since then, all states have recognized some form of post-conviction attack after direct appeal in the state courts has been exhausted. See generally Whitmore v. State, 299 Ark. 55, 771 S.W.2d 266 (1989), for a discussion of the costs of allowing state post-conviction proceedings and the problems involved in integrating state and federal post-conviction proceedings.

In state habeas proceedings, state law governs the extent to which claims can be raised and the procedures that must be followed in raising the claims. If a convicted person wins collateral relief in state court, further proceedings will be unnecessary. But failure to win in state court often will not bar a subsequent federal action to set aside a state conviction.

The remainder of this Chapter will focus on federal actions and two basic questions: (1) What issues should be cognizable in collateral actions? (2) Should it matter (and if so, why) whether the collateral action is brought by a person convicted in a state or federal court? Because this material involves, in part, complex questions of federal-state relations, only the surface is scratched here.

B. FEDERAL HABEAS CORPUS: THE PROCEDURAL FRAMEWORK

1. The Statutes

Federal habeas corpus remedies are available to challenge convictions rendered by both state and federal courts. The challenge must be brought by a person in custody—that person, who was originally the defendant in a criminal proceeding, is the "petitioner" in the habeas proceeding. The petitioner files a civil action in federal court, seeking a writ of habeas corpus on the ground that he is in custody in violation of federal law. Generally speaking, petitions for habeas corpus filed by state prisoners are governed by 28 U.S.C. § 2254 and are often referred to as section 2254 actions. Petitions in the nature of habeas corpus filed by federal prisoners are governed by 28 U.S.C. § 2255 and are often referred to as section 2255 actions.

On April 24, 1996, the President signed into law the Antiterrorism and Effective Death Penalty Act (hereinafter referred to as AEDPA). The AEDPA imposes significant limitations on the habeas corpus remedy in federal courts. Some of these limitations are directed specifically to state death-row claimants, and are conditioned on the state's implementation of a mechanism for appointing competent counsel for state post-conviction proceedings. Other limitations are directed more generally toward any state claimant seeking relief in the federal district court under the provisions of 28 U.S.C. § 2254. Limitations similar to these are imposed by AEDPA on federal prisoners seeking collateral relief under 28 U.S.C. § 2255.

What follows are the statutory provisions that are pertinent to the habeas corpus remedy, as amended by AEDPA. *AEDPA amendments are italicized.*

Section 2241

28 U.S.C.A. § 2241 et seq. sets forth the powers of federal judges to issue writs of habeas corpus and identifies the courts from which it may be sought.

§ 2241. Power to Grant Writ

(a) Writs of habeas corpus may be granted by the Supreme Court, any justice thereof, the district courts and any circuit judge within their respective jurisdictions. The order of a circuit judge shall be entered in the records of the district court of the district wherein the restraint complained of is had.

(b) The Supreme Court, any justice thereof, and any circuit judge may decline to entertain an application for a writ of habeas corpus and may transfer the application for hearing and determination to the district court having jurisdiction to entertain it.

(c) The writ of habeas corpus shall not extend to a prisoner unless—

(1) He is in custody under or by color of the authority of the United States or is committed for trial before some court thereof; or

(2) He is in custody for an act done or omitted in pursuance of an Act of Congress, or an order, process, judgment or decree of a court or judge of the United States; or

(3) He is in custody in violation of the Constitution or laws or treaties of the United States; * * *

* * *

Section 2244

Section 2244, as amended by AEDPA, essentially provides that a habeas petitioner gets one collateral attack. Successive petitions are virtually always to be dismissed. It also provides for a statute of limitations on habeas petitions.

28 U.S.C. § 2244. Finality of Determination

(a) No circuit or district judge shall be required to entertain an application for a writ of habeas corpus to inquire into the detention of a person pursuant to a judgment of a court of the United States if it appears that the legality of such detention has been determined by a judge or court of the United States on a prior application for a writ of habeas corpus *except as provided in Section 2255.*

(b)(1) A claim presented in a second or successive Habeas Corpus application under section 2254 that was presented in a prior application shall be dismissed.

(2) A claim presented in a second or successive Habeas Corpus application under section 2254 that was not presented in a prior application shall be dismissed unless—

(A) The applicant shows that the claim relies on a new rule of Constitutional law, made retroactive to cases on collateral review by the Supreme Court, that was previously unavailable; or

(B)(i) the factual predicate for the claim could not have been discovered previously through the exercise of due diligence; and

(ii) the facts underlying the claim, if proven and viewed in light of the evidence as a whole, would be sufficient to establish by clear and convincing evidence that, but for constitutional error, no reasonable factfinder would have found the applicant guilty of the underlying offense.

(3)(A) Before a second or successive application permitted by this section is filed in the district court, the applicant shall move in the appropriate court of appeals for an order authorizing the district court to consider the application.

(B) A motion in the court of appeals for an order authorizing the district court to consider a second or successive application shall be determined by a three-judge panel of the court of appeals.

(C) The court of appeals may authorize the filing of a second or successive application only if it determines that the

application makes a prima facie showing that the application satisfies the requirements of this subsection.

(D) The court of appeals shall grant or deny the authorization to file a second or successive application not later than 30 days after the filing of the motion.

(E) The grant or denial of an authorization by a court of appeals to file a second or successive application shall not be appealable and shall not be the subject of a petition for rehearing or for a Writ of Certiorari.

(4) A district court shall dismiss any claim presented in a second or successive application that the court of appeals has authorized to be filed unless the applicant shows that the claim satisfies the requirements of this section.

(c) In a habeas corpus proceeding brought in behalf of a person in custody pursuant to the judgment of a State court, a prior judgment of the Supreme Court of the United States on an appeal or review by a writ of certiorari at the instance of the prisoner of the decision of such State court, shall be conclusive as to all issues of fact or law with respect to an asserted denial of a Federal right which constitutes ground for discharge in a habeas corpus proceeding, actually adjudicated by the Supreme Court therein, unless the applicant for the writ of habeas corpus shall plead and the court shall find the existence of a material and controlling fact which did not appear in the record of the proceeding in the Supreme Court and the court shall further find that the applicant for the writ of habeas corpus could not have caused such fact to appear in such record by the exercise of reasonable diligence.

(d)(1) A 1-year period of limitation shall apply to an application for a writ of habeas corpus by a person in custody pursuant to the judgment of a State court. The limitation period shall run from the latest of—

(A) the date on which the judgment became final by the conclusion of direct review or the expiration of the time for seeking such review;

(B) the date on which the impediment to filing an application created by State action in violation of the Constitution or laws of the United States is removed, if the applicant was prevented from filing by such State action;

(C) the date on which the constitutional right asserted was initially recognized by the Supreme Court, if the right has been newly recognized by the Supreme Court and made retroactively applicable to cases on collateral review; or

(D) the date on which the factual predicate of the claim or claims presented could have been discovered through the exercise of due diligence.

(2)   The time during which a properly filed application for State post-conviction or other collateral review with respect to the pertinent judgment or claim is pending shall not be counted toward any period of limitation under this subsection.

Section 2253

Section 2253 limits the right of appeal from a district court's denial of a writ of habeas corpus.

28 U.S.C. § 2253. Appeal

(a)   In a habeas corpus proceeding or a proceeding under section 2255 before a district judge, the final order shall be subject to review, on appeal, by the court of appeals for the circuit in which the proceeding is held.

(b)   There shall be no right of appeal from a final order in a proceeding to test the validity of a warrant to remove to another district or place for commitment or trial a person charged with a criminal offense against the United States, or to test the validity of such person's detention pending removal proceedings.

(c)(1) Unless a circuit justice or judge issues a certificate of appealability, an appeal may not be taken to the court of appeals from—

> *(A)   the final order in a habeas corpus proceeding in which the detention complained of arises out of process issued by a State court; or*

> *(B)   the final order in a proceeding under section 2255.*

(2)   A certificate of appealability may issue under paragraph (1) only if the applicant has made a substantial showing of the denial of a constitutional right.

(3)   The certificate of appealability under paragraph (1) shall indicate which specific issue or issues satisfy the showing required by paragraph (2).

Section 2254

Section 2254 is the basic section governing review of state court convictions by a federal district court in a habeas corpus action. The AEDPA requires federal courts to give substantial deference to state court determinations of federal law. And it requires the petitioner to exhaust state remedies before seeking a habeas corpus petition in federal court. It also limits the ability of a state petitioner to receive an evidentiary hearing in the federal court.

28 U.S.C. § 2254. State Custody; Remedies in Federal Courts

(a) The Supreme Court, a Justice thereof, a circuit judge, or a district court shall entertain an application for a writ of habeas corpus in behalf of a person in custody pursuant to the judgment of a State court only on the ground that he is in custody in violation of the Constitution or laws or treaties of the United States.

(b)*(1) An application for a writ of habeas corpus on behalf of a person in custody pursuant to the judgment of a State court shall not be granted unless it appears that—*

> *(A) the applicant has exhausted the remedies available in the courts of the State; or*

> *(B)(i) there is an absence of available State corrective process; or*

>> *(ii) circumstances exist that render such process ineffective to protect the rights of the applicant.*

(2) An application for a writ of habeas corpus may be denied on the merits, notwithstanding the failure of the applicant to exhaust the remedies available in the courts of the State.

(3) A State shall not be deemed to have waived the exhaustion requirement or be estopped from reliance upon the requirement unless the State, through counsel, expressly waives the requirement.

(c) An applicant shall not be deemed to have exhausted the remedies available in the courts of the State, within the meaning of this section, if he has the right under the law of the State to raise, by any available procedure, the question presented.

(d) An application for a writ of habeas corpus on behalf of a person in custody pursuant to the judgment of a State court shall not be granted with respect to any claim that was adjudicated on the merits in State court proceedings unless the adjudication of the claim—

> *(1) resulted in a decision that was contrary to, or involved an unreasonable application of, clearly established Federal law, as determined by the Supreme Court of the United States; or*

> *(2) resulted in a decision that was based on an unreasonable determination of the facts in light of the evidence presented in the State court proceeding.*

(e)*(1) In a proceeding instituted by an application for a writ of habeas corpus by a person in custody pursuant to the judgment of a*

State court, a determination of a factual issue made by a State court shall be presumed to be correct. The applicant shall have the burden of rebutting the presumption of correctness by clear and convincing evidence.

(2) If the applicant has failed to develop the factual basis of a claim in State court proceedings, the court shall not hold an evidentiary hearing on the claim unless the applicant shows that—

(A) the claim relies on—

(i) a new rule of constitutional law, made retroactive to cases on collateral review by the Supreme Court, that was previously unavailable; or

(ii) a factual predicate that could not have been previously discovered through the exercise of due diligence; and

(B) the facts underlying the claim would be sufficient to establish by clear and convincing evidence that but for constitutional error, no reasonable factfinder would have found the applicant guilty of the underlying offense; and

(f) If the applicant challenges the sufficiency of the evidence adduced in such State court proceeding to support the State court's determination of a factual issue made therein, the applicant, if able, shall produce that part of the record pertinent to a determination of the sufficiency of the evidence to support such determination. If the applicant, because of indigency or other reason is unable to produce such part of the record, then the State shall produce such part of the record and the Federal court shall direct the State to do so by order directed to an appropriate State official. If the State cannot provide such pertinent part of the record, then the court shall determine under the existing facts and circumstances what weight shall be given to the State court's factual determination.

(g) A copy of the official records of the State court, duly certified by the clerk of such court to be a true and correct copy of a finding, judicial opinion, or other reliable written indicia showing such a factual determination by the State court shall be admissible in the Federal court proceeding.

(h) Except as provided in section 408 of the Controlled Substances Act, in all proceedings brought under this section, and any subsequent proceedings on review, the court may appoint counsel for an applicant who is or becomes financially unable to afford counsel, except as provided by a rule promulgated by the Supreme Court pursuant to statutory authority. * * *

(i)   The ineffectiveness or incompetence of counsel during Federal or State collateral post-conviction proceedings shall not be a ground for relief in a proceeding arising under section 2254.

Section 2255

Section 2255 is the main provision regulating habeas petitions by those who have been convicted in federal court. The AEDPA imposes a one-year statute of limitations on such petitions, and generally precludes successive petitions.

28 U.S.C. § 2255. Federal Custody; Remedies on Motion Attacking Sentence

A prisoner in custody under sentence of a court established by Act of Congress claiming the right to be released upon the ground that the sentence was imposed in violation of the Constitution or laws of the United States, or that the court was without jurisdiction to impose such sentence, or that the sentence was in excess of the maximum authorized by law, or is otherwise subject to collateral attack, may move the court which imposed the sentence to vacate, set aside or correct the sentence.

Unless the motion and the files and records of the case conclusively show that the prisoner is entitled to no relief, the court shall cause notice thereof to be served upon the United States attorney, grant a prompt hearing thereon, determine the issues and make findings of fact and conclusions of law with respect thereto. If the court finds that the judgment was rendered without jurisdiction, or that the sentence imposed was not authorized by law or otherwise open to collateral attack, or that there has been such a denial or infringement of the constitutional rights of the prisoner as to render the judgment vulnerable to collateral attack, the court shall vacate and set the judgment aside and shall discharge the prisoner or resentence him or grant a new trial or correct the sentence as may appear appropriate.

A court may entertain and determine such motion without requiring the production of the prisoner at the hearing.

An appeal may be taken to the court of appeals from the order entered on the motion as from the final judgment on application for a writ of habeas corpus.

An application for a writ of habeas corpus in behalf of a prisoner who is authorized to apply for relief by motion pursuant to this section, shall not be entertained if it appears that the applicant has failed to apply for relief, by motion, to the court which sentenced him, or that such court has denied him relief, unless it also appears that the remedy by motion is inadequate or ineffective to test the legality of his detention.

A 1-year period of limitation shall apply to a motion under this section. The limitation period shall run from the latest of—

> *(1)   the date on which the judgment of conviction becomes final;*

> *(2)   the date on which the impediment to making a motion created by governmental action in violation of the Constitution or laws of the United States is removed, if the movant was prevented from making a motion by such governmental action;*

> *(3)   the date on which the right asserted was initially recognized by the Supreme Court, if that right has been newly recognized by the Supreme Court and made retroactively applicable to cases on collateral review; or*

> *(4)   the date on which the facts supporting the claim or claims presented could have been discovered through the exercise of due diligence.*

> *Except as provided in section 408 of the Controlled Substances Act, in all proceedings brought under this section, and any subsequent proceedings on review, the court may appoint counsel, except as provided by a rule promulgated by the Supreme Court pursuant to statutory authority. * * **

> *A second or successive motion must be certified as provided in section 2244 by a panel of the appropriate court of appeals to contain—*

> *(1)   newly discovered evidence that, if proven and viewed in light of the evidence as a whole, would be sufficient to establish by clear and convincing evidence that no reasonable factfinder would have found the movant guilty of the offense; or*

> *(2)   a new rule of constitutional law, made retroactive to cases on collateral review by the Supreme Court, that was previously unavailable.*

Sections 2261–68

28 U.S.C. §§ 2261–68 are provisions added by AEDPA to limit collateral attacks by state death row inmates. Among other things, these sections: 1) limit the ability of death row inmates to obtain more than one stay of execution; 2) generally preclude considerations of claims that were not heard in state court because of the petitioner's failure to comply with a state procedural rule; 3) provide a "rocket docket" for expedited consideration of death penalty claims on habeas. To invoke these

provisions, the state must prove that it has established "by statute, rule of its court of last resort, or by another agency authorized by State law, a mechanism for the appointment, compensation, and payment of reasonable litigation expenses of competent counsel in State post-conviction proceedings brought by indigent prisoners whose capital convictions and sentences have been upheld on direct appeal to the court of last resort in the State or have otherwise become final for State law purposes. The rule of court or statute must provide standards of competency for the appointment of such counsel."

2. General Principles Concerning Habeas Relief After AEDPA

The innovations of AEDPA have raised some important questions about the extent of habeas corpus relief.

a. *Statute of Limitations*

The AEDPA imposes a statute of limitations for habeas corpus petitions: for most petitioners a petition must be filed within one year after the conviction becomes final., There is potentially an even stricter period for death row petitioners—if it is determined, under criteria provided in the statute, that the state provides competent counsel for state post-conviction proceedings, then a death row claimant must file a habeas petition within 180 days of the date his conviction becomes final, with a possible 30-day extension for cause. In Lonchar v. Thomas, 517 U.S. 314 (1996), the Court—applying pre-AEDPA law—held that there was no time limitation on an initial habeas petition, other than the equitable principle of laches. The Court in *Lonchar* declined to dismiss an initial petition filed just before the petitioner was scheduled to be executed six years after his conviction became final. But under the AEDPA, such a petition would have to be dismissed as untimely.[10]

Note that there the limitations period in AEDPA is tolled in section 2254 actions for the time taken to pursue state collateral relief. See Carey v. Saffold, 536 U.S. 214 (2002) (petition for state collateral review in California was "pending" in the time between the lower state court's decision and the filing of a new petition in a higher court, tolling the period for filing a federal habeas petition). See also Duncan v. Walker, 533 U.S. 167 (2001) (action for federal relief does not toll the AEDPA statute of limitations; section 2254 refers only to "state" collateral proceedings as tolling the limitations period).

---

[10] In Day v. McDonough, 547 U.S. 198 (2006), the Court held that a district court has the authority to raise an untimeliness defense *sua sponte*, but only in "exceptional circumstances." Thereafter in Wood v. Milyard, 566 U.S. 463 (2012), the Court held that an appellate court has a similar authority to raise an untimely defense *sua sponte,* but stated that the authority was somewhat more narrow than the district court's because the appellate court must consider the fact that the district court has already expended time and consideration on the merits.

Equitable Tolling: Holland v. Florida

In Holland v. Florida, 560 U.S. 631 (2010), the Court in an opinion by Justice Breyer held that the timeliness provision of AEDPA is subject to equitable tolling. While there is nothing in AEDPA about equitable tolling, Justice Breyer noted that the limitations period of AEDPA is not jurisdictional and stated that "a nonjurisdictional federal statute of limitations is ordinarily subject to a rebuttable presumption of equitable tolling." In the case of AEDPA, "the presumption's strength is reinforced by the fact that equitable principles have traditionally governed the substantive law of habeas corpus." Justice Breyer concluded as follows:

> The importance of the Great Writ, the only writ explicitly protected by the Constitution, Art. I, § 9, cl. 2, along with congressional efforts to harmonize the new statute with prior law, counsels hesitancy before interpreting AEDPA's statutory silence as indicating a congressional intent to close courthouse doors that a strong equitable claim would ordinarily keep open.

Justice Breyer stated that a petitioner is entitled to equitable tolling "only if he shows (1) that he has been pursuing his rights diligently, and (2) that some extraordinary circumstance stood in his way and prevented timely filing." Under the facts presented in *Holland,* the Court found that the limitations period was equitably tolled because Holland's lawyer (Collins)

> failed to file Holland's petition on time despite Holland's many letters that repeatedly emphasized the importance of his doing so. Collins apparently did not do the research necessary to find out the proper filing date, despite Holland's letters that went so far as to identify the applicable legal rules. Collins failed to inform Holland in a timely manner about the crucial fact that the Florida Supreme Court had decided his case, again despite Holland's many pleas for that information. And Collins failed to communicate with his client over a period of years, despite various pleas from Holland that Collins respond to his letters.

Justice Scalia, joined by Justice Thomas, dissented in *Holland.* Justice Alito wrote an opinion concurring in part and concurring in the judgment.

Relation Back: Mayle v. Felix

In Mayle v. Felix, 545 U.S. 644 (2005), the Court held that an amended habeas petition does not relate back (and thereby avoid AEDPA's one-year time limit) when it asserts a new ground for relief supported by facts that differ in both time and type from those set forth in the original timely pleading. The Court applied the relation-back provision of Rule 15(c)(2) of the Federal Rules of Civil Procedure (because habeas petitions are civil cases). The Court concluded that a limitation on relation-back principles was necessary to accommodate the intent of AEDPA which emphasized the importance of finality and federalism. Justice Souter, joined by Justice Stevens, dissented.

b.   *Effect on Supreme Court's Appellate Jurisdiction: Felker v. Turpin*

AEDPA requires dismissal of a claim presented in a state prisoner's federal habeas application if the claim was also presented in a prior application. The Act also compels dismissal of a claim that could have been but was not presented in a prior federal application, unless certain extremely rigorous conditions are met. These limitations are directed at the perceived problem of successive habeas petitions. To effectuate these strict standards, the Act creates a "gatekeeping" mechanism, under which a petitioner must move in the court of appeals for leave to file a second or successive habeas application in the district court. A three-judge panel then determines whether the petitioner has made a prima facie showing that the strict substantive requirements for successive applications have been met. The Act further declares that a panel's grant or denial of authorization to file "shall not be appealable and shall not be the subject of a petition for . . . writ of certiorari." Thus, the Act limits the appellate jurisdiction of the Supreme Court over successive habeas applications.

In Felker v. Turpin, 518 U.S. 651 (1996), the Court unanimously rejected a constitutional attack on this statutory limitation of Supreme Court appellate jurisdiction. Chief Justice Rehnquist, writing for the Court, declared that the AEDPA did not alter the Supreme Court's power to exercise *original* jurisdiction over a habeas petition, as provided for by 28 U.S.C. §§ 2241 and 2254. (It should be noted, however, that the Supreme Court has not granted relief on original jurisdiction over a habeas petition in more than 100 years.) On the jurisdictional question, Chief Justice Rehnquist concluded as follows:

> The critical language of Article III, § 2, of the Constitution provides that, apart from several classes of cases specifically enumerated in this Court's original jurisdiction, "in all the other Cases . . . the supreme Court shall have appellate Jurisdiction, both as to Law and Fact, with such Exceptions, and under such Regulations as the Congress shall make." Previous decisions construing this clause have said that while our appellate powers "are given by the constitution," "they are limited and regulated by the [Judiciary Act of 1789], and by such other acts as have been passed on the subject." The [AEDPA] does remove our authority to entertain an appeal or a petition for a writ of certiorari to review a decision of a court of appeals exercising its "gatekeeping" function over a second petition. But since it does not repeal our authority to entertain a petition for habeas corpus, there can be no

plausible argument that the Act has deprived this Court of appellate jurisdiction in violation of Article III, § 2.

On the merits, the Court refused, as an exercise of its original jurisdiction, to entertain Felker's claim for habeas relief on a successive petition. Felker challenged his conviction on the grounds of a *Brady* violation and an erroneous instruction on reasonable doubt. The Chief Justice set forth the standards for original jurisdiction, and the resolution of Felker's claims, in the following passage:

> [W]e now dispose of the petition for an original writ of habeas corpus. Our Rule 20.4(a) delineates the standards under which we grant such writs:
>
> > "* * * To justify the granting of a writ of habeas corpus, the petitioner must show exceptional circumstances warranting the exercise of the Court's discretionary powers and must show that adequate relief cannot be obtained in any other form or from any other court. These writs are rarely granted."
>
> Reviewing petitioner's claims here, they do not materially differ from numerous other claims made by successive habeas petitioners which we have had occasion to review on stay applications to this Court. Neither of them satisfies the requirements of the relevant provisions of the [AEDPA], let alone the requirement that there be "exceptional circumstances" justifying the issuance of the writ.

c.   *Certificate of Appealability*

The AEDPA limits the right to appeal from a district court's denial of a state defendant's petition for a writ of habeas corpus. The Act requires that the petitioner must obtain a "certificate of appeal" from a circuit judge. In Slack v. McDaniel, 529 U.S. 473 (2000), the Court set forth the standard that circuit judges are to apply in deciding whether to issue a certificate of appealability. It declared as follows:

> Where a district court has rejected the constitutional claims on the merits, the showing required to satisfy § 2253(c) is straightforward: The petitioner must demonstrate that reasonable jurists would find the district court's assessment of the constitutional claims debatable or wrong. The issue becomes somewhat more complicated where, as here, the district court dismisses the petition based on procedural grounds. We hold as follows: When the district court denies a habeas petition on procedural grounds without reaching the prisoner's underlying constitutional claim, a COA should issue when the prisoner shows, at least, that jurists of reason would find it debatable whether the petition states a valid claim of the denial of a constitutional right and that jurists of reason would find it debatable whether the district court was correct in its procedural ruling. This construction gives

meaning to Congress' requirement that a prisoner demonstrate substantial underlying constitutional claims and is in conformity with the meaning of the "substantial showing" standard * * * adopted by Congress in AEDPA. Where a plain procedural bar is present and the district court is correct to invoke it to dispose of the case, a reasonable jurist could not conclude either that the district court erred in dismissing the petition or that the petitioner should be allowed to proceed further. In such a circumstance, no appeal would be warranted.

See also Miller-El v. Cockrell, 537 U.S. 322 (2003) (finding that the petitioner met the *Slack* standard by providing circumstantial evidence that the prosecutor excused jurors on racial grounds in violation of Batson v. Kentucky, and remanding for a hearing of the appeal on the merits).

3. Factual Findings and Mixed Questions of Law and Fact

In a Section 2254 action, what deference does a federal court owe to the state court's determinations of law and fact? Before AEDPA, the Court had held that federal habeas courts were not required to defer to a state court's interpretations of federal law, nor to mixed questions of fact and law. See, e.g., Miller v. Fenton, 474 U.S. 104 (1985) (state court's decision that a confession was voluntary is a mixed question of fact and law which federal courts do not presume to be correct).

But as amended by AEDPA, section 2254 requires habeas courts to give substantial deference to *all* state court rulings in the case. AEDPA makes no definite distinction, in terms of deference, between questions of law and mixed questions of law and fact. The pertinent provision states as follows:

(d) An application for a writ of habeas corpus on behalf of a person in custody pursuant to the judgment of a State court shall not be granted with respect to any claim that was adjudicated on the merits in State court proceedings unless the adjudication of the claim—

(1) resulted in a decision that was contrary to, or involved an unreasonable application of, clearly established Federal law, as determined by the Supreme Court of the United States; or

(2) resulted in a decision that was based on an unreasonable determination of the facts in light of the evidence presented in the State court proceeding.

Guidelines on the Deferential Standard of Review in Section 2254(d): Williams v. Taylor

In Williams v. Taylor, 529 U.S. 362 (2000), the Court construed section 2254(d) as amended by the AEDPA, and set forth the standard for federal review of state court determinations, as mandated by that section. The case involved a claim on habeas that Williams's counsel had been ineffective at the penalty phase of his capital trial by failing to introduce evidence that Williams had been abused as a child and was borderline retarded. The State Supreme Court, applying Strickland v. Washington and subsequent Supreme Court cases, rejected Williams's ineffectiveness claim on the ground that Williams had not been prejudiced. Justice O'Connor, writing for the Court, analyzed the standard of review under AEDPA in the following passage:

> [F]or Williams to obtain federal habeas relief, he must first demonstrate that his case satisfies the condition set by § 2254(d)(1). That provision modifies the role of federal habeas courts in reviewing petitions filed by state prisoners.
>
> * * *
>
> The word "contrary" is commonly understood to mean "diametrically different," "opposite in character or nature," or "mutually opposed." The text of § 2254(d)(1) therefore suggests that the state court's decision must be substantially different from the relevant precedent of this Court. * * * A state-court decision will certainly be contrary to our clearly established precedent if the state court applies a rule that contradicts the governing law set forth in our cases. Take, for example, our decision in Strickland v. Washington. If a state court were to reject a prisoner's claim of ineffective assistance of counsel on the grounds that the prisoner had not established by a preponderance of the evidence that the result of his criminal proceeding would have been different, that decision would be "diametrically different," "opposite in character or nature," and "mutually opposed" to our clearly established precedent because we held in *Strickland* that the prisoner need only demonstrate a "reasonable probability that . . . the result of the proceeding would have been different." A state-court decision will also be contrary to this Court's clearly established precedent if the state court confronts a set of facts that are materially indistinguishable from a decision of this Court and nevertheless arrives at a result different from our precedent. Accordingly, in either of these two scenarios, a federal court will be unconstrained by § 2254(d)(1) because the state-court decision falls within that provision's "contrary to" clause.
>
> On the other hand, a run-of-the-mill state-court decision applying the correct legal rule from our cases to the facts of a prisoner's case would not fit comfortably within § 2254(d)(1)'s "contrary to" clause. Assume, for example, that a state-court decision on a prisoner's ineffective-assistance claim correctly identifies *Strickland* as the controlling legal authority and, applying that framework, rejects the

prisoner's claim. Quite clearly, the state-court decision would be in accord with our decision in *Strickland* as to the legal prerequisites for establishing an ineffective-assistance claim, even assuming the federal court considering the prisoner's habeas application might reach a different result applying the *Strickland* framework itself. * * * Although the state-court decision may be contrary to the federal court's conception of how *Strickland* ought to be applied in that particular case, the decision is not "mutually opposed" to *Strickland* itself.

So a state court decision cannot be overturned on habeas simply because it is incorrect—under the "contrary to" clause, the state court decision must be diametrically opposed to Supreme Court precedent in order to justify habeas relief.

Justice O'Connor next construed the "unreasonable application" clause of § 2254(d)(1):

First, a state-court decision involves an unreasonable application of this Court's precedent if the state court identifies the correct governing legal rule from this Court's cases but unreasonably applies it to the facts of the particular state prisoner's case. Second, a state-court decision also involves an unreasonable application of this Court's precedent if the state court either unreasonably extends a legal principle from our precedent to a new context where it should not apply or unreasonably refuses to extend that principle to a new context where it should apply.

A state-court decision that correctly identifies the governing legal rule but applies it unreasonably to the facts of a particular prisoner's case certainly would qualify as a decision "involv[ing] an unreasonable application of . . . clearly established Federal law."

Justice O'Connor noted that some lower courts had defined "unreasonable application of law" by determining whether any reasonable jurist would agree with the state court's determination—if so, this would preclude habeas relief. Justice O'Connor, however, rejected the "reasonable jurist" standard:

Defining an "unreasonable application" by reference to a "reasonable jurist" * * * is of little assistance to the courts that must apply § 2254(d)(1) and, in fact, may be misleading. Stated simply, a federal habeas court making the "unreasonable application" inquiry should ask whether the state court's application of clearly established federal law was objectively unreasonable. The federal habeas court should not transform the inquiry into a subjective one by resting its determination instead on the simple fact that at least one of the Nation's jurists has applied the relevant federal law in the same manner the state court did in the habeas petitioner's case. * * *

The term "unreasonable" is no doubt difficult to define. That said, it is a common term in the legal world and, accordingly, federal judges are familiar with its meaning. For purposes of today's opinion, the most important point is that an unreasonable application of federal law is different from an incorrect application of federal law. * * * In § 2254(d)(1), Congress specifically used the word "unreasonable," and not a term like "erroneous" or "incorrect." Under § 2254(d)(1)'s "unreasonable application" clause, then, a federal habeas court may not issue the writ simply because that court concludes in its independent judgment that the relevant state-court decision applied clearly established federal law erroneously or incorrectly. Rather, that application must also be unreasonable.

Justice O'Connor concluded as follows:

In sum, § 2254(d)(1) places a new constraint on the power of a federal habeas court to grant a state prisoner's application for a writ of habeas corpus with respect to claims adjudicated on the merits in state court. * * * Under the "contrary to" clause, a federal habeas court may grant the writ if the state court arrives at a conclusion opposite to that reached by this Court on a question of law or if the state court decides a case differently than this Court has on a set of materially indistinguishable facts. Under the "unreasonable application" clause, a federal habeas court may grant the writ if the state court identifies the correct governing legal principle from this Court's decisions but unreasonably applies that principle to the facts of the prisoner's case.

On the merits, a majority of the *Williams* Court held that the state court's decision was both "contrary to" and an "unreasonable application" of *Strickland*. The state court held that the *Strickland* prejudice prong did not focus on what the outcome might have been had defense counsel acted effectively—when in fact that is the very focus of the prejudice prong. The state court also ignored the impact that the substantial mitigating evidence might have had on the jury at the penalty phase.

Application of Deferential AEDPA Standards of Review and Rejection of Relief for "Unreasonable Failure to Extend" Existing Precedent: White v. Woodall

In White v. Woodall, 134 S.Ct. 1697 (2014), Justice Scalia wrote for the Court as it reversed the Sixth Circuit's grant of habeas relief to a state court defendant who brutally raped, slashed with a box cutter, and drowned a 16-year-old high-school student. The defendant pled guilty to murder, rape, and kidnaping, and was sentenced to death. The Kentucky Supreme Court affirmed the sentence, and the U. S. Supreme Court denied certiorari. Ten years later, the Sixth Circuit granted habeas relief on the ground that the state court had misapplied federal law.

At the penalty-phase trial, Woodall called character witnesses but declined to testify himself. Defense counsel asked the trial judge to instruct the jury that "[a] defendant is not compelled to testify and the fact that the defendant did not testify should not prejudice him in any way." The trial judge denied the request, and the Kentucky Supreme Court affirmed that denial. A federal district court ruled that the state judge's denial Woodard his Fifth Amendment self-incrimination right, and the Sixth Circuit agreed.

Justice Scalia examined the Court's precedents to find that Carter v. Kentucky, 450 U.S. 288 (1981), held that a non-inference instruction is required at the guilt stage of a case; Estelle v. Smith, 451 U.S. 454 (1981), concerned the introduction at the penalty phase of the results of an involuntary, un-*Mirandized* pretrial psychiatric examination; and Mitchell v. United States, 526 U.S. 314 (1999), disapproved a trial judge's drawing of an adverse inference from the defendant's silence at sentencing "with regard to factual determinations respecting the circumstances and details of the crime." From this he concluded that "[i]t is clear that the Kentucky Supreme Court's conclusion is not 'contrary to' the actual holding of any of these cases and did not amount to "an unreasonable application of" those cases." Justice Scalia noted that "*Mitchell* itself leaves open the possibility that some inferences might permissibly be drawn from a defendant's penalty-phase silence" and "suggests that *some* actual inferences might be permissible at the penalty phase."

Justice Scalia rejected the lower courts reasoning that Kentucky was "unreasonable in refusing to extend the governing legal principle to a context in which the principle should have controlled" and made clear that the AEDPA "does not require state courts to *extend* that precedent or license federal courts to treat the failure to do so as error." He identified "[t]he critical point" as being "relief is available under § 2254(d)(1)'s unreasonable-application clause if, and only if, it is so obvious that a clearly established rule applies to a given set of facts that there could be no fairminded disagreement on the question."

Justice Breyer, joined by Justices Ginsburg and Sotomayor, dissented and argued that *Carter* and *Estelle* "clearly establish that a criminal defendant is entitled to a requested no-adverse-inference instruction in the penalty phase of a capital trial."

Section 2254(d) Deference Requires the Federal Court to Review All Grounds for the State Decision: Wetzel v. Lambert

In Wetzel v. Lambert, 565 U.S. 520 (2012), the habeas petitioner challenged a 30 year-old conviction for robbery and murder on the ground that the government had suppressed a report that could be read to indicate that there was another suspect in the robbery (and related murder). The petitioner argued that the report was materially exculpatory evidence under *Brady*, for two reasons: 1) it could have created reasonable doubt that there was a different perpetrator; and 2) it could have impeached an important government witness. The state courts rejected both grounds: the first because the report was ambiguous on whether the other person was suspected of the robbery at issue or some other robbery, and the second because the witness was effectively impeached on other grounds. The federal appellate court granted the writ, ruling that the state court was plainly unreasonable in concluding that the suppressed report would not have been useful to impeach the government witness—saying nothing about the other argument (ambiguity of the report) that the state court relied upon as an alternative ground for dismissal.

The Court, in a per curiam opinion, reversed the federal court and held that it could not grant the writ unless it found that the state court was unreasonable on *each* ground upon which it relied. The Court explained as follows:

> Under § 2254(d), a habeas court must determine what arguments or theories supported the state court's decision; and then it must ask whether it is possible fairminded jurists could disagree that those arguments or theories are inconsistent with the holding in a prior decision of this Court.

> In this case, however, the Third Circuit overlooked the determination of the state courts that the notations [in the suppressed report] were, as the District Court put it, "not exculpatory or impeaching" but instead "entirely ambiguous." Instead, the Third Circuit focused solely on the alternative ground that any impeachment value that might have been obtained from the notations would have been cumulative. If the conclusion in the state courts about the content of the document was reasonable—not necessarily correct, but reasonable—whatever those courts had to say about cumulative impeachment evidence would be beside the point. * * *

Justice Breyer, joined by Justices Ginsburg and Kagan, dissented on the ground that the Court should not have granted certiorari as the case presented only "fact-specific questions about whether a lower court properly applied the well-established legal principles that it sets forth in its opinion."

4. Retroactivity

As discussed in Chapter 1, in a habeas action, a state court's determination of federal law is assessed as of the time the state conviction was finalized (i.e., direct review is over). Once the defendant's conviction has been finalized, he is not entitled to subsequent changes in legal doctrine that might work to his advantage. The Court established this principle in Teague v. Lane, set forth as a principal case in Chapter 1. The AEDPA essentially codified Teague v. Lane in section 2254(d), set forth above. The AEDPA's innovation is to treat the *Teague* concept not as one of retroactive application, but rather as a matter of deference to state court determinations. If the petitioner argues that a new rule should work to his benefit, this argument would be dismissed because new section 2254(d) requires a federal court to defer to a state court's determination of "clearly established" federal law. Arguing for a new rule on habeas is by definition prohibited because the state court decision is judged by whether it was contrary to clearly established law *at the time of the state court ruling.*

C. CLAIMS COGNIZABLE IN COLLATERAL PROCEEDINGS

Section 2254(a) makes it clear that a district court can only entertain an application for habeas corpus relief on behalf of a state prisoner if the prisoner alleges that state custody "is in violation of the Constitution or laws or treaties of the United States." In almost every case the prisoner claims that the state conviction was obtained in violation of the federal Constitution. Section 2255 allows an attack on a federal conviction alleged to be in violation of the Constitution or laws of the United States and adds other grounds for attack. But not every claim of a violation of federal law is cognizable on habeas. If that were so, the collateral remedy might serve as a substitute for appeal.

1. Non-Constitutional Claims

Federal Defendants

The courts have limited section 2255 relief to "substantial" violations of federal law that have resulted in significant harm to the petitioner. See Hill v. United States, 368 U.S. 424 (1962) (defendant denied opportunity to make a statement before sentencing; no attack permitted); United States v. Timmreck, 441 U.S. 780 (1979) (technical violation of rule establishing procedures for accepting guilty pleas; no attack permitted). As the Court in *Hill* put it, habeas review for federal statutory violations is not available for federal defendants under section 2255 unless the statutory violation qualifies as a "fundamental defect which inherently results in a complete miscarriage of justice, or an omission inconsistent with the rudimentary demands of fair procedure."

The Court applied the principles of *Hill* and *Timmreck* in Peguero v. United States, 526 U.S. 23 (1999). Peguero sought habeas relief from a federal conviction because the district court at sentencing failed to inform him of his right to appeal the sentence. This failure to notify was a violation of Fed.R.Crim.P. 32(a)(2). The Court, in an opinion by Justice Kennedy, relied on *Hill* and *Timmreck* and declared that as a general rule, "a court's failure to give a defendant advice required by the Federal Rules is a sufficient basis for collateral relief only when the defendant is prejudiced by the court's error." In this case, no prejudice could be found, because Peguero in fact had full knowledge of his right to appeal the sentence. Accordingly, he was not entitled to habeas relief.

State Defendants

In Reed v. Farley, 512 U.S. 339 (1994), the Court extended the "fundamental defect" test of *Hill* to claims of federal statutory violations brought by state defendants under section 2254. The statutory violation at issue in *Reed* concerned the Interstate Agreement on Detainers ("IAD"), a compact among 48 States, the District of Columbia, and the Federal Government. Article IV(c) of the IAD provided, among other things, that the trial of a prisoner transferred from one participating jurisdiction to another must commence within 120 days of the prisoner's arrival in the receiving State, and directed dismissal with prejudice when trial does not occur within the time prescribed. Reed's trial did not begin within this time limit. The trial court denied Reed's petition for discharge on the ground that the judge had previously been unaware of the 120-day limitation and that Reed had not earlier objected to the trial date or requested a speedier trial. Reed was convicted, and after unsuccessful appeals in the Indiana courts, he petitioned for a federal writ of habeas corpus under section 2254.

Justice Ginsburg, in an opinion for five Justices, rejected Reed's argument that the "fundamental defect" standard of *Hill* should not be applicable to habeas claims of state defendants brought under section 2254. She analyzed the issue as follows:

> [I]t is scarcely doubted that, at least where mere statutory violations are at issue, § 2255 was intended to mirror § 2254 in operative effect. Far from suggesting that the *Hill* standard is inapplicable to § 2254 cases, our decisions assume that *Hill* controls collateral review—under both §§ 2254 and 2255—when a federal statute, but not the Constitution, is the basis for the postconviction attack. * * *

> We see no reason to afford habeas review to a state prisoner like Reed, who let a time clock run without alerting the trial court, yet deny collateral review to a federal prisoner similarly situated.

The question remained whether the statutory violation suffered by Reed (i.e., the violation of the time limits of the IAD) rose to the level of a "fundamental defect" under *Hill*. Five members of the Court concluded that there was no "fundamental defect," but there was no majority opinion on this point. Justice Ginsburg, joined by Chief Justice Rehnquist and Justice O'Connor on this question, emphasized that Reed had not asserted his rights under the IAD in a timely manner. She did not, however, preclude the possibility that some violation of the IAD might be cognizable on section 2254 habeas review under the "fundamental defect" standard. She noted that the IAD's purpose of providing a nationally uniform means of transferring prisoners between jurisdictions "would be undermined if a State's courts resisted steadfast enforcement, with total insulation from § 2254 review."

Justice Scalia, in an opinion joined by Justice Thomas, concurred in Justice Ginsburg's determination that the "fundamental defect" standard was applicable to claims brought for federal statutory violations by state defendants under section 2254. He concurred only in the result, however, on the question of whether the IAD violation suffered by Reed rose to the level of a "fundamental defect." He argued, more broadly than Justice Ginsburg, that a violation of the IAD could never result in a "fundamental defect" warranting habeas review, and he implied even more broadly that there could never be a federal statutory violation that would justify review under the "fundamental defect" standard.

Justice Blackmun dissented in *Reed* in an opinion joined by Justices Stevens, Kennedy, and Souter. He argued that the "fundamental defect" test of *Hill* was too stringent to be applied to federal statutory claims brought by state prisoners under section 2254. He reasoned that section 2255 actions "cover the ground already covered by federal courts" and so error should be egregious before collateral relief is granted. In contrast " a primary purpose of § 2254 is to provide a federal forum to review a state prisoner's claimed violations of federal law." Thus, "where no federal court previously has addressed the § 2254 petitioner's federal claims, there is less reason to sift these claims through so fine a screen" as *Hill* provides.

State Law Violations as Due Process Violations: Estelle v. McGuire

Federal due process claims are clearly cognizable under §§ 2254 and 2255. State defendants are often therefore tempted to characterize a violation of some state law as tantamount to a due process violation. This ploy is not often successful, however. For example, in Estelle v. McGuire, 502 U.S. 62 (1991), McGuire was convicted in state court of the murder of his infant daughter. At the trial, the state offered medical evidence indicating that the infant had suffered severe injuries several weeks before her death. This evidence was offered to prove "battered child syndrome." The Ninth Circuit granted McGuire's habeas petition, reasoning that evidence of the child's prior injury was "incorrectly admitted pursuant to California law," and that the violation of a California rule of evidence also violated McGuire's due process rights.

The Supreme Court, in an opinion by Chief Justice Rehnquist, held that the alleged error did not "rise to the level of a due process violation" and reversed the grant of habeas relief. The Chief Justice concluded that "it is not the province of a federal habeas court to reexamine state court determinations on state law questions," and that "in conducting habeas review, a federal court is limited to deciding whether a conviction violated the Constitution, laws, or treaties of the United States." Thus it was irrelevant that the evidence of prior injuries may have been inadmissible under state law. The only question was whether admission of the evidence violated McGuire's right to due process, and the Court held that it did not. The Chief Justice reasoned that the prior injuries were admissible even if they were not linked to McGuire, because they tended to show that the infant's death "was the result of an intentional act by *someone,* and not an accident." As the evidence met the low threshold of relevance, any due process inquiry was at an end. The Chief Justice stated that "we need not explore further the apparent assumption of the court of appeals that it is a violation of the due process guaranteed by the Fourteenth Amendment for evidence that is not relevant to be received at a criminal trial."

2. Constitutional Claims Generally

From the foregoing it is apparent that federal habeas review is generally limited to constitutional claims. The next question is whether all constitutional claims can be raised in § 2254 and § 2255 proceedings. On the face of the statutes, the answer might appear to be "yes," but that would not be a correct statement of the current state of the law. Nor would it reflect the status of the writ through most of its history.

In the early days, as our brief historical exegesis noted, the writ was used most frequently to attack the jurisdiction of the court imposing judgment. However, in cases like Ex parte Lange, 85 U.S. (18 Wall.) 163 (1873) (permitting a challenge to a court's authority to impose sentence) and Ex parte Siebold, 100 U.S. 371 (1879) (permitting a challenge to the constitutionality of a statute), the writ was used more broadly for consideration of constitutional claims on the merits.

Consideration of Constitutional Claims: Brown v. Allen

In Brown v. Allen, 344 U.S. 443 (1953), claims of racial injustice in the South were at the heart of three consolidated cases involving collateral attacks on state convictions. Brown, convicted of rape and sentenced to death, alleged racial discrimination in the selection of the grand and petit juries and also the use of a coerced confession. Speller, also convicted of rape and sentenced to death, charged racial discrimination in the selection of the jury array in his case. Bernie and Lloyd Daniels were sentenced to death upon convictions for murder. They claimed that coerced confessions were used against them, that the procedure to determine the voluntariness of their confessions was invalid, and that there was racial bias in the selection of both grand and petit juries. Justice Reed delivered the opinion of the Court on most issues. The Reed opinion assumed that the lower federal courts had the power to issue writs of habeas corpus, even though there was no allegation of a jurisdictional defect in the state proceedings: "A way is left open to redress violations of the Constitution." The Court considered the merits of the Brown and Speller claims in affirming the denial of habeas corpus relief. But it held the Daniels's claims were barred because of the noncompliance with state procedures and the failure to file a timely appeal: "A failure to use a state's available remedy in the absence of some interference or incapacity * * * bars federal habeas corpus."

After Brown v. Allen, it appeared that all constitutional claims were cognizable in habeas corpus cases. No Justice actually argued otherwise in *Brown*. Kaufman v. United States, 394 U.S. 217 (1969), established that the same scope of review was available to § 2255 litigants.

Fourth Amendment Claims Not Cognizable on Habeas: Stone v. Powell

In the landmark case of Stone v. Powell, 428 U.S. 465 (1976), the Court held that Fourth Amendment claims are generally not cognizable on habeas review. Justice Powell, writing for the Court, reasoned that the primary purpose of the Fourth Amendment exclusionary rule is deterrence of illegal police conduct; as such, the rule operates to exclude reliable evidence and has nothing to do with protecting innocent people from unjust convictions, which is the goal of the writ. Justice Powell concluded that the benefits of extending the exclusionary rule to collateral review of Fourth Amendment claims were outweighed by the costs—not only the costs of losing reliable evidence, but also the dislocation costs associated with upsetting finalized criminal convictions and thereby increasing (1) the prosecutorial burdens on the government, (2) the sense of frustration of state and federal judges whose decisions are set aside, and (3) the general uncertainty costs associated with non-final judgments. Justice Powell concluded as follows:

> [W]here the State has provided an opportunity for full and fair litigation of a Fourth Amendment claim, a state prisoner may not be granted federal habeas relief on the ground that evidence obtained in an unconstitutional search or seizure was introduced at his trial. In this context the contribution of the exclusionary rule, if any, to the effectuation of the Fourth Amendment is minimal and the societal costs of the application of the rule persist with special force.

Justice Brennan, joined by Justice Marshall, dissented. He urged that the Court was rewriting jurisdictional statutes, those governing § 2254 and § 2255 cases, and arrogating Congressional power to itself. Justice White also dissented and argued that "[u]nder the amendments to the habeas corpus statute, which * * * represented an effort by Congress to lend a modicum of finality to state criminal judgments, I cannot distinguish between Fourth Amendment and other constitutional issues."

Full and Fair Opportunity

It is truly a rare case in which a state fails to meet the *Stone* requirement that it provide a full and fair opportunity for litigation of Fourth Amendment claims. The requirement has been held to mean that on factual issues the defendant had an opportunity to offer evidence, and that some appellate review was provided. See generally Willett v. Lockhart, 37 F.3d 1265 (8th Cir.1994) (en banc) (the only questions after *Stone* are whether the state has provided any corrective procedures at all, and whether an "unconscionable procedural breakdown" prevented the petitioner from using the corrective mechanism). The question is not whether state courts applied the Fourth Amendment correctly, but whether they provided sufficient *process* for the defendant to get some consideration of his Fourth Amendment claim. See also Capellan v. Riley, 975 F.2d 67 (2d Cir.1992) (summary affirmance of Fourth Amendment ruling, which was probably wrong on the merits, did not constitute an unconscionable breakdown in the state appellate process; claim barred on habeas).

Ineffective Assistance of Counsel: Kimmelman v. Morrison

In Kimmelman v. Morrison, 477 U.S. 365 (1986), Justice Brennan wrote for the Court as it held that Stone v. Powell did not bar a habeas petitioner from claiming ineffective assistance of counsel based upon his trial counsel's failure to file a timely motion to suppress evidence. The Court declined "to hold either that the guarantee of effective assistance of counsel belongs solely to the innocent or that it attaches only to matters affecting the determination of actual guilt." Justice Brennan reasoned as follows:

> Were we to extend *Stone* and hold that criminal defendants may not raise ineffective assistance claims that are based primarily on incompetent handling of Fourth Amendment issues on federal habeas, we would deny most defendants whose trial attorneys performed incompetently in this regard the opportunity to vindicate their right to effective trial counsel. We would deny all defendants whose appellate counsel performed inadequately with respect to Fourth Amendment issues the opportunity to protect their right to effective appellate counsel. * * * Thus, we cannot say, as the Court was able to say in *Stone,* that restriction of federal habeas review would not severely interfere with the protection of the constitutional right asserted by the habeas petitioner.

Justice Brennan also noted that unlike Fourth Amendment claims, there is usually no full and fair opportunity to bring ineffective assistance claims at trial or on direct review.

It should be noted that *Kimmelman* creates an anomaly when juxtaposed with *Stone*. If two defendants have the same meritorious Fourth Amendment claim, and both are prejudiced by the admission of the tainted evidence at trial, the defendant with the incompetent lawyer can reap the benefit of exclusion on habeas while the defendant with the competent lawyer cannot. See Friedman, A Tale of Two Habeas, 73 Minn.L.Rev. 247 (1988).

Miranda Claims: Withrow v. Williams

In Withrow v. Williams, 507 U.S. 680 (1993), the Court held that "*Stone*'s restriction on the exercise of federal habeas jurisdiction does not extend to a state prisoner's claim that his conviction rests on statements obtained in violation of the safeguards mandated by Miranda v. Arizona." Justice Souter wrote for the Court and began by noting that "*Stone's* limitation on federal habeas relief was not jurisdictional in nature, but rested on prudential concerns counseling against the application of the Fourth Amendment exclusionary rule on collateral review." He stressed that cases decided after *Stone* had read that case narrowly:

> Over the years, we have repeatedly declined to extend the rule in *Stone* beyond its original bounds. In Jackson v. Virginia, 443 U.S. 307 (1979), for example, we denied a request to apply *Stone* to bar habeas reconsideration of a Fourteenth Amendment due process claim of insufficient evidence to support a state conviction. We stressed that the issue was "central to the basic question of guilt or innocence," unlike a claim that a state court had received evidence in violation of the Fourth Amendment exclusionary rule, and we found that to review such a claim on habeas imposed no great burdens on the federal courts.

Justice Souter concluded that with respect to *Miranda* claims, "the argument for extending *Stone* again falls short." He explained this conclusion by stressing the difference between Fourth Amendment claims and *Miranda* claims:

> [T]he *Mapp* rule "is not a personal constitutional right," but serves to deter future constitutional violations; * * * the exclusion of evidence at trial can do nothing to remedy the completed and wholly extrajudicial Fourth Amendment violation. Nor can the *Mapp* rule be thought to enhance the soundness of the criminal process by improving the reliability of evidence introduced at trial. * * *

> *Miranda* differs from *Mapp* in both respects. * * * [I]n protecting a defendant's Fifth Amendment privilege against self-incrimination *Miranda* safeguards a fundamental *trial* right. * * *

> Nor does the Fifth Amendment "trial right" protected by *Miranda* serve some value necessarily divorced from the correct ascertainment of guilt. * * * By bracing against the possibility of unreliable statements in every instance of in-custody interrogation, *Miranda* serves to guard against the use of unreliable statements at trial.

Justice Souter also noted that barring *Miranda* claims on habeas "would not significantly benefit the federal courts in their exercise of habeas jurisdiction, or advance the cause of federalism in any substantial way." Justice Souter explained this assertion as follows:

> [E]liminating habeas review of *Miranda* issues would not prevent a state prisoner from simply converting his barred *Miranda* claim into a due process claim that his conviction rested on an involuntary confession. * * *

> If that is so, the federal courts would certainly not have heard the last of *Miranda* on collateral review. Under the due process approach, * * * courts look to the totality of circumstances to determine whether a confession was voluntary. Those potential circumstances * * * include the failure of police to advise the defendant of his rights to remain silent and to have counsel present during custodial interrogation. We could lock the front door against *Miranda,* but not the back.

Justice O'Connor, joined by the Chief Justice, dissented on the *Stone* issue and reasoned that confessions obtained in violation of *Miranda* are not necessarily untrustworthy. She recognized that reversal of a conviction on direct review because of a violation of the *Miranda* rule may be "an acceptable sacrifice for the deterrence and respect for constitutional values that the *Miranda* rule brings." But she concluded that "once a case is on collateral review, the balance between the costs and benefits shifts; the interests of federalism, finality, and fairness compel *Miranda*'s exclusion from habeas."

Justice Scalia, joined by Justice Thomas, also dissented on the *Stone* issue. Justice Scalia argued broadly that "[p]rior opportunity to litigate an issue should be an important equitable consideration in *any* habeas case, and should ordinarily preclude the court from reaching the merits of a claim, unless it goes to the fairness of the trial process or to the accuracy of the ultimate result."

D. LIMITATIONS ON OBTAINING HABEAS RELIEF

Even if the petitioner's claim is cognizable in a federal habeas proceeding, there are several important procedural limitations that must be overcome before habeas relief can be granted.

1. The Custody Requirement

Whether relief is sought under § 2254 or under § 2255, the applicant must be in custody. "Custody" is a term of art. Clearly if the petitioner is incarcerated at the time the habeas relief is sought, as a result of the conviction that he is challenging, he is in custody for purposes of the habeas statutes. But difficult questions arise if the petitioner has been released, or if he has completed his sentence for one crime and is serving a sentence on another.

In 1963, the Court found that parole was a custody status. Jones v. Cunningham, 371 U.S. 236 (1963). Subsequently, in Peyton v. Rowe, 391 U.S. 54 (1968), the Court held that habeas corpus could be used by a prisoner serving one sentence who wished to attack a consecutive sentence. In Carafas v. LaVallee, 391 U.S. 234 (1968), the Court held that a petitioner was in custody within the meaning of the statutes when he was incarcerated at the time the petition was filed, but released before his case was heard on the merits by the Supreme Court. Thus, discharge of a prisoner once properly before the court will not result in a finding of "no custody." The Court in *Carafas* noted that because of his conviction, the petitioner "cannot engage in certain businesses; he cannot serve as an official of a labor union for a specified period of time; he cannot vote in any election held in New York State; he cannot serve as a juror. Because of these disabilities or burdens which may flow from petitioner's conviction, he has a substantial stake in the judgment of conviction which survives the satisfaction of the sentence imposed on him."

Subsequently, the Court found custody in Hensley v. Municipal Court, 411 U.S. 345 (1973), where a defendant sentenced to prison for one year had his sentence stayed pending appellate and post-conviction attacks. After *Hensley,* release on bail has been held to constitute custody for purposes of federal habeas corpus. See. e.g., Campbell v. Shapp, 521 F.2d 1398 (3d Cir.1975). If a person is in custody in one jurisdiction and wishes to attack a conviction mandating future custody in another jurisdiction, Braden v. 30th Judicial Circuit Ct., 410 U.S. 484 (1973), suggests that any "detainer" or formal demand for custody by the expectant jurisdiction is "custody." In sum, "custody" is found even where the defendant is not incarcerated on the conviction he is challenging, so long as he is still suffering some significant harm from that conviction.

Collateral Harm and Mootness

In Lane v. Williams, 455 U.S. 624 (1982), the Court found that two defendants were not in custody for purposes of the habeas statutes. They pleaded guilty to burglary charges; each was incarcerated, released on parole, found to be a parole violator, and reincarcerated. When parole was revoked each challenged his guilty plea on the ground that he had not known of the mandatory parole requirement when he pleaded. But before the case reached the Supreme Court, each was released from custody. Because the parole terms had expired, Justice Stevens's opinion for the Court concluded that the case was moot. "No civil disabilities such as those present in *Carafas* result from a finding that an individual has violated parole. At most, certain non-statutory consequences may occur; employment prospects, or the sentence imposed in a future criminal proceeding, could be affected." Justice Marshall, joined by Justices Brennan and Blackmun, dissented, arguing that federal courts should presume the existence of collateral consequences to avoid the necessity of predicting how a state might use a conviction or parole revocation in future proceedings.

The Court reaffirmed the Lane v. Williams mootness principle in Spencer v. Kemna, 523 U.S. 1 (1998). Spencer's parole was revoked due to charges that he committed a rape. He attacked the parole revocation unsuccessfully in state courts, then brought a habeas proceeding. Largely due to state delay, the habeas petition was not considered until after Spencer's sentence had expired and he was released. Relying heavily on Lane v. Williams, the Court, in an opinion by Justice Scalia for eight Justices, held that the habeas petition was moot. The Court declared: "We adhere to the principles announced in *Lane*, and decline to presume that collateral consequences adequate to meet Article III's injury-in-fact requirement resulted from petitioner's parole revocation."

The Court rejected, as speculative, all the collateral harms asserted by Spencer. Spencer argued (1) that his parole revocation could be used to his detriment in a future parole proceeding; (2) that the revocation could be used to increase his sentence in a future sentencing proceeding should he violate the law and be caught and convicted; (3) that the parole revocation could be used to impeach him should he appear as a witness in future proceedings; and (4) that it could be used directly against him should he appear as a defendant in a criminal proceeding. According to the Court, none of these asserted harms were concrete enough to create a case or controversy.

Finally, Justice Scalia rejected the notion that an exception to the mootness limitation should apply when the delay leading to mootness is caused by the State. He reasoned as follows:

[M]ootness, however it may have come about, simply deprives us of our power to act; there is nothing for us to remedy, even if we were disposed to do so. * * * As for petitioner's concern that law enforcement officials and district judges will repeat with impunity the mootness-producing abuse that he alleges occurred here: We are confident that, as a general matter, district courts will prevent dilatory tactics by the litigants and will not unduly delay their own rulings; and that, where appropriate, corrective mandamus will issue from the courts of appeals.

Justice Stevens dissented.

Custody and AEDPA

As seen above, custody questions have usually arisen after the petitioner has been released and is arguing that his conviction is causing him some collateral harm. AEDPA has put a damper on such claims by imposing a one-year statute of limitations on habeas petitions. The year basically runs from the date on which a conviction becomes final. It is the rare habeas petitioner who has been freed from incarceration and yet is still arguably in custody within the one year AEDPA statutory period. It appears that many of the difficult custody questions have evaporated under AEDPA.

2. Exhaustion of State Remedies

A petitioner challenging a state conviction on habeas must establish that he has exhausted his state remedies before proceeding to federal court. The exhaustion requirement originated in Ex parte Royall, 117 U.S. 241 (1886), and it is now codified in 28 U.S.C.A. § 2254(b)–(c).

The Purpose of the Exhaustion Requirement

The exhaustion requirement is rooted in federal-state comity. It allows the states the first opportunity to apply controlling legal principles to the facts bearing on the constitutional claim of a defendant in a state criminal action. It thereby preserves for state courts a role in the application and enforcement of federal law and prevents interruption of state adjudication by federal habeas proceedings. Consequently, it is not enough that the petitioner has *been* to the state courts; he must have presented there the same ground he seeks to advance in his federal habeas corpus petition. See Byrnes v. Vose, 969 F.2d 1306 (1st Cir.1992) ("considerations of comity require that state courts be afforded the opportunity, in the first instance, to correct a constitutional violation before a federal court intervenes").

Which "Grounds" Have Been Exhausted?

Disputes arise when the petitioner's argument on habeas is different from that made in the state courts. The petitioner might argue that he exhausted his "claim" and the government argues that the claim he is making now was never made below. The petitioner's response is essentially "I did make that claim, and the state courts rejected it; I just made the claim in different words than I am using now." How to resolve this dispute?

The Court in Picard v. Connor, 404 U.S. 270, 278 (1971) provided the following basic definition: "the substance of a federal habeas corpus claim must first be presented to the state courts." Connor challenged the legality of an indictment, which had originally named John Doe, and then was amended to name him. In the state courts, he contended that the amending procedure did not comply with the Massachusetts statute, and therefore that he had not been lawfully indicted. In his habeas petition, he alleged a violation of equal protection. Justice Black, writing for the Court, concluded that the equal protection claim had not been exhausted in the state courts. He stated as follows:

> We emphasize that the federal claim must be fairly presented to the state courts. If the exhaustion doctrine is to prevent unnecessary conflict between courts equally bound to guard and protect rights secured by the Constitution, it is not sufficient merely that the federal habeas applicant has been through the state courts. The rule would serve no purpose if it could be satisfied by raising one claim in the state courts and another in the federal courts. * * *

> Until he reached this Court, respondent never contended that the method by which he was brought to trial denied him equal protection of the laws. * * * To be sure, respondent presented all the facts. Yet the constitutional claim * * * in those facts was never brought to the attention of the state courts. * * * [We] do not imply that respondent could have raised the equal protection claim only by citing book and verse on the federal constitution. We simply hold that the substance of a federal habeas corpus claim must first be presented to the state courts. The claim that an indictment is invalid is not the substantial equivalent of a claim that it results in an unconstitutional discrimination.

In Duncan v. Henry, 513 U.S. 364 (1995), Henry was convicted in a state court for child molestation, and on his state appeal he argued that the admission of testimony concerning an uncharged act of molestation was a violation of the California evidence code and was also a "miscarriage of justice" under the California Constitution. The state appellate courts denied relief. Subsequently, in his federal habeas petition, Henry argued that admitting the challenged testimony caused a fundamentally unfair trial, violating his federal due process rights. Relying on *Picard*, the Court, in a per curiam opinion, held that Henry had not exhausted that federal claim in the state courts. The Court concluded that Henry "did not apprise the state court of his claim that the evidentiary ruling of which he complained was not only a violation of state law, but denied him the due process of law guaranteed by the Fourteenth Amendment." While recognizing that the state law "miscarriage of justice" claim and the federal law "fundamental fairness" claim were *similar*, the Court stated that "mere similarity of claims is insufficient to exhaust." The Court noted that the state appellate court had "confined its analysis to the application of state law."

Justice Stevens dissented, accusing the majority of imposing "an exact labeling requirement." He called the majority's opinion "hypertechnical and unwise" because the state and Federal claims were substantially similar. Justice Stevens argued that where the state court has already denied a claim of fundamental unfairness, "nothing is to be gained by requiring the prisoner to present the same claim under a different label to the same courts that have already found it insufficient."

Mixed Petitions: Rose v. Lundy

What if a habeas petition contains a number of claims, some of which have been considered and denied by the state courts, and some of which have not? Such petitions are referred to as "mixed petitions"—containing both exhausted and unexhausted claims.

AEDPA provides that a district court faced with a mixed petition has three options:

1)   it can dismiss the entire petition without prejudice, requiring the petitioner to exhaust the unexhausted claims in state court—this procedure was set forth by the Court in the pre-AEDPA case of Rose v. Lundy, 455 U.S. 509 (1982);

2)   if the exhausted claims lack merit, the court can consider and dismiss them on the merits, then dismiss the unexhausted claims without prejudice so that the petitioner can bring them to state court; or

3)   in limited circumstances discussed infra, the court can enter a stay until the petitioner gets a state resolution on the unexhausted claims.

Under AEDPA, the district court does not have discretion to *grant* relief on the merits of exhausted claims that are included in mixed petitions. It only has discretion to deny relief on the merits.

As the Court in Rose v. Lundy made clear, the exhaustion requirement does not *preclude* habeas review; it merely *delays* habeas review. The exhaustion requirement is therefore unlike other limitations on collateral review (discussed later in this Chapter) such as the bar of procedural default in the state court, or the related bar of adequate state ground, both of which prevent claims from *ever* being heard on habeas.

Exhaustion and Multiple Habeas Petitions

What happens if a petitioner wants to split his claims, i.e., pursue the exhausted claims right now in federal court, then bring another habeas petition on the remaining claims once they were exhausted in the state court? This does not work, because the petitioner would run afoul of the severe limitations on successive habeas petitions that are found in AEDPA. See Burris v. Parke, 72 F.3d 47 (7th Cir.1995) ("A prisoner who decides to proceed only with his exhausted claims and deliberately sets aside his unexhausted claims risks dismissal of subsequent federal petitions.").

What happens if a habeas petition is dismissed because it contains unexhausted claims, then the petitioner exhausts the claims in state court and brings another federal habeas petition? Is this petition of now-exhausted claims considered "successive," and thus dismissed, within the meaning of AEDPA? In Stewart v. Martinez-Villareal, 523 U.S. 637 (1998), the Court, in an opinion by Chief Justice Rehnquist, held that such a petition setting forth claims previously dismissed as unexhausted could not be considered "successive" within the meaning of AEDPA, and therefore such a petition could be considered on the merits. The Chief Justice declared that "[t]o hold otherwise would mean that a dismissal of a first habeas petition for technical procedural reasons would bar the prisoner from ever obtaining federal habeas review." Justice Scalia and Justice Thomas dissented.

Mixed Petitions and the Statute of Limitations: Pliler v. Ford

In Pliler v. Ford, 542 U.S. 225 (2004), the Court considered the relationship between a mixed petition and the one-year statute of limitations applicable to habeas petitions under AEDPA. Justice Thomas, writing for the Court, noted the interplay:

> The combined effect of *Rose* and AEDPA's limitations period is that if a petitioner comes to federal court with a mixed petition toward the end of the limitations period, a dismissal of his mixed petition could result in the loss of all of his claims—including those already exhausted—because the limitations period could expire during the time a petitioner returns to state court to exhaust his unexhausted claims.

The case involved whether federal courts were required to notify pro se petitioners of this risk. The Court held that such notification was not required. Justice Thomas declared as follows:

> District judges have no obligation to act as counsel or paralegal to *pro se* litigants. * * * Explaining the details of federal habeas procedure and calculating statutes of limitations are tasks normally and properly performed by trained counsel as a matter of course. Requiring district courts to advise a *pro se* litigant in such a manner would undermine district judges' role as impartial decisionmakers.

Justices Ginsburg and Breyer dissented.

Staying a Mixed Petition to Allow Unexhausted Claims to Be Presented to the State Court: Rhines v. Weber

In Rhines v. Weber, 544 U.S. 269 (2005), the Court held that a federal court can, in narrow circumstances, enter a stay on a mixed petition; the stay will allow the petitioner to present his unexhausted claims to the state court in the first instance, and then to return to federal court for review of his perfected petition. The stay will protect the petitioner from having the AEDPA limitations period expire. Justice O'Connor, writing for the Court, noted that the "stay-and-abeyance" procedure was justified in certain cases because without it a petitioner with mixed claims would risk dismissal of the unexhausted claims due to the statute of limitations provision added by AEDPA. But the Court emphasized that the stay-and-abeyance procedure could be used only in limited circumstances. Justice O'Connor explained as follows:

> Because granting a stay effectively excuses a petitioner's failure to present his claims first to the state courts, stay and abeyance is only appropriate when the district court determines there was good cause for the petitioner's failure to exhaust his claims first in state court. Moreover, even if a petitioner had good cause for that failure, the district court would abuse its discretion if it were to grant him a stay when his unexhausted claims are plainly meritless.
>
> Even where stay and abeyance is appropriate, the district court's discretion in structuring the stay is limited by the timeliness concerns reflected in AEDPA. A mixed petition should not be stayed indefinitely. * * * [N]ot all petitioners have an incentive to obtain federal relief as quickly as possible. In particular, capital petitioners might deliberately engage in dilatory tactics to prolong their incarceration and avoid execution of the sentence of death. * * * Thus, district courts should place reasonable time limits on a petitioner's trip to state court and back. And if a petitioner engages in abusive litigation tactics or intentional delay, the district court should not grant him a stay at all.

On the other hand, it likely would be an abuse of discretion for a district court to deny a stay and to dismiss a mixed petition if the petitioner had good cause for his failure to exhaust, his unexhausted claims are potentially meritorious, and there is no indication that the petitioner engaged in intentionally dilatory litigation tactics. * * * In such a case, the petitioner's interest in obtaining federal review of his claims outweighs the competing interests in finality and speedy resolution of federal petitions. For the same reason, if a petitioner presents a district court with a mixed petition and the court determines that stay and abeyance is inappropriate, the court should allow the petitioner to delete the unexhausted claims and to proceed with the exhausted claims if dismissal of the entire petition would unreasonably impair the petitioner's right to obtain federal relief.

Justice Stevens, joined by Justices Ginsburg and Breyer, wrote a one-sentence concurring opinion. Justice Souter, joined by Justices Ginsburg and Breyer, wrote a short opinion concurring in part and concurring in the judgment.

Procedural Bars and Exhaustion of Claims

A petition is not a "mixed" petition within the meaning of Rose v. Lundy if the unexhausted claims are procedurally barred on other grounds. For example, if a petitioner fails to make an objection in the trial court, and state rules of procedure treat that failure as barring consideration on appeal, the defendant's claim is probably procedurally barred from consideration on habeas. (See the discussion of state procedural bars later in this Chapter). If the unexhausted claim is procedurally barred, "exhaustion is not possible because the state court would find the claims procedurally defaulted. The district court may not go to the merits of the barred claims, but must decide the merits of the claims that are exhausted and not barred." Toulson v. Beyer, 987 F.2d 984 (3d Cir.1993).

Waiver by the State

Before AEDPA, the state's failure to invoke the exhaustion requirement constituted a waiver and allowed the federal court to review an unexhausted claim. Granberry v. Greer, 481 U.S. 129 (1987). But this is no longer the case. Under the AEDPA the exhaustion requirement is not waived unless expressly by the state through counsel.

The Futility Exception to the Exhaustion Requirement

A habeas petitioner is not required to exhaust his claims in the state court if to do so would be futile—this futility exception, which was established by case law, has been retained in AEDPA. A good example of the futility exception is Harris v. DeRobertis, 932 F.2d 619 (7th Cir.1991). The district court dismissed Harris's habeas petition, holding that Harris had not exhausted the state post-conviction remedy established by an Illinois statute. Harris had failed to assert his constitutional claim in his state appeal. An Illinois statute allowed claims such as Harris's to be brought on collateral attack; but if the proceedings were commenced more than ten years after final judgment the petitioner had to prove that the delay was for some reason other than "culpable negligence." Harris's petition was filed twenty years after his conviction. The district court held that Harris could have tried to invoke the state remedy by demonstrating a lack of culpable negligence, and therefore his claim was unexhausted. The court of appeals disagreed. It noted that the Illinois statute had been in effect for more than forty years, and in that time "the Illinois courts have failed to produce even a single published opinion in which the court found a lack of culpable negligence." Based on the Illinois case law, the court found that "the culpable negligence standard is an exceptional means of relief which will be unavailable to virtually all prisoners." The court concluded as follows:

> We believe the better approach is to forego resort to the Illinois post-conviction process if a petition would be untimely, absent judicial precedent indicating that the culpable negligence exception would be met. Such a holding avoids the "merry-go-round procedure" * * * by which prisoners are shuttled back and forth between the state and federal courts before any decision on the merits is ever reached in order to exhaust meaningless remedies.

If, however, a state remedy is futile only because the petitioner has failed to comply with a rule of procedure, the question is no longer one of exhaustion or futility. The question is then whether the habeas petition is barred by the petitioner's failure to comply with the state rule. See Jones v. Jones, 163 F.3d 285 (5th Cir.1998).

Inexhaustible State Review and the Exhaustion Requirement: Castille v. Peoples

Suppose the state provides for collateral review without limitation as to number of petitions or the time in which they may be brought. Would it follow that a federal habeas petition could never be brought because the state post-conviction remedy is *never exhausted*? The Court in Castille v. Peoples, 489 U.S. 346 (1989), addressed this question. Justice Scalia wrote for a unanimous Court as follows:

> Title 28 U.S.C. § 2254(c) provides that a claim shall not be deemed exhausted so long as a petitioner "has the right under the law of the State to raise, by any available procedure, the question presented." Read narrowly, this language appears to preclude a finding of

exhaustion if there exists any possibility of further state-court review. We have, however, expressly rejected such a construction, holding instead that once the state courts have ruled upon a claim, it is not necessary for the petitioner to ask the state for collateral relief, based upon the same evidence and issues already decided by direct review. It would be inconsistent * * * to mandate recourse to state collateral review whose results have effectively been predetermined, or permanently to bar from federal habeas prisoners in States whose post-conviction procedures are technically inexhaustible.

Thus, the rule is that state collateral review is relevant for exhaustion purposes only if direct appeal has been bypassed and only if the collateral review process is meaningful and not itself inexhaustible.

Exhaustion and Discretionary Review in the State Supreme Court: O'Sullivan v. Boerckel

If the habeas petitioner has failed to include a constitutional claim in his petition for leave to appeal to the state supreme court, must the claim be dismissed in a federal habeas action for lack of exhaustion? This was the question addressed by the Court in O'Sullivan v. Boerckel, 526 U.S. 838 (1999). Boerckel appealed his state conviction to an intermediate appellate court, asserting six constitutional claims. After the claims were denied, Boerckel sought leave to appeal to the Supreme Court of Illinois. Review in that Court, as in the United States Supreme Court, is discretionary. In his motion, Boerckel included only three of his constitutional claims. He then sought habeas review for the three claims that he did not include in his petition to the Illinois Supreme Court. If Boerckel was required to bring those claims before the Illinois Supreme Court in order to satisfy the exhaustion requirement, his habeas petition would have to be dismissed. Moreover, it would have to be dismissed with prejudice, because the time to bring those claims to the Illinois Supreme Court had long since run out— meaning that he had committed a procedural default disentitling him from habeas review. However, if the exhaustion doctrine did not require him to bring those claims to the Illinois Supreme Court, then there was no bar to hearing them on habeas.

The Supreme Court, in an opinion by Justice O'Connor for six Justices, held that Boerckel had failed to exhaust his claims when he failed to bring them before the Illinois Supreme Court for discretionary review. She analyzed the rationale and application of the exhaustion requirement as follows:

> Because the exhaustion doctrine is designed to give the state courts a full and fair opportunity to resolve federal constitutional claims before those claims are presented to the federal courts, we

conclude that state prisoners must give the state courts one full opportunity to resolve any constitutional issues by invoking one complete round of the State's established appellate review process. Here, Illinois's established, normal appellate review procedure is a two-tiered system. Comity, in these circumstances, dictates that Boerckel use the State's established appellate review procedures before he presents his claims to a federal court.

Boerckel argued that if he were forced to bring all his constitutional claims before the Illinois Supreme Court, that Court would be inundated by claims that it could not meaningfully review and would have no interest in reviewing—thus undercutting the very comity interests that are behind the exhaustion requirement. Justice O'Connor responded to this argument in the following passage:

> We acknowledge that the rule we announce today—requiring state prisoners to file petitions for discretionary review when that review is part of the ordinary appellate review procedure in the State—has the potential to increase the number of filings in state supreme courts. We also recognize that this increased burden may be unwelcome in some state courts because the courts do not wish to have the opportunity to review constitutional claims before those claims are presented to a federal habeas court. * * * In this regard, we note that nothing in our decision today requires the exhaustion of any specific state remedy when a State has provided that that remedy is unavailable. * * * We hold today only that the creation of a discretionary review system does not, without more, make review in the Illinois Supreme Court unavailable.

Justice Souter concurred in *Boerckel*, noting that a state can avoid a flood of appeals to its State Supreme Court by making it plain "that it does not wish to require such applications before its petitioners may seek federal habeas relief." Justice Stevens, joined by Justices Ginsburg and Breyer, dissented in *Boerckel*. Justice Stevens concluded that the majority's application of the exhaustion requirement to state appellate court discretionary review "will impose unnecessary burdens on habeas petitioners; it will delay the completion of litigation that is already more protracted than it should be; and, most ironically, it will undermine federalism by thwarting the interests of those state supreme courts that administer discretionary dockets."

Justice Breyer wrote a separate dissenting opinion in *Boerckel*, joined by Justice Ginsburg. He noted that discretionary review is rarely granted by any of the State Supreme Courts, and "would presume, on the basis of Illinois's own rules and related statistics, and in the absence of any clear legal expression to the contrary, that Illinois does not mind if a state prisoner does not ask its Supreme Court for discretionary review prior to seeking habeas relief in federal court."

3. Procedural Default

Procedural default means that the habeas petitioner failed to comply with a rule of procedure during the trial or direct appeal. Like the exhaustion requirement, the procedural default doctrine is rooted in principles of federalism and comity. If the habeas remedy were always available despite the transgression of a state procedural rule, then state procedures—such as the requirement of a timely objection and the requirement of a timely notice of appeal—could be routinely disregarded. State defendants might not worry about complying if they could always seek habeas relief. Unlike the exhaustion requirement, however, which merely *delays* a collateral attack, the procedural default doctrine *precludes* it. The question, then, is whether and under what circumstances a habeas petitioner can be excused from a procedural default that was made in the state courts.

While the bar of procedural default is usually applied against state defendants, it is also applicable to federal defendants seeking habeas relief under section 2255. The reason is obvious: if the defendant violated a procedural rule that would bar *direct* review in the federal appellate court—such as failure to file timely notice of appeal—it would undermine that rule to excuse that default and allow collateral relief. This result is not, of course, due to federalism, but rather due to the respect for federal rules of procedure.

a. *Deliberate Bypass*

In Fay v. Noia, 372 U.S. 391 (1963), the Court created a very permissive test for lifting a state procedural bar to habeas relief. Noia brought a habeas petition, arguing that the confession admitted against him at trial was coerced. However, Noia had not brought an appeal on this or any other issue in the state courts; he had failed to a file a timely notice of appeal. Justice Brennan, writing for the Court, held that a procedural bar would be lifted unless it could be shown that the petitioner had *deliberately bypassed* a state procedural rule. Justice Brennan argued that lifting a procedural bar in all other cases—including where the default was caused by inadvertence or neglect—was necessary to effectuate federal interests. He asserted that petitioners would be unlikely to flaunt state procedural requirements and that state interests would not be unduly impaired. He reasoned as follows:

> A man under conviction for crime has an obvious inducement to do his very best to keep his state remedies open, and not stake his all on the outcome of a federal habeas proceeding which, in many respects, may be less advantageous to him than a state court proceeding. And if

because of inadvertence or neglect he runs afoul of a state procedural requirement, and thereby forfeits his state remedies, * * * those consequences should be sufficient to vindicate the State's valid interest in orderly procedure. Whatever residuum of state interest there may be under such circumstances is manifestly insufficient in the face of the federal policy, drawn from the ancient principles of the writ of habeas corpus, * * * of affording an effective remedy for restraints contrary to the Constitution.

Justice Clark dissented in *Fay,* contending that a deliberate bypass test was insufficient to protect legitimate interests of the states in their procedural rules. He argued that the majority had in effect substituted federal habeas corpus review for an appeal in state court. Justice Harlan also dissented in an opinion joined by Justices Clark and Stewart. He contended that the deliberate bypass standard "amounts to no limitation at all."

b. *A Required Showing of Cause and Prejudice*

Soon the Court began to cut back on Fay v. Noia, and ultimately it was overruled. In Francis v. Henderson, 425 U.S. 536 (1976), the petitioner challenged the make-up of his grand jury; but he had failed to comply with a state rule of procedure requiring that an objection to the composition of the grand jury must be made by motion prior to trial. The Court expressed deference to state procedures and held that habeas corpus relief was barred. It distinguished *Fay* as a case where the petitioner had defaulted on his entire appeal (by failing to file a timely notice of appeal) rather than a specific claim.

The majority in *Francis* stated that the procedural bar could be lifted only if the petitioner 1) could show good "cause" (i.e., a legitimate excuse) for the procedural default, and 2) could establish that the alleged violation of federal law had actually prejudiced his case.[11] *Francis* paved the way for the next case.

WAINWRIGHT V. SYKES
Supreme Court of the United States, 1977.
433 U.S. 72.

JUSTICE REHNQUIST delivered the opinion of the Court.

[Sykes was convicted of murder. At his trial, his confession was admitted. Sykes did not object and made no *Miranda* argument. Nor did he contend the confession was inadmissible in his appeals to the state courts. He then sought federal habeas relief, arguing that his *Miranda* rights were violated and his confession was erroneously admitted. The

---

[11] Justices Marshall and Stevens did not participate. Justice Brennan dissented.

district court granted habeas relief (finding no deliberate bypass) and the court of appeals affirmed.]

To the extent that the dicta of Fay v. Noia may be thought to have laid down an all-inclusive rule rendering state timely objection rules ineffective to bar review of underlying federal claims in federal habeas proceedings—absent a "knowing waiver" or a "deliberate bypass" of the right to so object—its effect was limited by *Francis*, which applied a different rule and barred a habeas challenge to the makeup of a grand jury. Petitioner Wainwright in this case urges that we further confine its effect by applying the principle enunciated in *Francis* to a claimed error in the admission of a defendant's confession.

* * *

* * * [I]t has been the rule that the federal habeas petitioner who claims he is detained pursuant to a final judgment of a state court in violation of the United States Constitution is entitled to have the federal habeas court make its own independent determination of his federal claim, without being bound by the determination on the merits of that claim reached in the state proceedings. This rule * * * is in no way changed by our holding today. Rather, we deal only with contentions of federal law which were *not* resolved on the merits in the state proceeding due to respondent's failure to raise them there as required by state procedure. We leave open for resolution in future decisions the precise definition of the "cause"-and-"prejudice" standard, and note here only that it is narrower than the standard set forth in dicta in Fay v. Noia, which would make federal habeas review generally available to state convicts absent a knowing and deliberate waiver of the federal constitutional contention. It is the sweeping language of Fay v. Noia, going far beyond the facts of the case eliciting it, which we today reject.

The reasons for our rejection of it are several. The contemporaneous-objection rule itself is by no means peculiar to Florida, and deserves greater respect than *Fay* gives it, both for the fact that it is employed by a coordinate jurisdiction within the federal system and for the many interests which it serves in its own right. A contemporaneous objection enables the record to be made with respect to the constitutional claim when the recollections of witnesses are freshest, not years later in a federal habeas proceeding. It enables the judge who observed the demeanor of those witnesses to make the factual determinations necessary for properly deciding the federal constitutional question. * * *

We think that the rule of Fay v. Noia, broadly stated, may encourage "sandbagging" on the part of defense lawyers, who may take their chances on a verdict of not guilty in a state trial court with the intent to raise their constitutional claims in a federal habeas court if their initial gamble does not pay off. The refusal of federal habeas courts to honor contemporaneous-objection rules may also make state courts themselves less stringent in their enforcement. Under the rule of Fay v. Noia, state appellate courts know that a federal constitutional issue raised for the first time in the proceeding before them may well be decided in any event by a federal *habeas* tribunal. Thus, their choice is between addressing the issue notwithstanding the petitioner's failure to timely object, or else face the prospect that the federal habeas court will decide the question without the benefit of their views.

* * *

We believe that the adoption of the *Francis* rule in this situation will have the salutary effect of making the state trial on the merits the "main event," so to speak, rather than a "tryout on the road" for what will later be the determinative federal habeas hearing. * * * If a criminal defendant thinks that an action of the state trial court is about to deprive him of a federal constitutional right there is every reason for his following state procedure in making known his objection.

The "cause"-and-"prejudice" exception of the *Francis* rule will afford an adequate guarantee, we think, that the rule will not prevent a federal habeas court from adjudicating for the first time the federal constitutional claim of a defendant who in the absence of such an adjudication will be the victim of a miscarriage of justice. Whatever precise content may be given those terms by later cases, we feel confident in holding without further elaboration that they do not exist here. Respondent has advanced no explanation whatever for his failure to object at trial, and, as the proceeding unfolded, the trial judge is certainly not to be faulted for failing to question the admission of the confession himself. The other evidence of guilt presented at trial, moreover, was substantial to a degree that would negate any possibility of actual prejudice resulting to the respondent from the admission of his inculpatory statement.

* * *

[The concurring opinions of CHIEF JUSTICE BURGER and JUSTICE STEVENS are omitted].

[The opinion of JUSTICE WHITE, concurring in the judgment, is omitted].

JUSTICE BRENNAN, with whom JUSTICE MARSHALL joins, dissenting.

* * *

Punishing a lawyer's unintentional errors by closing the federal courthouse door to his client is both a senseless and misdirected method of deterring the slighting of state rules. It is senseless because unplanned and unintentional action of any kind generally is not subject to deterrence; and, to the extent that it is hoped that a threatened sanction addressed to the defense will induce greater care and caution on the part of trial lawyers, thereby forestalling negligent conduct or error, the potential loss of all valuable state remedies would be sufficient to this end. And it is a misdirected sanction because even if the penalization of incompetence or carelessness will encourage more thorough legal training and trial preparation, the habeas applicant, as opposed to his lawyer, hardly is the proper recipient of such a penalty. * * *

Fay Overruled: Coleman v. Thompson

The Court finally overruled Fay v. Noia and its deliberate bypass standard in Coleman v. Thompson, 501 U.S. 722 (1991). Cases such as *Sykes* had limited *Fay* to its facts, so that the deliberate bypass standard essentially applied only when a state prisoner defaulted his entire appeal. That was the situation in *Coleman,* where the prisoner, by filing a late notice of appeal, defaulted his entire state post-conviction remedy. Justice O'Connor, writing for six members of the Court, recognized that the error in filing a late notice was "inadvertent" and the State conceded that Coleman had not deliberately bypassed his state post-conviction review. The Court nonetheless held that Coleman's habeas petition was barred in the absence of a showing of cause and prejudice. Justice O'Connor reasoned that the cause and prejudice standard was more compatible with interests of comity and finality than the deliberate bypass standard. She concluded as follows:

> In all cases in which a state prisoner has defaulted his federal claims in state court pursuant to an independent and adequate state procedural rule, federal habeas review of the claims is barred unless the prisoner can demonstrate cause for the default and actual prejudice as a result of the alleged violation of federal law, or demonstrate that failure to consider the claims will result in a fundamental miscarriage of justice. *Fay* was based on a conception of federal/state relations that undervalued the importance of state procedural rules. The several cases after *Fay* that applied the cause and prejudice standard to a variety of state procedural defaults represent a different view. We now recognize the important interest in finality served by state procedural rules, and the significant harm to the States that results from the failure of federal courts to respect them.

Justices Blackmun, Stevens, and Marshall dissented.

Cause and Prejudice for Federal Habeas Petitioners: United States v. Frady

United States v. Frady, 456 U.S. 152 (1982), holds that on collateral attack under § 2255 a petitioner convicted in federal court may not rely on the "plain error" doctrine of Fed.R.Crim.P. 52(b) to challenge an error as to which there was a procedural default. Frady, convicted in federal court of a vicious killing in 1963, moved to vacate his sentence on the ground that the jury instructions erroneously equated intent with malice and told the jury that the law presumes malice from the use of a weapon. He did not object to the instructions at trial. For the majority, Justice O'Connor wrote that the plain error standard, which is applicable on direct review and "was intended to afford a means for the prompt redress of miscarriages of justice," "is out of place when a prisoner launches a collateral attack against a criminal conviction after society's legitimate interest in the finality of the judgment has been perfected by the expiration of the time allowed for direct review or by the affirmance of the conviction on appeal." To prevail, Frady would have to meet the stricter standards of cause and prejudice under Wainwright v. Sykes. (Stricter even than the plain error standard, which is really saying something).

The *Frady* majority found, without reaching the question of cause, that Frady could not show prejudice. The Court noted that Frady had admitted the killing for which he had been convicted. Justice O'Connor stated that prejudice does not follow simply from the fact that a jury instruction was erroneous. Rather, prejudice must be evaluated by the effect of the error in the context of the whole trial. She concluded that a petitioner must show that errors at the trial "worked to his *actual* and substantial disadvantage, infecting his entire trial with error of constitutional dimensions." Frady had failed to contradict strong evidence in the record that he had acted with malice, and therefore the instruction was not prejudicial.[12]

Federal Defendant's Failure to Raise an Ineffective Assistance Claim on Direct Appeal; Is That a Procedural Default?: Massaro v. United States

In Massaro v. United States, 538 U.S. 500 (2003), the Court considered whether a federal defendant had procedurally defaulted an ineffective assistance of counsel claim by failing to assert it on direct review of his conviction. Justice Kennedy, writing for the Court, noted as "background" the general rule that claims not raised on direct appeal may not be raised on collateral review unless the petitioner shows cause and prejudice. He explained that "[t]he procedural default rule is neither a statutory nor a constitutional requirement, but it is a doctrine adhered to by the courts to

---

[12]   Justice Stevens concurred. Justice Blackmun concurred in the judgment. Justice Brennan dissented. Chief Justice Burger and Justice Marshall did not participate.

conserve judicial resources and to respect the law's important interest in the finality of judgments." But he found an exception to that general requirement for claims of ineffective assistance of counsel at trial. He noted that claims of ineffective assistance of counsel are not ordinarily—and not efficiently—made on direct review because a factual record of counsel's performance was never developed at trial. He explained as follows:

> Under Strickland v. Washington [discussed in Chapter 10], a defendant claiming ineffective counsel must show that counsel's actions were not supported by a reasonable strategy and that the error was prejudicial. The evidence introduced at trial, however, will be devoted to issues of guilt or innocence, and the resulting record in many cases will not disclose the facts necessary to decide either prong of the *Strickland* analysis. If the alleged error is one of commission, the record may reflect the action taken by counsel but not the reasons for it. * * * The trial record may contain no evidence of alleged errors of omission, much less the reasons underlying them. And evidence of alleged conflicts of interest might be found only in attorney-client correspondence or other documents that, in the typical criminal trial, are not introduced. Without additional factual development, moreover, an appellate court may not be able to ascertain whether the alleged error was prejudicial.

Justice Kennedy also noted that "[s]ubjecting ineffective-assistance claims to the usual cause-and-prejudice rule also would create perverse incentives for counsel on direct appeal. To ensure that a potential ineffective assistance claim is not waived—and to avoid incurring a claim of ineffective counsel at the appellate stage—counsel would be pressured to bring claims of ineffective trial counsel, regardless of merit." Justice Kennedy concluded as follows:

> We do not hold that ineffective-assistance claims must be reserved for collateral review. There may be cases in which trial counsel's ineffectiveness is so apparent from the record that appellate counsel will consider it advisable to raise the issue on direct appeal. There may be instances, too, when obvious deficiencies in representation will be addressed by an appellate court *sua sponte*. * * * We do hold that failure to raise an ineffective-assistance-of-counsel claim on direct appeal does not bar the claim from being brought in a later, appropriate [collateral] proceeding.

c. The Meaning of "Cause and Prejudice"

An Objection That Could Have Been Brought: Engle v. Isaac

One of the Court's first attempts to explain the "cause" part of the cause and prejudice standard is Engle v. Isaac, 456 U.S. 107 (1982). The

Court in *Engle* held that three habeas corpus petitioners could not collaterally challenge jury instructions given in a state criminal proceeding. The petitioners contended that Ohio had impermissibly shifted the burden of persuasion on self-defense issues to them, but none had objected at trial to the trial court's instructions. Without reaching the question of prejudice, the *Engle* Court found that there was no good cause for the petitioners' failure to object to the instructions in the state trial. The petitioners contended that their failure to raise the claim should be excused because the legal basis for an objection to the instructions was "novel" or unknown to them at the time of their trial. There was no clearly established law on point. But Justice O'Connor found that the basis of petitioners' constitutional claim (i.e., impermissible burden-shifting) had been apparent since *In re Winship,* decided before the petitioners were tried. (The Court in *Winship* held that due process requires the prosecution to prove every element of the crime beyond a reasonable doubt.)

The petitioners argued that the failure to invoke *Winship* had been justifiable, because *Winship* concerned the prosecution's burden to prove the *elements* of the crime, and did not specifically consider whether it was permissible to allocate to the defendant the burden of proof on affirmative defenses. But Justice O'Connor rejected this argument. She noted that *Winship* had been relied on by some lawyers making similar claims at that time. Thus, it could not be said that the petitioners had "lacked the tools to construct" an argument based on *Winship,* and consequently there was no good cause for failing to bring the argument. So long as the claim was "reasonably available" at the time of trial, there was no cause for the petitioners' failure to comply with the state's contemporary objection requirement. Justice O'Connor recognized that not "every astute counsel" would have made a constitutional objection in these circumstances. However, she concluded that the Constitution "does not insure that defense counsel will recognize and raise every constitutional claim."

Finally, Justice O'Connor rejected the petitioners' argument that an objection would have been "futile," because Ohio courts had routinely given the instruction shifting the burden of proving self-defense to the defendant. She stated that "the futility of presenting an objection to the state courts cannot alone constitute cause for a failure to object at trial." Justice O'Connor reasoned that a contemporary objection was required because "a state court that has previously rejected a constitutional argument may decide, upon reflection, that the contention is valid." Thus, the question for determining cause is not whether an objection would be "futile" but rather whether the objection was "reasonably available."[13]

---

[13] Justice Blackmun concurred in the result without opinion. Justice Stevens concurred in part and dissented in part in a brief opinion. Justice Brennan, joined by Justice Marshall, dissented.

Failure to Bring a Novel Claim as "Cause": Reed v. Ross

The Court examined the concept of "cause" again in Reed v. Ross, 468 U.S. 1 (1984). Ross was convicted of first-degree murder in 1969, *prior to* the Supreme Court's holding in *Winship* that the Due Process Clause requires the state to prove beyond a reasonable doubt all of the elements necessary to constitute the crime with which a defendant is charged. (Thus, the case differed from *Engle*, where *Winship* had already been decided at the time of the state trial). Jury instructions had imposed upon Ross the burden of showing that he lacked malice and that he acted in self-defense. Ross did not properly object to the instructions. Ross then sought federal habeas corpus relief.

The Supreme Court held, 5–4, in an opinion by Justice Brennan, that Ross had established cause for his failure to challenge the instructions. The state conceded that Ross had been prejudiced by the claimed violation—challenging only whether there was cause—so the Court concluded that the state procedural bar was lifted.

On the question of cause, Justice Brennan stated that "[c]ounsel's failure to raise a claim for which there was no reasonable basis in existing law does not seriously implicate any of the concerns that might otherwise require deference to a State's procedural bar" and that "if we were to hold that the novelty of a constitutional question does not give rise to cause for counsel's failure to raise it, we might actually disrupt state-court proceedings by encouraging defense counsel to include any and all remotely plausible constitutional claims that could, some day, gain recognition." The Court held, therefore, "that where a constitutional claim is so novel that its legal basis is not reasonably available to counsel, a defendant has cause for his failure to raise the claim in accordance with applicable state procedures." Justice Brennan concluded as follows:

> Whether an attorney had a reasonable basis for pressing a claim challenging a practice that this Court has arguably sanctioned depends on how direct this Court's sanction of the prevailing practice had been, how well entrenched the practice was in the relevant jurisdiction at the time of defense counsel's failure to challenge it, and how strong the available support is from sources opposing the prevailing practice.

Applying those standards to Ross's case, the Court looked to the law as it existed prior to *Winship* and found only scant, indirect support for the challenge that Ross mounted in his habeas corpus petition. So while Ross's claim of error was similar to that of the petitioners in *Engle,* those petitioners had the benefit of *Winship* in constructing their arguments at trial, while Ross did not. Therefore, Ross had cause for his procedural fault while the petitioners in *Engle* did not.

Justice Rehnquist dissented, joined by the Chief Justice and Justices Blackmun and O'Connor. He noted that the equating of novelty of claims with cause not to bring them "pushes the Court into a conundrum which it refuses to recognize. The more novel a claimed constitutional right, the more unlikely a violation of that claimed right undercut the fundamental fairness of the trial." In Justice Rehnquist's view, the majority's construction meant that if there was "cause" for not bringing a novel claim, there would by definition not be prejudice.

The Reed-Engle/AEDPA Whipsaw

Reed v. Ross holds that if a development in the law could not have been reasonably anticipated by the petitioner, then there is cause for not invoking the rule in the state proceedings. But can the petitioner then rely on that rule in habeas proceedings to show a violation of the Constitution? Recall the discussion of nonretroactivity of new rules on habeas, and particularly Teague v. Lane, in Chapter 1. Under *Teague*, new rules are generally inapplicable to habeas cases. A new rule is defined as any rule as to which reasonable minds could have differed before it was adopted, i.e., a rule that was not dictated by existing precedent. That standard was codified in AEDPA, which essentially prohibits federal courts from finding constitutional error if the state courts reasonably construed then-existing federal law as determined by the Supreme Court. How can the petitioner establish cause on grounds of "novelty" and yet argue that the state court decision was completely unreasonable because it failed to consider an admittedly novel federal claim? The "whipsaw" effect of *Ross* and the *Teague* principle is described by Professor Arkin in The Prisoner's Dilemma: Life in the Lower Federal Courts After Teague v. Lane, 69 No.Car.L.Rev. 371, 408 (1991):

> [I]f a petitioner is able to show that his claim is based on a "new" rule of law, the habeas court will excuse his state procedural default, assuming petitioner can show actual prejudice. But, having shown that the rule under which he seeks relief was not available to him at the time he should have raised it in the state courts, the petitioner may well have won the battle under *Wainwright* [v. Sykes] only to lose the war to *Teague*. Under most circumstances, the petitioner will have just shown that the very rule under which he seeks relief is not retroactive * * *.

See also Hopkinson v. Shillinger, 888 F.2d 1286 (10th Cir.1989) ("a holding that a claim is so novel that there is no reasonably available basis for it, thus establishing cause, must also mean that the claim was too novel to be dictated by past precedent").

Unavailability of Facts as Cause: Amadeo v. Zant

The *Ross* "reasonable availability" definition of cause can still have utility where the failure to assert a claim is due to a lack of *facts* that were not reasonably available to the defendant at the time of the state proceedings. A unanimous Supreme Court held in Amadeo v. Zant, 486 U.S. 214 (1988), that a state defendant who was convicted of murder and sentenced to death showed cause for a late challenge to the racial composition of the grand jury. The petitioner demonstrated that local officials had concealed a handwritten memorandum from the District Attorney to jury commissioners, which indicated that underrepresentation of black members of the grand jury was intentional. The memorandum was discovered by a lawyer in a civil suit challenging voting procedures. Amadeo's lawyer relied upon the report on direct appeal, but the state supreme court found that the challenge to the grand jury's composition came too late under state procedures.

Justice Marshall wrote for the Court as it found cause for the procedural default because the factual basis for the equal protection claim had been suppressed by the state. In articulating the meaning of "cause," the Court cited *Ross* and concluded as follows:

> If the District Attorney's memorandum was not reasonably discoverable because it was concealed by Putnam County officials, and if that concealment, rather than tactical considerations, was the reason for the failure of petitioner's lawyers to raise the jury challenge in the trial court, then petitioner established cause to excuse his procedural default under this Court's precedents.

Attorney Error Is Not Cause Unless It Constitutes Ineffective Assistance: Murray v. Carrier and Smith v. Murray

In Murray v. Carrier, 477 U.S. 478 (1986), Justice O'Connor wrote for the Court as it held that a federal habeas petitioner cannot show cause for a procedural default by establishing that competent defense counsel's failure to raise a claim of error was inadvertent rather than deliberate. In a rape and abduction case, the defendant's trial counsel had twice unsuccessfully requested an opportunity to review the victim's statements. Counsel failed to attack the trial judge's rulings in his petition for appeal, thus defaulting under a state court rule limiting judicial consideration on appeal to errors raised in the petition. The Court held that this failure to comply with the state procedure barred federal habeas corpus review even if it resulted from ignorance or inadvertence. Justice O'Connor wrote that "we discern no inequity in requiring [the defendant] to bear the risk of attorney error that results in a procedural default" by "counsel whose performance is not constitutionally ineffective." To establish cause for a procedural default, a prisoner must ordinarily "show that some objective factor external to the defense impeded counsel's efforts to comply with the State's procedural rule." Justice O'Connor elaborated as follows:

> Without attempting an exhaustive catalog * * *, we note that a showing that the factual or legal claim was not reasonably available to counsel * * *, or that some interference by officials * * * made compliance impracticable, would constitute cause under this standard.

> Similarly, if the procedural default is the result of ineffective assistance of counsel, the Sixth Amendment itself requires that responsibility for the default be imputed to the State [and it is therefore] cause for a procedural default.

Justice Stevens, joined by Justice Blackmun, concurred in the judgment. He argued that the cause and prejudice formula "is not dispositive when the fundamental fairness of a prisoner's conviction is at issue" and advocated an "overall inquiry into justice." Justice O'Connor responded that the Stevens approach would actually replace the cause requirement with a manifest injustice standard. She observed that the relationship of this standard to prejudice was uncertain. But in recognition of the fact that the cause and prejudice standard might produce a miscarriage of justice in some cases, Justice O'Connor stated that "in an extraordinary case, where a constitutional violation has probably resulted in the conviction of one who is actually innocent, a federal habeas corpus court may grant the writ even in the absence of a showing of cause for the procedural default." The Court remanded for an inquiry into whether the victim's statements contained material that would establish the defendant's innocence.

Justice Brennan, joined by Justice Marshall, dissented and argued that the cause and prejudice limitation, a judicial form of abstention not required by the language of the habeas corpus statute, should permit federal consideration of claims not raised because of inadvertence or ignorance.

Decided with Murray v. Carrier was Smith v. Murray, 477 U.S. 527 (1986), a capital case. Once again Justice O'Connor found no cause for a procedural default. A psychiatrist who examined Smith was called to testify by the state at the sentencing phase of the trial. He described, over Smith's objection, an incident that Smith had related to him. On appeal, Smith's counsel did not claim error in the use of the testimony, and so the claim was procedurally defaulted. In his habeas corpus petition, Smith claimed that the use of the statements violated his constitutional rights under the Fifth and Sixth Amendments. Justice O'Connor found that a deliberate decision had been made not to put the claim before the state supreme court and that, even if the decision was made out of ignorance of the claim's strength, this was not sufficient to demonstrate cause. She also concluded that the application of the cause and prejudice standard would not result in a fundamental miscarriage of justice, because "the alleged constitutional error neither precluded the development of true facts nor resulted in the admission of false ones."

Justice Stevens dissented in *Smith*, joined in full by Justices Marshall and Blackmun, and in part by Justice Brennan. He disagreed with the idea that only a claim implicating "actual innocence" could rise to the level of a miscarriage of justice, and argued that accuracy is not the only value protected by the Constitution.

Attorney Abandonment as Cause and Prejudice: Maples v. Thomas

In Maples v. Thomas, 565 U.S. 266 (2012), a state prisoner's pro bono attorneys left the law firm representing him without notifying either him or the court, thus causing him to miss the deadline for filing a notice of appeal in his state post-conviction case. The Court found that under these circumstances the prisoner demonstrated "cause" that excused the procedural default. Justice Ginsburg, writing for a seven-Justice majority, noted that "under agency principles, a client cannot be charged with the acts or omissions of an attorney who has abandoned him. Nor can a client be faulted for failing to act on his own behalf when he lacks reason to believe his attorneys of record, in fact, are not representing him." Reviewing the circumstances, the Court found that the prisoner's attorneys of record had abandoned him, thereby supplying the "extraordinary circumstances beyond his control" necessary to lift the state procedural bar to his federal petition. Justice Ginsburg concluded as follows:

> Through no fault of his own, Maples lacked the assistance of any authorized attorney during the 42 days Alabama allows for noticing an appeal from a trial court's denial of postconviction relief. As just observed, he had no reason to suspect that, in reality, he had been reduced to pro se status. Maples was disarmed by extraordinary circumstances quite beyond his control. He has shown ample cause, we hold, to excuse the procedural default into which he was trapped when counsel of record abandoned him without a word of warning.

Justice Alito, in a concurring opinion, summarized the confluence of eight factors that prevented the petitioner from filing the notice:

> Unbeknownst to petitioner, he was effectively deprived of legal representation due to the combined effect of no fewer than eight unfortunate events: (1) the departure from their law firm of the two young lawyers who appeared as counsel of record in his state postconviction proceeding; (2) the acceptance by these two attorneys of new employment that precluded them from continuing to represent him; (3) their failure to notify petitioner of their new situation; (4) their failure to withdraw as his counsel of record; (5) the apparent failure of

the firm that they left to monitor the status of petitioner's case when these attorneys departed; (6) when notice of the decision denying petitioner's request for state postconviction relief was received in that firm's offices, the failure of the firm's mail room to route that important communication to either another member of the firm or to the departed attorneys' new addresses; (7) the failure of the clerk's office to take any action when the envelope containing that notice came back unopened; and (8) local counsel's very limited conception of the role that he was obligated to play in petitioner's representation.

Justice Alito concluded that "[w]hat occurred here was not a predictable consequence of the Alabama system but a veritable perfect storm of misfortune, a most unlikely combination of events that, without notice, effectively deprived petitioner of legal representation. Under these unique circumstances, I agree that petitioner's procedural default is overcome."

Justice Scalia, joined by Justice Thomas, dissented on the ground that, although a procedural default may be excused when it is attributable to abandonment by his attorney, the petitioner failed to prove abandonment.

No Cause Based on Ineffectiveness of Counsel, Where There Is No Constitutional Right to Counsel: Coleman v. Thompson, Martinez v. Ryan, and Davila v. Davis

Carrier held that constitutionally ineffective assistance of counsel would establish the "cause" requirement that is part of the showing necessary to excuse a procedural default. In Coleman v. Thompson, 501 U.S. 722 (1991), Coleman had been convicted of capital murder; his direct appeals had been unsuccessful; he brought a petition in state court for relief under the *state* habeas corpus provisions; this petition was denied, and Coleman's counsel failed to file a notice of appeal from the denial. The failure to file the notice of appeal imposed a procedural bar to further relief. Coleman argued that his counsel's failure constituted ineffective assistance, and that the procedural bar was therefore lifted after Murray v. Carrier. Justice O'Connor, writing for the Court, rejected this argument. She relied on the line of right to counsel cases (discussed in Chapters 5 and 10), which hold that the defendant has no constitutional right to appointed counsel beyond the first appeal of right. She reasoned that because Coleman had no constitutional right to counsel in the state habeas proceedings, there could be no claim of constitutionally ineffective counsel. She concluded that "Coleman must bear the risk of attorney error that results in a procedural default."

Justice O'Connor also rejected the argument that cause to excuse a procedural default should be found whenever counsel was so ineffective as to violate the standards of Strickland v. Washington (discussed in Chapter 10), even though no Sixth Amendment claim is possible because the ineffectiveness did not occur at a stage of the proceedings in which there is a constitutional right to counsel. She stated that this argument "is inconsistent not only with the language of *Carrier,* but the logic of that opinion as well." She reasoned that "cause" must be something "external to the petitioner, something that cannot be fairly attributed to him." She asserted that the only type of attorney error for which the State must take responsibility independent of the petitioner is where the Sixth Amendment has been violated, i.e., where ineffectiveness occurs before or during the trial or in the first appeal. She explained as follows:

> Where a petitioner defaults a claim as a result of the denial of the right to effective assistance of counsel, the State, which is responsible for the denial as a constitutional matter, must bear the cost of any resulting default and the harm to state interests that federal habeas review entails. A different allocation of costs is appropriate in those circumstances where the State has no responsibility to ensure that the petitioner was represented by competent counsel. As between the State and the petitioner, it is the petitioner who must bear the burden of a failure to follow state procedural rules.

Justice Blackmun, joined by Justices Marshall and Stevens in dissent, attacked the majority's holding as "patently unfair." He argued that to permit a procedural default to preclude habeas review, when it was caused by attorney error egregious enough to constitute ineffective assistance of counsel, "in no way serves the State's interest in preserving the integrity of its rules and proceedings."

The alleged failure of counsel in *Coleman* was on *appeal* from an initial-review collateral proceeding, and in that initial proceeding the prisoner's claims had been addressed by the state habeas trial court. Subsequently, the Court in Martinez v. Ryan, 566 U.S. 1 (2012), modified "the unqualified statement in *Coleman* that an attorney's ignorance or inadvertence in a postconviction proceeding does not qualify as cause to excuse a procedural default." The Court, in an opinion by Justice Kennedy, qualified *Coleman* by recognizing "a narrow exception:

> Inadequate assistance of counsel at *initial-review* collateral proceedings may establish cause for a prisoner's procedural default of a claim of ineffective assistance at trial." (Emphasis added).

The Court explained that in *Coleman*, the substantive claim had already been addressed at the initial state collateral proceeding. In contrast, the substantive claim of the petitioner in *Martinez*—ineffective assistance of counsel at trial—had never been heard. Justice Kennedy explained as follows:

> Where, as here, the initial-review collateral proceeding is the first designated proceeding for a prisoner to raise a claim of ineffective assistance at trial, the collateral proceeding is in many ways the

equivalent of a prisoner's direct appeal as to the ineffective-assistance claim. This is because the state habeas court looks to the merits of the claim of ineffective assistance, no other court has addressed the claim, and defendants pursuing first-tier review are generally ill equipped to represent themselves because they do not have a brief from counsel or an opinion of the court addressing their claim of error.

Justice Kennedy concluded as follows:

[W]hen a State requires a prisoner to raise an ineffective-assistance-of-trial-counsel claim in a collateral proceeding, a prisoner may establish cause for a default of an ineffective-assistance claim in two circumstances. The first is where the state courts did not appoint counsel in the initial-review collateral proceeding for a claim of ineffective assistance at trial. The second is where appointed counsel in the initial-review collateral proceeding, where the claim should have been raised, was ineffective under the standards of Strickland v. Washington. To overcome the default, a prisoner must also demonstrate that the underlying ineffective-assistance-of-trial-counsel claim is a substantial one, which is to say that the prisoner must demonstrate that the claim has some merit.

Justice Scalia, joined by Justice Thomas, dissented, objecting to the modification of *Coleman,* on the ground that the majority had made "a radical alteration of our habeas jurisprudence that will impose considerable economic costs on the States and further impair their ability to provide justice in a timely fashion."

In Davila v. Davis, 137 S.Ct. 2058 (2017), the Court held that *Coleman* and not *Martinez* applied to a default of a claim allegedly caused by ineffectiveness of appellate counsel in state post-conviction proceedings. Therefore the defendant's procedural default—failure to raise a claim on appeal—was not excused and habeas relief was not available to him. The Court held that the *Martinez* Court provided a limited exception to the *Coleman* rule that precludes a finding of cause when counsel was ineffective in failing to raise the claim. The Court in *Martinez* did not intend to replace *Coleman* in the context of appellate ineffectiveness. Justice Thomas wrote the opinion for five Members of the Court. Justice Breyer, joined by Justices Ginsburg, Sotomayor, and Kagan, dissented.

Cause and Prejudice in the Context of a Brady Violation: Strickler v. Greene

The Court considered how the cause and prejudice standards apply to *Brady* violations in Strickler v. Greene, 527 U.S. 263 (1999). One of the major prosecution witnesses in Strickler's capital murder trial had made several statements to police that were flatly inconsistent with her very evocative and detailed trial testimony. The prosecutor had an open file policy, but despite this, the witness's pretrial statements were not turned over to the defense. Defense counsel, in light of the open file policy, made no pretrial request for *Brady* material. Nor did defense counsel pursue a *Brady* claim at trial or on state appellate and collateral review—this was understandable, however, because defense counsel had no reason to think that any exculpatory information had been suppressed.

Strickler conceded that he had procedurally defaulted the *Brady* claim; but he argued that the very suppression of the witness's statements constituted cause. As to prejudice, he argued that in order for information to be "material" under *Brady*, it has to be information strong enough to undermine confidence in the outcome of the trial. (See Chapter 8, supra, for a full discussion of this standard). So if suppression of information violates *Brady*, it should by definition satisfy the standard for "prejudice" under the procedural default doctrine.

Justice Stevens, writing for the Court, agreed in principle with Strickler that the factors supporting the finding of a *Brady* violation could also be the factors that would lead to a finding of cause. He focused on three factors in the case at bar:

> The documents were suppressed by the Commonwealth; the prosecutor maintained an open file policy; and trial counsel were not aware of the factual basis for the claim. The first and second factors— i.e., the non-disclosure and the open file policy—are both fairly characterized as conduct attributable to the State that impeded trial counsel's access to the factual basis for making a *Brady* claim. As we explained in Murray v. Carrier it is just such factors that ordinarily establish the existence of cause for a procedural default.

Justice Stevens found it unnecessary to decide, however, whether "cause" for a procedural default would be found if the prosecutor did not maintain an open file policy, and the defendant failed to make a *Brady* request before trial or a *Brady* claim on state court appeal.

On the question of prejudice, Justice Stevens agreed with Strickler that suppressing information important enough to rise to the level of *Brady* material would by definition satisfy the standard for prejudice under the procedural default doctrine. On the merits, however, the Court found that the suppression of the witness's statements did not constitute a *Brady* violation. Justice Stevens found that Strickler could not show that there was "a reasonable probability that his conviction or sentence would have been different had these materials been disclosed. He therefore cannot show materiality under *Brady* or prejudice from his failure to raise the claim earlier."

d. The Actual Innocence Exception

The Court in *Smith* and *Carrier* acknowledged that a procedural default could be lifted even in the absence of cause and prejudice, if the petitioner can show "actual innocence." This exception to the cause and prejudice requirement was described by the court in Johnson v. Singletary, 940 F.2d 1540 (11th Cir.1991) (en banc):

> [A]lthough factual inaccuracy in the guilt or sentencing context may well be *necessary* to a claim of actual innocence, factual inaccuracy is not *sufficient* unless the inaccuracy demonstrates, at least colorably, that the petitioner is * * * ineligible for either an adjudication of guilt or the sentence imposed. If prejudicial factual inaccuracy alone is enough to warrant review of a defaulted claim, then the actual innocence standard is meaningless.

Actual Innocence and the Death Penalty: Sawyer v. Whitley

In Sawyer v. Whitley, 505 U.S. 333 (1992), the Court applied the "actual innocence" exception to the cause and prejudice requirement in the context of a challenge to the death penalty. Chief Justice Rehnquist, writing for the Court, stated that in a habeas challenge to a death penalty, the petitioner will establish "actual innocence" only if he shows "by clear and convincing evidence that but for a constitutional error, no reasonable juror would have found the petitioner eligible for the death penalty under the applicable state law."

Sawyer and his accomplice Lane brutally murdered a woman; they beat her, scalded her with water, poured lighter fluid on her, and ignited the fluid. The victim died of her injuries two months later. At the sentencing phase, Sawyer's sister testified to Sawyer's mistreatment as a child. The jury found aggravating factors—that Sawyer was engaged in aggravated arson and that the murder was committed in an especially atrocious manner. It found no mitigating factors and sentenced Sawyer to death.

Sawyer brought two claims on habeas, both of which were procedurally barred, and neither of which satisfied the cause and prejudice requirement. One claim, a *Brady* claim, concerned exculpatory evidence relating to Sawyer's role in the offense, including evidence impeaching the credibility of a star prosecution witness, and an affidavit claiming that a child who witnessed the event had stated that Sawyer's accomplice had poured lighter fluid on the victim and ignited it, and that Sawyer had tried to stop him. The second claim was that Sawyer's trial lawyer had erred in failing to introduce at the sentencing phase the medical records from Sawyer's stays as a teenager in two mental hospitals.

The Chief Justice determined that there were three possible ways in which "actual innocence" might be defined in the death penalty context. The "strictest definition" would be to require the petitioner to show that the constitutional error negated an essential element of the capital offense of which he was convicted. The Chief Justice rejected this definition because the Court in Smith v. Murray had "suggested a more expansive meaning to the term of actual innocence in a capital case than simply innocence of the capital offense itself."

The "most lenient of the three possibilities" would be to allow the showing of actual innocence to extend to three factors: 1) the elements of the crime; 2) the existence of all aggravating factors; and 3) mitigating evidence "which bore, not on the defendant's eligibility to receive the death penalty, but only on the ultimate discretionary decision between the death penalty and life imprisonment." Put another way, "actual innocence" would be found under this view if the sentencer was presented with "a factually inaccurate sentencing profile." The Chief Justice rejected this definition, however, as too permissive. He reasoned that under this test, "actual innocence amounts to little more than what is already required to show prejudice." The majority therefore opted for a middle ground, and defined "innocent of the death penalty" as allowing a showing not only pertaining to innocence of the capital crime itself, but also permitting "a showing that there was no aggravating circumstance or that some other condition of eligibility had not been met." The Court noted that this test "hones in on the objective factors or conditions which must be shown to exist before a defendant is eligible to have the death penalty imposed." The Chief Justice concluded as follows:

> [T]he "actual innocence" requirement must focus on those elements which render a defendant eligible for the death penalty, and not on additional mitigating evidence which was prevented from being introduced as a result of claimed constitutional error.

Applying this test to Sawyer's claims, Chief Justice Rehnquist found that the medical records that Sawyer's attorney failed to introduce were not pertinent to actual innocence, as they were in the nature of mitigating evidence and so did not affect his death-eligibility. The fact that Sawyer had spent time in mental hospitals as a teenager was not relevant to an aggravating factor nor to an element of the crime.

As to the *Brady* material, the affidavit relating the statement of the child-eyewitness—to the effect that Sawyer had tried to stop the burning of the victim—was pertinent both to the crime and to the aggravating factor of arson. The Court concluded, however, that the affidavit, "in view of all the other evidence in the record, does not show that no rational juror would find that petitioner committed both of the aggravating circumstances found by the jury." The Court noted that the murder was atrocious and cruel "based on the undisputed evidence of torture before the jury quite apart from the arson" and that at any rate a reasonable juror could have discredited the affidavit in light of the other evidence. Thus, Sawyer had not established clear and convincing proof of his ineligibility for the death penalty.

Justice Stevens, joined by Justices Blackmun and O'Connor, concurred in the judgment. While agreeing that Sawyer had failed to establish "actual innocence," Justice Stevens took issue with the majority's definition of that standard. He argued that the majority's clear and convincing evidence standard imposed too severe a burden on the capital defendant. Justice Stevens found "no basis for requiring a federal court to be virtually certain that the defendant is actually ineligible for the death penalty, before merely entertaining his claim."

Justice Blackmun wrote a separate opinion concurring in the judgment. He launched a broad attack on the Court's habeas corpus jurisprudence. He criticized the "actual innocence" exception as assuming erroneously "that the only value worth protecting through federal habeas review is the accuracy and reliability of the guilt determination." He elaborated as follows:

> The accusatorial system of justice adopted by the Founders affords a defendant certain process-based protections that do not have accuracy of truth-finding as their primary goal. These protections * * * are debased, and indeed, rendered largely irrelevant, in a system that values the accuracy of the guilt determination above individual rights. Nowhere is this single-minded focus on actual innocence more misguided than in a case where a defendant alleges a constitutional error in the sentencing phase of a capital trial.

Actual Innocence of the Crime Itself: *Schlup v. Delo*

The Court distinguished *Sawyer,* and applied a more permissive standard to claims of actual innocence of the crime itself (as opposed to the death penalty), in Schlup v. Delo, 513 U.S. 298 (1995). Schlup was subject to the cause and prejudice requirements, which would have barred his *Brady* and *Strickland* claims. He argued, however, that the bar should be lifted because he had discovered new evidence that established his innocence of the crime. The lower courts held that Schlup's new evidence did not provide "clear and convincing" proof of his innocence as required by *Sawyer.* But the Supreme Court, in an opinion by Justice Stevens for a five-person majority, held that *Sawyer* was limited to challenges to the petitioner's sentence, and that "actual innocence" claims must be treated more permissively when the petitioner's challenge is to the conviction itself.

Justice Stevens explained the need to provide a more permissive standard of proof to claims of innocence of the crime:

> Claims of actual innocence pose less of a threat to scarce judicial resources and to principles of finality and comity than do claims that focus solely on the erroneous imposition of the death penalty. Though challenges to the propriety of imposing a sentence of death are routinely asserted in capital cases, experience has taught us that a substantial claim that constitutional error has caused the conviction of an innocent person is extremely rare. To be credible, such a claim requires petitioner to support his allegations of constitutional error with new reliable evidence—whether it be exculpatory scientific evidence, trustworthy eyewitness accounts, or critical physical evidence—that was not presented at trial. Because such evidence is obviously unavailable in the vast majority of cases, claims of actual innocence are rarely successful. * * *

> Of greater importance, the individual interest in avoiding injustice is most compelling in the context of actual innocence. The quintessential miscarriage of justice is the execution of a person who is entirely innocent. * * *

> The overriding importance of this greater individual interest merits protection by imposing a somewhat less exacting standard of proof on a habeas petitioner alleging a fundamental miscarriage of justice than on one alleging that his sentence is too severe. * * * Though the *Sawyer* standard was fashioned to reflect the relative importance of a claim of an erroneous sentence, application of that standard to petitioners such as Schlup would give insufficient weight to the correspondingly greater injustice that is implicated by a claim of actual innocence.

Justice Stevens concluded that in order to lift a procedural bar relating to a conviction as opposed to a sentence, in the absence of cause and prejudice, "the petitioner must show that it is more likely than not that no reasonable juror would have convicted him in the light of the new evidence." He noted that a habeas petitioner "is thus required to make a stronger showing than that needed to establish prejudice" but that, at the same time, the showing of "more likely than not" imposes a lower burden of proof than the "clear and convincing" standard required under *Sawyer*. The Court remanded for a determination of whether Schlup's new evidence met the more permissive standard.

Chief Justice Rehnquist wrote a dissenting opinion joined by Justices Kennedy and Thomas. The Chief Justice complained that the Court had added to the complexity of habeas corpus jurisprudence by creating two standards of proof for "actual innocence"—one for attacks on a conviction and one for attacks on a sentence. Justice Scalia wrote a separate dissent joined by Justice Thomas.

Actual Innocence and an Untimely Petition:
McQuiggin v. Perkins

In McQuiggin v. Perkins, 569 U.S. 383 (2013), the Court held that the "actual innocence" exception serves as a gateway through which a petitioner may pass whether the impediment is a procedural bar, as it was in Schlup v. Delo, or expiration of the AEDPA statute of limitations—as in this case, where the petitioner filed a habeas petition (alleging ineffective assistance of trial counsel) more than 11 years after his conviction became final. Justice Ginsburg, for five members of the Court, found no reason to distinguish between the statute of limitations and any other procedural bar when the petitioner could show actual innocence. Justice Ginsburg emphasized, however, that

> tenable actual-innocence gateway pleas are rare: a petitioner does not meet the threshold requirement unless he persuades the district court that, in light of the new evidence, no juror, acting reasonably, would have voted to find him guilty beyond a reasonable doubt. And in making an assessment of the kind Schlup envisioned, the timing of the petition is a factor bearing on the reliability of the evidence purporting to show actual innocence.

Justice Scalia filed a dissenting opinion joined in full by Chief Justice Roberts and Justice Thomas, and joined in part by Justice Alito. Justice Scalia argued that the AEDPA statute of limitations did not provide for an actual innocence exception. He concluded as follows:

> "Actual innocence" has, until today, been an exception only to judge-made, prudential barriers to habeas relief, or as a means of channeling judges' statutorily conferred discretion not to apply a procedural bar. * * * Where Congress has erected a constitutionally valid barrier to habeas relief, a court cannot decline to give it effect.

Actual Innocence and Invalid Guilty Pleas:
Bousley v. United States

The Court in Bousley v. United States, 523 U.S. 614 (1998), considered whether the actual innocence exception could apply to a procedurally defaulted attack on the validity of a guilty plea. Bousley pleaded guilty to drug crimes, as well as to a violation of a federal statute that prohibited "using" a firearm during the course of a drug transaction. At the time he pleaded guilty to the firearms offense, the local federal courts had construed "using" expansively, to cover basically any situation in which a defendant possessed a gun during the course of a drug offense. Bousley appealed his sentence, but did not challenge his guilty plea on direct appeal. His sentence was affirmed. Thereafter, the Supreme Court determined that the term "using" in the statute meant some kind of active use, such as brandishing or, of course, shooting. Bousley sought a writ of habeas corpus challenging the factual basis for his guilty plea to the firearms charge, on the ground that neither the "evidence" nor the "plea allocution" showed a "connection between the firearms in the bedroom of the house, and the garage, where the drug trafficking occurred."

The Supreme Court, in an opinion by Chief Justice Rehnquist for six Justices, held that Bousley would be entitled to a hearing on the merits of his involuntary guilty plea claim, if he could make the showing necessary to relieve the procedural default resulting from his failure to appeal his guilty plea. While he could not establish "cause" and "prejudice" under the circumstances, the Court held that Bousley would be entitled to relief if he could establish his actual innocence of the gun charge. However, the Court noted that the question of actual innocence was somewhat different in the context of an attack on a guilty plea. The Chief Justice elaborated:

> It is important to note in this regard that "actual innocence" means factual innocence, not mere legal insufficiency. In other words, the Government is not limited to the existing record to rebut any showing that petitioner might make. Rather, on remand, the Government should be permitted to present any admissible evidence of petitioner's guilt * * *. In cases where the Government has forgone more serious charges in the course of plea bargaining, petitioner's showing of actual innocence must also extend to those charges.

The Chief Justice rejected the argument made by Justice Scalia, in dissent, that the actual innocence inquiry will be unduly complicated by the absence of a trial transcript in the guilty plea context. He found this concern "overstated," because in federal courts, where this case arose, "guilty pleas must be accompanied by proffers, recorded verbatim on the record, demonstrating a factual basis for the plea."

Justice Stevens wrote a separate opinion dissenting from the majority's application of the actual innocence standard. He argued that it was unnecessary for Bousley to establish actual innocence, because under the Supreme Court's subsequent construction of the firearms statute, he had never been found guilty of any criminal conduct. This in itself was enough to require that his guilty plea be vacated.

Justice Scalia, joined by Justice Thomas, dissented. He asked: "How is the court to determine 'actual innocence' upon our remand in the present case, where conviction was based upon an admission of guilt? Presumably the defendant will introduce evidence (perhaps nothing more than his own testimony) showing that he did not 'use' a firearm in committing the crime to which he pleaded guilty, and the Government, eight years after the fact, will have to find and produce witnesses saying that he did. This seems to me not to remedy a miscarriage of justice, but to produce one."

Avoidance of Actual Innocence Determinations:
Dretke v. Haley

The Court in Dretke v. Haley, 541 U.S. 386 (2004), held that claims of actual innocence must be deferred if a habeas petition can be decided on other grounds. Haley received an enhanced sentence, and argued that this was in error because state law did not permit his prior crime to be used to enhance a sentence. Thus, he claimed that he was "actually innocent" of an enhanced sentence. He argued that this actual innocence excused his procedural default for failing to bring that claim in state court. But Haley also claimed that his state counsel was ineffective for failing to assert the claim that the enhancement did not apply. This ineffective assistance of counsel claim had not been defaulted. Under these circumstances the Court, in an opinion by Justice O'Connor, declared as follows:

> [A] federal court faced with allegations of actual innocence, whether of the sentence or of the crime charged, must first address all nondefaulted claims for comparable relief and other grounds for cause to excuse the procedural default. * * * To hold otherwise would be to license district courts to riddle the cause and prejudice standard with ad hoc exceptions whenever they perceive an error to be "clear" or departure from the rules expedient. Such an approach * * * would have the unhappy effect of prolonging the pendency of federal habeas applications as each new exception is tested in the court of appeals.

Justices Stevens and Kennedy wrote dissenting opinions.

4. Adequate and Independent State Grounds

A federal court is precluded from considering a habeas petition from a state prisoner—absent cause and prejudice or actual innocence—if the state decision rests on an adequate and independent state ground, such as a state procedural bar. The Supreme Court has stated that "in the habeas context, the application of the independent and adequate state ground doctrine is grounded in concerns of comity and federalism" and that without this doctrine "habeas petitioners would be able to avoid the exhaustion requirement by defaulting their federal claims in state court." Coleman v. Thompson, 501 U.S. 722 (1991).

The Court has recognized that it is often difficult to determine whether a state court has in fact relied on an adequate and independent state ground that would preclude review of any constitutional claim. In Harris v. Reed, 489 U.S. 255 (1989), the Court established the following presumption:

When a state court decision fairly appears to rest primarily on federal law, or to be interwoven with federal law, and when the adequacy and independence of any possible state law ground is not clear from the face of the opinion, we will accept as the most reasonable explanation that the state court decided the case the way it did because it believed that federal law required it to do so.

Thus, *Harris* requires the state court to make a plain statement that the ruling is based on state law, where it could fairly construed as resting on either federal or state law. But subsequent cases have found an adequate state ground in the absence of a plain statement.

Adequate State Ground Without an Explicit Statement: Coleman v. Thompson

The question in Coleman v. Thompson, 501 U.S. 722 (1991), was whether an adequate and independent state ground could be found in a state appellate court's summary order of dismissal. Coleman brought a state habeas proceeding alleging various federal constitutional errors. The trial court denied relief. Coleman's notice of appeal to the Virginia Supreme Court from the trial court's decision was untimely under Virginia law. The Commonwealth moved to dismiss the appeal on the sole ground that it was untimely. The Virginia Supreme Court delayed ruling on the motion to dismiss, and consequently briefs on both the motion and the merits were filed. Six months later, stating that it had considered all the briefs, the Virginia Supreme Court summarily granted the motion to dismiss the appeal and dismissed the petition for appeal. So the question was whether the Virginia court relied on the procedural bar to dismiss the action (in which case habeas relief would be denied), or relied instead on its interpretation of Coleman's constitutional claim.

Justice O'Connor, writing for the Court, found that the summary order rested on the adequate and independent state ground, i.e., the state law allowing dismissal of an appeal that was untimely filed. She rejected, for two reasons, Coleman's argument that the state court should be required to state explicitly that it is relying on an independent state ground in order to preclude federal habeas review. First, she asserted that an absolute requirement of an explicit statement misreads *Harris*, which requires an explicit statement only upon a predicate finding that the state decision "must fairly appear to rest primarily on federal law or to be interwoven with federal law." Second, the proposal for a per se plain statement rule would "greatly and unacceptably expand the risk" that federal habeas courts would review state decisions that were in fact based on adequate and independent state grounds.

Justice O'Connor explained that where it does not fairly appear that the state court decision is based primarily on federal grounds, "it is simply not true that the most reasonable explanation is that the state judgment rested on federal grounds," and that a conclusive presumption to that effect "is simply not worth the cost in the loss of respect for the State that such a rule would entail." She concluded that "we will not impose on state courts the responsibility for using particular language in every case in which a state prisoner presents a federal claim * * * in order that federal courts might not be bothered with reviewing state law and the record in the case." Rather, federal courts on habeas must consider the nature of the disposition and the surrounding circumstances of the order to determine whether the state court relied on an adequate state ground.

On the facts, the Court found that the Virginia Supreme Court's summary order did not "fairly appear" to rest on or to be interwoven with federal law. Justice O'Connor noted that the summary order granted the Commonwealth's motion to dismiss, which was based solely upon Coleman's failure to meet the time requirements for a notice of appeal. Federal law was not mentioned in the order. She recognized that the Virginia Supreme Court's explicit consideration of briefs discussing the merits "adds some ambiguity," but concluded that this did not override the "explicit grant of a dismissal motion based solely on procedural grounds."

Justice White wrote a concurring opinion in *Coleman*, emphasizing that he was not convinced that the Virginia Supreme Court followed a practice of waiving a procedural bar when constitutional issues are at stake.

Justice Blackmun, joined by Justices Marshall and Stevens, filed a lengthy dissent, criticizing the Court's "crusade to erect petty procedural barriers in the path of any state prisoner seeking review of his federal constitutional claims." He argued that the Court "is creating a Byzantine morass of arbitrary, unnecessary and unjustifiable impediments to the vindication of federal rights" and "subordinates fundamental constitutional rights to mere utilitarian interests."

Note that on the habeas corpus flow chart, the Court's finding that Virginia relied on a state rule to dismiss the appeal does not end the case. Rather, it means that the state applied a procedural bar. Coleman could still have his habeas petition heard—but only if he could establish cause and prejudice or actual innocence. As discussed above, Coleman could not do so. If the state procedural bar had not been applied, then Virginia would have ruled on the constitutional claims, there would have been no procedural defaults, and Coleman's habeas petition would have been heard.

Coleman and the Plain Statement Rule

After *Coleman,* is there anything left of the Harris v. Reed "plain statement" rule? Consider the views of Judge Williams, concurring in Young v. Herring, 938 F.2d 543 (5th Cir.1991) (en banc).

[The plain statement] requirement is to be applied narrowly— only in those cases where the state court considers both the procedural bar and explicitly the federal constitutional issue on the merits. The fact that the [state] court is fully aware of the presence of the federal constitutional issue is not enough even though the court does not clearly and expressly rely upon the procedural bar.

State Ground That Is Not Adequate

A state procedural bar will be deemed "adequate" to preclude habeas review only if it is *regularly followed* and *firmly established* in practice. See James v. Kentucky, 466 U.S. 341 (1984), where the defendant asked the judge to admonish the jury not to draw an inference from his failure to testify. The judge refused the request, and James appealed the refusal. The state supreme court held that a request for an admonition was not adequate to preserve a claim on appeal for a failure to give an instruction. But the U.S. Supreme Court stated that "for federal constitutional purposes, James adequately invoked his substantive right to jury guidance." The Court held that "Kentucky's distinction between admonitions and instructions is not the sort of firmly established and regularly followed state practice that can prevent implementation of federal constitutional rights."

In Ford v. Georgia, 498 U.S. 411 (1991), a unanimous Supreme Court held that a state procedural rule could not be applied retroactively to prevent federal review of a constitutional claim. Justice Souter's opinion for the Court concluded that a rule unannounced at the time of petitioner's trial could not have been firmly established at that time, and was thus "inadequate to serve as an independent state ground within the meaning of *James.*" See also Johnson v. Mississippi, 486 U.S. 578 (1988) (no adequate state ground where Mississippi law did not consistently require a claim such as the defendant's to be asserted on direct appeal).

Discretionary Rules as Adequate State Grounds: Beard v. Kindler

In Beard v. Kindler, 558 U.S. 53 (2009), the Court considered whether a discretionary state rule could ever be an adequate state ground, the violation of which would preclude federal habeas review of a state conviction. Kindler challenged his Pennsylvania state court conviction, but the state court exercised its discretion under the state's "fugitive dismissal rule" to dismiss the challenge because he had fled to Canada. Chief Justice Roberts, writing for the Court, set forth the issue:

> "Is a state procedural rule automatically 'inadequate' under the adequate-state-grounds doctrine—and therefore unenforceable on federal habeas corpus review—because the state rule is discretionary rather than mandatory?"

The Court answered that question in the negative. The Chief Justice explained the result as follows:

> We have framed the adequacy inquiry by asking whether the state rule in question was "firmly established and regularly followed." We hold that a discretionary state procedural rule can serve as an adequate ground to bar federal habeas review. * * * [A] discretionary rule can be "firmly established" and "regularly followed"—even if the appropriate exercise of discretion may permit consideration of a federal claim in some cases but not others.

> A contrary holding would pose an unnecessary dilemma for the States: States could preserve flexibility by granting courts discretion to excuse procedural errors, but only at the cost of undermining the finality of state court judgments. Or States could preserve the finality of their judgments by withholding such discretion, but only at the cost of precluding any flexibility in applying the rules.

> We are told that, if forced to choose, many States would opt for mandatory rules to avoid the high costs that come with plenary federal review. That would be unfortunate in many cases, as discretionary rules are often desirable. * * * The result would be particularly unfortunate for criminal defendants, who would lose the opportunity to argue that a procedural default should be excused through the exercise of judicial discretion.

Justice Alito took no part in the consideration of the case. Justice Kennedy, joined by Justice Thomas, wrote a concurring opinion.

Flexible Rules as Adequate State Grounds: *Walker v. Martin*

Most states set determinate time limits for collateral relief applications. But some like California apply a general "reasonableness standard" to judge whether a petition is timely filed. In Walker v. Martin, 562 U.S. 307 (2011), Martin raised claims on state collateral review five years after his conviction. The California Supreme Court denied relief on the ground that Martin was not reasonably timely under the state case law. The Supreme Court, in a unanimous opinion by Justice Ginsburg, held that California's timeliness requirement qualified as an independent state ground adequate to bar habeas corpus relief in federal court. Justice Ginsburg concluded that California's time rule, although discretionary and flexible, met the Beard v. Kindler "firmly established" criterion. The California Supreme Court framed the requirement in a trilogy of cases, instructing habeas petitioners to allege with specificity the absence of substantial delay, good cause for delay, or eligibility for one of four exceptions to the time bar. And California's case law made it plain that Martin's nearly five-year delay was "substantial." Justice Ginsburg observed that state ground may be found inadequate when a court has exercised its discretion in a surprising or unfair manner, but Martin made no such contention here.

State Law Rule Finding Procedural Default for Failure to Raise a Claim on Direct Appeal Is an Adequate and Independent State Ground: Johnson v. Lee

The Supreme Court, in the per curiam opinion in Johnson v. Lee, 136 S.Ct. 1802 (2016), took the Ninth Circuit to task for its failure to recognize that a California procedural rule was an adequate state ground that barred habeas review. The California "Dixon" rule provides that a defendant procedurally defaults a claim raised for the first time on state collateral review if he could have raised it earlier on direct appeal. Lee fell afoul of the rule, but the Ninth Circuit found that the Dixon rule was not an adequate ground to bar habeas relief, because it found the rule to be irregularly applied and not always cited by the California courts in dismissing a claim on collateral review. The Supreme Court found that the rule had been consistently applied by the state courts, and that the failure of a few California courts to specifically cite *Dixon* was of no moment. The Court stated that "every State shares this procedural bar in some form" and that "[f]or such well-established and ubiquitous rules, it takes more than a few outliers to show inadequacy."

"Exorbitant" Application of an Adequate State Ground: Lee v. Kemna

In Lee v. Kemna, 534 U.S. 362 (2002), the Court found an exception to procedural default on an adequate state ground, for "exceptional cases in which exorbitant application of a generally sound rule renders the state ground inadequate to stop consideration of a federal question" on habeas review. Lee, being tried for murder in Missouri, had produced alibi witnesses from California who would have testified that Lee was with them in California on the day of the murder. When it came time to present the witnesses, however, on the third day of trial, they were not in court and Lee's counsel did not know where they were. He asked for a day's continuance so that he could locate the witnesses, and assured the court that the witnesses had not left the jurisdiction because they had business to attend to locally. The trial judge refused to continue the trial, because he wanted to be with his daughter (who was having surgery) the next day, and had other trials to attend to after that. Lee presented no witnesses and was convicted. He brought a habeas petition, arguing that the trial court's refusal to grant a continuance violated his due process rights, and he presented affidavits from the alibi witnesses stating that they were not in the courtroom on the third day of trial because they had been informed by court personnel that they would not be testifying that day.

The state appellate court refused to consider the merits of Lee's due process argument, relying on a procedural bar: Missouri rules of procedure that require a motion for continuance to be submitted in writing with a supporting affidavit. The question for the Supreme Court was whether this procedural bar prohibited a habeas action in the absence of a showing of cause and prejudice or actual innocence.

Justice Ginsburg, writing for six Justices, declared that this case fit into the "limited category" of exceptional cases in which a generally sound state rule of procedure must be found inadequate. She summarized as follows:

> [W]hen the trial judge denied Lee's motion, he stated a reason that could not have been countered by a perfect motion for continuance. The judge said he could not carry the trial over until the next day because he had to be with his daughter in the hospital; the judge further informed counsel that another scheduled trial prevented him from concluding Lee's case on the following business day. Although the judge hypothesized that the witnesses had "abandoned" Lee, he had not a scintilla of evidence or a shred of information on which to base this supposition. * * * Lee's predicament, from all that appears, was one Missouri courts had not confronted before. * * * [A]nd most important, given the realities of trial, Lee substantially complied with Missouri's key Rule.

Justice Kennedy, joined by Justices Scalia and Thomas, dissented. Justice Kennedy argued that a regularly followed state rule had previously been found inadequate "only when the state had no legitimate interest in the rule's enforcement." The need to provide regulations on possibly spurious motions for continuance meant that the Missouri rules were "adequate" within the meaning of Supreme Court jurisprudence.

5. Abuse of the Writ

Even before enactment of AEDPA, successive habeas petitions—serial collateral attacks on the same judgment—ordinarily constituted "abuse of the writ," which generally precluded review regardless of the merits of the subsequent petitions. In McCleskey v. Zant, 499 U.S. 467 (1991), the Court held that a petitioner is generally not permitted to bring a successive habeas petition, but must ordinarily bring all claims in a single petition.

Justice Kennedy wrote the opinion for six members of the Court. The majority held that it was not necessary for the state to show that the petitioner had deliberately abandoned a claim in a prior habeas petition; a petitioner may also abuse the writ by failing to raise a claim through neglect.

Justice Kennedy accepted McCleskey's argument that the comity notions behind the procedural default doctrine were not applicable to successive federal habeas petitions. He responded as follows:

> Nonetheless, the doctrines of procedural default and abuse of the writ are both designed to lessen the injury to a State that results through reexamination of a state conviction on a ground that the State did not have the opportunity to address at a prior, appropriate time; and both doctrines seek to vindicate the State's interest in the finality of its criminal judgments.

The common purposes of "abuse of the writ" and "procedural default" led the Court in *McCleskey* to hold that a successive habeas petition could be entertained only if the petitioner could show cause and prejudice for failing to bring all claims together in a single petition, or, failing that, if he could show that the successive petition established his actual innocence.

Effect of AEDPA

AEDPA limits the use of successive petitions even further than the Court had done in *McCleskey*. The *McCleskey* Court held that a showing of cause and prejudice, or actual innocence, would permit a successive petition. AEDPA, in contrast, provides for absolute dismissal of claims identical to those previously brought (no exceptions), and dismissal of new claims with two minor exceptions: 1) if they are based on a new rule made retroactive to habeas cases by the Supreme Court (which essentially can never happen), or 2) if the claims were not included in the initial petition due to an unavailable factual predicate (as with the suppression of information that occurred in Amadeo v. Zant, supra). Moreover, assuming that one of these causes are shown, the petitioner then has to show by clear and convincing evidence that no reasonable factfinder could have convicted him. Thus, there is no actual innocence exception to excuse the cause requirement—the petitioner must establish not only cause, but also a standard of prejudice more rigorous than the actual innocence exception to the cause and prejudice requirement had been, i.e., clear and convincing evidence that but for the constitutional violation, no reasonable factfinder could have convicted the petitioner. Finally, the petitioner must obtain clearance from a three-member panel of the court of appeals (which must be satisfied of a prima facie case) before a successive petition can even be brought.

In Felker v. Turpin, 518 U.S. 651 (1996), the petitioner argued that the above provisions operate as a "suspension" of the writ of habeas corpus, in violation of Article I, section 9 of the Constitution. That clause provides that "the Privilege of the Writ of Habeas Corpus shall not be suspended, unless when in Cases of Rebellion or Invasion the public Safety may require it." But the Suspension Clause argument was unanimously rejected in an opinion by Chief Justice Rehnquist who viewed the statute as "a modified res judicata rule, a restraint on what is called in habeas corpus practice 'abuse of the writ.' "

Premature Claims and Successive Petitions: Stewart v. Martinez-Villareal

In Stewart v. Martinez-Villareal, 523 U.S. 637 (1998), Martinez brought a habeas petition challenging his capital conviction. The petition contained a number of claims; one claim was that Martinez was incompetent and therefore could not be executed. Such a claim is called a "*Ford*" claim, after Ford v. Wainwright, 477 U.S. 399 (1986) (holding that the Eight Amendment prohibits the execution of an incompetent person). The lower courts held that the *Ford* claim was procedurally premature, and the remaining claims were eventually dismissed on the merits. When the state proceeded to set a date certain for the execution, Martinez sought to reopen his *Ford* claim. The state argued that this was a successive petition, barred by the terms of AEDPA. But the Supreme Court, in an opinion by Chief Justice Rehnquist, held that the incompetence claim could not be treated as a successive petition because "[t]here was only one application for habeas relief, and the District Court ruled (or should have ruled) on each claim at the time it became ripe"; therefore the petitioner had the right to have it considered on the merits. The Chief Justice noted that if the government were correct, "the implications for habeas practice would be far-reaching and seemingly perverse" because "a dismissal of a first habeas petition for technical procedural reasons would bar the prisoner from ever obtaining federal habeas review."

Justices Scalia and Thomas dissented; each wrote separate opinions joined by the other. Both opinions made the point that however "perverse" the result, the plain meaning of AEDPA was that the revival of a petition dismissed or deferred on procedural grounds constitutes a successive petition, and is therefore prohibited, subject to the two very limited exceptions not at issue in this case.

Note that the *Martinez* rule would also apply in situations where a habeas claim is dismissed because the petitioner has not exhausted state remedies. If the petitioner then goes to state court and exhausts his remedies, but gets no relief, he can then refile his habeas petition. Such a petition is not "successive" within the meaning of AEDPA, because, like

Martinez, the petitioner never had his claims considered on the merits by the federal court. But it would be subject to another pitfall—the AEDPA statute of limitations. See the discussion of mixed petitions earlier in this Chapter.

6. Newly Discovered Evidence

Chief Justice Rehnquist wrote for the Court in Herrera v. Collins, 506 U.S. 390 (1993), as it rejected a habeas corpus challenge to a death penalty conviction based upon a claim of newly discovered evidence purporting to demonstrate innocence. Herrera was convicted of killing two police officers. He was identified by an eyewitness and in a dying declaration made by one of the officers. A note written by Herrera, implicating him in one of the murders, was found on his person when he was arrested. Forensic evidence also connected him to the crimes. Herrera filed a habeas corpus petition in state court. He did not contend that an error had been made at his trial. Rather, he contended that he had discovered new evidence proving that his brother Raul had actually killed the officers. He supported the petition with affidavits of Raul's lawyer and former cellmate, both relating inculpatory statements made by Raul, as well as an affidavit from Raul's son who purported to be an eyewitness to his father's murder of the officers. These affidavits were inconsistent with some details about the murders. Herrera's petition was filed 10 years after his conviction, and eight years after Raul's death.

Herrera's state habeas petition was dismissed as untimely by the Texas courts. He then filed a federal habeas petition asserting "that the Eighth and Fourteenth Amendments to the United States Constitution prohibit the execution of a person who is innocent of the crime for which he was convicted." In rejecting this assertion, the Chief Justice reasoned that innocence "must be determined in some sort of a judicial proceeding" and that when a defendant has been afforded a fair trial "and convicted of the offense for which he was charged, the presumption of innocence disappears." He stated that the writ of habeas corpus was not an appropriate vehicle for assessing factual innocence, in the absence of a claim of a constitutional violation in the proceeding—and Herrera made no such claim:

> Claims of actual innocence based on newly discovered evidence have never been held to state a ground for federal habeas relief absent an independent constitutional violation occurring in the underlying state criminal proceeding. * * * This rule is grounded in the principle that federal habeas courts sit to ensure that individuals are not imprisoned in violation of the Constitution—not to correct errors of fact.

Herrera relied on Sawyer v. Whitley, supra, where the Court held that a habeas petitioner who procedurally defaulted his claim may still have his federal constitutional claims heard if he makes a proper showing of actual innocence. But the Chief Justice distinguished *Sawyer* on the ground that it "makes clear that a claim of actual innocence is not itself a constitutional claim, but instead a gateway through which a habeas petitioner must pass to have his otherwise barred constitutional claim considered on the merits." The Chief Justice concluded that the "actual innocence" exception set forth in *Sawyer* did not extend to "freestanding claims of actual innocence." Compare Schlup v. Delo, 513 U.S. 298 (1995) (petitioner can rely on newly discovered evidence to establish actual innocence, where he claims—unlike Herrera—that there was a constitutional error at his trial).

In denying habeas relief, the Court relied on the fact that Herrera was not "left without a forum to raise his actual innocence claim." The Court noted that under Texas law, Herrera could seek executive clemency, and stated that clemency "is deeply rooted in our Anglo-American tradition of law, and is the historic remedy for preventing miscarriage of justice where judicial process has been exhausted."

Ultimately, the Court found it unnecessary to reach the question whether federal habeas relief would *ever* be available to prevent the execution of an innocent person when there is no possible state relief. The Chief Justice assumed *arguendo* that the Constitution prohibited such an execution; but he stated that, even if that were so, a defendant who claimed actual innocence after an error-free trial would have to make an "extraordinarily high" showing that the newly discovered evidence proved his innocence. This high threshold was required due to the "very disruptive effect that entertaining claims of actual innocence would have on the need for finality in capital cases, and the enormous burden that having to retry cases based on often stale evidence would place on the States."

The Court found that Herrera had not come close to satisfying an "extraordinarily high" threshold of proof of actual innocence. The Chief Justice stated that the evidence presented against Herrera at trial was strong, and that his purported evidence of innocence consisted of inconsistent and suspiciously-timed affidavits implicating a person who was now dead. He concluded that "coming 10 years after petitioner's trial, this showing of innocence falls far short of that which would have to be made in order to trigger the sort of constitutional claim which we have assumed, *arguendo,* to exist."

Justice O'Connor, joined by Justice Kennedy, wrote a concurring opinion and stated that she could "not disagree with the fundamental legal principle that executing the innocent is inconsistent with the Constitution." However, she found that Herrera was not "an innocent man on the verge of execution. He is instead a legally guilty one who, refusing to accept the jury's verdict, demands a hearing in which to have his culpability determined once again."

Justice Scalia, joined by Justice Thomas, concurred and argued that "[t]here is no basis in text, tradition, or even in contemporary practice (if that were enough) for finding in the Constitution a right to demand judicial consideration of newly discovered evidence of innocence brought forward after conviction."

Justice White concurred in the judgment. He assumed that a persuasive showing of actual innocence would bar execution, but found that Herrera had not made a sufficient showing of his innocence.

Justice Blackmun, joined by Justices Stevens and in large part by Justice Souter, dissented. He argued that the Eighth Amendment and the Due Process Clause forbid the execution of a person who can prove his innocence with newly discovered evidence. Justice Blackmun contended that the remedy of executive clemency is not adequate to satisfy the Constitution, because that remedy is too idiosyncratic and politicized to protect against the execution of an innocent person. He would "hold that, to obtain relief on a claim of actual innocence, the petitioner must show that he probably is innocent."

7.   Limitations on Obtaining a Hearing

What happens if a habeas petitioner claims that constitutional error occurred at his state trial, but the argument of error is dependent on a factual predicate that remains undeveloped? For example, if the defendant argues that the prosecutor exercised peremptory challenges in a discriminatory manner, certain factual issues will be important, e.g., how many were struck, who were they, what was said on voir dire, what rationale did the prosecutor give for striking the juror, etc.

If the facts supporting a habeas claim were not developed in the state court, the petitioner will need to move for an evidentiary hearing to develop his claims. However, if the petitioner should have developed the facts in the state system, and failed to do so, a question similar to that discussed in Wainwright v. Sykes, supra, arises—why should the petitioner be permitted an evidentiary hearing if he failed to develop the necessary facts in the state proceeding? Such a petitioner would seem to have run aground on a state procedural bar.

In Keeney v. Tamayo-Reyes, 504 U.S. 1 (1992), the Court relied on its procedural default cases such as Wainwright v. Sykes to hold that a petitioner who failed to develop facts in the state proceeding could be denied an evidentiary hearing in federal court (and thus, as a practical matter, denied habeas relief on the merits) unless he could establish "cause and prejudice" for the failure to develop the facts below. Tamayo-Reyes had pleaded nolo contendere to a charge of first-degree manslaughter. In his habeas action, he argued that his plea was not knowing and intelligent because his translator had not translated accurately and completely for him the *mens rea* element of the crime. He also contended that he did not understand the purposes of the plea form and the plea hearing, and that he thought he was agreeing to be tried for manslaughter rather than agreeing to plead guilty. The merits of his claim were obviously fact-dependent, but his counsel had failed to develop the necessary facts in state collateral proceedings. Justice White, writing for the Court, declared that "encouraging the full factual development in state court of a claim that state courts committed constitutional error advances comity by allowing a coordinate jurisdiction to correct its own errors in the first instance." He concluded that the state court "is the appropriate forum for resolution of factual issues in the first instance, and creating incentives for the deferral of factfinding to later federal-court proceedings can only degrade the accuracy and efficiency of judicial proceedings. This is fully consistent with and gives meaning to the requirement of exhaustion."

AEDPA Limitations on Obtaining a Hearing: *Williams v. Taylor* and *Schriro v. Landrigan*

After AEDPA, there are only a few reasons for which a habeas court can hold a factfinding hearing; the standards set forth in *Tamayo-Reyes* are restricted even further. As amended by AEDPA, 28 U.S.C. § 2254(e)(2)—the provision that controls whether a habeas petitioner may receive an evidentiary hearing in federal district court on claims that were not developed in the state court—provides as follows:

> If the applicant has failed to develop the factual basis of a claim in State court proceedings, the court shall not hold an evidentiary hearing on the claim unless the applicant shows that—
>
> (A) the claim relies on—
>
> (i) a new rule of constitutional law, made retroactive to cases on collateral review by the Supreme Court, that was previously unavailable; or
>
> (ii) a factual predicate that could not have been previously discovered through the exercise of due diligence; and
>
> (B) the facts underlying the claim would be sufficient to establish by clear and convincing evidence that but for constitutional error, no reasonable factfinder would have found the applicant guilty of the underlying offense.

The Court construed the AEDPA provisions concerning hearings in *Williams v. Taylor*, 529 U.S. 420 (2000). In his habeas petition, Williams sought an evidentiary hearing to develop three claims: 1) a claim under *Brady* that the prosecution failed to disclose a psychological report on the prosecution's star witness; 2) a claim that a juror had lied on voir dire by failing to disclose a source of bias; and 3) a related claim that the prosecutor committed misconduct because he knew that the juror was biased and failed to disclose that fact.

In the Supreme Court, Williams conceded that he could not satisfy the stringent standards for relief set forth in subdivision (B) of the statute (i.e., clear and convincing evidence of actual innocence). Resolution of the right to an evidentiary hearing therefore depended on whether Williams had "failed to develop" the basis of the factual claim in state court. The parties agreed that the facts necessary to support Williams's habeas claims had *not* been developed in the state court. Williams argued, however, that he had not *failed* to develop the claims, because he was *unable* to pursue the claims during the state court proceeding, i.e., he was not at fault. The government argued for a no-fault interpretation of the statutory term "failed", i.e., if the claims were not developed in the state court—no matter the reason—then there is no right to an evidentiary hearing to develop the claims in the federal district court.

The Court, in a unanimous opinion by Justice Kennedy, rejected the government's strict construction of the AEDPA term "failed", and held that the term "failed to develop" requires some "lack of diligence" on the petitioner's part. Justice Kennedy explained this ruling in the following passage:

In its customary and preferred sense, "fail" connotes some omission, fault, or negligence on the part of the person who has failed to do something. To say a person has failed in a duty implies he did not take the necessary steps to fulfill it. He is, as a consequence, at fault and bears responsibility for the failure. In this sense, a person is not at fault when his diligent efforts to perform an act are thwarted, for example, by the conduct of another or by happenstance. * * * We conclude Congress used the word "failed" in the sense just described. * * *

Under the opening clause of § 2254(e)(2), a failure to develop the factual basis of a claim is not established unless there is lack of diligence, or some greater fault, attributable to the prisoner or the prisoner's counsel. * * *

Justice Kennedy explained that the statute required the defendant and counsel to pursue factfinding with "diligence" in the state court:

For state courts to have their rightful opportunity to adjudicate federal rights, the prisoner must be diligent in developing the record and presenting, if possible, all claims of constitutional error. * * * Federal courts sitting in habeas are not an alternative forum for trying facts and issues which a prisoner made insufficient effort to pursue in state proceedings. Yet comity is not served by saying a prisoner "has failed to develop the factual basis of a claim" where he was unable to develop his claim in state court despite diligent effort. In that circumstance, an evidentiary hearing is not barred by § 2254(e)(2).

Justice Kennedy then applied the "diligence" test to the facts of the case. He found that Williams had not been diligent in pursuing his *Brady* claim, because the witness's psychological history had been disclosed at that witness's sentencing proceeding, well in time for Williams to use it in his state proceedings. Williams and his counsel were thus aware of the report and yet took no steps to have it produced. In contrast, Williams was *not* at fault for failing to develop the claim of juror bias and the related claim of prosecutorial misconduct in not disclosing it. The juror had misrepresented her background in answering a question on voir dire. There was no reason for Williams or his counsel to believe that the juror and the prosecutor were hiding anything. The Court noted that it would be "surprised, to say the least, if a district court familiar with the standards of trial practice were to hold that in all cases diligent counsel must check public records containing personal information pertaining to each and every juror."

In Schriro v. Landrigan, 550 U.S. 465 (2007), the Court found that a district court had not abused its discretion in refusing to grant a habeas petitioner's request for an evidentiary hearing to develop the facts supporting defense counsel's alleged ineffectiveness at a capital sentencing proceeding. Justice Thomas, writing for five members of the Court, found that the record in the instant case demonstrated that the defendant himself objected to pursuing any avenues of mitigating evidence.

Justice Stevens, joined by Justices Souter, Ginsburg and Breyer, dissented. He argued that the record was not as clear as the majority would have it, and that at any rate defense counsel's effectiveness was not dependent on the defendant's willingness to agree to foregoing favorable evidence.

8.   Harmless Error in Habeas Corpus Cases

A Less Onerous Standard of Harmlessness for the State to Meet: Brecht v. Abrahamson

In Brecht v. Abrahamson, 507 U.S. 619 (1993), the Court considered the standard that should be applied by a federal habeas court in assessing whether a constitutional error in a state court was harmless. The state urged as a standard that an error should be presumed harmless unless it had a "substantial and injurious effect on the verdict." This standard, which is employed by the Court for review of non-constitutional error on direct review, is referred to as the "*Kotteakos*" standard. See Kotteakos v. United States, 328 U.S. 750 (1946). The *Kotteakos* standard is less onerous for the state to meet—the error is less likely to create a reversal—than is the "harmless beyond a reasonable doubt" standard applied by the Court to constitutional errors on direct review. The more stringent test of harmlessness—understandably advocated by the petitioner in *Brecht*—is known as the "*Chapman*" standard. See Chapman v. California, discussed earlier in this Chapter in the section on harmless error on direct review.

The 5–4 majority in *Brecht* held that the *Chapman* standard was too stringent to be applied in a collateral attack of a state court conviction and that the more permissive *Kotteakos* test applied. The Court concluded that the "*Kotteakos* harmless-error standard is better tailored to the nature and purpose of collateral review than the *Chapman* standard, and application of a less onerous harmless-error standard on habeas promotes the considerations underlying our habeas jurisprudence."

Writing for the majority, Chief Justice Rehnquist emphasized the difference between collateral review and direct appeal:

> The reason most frequently advanced in our cases for distinguishing between direct and collateral review is the State's interest in the finality of convictions that have survived direct review within the state court system. We have also spoken of comity and federalism. * * * Finally, we have recognized that liberal allowance of the writ degrades the prominence of the trial itself, and at the same time encourages habeas petitioners to relitigate their claims on collateral review.

> * * * State courts are fully qualified to identify constitutional error and evaluate its prejudicial effect on the trial process under *Chapman,* and state courts often occupy a superior vantage point from which to evaluate the effect of trial error. For these reasons, it scarcely seems logical to require federal habeas courts to engage in the identical approach to harmless-error review that *Chapman* requires state courts to engage in on direct review.

The Chief Justice emphasized the following costs of "overturning final and presumptively correct convictions on collateral review because the State cannot prove that an error is harmless under *Chapman*":

1) the State's interest in finality and in sovereignty over criminal matters is undermined;

2) granting habeas relief "merely because there is a reasonable possibility that trial error contributed to the verdict is at odds with the historic meaning of habeas corpus—to afford relief to those whom society has grievously wronged"; and

3) the State suffers "social costs" due to the necessity to retry a case after a significant passage of time.

The Chief Justice was careful to note that the *Kotteakos* standard would be applied only to constitutional errors of the "trial type." If the constitutional error is "structural" in the sense that it tainted the entirety of the trial, then per se reversal is required whether the error is discovered on direct or habeas review. See the discussion earlier in this Chapter about errors that cannot be harmless.

Justice Stevens filed a concurring opinion in which he emphasized that, even under *Kotteakos,* the reviewing court must make a *de novo* examination of the trial record. He also emphasized that the reviewing court must focus on the effect of the error, not on whether it thinks that a defendant would have been convicted absent the error. He concluded that "the way we phrase the governing standard is far less important than the quality of the judgment with which it is applied."

Justice White dissented, joined by Justice Blackmun and in substantial part by Justice Souter. He argued that the *Chapman* standard was essential to the safeguard of constitutional rights. Justice O'Connor dissented in a separate opinion in which she argued that "the harmless-error standard is crucial to our faith in the accuracy of the outcome" of a state proceeding.

Burden of Proof as to Harmlessness: O'Neal v. McAninch

Who bears the burden on the harmlessness question in habeas cases? Must the defendant show that the error was harmful, or must the state show that the error was harmless? In O'Neal v. McAninch, 513 U.S. 432 (1995), the Court held that where a judge has "grave doubt" as to whether an error was harmless or not under the *Kotteakos* standard, the petitioner is entitled to habeas relief. Justice Breyer, writing for six Justices, defined "grave doubt" as arising when, "in the judge's mind, the matter is so evenly balanced that he feels himself in virtual equipoise as to the harmlessness of the error." Where "grave doubt" as to harmlessness exists, "the uncertain judge should treat the error, not as if it were harmless, but as if it affected the verdict."

Justice Breyer reasoned that allowing the petitioner to win in cases of "grave doubt" as to harmlessness was a result that was consistent with other harmless-error cases such as *Kotteakos* and *Chapman,* where the Court imposed the burden of showing harmlessness on the government. He contended that a rule "denying the writ in cases of grave uncertainty, would virtually guarantee that many, in fact, will be held in unlawful custody—contrary to the writ's most basic traditions and purposes." Justice Breyer recognized the state's interest in finality but declared that "this interest is somewhat diminished by the legal circumstance that the State normally bears responsibility for the error that infected the initial trial."

Justice Thomas, joined by Chief Justice Rehnquist and Justice Scalia, dissented. He argued that the burden should be placed on the petitioner, as it was the petitioner who was bringing the action. He emphasized that the habeas petitioner "comes to federal court as a plaintiff" and so "he naturally should be expected to bear the risk of failure of proof or persuasion." Justice Thomas also noted the limited impact that the majority's decision would have, because "cases in which habeas courts are in equipoise on the issue of harmlessness are astonishingly rare."